Psychotherapy Skills and Methods That Work

Psychotherapy Skills and Methods That Work

Edited by

Clara E. Hill and John C. Norcross

OXFORD
UNIVERSITY PRESS

OXFORD
UNIVERSITY PRESS

Oxford University Press is a department of the University of Oxford. It furthers the University's objective of excellence in research, scholarship, and education by publishing worldwide. Oxford is a registered trade mark of Oxford University Press in the UK and certain other countries.

Published in the United States of America by Oxford University Press
198 Madison Avenue, New York, NY 10016, United States of America.

Library of Congress Cataloging-in-Publication Data
ISBN 978–0–19–761101–2

DOI: 10.1093/oso/9780197611012.001.0001

Printed by Integrated Books International, United States of America

Dedicated to

Louis G. Castonguay
Exceptional researcher, gifted teacher, wonderful colleague

Contents

Preface

A warm welcome to *Psychotherapy Skills and Methods That Work*, a mammoth collaboration among dozens of scientist–practitioners and four professional organizations dedicated to improving the practice of psychotherapy. In this volume, we provide research and clinical evidence for what we know about the effectiveness of therapist skills and methods.

Psychotherapists must do *something* in their sessions—listen, reflect, question, encourage, challenge, interpret, guide, instruct. It would thus be helpful for psychotherapists across theoretical orientations to have evidence about when, how, under what conditions, and with whom to use these various skills and methods to guide their practice and training.

This book is a natural extension and complement to the three editions of *Psychotherapy Relationships That Work* (2002, 2011, 2019). In those volumes, John Norcross, Mike Lambert, and Bruce Wampold sought to combat the pervasive view that the treatment approach or "package" was the only thing that contributes meaningfully to psychotherapy outcome. They presented impressive research evidence that the therapeutic relationship and clients' transdiagnostic features, regardless of treatment package, contributed significantly to outcomes of psychotherapy, probably as much as, if not more than, the impact of the particular treatment approach. Hence, they sought to convince practitioners of the rightful place of evidence-based relationships and responsiveness alongside evidence-based treatments. Our goal in *Psychotherapy Skills and Methods That Work* is to continue in that tradition and present evidence of the rightful, research-substantiated place of evidence-based skills (e.g., questions, interpretations) and methods (e.g., cognitive restructuring, role induction).

Psychotherapy is a complex, multifactorial activity; reducing it to any single component does not do it justice and misleads clinical practice and training. We ought, to paraphrase Freud, consider all the components. Thus, our emphasis is on "alongside" rather than "instead of" or "better than."

As well, note two additional word choices: We use the terms *clients* and *patients* as well as *counseling* and *psychotherapy* interchangeably throughout the book. This pluralism is intended not only to avoid theoretical and professional disputes but also to model the complexity and inclusion of psychotherapy itself. We also strive to be sensitive to theoretical and cultural diversity and have thus asked our contributors to focus on the use of the skills/methods from different theoretical perspectives and with different patient populations.

Having proclaimed our mission, let us also articulate our exclusions. We focus solely on individual adult psychotherapy in this volume; we do not consider group psychotherapy, couple and family treatment, or pharmacotherapy. We sought to examine available research from around the world, but the majority of reviewed studies are from English-language journals. Given the hundreds of available treatment methods and skills in the psychotherapy multiverse, we also needed to restrict the skills and methods included in this volume to a manageable number.

The Task Force and Steering Committee

I (CEH) developed this project as my presidential initiative in 2021–2022 for the Society for the Advancement of Psychotherapy (SAP; Division 29 of the American Psychological Association [APA]) and invited John Norcross to co-lead the Task Force on Psychotherapy Skills and Methods That Work with me, given his extensive experience leading the previous task forces. We subsequently invited and gained co-sponsorship from the Society for Counseling Psychology (SCP; Division 17 of the APA), the Society for Psychotherapy Research (SPR), and the Society for the Exploration of Psychotherapy Integration (SEPI). These are, in our view, the premier organizations for psychotherapy research in the world. We are fortunate to have the collaboration and sponsorship of these major stakeholders in advancing the integration of practice and research in psychotherapy.

We asked each co-sponsoring organization of the Task Force to nominate one individual for our Steering Committee. We invited additional people with expertise in psychotherapy research, ensuring that we obtained gender, cultural, theoretical, and international representation on the Steering Committee. In addition to ourselves as Co-Chairs, the members of the Steering Committee were as follows (in alphabetical order):

Louis G. Castonguay, PhD, Pennsylvania State University, USA
Melanie M. Domenech Rodriguez, PhD, Utah State University, USA
Barry A. Farber, PhD, Columbia University, USA
Christoph Flückiger, PhD, University of Kassel, Switzerland (representing SPR)
Myrna L. Friedlander, PhD, University at Albany/State University of New York, USA
Beatriz (Betty) Gomez, PhD, Aigle Foundation, Argentina (representing SEPI)
Matthew J. Miller, PhD, Loyola University, USA (representing SCP)
Patricia T. Spangler, PhD, Uniformed Services University, USA (representing SAP)
Bernhard Strauss, PhD, University of Jena, Germany
Sigal Zilcha-Mano, PhD, University of Haifa, Israel

The principal tasks of Steering Committee members were fivefold. First, they recommended potential chapters and authors. Second, they reviewed the Introduction chapter and provided rich feedback about the foundation for the project. Third, they read completed chapters and evaluated the strength of the research evidence for the designated skill or method. Fourth, they reviewed the Conclusions chapter and provided incredibly helpful feedback about how to frame out findings. Finally, for those representing professional organizations, they communicated with their respective groups about the activities of the Task Force. We are grateful for their contributions.

Potential Audiences

We have designed *Psychotherapy Skills and Methods That Work* with four audiences in mind. Our first intended audience is practitioners of diverse theoretical orientations and professional disciplines who want to know which skills and methods have been shown to be effective in individual psychotherapy.

Our second and related audience is psychotherapy educators (trainers and supervisors). Deciding which skills and methods to teach requires a modicum (or more) of research evidence in addition to theory and experience. In addition, we need to teach trainees to think critically about how to gather and evaluate evidence about the effects of skills and methods.

Our third intended audience is policymakers—the people who set the requirements for practice and reimbursement. We hope that policymakers realize that we cannot simply mandate that mental health professionals implement evidence-based treatment packages; rather, the skills and methods in these treatment packages also need to be evidence-based in terms of immediate, intermediate, and distal outcomes.

Finally, we hope to influence the current and future generations of psychotherapy researchers to conduct more and better research. In addition to our current research designs, measures, and analyses, we need new and innovative strategies to help us understand the mysteries and complexities of psychotherapy.

We cannot continue to look cluelessly at the black box of the treatment method; we cannot continue to use as our only design the correlations between poorly defined skills/methods and distal outcomes; we cannot continue to ignore individual process and treatment outcomes in the research. We need to examine what works in terms of the entire treatment approach, the constituent therapy methods, and the associated skills for individual clients at specific moments within the context of the whole person of the client and therapist and their emergent relationship. The contributors to this volume have taken huge strides toward that lofty goal. But, as Jonas Salk reminds us, "The reward for work well done is the opportunity to do more."

Organization of the Book

We start with an introductory chapter on psychotherapist skills and methods: reviewing the controversies surrounding how to assess skills/methods, what contributes to success in psychotherapy, and how to link skills/methods to patient outcomes. This material provides the rationale and frame for our book. We then feature in Chapter 2 an updated summary of the research evidence on four skills/methods (affirmation, self-disclosure, immediacy, alliance rupture repairs) featured in the previous task forces on psychotherapy relationships that work.

In the first cluster of chapters, we focus first on specific therapist skills often included in helping skills textbooks: questions (Williams), Socratic questioning and guided discovery (Overholser and Beale), empathic reflections (Elliott et al.), metaphors (McMullen and Tay), interpretations (Zilcha-Mano et al.), paradoxical interventions (Peluso and Freund), advice/suggestions/recommendation (Hill et al.), integrating between-session homework (Ryum et al.), silences (Levitt and Morrill), and facilitating dyadic synchrony (Slonim et al.). Most of these therapist skills have been referred to as *verbal response modes* and typically are discrete pantheoretical behaviors that occur within sentences or speaking turns of sessions (except for between-session homework, which we put here to keep it next to advice, suggestions, and recommendations since they are related constructs).

The next cluster of chapters focuses on therapist methods that are typically more complex or extend over longer periods of time than the previous skills. These are broader multistep modules that fit within treatment packages. Although most were developed within particular theoretical traditions, all can be used by therapists across orientations. Representative transtheoretical methods are role induction (Swift et al.), collaborative assessment methods (Aschieri et al.), dream work (Spangler and Sim), routine outcome monitoring (Barkham et al.), and strength-based methods (Flückiger et al.). Representing more experiential and psychodynamic therapies, we present chapters on enhancing emotion regulation (Iwakabe et al.) and chairwork (Pascual-Leone and Baher). Representing more cognitive and behavioral therapies are chapters on mindfulness/meditation/acceptance (Goldberg et al.), behavioral activation (Cuijpers et al.), and cognitive restructuring (Ezawa and Hollon).

In the final chapter, we summarize the research evidence for the various skills and methods. With the guidance of our Steering Committee, we list the conclusions and recommendations of the Task Force on Psychotherapy Skills and Methods That Work. We also address training implications, therapeutic practices, and research directions grounded in the best of that research evidence.

The end result is a compilation of cutting-edge, practice-friendly research reviews about which therapy skills/methods work, which do not, and which lack enough research evidence to date to make a judgment about efficacy. We acknowledge up front that there are few research studies on several of the featured skills and methods; therefore, those chapters comprise a mix of research, practice, vision, and heuristics encouraging more research on each skill/method.

Chapter Guidelines

We developed detailed guidelines for the contributors of the skills and methods chapters to ensure standard section headings and similar chapter structures. We hope that this consistent format promotes comparability among the chapters and enhances the readers' experience of continuity throughout the volume, as well as provides the necessary information for readers to evaluate the evidence. The focus of the book is on the association between the skills/methods and immediate in-session, intermediate, and distal outcomes. Thus, although information about other aspects of the skills/methods (e.g., frequency of occurrence, description of subtypes, relation to other process variables) is important, such empirical data are not included in this book.

The chapter guidelines, in condensed fashion, are presented below as they were given to the contributors:

- *Introduction.* Introduce the method or skill in a few, reader-friendly paragraphs.
- *Definitions.* Define in theoretically neutral language the skill or method being reviewed. Identify any highly similar or equivalent constructs from diverse

theoretical traditions. Also cover briefly the theoretical background for the technique. If possible, present how the technique is viewed from two or three perspectives.

- *Clinical Description and Indications.* Operationalize the skill or method by describing how it is implemented in session. Also delineate specific patient characteristics, in-session markers, and clinical circumstances for which the skill/method is indicated versus contraindicated.
- *Assessment.* Review how the skill/method has typically been assessed. Then, review how the immediate within-session outcomes (e.g., client responses), the intermediate outcomes (e.g., post-session), and distal end-of-treatment outcomes (e.g., symptom change) have been assessed. Identify specific measures and their psychometric properties.
- *Clinical Examples.* Provide concrete examples of the skill/method, using de-identified or hypothetical transcripts, so that readers can understand how the skill/method is used in sessions.
- *Landmark Studies and Previous Reviews.* Walk readers through one or two landmark studies on the topic, describing the design, participants, and results. Then, if available, provide a quick synopsis of the findings of previous meta-analyses and systematic reviews on the skill or method.
- *Research Review.* Systematically compile all available empirical studies of the skill/method in individual psychotherapy written in the English language (and other languages, if possible). Each included study must link the skill/method to some kind of outcome (immediate, intermediate, distal) and can include case studies, qualitative studies, process studies, controlled trials, and quantitative studies, but exclude analogue studies or surveys. Divide the research review into three sections: (a) report on the link between the skill/method and immediate, in-session outcomes; (b) report on the link between the skill/method and intermediate (post-session, between sessions) outcomes; and (c) report on the link between the skill/method and distal, treatment-end outcomes.

  If possible, conduct an original meta-analysis of all available studies in each section, following guidelines in the Appendix of the seventh edition of the APA *Publication Manual*). If it is not possible to conduct a meta-analysis because there were not enough outcome studies, conduct a box-score analysis of the results in each study (positive, neutral, or negative associations). In addition, report on any evidence for moderators or mediators of the findings.
- *Possible Negative Effects and Harm.* Provide information about probable negative effects of this skill or method.
- *Diversity Considerations.* Describe the results related to diversity (e.g., gender, race/ethnicity, sexual orientation, socioeconomic status) and their intersection in the research evidence of the link between the skill/method and outcome.
- *Limitations of the Research.* Provide a brief description of the major limitations of the extant research linking the skill/method and outcome. Also give a concise paragraph or two on future research directions, particularly in terms of solutions to resolve persistent methodological problems.

- *Training Implications.* Explicate briefly the take-home points of the research review for clinical educators and supervisors.
- *Therapeutic Practices.* Provide in bullet form the evidence-based implications for practice.

Acknowledgments

We are grateful to the Society for the Advancement of Psychotherapy (APA Division 29) for encouraging us to pursue this Task Force and for supporting its multiple-year timeline. We appreciate our co-sponsoring organizations (SCP, SPR, SEPI) for joining us in this vital endeavor. The contributors endured multiple revisions of their chapters and faithfully followed demanding chapter guidelines. Our Steering Committee furnished timely research expertise, and Sarah Harrington at Oxford University Press provided editorial and publication expertise.

We also thank our patients who have taught us so much about using psychotherapy skills and methods. Likewise, we are indebted to our students and supervisees for challenging us to articulate and operationalize what we know about what works in psychotherapy. We especially recognize the community of psychotherapy scholars who have supported and encouraged us throughout our careers to think more deeply and reflectively about our craft. Finally, we acknowledge our families, who have provided us with a secure base from which to venture out and explore the COVID-plagued world.

Clara E. Hill and John C. Norcross

About the Editors

Clara E. Hill, PhD, earned her PhD at Southern Illinois University in 1974. She started her career in 1974 as an Assistant Professor in the Department of Psychology, University of Maryland, and has recently retired from there as a Professor. She has been President of the Society for Psychotherapy Research and of the Society for the Advancement of Psychotherapy (APA Division 29), Editor of the *Journal of Counseling Psychology*, and Co-Editor of *Psychotherapy Research*. Awards include the Leona Tyler Award (Society of Counseling Psychology), the Distinguished Psychologist Award (Society for the Advancement of Psychotherapy), the Distinguished Research Career Award (Society for Psychotherapy Research), and the Outstanding Lifetime Achievement Award (Section on Counseling and Psychotherapy Process and Outcome Research, Society for Counseling Psychology). Her major research interests are therapist skills, psychotherapy process and outcome, training and supervising therapists, dream work, meaning in life, and qualitative research. She has published more than 280 journal articles, more than 75 chapters in books, and 18 books (including *Helping Skills*, *Dream Work in Therapy*, *Essentials of Consensual Qualitative Research*, and *Meaning in Life*).

John C. Norcross, PhD, ABPP, is Distinguished Professor and Chair of Psychology at the University of Scranton, Clinical Professor of Psychiatry at SUNY Upstate Medical University, and a board-certified clinical psychologist. Author of more than 400 scholarly publications, he has co-written or edited 20 books, including *Psychotherapy Relationships That Work*, *Clinician's Guide to Evidence-Based Practice in Behavioral Health and Addictions*, *Self-Help That Works*, *Psychologists' Desk Reference*, *History of Psychotherapy*, *Leaving It at the Office: Psychotherapist Self-Care*, 13 editions of the *Insider's Guide to Graduate Programs in Clinical & Counseling Psychology*, and *Systems of Psychotherapy: A Transtheoretical Analysis*, now in its ninth edition. He was in part-time clinical practice for 35 years but now limits himself to consultation and supervision. He has served as President of the American Psychological Association (APA) Division of Clinical Psychology, the APA Division of Psychotherapy, Society for the Exploration of Psychotherapy Integration, and on the board of directors of the National Register of Health Service Psychologists. He has received multiple professional awards, such as APA's Distinguished Career Contributions to Education & Training Award, Pennsylvania Professor of the Year from the Carnegie Foundation, and election to the National Academies of Practice. An engaging teacher and clinician, he has conducted workshops and lectures in 40 countries.

Contributors

Christopher Anders, MA
Department of Psychological and Quantitative Foundations, University of Iowa

Filippo Aschieri, PhD
European Center for Therapeutic Assessment, Post-Graduate School of Psychology A. Gemelli, Catholic University of the Sacred Hearth
Therapeutic Assessment Institute

Dana Atzil-Slonim, PhD
Department of Psychology, Bar-Ilan University

Tabarak Baher, MA
Department of Psychology, University of Windsor

Jacques P. Barber, PhD
George F. Derner School of Psychology, Adelphi University

Michael Barkham, PhD
Clinical and Applied Psychology Unit, Department of Psychology, University of Sheffield

Eleanor Beale, MA
Department of Psychology, Case Western Reserve University
Psychology Department, Durham VA Medical Center

Mia Bennion, BA (Hons), PGCert, FHEA
Division of Nursing, Midwifery, and Social Work, University of Manchester

Arthur C. Bohart, PhD
Department of Psychology, California State University Dominguez Hills
School of Education and Counseling Psychology, Santa Clara University

Pim Cuijpers, PhD
Department of Clinical, Neuro and Developmental Psychology, Amsterdam Public Health Research Institute, Vrije Universiteit Amsterdam
Babes-Bolyai University, International Institute for Psychotherapy

Kim de Jong, PhD
Institute of Psychology, Leiden University

Jaime Delgadillo, PhD
Clinical and Applied Psychology Unit, Department of Psychology, University of Sheffield

A. C. Del Re, PhD
Department of Psychology, University of Kassel

Tohar Dolev-Amit, PhD
Department of Psychology, University of Haifa

Changming Duan, PhD
Department of Educational Psychology, University of Kansas

Robert Elliott, PhD
School of Psychological Sciences & Health, University of Strathclyde
Department of Psychology, University of Toledo

Catherine F. Eubanks, PhD
Gordon F. Derner School of Psychology, Adelphi University
Mount Sinai Beth Israel Psychotherapy Research Program, Icahn School of Medicine at Mount Sinai

Iony D. Ezawa, PhD
Department of Psychology, University of Southern California

Barry A. Farber, PhD
Program in Clinical Psychology, Teachers College, Columbia University

Hadar Fisher, PhD
Department of Psychology, University of Haifa

Christoph Flückiger, PhD
Department of Psychology, University of Kassel

Robert Freund, PhD
Department of Clinical Mental Health Counseling, Lynn University

Simon B. Goldberg, PhD
Department of Counseling Psychology, University of Wisconsin–Madison

Mathias Harrer, MSc
Technical University of Munich
Clinical Psychology and Psychotherapy, Friedrich-Alexander-University

Clara E. Hill, PhD
Department of Psychology, University of Maryland at College Park

Steven D. Hollon, PhD
Department of Psychology, Vanderbilt University

Zac E. Imel, PhD
Department of Educational Psychology, University of Utah

Shigeru Iwakabe, PhD
Department of Psychology, Ritsumeikan University

Jan H. Kamphuis, PhD
Department of Psychology, University of Amsterdam

Eirini Karyotaki
Department of Clinical, Neuro and Developmental Psychology, Amsterdam Public Health Research Institute, Vrije Universiteit Amsterdam

Nikolaos Kazantzis, BA (Hons), MA, PGDipClinPsych, PhD, FAPS, BICBT-CC
Cognitive Behavior Therapy Research Unit (Melbourne, Australia)
Beck Institute for Cognitive Behavior Therapy

John R. Keefe, PhD
Department of Psychiatry and Behavioral Sciences, Albert Einstein School of Medicine

D. Martin Kivlighan, III, PhD
Department of Psychological and Quantitative Foundations, University of Iowa

Sarah Knox, PhD
Department of Counselor Education & Counseling Psychology, Marquette University

Dale G. Larson, PhD
School of Education and Counseling Psychology, Santa Clara University

Heidi M. Levitt, PhD
Department of Psychology, University of Massachusetts Boston

Ailun Li, BS
Department of Psychology, Idaho State University

Wolfgang Lutz, PhD
Department of Psychology, University of Trier

Linda M. McMullen, PhD
Department of Psychology, University of Saskatchewan

Zenobia Morrill, PhD
Clinical Psychology Department, William James College

Thomas Munder, PhD
Department of Psychology, University of Zurich

Peter Muntigl, PhD
Department of Translation, Interpreting and Communication, University of Ghent
Faculty of Education, Simon Fraser University

J. Christopher Muran
Gordon F. Derner School of Psychology, Adelphi University
Mount Sinai Beth Israel Psychotherapy Research Program, Icahn School of Medicine at Mount Sinai

Kaori Nakamura, PhD
Faculty of Core Research, Ochanomizu University

John C. Norcross, PhD, ABPP
Department of Psychology, University of Scranton
Department of Psychiatry, SUNY Upstate Medical University

James C. Overholser, PhD, ABPP
Department of Psychology, Case Western Reserve University

Antonio Pascual-Leone, PhD
Department of Psychology, University of Windsor
Department of Psychiatry, University of Lausanne

Adar Paz, MA
Department of Psychology, Bar-Ilan University

Paul R. Peluso, PhD
Department of Counselor Education, Florida Atlantic University

Elizabeth A. Penix, MS
Department of Psychology, Idaho State University

Truls Ryum, PhD
Department of Psychology, Norwegian University of Science and Technology

Wonjin Sim
Department of Psychology, Towson University

Olga Smoliak, PhD
Department of Family Relations & Applied Nutrition, University of Guelph

Nili Solomonov, PhD
Institute of Geriatric Psychiatry, Weill Cornell Medicine

Christina S. Soma, PhD
Department of Educational Psychology, University of Utah

Patricia T. Spangler, PhD
Center for the Study of Traumatic Stress (CSTS), Contractor, Henry Jackson Foundation, under contract to CSTS
Department of Psychiatry, Uniformed Services University

Yvonne Stikkelbroek
Depression Expertise Centre-Youth, GGZ Oost Brabant
Department of Clinical Child and Family Studies, Faculty of Social and Behavioral Sciences, Utrecht University

Shannon L. Stuart-Maver, MA
Student Health and Counseling Services, University California, Davis

Joshua K. Swift, PhD
Department of Psychology, Idaho State University

Dennis Tay, PhD
Department of English and Communication, The Hong Kong Polytechnic University

Nathan C. Thoma, PhD
Department of Psychiatry, Weill Cornell Medical College

Arnold A. P. van Emmerik, PhD
Department of Psychology, University of Amsterdam

Carlijn J. M. Wibbelink, MSC
Department of Psychology, University of Amsterdam

Elizabeth Nutt Williams, PhD
Department of Psychology, St. Mary's College of Maryland

Xinyao Zhang, MA
Department of Educational Psychology, University of Utah

Sigal Zilcha-Mano, PhD
Department of Psychology, University of Haifa

1

Introduction to Psychotherapy Skills and Methods That Work

Clara E. Hill, John C. Norcross, and the Steering Committee

Imagine yourself sitting in a session with a psychotherapist. Of course, you want to feel safe in that setting, respect the therapist, enjoy a strong relationship, agree on treatment goals, and feel motivated to do the work. All well and good, and all predictive of and contributing to your eventual treatment success. But you also want the psychotherapist to *do* something to help you. It would rarely suffice for them to be only a nice, warm, real person (and even at that, they have to do something to make you think they are nice, warm, and real). You would probably want them to assess, listen, reflect, advise, interpret, support, challenge your irrational thoughts, be responsive to your cultural identities, provide new perspectives, offer feedback, teach you skills, or collaborate on between-session tasks.

Mental health professionals undergo extensive training and supervision to learn how to use these helping skills and methods. Students in doctoral health care psychology programs in the United States take an average of 6 years to complete their degree, accruing about 500 to 1,000 clinical hours pre-internship, 2,000 clinical hours during internship, and another 1,500+ postdoctoral hours before being licensed to practice independently. And many countries (e.g., England) require continued supervision throughout clinicians' careers. It could be that it takes that long for therapists to don the mantle of professionalism and come to believe that they have something credible to offer, and it could be the belief rather than the specific skills/methods used that matter (Frank & Frank, 1991). But trainers clearly believe they can teach mental health trainees how to *do* psychotherapy and become more effective over time (Hill et al., 2017).

The main thesis of this book is that skills and methods contribute substantially to the outcome of psychotherapy *in addition to* many other elements, such as the client, the therapist, their relationship, and external pressures. What therapists *do* makes a meaningful difference, although there are often a number of skills and methods that might prove helpful or hindering in any given situation. It is our hope that this book helps therapists implement skills and methods in a way that optimizes psychotherapy outcomes.

Whereas there is considerable research evidence for the overall effectiveness of psychotherapy (Wampold & Imel, 2015) and for the association between a strong therapeutic relationship and positive outcome (Norcross & Lambert, 2019), there is, surprisingly, less empirical support for the effectiveness of specific therapist skills and methods. In this volume, we strive to redress that deficiency by focusing on skills and methods that can be used across theoretical perspectives.

Clara E. Hill, John C. Norcross, and the Steering Committee, *Introduction to Psychotherapy Skills and Methods That Work*
In: *Psychotherapy Skills and Methods That Work*. Edited by: Clara E. Hill and John C. Norcross, Oxford University Press.
 DOI: 10.1093/oso/9780197611012.003.0001

We argue that the lack of research support is partially attributable to methodological pitfalls in the research endeavor, in that we have not developed adequate methods for studying the complexity and individuality of the therapeutic process. In addition, the dearth of research evidence for specific skills and methods is partially attributable to organizational and funding priorities that privilege investigating omnibus treatment approaches/packages for particular disorders rather than studying skills and methods. We suggest that now is a good time to step back and assess what we do and do not know and make recommendations for the future.

In this chapter, we begin by weighing in on the debates about what accounts for change in psychotherapy, namely whether it is the treatment approach, the relationship, characteristics of the therapist, characteristics of the client/patient, therapist responsiveness to client/patient needs, or client expectations that account for client outcomes. We then define and contextualize therapist skills and methods, especially in regard to other components of psychotherapy. Next, we take a deeper dive into how skills and methods are assessed, how outcomes (immediate in-session, intermediate, and distal) are assessed, how to link skills and methods with outcomes, and how to summarize the extant research on those skills and methods. Such research summaries naturally and ideally generate evidence-based therapeutic practices, which end all subsequent chapters in this volume. We conclude by outlining the purpose and process of the interorganizational Task Force that guides this book.

What Accounts for Change in Psychotherapy?

Multiple variables obviously contribute to change in psychotherapy: the therapy approach or package, treatment methods, the therapeutic relationship, the client, the clinician, external factors, common factors across approaches, and the context. The question is how much of the outcome variance is accounted for by each, a question that is difficult to answer given the complexity of the change process, the specific and unique nature of each course of psychotherapy, and our disinclination to focus on more than a single factor or two. Thus begat the debates about what accounts for change in psychotherapy. As asked by Norcross and Lambert (2019, p. 1), "Do treatments cure disorders, or do relationships heal people? Which is the most accurate version for practicing, researchers, and teaching psychotherapy?"

Medical Model (It's the Treatment Approach That Matters)

Probably the loudest and certainly the best-funded voice (the received view) has been from advocates of specific treatment packages, typically for specific disorders. They assert that the critical factor is the treatment itself, as researched in randomized clinical/controlled trials (RCTs). In the past, the vast majority of external funding for psychotherapy research has favored examining treatment packages for specific diagnoses (e.g., depression, anxiety), in part because of the need to demonstrate that psychotherapy works and that psychotherapists deserve reimbursement like other health care providers. Whether advocates are leading this charge intentionally or are following a system that requires a "gold standard" method in the form of a specific treatment packages is arguable (David & Cristea, 2018).

As evidence for this side, we have thousands of studies and hundreds of meta-analyses yielding evidence that psychotherapy in general is more effective than wait-list controls or no-treatment. Treatment package adherents have compiled and published lists of what were initially called *empirically validated psychotherapies*, later termed *empirically supported*, and are now called *evidence-based treatments* (Nathan & Gorman, 2015; Norcross et al., 2017). These lists are heavily weighted in favor of cognitive and behavioral treatments, probably because those approaches are brief, manualized, and lend themselves to behavioral assessments. Advantages of the treatment–medical model are that it fits with the biomedical model, aligns with most reimbursement demands, and is relatively clear-cut—that is, if the patient has such and such a disorder, provide such and such a treatment from the designated list.

But manifest limitations of this approach have been documented. First, there is minimal evidence for the specificity or superiority of the designated evidence-based psychotherapies for specific disorders (Wampold & Imel, 2015). Effect size differences between bona fide treatments conducted by competent therapists and containing a solid rationale are quite small (maximum of 0.20; Wampold & Imel, 2015), although perhaps still important (Lilienfeld, 2014). Second, a major methodological and interpretative problem of this approach is that the packages are large and multifaceted, involving a multitude of skills, methods, common factors, and relationship factors. Psychotherapists touting the efficacy of a particular treatment package rarely know what actually leads to therapeutic success. Third, rarely are the components of these treatment packages tested separately (i.e., dismantled), and most existing dismantling studies are seriously underpowered (Barkham & Lambert, 2021). And when they are tested separately, the proclaimed mechanism of change often ends up not being the core or necessary mechanism at all. Recent dismantling studies in cognitive restructuring (see Chapter 22), for example, reveal that neither of the putative essential methods routinely outperformed other methods.

Relationship Model (It's the Therapy Relationship That Matters)

Over the years, many have challenged the overreliance on the treatment approach, but perhaps the tipping point was the massive research evidence compiled by three task forces on the therapeutic relationship as a key healing component of psychotherapy. The product of these task forces was three editions of *Psychotherapy Relationships That Work* (Norcross, 2002, 2011; Norcross & Lambert, 2019; Norcross & Wampold, 2019). Evidence from this approach comes primarily from correlational process–outcome studies, rather than RCTs. Original meta-analyses provided considerable correlational evidence that relationship components (e.g., alliance, empathy) are robustly albeit moderately related to, and predictive of, treatment outcome. For example, a meta-analysis of 295 studies with more than 30,000 patients yielded a robust alliance–outcome association of 0.28 ($d = 0.57$; Flückiger et al., 2018). All told, relationship factors have been estimated to account for at least 15% to 20% of outcome variance (Norcross & Lambert, 2019), although it is not exactly clear how this estimate has been derived.

An advantage of this approach is that it validates the experience of many clients and therapists that the relationship is the most important component of treatment. A major limitation of the relationship model is that what constitutes the relationship is vague and largely subjective. Relationship factors are typically measured via self-report measures after sessions and thus are often confounded with the skills and methods, the client, client progress, and halo effects (Barber, 2009). In addition, measures of the relationship, such as empathy, often are conflated with and intermingle the effects of client, therapist, and relationship. And, of course, correlations cannot be interpreted as revealing causal effects, although mediation analyses (e.g., skills as mediated by changes in alliance in relation to outcome) and within-patient analyses (changes across times within patients) hold the possibility of getting us closer to causality (Crits-Christoph & Gibbons, 2021).

Client/Patient Factors (It's the Client/Patient That Matters)

In parallel, some researchers (Wampold & Imel, 2015) and theorists (e.g., Bohart & Tallman, 1999; Fuertes, 2022) have argued that clients are responsible for the lion's share of psychotherapy success (and failure). Such patient factors include motivation, disorder severity, psychological mindedness, functional impairment, expectancies, reactance level, attachment style, and readiness to change/stage of change. Of course, it makes sense that client factors are of major importance given that it is ultimately the clients who make the changes in their lives. In some ways, psychotherapy constitutes professionally coached client change (Goldfried & Davison, 1994). Research estimates place the client contribution to outcome at about 30% (Norcross & Lambert, 2019).

An advantage of this perspective is it shifts the focus to what we know about clients rather than blaming therapists for not having the perfect treatments. It also shifts the focus from seeing clients as passive recipients of treatments to seeing them as active agents of change. A major limitation, however, is that many of these client factors are static, largely beyond the immediate reach or influence of practitioners. Knowing that a client suffers from a chronic psychotic disorder or is in the precontemplation stage of change does not necessarily translate directly into prescriptive knowledge of which skills, methods, or treatments to use with them. Patients' trait-like characteristics cannot function as a mechanism of change, and without knowing the specific change mechanisms, we cannot adequately treat patients.

We highlight the impact of expectancies, hopes, and beliefs. These expectancies involve positive treatment expectations, a credible and socially sanctioned practitioner, the effort to attend and commit to therapy, and the multicomponent "placebo effect" (Benish et al., 2011; Evers et al., 2021; Wampold & Budge, 2012; Wampold et al., 2005). Careful research finds that treatment credibility (Constantino, Coyne et al., 2019) and positive outcome expectations (Constantino, Visla et al., 2019) do reliably predict, in a modest way, psychotherapy success. One estimate is that expectancy (placebo effect) accounts for 15% of the variance of improvement in psychotherapy (Norcross & Lambert, 2019). An advantage of this view is that it provides a target for clinician focus—cultivating positive expectations, enhancing therapist credibility, and leveraging realistic hope. A limitation is that the specific ways to capitalize on client expectations and hope are not yet well understood.

Therapist Effects (It's the Person of the Therapist That Matters)

Therapist effects are generally thought to account for about 5% to 8% of the variance in client outcomes, and these effects seem to be more pronounced with clients who are more challenging and distressed (Barkham et al., 2017). In other words, some therapists consistently achieve better client outcomes than others and better outcomes with some clients than others (Constantino et al., 2021). Although the amount of variance attributable to therapists is considerably smaller than that attributable to clients (recall again that patients are the ones who make the changes), it appears that therapists do indeed make a difference.

As noted above under client/patient factors, therapist expectancies can also influence therapist behaviors. Frank and Frank (1991) made a compelling argument that it is not so much what the therapist does that matters, but the therapist's belief—and corresponding client belief—in what they are doing. "Belief," as said in the film *A Monster Calls* (Bayona, 2016), "is half the cure."

An advantage of recognizing the therapist's contribution to outcome variance is that it recognizes the power of the individual therapist and, at the same time, positions the therapist as a relatively minor contribution. In addition, we can train people in the helping skills (e.g., Hill, 2020). A major limitation is that knowing there are therapist effects tells us little about what it is about therapists or what therapists do that matters. We still need to know what it is about the therapists that is more or less effective. Several possibilities present themselves: clinical experience, personality characteristics (e.g., attachment style, openness, flexibility), technical skills, relational abilities, cultural awareness, responsiveness to client needs, attentiveness to inner experiences, reflection about one's clinical work, and deliberate practice, but the evidence for all these remains elusive (Castonguay & Hill, 2017).

Personalizing (It's Responsiveness That Matters)

In this perspective, what matters is the therapist's responsiveness to the individual client—in the moment, session to session, or overall treatment. Different clients need and prefer different things at different times (Norcross & Cooper, 2021; Stiles et al., in press; Stiles & Horvath, 2017). As Frank and Frank (1991, p. xv) argued, "This position implies that ideally therapists should select for each patient the therapy that accords, or can be brought to accord, with the patient's personal characteristics and view of the problem."

The meta-analytic results for matching or personalizing psychotherapy to the transdiagnostic features of the patient have proven quite strong, more powerful on average than the effect sizes for the therapeutic relationship and therapist contribution and as powerful as the patient contribution (Norcross & Wampold, 2019). Among the effective ways to personalize the overall treatment is to tailor to clients' cultural identities, religious/spiritual commitments, strong preferences, reactance level, stage of change/readiness to change, and coping style (Norcross & Wampold, 2019). Furthermore, when the client loses motivation for treatment, to take an example of moment-to-moment personalizing, the therapist can try motivational interviewing skills to increase the client's motivation; or, when a rupture occurs, the therapist can use immediacy skills to repair the rupture (Constantino et al., in press).

The advantage of this personalizing or responsiveness is that it provides research-based evidence for psychotherapists to offer the best care when different situations arise and for particular patients. A limitation is that it does not take into account therapist personality and competence in delivering multiple in-session styles or various treatment packages. And unfortunately, we know of no reliable research estimating the percentage of outcome variance accounted for by therapist responsiveness (which would parallel the percentage figures provided in the other sections in this chapter).

Therapist Skills and Methods (It's What Therapists *Do* That Matters)

From this perspective, therapist skills (e.g., effective use of questions and interpretations) and methods (e.g., effective use of cognitive restructuring and role induction) matter, although in a complicated and nuanced interaction with therapist effects, client contributions, the therapeutic relationship, and evolving responsiveness (Hill, 2005; Gelso, 2005). As frequently lamented by psychotherapy trainees, what contributes to psychotherapy effectiveness "is messy"—it's a bunch of interdependent and iterative components. But the common denominator and sine qua non of all the perspectives on what accounts for psychotherapy outcome is that the therapist *does* something—skills and methods. There is no psychotherapy without therapist behavior; it is consequential and essential to the enterprise.

The effects of the hundreds of therapist skills and methods on psychotherapy outcome are admittedly complicated. As noted previously, skills and methods are not used in isolation but, rather, build on what has gone before. For example, therapists try to establish a working relationship and have clients explore before they move to action (Hill, 2020). That initial action or behavior change must then be maintained over time and generalized to other life situations. Furthermore, a variety of skills and methods can work at any given time, although all might lead to slightly different outcomes.

These skills and methods not only exert immediate impacts on session process but also interact with other skills and methods as well as extra-therapy experiences to influence more distal outcomes. These skills and methods are impacted by and impact other components of the psychotherapy process (and life outside of psychotherapy) such that it is difficult to tease out their unique contribution. It is, however, possible to study their impact if we remain aware of the complexity and interrelatedness of the multiple components of psychotherapy.

One cardinal advantage of this perspective is that we can disentangle the relative contribution of therapist behaviors if we can construct research paradigms and analytic methods for capturing the complexity of psychotherapy. Another advantage is that such research can direct practitioners in what to offer their patients and faculty in what to train their students. The major limitation is that such research is more complex and strains our current abilities; we hope to start the conversation about future research directions in this book.

Conceptualizing Therapist Skills and Methods

We conceptualize the overt behaviors of psychotherapists as occurring at four nested levels of abstraction. At the macro level are brand-name *treatment approaches* (or packages or theoretical orientations), such as psychodynamic, cognitive, experiential, and systemic. These psychotherapy systems or treatment packages are large and multifaceted, involving a multitude of skills and methods often applied by therapists in idiosyncratic ways. Although these overall approaches share some common factors (e.g., the therapeutic relationship, a credible rationale; Frank & Frank, 1991; Wampold & Imel, 2015), they also have some skills and methods that differentiate them (Blagys & Hilsenroth, 2000, 2002). Therapists generally identify with one or more theoretical approaches, with most mental health professionals integrating across orientations (Norcross & Goldfried, 2019).

At a second level of abstraction, between global theories and specific methods, are *change principles or processes*. Examples include raising awareness and counterconditioning, principles that cut across treatment packages. It is at this intermediate level that meaningful points of convergence are probably found among psychotherapy systems—such as enhancing the patient's awareness of the problem or defenses and teaching them skills that counter or inhibit the problem (Castonguay et al., 2019; Goldfried, 1980; Prochaska & Norcross, 2018). Indeed, some maintain that we should be teaching change principles, as opposed to global theoretical orientations (Castonguay et al., 2019).

At the next level of abstraction are *psychotherapy methods*, such as chair work, cognitive restructuring, dream work, and teaching mindfulness. (These have also been characterized as *techniques*, but we avoid that term here because it has also been used to characterize entire treatment packages.) Although methods were typically developed within a certain theoretical framework (e.g., relaxation within behavior therapy), they can be used pragmatically by therapists of all theoretical orientations to address specific client concerns; for instance, a cognitive–behavioral therapist might use an experiential exercise to arouse emotions and a psychodynamic therapist might teach relaxation or mindfulness to help the client manage their anxiety. These methods sometimes involve a well-defined sequence of steps; for instance, in dream work where therapists facilitate the exploration of individual images, help the client gain insight into the whole dream, and then encourage action through changing the dream and bridging the changes to waking life (Hill, 2004; see also Chapter 19, this volume). Other methods, such as strengths-based methods, involve a more flexible implementation of a variety of possible skills, depending on the client needs at the time.

At the micro level of abstraction are relatively discrete *therapist or helping skills*, such as reflections of feelings, interpretations, and immediacy. Therapists use skills (sometimes also called *verbal response modes*) to respond to or direct the client's behavior in the moment in sessions. These skills are readily taught, as is evident from the number of mental health training programs in existence (e.g., Carkhuff, 1969; Hill, 2020; Ivey et al., 2017) and from the evidence for the effectiveness of these training programs

Table 1.1 Four Levels of Overt Therapist Behavior

Level	Abstraction	Examples
High	Treatment packages/ theoretical orientations	Psychodynamic, cognitive–behavioral, experiential, systemic
High–medium	Change principles/processes	Consciousness raising, commitment, counterconditioning
Medium	Methods	Interpretation, behavioral activation, chair work, paradoxical intervention
Low	Skills	Questions, empathic reflections, affirmations, metaphors

(Knox & Hill, 2021). These skills are sometimes packaged into methods, but often they are used more loosely to accomplish specific goals/intentions for how the therapist wants the client to respond in the moment (e.g., express feeling, gain insight, practice new behavior).

Hence, in a complementary and hierarchical fashion, skills are nested within methods, which are in turn embedded within change principles or processes, which are embedded within treatment approaches or packages. Table 1.1 summarizes these four levels of overt therapist behaviors. Therapists behave at any given moment in terms of their overall treatment approach, their principles about what will promote change, their methods, and their moment-to-moment skills. Ideally, theory about the specific mechanism of change leads to the selection of methods and skills to help the client.

A clarification of import: Therapist methods and skills are frequently and erroneously conflated with entire treatment packages or psychotherapy systems. We have characterized this error as the *exclusivity myth* in psychotherapy—that certain processes or methods are the exclusive properties of particular therapy approaches (Norcross, 1995). We should, of course, acknowledge the theoretical origins of any given method, but all skills and methods as we have defined them can be effectively applied across theoretical approaches. No particular therapist and no single theory—integrative or otherwise—owns any particular therapist method or skill. They are decidedly pantheoretical and transdiagnostic.

A second clarification: In the preceding section, we have alluded only to the occurrence of therapists' behaviors at the four levels but have not considered competence. Clearly, it is not just whether a therapist behavior occurs but also how effectively it was implemented according to different perspectives (therapist, client, significant other, external judge).

Assessing Skills and Methods

Psychotherapist skills and methods have been assessed using a variety of approaches in research and training. The most frequent approaches are (a) overall estimates by trained judges of verbal response modes (and other skills) used within sessions; (b) quantitative ratings by therapists and clients of in-session behaviors via post-session or post-treatment report, or coding in in-session behaviors by trained judges/raters observing the video recording of sessions; (c) qualitative assessments of skills and methods; and (d) open-ended interviews of participants about the skills/methods. Here, we describe each approach and note their respective advantages and disadvantages.

Coding by Trained Judges of Verbal Response Modes

Starting soon after the invention of recording machines, coding systems were developed for counting therapist verbal response modes. A notable early example was Snyder's (1945) system for categorizing therapist and client behaviors into verbal response modes (VRMs), with more recent versions having been developed by Hill (1978, 2020) and Stiles (1979). These systems typically rely on trained judges coding VRMs in response units (e.g., grammatical sentences) from transcripts or videos of psychotherapy sessions. Some consistency has been found among category systems, indicating that a few VRMs can be reliably identified (Elliott et al., 1987).

An example comes from analyses of the well-known *Three Approaches to Psychotherapy* film series, popularly known as the Gloria films, which have been content analyzed for specific VRMS, such as minimal encouragers, questions, guidances, and interpretations. For example, Hill et al. (1979) found that Rogers used more restatements than did either Perls or Ellis (11% vs. 5% and 5%), whereas Ellis used more information than did either Perls or Rogers (30% vs. 12% and 7%).

An advantage of this approach is that the VRMs can be identified in sessions from watching videotapes or reading transcripts. Another advantage is that we know which skills "actually" transpired in sessions, as opposed to the distortions of subjective recall or self-report. A disadvantage is the reliance on overt behaviors rather than inner reactions. In addition, although it seems relatively straightforward to code therapist behaviors into a few discrete categories, an incredible number of skills fall into gray areas that prove difficult to judge. For example, "Are you sure?" is grammatically a closed question, but it might serve as a reflection or as a challenge. Moreover, each skill can be divided into multiple subcategories, which may exert differing effects. Consider that immediacy (i.e., talking in the here-and-now about the therapeutic relationship), for instance, can be used to establish a relationship, challenge the client, or repair a rupture; questions can be used to gather facts, explore thoughts or feelings, probe for insight, or probe for action ideas.

Compounding the complexity is that each therapist employs these skills in an individualized, probably idiosyncratic manner, such that there is no standardized VRM. Some therapists ask closed questions in a way that is inviting, whereas others ask in a clipped interview-like manner; some have a tentative tone to everything they say, whereas others most often make declarative statements. These individual differences and the complexity of psychotherapy make it difficult to collapse skills into a few categories; however, having too many response categories with only a few instances in some of the categories makes for difficulties in data analysis. As is perhaps not surprising, this approach is time- and labor-intensive (e.g., multiple judges are needed given relatively low agreement levels among judges). That leads to challenges in gathering sufficient data for analyses, particularly when nesting VRMs within sessions within clients within therapists within settings.

Retrospective Reports of In-Session Behaviors

Therapist skills and methods have frequently been assessed through post-session reports. Notable pantheoretical measures include the Comparative Psychotherapy Process Scale (Hilsenroth et al., 2005), the Multitheoretical List of Therapeutic Interventions (McCarthy & Barber, 2009), the Helping Skills Measure (Hill & Kellems, 2002), and the Psychotherapy Q-Set (Jones & Pulos, 1993). On these measures, clients, therapists, or trained judges estimate how often or how well the skills were used within a given session or treatment.

A major research advantage of post-session measurement is the ease of data collection—administration requires only a few minutes after a session or treatment. The patient's lived experience of psychotherapy is quickly captured; how they felt and responded to therapist behaviors. In addition, the results can easily be correlated with other post-session measures (e.g., of the therapeutic relationship) and with treatment outcome (e.g., changes in symptomatology), using sophisticated statistical methods such as multilevel modeling, structural equation modeling, and moderation/mediation analyses (Crits-Christoph & Gibbons, 2021).

Unfortunately, these retrospective ratings are often impressionistic summaries (halo effects) about what transpired across the entire session (e.g., how much therapist interpretation one estimates depends on a subjective judgment of how much is desired) rather than documentable records of what actually occurred. Some clients provide completely positive or negative ratings on post-session measures because they liked or disliked their therapist. Our own experience as psychotherapists completing these measures is that they prove valuable in gauging the patient's overall response, but that it is incredibly challenging to estimate how much or how well skills were used. Ratings of specific behaviors immediately after the session blur together, and memory is notoriously biased. Thus, although these measures provide a clear rating or number that can easily be statistically analyzed, they do not provide valid identification of skills nor do they link each skill with its specific consequences (e.g., assessing the effect of the therapist interpreting transference in a specific in-session moment).

Qualitative Assessments of Skills and Methods

Trained judges can observe sessions and conduct qualitative analyses of specific skills. For example, using a large team of trained judges, Hill and colleagues (2022) identified all therapist challenges in the initial, middle, and final sessions of one case. For each identified challenge, the researchers consensually assessed the type, manner of delivery, quality, and intent of the antecedents, challenge event, and consequences; they then aggregated across events to summarize when and why challenges were effective.

Advantages of this approach are that researchers can focus on one skill at a time within a given case and include multiple perspectives on the research team. Another plus is possessing multiple clinical judgments about the dynamics of the case, much as is done in case conferences, but with the advantage of having considerable data from the therapist and client. Disadvantages are the time-intensive nature of the process and the likelihood of clinical and theoretical biases.

Open-Ended Interviews of Participants

Clients and clinicians can be interviewed and asked to identify specific therapist skills or methods. For example, Knox and associates (1997) interviewed clients about their memories of salient therapist self-disclosures. These interviews are then typically analyzed utilizing rigorous qualitative approaches, such as critical–constructivist grounded theory (Levitt, 2021), descriptive–interpretive qualitative research (Elliott & Timulak, 2021), or consensual qualitative research (CQR; Hill & Knox, 2021).

An advantage of this approach is that therapists and clients are the ones who identify and locate the skill or method, so we know it registered with them. By contrast, even if the method appeared in a session transcript or in a video to an external observer, there is no guarantee that the client heard or absorbed it. Disadvantages are that interviews are often conducted long after the sessions were conducted; perspectives are thus altered by what occurred later in the session or after the treatment. It also often proves difficult to link the event described in the post-session interview with transcripts of what happened overtly in the session. For some participants, it is also challenging to know and articulate what they were experiencing at the time; in fact, the very process of talking about the events frequently alters their perceptions of the events (reactivity).

Overall Considerations

The different approaches to assessing therapist skills and methods likely yield quite different results, although few studies have tested this question empirically. In one study, a disturbingly low correlation was found between judge-rated post-session measures of therapists' skills and judges' coding of actual skills (VRMs) used within sessions (Heaton et al., 1995). These findings suggest that disparate results might emanate from differing measures and perspectives, raising concerns about validity and generalizability. Such cross-measure studies are difficult to conduct, and there is minimal payoff in our field for conducting such methodological studies given that they are not exciting and do not report on treatment outcomes.

One major unresolved question is whether to measure simply the presence of a therapist skill or method or to measure its quality or competence. Assessing presence is relatively easy (although we still do not obtain high levels of agreement), but assessing intensity, quality, or competence requires considerable clinical judgment and is prone to subjectivity. For example, theoretical orientation or personal preference might predispose judges to be critical about the quality of a given skill or method.

Determining the best approach for assessing therapist skill or method depends on the purpose of the study. If the purpose is to offer a broad-stroke estimate of what therapists did in sessions (e.g., comparing psychodynamic and cognitive–behavior therapies), then post-session measurement is probably adequate. But if the purpose concerns the effectiveness of the particular skills/methods, as is the purpose of this book, then we need a valid identification of the actual occurrence of the skill or method within the session. That way we can observe the context/antecedents and immediate client outcomes of the skill or method.

A final issue relates to reliability of judgments. Although most journals require evidence of the reliability of judgments, many researchers have experienced problems with requiring interrater reliability as a prerequisite for publication. Many of the behaviors that occur in psychotherapy fall into gray areas outside of well-defined categories. By insisting on high levels of reliability, judges must rely on very obvious observable cues and guess what other raters will think, rather than using their clinical wisdom to consider context, intention, and multiple interpretations. Within the qualitative research tradition, it is well known that multiple perspectives and the opportunity to talk over perceptions on the research team yield more valid data (Knox & Hill, 2020).

For this and additional reasons, we have evolved (across decades of conducting this genre of research) a definite, step-by-step approach to identifying and coding therapist skills and methods (Hill & Knox, 2021). A large team of trained judges watches the videotape of a session until a possible event emerges. They stop the video and each team member independently identifies what the skill was (and perhaps the quality or competence with which it was presented). They then discuss at length to arrive at a consensus judgment about the skill. This approach, in our experience, yields more clinically useful and consensually reliable data. As a bonus, it also proves more enjoyable for the judges.

Assessing *Outcomes* of Skills and Methods

Now we transition from assessing therapist skills and methods to assessing the effectiveness (or outcomes) of these skills and methods. But a basic question here, of course, is what we mean by "works" when we say psychotherapy skills and methods that work. What "works" is too binary for the complexity of psychotherapy as well as for the demands for specificity—what works for individual patients in singular situations.

Psychotherapy outcomes are, fundamentally, of three sorts: (a) proximal or immediate in-session outcomes (e.g., client's immediate response to a specific skill or method), (b) intermediate post-session or between sessions (e.g., client's appraisal of or satisfaction with an entire session, amount of homework completed, or ratings of completing homework at the beginning of subsequent sessions), and (c) distal end-of-treatment outcomes (e.g., changes in a client's symptoms or interpersonal functioning). Most practitioners and researchers would agree that all three types of outcomes are crucial and should be assessed (in some fashion), but they rarely are all assessed in the same research study. When they are, they frequently yield different effects (see Hill et al., 1988). Perspectives change over time given intervening events, so that follow-up results are often different than distal end-of-therapy results. And obviously, the different types of outcomes build on each other: An accumulation of immediate effects is associated with session-by-session effectiveness, which leads to more distal outcomes (although not typically in a direct or linear way).

Proximal or Immediate In-Session Outcomes

Immediate outcomes (or impacts) include the client response to the therapist skill or method as it occurs in a given session. This outcome is similar to clinicians observing how clients respond in the immediate moment to the therapist's intervention. Similarly, Basch (1980), a psychoanalyst, noted that the outcome of a good interpretation should be whether clients subsequently bring up new material (e.g., memories) that indicate that they have gained insight into their problems.

In the literature, immediate outcomes have most often been assessed by having trained judges code or rate some client observable behavior. For example, Town and associates (2012) studied clients' affect following therapists' use of confrontation, clarification, support, questions, self-disclosure, and information. For investigating the immediate effects of open questions, closed questions, restatements, and reflections of feelings, Anvari and colleagues (2020, 2022) examined changes in depth of affective exploration and depth of cognitive exploration. Prass and colleagues (2021) and Liposky and colleagues (in press) chose the outcome of changes in client collaboration. More recently, biomarkers are being used to assess physiological responses within session (see Chapter 19, this volume). Thus, there might be different immediate outcomes depending on the goals and intents of the particular skill or method. An advantage of this approach is that consistent criteria and consistent units of time (e.g., the first two client sentences, a 3-minute window after the skill occurs) can be used by judges across clients.

A second method (which can be termed immediate delayed) has been to have clients or therapists observe a recording of the session (when the session is fresh in their memory and not diluted by intervening events) and rate the helpfulness of each therapist speaking turn (e.g., "How helpful was this speaking turn?"). An advantage of this method is that the perceptions of the participants (the "insiders") can be obtained; a disadvantage is that these ratings are retrospective and thus susceptible to the influence of what came after the event in the session (e.g., if there was a rupture later, the patient would probably rate the event as less helpful).

A methodological choice arises in determining the optimal unit to assess the immediate consequences. One can look for the client response in the next sentence, the next speaking turn, the next 3-minute window, or the remainder of the session. Of course, we know that not all responses are exhibited immediately and vary across clients and situations. One esteemed colleague gave an example of how he finally understood an interpretation 25 years after it was delivered. Yet, for both practice and research, we need to connect the patient response to the specific skill or method—to determine what "works." If we use the remainder of the session as the unit, then the client could well be responding to something other than the designated skill or method. To be completely accurate, we would need access to the client's inner experience, and even that would change as they reflected on the skill/method over time.

The prime advantage of assessing immediate outcome is that a temporal link can be made between the skill/method and the outcome. We can then determine which therapist behaviors are associated with which client responses. The disadvantage is that it is time-intensive and costly to assess outcome this way, and the direct link is confounded by all the events that have occurred previously in the treatment (e.g., the outcome of a challenge probably depends on its timing and whether a positive relationship has been established). In addition, outcomes might be delayed rather than immediate (clients might initially not express a reaction but later say something), or outcomes could change over time (e.g., a therapist challenge might initially hurt, but the client might later realize its value). Finally, immediate outcomes might vary across client diagnoses and personality characteristics.

Intermediate Outcomes

Intermediate outcomes are typically assessed through ratings provided after sessions, between sessions, or before the next session. These outcomes can be assessed by clients, therapists, or trained judges using standardized, psychometrically sound questionnaires. Some typical post-session measures include the Session Rating Scale (Miller et al., 2005), the Working Alliance Inventory (Horvath & Greenberg, 1989), and the Session Evaluation Scale (Hill & Kellems, 2002). These assessments are typically evaluative and indicate overall session satisfaction. The outcome ratings reflect not only the personality and perspective of the evaluator but also a judgment of all that has transpired in treatment before and events outside of the psychotherapy. Between-session measures include behavioral recordings of homework. Session-to-session outcomes include client ratings on the Outcome Rating Scale (Miller & Duncan, 2000) at the beginning of sessions.

An advantage of using intermediate measures is their relative ease of administration and minimal intrusion into the therapy process. Practitioners also typically profit from obtaining session-level feedback from their clients, such as in routine outcome monitoring (see Chapter 15, this volume). A disadvantage is the inability for researchers to directly link specific skills or methods with intermediate outcomes. What therapists did a week or two ago does not easily or causally connect to patient success (or failure) this week.

Distal Post-Treatment Outcomes

Post-treatment outcomes are typically assessed through clients completing standardized, psychometrically sound self-report measures before beginning psychotherapy and then again at its completion. Examples of such distal measures include the Beck Depression Inventory (Beck et al., 1961), dozens of self-report symptom measures, and the Complementary Measure of Psychotherapy Outcome (Chui et al., 2021). Many researchers now also administer such measures before or after several sessions, say, every three or five sessions. In the vast majority of published RCTs comparing the relative efficacy of two or more treatment packages, measures of distal outcomes determine what works or which one works better. The difference in distress between the start and the end of treatment constitutes the primary index of success. In more sophisticated studies, the researchers account for the severity of the clients' initial distress and their ending distress (via residual change scores) and often consider all patients who began therapy (intent to treat) as opposed to only the treatment completers (who tend to inflate estimates of treatment success).

These measures share similar advantages and disadvantages as post-session measures (e.g., the relative ease of administration and minimal intrusion into the therapy process are offset by the inability to directly link specific skills/methods to outcomes). For better and for worse, the vast majority of distal outcomes in published research are patient self-reported symptoms or distress (Lambert, 2013). Notoriously, some clients rate themselves worse before treatment to show how badly they need therapy and better after therapy to show how much they have profited, called the *hello–goodbye* effect.

Overall Considerations

Much has been written about assessing outcomes (e.g., Lutz et al., 2021; Ogles, 2013), so we will not cover the entire terrain here. Rather, our aim is to identify outcomes that can be linked directly with specific therapist skills and methods. In that regard, we repeat that immediate outcomes have at least a temporal association with the skills/methods, whereas intermediate and distal outcomes cannot be directly linked with specific skills/methods, although they are more easily gathered and used in outcome research. Returning to our refrain of "it's messy" and adding "it depends," psychotherapists recognize that the impressive effects of psychotherapy are not all immediate, not all measurable, and not at all invariant. We hope that more effective ways will be developed to assess such varied outcomes.

Linking Skills and Methods to Outcomes

The complexity of psychotherapy process–outcome research has proven, at once, a boon and a burden. We have witnessed in the foregoing pages the multiple research models (e.g., medical model, relationship model, psychotherapist, patient, expectations, responsiveness, skills/methods), several levels of psychotherapy foci (treatment packages, change principles/processes, methods, skills) operating on at least three types of outcomes (immediate, intermediate, distal) using a plethora of research designs and methods. The possible number of research permutations is staggering.

We arrive now at our ultimate destination in this chapter: associating therapist skills and methods with psychotherapy outcomes. This is, simultaneously, the reward of process–outcome research and the bane of every psychotherapy investigator. How can we establish, with reasonable certainty, the causal link between what the psychotherapist does and patient improvement? Or how can we identify and disconfirm plausible rival explanations that account for patient improvement above and beyond what the therapist does?

Here, we concentrate on the most frequent approaches for associating therapist skills/methods with outcome: (a) correlations between the frequency of skills/methods with post-session or post-treatment outcome, (b) sequential analyses linking the skill/method with outcome, (c) qualitative analyses linking skills/methods with outcomes, (d) task analyses linking the skills/methods and outcome (or relatedly called event or episode analyses), and (e) conversation analyses. This list does not exhaust the possibilities, but it represents most of the current approaches.

Correlations Between Frequency of Skills/Methods and Outcomes

Much of the early process–outcome research involved linking the frequency (or proportion, to control for verbal fluency) of an isolated therapist skill with session or treatment outcome. Thus, researchers often correlated the proportion of the therapist skills/methods (divided by the total number of skills/methods to control for verbal activity) to post-session or post-treatment outcomes.

For example, Hill and colleagues (1988) correlated the proportion of therapist VRMs in sessions with client outcome. In terms of session outcome, they found that when therapists gave more interpretations and less information, clients rated the depth (quality) of sessions high. In contrast, the more confrontations therapists gave, the lower therapists rated the depth of sessions. In other words, clients and therapists disagreed on which skills led to deeper sessions. In terms of treatment outcome, Hill and colleagues found that the more open questions and paraphrases therapists provided, the more clients decreased in anxiety. In contrast, the more paraphrases and the fewer approval and closed questions therapists gave, the more the client increased in self-concept. Notably, even within a given study (and the same is generally true across studies), results differed across outcome measures, showing minimal consistency across measures and perspectives.

An advance on associating simple frequency or proportion of the skill/method with outcome is multilevel modeling. Here, researchers can separate out the effects of sessions, clients, and therapists (Crits-Christoph & Gibbons, 2021). Multilevel modeling thus removes variance associated with these effects but still is problematic in that frequency is being related to intermediate or distal outcome.

Stiles (1988; Stiles et al., 1998) has argued, however, that it makes little sense to correlate frequency of skills/methods with outcome given that more is not necessarily better. One good interpretation is obviously better than 10 poor interpretations. In fact, therapists might give more interpretations when clients are not responding to those already given. Or it may be that a moderate amount is necessary, and that amount might differ for various skills and diverse clients.

Likewise, we know that the quality or competency with which the skill/method was rendered obviously makes all the difference. Unfortunately, the field has not yet developed effective methods for doing so. In addition, what clients absorb from the skills is often different from what the therapist intended (e.g., the therapist might intend to encourage the client to explore feelings but the client might interpret as a demand to be less masculine). Is it the skill, the therapist intention, the client, or what?

Sequential Analyses Linking the Skill/Method with Immediate Outcome

Researchers can directly link therapist behavior with the immediate in-session outcome using sequential analyses, under the assumption that there is a temporal link between the two. Typically, this requires having one set of trained judges code the therapist skill/method and having another set of judges code the immediate client response (outcome). Again using the Hill and colleagues (1988) study as an example, a sequential analysis linked the judge-coded VRMs in the therapist speaking turns with the peak client experiencing levels as rated by trained judges in the subsequent speaking turn. Therapist self-disclosure was linked with the highest subsequent client experiencing, whereas confrontation was linked with the lowest subsequent client experiencing.

Valuable additions to this approach are to control for antecedent behavior when assessing the outcome of a skill/method. For example, when studying therapist advice, researchers could control for antecedent client collaboration when examining subsequent client collaboration (Liposky et al., in press; Prass et al., 2021). It is also important to nest events within clients and therapists to control for individual variability.

As noted above, an advantage of sequential analysis is that it gets closer to a direct outcome link given the temporal nature. The disadvantage is that it does not address concerns that client responses do not occur at a consistent interval, in that some are delayed or evolve. Furthermore, clients have different reactions to the same therapist behavior, and sequential analysis does not rule out or control for the impact of other variables (beyond the skill or method). Even when controlling for antecedent client variables, not all of the context can be included in this approach.

A variation of sequential analysis is to link the judged skill/method with participants' judgments of outcome (most often helpfulness ratings) based on post-session reviews (here considered immediate delayed outcome). Thus, researchers can determine how helpful clients or therapists thought a specific skill or method was. In the study cited above (Hill et al.,1988), therapists and clients watched the videotape of a session immediately after its conclusion and rated the helpfulness of each therapist speaking turn. Researchers then computed the average helpfulness ratings for each skill. In that analysis, clients rated therapist self-disclosures as the most helpful, whereas open questions, closed questions, and direct guidance were rated the least helpful. In contrast, therapists rated their interpretations as the most helpful and their self-disclosures as the least helpful.

Advantages of this approach are that participants can evaluate the specific skills or disclose inner experiences, and these can be linked to the coded VRMs. Disadvantages are that the method is time-consuming and intrusive into the treatment process. The video review also needs to be completed within about 24 hours after the session so that memories are fresh. Finally, post-session evaluations tend to render different results than in-session experiences (Hill et al., 1994).

Qualitative Approaches to Linking Skills/Methods and Outcomes

A more recent approach has been to have a team of experienced judges view the skill/method within the context of the entire session and case and consensually determine the consequences (outcomes) of skills or methods. One exemplar is consensual qualitative research—cases (CQR-C; Hill & Knox, 2021). In the study of therapist challenges described above, for instance, judges not only identified when challenges occurred but also examined their antecedents and consequences (Hill et al., 2022). Thus, researchers relied on clinical judgment to determine the outcomes for each challenge given the context of the case. Results indicated that in the presence of a strong therapeutic alliance when the client was less defended, a clear and empathic therapist challenge led the client to become more open and reflective. By contrast, when the client was defensive and the therapist challenge was of lower quality, the client became even more defended and closed. Sophisticated qualitative research can thus generate the elusive when–then guidance that practitioners and researchers crave.

Advantages of this approach are that multiple perspectives among judges can be included and considered, with the hope that these will lead to more valid conclusions. In addition, researchers can use their clinical judgment and consider the dynamics of the entire case. Disadvantages are the time-intensive nature of the process, the inevitable problems in establishing causality, and the likelihood of biases.

Task Analysis Linking Skills/Methods with Outcome

Task analysis (or event/episode analysis) examines outcomes after longer sequences of psychotherapist and patient behavior (Greenberg, 2007; Pascual-Leone et al., 2009). In the discovery stage, researchers identify the theorized steps of some method (e.g., rupture repair), watch multiple events to see how the process actually unfolds in psychotherapy, and then merge those observational results into a model of the change process that differs for successful and unsuccessful cases. In the validation stage, researchers test the model by having judges rate the client and therapist behaviors in each step using standardized measures that fit the description of that stage (e.g., client experiencing for a step of exploration, resolution for the final step) on a new sample of clients and therapists. The model is iteratively modified based on the results.

By comparing replicated results across successful and unsuccessful cases, researchers can determine what probably leads to successful outcomes across cases. The usual problems with establishing conclusive causality between the therapy method and patient outcome persist, but at least the temporal linkages are consistent across multiple patients.

Conversation Analysis

Conversation analysts (e.g., Hepburn & Potter, 2021) study both verbal and nonverbal conduct in social interactions, including psychotherapy. Conversation analysis yields a detailed description of not only the sequential steps of a method but also the surrounding interactions between clinician and client, given that the same statement said in different ways can produce profoundly varying meanings and impacts (Wachtel, 2011). This method allows researchers to consider interactional nuances and, further, separates competing causal processes. Hence, conversational analysis offers reasonable approximations to causal sequences. Chapter 5 provides an excellent example of how this method can be applied to investigate empathic reflections.

Overall Considerations

Alas, studies using different research approaches for associating therapist skills/methods with outcome frequently do not yield consistent results. In Hill and colleagues' (1988) study, for example, different results were obtained from (a) correlating judgments of verbal response modes with immediate judgments of subsequent client behavior, (b) comparing the average client-rated and therapist-rated helpfulness of the therapist skills, and (c) correlating the occurrence of the skills with post-session or post-treatment outcomes. Depending on the research approach, the most effective therapist skill was interpretation, open question, paraphrase, or self-disclosure; by contrast, the least effective therapist skill was confrontation, approval, closed question, self-disclosure, or direct guidance. It's messy and it depends, indeed!

Qualitative methods, task analyses, and conversation analysis may be more clinically useful for studying process–outcome relations given that contextual variables can be included in the models, but they prove more intensive and typically involve just a few clients. Similarly, multilevel modeling can account for therapist, client, session, and event effects, but it fails to consider the clinical and contextual variables. We suspect if results were compared across all of these approaches for a common data set, even fewer consistencies would appear.

Researchers currently struggle to take the complexity of psychotherapy and the sequencing of skills/methods into account. To do so requires that we consider the antecedents of skills/methods (e.g., in what circumstances are they helpful or hindering), therapist and client variables (e.g., personality, attachment style, diagnosis, motivation, social support), stage of treatment, as well as an assortment of immediate and distal outcomes. The impact of skills/methods cannot be examined in isolation because they occur in the context of what has gone before and what transpires after, as well as what transpires outside of therapy. Qualitative, conversation, and task analytic approaches probably have the best chances of successfully determining the sequence of several steps in context.

As should be apparent at this point in the chapter, we strongly assert that the association between therapist skills/methods and outcome has not received adequate attention in the research literature. In part, this neglect is undoubtedly due to the time-intensive nature of the phenomenon. In part, it is also attributable to the dominant funding mechanisms and research paradigms that favor comparing the relative efficacy of brand-name treatment packages for specific diagnoses. As is frequently said in evidence-based practice, "the absence of evidence is not evidence of absence."

Reviewing and Summarizing the Research

The most widely accepted method for reviewing and aggregating results across quantitative research studies is meta-analyses (Appelbaum et al., 2018). In parallel, the most accepted method for summarizing qualitative studies is meta-synthesis or qualitative meta-analyses (Levitt et al., 2018; Timulak & Creaner, 2023). In this book, when possible, we asked contributors to conduct an original quantitative or qualitative meta-analysis to summarize the research evidence on the association between their respective therapist skill/method and immediate, intermediate, and distal outcomes.

Unfortunately, not much research exists on the immediate in-session outcomes for many of the skills and methods featured in this book. As a result, it was not always possible for contributors to conduct quantitative or qualitative meta-analyses on the relation between particular skills/methods and immediate outcomes.

The alternative we proposed was for contributors to calculate box scores to summarize the limited research evidence. *Box scores* reflect the judgment of the chapter authors based on the evidence of the outcomes. By a process of designating criteria and discussion among themselves, authors determined whether the association between the skill/method and each outcome in a given study was positive (+), neutral (0, =), or negative (−). They then aggregated across outcomes to derive a summary box score (when appropriate) for each measure, outcome, and study. In this manner, contributors summarized the overall pattern of their research results.

When the sample sizes varied substantially across studies (e.g., a single case study vs. a sample of 100 clients), we encouraged authors to weight the box scores. They did so by the sample size; for instance, consider a + to be 1, = to be 0, − to be −1; multiply each finding by the sample size, and then divide by the total sample size across studies. This weighting procedure, in a rough sense, accounted for the sample sizes in individual studies.

Such box scores are less than ideal compromises to formal meta-analyses or meta-syntheses but probably superior to narrative reviews alone. Author bias and researcher allegiance can certainly enter into the coding and interpretation of box scores, which is why we asked authors to establish criteria and discuss to consensus. Ideally, the research reviews in this book will stimulate new research so that meta-analyses can be conducted on all the therapist skills and methods featured in the next edition of *Psychotherapy Skills and Methods That Work*.

Although there was minimal research on the connection between skills/methods and *immediate in-session* outcomes, there was more research on the relation between skills/methods and *intermediate* and *distal (treatment)* outcomes. Hence, we present this evidence in this volume to communicate the state of the evidence for these important skills/methods. We do so with the painful awareness of the problems (as detailed previously in this chapter) in connecting skills/methods with distal outcomes given the lack of a temporal connection, the lack of contextual specificity, and the multitude of confounding variables.

In the absence of research evidence on the immediate in-session outcomes of therapist skills and methods, practitioners are frequently left to extrapolate from the global results of RCTs and effectiveness studies using those skills and methods as part of a larger treatment package. Those interested in the effectiveness of, for example, mindfulness (see Chapter 20) or cognitive restructuring methods (see Chapter 22) will look at the effectiveness of entire mindfulness treatments or a course of cognitive therapy to indirectly glean some information on the usefulness of the constituent methods. Such research evidence is presented in this book as a complement to the specific and superior evidence provided on the methods themselves.

Although obviously useful, such outcome research on entire treatment packages suffers from numerous limitations. First, as explained previously, those research results do not determine which components of the treatment package prove efficacious. Was it the particular skill/method, the therapeutic relationship, the patient, the expectation, or the responsiveness? Second, clinical trials focus primarily on the distal, end-of-treatment outcomes, which are insensitive for identifying the impacts of skills or methods offered months ago. More researchers, however, are now examining such changes on a session-by-session basis so that they can examine the trajectory of change over time.

In the End, Training Implications and Therapeutic Practices

The natural end results of the psychotherapy research summaries in this book and elsewhere are research-supported training and clinical practice. The cumulative research on a skill/method ideally yields or generates actionable guidance for trainers on how to enhance student competence and for psychotherapists on how to provide better therapy. All subsequent chapters in *Psychotherapy Skills and Methods That Work* thus conclude with such training implications and therapeutic practices.

In this regard, we intend the volume as translational research: to move research discoveries into established practice and training. We aim to move the science to service, from the research lab to the consulting room (Norcross et al., 2017).

What will practitioners gain from reading this book? Our summaries of the research evidence will certainly guide and advise clinicians. Sometimes, that research will lead to adopting a particular skill/method because the research is supportive and sometimes to using the skill/method in particular clinical circumstances or with specific patients. Other times, the researchers cannot recommend whether or when the skill/method should be adopted because the volume or quality of the research is insufficient. On rare times, the research evidence will suggest that the routine use of the skill/method should be avoided.

We hope that practitioners will actively engage in the dialogue, too, telling us where the research is wrong-headed and what we ought to be looking at instead (Tasca et al., 2015). Collaboration between practitioners and researchers will lead to better research methods and more practice-friendly results (Castonguay et al., 2010).

The final chapter in this volume contains a tabular summary of the research evidence for each skill/method by type of outcome (immediate, intermediate, distal). That chapter also presents the consensual judgments of the Task Force Steering Committee about the effectiveness of the reviewed psychotherapy skills and methods. We conclude with recommendations for training, clinical practice, and research.

The Interorganizational Task Force

The interorganizational Task Force was commissioned to identify, compile, and disseminate the research evidence on psychotherapist skills and methods used across theoretical orientations. This Task Force was initiated by the Society for the Advancement of Psychotherapy (APA Division of Psychotherapy) and co-sponsored by the Society of Counseling Psychology (APA Division of Counseling Psychology), the Society for Psychotherapy Research, and the Society for the Exploration of Psychotherapy Integration. All these professional organizations promote the integration of the science and practice of psychotherapy.

As detailed in the Preface, the authors of each chapter reviewed the research evidence on the outcomes of a specific skill or method, following a thorough and demanding chapter structure (presented in the Preface). Based on that research evidence, the authors concluded their respective chapters with diversity considerations, training implications, and therapeutic practices.

The first challenge for the Task Force was to determine which skills and methods to include. We struggled to differentiate skills and methods from total treatment packages (e.g., psychodynamic approaches), on the one hand, and the therapeutic relationship (e.g., warmth, alliance), the person of the therapist (e.g., authoritarian), and the person of the client (e.g., motivated, depressed), on the other hand. We regret that we could not include all of the possible skills and methods in this text. We especially miss chapters on therapist challenges, development of mentalization, working with cultural diversity, and exposure methods. It is hoped that these can be included in future editions. We also note that some evidence about four specific skills and methods was included in *Psychotherapy Relationships That Work.* Rather than commissioning new chapters on these four, we summarize the findings briefly in Chapter 2.

Contributors compiled the available research evidence about the association between therapist skills and methods and immediate (within-session), intermediate, and distal (post-treatment) outcomes. The evidence is based on actual psychotherapy (rather than analogue) conducted with adults in individual format (thus excluding group, couples, child/adolescent, and family therapy). When available, the research was reviewed for what works and with whom under what conditions (moderators)—the ultimate quest for process–outcome research.

The chapters were peer-reviewed by the two editors and subsequently underwent at least three revisions. When the chapters were finalized, at least three psychotherapy experts from the 12-person Steering Committee reviewed and rated the evidentiary strength of each skill and method. In this way, we reached an expert consensus on which skills and methods work, which do not, and which have not yet been sufficiently researched. That consensus informed and fueled the Task Force's conclusions and recommendations (see Chapter 23).

The Goal Revisited

We end this chapter by returning to the prime goal of our Task Force: to expand the research evidence and clinical practices on psychotherapy skills and methods, those pantheoretical behaviors clinicians use within sessions. There are hundreds of books published on how to conduct particular psychotherapy skills and methods; however, to our knowledge, none of them are explicitly grounded in and guided by the research evidence on what works for whom (Roth & Fonagy, 2005). In this respect, we hope that *Psychotherapy Skills and Methods That Work* will prove a singular and productive work.

At the same time, we ardently hope that corrective attention to these psychotherapist behaviors will be conceptualized and employed *in addition to* what already demonstrably works in psychotherapy—the therapeutic relationship, the treatment package, the person of the therapist, the contribution of the patient, and the like. In the integrative or pluralistic tradition, we consider the fruits of this book as not either/or but as both/and. Many things contribute to change in psychotherapy; let us cherish and practice them all! We on this Task Force are committed to ending the culture wars in psychotherapy by harvesting the research evidence and then practicing what works across the magnificent complexity and the impressive efficacy of psychotherapy.

References

Anvari, M. S., Dua, V., Lima Rosas, J., Hill, C. E., & Kivlighan, D. M., Jr. (2022). Facilitating exploration in psychodynamic psychotherapy: Therapist skills and client attachment. *Journal of Counseling Psychology, 69*(3), 348–360. https://doi.org/10.1037/cou0000582

Anvari, M. S., Hill, C. E., & Kivlighan, D. M., Jr. (2020). Therapist skills associated with client emotional expression in psychodynamic psychotherapy. *Psychotherapy Research, 30*(7), 900–911. https://dx.doi.org/10.1080/10503307.2019.1680901

Appelbaum, M., Cooper, H., Kline, R. B., Mayo-Wilson, E., Nezu, A. M., & Rao, S. M. (2018). Journal article reporting standards for quantitative research in psychology: The APA Publications and Communications Board task force report. *American Psychologist, 73*(1), 3–25. https://doi.org/10.1037/amp0000191

Barber, J. P. (2009). Toward a working through of some core conflicts in psychotherapy research. *Psychotherapy Research, 19*(1), 1–12. http://dx.doi.org/10.1080/10503300802609680

Barkham, M., & Lambert, M. J. (2021). The efficacy and effectiveness of psychological therapies. In M. Barkham, W. Lutz, & L. G. Castonguay (Eds.), *Bergin and Garfield's handbook of psychotherapy and behavior change* (50th anniversary ed., pp. 135–189). Wiley.

Barkham, M., Lutz, W., Lambert, M. J., & Saxon, D. (2017). Therapist effects, effective therapists, and the law of variability. In L. G. Castonguay & C. E. Hill (Eds.), *How and why are some therapists better than others? Understanding therapist effects* (pp. 13–36). American Psychological Association.

Bayona, J. A. (Director). (2016). *A monster calls* [Film]. Participant.

Beck, A. T., Ward, C. H., Mendelson, J., Mock, J., & Erbaugh, J. (1961). An inventory for measuring depression. *Archives of General Psychiatry, 4*(6), 561–571. https://doi.org/10.1001/archpsyc.1961.01710120031004

Benish, S. G., Quintana, S., & Wampold, B. E. (2011). Culturally adapted psychotherapy and the legitimacy of myth: A direct-comparison meta-analysis. *Journal of Counseling Psychology, 58*(3), 279–289. https://doi.org/10.1037/a0023626

Blagys, M. D., & Hilsenroth, M. J. (2000). Distinctive of short-term psychodynamic–interpersonal psychotherapy: A review of the comparative psychotherapy process literature. *Clinical Psychology: Science and Practice, 7*(2), 167–189. http://dx.doi.org/10.1093/clipsy/7.2.167

Blagys, M. D., & Hilsenroth, M. J. (2002). Distinctive activities of cognitive–behavioral therapy: A review of the comparative psychotherapy process literature. *Clinical Psychology Review, 22*(5), 671–706. https://dx.doi.org/10.1016/S0272-7358(01)00117-9

Bohart, A. C., & Tallman, K. (1999). *How clients make therapy work: The process of active self-healing.* American Psychological Association.

Carkhuff, R. R. (1969). *Human and helping relations* (Vols. 1 and 2). Holt, Rinehart and Winston.

Castonguay, L. G., Boswell, J. F., Zack, S. E., Baker, S., Boutselis, M. A., Chiswick, N. R., Damer, D. D., Hemmelstein, N. A., Jackson, J. S., Morford, M., Ragusea, S. A., Roper, J. G., Spayd, C., Weiszer, T., Borkovec, T. D., & Holtforth, M. G. (2010). Helpful and hindering events in psychotherapy: A practice research network study. *Psychotherapy, 47*(3), 327–344.

Castonguay, L. G., Constantino, M. J., & Beutler, L. E. (Eds.). (2019). *Principles of change: How psychotherapists implement research in practice.* Oxford University Press.

Castonguay, L. G., & Hill, C. E. (2017). *How and why are some therapists better than others? Understanding therapist effects.* American Psychological Association.

Chui, H., Chong, E. S. K., Atzil-Slonim, D., Sahin, Z., Solomonov, N., Minges, M. V., Kuprian, N., & Barber, J. P. (2021). Beyond symptom reduction: Development and validation of the Complementary Measure of Psychotherapy Outcome (COMPO). *Journal of Counseling Psychology, 68*(5), 550–561.https://doi.org/10.1037/cou0000536

Constantino, M. J., Boswell, J. F., Coyne, A. E., Swales, T. P., & Kraus, D. R. (2021). Effect of matching therapists to patients vs. assignment as usual on adult psychotherapy outcomes: A randomized clinical trial. *JAMA Psychiatry, 78*(9), 960–969. https://doi.org/10.1001/jamapsychiatry.2021.1221

Constantino, M. J., Coyne, A. E., Boswell, J. F., Goldfried, M. R., & Castonguay, L. G. (in press). Training on context-responsive psychotherapy integration: An evidence-informed framework. In L. G. Castonguay & C. E. Hill (Eds.), *Being and becoming a psychotherapist: Training and supervision*. American Psychological Association.

Constantino, M. J., Coyne, A. E., & Boswell, J. F., & Visla, A. (2019). Promoting treatment credibility. In J. C. Norcross & M. J. Lambert (Eds.), *Psychotherapy relationships that work* (3rd ed., pp. 495–521). Oxford University Press.

Constantino, M. J., Visla, A., Coyne, A. E., & Boswell, J. F. (2019). Cultivating positive outcome expectation. In J. C. Norcross & M. J. Lambert (Eds.), *Psychotherapy relationships that work* (3rd ed., pp. 461–494). Oxford University Press.

Crits-Christoph, P., & Gibbons, M. B. C. (2021). Psychotherapy process-outcome research: Advances in understanding causal connections. In M. Barkham, W. Lutz, & L. G. Castonguay (Eds.), *Bergin and Garfield's handbook of psychotherapy and behavior change* (pp. 263–295). Wiley.

David, D., & Cristea, I. (2018). The new great psychotherapy debate: Scientific integrated psychotherapy vs. plurality. Why cognitive–behavior therapy is the gold standard in psychotherapy and a platform for scientific integrated psychotherapy. *Journal of Evidence-Based Psychotherapies*, *18*(2), 1–17. https://doi.org/10.24193/jebp.2018.2.11

Elliott, R., Hill, C. E., Stiles, W. B., Friedlander, M. L., Mahrer, A. R., & Margison, F. R. (1987). Primary therapist response modes: Comparison of six rating systems. *Journal of Consulting and Clinical Psychology*, *55*, 218–223. https://dx.doi.org/10.1037/0022-006X.55.2.218

Elliott, R., & Timulak, L. (2021). *Essentials of descriptive–interpretive qualitative research: A generic approach*. American Psychological Association.

Evers, A. W. M., Colloca, L., Blease, C., Gaab, J., Jensen, K. B., Atlas, L. Y., Beedie, C. J., Benedetti, F., Bingel, U., Büchel, C., Bussemaker, J., Colagiuri, B., Crum, A. J., Finniss, D. G., Geers, A. L., Howick, J., Klinger, R., Meeuwis, S. H., Meissner, K., . . . Kirsch, I. (2021). What should clinicians tell patients about placebo and nocebo effects? Practical considerations based on expert consensus. *Psychotherapy and Psychosomatics*, *90*(1), 49–56. https://doi.org/10.1159/000510738

Flückiger, C., Del Re, A. C., Wampold, C. E., & Horvath, A. O. (2018). The alliance in adult psychotherapy: A meta-analytic synthesis. *Psychotherapy*, *55*, 316–340. https://psycnet.apa.org/fulltext/2018-23951-001.html

Frank, J. D., & Frank, J. B. (1991). *Persuasion and healing: A comparative study of psychotherapy* (3rd ed.). Johns Hopkins University Press.

Fuertes, J. N. (Ed.). (2022). *The other side of psychotherapy: Understanding clients' experiences and contributions to psychotherapy*. American Psychological Association.

Gelso, C. J. (2005). Introduction to special issue. *Psychotherapy: Theory, Research, Practice, Training*, *42*(4), 419.

Goldfried, M. R. (1980). Toward the delineation of therapeutic change principles. *American Psychologist*, *35*(11), 991.

Goldfried, M. R., & Davison, G. C. (1994). *Clinical behavior therapy* (expanded ed.). Wiley.

Greenberg, L. S. (2007). A guide to conducting a task analysis of psychotherapeutic change. *Psychotherapy Research*, *17*, 15–30. https://dx.doi.org/10.1080/10503300600720390

Heaton, K. J., Hill, C. E., & Edwards, L. A. (1995). Comparing molar and molecular methods of judging therapist techniques. *Psychotherapy Research*, *5*(2), 141–153. https://dx.doi.org/10.1080/10503309512331331266

Hepburn, A., & Potter, J. (2021). *Essentials of conversation analysis*. American Psychological Association.

Hill, C. E. (1978). Development of a counselor verbal response category system. *Journal of Counseling Psychology*, *25*(6), 461–468. https://doi.org/10.1037/0022-0167.25.5.461

Hill, C. E. (Ed.). (2004). *Dream work in therapy: Facilitating exploration, insight, and action*. American Psychological Association.

Hill, C. E. (2005). Therapist techniques, client involvement, and the therapeutic relationship: Inextricably intertwined in the therapy process. *Psychotherapy: Theory, Research, Practice, Training, 42*, 431–442. https://doi.org/10.1037/0033-3204.42.4.431

Hill, C. E. (2020). *Helping skills: Facilitating exploration, insight, and action* (5th ed.). American Psychological Association.

Hill, C. E., Helms, J. E., Tichenor, V., Spiegel, S. B., O'Grady, K. E., & Perry, E. S. (1988). Effects of therapist response modes in brief psychotherapy. *Journal of Counseling Psychology, 35*(3), 222–233. https://dx.doi.org/10.1037/0022-0167.35.3.222

Hill, C. E., & Kellems, I. S. (2002). Development and use of the Helping Skills Measure to assess client perceptions of the effects of training and of helping skills in sessions. *Journal of Counseling Psychology, 49*(2), 264–272. https://doi.org/10.1037/0022-0167.49.2.264

Hill, C. E., & Knox, S. (2021). *Essentials of consensual qualitative research*. American Psychological Association.

Hill, C. E., Morales, K., Gerstenblith, J. A., Bansal, P., An, M., Rim, K., & Kivlighan, D. M., Jr. (2022). Therapist challenges and client responses in psychodynamic psychotherapy: An empirically-supported case study. *Psychotherapy, 59*(1), 74–83. https://dx.doi.org/10.1037/pst0000424

Hill, C. E., O'Grady, K. E., Balenger, V., Busse, W., Falk, D., Hill, M., Rios, P., & Taffe, R. (1994). A methodological examination of videotape-assisted reviews in brief therapy: Helpfulness ratings, therapist intentions, client reactions, mood, and session evaluation. *Journal of Counseling Psychology, 41*, 236–247. https://dx.doi.org/10.1037/0022-0167.41.2.236

Hill, C. E., Spiegel, S. B., Hoffman, M. A., Kivlighan, D. M., Jr., & Gelso, C. J. (2017). Expertise in psychotherapy revisited. *The Counseling Psychologist, 45*, 7–53. https://dx.doi.org/10.1177/0011000016641192

Hill, C. E., Thames, T. B., & Rardin, D. K. (1979). Comparison of Rogers, Perls, and Ellis on the Hill Counselor Verbal Response Category System. *Journal of Counseling Psychology, 26*, 198–203.

Hilsenroth, M. J., Blagys, M. D., Ackerman, S. J., Bonge, D. R., & Blais, M. A. (2005). Measuring psychodynamic–interpersonal and cognitive–behavioral techniques: Development of the Comparative Psychotherapy Process Scale. *Psychotherapy: Theory, Research, Practice, Training, 42*(3), 340–356. https://doi.org/10.1037/0033-3204.42.3.340

Horvath, A. O., & Greenberg, L. S. (1989). Development and validation of the Working Alliance Inventory. *Journal of Counseling Psychology, 36*(2), 223–233. https://doi.org/10.1037/0022-0167.36.2.223

Ivey, A. E., Ivey, M. B., & Zalaquette, L. P. (2017). *Intentional interviewing and counseling: Facilitating client development in a multicultural society* (9th ed.). Cengage.

Jones, E. E., & Pulos, S. M. (1993). Comparing the process in psychodynamic and cognitive–behavioral therapies. *Journal of Consulting and Clinical Psychology, 61*(2), 306–316. https://doi.org/10.1037/0022-006X.61.2.306

Knox, S., Hess, S., Petersen, D., & Hill, C. E. (1997). A qualitative analysis of client perceptions of the effects of helpful therapist self-disclosure in long-term therapy. *Journal of Counseling Psychology, 44*(3), 274–283. https://doi.org/10.1037/0022-0167.44.3.274

Knox, S., & Hill, C. E. (2021). Training and supervision in psychotherapy: What we know and what we need to know. In M. Barkham, W. Lutz, & L. G. Castonguay (Eds.), *Bergin and Garfield's handbook of psychotherapy and behavior change* (50th anniversary ed., pp. 327–349). Wiley.

Lambert, M. J. (2013). The efficacy and effectiveness of psychotherapy. In M. J. Lambert (Ed.), *Bergin and Garfield's handbook of psychotherapy and behavior change* (6th ed., pp. 169–218). Wiley.

Levitt, H. M. (2021). *Essentials of critical-constructivist grounded theory research*. American Psychological Association.

Levitt, H. M., Bamberg, M., Creswell, J. W., Frost, D. M., Josselson, R., & Suárez-Orozco, C. (2018). Journal article reporting standards for qualitative primary, qualitative meta-analytic, and mixed methods research in psychology: The APA Publications and Communications Board task force report. *American Psychologist, 73*(1), 26–46. https://doi.org/10.1037/amp0000151

Lilienfeld, S. O. (2014). The Dodo bird verdict: Status in 2014. *The Behavior Therapist, 37*(4), 91–95.

Liposky, H., Hill, C. E., & Kivlighan, D. M., Jr. (in press). Advice-giving in final sessions of psychodynamic psychotherapy: Is it advised? *Psychotherapy Research*. https://doi.org/10.1080/09515070.2022.2095617

Lutz, W., de Jong, K., Rubel, J. A., & Delgadillo, J. (2021). Measuring, predicting, and tracking change in psychotherapy. In M. Barkham, W. Lutz, & L. G. Castonguay (Eds.), *Bergin and Garfield's handbook of psychotherapy and behavior change* (50th anniversary ed., pp. 89–134). Wiley.

McCarthy, K. S., & Barber, J. P. (2009). The Multitheoretical List of Therapeutic Interventions (MULTI): Initial report. *Psychotherapy Research, 19*(1), 96–113. https://doi.org/10.1080/10503300802524343

Miller, S. D., & Duncan, B. L. (2000). *The Outcome Rating Scale*.

Miller, S. D., Duncan, B. L., Sorrell, R., & Brown, G. S. (2005). The Partners for Change Outcome Management System. *Journal of Clinical Psychology, 61*, 199–208.

Nathan, P. E., & Gorman, J. M. (Eds.). (2015). *A guide to treatments that work* (4th ed.). Oxford University Press.

Norcross, J. C. (1995). Dispelling the Dodo bird verdict and the exclusivity myth in psychotherapy. *Psychotherapy, 32*(3), 500–504. https://doi.org/10.1037/0033-3204.32.3.500

Norcross, J. C. (Ed.). (2002). *Psychotherapy relationships that work*. Oxford University Press.

Norcross, J. C. (Ed.). (2011). *Psychotherapy relationships that work* (2nd ed.). Oxford University Press.

Norcross, J. C., & Cooper, M. (2021). *Personalizing psychotherapy: Assessing and accommodating patient preferences*. American Psychological Association.

Norcross, J. C., & Goldfried, M. R. (Eds.). (2019). *Handbook of psychotherapy integration* (3rd ed.). Oxford University Press.

Norcross, J. C., Hogan, T. P., Koocher, G. P., & Maggio, L. A. (2017). *Clinician's guide to evidence-based practices: Behavioral health and addictions* (2nd ed.). Oxford University Press.

Norcross, J. C., & Lambert, M. J. (2019). Evidence-based psychotherapy relationships: The third task force. In J. C. Norcross & M. J. Lambert (Eds.), *Psychotherapy relationships that work: Volume 1. Evidence-based therapist contributions* (pp. 1–23). Oxford University Press.

Norcross, J. C., & Wampold, B. E. (Eds.). (2019). *Psychotherapy relationships that work: Volume 2. Evidence-based responsiveness*. Oxford University Press.

Ogles, B. M. (2013). Measuring change in psychotherapy. In M. J. Barkham (Ed.), *Bergin and Garfield's handbook of psychotherapy and behavior change* (50th anniversary ed., pp. 134–166). Wiley.

Pascual-Leone, A., Greenberg, L. S., & Pascual-Leone, J. (2009). Developments in task analysis: New methods to study change. *Psychotherapy Research, 19*(4–5), 527–542. https://dx.doi.org/10.1080/10503300902897797

Prass, M., Ewell, A., Hill, C. E., & Kivlighan, D. M., Jr. (2021). Solicited and unsolicited advice-giving in psychotherapy: Is it advised? *Counselling Psychology Quarterly*, [*34*(2)], 253–274. https://dx.doi.org/10.1080/09515070.2020.1723492

Prochaska, J. O., & Norcross, J. C. (2018). *Systems of psychotherapy: A transtheoretical analysis* (9th ed.). Oxford University Press.

Roth, A., & Fonagy, P. (2005). *What works for whom: A critical review of psychotherapy research* (2nd ed.). Guilford.

Snyder, W. U. (1945). An investigation of the nature of nondirective psychotherapy. *Journal of General Psychology, 33*, 193–223. https://doi.org/10.1080/00221309.1945.10544506

Stiles, W. B. (1979). Verbal response modes and psychotherapeutic technique. *Psychiatry, 42*, 49–62.

Stiles, W. B. (1988). Psychotherapy process–outcome correlations may be misleading. *Psychotherapy, 25*(1), 27–35. https://dx.doi.org/10.1037/h0085320

Stiles, W. B., Bate, J., & Anderson, T. (in press). Building a theory of responsiveness training. In L. G. Castonguay & C. E. Hill (Eds.), *Being and becoming a psychotherapist: Training and supervision*. American Psychological Association.

Stiles, W. B., Honos-Webb, L., & Surko, M. (1998). Responsiveness in psychotherapy. *Clinical Psychology*, *5*(4), 439–458. https://dx.doi.org/10.1111/j.1468-2850.1998.tb00166.x

Stiles, W. B., & Horvath, A. O. (2017). Appropriate responsiveness as a contribution to therapist effects. In L. G. Castonguay & C. E. Hill (Eds.), *How and why are some therapists better than others? Understanding therapist effects* (pp. 71–84). American Psychological Association.

Tasca, G. A., Sylvestre, J., Balfour, L., Chyurlia, L., Evans, J., Fortin-Langelier, B., Francis, K., Gandhi, J., Huehn, L., Hunsley, J., Joyce, A., Kinley, J., Koszycki, D., Leszcz, M., Lybanon-Daigle, V., Mercer, D., Ogrodniczuk, J., Presniak, M., Ravitz, P., . . . Wilson, B. (2015). What clinicians want: Findings from a psychotherapy practice research network survey. *Psychotherapy*, *52*(1), 1–11. https://doi.org/10.1037/a0038252

Timulak, L., & Creaner, M. (2023). *Essentials of qualitative meta-analysis*. American Psychological Association.

Town, J. M., Hardy, G. E., McCullough, L., & Stride, C. (2012). Patient affect experiencing following therapist interventions in short-term dynamic psychotherapy. *Psychotherapy Research*, *22*(2), 208–219. https://doi.org/10.1080/10503307.2011.637243

Wachtel, P. L. (2011). *Therapeutic communication: Knowing what to say when*. Guilford.

Wampold, B. E., & Budge, S. L. (2012). The 2011 Leona Tyler Award address: The relationship—and its relationship to the common and specific factors of psychotherapy. *The Counseling Psychologist*, *40*, 601–643.

Wampold, B. E., & Imel, Z. E. (2015). *The great psychotherapy debate: The evidence for what makes psychotherapy work*. Routledge.

Wampold, B. E., Minami, T., Tierney, S. C., Baskin, T. W., & Bhati, K. S. (2005). The placebo is powerful: Estimating placebo effects in medicine and psychotherapy from randomized clinical trials. *Journal of Clinical Psychology*, *61*(7), 835–854.

2

Affirmation/Validation, Self-Disclosure, Immediacy, and Rupture Repairs

Barry A. Farber, Clara E. Hill, Sarah Knox, Catherine F. Eubanks, J. Christopher Muran, and John C. Norcross

There is a deep and abiding synergy between psychotherapy methods and the therapeutic relationship. They constantly shape and inform each other. The relationship does not exist apart from what the therapist does, and we cannot imagine any treatment method that does not exert some relational impact (Norcross & Lambert, 2019b). Put differently, therapist skills and methods are relational acts (Safran & Muran, 2000).

For historical reasons and research convenience, the field has distinguished between the therapeutic relationship and therapist skills/methods. Words such as "relating" and "interpersonal behavior" are used to describe *how* therapists and clients feel about and behave toward each other. By contrast, terms such as "skill," "method," and "technique" are used to describe *what* is done by the therapist. In research and theory, we often treat the how and the what—the relationship and the method, the interpersonal and the instrumental—as separate categories. In reality, of course, what one does and how one does it are complementary and nearly inseparable (Gelso, 2005; Norcross & Lambert, 2019; Orlinsky et al., 2004).

The members of the task forces behind the three editions of *Psychotherapy Relationships That Work* struggled to establish the inclusion and exclusion criteria for elements of the therapy relationship, especially in their intersection with therapist methods and skills. We readily agreed that discrete, relatively nonrelational methods (e.g., cognitive restructuring) were not part of our purview, but that several explicitly relationship-oriented methods would be included. We featured in those books several "relational" methods—for example, conducting routine outcome monitoring (Lambert et al., 2019; updated and appearing in this volume), repairing alliance ruptures (Eubanks et al., 2019), expressing immediacy and self-disclosing (Hill et al., 2019), and offering positive regard or affirmation (Farber et al., 2019).

Rather than commissioning new chapters when minimal research has been conducted since these chapters were published, we summarize here the research evidence initially presented in *Psychotherapy Relationships That Work* (Norcross & Lambert, 2019a) on the clinical effectiveness of the latter four therapist behaviors: affirmation/validation, self-disclosure, immediacy, and rupture repairs. For each therapist behavior, we provide a definition of the skill or method, a review of the research evidence, training implications, and therapeutic practices.

The following sections are thumbnail sketches of the longer chapters and the detailed meta-analyses. We strongly recommend interested readers return to the original sources

Barry A. Farber, Clara E. Hill, Sarah Knox, Catherine F. Eubanks, J. Christopher Muran, and John C. Norcross, *Affirmation/Validation, Self-Disclosure, Immediacy, and Rupture Repairs* In: *Psychotherapy Skills and Methods That Work*. Edited by: Clara E. Hill and John C. Norcross, Oxford University Press. © Clara E. Hill and John C. Norcross 2023. DOI: 10.1093/oso/9780197611012.003.0002

(Eubanks et al., 2019; Farber et al., 2019; Hill et al., 2019) for the complete presentation and additional information, such as clinical examples, landmark studies, moderator analyses, research limitations, patient contributions, and diversity considerations.

Affirmation/Validation

Definition

> To the extent that the therapist finds himself experiencing a warm acceptance of each aspect of the client's experience as being a part of that client, he is experiencing unconditional positive regard . . . it means there are no conditions of acceptance . . . it means a "prizing" of the person . . . it means a caring for the client as a separate person.
>
> —Rogers (1957, p. 101)

From the beginning of his efforts to explicate the essential elements of person-centered therapy, Carl Rogers focused on positive regard and warmth. For Rogers, a therapist's provision of positive regard was a crucial counterbalance to the *conditions of worth* typically imposed by parents on their children. Implicit too in Rogers' quote is his disapproval of what he perceived as the arrogance of the psychoanalytic community at that time, including the tendency of its practitioners to accord hierarchical distinctions between themselves and their patients. Rogers did not believe that anyone, including a psychotherapist, could be more expert or knowledgeable about a client than the client themself. Instead, he believed that treating clients in a consistently warm, caring, highly regarding manner would inevitably allow them to grow psychologically, to fulfill their potential.

Rogers (1959) offered another definition of unconditional positive regard:

> If the self-experiences of another are perceived by me in such a way that no self-experience can be discriminated as more or less worthy of positive regard than any other, then I am experiencing unconditional positive regard for this individual. . . . Putting this in simpler terms, to feel unconditional positive regard towards another is to "prize" him [sic]. . . . This means to value the person, irrespective of the differential values which one might place on his [sic] specific behaviors. (p. 208)

Here, Rogers offers a single synonym ("prizing") as a stand-in for positive regard.

Rogers' written and spoken statements consistently maintain that a core feature of positive regard is the therapist's affective behavior toward their clients; he consistently invoked words such as warmth, liking, affirmation, nonpossessive love, and affection in referring to this therapist behavior and facilitative condition (Farber et al., 2022). Thus, in making decisions regarding the studies to include in our meta-analysis, we chose to exclude those studies that investigated therapist *respect* and *support*; both these concepts (which were studied as single variables only rarely) have something in common with Rogers' ideas about positive regard, but in our view they omit an essential affective component—warmth or liking for the client.

To this day, agreeing on a single phrase to refer to this therapist behavior remains problematic. It is most often termed *positive regard*, but early studies and theoretical writings preferred the phrase *nonpossessive warmth*. Some contemporary person-centered theorists continue to prefer the term *unconditional positive regard* and/or to distinguish between this term (with its emphasis on acceptance) and *positive regard* per se (with its emphasis on support and caring). Some reviews of the research on "acceptance, nonpossessive warmth, or positive regard" (Orlinsky et al., 1994, p. 326) grouped them under the category of *therapist affirmation*. We use the term *affirmation* to refer to the general constellation of therapist behaviors encompassed by this and similar phrases.

We also include therapist *validation*, which, according to Linehan (1997), can be seen as a form of positive regard: "The person, rather than the constructs brought to the interaction by the therapist, is seen and countenanced. Validation used in this sense perhaps comes closest to the meaning of the term 'unconditional positive regard' used by Rogers (1959)" (p. 357). Thus, Farber et al. (2019) included validation as a term in their meta-analysis, specifically when this variable was assessed via a measure typically used to assess positive regard.

Carl Rogers, Marsha Linehan, and others constructed the theoretical foundation underlying the therapist behaviors of affirmation and validation. Without the larger aim or condition of positive regard, the observable therapist behaviors would prove shallow. We believe this conceptualization would align with that of Rogers: Affirmation/validation is the observable manifestation of the underlying positive regard. These therapist skills are used, assessed, and indeed taught in terms of positive regard.

Still, several problems with the concept of positive regard have been identified (e.g., Lietaer, 1984). One is that it is unlikely that any mental health practitioner can provide constant doses of unconditional positive regard inasmuch as we all reinforce selectively. We reinforce certain actions and not others, and even those actions that we strive to continually reinforce through positively regarding statements or behaviors are subject to the vagaries of our moods or circumstances and the shifting behaviors of those we encounter.

Research Review

To find studies that documented a relation between positive regard and outcome in psychotherapy, Farber et al. used the PsycInfo database. Main root terms searched in the title or the abstract were *positive regard*, *warmth*, *nonpossessive warmth*, *therapist affirmation*, *unconditional positive regard*, *acceptance*, *validation*, and *unconditional regard*. All these terms were crossed with *psychotherapy*, *psychotherapist*, and *psychotherapeutic*. Additional studies were located by running a search with the root term "*Barrett-Lennard*" given that he developed the most widely used instrument to assess positive regard. Furthermore, all meta-analyses and review articles yielded by these searches were reviewed for eligible empirical studies. Farber et al. generally excluded non-English articles from consideration, with the exception of a few papers that were translated (by a colleague) from German.

The specific inclusion criteria were as follows: (a) The study identified positive regard as unconditional regard, positive regard, warmth, nonpossessive warmth, affirmation, acceptance, or validation; (b) positive regard (in any of these forms) was considered as a predictor of outcome in the study; (c) the study reported quantitative outcome data and relevant statistics (e.g., correlations between positive regard ratings and treatment outcome or mean outcome comparisons between groups with differential positive regard ratings) that could be used to calculate effect sizes; and (d) treatment was individual, family, or group psychotherapy.

Farber et al. (2019) did not immediately exclude studies encountered through the search parameters described above that looked at positive regard as part of a "composite" factor—typically as part of the constellation of Rogerian facilitative conditions. Farber et al. obtained disaggregated raw data through correspondence with the authors of three studies, but in most cases this was not possible. Because investigating the facilitative conditions in aggregate is a relatively common practice in both early and more recent studies—a practice justified by the strong intercorrelations among positive regard, empathy, and congruence/genuineness—Farber et al. included these composite variables with the goal of testing for a moderating effect when positive regard is assessed singly versus in aggregate form. A total of 24 studies using composite scores (typically from the Truax rating scales or Barrett-Lennard inventory) were included in the meta-analysis. Only those studies in which the composite predictor (typically, the three facilitative conditions) was coherently defined with an overall clear relation to positive regard were included, whereas studies that aggregated positive regard with an excessively large or unwieldy group of variables were excluded. Finally, Farber et al. excluded studies that explicitly reported that participants in the low and high facilitative conditions groups did not have significantly different ratings of positive regard.

After scanning the literature with these criteria in mind, more than 100 studies were selected for review. In the end, 64 were found to be entirely consistent with these criteria and thus were included in the meta-analysis.

Because the purpose of this meta-analysis was to examine the relation between therapist positive regard and treatment outcome, effects sizes were collected for each analysis that included positive regard and an outcome variable. Since each study reported effects using different types of effect sizes, Farber et al. (2019) converted all effect sizes to Hedges' *g* (per Cooper et al., 2009). When computing Hedges' *g*, each effect size accounts for the sample size of each study-based analysis; thus, Hedges' *g* offers an unbiased estimator of *d* since the effect size estimate *d* tends to have a small overestimation bias that can be removed using a correction formula. A statistical package available online aided in the statistical analysis for this project (see Del Re, 2010; Del Re & Hoyt, 2010).

A total of 369 effect sizes within 64 studies, comprising 3,528 patients, were included in the overall analysis. Using a random effects model, the aggregate effect size was $g = .28$, indicating that positive regard has a small association with psychotherapy outcomes. In addition, the 95% confidence interval (CI) did not include zero (CI = 0.25, 0.31), indicating that the effect of positive regard on outcome is significantly different from zero.

To assess whether there was variability among these 64 studies above and beyond what would be expected by chance, a homogeneity test was conducted. Using the homogeneity statistics, Q and I^2 (Hedges, 1982), the assumption that the studies selected were sampled from the same population (i.e., were homogenous) was rejected (Q ($df = 368$) = 1132.56, $p < .0001$; $I^2 = 67.51\%$). This finding indicated that there a large amount of heterogeneity of effects among these studies, suggesting that there may be moderators of the effects produced.

To assess for publication bias or the "file drawer problem," Farber et al. (2019) conducted an Orwin's fail-safe *N* analysis. The analysis found that a total of 2,049 studies that are not significant at the .05 level would be needed to negate the strength of the aggregated effect. However, the funnel plot of included studies indicated the possibility of publication bias: The substantial asymmetry around the mean may be evidence that included studies disproportionally report elevated effect sizes, The studies that had effect sizes of $g > 1.0$ tended to be published before 1995 and have an n of less than 50, with two exceptions (Murphy & Cramer, 2010; Cordaro et al., 2012).

Since 369 effect sizes were nested within 64 studies, the assumption of independence was managed via stipulating a correlation between outcome measures of .5 (Wampold et al., 1997). To account for this issue statistically, Farber et al. (2019) employed a multilevel random effects meta-analysis in which effect sizes were nested within individual study samples (Konstantopoulos, 2011). This analysis accounted for the fact that some studies utilized the same data set to report multiple correlations of positive regard and outcome. Controlling for nesting within samples, the multilevel analysis yielded a larger effect than the random effects model, with an aggregate effect size of $g = .36$ (CI = 0.28, 0.44), and the same heterogeneity (Q ($df = 368$) = 1132.56, $p < .001$).

Seventy-five percent ($k = 48$, 369 effect sizes) of the studies included in the meta-analysis pertained to individual psychotherapy. The effect size (g) of those studies was .40 (with a 95% CI of 0.32 to 0.49).

Training Implications

The results of the meta-analysis suggest that therapist trainees of all theoretical persuasions should be taught adopt an attitude of positive regard—and display the behaviors of affirmation and validation—toward their clients. Farber et al. (2019) suggested that including Rogers' writings on the helping skills would contribute greatly to every beginning practica in graduate training programs regardless of the theoretical orientation of that course. They also suggested that practica instructors remind students that practices that encourage therapists to approach patients through a lens of detachment and neutrality, or through exclusively dispassionate, technically driven interventions, are contraindicated by research evidence.

In addition, there is value in monitoring the quality and consistency of positive regard that supervisees offer their clients. Although this may be partially accomplished through supervisory discussions of countertransference (i.e., of therapists' emotional attitudes toward patients), Farber et al. (2019) suggested that supervisors focus, at least occasionally, on the specific behaviors in which trainees' acceptance, validation, liking, and caring for their clients have been conveyed (or not) in sessions and what the clinical consequences of these actions have been. Supervisors would do well to find out what and why their supervisees convey certain affirming behaviors and adopt certain words and phrases but omit others. Such discussion might lead to profitable supervisory discussions regarding the state of the therapeutic alliance and/or the possibility of alliance ruptures within supervisees' caseloads.

Last, viewing "Gloria" is not enough given that many students' knowledge of Rogers begins and ends with seeing this film. It is a perfectly good introduction to Rogers' work and therapeutic philosophy, but based only on viewing this film, many students are left with the wrong impression of what an overall attitude of positive regard or affirmation entails. Watching multiple videos of Rogers' work, reading summaries or transcripts of his sessions (Farber et al., 1996), and/or observing others (e.g., Linehan, 1993, 1997) put into practice similar concepts (i.e., validation) are all likely to greatly expand students' understanding of the broad meanings and implications of demonstrating positive regard in their clinical work.

Therapeutic Practices

The provision of positive regard or affirmation significantly predicts and relates to success in individual psychotherapy. The meta-analysis indicates a moderate association, suggesting that positive regard is an important but not exhaustive part of the process–outcome equation. Extrapolating from the meta-analysis, the following recommendations are offered for clinical practice:

- Provide validation and affirmation in sessions. At a minimum, it "sets the stage" for other mutative interventions and, at least in some cases, may prove sufficient to effect positive change. In fact, there is virtually no research-driven reason to withhold positive regard.
- Keep in mind that affirming patients serves many valuable functions. It strengthens the client's sense of self or agency and belief in their capacity to be engaged in an effective relationship; functions as a positive reinforcer for clients' engagement in the therapeutic process, including difficult self-disclosures; and facilitates growth and resilience.
- Avoid the tendency to be content with feeling good about patients; instead, allow yourself to express positive feelings to clients. The therapist's conveyance of affirmation or positive regard does not have to translate to a stream of compliments or to a gushing of positive sentiment that may overwhelm or even terrify some clients; rather, therapists can communicate care and respect that affirms a client's sense of worth. To most clients, the conviction that "my therapist really cares about me" likely serves a critical function, especially in times of stress.
- Convey regard through multiple channels: offering reassuring, caring words; creating positive narratives; practicing active listening; allowing flexibility in scheduling; speaking in a gentle tone of voice; establishing responsive eye contact; and maintaining positive body language.

- Monitor your affirmation and adjust it as a function of particular patients and specific situations. The research demonstrates that clients vary in the extent to which they need, elicit, and/or benefit from it.

Self-Disclosure and Immediacy

Definition

Psychotherapist use of self-disclosure (TSD) and immediacy (IM) has long been controversial. Psychoanalytic theorists (Curtis, 1981, 1982; Greenson, 1967) traditionally urged analysts to remain neutral blank screens, allowing clients to project their material onto the clinician. More recent relational psychoanalysts (Eagle, 2011; Levenson, 2010; McWilliams, 2004), by contrast, have suggested that therapists can facilitate the therapeutic process by disclosing and talking about the relationship. Humanistic theorists (Bugental, 1965; Farber, 2006; Jourard, 1971), advocating for therapist transparency and genuineness, have typically viewed TSD and IM as curative elements of the therapeutic process. Many cognitive therapists (e.g., Beck et al., 1979) view the use of TSD and IM as beneficial to address problems that arise in the relationship.

TSD can be defined as "therapist statements that reveal something personal about the therapist" (Hill & Knox, 2002, p. 256). This definition can be further narrowed to involve a *verbal* revelation about the therapist's life or person *outside of therapy*, and to exclude nonverbal self-disclosures (e.g., a family photo on the desk) to focus on verbal statements that therapists share with clients. TSDs can be about feelings (e.g., "I get angry when someone pushes in front of me like that"), similarities (e.g., "I also had an anxiety disorder"), insight (e.g., "I realized that I have difficulty forming a relationship because my parents had such a bad relationship"), or strategies (e.g., "I try to eat fruits and vegetables and walk every day"). Therapists use TSD to establish a bond, to help clients feel normal or understood, and to encourage more client disclosure (Hill, 2020). Other terms used to describe this skill are self-revealing disclosures, extra-therapy disclosures, and transparency.

IM can be defined as the therapist and client processing the therapeutic relationship in the here-and-now (Hill, 2020) or "any discussion within the therapy session about the relationship between therapist and patient that occurs in the here-and-now, as well as any processing of what occurs in the here-and-now patient–therapist interaction" (Kuutmann & Hilsenroth, 2011, p. 188). IM occurs when therapists talk about the therapy relationship in the present moment. IM can include asking the client about immediate feelings and thoughts (e.g., "How are you feeling talking about this with me?"), expressing immediate therapist feelings (e.g., "I'm feeling annoyed that you are frequently late for sessions"), drawing parallels with other relationships (e.g., "You mentioned that no one seems to care about you . . . I wonder if you feel that I don't care about you?"), making the covert overt (e.g., "You seem so quiet . . . I wonder how you feel about being here?"), and acknowledging a breach in the relationship (e.g., "We seem to have reached an impasse"). Intentions for IM include encouraging the client to express unstated feelings; attempting to negotiate, enhance, or repair the therapy relationship;

and modeling appropriate ways to interact with others during conflict (Hill, 2020). Other terms that have been used to describe this skill include metacommunication, relational events, processing the therapy relationship, discussions about the here-and-now in the here-and-now, and present-focused work.

In both TSD and IM, therapists disclose about themselves during the treatment. With TSD, therapists disclose information or facts about themselves; with IM, therapists disclose about their experiences of the therapy process or relationship. In both TSD and IM, therapists may feel vulnerable bringing themselves into the relationship instead of focusing exclusively on the client.

Research Review

The task was to systematically review the literature on the clinical consequences of TSD and IM in therapy. In their review, Hill et al. (2019) included only studies published in English. They used five steps to identify possible studies: (a) included studies identified in earlier reviews; (b) manually examined the past 15 years of *Journal of Counseling Psychology*, *Journal of Consulting and Clinical Psychology*, *The Counseling Psychologist*, *Psychotherapy Research*, *Psychotherapy*, and *Counselling Psychology Quarterly*; (c) searched reference lists of relevant published articles; (d) conducted several PsycInfo searches using the following terms: disclosure, self-disclosure, self-revealing disclosure, self-disclosing disclosure, extra-therapy disclosure, transparency, immediacy, metacommunication, relational events, therapeutic processes, here and now, and present focus; and (e) sent a query to the listservs of the Society for Psychotherapy Research and the Society for Counseling Psychology, as well as to specific authors who had conducted research in these areas, asking for published or unpublished studies in this area written in English. In terms of unpublished data, they identified and included data about unhelpful TSDs that had not been published in the Knox et al. (1997) article and another study that has since been published (Pinto-Coelho et al., 2016).

To be included in the pool of studies, TSD and/or IM had to be specifically identified as occurring in psychotherapy sessions using one of two methods: (a) coded by trained judges or (b) clients or therapists were interviewed/surveyed and asked to identify specific TSDs or IMs that they recalled from therapy sessions. Only if specific TSDs and IMs were identified could their clinical consequences be specifically linked to the methods.

Each study also had to include clear statements about the number of participants for whom the consequences applied (e.g., "78% of the clients reported . . ." vs. a vague statement suggesting that TSD/IM was helpful without identifying for how much of the sample such a statement was true). The clinical consequences did not need to be immediate, given that the influence of TSD and IM could be evidenced beyond the immediate speaking turn.

Exclusion criteria included analogue designs, in which nonclients (e.g., typically psychology undergraduate students) read a transcript or watched a video portrayal of a therapist offering a TSD or IM and rated how much they liked it or how helpful it would be (e.g., Dowd & Boroto, 1982; McCarthy & Betz, 1978). Similarly, studies that asked about general attitudes toward TSD/IM (e.g., preference for using or receiving TSD) were excluded. Also excluded were correlational studies of the association between the frequency of TSD/IM and session or treatment outcome (e.g., Kuutman & Hilsenroth, 2011; Lingiardi et al., 2011), because there is no reliable way of knowing in correlational studies that the session or treatment outcomes are specifically linked with any particular TSD or IM.

Because almost all of the studies in the final database of 21 studies used qualitative designs, Hill et al. (2019) could not conduct a quantitative meta-analysis. Therefore, they conducted a qualitative meta-analysis (QMA; Hill et al., 2012; Hill & Knox, 2021), converting results from the three quantitative studies into qualitative results so that they could include them in the QMA. They linked TSD and IM with proximal or immediate clinical consequences, typically those that occurred within the session (we did not expect the influence of TSD or IM to be distal or last until the end of treatment).

All decisions were made via consensus of the authors. This consensus procedure involved considerable discussion and checking/rechecking the data to ensure that data were tabulated and interpreted as consistently as possible. They first recorded clinical consequences (e.g., gained insight) listed as being associated with specific TSDs/IMs for each study, using the authors' words as much as possible to describe these consequences. Based on the recorded data, Hill et al. (2019) then developed categories of clinical consequences (e.g., enhanced therapy relationship). As a team, they next consensually coded each consequence listed in each study into one of the categories. They revised the categories frequently throughout this process, trying to make them as clear as possible. After all consequences were coded, they collapsed categories that appeared to involve similar constructs, particularly to eliminate categories that seldom occurred.

As they proceeded, Hill et al. (2019) developed several decision rules. First, each clinical consequence could count only once per participant, even if several examples of the consequence were given and different terms were used for the consequences within a given category. Second, when they collapsed categories, they sometimes had the problem that different numbers of participants endorsed examples within categories. Their rule was to use the largest number rather than averaging across examples, because doing so provided the best representation of how many clients fit the overall category. Third, because several studies involved single cases and others involved multiple participants, it would not be fair to average across studies because doing so would assign disproportionally greater weight to studies with fewer participants. Instead, they counted the number of cases to which each clinical consequence applied in each study, as well as tabulated the total number of participants for each study.

Hill et al. (2019) tallied the results across studies for each clinical consequence. For example, using a hypothetical example of consequence X in four studies: X is mentioned once in a case study (so we coded 1/1), 9 times out of 13 cases in a qualitative study (9/13), 0 times in a qualitative study of 15 people (0/15), and a medium effect in a study of 30 (22/30). Thus, we could conclude that of the 59 participants, 32 (.54 or 54%) experienced consequence X.

They determined which clinical consequences occurred most frequently across all studies, reporting in this chapter on all those consequences that occurred for more than 30% of the total. To determine if some categories occurred more often than others, we a priori agreed to use Ladany et al.'s (2012) criterion that categories had to differ by at least 30% to be considered different (e.g., categories that were endorsed 70% vs. 40% would be considered different).

Self-Disclosure and Immediacy Combined

For the 21 studies that included a combined category of TSD and IM (total sample of 184 cases), the most frequently occurring clinical consequences were enhanced therapy relationship (60%), improved client mental health functioning (42%), client gained insight (38%), overall helpful for client (36%), and client opened up (33%). From this analysis, we conclude that the clinical consequences of TSDs and IMs are generally positive, in that the therapy relationship was enhanced, the clients had better mental health functioning, and the methods were overall perceived to be helpful. Furthermore, the negative clinical consequences were minimal. These results are consistent with previous reviews (Hill & Knox, 2002, 2009), but they provide a more sophisticated analysis of the findings. It is also interesting to think about the clinical consequences that were not found. None of the studies reported client resistance (e.g., avoidance, interrupting, or changing the topic), lack of involvement, direct expression of emotions (e.g., crying, laughter, or sighing), or action (e.g., behavior change).

The wide heterogeneity of studies included in this analysis, however, suggests caution in interpreting these results. The biggest difference was between TSD and IM, so these were analyzed separately.

TSD Linked with Immediate Outcome

In five studies that focused on TSD as a unique skill (not combined with IM, total of 99 cases), the four most frequently occurring clinical consequences were enhanced therapy relationship (64%), client gained insight (46%), client mental health functioning improved (45%), and overall helpful for client (37%). These results closely parallel the overall analysis of 21 studies, with the exception that the category of clients using IM never occurred in this sample, whereas it had in the overall sample (because of the IM studies). These results should be viewed with caution because there were only five studies that focused solely on TSD. These studies varied in terms of type (reciprocal, historical, philosophical, emotional, and unspecified), method of analysis (experimental, phenomenological, grounded theory, and consensual qualitative research), and perspective (client ratings after session, interviews of clients, and interviews of therapists).

IM Linked with Immediate Outcome

In the 15 studies that focused on IM as a unique skill (not combined with TSD, total of 78 cases), the most frequently occurring clinical consequences were enhanced therapy relationship (40%), client opened up (40%), and overall not helpful (39%). Thus, there were mostly positive consequences for the therapy relationship and for the client opening up, but also some negative consequences of not being helpful and the client not feeling understood.

As with the findings for TSD, however, Hill et al. (2019) recommended caution in interpreting these data because of the considerable heterogeneity among the 15 studies in terms of samples, events, and analyses. Fortunately, given that there were 15 IM studies, they could investigate some sources of heterogeneity, and we turn next to these subsample analyses of a set of five studies involving positive outcomes of rupture repairs and then six qualitative studies of a range of IM events. Differences between the two sets of studies were therapist experience level (therapists in the task analyses were all experienced, whereas 16 of the 25 therapists in the qualitative studies were doctoral students and only 9 were experienced) and valence of the events (only positive events were coded in the first set, but all events within therapy were coded in the qualitative analyses so that there were both positive and negative events).

For the 16 cases in the task analyses of repaired ruptures, the most frequently occurring categories were all positive: client opening up (100%), improvements in client mental health functioning (62%), gains in insight (56%), client used immediacy (38%), and enhanced therapy relationship (38%). Interestingly, judges observed no negative consequences for IM in these events, perhaps because only exemplar positive events were selected so that researchers could determine mechanisms of change. An alternate explanation is that clients and therapists were not interviewed about these events, and judges may not have been aware of some of the negative reactions of clients and therapists.

For the six qualitative studies on the range of IM events (total sample = 25), the most frequently occurring consequences were client opened up (60%), client used immediacy (55%), overall not helpful (50%), and gains in insight (41%). Thus, the clinical consequences for IM as used by mostly doctoral student therapists-in-training (16 of the 25 therapists) were mostly positive (client opening up, using immediacy, and gaining insight), although there were some negative clinical consequences.

If we directly compare the results for the five studies that involved trained judges coding IM as used by experienced therapists in positive events (repaired ruptures) with the results for the six studies that examined IM as used by therapists ranging in experience levels in both positive and negative events, again coded by trained judges, there were three meaningful differences (>30%). Studies examining only positive events had more improved mental health functioning (62% vs. 9%), more client opened up (100% vs. 60%), and less overall not helpful (0% vs. 50%). Thus, it appears (not surprisingly) that studying only positive events (repaired ruptures) in cases with experienced therapists provides a different and more positive perspective on the consequences of IM than does studying a range of positive and negative events with less experienced therapists. Although the experienced therapists in the task analyses also may have had negative IM events in their cases, these were not included in the studies because the researchers examined only repaired ruptures.

Comparison of TSD and IM

Hill et al. (2019) also compared the results of the five studies that focused on TSD and the six qualitative studies that focused on IM in a range of events. Studies in the two subsamples were similar in that all included both positive and negative events, although they varied in other ways (of the TSD studies, two involved client interviews, two involved interviews with experienced therapists, and one involved an experimental manipulation with doctoral-student therapists; all of the six IM studies involved trained judges coding in-session therapist behaviors and a range of experience levels of therapists). Hence, in addition to differences in findings between samples being due to the type of method (TSD vs. IM), differences could have been due to differences in the experience level of therapists, research approach (interviews vs. coding of behavior), or perspective (judges, therapists, and clients). With these limitations in mind, Hill et al. tentatively explored differences between the two subsamples.

They found five meaningful differences (>30%). TSD, as compared with IM, resulted in more improved mental health functioning (45% vs. 9%), more overall helpful for client (37% vs. 5%), more enhanced therapy relationship (64% vs. 23%), but less client opened up (27% vs. 60%) and less client using immediacy (0% vs. 55%). Perhaps the differences in consequences are related to differences in intent. With TSDs, therapists typically focus mostly on clients and use themselves to facilitate more client exploration (e.g., "When I have been in your situation, I felt angry. I wonder if you feel that way") and are likely to foster understanding and better mental health functioning. In contrast, IMs are often used because of problems in the relationship and are likely to reveal underlying stresses (e.g., "I am feeling bored right now, and I wonder what is going on with you?").

Training Implications

Given the QMA findings that TSD and IM lead to mostly positive consequences, training is needed to help therapists use these methods competently. In our years of training novice therapists, these are among the most difficult skills to learn to use effectively. In fact, doctoral-student therapists described self-disclosure and immediacy as difficult, advanced skills that were acquired only after considerable practice (Hill et al., 2015). Much of their challenge arises because they require so much of therapists personally, and it is difficult for novice therapists to set boundaries on what is and is not appropriate to share with clients.

Role-playing and deliberate practice (e.g., Hill et al., 2020) might prove helpful. Trainees would bring to supervision specific times that they could have used TSD or IM. They then would practice such skills in a safe, supportive environment. Next, they would use them in sessions with the target client and watch the videotaped results. By repeatedly practicing with the specific client and with supervisor feedback, trainees may be more likely to use these methods effectively with that client and, it is hoped, transfer such learning to future clients.

One study (Spangler et al., 2014), in fact, found that instruction, modeling, feedback, and practice were all effective in helping undergraduates learn to use immediacy, but practice was particularly effective. These findings again demonstrate that novice therapists may need extensive rehearsal in using these skills, perhaps in a number of different formats. Learning IM in a controlled training setting does not mean that trainees can apply it effectively in a clinical setting. In addition, intriguing qualitative findings in that same study pointed to the influence of culture in affecting students' ability to learn and use IM. Students from cultures that discourage direct communication, for example, found it more difficult to use IM, whereas students whose families encouraged open and direct communication found it easier to use the skill.

In a recent study (Pinto-Coelho et al., 2018), experienced therapists reported a lack of formal training in TSD. The practitioners suggested that trainers include explicit education about TSD in their curricula. Pinto-Coelho et al. reported that experiencing successful TSD in supervision, being paired with more experienced therapists (e.g., co-therapy and group therapy), and experiencing TSD in their own personal therapy were the most compelling training experiences. Development of a pre-TSD decision-making tool or a post-TSD measure could assist trainees in deciding when to disclose in a specific situation.

Therapeutic Practices

Both TSD and IM typically produced positive clinical consequences for clients, suggesting that therapists might consider using them in sessions. Given that previous research (e.g., Hill et al., 1988, 2014), however, has shown that both are relatively infrequent in psychotherapy, therapists need to use them sparingly for appropriate intentions or reasons.

- Consider using TSD when clients feel alone, vulnerable, and in need of support.
- Recall that TSD is typically a "safe" method when done skillfully and thoughtfully.
- Use these methods to facilitate client exploration, which fosters their understanding and better mental health functioning.
- Consider using IM to negotiate the relationship and when there are problems in the relationship.
- Beware that using IM to help clients open up and talk about feelings, especially when negotiating the therapeutic relationship, raises the potential for volatility.
- Be prepared to address your own and clients' reactions when using IM.
- Maintain the focus on the client rather than using these skills for therapist self-gratification.
- Evaluate how clients might respond and whether TSD is likely to help them.
- Make sure the therapeutic relationship is strong before using TSD.
- Keep the disclosure brief with few details, and disclose resolved rather than unresolved material.
- Make the TSD relevant to client material, especially emphasizing similarities between therapist and client.
- Turn the focus back to the client after delivering the TSD or IM, and observe the client's reactions and responses to the skills.
- Assess the skills' effectiveness and determine whether it would be advisable to use them again with this client.
- Be aware that therapist immediacy frequently generates increased client immediacy; if you desire clients to be more immediate, then consider being more immediate yourself.
- Recognize that therapist IM typically "raises the temperature in the room" and can prove challenging for therapists and clients uncomfortable with having open discussions about the relationship.

- Implement TSD and IM skillfully in routine practice by watching videotapes of session segments in which they had positive and problematic consequences, examining your countertransference needs, and engaging in deliberate practice.

Rupture Repairs

Definition

The growing literature on the therapeutic alliance (Norcross & Lambert, 2019b) underscores the importance of building a strong working relationship with patients. However, across therapies, there are moments when the alliance needs to be more figure than ground in order to keep the psychotherapy alive: when there is a rupture in the alliance.

Much of the alliance rupture literature draws on Bordin's (1979) conceptualization of the *alliance* as composed of (a) agreement between patient and therapist on the goals of treatment, (b) collaboration between patient and therapist on the tasks of treatment, and (c) an affective bond between the patient and therapist. A *rupture* is a deterioration in this alliance, manifested by a disagreement between the patient and therapist on the goals, a lack of collaboration on tasks, or a strain in the emotional bond (Eubanks-Carter et al., 2010; Safran & Muran, 2000). Although the term rupture may connote a dramatic breakdown in the therapeutic relationship, many studies of alliance ruptures also regard subtle tensions and minor misattunements as markers of ruptures.

A number of other terms have been used in the literature to describe problems or difficulties in the alliance. These include weakenings (e.g., Lansford, 1986), threats (e.g., Bennett et al., 2006), misattunements (e.g., Beebe & Lachmann, 2002), challenges (e.g., Agnew et al., 1994), misunderstandings (Rhodes et al., 1994), and impasses (Hill et al., 1996; Safran & Muran, 2000). Alliance ruptures are also related to constructs such as ambivalence and resistance (e.g., Hara et al., 2015; for a review, see Muran, 2019).

At an implicit level, ruptures can also be understood as (a) breakdowns in the continuous negotiation of therapists' and patients' respective needs and (b) negations due to power differences between therapists' and patients' respective identities (Muran & Eubanks, 2020). The former has been defined by the dialectical tension experienced as both therapist and patient pursue their own motivational needs for agency and communion (Safran & Muran, 2000); the latter by the dialectical tendency to objectify the other by culturally informed categories in the existential struggle toward mutual recognition of respective subjectivities. These dialectics are inherent to understanding ruptures and their ubiquity (Muran et al., 2022).

Ruptures appear in two main subtypes: withdrawal and confrontation ruptures (Harper, 1989a, 1989b; Safran & Muran, 2000). In withdrawal ruptures, the patient moves away from the therapist or the work of therapy, for example, by avoiding the therapist's questions or by hiding their dissatisfaction with therapy by being overly appeasing. In confrontation ruptures, the patient moves against the therapist or the work of therapy by expressing anger or dissatisfaction with the therapist or treatment, or by trying to pressure or control the therapist. Ruptures can also include elements of both withdrawal and confrontation.

A rupture is generally deemed to be repaired or resolved when the patient and therapist resume collaborating on the work of therapy with a strong affective bond. Strategies for resolving alliance ruptures include *direct* strategies, which involve the therapist and patient explicitly acknowledging the rupture, and *indirect* strategies, whereby the rupture is resolved without being explicitly acknowledged. Direct strategies have been understood with regard to the principle of metacommunication (Kiesler, 1996; Safran & Muran, 2000), which involves a collaborative inquiry into the respective subjectivities and contributions of both patient and therapist to the immediacy of the rupture experience.

Resolution strategies can also be conceptualized in terms of three pathways to repair (Muran & Eubanks, 2020). The first pathway involves reattuning to the patient via simple clarifications or validations of feelings and intentions; in other words, in the face of a rupture, the therapist continues to engage in alliance-building and alliance-maintaining behaviors by consistently approaching the patient with empathy, curiosity, and validation. The second involves the use of *immediate* strategies, such as explaining or modifying a therapy task, which are focused on repairing the rupture expeditiously and re-engaging in the work of therapy that the dyad was engaged in prior to the rupture. The third pathway consists of *expressive* strategies such as metacommunication that aim to shift the focus of the therapy session to exploring the rupture and the patient's needs or concerns that underlie it. Task analyses of immediate strategies for renegotiating therapy tasks or goals (Muran et al., 2023) and expressive strategies for exploring ruptures (Safran & Muran, 1996) provide some empirical support for these latter two pathways to repair. (For additional contributions to the rupture repair literature across multiple treatments, see Eubanks et al., 2022.)

Research Review

Eubanks et al. (2019) conducted a meta-analysis focused on the effects of repairing ruptures in individual psychotherapy. In an effort to capture all relevant studies, including studies they may have missed in their prior review (Safran et al., 2011), they set fewer limits on their literature search. They did not limit their search to studies published in English, nor to studies of only therapy with adults. In addition to the primary systematic search described below, which was conducted by the first author (CFE), supplementary searches were conducted by the second author (JCN) and by an advanced graduate student. The contributions of these additional searches are noted below.

The primary search involved a computerized search of the PsycInfo database. Using the search terms *alliance* and *rupture*, *alliance patterns*, and *alliance* (must be mentioned in the abstract) and *outcome*, a list of 1,749 peer-reviewed publications was generated on July 24, 2017. Removal of duplicates resulted in 1,700 publications. Eubanks et al. (2019) also conducted a PsycInfo search of publications that cited their prior meta-analysis in both forms in which it was published (Safran et al., 2011), yielding an additional 159 studies, resulting in a total of 1,859 publications. Finally, in order to ensure that they included studies that had been published in advance form online but had not yet appeared in a journal volume or in PsycInfo, they conducted a search of advance online publications in the journal *Psychotherapy Research* and identified five additional publications. The independent searches of the second author (JCM) and the graduate research assistant yielded 15 additional studies.

The abstracts of these publications were inspected for studies meeting the following criteria: (a) The publication must concern the alliance in psychotherapy (as opposed to other settings such as primary medical care or schools); (b) the publication must be an empirical study with quantitative measures of treatment or session-level outcome, not a review or theoretical paper; and (c) the study must investigate either alliance ruptures, identified using quantitative criteria, or rupture resolution training, which must feature a specific focus on helping therapists manage alliance ruptures and include a comparison group.

In order to capture all studies of alliance fluctuations that can be identified as ruptures and repairs, Eubanks et al. (2019) also included any study with multiple (three or more) measurements of the alliance across therapy, even if that study did not specifically use the term rupture in the title or abstract. Their hope was to capture studies that identified ruptures but possibly used other terms (e.g., alliance weakenings) to describe them. They chose a minimum of three alliance measurements because this is necessary for identifying a V-shaped high–low–high pattern. In cases in which they could not determine from the abstract whether or not the alliance was rated at least three times, they erred on the side of inclusivity and selected the study.

These cumulative selection processes yielded 388 studies that underwent full-text review. Based on this review, 17 studies were selected for inclusion in the meta-analyses, and 371 studies were rejected. Reasons for rejection were as follows: The study did not include a quantitative measurement of ruptures or rupture resolution training (339), the study did not link rupture-repair or rupture resolution training to outcome (17), the study used the same data set as another study in the meta-analysis (5), the study was a task analysis or case study (6), the study provided rupture resolution training but lacked a bona fide comparison group (3), and the study did not report information needed to calculate effect sizes (1).

Eubanks et al. (2019) received additional data necessary for calculating effect sizes from the authors of five studies. In addition, they utilized data obtained previously from the author of one of the studies included in their prior meta-analysis (Safran et al., 2011). Finally, they included data from two studies (Eubanks, Lubitz, et al., 2019; Lipner et al., 2022) that were in preparation at the time of the search and were conducted by our research team. These two studies had 10 overlapping cases, so effect sizes were recalculated excluding those 10 cases from Lipner et al. (2022) to ensure that no cases would be included twice in the meta-analysis. In sum, their search efforts yielded 11 studies that were selected for inclusion in the meta-analysis of ruptures, repairs, and outcome, and six studies for the analysis of rupture resolution training.

Studies that met inclusion criteria were coded for the following: descriptive study information and sample characteristics including type of treatment, length of treatment, prevalence of personality disorder diagnoses in the sample, method used to measure alliance ruptures and repairs, timing of measurement of alliance ruptures and repairs, number of patients, number of therapists, comparison groups, frequency of ruptures and repairs in the sample, and data for the calculation of effect sizes. All studies were coded by the first author (CFE), and 58% of randomly selected studies were coded by an additional coder, either the second author (JCN) or a graduate research assistant.

Coders showed a high level of agreement (95.4%) across all variables. Differences were resolved through discussion and consensus.

Effect sizes were recalculated for all studies. Standardized mean differences were calculated based on means and standard deviations or *F* ratios provided in the articles or directly from the authors. These standardized mean scores were then converted into *r* and *d* effect sizes. When studies reported more than one measure of treatment outcome, effect sizes were calculated for each outcome measure and then averaged to form one effect size per study. Comprehensive Meta-Analysis Version 3.3.07 was used for all analyses using random effect models.

When studies reported findings for more than one comparison group, Eubanks et al. (2019) selected one comparison group to focus on. Specifically, for the analysis of ruptures, repairs, and outcome, some studies compared patients with rupture–repair episodes to patients without rupture–repair episodes, thereby lumping together patients with unrepaired ruptures and patients with no ruptures. Other studies distinguished between repaired, unrepaired, and no rupture groups. To highlight the clinical importance of repairing a rupture over against leaving it unrepaired, they chose to focus on the comparison between repaired and unrepaired ruptures. However, they also ran analyses comparing patients with repaired ruptures to patients with no ruptures and report those findings below.

Eubanks et al. (2019) conducted two meta-analyses. The first meta-analysis examined the association between alliance rupture–repair and outcome in the 11 studies that provided sufficient data for this analysis. These studies, involving 1,318 patients, consisted of investigations of the relation between rupture resolution (measured by self-report or observer coding) and distal outcome (operationalized as completion of therapy vs. premature dropout, or as change in symptom measures from intake to termination), studies that compared the outcomes of patients with rupture–repair episodes to patients who did not have rupture–repair episodes, and studies that compared the outcomes of patients with rupture–repair episodes to patients with ruptures that were not repaired. The first meta-analysis yielded an effect size of $r = .30$, $d = .62$, $z = 2.96$, 95% CI (.10, .47), $p = .003$, indicating a statistically significant, moderate relation between rupture resolution and positive patient outcome. The fail-safe *N* was 182. Given that some studies included comparisons across three types of cases—repaired ruptures, unrepaired ruptures, and no ruptures—they also ran the analysis using the comparison of patients with rupture–repair episodes to patients with no ruptures and obtained similar results: $r = .25$, $d = .51$, $z = 4.45$, 95% CI [.14, .35], $p < .001$.

Our second meta-analysis examined the impact of rupture resolution training or supervision on patient outcome. This analysis encompassed six studies, 276 trainees/supervisees, and approximately 407 patients treated by those trainees/supervisees. The aggregated correlation was $r = .11$, $d = .22$, $z = 1.08$, 95% CI (−.09, .30), $p = .28$, suggesting that rupture resolution training had only a small, statistically nonsignificant impact on patient outcomes in the present sample. Of course, with a larger number of studies and greater power, such a modest effect may have proven statistically significant, as it was in their previous meta-analysis.

Mean weighted effect sizes across the six studies were significantly heterogeneous, $Q(5) = 17.19$, $p = .004$, $I^2 = 70.92$. Thus, Eubanks et al. (2019) examined several potential moderators (patient, trainee/therapist, and training characteristics) that might explain this variability, and found two significant moderators. First, they entered the percentage of patients in the study with a personality disorder diagnosis as a continuous variable in a meta-regression and found that personality disorder diagnosis was a significant moderator, $B = -.007$, standard error = .0021, 95% CI (–.0106, –.0024), $z = -3.12$, $p = .002$. The greater the percentage of patients with personality disorder diagnoses, the smaller the correlation between rupture resolution training and patient outcome. Second, when they grouped studies according to whether the rupture resolution training condition was more closely aligned with cognitive–behavioral therapy (CBT) or with psychodynamic therapy, they found a significant difference, $Q(1) = 13.57$, $p < .001$. For more CBT treatments, rupture resolution training was associated with better patient outcome, $r = .28$, $z = 3.96$, $p < .001$, but not for psychodynamic treatments.

There were several landmark studies in the rupture literature that did not meet inclusion criteria for either of the two meta-analyses due to their designs, but they offer promising support for rupture repair strategies and/or training. In a series of single-case studies ($N = 8$, two sessions per case), Safran and Muran (1996; Safran et al., 1990, 1994) applied the task analytic method to define a four-stage model of the rupture resolution process (related to session-level outcome): (a) The therapist recognizes and draws the patient's attention to the rupture; (b) the patient and therapist explore the rupture collaboratively; (c) if the patient becomes uncomfortable exploring the rupture, the therapist encourages an exploration of the patient's avoidance maneuvers and their function; and (d) the therapist and patient focus on clarifying the patient's core relational wish or fear that underlies the rupture. Task analyses by other research teams have provided additional support for the value of therapists recognizing ruptures and then addressing them via collaborative exploration of the rupture (Agnew et al., 1994; Bennett et al., 2006; Daly et al., 2010; Swank & Wittenborn, 2013). A recent task analysis of rupture repair in CBT for personality disorders via renegotiation of tasks or goals (Muran et al., 2023) yielded a rational–empirical model that identified a variety of repair strategies that therapists can employ, including explaining the rationale for a task or goal, clarifying obstacles to a task or goal, and changing or modifying the task or goal. Similar findings highlighting the value of therapists responsively changing a task to meet a patient's concerns were obtained in two other task analyses of rupture repair in CBT (Aspland et al., 2008; Cash et al., 2014).

The strongest empirical support for training therapists to recognize and address alliance ruptures comes from a randomized controlled trial of the additive effect of alliance-focused training on CBT for personality disorders (Muran et al., 2018). In this study, which utilized a multiple baseline design, therapist trainees began conducting a case in CBT with CBT supervision. Therapists were randomly assigned to switch from CBT supervision to alliance-focused training after either 8 or 16 sessions. As predicted, after switching from CBT to alliance-focused training, therapist trainees demonstrated decreases in blaming behaviors (e.g., criticizing the patient) and directiveness (e.g., directing the patient how to behave), and patients demonstrated complementary decreases in dependent behaviors (e.g., following, accepting, and relying on the direction of the other). Both therapists and patients demonstrated increases in expressiveness (e.g., disclosing, expressing one's innermost self) and affirming behaviors (e.g., understanding the other, providing emotional support, and encouraging autonomy) following the switch from CBT to alliance-focused training. Analyses indicated that several of the changes in therapist behavior were linked to positive treatment outcome.

Training Implications

Eubanks et al.'s (2019) meta-analysis found a medium-size effect for the positive impact of rupture resolution in session on distal patient outcome and a small, nonsignificant effect for rupture resolution training on patient outcomes. There is also promising evidence that alliance-focused training can lead to improvements in how therapists interact with patients (Muran, 2019; Muran et al., 2018). Critical components of alliance-focused training include increasing therapist awareness of ruptures and improving therapists' abilities to regulate their emotions around ruptures. Generally, therapists cannot resolve ruptures that they cannot recognize or tolerate (Muran & Eubanks, 2020). Therapist recognition of ruptures has been associated with improvements in client functioning, even when therapists identify ruptures that clients did not (Chen et al., 2018).

Ruptures can be emotionally challenging experiences for therapists, so supervisors need to build a strong supervisory alliance to create a safe space for trainees to share their experiences of ruptures, while also challenging them to approach rather than avoid ruptures (Eubanks-Carter et al., 2015; Muran et al., 2010; Urmanche et al., 2021). Supervisors can model responsiveness to ruptures that emerge in the supervisory alliance, particularly because subtle, passive withdrawal in response to perceived supervisor criticism may be more common than direct confrontation (Friedlander, 2015).

Moderator analysis revealed that rupture resolution training was particularly valuable for cognitive behavior therapists, many of whom may not have received explicit training in processing relationship dynamics with their patients. Eubanks et al. (2019) recommended rupture resolution training for all therapists, but proposed that it may be especially important for therapists with less experience and training in negotiating the therapeutic alliance.

Eubanks et al. (2019) argued that the aim of alliance-focused training is not to teach therapists a prescription of exactly how to handle a rupture but, rather, to equip them with skills that prepare them to derive their own personalized solutions to specific ruptures when they arise. Therapists need to recognize ruptures; tolerate the difficult emotions they evoke; and respond to their patients in an empathic, genuine, flexible way that is responsive to patients' needs.

The training techniques used to facilitate these skills include videotape analysis of rupture moments, awareness-oriented role plays, and mindfulness training. Videotape analysis should focus on closely attending to moments of rupture and encouraging trainees to become more aware and accepting of what they were experiencing during the rupture. Awareness-oriented role plays in which trainees take turns playing the roles of patient and therapist can help them become more aware of feelings that were contributing to the rupture and actively engage with any concerns they have about addressing the rupture with the patient. Eubanks et al. (2019) encouraged trainees to develop mindfulness practices incorporate mindfulness exercises into supervision sessions in order to enhance trainees' ability to attend to the here and now with an attitude of curiosity and nonjudgmental acceptance. In addition to these key features, alliance-focused training can also include readings, watching tapes of experienced therapists, and training in process measures such as the Rupture Resolution Rating System or 3RS (Eubanks et al., in press; Muran & Eubanks, 2020).

Therapeutic Practices

The research reviewed here demonstrates that alliance rupture repair is associated with positive outcome. Eubanks et al. (2019) described research-supported practices for addressing and repairing ruptures in the alliance.

- Be attuned to indications of ruptures in the therapeutic relationship. Be alert to the presence of confrontation ruptures, in which patients express dissatisfaction or hostility, as well as more subtle markers of withdrawal, which may take the form of patients evading or appeasing the therapist in an effort to move away from the therapist or the work.
- Be alert as well to one's own engagement in rupture behaviors, such as becoming overly defensive or controlling (confrontation markers) or filling the session with abstract, intellectualized talk (withdrawal marker).
- Acknowledge the rupture directly. If the bond is not strong enough for a direct exploration of the rupture, or if direct exploration would take the focus away from a therapeutic task that needs to be prioritized to alleviate great distress, then address ruptures in an indirect, immediate manner, by responsively changing the tasks or goals of therapy in the direction of the patient's concerns.
- Invite patients, openly and nondefensively, to explore their experience of the rupture.
- Empathize with patients' expression of negative feelings about the therapist or the therapy.
- Validate patients for broaching a difficult and potentially divisive topic in the session.
- Accept responsibility for one's own participation in the rupture, and do not blame patients for misunderstanding or failing to comply with the therapist's wishes.
- Consider linking ruptures in session to interpersonal patterns in the patient's life outside of sessions to engage a patient who is withdrawing from a focus on the rupture.
- Be alert at the same time to the possibility that you—and your patients—may feel pulled to link the rupture to other relationships in order to escape a painful exploration of how the therapist is disappointing the patient.
- Anticipate that ruptures can evoke feelings of confusion, ambivalence, incompetence, and guilt in therapists.
- Develop your abilities to recognize, tolerate, validate, and empathically explore your own negative feelings so that you can do the same for your patients.

References

Agnew, R. M., Harper, H., Shapiro, D. A., & Barkham, M. (1994). Resolving a challenge to the therapeutic relationship: A single case study. *British Journal of Medical Psychology*, *67*, 155–170. https://doi.org/10.1111/j.2044-8341.1994.tb01783.x

Aspland, H., Llewelyn, S., Hardy, G. E., Barkham, M., & Stiles, W. (2008). Alliance ruptures and rupture resolution in cognitive–behavior therapy: A preliminary task analysis. *Psychotherapy Research*, *18*, 699–710.

Beck, A. T., Rush, J. A., Shaw, B. R., & Emery, G. (1979). *Cognitive therapy of depression*. Guilford.

Beebe, B., & Lachmann, F. M. (2002). *Infant research and adult treatment: Co-constructing interactions*. Taylor & Francis.

Bennett, D., Parry, G., & Ryle, A. (2006). Resolving threats to the therapeutic alliance in cognitive analytic therapy of borderline personality disorder: A task analysis. *Psychology and Psychotherapy, 79*, 395–418. https://doi.org/10.1348/147608305X58355

Bordin, E. (1979). The generalizability of the psychoanalytic concept of the working alliance. *Psychotherapy, 16*, 252–260. https://doi.org/10.1037/h0085885

Bugental, J. F. T. (1965). *The search for authenticity*. Holt, Rinehart & Winston.

Cash, S. K., Hardy, G. E., Kellett, S., & Parry, G. (2014). Alliance ruptures and resolution during cognitive behaviour therapy with patients with borderline personality disorder. *Psychotherapy Research, 24*(2), 132–145. https://doi.org/10.1080/10503307.2013.838652

Chen, R., Atzil-Slonim, D., Bar-Kaila, E., Hasson-Ohayon, I., & Refaeli, E. (2018). Therapists' recognition of alliance ruptures as a moderator of change in alliance and symptoms. *Psychotherapy Research, 28*, 560–570. https://doi.org/10.1080/10503307.2016.1227104

Cooper, H., Hedges, L. V., & Valentine, J. C. (Eds.). (2009). *The handbook of research synthesis and meta-analysis* (2nd ed.). Russell Sage Foundation.

Cordaro, M., Tubman, J. G., Wagner, E. F., & Morris, S. L. (2012). Treatment process predictors of program completion or dropout among minority adolescents enrolled in a brief motivational substance abuse intervention. *Journal of Child & Adolescent Substance Abuse, 21*, 51–68. https://doi.org/10.1080/1067828X.2012.636697

Curtis, J. M. (1981). Indications and contraindications in the use of therapist's self-disclosure. *Psychological Reports, 49*, 499–507. https://doi.org/10.2466/pr0.1981.49.2.499

Curtis, J. M. (1982). Principles and techniques of non-disclosure by the therapist during psychotherapy. *Psychological Reports, 51*, 907–914. https://doi.org/10.2466/pr0.1982.51.3.907

Daly, A.-M., Llewelyn, S., McDougall, E., & Chanen, A. M. (2010). Rupture resolution in cognitive analytic therapy for adolescents with borderline personality disorder. *Psychology & Psychotherapy: Theory, Research & Practice, 83*(3), 273–288. https://doi.org/10.1348/147608309X481036

Del Re, A. C. (2010). *RcmdrPlugin.MAc: Meta-analysis with correlations (MAc) Rcmdr Plug-in* (R package version 1.0.7). http://CRAN.R-project.org/package=MAc

Del Re, A. C., & Hoyt, W. T. (2010). *MAc: Meta-Analysis with correlations* (R package version 1.0.6). https://CRAN.R-project.org/package=MAc

Dowd, E. T., & Boroto, D. R. (1982). Differential effects of therapist self-disclosure, self-involving statements, and interpretation. *Journal of Counseling Psychology, 29*, 8–13. https://doi.org/10.1037/0022-0167.29.1.8

Eagle, M. N. (2011). *From classical to contemporary psychoanalysis: A critique and integration*. Routledge.

Eubanks, C. F., Lubitz, J., Muran, J. C., & Safran, J. D (2019). Repairing alliance ruptures. In J. C. Norcross & M. J. Lambert (Eds.), *Psychotherapy relationships that work: Volume 1. Evidence-based therapist contributions* (3rd ed., pp. 549–579). Oxford University Press.

Eubanks, C. F., Muran, J. C., & Samstag, L. W. (in press). Alliance-focused training: Teaching therapists to navigate alliance ruptures. In L. G. Castonguay & C. E. Hill (Eds.), *Advancing training and supervision in psychotherapy*. American Psychological Association.

Eubanks, C. F., Samstag, L. W., & Muran, J. C. (2022). *Rupture & repair in psychotherapy: A critical process for change*. American Psychological Association.

Eubanks-Carter, C., Muran, J. C., & Safran, J. D. (2010). Alliance ruptures and resolution. In J. C. Muran & J. P. Barber (Eds.), *The therapeutic alliance: An evidence-based approach to practice and training* (pp. 74–94). Guilford.

Eubanks-Carter, C., Muran, J. C., & Safran, J. D. (2015). Alliance-focused training. *Psychotherapy, 52*, 169–173. https://doi.org/10.1037/a0037596

Farber, B. A. (2006). *Self-disclosure in psychotherapy*. Guilford.

Farber, B. A., Brink, D. C., & Raskin, P. M. (1996). *The psychotherapy of Carl Rogers: Cases and commentary*. Guilford.

Farber, B. A., Suzuki, J. Y., & Lynch, D. A. (2019). Positive regard and affirmation. In J. C. Norcross & M. J. Lambert (Eds.), *Psychotherapy relationships that work: Volume 1. Evidence-based therapist contributions* (3rd ed., pp. 288–322). Oxford University Press.

Farber, B. A., Suzuki, J. Y., & Ort, D. (2022). *Understanding and enhancing positive regard in psychotherapy: Carl Rogers and beyond*. American Psychological Association.

Friedlander, M. L. (2015). Use of relational strategies to repair alliance ruptures: How responsive supervisors train responsive psychotherapists. *Psychotherapy, 53*, 214–225. https://doi.org/10.1037/a0037044

Gelso, C. J. (2005). Introduction to special issue. *Psychotherapy, 42*, 419–420. https://doi.org/10.1037/0033-3204.42.4.419

Greenson, R. R. (1967). *The technique and practice of psychoanalysis* (Vol. 1). International Universities Press.

Hara, K. M., Westra, H. A., Aviram, A., Button, M. L., Constantino, M. J., & Antony, M. M. (2015). Therapist awareness of client resistance in cognitive–behavioral therapy for generalized anxiety disorder. *Cognitive Behavior Therapy, 44*, 162–174. https://doi.org/10.1080/16506073.2014.998705

Harper, H. (1989a). *Coding guide I: Identification of confrontation challenges in exploratory therapy*. University of Sheffield.

Harper, H. (1989b). *Coding guide II: Identification of withdrawal challenges in exploratory therapy*. University of Sheffield.

Hedges, L. V. (1982). Estimating effect sizes from a series of independent experiments. *Psychological Bulletin, 92*, 490–499. https://doi.org/10.1037/0033-2909.92.2.490

Hill, C. E. (2020). *Helping skills: Facilitating exploration, insight, and action*. American Psychological Association.

Hill, C. E., Baumann, E., Shafran, N., Gupta, S., Morrison, A., Peres Rojas, A., Spangler, P. T., Griffin, S., Pappa, L., &. Gelso, C. J. (2015). Is training effective? A study of counseling psychology doctoral trainees in a psychodynamic/interpersonal training clinic. *Journal of Counseling Psychology, 62*, 184–201. https://doi.org/10.1037/cou0000053

Hill, C. E., Gelso, C. J., Chui, H., Spangler, P., Hummel, A., Huang, T., Jackson, J., Jones, R., Palma, B., Bhatia, A., Gupta, S., Ain, S., Klingaman, B., Lim, R., Liu, J., Hui, K., Jezzi, M., & Miles, J. R. (2014). To be or not to be immediate with clients: The use and perceived effects of immediacy in psychodynamic/interpersonal psychotherapy. *Psychotherapy Research, 3*, 299–315. https://doi.org/10.1080/10503307.2013.812262

Hill, C. E., Helms, J. E., Tichenor, V., Spiegel, S. B., O'Grady, K. E., & Perry, E. S. (1988). The effects of therapist response modes in brief psychotherapy. *Journal of Counseling Psychology, 35*, 222–233. https://doi.org/10.1037/10412-004

Hill, C. E., Kivlighan, D. M., III, Rousmaniere, T., Kivlighan, D. M., Jr., Gerstenblith, J. A., & Hillman, J. W. (2020). Deliberate practice: Effects on doctoral student therapists and clients. *Psychotherapy, 57*, 587–597. https://doi.org/10.1037/pst0000247

Hill, C. E., & Knox, S. (2002). Self-disclosure. In J. C. Norcross (Ed.), *Psychotherapy relationships that work: Therapist contributions and responsiveness to patient needs* (pp. 249–259). Oxford University Press.

Hill, C. E., & Knox, S. (2009). Processing the therapeutic relationship. *Psychotherapy Research, 19*, 13–29. https://doi.org/10.1080/10503300802621206

Hill, C. E., & Knox, S. (2021). *Essentials of consensual qualitative research*. American Psychological Association.

Hill, C. E., Knox, S., & Hess, S. (2012). *Qualitative meta-analysis*. In C. E. Hill (Ed.), *Consensual qualitative research: A practical resource for investigating social science phenomena* (pp. 159–172). American Psychological Association.

Hill, C. E., Knox, S., & Pinto-Coelho, K. G. (2019). Self-disclosure and immediacy. In J. C. Norcross & M. J. Lambert (Eds.). Psychotherapy relationships that work Volume i: Evidence-based therapist contributions (3rd ed., pp 379-420. Oxford University Press. *Psychotherapy, 55*, 445–460. https://doi.org/10.1037/pst0000182

Hill, C. E., Knox, S., & Pinto-Coelho, K. G. (2019). Self-disclosure and immediacy. In J. C. Norcross & M. J. Lambert (Eds.), *Psychotherapy relationships that work: Volume 1. Evidence-based therapist contributions* (3rd ed., pp. 379–420). Oxford University Press.

Hill, C. E., Nutt-Williams, E., Heaton, K. J., Thompson, B. J., & Rhodes, R. H. (1996). Therapist retrospective recall of impasses in long-term psychotherapy: A qualitative analysis. *Journal of Counseling Psychology, 43*, 207–217. https://doi.org/10.1037/0022-0167.43.2.207

Jourard, S. M. (1971). *The transparent self.* Van Nostrand.

Kiesler, D. J. (1996). *Contemporary interpersonal theory and research: Personality, psychopathology, and psychotherapy.* Wiley.

Knox, S., Hess, S., Petersen, D., & Hill, C. E. (1997). A qualitative analysis of client perceptions of the effects of helpful therapist self-disclosure in long-term therapy. *Journal of Counseling Psychology, 44*(3), 274–283. https://doi.org/10.1037/0022-0167.44.3.274

Konstantopoulos, S. (2011). Fixed effects and variance components estimation in three-level meta-analysis. *Research Synthesis Methods, 2*, 61–76. https://doi.org/10.1002/jrsm.35

Kuutmann, K., & Hilsenroth, M. J. (2011). Exploring in-session focus on the patient–therapist relationship: Patient characteristics, process and outcome. *Clinical Psychology and Psychotherapy, 19*, 187–202. https://doi.org/10.1002/cpp.743

Ladany, N., Thompson, B. J., & Hill, C. E. (2012). Cross analysis. In C. E. Hill (Ed.), *Consensual qualitative research: A practical resource for investigating social science phenomena* (pp. 117–134). American Psychological Association.

Lambert, M. J., Whipple, J. L., & Kleinstäuber, M. (2019). Collecting and delivering client feedback. In J. C. Norcross & M. J. Lambert (Eds.), *Psychotherapy relationships that work: Volume 1. Evidence-based therapist contributions* (3rd ed., pp. 580–630). Oxford University Press.

Lansford, E. (1986). Weakenings and repairs of the working alliance in short-term psychotherapy. *Professional Psychology: Research and Practice, 1*, 364–366. https://doi.org/10.1037/0735-7028.17.4.364

Levenson, H. (2010). *Brief dynamic therapy.* American Psychological Association.

Lietaer, G. (1984). Unconditional positive regard: A controversial basic attitude in client-centered therapy. In R. F. Levant & J. M. Shlien (Eds.), *Client-centered therapy and the person-centered approach* (pp. 41–58). Praeger.

Linehan, M. M. (1993). *Cognitive behavioral treatment of borderline personality disorder.* Guilford.

Linehan, M. M. (1997). Validation and psychotherapy. In A. Bohart & L. Greenberg (Eds.), *Empathy reconsidered: New directions in psychotherapy* (pp. 353–392). American Psychological Association. https://doi.org/10.1037/10226-016

Lingiardi, V., Colli, A., Gentile, D., & Tanzilli, A. (2011). Exploration of session process: Relationship to depth and alliance. *Psychotherapy, 48*, 391–400. https://doi.org/10.1037/a0025248

Lipner, L. M., Muran, J. C., Eubanks, C. F., Gorman, B., & Winston, A. (2022). Operationalizing alliance rupture–repair events using control chart methods. *Clinical Psychology & Psychotherapy, 29*, 339–350. https://doi.org/10.1002/cpp.2606

McCarthy, P. R., & Betz, N. E. (1978). Differential effects of self-disclosing versus self-involving counselor statements. *Journal of Counseling Psychology, 25*, 251–256. https://doi.org/10.1037/0022-0167.25.4.251

McWilliams, N. (2004). *Psychoanalytic psychotherapy: A practitioner's guide* (pp. 180–189). Guilford.

Muran, J. C. (2007). A relational turn on thick description. In J. C. Muran (Ed.), *Dialogues on difference: Diversity studies of the therapeutic relationship* (pp. 257–274). American Psychological Association.

Muran, J. C. (2019). Confessions of a New York rupture researcher: An insider's guide and critique. *Psychotherapy Research, 29*, 1–14. https://doi.org/10.1080/10503307.2017.1413261

Muran, J. C., & Eubanks, C. F. (2020). *Therapist performance under pressure: Negotiating emotion, difference, and rupture.* American Psychological Association.

Muran, J. C., Eubanks, C. F., Lipner, L. M., & Bloch-Elkouby, S. (2023). Renegotiating tasks or goals as rupture repair: A task analysis in a cognitive–behavioral therapy for personality disorder. *Psychotherapy Research, 33*(1), 16–29. https://doi.org/10.1080/10503307.2022.2079439

Muran, J. C., Eubanks, C. F., & Samstag, L. W. (2022). Rupture in a wicked and wonderful world. In C. F. Eubanks, L. W. Samstag, & J. C. Muran (Eds.), *Rupture & repair in psychotherapy: A critical process for change* (pp. 3–20). American Psychological Association.

Muran, J. C., Safran, J. D., & Eubanks-Carter, C. (2010). Developing therapist abilities to negotiate alliance ruptures. In J. C. Muran & J. P. Barber (Eds.), *The therapeutic alliance: An evidence-based guide to practice*. (pp. 320–340). Guilford.

Muran, J. C., Safran, J. D., Eubanks, C. F., & Gorman, B. S. (2018). The effect of alliance-focused training on a cognitive–behavioral therapy for personality disorders. *Journal of Consulting and Clinical Psychology*, *86*, 384–397. https://doi.org/10.1037/ccp0000284

Murphy, D., & Cramer, D. (2010, July). Mutuality as relational empowerment [Paper presentation]. World Association for Person-Centered and Experiential Psychotherapy and Counselling, Rome, Italy.

Norcross, J. C., & Lambert, M. J. (2019a). *Psychotherapy relationships that work: Volume 1. Evidence-based therapist contributions* (3rd ed.). Oxford University Press.

Norcross, J. C., & Lambert, M. J. (2019b). Evidence-based psychotherapy relationships: The Third Task Force. In J. C. Norcross & M. J. Lambert (Eds.), *Psychotherapy relationships that work: Volume 1. Evidence-based therapist contributions* (3rd ed., pp. 1–23). Oxford University Press.

Orlinsky, D. E., Grawe, K., & Parks, B. K. (1994). Process and outcome in psychotherapy—Noch einmal. In A. E. Bergin & S. L. Garfield (Eds.), *Handbook of psychotherapy and behavior change* (4th ed., pp. 27–376). Wiley.

Orlinsky, D. E., Ronnestad, M. H., & Willutzki, U. (2004). Fifty years of psychotherapy process-outcome research: Continuity and change. In M. J. Lambert (Ed.), *Bergin and Garfield's handbook of psychotherapy and behavior change* (pp. 307–389). Wiley.

Pinto-Coelho, K. G., Hill, C. E., Kearney, M. S., Sauber, E., Sarno, E. L., Brady, J., Baker, S. M., Ireland, G. W., Hoffman, M. A., Spangler, P. T., & Thompson, B. J. (2018). When in doubt, sit quietly: A qualitative investigation of experienced therapists' perceptions of self-disclosure. *Journal of Counseling Psychology*, *65*, 440–452. https://doi.org/10.1037/cou0000288

Pinto-Coelho, K., Hill, C. E., & Kivlighan, D. (2016). Therapist self-disclosures in psychodynamic psychotherapy: A mixed methods investigation. *Counselling Psychology Quarterly*, *29*, 29–52. https://doi.org/10.1080/09515070.2015.1072496

Rhodes, R., Hill, C. E., Thompson, B. J., & Elliott, R. (1994). Client retrospective recall of resolved and unresolved misunderstanding events. *Journal of Counseling Psychology*, *41*, 473–483. https://doi.org/10.1037/0022-0167.41.4.473

Rogers, C. R. (1957). The necessary and sufficient conditions of therapeutic personality change. *Journal of Consulting Psychology*, *21*, 95–103. https://doi.org/10.1037/h0045357

Rogers, C. R. (1959). A theory of therapy, personality, and interpersonal relationships: As developed in the client-centered framework. In S. Koch (Ed.), *Psychology: A study of a science. Study 1, Volume 3* (pp. 184–256). McGraw-Hill.

Safran, J. D., Crocker, P., McMain, S., & Murray, P. (1990). The therapeutic alliance rupture as a therapy event for empirical investigation. *Psychotherapy: Theory, Research and Practice*, *27*, 154–165.

Safran, J. D., & Muran, J. C. (1996). The resolution of ruptures in the therapeutic alliance. *Journal of Counseling and Clinical Psychology*, *64*, 447–458. https://doi.org/10.1037/0022-006X.64.3.447

Safran, J. D., & Muran, J. C. (2000). *Negotiating the therapeutic alliance: A relational treatment guide*. Guilford.

Safran, J. D., Muran, J. C., & Eubanks-Carter, C. (2011). Repairing alliance ruptures. In J. C. Norcross (Ed.), *Psychotherapy relationships that work* (2nd ed., pp. 224–238). Oxford University Press.

Safran, J. D., Muran, J. C., & Samstag, L. W. (1994). Resolving therapeutic alliance ruptures: A task analytic investigation. In A. O. Horvath & L. S. Greenberg (Eds.), *The working alliance: Theory, research, and practice* (pp. 225–255). Wiley.

Spangler, P. T., Hill, C. E., Dunn, M. G., Hummel, A., Walden, T., Liu, J., Jackson, J., Ganginis, H. V., & Salahuddin, N. (2014). Training undergraduate students to use immediacy. *The Counseling Psychologist*, *42*, 729–757. https://doi.org/10.1177/0011000014542835

Swank, L. E., & Wittenborn, A. K. (2013). Repairing alliance ruptures in emotionally focused couple therapy: A preliminary task analysis. *American Journal of Family Therapy*, *41*(5), 389–402. https://doi.org/10.1080/01926187.2012.726595

Urmanche, A., Minges, M., Eubanks, C. F., Gorman, B. S., & Muran, J. C. (2021). Deepening the group training experience: Group cohesion and supervision impact in alliance-focused training. *Group Dynamics*, *25*, 59–73. https://doi.org/10.1037/gdn0000134

Wampold, B. E., Mondin, G. W., Moody, M., Stich, F., Benson, K., & Ahn, H. (1997). A meta-analysis of outcome studies comparing bona fide psychotherapies: Empirically, "all must have prizes." *Psychological Bulletin*, *122*, 203–215. https://doi.org/10.1037/0033-2909.122.3.203

3
Questions

Elizabeth Nutt Williams

Author's Note: I thank Lynx Gabinet-Bethoulle and MacKenzie Brooks for their assistance.

Questions are a basic form of communication and a way for us to learn more about another person or a particular subject. We learn to use questions from a very early age (Brown, 1968; Piaget, 1926) to ask for what we want and to develop our understanding of the world around us. We learn to refine our use of questions over time, and it has been suggested that "well-crafted questions lead to new insights, generate discussion, and promote the comprehensive exploration of subject matter" (Tofade et al., 2013, p. 1).

Indeed, questions (particularly well-crafted questions) are foundational to psychotherapy (Hill, 2020; McCarthy et al., 2021). Some have even suggested that it is "inconceivable" not to have questions in therapy (L. Thompson et al., 2016, p. 40). Yet others consider questions to be intrusive (Brodsky & Lichtenstein, 1999) and have actively discouraged their use (Patterson, 1985). Some simply have suggested not overusing questions in therapy (E. Williams, 2002).

The goal of this chapter is to explore the effectiveness of questions in individual psychotherapy. Unfortunately, there is surprisingly little empirical research on questions given their foundational nature to the field. Indeed, researchers have noted that the research on questions is "scant" (Renger, 2021), "limited" (McCarthy et al., 2021), and "scarce" (Neipp et al., 2021). Thus, this chapter reviews the available research and explore how questions might be used in treatment and in training.

Definitions

The *Merriam-Webster Dictionary* defines *questions* as interrogative sentences or clauses, such as grammatical expressions beginning with "who," "what," or "which" that are designed to elicit information (e.g., "How are you?" "What was that experience like?" "Did you feel successful in completing that task?"). Questions in psychotherapy have usually been defined by the syntax or grammatical structure of speech. If, for example, a statement ends with a question mark, it usually suggests that a question has been asked.

Typically, questions have been divided into open and closed questions. *Open questions* tend to facilitate a client's exploration with "no right answer in mind" (Hill, 2020, p. 138). Open questions do not have a simple answer, may elicit a broad and extensive response, and tend to use the wh– stem: who, what, when, why (and how).

Elizabeth Nutt Williams, *Questions* In: *Psychotherapy Skills and Methods That Work*. Edited by: Clara E. Hill and John C. Norcross, Oxford University Press. © Clara E. Hill and John C. Norcross 2023. DOI: 10.1093/oso/9780197611012.003.0003

A therapist might ask, "How did that make you feel?" or "What happened next?" *Closed questions*, on the other hand, typically ask for more specified and defined answers. For example, questions that involve a yes or no response, or a brief answer, are typically considered to be closed questions (Hill, 2020). A therapist might ask, "Were you able to complete the homework assignment this week?" or "What is your brother's name?"

This distinction may not, in fact, be the most important element of the question. It may simply have been the easiest and most reliable way of coding questions in the research. There are a number of other elements of questions that might be more or equally important to consider when assessing the effectiveness of the skill in individual psychotherapy, such as tone, timing, focus, context, and culture. For example, is the question asked briskly or warmly or does the question occur at the beginning of the session or during an emotional exploration in the middle of treatment? What is happening at the time the question is asked (e.g., when the client is crying)? Is the question focused on facts, exploration, insight, or action? How do the therapist and the client's cultural backgrounds and social identities impact the questions asked and how they are received?

Clinical Description and Indications

Research suggests that questions are used with moderate frequency in psychotherapy but vary depending on the type of question (open vs. closed) and stage of therapy (intake vs. ongoing). Closed questions appear to be used more often than open questions, particularly in intake sessions (Hill, 1978; Kivlighan, 1989; A. Thompson, 1986). Closed questions are used on average 15% of the time (with a range of 4–23%; Hill et al., 1981, 1983, 1988; A. Thompson, 1986), whereas open questions are used less frequently—on average 10% of the time (with a range of 3–15%; Hill et al., 1983). Taken together, questions are typically used in moderate amounts (Cunha et al., 2012; Elliott et al., 1987; Hill et al., 1979; Kivlighan, 1989).

As a basic helping skill (Gelso & Williams, 2022), questions are used across theoretical orientations, from psychodynamic, cognitive–behavioral, humanistic, and feminist multicultural orientations to integrative approaches. A number of specific types of questions have been used in individual psychotherapy, such as rhetorical questions (García Pérez de León, 2018), Socratic questions (J. Beck, 2011; Wharne, 2022), and hypothetical/what if questions (Newman, 2002). One particular type of hypothetical question, the miracle question, has gained interest particularly among therapists who use a solution-focused brief therapy approach (de Shazer et al., 1986; Neipp et al., 2021). Questions are typically used to gather information, but questions can also be used to focus on thoughts, feelings, insight, and action, as well as to clarify information and encourage exploration (Hill, 2020). For example, therapists might use questions to obtain information about facts (such as at intake) or about a client's emotional, cognitive, or behavioral reactions throughout psychotherapy.

Questions may also differ based on the intentions of the individual therapist (Hill et al., 1988; Hill & O'Grady, 1985; Kivlighan, 1989). For example, a therapist might ask how a client spent their weekend not as a way to gather information but, rather, as a way to ease the client into the process of therapy (helping them practice being expressive).

Another therapist might ask a question to demonstrate or strengthen the alliance between the client and therapist. A therapist might ask a question as a way to challenge their client. Or they may simply need to ask a question to obtain a fact to help them fully understand the client's story.

Although I am aware of no research that contraindicates the use of a question (see section on Possible Negative Effects and Harm), the research does suggest that there are elements to be considered when deciding to use a question in session. Are there better times to use certain structures (open vs. closed questions), different words, or different deliveries of the question? I would imagine so, but there is unfortunately limited research on these topics. Clinical wisdom suggests, however, that using questions in therapy should be about meeting the client where they are and personalizing the approach (Norcross & Cooper, 2021).

Assessment

The ways in which questions in psychotherapy, as well as their effectiveness, have been measured are detailed next.

Measures of Therapists' Use of Questions

An important element of the research to consider is how questions have been operationalized and coded. Most typically, psychotherapy process studies have examined a range of therapist skills and methods, often referred to as *helping skills* or *verbal response modes*. Elliott et al. (1987) reviewed six systems for coding verbal response modes (of which questions are one). Within the research on individual psychotherapy, three systems appear to have been used most often (see the Research Review section): The Helping Skills System (HSS; Hill, 2020), previously called the Hill Counselor Verbal Response Category System (Hill, 1978); the Response Mode Rating System (Elliott, 1985); and the Verbal Response Mode System (Stiles, 1978). Elliott et al. (1987) suggested that the different systems, while not identical, reflect "a set of fundamental response-mode categories or dimensions" (p. 222), all of which included questions. The approach to coding is also consistent across systems, using session transcripts coded by observers (ranging from trained undergraduates and doctoral students to professional psychotherapists).

In the most frequently used system, the HSS (Hill, 2020), the coding of questions has expanded from simply open and closed questions to a more nuanced approach. The HSS allows for the coding of open questions with a specific focus on thoughts, feelings, insight, or action, and of closed questions with a specific focus on facts, clarification, exploration, insight, or action (Hill, 2020). Most recently, probes for insight—defined as methods that "invite clients to think about deeper meanings for their thoughts, feelings, or behaviors" (Hill, 2020, p. 252)—have been examined as a subcategory of open questions with a focus on insight (Hill et al., 2020). Thus, the most recent coding system for questions includes both grammatical structure and the focus of the question content.

Measures of Outcome

In order to establish the effectiveness of questions, various measures of immediate and intermediate outcome have been used. The measures themselves can be divided into three groups: (a) *observer-coded* (measures coded by observers through transcripts or videotapes of sessions), (b) *client pre–post* (measures completed by clients pre, post, or pre and post session), and (c) *client and therapist post-session review* (measures completed by clients in post-session review of the videotape, typically at speaking turns).

Of the observer-coded measures of immediate outcomes, the most common have been measures of client emotional arousal (e.g., Client Emotional Arousal Scale; Machado et al., 1999), client experiencing (e.g., the Experiencing Scale; Klein et al., 1986), and client self-references or use of emotional language [e.g., self-referencing pronouns (Tausczik & Pennebaker, 2010) and self-referring emotion words (Mergenthaler, 1996)]. All of these measures attempt to assess the extent to which questions increase client expressiveness and openness to the treatment.

In terms of client pre–post measures to assess slightly more distal outcome, the most common measures appear to be symptom reduction or improvement, such as reductions in anxiety (Beck Anxiety Inventory; A. Beck & Steer, 1990) or general symptoms (Symptom Checklist-90–Revised; Derogatis et al., 1976). These types of outcome measures are useful but also limited in assessing the effectiveness of questions, as it is not clear whether it is the use of questions per se that impacts the overall outcome. Other studies have examined client personality factors such as attachment style as a pretest (e.g., Experience in Close Relationships Scale; Brennan et al., 1998), as well as post-session outcomes such as alliance (Working Alliance Inventory–Short Revised; Hatcher & Gillaspy, 2006) and session depth and smoothness (e.g., Session Evaluation Questionnaire; Stiles & Snow, 1984). Measures such as these increase the probability of showing the impact of client factors on the use of questions as well as the immediate impact of session-level process.

The link between questions and session outcomes may be important, but it may prove most useful to study the microprocesses of psychotherapy to understand the immediate impact of questions. Thus, client and therapist post-session review measures have been used to focus on micro-level processes, most typically using measures of helpfulness of particular skills, such as questions (e.g., the Helpfulness Scale; Elliott, 1985). These types of immediate measures of impact may be useful to explore further with additional refinements to the measurement of questions (see section on Limitations of the Research).

Clinical Examples

To illustrate the use of questions in individual psychotherapy and to highlight three important considerations (diversity, timing, and focus), three brief hypothetical examples are provided.

Example 1: Considering Diversity

In this example, a White cisgender 50-year-old male therapist (T) is working with an African American transfemale 20-year-old client (C). The therapist has been seeking supervision to ensure that he is fully aware of his own reactions to race and gender in therapy but has not had much experience with transgender clients or with clients of different racial backgrounds. In the last session, he could tell that he had offended his client and wanted to repair the rupture in the next session. Questions are italicized.

T: Before we get started with our usual work today, I wanted to take a moment to address something that happened in our last session. I may be wrong, but it felt to me that you pulled back after I asked about your experiences as a Black woman in the trans community. I would really like to understand your experiences, but I am worried that I unintentionally offended you in how I brought it up. *Would you feel comfortable talking about this issue today?*

C: Yes, I would be comfortable with that. I am not sure where to start.

T: I'd really like to understand your experience. *What was it like for you when I asked about your experiences in the trans community?*

In this example, the therapist provides context for where they want to go with the exploration of the rupture and then asks a "closed" question ("Would you feel comfortable talking about your reaction in our last session?"). The client responds briefly but in the affirmative, and the therapist follows with an open-ended question, allowing the client to take the conversation in the direction she chooses. The success of this approach may depend less on whether the questions were open or closed and more on the intention of the therapist (e.g., to acknowledge a microaggression, provide an apology, and reconnect with the client) and the tone of the question itself.

Example 2: Considering Timing

In this example, a Latinx female 70-year-old therapist is working with a White male 40-year-old client. They have been working on the client's relationship concerns.

C: I guess I just don't get it. Why would she respond to me that way?

T: *What is your sense of why she would respond that way?*

C: I don't know! That's why I am here.

T: We've been working together for a while now. *What is it that you wish I understood better about your relationship concerns?*

C: I wish I knew. I wish I could articulate it better. I wish you could just wave a magic wand and make it better.

T: (laughs) Me, too! That would be lovely. But my wand is the in shop. (Client chuckles) *Do you think we are experiencing the same communication problems that you experience with other women in your life?*

C: (silent for a minute) Actually, yeah. That seems really important. I guess we could talk about that.

In this example, the therapist starts with an open question, but the client is not sure how to respond. Following a moment of levity, the therapist asks a closed question that seems to have a strong impact on the client. This provides an example of how closed questions (that one could answer with a yes/no or very brief response) have the ability to challenge the client and may open up new avenues for exploration. The therapist also clearly takes into account tone (humorous), timing, and her intention to challenge the client within a supportive framework.

Example 3: Considering Focus

In this example, a 35-year-old Black female therapist is working with a 60-year-old Asian male client who is experiencing conflict with his son. This exchange occurs in the intake session.

T: *Can you say more about what happened with your son?*
C: I told him he was disrespectful and now he won't return my calls.
T: *How long ago did this happen?*
C: About 6 months ago. We used to talk almost every day.
T: I see you are tearing up a bit. *How are you feeling?*
C: I am fine. I just want to learn what to do to fix this problem.
T: I understand. *Do you want to start with telling me about how things used to be between you?*
C: Ok. (pauses)
T: It might be hard, given how close you used to be, but I'd really like to understand. *What was your relationship with your son like before this situation occurred?*
C: It was great. I really miss him. I relied on him for many things. I just really miss him now. (pauses for a minute) I think you are right. I do have a lot of emotions about this situation, but I am not sure what do with them.
T: I can see how much he means to you. *What feels most important for you to tell me about your relationship or about the situation?*

In this example, the therapist starts with both closed and open questions that, like many intake sessions, are designed to elicit information. When the therapist focuses on feelings after acknowledging the client's nonverbal behavior, the client pushes back. The therapist reverses course and asks a closed question about how the relationship was prior to the rupture. When the client does not seem to know what to do, the therapist provides context and asks an open question. The therapist's comfort and respect for the client's feelings and wishes allow the client to see that he has many emotions rising to the surface. In response to the client's emotions and sense of uncertainty with how to proceed, the therapist allows the client, with an open question, to choose the course of the next steps of the interview.

Landmark Studies and Previous Reviews

No previous systematic reviews were found that specifically examined the use of questions in individual psychotherapy. The closest review identified was the Orlinsky et al. (1994) review of process and outcome, which included one table on "exploration." They noted that their review of exploration (or what they parenthetically refer to as "open-ended questioning," p. 307) resulted in mixed findings vis-à-vis psychotherapeutic outcome. Most findings showed no impact on distal treatment outcome, and approximately 40% of findings showed positive impact (with only one finding that showed negative impact).

Although there is not a lot of empirical research on the effectiveness of questions in individual psychotherapy, one study set the bar for future process–outcome research. One of the most comprehensive studies of therapist responses, including questions, was Hill and colleagues' (1988) classic study of eight cases of psychotherapy. Hill et al. examined the effects of therapist response modes on immediate (proximal) outcomes as well as (distal) treatment outcomes. They asked 50 therapists to nominate the 10 best psychotherapists in a geographic area. Eight therapists agreed to participate, meeting with a randomly assigned client for 12–20 sessions.

Every session was videotaped, transcribed, and coded for therapist responses (using the Hill Counselor Verbal Response Modes Category System; Hill, 1986) and for client experiencing (using the Client Experiencing Scale; Klein et al., 1986). Immediately following each session, therapists and clients completed the Session Evaluation Questionnaire (Stiles & Snow, 1984) and participated in a post-session video review in which therapists completed the Therapist Intentions List (Hill & O'Grady, 1985), clients completed the Client Reactions System (Hill et al., 1988), and both therapists and clients rated the helpfulness of each therapist speaking turn (using the Helpfulness Scale; Elliott, 1985). The clients also completed (distal) treatment outcome measures [the Symptom Checklist-90 (Derogatis et al., 1976) and the Tennessee Self-Concept Scale (Fitts, 1965)] at pretreatment and 1 or 2 weeks after termination.

Focusing here only on the results for questions, the researchers found that closed questions (19%) were used more often than open questions (13%) (with closed questions used more frequently with depressed clients) and that clients rated closed questions as more helpful than open questions (although therapists had the opposite pattern). The proportion (frequency of occurrence) of open questions was negatively related to the smoothness of the session but positively related to symptom reduction at termination. Using an interesting approach that has not been used much in subsequent years, Hill et al. (1988) found that therapist response modes and intentions covaried systematically. For example, closed questions were associated with the intentions of "get information" and "clarify," whereas open questions were associated with the intentions of "get information," "focus," "clarify," and "feelings." When therapists used closed questions, clients reported "no reaction" most frequently. When therapists used open questions, clients reported feeling "challenged" or "negative," which is similar to clients' lower ratings of helpfulness.

Using a small sample, Hill et al. (1988) cautioned that there were large individual differences in the use of response modes and that more research was necessary. In particular, an important finding that seems to have been left behind in much of the subsequent research was that "therapist intentions accounted for more of the unique variance than did response modes" (p. 231). Hill and colleagues concluded, "We recommend that further research on the effects of therapist interventions take into account context, timing, and individual differences between clients" (p. 232).

A more recent study has attempted to address many of the methodological limitations of the past research in this area. Freites and colleagues (2022) examined the antecedents and consequences of open and closed questions in individual psychotherapy intake sessions. Studying the intake sessions of 88 clients with 33 doctoral student therapists (using a nested design), they examined the immediate outcomes of particular questions (using the HSS; Hill, 2020) by highlighting the client's subsequent use of self-referring pronouns (Tausczik & Pennebaker, 2010), self-referring emotion words (Mergenthaler, 1996), and total number of words used, controlling for the antecedent use of these behaviors.

Some of the improvements to methodology Freites et al. (2022) included were to include only those therapist speaking turns in which a question was the only intervention (i.e., not paired with another skill, such as reflection of feeling) and to more narrowly define subtypes of open and closed questions. The researchers coded for open questions for thoughts (OQT) and open questions for feelings (OQF) and for closed questions for facts (CQF) and closed questions other (CQO). Once intake sessions were completed, the videos were transcribed and trained undergraduate students coded the sessions for questions, pronouns, and emotion words.

Freites et al. (2022) found that, indeed, not all closed questions are the same. Many closed questions operate similarly to open questions (with the exception of closed questions for facts). Specifically, the researchers found that when clients were using a high number of self-referring pronouns and emotion words, therapists were more likely to ask open questions (focusing on thoughts when there were more self-referring pronouns and focusing on feelings when there were more self-referring emotion words as antecedents). In terms of the consequences or immediate outcome of asking questions, the researchers found that clients spoke less and used fewer self-referring pronouns after closed questions for facts and used more self-referring emotion words after open questions for feelings.

This study helps extend (and, frankly, may revitalize) the limited research on questions in psychotherapy. The examination of subtypes of questions (e.g., open questions for feeling, closed questions for facts) is an advancement of the research. It is interesting that Freites et al. (2022) focused on speaking turns with just questions; however, more research is needed to help tease apart the more common method in ongoing psychotherapy of using combinations of skills (e.g., questions with reflections of feeling) in the same speaking turn. In addition, it is important to note that the study focused on intake sessions. More research is needed to study ongoing treatment, as questions at intake may more heavily rely on closed questions for facts (in this study, 47.6% of the questions asked were closed questions for facts).

Research Review

A computerized literature search was conducted in September 2021 using the search terms "question*" and "psychotherap*" (with subject term "psychotherapy outcomes") to find empirical studies in PsycInfo. Because the term "question" gets used in many ways that have nothing to do with the focus of this research review (and because many studies of "questions" are actually coded as probes, exploration, or response modes), I altered the approach to using the term "response modes" in the search and then carefully examined the studies for an investigation of questions specifically. The inclusion criteria were published empirical studies of individual psychotherapy, in English language, that investigated in-session therapist questions with adult clients and contained one or more measures of client impact/outcome or session quality.

A total of 78 studies were initially located, but 68 were excluded based on the following criteria: studies not of individual therapy, analogue studies, dissertations, non-English language studies, non-empirical articles, case studies, articles with no outcome measures, and studies that did not separately identify questions as a focus of study. The remaining 10 studies were included in the research review (Table 3.1). Only one study (Hill et al., 1988) was identified that linked therapist in-session questions to distal, end-of-treatment outcomes (e.g., symptom reduction). Because that was the only distal outcome identified, it was not included in Table 3.1.

Table 3.1 summarizes 10 empirical studies of the immediate impact of questions in individual psychotherapy with more than one client. These 10 studies (including a total of 328 clients and 176 therapists) provided a total of 16 measures of immediate impact on the client or session (e.g., client expressiveness, client-rated therapist empathy, helpfulness, alliance). Each outcome measure examined received an overall summary or box score for a positive, neutral, or negative association between therapist questions and immediate impact. As Table 3.1 shows, the research results are mixed. Approximately one-third (5) of the outcomes reviewed were positive, approximately one-third (5) of the outcomes were neutral, and approximately one-third (6) of the outcomes were negative. I review below the specific positive and negative findings regarding questions and immediate psychotherapeutic impacts.

Positive Impacts

It is interesting that psychotherapists tend to use fewer open than closed questions (Cunha et al., 2012; Hill et al., 1988; Huang et al., 2013) yet open questions (as compared to closed questions) seem to have more positive impacts on the process of therapy, in the current research review and in both single-session and ongoing therapy. For example, Goates-Jones et al. (2009), while not finding much impact of questions in single session, did find that approximately one-third of their sample engaged in more narrative processing when asked questions. They suggested that research should "investigate variables that moderate the client internal narrative process" (p. 229) given that some of the clients responded very well to questions. This result further suggests that individual variables, such as cognitive complexity, may help deepen our understanding of the impact of questions.

Recent work has examined more nuanced approaches to therapist use of skills in relation to client variables in ongoing psychotherapy (e.g., by nesting client and therapist data and by excluding speaking turns that include more than one therapeutic skill). For example, Freites et al. (2022) found that clients had more self-referring pronouns and emotion words in response to open questions about feelings, suggesting that open

Table 3.1 Studies of Immediate Outcomes of Therapist Questions

Study	Sample (*N*)	Variables	Results	Box Score
Anvari et al. (2020)	22 therapists seeing 36 clients in ongoing treatment	Open questions (focused on thoughts and feelings) Client emotional expression Client attachment style	Regardless of attachment style, clients demonstrated the highest level of emotional expression following open questions for feelings.	+
Anvari et al. (2022)	26 therapists seeing 62 clients in ongoing treatment	Open questions (focused on thoughts and feelings) Client cognitive–behavioral exploration and affective exploration Client attachment style	Clients displayed higher affective exploration following open questions for feelings.	+
			Therapist use of open questions for feelings was related to increased cognitive–behavioral exploration.	+
			No differences found between open questions for feelings and reflections of feelings in terms of subsequent affective exploration.	=
Barkham & Shapiro (1986)	6 counselors seeing 24 clients (with half assessed at initial session and half assessed during ongoing treatment)	Open and closed questions Empathy	Clients' ratings of counselor empathy were negatively related to use of closed questions in both initial and ongoing sessions and to use of open questions in initial sessions.	–
Elliott et al. (1982)	16 therapists seeing 16 clients in ongoing treatment	Questions Helpfulness	Questions were the least helpful response mode [but could be seen as "slightly helpful" (p. 359) rather than unhelpful].	–
Fitzpatrick et al. (2001)	17 expert therapists seeing 21 clients in a single session (archival)	Information seeking (questions) Alliance Good moments in therapy	Therapists asked more questions when there were good moments in the context of low alliance.	=
Freites et al. (2022)	33 therapists seeing 88 clients at intake	Open questions (for thoughts, feelings, insight, action) Closed questions (for facts, thoughts, feelings, clarification, insight, action, and other) Subsequent client responses (number of words, self-referring pronouns and emotion words)	Clients had more self-referring pronouns and emotion words in response to open questions about feelings.	+
			Clients spoke less after closed questions about facts and expressed fewer self-referring pronouns.	–

Table 3.1 Continued

Study	Sample (*N*)	Variables	Results	Box Score
Goates-Jones et al. (2009)	13 therapists seeing 26 clients for a single session (intake)	Open questions about thoughts and feelings Anxiety Helpfulness Narrative process	No difference (in terms of client response or rated helpfulness) whether therapists used open questions about thoughts or open questions about feelings.	=
			Clients responded with internal narrative processing when therapists asked open questions about feelings (but this finding was true for less than one-third of the cases).	+
Hill et al. (1988)	8 therapists seeing 8 clients for ongoing treatment	Open and closed questions Therapist intentions Client reactions Helpfulness Session evaluation (depth and smoothness)	Clients rated closed questions as more helpful than open questions (although therapists had the opposite pattern).	=
			Open questions were negatively related to the smoothness of the session.	–
			When therapists used closed questions, clients reported no reaction most frequently. When therapists used open questions, clients reported feeling challenged or negative.	–
Huang et al. (2013)	4 therapists seeing 16 clients (8 engagers who continued for at least 8 sessions; and 8 non-engagers who did not return after intake)	Closed question and open question for thoughts	Therapists did not significantly differ in their use of questions with engagers versus non-engagers.	=
Wiser & Goldfried (1998)	31 therapists seeing 31 clients in ongoing treatment	Open and closed questions Client experiencing	Questions were associated with decreases in client experiencing.	–

questions facilitate exploration. Relatedly, Anvari et al. (2020) found greater client emotional expression in response to questions when clients had been expressing fewer emotions. They suggested that therapists may use open questions with clients who are "not into their feelings" (p. 908) to prompt more emotional exploration, whereas with clients already expressing feelings, therapists used more reflection of feeling or paraphrase to help the clients continue a process already started.

In a follow-up study, Anvari et al. (2022), in studying the focus (thoughts vs. feelings) of questions and the role of client attachment, found, contrary to their hypotheses, that clients engaged in more cognitive–behavioral exploration when asked open questions about feelings, a finding particularly true for clients low in attachment anxiety. Examining the 10th session of psychodynamic therapy in a community clinic, the researchers found that therapists focused more on thoughts than feelings. However, therapists did focus more on affect when clients were already expressing their emotions (in contrast to Anvari et al., 2020).

Overall, most of the immediate outcomes for questions have been positive or neutral (10 out of the 16 box score results; see Table 3.1). In particular, directing clients to focus on feelings resulted in greater emotional processing. Yet, among the neutral findings (see Table 3.1), there appear to be few differences between asking open questions for feelings and providing reflections of feelings in terms of affective exploration. However, although clients rated open questions for feelings and for thoughts as equally helpful, use of open questions for feelings resulted in greater cognitive expression in clients, particularly clients who were low in attachment anxiety. These findings highlight not only the complexity of process research but also the potential importance of including client factors (e.g., attachment style) in the research.

Negative Impacts

While several studies have emphasized the positive and neutral impacts of questions, a few studies have also highlighted the potential negative effects of questions, particularly closed questions. Generally speaking, closed questions have been associated with more negative client outcomes and are considered less helpful (even "boring") by clients (Hill et al., 1988). In addition, Barkham and Shapiro (1986) found that client-rated therapist empathy was lower when therapists asked questions, particularly in initial sessions. They found that therapists used more open questions in earlier sessions, suggesting the importance of examining therapist verbal response modes at different stages of therapy.

Overall, the negative impacts of questions relate mostly to client perceptions of the therapist (as less empathic or less helpful; Barkham & Shapiro, 1986; Elliott et al., 1982), of the session (as less smooth; Hill et al., 1988), or of their own reactions as negative (Hill et al., 1988). There is also some evidence that questions may occasionally be related to less client experiencing (Wiser & Goldfried, 1998), particularly in terms of emotional articulation following closed questions about facts in intake sessions (Freites et al., 2022).

In summary, there is evidence that questions can have a positive impact on the process and immediate outcome of psychotherapy, especially increased client emotional expressiveness and affective exploration. At the same time, the research findings remain mixed, and more targeted research is needed to clarify when questions are helpful and when they are not. (See Table 3.1 for the box scores for immediate outcome: 5 positive, 5 neutral, and 6 negative.) Finally, there is almost no research evidence on the link between therapist in-session use of questions and the end-of-treatment, distal patient outcomes (for one example, see Hill et al., 1988; see also the Landmark Studies and Previous Reviews section).

Possible Negative Effects and Harm

Although 10 of the 16 empirical findings were positive or neutral in the research review, a number of negative impacts have also been identified in the broader literature. These include reports of lower empathy and helpfulness ratings, less emotional experiencing, and occasionally negative process (Barkham & Shapiro, 1986; Thrasher et al., 2006; Tollison et al., 2008; Wiser & Goldfried, 1998). Although the possible negative impacts seem limited and questions do not seem harmful per se, one might need to consider variables related to the questions themselves to consider where harm or therapeutic errors may come into play. For example, therapists might want to consider the timing of the question (e.g., Hill et al., 1988); the structure and word choices of the question (e.g., Heritage et al., 2007); their intention in asking the question (e.g., Hill & O'Grady, 1985); and elements of the client, therapist, and therapeutic relationship that contextualize the use of the question at any particular time in therapy (e.g., Leutritz et al., 2020).

As one example, therapists' own emotional reactions and emotion regulation may affect the impact of a question in therapy (Chui & Liu, 2021). Asking a question that is highly charged emotionally may have differential effects depending on therapist's own emotional experience, such as whether a therapist has become tearful (Morgan & Williams, 2021). Clients' emotional reactivity may also impact their response to questions, particularly for specific attachment styles (Leutritz et al., 2020). Thus, considering one's own and the client's emotional context should be part of a therapist's decision-making about the appropriateness of an intervention, including asking a question, in order to avoid harm or negative effects.

Diversity Considerations

Although we have found no research evidence about diversity related specifically to therapist questions, it seems logical to assume that diversity and social identity would be important to consider in the effectiveness of questions in individual psychotherapy. For example, there is research which suggests that racial microaggressions occur in therapy (Yeo & Torres-Harding, 2021) and that the therapist's sense of cultural comfort is an important determinant in how they interact with clients (Bartholomew et al., 2021). If a therapist has a low level of cultural comfort, how might they inquire about racial microaggressions as a way to repair a rupture? Would they even do so, or would they avoid the question? How might such a question be phrased? For example, how one interprets gaze may be related to cultural issues (Hill, 2020), and looking away may be perceived as a signal of insincerity (J. Williams et al., 2009). It might be helpful for a therapist to take nonverbal indicators into consideration when deciding how to best ask a question.

In addition, social identity variables may be considered basic elements in choosing and using particular questions. Does the gender of the therapist and client matter in the asking of questions? Some research has found that gender may not have broad impact on an individual's responses to questions, except perhaps with highly sensitive or intimate topics (Hancock & Rubin, 2015). There has not been enough research on gender in psychotherapy process to establish its effect on question asking, but additional research would be interesting and potentially useful. There is, however, a growing body of research on racial ethnic issues in the process of psychotherapy (e.g., Casas et al., 2017; Leong, 2014; Sue et al., 2019) that could be expanded to focus more specifically on the use and impact of questions.

Beyond gender and race, there are many other social identity variables that might be important to consider in the use and framing of questions, including sexual orientation, social class, and religion. In addition, individual variables such as attachment style and emotional regulation (Leutritz et al., 2020) can impact responses to questions.

Limitations of the Research

Recent research (e.g., Anvari et al., 2020, 2022; Freites et al., 2022) has attempted to correct previous methodological limitations, such as identifying therapist use of questions that is not in combination with other skills (Freites et al., 2022), controlling for overall verbal activity of the therapist (Huang et al., 2013), and narrowing the focus of the questions (e.g., examining open questions for feelings and closed questions for facts rather than simply open and closed questions) (Anvari et al., 2020, 2022; Freites et al., 2022). However, most of the research on the effectiveness of questions in individual psychotherapy has continued to focus on the frequency of use of questions. Yet frequency alone may not be the best way to operationalize or understand the effectiveness of the question in psychotherapy. Why should frequency matter? And are there other ways to define the structure of questions (beyond a narrowing of open questions to open questions for feelings, as one example)? Future research could address these issues by examining the particular wording of questions, the therapists' intentions behind asking particular questions, and various individual variables related to therapists and clients. In addition, more studies of ongoing treatment will be potentially more useful than studies of single sessions.

Several methodological approaches may be helpful to consider for future research. In particular, the research on questions in therapy might benefit from taking a client-focused perspective (Fuertes & Williams, 2017) and use qualitative methods to identify the elements of questions that seem important to clients, both in therapeutic process and outcome. In addition, it would also be interesting to explore lesser used methodologies in the field, such as conversation analysis (Cannon et al., 2020), to further explore the effectiveness of questions.

Although the typical focus for research on questions has been both frequency of use and the structure of the question (e.g., open vs. closed), other elements of questions could have greater therapeutic impact. For example, how much does specific word choice matter? As an example from the medical field, Heritage et al. (2007) examined the difference between asking a patient, "Is there *anything* else you want to address in the visit today?" compared with "Is there *something* else you want to address in the visit today?" Among 224 patients randomly assigned to be asked one of the two questions at the end of their intake visit, the question using the term "something" significantly reduced the number of unmet concerns among the patients on a post-session survey (and neither question significantly increased the time spent with the patient, a concern for physicians). Heritage and colleagues also examined a number of other linguistic issues, including the use of the term "concerns" versus "questions" (i.e., "Do you have any other questions?"); they found that physicians asking about concerns rather than questions elicited more information from the patients.

Similarly, McGee et al. (2005), suggesting that "asking a question is not a benign act" (p. 382), reviewed various approaches to therapeutic questions using a conversation analysis. They suggested that all questions involve presuppositions or assumptions. For example, asking a patient what made them "decide" to do something assumes a sense of agency and responsibility, whereas a question about what "prevented" them from a behavior provides a different assumption (and presumably different answers from the patient). In fact, Richmond et al. (2014) found, perhaps not surprisingly, that asking solution-focused questions at intake generated more solutions and fewer problems than asking problem-focused questions. Similar to McGee et al. (2005), Richmond et al. (2014) suggested that questions are not neutral, even at intake. Thus, the words we use to construct our questions may significantly impact the information we receive. Perhaps more studies at this level of microanalysis of word choice will help us better understand the impacts of questions in psychotherapy.

It also seems fruitful to examine therapist factors in the use of questions, including the intention behind the use of particular questions (García Pérez de León, 2018; Renger, 2021), as well as the impact of therapist personality factors on outcome. For example, does a therapist's level of introversion or extraversion impact use of questions [as Huang et al. (2013) suggested that overall verbal activity be controlled for in studying use of questions]? Other therapist personality variables to consider might be humility in assessing one's alliance-building skills (Coyne et al., 2022), cultural humility (Hook et al., 2017), and the use of questions in cross-cultural contexts (Aafjes-van Doorn et al., 2018; Ito, 2017; Li et al., 2018).

In addition to therapist factors, client factors, such as the ability to handle cognitive complexity, may be useful in furthering our understanding of the effectiveness of questions. For example, in a nontherapeutic interview study, Hanway and colleagues (2021) experimentally manipulated the use of low, moderate, and high cognitive load questions and found that moderate and high cognitive load had a negative impact on interviewer's performance. Specifically, interviewers who were asked to do more (e.g., understand what the interviewee was communicating *and* identify follow-up questions to ask *and* think about the wording of their questions and the order in which they should be asked) recalled less of the interview. Although the study was related to police interviewing (and used non-expert participants in an analogue setting), the connection to psychotherapy is interesting because therapists must manage this type of cognitive load as well.

But what about the clients? What is the impact of asking cognitively loaded questions of the client? For example, there is some evidence that clients with higher cognitive abilities prefer open questions (Rautalinko, 2013). Cognitively complex questions may work well with some clients and less well with others, but we know very little about this issue. As Brubacher et al. (2020) suggested, answering open questions involves a deeper processing and memory search, which may relate to how "helpful" clients find open and closed questions. In summary, we need more research on questions to help us more effectively personalize therapy for each client (Coyne et al., 2022; Norcross & Cooper, 2021; Norcross & Wampold, 2018).

Training Implications

Asking useful questions in psychotherapy is important, and learning how to do so requires therapists to understand not only the structure of the questions but also, as previously highlighted, the contextual, interpersonal, and nonverbal elements of therapy. Thus, training that highlights the therapeutic alliance, empathy, and cultural humility may provide helpful context for learning to effectively use questions in psychotherapy.

Most novice psychotherapists begin by asking a lot of questions, as questioning is a therapeutic skill with which many have experience. For example, early process research (Hill et al., 1981; Kivlighan, 1989) suggested that particularly in initial sessions (prior to a semester of intense training), questions were used frequently (23–29% of the time), whereas that percentage dropped after training (to 15–18% of the time). Overall, it appears that trainees ask more questions early in their training but reduce their use of questions over time.

One way for trainees to review their use of questions is by studying audio/video recordings of their sessions. They can then assess whether they ask more closed than open questions. How effective have their questions been? What were their intentions behind each question asked? What is the effectiveness of using particular words in their questions? What do they learn about the varying effectiveness of their tone, pitch, and clarity? Studying one's own conversation approach is critical to understanding one's normative style and to identify whether the therapist wants to try different approaches (in question structure, word choice, or tone).

It would also be useful for trainees to examine their own social identities and where they feel comfort and discomfort asking certain questions. If they are asking many fact-gathering questions, are they uncomfortable and are there other ways of learning the information? Could they intersperse information-seeking questions with those designed to build alliance? What are the therapist's intentions behind the questions, and have they considered cultural and social identity in how they ask the questions and how their clients have responded?

Finally, trainees might consider engaging in deliberate practice (Miller et al., 2020). It is helpful to make mistakes in a practice context. Without mistakes, there may be little growth. What happens when a question evokes a negative client reaction? Can the trainee distinguish between a clinical mistake and a necessary challenge (that happens to evoke negative reactions)? Helping trainees consider (and practice) what to do when they do make a mistake in therapy, as well as how to work with the client to repair ruptures (MacDonald & Muran, 2021; Yeo & Torres-Harding, 2021), is an important part of psychotherapy training and may help trainees refine their use of questions in psychotherapy.

Therapeutic Practices

In conclusion, despite relatively little empirical research on the effectiveness of questions in psychotherapy, the research does suggest some ways to use questions that might prove useful in practice:

- Use open questions to encourage clients to explore thoughts and feelings and to consider change.
- Ask questions to prompt exploration in clients high in cognitive ability or low in attachment anxiety.
- Use fewer questions when clients are already expressing thoughts and feelings.
- Limit fact-finding closed questions when possible.
- Consider social identity variables in the use of questions, as with other elements of psychotherapy process.
- Deliberately practice and refine (rinse and repeat!) the use of questions.

References

* Studies included in the research review and box score.

Aafjes-van Doorn, K., Klinar Alfaro, D., Fialová, M., & Kamsteeg, C. (2018). Psychotherapy integration training around the globe: A personal and empirical perspective. *Journal of Psychotherapy Integration*, *28*(4), 505–520. https://doi.org/10.1037/int0000135

*Anvari, M. S., Dua, V., Lima-Rosas, J., Hill, C. E., & Kivlighan, D. M., Jr. (2022). Facilitating exploration in psychodynamic psychotherapy: Therapist skills and client attachment style. *Journal of Counseling Psychology*, *69*(3), 348–360. https://doi.org/10.1037/cou0000582" https://doi.org/10.1037/cou0000582

*Anvari, M., Hill, C. E., & Kivlighan, D. M. (2020). Therapist skills associated with client emotional expression in psychodynamic psychotherapy. *Psychotherapy Research*, *30*(7), 900–911. https://doi.org/10.1080/10503307.2019.1680901

*Barkham, M., & Shapiro, D. A. (1986). Counselor verbal response modes and experienced empathy. *Journal of Counseling Psychology*, *33*(1), 3–10. https://doi.org/10.1037/0022-0167.33.1.3

Bartholomew, T. T., Pérez-Rojas, A. E., Bledman, R., Joy, E. E., & Robbins, K. A. (2021). "How could I not bring it up?" A multiple case study of therapists' comfort when Black clients discuss anti-Black racism in sessions. *Psychotherapy*. Advance online publication. https://doi.org/10.1037/pst0000404

Beck, A. T., & Steer, R. A. (1990). *Beck Anxiety Inventory manual*. Psychological Corporation.

Beck, J. S. (2011). *Cognitive behavior therapy*. Guilford.

Brennan, K. A., Clark, C. L., & Shaver, P. R. (1998). Self-report measurement of adult attachment: An integrative overview. In J. A. Simpson & W. Rholes (Eds.), *Attachment theory and close relationships* (pp. 46–76). Guilford.

Brodsky, S. L., & Lichtenstein, B. (1999). Don't ask questions: A psychotherapeutic strategy for treatment of involuntary clients. *American Journal of Psychotherapy*, *53*(2), 215–224. https://doi.org/10.1176/appi.psychotherapy.1999.53.2.215

Brown, R. (1968). The development of Wh questions in child speech. *Journal of Verbal Learning and Behavior*, *7*, 279–290. doi:10.1016/S0022-5371(68)80002-7

Brubacher, S., Sharman, S., Scoboria, A., & Powell, M. B. (2020). The effect of question type on resistance to misinformation about present and absent details. *Applied Cognitive Psychology*, *34*(6), 1323–1334. https://doi.org/10.1002/acp.3742

Cannon, C., Meredith, J., Speer, S., & Mansell, W. (2020). A conversation analysis of asking about disruptions in method of levels psychotherapy. *Counselling and Psychotherapy Research, 20*, 154–163. https://doi.org/10.1002/capr.12243

Casas, J. M., Suzuki, L. A., Alexander, C. M., & Jackson, M. A. (2017). *Handbook of multicultural counseling* (4th ed.). SAGE.

Chui, H., & Liu, F. (2021). Emotional experience of psychotherapists: A latent profile analysis. *Psychotherapy, 58*(3), 401–413. https://doi.org/10.1037/pst0000379

Coyne, A. E., Constantino, M. J., Boswell, J. F., & Kraus, D. R. (2022). Therapist-level moderation of within- and between-therapist process–outcome associations. *Journal of Consulting and Clinical Psychology, 90*(1), 75–89. https://doi.org/10.1037/ccp0000676" https://doi.org/10.1037/ccp0000676

Cunha, C., Gonçalves, M. M., Hill, C. E., Mendes, I., Ribeiro, A. P., Sousa, I., Angus, L., & Greenberg, L. S. (2012). Therapist interventions and client innovative moments in emotion-focused therapy for depression. *Psychotherapy, 49*(4), 536–548. https://doi.org/10.1037/a0028259

Derogatis, L. R., Rickels, K., & Rock, A. F. (1976). The SCL-90 and the MMPI: A step in the validation of a new self-report scale. *British Journal of Psychiatry, 128*, 280–289.

De Shazer, S., Berg, I. K., Lipchik, E., Nunnally, E., Molnar, A., Gingerich, W., & Weiner-Davis, M. (1986). Brief therapy: Focused solution development. *Family Process, 25*, 207–221.

Elliott, R. (1985). Helpful and nonhelpful events in brief counseling interviews: An empirical taxonomy. *Journal of Counseling Psychology, 32*, 307–322.

*Elliott, R., Barker, C. B., Caskey, N., & Pistrang, N. (1982). Differential helpfulness of counselor verbal response modes. *Journal of Counseling Psychology, 29*(4), 354–361.

Elliott, R., Hill, C. E., Stiles, W. B., Friedlander, M. L., Mahrer, A. R., & Margison, F. R. (1987). Primary therapist response modes: Comparison of six rating systems. *Journal of Consulting and Clinical Psychology, 55*(2), 218–223. doi:10.1037/0022-006X.55.2.218

Fitts, W. H. (1965). *Manual for the Tennessee Self Concept Scale*. Counselor Recordings and Tests.

*Fitzpatrick, M. R., Stalikas, A., & Iwakabe, S. (2001). Examining counselor interventions and client progress in the context of the therapeutic alliance. *Psychotherapy, 38*(2), 160–170.

*Freites, E., Hill, C. E., Seo, A., Milheim, E., Williams, J., & Kivlighan, D. M. (2022). Antecedents and consequences of open and closed questions in intake sessions of psychodynamic therapy. *Psychotherapy Research*. Advance online publication: doi:10/1080/10503307.2022.2081100

Fuertes, J. N., & Williams, E. N. (2017). Client-focused psychotherapy research. *Journal of Counseling Psychology, 64*(4), 369–375.

García Pérez de León, C. (2018). "What was I thinking?!" Rhetorical questions as a technique to identify and explore impasses in therapy. *Australian and New Zealand Journal of Family Therapy, 39*(1), 21–37. https://doi.org/10.1002/anzf.1283

Gelso, C. J., & Williams, E. N. (2022). *Counseling psychology* (4th ed.). American Psychological Association.

*Goates-Jones, M. K., Hill, C. E., Stahl, J. V., & Doschek, E. E. (2009). Therapist response modes in the exploration stage: Timing and effectiveness. *Counselling Psychology Quarterly, 22*(2), 221–231.

Hancock, A. B., & Rubin, B. A. (2015). Influence of communication partner's gender on language. *Journal of Language and Social Psychology, 34*(1), 46–64.

Hanway, P., Akehurst, L., Vernham, Z., & Hope, L. (2021). The effects of cognitive load during an investigative interviewing task on mock interviewers' recall of information. *Legal and Criminological Psychology, 26*, 25–41. https://doi.org/10.1111/lcrp.12182

Hatcher, R. L., & Gillaspy, J. A. (2006). Development and validation of a revised short version of the working alliance inventory. *Psychotherapy Research, 16*, 12–25. doi:10.1080/10503300500352500

Heritage, J., Robinson, J. D., Elliott, M. N., Beckett, M., & Wilkes, M. (2007). Reducing patients' unmet concerns in primary care: The difference one word can make. *Journal of General Internal Medicine, 22*, 1429–1433.

Hill, C. E. (1978). Development of a counselor verbal response category system. *Journal of Counseling Psychology*, *25*(5), 461–468.
Hill, C. E. (1986). An overview of the Hill counselor and client verbal response modes category system. In L. Greenberg & W. Pinsof (Eds.), *The psychotherapeutic process: A research handbook* (pp. 131–160). Guilford.
Hill, C. E. (2020). *Helping skills: Facilitating exploration, insight, and action* (5th ed.). American Psychological Association.
Hill, C. E., Carter, J. A., & O'Farrell, M. K. (1983). A case study of the process and outcome of time-limited counseling. *Journal of Counseling Psychology*, *30*(1), 3–18.
Hill, C. E., Charles, D., & Reed, K. G. (1981). A longitudinal analysis of changes in counseling skills during doctoral training in counseling psychology. *Journal of Counseling Psychology*, *28*, 428–436.
*Hill, C. E., Helms, J. E., Tichenor, V., Spiegel, S. B., O'Grady, K. E., & Perry, E. S. (1988). Effects of therapist response modes in brief psychotherapy. *Journal of Counseling Psychology*, *35*, 222–233.
Hill, C. E., Lu, Y., Gerstenblith, J. A., Kline, K. V., Wang, R. J., & Zhu, X. (2020). Facilitating client collaboration and insight through interpretations and probes for insight in psychodynamic psychotherapy: A case study of one client with three successive therapists. *Psychotherapy*, *57*(2), 263–272. doi:10.1037/pst0000242
Hill, C. E., & O'Grady, K. E. (1985). List of therapist intentions illustrated in a case study and with therapists of varying theoretical orientations. *Journal of Counseling Psychology*, *32*, 3–22.
Hill, C. E., Thames, T. B., & Rardin, D. K. (1979). Comparison of Rogers, Perls, and Ellis on the Hill Counselor Verbal Response Category System. *Journal of Counseling Psychology*, *26*(3), 198–203.
Hook, J. N., Davis, D., Owen, J., & DeBlaere, C. (2017). *Cultural humility: Engaging diverse identities in therapy*. American Psychological Association.
*Huang, T., Hill, C., & Gelso, C. (2013). Psychotherapy engagers versus non-engagers: Differences in alliance, therapist verbal response modes, and client attachment. *Psychotherapy Research*, *23*(5), 568–577. https://doi.org/10.1080/10503307.2013.807378
Ito, T. (2017). Points to consider when using questions in solution-focused brief therapy: A qualitative study of interviews with proficient therapists. *Japanese Journal of Educational Psychology*, *65*(1), 37–51. https://doi.org/10.5926/jjep.65.37
Kivlighan, D. M. (1989). Changes in counselor intentions and response modes and in client reactions and session evaluation after training. *Journal of Counseling Psychology*, *36*(4), 471–476. https://doi.org/10.1037/0022-0167.36.4.471
Klein, M. H., Mathieu-Coughlan, P., & Kiesler, D. J. (1986). The Experiencing scales. In L. Greenberg & W. Pinsof (Eds.), *The psychotherapeutic process: A research handbook* (pp. 21–72). Guilford.
Leong, F. T. L. (Ed.). (2014). *APA handbook of multicultural psychology*. American Psychological Association.
Leutritz, A. L., Colic, L., Borchardt, V., Cheng, X., Zhang, B., Lison, S., Frommer, J., Buchheim, A., Strauss, B., Fonagy, P., Nolte, T., & Walter, M. (2020). Attachment-specific speech patterns induce dysphoric mood changes in the listener as a function of individual differences in attachment characteristics and psychopathology. *Psychology and Psychotherapy: Theory, Research and Practice*, *93*, 754–776. https://doi.org/10.1111/papt.12258
Li, X., Kivlighan, D. M., Jr., Hill, C. E., Hou, Z.-J., & Xu, M. (2018). Helping skills, working alliance, and session depth in China: A multilevel analysis. *The Counseling Psychologist*, *46*(3), 379–405.
Macdonald, J., & Muran, C. J. (2021). The reactive therapist: The problem of interpersonal reactivity in psychological therapy and the potential for a mindfulness-based program focused on "mindfulness-in-relationship" skills for therapists. *Journal of Psychotherapy Integration*, *31*(4), 452–467. https://doi.org/10.1037/int0000200

Machado, P. P., Beutler, L. E., & Greenberg, L. S. (1999). Emotion recognition in psychotherapy: Impact of therapist level of experience and emotional awareness. *Journal of Clinical Psychology, 55*, 39–57. doi:10.1002/1097-4679/jcp199901

McCarthy, J., Shannon, E., & Bruno, M. (2021). Creative question-framing: 12 ideas for counselors-in-training. *Journal of Creativity in Mental Health, 16*(4), 499–510.

McGee, D., Vento, A. D., & Bavelas, J. B. (2005). An interactional model of questions as therapeutic interventions. *Journal of Marital and Family Therapy, 31*(4), 371–384. https://doi.org/10.1111/j.1752-0606.2005.tb01577.x

Mergenthaler, E. (1996). Emotion–abstraction patterns in verbatim protocols: A new way of describing psychotherapeutic processes. *Journal of Consulting and Clinical Psychology, 64*(6), 1306–1315. https://doi.org/10.1037/0022-006X.64.6.1306

Miller, S. D., Hubble, M. A., & Chow, D. (2020). *Better results: Using deliberate practice to improve therapeutic effectiveness*. American Psychological Association.

Morgan, E., & Williams, E. N. (2021). A qualitative study of psychotherapists' in-session tears. *Psychotherapy, 58*(1), 150–159. doi:10.1037/pst0000298

Neipp, M., Beyebach, M., Sanchez-Prada, A., & del Carmen Delgado Alvarez, M. (2021). Solution-focused versus problem-focused questions: Differential effects of miracles, exceptions and scales. *Journal of Family Therapy, 43*(4), 728–747. doi.org/10.1111/1467-6427.12345

Newman, C. F. (2002). Hypotheticals in cognitive psychotherapy: Creative questions, novel answers, and therapeutic change. In R. L. Leahy & E. T. Dowd (Eds.), *Clinical advances in cognitive psychotherapy: Theory and application* (pp. 311–324). Springer.

Norcross, J. C., & Cooper, M. (2021). *Personalizing psychotherapy: Assessing and accommodating patient preferences*. American Psychological Association.

Norcross, J. C., & Wampold, B. E. (2018). A new therapy for each patient: Evidence-based relationships and responsiveness. *Journal of Clinical Psychology, 74* (11), 1889–1906. https://doi.org/10.1002/jclp.22678

Orlinsky, D. E., Grawe, K., & Parks, B. K. (1994). Process and outcome in psychotherapy—Noch einmal. In A. E. Bergin & S. L. Garfield (Eds.), *Handbook of psychotherapy and behavior change* (4th ed., pp. 207–376). Wiley.

Patterson, C. H. (1985). *The therapeutic relationship: Foundations for an eclectic psychotherapy*. Brooks/Cole.

Piaget, J. (1926). *The language and thought of the child*. Harcourt Brace.

Rautalinko, E. (2013). Reflective listening and open-ended questions in counselling: Preferences moderated by social skills and cognitive ability. *Counselling & Psychotherapy Research, 13*(1), 24–31.

Renger, S. (2021). Therapists' views on the use of questions in person-centered therapy. *British Journal of Guidance & Counselling*, 1–13.

Richmond, C. J., Jordan, S. S., Bischof, G. H., & Sauer, E. M. (2014). Effects of solution-focused versus problem-focused intake questions on pre-treatment change. *Journal of Systemic Therapies, 33*(1), 33–47.

Stiles, W. B. (1978). Verbal response modes and dimensions of interpersonal roles: A method of discourse analysis. *Journal of Personality and Social Psychology, 36*, 693–703.

Stiles, W. B., & Snow, J. S. (1984). Counseling session impact as viewed by novice counselors and their clients. *Journal of Counseling Psychology, 31*, 3–12.

Sue, D. W., Sue, D., Neville, H. A., & Smith, L. (2019). *Counseling the culturally diverse: Theory and practice*. Wiley.

Tausczik, Y. R., & Pennebaker, J. W. (2010). The psychological meaning of words: LIWC and computerized text analysis methods. *Journal of Language and Social Psychology, 29*(1), 24–54. https://doi.org/10.1177/0261927X09351676

Thompson, A. P. (1986). Changes in counseling skills during graduate and undergraduate study. *Journal of Counseling Psychology, 33*, 65–72.

Thompson, L., Howes, C., & McCabe, R. (2016). Effect of questions used by psychiatrists on therapeutic alliance and adherence. *British Journal of Psychiatry, 209*(1), 40–47.

Thrasher, A. D., Golin, C. E., Earp, J. L., Tien, H., Porter, C., & Howie, L. (2006). Motivational interviewing to support antiretroviral therapy adherence: The role of quality counseling. *Patient Education and Counseling, 62*, 64–71.

Tofade, T., Elner, J., & Haines, S. T. (2013). Best practices strategies for effective use of questions as a teaching tool. *American Journal of Pharmaceutical Education, 77*(7), 1–9. doi:10.5688/ajpe.777155

Tollison, S. J., Lee, C. M., Neighbors, C., Neil, T. A., Olson, N. D., & Larimer, M. E. (2008). Questions and reflections: The use of motivational interviewing microskills in a peer-led brief alcohol intervention for college students. *Behavior Therapy, 39*(2), 183–194.

Wharne, S. (2022). Socratic questioning and irony in psychotherapeutic practices. *Journal of Contemporary Psychotherapy, 52*, 137–144.

Williams, E. N. (2002). Therapist techniques. In G. S. Tryon (Ed.), *Counseling based on process research: Applying what we know* (pp. 232–264). Allyn & Bacon.

Williams, J. A., Burns, E. L., & Harmon, E. A. (2009). Insincere utterances and gaze: Eye contact during sarcastic statements. *Perceptual and Motor Skills, 108*(2), 565–572.

*Wiser, S., & Goldfried, M. R. (1998). Therapist interventions and client emotional experiencing in expert psychodynamic–interpersonal and cognitive–behavioral therapies. *Journal of Consulting & Clinical Psychology, 66*, 634–640.

Yeo, E., & Torres-Harding, S. R. (2021). Rupture resolution strategies and the impact of rupture on the working alliance after racial microaggressions in therapy. *Psychotherapy, 58*(4), 460–471. https://doi.org/10.1037/pst0000372

4
Socratic Questioning and Guided Discovery

James C. Overholser and Eleanor Beale

Socratic questioning is based on a thoughtful integration of ancient philosophy and contemporary psychotherapy with a particular reliance on cognitive therapy (Kazantzis et al., 2019). The broader Socratic method encourages people to view their thoughts as hypotheses to be tested and revised as needed in order to remain consistent with adaptive life perspectives. The philosophical underpinnings of the Socratic method, first started by Socrates, rely on a cooperative dialogue in the form of questions and answers to bring out contradictions in thinking and to uncover definitions that support a person's beliefs. This style of conversation focuses on self-discovery and the refutation of false knowledge and erroneous beliefs.

The Socratic method derives from the dialogues of Plato, a series of stories presented as public conversations and open forum debates in ancient Greece. Throughout these dialogues, Socrates relied on a series of questions to explore abstract topics. The discussion usually revealed the inadequate answers provided by politicians, generals, and religious leaders of his time. Socrates was contrasted with the Sophists, professed teachers who were seen as manipulating another person's answers to force them to arrive at the predetermined conclusion. In contrast, the Socratic method is an interactive discussion that remains open to a range of possible answers, in a collaborative search for useful beliefs.

Socratic questions can be used in many forms of psychotherapy. Extending beyond the narrow focus of symptom reduction, Socratic questions are used to promote the client's self-awareness and self-improvement. The systematic use of questions allows the therapist to serve as a knowledgeable guide, assisting clients to discover their own solutions or adopt new ways of thinking (Overholser, 2018). The therapist remains supportive and curious, while avoiding the role of expert.

Definitions

There has been confusion and disagreement about the terms related to Socratic questioning (Carey & Mullan, 2004). In this chapter, we propose a definition of Socratic questions as the use of *open-ended exploratory questions, often integrated with guided discovery*. Thus, in this chapter, Socratic questions (Overholser, 1993a) are integrated with guided discovery (Overholser, 2013) whereby the therapist directs the conversation toward the uncovering of core beliefs that underlie most forms of psychotherapy (Overholser et al., 2010). *Socratic questions* aim to help clients think about their situation from a new perspective. *Guided discovery* is a process whereby the therapist works

James C. Overholser and Eleanor Beale, *Socratic Questioning and Guided Discovery* In: *Psychotherapy Skills and Methods That Work*. Edited by: Clara E. Hill and John C. Norcross, Oxford University Press. © Clara E. Hill and John C. Norcross 2023.
DOI: 10.1093/oso/9780197611012.003.0004

with the client to appreciate one or more core beliefs related to adaptive functioning. The specific strategies of Socratic questioning and guided discovery can be used within many approaches to psychotherapy.

Clinical Description and Indications

Guided discovery and Socratic questioning can be applied with a wide range of psychotherapy clients. However, effective application of Socratic questions requires at least a modest level of cognitive complexity on the part of the client and patience on the part of the therapist. The Socratic therapist avoids assuming the role of expert or teacher, and shuns the tendency to share information with clients through a semi-educational format. Instead, a Socratic therapist struggles to understand the client's view and works to search for new ideas and possible solutions (Lear, 2006).

In general, Socratic questioning and guided discovery may be beneficial for clients who are struggling with persistent emotional problems, especially related to anxiety or depression. Also, the approach seems useful when helping clients understand and change their dysfunctional personality styles. Depressed clients are most likely to benefit from a Socratic style if they display a tendency for pessimistic beliefs and if they are not otherwise being treated with medications (Vittorio et al., 2021). The assessment of patterns and the uncovering of beliefs are useful with clients who are open to the process of self-discovery and able to take a curious stance regarding their own struggles. However, Socratic questions may be too subtle or indirect for clients who are struggling with a psychotic disorder, developmental delays, cognitive impairment, or a lack of insight.

Socratic Questioning

Socratic questions are used to facilitate new ways of viewing life and interpreting situations (Padesky, 1993). In the process, the therapist deliberately asks the client a series of interrelated questions that are phrased in an open manner with the therapist having no predetermined answer. The therapist uses questions to awaken the client's "slumbering intellect" (Howard, 2011). Clients often have a more adaptive view of problems and their solutions when they have been encouraged to stop to review their options. The therapist plays an active role in the discussion, pushing clients to see their struggles from a different point of view. The goal is to confront an important topic, explore several possibilities, and help guide the client toward rational decision-making.

Socratic questions can be applied across theoretical orientations. Specific application of Socratic questioning has been used to encourage dialectic thinking in dialectical behavioral therapy (Bonavitacola et al. 2019), to support cognitive restructuring in cognitive therapy (Beck & Dozois, 2011), to debate irrational cognitions in rational–emotive behavior therapy (David et al., 2021), to emphasize learning principles in exposure therapy (Craske et al., 2014), and to challenge awareness of rumination in metacognitive therapy (Callesen et al., 2014).

The use of Socratic questioning has evolved into different styles, according to therapist preferences. One main style derives from Beck's cognitive therapy (Beck & Emery, 1985; Beck et al., 1979), using a supportive, collaborative style linked to guided discovery (J. Beck, 2020; Kazantzis et al., 2014; Froján-Parga et al., 2018; Padesky, 1993; Padesky & Beck, 2003). A different approach is more aligned with Ellis' rational–emotive behavior therapy (David et al., 2021; Ellis, 1994) and retains a more directive and confrontational style (Froján-Parga et al., 2018). The current review includes research from both camps. Both styles are useful, and this review aims to integrate the two styles of Socratic questioning.

Padesky (1993) proposed that Socratic questions involve four components: (a) The client has the knowledge needed to answer the questions, (b) the questions focus the client's attention on a relevant issue, (c) the questions move from concrete issues to abstract topics, and (d) the questions help the client create a new understanding of their problems. These criteria provide a useful starting point upon which we will expand (Table 4.1).

Questions Help Focus Attention

The therapist poses questions that focus the client's attention on a specific topic relevant to therapeutic goals. Questions may focus on identifying client competencies, exploring the client's goals, or reinterpreting events from a more positive perspective (Flückiger et al., 2014). The therapist works on the belief that the client has the information to answer the questions, and that the questions will help the client notice or remember relevant information (Padesky, 1993). Socratic questions uncover information held by the client that may have been neglected, rejected, or discounted (Kennerly, 2007; Padesky, 1993).

Questions Occur in a Brief Sequence

The therapist relies on a series of questions presented in a brief sequence that often is limited to a few minutes. There is no expectation that each therapy session will be overflowing with questions from the therapist. At times, the therapist may shift into a more directive style, redirecting the conversation onto useful topics.

Questions Are Part of a Collaborative Search for New Information

The therapist's questions may encourage clients to search for new ways of viewing their struggles or their coping options. The search is conducted in a collaborative manner by exploring strategies the client has tried before, strategies that have been recommended by others, and strategies the client may like to try for a new approach.

Questions Follow a Bifurcated Style

Some of the therapist's questions present two equally valid options and allow the client to decide which choice fits their beliefs. For example, if a therapist poses the question, "Do you think this strategy would help?" it implies the therapist believes the new strategy will help. In contrast, if two options are presented ("Do you think this strategy would make things better or could it complicate things and even make the situation worse?"), then clients are encouraged to anticipate the likely impact of their actions. Some questions offer an alternative interpretation and ask for the client's reaction. For

Table 4.1 Socratic Questions and Guided Discovery Rating Scale

Socratic Questions/Guided Discovery Rating Scale	Not at all	Occasionally	Frequently
1. The therapist asks a question for which the client has the knowledge needed to answer the question, even if it forces the client to stop and confront important ideas or painful memories.	0	1	2
2. The therapist uses questions to focus the client's attention on a relevant issue that could help therapy confront important nontrivial issues.	0	1	2
3. The therapist uses questions to move the discussion from concrete issues to abstract topics, personal values, or major life goals.	0	1	2
4. The therapist uses questions to shift the client's perspective, viewing their troubles from a new and useful vantage point.	0	1	2
5. The therapist's questions occur in a brief sequence, interlaced with more directive comments and general discussions.	0	1	2
6. The therapist uses questions in a collaborative search for new information, seeking a different and more useful way of viewing the client's problems.	0	1	2
7. The therapist's question presents two equally valid options and the client is asked to choose one as their preferred answer.	0	1	2
8, The therapist's question relies on curiosity to seek honest answers so both client and therapist collaborate on the search for useful information.	0	1	2
9. The therapist's question avoids specific directions, but nonetheless may push the client to confront difficult decisions.	0	1	2
10. Openly or implicitly, the therapist expresses a general attitude, such as: a. All clients are capable of making adaptive changes in their lives. b. Effective change is often a process that develops gradually over time. c. Most people benefit by making adaptive changes in their activities and attitudes. d. Negative life events often turn out better than first expected. e. Difficult life circumstances can provide opportunities for growth. f. Change is often a gradual process that involves new actions and new attitudes. g. Past events do not need to create everlasting emotional turmoil.	0	1	2

(continued)

Table 4.1 Continued

Socratic Questions/Guided Discovery Rating Scale	Not at all	Occasionally	Frequently
11. The therapist seems to have a plan for each session, usually trying to help the client see the benefit of the core beliefs described in item 10.	0	1	2
12. The therapist relies on inductive reasoning to help search for general patterns or potential causes related to the client's problem areas.	0	1	2
13. The therapist serves as a supportive guide, minimizing the importance of book knowledge and avoiding the role of expert.	0	1	2
14. The therapist encourages the collaborative use of hypothesis testing as a mean of evaluating the utility or validity of the client's beliefs and expectations.	0	1	2

example, the therapist may ask, "Does this situation seem like a horrible catastrophe, or would it be more helpful to view it as an annoyance?"

Questions Rely on Curiosity

Socratic questions rely on the therapist's curiosity while exploring topics of interest (Paul & Elder, 2007). Many questions are presented as open-ended topics, and clients are encouraged to support their views while saying only what they believe to be true. For example, if a therapist asks, "What can you do to improve this situation?" it may result in an empty response, such as "I don't know." Instead, it may be better to ask a short series of questions, such as "How did you react when this happened?" (pause for client response); "If it happens again, how would you *like* to respond?" (pause for client response); and "Have you thought about ways that your best friend would deal with this type of problem?" (pause for client response).

Questions Avoid Specific Directions

Socratic questions avoid the tendency to provide clients with a new strategy and request their approval. For example, "Do you think it would help to talk to your wife about your concerns?" includes an implied directive, implicitly conveying the notion that "I think this is a good idea." Socratic questions often push the client forward to make adaptive changes, while expecting the client to steer the direction of the conversation and make rational decisions.

Guided Discovery

Socratic questions are integrated with guided discovery. First proposed as a therapeutic process by Aaron Beck as part of cognitive therapy (Beck et al., 1979; Beck & Emery, 1985), guided discovery relies on a process of shaping (Calero-Elvira et al., 2013) whereby the discussion gently flows increasingly closer toward meaningful issues and useful strategies. Instead of trying to solve a specific problem for the client, the therapist helps clients learn to solve problems by cultivating general attitudes that underlie emotional stability and effective coping (Overholser, 2013).

Common Destinations for the Conversation

Core beliefs are adaptive attitudes that are likely to be accepted by most therapists (Overholser et al., 2010), and these broad attitudes may underlie the goals for the conversation (see Table 4.1, item 10). During therapy sessions, the therapist may strongly encourage clients to consider one of these core beliefs.

Planful Strategy

Guided discovery uses questions to keep the conversation focused on adaptive functioning. Questions can be used to confront the client's logical reasoning, aiming to highlight logical fallacies that underlie the client's approach to problem situations (Elder & Paul, 2007). Therapists guide clients in exploring areas for possible improvement in attitudes or behaviors.

Inductive Reasoning

When discussing a current problem, the therapist may attempt to collect a string of examples to search for recurrent patterns or general themes. Inductive reasoning helps clients learn from their own life experiences (Overholser, 1993b). Guided discovery encourages a methodical search for the possible causes of their struggles, systematically ruling out factors that seem nonessential. The goal is to identify factors that could be avoided, managed, or altered in some way.

Disavowal of Knowledge

In guided discovery, the therapist respects the knowledge the client has regarding their own subjective experience, personal goals, and moral values (Overholser, 1995). This is perhaps the most controversial aspect of applying the Socratic approach. Therapists must disavow their own knowledge and prioritize the client's perspective. By viewing clients as experts about their own life, thoughts, emotions, struggles, secrets, and personal relationships, therapists direct the discussion away from solving problems and toward broader client empowerment.

Hypothesis Testing

Guided discovery often relies on hypothesis testing to explore the evidence base for various beliefs. Together, the therapist and client sort through the available evidence, find unconsidered counter-evidence, and search for connections and patterns. Behavioral activities and tracking measures can provide data to support or refute various beliefs.

The Process and Content of Sessions

The *content* of therapy sessions involves using Socratic questioning in small doses and brief intervals scattered across sessions. The therapist may ask the client 40–60 questions per session. However, each session also includes interludes of discussion and explanation to avoid the feel of a rapid-fire interrogation.

The *process* of guided discovery centers on the therapist's intellectual modesty to demonstrate a willingness to approach opinions and expectations as thoughts instead of facts and listen to the client's response. In a study of four depressed patients, metacognitive therapy was combined with a Socratic dialogue to challenge beliefs about the benefits of rumination (Callesen et al., 2014). Through modesty, both therapist and client can effectively explore the benefits and downfalls of certain ways of thinking. Socratic questions such as "How have you arrived at that belief? What led you to that conclusion?" can help clients refine their own perspective (Wells, 2007).

Assessment

Assessing Socratic Questioning and Guided Discovery

Given the limited research conducted on Socratic questioning, only two strategies of formal assessment have been applied (Braun et al., 2015; Froján-Parga et al., 2011). Each of these assessment strategies focuses on ratings provided by trained judges after they watched or listened to recordings of therapy sessions. We know of no self-report questionnaires or therapist self-evaluation rating forms that assess the use of Socratic questions or guided discovery. There is a risk that different investigators will be studying different styles, based on their own preconceived views of Socratic questioning, without a strong foundation in the historical figure Socrates as reported in the *Dialogues of Plato*.

Guided discovery has been assessed by a single item on the Cognitive Therapy Rating Scale (Young & Beck, 1980) and its revised version (Blackburn et al., 2001). In both versions, the item is used to evaluate the degree to which the therapist relied on guided discovery during a given therapy session. The rating instructions highlight the use of questions to help clients seek new perspectives on their problems, explore different ideas, and test assorted hypotheses. The item is scored from 0 (poor: a debate style of interview) to 6 (excellent: skillful use of questions to draw out new ideas), and a rating is provided after listening to an entire therapy session.

The only studies that have assessed Socratic questioning have examined the amount of Socratic questioning used within the current session (Froján-Parga et al., 2011, 2018) or the previous session (Braun et al., 2015; Vittorio et al., 2021).

Froján-Parga and colleagues (2011, 2018) examined videotaped recordings of therapy sessions, coding therapist verbal statements into seven functions identified by the researchers based on basic behavioral operations. Therapist verbalizations were coded for statements or questions that appeared to focus on assorted therapist functions, including reinforcement (agreement with and acceptance of something the client has said), punishment (disagreement and disapproval of a client's statement), instruction (providing the client with guidance for conducting behavior outside the therapy room), providing information, and motivating the client by highlighting the advantages of new behavior or the disadvantages of current dysfunctional behavior. Client verbalizations were coded for their degree of alignment with the therapist's goals and agreement with the therapist's most recent statement. The assessment system focuses on observable changes in client verbalizations that occur within a given session.

Using different assessment methods, by Braun and colleagues (Braun et al., 2015; Vittorio et al., 2021), audiotaped therapy sessions were rated on the Socratic Questioning Scale (SQS), a 5-item measure that applies a 7-point Likert scale to the following questions:

How frequently did the therapist ask questions of the client in the service of using (any) cognitive behavioral strategies?

How frequently did the therapist ask questions of the client in the service of using cognitive strategies focused on developing alternative perspectives?

When the therapist worked with the client to develop alternative perspectives, was this work focused on key cognitions (cognitions central to strong emotional reactions)?

When dealing with a specific automatic thought, how many questions did the therapist typically ask?

Did the therapist ask open-ended questions that require thoughtful reflection (related to developing alternative responses)?

Higher scores on the SQS represent greater therapist use of Socratic questioning. The SQS showed satisfactory interrater reliability and acceptable internal consistency, in addition to capturing a fairly global view of therapy sessions.

Assessing Within-Session Outcomes

Froján-Parga and colleagues (2011, 2018) examined any changes that occurred in the therapist and client verbal exchange. The coding system relies on a functional analysis of therapy sessions and is aligned with an operant conditional view of therapeutic interactions. In addition, the assessment method identified an unfolding of a stimulus–response exchange throughout a session.

Assessing End-of-Treatment Outcomes

Braun et al. (2015) assessed symptom reduction using two standardized depression scales, the Beck Depression Inventory–II (BDI-II; Beck et al., 1996) and the Hamilton Rating Scale for Depression (Hamilton, 1967). Vittorio et al. (2021) used the BDI-II to assess decrease in depression symptomatology, and Strunk et al. (2006) used the Life Events Prediction Task to assess the role of cognitive bias as a moderator on the reduction of depression symptoms resulting from higher use of Socratic questioning.

Based on the concepts and definitions presented in this chapter, we suggest that Socratic questioning does not directly aim for a reduction of the client's symptoms or an amelioration of the client's emotional distress. Instead, the use of Socratic questioning often aims to develop a balanced view of life, and this outlook may require a philosophical shift of perspective. Discussions may center around broad goals for life improvement, such as increasing a client's social maturity; helping a client rely on rational decision-making when confronted with common problems involving loss, conflict, or rejection; improving tolerance for oneself and other people; and developing a general attitude of creative flexibility when confronted with obstacles toward personal goals. Thus, the outcome of these discussions would ideally lead to an increase in the client's ability to engage in these explorations independently and openly. Then, there is movement toward self-regulation whereby the client learns to control urges, emotions, and maladaptive habits through cognitive reasoning and logical thinking. Clients can feel empowered when they begin to appreciate that they are capable of controlling their behaviors as well as their emotions. Unfortunately, again, we know of no such measures that assess these targeted outcomes of Socratic questioning at either the immediate in-session or the end-of-treatment time points.

Clinical Examples

During one session, a depressed client complained that her life was "in the toilet." [Although the client signed a release, the client's situation and identity have been changed to protect confidentiality.] When asked to explain such an extreme view, she focused on a recent conflict and ongoing troubles with her romantic partner. The psychotherapist asked a short series of Socratic questions to help the client clarify the situation, her goals, and realistic options: "Where do you see this relationship going from here?" "What do you think the romance will be like in 6 months?" "How realistic is it to expect your partner to make these changes?" and "What can *you* do to help create the future that you hope to see?" The client replied that she hoped to maintain the romance but wanted her partner to be more attentive at home, less critical about household chores, and more cooperative with the extended family. She had become focused on possible changes in her partner, overlooking her own role in the ongoing struggles experienced by the couple. The therapist was trying to push her toward a general sense of personal responsibility and self-control over the situation, as well as assessing the viability of the relationship and searching for realistic changes that could be implemented.

Sometimes the therapy dialogue will explore the developmental antecedents that appear related to adult emotional struggles. To protect client confidentiality, the following example is an amalgamation of dialogue that occurred across several sessions with several clients struggling with similar problems.

An adult male client was struggling with emotional scars from his cold and critical father. Even though the client had reached mid-life, and his father had died years earlier, he was still bothered by painful memories and a tendency for self-recrimination. In session, the therapist (T) asked the client (C) a series of questions to guide him along a path of self-discovery:

T: Tell me about your parents.

C: Well, my mother was a homemaker, and my father worked a factory job. He usually came home tired, frustrated, and spent the evening scolding me about stupid little things.

T: What is your understanding—why do you think your father became so upset on a regular basis?

C: I think he was a jerk. No. I think he hated his job and took it out on us kids, primarily me.

T: Do you feel his anger was linked to the stress he was under at the time?

C: I guess so. I don't know. I never thought about it.

T: Was your father critical of your sisters too, or was he primarily focused on you?

C: I think he dealt with them differently. They were younger and he didn't have as much to do with them because they were girls. It sure seemed like he focused on me. [During a subsequent session, the childhood events were explored in more context.]

T: What do you know about your father's upbringing?

C: His parents, my grandparents, were immigrants. His father was a skilled craftsman, but worked a lot and never really climbed up to a level where he had his own shop.

T: Do you know much about your father's childhood?

C: I have heard stories that my grandfather had a temper. He would use a switch to punish the kids whenever they misbehaved. That was the way back then.

T: Because your father grew up in a different time, when corporal punishment was common, do you feel that shaped his view of parenting?

C: Sure. I guess it was pretty common back then.

T: If your father's parents were verbally harsh or physically abusive, how did these factors influence your father as a person and as a parent?

C: I don't know. I guess it taught him how parenting works; spare the rod and spoil the child.

T: Are some of the pieces starting to fit together?

C: What do you mean?

T: Are you getting a different view of your father; maybe a different understanding of why he behaved the way he did?

C: Maybe. I guess so.

T: Does it help you in any way to gain a better understanding of your father and how he was raised?

C: I guess so. Maybe he wasn't just picking on me. Maybe he thought he was doing his job as a parent.

In order to reduce the feeling of an interrogation, questions can be packaged with a brief explanation, apology, or simple review of the topics being discussed. Thus, it can be helpful to precede the question with simple phrases, such as "This might be a hard question . . .," "What's your best guess . . .," "If we stop for a moment . . .," or "As we sit here now . . .". Some of the therapist's questions appear quite leading, but in general the therapist is hoping to push the client to confront a new way of looking at his father and the events from many years ago. By viewing the events from a different vantage point, it was hoped the client may become capable of letting go of his persistent negative emotions:

T: I have come to believe that people often go down one of two paths. Many people say: "That's how I was raised, so that's how it should be done." However, others choose the opposite path, and state "That's how I was raised, and I will not behave that way toward my own children." Now, it seems like your father took the first path, but you have chosen the second path. Does that make sense or am I way off base?

C: So I turned my back on violence? I guess I try to not let anger get the better of me.

T: Have you reached a point where you can forgive and forget the conflict you experienced with your father?

C: No. I don't think so. The pain runs too deep.

T: We are not trying to erase the events that happened years ago, but can we balance things out with memories of a few positive moments you had with your father?

C: I liked hiking and fishing. Sometimes we would go out and rent a boat to fish on the lake. That was usually a lot of fun.

T: We have focused a lot on the intense disagreements you've had with your father. Do you think it will be possible to reach a point of forgiveness toward your father?

C: No. I feel like things are too broke to fix.

T: Really? Do you believe things are too broken to fix here? Well, I don't and I'll go so far as to say it is entirely under your control. You have the power to forgive your father, right here and right now. Do you agree?

C: Yes.

T: Okay, so what can you do to reach 100 percent forgiveness from your side of the events?

C: No idea.

T: Earlier, you said that "you are who you are" and you are at peace with that. So you accept yourself, even with your flaws and faults. Is that right?

C: I don't know. Maybe.

T: I believe that all people include a mix of good and bad qualities, and I believe that all memories of people can include a mix of good and bad memories. Do you agree?

C: Yeah, sure.

T: Can we apply these notions onto memories of your father?

C: Yeah, I guess he had a lot of positive qualities. He worked hard, supported the family, and seemed popular at the local bar.

T: You had said you could understand why people 100 years ago ruled with an iron fist. I get it. It was a different time and people behaved differently than they do today. Can we apply this notion to your father? It seems like he lived in a different social environment, and parents raised their children with more rules, strict enforcement, and disinterest. Do these societal changes help you to see your father's behavior a little differently?

In the following session, the therapist returned to these issues:

T: After our last session, I had a few lingering thoughts about our discussion. How about you—did you continue to think about the issues we discussed last week?

C: Yes, I had an epiphany. Because my father is gone, I assumed these issues were locked in place. It was eye opening to think that I could still reach a point of reconciliation.

T: Great. I agree there is a lot you can do to work through these painful memories. [At the end of one session, the client was asked to visit the cemetery where his parents are buried. A small family gathering had been scheduled so his siblings could celebrate Father's Day by visiting the cemetery together.]

T: What was it like for you when you attended the memorial service?

C: I had a lot of thoughts stirring in my head, but I didn't say much and I tried to not show my emotions, but when I approached the grave, I got really choked up.

T: What was going on inside of you at that moment—what did you notice in your feelings and your thoughts?

C: It was odd. I felt sad but I also felt angry.

T: Did you speak up at the family gathering when you got back to your sister's home?

C: No. I tried to be polite, so I didn't say much.

T: What held you back?

C: I know everyone there thought he was a great guy. I was having too many thoughts about all of the things he didn't do, and I felt he was not much of a father.

T: If you had said something, what might you have said?

C: I was afraid I would tell everyone how he was always critical of me, how nothing was ever good enough for him, and how he made me feel like a loser.

T: How would your life have been different if your father had been nicer to you when you were young?

C: I guess life would have been easier. Maybe I would have had more enjoyment.

T: How would *you* be different?

C: I don't know. I guess I'd be different. I'm not sure if that would be a good thing or a bad thing. I'd have to think about it.

T: Moving forward, would life be better if you could somehow forget these events?

C: Maybe not forget . . . but stop dwelling on them and letting them drag me down so much.

T: And do you feel you could make that change, control how much you let these memories drag you down?

C: Yeah, sure, . . . I'm pretty sure.

Several goals were pursued in these sessions. First, the client was encouraged to gain distance from a self-critical attitude, hearing the criticism he had internalized from his father. Second, the client was encouraged to debate these critical attitudes instead of automatically accepting the criticism as if it were an accurate appraisal and a fair evaluation of the client. Third, the client was later encouraged to understand his father, reflecting upon his knowledge of the father's upbringing. Additional questions were used to help the client gain insight into the developmental origins of the father's negativity, arising from the criticism with which the father had been raised, the societal morals of the time, the parenting styles of a previous generation, family reliance on corporal punishment, and the priority of work when serving as the sole breadwinner for a family. Fourth, the client was asked to understand the father's role, reactions, and reasons for the criticism. These are complex questions, and they should be used carefully in a therapy session.

The transcript shows a rapid transition between a series of questions and a more directive approach to the issues. At times, the therapist used leading questions to push the client to confront his long-standing tendencies to blame his father and maintain his anger over a span of many years. The therapist was not trying to tell the client what to do or how to feel but, rather, was pushing the client to realize that past events do not need to continue to haunt him and to accept the fact that forgiveness and emotional equanimity are under his control. The client learned to let go of troubled memories to embrace the present moments of daily life.

Landmark Studies and Previous Reviews

Most previous publications on the Socratic method and Socratic questions have relied on anecdotal evidence (Kazantzis et al., 2014) or surveys of experts (Clark & Egan, 2018; Kazantzis et al., 2018). We consider the handful of research studies in the subsequent "Research Review" section.

In their narrative review of the literature, Clark and Egan (2015) concluded that research on the Socratic method has been plagued by a lack of clarity in terminology and operational definitions of the strategies. To our knowledge, there are no quantitative reviews of the research evidence on the association between therapist use of Socratic questioning and guided discovery and patients' subsequent psychotherapy outcomes.

Research Review

Because minimal empirical research has been conducted on the effectiveness of Socratic questioning (Clark & Egan, 2015), it is not possible to conduct a meta-analysis of such research. Even in the few studies that have been conducted, the participants and methodology have varied greatly, making direct comparisons less meaningful. In addition, as noted in the "Assessment" section, there is little consensus on how to define Socratic questioning. Thus, the critical evaluation of Socratic questions remains limited to a narrative review of a few studies.

Using both MEDLINE and Google Scholar, we searched the literature since the year 2000 (only theoretical papers were published on these topics prior to the year 2000) using the terms "Socratic" and "Socrates" combined with "psychotherapy," "psychological," and "treatment." We also reviewed the reference list from each of the identified publications. Our inclusion criteria were published journal articles in the English language involving actual psychotherapy (not analogues) investigating the process or effectiveness of the Socratic method or Socratic questioning. After removing philosophical articles, review papers, and articles about teaching, we identified eight studies of interest.

These studies (Table 4.2) typically involved small samples of patients (ranging from 1 to 55 clients) being treated by a handful of therapists (ranging from one to six therapists). All eight studies were conducted by the same two groups of investigators discussed in the "Assessment" section. The first group (Calero-Elvira et al., 2013; Froján-Parga et al., 2009, 2011, 2018; Pardo-Cebrián et al., 2021) has studied the process of using Socratic questioning during therapy sessions based on operant conditioning principles, and their work does not examine distal patient outcomes. The second group of investigators (Braun et al., 2015; Vittorio et al., 2021) has assessed the impact of Socratic questioning (using the SQS) on client depression. The specifics of these two lines of study are described here. In Table 4.2, we provide a box score for each study, using the simple rating of + to indicate the use of Socratic questions had a positive impact on the

Table 4.2 Summary of Research Studies That Examined the Process and Effectiveness of Socratic Questions in Psychotherapy Sessions

Study	Sample	Measures	Results
		Process of Socratic Questioning	
Froján-Parga et al. (2009)	Video recordings of 5 conversation fragments 4 outpatient clinical sessions 1 client (29-year-old woman) 1 therapist (behavioral psychologist)	Measure of verbal interactions 7 categories based on basic behavioral operations (discriminative, evocative, reinforcement, punishment, instructional, motivational, informative, and other) A three-term sequence of stimulus–response–consequence was used to analyze change in therapist's client-directed verbalizations as the debate evolved Measure of client's verbalizations/cognitions Client verbalizations that the therapist challenged	Process findings Client–therapist interactions fell into four types: (a) Therapist evoked a response from the client without reinforcement/punishment; (b) therapist evoked a response from the client with reinforcement; (c) therapist evoked a response from client with punishment; and (d) any previous type with preceding informative, motivational, or instructional statement. Therapist directed changes using three methods: (a) The objective is not met, the therapist punishes (or does not reinforce) the client's verbal behavior, and a change is made; (b) the therapist's partial or final objective is met, reinforcement may be delivered, and a change is made to confirm what has been achieved or to move on with the therapy; and (c) the client changes topic of conversation and the therapist engages in the debate for a while, digressing from the strategy the therapist was following. Box score: +

(*continued*)

Table 4.2 Continued

Study	Sample	Measures	Results
Froján et al. (2010)	Video recordings of 16 clinical sessions 4 clients (age range: 19–53 years;, 2 males and 2 females) 3 behavioral therapists (with either 8 or 15 years of experience)	Measure of therapist's verbal behavior 8 behavioral categories (reinforcement, punishment, discriminative stimulus, elicitation, information, motivation, instruction, other) and duration of verbalization Measure of therapeutic stage 4 stages identified from the main goals of psychological interventions (assessment, explanation of functional analysis and treatment proposal, treatment, and consolidation of therapeutic change)	Process findings In the phase of assessment, there was a predominance of point-event categories (mainly discriminative stimulus and reinforcement) while there were hardly any verbalizations with informative, instructional, and/or motivational contents. In the phase of functional analysis and treatment proposal, there was a prevalence of state-event categories, particularly information occupied more than 50% of the session time analyzed. The phases of treatment and change consolidation differed from assessment in having a greater percentage of time on information, motivation, and instruction. They also had significantly less time in these areas compared to the phase of explanation of the functional analysis and treatment proposal. Box score: +
Froján-Parga et al. (2011)	Video recordings of 18 sequences 16 sessions 8 clients (age range: 16–50 years; 1 male and 8 females) 6 CBT therapists (ranging from 1 to >15 years of experience)	Measure of therapist verbal behavior 7 categories based on behavioral operations (discriminative, evocative, reinforcement, punishment, instructional, motivational, informative, and other) A three-term sequence of stimulus–response–consequence was used to analyze change in therapist's client-directed verbalizations as the debate evolved	Process findings The most frequent event functions during debate were the hypothesized discriminative (41.33%) and reinforcement (18.15%) function. The most salient of the state functions was the informative function, with an average frequency of 21.30% and a mean duration of 35.20%. The motivational and instructional functions had a low frequency of occurrence (instructional: 4.17%; motivational: 2.71%) and a very short duration compared to the overall duration of the segments (instructional: 4.60%; motivational: 3.20%). Three states of the Socratic method segments were found: start, course, and end. Functions progressed in this order: discriminative, reinforcement, and punishment → informative and instruction → motivational. At the end, a sequence similar to the initial one takes place, with verbalizations with discriminative, reinforcement, and punishment functions. Box score: +

Calero-Elvira et al. (2013)	Video recordings of 65 conversation fragments 7 clients (age range: 29–34 years) 1 therapist (cognitive–behavioral therapist with 16 years of experience)	Measure of therapist verbal behavior 4 categories based on basic behavioral operations (cue, approval, disapproval) Measurement of client verbal behavior 4 categories (pro-therapeutic verbalizations, verbalizations approaching the therapeutic objective, verbalizations intermediate with respect to the therapeutic objective, verbalizations opposing the therapeutic objective) Measure of verbal effectiveness Verbal Effectiveness Scale, which categorizes a Socratic fragment into a failure, a partial success, or a total success	Process findings 39 Socratic fragments were classified as a total success, 21 as a partial success, and 5 as a failure. The therapist delivered approval versus disapproval after the patient's verbalizations depending on their compatibility with therapeutic goals. Socratic fragments were more or less effective in terms of overall verbal adjustment, depending on the relations between the patient's responses and subsequent approval/disapproval. Box score: +
Froján-Parga et al. (2018)	Video recordings of 10 sessions 1 clinical case (32-year-old woman) 1 therapist (>15 years of experience) using cognitive–behavioral marital therapy	Measure of therapist verbal behavior 7 categories based on behavioral operations (discriminative, evocative, reinforcement, punishment, instructional, motivational, informative, and other) A three-term sequence of stimulus–response–consequence was used to analyze change in therapist's client-directed verbalizations as the debate evolved Measurement of client's verbal behavior 4 categories (pro-therapeutic verbalizations, verbalizations approaching the therapeutic objective, verbalizations intermediate with respect to the therapeutic objective, and verbalizations opposing the therapeutic objective)	Process findings 6 types of behavioral chains amounted to 40% of all interactions during the session. 60% of all interactions were heterogeneous and corresponded to activities such as informing, giving instructions regarding tasks to be completed, or motivating the client to change. Client verbalizations approached the therapeutic objective in three types of sequences: (a) Therapist emitted discriminative verbalizations before and after the client's emission of VAT, (b) therapist emitted discriminative verbalizations before and reinforcing verbalizations after the client's response, and (c) therapist first discriminated and then emitted other kind of verbalizations. The most common sequences related to verbalizations opposed to the therapeutic objective (VOT) were discriminating before and after the client's response, discriminating before and punishing after, and discriminating before and emitting other kind of verbalizations after. Box score: +

(continued)

Table 4.2 Continued

Study	Sample	Measures	Results
Pardo-Cebrián et al. (2021)	Video recordings of 113 segments of Socratic questioning 18 adult outpatients (77.7% women with mean age of 28.7 years) 11 behavioral therapists (ranging from an averaging 10.3 years for experiences and 1.3 years for inexperienced therapists)	Measurement of therapist verbal behavior The Therapist System of Categories (7 categories based on behavioral operations (discriminative, evocative, reinforcement, punishment, instructional, motivational, informative, and other) Measurement of patient verbal behavior The Patient System of Categories (4 categories—pro-therapeutic verbalizations, verbalizations approaching the therapeutic objective, verbalizations intermediate with respect to the therapeutic objective, verbalizations opposing the therapeutic objective, and other) Measure of verbal effectiveness Verbal Effectiveness Scale, which categorizes a Socratic fragment into a failure, a partial success, or a total success	Process findings The main types of therapist verbalizations in the Socratic method are explaining and questioning. The most used questions are aimed at questioning the validity of client utterances. As the Socratic method evolves, questions about validity decrease and questions about utility increase. Debate questions preceded by other verbalizations such as using analogies, explaining in a technical manner, and motivating lead to patient responses closer to therapeutic objectives compared to when debate questions are used without such verbalizations. Box score: +
Effectiveness of Socratic Questioning			
Braun et al. (2015)	Video recordings of 55 depressed outpatient adults (89% White; 53% women; age range: 18–69 years) 16-week course of cognitive therapy 4 advanced graduate student therapists with 1–2 years of clinical experience	Measure of depression Beck Depression Inventory–II and the Hamilton Rating Scale for Depression Measure of therapeutic alliance Working Alliance Inventory Measure of Socratic questioning • 5-item Socratic Questioning Scale that uses a 7-point Likert scale reflecting the amount that a therapist uses Socratic questioning in a given session, where higher scores represent greater therapist use	Outcomes The average on the SQS ranged from 1.16 to 2.68 (standard deviations ranging from .77 to .91). The amount of Socratic questioning within each session significantly predicted session-to-session decrease in depression symptoms. This finding remained significant when accounting for within-patient variability. Box score: +

Vittorio et al. (2021)	Video recordings of 55 depressed outpatient adults (89% White; 53% women; age range: 18–69 years) 16-week course of cognitive therapy 4 advanced graduate student therapists with 1–2 years of clinical experience	Measure of depression Beck Depression Inventory–II Measure of pessimistic bias Life Events Prediction Task prompts participants to predict the probability that 40 events will occur over a 1-week period. Bias scores range from –1 to 1, where negative values reflect pessimistic bias and positive scores reflect optimistic bias. Measure of dysfunctional attitudes Dysfunctional Attitudes Scale is a 40-item self-report inventory of maladaptive beliefs. Measure of Socratic questioning 5-item Socratic Questioning Scale that uses a 7-point Likert scale reflecting the amount that a therapist uses Socratic questioning in a given session, where higher scores represent greater therapist use	Outcomes Individuals with a greater pessimistic bias experienced greater symptom improvement at the next session as a function of within-person Socratic questioning. Individuals not on medication experienced greater symptom improvement at the next session as a function of within-person Socratic questioning. Box score: +

CBT, cognitive–behavioral therapy; SQS, Socratic Questioning Scale; VAT, verbalization that approximates the therapeutic goal of the Socratic method; VOT, verbalization that opposes the therapeutic objective of the Socratic method.

client, 0 to reflect a neutral impact, and – to denote a detrimental impact. Although therapeutic changes were modest, there were no detrimental effects seen from the use of Socratic questions.

Immediate Outcomes Based on Operant Conditioning Principles

Froján-Parga and colleagues (2009) examined videotaped recordings from five therapy sessions provided to a single adult client. The therapist had 20 years of professional experience, and the client was a 29-year-old woman struggling with low mood. The recordings were rated using the authors self-developed Therapist System of Categories coding system, scoring verbal statements for indicators of reinforcement, punishment, information, instruction, and motivational encouragement. The results identified a shaping procedure in which the therapist's statements used verbal reinforcement and punishment to guide the client toward a therapeutic goal. Early in the session, the client expressed views that she lacked self-esteem at work. The therapist explained the final goal for their discussion was to examine, challenge, and support the view that she is a successful woman. Despite the reliance on a single case, this study set the stage for subsequent research on the process of Socratic questioning by this group of investigators (e.g., Frojan et al., 2010).

Froján-Parga and colleagues (2011) expanded their protocol to examine videotaped recordings from eight clients treated by six different therapists. Clients were seeking treatment for assorted problems, including depression, eating disorders, and relationship concerns. The same coding procedures were used, and similar findings were obtained. The investigation showed that therapists used differential reinforcement of the client's statements to gradually move the client toward the target verbalization, defined as the statement the therapist wanted the client to state by the end of their discussion. The debate was focused on client verbalizations that caused discomfort for the client. At times, the therapist highlighted the benefits of a different attitude. At other times, the therapist proposed more adaptive views and asked assorted questions to check on the client's understanding and degree of agreement with the new attitude. The authors concluded that Socratic questions rely on a shaping procedure and described their approach to questioning as more directive than the Socratic style proposed by Beck, Ellis, and Padesky and the definitions proposed in this chapter. The researchers (Froján-Parga et al., 2011) describe their approach to the Socratic method as aligned with operant conditioning strategies aimed toward a predetermined goal response.

This line of research continued with Calero-Elvira and colleagues (2013), examining sessions from seven clients working with a single therapist. The investigation rated the therapist's statements, questions, and responses to the client, sometimes evaluating whether the client's answers were believed to reflect dysfunctional attitudes. The therapist's verbal behavior was categorized as a cue, an approval, a disapproval, or other, in line with operant definitions. Client verbalizations were similarly categorized as pro-therapeutic verbalizations, verbalizations approaching the therapeutic objective, verbalizations intermediate with respect to the therapeutic objective, verbalizations opposing the therapeutic objective, and other. Results showed that the Socratic approach encouraged a gradual increase in client statements that aligned with the therapist's view of adaptive attitudes. The authors concluded that the Socratic method relies on a process of verbal shaping whereby the therapist deftly guides the client toward answers that are deemed acceptable and adaptive. The researchers continued to promote a focus on operant conditioning principles as applied to changes seen in the debate between therapist and client.

Similarly, the same group of researchers (Froján-Parga et al., 2018) published a detailed case study in which they assessed 10 therapy sessions provided to a 32-year-old woman who was struggling with relationship problems. Videotaped sessions were coded for the therapist's verbal behavior. Statements were marked as indicating reinforcement or punishment in response to the client's statements, or providing information, motivational advice, or general instructions. In line with their prior work, the results supported the view that the Socratic dialog relies on processes of chaining and shaping to encourage changes in the client's statements. In a subsequent study by the same group, two categorical systems for therapist and client were developed from the already described outcomes and used to assess the strategic functions within the Socratic method (Pardo-Cebrián et al., 2021). The study used a problem-solving framework in which questions were used to challenge the evidence and logic supporting the client's beliefs, as well as using questions to debate the validity or utility of certain beliefs. Results suggested that a therapist may use questions and an active debating style of discussion to subtly direct the flow of the conversation. In general, these studies focused on measuring changes in the client's verbalizations that occurred within a specific therapy session. The goal was to map the topography of sessions that relied on Socratic questions.

Distal Outcomes on Depression

In an alternative line of study, Braun and colleagues (2015) have conducted research into Socratic questioning by coding audiotaped therapy sessions. Fifty-five depressed adult outpatients underwent a 16-week course of cognitive therapy and depression symptoms were assessed using the BDI-II (Beck et al., 1996) and the Hamilton Rating Scale for Depression (Hamilton, 1967). Results revealed that among the 44 patients who completed treatment, the more frequent use of Socratic questions (as assessed using the SQS) was associated with greater therapeutic gains as seen in a greater reduction of depressive symptoms (as assessed using the BDI-II) at the subsequent therapy session. This research was extended by Vittorio and colleagues (2021), who examined pretreatment predictors of treatment response using data from the same 55 depressed adults. Results showed that Socratic questions had the strongest beneficial impact on depressed clients who were not being treated with antidepressant medication. Also, Socratic questioning was found especially helpful for depressed clients who reported high levels of pessimistic attitudes at the start of treatment, as measured using the Life Events Prediction Task (Strunk et al., 2006). Both findings seem aligned with clinical practice in deciding which depressed clients may be well-suited for cognitive therapy using Socratic questioning. However, the outcome changes were limited to modest reductions in self-reported depression scores from one session to the next.

One last study examined the clinical utility of guided discovery in the treatment of adult psychiatric patients. Hoffart and colleagues (2002) evaluated the treatment of 32 patients with agoraphobia with panic disorder, 2 patients with agoraphobia without panic disorder, and 1 patient with panic disorder without agoraphobia. In addition, 21 patients met criteria for a cluster C personality disorder. Therapy was provided in group format, distributed across 11 sessions, and aimed to address agoraphobia as well as personality dysfunction. The use of guided discovery was rated by therapists after each session using a 0–100 scale: "How well do you think you helped the patient discover new ways of seeing his/her problems?" Results suggested that guided discovery did not have a significant impact on changes in emotional distress from session 1 to session 3.

Summary

There is modest support for the effectiveness of using Socratic questions in individual psychotherapy. Socratic questioning has been shown to guide the client's verbalizations toward more adaptive attitudes (Froján-Parga et al., 2018; Pardo-Cebrian et al., 2021) and to significantly reduce symptoms of depression from one session to the next (Braun et al., 2015), particularly when working with individuals who have a pessimistic cognitive bias (Vittorio et al., 2021). Thus, the available research has found positive immediate and intermediate effects for Socratic questioning.

Possible Negative Effects and Harm

There is no research available specifically assessing the possible negative effects and harm that might result from the application of the Socratic method broadly, or guided discovery and Socratic questioning particularly. There have also been no anecdotal reports of negative effects caused by Socratic questioning. However, the Socratic approach could become overly abstract for some clients who may struggle with cognitively complex issues. Furthermore, if used exclusively throughout a therapy session, the client may feel interrogated, and the discussion may ramble on obtuse issues that lack any direct application to the client's life or struggles.

Diversity Considerations

The use of Socratic questions seems well-suited for discussing topics related to diversity. However, no research exists on the relation between guided discovery or Socratic questioning and diversity considerations. Because of the interrogative nature of a Socratic dialogue, the process may need to be adapted to align with different cultural patterns of communication. Throughout the process of guided discovery, it is hoped that therapists remain open to new ideas and different values, respecting the client's personal background, beliefs, and identities. Similarly, it is hoped that therapists remain willing to learn about new beliefs and values that derive from different life experiences, whether related to a person's race, religious beliefs, sexual interests, gender identity, or country of origin.

Limitations of the Research

Despite numerous references to a Socratic approach to psychotherapy, it has been applied in different ways, making it difficult to generalize across studies and practitioners. Similarly, in their survey of 15 expert cognitive–behavioral therapy (CBT) researchers, Clark and Egan (2018) found that some experts believed that the Socratic method was a central feature of most applications of CBT, whereas other experts believed the Socratic approach was best used sparingly. These differences in definition, opinion, and application complicate the history of research on Socratic questioning and guided discovery.

Research on Socratic questioning and guided discovery has been extremely limited. The research reviewed relied on small samples or case studies, and the investigators used different research methodologies. Application of Socratic questions and guided discovery in therapy has been primarily supported by clinical experience. Although this limits the widespread acceptance of these techniques, it makes sense given Socrates' tendency to focus on logical consistency across a set of beliefs and opinions. Another limitation is the severe lack of evidence-based definitions, constructs, and assessment measures for Socratic questioning, guided discovery, and patient-related outcomes when using these skills. Different strategies have been used to define Socratic questioning, which creates confusion between different investigators. The importance of agreed upon definitions and guidelines for Socratic questioning and guided discovery will be key to producing the necessary research to determine their effectiveness.

It would be helpful for investigators to investigate the immediate outcomes of Socratic questions and guided discovery compared with other established therapeutic skills. Qualitative research may be particularly useful for exploring the benefits of Socratic questioning and guided discovery as a means of learning from small samples of clients or their therapists. At the heart of applying Socratic questioning and guided discovery is the interaction and dynamic between therapist and client. Qualitative research might provide support from the perspective of the client for the effectiveness of applying these skills to help shift client perspectives and build a sense of empowerment in their lives. It could be useful to interview therapists and clients after several sessions that were laced with Socratic questions in order to evaluate the subjective experience and potential benefit of these skills.

Training Implications

Although there has been no empirical research conducted on training therapists on Socratic questioning or guided discovery specifically, some guidelines can be suggested from clinical experience. The skills and attitudes that underlie the use of Socratic questions are probably enhanced when trainees are well-versed in the Platonic dialogues (Dinkins & Cangelosi, 2019; Wharne, 2022). Learning the Socratic approach probably relies on small incremental changes through a combination of patience, curiosity, and a sincere desire to understand each client (Waltman, 2020). Trainees can learn about Socratic questioning and guided discovery from published books and articles. Role-played interactions can be used to demonstrate a series of questions that avoid the feel of an interrogation. For training purposes, we particularly recommend the comprehensive books by Overholser (2018) and Waltman and colleagues (2020). Supervisors can observe sessions using videotape recordings and rate the therapist according to the 14 criteria described in Table 4.1. The application of Socratic questions can be modeled during supervisory meetings as a supervisor guides the supervisee in a similar way as therapists guide clients (Waltman & Codd, 2021). Supervision can include concrete experiences, reflective observations, abstract conceptualization, and active experimentation (Codd & Waltman, 2021). The improper use of Socratic questions can be highlighted by a supervisor by pointing out examples of excessive reliance on therapist knowledge or instances that lack a genuine curiosity in searching out new ideas. Creativity, patience, pragmatism, and empathy are central to understanding and applying guided discovery and Socratic questioning.

Therapeutic Practices

Although the empirical research on its effectiveness is limited, the immediate results of using Socratic questioning and guided discovery in psychotherapy (see Table 4.2) tend to be positive. We advance the following therapeutic practices based on an integration of the limited research evidence, ancient philosophy, and contemporary cognitive therapy:

- Consider Socratic questions especially for clients struggling with depression, despair, and hopelessness.
- Adopt the overarching collaborative, empowering, and respectful open-minded stance provided by guided discovery.
- Consider Socratic questioning for clients who enter psychotherapy with a pessimistic outlook and who are not being treated via psychotropic medications.
- Use questions that help gradually promote a shift of attitudes, guiding the client toward some core beliefs that underlie successful management of life struggles.
- Avoid an excessive focus on instructional methods or didactic information change, which tends to minimize patient input.
- Adapt Socratic questions to each patient's cultural identity, with the therapist respecting each client's personal background, life experiences, and values.

References

* Studies included in the research review.

Beck, A. T., & Dozois, D. (2011). Cognitive therapy: Current status and future directions. *Annual Review of Medicine*, *62*, 397–409.

Beck, A. T., & Emery, G. (1985). *Anxiety disorders and phobias: A cognitive perspective.* Basic Books.

Beck, A. T., Rush, A. J., Shaw, B., & Emery, G. (1979). *Cognitive therapy of depression*. Guilford.

Beck, A. T., Steer, R. A., & Brown, G. K. (1996). *Beck Depression Inventory manual* (2nd ed.). Psychological Corporation.

Beck, J. (2020). *Cognitive therapy: Basics and beyond* (3rd ed.). Guilford.

Blackburn, I., James, I., Milne, D., Baker, C., Standart, S., Garland, A., & Reichelt, F. (2001). The Revised Cognitive Therapy Scale (CTS-R): Psychometric properties. *Behavioural and Cognitive Psychotherapy*, *29*, 431–446.

Bonavitacola, L., Miller, A., McGinn, L., & Zoloth, E. (2019). Clinical guidelines for improving dialectical thinking in DBT. *Cognitive and Behavioral Practice*, *26*(3), 547–561.

*Braun, J., Strunk, D., Sasso, K., & Cooper, A. (2015). Therapist use of Socratic questioning predicts session-to-session symptom change in cognitive therapy for depression. *Behavior Research and Therapy*, *70*, 32–37.

*Calero-Elvira, A., Frojan-Parga, M., Ruiz-Sancho, E., & Alpanes-Freitag, M. (2013). Descriptive study of the Socratic method: Evidence for verbal shaping. *Behavior Therapy*, *44*, 625–638.

Callesen, P., Jensen, A., & Wells, A. (2014). Metacognitive therapy in recurrent depression: A case replication series in Denmark. *Scandinavian Journal of Psychology*, *55*(1), 60–64.

Carey, T., & Mullan, R. (2004). What is Socratic questioning? *Psychotherapy*, *41*(3), 217–226.

Clark, G., & Egan, S. (2015). The Socratic method in cognitive behavioural therapy: A narrative review. *Cognitive Therapy and Research*, *39*, 863–879.

Clark, G., & Egan, S. (2018). Clarifying the role of the Socratic method in CBT: A survey of expert opinion. *International Journal of Cognitive Therapy*, *11*(2), 184–199.

Codd, T., & Waltman, S. (2021). Socratic strategies for teaching Socratic strategies. In S. Waltman, R. Codd, L. McFarr, & B. Moore (Eds.), *Socratic questioning for therapists and counselors: Learn how to think and intervene like a cognitive behavioral therapist* (pp. 256–265). Routledge.

Craske, M., Treanor, M., Conway, C., Zbozinek, T., & Vervliet, B. (2014). Maximizing exposure therapy: An inhibitory learning approach. *Behaviour Research and Therapy*, *58*, 10–23.

David, O., Cîmpean, A., Costescu, C., DiGiuseppe, R., Doyle, K., Hickey, M., & David, D. (2021). Effectiveness of outpatient rational emotive behavior therapy over one decade. *American Journal of Psychotherapy*, *74*(4), 157–164.

Dinkins, C., & Cangelosi, P. (2019). Putting Socrates back in the Socratic method: Theory-based debriefing in the nursing classroom. *Nursing Philosophy*, *20*, e12240.

Elder, L., & Paul, R. (2007). Critical thinking: The art of Socratic questioning. *Journal of Developmental Education*, *31*(2), 32–33.

Ellis, A. (1994). *Reason and emotion in psychotherapy* (rev. ed.). Birch Lane Press.

Flückiger, C., Zinbarg, R., Znoj, H., & Ackert, M. (2014). Resource activation in generalized anxiety—An observer-based microprocess analysis of patients' in-session outcomes. *Psychotherapy*, *51*(4), 535–545.

*Froján, M., Montano, M., & Calero, A. (2010). Therapeutic verbal behavior analysis: A descriptive approach to the psychotherapeutic phenomenon. *Spanish Journal of Psychology*, *13*(2), 914–926.

*Froján-Parga, M., Calero-Elvira, A., & Montaño-Fidalgo, M. (2009). Analysis of the therapist's verbal behavior during cognitive restructuring debates: A case study. *Psychotherapy Research*, *19*(1), 30–41.

*Froján-Parga, M., Calero-Elvira, A., & Montaño-Fidalgo, M. (2011). Study of the Socratic method during cognitive restructuring. *Clinical Psychology and Psychotherapy*, *18*, 110–123.

*Froján-Parga, M., Calero-Elvira, A., Pardo-Cebrián, R., & Núñez de Prado-Gordillo, M. (2018). Verbal change and cognitive change: Conceptual and methodological analysis for the study of cognitive restructuring using the Socratic dialog. *International Journal of Cognitive Therapy*, *11*(2), 200–221.

Hamilton, M. (1967). Development of a rating scale for primary depressive illness. *British Journal of Social and Clinical Psychology*, *6*, 278–296.

*Hoffart, A., Versland, S., & Sexton, H. (2002). Self-understanding, empathy, guided discovery, and schema belief in schema-focused cognitive therapy of personality disorders: A process–outcome study. *Cognitive Therapy and Research*, *26*(2), 199–219.

Howard, A. (2011). Socrates as a role model for counsellors. *Practical Philosophy*, *2*(1), 15–17.

Kazantzis, N., Beck, J., Clark, D., Dobson, K., Hofmann, S., Leahy, R., & Wong, C. (2019). Socratic dialogue and guided discovery in cognitive behavioral therapy: A modified Delphi panel. *Journal of Cognitive Therapy*, 11(2), 140–157.

Kazantzis, N., Fairburn, C., Padesky, C., Reinecke, M., & Teesson, M. (2014). Unresolved issues regarding the research and practice of cognitive behavior therapy: The case of guided discovery using Socratic questioning. *Behaviour Change, 31*(1), 1–17.

Kennerly, H. (2007). *Socratic method.* Cognitive Therapy Centre.

Lear, J. (2006). The Socratic method of psychoanalysis. In S. Ahbel-Rappe & R. Kamtekar (Eds.), *A companion to Socrates* (pp. 442–461). Blackwell.

Overholser, J. C. (1993a). Elements of the Socratic method: I. Systematic questioning. *Psychotherapy, 30*(1), 67–74.

Overholser, J. C. (1993b). Elements of the Socratic method: II. Inductive reasoning. *Psychotherapy, 30*(1), 75–85.

Overholser, J. C. (1995). Elements of the Socratic method: IV. Disavowal of knowledge. *Psychotherapy, 32*(2), 283–292.

Overholser, J. C. (1996). Elements of the Socratic method: V. Self-improvement. *Psychotherapy, 33*(4), 549–559.

Overholser, J. C. (2013). Guided discovery: Problem-solving therapy integrated within the Socratic method. *Journal of Contemporary Psychotherapy, 43*(2), 73–82.

Overholser, J. C. (2018). *The Socratic method of psychotherapy.* Columbia University Press.

Overholser, J. C., Braden, A., & Fisher, L. (2010). You've got to believe: Core beliefs that underlie effective psychotherapy. *Journal of Contemporary Psychotherapy, 40,* 185–194.

Padesky, C. (1993). Socratic questioning: Changing minds or guiding discovery? Keynote address delivered at the European Congress of Behavioural and Cognitive Therapies, London.

Padesky, C., & Beck, A. T. (2003). Science and philosophy: Comparison of cognitive therapy and rational emotive behavior therapy/ *Journal of Cognitive Psychotherapy, 17*(3), 211–224.

*Pardo-Cebrián, R., Calero-Elvira, A., Guerrero-Escagedo, M., & López-Gómez, A. (2021). What works in the Socratic debate? An analysis of verbal behaviour interaction during cognitive restructuring. *Behavioural and Cognitive Psychotherapy, 49,* 513–525.

Paul, R., & Elder, L. (2007). Critical thinking: The art of Socratic questioning. *Journal of Developmental Education, 31*(1), 36–37.

Strunk, D., Lopez, H., & DeRubeis, R. (2006). Depressive symptoms are associated with unrealistic negative predictions of future life events. *Behavior Research and Therapy, 44,* 861–882.

*Vittorio, L., Braun, J., Cheavens, J., & Strunk, D. (2021). Cognitive bias and medication use moderate the relation of Socratic questioning and symptom change in cognitive behavioral therapy of depression. *Cognitive Therapy and Research*, 45, 1235–1245.

Waltman, S. (2020). Rethinking how we teach Socratic questioning. *Psychotherapy Bulletin, 55*(4), 18–22.

Waltman, S. H., Codd III, R. T., McFarr, L. M., & Moore, B. A. (2020). *Socratic questioning for therapists and counselors: Learn how to think and intervene like a cognitive behavior therapist.* Routledge.

Waltman, S., & Codd, R. (2021). A framework for Socratic questioning: Beckian Socratic dialogue. In S. Waltman, R. Codd, L. McFarr, & B. Moore (Eds.), *Socratic questioning for therapists and counselors: Learn how to think and intervene like a cognitive behavioral therapist* (pp. 55–69). Routledge.

Wells, A. (2007). Cognition about cognition: Metacognitive therapy and change in generalized anxiety disorder and social phobia. *Cognitive and Behavioral Practice, 14*(1), 18–25.

Wharne, S. (2022). Socratic questioning and irony in the psychotherapeutic process. *Journal of Contemporary Psychotherapy, 52*(2), 137–144.

Young, J., & Beck, A. T. (1980). *Cognitive Therapy Rating Scale manual.* Psychotherapy Research Unit, University of Pennsylvania.

5
Empathic Reflection

Robert Elliott, Arthur C. Bohart, Dale G. Larson, Peter Muntigl, and Olga Smoliak

Authors' Note: We are grateful to Gerald Goodman and William Miller for useful discussions.

Therapist empathic reflections are a class of therapist response modes whose primary expressed intention is to "reflect back" or share the therapist's understanding of the client's communications and underlying experiences. They are the primary tool of person-centered and experiential approaches to psychotherapy (Elliott et al., 2004; Goodman & Esterly, 1988; Murphy, 2019), but they have been widely adopted and are a core part of basic communication skills training programs (e.g., Hill, 2020; Ivey et al., 2022; Miller & Rollnick, 2013).

Although the word *skill* is used in the title of this book, we regard empathic reflection as a type of therapist *response mode* (or speech act) rather than a *skill* in the ordinary language sense of expertise or ability to do something well (*Oxford English Dictionary*; Simpson & Wiener, 1989). In fact, Carl Rogers (1975) did not like the idea of empathic responding as a "skill," famously claiming that he was never trying to reflect feelings. Instead, he saw himself as checking his understanding of the client. It was only in the 1960s and 1970s that writers such as Carkhuff and Berenson (1977), Goodman and Dooley (1976), and others began to describe empathic reflection as a "skill" that could be taught. Since then, the teaching of empathic reflection as a skill has grown and is typically a core part of curricula for the training of counselors, as well as for a wide range of other helpers.

In our review, we examine the effectiveness of empathic reflection as a response mode without regard to how well or poorly it is carried out. In any case, there is almost no research on the skillful or unskillful delivery of empathic reflections. Instead, it is our view that the quality of skillful empathic reflection is best described as *empathy*, which has already been evaluated in a series of reviews (Bohart et al., 2002; Elliott et al., 2011, 2019).

In this chapter, we begin with definitions and subtypes of empathic reflections and provide clinical examples. We report an original meta-analysis of quantitative research, along with narrative reviews of qualitative and conversation analysis (CA) research. We also examine the limitations of the research reviewed, before concluding with diversity considerations, training implications, and recommended therapeutic practices.

Robert Elliott, Arthur C. Bohart, Dale G. Larson, Peter Muntigl, and Olga Smoliak, *Empathic Reflection* In: *Psychotherapy Skills and Methods That Work*. Edited by: Clara E. Hill and John C. Norcross, Oxford University Press. © Clara E. Hill and John C. Norcross 2023.
DOI: 10.1093/oso/9780197611012.003.0005

Definitions

At the outset, we note that the term *reflection* is somewhat misleading. The term connotes a simple mirroring or paraphrasing of what the other person says; however, many empathic reflections are more complex than this. Accordingly, proponents of the person-centered tradition (e.g., Brodley, 2006; Mearns et al., 2013; Rogers, 1975) prefer *empathic understanding* responses or *empathic following responses*. Following Goodman and Dooley (1976) and others, we define empathic reflections primarily in terms of their expressed intent. Carl Rogers (1951) saw reflections as having the purpose of "trying to understand from the client's point of view and to communicate that understanding" (p. 452). This response mode is distinguished from, for instance, interpretations, whose primary expressed intent is to "bring news" to the client (Goodman & Esterley, 1988, p. 71). Empathic reflections are also distinct from advice aimed at offering guiding information to the client, and questions focused on eliciting information from the client. Furthermore, *expressed intention* (communicating understanding) can be distinguished from the *form* (reflection or paraphrase) of a therapist's response (Goodman & Dooley, 1976; see also Stiles, 1986).

By calling them *empathic reflections*, we highlight the connection of this form of response with *empathy*, while still distinguishing between the two concepts. That is, empathic reflections refer to responses primarily intended to convey the therapist's empathic understanding of the client (Goodman & Esterley, 1988).

On the other hand, we use *empathy* to denote the quality or skillfulness of empathic reflections and related therapist empathic responses (e.g., claims of understanding such as "mhm" responses or nonverbal expressions of understanding). Similarly, Hill (2020) noted, "Empathy is not a specific response type or skill; rather, it is an attitude or manner of responding with genuine caring and a lack of judgment" (p. 434). The classic definition of empathy is that of Carl Rogers (1957): "To sense the client's private world as if it were your own, but without ever losing the 'as if' quality" (p. 99). Relatedly, Hill (2020) defined empathy as "understanding clients at both a cognitive level (their thoughts and expressions) and an affective level (their feelings)" (p. 434). In fact, we see empathy as a complex cognitive–affective–perceptual–somatic process of trying to enter or sense the phenomenological world of another person in order to get in touch with how they see and experience the world. Furthermore, empathy cannot be reduced to saying back or paraphrasing what the client has said, or simply noting that the client is feeling a certain feeling. Instead, it is trying to *understand* what the client is getting at, which often goes beyond the spoken words to capture implicit meanings. For Brodley (2001), "The therapist's sole goal in acceptant empathic understanding is to *understand* the client in a manner that is likely to result in the client having *the experience of being understood*" (p. 18).

In any case, as used in contemporary practice, empathic reflections are not necessarily either simple mirroring or paraphrasing responses, although they may be. They often involve trying to *infer* what the client is getting at, and they also involve resonating (emotionally and bodily) with the client's often implicit experience (Elliott & Greenberg, 2021). Therefore, empathic reflections may have a *depth* dimension (Gendlin, 1968) and may be "additive" (Hammond et al., 1977). However, the degree of inference does not go beyond what the client presumably has available to conscious awareness.

From the point of view of conversational analysis (CA; Sacks, 1995; Sidnell & Stivers, 2013), empathic reflections would be considered one form of *empathic response* (Muntigl, Knight, & Watkins, 2014). (CA researchers do not use the term "empathic reflection.") Empathic responses reveal the recipient's (i.e., therapist's) understanding and appreciation of the teller's (i.e., client's) troubles and emotional experience (Weiste & Peräkylä, 2014), and they may be distinguished from non-empathic responses that do not address clients' perspectives or substantially depart from and alter clients' understandings of their experience (e.g., Ruusuvuori, 2005, 2007; Voutilainen et al., 2010). Prior CA studies identified various conversational methods used to convey empathy. According to Hepburn and Potter (2007), empathic responses are speaking turns that (a) formulate or describe/reference the other's perspective or experience and (b) acknowledge the client's "expert" authority to know and describe their experience. In CA, *formulations* overlap substantially with what we are referring to as empathic reflections, displaying understanding by summarizing or providing an upshot of prior talk (e.g., Antaki, 2008; Heritage & Watson, 1979).

Consistent with this CA perspective, empathy and empathic responses do not occur in isolation but, rather, are part of larger "empathy sequences" (Muntigl, Knight, & Watkins, 2014) in which clients attempt to make themselves understood, therapists offer understandings (commonly via empathic responses or formulations), and clients provide feedback about the accuracy or appropriateness of those understandings. The focus is on the sequential organization of jointly accomplished and negotiated *displays* of affect and understanding, critiquing a more conventional view of empathy as a one-way therapist intervention or discrete speech act (e.g., Heritage, 2011; Ruusuvuori, 2007).

Finally, although the intent of empathic reflections is to convey empathy to clients, it is not the case that empathic reflections are the only therapist responses that result in clients feeling understood. For example, Elliott et al. (1982) studied two samples of clients. In the first sample, they found that in single-session interventions there was a medium effect size relation between empathic reflections and clients feeling understood. However, in the second sample, from ongoing therapy, there was no relation. That is, clients could feel understood from any response form that displayed or revealed therapist understanding, including questions and advice.

Types of Empathic Reflection

Contemporary psychotherapists have identified various kinds of empathic reflection. We briefly summarize some of their distinctions. Hill's (2020) helping skills system includes two types of empathic reflection responses, primarily based on their target or content. *Reflections of feeling* can repeat, rephrase, or identify the client's feelings, or they may be more inferentially arrived at from nonverbal behavior or other aspects of the client's situation or verbal communication. *Restatements* paraphrase content and meaning, and they can reference material in the moment, earlier in a session, or even earlier in therapy. Ivey and Authier's (1978) microskill taxonomy includes several types of empathic reflections: *encouraging* (repeating what the client said), *paraphrasing*, *summarizing*, *reflection of feelings*, *reflection of meaning*, and *empathic self-disclosure* (where the therapist demonstrates understanding by sharing a relevant personal experience). To these, Larson (2020) adds *first-person responses*. In a first-person response, the therapist speaks from the point of view of the client, using the first person (e.g., "So I hear a part of you saying, 'I can't stand this job anymore!' ").

Within motivational interviewing (MI; Miller & Rollnick, 2013), many kinds of reflection have been described and studied (Amrhein et al., 2008, Moyers et al., 2014). Broadly, reflections can be either *simple* (restating what the person has just said with little or no added meaning) or *complex* (where a guess is made about previously implicit meaning, or meaning or emphasis is added). MI then distinguishes among content of reflections: *change talk* (e.g., desire or reasons to change), *sustain talk* (difficulties in changing or reasons not to change), *commitment language*, and *other* (everything else). Beyond this, MI specifies an ever-expanding range of reflections—for example, *continuing the paragraph* (a complex reflection where the therapist says what might follow from what the client said), *double-sided* (where the interviewer states both sides of a client's ambivalence), and *summary* (which brings together multiple contents the client has expressed).

In their study of client-centered therapy drawing on a CA perspective, Muntigl, Knight, and Watkins (2014) identified varying types of empathic responses, providing a useful perspective on the types of empathic reflection described above: *Gist formulations* summarize the client's prior talk, *upshot formulations* deliver the implications of the client's talk, *naming another's feelings* formulates the client's emotional state, and *co-completions* complete the client's prior incomplete utterance. Formulations have also been found to vary in the extent to which they convey empathy. Furthermore, in comparing cognitive–behavioral therapy and psychoanalysis, Weiste and Peräkylä (2013) found that *highlighting* and *rephrasing* formulations remain closest to clients' talk (i.e., most empathic and consistent with what we are calling empathic reflections), whereas *relocating* and *exaggerating* significantly transform or challenge clients' prior talk and are therefore unlikely to function as empathic reflections.

Finally, in order to help therapists broaden the range of their empathic reflections, Elliott and Greenberg (2021, pp. 53–56) identified nine types of empathic reflections, based on different client micro-markers and corresponding aspects or tracks of client experience. Table 5.1 describes and contains examples of each type: *empathic repetition*, *empathic reflection* (of the main content or feeling the client is communicating), *empathic affirmation* (gentle reflections of emotional pain), *empathic formulation* (used in a narrower sense than in the CA literature, here referring to translating client communication or experience into psychological terms or a useful narrative), *empathic refocusing* (reflecting back toward avoided experiences), *evocative reflection* (heightening emotion by vivid imagery or first-person presentation), *exploratory reflection* (tentative and aimed at unclear experiences), *process reflection* (nonconfrontational description of client verbal or nonverbal action), and *empathic conjecture* (tentative guesses about client unspoken experience).

Table 5.1 Nine Types of Empathic Reflection Responses

Type	Content/Target/Micro-Marker (What the Therapist Is Listening For)	Examples
Empathic repetition (repeats a word or phrase verbatim to help client stay with or elaborate)	*Key words*: Potentially important word or phrase	C: "Sometimes I feel like I'm too sensitive." T: "Too sensitive."
Empathic reflection (feeds back main points or content to make sure it has been heard correctly)	*Central content*: The gist or main point; central idea; essence; substance; crux	"OK, so the point is that the whole family was there for once. Is that what you're saying?"
Evocative reflection (uses vivid words, images, or manner to open up experience; includes speaking in the first person as if they were the client)	*Emerging emotion*: Poignant, touching, emotionally alive experiencing	"Sort of feeling like, 'I'm *drowning* here!' "
Empathic affirmation (offers empathy and support; generally delivered with gentle, compassionate voice)	*Vulnerable emotion*: What is tender, fragile, or painful	"I guess it just hurts to see that."
Exploratory reflection (tentatively leaves an open edge to model self-exploration)	*Edge of awareness*: Important, emerging, unclear experiencing	"So the feeling is almost kind of like bitterness, but not quite?"
Process reflection (describes what client is doing right now in the session, including nonverbals)	*Client process*: Immediate client experience, task, action, manner, including different aspects of the person	"There's a tear there." "Right now you're maybe just remembering what happened with your partner."
Empathic formulation (collaborates with client to identify their experience and to translate it into a useful narrative about their process)	*Person*: General shared understandings of person, their context, or their process	"So from what you've said, it sounds like, first you start feeling sad, then you get scared of the sadness."
Empathic conjecture (makes an empathy-based guess about what client may be experiencing but has not yet said out loud)	*Implicit experience*: Unspoken but possibly present experiencing	"As you speak, I'm getting a heavy feeling, almost sadness, in my stomach. Does that fit for you?"
Empathic refocusing (offers client opportunity to return to uncomfortable experience the client has introduced, then moved away from)	*Bypassed experience*: Avoided, minimized, ignored, side-tracked experiencing	"So it seems to you that you drink less than your friends, but I guess I also hear that a part of you is still worried that you might be drinking more than you really want to be."

Clinical Description and Indications

Therapeutic Functions of Empathic Reflections

Although the most obvious function of empathic reflections is to convey empathic understanding, a variety of other functions have been proposed. Broadly, reflections are affiliative responses that act to support, validate, or help clients feel that they make sense (Heritage, 2011). In addition, a wide range of more specific functions have been proposed to (a) help clients access feelings and experience (Martin, 2016); (b) foster emotion regulation (Watson, 2002); (c) help clients reflect on their experience (Rennie, 1998); (d) help clients articulate, symbolize, and carry forward their experiencing (Gendlin, 1968); (e) help clients differentiate and integrate information (Wexler, 1974); (f) help clients deconstruct old ideas (Watson, 2002); (g) foster higher order thinking and facilitate client creativity (Bohart, 2021); (h) orient clients toward present feelings or toward future possibilities (Bohart et al., 1993); (i) strengthen the self and foster positive introjects (Watson, 2002); (j) help clients access and work through ambivalence by fostering change talk (Miller & Rollnick, 2013); and (k) draw attention to therapeutically relevant meanings in what the client has said (Antaki, 2008).

General Indications for Empathic Reflection

Clients' displays of emotion offer opportunities, what Suchmann et al. (1997) call *empathic opportunities*, for therapists to respond with empathy. These typically take the form of a client's report of a distressing experience or situation, referred to colorfully as *troubles telling* (Jefferson, 1988). Empathic opportunities also encompass client talk that often extends beyond factual reporting of events to disclosures of feelings or thoughts about events and people in their lives (e.g., becoming surprised or disappointed). Through these affective descriptions, clients display a *stance* (Stivers, 2008) toward these events. CA distinctly focuses on the client's frame of reference as displayed or made recognizable for the recipient (therapist). An affective stance can be achieved lexically (through words) and grammatically but also kinetically (through body movement) and prosodically (through speech intonation and rhythm; Muntigl et al., 2012; Suchman et al., 1997). A stance may evolve (rather than being static) throughout a troubles' telling, providing a moving target for the therapist to respond to (Muntigl et al., 2012).

Indications for Types of Empathic Reflection

The different forms and functions of empathic reflection raise the issue of when and how to offer them. What are the indicators or micro-markers that point to particular types of reflection? For example, in motivational interviewing, reflections are generally seen as most helpful when capturing *change talk*—that is, client speech favoring client movement toward a specific goal (Miller & Rollnick, 2013). For the most part, however, there is little differential information about when and how to use empathic reflections. It may be that the lack of consensus on how to operationalize and use empathic reflections in clinical practice plays a role in the empirical conclusions we draw later. As an example of what might be possible, Table 5.1 provides, for each of a set of types of empathic reflections, a recommended target micro-marker that the therapist is listening for and which is hypothesized to be the optimal context for the corresponding reflection response.

Assessment

Assessment of Empathic Reflections

There are several systems for classifying therapist response modes that include empathic reflections. Hill's system (in its various versions: e.g., Hill, 1978, 1986, 2020) has probably been used over the longest time period. However, during the past 20 years, the most frequently used approach has been based on motivational interviewing, including the Motivational Interviewing Skill Code (Amrhein et al., 2008) and the Motivational Interviewing Treatment Integrity Coding Manual (MITI; e.g., Moyers et al., 2005, 2014). Empathic reflections are also included in the coding systems of Stiles (1992) and Elliott (1985). Beyond this, psychodynamic therapy researchers have sometimes assessed empathic reflection, although commonly referred to as *clarification* (e.g., McCullough et al., 1991).

An especially important but tricky issue is distinguishing between empathic reflection and interpretation. Thus, reflections can pick up client experiences that are at the edges of awareness but which have not yet been put into words. This means that it is not always easy to determine the difference between a "deep" empathic reflection and an interpretation, leading to disagreements among researchers.

The confusion with interpretation underscores the broader question of how reliably one can identify empathic reflections. Identifying reflections *within* different coding systems can be done reliably (e.g., Elliott et al., 1987; Hill, 1986; Lietaer & Gundrum, 2018; Stiles, 1986). However, there are problems with identifying reflections *across* coding systems. This is most likely in part due to the varying ways that empathic reflections are defined. For example, Ivey et al.'s (1987) system scores deeper empathic reflections as interpretations (e.g., Weinrach, 1990), whereas Hill's (1986) coding definition (as well as the system developed by Brodley; see Moon, 2018) sticks closer to the person-centered/experiential tradition, which has a more expansive definition of reflections, including deeper, more exploratory empathic responses (e.g., referred to in Table 5.1 as evocative, exploratory and process reflections, plus empathic conjectures, empathic formulations, and empathic refocusing). Despite these differences, Elliott et al. (1987) found convergence between six response mode scoring systems used to rate a common set of sessions with seven psychotherapists. Depending on how one interprets this, one can conclude that there is some relation across systems as to what a reflection is, but there is also some disagreement.

Assessment of the Effects of Empathic Reflections

Different research approaches point to different ways of assessing the effects or effectiveness of empathic reflections. Therefore, we briefly review them here.

The most widely used of these is the *process–outcome* criterion, in which researchers measure both a within-session process (e.g., a particular type of empathic reflection, typically aggregated as a total or proportion across a whole session) and a post-session or post-treatment outcome. At the post-session level, measures might include relationship quality (e.g., the Working Alliance Inventory; cf. Boardman et al., 2006) or client continuation of therapy versus dropping out (e.g., Huang et al., 2013). At the treatment level, measures might include client post-therapy abstinence from substance misuse (e.g., Palfai et al., 2016) or amount of pre–post symptom reduction (e.g., Brief Symptom Inventory; Milbrath et al., 1999). Such studies are intuitively appealing but suffer from causal inference problems, such as reverse- or third-variable causation (e.g., Stiles & Shapiro, 1994).

Another, increasingly popular, approach to change process research is the *sequential process* paradigm (Elliott, 2010). In these studies, researchers identify examples of a particular therapy process, such as empathic reflection, and then look at what the client does next in the session, using measures of productive (e.g., client experiencing; Hill et al., 1983) or unproductive (e.g., counterchange talk in motivational interviewing; Moyers et al., 2009) process. The chief strength of this design is that it comes closer to warranting causal inference because we can directly see whether what the client says next is ostensibly a response to what the therapist just said, as opposed to an evasion or change of topic.

A less robust version of the sequential process paradigm throws out the sequential information. In *process–process correlational* research, the client process variable (e.g., observer ratings of client engagement) is aggregated over a time period, most often the whole session (e.g., Boardman et al., 2006), and correlated with the therapist process measure aggregated over the same time period.

A less often used approach, *sequential experiential* research, has clients review recordings of sessions and rate the immediate within-session impact of particular empathic reflections using interpersonal process recall (Elliott, 1986). Immediate impacts are most often helpfulness (e.g., Elliott et al., 1982) but sometimes involve particular immediate reactions such as feeling understood (e.g., Elliott, 1985).

In addition, qualitative researchers (e.g., Bachelor, 1988) have interviewed clients about their experiences of therapy, and these clients sometimes talk about therapist empathic reflections. Finally, CA has provided a rich account of how clients affiliate or disaffiliate with therapist empathic reflections (Muntigl et al., 2013; Muntigl & Horvath, 2014).

Clinical Examples

We present two contrasting segments of emotion-focused therapy taken from Muntigl et al.'s (2012, 2013) CA studies, one successful, the other unsuccessful. Each of these examples includes the sequential structures within which empathic reflections are located (discussed in more detail later in this chapter). In order to convey important details about these interactions, CA uses special transcription conventions (Table 5.2; see also Hepburn & Bolden, 2017; Jefferson, 2004), similar to a musical score. We invite the reader to study these transcripts for the valuable level of relevant detail about the verbal and nonverbal means used by client and therapist to construct each of the two empathy sequences. (Key expressions of judgment and affect are in bold; annotations of important nonverbals are in italics.)

The first extract portrays a standard, successful empathic reflection. Near the end of therapy, the client Paula is reporting on how she has acted in ways that are contrary to her prior patterns of behavior by taking more control of her actions: Rather than

Table 5.2 Conversation Analysis Transcription Notation

Symbol	Meaning
[	Starting point of overlapping talk
]	Endpoint of overlapping talk
(1.5)	Silence measured in tenths of seconds
(.)	Hearable untimed pause <0.2 seconds
.	Falling intonation at end of utterance
,	Continuing intonation at end of utterance
wor-	Truncated, cut-off speech
wo:rd	Prolongation of sound
word=word	Latching (no audible break between words)
↑word	Markedly upward shift in pitch
.hhh	Audible inhalation, # of h's indicate length
hhh	Audible exhalation, # of h's indicate length
heh/huh/hah/hih	Laugh particles
((cough))	Audible nonspeech sounds
Italics (blue)	Nonverbal behavior (actor indicated by initial)
Bold	Examples of key activities

withdrawing from certain uncomfortable situations, she has confronted others and stood up for herself:

Extract 1: 312.16(03) [13:28]/Muntigl et al. 2013, p. 4

1) Client's troubles telling + affective stance display

01 Paula: I: think at one point in time I was saying, like (0.7) u:m,
02 (1.3)
03 Paula: i- it's kind of like starting to- (.) to change and like first
p *hands circling over each other in front of body*
04 it was kind of like **a little bit on the aggressive side**
05 **of things** .hh=
06 Ther: =↑mm:.
07 (0.7)
08 Paula: and that I ↑really wanted like (.) you know like to get into
p *taps hands down/ holds hands up*
09 this:, (1.0) well I guess what you would call **assertiv:e** (.)
p *chops hands forward*

10 **behaviour , (.) [mode.]**
11 Ther: [mm hm] mm hm
p *pulses hands forward*
13 (0.4)
14 Paula: a:n- (0.9) yea:h, (0.9) u- and for some time I was ↑kind of a
15 **little bit worried** .hh that I wouldn't be able like
16 to:, (.) to find that balance but, (0.4)
17 **it's comin:g (0.4) alo:ng (0.7) alright (h)e he he.**=
p *slow shallow multiple nods*
t *shallow nod*

2) Therapist's empathic reflection [gist formulation]

18 Ther: =so you're finding a way (.) to do it but also not to do it
19 too aggressive[ly,]
20 Paula: [.hh]
21 Ther: to do it in a way that's, (0.4) works socially, works for
p *multiple nods ------------------------------> fast...*
22 you, works for them.
p *multiple nods----->*

3) Client's response [confirmation]

23 Paula: ((lip smack))) ↑yeah.
p *fast deep multiple nods*
t *multiple shallow nods*
24 (0.3)
p *fast multiple nods*
25 Ther: and isn't, (0.3) you know turning off everyone you
p *fast multiple nods------------------------->*
t *Smiling*
26 Paula: [thet's-]
27 Ther: [meet,]kind of
p nods----------->
28 Paula: that's right. [that's] right,=
29 Ther: [yeah,]
t *double nod*
p *multiple nods*

The second extract shows a short sequence with the same client but from an earlier session. Here, the therapist's effort at recasting Paula's stance is rejected, resulting in a disaffiliative sequence. The transcript shows not only how the therapist's attempt at connecting with the client's expressed stance seems to miss the mark, resulting in *failed empathy*, but also how the therapist secures re-affiliation with Paula by mobilizing a number of key interactional resources: producing nods in direct response to Paula's stance displays and later by showing understanding of Paula's alternative position:

Extract 2: 312.09(08)/ taken from Muntigl et al. 2012, p.126

1) Client's affective stance display
01 Paula: and it's just **really hard**, (0.8) to say oka:y
(1.3)
02 this person (2.0) doesn't make me feel **good,**
03 (3.4)
04 a:n- (.) like jus- (.) just to leave it like
just to sa::y,
05 **like f::- (.) ↑f:orget it. like just drop it**
an- and move o:n.
06 **like it doesn't work.**
07 (2.5)
2) Therapist's empathic reflection/conjecture
08 Ther: and is there (.) a feeling of somehow,
09 (0.9)
10 I **fa:iled** if tha- I do that or I-
3) Client's response [disconfirmation]
11 (1.1)
12 Paula: .hhh::: hhh:::
13 (8.8)
14 Paula: I- euh no:. like-
15 (.)
4) Re-affiliation/ Mutual consensus
16 Paula: w- what ↑I'm wondering about like wis this-
(0.8) particular man.
17 like why: (.) am I **so: hung up** on him. (0.3)
t *shallow multiple nods.*
18 like why do I **have to try:,** (1.2)↑**so hard,**
(0.5)
t *slow double nod-----------> shallow nod*
19 and at the same time like it's almost like he
doesn't ca:re.
20 (1.5)
t *deep nod. slow nod.*
21 Paul: and why do, (0.4) why do I **keep,** (3.9)
↑**running.**
t *slow nod*
22 (1.6)
t *multiple nods→*
23 Paula: uh(hh) (.) and why does he say certain things,
(0.3) which kind of me
t -->
24 make ↑thi:nk (.) that he **cares,** but then (0.8)
in his behavior
p *double nod*

25 he **doesn't really-** (.) **live up to it.** uh(hh)
p *Smiles*
t *Nod*
26 Ther: so you feel **very confused** by his behavior
27 (1.0)
28 Paula: oh ↑yeah. (h)he he he!
p *rolls eyes to side*
t *shallow nod*

We are aware that it can take some effort to fully appreciate transcripts as complex as these, but we believe the standard simplified transcripts omit important interactional detail and, as a result, grossly underestimate the interpersonal complexity and collaborative nature of the empathic reflection process. In particular, lines 11–15 of extract 2 provide a classic example of how clients signal that a reflection has failed to capture their experience. (Later, we provide a targeted elaboration of what is going on in these examples.)

Landmark Studies and Previous Reviews

Landmark Studies

In this section, we briefly describe four studies that illustrate the main types of evidence to be reviewed in our meta-analysis. These studies correspond to the different criteria for assessing the effectiveness of empathic reflections introduced earlier.

Process–Outcome

In a study of psychodynamic therapy for bereavement, Milbrath et al. (1999) examined two kinds of empathic reflection, corresponding to what are referred to more commonly as reflections of content (referred to by these authors as *clarification*) or emotion (*reflection*). Their effectiveness variables included client improvement on three outcome measures (e.g., Brief Symptom Inventory), generating a total of six process–outcome correlations. Four were reported as not statistically significant and therefore estimated as zero; the other two correlations (both involving reflection of feeling) were large (r = .61 and .48), yielding a study-level average process–outcome correlation for reflection of feeling of .39 (calculated using the Fisher r-to-z transformation), while the process–outcome correlation for reflection of content was estimated at zero (based on being reported as statistically nonsignificant).

Sequential Process

In a study of the change process in motivational interviewing for alcohol misuse, Moyers et al. (2009) studied three kinds of reflection: *reflection of client change talk* (e.g., talking about reasons to change), *reflection of client counterchange talk* (e.g., difficulty of changing), and *reflection of other change talk* (or neutral or balanced change/counterchange talk). They evaluated how often these three kinds of reflections were followed by client change talk (previously found to lead to post-therapy client change and therefore considered to be a productive client in-session process) or client counterchange talk (considered to be an unproductive client process likely to interfere with client change). As they expected, the researchers found that reflections of client change talk appeared to lead to client change talk (phi = .215) but did not suppress client counterchange talk. On the other hand, reflections of counterchange talk did not affect client change talk but did enhance client counterchange talk (phi = .175, reversed to −.175 to reflect this as a negative effect). Reflections of neutral or balanced change talk had no effect on either client change or counterchange talk. These results support the MI change process model but were small. Furthermore, the picture was complicated by the presence of reverse causation (i.e., client change talk led to therapist reflections of change talk) and third variable causation (i.e., chains of client self-generated change talk).

Process–Process Correlational Research

In a study of MI for smoking cessation, Boardman et al. (2006) evaluated two kinds of reflections: *simple reflections* (defined as briefer responses paraphrasing or rephrasing of either content or emotion) and *summaries* (longer, more complex reflections referring to two or more client responses). Rates of these for whole sessions were calculated and correlated with observer session ratings on the Working Alliance Inventory and the Client Engagement subscale of the Vanderbilt Psychotherapy Process Scale. Summary reflections were slightly better at predicting the two measures of good process (mean $r = .19$) than simple reflections (mean $r = .05$). However, the causal relation between average reflection ratings and good process measures could as easily run in reverse or even be circular.

Sequential Experiential

Elliott et al. (1982) reported on two studies of empathic reflections evaluated by raters, clients, or therapists: one study of brief, laboratory-based therapy sessions, the other involving clients in ongoing therapy. After each session, clients reviewed the recordings of their sessions and rated the helpfulness of therapist responses. None of the correlations between perceived empathic reflection and client-rated helpfulness were statistically significant (range: −.05 to .09). Exploratory analyses pointed to the possibility that "for each mode, significantly helpful and nonhelpful instances can be found, so that the overall effect is that the ratings cancel each other out" (p. 360).

Previous Reviews

Orlinsky et al. (2004) summarized the results of 14 previous process–outcome studies of therapist reflection using the old-fashioned box score method: 8 of these studies reported no association between reflections and outcome, 5 reported negative correlations, whereas only 1 reported a positive correlation. We are not aware of any previous quantitative meta-analyses of research on the effectiveness of empathic reflections.

In contrast, a cumulative series of meta-analyses of process–outcome research on therapist *empathy* have been published (Bohart et al., 2002; Elliott et al., 2011, 2019). These reviews are consistent in finding a moderate association between therapist empathy and client post-therapy outcome ($r = .28$; equivalent to $d = .58$). There is, however, little or no overlap between the studies in these previous meta-analyses and the following research review on empathic reflection.

Research Review

Meta-Analysis of Quantitative Research

In this section, we report the results of an original meta-analysis of available research relating therapist empathic reflections to measures of their effectiveness. We started with a general question: How effective are therapist empathic reflections? We operationalized this by searching for studies that provided evidence of empathic reflections having had helpful or hindering effects. This search yielded a more refined question: What associations are there between empathic reflections and measures of their effectiveness? We were also interested in a range of potential moderators of the effectiveness of empathic reflection, which generated further research questions: (a) Do different *effectiveness criteria* (as described earlier; e.g., process–outcome) produce similar or different sized effects? (b) Are some *types of reflection* (e.g., complex vs. simple) more effective than others? (c) Does the *content of reflections* (e.g., feeling vs. content) make a difference for their effectiveness? Importantly, our review deals with the presence or absence of reflections (including their quantity) rather than *quality* of reflections.

Search Strategy

Because of the multiple meanings of the word *reflection* in the psychological literature and because most measures of empathic reflection are embedded in broader systems of therapist response modes, we started with a recent systematic review of measures of therapist verbal response modes (Gumz et al., 2015). From this, we identified the major approaches to measuring therapist response modes, including those described earlier. For each, we identified one or two original or key references; for MI, we used Amrhein et al. (2008) and Moyers et al. (2005); for general response mode rating systems, we used Hill (1978), Hill et al. (1981), Stiles (1979, 1992), Elliott et al. (1982), and Elliott (1985); and for psychodynamic response rating systems, we used Gumz et al. (2015). Using the cited source function in PsycInfo, this gave us a starter set of 1,075 sources; after screening these via their abstracts, we were left with 60 possible sources to retrieve. From here, we checked reference lists to identify more studies; this resulted in a further 32 sources to check. After retrieval and analysis of these additional studies, we added 12 more, for a total of 45 studies involving 49 samples of clients (4 studies each contained 2 samples). However, 6 experimental process studies (e.g., Waskow, 1962) were judged to be outside the parameters of this review, resulting in 39 studies involving 43 samples of clients. Table 5.3 provides the Preferred Reporting Items for Systematic Reviews and Meta-Analyses (PRISMA) information.

Characteristics of the Studies

Table 5.4 summarizes the 43 samples (from 39 studies) and 214 effects (n = 2,710 clients, 573+ therapists) used in the meta-analysis. Research on the effectiveness of empathic reflections has burgeoned during the past 20 years, driven largely by research on MI for substance misuse, which is now the most-studied treatment approach and client presenting problem in this literature. Client ethnicity was reported for only 18 (42%) of the 43 samples; only 5 studies reported therapist ethnicity. Of studies that reported client ethnicity (most of which were on MI), mean non-European ethnicity

Table 5.3 PRISMA Information for Meta-Analysis

Stage	No. of Sources Included	No. of Sources Excluded	Notes
1. Search result:	1,075		Date of search: January 2022
2. Abstract screening stage: Possible empathic reflection effectiveness studies	60	1,015	
3. Original search full text retrieval, review, and analysis	33	27	Unable to retrieve full text Failed exclusion criteria Combined with another study at full text review or analysis
4. Sources added via branching bibliographies	12	20	Combined Failed exclusion criteria
5. Final sample	39 (27 + 12) studies 43 samples in main study	6	4 studies contained 2 samples each 6 experimental process samples/studies dropped

was 60% (range: 0–100%). Reflection was overwhelmingly assessed by nonparticipant observers; most often, raters did not distinguish between different types and contents of reflections. Reflections were most frequently coded at the therapist speaking turn level, but often then aggregated to the session level (e.g., proportion of reflections out of the total number of speaking turns). Effectiveness evaluation most often involved observer ratings of good client process or client ratings (e.g., of outcome or helpfulness). The most common index of effectiveness was client next speaking turn good process (e.g., client change talk), but client post-therapy outcome measure scores were also common. Sequential process and post-therapy process–outcome effectiveness criteria were most common in our data set.

Estimation of Effect Size

We used Pearson correlations as our main metric of effect size. Our strategy was to extract all possible effects. Therefore, we used the following conventions to estimate *r*: First, if the result was nonsignificant, but we had enough information to calculate a *t* and then convert, we did so. If we had no other information than that the effect was nonsignificant, we set *r* at 0. We converted standardized difference and odds ratio effect sizes to correlations using standard formulas. For transition probabilities in sequential process design studies, we calculated phi coefficients, which are equivalent to correlation coefficients for 2 × 2 tables. We also report results as standardized differences (Cohen's *d*).

Coding Procedure and Analyses

As summarized in Table 5.4 and in keeping with the exploratory nature of this meta-analysis, we coded multiple features of each study: therapy approach/orientation, format/modality, setting, client presenting problem, treatment length, sample size, and experience level of therapists. For reflection measures, we coded rater perspective (e.g.,

Table 5.4 Selected Study Characteristics

Parametric Characteristics	*N*	*M*	*SD*	Range
Sample size: Studies/samples	43 samples 39 studies	63.0	68.0	
Clients (for 43 samples)	2,710	(median: 37)		1–327
Therapists (for 39 samples)	573	(median: 8)		1–131
Length of therapy (sessions)	40	6.6 (median: 2)	10.2	1–47
Effects per study	43	5.0	4.3	1–18

Categorical Characteristics	*N*	Selected Categories	*n*
Year of publication	43	1981–2000	12
		2001–2021	31
Theoretical orientation	43	Motivational Interviewing	21
		Psychodynamic	8
		Humanistic–experiential	2
		Mixed, eclectic, or unknown	13
Treatment format	43	Individual in person	41
Client presenting problem	43	Substance misuse	17
		Normal/minor disturbance	7
		Mixed clinical	16
		Physical health problems	3
Client ethnicity	18	Non-European origin (mean %)	60%
Therapist experience level	42	Paraprof/early grad student	6
		Master's level/advance grad student	22
		Recent/experienced PhD	14
Reflection assessment	214	Observer	211
Perspective		Client/therapist	3
		General/broad	146
Target/content		Content/meaning	12
		Feeling/emotion	6
		Change-related	40
		Summary	5
		General/broad	131
Type of reflection		Simple/basic	22
		Complex/deeper/feeling/summary	61
Effectiveness assessment	214	Observer	95
Perspective		Client	108
Effectiveness criterion	214	Process–outcome: Post-therapy	67 (14)[a]
		Process–outcome: Post-session	11 (7)
		Sequential process	82 (17)
		Process–process correlational	12 (5)
		Sequential experiential	42 (4)

[a]Numbers in parentheses refer to the number of samples using each change process effectiveness criterion; some samples used multiple criteria.

observer), target/content of reflection (e.g., feeling, change talk), type of reflection (e.g., simple, complex), and reflection measurement unit (e.g., speaking turn, 2- to 5-minute segment). For effectiveness measures, we coded perspective (therapist, client), variable type (e.g., client next turn good process; client post-therapy outcome), and measure timing (e.g., client next turn good/poor process). Finally, we coded effect size calculation method and change process effectiveness criterion.

We conducted two sets of analyses. First, we analyzed the 214 separate effects to examine the impact of reflection and effectiveness criterion parameters, with and without inverse weighting for the number of effects within studies to control for nonindependence of effects from the same sample. Second, study-level analyses averaged individual effects within client samples before further analysis, thus avoiding problems of nonindependence and eliminating bias due to variable numbers of effects reported in different studies (Lipsey & Wilson, 2001).

For analyses across studies, including overall effects, effectiveness criteria, and moderator variable analyses, we used Fisher's r-to-z transformation, weighted studies by inverse error ($n - 3$), analyzed for heterogeneity of effects using Cochrane's Q, and used a restricted maximum likelihood random effects model [calculated using Wilson's (2021) updated macros for SPSS]. We also calculated I^2, an estimate of the proportion of variation due to true variability as opposed to random error (Higgins et al., 2003) and generated a funnel plot. (We were unable to calculate a fail-safe number.) In subgroup and moderator analyses, given the overall baseline of zero effect size, we have interpreted small effects (mean $r_w \geq |.1|$) as potentially meaningful or promising, even when because of small sample size these were not statistically significant.

Results

Overall Effectiveness

We calculated the overall effectiveness for empathic reflections in three ways (Table 5.5), all with virtually identical findings of around zero (the largest was Model 2, with mean $r_w = .02$, equivalent to $d = .04$). Overall, we found *no* relation between therapist empathic reflections and effectiveness with clients. Furthermore, these effects were relatively homogeneous: Higgins I^2 values were generally low (where they could be calculated at all), and only the effects level Model 1 analysis had a significant Cochrane's Q, no doubt because degrees of freedom were inflated using multiple effects from each study.

The null effect here obviates the usual bias checks, such as funnel plots and fail-safe numbers, although we did find some evidence of bias in the form of a medium-sized correlation of .33 ($p < .05$) between effect size (r) and standard error of r (see funnel plot in Figure 5.1). This might mean that our estimate of mean weighted $r = .02$ is, if anything, overly optimistic. As the lower part of Table 5.5 shows, our null results were remarkably consistent across all three levels of effectiveness: within-session, post-session, and post-therapy.

Immediate Within-Session Effectiveness

Within-session effectiveness included results using three criteria (sequential process, sequential experiential, and process–process correlational); because studies often included measures using different criteria, only effects-level data could be analyzed (k = 136 effects; 24 studies; 1,217 clients), although analyses controlled for number of effects

Table 5.5 Empathic Reflection–Effectiveness Correlations: Overall and Three-Level Summary Statistics[a]

	Effects Level, Model 1 ($k = 214$)	Effects Level, Model 2 ($k = 214$)	Sample level ($k = 43$)
	M (95% CI)	*M* (95% CI)	*M* (95% CI)
Overall (Excluding Experimental)			
Weighted mean *r* [*d*]	.019 (–.004, .042) [.04]	.020 (–.024, .065) [.04]	.014 (–.025, .052) [.03]
Cochrane's *Q*	290.7*	74.3 (NS)	23.8 (NS)
I^2	27%	—	—
Within-Session Effectiveness ($k = 136$) (24 Studies; 1,217 Clients)			
Weighted mean *r* [*d*]	.020 (–.013, .053) [.04]	.024 (–.044, .093) [.05]	—
Cochrane's *Q*	157.3	42.2 (NS)	
I^2	14%	—	
Post-Session Effectiveness ($k = 11$) (3 Studies; 72 Clients)			
Weighted mean *r* [*d*]	.003 (–.150, .157) [.01]	.019 (–.221, .185) [–.04]	—
Cochrane's *Q*	3.0	2.1 (NS)	
I^2	—	—	
Post-Therapy Effectiveness ($k = 67$) (22 Studies; 1,734 Clients)			
Weighted mean *r* [*d*]	.019 (–.0143, .053) [.04]	.020 (–.040, .079) [.04]	—
Cochrane's *Q*	129.2	29.6 (NS)	
I^2	49%	—	
Between groups Q	.4 ($df = 2, 211$)	.2 ($df = 2. 211$)	—

[a]Random effects model, restricted maximum likelihood with Fisher *r*-to-*Z* transformations; inverse variance weights except where noted. Effects level, Model 1 ignores number of effects calculated per study (violates non-independence assumption). Effects level, Model 2 uses additional weighting by number of effects per study (weight = [*n* clients – 3]/number of effects per study). Fail-safe numbers could not be calculated.

95% CI, 95% confidence interval; NS, not significant.

*$p < .001$.

per study. Empathic reflections did not predict within-session effectiveness; Table 5.5 presents additional details.

Breaking down within-session effectiveness further, we looked separately at sequential process, sequential experiential, and process–process correlational designs. These results are summarized in Table 5.6. For sequential process ($k = 82$) and sequential experiential ($k = 42$) effects, mean r_w was –.01 ($d = –.03$) and .04 ($d = .08$), respectively, again indicating no relation between empathic reflections and immediate within-session

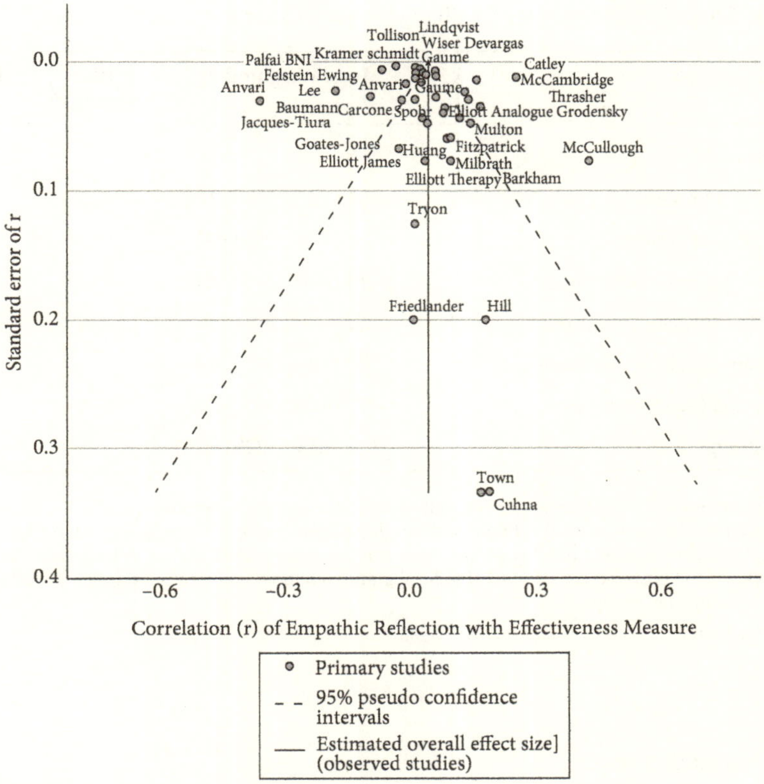

Figure 5.1 Funnel plot of empathic reflection–effectiveness effects by standard error: study-level effects.

effectiveness. On the other hand, process–process correlation designs (k = 12 effects) produced variable (I^2 = 53%) but slightly favorable results marginally supporting the effectiveness of empathic reflections [mean r_w =.14; 95% confidence interval (CI): –.08, .35; d = .28]. This result suggests that therapist empathic reflections show a small tendency to be associated within sessions with higher rates of client productive process (e.g., proportion of client change talk; Catley et al., 2006). However, the direction of causal influence is not clear in these studies, so this effect might be inflated by unmeasured reverse or circular causal processes.

Post-Session Effectiveness

We found no effect for post-session effectiveness measures [Tables 5.5 and 5.6; k = 11 effects; 3 studies; 72 clients; r_w = .01; CI: –.22, .19; d = .02; Q = 2.1, not significant (NS)]. Although the sample was small, the effects are consistent, suggesting that rates of empathic reflection are generally unrelated to global measures of good session outcome or process, including client ratings of session or relational quality (e.g., Barkham & Shapiro, 1986), observer ratings of client insight gain over the course of the session (Baumann & Hill, 2008), composite ratings of good versus bad sessions (Friedlander et al., 1985), and client post-session engagement in treatment (e.g., Huang et al., 2013).

Table 5.6 Effect-Level Effects Across Change Process Criteria[a]

Research Design	k	Mean Weighted r [d]	Within Group Q	I^2 (%)
Within-session				
Sequential process	82	−.01 (−.13, .10) [−.03]	14.7	—
Sequential experiential	42	.04 (−.19, .27) [.08]	0.8	—
Process–process correlational	12	.14 (−.08, .35) [.28]	23.4*	53
Post-session (process–outcome)	11	*.01 (−.27, .29) [.02]*	2.1	—
Post-therapy (process–outcome)	67	*.03 (−.06, .13) [.06]*	29.6	—
Experimental (process–process)	21	−.17 (−.37, .05) [−.34]	35.7*	—
Between groups Q		4.37 (df = 5, 229) (NS)		

[a]Mean correlations and significance tests (vs. null hypothesis $r = 0$) for subgroups calculated using Fisher's z scores and a restricted maximum likelihood random effects model using Wilson's (2021) macros for SPSS and weighting by inverse error and number of effects per study (= Effects level, Model 2). Italics indicates results for post-session and post-therapy effects that differ slightly from those reported in Table 5.5; this is because of the differing number of groups.

NS, not significant.

*$p < .05$.

Post-Therapy Effectiveness

Similarly, we found no effect for empathic reflections on measures of post-therapy outcome ($k = 67$ effects; 22 studies; 1,734 clients), despite the more robust sample and high consistency. The Model 2 mean r_w was .03 ($d = .06$; $Q = 29.6$, NS). Thus, frequency of empathic reflections appears to be unrelated to treatment outcome. As with immediate within-session effectiveness, these effects were significantly and consistently smaller than $r = .1$, generally considered to be a small effect; this justifies an inference of a null or no-difference effect.

Moderator Analyses

The lack of heterogeneity made it unlikely that we would find substantial effects for moderator variables, while at the same time raising the question of what might make reflections helpful or unhelpful. For this reason, we carried out exploratory analyses on a range of potential moderators.

Type of Reflection

The most common distinction we encountered in the literature was simple, brief reflections versus more complex, ambitious reflections—a distinction described variously as additive (Hammond, 1977), change-focused, deeper or complex (e.g., Amrhein et al., 2008), and exploratory (e.g., Barkham & Shapiro, 1986). However, as Table 5.7 indicates, we found no overall difference in effects between (a) undifferentiated general reflections, (b) simple reflections, and (c) more complex reflections, with all effects

Table 5.7 Effect-Level Effects Across Reflection Type[a]

Reflection Type	*N*	Mean Weighted *r* [*d*]	Within Group Q	I^2 (%)
General/broad	131	.02 (–.05, .09) [.04]	49.2	0
Simple/basic	22	–.00 (–.12, .12) [.04]	15.2	0
"Reflection-plus" (complex/ deeper/etc.)	61	.03 (–.04, .11) [.06]	9.4	0
Between groups Q		.04 (*df* = 2, 211) (NS)		

[a]See note for Table 5.6. No mean weighted *r* values were statistically significant.
NS, not significant.

hovering around zero. Perhaps complexity or ambitiousness of reflections is still too undifferentiated a concept; furthermore, adding more of a speculative element to a reflection may simply mean that the therapist is more likely to get it wrong.

Target/Content of Reflection

A more fine-grained and potentially promising approach has been to examine the specific contents of reflections—that is, what they refer to. This is certainly the rationale behind the common distinction between reflections of content and feeling (e.g., Hill, 1978), as well as the proliferation of the different types of change-related reflections in MI (e.g., Amrhein et al., 2008). As Table 5.8 shows, we found two small, statistically nonsignificant but intriguing effects favoring change talk reflections (k = 13; mean r_w = .12; CI: –.08, .31; NS; d = .24) and session summary reflections (k = 5; mean r_w = .15; CI: –.22, .48; NS; d = .30). These effects also help explain the general null effect, which may be the result of watering down slightly helpful reflection contents with contents that have no relation to effectiveness.

Other Moderators

Looking at sample level effects (k = 43), we found no differences or significant effects for type of therapy (MI, psychodynamic, mixed/unspecified), therapist experience, client presenting difficulty, client ethnicity (non-European origin), or decade in which the study was conducted. Similarly, for effect-level effects (k = 214), we found highly consistent null results across a wide range of effectiveness variables, including client interpersonal process recall (IPR) turn-ratings, client next-turn productive process, client or observer post-session ratings, client post-therapy outcome or status, and therapist turn-level or post-session ratings.

Review of Qualitative Research

We located only four qualitative studies specifically examining the effectiveness of psychotherapist empathic reflections. Bohart and Boyd (1997) found evidence that clients interpreted empathic reflections in terms of what they were looking for. One

Table 5.8 Effect-Level Effects Across Reflection Target/Content[a]

Reflection Target/Content	N	Mean Weighted *r* [*d*]	Within Group Q	I^2 (%)
General/broad	146	.02 (−.02, .07) [.05]	42.4	0
Content/meaning	12	−.05 (−.18, .07) [−.11]	10.8	75
Feeling/emotion	6	.08 (−.36, .49) [.16]	0.2	0
Change talk	13	.12 (−.08, .31) [.24]	1.53	0
Counterchange talk	12	−.03 (−.16, .10) [−.06]	14.52	24
Neutral/balanced talk	9	−.01 (−.22, .20) [−.02]	0.67	0
Commitment language	6	.03 (−.42, .47) [.07]	0.07	0
Unrelated to change	5	−.08 (−.50, .36) [−.18]	0.01	0
Summary	5	.15 (−.22, .48) [.30]	.31	0
Between groups Q		3.78 (df = 8, 205) (NS)		

[a]See note for Table 5.6. No mean weighted *r* values were statistically significant.
NS, not significant.
$^{**}p < .01$.

client, looking for support, interpreted her therapist's empathic reflections in terms of providing support. Another client, looking for insight, interpreted her therapist's empathic reflections as offering insight. Myers (2000) interviewed 5 female clients after their experiences with two therapists. Clients mentioned that paraphrasing, clarifying, and summarizing helped them feel understood; they specifically mentioned the value of the therapist summing up and saying back some of what they had said, and they valued hearing their own words fed back to them in a different way. In Bachelor (1988), 27 clients described a situation in which their therapist had been empathic. She found that empathy was not tied to a particular response form or therapist behavior. Finally, in a grounded theory analysis of clients' reports on experiences of empathy in therapy (MacFarlane et al., 2017), simple reflections were associated with client experiences of cognitive empathy, which appeared to lead to improved client self-understanding. Emotional empathy was communicated through therapist nonverbals and self-disclosures.

In summary, a common theme across the four studies was that empathic reflections were not uniquely associated with specific client effects. They can be interpreted by clients in different ways, and they are not the only responses that lead to clients' experiences of empathy. However, three of the four studies did find that reflections are one response form associated with an increase in client self-understanding.

Review of Conversation Analysis Studies

The key premise of CA is that social interaction is sequentially organized and accomplished through speakers' shared methods of action and reasoning (Stivers &

Sidnell, 2013). One key line of CA investigation is identifying and describing commonly occurring sequences of responsive actions (e.g., question–answer, storytelling–response) for how they are "done" or accomplished in interaction both vocally (e.g., lexico-grammar, prosody) and nonvocally (e.g., gesture, gaze). There is a growing body of CA work on empathic responses in psychotherapy and related helping interactions, most of which address what we are referring to as empathic reflection (e.g., Elliott et al., 2000; Muntigl, Knight, & Watkins, 2014) (The 21 CA studies specifically focused on psychotherapy are marked with "+" in the reference list. These studies involved roughly 1,150 segments of therapy and an unknown number of clients; a summary table of CA findings, with more information, is available from the first author.)

Muntigl, Knight, & Watkins (2014) observed a three-part sequence in psychotherapy in which therapist empathic responses (i.e., reflections) are regularly used to display empathy: (a) The client reports a distressing experience or situation, (b) the therapist provides an empathic reflection or displays understanding of the client's experience, and (c) the client responds (e.g., confirmation, disconfirmation) to the therapist's empathic reflection. We refer back to the two CA transcripts with the client Paula presented earlier under the Clinical Examples section to illustrate how CA research has shed light on how empathic reflections feature in accomplishing and negotiating empathy sequences in therapy.

Successful Empathy (Example 1)

Empathic Opportunities: Client Troubles Telling + Affective Stance Displays

Conversational analysis research indicates that empathy sequences begin with clients providing the therapist with detailed, incremental access to their troubles and their progress in dealing with those troubles, as well as their affective stance toward those troubles (i.e., how they feel about them). This offers an empathic opportunity for therapists to show their understanding and support (e.g., Kupetz, 2014; Muntigl, Knight, & Watkins, 2014). In Example 1, lines 01–10 illustrate how clients can develop an affective stance, first through descriptions of being "a little bit on the aggressive side of things" and adopting an "assertiv:e behaviour , mode.", and then by stating a "worry" in which she is unsure as to whether she will be able to find a balance of taking control while not exceeding boundaries (lines 14–17). In line 17, Paula conveys some tentative self-reassurance via a positive assessment "it's comin:g (0.4) alo:ng (0.7) alright" and a series of slow successive nods. The therapist, in turn, nods in unison, thus displaying token affiliation (= the minimum required) with Paula's assessment. Paula's stance is also built up through a number of nonvocal, mainly gestural, resources. For example, in line 03, her circular hand movement reinforces her claim that her behavior is "starting to- (.) to change", making this visually accessible to the therapist. Paula's tapping hand movements in line 08 further emphasize her desire to change her ways ("I ↑really wanted"), and her chopping/tapping hand movements provide further visual access into her having taken on a more assertive behavioral mode. The affective stance components of Paula's turn include descriptions of having been aggressive/assertive, claims of desiring change, worry, positive assessment that she will find a balance, and gestural resources to accompany and strengthen Paula's stance.

Therapist Formulation Response

Conversational analysis research shows how therapists respond to empathic opportunities with formulation responses (empathic reflections; e.g., Davis, 1986; Voutilainen et al., 2019). In lines 18–22, we see the therapist offering a summary formulation (= reflection) that captures the gist of the client's prior talk. The formulation is produced without any intervening pauses (i.e., contiguous to Paula's prior turn, which often conveys affiliation or "being in agreement") and highlights how Paula is able to achieve a "healthy" balance between competing needs: "taking control/standing up for herself" versus "not imposing on others" ("do it too aggressively"). Then, in lines 25–27, the therapist continues her turn by downplaying the possible negative effects of Paula taking control and being assertive ("isn't, . . . turning off everyone you meet"). In common with other CA studies (e.g., Weiste et al., 2016), the therapist's formulation here works empathically in the following ways: (a) It demonstrates their understanding of the client's dilemma by summarizing her affective stance and thus by staying close to the client's own descriptions of her personal experience; (b) it invites confirmation from the client, thus allowing her to maintain "ownership of experience" and to validate her expert role by confirming or disagreeing with the therapist's response; and (c) it supports and thus affiliates with the client's emotional meanings, but without identifying with or intruding on the client's feelings as, for example, through sympathy. Such subtleties are difficult to capture in standardized measures of therapist empathic reflection such as used in the research reviewed earlier.

Client Confirmation

Responses to therapist formulations/empathic reflections, which constitute the third position of empathy sequences, have been shown to be either affiliative or disaffiliative (e.g., Muntigl & Horvath, 2014). Whereas affiliative responses display varying degrees of agreement with the therapist's proffered empathy, disaffiliative responses convey disagreement (e.g., Elliott et al., 2000), often as either a form of direct opposition or as communicating disengagement such as refraining from answering (cf., Eubanks et al., 2018 on "confrontation" vs. "withdrawal" in alliance ruptures). Strong forms of client affiliation have been noted to co-accomplish what has been termed *empathic moments* in the CA literature (Heritage, 2011). During these moments, therapists and clients display interactional synchrony at both the vocal and nonvocal (e.g., synchronous nodding) levels and display (prosodically) upgraded, overlapping confirmation, as seen in Example 1, lines 21–29.

Failed Empathy and Re-affiliation (Example 2)

Moments of disaffiliation occur when clients do not communicate agreement with the prior therapist formulation (e.g., Guxholli et al., 2021; Muntigl et al., 2013). Example 2 shows a short sequence with the same client in which the therapist's effort at recasting Paula's stance is rejected, resulting in a disaffiliative sequence. The transcript shows not only how the therapist's attempt seems to miss the mark, resulting in *failed empathy*, but also how the therapist secures re-affiliation with Paula by producing nods in direct response to Paula's stance displays and later by showing understanding of Paula's alternative position:

Missed empathic opportunity

Lines 01–07 provide an illustration of a missed empathic opportunity that the therapist's reflection fails to pick up [Wynn and Wynn (2006) offer another example of failed empathy]. Paula's initial troubles telling highlight her dissatisfaction and frustration with her current boyfriend and the relationship. Her unhappiness is conveyed through negative assessments such as "it's just really hard" and "this person (2.0) doesn't make me feel good," and a sense of hopelessness for and frustration of the relationship situation as communicated via expressions such as "like f::- (.) ↑f:orget it. like just drop it an- and move o:n." Various prosodic features (i.e., stress, rise/falling intonation, syllable lengthening) also consistently work to upgrade her feelings of frustration and stuckness.

Therapist failed attempt at empathic response

CA studies have described how empathic responses that rephrase or transform are inherently risky, in the sense that they are more likely to be disconfirmed by the client (e.g., Antaki, 2008; Weiste & Peräkylä, 2013). In Example 2, lines 08–10, rather than summarizing or highlighting the client's frustration, the therapist's empathic response draws attention to a possible reason (feelings of failure) that could explain why the client finds it difficult to move on. Thus, it is not the client's displayed affect as such that the therapist orients to (negative affect toward the boyfriend and relationship) but, rather, the possibility that the client might blame herself if the relationship fails. This inferential leap, going significantly beyond what the client had said, is certainly a plausible (and perhaps even insightful) display of understanding of the client's troubles. But it is offered without making an explicit connection, or show of support/affiliation, with what the client had said, which increases the risk of disconfimation (e.g., Voutilainen et al., 2010). The client might not, in turn, recognize this new understanding as her own.

Client disconfirmation

The defining feature of a failed empathy sequence is client disaffiliation (disconfirmation; e.g., Muntigl, 2020; Weiste, 2015). Lines 11–15 provide a graphic illustration of client disaffiliation/disconfirmation/disagreement. Perhaps for the reasons mentioned above, the client disaffiliates with what the therapist had put forward and instead works to clarify her original position. Her disaffiliation at lines 12 onwards can be immediately inferred from the transcript: First, there is a significant silence following the therapist's turn completion (line 11), which implicates that confirmation may not be provided (see Pomerantz, 1984). Second, she utters a pronounced sigh, as expressed via a deep in- and out-breath (".hhh::: hhh:::"), which also signals potential disagreement in this sequential position (Hoey, 2014). Third, following another lengthy pause of 8.8 seconds, she expresses explicit disagreement, "no:" in line 14. After having rejected the therapist's attempt at focusing on "feelings of failure" as an explanatory construct for her frustration, the client continues by critically questioning her excessive feelings for the boyfriend and her effort in keeping the relationship going (I so: hung up on him; I have to try:, ↑so hard; I keep, ↑running) with the boyfriend's lack of interest (he doesn't ca:re).

Therapist re-affiliation

CA researchers have long documented how dispreferred responses as illustrated by Example 2 lead to attempts to repair the disaffiliation (e.g., Muntigl & Horvath, 2014).

For instance, in lines 16–28, during the client's next speaking turn (in which she criticizes herself and her boyfriend), the therapist nods at strategic places within Paula's turn that involve criticism. These nods communicate the therapist's affiliation with the client's new divergent position and, by indicating support, encourage her to continue developing her position until they reach the point where the therapist can offer a suitable formulation/empathic reflection to secure their re-affiliation. This empathic display seems to resonate well with Paula, as it results in a successful re-affiliative episode: Paula offers strong confirmation in line 28 (oh ↑yeah.).

In summary, this interaction in Example 2 may be interpreted as at best a mixed success: Re-affiliation between therapist and client was achieved and maintained, preventing a worse in-session outcome, but the therapist's possible immediate agenda of developing the client's stance in a different, potentially relevant direction (e.g., through two-chair work on a self-critical process) was not. Thus, the two examples illustrate how empathic reflections appear to succeed or fail through the operation of multiple complex and nuanced moment-by-moment processes. The chief value of this CA literature is to document the existence of some of these processes, something that is not currently reflected in the quantitative research literature or measures.

Summary and Implications of Research Review

In our meta-analysis of the quantitative literature, we found empathic reflections in general appear to have no relation to a wide range of measures of effectiveness. At the same time, we found a few small, nonstatistically significant positive effects for (a) reflections of client desire or reasons for change ("change talk"; Moyers et al., 2009), possibly because they encourage the client or offer a direction forward for the client; and (b) summary reflections (e.g., Boardman et al., 2006), possibly because they begin to offer the client a narrative for their process or provide closure for the session and a direction forward.

We can make sense of this reliably null effect (i.e., statistically significantly less than a small effect $< |.1|$) with four, probably overlapping, theories. The first (*filler theory*) suggests that empathic reflections are therapeutically inert filler. The second (*nudge theory*) suggests that empathic reflections are "nudges" (Thaler & Sunstein, 2008)—that is, small opportunities for clients to explore further, generally imperceptible in their effects, which are likely to be indirect and contextual. The third (*cancellation theory*) suggests that some reflections are likely to be helpful, but these are rare and probably cancelled out by unhelpful or even hindering reflections. Finally, there is *quality theory*, which suggests that the empathy, timing, and manner of reflections are essential for them to be effective.

The small set of qualitative studies reviewed points to two main conclusions: (a) that empathic reflections are not uniquely associated with specific effects, and (b) that reflections do appear to be regularly associated with enhanced client self-understanding.

The CA research begins to highlight the intricacy and complexity of what goes into empathic reflections in the joint achievement of both "empathic moments" (as in Extract 1) and instances of "failed empathy" (as in Extract 2). Specifically, CA research points to the importance of therapists recognizing and responding to empathic opportunities (referred to as "markers" in emotion-focused therapy; Elliott et al., 2004) afforded by troubles telling. Furthermore, CA highlights the importance of the form and delivery of responses for them to be heard as empathic (vs. less empathic or non-empathic). It also directs the attention to the third part of the empathic sequence—the client's response (i.e., how the client receives the therapist's response) as offering opportunities for stronger empathic responses or to repair failed empathy by re-affiliating.

Possible Negative Effects and Harm

Based on the CA literature, illustrated by Example 2, empathic reflections are likely to have negative effects under the following conditions: (a) when reflections deviate too far from client experience, especially when not expressed tentatively enough or with enough empathy or affiliation from the therapist (e.g., Muntigl et al., 2020); (b) when reflections fail to adequately represent clients' affective stance, including the intensity or strength of their feelings ("underreflecting"; e.g., Jefferson, 1988); or (c) when therapists fail to take back or repair reflections after clients subtly signal disagreement (e.g., Example 2).

At the same time, Miller and Rollnick (2013) wrote that it is unlikely that an empathic reflection will cause any harm. We understand this statement to mean that the capacity for harm is substantially less than for more directive responses such as challenge, criticism, or advice-giving (Miller et al., 1993).

Diversity Considerations

Client ethnicity was reported for only 18 (42%) of the samples in our meta-analysis and then mostly for studies on MI, which often involved Black or Hispanic populations (itself a reflection of cultural bias; cf. Substance Abuse and Mental Health Services Administration, 2019). Some MI research explicitly addressed sociocultural dimensions of people's experiences and identities (e.g., Carcone et al., 2013; Feldstein Ewing et al., 2015; Jacques-Tiura et al., 2017), suggesting the overall null effects we found for empathic reflections are likely to hold across several dimensions of diversity (e.g., gender, race/ethnicity, sexual orientation, socioeconomic status). In fact, we found no relation between the proportion of non-European clients in the studies reporting ethnicity and the effectiveness of empathic reflections. None of the small number of qualitative studies included non-European-origin clients, but we are unaware of any studies that systematically studied differences in response to empathic reflection across different cultural identities.

Nevertheless, Rimal et al. (2021) discussed the translation of MI concepts such as reflective listening into Nepali, noting that Indigenous trainees believed it would be impolite to offer empathic reflections as statements, preferring instead to add tag-questions to make them more tentative (cf. exploratory reflection, Table 5.1). Miller and others in the MI community have argued that reflections are useful for working with clients from various social positionalities (e.g., Miller & Rollnick, 2013). On the other hand, we are also aware that in some cultures, attitudes toward authority lead clients (e.g., in

East Asia) to expect therapists to take the lead and give advice (e.g., Sue et al., 2022). A "pure" nondirective style of a steady diet of empathic reflections might backfire with such clients, along with many in Western cultures. Obviously, more reporting of ethnicity data and research on empathic reflections in diverse populations is needed.

Limitations of the Research

Although empathy is considered a critical change process in psychotherapy (e.g., Bohart & Greenberg, 1997; Elliott et al., 2019), little work has been done to show how empathy is achieved within sessions at an interactional level (Wynn & Wynn, 2006), for example, via therapist empathic reflections and the client and therapist actions that precede and follow them. Historically, research on empathy and empathic reflections has focused largely on its cognitive components and relied primarily on retrospective self-report or behavioral coding systems. These methods lack the specificity and contextual sensitivity needed for clarifying when and how (i.e., using which communicative resources) empathic reflections and the empathy sequences in which they are embedded are most likely to succeed or fail. Existing measures and methods for studying empathy and empathic reflections are also limited in their potential for clarifying how empathy can be interactionally brought off and jointly achieved by therapists and clients (Pudlinski, 2005). CA research focuses on empathy as process and *inter-action* and extends the therapy literature by locating abstract concepts (e.g., empathy, emotion, understanding, frame of reference) in concrete practices. It challenges the notion of therapists as the sole and unilateral empathy providers and of clients as passive empathy recipients, highlighting the interconnectedness and sequential nature of therapy participants' inter-actions. Note also CA researchers have evaluated the success or failure of the therapist's empathic reflections based on the commonsense criteria of client affiliation/disaffiliation and progress on therapeutic work, evaluative standards that were not used in *any* of the 37 studies in our meta-analysis.

It seems premature to dwell too much on the causal status of these tentative findings. However, we do note that different change process research designs vary in the kinds of causal claims they support. For example, as appealing as process–outcome studies are, they do not address the complex mediational process needed to explain how empathy sequences unfold within sessions to link therapy process to outcome. These causal gaps are a major limitation of these designs. The gap is narrowed in process–process correlational designs, but because these ignore the sequential nature of the therapy process, they lose any reasonable basis for untangling the direction of causality when correlations are found. This leaves us with sequential process and sequential experiential designs, which capitalize on direct sequential links between client and therapist process. In these designs, we can look at specific therapist responses and see what the client does next (sequential process, using observer coding systems such as MITI) or what they experience next (sequential experiential, using IPR to ask clients). Furthermore, these designs allow us to separate out competing causal processes, such as client self → self and client → therapist influences (e.g., Moyers et al., 2009), and thus lend themselves to demonstrating precedence, plausibility, and internal validity (cf. Elliott et al., 2019).

These sequential designs sound promising; however, our results make clear that we do not yet have a clear account of what kinds of reflections, in what kinds of within-session contexts, have what kinds of helpful and hindering effects. The preliminary work needed for a fuller understanding of how and when empathic reflections work has not been addressed by any of the six change process research designs included in our meta-analysis. This suggests that psychotherapy researchers have attempted to quantify empathic reflections before fully understanding how and when they work, which we refer to as "premature quantification."

We are critical of most of the existing research on therapist empathic reflections, on multiple grounds. For example, each of the different change research designs has significant flaws that seriously compromise the validity of findings. Furthermore, as the CA literature highlights, the existing rating systems for therapist empathic reflections are blunt instruments that ignore important aspects of client context (e.g., empathic opportunities), fail to account for nonverbal and paralinguistic factors, and do not assess client next turn affiliation/disaffiliation and therapist ability to attend to and use this kind of client feedback.

It strikes us that we can begin to remedy this problem of premature quantification by carrying out the missing careful observational and descriptive research on empathic reflections and empathy sequences. A long time ago, the first author of this chapter told the first editor of this book a parable about how to study the silver fox, a rare, shy creature that lives in the forest. It went something like this:

> If we go crashing through the bushes with our usual methods, like quantitative rating scales and rigidly fixed category systems, we will scare her and we will never see her because she will hide from us. Instead, we must go quietly and respectfully through the forest, there to settle down amid the weeds and wildflowers of a sunny meadow. In that meadow we must wait quietly, patiently, and in a humble, nonthreatening manner. Then, if we are lucky, she will eventually emerge. And when she does come into that meadow we will watch carefully, observe what we can see, and learn from her. (Update: If we are technologically sophisticated, we might set up a camera to take pictures automatically and nonintrusively when she happens by.)

We are saying that researchers now need to go back to that preliminary step. We believe that one important method for coming to know the silver fox of empathic reflections is CA, particularly if it is applied with a significant events approach focusing on empathic moments or failed empathy. To complement the observational perspective of CA, a phenomenological perspective focused on clients' subjective experiences of empathic reflections is also needed (Myers, 2000).

Most critically, in our meta-analysis we did not set out here to review research on the *quality* of empathic reflections. Instead, our focus was on the response mode itself—that is, its presence or absence in a given speaking turn, or its frequency or proportion within a session. We also explored types and contents of empathic reflection. In general, "empathy" is our best candidate for describing the quality of empathic reflections and is clearly related to outcome (Elliott et al., 2019); however, it obviously covers a broader range of responses. We are missing a clear account of what makes some reflections more or less skillful than others. In this review, we have seen attempts to address this in terms of specific types or contents of reflections (e.g., reflections of change talk or summary reflections), but ignoring client context and therapist manner is unlikely to produce anything more than the small effects we have seen here. The specification of markers for different reflection responses (cf. Table 5.1) is consistent with a broader trend in contemporary therapy theory and practice (Watson & Wiseman, 2021). For empathic reflections, quality probably includes such things as how attuned the reflection is to the client's experience (Bohart & Greenberg, 1997), how responsive it is to the empathic opportunity and affective stance offered by the client (as the CA literature shows), how emotionally and experientially engaging it is (Gendlin, 1968), and so on.

Another suggestion for further research includes studying what makes *unhelpful reflections* counterproductive: Are they too obvious, too slow, too intrusive, too awkward, cliched ("wooden"), distracting, attention-seeking, or just plain wrong? Reflections look easy, but in our experience they are difficult to do well; people often think they are already good at them when they are not. Thus, we need to study unhelpful reflections to be able to identify them and the contexts in which they are more likely to occur, and also to teach therapists to avoid or repair them. We could also study *significant reflection events*: Some reflections (e.g., at particular *empathic moments*) might be important, useful, or even transformative, enabling clients to feel deeply understood, accepted, validated, or accompanied. Learning from such moments can tell us how to better facilitate them.

Training Implications

Training programs that teach empathy and empathic reflection go back to Carl Rogers' training courses in the 1940s (documented in Kirschenbaum, 2008); however, they expanded rapidly in the 1970s with the work of Ivey, Goodman, and others. Meta-analyses (e.g., Ngo, 2022; Teding van Berkhout & Malouff, 2016) suggest that such training programs are generally effective in imparting empathy and empathic reflection skills, and that both didactic and skill practice components contribute to this effectiveness. Unfortunately, the impact of such trainings on client outcome is unknown; furthermore, their curricula have often promulgated simplistic ideas about empathic reflections and frequently led to their indiscriminate use. We suspect that this is largely due to a kind of fetishization of therapist empathic reflections at the expense of attention to their optimal contexts, common client responses, and alternate modes of expression.

In fact, CA studies of empathy sequences and empathic reflection/formulation can inform therapy practice and training. First, therapists informed by CA work can be taught to better recognize *opportunities for empathy* and discern the client's affective stance toward described events. An affective stance can be developed to varying degrees. Supervisors can help students attend to opportunities for clients to further develop their stance and unpack or detail their experiences before producing more conjectural empathic responses. This would help therapists improve the timing and accuracy of their empathic reflections by clarifying the relevant micro-markers and subtle nuances in client talk.

Second, in teaching about *empathic reflections*, trainers can draw on existing CA work to help their supervisees learn about multiple, multimodal ways to display an understanding of clients' troubles, including both empathic reflections and other interactional resources for expressing empathy. For example, supervisors can point out prosodic continuity and discontinuity (e.g., matching or nonmatching the client in speech rhythm or pitch) and how these may play a role in whether an utterance is heard by the client as more or less empathic (Weiste & Peräkylä, 2014). CA studies can also highlight that therapists' responses may convey different degrees of empathic strength or intensity (Jefferson, 1988). For example, a nod at the end of the trouble telling may convey insufficient empathy (Stivers, 2008), whereas the therapist's disclosure of second stories (e.g., "The same thing also happened to me") may indicate too much personal involvement on the part of the therapist (Ruusuvuori, 2005, 2007). Supervisors can also help therapists recognize that the more their empathic responses depart from clients' original descriptions, the more caution or tentativeness they may want to adopt in delivering them (Muntigl, 2020; Weiste et al., 2016).

Finally, in evaluating *empathic receipts*, trainers and supervisors can direct supervisees' attention to clients' responses and recognize when empathic reflections are not (strongly) confirmed by clients and make efforts to re-affiliate or adjust their responses in order to elicit a stronger endorsement from clients. For example, a CA-trained therapist in Extract 2 would probably have recognized Paula's expressive sigh and silence as signaling disagreement—that is, disaffiliation with her therapist's empathic conjecture. Similarly, as trainers, we must confess that we have generally downplayed clients' immediate affiliation or disaffiliation to reflections, robbing ourselves and our students of the opportunity to learn from clients on a response-by-response level. In the process, we have ignored the most important form of deliberate practice: learning how to learn from our clients' immediate reactions to what we have offered them.

Therapeutic Practices

Based on our research review, as well as clinical experience, we suggest that therapists do the following:

- Listen for and reflect client change talk (e.g., desire for change), especially with clients struggling with ambivalence about self-damaging activities. [Source: reflection meta-analysis]
- Offer summary reflections that pull together what you and the client have talked about, where possible formulating client experience into narratives about how their difficulties unfold. [Source: reflection meta-analysis]
- Base empathic reflections on genuine empathy and positive regard for the client and allow yourself to convey this to them [Source: empathy meta-analysis]
- Offer empathic reflections when clients offer empathic opportunities—for instance, when they express emotion in the context of telling about their troubles (or other important experiences). [Source: CA review]
- Offer empathic reflections particularly when patients are confused or uncertain about their feelings; such reflections seem to regularly enhance their self-understanding. [Source: review of qualitative research]

- Reflect not only what the client is saying and feeling but also how intensely they are saying or feeling it, and try to match this intensity in the manner of your reflection. [Source: CA review]
- Match the delivery of your reflections to their distance from your client's main message: The further away a reflection is from the client's expressed experience, the more careful, tentative, or humble you will want to be in offering it. [Source: CA review]
- Pay close attention to how clients immediately respond to your reflections; make sure to reflect hesitation and lukewarm agreement nondefensively as indicating you have missed the client's meaning. [Source: CA review]
- Correct your empathic reflections when this happens, and perhaps acknowledge that you initially missed the client's meaning or experience. [Source: CA review]

References

* Sources used in meta-analysis; + psychotherapy research sources used in conversational analysis review.

Amrhein, P., Miller, W. R., Moyers, T., & Ernst, D. (2008). *Manual for the Motivational Interviewing Skill Code (MISC)* (Article 27). Department of Psychology Faculty Scholarship and Creative Works. https://digitalcommons.montclair.edu/psychology-facpubs/27

+Antaki, C. (2008). Formulations in psychotherapy. In A. Peräkylä, C. Antaki, S. Vehviläinen, & I. Leudar (Eds.), *Conversation analysis and psychotherapy* (pp. 26–42). Cambridge University Press.

*Anvari, M., Hill, C. E., & Kivlighan, D. M. (2020). Therapist skills associated with client emotional expression in psychodynamic psychotherapy. *Psychotherapy Research, 30*(7), 900–911. https://doi.org/10.1080/10503307.2019.1680901

*Anvari, M. S., Dua, V., Lima-Rosas, J., Hill, C. E., & Kivlighan, D. M., Jr. (2022). Facilitating exploration in psychodynamic psychotherapy: Therapist skills and client attachment style. *Journal of Counseling Psychology, 69*(3), 348–360. http://dx.doi.org/10.1037/cou0000582

Bachelor, A. (1988). How clients perceive therapist empathy: A content-analysis of received empathy. *Psychotherapy, 25*, 227–240. doi:10.1037/h0085337

*Barkham, M., & Shapiro, D. A. (1986). Counselor verbal response modes and experienced empathy. *Journal of Counseling Psychology, 33*, 3–10.

*Baumann, E., & Hill, C. E. (2008). The attainment of insight in the insight stage of the Hill dream model: The influence of client reactance and therapist interventions. *Dreaming, 18*(2), 127–137. https://doi.org/10.1037/1053-0797.18.2.127

+Bercelli, F., Rossano, F., & Viaro, M. (2008). Clients' responses to therapists' reinterpretations. In A. Peräkylä, C. Antaki, S. Vehviläinen, & I. Leudar (Eds.), *Conversation analysis and psychotherapy* (pp. 43–61). Cambridge University Press. https://doi.org/10.1017/CBO9780511490002.004

*Boardman, T., Catley, D., Grobe, J., Little, T., & Ahluwalia, J. (2006). Using motivational interviewing with smokers: Do therapist behaviors relate to engagement and therapeutic alliance? *Journal of Substance Abuse Treatment, 31*, 329–339.

Bohart, A. C. (2021). *The art of Bohart*. PCCS Books.

Bohart, A. C., & Boyd, G. (1997, December). Clients' construction of the therapy process: A qualitative analysis [Poster presentation]. Meeting of the North American Chapter of the Society for Psychotherapy Research, Tucson, AZ.

Bohart, A. C., Elliott, R., Greenberg, L. S., & Watson, J. C. (2002). Empathy. In J. Norcross (Ed.), *Psychotherapy relationships that work* (pp. 89–108). Oxford University Press.

Bohart, A. C., & Greenberg, L. S. (1997). Empathy and psychotherapy: An introductory overview. In A. Bohart & L. S. Greenberg (Eds.), *Empathy reconsidered: New directions in psychotherapy* (pp. 3–31). American Psychological Association.

Bohart, A. C., Humphrey, A., Magallanes, M., Guzman, R., Smiljanich, K., & Aguallo, S.. (1993). Emphasizing the future in empathy responses. *Journal of Humanistic Psychology*, *33*, 12–29.

Brodley, B. T. (2001). Observations of empathic understanding in client-centered practice. In S. Haugh & T. Merry (Eds.), *Empathy* (pp. 16–37). PCCS Books.

Brodley, B. T. (2006). Non-directivity in client-centered therapy. *Person-Centered & Experiential Psychotherapies*, *5*, 36–52. doi:10.1080/14779757.2006.9688391

*Carcone, A. I., Naar-King, S., Brogan, K. E., Albrecht, T., Barton, E., Foster, T., Martin, T., & Marshall, S. (2013). Provider communication behaviors that predict motivation to change in Black adolescents with obesity. *Journal of Developmental & Behavioral Pediatrics*, *34*(8), 599–608. https://doi.org/10.1097/DBP.0b013e3182a67daf

Carkhuff, R. R., & Berenson, G. G. (1977). *Beyond counselling and psychotherapy* (2nd ed.). Holt, Rinehart & Winston.

*Catley, D., Harris, K. J., Mayo, M. S., Hall, S., Okuyemi, K. S., Boardman, T., & Ahluwalia, J. (2006). Adherence to principles of motivational interviewing and client within-session behavior. *Behavioural and Cognitive Psychotherapy*, *34*, 43–56.

*Cunha, C., Gonçalves, M. M., Hill, C. E., Mendes, I., Ribeiro, A. P., Sousa, I., Angus, L., & Greenberg, L. S. (2012). Therapist interventions and client innovative moments in emotion-focused therapy for depression. *Psychotherapy*, *49*(4), 536–548. https://doi.org/10.1037/a0028259

+Davis, K. (1986). The process of problem (re)formulation in psychotherapy. *Sociology of Health & Illness*, *8*(1), 44–74.

*DeVargas, E. C., & Stormshak, E. A. (2020). Motivational interviewing skills as predictors of change in emerging adult risk behavior. *Professional Psychology*, *51*(1), 16–24. https://doi.org/10.1037/pro0000270

*Elliott, R. (1985). Helpful and nonhelpful events in brief counseling interviews: An empirical taxonomy. *Journal of Counseling Psychology*, *32*, 307–322.

Elliott, R. (1986). Interpersonal process recall (IPR) as a psychotherapy process research method. In L. Greenberg & W. Pinsof (Eds.), *The psychotherapeutic process* (pp. 503–527). Guilford.

Elliott, R. (2010). Psychotherapy change process research: Realizing the promise. *Psychotherapy Research*, *20*(2), 123–135. doi:10.1080/10503300903470743

*Elliott, R., Barker, C. B., Caskey, N., & Pistrang, N. (1982). Differential helpfulness of counselor verbal response modes. *Journal of Counseling Psychology*, *29*, 354–361.

Elliott, R., Bohart, A. C., Watson, J. C., & Greenberg, L. S. (2011). Empathy. In J. Norcross (Ed.), *Psychotherapy relationships that work* (2nd ed., pp. 132–152). Oxford University Press.

Elliott, R., Bohart, A. C., Watson, J. C., & Murphy, D. (2019). Empathy. In J. C. Norcross & M. J. Lambert (Eds.), *Psychotherapy relationships that work: Evidence-based therapist contributions* (3rd ed., Vol. 1, pp. 245–287). Oxford University Press.

Elliott, R., & Greenberg, L. S. (2021). *Emotion-focused counselling in action*. SAGE.

Elliott, R., Hill, C. E., Stiles, W. B., Friedlander, M. L., Mahrer, A., & Margison, F. (1987). Primary therapist response modes: A comparison of six rating systems. *Journal of Consulting and Clinical Psychology*, *55*, 218–223.

*Elliott, R., James, E., Reimschuessel, C., Cislo, D., & Sack, N. (1985). Significant events and the analysis of immediate therapeutic impacts. *Psychotherapy*, *22*, 620–630.

+Elliott, R., Slatick, E., & Urman, M. (2000). "So the fear is like a thing . . .": A significant empathic exploration event in process–experiential therapy for PTSD. In J. Marques-Teixeira & S. Antunes (Eds.), *Client-centered and experiential psychotherapy* (pp. 179–204). Vale & Vale.

Elliott, R., Watson, J. C., Goldman, R. N., & Greenberg, L. S. (2004). *Learning emotion-focused therapy: The process–experiential approach to change*. American Psychological Association.

Eubanks, C. F., Muran, J. C., & Safran, J. D. (2018). Alliance rupture repair: A meta-analysis. *Psychotherapy*, *55*(4), 508–519. https://doi.org/10.1037/pst0000185

*Feldstein Ewing, S. W., Gaume, J., Ernst, D. B., Rivera, L., & Houck, J. M. (2015). Do therapist behaviors differ with Hispanic youth? A brief look at within-session therapist behaviors and youth treatment response. *Psychology of Addictive Behaviors, 29*(3), 779–786. https://doi.org/10.1037/adb0000079

*Fitzpatrick, M. R., Stalikas, A., & Iwakabe, S. (2001). Examining counselor interventions and client progress in the context of the therapeutic alliance. *Psychotherapy, 38*(2), 160–170. https://doi.org/10.1037/0033-3204.38.2.160

*Friedlander, M. L., Thibodeau, J. R., & Ward, L. G. (1985). Discriminating the "good" from the "bad" therapy hour: A study of dyadic interaction. *Psychotherapy, 22*(3), 631–642. https://doi.org/10.1037/h0085549

*Gaume, J., Bertholet, N., Faouzi, M., Gmel, G., & Daeppen, J. B. (2010). Counselor motivational interviewing skills and young adult change talk articulation during brief motivational interventions. *Journal of Substance Abuse Treatment, 39*(3), 272–281. https://doi.org/10.1016/j.jsat.2010.06.010

*Gaume, J., Gmel, G., & Daeppen, J. B. (2008). Brief alcohol interventions: Do counsellors' and patients' communication characteristics predict change? *Alcohol and Alcoholism, 43*(1), 62–69. https://doi.org/10.1093/alcalc/agm141

Gendlin, E. T. (1968). The experiential response. In E. Hammer (Ed.), *Use of interpretation in treatment* (pp. 208–227). Grune & Stratton. http://previous.focusing.org/gendlin/docs/gol_2156.html

*Goates-Jones, M. K., Hill, C. E., Stahl, J. V., & Doschek, E. E. (2009). Therapist response modes in the exploration stage: Timing and effectiveness. *Counselling Psychology Quarterly, 22*(2), 221–231. https://doi.org/10.1080/09515070903185256

Goodman, G., & Dooley, D. (1976). A framework for help-intended communication. *Psychotherapy, 13*, 106–117.

Goodman, G., & Esterly, G. (1988). *The talk book: The intimate science of communicating in close relationships*. Ballantine.

*Grodensky, C., Golin, C., Parikh, M. A., Ochtera, R., Kincaid, C., Groves, J., Widman, L., Suchindran, C., McGirt, C., Amola, K., & Bradley-Bull, S. (2017). Does the quality of SafeTalk motivational interviewing counseling predict sexual behavior outcomes among people living with HIV? *Patient Education and Counseling, 100*(1), 147–153. https://doi.org/10.1016/j.pec.2016.08.014

Gumz, A., Treese, B., Marx, C., Strauss, B., & Wendt, H. (2015). Measuring verbal psychotherapeutic techniques: A systematic review of intervention characteristics and measures. *Frontiers in Psychology, 6*(1705), 1–25. doi:10.3389/fpsyg.2015.01705

+Guxholli, A., Voutilainen, L., & Peräkylä, A. (2021). Safeguarding the therapeutic alliance: Managing disaffiliation in the course of work with psychotherapeutic projects. *Frontiers in Psychology, 11*, 596972.

+Hak, T., & de Boer, F. (1996). Formulations in first encounters. *Journal of Pragmatics, 25*(1), 83–99. https://doi.org/10.1016/0378-2166(94)00076-7

Hammond, D. C., Hepworth, D. H., & Smith, V. G. (1977). *Improving therapeutic communication: A guide for developing effective techniques*. Wiley.

Hepburn, A., & Bolden, G. B. (2017). *Transcribing for social research*. SAGE. https://doi.org/10.4135/9781473920460

Hepburn, A., & Potter, J. (2007). Crying receipts: Time, empathy, and institutional practice. *Research on Language and Social Interaction, 40*, 89–116. https://doi.org/10.1080/08351810701331299

Heritage, J. (2011). Territories of knowledge, territories of experience: Empathic moments in interaction. In T. Stivers, L. Mondada, & J. Steensig (Eds.), *The morality of knowledge in conversation* (pp. 159–183). Cambridge University Press.

Heritage, J., & Watson, R. (1979). Formulations as conversational objects. In G. Psathas (Ed.), *Everyday language* (pp. 123–162). Irvington.

Higgins, J. P. T., Thompson, S. G., Deeks, J. J., & Altman, D. G. (2003). Measuring inconsistency in meta-analyses, *British Journal of Medicine, 327*, 557–560.

Hill, C. E. (1978). The development of a system for classifying counselor responses. *Journal of Counseling Psychology*, *25*, 461–468.

Hill, C. E. (1986). An overview of the Hill counselor and client verbal response modes category systems. In L. S. Greenberg & W. M. Pinsof (Eds.), *The psychotherapeutic process: A research handbook* (pp. 131–160). Guilford.

Hill, C. E. (2020). *Helping skills: Facilitating exploration, insight, and action* (5th ed.). American Psychological Association.

*Hill, C. E., Carter, J. A., & O'Farrell, M. K. (1983). A case study of the process and outcome of time-limited counseling. *Journal of Counseling Psychology*, *30*(1), 3–18. https://doi.org/10.1037/0022-0167.30.1.3

Hill, C. E., Greenwald, C., Reed, K. G., Charles, D., O'Farrell, M. K., & Carter, J. A. (1981). *Manual for the counselor and client verbal response category system*. Marathon.

*Hill, C. E., Helms, J. E., Tichenor, V., Spiegel, S. B., O'Grady, K. E., & Perry, E. S. (1988). Effects of therapist response modes in brief psychotherapy. *Journal of Counseling Psychology*, *35*(3), 222–233. https://doi.org/10.1037/0022-0167.35.3.222

Hoey, E. M. (2014). Sighing in interaction: Somatic, semiotic, and social. *Research on Language and Social Interaction*, *47*(2), 175–200. https://doi.org/10.1080/08351813.2014.900229

*Houck, J. M., & Moyers, T. B. (2015). Within-session communication patterns predict alcohol treatment outcomes. *Drug and Alcohol Dependence*, *157*, 205–209. https://doi.org/10.1016/j.drugalcdep.2015.10.025

*Huang, T., Hill, C., & Gelso, C. (2013). Psychotherapy engagers versus non-engagers: Differences in alliance, therapist verbal response modes, and client attachment. *Psychotherapy Research*, *23*(5), 568–577. https://doi.org/10.1080/10503307.2013.807378

Ivey, A. E., & Authier, J. (1978). *Microcounseling: Innovations in interviewing, counseling, psychotherapy, and psychoeducation* (2nd ed.). Charles C Thomas.

Ivey, A. E., Ivey, M. B., & Simek-Downing, L. (1987). *Counseling and psychotherapy: Skills, theories, and practice* (2nd ed.). Prentice-Hall.

Ivey, A. E., Ivey, M. B., & Zalaquett, C. P. (2022). *Intentional interviewing and counselling: Facilitating client development in a multicultural society* (10th ed.). Cengage.

*Jacques-Tiura, A. J., Carcone, A. I., Naar, S., Brogan Hartlieb, K., Albrecht, T. L., & Barton, E. (2017). Building motivation in African American caregivers of adolescents with obesity: Application of sequential analysis. *Journal of Pediatric Psychology*, *42*(2), 131–141. https://doi.org/10.1093/jpepsy/jsw044

Jefferson, G. (1988). On the sequential organization of troubles talk in ordinary conversation. *Social Problems*, *35*, 418–442. https://doi.org/10.2307/800595

Jefferson, G. (2004). Glossary of transcript symbols with an introduction. In G. Lerner (Ed.), *Conversation analysis: Studies from the first generation* (pp. 13–31). Benjamins.

Kirschenbaum, H. (2008). *The life and work of Carl Rogers*. American Counseling Association.

*Kramer Schmidt, L., Moyers, T. B., Nielsen, A. S., & Andersen, K. (2019). Is fidelity to motivational interviewing associated with alcohol outcomes in treatment-seeking 60+ year-old citizens? *Journal of Substance Abuse Treatment*, *101*, 1–11. doi:10.1016/j.jsat.2019.03.004

Kupetz, M. (2014). Empathy displays as interactional achievement–Multimodal and sequential aspects. *Journal of Pragmatics*, *61*, 4–34. https://doi.org/10.1016/j.pragma.2013.11.006

Larson, D. (2020). *The helper's journey: Empathy, compassion, and the challenge of caring* (2nd ed.). Research Press.

*Lee, D. Y., Uhlemann, M. R., & Haase, R. F. (1985). Counselor verbal and nonverbal responses and perceived expertness, trustworthiness, and attractiveness. *Journal of Counseling Psychology*, *32*(2), 181–187. https://doi.org/10.1037/0022-0167.32.2.181

Lietaer, G., & Gundrum, M. (2018). His master's voice: Carl Rogers' verbal response modes in therapy and demonstration sessions throughout his career: A quantitative analysis and some qualitative-clinical comments. *Person-Centered & Experiential Psychotherapies*, *17*(4), 275–333. doi:10.1080/14779757.2018.1544091

*Lindqvist, H., Forsberg, L., Enebrink, P., Andersson, G., & Rosendahl, I. (2017). The relationship between counselors' technical skills, clients' in-session verbal responses, and outcome in smoking cessation treatment. *Journal of Substance Abuse Treatment*, *77*, 141–149. https://doi.org/10.1016/j.jsat.2017.02.004

Lipsey, M. W., & Wilson, D. B. (2001). *Practical meta-analysis*. SAGE.

MacFarlane, P., Anderson, T., & McClintock, A. S. (2017). Empathy from the client's perspective: A grounded theory analysis. *Psychotherapy Research*, *27*, 227–238.

Martin, D. C. (2016). *Counseling and therapy skills* (4th ed.). Waveland.

*McCambridge, J., Day, M., Thomas, B. A., & Strang, J. (2011). Fidelity to motivational interviewing and subsequent cannabis cessation among adolescents. *Addictive Behaviors*, *36*(7), 749–754. https://doi.org/10.1016/j.addbeh.2011.03.002

*McCullough, L., Winston, A., Farber, B. A., Porter, F., Pollack, J., Vingiano, W., Laikin, M., & Trujillo, M. (1991). The relationship of patient–therapist interaction to outcome in brief psychotherapy. *Psychotherapy*, *28*(4), 525–533. https://doi.org/10.1037/0033-3204.28.4.525

Mearns, D., Thorne, B., & McLeod, J. (2013). *Person-centred counselling in action* (4th ed.). SAGE.

*Milbrath, C., Bond, M., Cooper, S., Znoj, H. J., Horowitz, M. J., & Perry, J. C. (1999). Sequential consequences of therapists' interventions. *Journal of Psychotherapy Practice and Research*, *8*(1), 40–54.

Miller, W. R., Benefield, R. G., & Tonigan, J. S. (1993). Enhancing motivation for change in problem drinking: A controlled comparison of two therapist styles. *Journal of Consulting and Clinical Psychology*, *61*, 455–461.

Miller, W. R., & Rollnick, S. (2013). *Motivational interviewing: Preparing people for change* (3rd ed.). Guilford.

Moon, K. (2018). A client-centered commentary on Lietaer and Gundrum's verbal response modes. *Person-Centered & Experiential Psychotherapies*, *17*(4), 334–341.

Moyers, T. B., Manuel, J. K., & Ernst, D. (2014). Motivational interviewing treatment integrity coding manual 4.1 [Unpublished manual]. University of New Mexico.

*Moyers, T. B., Martin, T., Houck, J. M., Christopher, P. J., & Tonigan, J. S. (2009). From in-session behaviors to drinking outcomes: A causal chain for motivational interviewing. *Journal of Consulting and Clinical Psychology*, *77*(6), 1113–1124. https://doi.org/10.1037/a0017189

Moyers, T. B., Martin, T., Manuel, J. K., Hendrickson, S. M., & Miller, W. R. (2005). Assessing competence in the use of motivational interviewing. *Journal of Substance Abuse Treatment*, *28*(1), 19–26. https://doi.org/10.1016/j.jsat.2004.11.001

*Multon, K. D., Ellis-Kalton, C. A., Heppner, M. J., & Gysbers, N. C. (2003). The relationship between counselor verbal response modes and the working alliance in career counseling. *Career Development Quarterly*, *51*(3), 259–273. https://doi.org/10.1002/j.2161-0045.2003.tb00606.x

+Muntigl, P. (2020). Managing distress over time in psychotherapy: Guiding the client in and through intense emotional work. *Frontiers in Psychology*, *10*, 3052. https://doi.org/10.3389/fpsyg.2019.03052

+Muntigl, P., & Horvath, A. O. (2014). The therapeutic relationship in action: How therapists and clients co-manage relational disaffiliation. *Psychotherapy Research*, *24*(3), 327–345. https://doi.org/10.1080/10503307.2013.807525

+Muntigl, P., Knight, N., & Angus, L. (2014). Targeting emotional impact in storytelling: Working with client affect in emotion-focused psychotherapy. *Discourse Studies*, *16*(6), 753–775. https://doi.org/10.1177/1461445614546255

+Muntigl, P., Knight, N., Horvath, A. O., & Watkins, A. (2012). Client attitudinal stance and therapist–client affiliation: A view from grammar and social interaction. *Research in Psychotherapy: Psychopathology, Process and Outcome*, *15*(2), 117–130. https://doi.org/10.4081/RIPPPO.2012.119

+Muntigl, P., Knight, N., & Watkins, A. (2014). Empathic practices in client-centered psychotherapies. In E. M. Graf, M. Sator, & T. Spranz-Fogasy (Eds.), *Discourses of helping professions* (pp. 33–57). Benjamins.

+Muntigl, P., Knight, N., Watkins, A., Horvath, A. O., & Angus, L. (2013). Active retreating: Person-centered practices to repair disaffiliation in therapy. *Journal of Pragmatics*, *53*, 1–20. https://doi.org/10.1016/j.pragma.2013.03.019

Murphy, D. (2019). *Person-centred experiential counselling for depression* (2nd ed.). SAGE.

Myers, S. (2000). Empathic listening: Reports on being heard. *Journal of Humanistic Psychology, 40*(2), 148–172.

Ngo, H. L. (2022). Instructional components and their combinations for teaching empathy to mental health practitioners and trainees: Pairwise and network meta-analyses [Unpublished master's thesis]. Graduate Department of Applied Psychology and Human Development, University of Toronto.

Orlinsky, D. E., Rønnestad, M. H., & Willutzki, U. (2004). Process and outcome in psychotherapy. In M. J. Lambert (Ed.), *Bergin and Garfield's handbook of psychotherapy and behavior change* (5th ed., pp. 307–389). Wiley.

*Palfai, T. P., Cheng, D. M., Bernstein, J. A., Palmisano, J., Lloyd-Travaglini, C. A., Goodness, T., & Saitz, R. (2016). Is the quality of brief motivational interventions for drug use in primary care associated with subsequent drug use? *Addictive Behaviors, 56*, 8–14. https://doi.org/10.1016/j.addbeh.2015.12.018

+Peräkylä, A. (2019). Conversation analysis and psychotherapy: Identifying transformative sequences. *Research on Language and Social Interaction, 52*(3), 257–280.

Pomerantz, A. (1984). Agreeing and disagreeing with assessments: Some features of preferred/dispreferred turn shaped. In J. M. Atkinson & J. Heritage (Eds.), *Structures of social action: Studies in conversation analysis* (pp. 57–101). Cambridge University Press.

Pudlinski, C. (2005). Doing empathy and sympathy: Caring responses to troubles telling on a peer support line. *Discourse Studies, 7*, 267–288. https://doi.org/10.1177/1461445605052177

Rennie, D. L. (1998). *Person-centred counselling: An experiential approach*. SAGE.

Rimal, P., Khadka, S., Bogati, B., Chaudhury, J., Rawat, L., Bhat, K., Manandhar, P., Citrin, D., Maru, D., Ekstrand, M., Swar, S., Aryal, A., Kohrt, B., Shrestha, S., & Acharya, B.. (2021). Cross-cultural adaptation of motivational interviewing for use in rural Nepal. *BMC Psychology, 9*, 52. https://doi.org/10.1186/s40359-021-00557-y

*Rodriguez, M., Walters, S. T., Houck, J. M., Ortiz, J. A., & Taxman, F. S. (2018). The language of change among criminal justice clients: Counselor language, client language, and client substance use outcomes. *Journal of Clinical Psychology, 74*(4), 626–636. https://doi.org/10.1002/jclp.22534

Rogers, C. R. (1951). *Client centered therapy*. Houghton Mifflin.

Rogers, C. R. (1957). The necessary and sufficient conditions of therapeutic personality change.. *Journal of Consulting Psychology, 21*, 95–103.

Rogers, C. R. (1975). Empathic: An unappreciated way of being. *Counseling Psychologist, 5*(2), 2–10.

Ruusuvuori, J. (2005). "Empathy" and "sympathy" in action: Attending to patients' troubles in Finnish homeopathic and general practice consultations. *Social Psychology Quarterly, 68*, 204–222. https://doi.org/10.1177/019027250506800302

Ruusuvuori, J. (2007). Managing affect: Integrating empathy and problem solving in two types of health care consultation. *Discourse Studies, 9*, 597–622. https://doi.org/10.1177/1461445607081269

Sacks, H. (1995). *Lectures on conversation*. Blackwell.

Sidnell, J., & Stivers, T. (Eds.). (2013). *The handbook of conversation analysis*. Wiley-Blackwell.

Simpson, J. A., & Weiner, E. S. C.. (1989). *The Oxford English dictionary*. Clarendon Press.

*Spohr, S. A., Taxman, F. S., Rodriguez, M., & Walters, S. T. (2016). Motivational interviewing fidelity in a community corrections setting: Treatment initiation and subsequent drug use. *Journal of Substance Abuse Treatment, 65*, 20–25. https://doi.org/10.1016/j.jsat.2015.07.012

Stiles, W. B. (1979). Verbal response modes and psychotherapeutic technique. *Psychiatry, 42*, 49–62.

Stiles, W. B. (1986). Development of a taxonomy of verbal response modes. In L. S. Greenberg & W. M. Pinsof (Eds.), *The psychotherapeutic process: A research handbook* (pp. 161–200). Guilford.

Stiles, W. B. (1992). *Describing talk: A taxonomy of verbal response modes*. SAGE.

Stiles, W. B., & Shapiro, D. A. (1994). Disabuse of the drug metaphor: Psychotherapy process–outcome correlations. *Journal of Consulting & Clinical Psychology, 62*, 942–948.

Stivers, T. (2008). Stance, alignment, and affiliation during storytelling: When nodding is a token of affiliation. *Research on Language and Social Interaction*, *41*, 31–57. https://doi.org/10.1080/08351810701691123

Stivers, T., & Sidnell, J. (2013). Introduction. In J. Sidnell & T. Stivers (Eds.), *The handbook of conversation analysis* (pp. 1–8). Wiley.

Substance Abuse and Mental Health Services Administration. (2019). 2018 National Survey on Drug Use and Health *detailed tables*. https://www.samhsa.gov/data/report/2018-nsduh-detailed-tables

Suchman, A. L., Markakis, K., Beckman, H. B., & Frankel, R. (1997). A model of empathic communication in the medical interview. *Journal of the American Medical Association*, *277*(8), 678–682. https://doi.org/10.1001/jama.1997.03540320082047

Sue, D. W., Sue, D., Neville, H. A., & Smith, L. (2022). *Counselling the culturally diverse: Theory and practice* (9th ed.). Wiley.

Teding van Berkhout, E., & Malouff, J. M. (2016). The efficacy of empathy training: A meta-analysis of randomized controlled trials. *Journal of Counseling Psychology*, *63*(1), 32–41. https://doi.org/10.1037/cou0000093

Thaler, R. H., & Sunstein, C. R. (2008). *Nudge: Improving decisions about health, wealth, and happiness*. Yale University Press.

*Thrasher, A. D., Golin, C. E., Earp, J. A., Tien, H., Porter, C., & Howie, L. (2006). Motivational interviewing to support antiretroviral therapy adherence: The role of quality counseling. *Patient Education and Counseling*, *62*(1), 64–71. https://doi.org/10.1016/j.pec.2005.06.003

*Tollison, S. J., Lee, C. M., Neighbors, C., Neil, T. A., Olson, N. D., & Larimer, M. E. (2008). Questions and reflections: The use of motivational interviewing microskills in a peer-led brief alcohol intervention for college students. *Behavior Therapy*, *39*(2), 183–194. https://doi.org/10.1016/j.beth.2007.07.001

*Tollison, S. J., Mastroleo, N. R., Mallett, K. A., Witkiewitz, K., Lee, C. M., Ray, A. E., & Larimer, M. E. (2013). The relationship between baseline drinking status, peer motivational interviewing microskills, and drinking outcomes in a brief alcohol intervention for matriculating college students: a replication. *Behavior Therapy*, *44*(1), 137–151. https://doi.org/10.1016/j.beth.2012.09.002

*Town, J. M., Hardy, G. E., McCullough, L., & Stride, C. (2012). Patient affect experiencing following therapist interventions in short-term dynamic psychotherapy. *Psychotherapy Research*, *22*(2), 208–219. https://doi.org/10.1080/10503307.2011.637243

*Tryon, G. S. (2003). A therapist's use of verbal response categories in engagement and nonengagement interviews. *Counselling Psychology Quarterly*, *16*(1), 29–36. https://doi.org/10.1080/0951507021000050168

*Villarosa-Hurlocker, M. C., O'Sickey, A. J., Houck, J. M., & Moyers, T. B. (2019). Examining the influence of active ingredients of motivational interviewing on client change talk. *Journal of Substance Abuse Treatment*, *96*, 39–45. https://doi.org/10.1016/j.jsat.2018.10.001

+Voutilainen, L. (2012). Responding to emotion in cognitive psychotherapy. In A. Peräkylä & M.-L. Sorjonen (Eds.), *Emotion in interaction* (pp. 235–255). Oxford University Press.

Voutilainen, L., Henttonen, P., Stevanovic, M., Kahri, M., & Peräkylä, A. (2019). Nods, vocal continuers, and the perception of empathy in storytelling. *Discourse Processes*, *56*(4), 310–330. https://doi.org/10.1080/0163853X.2018.1498670

+Voutilainen, L., Peräkylä, A., & Ruusuvuori, J. (2010). Recognition and interpretation: Responding to emotional experience in psychotherapy. *Research on Language and Social Interaction*, *43*, 85–107. https://doi.org/10.1080/08351810903474799

*Wampold, B. E., & Kim, K.-H. (1989). Sequential analysis applied to counseling process and outcome: A case study revisited. *Journal of Counseling Psychology*, *36*(3), 357–364. https://doi.org/10.1037/0022-0167.36.3.357 [reanalysis of Hill et al., 1983]

*Waskow, I. E. (1962). Reinforcement in a therapy-like situation through selective responding to feelings or content. *Journal of Consulting Psychology*, *26*(1), 11–19. https://doi.org/10.1037/h0039889

Watson, J. C. (2002). Re-visioning empathy. In D. Cain & J. Seeman (Eds.), *Humanistic psychotherapies: Handbook of research and practice* (pp. 445–471). American Psychological Association.

Watson, J. C., & Wiseman, H. (Eds.). (2021). *The responsive psychotherapist: Attuning to clients in the moment*. American Psychological Association.

Weinrach, S. G. (1990). Rogers and Gloria: The controversial film and the enduring relationship. *Psychotherapy*, *27*(2), 282–290. https://doi.org/10.1037/0033-3204.27.2.282

+Weiste, E. (2015). Describing therapeutic projects across sequences: Balancing between supportive and disagreeing interventions. *Journal of Pragmatics*, *80*, 22–43.

+Weiste, E., & Peräkylä, A. (2013). A comparative conversation analytic study of formulations in psychoanalysis and cognitive psychotherapy. *Research on Language and Social Interaction*, *46*, 299–321. https://doi.org/10.1080/08351813.2013.839093

+Weiste, E., & Peräkylä, A. (2014). Prosody and empathic communication in psychotherapy interaction. *Psychotherapy Research*, *24*, 687–701. https://doi.org/10.1080/10503307.2013.879619

+Weiste, E., Voutilainen, L., & Peräkylä, A. (2016). Epistemic asymmetries in psychotherapy interaction: therapists' practices for displaying access to clients' inner experiences. *Sociology of Health & Illness*, *38*, 645–661. https://doi.org/10.1111/1467-9566.12384

Wexler, D. A. (1974). A cognitive theory of experiencing, self-actualization, and therapeutic process. In D. A. Wexler & L. N. Rice (Eds.), *Innovations of client-centered therapy* (pp. 49–116). Wiley.

Wilson, D. B. (2021). *SPSS meta-analysis macro* [Computer software]. http://mason.gmu.edu/~dwilsonb/MetaAnal.html

*Wiser, S., & Goldfried, M. R. (1998). Therapist interventions and client emotional experiencing in expert psychodynamic–interpersonal and cognitive–behavioral therapies. *Journal of Consulting & Clinical Psychology*, *66*(4), 634–640. https://doi.org/10.1037/0022-006X.66.4.634

+Wu, Y. (2019). Empathy in psychotherapy: Using conversation analysis to explore the therapists' empathic interaction with clients. *Southern African Linguistics & Applied Language Studies*, *37*(3), 232–246. https://doi.org/10.2989/16073614.2019.1671881

+Wynn, R., & Wynn, M. (2006). Empathy as an interactionally achieved phenomenon in psychotherapy: Characteristics of some conversational resources. *Journal of Pragmatics*, *38*(9), 1385–1397. https://doi.org/10.1016/j.pragma.2005.09.008

6
Metaphors

Linda M. McMullen and Dennis Tay

Metaphors are ubiquitous in everyday talk. Most often, these nonliteral expressions have become such a common way of speaking that we no longer recognize them as metaphorical. For example, in English we routinely speak of *the legs of a chair*, of *a hot tip*, and as *not seeing the forest for the trees*. Those who are familiar with such phrases understand that a chair does not literally have legs as humans and animals do, that a tip cannot literally register a temperature, and that we are not actually speaking of trees and forests when referring to a focus on parts and wholes.

On some occasions, speakers introduce new expressions that can expand the listener's way of thinking and understanding. For example, as a way of capturing the fragility of living, one might describe one's life as *a thread ready to break*. Such fresh expressions often stand out for the listener and can demand more attention in order to unravel and flesh out the range of meanings.

Psychotherapy has been described as "the talking cure," so it is perhaps not surprising that much has been said about the use of metaphor as a facilitator of client change. In this chapter, we focus on varied uses of metaphor in individual psychotherapy and review the research evidence on their effectiveness. We consider such questions as "How might a therapist introduce a metaphor into a session with a client?" and "Do metaphors matter in terms of client in-session and end-of-therapy outcomes?" We conclude by advancing research-informed diversity considerations, training implications, and therapeutic practices.

Definitions

Metaphor has been defined in a variety of nuanced ways. A standard dictionary definition is "the application of a word or phrase to something that it does not apply to literally, in order to indicate a comparison with the literal usage" (*Oxford Paperback Dictionary*, 1994, p. 506). In this case, metaphor's distinction from, and comparison with, the literal is highlighted. Other definitions highlight comparison, as in "understanding and experiencing one kind of thing in terms of another" (Lakoff & Johnson, 1980, p. 5) or "describing and potentially thinking about something in terms of something else" (Semino, 2008, p. 2). Still other definitions of metaphor explicitly invoke relations between different domains, as in "a linguistic expression using words from a *source* domain to talk and refer to something different in a *target* domain" (Gelo & Mergenthaler, 2012, p. 159). Here, the target refers to the concept being described (e.g., a chair or a tip), and the source to the conceptual knowledge that structures our

Linda M. McMullen and Dennis Tay, *Metaphors* In: *Psychotherapy Skills and Methods That Work*. Edited by: Clara E. Hill and John C. Norcross, Oxford University Press. © Clara E. Hill and John C. Norcross 2023. DOI: 10.1093/oso/9780197611012.003.0006 understanding of the target (e.g., the human body or temperature; Tay, 2016a). What is common to these definitions is the notion of using language flexibly.

Beyond these generic definitions, other distinctions have been proposed in the context of metaphor use in psychotherapy. Much has been made of the distinction between what are called conventional, frozen, or dead metaphors and what are called nonconventional, novel, or living metaphors. The former are used without effort to talk about common things and which, through constant use, have lost any sense of the original image and have given up any association to anything other than the literal meaning which we now ascribe to them. The latter metaphors are originally created or newly minted and which can surprise us into new awareness (Bayne & Thompson, 2000; Gelo & Mergenthaler, 2012). It is these that have often been proposed as most important for the tasks of therapy.

Key metaphors have also been distinguished in the therapy literature (Siegelman, 1990). These expressions are often metaphors for the self or whole person (Long & Lepper, 2008), as in *I'm fragmented or broken*, and are thought to encapsulate important themes and to serve as markers of change. Therapists and clients can, then, use such metaphors to chart the course and progress of therapy.

Metaphor in the context of psychotherapy has also been used synonymously with the more inclusive category of figurative language (e.g., analogies, similes, idioms, puns, allegories, anecdotes, narratives) and with the employment of various literary and artistic forms and practices (e.g., tasks, objects, artistic creations) during therapy. Such extensions of the term, again, underscore the significance of going beyond literal language—and even beyond language itself—as a way of engaging the client in new ways of experiencing. Even key therapeutic processes, such as transference, have been conceptualized as metaphoric. In this case, the focus is not so much on the therapist's (or client's) use of metaphor as a discursive device but, rather, on the benefits of understanding such processes in novel ways (Tay, 2016b).

Stock metaphors also appear in the literature on metaphor in psychotherapy. In this case, what are considered standard source concepts have been prepared and mapped beforehand onto corresponding concepts, which therapists can use prescriptively (Blenkiron, 2010; Stott et al., 2010). For example, a therapist might advise an anorexic client that trying to live with anorexia is like trying to drive a car without gas (Stott et al., 2010). In addition, metaphors have been proposed as a way of structuring therapy, itself, and as a form of therapy, as in externalizing metaphors therapy (McGuinty et al., 2014).

Recognition of the potential utility of metaphor in psychotherapy is evident in the ubiquity with which it is conceptualized in multiple therapeutic approaches. For example, metaphors are discussed in psychoanalysis and other depth therapies (Kopp, 1995; Siegelman, 1990); Ericksonian approaches (Close, 1998; Combs & Freedman, 1990); cognitive–behavioral approaches (Muran & DiGiuseppe, 1990); process–experiential therapy; and embodied, relational-centered therapy (Finlay, 2015).

For example, in psychoanalysis, metaphors are thought to symbolically encapsulate a person's problems (Dwairy, 2009), character structure, defenses, and unconscious fantasies (Forrest, 1973). Because the client's use of metaphor is considered to be derived, via association, from the client's unconscious, these metaphors are theorized as providing important insights around which therapists can structure their interpretations (Long & Lepper, 2008). Other theorists in the depth tradition (e.g., Kopp, 1995;

Siegelman, 1990) have emphasized metaphor's power for communicating and working with emotions and other sensorimotor states. A client's communication of strong affect via metaphor (e.g., *I stab people with my voice*) is conceptualized as possibly signaling material that is actively defended against or difficult for the client to verbalize in literal language. It can also provide the therapist with a point of entry for deepening the client's exploring of the meaning of the metaphor, experiencing of affect, and gaining of insight.

In contrast, cognitive theorists propose metaphor as a heuristic and epistemic device (Muran & DiGiuseppe, 1990) that can alter clients' unhelpful ways of thinking (negative schemas). In cognitive–behavioral approaches, the meaning of a metaphor is often made more explicit than in depth or Ericksonian practices and is usually deconstructed to maximize the possibility of making a particular point (Blenkiron, 2005). Some advocates of cognitive–behavioral therapy promote a collaborative approach to metaphor in which therapists pay particular attention to clients' metaphors; use Socratic questioning to open up these metaphors; and engage in back-and-forth exchanges in which the client and the therapist incorporate, extend, and alter each other's metaphors (Mathieson et al., 2015; Stoddard & Afari, 2014). Metaphors are thought to assist the client and the therapist in identifying problematic ways of thinking, enable the client to develop new perspectives, aid in the development of tasks, and forge a common therapy language.

Other practitioners have focused more centrally on the embodied sensations of metaphor for how they make sense of their clients' worlds. As illustrated through case studies of relational-centered therapy, metaphors may engage different senses in multiple ways (Finlay, 2015). Similarly, engagement of diverse senses is theorized as occurring through nonverbal, metaphoric communications in the form of therapy tasks (e.g., see case studies by Hamburg, 2017).

Clinical Description and Indications

One option available to psychotherapists is the creation of their own metaphors. They can choose to fashion metaphors spontaneously or deliberately in their work with clients. For example, they can rely on what they consider to be a particularly apt stock metaphor (Blenkiron, 2005) or can employ novel metaphors (e.g., allegories) that can enable the client to work out new ways of thinking, feeling, being, and acting. Alternatively, they can respond with a metaphor of their own that is isomorphic to the client's metaphor in order to reframe the problem.

However, some of the most detailed documentation and development of therapists' use of metaphor has focused on what therapists do when they take up a metaphor—often a metaphor introduced by the client—in the course of therapy. The first step is that the therapist must notice or identify a word or phrase as metaphoric. This act might be easier for some therapists than for others, and for some metaphors than others. That is, some therapists might easily hear even a conventional metaphor as metaphoric, whereas others might not notice a novel metaphoric word or expression. The second step is for the therapist to decide whether to take up a particular metaphor. We know little about how such decisions are made, although we might speculate that those metaphors deemed relevant to, for example, the client's sense of self, ways of being with others, and the major themes or tasks of therapy could be ones that become the focus of a therapist's attention.

Having heard a word or phrase as metaphoric and having decided to take it up, the therapist must then decide *how* to take it up. Options include ratification—that is, repeating the metaphor vehicle by using the same or similar words; commenting on the use of the word or phrase; or using an associated word in later therapeutic talk. For example, to a client who describes their vitality and youthfulness as *a fountain that constantly gives freshness*, a therapist might respond, "Ah, *fountain, fountain, fountain*, good description! Are those bad feelings far away from us now?" Such a move can sometimes be sufficient to draw the client's attention to the metaphor and to encourage further development of it.

Rephrasing of the metaphor vehicle using a synonym, a different metaphor, or simple metaphorical expansion via an associated word or phrase is another option. For example, in response to a client who says "I put up *a mirror* and people interact and *see what they want to see* in me. That I'm behind that *mirror* and they never really *see* me," the following exchange between the therapist (T) and the client (C) might occur:

T: They *see certain aspects of you.*

C: Yeah. When I use the word "mirror," I mean I *reflect* what they want to *see* so therefore . . .

T: You *show them the parts of you that fit them* but they're *looking* for it.

In this exchange, the therapist initially expands the metaphor of the mirror by focusing on the viewer's perspective, which is followed by a further back-and-forth clarification and elaboration of the metaphor from the perspective of the client.

Occasionally, a therapist might choose to clarify the meaning of a metaphor to create a shared understanding. In this case, the response to a client's metaphor does not have to include metaphoric language. For example, a client might say, "Maybe everything I do is quite immature. Like a *small tree*, or a *seedling*. Maybe everyone else is a *big tree* but I am just a *seedling*," to which a therapist could reply, "Okay. What do you think the *seedling* is like?"

Another option is to explicate what is implicit in the metaphor (Mathieson et al., 2015; Strong, 1989). In this case, the therapist works to draw out the unstated features of the metaphoric image (the source domain) so that the comparisons to, and implications for, the client's present life (the target domain) can be explicitly fleshed out. This work can be achieved through reflective listening, focusing on the words themselves, and helping the client stay with their experience. For example, a client might metaphorically characterize instances of emotional instability as "[talking with people] *takes my mind away* from what I'm doing"; "from one song on the radio to the next, my mood *shifts*, sometime almost *180 degrees*"; "like a *feather in a rapid stream*"; and "the more I concentrate on them [her emotions], the more likely I am to *force them to move rapidly in one direction or another*." In an attempt to draw out one unstated commonality in these metaphors, a therapist might respond, "Now there's something frightening about being so vulnerable to being affected by *outside things*. Like talking to somebody else or a song *shifting* you." In this example, the metaphor of *outside things* can serve as a possible connector between what might be seen as diverse metaphor source domains.

Modifying, extending, and elaborating a particularly salient metaphor are additional ways in which a therapist can work with a client's metaphor. For example, a therapist might engage the client in building up the metaphoric image (Kopp & Craw, 1998), in playing with possibilities, in weaving a web of correspondences, in teasing out additional dimensions and ramifications (Ferrara, 1994), in marking and selecting parts of the metaphor for in-depth expansion, and in connecting with the current situation and making connections to the future (Sims, 2003). Such work can be collaborative in that both the client and the therapist take up and work the metaphor, typically through the combined use of literal and metaphoric language.

Little has been said about the lack of a therapist's response to a metaphor in psychotherapy. Consider three possible "non" responses to metaphors and the reasons that might account for the relative absence of attention to such responses in the literature. First, a therapist might not notice or recognize a word or phrase as metaphoric, particularly if it is a conventional metaphor that is commonly used, such as *I feel down*, and this lack of recognition might not be considered consequential for the course of therapy. Second, a therapist might comprehend a word or phrase as metaphoric but deliberately decide not to comment on it. At present, we know little about such decisions. Third, a therapist might comprehend a word or phrase as metaphoric, provide no immediate response to it, but make a note of it for future reference and possible use (Bayne & Thompson, 2000). Again, we know little about these decisions and possible future actions. We draw attention to these categories of responses to foreshadow notions to which we will return, specifically that some therapists might benefit from training in how to recognize and respond to client metaphors; that some conventional metaphors can, on occasion, be opened up in productive ways; and that research that attempts to unpack clients' and therapists' reactions to and decisions about metaphor use over a course of therapy might prove informative.

Other response categories identified in the literature, but about which little has been said, include failure to comprehend or understand the point of a client's metaphor (Ferrara, 1994), therapists' use of explicit praise of or agreement with a metaphor (Mathieson et al., 2015), and therapists' rejection of a client's metaphor (Tay, 2021). Any of these moves could constitute opportunities for productive therapeutic engagement or moments of rupture. Again, we highlight them in order to reinforce the point that not all therapists' uses of metaphor can be neatly packaged into what might be taken at face value as productive engagement.

Little is known about the specific client characteristics, in-session markers, and clinical circumstances for which therapists' use of metaphor is indicated or contraindicated. The few studies in which this topic is addressed are based on speculative connections to client diagnoses, such as psychosis and borderline personality disorder. In a systematic review of the use of metaphor for understanding and managing psychotic experiences, none of the studies empirically measured the helpfulness of metaphors (Mould et al., 2010). Similarly, a study on the use of metaphor in psychodynamic psychotherapy with clients labeled "borderline" or "non-borderline" focused on the type of symbolic processing adopted by the clients and concluded that the so-called borderline clients adopted a literal mode of symbolic processing (a concrete, here-and-now level) while so-called non-borderline clients adopted a representational mode of symbolic processing (a shifting between concrete and symbolic aspects in which meaning was collaboratively developed; Rasmussen & Angus, 1996). No conclusions on the relation of such modes of symbolic processing and therapy outcome were drawn.

Assessment

In the context of research studies, therapists' use of metaphor is typically assessed through the judgment of external observers/raters who have been trained to identify metaphors and possibly to distinguish between novel and conventional forms. Several training manuals are available to identify metaphors (e.g., Barlow et al., 1971; Gelo, 2008). Typically, these manuals focus on introducing raters to what constitutes a metaphor (or figurative language more generally), engaging with a potential source of data (e.g., reading transcripts of psychotherapy sessions to develop an initial sense of the sessions; detailed re-reading of the same transcripts to identify metaphoric words or sequences), distinguishing novel from conventional expressions, and reaching consensus on the presence of a metaphor if multiple raters are used.

Metaphor identification procedures are also available from the related field of linguistics [e.g., Pragglejaz Group's (2007) metaphor identification procedure; Cameron and Maslen's (2010) discourse dynamics approach]. These are not uniquely focused on psychotherapy language but tend to have more stringent linguistic criteria, such as what constitutes a word/clause, and the use of dictionaries to determine whether meanings in context deviate from their basic meanings. As far as practicable, we advise researchers to consider making use of both—the former for its specific attention to therapeutic factors and the latter for greater sensitivity to linguistic forms and structures (see Tay, 2017).

Although the quality of therapists' use of metaphor is not typically assessed, whether and how therapists initiate or take up a metaphor are most often the focus in research studies. Frequency counts of therapists' use of metaphor, often in relation to the frequency of clients' use of metaphor, have been used as a simple indication of who in the therapeutic dyad is engaging in greater or lesser use of metaphor.

What a therapist does with a metaphor (their own or those produced by the client) can be coded using the response categories detailed in the section on Clinical Description and Indications (e.g., constructing a novel metaphor; repeating, clarifying, elaborating a client's metaphor; no response; Mathieson et al., 2015; Strong, 1989) and/or can be interpreted by a researcher or by the therapist who conducted the psychotherapy. Such interpretations typically consist of detailed qualitative accounts. In these accounts, metaphoric expressions or sequences of metaphor are excerpted from transcripts of psychotherapy sessions. Researchers typically connect the expressions or sequences with an interpretation of what is occurring and possibly being accomplished in the client–therapist interaction at the moment of metaphor use. Therapists' assessment of their own use of metaphor can consist of retrospective narrative accounts of, for example, what they were thinking, intending, feeling, sensing, and doing when using a metaphor. The construction of such accounts sometimes occurs through post-session inquiry interviews or interpersonal process recall (Kagan, 1975). Similar assessments of what clients have to say about their therapists' use of metaphor can also be determined through such interviews and recall processes. Here, the focus is typically on what clients were thinking, feeling, or otherwise experiencing during the therapists' and their own metaphoric segments in the moment the segment was occurring and/or upon later reflection.

Immediate, Within-Session Outcomes and Delayed, Immediate Post-Session Outcomes

Attempts to connect therapists' metaphors to immediate within-session client responses have typically focused on affective experiencing and cognitive engagement. Affective experiencing can be assessed with standardized scales (e.g., the Experiencing Scale; Klein et al., 1986), client self-reports of subjective experiencing, client use of emotionally toned words, or third-party observations and interpretations either during the client's subsequent use of the therapist's metaphor or during the client's use of their own metaphor, or via literal language.

Client cognitive engagement has also been used to assess responses to therapists' use of metaphor. Specific responses have included the expression of insight as judged by external raters (Barlow et al., 1977) and cognitive mastery as evidenced by the use of abstract nouns (Gelo & Mergenthaler, 2012). It is not uncommon, however, for cognitive engagement to be paired with emotional regulation as an in-session marker of client responses. Examples include the notion of mentalization, defined as "a sophisticated kind of affective regulation involving self-reflection and interest in one's mind" (Long & Lepper, 2008, p. 346).

Whether and how clients and therapists work together to co-construct metaphors is another potential within-session or across-session outcome of interest. Here, the focus is on key metaphors—those that encapsulate central themes of the therapy—and on metaphor change talk that often consists of entailments that cohere around a conceptual metaphor such as CHANGE AS A JOURNEY (Sarpavaara & Koski-Jännes, 2013). What matters with co-constructed metaphoric sequences is not who initiated the metaphor but, rather, that a therapist-initiated metaphor is taken up and worked by the client, and a client-initiated metaphor is taken up and worked by the therapist. However, co-construction of a metaphor, in and of itself, does not necessarily indicate a productive process (Mathieson et al., 2015); rather, it is how the metaphor is worked that matters. In the case of metaphor change talk, it is possible for such talk to be used, for example, to capture the consolidation of accomplishments reached by the client and therapist, optimism about facing life after therapy, and the reality of confronting new challenges in life (Råbu et al., 2013). Assessing whether and the extent to which co-construction of a metaphor signifies a productive process is typically achieved through the use of post-session inquiry interviews with clients and therapists as well as through the tracking of metaphor use over time.

Distal, End-of-Treatment Outcomes

End-of-treatment client outcomes in metaphor research are typically assessed through standard outcome measures. These measures have included (a) self-reported assessments relevant to the client's distress (e.g., measures of dysphoria), (b) ratings of target complaints, (c) assessment of the client–therapist relationship or working alliance, (d) global change ratings or assessment of functioning, (e) behavioral changes, and (f) clients' and therapists' post-therapy assessments of the therapy experience.

Although such measures have been useful for assessing therapeutic change, tying such assessments to a therapist's use of metaphor has been elusive and has led to the conclusion that a simple relation between such measures and the use of metaphor is unlikely to exist (McMullen, 1989). Currently, the best clinical evidence of a link between therapists' use of metaphor and end-of-treatment outcomes is probably its spontaneous construction by clients—that is, the unprompted disclosure of the significance and helpfulness of such use.

Clinical Examples

The following examples, extracted from transcripts of real psychotherapy sessions with actual clients, illustrate a few of the ways psychotherapists use metaphors. Italicized portions accentuate the metaphors.

Therapist's Spontaneous Use of Metaphors

In this example, the therapist (T; female, American, aged 31–40 years), speaking to her international student client (C; female, Portuguese, aged 21–30 years), spontaneously uses and elaborates a bomb disposal metaphor to illustrate the high, and perhaps unrealistic, expectations that are causing anxiety for the client.

T: I think it's the expectation and the demands that may cause you anxiety. Like being in that school in [name of country] then being sent here, knowing that your company sent you—and what would it look like if you returned back home? Would you be a failure? You know, here you are, you're [with them], wanted them for your school—and you have all these other smart folks around you. And you're not the same star that you were back in your country. And you're afraid the same thing may happen that happened in [name of country].

C: Yeah.

T: So with those things in the background, why wouldn't someone be anxious about an exam or about material or whatever the case is? If you have this huge—you know, it's kind of like even an example—and we have to begin wrapping up. But like—you know, like *a person—the people who have to disbomb bombs*? You know—I forget what they call them, but *if a building even called, the bomb squad comes in*, right? And it's *one person who has to realize—figure out which wires to disconnect*. And *you see the clock—it's ticking* and it's *down to three seconds or whatever*, and *you've got to figure out which wire to pull*.

C: Mm hmm.

T: And they know that if they don't get the—*if they don't pull the right cord, the whole building—the whole city's going to be bombed and everything. That's a lot of pressure*, right? And so that can be—if that person had so much anxiety at that point to say,

"Uh, I can't do this." You know—whereas the bomb trainers—thankfully, they're not like that, you know? They can *think under pressure and put that anxiety aside and not think about all of this stuff when they're doing that*, right? So if you have *all this pressure behind you, in the background, when you take a test or you sit down and read something, that can affect your performance as well.*

Despite the spontaneous nature of the above metaphor, the therapist articulates the correspondences between source and target elements in a way that has the potential to benefit the client's understanding of her situation. The client responds intermittently with markers of understanding and affirmation ("Mm hmm," "yeah"), possibly indicating her appreciation of the spontaneous metaphor.

Therapist Extending a Client's Metaphor

In this example, the client (male, American, aged 31–40 years) spontaneously characterizes thinking about negative emotions as a process involving physical space and movement, *wandering around* and *going down* to a lower place.

C: As I kind of *go down each step* I can see it. And I can see how like it negates who I do it to, too. You know, how it's like this insult when I start seeing you as this somebody I need to have to have care for me and be, like and be my friend, right, you know? You just, you can't be [name of friend]. You have to be my friend otherwise therapy isn't successful or then it's just blah, blah, blah, you know? I think well I have to keep—I have to greet you, [name of friend]. *Get more space*, too. It seems like that's part of it. And you start goofing *the center of where you are*, so you have to *go wandering around* for it more.

T: Yeah.

C: *I almost don't want to go down there.* You know, there's something in me that's released and I keep on getting ideas about, and *instead of going really down . . .*

T: Yeah.

C: Because . . .

T: Yeah. Maybe you ought to *come back up for a moment and* sort of *walk your way back up the steps for a minute* because, and sort of *feel the reversal* too, before you go completely.

C: I don't know. It's like people can feel when there isn't self-concern and they're scared of it, you know? Because I know . . . when the *shit hits the fan*, unless you take care of yourself nobody really is going to. So if they like find this person whose energy is getting all gone out there and they get, you know . . .

T: Yeah. Yeah. Like you're seeing, you're getting some kind of clearer sense of how you seem to other people *in the dark*.

C: Yeah. Yeah, I'm really feeling, I'm just getting, I mean I'm only saying one-tenth of the flashes I'm getting.

The therapist (male, American, aged 31–40 years) appears to recognize the inferential potential of this metaphor and extends the idea of downward movement by suggesting the client *come back up for a moment*. In doing so, a metaphorically framed course of action is offered to the client.

Therapist Changing a Client's Metaphor

Here, the client (male, New Zealander, aged 41–50 years) produces a spontaneous metaphor of a *diversion device* that is used to *block out* rumination.

T: Ok. That's where you started. What happened to your thoughts? How did your thoughts get going? How did the rumination get going?
C: Actually, um, they just appeared.
T: Mmhmm. Yep. And what did you do with them once they appeared?
C: Again, I tried to *block them out* with my *attention diversion device*.
T: Yeah. And what happened when you *blocked it out*?
C: I spend all the time, um, *rotating between the device and the rumination*.
T: Rumination. *I have this mental image of you kind of fighting. You come up to you and you can put your shield up.*

Although the initial exchanges recognize and stay with this metaphor, the therapist (female, New Zealander, aged 41–50 years) switches to a minimally related metaphor of the client *fighting* and *putting up a shield* against the rumination, perhaps in an attempt to make the metaphor more realistic and grounded in actual physical experience. The client appears to accept this change of metaphor as the next few turns focus on a more literal description of how he physically struggles with the discomfort and loss of sleep.

Therapist's Use of Stock or Prepared Metaphors

In this session, which is near the beginning of treatment, the therapist (female, New Zealander, aged 41–50 years) is explaining to the client (male, New Zealander, aged 41–50 years) how rumination is understood within that therapy approach. As a way of providing the client with an explanatory tool, the therapist communicates a prepared metaphor, in the form of a well-structured analogy that depicts thoughts as misbehaving children on a school bus.

T: And this is the other one that I quite like. So, *there's a school bus and you are the driver. On this bus we have a bunch of school kids. The bus represents the direction you are taking in your life, and the school kids represents thoughts, feelings, bodily states, memories, other aspects and experience*. What happens is that *you're driving along and the school kids start calling out to you telling you what you have to do and where you have to go. So you have to make a left turn, you've got to make a turn right, you've got to speed up, got to slow down. They start calling you names, they start threatening you. Sometimes they even start throwing things at you. Even though the school kids are unpleasant, annoying, distracting, they don't actually hurt you. The trick is to keep on driving the bus in the direction you want despite the antics of the school kids in the back. Accept the noisy school kids as just being something that comes with being a bus driving and eventually they get tired and stop misbehaving. So, identifying there if you've got all this distracting, horrible, negative stuff at the back of the bus my job is to just keep on driving my bus and keep going in the direction I want.*

C: Ignore them and they will go away.

T: Ignore them and they will go away. So are these analogies helping kind of explain where we are going?

C: Yeah.

The stock nature of the metaphor is explicitly indicated by the therapist at the beginning of this segment ("this is the other one that I quite like"). The client responds by proactively summarizing the gist of the analogy ("Ignore them and they will go away") and indicates that the analogy is helpful in explaining and preparing him for the therapy approach.

Landmark Studies and Previous Reviews

Two metaphor studies with the highest impact, as measured by citation counts, are Angus and Rennie (1988) and Martin et al. (1992). Differences in research questions, designs, and outcomes between these two studies underscore the diversity of research in this area.

Angus and Rennie (1988) aimed to "discover and describe how therapists and clients construct, express, and apprehend metaphors" (p. 553). The study was qualitative in design and involved the analysis of sequences of repeated use of metaphor in one session for each of four pairs of therapists and clients (a total of five client-generated and six therapist-generated metaphors), coupled with verbal accounts of subjective experiencing by the clients and therapists via post-session inquiry interviews. The researchers prepared summaries of moment-by-moment accounts from the clients' and therapists' post-session recalled experiences during each metaphoric interchange, together with observations of the inquiry interviewer/researcher. These summaries were then combined with descriptions of the characteristics or properties of each metaphoric expression and sorted into themes. One set of relations among the themes was characterized by two patterns of metaphoric communication that were illustrated with excerpts of therapy talk. One pattern was labeled *meaning conjunction* and was described as "a discovery-oriented, collaborative process associated with a mutually shared understanding of the meaning of a metaphor" (p. 552). The other pattern was labeled *meaning disjunction* and described as "a noncollaborative process of meaning derivation frequently associated with a joint misunderstanding of the meaning of a metaphor" (p. 552). This study showed that an in-depth qualitative analysis of how therapists and clients used metaphors in-session provided evidence of both productive and not-so-productive processes.

In contrast, Martin et al. (1992) conducted a study designed to address questions on the memorability and helpfulness of therapists' metaphors. Three therapists, who were trained in the intentional use of metaphor, engaged with four clients for a total of 41 sessions of experiential psychotherapy. Clients and therapists completed the Episodic Memory Questionnaire after each session and rated the helpfulness of each session. Results indicated that clients recalled therapists' intentional metaphors approximately two-thirds of the time, and that in almost all of these instances the metaphors recalled by the clients were initiated or developed through a collaborative participation of both partners, a finding that builds on one of the patterns described by Angus and Rennie (1988). In addition, clients rated sessions from which they recalled therapists' metaphors as more helpful than sessions from which they recalled events other than therapists' intentional use of metaphor.

Participants' responses were interpreted by the researchers as suggesting that these metaphors served the therapeutic functions of (a) enhancing emotional awareness and understanding and (b) conceptual "bridging," and the motivational functions of (a) enhanced relationship with the therapist and (b) goal clarification. However, due to the small number of dyads, the high educational level of the clients, and the single theoretical orientation of the therapists, the researchers cautioned against interpreting their findings as more than exploratory and suggestive.

A 2008 review of the research literature on the use of metaphor in psychotherapy (McMullen, 2008) yielded few solid conclusions to formulate practice recommendations. For example, the frequency of use, even of novel metaphors, was not found to be consistently related to outcome. Similarly, metaphoric communication between clients and therapists was not consistently found to be a marker of productive therapy processes. Of more promise was the potential for specific metaphors to capture the central themes of psychotherapy in a particular case and to serve as markers of change. The difficulty in drawing conclusions and formulating recommendations from this literature was attributed, in part, to the absence of replication and little use of common research strategies across studies and, in part, to the lack of sufficient attention to the highly contextualized nature of metaphor. McMullen called for a more contextualized research approach in which the use of metaphors is analyzed over time and in which the analysis includes other cues (e.g., emphases, intonation, crying) that figure into how the metaphor is received.

Research Review

In this review, we limited our selection of studies to those in which psychotherapists' use of metaphor was specifically linked to client outcomes, either within-session or end-of-treatment. Using the key phrases "figurative language in psychotherapy" and "therapists' use of metaphor in psychotherapy," we searched PsycInfo and Google Scholar for relevant articles. To this initial list, we added other sources of which we were knowledgeable from our work on the topic. Our initial list comprised 65 articles, books, and chapters. We excluded sources that were non-empirical or reviews, were focused only on clients' use of metaphor, or did not investigate therapists' use of metaphor in relation to client outcomes. In the end, 14 studies remained.

Table 6.1 presents the 14 studies and their characteristics. These studies, in total, encompass 47 therapists and 101 clients.

Because of the small number of both qualitative and quantitative studies, it was not possible to conduct either a meta-synthesis or a meta-analysis; rather, we opted for a box score analysis. Box scores for each outcome in each of the 14 studies were initially assigned by the first author (LM) and subsequently verified by the second author (DT).

Table 6.1 Studies of Immediate and Distal Treatment Outcomes of Psychotherapists' Use of Metaphor

Study	Sample	Focus of Analysis and Measures of Outcome	Results
		Immediate Outcomes	
Pollio & Barlow (1975)	1 hour of 1 case of successful Gestalt therapy with a 38-year-old woman and a male therapist	Novel vs. frozen instances of figurative language Immediate outcome: Client problem-setting and problem-solving as interpreted by the researchers in the context of figurative themes produced by the client	Client's use of novel figures tended to occur in bursts and was associated with problem-setting/solving; therapist encouraged client to respond in general, then focused on specific areas to be discussed metaphorically, and finally helped the client out of the metaphor and back to the demands of real life. Box score: 1 positive
Barlow et al. (1977)	1 session of psychotherapy with (1) a male client and (2) a female client	(1) Novel figurative language; (2) Novel and frozen instances of figurative language Immediate outcome: Regions of therapeutic insight, as (1) qualitatively interpreted by researchers or (2) coded by trained judges from transcripts and quantitatively analyzed	(1) Therapist and client repeatedly used, responded to, and built upon each other's metaphors; co-occurrence of metaphoric language and insight; (2) one pattern in which novel figurative language tended to co-occur significantly with regions of insight and a second pattern in which literal statements expressing insight followed upon high frequency of novel metaphors, which in turn triggered new bursts of metaphoric activity. Box score: 1 positive
Angus & Rennie (1988)	1 session of therapy with each of 4 clients (3 women and 1 man); 4 male therapists with varying years of experience and theoretical orientations	Five client-generated and 6 therapist-generated metaphoric sequences selected across the 4 sessions Immediate outcome: Verbal reports of subjective experiencing by each client and therapist based on post-session audiotape review of the metaphoric sequences, coupled with observations of the researcher	Two dyads engaged in a discovery-oriented, collaborative process associated with the development of a mutually shared understanding of the meaning of a metaphor; 2 dyads engaged in a noncollaborative process that was associated with a joint misunderstanding of the meaning of a metaphor. Box scores: 1 positive, 1 negative

Hill & Regan (1991)	Single case of brief psychotherapy with a female client and a male therapist based in a combination of Gestalt, Rogerian, and cognitive approaches	Therapist's use of metaphors and self-rated intentions to encourage insight on the part of the client and to provide support Immediate outcome: Client ratings of therapist interventions	Therapist's use of metaphors co-occurred with his self-rated intention to encourage insight; therapist interventions involving metaphors rated as more helpful by client than other interventions. Box scores: 2 positive
Martin et al. (1992)	41 sessions of experiential psychotherapy across 4 client–therapist dyads	Therapists' reports of any metaphors they attempted to initiate and/or develop intentionally in each session Immediate outcome: Clients' and therapists' post-session responses on the Episodic Memory Questionnaire; clients' and therapists' ratings of session helpfulness on a 5-point scale	Clients rated sessions in which they recalled therapists' intentional use of metaphor as more helpful than sessions in which they recalled other therapeutic events. Box score: 1 positive
Rasmussen & Angus (1996)	1 session from each of 4 client–therapist dyads; 2 clients (ages 24 and 38 years) were described as "non-borderline" and 2 (ages 27 and 29 years) as "borderline"; 2 therapists (1 psychodynamically oriented and 1 psychoanalytically oriented) were treating one client from each category	Metaphoric segments that seemed to convey important aspects of the session as judged by the researcher Immediate outcome: Clients' and therapists' reports of what they were thinking/feeling/experiencing during the metaphoric segments and upon reflection of the playback of the segment during post-session open-ended interviews Moderator: Diagnostic label assigned to client	Metaphors were part of either a symbolic (representational) mode of interaction in which their meanings were negotiated by the client and the therapist and contributed to a shared therapy vocabulary or a literal mode of interaction in which negotiated meanings and a shared therapy vocabulary were absent. Dyads with a non-borderline client were characterized by a symbolic mode of interaction, whereas dyads with a borderline client were characterized by a literal mode of interaction. Box scores: 1 positive, 1 negative

(*continued*)

Table 6.1 Continued

Study	Sample	Focus of Analysis and Measures of Outcome	Results
Rasmussen (2000)	Same data as in Rasmussen & Angus (1996)	One therapist metaphor segment selected from each of the 4 sessions Immediate outcome: Clients' and therapists' reports of what they were thinking/feeling/experiencing during the metaphoric segment and upon reflection of the playback of the segment during post-session open-ended interviews Moderator: Diagnostic label assigned to client	One successful resonance of therapist's metaphor with a non-borderline client's experience. Three unsuccessful results: Therapist's metaphor misunderstood by one non-borderline client; therapist's metaphor with each of the 2 borderline clients appeared to be empathic failures. Box score: 1 negative
Long & Lepper (2008)	1 transcript from an early, middle, and late session of psychoanalytic therapy with 4 clients (2 women and 2 men aged 32–61 years; 3 with clinically significant improvement), all with the same therapist	All instances of figurative language, including key, novel, and conventional figures Immediate outcome: Mentalizing exchanges between client and therapist (therapist doing or facilitating affective regulation involving self-reflection and interest in one's mind for the client)	Significantly more instances of figurative language (and of novel figurative language) in mentalizing exchanges than in non-mentalizing exchanges; this pattern was particularly marked for the 2 clients showing the most clinical improvement. Box score: 1 positive
Gelo & Mergenthaler (2012)	42 sessions (1st year of treatment) of metacognitive interpersonal therapy with an Italian woman aged 25 years	Unconventional metaphors as identified by trained raters Immediate outcome: 4 patterns of emotional–cognitive regulation formed by combinations of emotionally toned words (ET) and abstract nouns (AB): relaxing (low ET, low AB), reflecting (low ET, high AB), experiencing (high ET, low AB), and connecting (high ET, high AB); phases of therapeutic engagement as defined by the therapeutic cycles model	Dyad results: Significantly more metaphors in moments of connecting and significantly fewer during moments of relaxing compared with other patterns; significantly more metaphors in moments of reflecting and significantly fewer during experiencing compared with other patterns; significantly more metaphors in phases characterized by therapeutic engagement. Box score: 1 positive

		End-of-Treatment Outcomes	
Amira (1983)	10 cases (all male clients aged 18–22 years); 1 successful and 1 unsuccessful case treated by each of 5 therapists (2 humanistically oriented and 3 analytically oriented)	Rate of production and frequency of instances of novel figurative language End-of-treatment outcomes: Global change ratings by clients, therapists, and independent clinicians on a scale from −5 to +5; changes between pre- and post-therapy scores on MMPI depression, psychasthenia, and social introversion scales	Measures of novel figurative language failed to discriminate between high- and low-change patients, therapists, or dyads. Box score: 1 neutral
McMullen (1985)	1 case of significant improvement (woman, aged 41 years) and 1 case of minimal improvement (woman, aged 27 years), each treated by a male therapist	Instances of novel figurative language from 15-minute segments from the first two, median two, and last two available sessions from each case End-of-treatment outcome: Determined by an external judge on the basis of therapists' descriptions of the course of therapy and their judgments of the overall degree of improvement made by the client	Significant improvement case: Content of client's novel figures related to troubling experiences and problems; client repeated figures originally used by the therapist; significantly more instances of client's figures were followed by therapist's use of such language. Minimal improvement case: Content of client's novel figures focused on external circumstances; therapist responded less often to client's novel figures. Box score: 1 positive
McMullen (1989)	1 successful and 1 unsuccessful case (all men) treated by each of 3 therapists (all men) in short-term, psychodynamically oriented therapy	Repeated instances of novel and conventional figurative language used in the expression of major therapy themes plus single instances conceptually related to these themes from 95 sessions End-of-treatment outcomes: Scores on the MMPI, global change ratings, ratings of target complaints, and clients' retrospective accounts of their therapy experience	Compared to their less successful counterparts, clients in successful cases produced (primarily conventional) instances of figurative language that cohered around a central metaphor(s) related to a salient theme in therapy, whereas therapists in the successful cases took up instances related to the central metaphor(s) in some form, be it simple repetition of the client's instances, extensive use of a particular client-generated metaphor, or use of their own instances related to the theme encapsulated by the client's metaphor. Box score: 1 positive

(*continued*)

Table 6.1 Continued

Study	Sample	Focus of Analysis and Measures of Outcome	Results
Råbu et al. (2013)	12 cases (10 women, 2 men clients, aged 25–52 years; 5 women and 3 men therapists, aged 49–68 years) that had reached a "good enough" outcome	Metaphors on therapeutic improvement and ending identified in therapy sessions, post-session interviews with clients and therapists, and post-session notes provided by clients and therapists End-of-treatment outcomes: Ratings on Outcome Questionnaire and the Inventory of Interpersonal Problems	Categories of metaphors that captured therapeutic improvement and ending (initiated by either the client or the therapist) were part of the material of a joint, tailor-made language developed by the client and the therapist that appeared to offer the possibility of the therapeutic relationship continuing to exist as a model for the future. Box score: 1 positive
McGuinty et al. (2017)	50 post-secondary students (aged 18–30 years) receiving treatment at university counseling centers from 14 (13 female) MA- and PhD-level therapists	Comparison of participants receiving externalizing metaphors therapy vs. a small number of participants receiving treatment-as-usual End-of-treatment outcomes: pre–post changes in measures of depression, anxiety, and stress (Depression Anxiety Stress Scale–21) and trait anxiety (State–Trait Anxiety Inventory)	No significant pre–post differences between the treatment and the control group on any of the 4 outcomes. Box score: 4 neutral

MMPI, Minnesota Multiphasic Personality Inventory.

A positive score denotes a positive effect, a neutral score indicates no effect, and a negative score indicates a negative effect.

Links Between Metaphor Use and Immediate, Within-Session Outcomes

Most of the research on the relation of therapists' use of metaphor to immediate, within-session outcomes has been focused on clients' cognitive processes. In one case study, the therapist's and client's mutual use of novel figurative language was found to occur in extended bursts and be related to problem-setting and problem-solving (Pollio & Barlow, 1975), yielding one positive box score. A report of two case studies also showed that in each case, figurative language co-occurred with therapeutic insight (i.e., when vague, impressionistic felt meanings were made explicit or when novel and revealing disclosures occurred). In addition, in one of these case studies, literal statements expressing insight were found to follow upon high frequency of novel metaphors that, in turn, triggered new bursts of metaphoric activity (Barlow et al., 1977), yielding one positive box score. In an additional case study, the therapist's use of metaphor was found to co-occur with his self-rated intention to encourage insight on the part of the client (Hill & Regan, 1991), which resulted in an additional positive box score. In sum, these three studies with three positive, no neutral, and no negative box scores provide preliminary support for a positive connection between metaphor use and positive in-session cognitive processes.

A focus on cognitive–affective regulation, as defined by mentalizing exchanges between clients and therapists (i.e., the therapist doing or facilitating affective regulation involving self-reflection and interest in one's mind for the client; Long & Lepper, 2008), showed that significantly more metaphors were co-elaborated in mentalizing versus non-mentalizing exchanges (one positive box score). Patterns of emotional–cognitive regulation as defined by combinations of emotionally toned words (ET) and abstract nouns (AB)—that is, relaxing (low ET, low AB), reflecting (low ET, high AB), experiencing (high ET, low AB), and connecting (high ET, high AB)—have also been found to relate to metaphor use (Gelo & Mergenthaler, 2012). An analysis of unconventional (novel) metaphor use by the therapist–client dyad showed that, as predicted, more of these metaphors were found in moments of emotional–cognitive integration (i.e., in connecting), in phases of dyadic abstract reflection, and in phases characterized by therapeutic engagement, whereas fewer were found in processes of relaxing, yielding one positive box score. In total, we assigned two positive box scores to the findings from these two studies. However, given that the evidence for a positive relation between emotional–cognitive regulation and metaphor use is based on only two studies, this relation must be considered preliminary.

Links Between Metaphor Use and Delayed, Immediate Post-Session Outcomes

Post-session helpfulness ratings have shown that the client rated the therapist's metaphors as more helpful than methods not involving metaphors (Hill & Regan,

1991; one positive box score) and that clients rated sessions in which they recalled the therapists' use of metaphors as more helpful than sessions in which they recalled other therapeutic events, especially when these metaphors were developed collaboratively and repetitively (Martin et al., 1992; one positive box score). Although these two studies yielded a total of two positive, no neutral, and no negative box scores, the research evidence on helpfulness must be viewed as preliminary, given the small number of studies.

A link between how metaphors are developed by clients and psychotherapists in-session and the style of communication or interaction that characterizes the dyad has also been demonstrated. A qualitative analysis of metaphoric sequences coupled with post-session inquiry interviews with clients and therapists showed that metaphoric communication signaled either a collaborative process of meaning negotiation and the development of a common therapy vocabulary ("meaning conjunction") or a noncollaborative process of meaning derivation often associated with a joint misunderstanding of the meaning of a metaphor ("meaning disjunction"; Angus & Rennie, 1988), yielding one positive and one negative box score. A similar analysis to that of Angus and Rennie (1988) also showed that metaphoric communication by psychotherapists and clients can contribute to negotiated meanings that are part of a shared therapeutic vocabulary (labeled a "representational mode of interaction") or, conversely, can fail to contribute to negotiated meanings and to provide thematic structure to a session (labeled a "literal mode of interaction"; Rasmussen & Angus, 1996), again yielding one positive and one negative box score. However, a subsequent analysis of therapists' metaphors that conveyed an important aspect of a session from Rasmussen and Angus (1996) showed that in only one of the four dyads was a metaphor used by the therapist as an attempt to convey his understanding and empathic resonating with the client also evaluated by the client as a powerful and appropriate image. In the other three dyads, the therapists' attempts to use metaphor to forge an integration, to highlight a conflict, or to assist the client to examine affect that the therapist thought was active in the transference were met by the client with confusion, misunderstanding, or a possible sense of being overwhelmed (Rasmussen, 2000). We assigned a negative box score to this latter study. Taken together, these three studies with a total of two positive, no neutral, and three negative box scores provide preliminary evidence that use of metaphor can be associated with productive and not-so-productive styles of psychotherapist–client interaction and client responses.

The only studies in which a possible moderating variable—client diagnosis—was considered revealed inconsistent patterns. Mode of interaction between therapists and clients (representational vs. literal) was found to vary with a client diagnosis of "non-borderline" or "borderline" (Rasmussen & Angus, 1996). Specifically, the non-borderline dyads were characterized by a representational mode of interaction in which the negotiating of meanings of clients' metaphors was collaboratively developed, whereas the borderline dyads were characterized by a literal mode in which interaction was at a concrete, here-and-now level and the meanings of metaphors were not negotiated. However, a subsequent analysis of the same data showed mixed results in terms of client diagnosis and the impact of metaphoric sequences on the clients and the therapeutic process (Rasmussen, 2000). In only one of the two dyads with a client labeled non-borderline was the therapist's metaphor met with a positive response by the client.

In summary, the existing studies focused on possible links between therapists' use of metaphor and immediate, within-session outcomes and delayed, immediate post-session outcomes are based in differently constituted samples, diverse indicators of therapists' use of metaphor, and different measures of within-session outcomes. Thus, drawing firm conclusions about these possible links is challenging. With this caveat, we offer the following observations:

1. Given that the existing studies were situated in a variety of theoretical orientations, including Gestalt, person-centered, experiential, psychodynamic, cognitive, and meta-cognitive interpersonal, the use of metaphors by therapists and its link to productive within-session outcomes are probably pantheoretical.
2. Most research has focused on investigating the links between metaphor use and client cognitive processes, such as problem-setting/-solving and insight, and client cognitive–affective regulation, as measured by mentalizing processes such as reflecting and connecting (five positive, no neutral, and no negative box scores). These positive links are tentatively established.
3. Preliminary evidence indicates that psychotherapists' use of metaphor can be associated with higher client helpfulness ratings (two positive, no neutral, and no negative box scores), but also with both productive and not-so-productive modes of therapist–client interaction (two positive, no neutral, and three negative box scores).
4. Although one moderator (client diagnosis) has been studied, no conclusions can be drawn about mediators and moderators of immediate outcomes.

Links Between Metaphor Use and Distal, End-of-Treatment Outcomes

To date, no studies focused on determining causal links between therapists' use of metaphor and distal, end-of-treatment outcomes as assessed by standard measures have been conducted. Thus, only correlational relations can be determined from the extant evidence.

However, some useful findings have emerged from these studies. An analysis of frequency counts of the use of novel figures in five high-change and five low-change cases as assessed by a combination of (a) global change ratings by clients, therapists, and independent clinicians, (b) ratings of target complaints, and (c) changes between pre- and post-therapy scores on the depression, psychasthenia, and social introversion scales of the Minnesota Multiphasic Personality Inventory (MMPI) revealed no differences between high- and low-change clients, therapists, or dyads (Amira, 1983; one neutral box score). This finding casts doubt on the notion that a simple relation between the quantity of therapists' metaphor use—even novel metaphor use—and end-of-treatment outcomes exists.

In qualitative studies, various patterns of sharing metaphors by clients and therapists—particularly those related to clients' troubling experiences and the major therapy themes—differentiated cases of poor versus good outcomes. Outcomes in one study (McMullen, 1985) were determined by an external judge on the basis of therapists' descriptions of the course of therapy and their judgments of the overall degree of improvement made by the client. Outcomes in a second study (McMullen, 1989) were determined by changes between pre- and post-therapy scores on MMPI depression, psychasthenia, and social introversion scales; global change ratings; ratings of target complaints; and clients' retrospective accounts of their therapy experience. Specifically, what differentiated poor from good outcome cases was not the absolute frequency of reciprocal exchanges or in-the-moment co-elaboration of metaphors. Rather, it was that compared to their less successful counterparts, clients in successful cases produced instances of figurative language (e.g., words such as *burned*, *fried*, and *scarred*) that cohered around a central metaphor(s) [e.g., HUMAN ACTIONS (OR REACTIONS) PRODUCE PHYSICAL HARM] related to a salient theme in therapy (e.g., relationships with others) and that the therapists took up instances related to the central metaphor(s) in some form. We assigned one positive box score to each of these two studies. Another study in which outcome was measured by ratings on the Outcome Questionnaire and the Inventory of Interpersonal Problems found that metaphors capturing therapeutic improvement and ending contributed to a joint (client–psychotherapist), tailor-made language in cases that had reached "a good enough outcome" (Råbu et al., 2013; one positive box score).

Finally, a comparison of a form of metaphor therapy with treatment-as-usual found no differences in pre–post ratings on the depression, anxiety, and stress scales of the Depression Anxiety Stress Scales–21 and on trait anxiety on the State–Trait Anxiety Inventory between participants receiving the metaphor therapy and those receiving treatment-as-usual (McGuinty et al., 2017; four neutral box scores). This study provides a further note of caution with regard to the prescriptive use of metaphor by therapists.

In summary, the five studies focused on distal outcomes provide some evidence that joint (client and psychotherapist) development of metaphors related to therapy-relevant themes can be associated with positive change (three positive box scores), but they also indicate that simple relations between amount of metaphor use and end-of-treatment outcomes are unlikely to exist (five neutral box scores). Of note is that there has been no consistency in which distal outcomes have been examined.

Summary of Links Between Metaphor Use and Outcomes

Of more promise than distal, end-of-treatment outcomes is the assessment of the impact of therapists' use of metaphor via more immediate outcomes. In particular, outcomes such as cognitive engagement and cognitive–affective regulation expressed through metaphoric or literal language that are evident in-the-moment during a session or upon post-session recall appear to be the best way, at present, of determining the effectiveness of therapists' metaphors. It seems more likely, then, that metaphors influence immediate interactions than long-term outcomes, although one could imagine clients taking away a central metaphor as something they use to adjust their thinking.

Possible Negative Effects and Harm

Possible negative effects or harms of therapists' use of metaphor have received relatively little attention in the research. One study (Billow et al., 1987; cited in McCurry &

Hayes, 1992) provided evidence that metaphors high in affect were less comprehensible for persons suffering from schizophrenia than those low in emotional content. Other researchers (e.g., Tay, 2016c) have similarly speculated that metaphors might play a role in the onset of delusional thinking. For example, delusional "literal" thoughts such as believing oneself to be the devil might partly result from overextending originally metaphorical ideas or experiences (e.g., being compared to a devil).

Differential receptiveness toward metaphoric talk among clients might also affect how certain clients react to therapists' use of metaphor. For example, some clients might relish such use by a therapist, whereas others could find it off-putting or confusing and could judge metaphoric language as less efficient, direct, focused, or concrete than literal language (Tay, 2020).

Diversity Considerations

Considerations of diversity, such as gender, race/ethnicity, and sexual orientation, do not figure prominently in the literature on metaphors in psychotherapy. The one exception is some initial attention to culture and religion in case examples. For example, an analysis of the use of metaphor therapy with a young, adult male, Arab-Muslim client illustrated how a therapist worked at a nonliteral level with the client. Rather than dealing directly with the client's anger toward his family and possibly revealing forbidden feelings, the therapist focused on the client's metaphors that encapsulated these (and other) feelings. Specifically, the therapist asked the client to describe the metaphors he used for his experiences (e.g., *a blocked floodgate* that symbolized the built-up pressure and pain in his chest from unexpressed anger), stayed with the client's metaphor, asked what the solutions to the metaphorically presented problems were (e.g., *the water finding outlets that allow the pressure to be lowered without flooding the surrounding area*), and encouraged the client to imagine and describe the solution (Dwairy, 2009). The client was also encouraged to continue to develop and elaborate the metaphors between sessions. Among the changes noted by the therapist were that the client started to be "more open in his communication with people," was "ready to talk more freely about his anger towards his parents," and gradually came to "connect to his feelings and learn new ways of coping." Such changes were, in part, attributed to the indirect focus on the client's salient problems afforded by the use of metaphor. Clearly, more research that attends to diversity considerations is needed.

Limitations of the Research

Thirty years ago, the research on metaphor in psychotherapy was characterized as "largely unsystematic and anecdotal" (McCurry & Hayes, 1992). The current review provides evidence of some progress away from the anecdotal and toward research strategies linked to immediate (e.g., cognitive processes such as insight, problem-setting, reflecting, and cognitive–affective integration) and distal outcomes (e.g., global change ratings; scores on measures of interpersonal problems, anxiety, depression, and stress). However, the research evidence remains limited, and little continuity exists across studies, with virtually no efforts at replication. The body of research is, then, a set of "one-off" studies.

We still know relatively little about how psychotherapists use metaphors, the many ways in which they do so, and their effects on clients. For example, when do therapists decide to focus on a particular client metaphor and how do they do so within and across sessions? To what extent and in what ways do therapists modulate paralinguistic cues, such as tone of voice, emphases, and gestures, in their delivery of metaphors? When do they decide to introduce their own metaphors and how do they construct them? What client cues guide therapists when deciding to continue or discontinue use of a metaphor? Such questions point to the need for a much more in-depth focus on the process of using metaphors in and between sessions.

One direction for future research is to hypothesize a specific sequence that occurs in a successful use of metaphors. For example, the client might initiate a metaphor; the therapist might pick up on it and ask the client to describe the image, articulate the emotions attached to the image, associate to the image, and link to life outside of therapy. Task analysis could then be used to test and refine the model.

In general, we suggest that researchers in this area could focus on (a) going beyond the content of metaphors to include more fine-grained analyses of paralinguistic features (e.g., intonation, pauses, gestures); (b) being cognizant of the development of metaphors over time and tracking use over a session of therapy and over the course of therapy as a whole; (c) going beyond the analysis of short, isolated extracts of metaphors to consider how metaphoric meaning is developed in conjunction with literal language; (d) seeking systematic input from practitioners on the import of linguistic and discursive elements; and (e) engaging researchers, practitioners, and clients as co-researchers who can inform the development of research questions, selection of methodological approaches, and choice of methods and measures. Such programs of research have the potential advantage of both continuity and adaptability—of building on what seems to work and of responding innovatively to new knowledge.

Training Implications

Psychotherapy educators and clinical supervisors might consider a variety of training strategies to promote the use of metaphors in sessions. A first step is to assist trainees in recognizing when the client is speaking figuratively through attentive listening for such language. Such recognition is likely to be easier for novel than conventional metaphors, so more focus might need to be placed on sensitizing trainees to hear the latter. A subsequent step is to assist trainees in deciding whether to respond immediately and actively to the metaphor. Such decisions are not easy and might depend, for example, on how evocative the metaphor is, how often it and its entailments have been used, whether it seems to be related to major themes, or how ready the client seems to be to go further with it. Trainees should then be equipped with a repertoire of possible responses, including showing genuine curiosity about the client's associations, explicating what is implicit in a metaphor, therapeutically extending or modifying it, creating and delivering a therapist-generated metaphor, and recognizing and remembering a client's metaphor for future use (Bayne & Thompson, 2000; Strong, 1989).

Learning how to extend or modify a metaphor via co-elaboration with a client might be assisted by first instructing new therapists in its two-part structure: (a) the target (the concept being described; e.g., depression) and (b) the source (the conceptual knowledge that structures our understanding of the target through the mapping of relevant entities, attributes, and relations; e.g., *descent*, *darkness*). Trainees can be taught how to probe inferences from source domains and how to map these instances back to the target in ways that involve clients in a collaborative process. Helping develop a sensitivity toward the existence of strategic junctures within each instance of metaphoric elaboration, and how to appropriately flag such junctures, can be another focus for training (Tay, 2011).

Resources on the use of metaphor in psychotherapy are often in the form of books (e.g., Blenkiron, 2010; Siegelman, 1990; Stott et al., 2010). An exception is the development and evaluation of a training workshop in cognitive–behavior therapy (Mathieson et al., 2018). This workshop included introductions to metaphor theory, identification of metaphors, the functions of metaphors in psychotherapy, the model of metaphor in cognitive–behavioral therapy, as well as homework assignments and practice sessions. Evaluation of the workshop indicated that participating therapists reported having developed an increased awareness of, and confidence in using, metaphors, as well as having spent increased time elaborating client metaphors in-session.

Therapeutic Practices

The preliminary research evidence suggests that psychotherapists' co-elaboration of metaphors with clients is linked with improved cognitive processes and cognitive–affective regulation in session. Careful listening to the figurative language in therapy can inform the practitioner about the client's concerns, self-image, relationships, perceptions, affective experiences, and changes in these domains. From this sparse evidence base, we draw the following practices:

- Pay particular attention to key metaphors repeated by the client or appearing in extended bursts.
- Work with the client on those metaphors particularly relevant to the themes and processes of therapy.
- Respond naturally to clients' metaphors in a variety of ways—for example, simple repetition, modifying and elaborating, and delayed response.
- Adopt a collaborative style of co-elaborating metaphors with clients.
- Avoid a didactic, coercive style when delivering one's own metaphor to a client.
- Refrain from the overzealous use of *stock* metaphors (pre-prepared metaphors that can be used prescriptively when appropriate).
- Do not assume a shared, mutual understanding of meaning for any metaphor; check with the client for their interpretation and experience.
- Assess clients' within-session and across-session responsiveness to metaphors, particularly in terms of the impacts on cognitive processes and on cognitive–affective regulation.
- Adapt one's metaphors to cultural histories, locations, and allegiances.

- Recognize that metaphors can be easily misinterpreted or taken as offensive by clients whose first language is not English.

References

* Studies included in the research review.

*Amira, S. A. (1983). Figurative language and metaphor in successful and unsuccessful psychotherapy [Doctoral dissertation, Vanderbilt University, 1982]. *Dissertation Abstracts International, 43*, 1244B.

*Angus, L. E., & Rennie, D. L. (1988). Therapist participation in metaphor generation: Collaborative and noncollaborative styles. *Psychotherapy: Theory, Research, Practice, Training, 25*(4), 552–560.

Barlow, J. M., Kerlin, J. R., & Pollio, H. R. (1971). *Training manual for identifying figurative language* (Tech. Rep. No. 1). University of Tennessee.

*Barlow, J. M., Pollio, H. R., & Fine, H. J. (1977). Insight and figurative language in psychotherapy. *Psychotherapy, 14*(3), 212–222.

Bayne, R., & Thompson, K. L. (2000). Counsellor response to clients' metaphors: An evaluation and refinement of Strong's model. *Counselling Psychology Quarterly, 13*(1), 37–49. https://doi.org/10.1080/09515070050011051

Billow, R. M., Rossman, J., Lewis, N., Goldman, D., Kraemer, S., & Ross, P. (1987). Metaphoric communication and miscommunication in schizophrenic and borderline states. In R. E. Haskell (Ed.), *Cognition and symbolic structures: The psychology of metaphoric transformation* (pp. 141–162). Ablex.

Blenkiron, P. (2005). Stories and analogies in cognitive behaviour therapy: A clinical review. *Behavioural and Cognitive Psychotherapy, 33*(1), 45–59. https://doi.org/10.1017/S1352465804001766

Blenkiron, P. (2010). *Stories and analogies in cognitive behaviour therapy*. Wiley.

Cameron, L., & Maslen, R. (2010). *Metaphor analysis: Research practice in applied linguistics, social sciences and the humanities*. Equinox.

Close, H. T. (1998). *Metaphor in psychotherapy: Clinical applications of stories and allegories*. Impact.

Combs, G., & Freedman, J. (1990). *Symbol, story, and ceremony: Using metaphor in individual and family therapy*. Norton.

Dwairy, M. (2009). Culture analysis and metaphor psychotherapy with Arab-Muslim clients. *Journal of Clinical Psychology, 65*(2), 199–209. https://doi.org/10.1002/jclp.20568

Ferrara, K. W. (1994). *Therapeutic ways with words*. Oxford University Press.

Finlay, L. (2015). Sensing and making sense: Embodying metaphor in relational-centered psychotherapy. *The Humanistic Psychologist, 43*(4), 338–353.

Forrest, D. V. (1973). On one's own onymy. *Psychiatry, 36*(3), 266–290. https://doi.org/10.1080/00332747.1973.11023763

Gelo, O. (2008). *Metaphor and emotional-cognitive regulation in psychotherapy: A single case study*. Ulmer Textbank.

*Gelo, O. C. G., & Mergenthaler, E. (2012). Unconventional metaphors and emotional-cognitive regulation in a metacognitive interpersonal therapy. *Psychotherapy Research, 22*(2), 159–175. https://doi.org/10.1080/10503307.2011.629636

Hamburg, S. R. (2017). Metaphoric tasks in psychotherapy: Case studies of "Margie's" self-image and "Amy's" pain. *Pragmatic Case Studies in Psychotherapy, 13*(4), 284–328. https://doi.org/10.14713/pcsp.v13i4.2020

*Hill, C. E., & Regan, A. M. (1991). The use of metaphors in one case of brief psychotherapy. *Journal of Integrative and Eclectic Psychotherapy, 10*(1), 56–67.

Kagan, J. (1975). Interpersonal process recall: A method for influencing human interaction [Unpublished manuscript].

Klein, M. H., Mathieu-Coughlan, P., & Kiesler, D. J. (1986). The experiencing scales. In L. S. Greenberg & W. M. Pinsoff (Eds.), *The psychotherapeutic process: A research handbook* (pp. 21–71). Guilford.

Kopp, R. R. (1995). *Metaphor therapy: Using client-generated metaphors in psychotherapy.* Brunner/Mazel.

Kopp, R. R., & Craw, M. J. (1998). Metaphoric language, metaphoric cognition, and cognitive therapy. *Psychotherapy: Theory, Research, Practice, Training, 35*(3), 306–311.

Lakoff, G., & Johnson, M. (1980). *Metaphors we live by.* University of Chicago Press.

*Long, P. S., & Lepper, G. (2008). Metaphor in psychoanalytic psychotherapy: A comparative study of four cases by a practitioner–researcher. *British Journal of Psychotherapy, 24*(3), 343–364. https://doi.org/10.1111/j.1752-0118.2008.00090.x

*Martin, J., Cummings, A. L., & Hallberg, E. T. (1992). Therapists' intentional use of metaphor: Memorability, clinical impact, and possible epistemic/motivational functions. *Journal of Consulting and Clinical Psychology, 60*(1), 143–145.

Mathieson, F., Jordan, J., Bennett-Levy, J., & Stubbe, M. (2018). Keeping metaphor in mind: Training therapists in metaphor-enhanced cognitive behaviour therapy. *The Cognitive Behaviour Therapist, 11*, e8. https://doi.org/10.1017/S1754470X18000077

Mathieson, F., Jordan, J., Carter, J. D., & Stubbe, M. (2015). The metaphoric dance: Co-construction of metaphor in cognitive behaviour therapy. *The Cognitive Behaviour Therapist, 8*, e24. https://doi.org/10.1017/S1754470X15000628

McCurry, S. M., & Hayes, S. C. (1992). Clinical and experimental perspectives on metaphorical talk. *Clinical Psychology Review, 12*(7), 763–785. https://doi.org/10.1016/0272-7358(92)90023-2

McGuinty, E., Armstrong, D., & Carrière, A.-M. (2014). A clinical treatment intervention for dysphoria: Externalizing metaphors therapy. *Clinical Psychology & Psychotherapy, 21*(5), 381–393. https://doi.org/10.1002/cpp.1844

*McGuinty, E., Bird, B. M., Carlson, A., Yarlasky, K., Morrow, D., & Armstrong, D. (2017). Externalizing Metaphors Therapy: Outcomes related to a three-session treatment model for anxiety and depression. *Journal of Systemic Therapies, 36*(3), 52–71. https://doi.org/10.1521/jsyt.2017.36.3.52

*McMullen, L. M. (1985). Methods for studying the use of novel figurative language in psychotherapy. *Psychotherapy: Theory, Research, Practice, Training, 22*(3), 610–619.

*McMullen, L. M. (1989). Use of figurative language in successful and unsuccessful cases of psychotherapy: Three comparisons. *Metaphor and Symbol, 4*(4), 203–225. https://doi.org/10.1207/s15327868ms0404_1

McMullen, L. M. (2008). Putting it in context: Metaphor and psychotherapy. In R. W. Gibbs, Jr. (Ed.), *The Cambridge handbook of metaphor and thought* (pp. 397–411). Cambridge University Press.

Mould, T. J., Oades, L. G., & Crowe, T. P. (2010). The use of metaphor for understanding and managing psychotic experiences: A systematic review. *Journal of Mental Health, 19*(3), 282–293. https://doi.org/10.3109/09638231003728091

Muran, J. C., & DiGiuseppe, R. A. (1990). Towards a cognitive formulation of metaphor use in psychotherapy. *Clinical Psychology Review, 10*, 69–86. https://doi.org/10.1016/0272-7358(90)90107-L

Oxford paperback dictionary (4th ed.). (1994). Oxford University Press.

*Pollio, H. R., & Barlow, J. M. (1975). A behavioural analysis of figurative language in psychotherapy: One session in a single case study. *Language and Speech, 18*(3), 236–254. https://doi.org/10.1177/002383097501800306

Pragglejaz Group. (2007). MIP: A method for identifying metaphorically used words in discourse. *Metaphor and Symbol, 22*(1), 1–39. doi:10.1207/s15327868ms2201_1

*Råbu, M., Haavind, H., & Binder, P. E. (2013). We have travelled a long distance and sorted out the mess in the drawers: Metaphors for moving towards the end in psychotherapy. *Counselling and Psychotherapy Research, 13*(1), 71–80. https://doi.org/10.1080/14733145.2012.711339

*Rasmussen, B. (2000). Poetic truths and clinical reality: Client experience of the use of metaphor by therapists. *Smith College Studies in Social Work, 70*(2), 355–373. https://doi.org/10.1080/00377310009517597

*Rasmussen, B., & Angus, L. (1996). Metaphor in psychodynamic psychotherapy with borderline and non-borderline clients: A qualitative analysis. *Psychotherapy: Theory, Research, Practice, Training, 33*(4), 521–530.

Sarpavaara, H., & Koski-Jännes, A. (2013). Change as a journey: Clients' metaphoric change talk as an outcome predictor in initial motivational sessions with probationers. *Qualitative Research in Psychology, 10*(1), 86–101. https://doi.org/10.1080/14780887.2011.586256

Semino, E. (2008). *Metaphor in discourse*. Cambridge University Press.

Siegelman, E. Y. (1990). *Metaphor and meaning in psychotherapy*. Guilford.

Sims, P. A. (2003). Working with metaphor. *American Journal of Psychotherapy, 57*(4), 528–536. https://doi.org/10.1176/appi.psychotherapy.2003.57.4.528

Stoddard, J. A., & Afari, N. (2014). *The big book of ACT metaphors: A practitioner's guide to experiential exercises and metaphors in acceptance and commitment therapy*. New Harbinger.

Stott, R., Mansell, W., Salkovskis, P., Lavender, A., & Cartwright-Hatton, S. (2010). *Oxford guide to metaphors in CBT: Building cognitive bridges*. Oxford University Press.

Strong, T. (1989). Metaphors and client change in counselling. *International Journal for the Advancement of Counselling, 12*(3), 203–213. https://doi.org/10.1007/BF00120585

Tay, D. (2011). Discourse markers as metaphor signaling devices in psychotherapeutic talk. *Language & Communication, 31*(4), 310–317. https://doi.org/10.1016/j.langcom.2011.02.001

Tay, D. (2016a). Finding the middle ground between therapist-centred and client-centred metaphor research in psychotherapy. In M. O'Reilly & J. Lester (Eds.), *The Palgrave handbook of adult mental health* (pp. 558–576). Palgrave Macmillan.

Tay, D. (2016b). Metaphor and psychological transference. *Metaphor and Symbol, 31*(1), 11–30. https://doi.org/10.1080/10926488.2016.1116903

Tay, D. (2016c). Using metaphor in healthcare: Mental health. In E. Semino & Z. Demjén (Eds.), *The Routledge handbook of metaphor and language* (pp. 371–384). Routledge.

Tay, D. (2017). Quantitative metaphor usage patterns in Chinese psychotherapy talk. *Communication & Medicine, 14*(1), 51–68. https://doi.org/10.1558/cam.27688

Tay, D. (2020). Surveying views of metaphor vs. literal language in psychotherapy: A factor analysis. *Metaphor and the Social World, 10*(2), 273–291. https://doi.org/10.1075/msw.00007.tay

Tay, D. (2021). Metaphor response categories and distribution between therapists and clients: A case study in the Chinese context. *Journal of Constructivist Psychology, 34*(4), 378–394. https://doi.org/10.1080/10720537.2019.1697913

7

Interpretations

Sigal Zilcha-Mano, Hadar Fisher, Tohar Dolev-Amit, John R. Keefe, and Jacques P. Barber

Interpretations are a fundamental component of most psychodynamic treatments and a common feature of other forms of psychotherapy. In psychodynamic work, interpretations address a central conflictual theme that the therapist believes is likely responsible for the pain and suffering of the individual (Crits-Christoph et al., 1988). Therapists use interpretations to increase patients' insight concerning unconscious and preconscious elements in their lives (Nunberg, 1948), and many theorists consider them to be at the top of the hierarchy of psychodynamic methods (Bibring, 1954). Repeated use of interpretations is expected to bring lasting ("structural") change in the individual through a process of uncovering unconscious themes and increasing self-understanding ("aha" moments) and result in improved mental health and reduced symptoms (Horwitz, 1974).

Despite the importance of interpretation, both in theoretical and clinical psychodynamic literature, research studies in this area have been more limited than one would expect for such a key method. To the best of our knowledge, this is the first systematic review to synthesize the research evidence on the association between psychotherapists' interpretations and outcome at three time frames: immediate (in-session), intermediate (measured after sessions), and distal (symptom reduction at the end of treatment).

If the aim of interpretations is raising insight, then insight can be seen as its immediate or intermediate outcome. *Insight* is commonly defined as awareness of one's recurring emotional, cognitive, behavioral, and interpersonal patterns (Connolly Gibbons et al., 2007), manifested as a conscious shift in meaning involving the creation of new connections that can be seen as enabling more adaptive coping (Hill et al., 2007). For example, in many psychodynamic treatments, such new understandings may refer to potential associations between past and present experiences, shedding light on how past experiences may affect current tendencies to perceive intrapersonal and interpersonal situations and behave in certain ways. Gains in insight were found to be associated with better treatment outcomes in a recent meta-analysis (Jennissen et al., 2018), especially in psychodynamic treatments (Barber et al., 2021).

The process of raising awareness and understanding of recurring maladaptive patterns is transtheoretical, although manifesting differently across theoretical orientations (Wampold et al., 2007). For example, in cognitive treatments, identifying and challenging automatic thought distortions and their underlying negative personal schemas (Beck, 1976; Leahy, 2017) have some similarities to psychodynamic

Sigal Zilcha-Mano, Hadar Fisher, Tohar Dolev-Amit, John R. Keefe, and Jacques P. Barber, *Interpretations*
In: *Psychotherapy Skills and Methods That Work*. Edited by: Clara E. Hill and John C. Norcross, Oxford University Press.
 DOI: 10.1093/oso/9780197611012.003.0007

interpretations. The same is true regarding schema therapy, in which the therapists and the patients may engage in identifying and exploring the origin of maladaptive schemas, which are self-defeating emotional and cognitive patterns established in childhood and repeated throughout life (Young et al., 2003).

Definitions

In the context of psychodynamic treatment, *interpretation* refers to a psychotherapist skill in which the psychotherapist recognizes, and then seeks to raise, the patients' awareness and understanding of recurrent maladaptive patterns (Gabbard, 2009; Summers & Barber, 2010). A broader, transtheoretical definition of interpretation is "a statement that goes beyond what the patient has overtly stated or recognized and gives a new meaning, reason, or explanation for behaviors, thoughts, or feelings so that the patient can see problems in a new way" (Hill, 2020, p. 255). Awareness of such maladaptive patterns, when it is not only intellectual but also emotionally involved and experience-near, is expected to raise insight, which in turn is expected to result in cognitive and behavioral change, symptom reduction, and an increase in well-being (Kuncewicz et al., 2014).

Some interpretations focus on *intrapersonal*, others on *interpersonal* conflicts or maladaptive recurring patterns. From the ego psychology perspective, intrapersonal conflict commonly refers to a conflict between the ego and the superego, and between the ego and the id. For example, therapists may recognize and interpret the patient's use of less mature defenses to handle internal and external stressors, viewing defenses as expressions of unconscious conflicts, needs, and motivations (Freud, 1955). From a relational perspective, intrapersonal conflict commonly refer to aspects of the self or "inner voices" that have different and at times conflicting needs (Bromberg, 2003). In contrast, interpersonal conflict commonly refers to a conflict between the individual's interpersonal wishes (what the individual wants and needs in interpersonal relationships) and the response of the others to those wishes (Luborsky, 1984). Interpretations focusing on interpersonal conflict and maladaptive patterns can be divided into those concerning the patients' interpersonal relationships outside of treatment and those concerning enactments of these patterns in the relationship with the therapist, also referred to as *transference interpretations* (Foelsch & Kernberg, 1998). Interpretations also differ in the extent to which they are viewed as objective information that the therapist delivers to the patient, as a hypothesis to consider or prompt for further reflection, or as a collaborative task that both the patient and the therapist engage in, with the result of the patient understanding the therapist's subjectivity and feeling understood by the therapist (Aron, 1992).

Clinical Description and Indications

According to some psychodynamic perspectives, therapists are advised to start with an empathic statement, move to a tentative hypothesis regarding the identified maladaptive pattern, then conclude again with empathy (Summers & Barber, 2010). For example, a therapist may say,

> You feel so alone, with no one being there for you. I think that maybe you are so afraid of being left alone that you are clinging to those who mean so much to you, in a way that may make it hard for them to stay, then at the end you really find yourself alone, sad, and angry. All this makes you feel that no matter what you do, you will not get the help and intimacy that you want so much from others.

After an interpretation is provided, the therapist can carefully explore the patient's reaction: Does it lead to greater emotional openness and greater disclosure of emotions (Basch, 1980)? Does it lead to rupture in the alliance (Milbrath et al., 1999)? Clinical experience and a few research studies (e.g., Basch, 1980; Leibovich et al., 2020) advise offering interpretations as a tentative hypothesis to facilitate further explorations, rather than as an objective truth (Leibovich et al., 2020; Wachtel, 1993). It has also been suggested that it is advisable to be flexible in use of interpretations and make the rationale on which they are based clear (Katz et al., 2019; Owen & Hilsenroth, 2014).

Other clinical suggestions, requiring empirical support, indicate that the recommended number of interpretations differ from patient to patient and from one stage of treatment to the other, but it is generally not high, especially for transference interpretations. The rule of thumb is about one or two transference interpretations per session (Høglend et al., 2008) when their content is close to the surface of consciousness (Speisman, 1959).

Another rule of thumb concerns the timing of interpretations and states that it is generally more advisable to provide the interpretation in the middle of the session. Providing it at the end of a session may preclude the opportunity to work through its potential meanings, and providing it too early may prevent establishing a strong enough alliance to serve as a supportive environment for the interpretation (Gabbard, 2006; Leibovich et al., 2020). The same is true about offering interpretations too early in the course of treatment before a sufficiently strong alliance has been formed (Summers & Barber, 2010).

In addition, some theorists have argued that transference and nontransference interpretations have different recommended timing. That is, it is advisable to first increase the patients' curiosity about maladaptive patterns outside the relationship with the therapist, as well as their insight into such patterns, and only then interpret them as part of the transference toward the therapist (Book, 1998). Others, however, have noted the importance of offering transference interpretations early in treatment (Davenloo, 2000; Kernberg, 1975). The rationale here is that interpreting defenses early in the process of therapy will create pressure that will allow warded-off feelings to be experienced and processed as quickly and completely as possible (Davanloo, 2000).

There is an ongoing debate regarding the characteristics of the patients who may benefit most from interpretation. Some studies suggest that the use of transference and nontransference interpretations is related to better treatment outcomes for patients with more, rather than fewer, interpersonal problems (e.g., Høglend et al., 2008; Keefe et al., 2019). Other studies report an opposite pattern of findings, with a greater number of transference and nontransference interpretations being related to better treatment outcomes in patients with fewer, rather than more, interpersonal problems (e.g., Connolly et al., 1999; Jacobs & Warner, 1981; Ogrodniczuk et al., 1999).

Several potential explanations may shed light on these mixed research reports. It may be that different measures of interpersonal competence capture different constructs that show distinct associations with interpretations in predicting outcome. Alternatively, similar to the interaction between interpersonal problems and therapeutic alliance (Zilcha-Mano & Fisher, 2022), the effect on the outcome of the interaction between interpretations and the patients' interpersonal characteristics may run in opposite directions for between-patients versus within-patient effects. The *between-patients* level refers to differences between patients in the extent to which their therapists generally tended to use interpretations in their treatments. In contrast, the *within-patient* level refers to changes in the use of interpretations in sessions with the same patient. Thus, for individuals with more severe interpersonal problems, the association between interpretations and outcome may be positive at the between-patients level but negative at the within-patient level. At the between-patients level, a general use of a low-intermediate amount of interpretation over the course of treatment may be more beneficial than a high amount. By contrast, at the within-patient level, a gradual increase in the amount of interpretation may be more beneficial than a stable amount of interpretations or a reduction in the amount.

Assessment

Measures assessing the occurrence of interpretations in an entire session can be divided into those estimating the extent to which interpretations were a characteristic of the session (e.g., McCarthy et al., 2016) and those focusing on the frequency of interpretations used in a session (e.g., Crits-Christoph et al., 1988). Measures assessing the occurrence of interpretations within each therapist sentence or speaking turn in sessions can be divided into those measuring whether interpretations occur or do not occur (e.g., Piper et al., 1991) and those assessing the accuracy and quality of the interpretations (e.g., Silberschatz et al., 1986). The potential validity of the patients' perspective depends on the extent to which they are capable of recognizing particular technical processes occurring within their psychotherapy (DeFife et al., 2008) and on their internal scaling of the extent to which such interpretations were used. These abilities and tendencies may be affected by a variety of factors, such as personality disorders (Lipsitz-Odess et al., 2021).

Regarding within-sessions measures of interpretations, researchers code the occurrence of interpretation in each therapist's speech turn. An example is the revised Hill Counselor Verbal Response Modes Category System (HCVRMCS; Hill, 1985, 1986), which includes nine pantheoretical, nominal, mutually exclusive therapist verbal response modes, including interpretation. Judges code the response modes using transcripts of sessions and calculate the proportions of response modes (number of interpretations divided by the total number of therapist verbal response modes used in the session). In the Helping Skills System (Hill, 2020), a revision of the HCVRMCS, interpretations (and the other response modes) are coded by judges both on video and in transcripts of sessions.

The Psychodynamic Intervention Rating Scale (Cooper et al., 2002) includes codes for interpretative interventions (including defense and transference interpretations) and non-interpretive interventions (including direct questions, clarifications, supportive and work-enhancing statements, associations, acknowledgments, reflections, and contractual arrangements). Judges code both on the basis of video and transcripts of the sessions.

Measures assessing outcome can be divided into those focusing on immediate in-session outcomes, such as the extent to which the patient becomes more open and collaborative (e.g., Hill et al., 2020); intermediate or post-session outcome (e.g., depth of experience in the session; Stiles & Snow, 1984); and distal treatment outcome, such as end-of-treatment symptom change (e.g., Gaston et al., 1994). Regarding measures of immediate outcome, based on the theoretical assumptions that interpretations aim to foster patients' insight, previous researchers explored whether patients exhibited greater insight following therapists' interpretation. Insight in this regard was coded using the following definition: "Client expresses an understanding of something about him/herself and can articulate patterns or reasons for behaviors, thoughts, or feelings" (Hill et al., 2020, p. 265). Another study coded the maturity of patients' defense mechanism as the immediate outcome based on the idea that some of these insights involve increased clarity regarding the use of maladaptive defense mechanisms, which may result in patients adapting more mature defense mechanisms (Drapeau et al., 2008).

Clinical Examples

The three examples below are based on a composite clinical case; informed consent was obtained from the patients (P) and therapists (T). The first interpretation refers to an interpersonal conflict outside the therapy room, the second is an intrapersonal conflict, and the third is a transference interpretation. Interpretations are italicized.

Example 1: Interpersonal Interpretation—Outside the Therapy Room

T: *From what you tell, it seems you really needed her support.*

P: That's interesting. I didn't think of it that way. What do you mean?

T: *I noticed that with your friend, too, like what you said about your partner, you felt you really needed her support, but at the same time you felt that she was too busy with herself, not paying attention to you, and not seeing how much you were in need. In response, you are not sure what to say to her and eventually decide that there's no point in trying at all, then withdraw into yourself and feel lonely.*

P: I didn't think of that. Hearing you saying that, it sounds right to me . . . and that loneliness is so painful. The loneliness of being without hope (crying). That there's no chance that it will ever be different.

T: *I think that we are identifying together a pattern that manifests in various relationships that are important to you, and this pattern appears to hurt you.* I think it makes sense for us to try to understand it, where it comes from, and how it can be changed.

Example 2: Intrapersonal Interpretation

P: I prefer to manage on my own. I'm much better off alone. What do I need all these disappointments over and over again for? It's time I learn my lesson and stop trying all the time.

T: *I hear that now you feel like you just want to be on your own. Thinking about what you told me so far, it seems like on one hand, part of you would like you to manage on your own, so that you will never have to feel helpless and dependent on other people's good will anymore, and on the other hand, another part is not willing to give up on the possibility that there's someone who will care about you and attend to you.*

P: True. And I'm fed up. If in any case nobody cares and people think only of themselves, then it's better for me already to stop expecting and be disappointed.

T: *You'd like to silence the voice that needs someone else, because right now it only hurts you, only increases the disappointment, but maybe you're also worried about what you'll be left with if you give it up.*

Note that whereas the conflict the patient described may seem interpersonal, the interpretation the therapist gave focused on the intrapersonal aspects of this conflict.

Example 3: Transference Interpretation

T: *A moment ago you were telling me in great detail about what happened yesterday, and suddenly you seem to be inert, distant. I'm asking myself what happened between us now. Did I do something to drive you away?*

P: I don't know. Suddenly I feel like I don't have much to say.

T: How do you feel?

P: I don't know. Suddenly I get, like, a distressing feeling. What's the point of talking about all this?

T: *I hear the distress you feel, and you suddenly seem to me closed and alone. I wonder if it has anything to do with the fact that I just looked at the clock?*

P: Don't know. Maybe.

T: *Maybe you felt like I was not interested in you? That when you need my support so much, I'm preoccupied with how much time of the meeting is left, and I'm not available to be with you?*

P: It was so important for me to tell you what happened yesterday, and I was really offended when I saw you looking at the clock.

T: *I wanted to make sure we had enough time to work on the important things you are revealing. This is why I looked at the clock. I understand now that it hurt you and gave you the impression that I don't see you and don't understand how much you need me. I'm sorry about that. I ask myself whether what happened between us now is related to the things you and I talked about, that sometimes happen to you in relationships with people who are important to you?*

P: I kind of understand, but I'm not sure I completely understand. Can you say more?

T: *I wonder maybe you felt like you felt with your parents. Like them, I am too busy with other important stuff to listen to you. Immediately you felt unimportant as you described you felt with your father.*

Landmark Studies and Previous Reviews

Landmark Studies

Høglend and colleagues (Høglend, 1993; Høglend et al., 2008) used randomized controlled trials to evaluate the effect of transference interpretations on distal treatment outcomes. In one study, 43 patients were randomized to a psychodynamic treatment with high versus no transference interpretations. Patients in the high transference interpretation condition showed poorer outcomes than those in the no transference condition (Høglend, 1993). In the other study, 100 patients were randomized to a psychodynamic treatment with low to moderate versus no transference interpretations. No significant group differences in distal outcomes were found between the two conditions. Analyses on differences between patients, however, revealed that those with more interpersonal difficulties, as evident by the poor quality of their object relations, showed better psychodynamic functioning in the low to moderate transference interpretation condition than did those in the condition without transference interpretation (Høglend et al., 2008). Further analyses explored whether this effect was mediated by change in insight and tolerance for affects. A significant mediation effect was found, suggesting that interpretations may result in better outcome through gains in insight and improved affect awareness (Høglend & Hagtvet, 2019). Specifically, transference interpretations for patients with poor quality of their object relations was mediated by both change in insight and tolerance of affect.

Case studies have been used to zoom in and understand the nuances and immediate outcomes of interpretations. For example, in a landmark study, Hill and colleagues (2020) found that probes for insight (i.e., open questions that invite patients to think about different meanings for their thoughts, feelings, or behaviors) led to more patient collaboration than did interpretations. At the same time, there was no significant difference between interpretations and probe for insight in predicting subsequent insight.

Previous Reviews

Several reviews have evaluated the association between psychodynamic skills assessed directly from therapy process ratings and treatment outcome. Crits-Christoph et al. (2013) and Crits-Christoph and Gibbons (2021) found that higher frequency of psychodynamic interpretations in general predicted better treatment outcome and that higher frequency of transference interpretations predicted poorer treatment outcomes for subsets of patients. They also found that higher levels of accuracy in interpretations significantly predicted outcome, but they could not demonstrate a causal pathway. Furthermore, they concluded that the adverse effect of transference interpretations is more pronounced for patients with a low quality of object relations. Relatively more favorable treatment outcomes were obtained when therapists accurately addressed central aspects of patients' interpersonal dynamics.

Research Review

We conducted a search in May 2021 of the PubMed, PsycInfo, and MEDLINE databases between January 1970 and May 2021, with the following search terms: psychotherapy, therapy or treatment, and technique, intervention or interpretation, psychodynamic or psychoanalytic or dynamic or supportive-expressive or insight-oriented, and psychotherapist or therapist. We excluded studies that measured adherence to psychodynamic treatment rather than focusing only on interpretations. If studies used the same data in multiple reports, we included their data only once.

The criteria for inclusion in the research review were as follows: (a) The authors referred to the therapy method or skill as interpretation, or to psychotherapeutic treatment that specifically included interpretations; (b) the authors provided data on outcome (immediate, intermediate, and/or distal) measures; (c) the data reported were such that it is was possible to evaluate the association between interpretations and outcome; (d) the treatment was individual psychotherapy, rather than group, couple, or family therapy; (e) the patients were adults (older than age 18 years); and (f) reports were written in English.

We identified 53 studies in which interpretations were measured and their associations with outcome (immediate, intermediate, distal) assessed. Of these 53 articles, 18 met the criterion of interpretation provided by the therapist during a psychotherapy session and tested its association with outcome. Tables 7.1 and 7.2 summarize these studies. The total number of patients was 1,011, and the total number of psychotherapists was 316 across the 18 studies.

The small number of studies in each of the outcome categories (six immediate, four intermediate, 12 distal; some studies addressed more than one level of outcome) and their diversity precluded conducting a quantitative meta-analysis. Thus, following Hill et al. (Chapter 9, this volume), we conducted a box score analysis of the association between interpretations and outcomes. We employed our judgment based on the reported effects in the original studies to aggregate the effects across the 18 studies. We gave each effect a box score in terms of positive associations (positive score), neutral association (neutral score), or negative associations (negative score).

Measures of interpretations in psychotherapy varied. In the studies included in the current research review, the majority (38.89%) assessed the degree to which interpretations were a characteristic of the session based on post-session self-report ratings or ratings by trained judged. Other studies (27.78%) assessed the frequency of interpretations used in a session as coded by trained judges, and two studies (11.11%) assessed the accuracy and quality of the interpretations (Crits-Christoph et al., 1988; Silberschatz et al., 1986).

Table 7.1 Summary of Studies on Immediate and Intermediate Outcomes of Psychotherapist Interpretations

Study	Sample	Measures of Interpretation, Outcome, and Moderators	Results
		Immediate Outcome	
Drapeau et al. (2008)	First session of brief psychodynamic intervention (Gillieron, 1989) for 32 (17 female) adult patients nested within 6 (2 female) therapists. One licensed psychologist; the others were licensed psychiatrists.	Measure of interpretation: Interpretation category of the PIRS (Cooper et al., 2002). Defense and transference interpretations were folded into one category ("Interpretations"). Measures of immediate outcome: Defense Mechanisms Rating Scale (Perry, 1990) Measure of moderators: None	No significant sequence was found for therapist interpretations followed by change in the patients' level of defensive functioning. Box score: 1 neutral
Hill, Helms, Tichenor, et al. (1988)	Multiple case studies of 8 adult females presenting symptoms of depression, anxiety, self-esteem, and relationship problems. Patients underwent 12-session psychotherapy with 8 experienced therapists (4 male) from a range of theoretical orientations.	Measure of interpretation: Category in HCVRMCS (Hill, 1978) as coded by trained judges from transcripts Measures of immediate outcome based on a post-session videotape review: (a) Helpfulness was rated by therapist and patient on a 9-point scale (1 = extremely unhelpful, 9 = extremely helpful); (b) Patient Reactions System (Hill, Helms, Spiegel, et al., 1988): supported, therapeutic work, challenged, negative reactions, no reaction; coded by patients. Measures of immediate outcome based on ratings by trained coders: Patients' emotional experience as rated on the EXP (Klein et al., 1986) Measures of moderators: None	For helpfulness, compared to other skills, interpretation was rated as most helpful by therapists and second most helpful by patients. For patient reactions, interpretation was more often followed by therapeutic work reactions (better understanding of thoughts and feelings and new ways to behave) than expected by chance. Interpretation was associated with higher levels of patient emotional experience. Box scores: 4 positive

(*continued*)

Table 7.1 Continued

Study	Sample	Measures of Interpretation, Outcome, and Moderators	Results
Hill et al. (2020)	Case study of 18 sessions of 192 middle-aged, White men paired with 3 doctoral student therapists in psychodynamic psychotherapy. Six sessions with the highest post-session therapist-rated patient insight for each of the 3 cases.	Measure of interpretation: Category in the Helping Skills System (Hill, 2014) as coded by trained judges from videotapes and transcripts. Therapists' interpretations were compared to therapists' probe for insight intervention (i.e., open questions that invite patients to think about different meanings for their thoughts, feelings, or behaviors). Measures of immediate outcome: (a) Patient collaboration rated by trained judges using the Use of Therapist Interventions Scale (Allen et al., 1990); (b) patient insight was rated by trained judges using the Judge-Rated Insight Scale (Hill et al., 1992). Measures of moderators: None	For patient collaboration, probe for insight was associated with more gains in collaboration than were interpretations, although only tending toward statistical significance ($b = -0.47, p = .059$). For patient insight, controlling for antecedent patient collaboration and insight, no significant differences were found between interpretations and probe for insight ($b = -0.15, p = 0.69$). Box scores: 2 neutral
Locati et al. (2019)	Three first sessions of 24 patients (17 female) nested within 12 therapists (8 female) in psychodynamic supportive therapy.	Measure of interpretation: Category in the PIRS (Cooper et al., 2002) Measures of immediate outcome: Therapeutic alliance was measured using the Collaborative Interaction Scale (Colli & Lingiardi, 2009). Measures of moderators: None	Positive alliance was not associated with defense interpretation (adj = 0.32, $p = .75$) or transference interpretation (adj = −1.26, $p = .21$). Neutral alliance was negatively associated with defense interpretations (adj = −3.25, $p < .01$) and with transference interpretations (adj = −4.4, $p < .01$). Negative alliance was positively associated with defense interpretations (adj = 5.18, $p < .01$) and with transference interpretations (adj = 9.62, $p < .01$). Box scores: 4 negative, 2 neutral [the authors suggest that neutral alliance can be seen as positive process that is "the grounds for establishing a more positive alliance" (p. 119).]

Milbrath et al. (1999)	The fourth session of 20 patients in a psychotherapy for pathological grief reactions, treated by 9 therapists (5 female). Four therapists were clinical psychologists, 3 were psychiatrists, and 2 were psychiatric social workers.	Measure of interpretation: Category in the PIRS (Cooper et al., 2002) Measures of immediate outcome: Measure of patient's elaboration and dyselaboration (Horowitz et al., 1993). Elaboration includes convey facts, convey emotionality, and convey significance. Dyselaboration includes peripheral talk and distort significance. Measures of moderators: None	Defense interpretations were followed by disclosure of emotion (lag 1: $Z = 8.34$; lag 2: $Z = 5.01$; lag 3: $Z = 3.30$). Defense interpretations were also followed by conveying significance and making connections between different topics and the self for lags 1 and 3 (lag 1: $Z = 3.27$; lag 3: $Z = 2.11$). Defense interpretations were followed by a decrease in conveying facts (lag 1: $Z = -9.71$; lag 2: $Z = -5.30$; lag 3: $Z = -4.05$; lag 5: $Z = -2.16$). Transference interpretations were followed by conveying significance and making connections for up to 5 sequences after the therapist's intervention (lag 1: $Z = 7.96$; lag 2: $Z = 4.32$; lag 3: $Z = 3.29$; lag 4: $Z = 4.07$; lag 5: $Z = 4.36$). Transference interpretations were followed by a decrease in conveying facts (lag 1: $Z = -2.24$; lag 4, $Z = -2.00$; lag 5: $Z = -2.23$). Box scores: 5 positive
Silberschatz et al. (1986)	3 patients diagnosed with depression or dysthymic disorder were randomly selected from a larger sample. Case 1 showed an excellent outcome, Case 2 showed a moderately good outcome, and Case 3 showed a poor outcome. The therapists were all experienced psychologists and psychiatrists with a psychodynamic orientation.	Measure of interpretation: The typology devised by Malan (1963), which distinguishes between interpretation and transference interpretation. The accuracy of interpretation was measured using the Plan Compatibility of Interventions Scale (Caston, 1986). Both were measured by clinical judges. Measures of immediate outcome: The EXP Klein et al., 1986) Measures of moderators: None	No significant differences were found between transference and no transference interpretations on the residualized EXP scores (Case 1: $t = -3.41$, $p < .05$; Case 2: $t = 1.03$, NS; Case 3: $t = 0.62$, NS). The accuracy of interpretations was positively associated with increased EXP score (Case 1: $r = 0.54$, $p < .001$; Case 2: $r = .28$, $p < .01$; Case 3: $r = .25$, $p < .01$). Box scores: 1 positive, 1 neutral

(*continued*)

Table 7.1 Continued

Study	Sample	Measures of Interpretation, Outcome, and Moderators	Results
		Intermediate Outcome	
Datz et al. (2019)	20 clients at various stages of their respective therapeutic journeys were interviewed. For each patient, one session was recorded; 2 of the 20 patients were recorded during two sessions; in total, 22 psychotherapeutic sessions were analyzed.	Measure of interpretation: The interpretive techniques category of the Psychodynamic Interventions List (Gumz et al., 2014) as coded from transcribed sessions Measures of outcome: Working Alliance Inventory–Short Revised (Munder et al., 2010) as rated by the client	Interpretative forms of intervention were associated with higher WAI scores than were supportive forms (Mann–Whitney $U = 2283.5$, $p = 0.000$, $d = 0.67$). Box score: 1 positive
Lingiardi et al. (2011)	60 clients (40 female), treated by 60 (28 female) therapists (experienced psychiatrists and psychologists). All clients were treated with three theoretical approaches: psychodynamic ($n = 35$), cognitive–behavioral ($n = 17$), and integrative ($n = 8$). Patients and sessions were chosen randomly.	Measure of interpretation: PQS (Jones, 1985) as coded by trained judges from videotapes and transcripts Measures of outcome: (a) WAI-O (Horvath & Greenberg, 1989) as coded by trained judges from videotapes and transcripts; (b) SEQ-D (Stiles & Snow, 1984) as coded by trained judges from videotapes and transcripts	The following PQS items were positively correlated to the WAI-O: "Therapist makes connections between the therapeutic relationship and other relationships" ($r = .40$, $p < .05$) and "Therapist identifies a recurrent theme in the patient's experience or conduct" ($r = .36$, $p < .05$). The following PQS items were correlated to the SEQ-D: "Therapist identifies a recurrent theme in the patient's experience or conduct" ($r = .61$, $p < .05$); "Therapist points out patient's use of defensive maneuvers (e.g., undoing, denial)" ($r = .42$, $p < .05$); and "Therapist interprets warded-off or unconscious wishes, feelings, or ideas" ($r = .33$, $p < .05$). Nonsignificant correlations were not reported. However, at least 8 potential correlations (4 reported items and 2 outcome measures). Box scores: 5 positive and 3 neutral

Ogrodniczuk et al. (2000)	144 clients (61% female), treated by 8 therapists (5 female), 3 psychologists, 2 social workers, 2 occupational therapists, and 1 psychiatrist. Each patient received either interpretive or supportive therapy.	Measure of interpretation: PTS as rated by the client and the therapist Measures of outcome: Therapeutic alliance, as rated by the client, defined as the working relationship between the patient and the therapist. An overall alliance score was derived by calculating the average of the 6 items, and a summary of the entire course of therapy was used.	In interpretive therapy, there was a significant correlation between alliance and the patient-rated interpretive subscale of the PTS ($r[68] = 0.54$, $p = 0.00$) and between alliance and the therapist-rated interpretive subscale of the PTS ($r[70] = 0.30$, $p = 0.01$). These associations were not significant in supportive therapy. Box scores: 2 positive, 2 neutral
Piper et al. (1991)	64 clients (62% female), treated by 8 therapists (3 psychiatrists, 1 psychologist, and 4 social workers). All clients received dynamically oriented treatment.	Measure of interpretation: TIRS (Piper, Debbane, de Carufel & Bienvenu, 1987), as coded by trained judges from videotapes Measures of outcome: Therapeutic alliance, defined as the nature of the working relationship between the client and the therapist, rated separately by the client and the therapist. Four items rated the immediate impression, and 2 items rated the reflective impression. An overall score of the 6 items was calculated.	The proportion of transference interpretations was negatively correlated with the client-rated alliance ($r = -.21$, $p < .10$), with the therapist-rated immediate impression of the alliance ($r = -.33$, $p < .10$), and with the therapist-rated reflective impression of the alliance ($r = -.32$, $p < .10$). Box scores: 3 negative

EXP, Experiencing scale; HCVRMCS, Hill Counselor Verbal Response Modes Category System; NS, not significant; PIRS, Psychodynamic Intervention Rating Scale; PQS, Psychotherapy Q-Sort; PTS, Perception of Technique Scale; SEQ-D, Depth scale of the Session Evaluation Questionnaire; TIRS, Therapist Intervention Rating System; WAI-O, Working Alliance Inventory–Observer.

Table 7.2 Summary of Studies on Distal Treatment Outcomes of Psychotherapist Interpretations

Study	Sample and Methods	Measures of Interpretations and Outcome	Interpretation–Outcome Association	Moderator Results
Crits-Cristoph et al. (1988)	43 patients (30 female) were treated by 28 therapists. Accuracy was assessed based on therapists' interpretations of two early in-treatment sessions of dynamic therapy.	Measure of interpretation: CCRT (Luborsky, 1977) coded by trained judges from transcribed sessions. Measures of outcome: (a) Residual gain (general adjustment ratings made by the patient and a clinical observer, which were obtained pre- and post-therapy and were statistically adjusted for the effects of the patient's initial level of functioning); and (b) therapy benefits (ratings by the patient and the therapist assessing actual change).	The accuracy of the wish and a response from the CCRT "other" were significantly associated with residual gain ($r = .44, p < .01$) and with rated benefits ($r = .38, p < .05$). The accuracy of the response of the CCRT "self" was not related to residual gain ($r = .07$, NS) and was not associated with rated benefits ($r = .16$, NS). Box scores: 2 positive, 2 neutral	
Connolly et al. (1999)	29 patients (76% female) underwent brief supportive–expressive therapy. Four PhD-level therapists had at least 5 years of postdoctoral clinical experience with dynamic psychotherapy. Therapist speaking turns from three early sessions (2, 3, and 4) of psychotherapy were coded by three independent judges for each patient.	Measure of interpretation: Each therapist statement was rated as an interpretation, a clarification, a question, or other statement. Statements that were rated as interpretations by the coders were rated by 3 other independent coders who decided the type of interpretation (transference/nontransference). Measures of outcome: (a) BDI (Beck, Ward, Mendelson, Mock, & Erbaugh, 1961); (b) HAM-D (Hamilton, 1960). Both measures were completed at treatment intake and termination. Measures of moderators: The quality of interpersonal relationships was assessed using the global rating from the Health–Sickness Rating Scale (Luborsky & Bachrach, 1974). A clinician rated each patient before treatment on a scale from 0 to 100 assessing "the quality of the patient's interpersonal relationships."	Average percentage of transference interpretations did not predict post-treatment symptoms controlling for pre-treatment symptoms. Box scores: 2 neutral	Significant interaction was found between average percentage of transference interpretations and quality of interpersonal relationships in the prediction of symptom change (both BDI and HAM-D). High levels of transference interpretations were significantly associated with poor treatment outcome for patients with poor interpersonal functioning.

Gaston et al. (1998)	120 patients (66.67% female), older adults with depression, were treated by 10 therapists with at least 1 year of postdoctoral training in the specific therapy. Each patient was randomly assigned to one of four conditions: behavioral therapy, cognitive therapy, brief dynamic therapy, and a delayed treatment control group.	Measure of interpretation: The exploratory interventions subscale of the Inventory of Therapeutic Strategies (Gaston and Ring, 1992) coded by trained judges from videotapes. Measures of outcome: (a) Depressive symptoms measured by both the BDI (Beck et al., 1961, and the HRSD (Hamilton, 1960). Measure of moderators: California Therapeutic Rating Scale (Marmar, Weiss, & Gaston, 1989) measured the alliance and comprised four scales.	Exploratory interventions across therapy sessions predicted lower post-treatment HRSD scores only in cognitive therapy (R^2 increment =12%). Exploratory interventions did not predict post-treatment BDI scores. Box scores: 1 positive, 7 neutral	Across sessions, no significant interaction was found between exploratory interventions and alliance. But when sessions were analyzed separately, a significant interaction was found at session 10 for behavioral and cognitive therapies. Fewer exploratory interventions provided in cases of better alliance were predictive of less depressive symptomatology at termination. Conversely, more exploratory interventions provided in cases of poorer alliance were predictive of less depressive symptomatology at termination.
Glock et al. (2018)	34 patients (27 female) sought treatment for anxiety symptoms as their primary concern. The time of measurement was not specified. Details on the type of psychotherapy were not provided.	Measure of interpretation: CPPS (Hilsenroth et al., 2005). Item 13, "The therapist suggests alternative understanding not previously recognized by the patient." Patients rated their perceptions on how helpful the interventions were during their treatment. Measure of outcome: Overall improvement in psychotherapy. Patients were asked to rate the following item: "Overall, how much did you improve during the therapy?"	The interpretation item had the highest group mean ($M = 6.9$)—that is, it was rated as the most helpful intervention. This item was marginally associated with the measure of overall improvement ($r = .320$, $p = .065$). Box scores: 2 positive	

(*continued*)

Table 7.2 Continued

Study	Sample and Methods	Measures of Interpretations and Outcome	Interpretation–Outcome Association	Moderator Results
Hendriksen et al. (2011)	147 patients with depression (70% female) were allocated to short-term psychoanalytic supportive psychotherapy or combined therapy (psychotherapy and medication).	Measure of interpretation: Therapist Evaluation Form assessed the therapist's appraisal of the applied technique during treatment (5 categories from only supportive to only expressive), as rated by the therapists. Measures of outcome: HAM-D (Hamilton, 1960). Measurement of moderators: The patient's defense style based on Vaillant's (1971) hierarchy of ego defense mechanisms (immature, neurotic, or mature).	Expressive techniques were associated with a decrease in post-treatment HAM-D controlling for pretreatment HAM-D ($B = -2.38, p < 0.01$). Box score: 1 positive	No significant interaction effect was found between expressive techniques and maturity of defense style on HAM-D.
Hill et al. (1988)	8 patients (all female) older than age 25 years with self-esteem and relationship problems were treated by 8 therapists (4 female). Type of treatment was not provided.	Measure of interpretation: HCVRMCS (Hill, 1985, 1986) as coded by trained judges from transcribed sessions. Measures of outcome: (a) The Anxiety and Depression scales of the SCL-90-R (Derogatis et al., 1976); (b) the Depression scales of the SCL-90-R; and (c) the TSCS (Fitts, 1965), all rated by the patients. Change was determined by using squared-difference scores and retaining the signs between pre- and post-administrations.	Interpretation on the HCVRMCS did not correlate significantly with the SCL-R Anxiety scale ($r = .17$, NS), the SCL-R Depression scale ($r = .38$, NS), or the TSCS ($r = .55$, NS). Box scores: 1 positive, 2 neutral	
Jacobs & Warner (1981)	161 patients (66.66% female) were treated by 21 therapists (77% female). All patients were treated with dynamic-oriented psychotherapy.	Measure of interpretation: The uncovering subscale of the Staff Attitudes and Therapeutic Style, a therapist self-report questionnaire developed for this study. This subscale consists of scores for recognizing feelings and connecting temporal associations (clarifications and interpretations). Measure of outcome: GIS, answered on a 7-point scale ranging from "very much worse" to "very much improved," as rated by the patient.	The association between the uncovering subscale and the GIS was insignificant ($F = 1.96$, NS). Box score: 1 neutral	There was a significant interaction effect with the severity of clinical diagnosis ($F = 4.19, p < .05$). High levels of uncovering appear to have been associated with poor outcomes on the GIS in the more seriously disturbed group ($r = -.36$; p was not reported).

		Measurement of moderators: Severity of clinical diagnosis. Clinical diagnoses represented four main categories: neuroses (49%), personality trait disorders (25%), borderline conditions (15%), and psychoses (11%). Based on severity, the first two categories reflected a group of mild to moderate disorders, whereas the second two characterized the seriously disturbed group.		
Levy et al. (2015)	76 patients (55 female) were treated by 26 therapists with psychodynamic psychotherapy at a university-based outpatient clinic. Therapists were advanced doctoral students (13 female).	Measure of interpretation: Item 13, "The therapist suggests an alternative understanding not previously recognized by the patient" from the CPPS (Hilsenroth et al., 2005) as coded by trained judges from videotapes. Measure of outcome: GSI is an index of global distress derived as a summary score from the BSI (Derogatis, 1993). Measurement of moderators: (a) Alliance was measured with the Combined Alliance Short Form–Patient Version (Hatcher & Barends, 1996) as rated by the patient; (b) object relatedness was measured with Social Cognition and Object Relations Scale (Westen, 1995). Independent raters completed the measure based on narratives told during assessment and the first two treatment sessions.	In multilevel model accounting for therapist effects, and including patients' personality disorder, insight, alliance, object relations, and GSI at pretreatment evaluation, early session use of interpretation ($b = 0.81$, SE = 0.28, $p = 0.01$) was significantly related to a reliable change in GSI. Box score: 1 positive	There was no significant interaction between interpretations and alliance or interpretations and object relatedness on GSI.

(*continued*)

Table 7.2 Continued

Study	Sample and Methods	Measures of Interpretations and Outcome	Interpretation–Outcome Association	Moderator Results
Lilliengren et al. (2019)	10 good and 10 poor outcome cases were obtained from a randomized trial comparing cognitive therapy and STPP for cluster C personality disorders. Each outcome group included 5 cases from the CT group and 5 from the STPP group.	Measure of interpretation: Psychotherapy Process Q-Set (Jones, 1985), which yields ipsative scores. After watching a treatment session (or reading a session transcript), the rater sorts the 100 items into nine piles according to how characteristic of the session they are. Item 67, "Therapist interprets warded-off or unconscious wishes, feelings or ideas," refers to interpretation. Measure of outcome: Successful and unsuccessful cases were defined based on their respective amount of change in self-reported psychiatric symptoms, as assessed with the SCL-90-R (Derogatis et al., 1973).	Therapists in the unsuccessful cases showed significantly greater use of interpretations (successful: $M = 5.41$, $SD = 0.73$; unsuccessful: $M=6.35$, $SD=0.88$, $t = -2.703$, $p = .015$). Box score: 1 negative	
Milbrath et al. (1999)	20 bereaved patients (all female), ranging from normal to pathological grief reaction, were treated by 9 therapists (5 female; 4 clinical psychologists, 3 psychiatrists, and 2 psychiatric social workers). All patients were treated with brief dynamic psychotherapy for stress response symptoms. Process variables were derived from session 4, and the outcome was measured from pre- to post-treatment.	Measure of interpretation: Psychodynamic Intervention Rating Scale (Cooper & Bond, 1992) as coded by trained judges from transcribed sessions. Measure of outcome: Depression subscales of the BSI (Derogatis & Melisaratos, 1983).	The defense interpretation score was associated with lower symptoms, controlling for pretreatment symptoms ($r = -0.48$, $p < 0.05$). Box score: 1 positive	

Ogrodniczuk et al. (2000)	144 patients (61% female) were treated by 8 therapists (5 female; 3 psychologists, 2 social workers, 2 occupational therapists, and 1 psychiatrist. Each patient received either interpretive or supportive therapy.	Measure of interpretation: PTS as rated by the patient and the therapist. Measures of outcome: A set of outcome measures was reduced to three factors: (a) general symptomatology and dysfunction, (b) social–sexual maladjustment, and (c) non-use of mature defenses and family pathology.	Patient ratings on the interpretive subscale of the PTS-P were associated with poorer outcomes in the area of social–sexual functioning ($r[64] = 0.34$, $p = 0.01$). No other significant associations were found. Box scores: 2 neutral, 1 negative	
Piper et al. (1991)	64 patients (62% female) were treated by 8 therapists (3 psychiatrists, 1 psychologist, and 4 social workers). All patients received dynamically oriented treatment.	Measure of interpretation: TIRS (Piper et al., 1987) coded by trained judges from videotapes. Measures of outcome: A set of outcome variables was reduced to four factors—(a) interpersonal functioning, (b) psychiatric symptoms, (c) self-esteem, and (d) life satisfaction—as rated by the patient, therapist, and an independent assessor. Measurement of moderators: Quality of Object Relations, assessed before the start of therapy by an unstructured interview by a trained interviewer, other than the therapist.	The proportion of transference interpretations on the TIRS was positively correlated with higher patient-rated general symptoms and dysfunction ($r = .34$, $p < .01$). Nonsignificant correlations were found between the TIRS and the three other factors: psychiatric symptoms ($r = .17, p < .18$), self-esteem ($r = .09, p < .48$), and life satisfaction ($r = .08, p < .50$). Box scores: 1 negative, 3 neutral	The proportion of transference was significantly (or near significantly) correlated with poorer interpersonal functioning and psychiatric outcome for high QOR patients. None of the correlations for low QOR patients were significant.

BDI, Beck Depression Inventory; BSI, Brief Symptom Inventory; CCRT, core conflictual relationship theme; CPPS, Comparative Psychotherapy Process Scale; CT, Cognitive Therapy; GIS, Global Improvement Scale; GSI, Global Severity Index; HAM-D, Hamilton Rating Scale for Depression; HCVRMCS, Hill Counselor Verbal Response Modes Category System; NS, not significant; PTS, Perception of Technique Scale; QOR, Quality of Object Relation; SCL-90-R, Symptom Checklist-90–Revised; STPP, Short Term Psychodynamic Psychotherapy; TIRS, Therapist Intervention Rating System; TSCS, Tennessee Self-Concept Scale.

The perspective of the assessor also varied. The vast majority of research (77.78%) focused on the perspective of an external observer (e.g., Drapeau et al., 2008), 11.11% on the therapists' perspective (e.g., Hendriksen et al., 2011), and only 5.55% on the patients' perspective (e.g., Glock et al., 2018). One study (6.5%) focused on both patients' and therapists' perspectives (Ogrodniczuk et al., 2000).

Of the six studies assessing immediate in-session outcome (see Table 7.1), two (33.33%) focused on patients' collaboration or alliance, two (33.33%) on the quality of the patients' therapeutic work (e.g., elaborating on important topics), and two (33.33%) on improved emotional processing. Additional types of in-session outcomes were patients' maturity of defense mechanism, insight, and emotional processing, with a single study focusing on each. Some of the studies used several outcomes. All four studies focusing on intermediate session outcome assessed the alliance (e.g., Datz et al., 2019). In addition, one study assessed session depth (e.g., Lingiardi et al., 2011).

Of the 12 studies assessing distal treatment outcome (see Table 7.2), 41.67% assessed severity of depression (e.g., Connolly et al., 1999), 33.33% general symptom severity (e.g., Levy et al., 2015), and 41.66% general life satisfaction and level of functioning (e.g., Bush & Meehan, 2011) or problem improvement (e.g., Jacobs & Warner, 1981) as the outcome. The types of assessment do not amount to 100% because three studies included more than one outcome measure. For example, one study assessed the severity of anxiety, the severity of depression, and the level of self-concept as outcomes (Hill, Helms, Tichenor, et al., 1988).

The perspective of the assessor in all outcome measures varied, with 27.78% focusing on the patients' perspective (e.g., Pesale & Hilsenroth, 2009) and 33.33% on the perspective of the external evaluator coding the session (e.g., Lingiardi et al., 2011). Other studies focused on more than one perspective, with 27.78% focusing on patients' and therapists' perspectives, 11.11% focusing on patients' and external evaluators' perspectives, and 6.25% combining all three perspectives into one factor.

Associations Between Interpretations and Immediate Outcomes

There were six studies with 88 patients, testing the association between the use of interpretations and a variety of immediate outcomes. In terms of positive immediate outcomes, Hill, Helms, Tichenor, et al. (1988) compared the patient- and therapist-rated helpfulness of interpretations with other types of interventions, such as closed or open questions, self-disclosure, and direct guidance. Based on a sample of eight patients, they found that interpretations were rated as most helpful by therapists and second most helpful (after self-disclosure) by patients. Furthermore, following the use of interpretation, patients indicated a therapeutic work reaction—that is, achieving better understanding of their feelings and thoughts and adopting new ways to behave. Similarly, patients presented greater emotional processing following interpretations (Hill, Helms, Tichenor, et al., 1988; Silberschatz et al., 1986). In addition, the frequency of defense interpretations (i.e., therapists' interventions on patients' defense mechanisms) in a sample of 20 patients with pathological grief reaction was followed by greater disclosure of emotions, conveying significant information about oneself and making new connections between important themes, and by a decrease in conveying factual statements that do not facilitate the therapeutic work (Milbrath et al., 1999). The use of transference interpretations was also followed by conveying significant information about oneself and making new connections, and by a decrease in conveying factual statements (Milbrath et al., 1999). We thus assigned 10 positive box scores in this section (see Table 7.1).

In terms of negative immediate outcomes, some potential adverse effects of defense and transference interpretations were found in the only study that tested the association between interpretations and alliance (Locati et al., 2019). In that study, both defense and transference interpretations were positively associated with immediate negative alliance and negatively associated with aspects of good alliance, as indicated by coding of direct and indirect rupture markers. We thus assigned four negative box scores in this section.

In terms of neutral immediate outcomes, other studies found no significant effects of interpretations on patients' defense mechanisms (Drapeau et al., 2008), and interpretation was not followed by greater patients' collaboration or insight than in the case of open questions inviting the patient to explore their thoughts, feelings, or behaviors (Hill et al., 2020). Furthermore, interpretation was not followed by some positive aspects of alliance (Locati et al., 2019). We thus assigned six neutral box scores in this section (see Table 7.1).

In summary, there were 10 positive, six neutral, and four negative box scores. Thus, the majority of the associations between interpretations and immediate outcome were positive, indicating that clients typically reacted positively to therapist interpretations in that immediate session.

Associations Between Interpretations and Intermediate Outcomes

In four studies with 288 patients, researchers examined the association between the use of interpretations and a variety of intermediate outcomes, such as alliance strength and session depth (as measured after or between sessions).

Of the four studies that examined the relation between the use of interpretations and alliance, three studies found a favorable effect on alliance strength, two for patient-rated alliance (Datz et al., 2019; Ogrodniczuk et al., 2000), and one for alliance as rated by external judges based on the videotapes and transcripts of the sessions (Lingiardi et al., 2011). We thus assigned five positive scores in this section (see Table 7.1).

A negative relation between frequency of interpretations and post-session alliance strength was found in only one study (Piper et al., 1991). That study found that a greater proportion of transference interpretations (of all the methods used in the session) was associated with poorer alliance as rated by both patients and two aspects of alliance rated by the therapists. We thus assigned three negative box scores in this section (see Table 7.1). One potential post hoc explanation is that transference interpretations may have an adverse effect when provided in a high dose. However, given that no causality can be established between transference interpretations and alliance in this study, it is also possible that higher levels of negative transference resulted in both poorer alliance and greater use of transference interpretation by the therapists.

Lingiardi et al. (2011) focused on session depth as coded by judges based on session videotapes and transcripts, and they found that greater use of interpretations was associated with the session being coded as deeper. We assigned three positive box scores for this study (see Table 7.1).

In summary, there were eight positive, five neutral, and three negative box scores. Thus, half of the associations between the frequency of interpretations and intermediate outcomes were positive.

To the best of our knowledge, no study investigated the existence of moderators of the effect of interpretations on intermediate outcome.

Associations Between Interpretations and Distal Outcomes

Twelve studies with 866 patients investigated the association between the frequency or accuracy of interpretations and distal outcome (changes in symptom severity throughout treatment).

In terms of positive associations, seven out of 12 studies found positive association between higher frequency or accuracy of interpretations and better outcome (Crits-Cristoph et al., 1988; Gaston et al., 1998; Glock et al., 2018; Hendriksen et al., 2011; Hill, Helms, Tichenor, et al., 1988; Levy et al., 2015; Milbrath et al., 1999). For example, Levy et al. (2015) found that a greater use of interpretations early in treatment was associated with greater likelihood of the patients showing reliable change on a global severity index. A similar association was found in a study correlating the frequency of defensive interpretations and reduction in symptom severity in a sample of 20 bereaved patients (Milbrath et al., 1999). A tendency toward a significant beneficial of interpretations on outcome was also found in Glock et al. (2018), in which 34 patients were asked to rate the extent to which they found the therapists' use of interpretations to be helpful. Interpretation was rated as the most helpful intervention. In addition, there was a marginally significant association, with patients who rated their therapist's use of interpretations as more helpful also showing better treatment outcome. We thus assigned nine positive box scores in this section (see Table 7.2).

In terms of neutral or negative associations between the frequency of interpretation and distal outcome, Jacobs and Warner (1981) found neutral results between the frequency of interpretation in psychodynamic treatment and patients' ratings on the Global Improvement Scale. Ogrodniczuk et al. (2000) found no significant association between interpretation and symptom reduction but an adverse association on social and sexual functioning. Piper et al. (1991) found an adverse effect of interpretations, but this time on general symptom reduction, whereas the effect on psychiatric symptoms, social and sexual functioning, was not significant. Similarly, Lilliengren et al. (2019) found a greater use of interpretations in 10 cases with a poor outcome than in 10 cases with a good outcome. Overall, we assigned 19 neutral box score (seven of them drawn from one study) and three negative box scores (see Table 7.2).

In summary, we assigned nine positive, 19 neutral, and three negative scores. Thus, the results linking the frequency of interpretations to distal outcome are mixed.

Moderators of Distal Outcomes

Although most of the associations reported in the studies demonstrated a neutral association (19 of 32 box score; see Table 7.2), findings did show considerable variability as a function of the type of interpretations, type of distal outcomes, type of treatment, patients' symptoms, and object relations. With regard to type of interpretation, Crits-Cristoph et al. (1988) found that a greater accuracy of interpretations focusing on the individual's interpersonal unmet wishes and perceived responses of the others to these wishes was associated with greater symptom reduction by the end of treatment. But that was not the case with respect to the accuracy of the therapists' interpretations regarding the individual's own responses to others, which did not have a significant association with outcome.

With regard to variability in the type of outcome, Hill, Helms, Tichenor, et al. (1988) found no significant relation between interpretations on changes in symptoms of anxiety and depression in a sample of eight patients. Nevertheless, the authors found a nonsignificant but moderate (r =. 55) association with changes in patient-rated self-concept (one's thoughts and feelings about the self that contribute to a sense of identity).

With regard to variability in type of treatment, a study that examined the effect of interpretations in different types of psychotherapy found that interpretations had a significant association with therapist-rated outcome in cognitive therapy but not in psychodynamic therapy (Gaston et al., 1998).

We located one study that found a moderating relation of the severity of clinical diagnosis (Jacobs & Warner, 1981). Patients with more severe clinical diagnosis who received more interpretations, as rated by the therapists, reported poorer outcome than those with a less severe clinical diagnosis.

Three studies focused on the patients' maturity and style of object relation. Levy et al. (2015) focused on clinician-rated affective and cognitive aspects of an individual's object relations and found no significant moderation. Connolly et al. (1999) found that high levels of transference interpretations were significantly associated with poor treatment outcome for patients with poor interpersonal functioning. By contrast, Piper et al. (1991) found that the proportion of transference interpretations was significantly correlated with poorer interpersonal functioning and psychiatric outcome in patients with a high quality of object relation, whereas no significant effect of interpretation on outcome was found for those with low quality of object relation.

Neither of two studies examining a potential moderation of alliance strength (measured post-session) on the interpretation–outcome association found a moderating effect in psychodynamic treatment (Gaston et al., 1998; Levy et al., 2015). In one of these studies, such a moderating effect was tested at sessions 5, 10, and 15 and found only for cognitive therapy and only in a particular session (Gaston et al., 1998). One study focused on the ability of the level of maturity of defense style to moderate the interpretations–outcome association, and it found no significant effect (Hendriksen et al., 2011).

In summary, individual studies have found greater effect of interpretation on distal outcome when interpretations focused on the individual's interpersonal unmet wishes and perceived responses of the others to these wishes (one study), when the outcome was self-concept rather than symptoms (one study), in cognitive therapy rather than psychodynamic therapy (one study), and when patients' showed a less severe clinical diagnosis (one study). To our knowledge, none of these patterns have been replicated in any published studies to date. In addition, mixed results were found in regard to patient object relations.

Therapist Effects on Distal Outcomes

Whether some psychotherapists are better than others in their interpretations has seldom been studied. Some evidence suggests that more interpretations are associated with a reduction in the patients' maladaptive defense only for those therapists who experienced good parental care and negative introjection (Hersoug, 2004). Moreover, a negative relation between frequency of transference interpretations and outcome was found when therapists experienced an increase in feeling inadequate and disengaged during therapy (Dahl et al., 2016, 2017).

In the current review, the few studies that accounted for therapist effects suggested that the interpretation–outcome association remained statistically significant even after accounting for the therapist effect; that is, interpretation in these studies was effective regardless of who provided the interpretation (Katz et al., 2019; Keefe et al., 2019; Levy et al., 2015). Still, some therapist variable may affect the interpretation–outcome association.

With regard to the professional background of the psychotherapist, a potential explanation of the negative interpretation–outcome association found in two studies (Ogrodniczuk et al., 2000; Piper et al., 1991) is the training of the therapists. The therapists in these studies varied in their professional background (e.g., social workers, occupational therapists), compared to the relatively more homogeneous training in the other nine studies, in which participating therapists received training mostly as clinical psychologists or psychiatrists. If future studies support such an explanation, it may point to the need to systematically investigate how the type of training received may affect the competence and manner in which interpretations are delivered and their subsequent outcomes.

Summary of the Research Review

Half the findings suggest a positive association between interpretation and in-session immediate outcomes (10 positive, six neutral, and four negative box scores) as well as intermediate outcomes (eight positive, five neutral, and three negative box scores). By contrast, the associations between interpretations and distal treatment outcomes were mixed (nine positive, 19 neutral, and three negative box scores), with findings varying according to the type of interpretation and the type of outcome.

The few available studies that tested moderators of the association between the frequency of interpretations and distal outcome suggest that the patients' object relation may be of importance on who benefits most from interpretations. However, based on the literature, the direction of this association is not consistent. Some studies showed that individuals with better object relation benefit more from interpretations, whereas others found the opposite or did not find any association. The only study that used an experimental design in which individuals were randomized to receive a treatment with or without interpretations found that individuals with poorer object relation benefited more from interpretation than did those with high-quality object relation.

An interesting pattern of results was found for the few studies focusing on the effect of interpretation on alliance for the immediate versus intermediate outcomes. For immediate in-session outcome, measured at several time points during the session, interpretations were associated with poorer alliance. By contrast, for intermediate end-of-session outcome, most of the studies found that interpretations were associated with stronger alliance.

Possible Negative Effects and Harm

Although the potential side effects of interpretations have not received much research attention, many agree that rigidly adhering to interpretations (or any other skill) may cause harm to patients (Summers & Barber, 2010). Some evidence suggests that interpretations that are not accurate are not helpful (Crits-Christoph et al., 1988; Silberschatz, 2017).

Studies focusing on adherence to psychodynamic treatment in general (rather than on interpretations alone) point to the potential importance of paying attention to the amount of interpretations. One study that sought to identify the right "dose" of interpretation (the number of interpretations provided in a session) found that a moderate dose, rather than a high dose, is recommended (McCarthy et al., 2016). Many explanations can be provided for the potentially adverse effect of a high dose of interpretation, especially transference interpretation, including patients' feeling attacked, accused, and misunderstood. Thus, many theorists have stressed the care with which interpretations should be used, referring to them as "high-risk, high-gain" methods (Gabbard, 2006, p. 1668).

Our research review on the association between interpretation and alliance may shed some light on providing interpretations in the right manner and at the appropriate time. The review of intermediate outcome revealed a positive association between interpretations and alliance in three of four studies so that greater use of interpretation was associated with stronger alliance. Interestingly, the one study that found a negative association (more interpretations were associated with poorer alliance) focused on more direct transference interpretations (Piper et al., 1991). A potential explanation is the possible adverse effect of a high proportion of transference interpretations on the working alliance. This explanation is supported by the only study that associated interpretation and alliance as an immediate outcome (as measured during the session) and also found a negative association. Yet, the explanation should be considered with caution because the available findings are based on between-individual differences, whereas the phenomenon of interest is a within-individual one. Thus, alternative explanations, such as reverse causation, where poor alliance results in more transference work, cannot be ruled out. For example, it could be that therapists who recognized a disruption in the alliance may have used transference interpretation to understand this disruption in the context of the patient's core pain or conflict (Foelsch & Kernberg, 1998).

Diversity Considerations

There has been limited research to date on the effectiveness of interpretations as a function of the individual's gender, race/ethnicity, sexual orientation, and socioeconomic status. As a result, there are no research-based guidelines on how to implement interpretations across diverse patients, except for the general guideline of acting in a responsive and sensitive manner.

In offering interpretations, therapists can become familiar with the patient's cultural background as well as one's own, and acknowledge and explore the differences between them (Connolly Gibbons et al., 2012; Leichsenring & Schauenburg, 2014). However, when offering interpretations that go beyond what the patient is saying and presenting new perspectives, therapists should be careful not to impose their own worldview on the patient. Therapists are expected to show multicultural competence, as manifested in expanding their knowledge of patients' cultural background and worldview and of the corresponding methods to be used, and gaining awareness of their own assumptions, beliefs, and values that may affect their work with each patient (Sue et al., 1992; Tao et al., 2015). Therapists are also expected to be knowledgeable and open to discuss issues related to their and their patients' sexual identity (Quiñones et al., 2017).

Limitations of the Research

A major limitation of the current findings is the reliance, in most studies, on the correlation between frequency (rather than accuracy or quality) of interpretations and outcome. More is not necessarily better, and in fact, it could be that psychotherapists use more interpretations when the patient is not receptive or understanding of the interpretations. It is more appropriate to examine the accuracy or quality of the interpretations in association with immediate in-session outcome than intermediate or distal outcome so that we can link the interpretations directly with how the patient responds.

Most of the available research on intermediate and distal outcomes is based on between-individuals associations, most commonly being limited to a single time in treatment when the interpretations were evaluated. Therefore, most of the available findings mix the general levels of interpretation provided by the therapist to a given patient with deviations from this general level in a given session. This is a severe limitation because it is not possible to draw inferences about within-individual effects from between-individuals effects (Fisher et al., 2018).

One of the main factors contributing to the focus on a single session per patient is the labor-intensive process of coding in-session processes for each session, which limits dramatically the number of sessions that can be coded. Thus, some studies have focused on patients' and therapists' self-reports, which can be administered repeatedly throughout treatment, even on a session-by-session basis. Self-report measures have their own limitations, however, including their subjectivity and their restriction to what the patients and therapists are aware of and interested in reporting.

The greatest advantage of the research literature is also its greatest limitation: the great diversity of measures (various aspects of the skill from different informants), designs (randomized controlled trials, effectiveness studies), treatment types and durations (e.g., long-term psychoanalysis vs. short-term psychodynamic treatment), and statistical methods (e.g., disentangling between- and within-therapist as well as between- and within-patient variances vs. using raw scores). This great variability has the potential to serve as a rich source for identifying who may benefit most from each type of interpretation for each type of outcome. However, the small number of studies makes it difficult to study the effect of any single moderator.

One direction for future research is the development of artificial intelligence algorithms that can mimic observer coding (Imel et al., 2019) based on videotaped sessions or transcripts. Automated coding of interpretations can be especially instrumental in providing therapists with real-time feedback on their methods. Similarly, automatic measures can be collected during the session to provide insight into patients' and therapists' moment-to-moment experiences before, during, and after the therapists provide an interpretation (e.g., facial microexpressions; Arango et al., 2019).

To enhance clinical practice and research, it is important to move from context-free questions of whether interpretations are effective to questions of for whom, when, and in which manner interpretations can be effective. Such questions can be addressed in many ways, including data-driven machine learning for identifying the optimal use of interpretation for each individual or subpopulation of individuals (Cohen et al., 2021). In addition, theory-driven moderated mediation models can identify between-individuals moderators (the patients who benefit most) and within-individual ones (the optimal timing of interpretations) in a within-patient mediation model of the effect of specific therapists training or type of treatment on the methods used, which in turn predicts treatment outcome.

Few researchers have distinguished within-patient from between-patients effects. Disentangling these two effects is of critical importance because within-patient effect (rather than between-patients effect) can indicate the ability of interpretations to serve as a mechanism of change in treatment (Zilcha-Mano, 2021). Between-patients effect may indicate that patients who generally received more interpretations than other methods showed better outcomes. But this association may be a product of therapists' responsiveness: the tendency to provide more interpretations to some patients than to others (Stiles, 1988).

Training Implications

Numerous clinical training resources are available for offering skillful interpretations (e.g., Book, 1998; Malan, 1979; McCullough, 2003; Safran & Muran, 2000; Summers & Barber, 2010; Wachtel, 2011). None of these training programs have been subjected to empirical research on their effectiveness, to our knowledge, with the exception of training in repairing alliance ruptures (see Chapter 2, this volume).

Based on the clinical and theoretical knowledge, to skillfully implement interpretations, we recommend that trainees (a) be familiar with the theoretical models for each type of interpretation (intrapersonal conflict, interpersonal transferential, and nontransferential repetitive patterns); (b) master concrete procedures to formulate patients' problems and deliver interpretations addressing those issues (e.g., the core conflictual relationship theme guidelines for constructing and delivering interpretations); and (c) receive supervision with detailed feedback on the manner in which they deliver the interpretations. In supervision, it is possible to teach how to take into account the many factors that may affect the effectiveness of the interpretations, including the patient's quality of object relation, strength of therapeutic alliance, and phase of therapy (Spiegel & Hill, 1989).

Preferably, videotaped sessions will be used to enable supervision that takes into account the moment-to-moment unfolding of the session. In the future, automatic feedback about the skillful implementation of interpretations within the sessions may also become available (Weck et al., 2021).

Therapeutic Practices

Although it is too early to formulate research-based guidelines for the skillful use of interpretations, the following practices can be recommended based on a synthesis of clinical experience and empirical research:

- Observe the immediate and intermediate outcomes of an interpretation (Do the patients reject the interpretation, accept it passively and not act on it, or embrace it and make it their own, using it to deepen the therapeutic work?).
- Check with patients about how they feel about the interpretation and be responsive to patients' verbal and nonverbal reactions.
- Prioritize the accuracy and experience-nearness of your interpretations over their simple frequency.
- Take into account the patient's sociocultural context, psychological history, and readiness for interpretation.
- Monitor the strength of the alliance before, during, and after you provide interpretations.
- Repair any alliance ruptures resulting from the negative effects of interpretations.
- Attend to patients' quality of object relations when considering whether to use interpretations. Patients with poorer object relations may benefit more from interpretations compared to patients with high quality of object relations.
- Be aware that interpretations may not be beneficial, and in some cases, they may prove harmful if not provided at the right time and if not attuned to the patient.

References

* Studies included in the research review.

Allen, J. G., Gabbard, G. O., Newsom, G. E., & Coyne, L. (1990). Detecting patterns of change in patients' collaboration within individual psychotherapy sessions. *Psychotherapy: Theory, Research, Practice, Training, 27*(4), 522–530.

Arango, I., Miranda, E., Ferrer, J. C. S., Fresán, A., Ortega, M. A. R., Vargas, A. N., Barragán, S., Villanueva-Valle, J., Munoz-Delgado, J., & Robles, R. (2019). Changes in facial emotion expression during a psychotherapeutic intervention for patients with borderline personality disorder. *Journal of Psychiatric Research, 114*, 126–132.

Aron, L. (1992). Interpretation as expression of the analyst's subjectivity. *Psychoanalytic Dialogues, 2*(4), 475–507.

Barber, J. P., Muran, J. C., McCarthy, K. S., Keefe, J. R., & Zilcha-Mano, S. (2021). Research on dynamic therapies. In M. Barkham, W. Lutz, & L. Castonguay (Eds.), *Bergin and Garfield's handbook of psychotherapy and behavior change* (7th ed., pp. 387–420). Wiley.

Basch, M. F. (1980). *Doing psychotherapy*. Basic Books.

Beck, A. T. (1976). *Cognitive therapy and the emotional disorders*. International Universities Press.

Beck, A. T., Ward, C. H., Mendelson, M., Mock, J., & Erbaugh, J. (1961). An inventory for measuring depression. *Archives of General Psychiatry, 4*(6), 561–571.

Bibring, E. (1954). Psychoanalysis and the dynamic psychotherapies. *Journal of the American Psychoanalytic Association, 2*(4), 745–770.

Book, H. E. (1998). *How to practice brief psychodynamic psychotherapy: The core conflictual relationship theme method*. American Psychological Association.

Bromberg, P. M. (2003). One need not be a house to be haunted: On enactment, dissociation, and the dread of "not-me"—A case study. *Psychoanalytic Dialogues, 13*(5), 689–709.

Bush, M., & Meehan, W. (2011). Should supportive measures and relational variables be considered a part of psychoanalytic technique? Some empirical considerations. *International Journal of Psychoanalysis, 92*(2), 377–399.

Caston, J. (1986). The reliability of the diagnosis of the patient's unconscious plan. In J. Weiss, H. Sampson, & the Mount Zion Psychotherapy Research Group (Eds.), *The psychoanalytic process: Theory, clinical observations, and empirical research* (pp. 241–255). Routledge.

Cohen, Z. D., Delgadillo, J., & DeRubeis, R. J. (2021). Personalized treatment approaches. In M. Barkham, W. Lutz, & L. Castonguay (Eds.), *Bergin and Garfield's handbook of psychotherapy and behavior change* (7th ed., pp. 673–703). Wiley.

Colli, A., & Lingiardi, V. (2009). The Collaborative Interactions Scale: A new transcript-based method for the assessment of therapeutic alliance ruptures and resolutions in psychotherapy. *Psychotherapy Research, 19*(6), 718–734.

*Connolly, M., Crits-Christoph, P., Shappell, S., Barber, J., Luborsky, L., & Shaffer, C. (1999). Relation of transference interpretations to outcome in the early sessions of brief supportive–expressive psychotherapy. *Psychotherapy Research, 9*(4), 485–495.

Connolly Gibbons, M. B., Crits-Christoph, P., Barber, J. P., & Schamberger, M. (2007). Insight in psychotherapy: A review of empirical literature. In L. G. Castonguay & C. Hill (Eds.), *Insight in psychotherapy* (pp. 143–165). American Psychological Association.

Connolly Gibbons, M. B., Thompson, S. M., Scott, K., Schauble, L. A., Mooney, T., Thompson, D., Green, P., MacArthur, M. J., & Crits-Christoph, P. (2012). Supportive–expressive dynamic psychotherapy in the community mental health system: A pilot effectiveness trial for the treatment of depression. *Psychotherapy, 49*(3), 303–316.

Cooper, S., & Bond, M. (1992). *Psychodynamic Interventions Rating Scale* [Unpublished manuscript].

Cooper, S., Bond, M., Audet, C., Boss, K., & Csank, P. (2002). *The psychodynamic intervention rating scale* (4th ed.). McGill University.

*Crits-Christoph, P., Cooper, A., & Luborsky, L. (1988). The accuracy of therapists' interpretations and the outcome of dynamic psychotherapy. *Journal of Consulting and Clinical Psychology, 56*(4), 490–495.

Crits-Christoph, P., & Gibbons, M. B. C. (2021). Psychotherapy process–outcome research: Advances in understanding causal connections. In M. Barkham, W. Lutz, & L. G. Castonguay (Eds.), *Bergin and Garfield's handbook of psychotherapy and behavior change* (7th ed., pp. 263–296). Wiley.

Crits-Christoph, P., Gibbons, M. B. C., & Mukherjee, D. (2013). The efficacy and effectiveness of psychotherapy. In Michael J. Lambert (Ed.), *Bergin and Garfield's handbook of psychotherapy and behavior change* (6th ed., pp. 298–340). Wiley.

Dahl, H. J., Høglend, P., Ulberg, R., Amlo, S., Gabbard, G. O., Perry, J. C., & Christoph, P. C. (2017). Does therapists' disengaged feelings influence the effect of transference work? A study on countertransference. *Clinical Psychology & Psychotherapy, 24*(2), 462–474.

Dahl, H. J., Ulberg, R., Friis, S., Perry, J. C., & Høglend, P. A. (2016). Therapists' inadequate feelings and long-term effect of transference work. *Psychotherapy and Psychosomatics, 85*(5), 309–311.

*Datz, F., Wong, G., & Löffler-Stastka, H. (2019). Interpretation and working through contemptuous facial micro-expressions benefits the patient–therapist relationship. *International Journal of Environmental Research and Public Health, 16*(24), 4901.

Davanloo, H. (2000). *Intensive short-term dynamic psychotherapy: Selected papers of Habib Davanloo, MD.* Wiley-Blackwell.

DeFife, J. A., Hilsenroth, M. J., & Gold, J. R. (2008). Patient ratings of psychodynamic psychotherapy session activities and their relation to outcome. *Journal of Nervous and Mental Disease, 196*(7), 538–547.

Derogatis, L. R. (1993). *Brief Symptom Inventory: BSI.* Pearson.

Derogatis, L. R., Lipman, R. S., & Covi, L. (1973). SCL-90: An outpatient psychiatric rating scale—Preliminary report. *Psychopharmacology Bulletin, 9*(1), 13–28.

Derogatis, L. R., & Melisaratos, N. (1983). The Brief Symptom Inventory: An introductory report. *Psychological Medicine, 13*(3), 595–605.

Derogatis, L. R., Rickels, K., & Rock, A. F. (1976). The SCL-90 and the MMPI: A step in the validation of a new self-report scale. *British Journal of Psychiatry, 128*(3), 280–289.

*Drapeau, M., de Roten, Y., Beretta, V., Blake, E., Koerner, A., & Despland, J. N. (2008). Therapist technique and patient defensive functioning in ultra-brief psychodynamic psychotherapy: A lag sequential analysis. *Clinical Psychology & Psychotherapy, 15*(4), 247–255.

Fisher, A. J., Medaglia, J. D., & Jeronimus, B. F. (2018). Lack of group-to-individual generalizability is a threat to human subjects research. *Proceedings of the National Academy of Sciences of the USA, 115*(27), E6106–E6115.

Fitts, W. H. (1965). *Tennessee Self Concept Scale manual, recordings and tests.* Counselor Recordings and Tests.

Foelsch, P. A., & Kernberg, O. F. (1998). Transference-focused psychotherapy for borderline personality disorders. *Psychotherapy in Practice, 4*(2), 67–90.

Freud, S. (1955). Studies on hysteria. In S. Freud & J. Strachey (Eds.), *The standard edition of the complete psychological works of Sigmund Freud: Vol. 2 (1893–1895)* (pp. 3–181). Hogarth Press and the Institute of Psycho-Analysis.

Gabbard, G. O. (2006). When is transference work useful in dynamic psychotherapy? American Journal of Psychiatry, *163*(10), 1667–1669.

Gabbard, G. O. (2009). Techniques of psychodynamic psychotherapy. In *Textbook of psychotherapeutic treatments* (pp. 43–67). American Psychiatric Publishing.

Gaston, L., Piper, W., Debbane, E., Bienvenu, J. P., & Garant, J. (1994). Alliance and technique for predicting outcome in short- and long-term analytic psychotherapy. *Psychotherapy Research, 4*(2), 121–135.

Gaston, L., & Ring, J. M. (1992). Preliminary results on the inventory of therapeutic strategies. *Journal of Psychotherapy Practice and Research, 1*(2), 135.

*Gaston, L., Thompson, L., Gallagher, D., Cournoyer, L. G., & Gagnon, R. (1998). Alliance, technique, and their interactions in predicting outcome of behavioral, cognitive, and brief dynamic therapy. *Psychotherapy Research, 8*(2), 190–209.

Gillieron, E. (1989). Short psychotherapeutic interventions (four sessions). *Psychotherapy and Psychosomatics, 51*(1), 32–37.

*Glock, G., Hilsenroth, M., & Curtis, R. (2018). Therapeutic interventions patients with anxiety problems find most helpful: A case for integration? *Journal of Psychotherapy Integration, 28*(2), 233–241.

Gumz, A., Horstkotte, J. K., & Kaestner, D. (2014). The techniques of the psychodynamic therapist: Verbal interventions from a theoretical and practice-oriented perspective. *Zeitschrift fur Psychosomatische Medizin Und Psychotherapie, 60*(3), 219–237.

Hamilton, M. (1960). A rating scale for depression. *Journal of Neurology, Neurosurgery, and Psychiatry, 23*(1), 56–62.

Hatcher, R. L., & Barends, A. W. (1996). Patients' view of the alliance in psychotherapy: Exploratory factor analysis of three alliance measures. *Journal of Consulting and Clinical Psychology, 64*(6), 1326–1336.

*Hendriksen, M., Van, H. L., Schoevers, R. A., De Jonghe, F. E., Van Wijk, C. M. G., Peen, J., & Dekker, J. J. (2011). Therapist judgment of defense styles and therapeutic technique related to outcome in psychodynamic psychotherapy for depression. *Psychotherapy and Psychosomatics, 80*(6), 377–379.

Hersoug, A. G. (2004). Assessment of therapists' and patients' personality: Relationship to therapeutic technique and outcome in brief dynamic psychotherapy. *Journal of Personality Assessment, 83*(3), 191–200.

Hill, C. E. (1978). Development of a counselor verbal response category. *Journal of Counseling Psychology, 25*(5), 461–468.

Hill, C. E. (1985). Manual for the Hill Counselor Verbal Response Modes Category System (Rev. ed.) [Unpublished manuscript]. University of Maryland.

Hill, C. E. (1986). An overview of the Hill Counselor and Client Verbal Response Modes Category Systems. In L. Greenberg & W. Pinsof (Eds.), *The psychotherapeutic process: A research handbook* (pp. 131–160). Guilford.

Hill, C. E. (2014). *Helping skills: Facilitating exploration, insight, and action* (4th ed.). American Psychological Association.

Hill, C. E. (2020). *Helping skills: Facilitating exploration, insight, and action* (5th ed.). American Psychological Association.

Hill, C. E., Castonguay, L. G., Angus, L., Arnkoff, D. B., Barber, J. P., Bohart, A. C., Borkovec, T. D., Bowman, E. A., Caspar, F., Gibbons, M. B. C., Crits-Christoph, P., Cruz, J. M., Elliott, R., Friedlander, M. L., Gelso, C. J., Glass, C. R., Goldfried, M. R., Greenberg, L. S., Holtforth, M. G., . . . Wampold, B. E. (2007). Insight in psychotherapy: Definitions, processes, consequences, and research directions. In L. G. Castonguay & C. E. Hill (Eds.), *Insight in psychotherapy* (pp. 441–454). American Psychological Association.

Hill, C. E., Corbett, M. M., Kanitz, B., Rios, P., Lightsey, R., & Gomez, M. (1992). Client behavior in counseling and therapy sessions: Development of a pantheoretical measure. *Journal of Counseling Psychology, 39*, 539–549.

Hill, C. E., Helms, J. E., Spiegel, S. B., & Tichenor, V. (1988). Development of a system for categorizing client reactions to therapist interventions. *Journal of Counseling Psychology, 35*(1), 27–36.

*Hill, C. E., Helms, J. E., Tichenor, V., Spiegel, S. B., O'Grady, K. E., & Perry, E. S. (1988). Effects of therapist response modes in brief psychotherapy. *Journal of Counseling Psychology, 35*(3), 222–233.

*Hill, C. E., Lu, Y., Gerstenblith, J. A., Kline, K. V., Wang, R. J., & Zhu, X. (2020). Facilitating client collaboration and insight through interpretations and probes for insight in psychodynamic psychotherapy: A case study of one client with three successive therapists. *Psychotherapy, 57*(2), 263–272.

Hilsenroth, M. J., Blagys, M. D., Ackerman, S. J., Bonge, D. R., & Blais, M. A. (2005). Measuring psychodynamic-interpersonal and cognitive-behavioral techniques: Development of the Comparative Psychotherapy Process Scale. *Psychotherapy: Theory, Research, Practice, Training, 42*(3), 340–356.

Høglend, P. (1993). Transference interpretations and long-term change after dynamic psychotherapy of brief to moderate length. *American Journal of Psychotherapy, 47*(4), 494–507.

Høglend, P., Bøgwald, K.-P., Amlo, S., Marble, A., Ulberg, R., Sjaastad, M. C., Sørbye, Ø., Heyerdahl, O., & Johansson, P. (2008). Transference interpretations in dynamic psychotherapy: Do they really yield sustained effects? *American Journal of Psychiatry, 165*(6), 763–771.

Høglend, P., & Hagtvet, K. (2019). Change mechanisms in psychotherapy: Both improved insight and improved affective awareness are necessary. *Journal of Consulting and Clinical Psychology, 87*(4), 332–344.

Horowitz, M., Milbrath, C., Reidbord, S., & Stinson, C. (1993). Elaboration and dyselaboration: Measures of expression and defense in discourse. *Psychotherapy Research, 3*(4), 278–293.

Horvath, A. O., & Greenberg, L. S. (1989). Development and validation of the Working Alliance Inventory. *Journal of Counseling Psychology, 36*(2), 223–233.

Horwitz, L. (1974). *Clinical prediction in psychotherapy*. Aronson.

Imel, Z. E., Pace, B. T., Soma, C. S., Tanana, M., Hirsch, T., Gibson, J., Georgiou, P., Narayanan, S., & Atkins, D. C. (2019). Design feasibility of an automated, machine-learning-based feedback system for motivational interviewing. *Psychotherapy, 56*(2), 318–328.

*Jacobs, M. A., & Warner, B. L. (1981). Interaction of therapeutic attitudes with severity of clinical diagnosis. *Journal of Clinical Psychology, 37*(1), 75–82.

Jennissen, S., Huber, J., Ehrenthal, J. C., Schauenburg, H., & Dinger, U. (2018). Association between insight and outcome of psychotherapy: Systematic review and meta-analysis. *American Journal of Psychiatry, 175*(10), 961–969.

Jones, E. E. (1985). *Psychotherapy* Process Q-Set *coding manual*. University of California, Berkeley.

Katz, M., Hilsenroth, M. J., Gold, J. R., Moore, M., Pitman, S. R., Levy, S. R., & Owen, J. (2019). Adherence, flexibility, and outcome in psychodynamic treatment of depression. *Journal of Counseling Psychology, 66*(1), 94–103.

Keefe, J. R., Solomonov, N., Derubeis, R. J., Phillips, A. C., Busch, F. N., Barber, J. P., Chambless, D. L., & Milrod, B. L. (2019). Focus is key: Panic-focused interpretations are associated with symptomatic improvement in panic-focused psychodynamic psychotherapy. *Psychotherapy Research, 29*(8), 1033–1044.

Kernberg, O. F. (1975). Transference and countertransference in the treatment of borderline patients. *Journal of the National Association of Private Psychiatric Hospitals, 7*(2), 14–24.

Klein, M. H., Mathieu-Coughlan, P., & Kiesler, D. J. (1986). The experiencing scales. In L. S. Greenberg & W. M. Pinsof (Eds.), *The psychotherapy process: A research handbook* (pp. 21–71). Guilford.

Kuncewicz, D., Lachowicz-Tabaczek, K., & Załuski, J. (2014). Why insight in psychotherapy does not always lead to behaviour change? *Polish Journal of Applied Psychology, 12*(2), 99–122.

Leahy, R. L. (2017). *Cognitive therapy techniques: A practitioner's guide*. Guilford.

Leibovich, L., Wachtel, P. L., Nof, A., & Zilcha-Mano, S. (2020). "Take a sad song and make it better": What makes an interpretation growth facilitating for the patient? *Psychotherapy, 57*(3), 400–413.

Leichsenring, F., & Schauenburg, H. (2014). Empirically supported methods of short-term psychodynamic therapy in depression—Towards an evidence-based unified protocol. *Journal of Affective Disorders, 169*, 128–143.

*Levy, S. R., Hilsenroth, M. J., & Owen, J. J. (2015). Relationship between interpretation, alliance, and outcome in psychodynamic psychotherapy: Control of therapist effects and assessment of moderator variable impact. *Journal of Nervous and Mental Disease, 203*(6), 418–424.

*Lilliengren, P., Philips, B., Falkenström, F., Bergquist, M., Ulvenes, P., & Wampold, B. (2019). Comparing the treatment process in successful and unsuccessful cases in two forms of psychotherapy for cluster C personality disorders. *Psychotherapy, 56*(2), 285–296.

*Lingiardi, V., Colli, A., Gentile, D., & Tanzilli, A. (2011). Exploration of session process: Relationship to depth and alliance. *Psychotherapy, 48*(4), 391–400.

Lipsitz-Odess, I., Fisher, H., Kartaginer, O., Leibovich, L., & Zilcha-Mano, S. (2021). When less is more: The perception of psychotherapy techniques as a function of patient personality disorder. *Psychology and Psychotherapy, 94*(4), 929–951.

*Locati, F., Rossi, G., & Parolin, L. (2019). Interactive dynamics among therapist interventions, therapeutic alliance and metacognition in the early stages of the psychotherapeutic process. *Psychotherapy Research, 29*(1), 112–122.

Luborsky, L. (1977). Measuring a pervasive psychic structure in psychotherapy: The core conflictual relationship theme. In N. Freedman & S. Grand (Eds.), *Communicative structures and psychic structures* (pp. 367–395). Springer.

Luborsky, L. (1984). *Principles of psychoanalytic psychotherapy: A manual for supportive-expressive treatment*. Basic Books.

Luborsky, L., & Bachrach, H. (1974). Factors influencing clinician's judgments of mental health: Eighteen experiences with the Health–Sickness Rating Scale. *Archives of General Psychiatry, 31*(3), 292–299.

Malan, D. H. (1963). *A study of brief psychotherapy*. Tavistock.

Malan, D. H. (1979). *Individual psychotherapy and the science of psychodynamics*. Butterworth.

Marmar, C. R., Weiss, D. S., & Gaston, L. (1989). Toward the validation of the California Therapeutic Alliance Rating System. *Psychological Assessment, 1*(1), 46.

McCarthy, K. S., Keefe, J. R., & Barber, J. P. (2016). Goldilocks on the couch: Moderate levels of psychodynamic and process–experiential technique predict outcome in psychodynamic therapy. *Psychotherapy Research, 26*(3), 307–317.

McCullough, J. P., Jr. (2003). *Treatment for chronic depression: Cognitive Behavioral Analysis System of Psychotherapy (CBASP)*. Educational Publishing Foundation.

*Milbrath, C., Bond, M., Cooper, S., Znoj, H. J., Horowitz, M. J., & Perry, J. C. (1999). Sequential consequences of therapists' interventions. *Journal of Psychotherapy Practice and Research, 8*(1), 40–54.

Munder, T., Wilmers, F., Leonhart, R., Linster, H. W., & Barth, J. (2010). Working Alliance Inventory–Short Revised (WAI-SR): Psychometric properties in outpatients and inpatients. *Clinical Psychology & Psychotherapy, 17*(3), 231–239.

Nunberg, H. (1948). *Practice and theory of psychoanalysis*. International University Press.

Ogrodniczuk, J. S., Piper, W. E., Joyce, A. S., & McCallum, M. (1999). Transference interpretations in short-term dynamic psychotherapy. *Journal of Nervous and Mental Disease, 187*(9), 571–578.

*Ogrodniczuk, J. S., Piper, W. E., Joyce, A. S., & McCallum, M. (2000). Different perspectives of the therapeutic alliance and therapist technique in 2 forms of dynamically oriented psychotherapy. *Canadian Journal of Psychiatry, 45*(5), 452–458.

Owen, J., & Hilsenroth, M. J. (2014). Treatment adherence: The importance of therapist flexibility in relation to therapy outcomes. *Journal of Counseling Psychology, 61*(2), 280–288.

Perry, J. C. (1990). Defense mechanism rating scale (5th ed.). Harvard School of Medicine.

Pesale, F. P., & Hilsenroth, M. J. (2009). Patient and therapist perspectives on session depth in relation to technique during psychodynamic psychotherapy. *Psychotherapy: Theory, Research, Practice, Training, 46*(3), 390–396.

*Piper, W. E., Azim, H. F. A., Joyce, A. S., & McCallum, M. (1991). Transference interpretations, therapeutic alliance, and outcome in short-term individual psychotherapy. *Archives of General Psychiatry, 48*(10), 946–953.

Piper, W. E., Debbane, E. G., de Carufel, F. L., & Bienvenu, J. P. (1987). A system for differentiating therapist interpretations from other interventions. *Bulletin of the Menninger Clinic, 51*(6), 532–550.

Quiñones, T. J., Woodward, E. N., & Pantalone, D. W. (2017). Sexual minority reflections on their psychotherapy experiences. *Psychotherapy Research, 27*(2), 189–200.

Safran, J. D., & Muran, J. C. (2000). *Negotiating the therapeutic alliance*. Guilford.

Silberschatz, G. (2017). Improving the yield of psychotherapy research. *Psychotherapy Research, 27*(1), 1–13. https://doi.org/10.1080/10503307.2015.1076202

*Silberschatz, G., Fretter, P. B., & Curtis, J. T. (1986). How do interpretations influence the process of psychotherapy? *Journal of Consulting and Clinical Psychology, 54*(5), 646–652.

Speisman, J. C. (1959). Depth of interpretation and verbal resistance in psychotherapy. *Journal of Consulting Psychology, 23*, 93–99.

Spiegal, S. B., & Hill, C. E. (1989). Guidelines for research on therapist interpretation: Toward greater methodological rigor and relevance to practice. *Journal of Counseling Psychology, 36*(1), 121–129.

Stiles, W. B. (1988). Psychotherapy process–outcome correlations may be misleading. *Psychotherapy: Theory, Research, Practice, Training, 25*(1), 27–35.

Stiles, W. B., & Snow, J. S. (1984). Dimensions of psychotherapy session impact across sessions and across clients. *British Journal of Clinical Psychology, 23*(1), 59–63.

Sue, D. W., Arredondo, P., & McDavis, R. J. (1992). Multicultural counseling competencies and standards: A call to the profession. *Journal of Counseling & Development, 70*(4), 477–486.

Summers, R. F., & Barber, J. P. (2010). *Psychodynamic therapy: A guide to evidence-based practice*. Guilford.

Tao, K. W., Owen, J., Pace, B. T., & Imel, Z. E. (2015). A meta-analysis of multicultural competencies and psychotherapy process and outcome. *Journal of Counseling Psychology*, *62*(3), 337–350.

Vaillant, G. E. (1971). Theoretical hierarchy of adaptive ego mechanisms: A 30-year follow-up of 30 men selected for psychological health. *Archives of General Psychiatry*, *24*(2), 107–118.

Wachtel, P. L. (1993). *Therapeutic communication: Principles and effective practice*. Guilford.

Wachtel, P. L. (2011). *Therapeutic communication: Knowing what to say when*. Guilford.

Wampold, B. E., Imel, Z. E., Bhati, K. S., & Johnson-Jennings, M. D. (2007). Insight as a common factor. In L. G. Castonguay & C. Hill (Eds.), *Insight in psychotherapy* (pp. 119–139). American Psychological Association.

Weck, F., Junga, Y. M., Kliegl, R., Hahn, D., Brucker, K., & Witthöft, M. (2021). Effects of competence feedback on therapist competence and patient outcome: A randomized controlled trial. *Journal of Consulting and Clinical Psychology*, *89*(11), 885–897.

Westen, D. (1995). *Social Cognition and Object Relations Scale: Q-Sort for Projective Stories (SCORS-Q)* [Unpublished manual]. Cambridge Hospital and Harvard Medical School, Cambridge, MA.

Young, J. E., Klosko, J. S., & Weishaar, M. E. (2003). *Schema therapy: A practitioner's guide*. Guilford.

Zilcha-Mano, S. (2021). Toward personalized psychotherapy: The importance of the trait-like/state-like distinction for understanding therapeutic change. *American Psychologist*, *76*(3), 516–528.

Zilcha-Mano, S., & Fisher, H. (2022). Distinct roles of state-like and trait-like patient–therapist alliance in psychotherapy. *Nature Reviews Psychology*, *1*(4), 194–210.

8
Paradoxical Interventions

Paul R. Peluso and Robert Freund

The origins of paradoxes arise from ancient philosophy, with the word *paradox* derived from the Greek meaning "beyond belief." For example, Epimenides of Crete (600 BC) was reported to have said, "All Cretans are liars." This statement is paradoxical because, himself being Cretan, he should be lying. However, if Epimenides lies, then his statement about "*all* Cretans are liars" cannot be true (and so on and so on). Paradoxes, by their nature, can go from being maddeningly absurd to amusingly witty.

Paradoxical interventions (PIs) are intended to help clients become more flexible, or at least open to thinking about their problems from a new perspective. Among the potential benefits of PIs are that they often produce rapid behavioral change on the second-order level (i.e., change on a systemic or structural level of functioning). Clients often experience feelings ranging from relief that a new option is available that allows them to stop struggling with their problem to frustration at having to make a choice to continue a behavior without the "cover" of their previous explanation for it (Ascher, 1989; Peluso, 2023a; Weeks & L'Abate, 1982).

Because of some of these reactions, PIs are often considered potentially unethical because they can be deceptive or manipulative. However, when used appropriately, they can be demonstrably effective (Browning & Hull, 2021; Hill, 1987; Lambert, 2004). According to Browning and Hull (2021), the bias against PIs may be the result of practitioners who used directional PIs to gain compliance from a client. The motivation behind these tactics is power dynamics on the part of the therapist that are not specific to the use of PIs and are neither therapeutic nor supported by the research on creating an effective psychotherapeutic relationship (Browning & Hull, 2021; Norcross & Lambert, 2019). By contrast, effective PIs are nondirectional and encourage change by giving clients a choice between the options (Browning & Hull, 2021).

In this chapter, we examine the clinical indications and evidence base for the use of PIs. We also provide clinical examples; diversity considerations; training recommendations; and, based on the research findings, therapeutic practices. First, we discuss some basic definitions.

Definitions

The *Merriam-Webster Dictionary* defines a paradox as "a statement or proposition seemingly self-contradictory or absurd, and yet explicable as expressing a truth" ("Paradox," n.d.). This definition can be thought of as the practitioner's definition. That is, an explicit PI consists of seemingly self-contradictory and sometimes even absurd therapeutic

Paul R. Peluso and Robert Freund, *Paradoxical Interventions* In: *Psychotherapy Skills and Methods That Work*. Edited by: Clara E. Hill and John C. Norcross, Oxford University Press. © Clara E. Hill and John C. Norcross 2023. DOI: 10.1093/oso/9780197611012.003.0008 perspectives about a client's circumstances. The use of opposite meanings, or defying a client's expectations about what a therapist *should* say, may also be humorous. However, the element of truth that is present makes PIs *real* and unavoidable, rather than an elaborate joke that can be easily dismissed (Ascher, 1989; Peluso, 2023a).

Another definition is that a paradox is a "statement or situation that contains two true elements that cannot simultaneously coexist" (Peluso, 2023a, p. 67), which is counterintuitive or defies logic. This additional definition of paradox can be thought of as the client's perspective or experience of the paradox. Although they are seemingly self-contradictory or even absurd, paradoxical comments contain an element of truth that leads the client to reconsider how they viewed the problem originally. The clinical usefulness of PIs is that they invite the client to think about a problem in a different way, take an action that is contrary to what they may have done before, and/or feel differently about their particular circumstances.

Dialectics

In order to understand the therapeutic use of PIs, it is important to consider the concept of *dialectics*. Dialectics is the process of contrasting a thing with its *opposite* in order to create a new meaning (Watzlawick et al., 1974). The dialectic process involves looking for an opposite meaning contained in what it is that a client is describing as problematic (i.e., seeing the bad in the good and the good in the bad):

> From the dialectical perspective, a problem can occur when one believes the solution to a difficulty is the implementation of that difficulty's opposite polarity. An "either/or" view of reality is a trap which denies us the ability to move to different frames of reference to multiple alternatives . . . dialectical thinking means looking at both the positive and negative aspects of symptoms in terms of their antecedents and consequence. It must be recognized that symptoms serve a positive function. (Weeks & L'Abate, 1982, p. 90)

As a result, PIs may prove therapeutically effective because the dialectical approach mirrors the tension of a client's ambivalence or dilemma (i.e., "either/or" thinking). When a client is confronted with an external life circumstance, or an internal demand where the individual feels vulnerable, a "dialectical tension" is created and the client often feels trapped (Peluso, 2023a). Another, closely related element to dialectics in understanding PIs is *reframing*. Reframing is a way of redefining the client's perspective to provide new meaning for a problematic concern. According to Watzlawick et al. (1974),

> To reframe . . . means to change the *conceptual and/or emotional setting or viewpoint* [italics added] in relation to which a situation is experienced and to place it in another frame which fits the "facts" of the same concrete situation equally well or even better, and thereby changes its entire meaning. (p. 95)

Often, a reframe is unexpected and requires clients to reappraise their conceptualization in a different and more positive way (hence its connection to dialectics above and PIs in general).

A final element to help define the use of PIs is *double-binds*, which refer to implicit communications between two people that keep one of the two subservient to the other. For a double-bind to be enacted, there are two (or three) levels of directives or "injunctions" placed on the recipient by the "superior" person(s) that involve threats of punishment under the pretext of love or obligation (Gibney, 2006). Then, a "secondary injunction" is imposed on the recipient, which conflicts with the first but at a higher or more abstract level implying autonomy, using relational obligation as a driving source for the "victim's" decision-making. The threats imply that the relationship will be damaged or lost if the injunction is not complied with. If needed, the "superior" individual(s) issues a third injunction that implies damage to someone else if the victim does not comply with the primary injunction; this typically involves direct threats of harm, abandonment, and so forth. The essence of a double-bind is two or three conflicting demands, *each on a different logical level*, none of which can be ignored or escaped. In other words, the client is placed in a paradoxical, "no-win" situation, which is often the origin of a client's problematic behavior or is the factor that maintains it (Gibney, 2006; Watzlawick et al., 1974).

Whereas a *pathogenic* double-bind places a person in a no-win predicament, a PI can act as a *therapeutic* double-bind (Browning & Hull, 2021; Peluso, 2023a), placing a client in a "no-lose" situation. In the case of symptom prescription, for example, the behavior the client wants to change or eliminate is actually encouraged by the therapist, effectively utilizing therapeutic double-binds as a PI to create cognitive dissonance, ultimately undermining the client's problematic behavior (Fisch et al., 1982; Watzlawick et al., 1974).

Early Paradoxical Techniques

Alfred Adler first used PIs similar to what is known today as "prescribing the symptom," which may have led to the notion that all PIs are merely reverse psychology (Browning & Hull, 2021). Because Adler believed that there was an interpersonal dynamic (or purpose) to the client's depressive symptoms, he tried to avoid being placed in the position of an authority who (albeit benignly) was trying to get the patient to change against their will, hence arousing resistance (Carlson et al., 2006; Weeks & L'Abate, 1982). Adler (1956), would advise the patient to

> "Never do anything you don't like." This seems to be a very modest request, but I believe it goes to the root of the whole trouble. If a depressed person is able to do anything he wants, who can he accuse? What has he got to revenge himself for? "If you want to go to the theatre," I tell him, "or go on a holiday, do it. If you find on the way that you don't want to, stop it." (pp. 346–347)

The goal was to avoid power struggles, which would be destructive to the therapeutic relationship, and to have clients experience their own agency or power. Specifically, Adler stated, "I know, that if I allow it, he will no longer want to do it. I know that if I hinder him, he will start a war" (p. 347). The result of the PI is to shift the patient from being uncooperative toward being cooperative and to becoming an active participant in the therapy (Bornstein et al., 1989; Weeks & L'Abate, 1982).

Whereas Adler's approach to the use of paradoxes in therapy was nonspecific, Viktor Frankl's approach was targeted toward symptoms related to anxiety, obsessive–compulsive disorders, and phobias (Ascher, 1989; Browning & Hull, 2021). He reasoned that these disorders were the result of feedback mechanisms: "A given symptom is responded to by a phobia, the phobia triggers the symptom, and the symptom, in turn, reinforces the phobia" (Frankl, 1959, p. 130). The PIs that Frankl employed were designed to disrupt the circular causal loop by prescribing the symptom itself, even going so far as to encourage the most extreme version of the symptom. By doing this, the patient would see (a) how absurd either the fear or the response to the fear was (because enacting it put the concern into proper perspective), (b) how much control the individual had over the symptom (because they could conjure it at will), or (c) both. For example, if a client was afraid of failing at some task, Frankl would encourage the patient to *try* to fail, and to do so with the most intensity while imagining the most extreme consequences. This task would allow the patient to relax and begin to consider alternative explanations or behaviors (Frankl, 1975; Weeks & L'Abate, 1982).

Recent Therapeutic Approaches to Paradoxes

In 1989, S. Hayes and Melancon wrote about the paradoxical nature of their approach to treating emotional avoidance, which would eventually be retitled acceptance and commitment therapy (ACT). They speculated that emotional avoidance—that is, the client's attempts to avoid unpleasant thoughts, feelings, or activities—was more often the client's central problem. They drew on communications theory approaches, along with relational-frame theory, to de-couple the problematic social–verbal contexts by creating what they called "creative hopelessness," encouraging the client to let go of their struggle and eventually make a commitment to action (S. Hayes et al., 2021).

Similarly, Linehan and associates, in treating individuals diagnosed with borderline personality disorder, created dialectical–behavioral therapy (DBT). In DBT, the focus of the dialectical approach is in the synthesis of the client's original position (thesis) and the therapist's presentation of the opposite idea (antithesis); this combination creates a new perspective and action to be taken. All of the skills that are central to DBT—interpersonal effectiveness, emotion regulation, and distress tolerance—have dialectical and/or paradoxical elements to them (Linehan, 2014; Shearin & Linehan, 1989).

Selvini-Palazzoli and colleagues (collectively referred to as the "Milan Group") expanded and refined the use of PIs with entire families. First, they grounded the ideas of paradoxical change in the underpinnings of cybernetics and communication. Next, they believed that interactions among family members were expressions of behavior that were governed by a set of rules. They called the dysfunctional family's interactions a "game," in which each individual is trying to keep other individuals' behavior under control, theorizing, "The power is only in the rules of the game" (Selvini-Palazzoli et al., 1978, p. 6). As a result, they found that the family "sustains its game through an intricacy of paradoxes which can only be undone by counterparadoxes in the context of therapy" (p. 8). One of their primary PIs is *positive connotation* (Selvini-Palazzoli et al., 1978). To identify the positive connotation, the practitioner asks, "What is something *positive* that the family member's symptom accomplishes? Does it help a client to avoid, excuse, postpone, achieve a private sense of triumph (albeit at a price)?" By identifying the positive connotation for the systematic behavior, family members are placed at the same level (rather than levels of "good and bad" or "sick and well"). In addition, the positive connotation introduces a novel/absurd element ("X" symptom is not really a problem but is good/beneficial) and sets the stage for accepting any paradoxical suggestion or intervention, such as suggesting that the family should enact some other pattern of relating to one another.

Clinical Description and Indications

A recent approach has categorized PIs based on the psychotherapist's strategy for achieving second-order change (Peluso, 2023a). The specific strategies are neutralizers, tranquilizers, energizers, and challengers.

Neutralizers are utilized to reduce the oppositional impact of client comments and behaviors in therapy. Tactically, a clinician avoids the opportunity to engage in a conflict with a client, instead responding with joining humor, curiosity, validation, and positional neutrality. By denying the client the opportunity to spar or place the clinician in an elevated or diminished status, the therapeutic relationship and process remains intact (Peluso, 2023b).

Tranquilizers help restore emotional equilibrium to clients whose behavior is getting in the way of solving their problems. Strategically, tranquilizers help clients "push the reset button" and stop "trying" to solve the problem in a way that has the opposite effect. These may take the form of giving clients permission to experience their struggles without suffering (i.e., prescribing the symptom), postponing difficult decisions or processes, prohibiting desired behaviors in order to encourage their enaction, and advocating for symptomatic behavior in order for it to be accepted and therefore open to change (Peluso, 2023a).

Energizers are intended to stimulate action when clients have become locked into a particular pattern of emotional paralysis or clinical unproductivity. The central strategy is to encourage clients to reappraise their circumstances and move toward new solutions. Tactically, energizers may be accomplished by reframing problematic behavior with prosocial dimensions (i.e., positive connotation); recommending clients practice problematic behaviors for benign purposes; or inviting clients to educate clinicians on the logic underlying their problematic behaviors, as they understand it (Peluso, 2023a).

Last, *challengers* get clients to stop doing something destructive that they believe is the *only* option by directly raising their awareness. Although they are the most therapeutically "risky" methods, challengers prompt clients to react and disengage from the problematic behavioral solutions in favor of more adaptive functioning. Tactically, this can be done through symptom prescription, predicting cause and effect based on knowledge of client schemas, exaggeration of distorted thought process, or with gentle and supportive confronting (Peluso, 2023a).

Paradoxical interventions can be used in a number of clinical circumstances, especially with highly reactant individuals and highly resistant families (Beutler et al., 2002; Shoham-Salomon & Rosenthal, 1987). Clients who are trapped in ambivalence, engaged in a toxic double-bind, or utilizing maladaptive thought processes with rigid applications may respond well to PIs. Some have proposed that client behaviors can guide the clinician in deciding which PI strategy to use: Negativistic client behavior would probably respond to neutralizing PIs, emotionally overactivated clients would probably benefit more from tranquilizing PIs, clients who are immobilized by their circumstances probably call for energizing PIs, and clients with persistently entrenched (and destructive) behaviors may necessitate the use of challenging PIs (Katz, 1984; Martinez-Taboas, 1990; Peluso, 2023a; Rohrbaugh et al., 1981; Tennen et al., 1981). Note, however, that these clinical recommendations have not yet been empirically tested.

Assessment

To date, there are no measures of the occurrence and quality of PIs in psychotherapy. On the one hand, the most typically mentioned PIs in the literature are symptom prescription and positive connotation, but they have not been well-defined or operationalized. As a result, researchers must either rely on therapist assertion that a PI was used or use judgments based on observations.

One measure that has been used to assess immediate in-session effects of PIs is the Penman Coding System (Penman, 1980), which evaluates communications between people along manifest (surface) and latent (deeper) levels, with nine and 16 codes for each of the respective levels. Holloway et al. (1990) chose the Penman system to assess the immediate impact of PIs because it is derived from the communication theory of Watzlawick et al. (1967), which is one of the theoretical origins for the use of PIs. Unfortunately, although the Penman Coding System seems like a useful way to ascertain the immediate effect of PIs, this system has not been used in a published study since Holloway et al. (1990), perhaps due to the time and labor demands of observational coding that have been noted in the literature (Baker et al., 2022; Imel et al., 2019).

Clients may respond to a PI with a variety of emotional responses, ranging from the more benign (puzzlement, humor, etc.) to the more turbulent (anger, hurt, etc.), perhaps as a function of the amount of reactance aroused in the client (Browning & Hull, 2021). Clinicians can look for shifts in perception and processing that accompany the emotional responses as a sign that the PI is having the desired effect (Peluso, 2023a). Unfortunately, to date, no measures have been developed to specifically assess the emotional responses. Measures for assessing client reactivity could also be used to assess its moderating effects on the relation between PIs and client receptiveness. For example, the Therapeutic Reactance Scale (TRS; Dowd et al., 1991) could be used to asses changes in reactance as a precursor to making changes to behavior. Examples of TRS items are the following: "I am not very tolerant of others' attempts to persuade me," "I am very stubborn and set in my ways," and "I am very open to solutions to my problems from others" (Dowd et al., 1991, p. 543).

In terms of distal outcome, most studies in the literature have used measures of symptom change. These include the Beck Depression Inventory (A. Beck et al., 1996) and the Symptom Checklist (Derogatis & Savitz, 1999).

Although some immediate shifts in symptom presentation may occur (particularly in response to interventions such as symptom prescription), this type of first-order change alone (symptom reduction) does not indicate that the paradox has been effective. However, paradigms that track rapid symptom change (from session to session) may be useful in tracking the effectiveness of PIs (Lemmens et al., 2021; Tang & DeRubeis, 1999). This suggestion is related to the systemic destabilization and reorientation that it is hoped takes place during the implementation of a PI, consistent with Tang and DeRubeis' (1999) thesis regarding sudden gains in psychotherapeutic process.

Because PIs function to subvert established patterns, it is important to assess not only first-order but also second-order changes to find evidence about whether the client has reoriented themselves. Although second-order change is difficult to measure directly, it can be inferred from coding of specific behavioral changes, such as increased "change talk" by the client (immediate outcome), change in mood (immediate outcome), decreased symptomatology (distal outcome), or openness to new behaviors (either immediate or distal outcomes). In addition, the Client Evaluation of Motivational Interviewing Scale can be used to evaluate effects of PIs (Madson et al., 2015).

Clinical Examples

First, we give a fictional example of a neutralizing paradox. A young man was brought to treatment by his partner, after he discovered emotional infidelity on her part. He expressed his resentment for being in treatment in the initial session ("I'm not sure what I am doing here; she's the one with the issue!") along with his ambivalence regarding whether he even wanted to remain in his marriage. The therapist responded,

> I agree with you 100%. And I don't believe it's effective to provide therapy when my client is unsure if change is what *they* want. I sense too that you want to explore the potential of staying in your marriage, but aren't ready to commit to a long-term repair attempt. I wouldn't be willing to commit to a long-term treatment plan if you weren't sure that it was what you wanted. I'd be willing to offer you three sessions at a time though, during which we can explore what is possible for the relationship and what you really want to do with all this.

The young man, seeming relieved, stated that he could agree to that plan.

In this example, the therapist neutralized the client's potentially disruptive ambivalence toward treatment by removing the points of opposition: commitment and time. By making it the client's decision, the therapist removed the client's need to take ownership of a particular outcome.

Second, we present an example of a tranquilizer paradox based on a composite of clinical interactions. A woman sought consultation on her marriage, unsure if she should remain or file for a divorce. After spending time questioning her sexuality, the client realized that she was a lesbian and thus did not feel she could remain in her current relationship. In her anxiety and ambivalence, she was frequently snapping at her husband and picking fights. Ultimately, she described feeling like she needed to "get out of the marriage" but was weighing the impact divorce would have on her two daughters.

She did not know if it would be better to stay closeted in a "sham" marriage or to be completely transparent with her family. The clinician offered the following:

> There are two concepts of time in Greek philosophy. Chronos, our current sense of time, is moments marching forward. Kairos, however, is time at its most opportune moment for something to take place. Perhaps your difficulty deciding what to do is because your Chronos hasn't caught up with Kairos. It may not be the opportune time for you to decide. What would it be like to let yourself sit with the question for some time without needing to choose?

Accepting this as a therapeutic homework, and agreeing with the therapist's perspective, the client reduced her expectations for immediate decisions.

In this example, the clinician tranquilized the client's panic and distress about needing to make a decision. By reframing the decision-making process into something organically larger than herself, the therapist offered the client the freedom to be in the present moment and allowed her to postpone making a decision for which she was clearly not ready. Her ego-dystonic pressure lessened, and the therapeutic energies could shift to the actual solutions.

Landmark Studies and Previous Reviews

In one landmark study, Holloway et al. (1990) investigated the use of PIs in the course of a video-recorded session of couples therapy conducted by Gerald Weeks, an acknowledged expert in the use of PIs. The couple was being seen for wife's insomnia, and Weeks reconceptualized the condition as related to the couple's dynamic (rather than just the wife's disorder). Weeks reported that he had previously used PI with the wife (symptom prescription for insomnia), which was effective when she employed it (approximately two nights a week), but was frustrated because she did not consistently use the intervention. Weeks realized that the insomnia maintained the status quo for the couple (who were at odds about getting married, despite having been in a committed relationship for a number of years). This understanding became the basis for his PI used in the session with both partners, as he reframed the insomnia as beneficial for the couple because it allowed them to postpone a decision on marriage and the future of the relationship. Interactions between the male and female client, between the female client and therapist, and between the therapist and male client were coded using the Penman Coding System (described above). In the study, the session was divided into three segments: before, during, and after the PI.

The sequential analysis of these codes revealed that prior to the PI, there were power struggles between the male client and the therapist, but the male client became more supportive and positive following the introduction of the PI, and the negative interaction pattern between the male client and female client dissipated by the end of the session (Holloway et al., 1990). The authors concluded that the PI had an immediate impact on the couple and recommended that sequential analyses could be beneficial in better understanding how PIs effect change at the process level as well as at the behavioral level.

A few meta-analyses have been conducted on the end-of-treatment outcomes of treatment packages featuring PIs. In a meta-analysis of 15 studies on PI treatments in relation to treatment outcomes, Hill (1987) reported a mean effect size of 0.99 for paradoxical treatments compared to no-treatment controls ($k = 39$), and a mean effect size of 0.56 compared to placebo control groups ($k = 60$). He concluded that, on average, clients receiving PIs were better off than 84% of clients in no-treatment groups and 72% of those in placebo control groups. In addition, he reported a nonstatistical comparison between paradoxical and nonparadoxical cognitive–behavioral therapy (CBT), concluding that paradoxical treatments scored higher on 32 of 33 comparisons, suggesting that paradoxical treatments were more effective.

In Shoham-Salomon and Rosenthal's (1987) meta-analysis of 12 separate articles, they found a significant weighted effect size of $r = .42$ for paradoxical treatments compared to control groups, but also found a small, nonsignificant effect size of $r = .13$ for comparisons with nonparadoxical treatments. In five studies in which follow-up assessments were made, Shoham-Salomon and Rosenthal reported that the strength of the effect of paradoxical treatments increased more over time than did that of nonparadoxical treatments. That finding suggested that there may have been a "sleeper effect in which paradoxical interventions require an incubation period before they can produce a superior effect" (p. 26). Note that they explicitly stated that they "accepted the authors' definition of paradoxical interventions" (p. 23) and did not otherwise verify that PIs were used.

DeBoard (1989) conducted a review of 25 studies of psychotherapy that used PIs (mostly symptom prescription) and concluded that 92% of the studies demonstrated "at least some form of therapeutic improvement" (p. 397). However, this was a more descriptive summary rather than a formal meta-analysis of the overall effect.

More recently, meta-analyses or systematic reviews of nonpharmacological interventions for insomnia and depression have included studies of PI treatments (Gee et al., 2019; Jansson-Fröjmark & Norell-Clarke, 2018; van der Zweerde et al., 2019). These studies suggested the overall effectiveness of PIs, although separate effect sizes were not calculated.

Finally, Morin and colleagues (1999, 2006), as part of a larger systematic review of nonpharmacological treatments of chronic insomnia, found evidence that treatments employing PIs (again, primarily symptom prescription) were effective. In fact, they noted that PIs, as a treatment method for insomnia, had met the American Psychological Association Division 12 criteria for evidence-based treatments (Morin et al., 2006).

Research Review

In the literature, we found no studies of the immediate in-session outcomes of PI. In other words, how patients respond immediately to therapist use of PI has not been investigated. Hence, the studies we review have all involved treatments that included PI (although none of these actually assessed the frequency and quality of the PI). We first report two original meta-analyses with large samples reporting distal, end-of-treatment patient outcomes. We then consider the results of case studies using a narrative review.

Meta-Analytic Review

We followed the examples of previous meta-analyses (Hill, 1987; Shoham-Salomon & Rosenthal, 1987) and conducted two meta-analyses of the available research on the link between treatments involving PI and distal outcomes. The first was a comparison of treatments involving PIs to placebo control groups, wait-list control groups, or pre-post measures within subjects. The second meta-analysis was a comparison between the effects of treatments involving PIs and nonparadoxical interventions in the same studies.

Inclusion Criteria

We searched PsycInfo, MEDLINE, and Google Scholar using terms such as "paradox," "paradoxical intention," "positive connotation," and "paradoxical technique." We included variations on these terms to refine our search as we identified potential articles. We also reviewed previous meta-analyses and systematic reviews for potential articles (DeBoard, 1989; Gee et al., 2019; Hill, 1987; Jansson-Fröjmark & Norell-Clarke, 2018; Morin et al., 2006; Shoham-Salomon & Rosenthal, 1987; van der Zweerde et al., 2019). In many cases, the effect sizes reported in the meta-analyses were recomputed to obtain standard errors and inverse variance weights not previously reported. In the process of reviewing articles, we identified additional articles of interest and continued an iterative process of seeking additional sources of published, unpublished, and in press articles until the relevant literature was exhausted.

All articles were in English and presented actual individual psychotherapy studies (not analogues). We did not constrain the time frame for publication, although the majority of articles were published between 1979 and 2013. Dissertations and unpublished materials were excluded.

Initially, our search yielded 80 articles that showed promise for inclusion in one of the two meta-analyses. Further review and coding by both authors eliminated 63 articles due to a lack of appropriate reporting of statistical findings, a focus on variables not of interest to the topic, or use of clinical simulations. In all, the studies considered were only/primarily in English, of individual psychotherapy. The final sample consisted of 17 studies, 21 effect sizes, encompassing 471 patients/participants. Figure 8.1 presents a Preferred Reporting Items for Systematic Reviews and Meta-Analyses (PRISMA) flowchart.

In terms of participant demographics, only 32% of the studies reported therapist demographics. Male therapists outnumbered female therapists by a ratio of more than 3:1, whereas female clients outnumbered male clients by a ratio of 2.5:1. The studies overwhelmingly targeted specific disorders (insomnia, phobias, procrastination, and depression), and all but one study had either a head-to-head comparison with another treatment (i.e., stimulus control) or a baseline comparison (e.g., pretreatment rating of symptoms). In terms of diagnoses, insomnia was the focus of more than 30% of the studies, with anxiety, procrastination, and depression each comprising 13% of the studies. Furthermore, symptom prescription and positive connotation were the specific techniques most often studied (more than 55% of the studies), with various measures of symptom reduction (ranging from measures such as the Beck Depression Inventory to checklists of symptoms and patient-rated perceptions of change) utilized

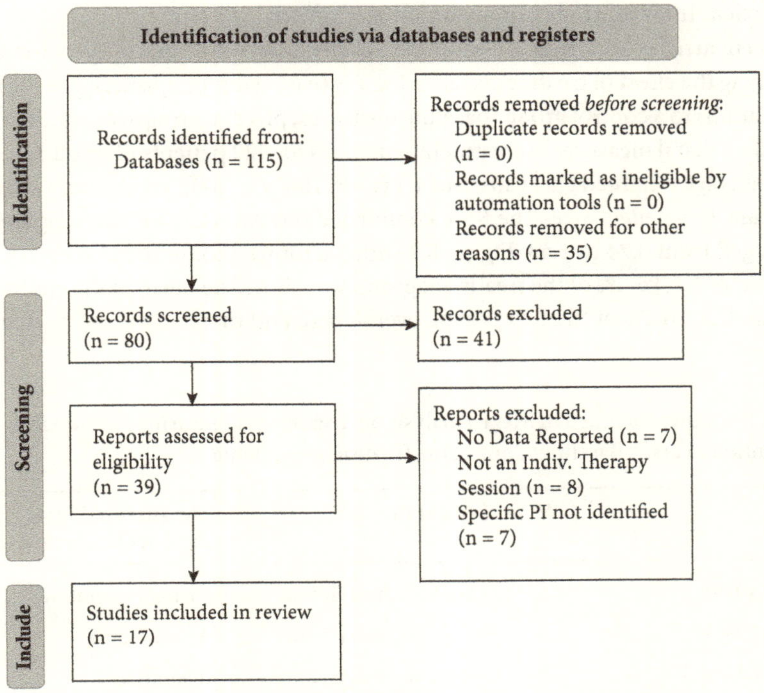

Figure 8.1 PRISMA flowchart of articles identified and used in meta-analyses.

as the indicator of success. Last, most studies did not adequately report ethnicity, but when ethnicity was reported, participants were predominately White/European American.

Preparation of Data

If a study reported more than one effect size, these were averaged (Hunter & Schmidt, 2004) within studies. Negative correlations were examined for whether the finding was consistent with improvement (i.e., reduction of symptoms). If the negative correlation indicated improvement, then the sign was reversed and entered as a positive correlation for the purposes of the analysis (Borenstein et al., 2009).

Mean differences and pooled standard deviations were calculated to create an initial *d* coefficient effect size. However, due to the fact that most of the studies had small sample sizes, which can artificially inflate the effect size estimates, Hedges correction was applied to create an unbiased effect size estimate (Borenstein et al., 2009; Lipsey & Wilson, 2001). We employed a random effects model (Hedges & Olkin,1985) and computed a weighted effect size, standard error, and inverse variance weight for each analysis (Borenstein et al., 2009; Diener et al., 2009; Lipsey & Wilson, 2001). *Z* tests for significance of the overall weighted mean effect size, as well as *Q* statistic and I^2 for testing homogeneity, were conducted for both meta-analyses. Last, a fail-safe *N* was calculated, which identifies the number of studies needed to reduce the effect size down to below 0.10, which is a minimum threshold for a small effect (Cohen, 1988; Norcross & Lambert, 2019).

Paradoxical Interventions Versus Baseline/Control

Seventeen articles reported 21 separate results that were appropriate for analysis comparing the effect of treatments featuring PIs (e.g., symptom prescription or positive connotation) to a control group (baseline measures, placebo groups, or wait-list control groups) on distal measures of treatment outcomes for 422 patients (Table 8.1).

The average weighted effect size was 1.1 ($z = 6.166, p < .000$), producing a statistically significant large effect size. The 95% confidence interval (CI) for the weighted effect size ranged from 0.74 to 1.43. Figure 8.2 shows a funnel plot of the effect sizes. With a Cohen's *d* of 1.1, 86.4% of the treatment group was above the mean of the control group (Cohen's U_3), 58.2% of the two groups overlapped, and there was a 78.2% chance that

Table 8.1 Studies Included in Meta-Analysis on Treatments Featuring Paradoxical Interventions Versus Baseline/Control on Treatment Outcome

Study	*N*	Type of PI	Measures of Distal Patient Outcome	Effect Size[a]
Ascher (1979)	5	Symptom prescription	Urinary retention	2.52
Ascher (1981)	5	Symptom prescription	Agoraphobia	4.70
Ascher & Efran (1978)	5	Symptom prescription	Insomnia	1.87
Ascher & Turner (1979)	20	Symptom prescription	Insomnia	1.03 1.83
Ascher & Turner (1980)	20	Symptom prescription	Insomnia	0.88 0.83
Beck & Strong (1982)	20	Positive connotation	Depression	1.61
Broomfield & Espie (2003)	32	Symptom prescription	Insomnia	0.48
Conoley & Garber (1985)	38	Reframing	Loneliness and depression	0.20
Espie et al. (1989)	27	Symptom prescription	Insomnia	0.15 0.31
Feldman et al. (1982)	20	Symptom prescription and positive connotation	Depression	0.70
Hills et al. (1985)	29	Symptom prescription	Loneliness and depression	1.32
Hsu & Lieberman (1982)	8	Symptom prescription	Anorexia nervosa	2.46
Lacks et al. (1983)	30	Symptom prescription	Insomnia	0.05
Lopez & Wambach (1982)	22	Symptom prescription	Procrastination	0.66
Ott et al. (1983)	28	Symptom prescription	Insomnia	1.27
Turner & Ascher (1979)	20	Symptom prescription	Insomnia	0.74 1.31
Wright & Strong (1982)	20	Symptom prescription	Procrastination	2.63

[a]Effect sizes are averaged when more than one is reported in a single study, except where indicated (Diener et al., 2009).

PI, paradoxical intervention.

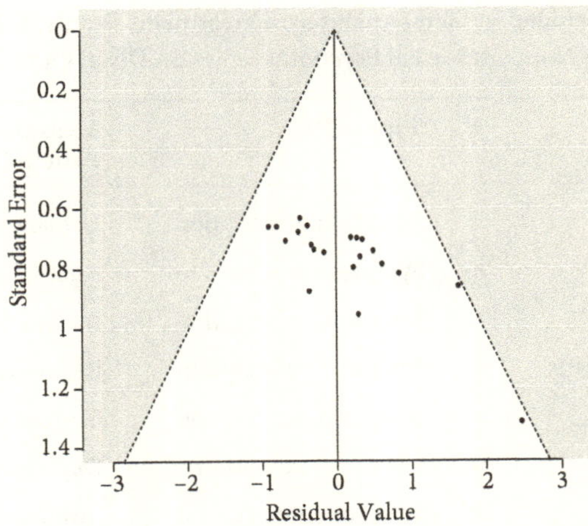

Figure 8.2 Funnel plot of effect sizes for treatments featuring paradoxical interventions compared to pre–post scores, control groups, and placebo groups.

a patient receiving a treatment involving PI had a higher score than a patient picked at random from the control group (probability of superiority). Last, in order to have one more favorable outcome in the treatment group compared to the control group, only 2.49 people would need to be treated (Magnusson, n.d.).

Cochrane's Q, which we used to check for heterogeneity, rejected the null hypothesis ($Q = 54.405$, $df = 20$, $p = .0001$). Thus, any variability among the effect sizes investigated was probably due to factors other than sampling error. I^2 equaled 61%, indicating that with the random effects model, there was moderate variation among the studies due to heterogeneity (considered further below). For the fail-safe *N* calculation, approximately 167 studies with an effect size of 0 would need to be published in order to bring the weighted mean effect size below 0.10, or practical significance.

Paradoxical Interventions Versus Nonparadoxical Interventions

Seventeen articles reported 20 separate results that were analyzed in the meta-analysis comparing the effect of treatments involving PI and non-PI on distal treatment outcomes for 471 patients (Table 8.2). Fifteen of the 17 reviewed studies used some form of random assignment, thereby affording a causal link to overall distal outcomes.

The average weighted effect size was 0.49 ($z = 3.318$, $p = .009$), a statistically significant medium effect size. The 95% CI for the weighted effect size ranged from .20 to .77. Figure 8.3 shows a funnel plot of the effect sizes. With a Cohen's *d* of 0.49, 68.8% of the treatment group was above the mean of the control group (Cohen's U_3), 80.6% of the two groups overlapped, and there was a 63.6% chance that a patient receiving a PI had a higher score than a patient picked at random from the control group (probability of superiority). In addition, to have one more favorable outcome in the treatment group compared to the control group, 6.15 people would need to be treated (Magnusson, n.d.).

We computed Cochrane's Q to check for heterogeneity and rejected the null hypothesis ($Q = 30.20$, $df = 19$, $p = .05$). Hence, any variability among the effect sizes investigated was probably due to factors other than sampling error. The I^2 of 37.5% indicated that there was small to medium variation due to heterogeneity (considered

Table 8.2 Studies Included in Meta-Analysis on Treatments Featuring Paradoxical Interventions Versus Nonparadoxical Psychotherapies on Distal Outcome

Study	*N*	Type of PI	Measures of Distal Patient Outcome	Effect Size[a]
Ascher (1979)	5	Symptom prescription	Urinary retention	0.91
Ascher (1981)	5	Symptom prescription	Agoraphobia	2.07
Ascher & Efran (1978)	5	Symptom prescription	Insomnia	5.69
Ascher & Schotte (1999)	20	Symptom prescription	Recursive anxiety	2.46
Ataoglu et al. (2003)	30	Symptom prescription	Conversion reaction	0.83
Beck & Strong (1982)	20	Positive connotation	Depression	1.25
Espie et al. (1989)	26	Symptom prescription	Insomnia	0.31 0.08
Feldman et al. (1982)	20	Symptom prescription and positive connotation	Depression	0.34
Horvath & Goheen (1990)	41	Symptom Prescription	Insomnia	0.85
Kraft et al. (1985)	45	Reframing and positive connotation	Depression	0.60
Lacks et al. (1983)	20	Symptom prescription	Insomnia	0.00 0.00
Lopez & Wambach (1982)	28	Symptom prescription	Procrastination	0.07
Ott et al. (1983)	20	Symptom prescription	Insomnia	0.90
Shoham-Salomon et al. (1989)	20	Reframing and symptom prescription	Procrastination	0.99
Turner & Ascher (1979)	20	Symptom prescription	Insomnia	0.14
Wright & Strong (1982)	20	Symptom prescription	Procrastination	0.56

[a]Effect sizes are averaged when more than one is reported, except where indicated (Diener et al., 2009).
PI, paradoxical intervention.

further below). The fail-safe *N* indicated that approximately 65 studies with an effect size of 0 would need to be published to bring the weighted mean effect size below 0.10, or practical significance.

Moderators

Because of the significant *Q* statistics and the I^2 findings in both meta-analyses, we investigated potential moderators and mediators that might explain the variability. The first analysis concerned comparisons between PIs and wait-list controls, pre- and post-test measures, or placebo interventions. A majority of effect sizes reported ($k = 11$ of 21) were from wait-list or control groups. As a moderator variable, wait-list or control groups was not statistically significant ($Q = 13.472$, $df = 10$, $p = .198$). The weighted mean effect size was 0.96 (95% CI = −0.25, 0.58), which was significant ($z = 5.327$, $p < .0001$) and slightly lower than the reported effect size above, although still considered large. The next group of effect sizes reported ($k = 5$) used placebo interventions compared to

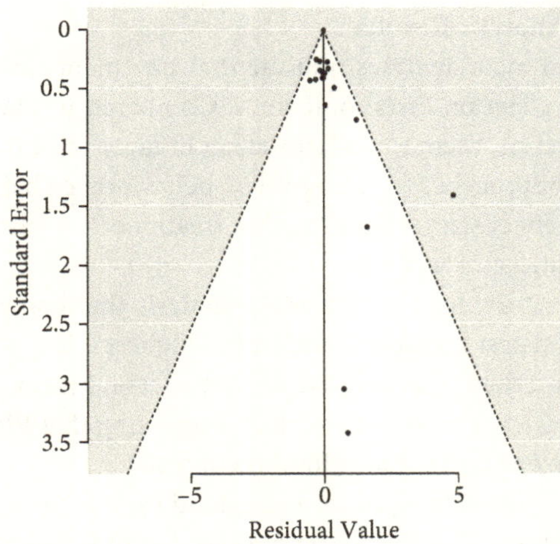

Figure 8.3 Funnel plot of effect sizes for treatments featuring paradoxical interventions compared to stimulus control, progressive relaxation, and cognitive–behavioral therapy.

PIs. These studies evidenced a much lower effect size, 0.52 (95% CI = −0.0036, 1.03), which was not significant ($z = 1.94$, $p = .0516$), and the test for homogeneity was not significant ($Q = 2.26$, $df = 4$, $p = .687$). The final group of studies ($k = 5$) used pre- and post-treatment comparisons using PI. This analysis resulted in a much larger effect size, 2.18 (95% CI = 1.5, 3.0), which was statistically significant ($z = 5.943$, $p = .0001$), and the test for homogeneity was not significant ($Q = 6.64$, $df = 4$, $p = .156$). Not surprisingly, the strongest effect was between pre- and post-test, followed by a wait-list or control group.

The second meta-analysis compared the use of PI treatments against other therapeutic approaches. A majority of studies ($k = 9$ of 17) used CBTs as the comparison. As a moderator variable, CBT was significant ($Q = 13.92$, $df = 8$, $p = .02$). The weighted mean effect size was 0.88 (95% CI = 0.54, 1.2), which was significant ($z = 5.14$, $p = .0001$) and considerably higher than the reported medium effect size above. The next largest group of comparison methods ($k = 7$) used stimulus control compared to PIs. These studies evidenced a much lower effect size, 0.12 (95% CI = −0.23, 0.46), which was not significant ($z = 0.6758$). The test for homogeneity was also not significant ($Q = 0.3921$, $df = 6$, $p = .998$). The final group of interventions ($k = 3$) used progressive relaxation compared to PIs. These studies also evidenced a much lower effect size, 0.14 (95% CI = −0.31, 0.58), which was not significant ($z = 0.601$). The test for homogeneity was also not significant ($Q = 0.333$, $df = 2$, $p = .8465$).

We found no statistical significance for several other moderator analyses: patient diagnosis, theoretical orientation, and type of outcome measure, which was similar to Hill's (1987) overall finding. Shoham-Salomon and Rosenthal (1987) reported significant effects for the type of PI (positive connotation, symptom prescription), but often these relied on comparison between a small number of studies, and they did not compute Cochrane's Q statistic or I^2, making direct comparison of these variables as moderators difficult. Additional moderator analyses were contemplated (e.g., client gender), but not enough studies reported these demographic variables to yield a useful analysis, so these were abandoned.

Summary of Meta-Analytic Results

The results of the two meta-analyses indicate that treatments involving PIs had a demonstrable, positive effect on distal outcomes. Compared to placebo group, wait-list control group, or baseline, there was a large effect in favor of PI treatments. Compared to other therapeutic approaches (e.g., cognitive–behavioral or behavioral approaches), we found a medium effect size, suggesting that treatments involving PIs may be superior to other therapeutic approaches.

In terms of moderators, for the first meta-analysis that compared PIs to wait-list controls, pre- and post-test measures yielded the highest effect size, followed by wait-list control groups, and then placebo groups. In the second meta-analysis, only studies using CBT had a significant moderating effect, suggesting that PIs were more effective than CBT but not more effective than stimulus control.

The current results generally replicate and extend the conclusions of previous meta-analyses. The magnitude of the effect sizes observed in the current analysis comparing PIs to placebo or control groups was similar to those reported by both Hill (1987) and Shoham-Salomon and Rosenthal (1987). However, unlike Shoham-Salomon and Rosenthal's meta-analysis, the head-to-head comparison was significant (although the magnitude was similar). This may have been a function of having more studies in our sample.

Research Review of Case Studies

In our review of the literature, we identified several small *N* and single-case design studies that did not report statistical results sufficient to include in the meta-analyses but did include interesting data. In several studies, authors reported session-to-session changes following therapist use of treatment packages featuring PIs, where patients behave differently out of session, to disrupt some problematic behavioral sequence. For example, in a study of insomnia, the PI suggested by the therapist was for the client to try *not* to fall asleep and to stay awake as long as possible (Ascher & Efran, 1978). These types of PIs cannot be carried out in the therapeutic session; they must be conducted outside of therapy. We review these articles in this section using box scores based on whether client symptoms were reported as improved, neither improved nor worsened, or worsened. Table 8.3 summarizes these 12 individual therapy studies, with a total of 35 patients.

Our box score analysis showed positive scores for all 12 studies along with a negative score in one study (see Table 8.3). Of course, this pattern might prove in part a function of publishing novel and "significant" findings, as opposed to pedestrian or nonsignificant results. At the same time, the pattern does generally dovetail with the distal results in the meta-analyses.

One case study indicated that the therapist's ability to communicate a rationale is important (Hsu & Lieberman, 1982). Hsu and Lieberman described the treatment of eight inpatient clients who were being treated for anorexia nervosa. The PIs consisted of suggesting that it was better for the patients to keep the disorder, that the patients found that there were some benefits to the disorder, and that changing or curing the disorder could make them unhappy. These suggestions were all made in the context of the

Table 8.3 Case Studies Using Paradoxical Intervention and Reported Outcome

Study	*N*	Type of PI	Measures of Distal Patient Outcome	Box Score or Reported Outcome[a]
Adshead et al. (1988)	1	Symptom prescription	Obsessive–compulsive disorder	+
Ascher (1979)	5	Symptom prescription	Urinary retention	+
Ascher (1981)	5	Symptom prescription	Agoraphobia	+
Ascher & Efran (1978)	5	Symptom prescription	Insomnia	+
Bornstein et al. (1981)	1	Symptom prescription	Recursive anxiety	+
Chapleau et al. (2013)	1	Symptom prescription	Conversion disorder	+
Chase et al. (1984)	4	Symptom prescription	Malingering	+
Hsu & Lieberman (1982)	8	Positive connotation	Anorexia nervosa	7 patients: + 1 patient: –
Kolko & Milan (1983)	1	Positive connotation	Youth delinquency	+
Kolko (1984)	1	Symptom prescription	Agoraphobia	+
Shackel & Zarske (1982)	1	Symptom prescription	Child tantrums	+
Vandereyken (1982)	2	Symptom prescription	Sexual dysfunction	+

[a]Patient improved, +; no change, 0; worsened, –.
PI, paradoxical intervention.

treatment that they were receiving in the hospital, where their health was being continually monitored. Outcome was improvement on measures of weight gain and physical health for all eight patients.

Kolko and Milan (1983) reported on the use of a PI on three early teenage students who had significant school absences. Using multiple baselines to determine the number of class periods attended, the clinician reframed the children's behavior as a normal phase of development and that the children were not yet as mature as their peers, but that they should not interrupt this phase. Instead, they were to *not* go to school or fight the urge to misbehave until the phase had passed. They reported that within the first week, this PI was successful in improving students' attendance, as well as their in-class behavior and participation, based on teacher report (long-term outcomes).

Possible Negative Effects and Harm

Perhaps no other psychotherapy method has attracted more concern about its potential harm than PIs. The primary concern is that they are "manipulative." However, as Jay Haley (1987) famously asserted, everything in therapy is, to some degree, manipulative because it deals with ideas, constructs, or interventions that are outside the client's awareness. Some of the traditional critiques include whether PIs are *unnecessarily* manipulative (Weeks & L'Abate, 1982). In addition, many theorists caution therapists about using PIs as a gimmick, without sufficient training or a thorough understanding of the client and their unique circumstances (Peluso, 2023a). None of the empirical research we reviewed for this chapter listed any negative effects that resulted from PIs. However, to ignore concerns that have been reflected in the literature would seem like an oversight to us. As a result, we briefly review some of these concerns and cautions here.

Weeks and L'Abate (1982) outlined three areas of concern regarding manipulation. The first is when the therapist defines the problem and the goals of therapy without client input. They suggest that this can be overcome by engaging the client in the assessment and goal-setting process. The second, related area of concern is when PIs are used without informed consent. Here, there is some disagreement about whether PIs would work if they were fully explained, and whether the lack of explanation of the method prior to it being utilized would decrease its effectiveness (Browning & Hull, 2021; Peluso, 2023a). Third is the concern of selecting a PI that is restrictive, controlling, or intrusive. Weeks and L'Abate (1982), Ascher (1989), and others have consistently stated that PIs that incorporate any of those elements (e.g., interventions that rely on punishment) are decidedly problematic, probably ineffective, and likely unethical.

Peluso (2023a) examined PIs through the lens of six ethical principles: autonomy, fidelity, nonmaleficence, justice, beneficence, and veracity. Guidelines for the ethical practice of PIs require the practitioner to be mindful of each principle. Ironically, authors have speculated that by reframing the issues as injunctions of double-binds, PIs can be used to help resolve ethical dilemmas, although this has yet to be investigated empirically (Ascher, 1989; Browning & Hull, 2021; Peluso, 2023a).

Diversity Considerations

Serious drawbacks in most of the studies in this meta-analysis were (a) the lack of reporting of client and clinician diversity and (b) the paucity of actual diversity in clients intersecting dimensions of cultural identities (when ethnicity was reported, participants were Caucasian). As a result, the generalizability of the findings of the present meta-analyses for non-White populations may be limited. We recommend that researchers implement sampling procedures that increase the inclusion of participants in research and seek out more ethnically diverse clinical samples (J. Hayes et al., 2016).

Limitations of the Research

One major limitation of the current investigation is the lack of measures and methods to assess the immediate outcomes of PIs. Most studies relied on distal measures of symptom reduction, although some were intersession measures. What this fails to address is the direct impact of the PI in the immediate moment, as well as later within the same session. Observational approaches may provide a possible method, but there are (as yet) no measures that we know of to assess either the occurrence of PI or its immediate outcomes.

There is some guidance in the literature about what these immediate effects would look like in session. The client's immediate reaction to the PI may often serve as an indication of the positive effect of the intervention (Ascher, 1989). Reactions can include shock, surprise, or confusion, and they are easily detected. Verbal and nonverbal emotional reactions (e.g., startle reflexes, looks of surprise, genuine or Duchenne smiles) can be captured by video or perhaps even using automated techniques to assess these successful moments. In addition, studies that employ more sophisticated statistical designs (e.g., lagged correlations, structural equations, unconfounded regressions, multilevel modeling, growth curve studies) have not yet been employed.

Another limitation of the research on PIs is that not many *client* factors have been systematically explored to determine their impact on effectiveness. One example of research on client factors is a study conducted by Shoham-Salomon and colleagues (1989). They found that reactance seemed to attenuate the effectiveness of PIs. Individuals with higher levels of reactance tended to respond *better* to PIs than did individuals with lower levels of reactance. Likewise, Horvath and Goheen (1990) examined reactance level on the efficacy of PIs treatment outcomes. Whereas in head-to-head comparisons between stimulus control and PIs both low and high reactant clients improved equally, at follow-up, more reactive clients who received the PIs continued to show improvement.

In addition, although there was diversity of disorders represented in the studies included for the present meta-analyses, insomnia and other anxiety disorders were overrepresented. As a result, the results may not necessarily be applicable to other disorders and diagnoses. Future research into PIs that focuses on client factors (e.g., personality traits, attachment style) or types of disorders that may moderate or mediate the overall effect could help clinicians select the best interventions that will be most beneficial to clients, as well as increase the persistence of change over time following treatment using PIs.

Perhaps the major limitation to the meta-analyses was the relative lack of recent research on PIs. Although there were enough studies to conduct the meta-analyses, given the demonstrated effectiveness of PIs, it is noteworthy that the majority of articles are from the 1980s, and there are very few after 2000. This may be due to the fact that studying therapeutic methods as they occur in a given session is difficult and that research on therapeutic processes is time-consuming and complicated (Begley & Ioannidis, 2015; Cook et al., 2017; Wampold & Imel, 2015). Future studies that either replicate the previous findings or apply PIs in settings that have not been previously investigated (e.g., substance abuse treatment) would lend greater weight to the efficacy of PIs.

There are several promising directions for research at the therapist level, client level, and process level. First, at the therapist level, an investigation of the role of therapist use of PIs would be important to discover how different therapists conceptualize and implement them. Are some therapists better than others in executing PIs? Can these elements be taught? Using observational approaches, combined with advances in computer vision, artificial intelligence, and other technologies, researchers can better track the implementation of PIs, as well as any preceding and anteceding actions, emotions, and behaviors of the therapist and client, to better understand the mechanisms of their effectiveness (Baker et al., 2022; Gibilisco et al., 2018; Goldberg et al., 2020; Imel et al., 2019). Last, we suspect that there might be an element of mediation between how experience and mastery affect the use of PIs and their impact on clinical outcomes (Peluso, 2023a).

Finally, at the process level, the relation between PIs and the therapeutic relationship has not been explored. Some researchers found that clients receiving PIs rated their therapists as more competent and that the relationship was more positive (Horvath & Goheen, 1990; Shoham-Salomon et al., 1989), whereas other researchers have surmised that the relationship with the therapist might not be as important in order to be effective (Beutler et al., 2002; Weeks & L'Abate, 1982). However, to be thoroughly answered, more sophisticated dismantling studies or mediation studies are required.

Training Implications

Writing back in 1982, Weeks and L'Abate acknowledged that there were only a few programs in the United States that taught the use of PIs. They suggested that if a clinician was not trained in their formal education setting, they could learn through postgraduate training or externships, or they could seek out a clinical supervisor who was trained in their use.

Some contemporary scholars have begun to endorse the use of PIs (Browning & Hull, 2021) and have developed textbooks that can systematically train clinicians in the use of PIs (e.g., Peluso, 2023a, 2023b). Other texts have discussed important elements related to PIs, such as second-order change (Fraser & Solovey, 2007), whereas approaches such as DBT and ACT embrace the use of dialectics (for recent training texts, see Chapman & Dixon-Gordon, 2020; S. Hayes, 2016) but do not explicitly teach PIs. In addition, we are unaware of any formal training programs or processes for PIs that have been formally tested for their effectiveness.

Therapeutic Practices

Treatments involving PIs, compared to baseline or control groups, demonstrated a large effect on distal treatment outcomes, although we have minimal indication of their immediate in-session impact. As a result, we tentatively recommend that practitioners do the following:

- Consider using paradoxes once the therapeutic relationship is stable and the clinician has the skill to repair an alliance rupture (should one occur).
- Use PIs such as prescribing the symptom, positive connotation, or reframing to demonstrate that a symptom is in a client's control or to reduce client pressure to take action for which they are not ready.
- Consider paradoxes particularly for anxiety and sleep difficulties and highly reactant patients because the research evidence is strongest in these areas.
- Tailor the type of PI to the client: Directional or compliance-based paradoxes (e.g., recommending continue to engage in the behavior they seek to change) are less of a threat to the therapeutic relationship, but they are not likely to be as effective with highly reactant clients. Conversely, defiance-based paradoxes (e.g., "prohibiting" the client from doing something that is actually beneficial) may be effective, but they can elicit reactance from the client and risk therapeutic ruptures.

- Engage the client in feedback about the experience and the effect of the PI. There may be times when the immediate experience of the method might not be positive, but it later helps change behavior.
- Obtain consent from clients regarding paradox. Deception is not necessary for PIs to succeed.
- Explore with clients what it will mean to have their concept of what their problem is and what the solution might entail.
- Frame for some patients that a therapeutic double-bind (PI) provides an alternative way to define their circumstances in a more productive way. That will likely minimize ethical concerns about deception and manipulation.

References

* Studies included in the meta-analyses.

Adler, A. (1956). *The individual psychology of Alfred Adler*. Basic Books.

*Adshead, G., Drummond, L. M., & Mercer, S. (1988). Paradoxical intention and anti-exposure in a non-compliant, obsessive–compulsive ritualiser. *British Journal of Psychiatry, 153*, 821–823. https://doi.org/10.1192/bjp.153.6.821

*Ascher, L. M. (1979). Paradoxical intention in the treatment of urinary retention. *Behaviour Research and Therapy, 17*, 267–270. https://doi.org/10.1016/0005-7967(79)90042-1

*Ascher, L. M. (1981). Employing paradoxical intention in the treatment of agoraphobia. *Behaviour Research and Therapy, 19*, 533–542. https://doi.org/10.1016/0005-7967(81)90080-2

Ascher, L. M. (1989). *Therapeutic paradox*. Guilford.

*Ascher, L. M., & Efran, J. S. (1978). Use of paradoxical intention in a behavioral program for sleep onset insomnia. *Journal of Consulting and Clinical Psychology, 46*, 547–550. https://doi.org/10.1037/0022-006X.46.3.547

*Ascher, L. M., & Schotte, D. E. (1999). Paradoxical intention and recursive anxiety. *Journal of Behavior Therapy and Experimental Psychiatry, 30*, 71–79. https://doi.org/10.1016/S0005-7916(99)00009-9

*Ascher, L. M., & Turner, R. M. (1979). Paradoxical intention and insomnia: An experimental investigation. *Behaviour Research and Therapy, 17*, 408–411. https://doi.org/10.1016/0005-7967(79)90015-9

*Ascher, L. M., & Turner, R. M. (1980). A comparison of two methods of the administration of paradoxical intention. *Behaviour Research and Therapy, 18*, 121–126. https://doi.org/10.1016/0005-7967(80)90106-0

*Ataoglu, A., Ozcetin, A., Icmeli, C., & Ozbulut, O. (2003). Paradoxical therapy in conversion reaction. *Journal of Korean Medical Science, 18*(4), 581–584. https://doi.org/10.3346/jkms.2003.18.4.581

Baker, A., Peluso, P. R., Freund, R., Diaz, P., & Ghaness, A. (2022). Using dynamical systems mathematical modelling to examine the impact of emotional expression on the therapeutic relationship: A demonstration across three psychotherapeutic theoretical approaches. *Psychotherapy Research, 32*(2), 223–237. doi:10.1080/10503307.2021.1921303

Beck, A. T., Steer, R. A., & Brown, G. (1996). *Beck Depression Inventory–II (BDI-II)* [Database record]. APA PsycTests. https://doi.org/10.1037/t00742-000

*Beck, J. T., & Strong, S. R. (1982). Stimulating therapeutic change with interpretations: A comparison of positive and negative connotation. *Journal of Counseling Psychology, 29*, 551–559. https://doi.org/10.1037/0022-0167.29.6.551

Begley, C. G., & Ioannidis, J. P. A. (2015). Reproducibility in science: Improving the standard for basic and preclinical research. *Circulation Research, 116*, 116–126. doi:10.1161/CIRCRESAHA.114.303819

Beutler, L. E., Moleiro, C., & Talebi, H. (2002). Resistance in psychotherapy: What conclusions are supported by research. *Journal of Clinical Psychology*, *58*(2), 207–217. doi:10.1002/jclp.1144

Borenstein, M., Hedges, L. V., Higgins, J. P. T., & Rothstein, H. R. (2009). *Introduction to meta-analysis*. Wiley.

Bornstein, P. H., Krueger, H. K., & Cogswell, K. (1989). Principles and techniques of couples paradoxical therapy. In L. M. Ascher (Ed.), *Therapeutic paradox* (pp. 298–310). Guilford.

*Bornstein, P. H., Sturm, C. A., Retzlaff, P. D., Kirby, K. L., & Chong, H. (1981). Paradoxical instruction in the treatment of encopresis and chronic constipation: An experimental analysis. *Journal of Behavior Therapy and Experimental Psychiatry*, *12*(2), 167–170. https://doi.org/10.1016/0005-7916(81)90012-4

*Broomfield, N. M., & Espie, C. A. (2003). Initial insomnia and paradoxical intention: An experimental investigation of putative mechanisms using subjective and actigraphic measurement of sleep. *Behavioural and Cognitive Psychotherapy*, *31*(3), 313–324. https://doi.org/10.1017/S1352465803003060

Browning, S., & Hull, R. (2021). Reframing paradox. *Professional Psychology*, *52*(4), 360–367. http://dx.doi.org/10.1037/pro0000384

Carlson, J., Watts, R. E., & Maniacci, M. (2006). *Adlerian therapy: Theory and practice*. American Psychological Association.

*Chapleau, K. M., Landsberger, S. A., Povlinski, J., & Diaz, D. R. (2013). Using paradoxical intention therapy to treat refractory nonepileptic events. *Psychosomatics*, *54*(4), 398–401. https://doi.org/10.1016/j.psym.2012.12.003

Chapman, A. L., & Dixon-Gordon, K. L. (2020). Dialectical behavior therapy. American Psychological Association. https://doi.org/10.1037/0000188-000

*Chase, J. L., Shea, S. J., & Dougherty, F. I. (1984). The use of paradoxical interventions within a prison psychiatric facility. *Psychotherapy: Theory, Research, Practice, Training*, *21*(2), 278–281. https://doi.org/10.1037/h0085984

Cohen, J. (1988). *Statistical power analysis for the behavioral sciences*. Routledge.

*Conoley, C. W., & Garber, R. A. (1985). Effects of reframing and self-control directives on loneliness, depression, and controllability. *Journal of Counseling Psychology*, *32*, 139–142. https://doi.org/10.1037/0022-0167.32.1.139

Cook, S. C., Schwartz, A. C., & Kaslow, N. J. (2017). Evidence-based psychotherapy: Advantages and challenges. *Neurotherapeutics*, *14*(3), 537–545. doi:10.1007/s13311-017-0549-4

DeBoard, J. B. (1989). Paradoxical interventions: A review of the recent literature. *Journal of Counseling and Development*, *67*, 394–398. https://doi.org/10.1002/j.1556-6676.1989.tb02099.x

Derogatis, L. R., & Savitz, K. L. (1999). The SCL-90-R, Brief Symptom Inventory, and Matching Clinical Rating Scales. In M. E. Maruish (Ed.), *The use of psychological testing for treatment planning and outcomes assessment* (pp. 679–724). Erlbaum.

Diener, M. J., Hilsenroth, M. J., & Weinberger, J. (2009). A primer on meta-analysis of correlation coefficients: The relationship between patient-reported therapeutic alliance and adult attachment style as an illustration. *Psychotherapy Research*, *19*(4–5), 519–526. doi:10.1080/10503300802491410

Dowd, E. T., Milne, C. R., & Wise, S. L. (1991). The Therapeutic Reactance Scale: A measure of psychological reactance. *Journal of Counseling and Development*, *69*(6), 541–545. https://doi.org/10.1002/j.1556-6676.1991.tb02638.x

*Espie, C. A., Lindsay, W. R., Brooks, D. N., Hood, E. M., & Turvey, T. (1989). A controlled comparative investigation of psychological treatments for chronic sleep-onset insomnia. *Behaviour Research and Therapy*, *27*(1), 79–88. https://doi.org/10.1016/0005-7967(89)90123-x

*Feldman, D. A., Strong, S. R., & Danser, D. B. (1982). A comparison of paradoxical and nonparadoxical interpretations and directives. *Journal of Counseling Psychology*, *29*, 572–579. https://doi.org/10.1037/0022-0167.29.6.572

Fisch, R., Weakland, J. H., & Segal, L. (1982). *The tactics of change: Doing therapy briefly*. Jossey-Bass.

Frankl, V. E. (1959). *Man's search for meaning*. Hodder & Staughton.

Frankl, V. E. (1975). Paradoxical intention and dereflection. *Psychotherapy*, *12*, 226–237. https://doi.org/10.1037/h0086434

Fraser, J. S., & Solovey, A. D. (2007). *Second-order change in psychotherapy: The golden thread that unifies effective treatments*. American Psychological Association.

Gee, B., Orchard, F., Clarke, E., Joy, A., Clarke, T., & Reynolds, T. (2019). The effect of non-pharmacological sleep interventions on depression symptoms: A meta-analysis of randomised controlled trials. *Sleep Medicine Reviews*, *43*, 118–128. https://doi.org/10.1016/j.smrv.2018.09.004

Gibilisco, H., Laubenberger, M., Spiridonov, V., Belga, J., Hallstrom, J. O., & Peluso, P. R. (2018). A multi-modal approach to sensing human emotion. In 2018 IEEE International Conference on Big Data (Big Data), *Seattle, WA* (pp. 2499–2502). IEEE. doi:10.1109/bigdata.2018.8622451

Gibney, P. (2006). The double bind theory: Still crazy-making after all these years. *Psychotherapy in Australia*, *12*(3), 48–55. https://search.informit.org/doi/10.3316/informit.545822294870607

Goldberg, S. B., Flemotomos, N., Martinez, V. R., Tanana, M. J., Kuo, P. B., Pace, B. T., Villatte, J. L., Georgiou, P. G., Van Epps, J., Imel, Z. E., Narayanan, S. S., & Atkins, D. C. (2020). Machine learning and natural language processing in psychotherapy research: Alliance as example use case. *Journal of Counseling Psychology*, *67*(4), 438–448. https://doi.org/10.1037/cou0000382

Haley, J. (1987). *Problem-solving therapy: New strategies for effective family therapy*. Jossey-Bass.

Hayes, J. A., McAleavey, A. A., Castonguay, L. G., & Locke, B. D. (2016). Psychotherapists' outcomes with White and racial/ethnic minority clients: First, the good news. *Journal of Counseling Psychology*, *63*(3), 261–268. https://doi.org/10.1037/cou0000098

Hayes, S. C. (2016). *The act in context: The canonical papers of Steven C. Hayes* (pp. 117–126). Routledge.

Hayes, S. C., Law, S., Assemi, K., Falletta-Cowden, N., Shamblin, M., Burleigh, K., Olla, R., Forman, M., & Smith, P. (2021). Relating is an operant: A fly over of 35 years of RFT research. *Perspectivas Em Análise Do Comportamento*, *12*(1), 005–032. https://doi.org/10.18761/PAC.2021.v12.RFT.02

Hayes, S. C., & Melancon, S. M. (1989). Comprehensive distancing, paradox, and the treatment of emotional avoidance. In M. Ascher (Ed.), *Paradoxical procedures in psychotherapy* (pp. 184–218). Guilford.

Hedges, L. V., & Olkin, I. (1985). *Statistical methods for meta-analysis*. Academic Press.

Hill, K. A. (1987). Meta analysis of paradoxical interventions. *Psychotherapy*, *24*, 266–270. https://doi.org/10.1037/h0085714

*Hills, H. I., Gruszkos, J. R., & Strong, S. R. (1985). Attribution and the double bind in paradoxical interventions. *Psychotherapy: Theory, Research, Practice, Training*, *22*(4), 779–785. https://doi.org/10.1037/h0085569

Holloway, E. L., Wampold, B. E., & Nelson, M. L. (1990). Use of a paradoxical intervention with a couple: An interactional analysis. *Journal of Family Psychology*, *3*(4), 385–402. https://doi.org/10.1037/h0080552

*Horvath, A. O., & Goheen, M. D. (1990). Factors mediating the success of defiance- and compliance-based interventions. *Journal of Counseling Psychology*, *37*(4), 363–371. https://doi.org/10.1037/0022-0167.37.4.363

*Hsu, L. G., & Lieberman, S. (1982). Paradoxical intention in the treatment of chronic anorexia nervosa. *American Journal of Psychiatry*, *139*(5), 650–653. https://doi.org/10.1176/ajp.139.5.650

Hunter, J. E., & Schmidt, F. L. (2004). *Methods of meta-analysis: Correcting error and bias in research findings* (2nd ed.). SAGE.

Imel, Z. E., Pace, B. T., Soma, C. S., Tanana, M., Hirsch, T., Gibson, J., Georgiou, P., Narayanan, S., & Atkins, D. C. (2019). Design feasibility of an automated, machine-learning based feedback system for motivational interviewing. *Psychotherapy*, *56*(2), 318–328. https://doi.org/10.1037/pst0000221

Jansson-Fröjmark, M., & Norell-Clarke, A. (2018). The cognitive treatment components and therapies of cognitive behavioral therapy for insomnia: A systematic review. *Sleep Medicine Reviews*, *42*, 19–36. https://doi.org/10.1016/j.smrv.2018.05.001

Katz, J. (1984). Symptom prescription: A review of the clinical outcome literature. *Clinical Psychology Review*, *4*(6), 703–717. https://doi.org/10.1016/0272-7358(84)90013-8

*Kolko, D. J. (1984). Paradoxical instruction in the elimination of avoidance behavior in an agoraphobic girl. *Journal of Behavior Therapy and Experimental Psychiatry*, *15*(1), 51–57. https://doi.org/10.1016/0005-7916(84)90123-X

*Kolko, D. J., & Milan, M. A. (1983). Reframing and paradoxical instruction to overcome "resistance" in the treatment of delinquent youths: A multiple baseline analysis. *Journal of Consulting and Clinical Psychology*, *51*(5), 655–660. https://doi.org/10.1037/0022-006X.51.5.655

Kraft, R. G., Claiborn, C. D., & Dowd, E. T. (1985). Effects of positive reframing and paradoxical directives in counseling for negative emotions. *Journal of Counseling Psychology*, *32*(4), 617–621. http://dx.doi.org/10.1037/0022-0167.32.4.617

*Lacks, P., Bertelson, A. D., Gans, L., & Kunkel, J. (1983). The effectiveness of three behavioral treatments for different degrees of sleep onset insomnia. *Behavior Therapy*, *14*, 593–605. https://doi.org/10.1016/S0005-7894(83)80052-5

Lambert, M. J. (2004). *Bergin and Garfield's handbook of psychotherapy and behavioral change* (5th ed.). Wiley.

Lemmens, L., DeRubeis, R. J., Tang, T. Z., Schulte-Strathaus, J., & Huibers, M. (2021). Therapy processes associated with sudden gains in cognitive therapy for depression: Exploring therapeutic changes in the sessions surrounding the gains. *Frontiers in Psychiatry*, *12*, 576432. https://doi.org/10.3389/fpsyt.2021.576432

Linehan, M. M. (2014). *DBT skills training manual* (2nd ed.). Guilford.

Lipsey, M. W., & Wilson, D. B. (2001). *Practical meta-analysis*. SAGE.

*Lopez, F. G., & Wambach, C. A. (1982). Effects of paradoxical and self control directives in counseling. *Journal of Counseling Psychology*, *29*, 115–124. https://doi.org/10.1037/0022-0167.29.2.115

Madson, M. B., Mohn, R. S., Schumacher, J. A., & Landry, A. S. (2015). Measuring client experiences of motivational interviewing during a lifestyle intervention. *Measurement and Evaluation in Counseling and Development*, *48*(2), 140–151. https://doi.org/10.1177/0748175614544687

Magnusson, K. (n.d.). *Interpreting Cohen's d effect size*. http://rpsychologist.com/d3/cohend

Martinez-Taboas, A. (1990). Controlled outcome research with paradoxical interventions: A review for clinicians. *Psychotherapy*, *27*, 468–474. https://doi.org/10.1037/0033-3204.27.3.468

Morin, C. M., Bootzin, R. R., Buysse. D. J., Edinger, J. D., Espie, C. A., & Lichstein, K. L. (2006). Psychological and behavioral treatment of insomnia: Update of the recent evidence (1998–2004). *Sleep*, *29*(11), 1398–1414. doi:10.1093/sleep/29.11.1398

Morin, C. M., Hauri, P. J., Espie, C. A., Spielman, A. J., Buysse, D. J., & Bootzin, R. R. (1999). Nonpharmacologic treatment of chronic insomnia. An American Academy of Sleep Medicine review. *Sleep*, *22*(8), 1134–1156. https://doi.org/10.1093/sleep/22.8.1134

Norcross, J. C., & Lambert, M. J. (2019). Evidence-based psychotherapy relationships: The Third Task Force. In J. C. Norcross & M. J. Lambert (Eds.), *Psychotherapy relationships that work: Volume 1. Evidence based therapist contributions* (3rd ed., pp. 1–23). Oxford University Press.

*Ott, B. D., Levine, B. A., & Ascher, L. M. (1983). Manipulating the explicit demand of paradoxical intention instructions. *Behavioural Psychotherapy*, *11*, 25–35. https://doi.org/10.1017/S014134730000879X

Paradox. (n.d.). *Merriam-Webster.com dictionary*. Merriam-Webster. Retrieved December 22, 2021, from https://www.merriam-webster.com/dictionary/paradox

Peluso, P. R. (2023a). *Advanced principles of counseling and psychotherapy: Learning, integrating, and consolidating the nonlinear thinking of master practitioners* (2nd ed.). Routledge.

Peluso, P. R. (2023b). *Principles of counseling and psychotherapy: Learning the essential domains and nonlinear thinking of master practitioners* (3rd ed.). Routledge.

Penman, R. (1980). *Communication processes and relationships*. Academic Press.

Rohrbaugh, M., Tennen, H., Press, S., & White, L. (1981). Compliance, defiance, and therapeutic paradox: Guidelines for strategic use of paradoxical interventions *American Journal of Orthopsychiatry*, *51*, 454–467. doi:10.1111/J.1939-0025.1981.Tb01393.X

Selvini-Palazzoli, M., Boscolo, L., Cecchin, G., & Prata, G. (1978). *Paradox and counter paradox.* Aronson.

*Shackel, J. A., & Zarske, J. A. (1982). The treatment of temper tantrums in a cerebral palsied child: A paradoxical intervention. *School Psychology Review, 11*(3), 324–328. doi:10.1080/02796015.1982.12084981

Shearin, E. N., & Linehan, M. M. (1989). Dialectics and behavior therapy: A metaparadoxical approach to the treatment of borderline personality disorder. In L. M. Ascher (Ed.), *Therapeutic paradox* (pp. 255–288). Guilford.

Shoham-Salomon, V., Avner, R., & Neeman, R. (1989). You're changed if you do and changed if you don't: Mechanisms underlying paradoxical interventions. *Journal of Consulting and Clinical Psychology, 75*, 590–598. https://doi.org/10.1037/0022-006X.57.5.590

Shoham-Salomon, V., & Rosenthal, R. (1987). Paradoxical interventions: A meta-analysis. *Journal of Consulting and Clinical Psychology, 55*, 22–27. https://doi.org/10.1037/0022-006X.55.1.22

Tang, T. Z., & DeRubeis, R. J. (1999). Sudden gains and critical sessions in cognitive–behavioral therapy for depression. *Journal of Consulting and Clinical Psychology, 67*(6), 894–904. https://doi.org/10.1037//0022-006x.67.6.894

Tennen, H., Press, S., Rohrbaugh, M., & White, L. (1981). Reactance theory and therapeutic paradox: A compliance–defiance model. *Psychotherapy, 18*(1), 14–22. https://doi.org/10.1037/h0085955

*Turner, R. M., & Ascher, L. M. (1979). Controlled comparison of progressive relaxation, stimulus control, and paradoxical intention therapies for insomnia. *Journal of Counseling and Clinical Psychology, 47*, 500–508. https://doi.org/10.1037/0022-006X.47.3.500

*Vandereyken, W. (1982). Paradoxical strategies in blocked sex therapy. *American Journal of Psychotherapy, 36*(1), 103–108. doi:10.1176/appi.psychotherapy.1982.36.1.103

van der Zweerde, T., Bisdounis, L., Kyle, S. D., Lancee, J., & van Straten, A. (2019). Cognitive behavioral therapy for insomnia: A meta-analysis of long-term effects in controlled studies. *Sleep Medicine Reviews, 48*, 101208. https://doi.org/10.1016/j.smrv.2019.08.002

Wampold, B. E., & Imel, Z. (2015). *The great psychotherapy debate* (2nd ed.). Erlbaum.

Watzlawick, P., Beavin, J. J., & Jackson, D. D. (1967). *Pragmatics of human communication: A study of interactional patterns, pathologies and paradoxes.* Norton.

Watzlawick, P., Weakland, J., & Fisch, R. (1974). *Change: Principles of problem formulation and problem resolution.* Norton.

Weeks, G. R., & L'Abate, L. (1982). *Paradoxical psychotherapy: Theory and practice with individuals, couples, and families.* Brunner/Mazel.

*Wright, R. M., & Strong, S. R. (1982). Stimulating therapeutic change with directives: An exploratory study. *Journal of Counseling Psychology, 29*, 199–202. https://doi.org/10.1037/0022-0167.29.2.199

9

Advice, Suggestions, Recommendations

Clara E. Hill, Sarah Knox, and Changming Duan

Authors' Note: We are grateful to Charles J. Gelso, Kristen Pinto-Coelho, Michael J. Scheel, Barbara Thompson, and Barbara Vivino for reviewing drafts of this chapter and helping us improve it.

Advice, suggestions, and recommendations (ASR) are all ways in which psychotherapists gently encourage their clients to do something in the hope of facilitating change. Psychotherapists might suggest, for example, that clients think more deeply about their motivations, note when they feel angry, or pay attention to their breathing when with their partner. Given that ASR are used across theoretical orientations and may have the potential for both helping and harming clients, we need to know more about their actual effectiveness.

In this chapter, we examine the immediate (assessed in-session), immediate delayed (assessed at post-session), and intermediate (assessed at the beginning of subsequent sessions) effects of ASR in individual psychotherapy. We provide definitions, clinical examples, and clinical indicators for ASR as well. We conclude with diversity considerations, training implications, and therapeutic practices related to ASR.

Definitions

The term most often used in the literature when describing such skills is *direct guidance* (DG), defined as "making suggestions, giving directives, or providing advice for what helpers think clients might do outside of helping sessions" (Hill, 2020, pp. 340–341). Researchers have also used terms such as recommendations (e.g., Scheel et al., 1999), directives (e.g., Duan et al., 2012), homework (e.g., Chapter 10, this volume), or advice (e.g., Prass et al. 2021). The definitions for all these terms are vague, so their overlap is difficult to determine.

DG exists on a continuum, ranging from implicit and indirect to very direct. At the implicit and often unstated end of the continuum is one's overall philosophy (e.g., psychotherapy/introspection is effective, change is good, emotions are beneficial, kindness/morality are good, and one must follow the rules/laws of one's society) that undoubtedly influences therapists' behaviors in session, including provision of implicit advice (e.g., implying that clients should introspect or talk about emotions) without explicitly stating such recommendations. Because advice and suggestions are also generally more tentative and nonprescriptive, they are on the more indirect end of the continuum. Recommendations and directives seem to fall in the middle of the continuum.

Clara E. Hill, Sarah Knox, and Changming Duan, *Advice, Suggestions, Recommendations* In: *Psychotherapy Skills and Methods That Work*. Edited by: Clara E. Hill and John C. Norcross, Oxford University Press. © Clara E. Hill and John C. Norcross 2023.
DOI: 10.1093/oso/9780197611012.003.0009

Homework involves even more of a demand on the client to enact the proposed action, and so it is on the most directive end of the continuum. Other scholars have similarly distinguished between indirect (a metaphorical task, a therapeutic suggestion) and direct (assignment of a task or homework) therapeutic tasks (e.g., Brown-Standridge, 1989).

An example of advice is a psychotherapist suggesting that it might prove helpful if a client were to notice when they beat themselves up during the week, without necessarily following up in subsequent sessions about whether the client implemented the advice. A recommendation might be to see a physician for medications. An example of a homework assignment is a psychotherapist telling a client to write every time they felt like beating themself up during the week and to bring that list back to the next session, then following up with the client to ascertain how the homework went, and modifying the homework to fit the client's needs.

For this chapter, we focus on advice, suggestions, and recommendations, or the indirect end of the continuum of DG. Thus, we exclude literature that focused explicitly on homework, although we acknowledge that homework could have been included in some of the studies that used the umbrella term of DG (although most of these studies came from a psychodynamic/humanistic framework and so were not likely to involve homework).

Depending on many factors (e.g., theoretical orientation, cultural background, personality, client characteristics), therapists may use ASR with greater or lesser frequency. Those from psychoanalytic traditions, for instance, are typically hesitant to give ASR (and rarely offer the more directive forms of assigning homework), fearing that doing so would make clients dependent on them or impair clients' ability to gain insight on their own (Abraham, 1925/1955; Gaylin, 2000). Other psychodynamic theorists have argued, however, that ASR is used more frequently in psychodynamic therapies than might be imagined, such as when clinicians suggest that clients record their dreams or initiate topics for discussion (Stricker, 2006). Indeed, ASR is inherently present in psychodynamic psychotherapy, and psychotherapists ignore it as a potentially useful method at their peril (Nichols & Paolino, 1986).

Client-centered clinicians also reflect differing opinions regarding the use of ASR. In seeking to nurture clients' "vast resources for self-understanding and for altering their self-concepts, basic attitudes, and self-directed behavior" (Rogers, 1980, p. 115), some client-centered psychotherapists aspire to be relatively nondirective (Brodley, 2006) and avoid intentionally or unintentionally directing client attention to content or processes dictated by the psychotherapist. Instead, psychotherapists try to follow the client's lead and accept their way of communicating about their experiences. Thus, they try not to ask clients to engage in particular actions or activities, for doing so presumes that the psychotherapist is the expert and may undermine clients' self-determination, empowerment, and safety (Brodley, 2006). Others within this tradition, however, have suggested that ASR are integral to psychotherapy and may be viewed as a client-centered endeavor depending on how they are delivered (Rita & John, 1999).

Those adhering to cognitive–behavioral therapy (CBT) frequently offer ASR and homework assignments, for they view the therapist's role as taking the lead in guiding clients to address specific concerns in session and serving as a guide or Socratic educator (Clark & Egan, 2015). Indeed, some (e.g., Walborn, 1996) have suggested that failure to use ASR could harm the therapeutic relationship if clients perceive the clinician as uncaring or unconcerned. Lazarus (1996) stated that in short-term psychotherapy, waiting until clients achieve understanding or decide on a course of action before offering useful ASR is an unwise luxury. In contrast, some CB psychotherapists lament what they perceive as an "overly prescriptive orientation" (Silverman, 1999, p. 317), in which clinicians have rendered "verbal prescription providers" (Silverman, 1999, p. 318).

Finally, in the integrative helping skills model (Hill, 2020), psychotherapists are advised to use ASR after helping clients explore and gain insight into the target problem. Psychotherapists are trained to attend to and reflect upon "pulls" to give ASR (e.g., in response to questions or requests from clients or from a personal need to be overly helpful). They are taught to use ASR intentionally and nonjudgmentally, to determine when clients are receptive to ASR, to work collaboratively with clients to develop action strategies rather than imposing them, and to observe client reactions to determine the effectiveness of their skills. Thus, therapists are taught not that ASP are in general effective or ineffective but, rather, that they can be effective or ineffective depending of what the client needs at the time.

Clinical Description and Indications

Some theorists suggest that ASR, and DG more broadly, are optimally used to help clients make behavior changes after the therapeutic relationship has been established and there has been sufficient exploration and insight work (e.g., Egan, 1994; Hill, 2020; Prochaska et al., 1992). The rationale is that psychotherapists need to help clients explore their concerns, experience the underlying emotions, and understand what is going on within themselves before helping clients begin to alter their behavior or environment.

On the other hand, some clients request advice and might even leave treatment if they do not receive it, even before a therapist perceives that a relationship has been established or before sufficient exploration and insight have been achieved. In some cases, providing such advice is helpful, whereas for others giving advice would constitute a therapeutic error. Thus, psychotherapists must be responsive to what their clients seek while also assessing what their clients clinically need. Psychotherapists can encourage some clients to be curious about why they want advice, support change attempts on their part, and help them become more active agents of their own lives.

In addition to these client factors, therapist beliefs about the change process undoubtedly dictate their degree of directiveness: If psychotherapists believe that they are the experts whose role is to diagnose and solve problems, then they are more likely to prescribe actions. In contrast, if psychotherapists believe that they function more like facilitators and fellow journeyers with clients being the active agents of change (e.g., Bohart & Tallman, 1999), they are more likely to eschew giving explicit advice.

Beginning psychotherapist trainees tend to offer advice to their clients, as advice-giving in interpersonal relationships is common in U.S. culture (MacGeorge & Van Swol, 2018). Americans often seek advice, and "experts" (e.g., Dear Abby, Ask Amy) frequently give it. For many trainees, a major shift is using less advice with clients than they do with friends and family and to shift from feeling invested in changing the client to valuing clients taking responsibility for their own changes (Hill, 2020).

Assessment

Assessment of ASR

Advice, suggestions, and recommendations can be assessed through judgments about perceived frequency of occurrence in an entire session. For example, an item on the therapist-rated Complementary Measure of Psychotherapy Outcome, which is completed after sessions, reads, "I gave explicit advice or direct suggestion to the patient" (Hilsenroth et al., 2005). However, such assessments yield only a general estimate of how much ASR was given in the session, rather than capturing the occurrence of specific instances of ASR.

To understand the effect of a skill, researchers must locate and examine specific occurrences within sessions. We suggest that the most accurate estimate of the occurrence of ASR involves having trained judges code whether ASR occurred within each therapist sentence or speaking turn within sessions. Judgments by trained observers do not necessarily reflect what psychotherapists intend or covertly communicate, nor do they necessarily reflect what clients hear nor how they absorb the communication; however, they do provide a clear operationalization of observable in-session therapist behavior.

An example of a microprocess measure of verbal response modes is the Hill Counselor Verbal Response Modes Category System (HCVRMCS; Hill, 1978), now called the Helping Skills System (Hill, 2020), which includes ASR as a subcategory of DG. A similar category of advisement can be found in Stiles (1979), and of general advisement in Elliott (1985). A comparison of six measures of advisement (including the above three) on a common set of seven transcripts from across a range of theoretical orientations found moderate convergence for codings of advisement.

Alternatively, researchers have asked psychotherapists and clients to list all the directives or recommendations that occurred within a session (Duan et al., 2012; Scheel et al., 2004). We suspect, however, that participants are most likely to remember the most salient instances rather than all instances.

Assessment of Outcomes of ASR

When examining the effects of skills, psychotherapy outcome researchers have focused primarily on distal (big O) outcomes (post-therapy treatment outcomes). In contrast, many process–outcome researchers (e.g., Rice & Greenberg, 1984) prefer in-session, immediate (small o) outcomes to better capture the effects of specific contextualized skills. It seems crucial for outcomes to be directly and temporally linked to the skill or method (e.g., how the client responded immediately to therapist ASR). A direct connection is typically not discernable with big O post-therapy outcomes because such outcomes reflect a combination of many in-session and extra-therapy experiences. We suggest, then, that the clearest estimates of ASR effects are client in-session behaviors, given that they occur immediately after the ASR and are thus temporally and sequentially linked to the skill (although other antecedent or concomitant variables also contribute to the impact).

In this chapter, we refer to *immediate in-session outcomes* as those assessed in the immediate sentences, speaking turns, or minutes after the ASR (e.g., client collaboration, client experiencing, 3-minute time window). *Immediate delayed outcomes* refer to assessments made later in sessions (e.g., intent to act) or right after sessions based on reviews of videotapes (e.g., client helpfulness ratings), as these are all assessments based on the specific therapist skills. *Intermediate outcomes* are those assessed after sessions as global estimates of effectiveness (e.g., using post-session measures such as the Session Evaluation Scale; Hill & Kellems, 2002) or at the beginning of subsequent sessions (e.g., implementation of recommendations).

In the research review (below), we examined these three time points because outcomes probably differ depending on when and how they are assessed. In regard to "when," clients might initially react positively to the ASR but then become more negative after further reflection, or might not take action because of intervening events after the session. In regard to "how," client immediate in-session response differs from global estimates of satisfaction because of the different focus.

Outcomes also depend on who conducts the assessment. Clients, psychotherapists, and trained judges all have different perceptions of the outcome based on their roles (client as the receiver, psychotherapist as the giver, and judges as outsiders). Outcomes could also differ based on the demands of the situation. For example, clients could indicate in session an intent to act to please the psychotherapist but have no intention of carrying out the ASR or run into obstacles in attempting to implement it. Similarly, judges could react according to how they might personally perceive the skill rather than attending to how the client responds.

Clinical Examples

Here, we present multiple examples of ASR provided by doctoral-student psychotherapists in initial sessions of open-ended psychodynamic psychotherapy (Prass et al., 2021, p. 273):

> "I would recommend to be honest and live in the reality, which might be hard for you."
>
> "Over the next week, notice what's happening and be aware of it . . . write down what thoughts jump into your head."
>
> "As thoughts and feelings come to mind that you would like to share with me, write them down."
>
> "My suggestion is that you go to the party and meet his friends . . . but you have every right to leave early and go home."
>
> "How about taking care of you?"
>
> "I wonder if you could continue working on your boundaries, if you could begin to say this is how I feel and take ownership of your feelings."
>
> "I want you to think about being easy on yourself about that. Think of the resources you have to be able to do that."
>
> "I would definitely apply for unemployment . . . it can't hurt to try."
>
> "Journaling when you're in therapy can be a really helpful thing."

Landmark Studies and Previous Reviews

Landmark Studies

Hill et al. (1988): Multiple Case Studies

Building on two earlier case studies (Hill et al., 1983; O'Farrell et al., 1986), Hill and colleagues (1988) examined the immediate impacts of therapist verbal response modes (VRMs; Hill, 1978) in eight cases of 12-session psychotherapy (four White male and four White female experienced psychotherapists with adult female clients presenting with depression, anxiety, low self-esteem, and problems with relationships). While reviewing videotapes after every session, clients rated the helpfulness of each therapist speaking turn and indicated up to three reactions (e.g., learned new ways to behave) for that speaking turn; psychotherapists correspondingly indicated their intentions (e.g., to promote change) and rated the helpfulness of each of their speaking turns. A team of trained judges rated the client experiencing level (i.e., level of emotional arousal, involvement, insight, and mastery) of every client speaking turn. Compared to other therapist VRMs, ASR were rated by therapists as moderately helpful, were rated by clients as least helpful, were associated with the lowest level of client experiencing, and were not associated with any particular client reactions.

Prass et al. (2021): Solicited or Unsolicited Advice in Early Sessions

Prass and associates (2021) investigated the first instance of when clients solicited advice and whether psychotherapists gave advice, as well as the first instance of unsolicited advice (defined as making a recommendation about what to do, think, or feel in response to a problem or need). Their sample was 98 adult clients (62 females, 36 males; 61 White, 37 persons of color) seen by 30 doctoral-student psychotherapists (21 females, nine males; 17 White/European American, 13 persons of color) in the first 20 sessions of psychodynamic psychotherapy (Prass et al., 2021). Sixty-nine percent of clients solicited advice at least once, and 61% had at least one instance of unsolicited advice (there was overlap in 31 cases). Client collaboration (similar to in-session working alliance) was rated by trained judges for the antecedent and subsequent 3 minutes surrounding the advice event, and the content of the advice (for outside of therapy vs. therapy-related) was coded.

When clients solicited advice, 84% of the requests involved problems outside of therapy (e.g., what to do about a relationship). In contrast, 16% of the requests involved therapy-related requests (e.g., what they should talk about, whether they should continue therapy), all occurring on average in the fourth or fifth session of psychotherapy.

Considering only the cases involving problems outside of therapy (the most typical type of solicited advice), clients solicited more advice when antecedent client collaboration was high, so they were already engaged in the therapeutic process. In these instances, the psychodynamic psychotherapists more often did *not* give advice than gave it (56% vs. 44%), indicating that they were cautious about automatically giving advice. Psychotherapists who were anxiously attached gave more advice to clients who were also anxiously attached, whereas psychotherapists who were less anxiously attached gave more advice to clients who were less anxiously attached, suggesting that similarity of attachment style may have influenced their use of the skill. If either the psychotherapist or the client was highly avoidantly attached, less advice was given, suggesting that avoidant attachment for either participant signaled psychotherapists to refrain from giving advice.

Subsequent client collaboration was higher when psychotherapists did *not* give advice than when they did, suggesting that clients engaged more in therapy when psychotherapists did not give advice. Some examples of what psychotherapists did instead of providing advice were admitting not having advice to offer, reflecting client feelings of distress, or asking open questions about feelings, thus perhaps facilitating client exploration so that clients could come to their own decisions.

In contrast, in the 11 instances in which clients solicited advice about therapy-related concerns, antecedent client collaboration was low, indicating that clients were asking for help in terms of the therapy itself. These psychotherapists more often did *not* give advice than gave it (73% vs. 27%), indicating that psychotherapists were even more cautious about giving advice when clients asked for guidance regarding the therapy process itself than when they sought advice regarding problems outside of therapy. Similarly, subsequent client collaboration was higher when psychotherapists did *not* give advice than when they did, suggesting that clients engaged more in therapy when therapists did not give this type of advice. The researchers could not analyze for the moderating effects of attachment styles given the small number of cases.

Psychotherapists were more likely to give unsolicited than solicited advice (62% vs. 29%). Subsequent client collaboration was lower after psychotherapists gave advice, suggesting again that clients became less engaged in therapy after therapist advice. For unsolicited advice, psychotherapists who were avoidantly attached were less likely to give advice to clients who were anxiously attached, suggesting that perhaps they were reluctant to give advice when clients became clingy and needy.

Hence, across three subsamples, client collaboration (controlling for antecedent client collaboration) decreased after advice. Interestingly, although the average client collaboration decreased following both the solicited and unsolicited advice, client collaboration increased in 7% of solicited advice events and 10% of unsolicited advice events, suggesting that advice is at least occasionally helpful.

Previous Reviews

Duan and colleagues (2018) conducted a narrative review of the literature related to advice-giving in psychotherapy, noting that it has mostly been studied under the umbrella term of *direct guidance*. In the empirical studies reviewed therein, DG accounted for 4–20% of all therapist responses in early sessions or in brief therapy (e.g., Elliott et al., 1987; Friedlander, 1982; Hill, 1978; Hill et al., 1988), and it was used more often in CBT than in psychodynamic or person-centered therapy (e.g., Elliott et al., 1987; Hill et al., 1979; Stiles et al., 1988). As outcomes, researchers used client ratings of helpfulness based on reviews of recordings immediately after the session (e.g., Elliott, 1985; Hill et al., 1988; Murphy et al., 1984), observed/judged client responses/behaviors following the advice (e.g., Allen et al., 1996; Hill, 1983; Hill et al., 1988), session level or treatment evaluations (e.g., Allen et al., 1996), or symptom reduction (e.g., Hill et al., 1988). The research on the relation between therapist use of DG and patient outcomes was reported as limited and inconsistent.

We are not aware of any meta-analyses on the effectiveness of ASR in psychotherapy. There are, however, several meta-analyses on the distal treatment outcomes of therapist directiveness as a function of client reactance (defined as being easily provoked and responding oppositionally to external demands). In a meta-analysis of 13 studies (1,208 patients), Beutler and colleagues found a large effect size ($d = .78$) for matching therapist directiveness to patient reactance (Edwards et al., 2019). Highly reactant clients benefited more from self-control, minimal direction, and paradoxical interventions, whereas lowly reactant clients benefited more from therapist directiveness and explicit guidance.

Research Review

Search Strategy and Inclusion Criteria

Our inclusion criteria were actual psychotherapy studies (no analogues), conducted in an individual format, and published in English language. The study must have reported at least one outcome that could be directly tied to ASR.

We searched PsycInfo in January 2021 using the following terms: counseling or therapy advice, advice, psychotherapy advice, therapist advice, advice from therapist, advice-giving, advice-giving psychotherapy, advice-giving therapist, direct guidance therapist, direct guidance therapy, direct guidance, counseling, outcome direct guidance therapist, therapist directives, therapist prescriptions, therapist, suggestions, and therapist recommendations. We also asked colleagues for articles and searched reference lists of articles for ones that might have been missed in the search. These methods produced a total of 45 potential studies in which ASR, broadly defined, might have been investigated in relation to any type of outcome. After a review by the three authors, seven studies met all of the inclusion criteria. Table 9.1 summarizes these seven studies (327 clients and 131 therapists). Five studies included measures of immediate in-session outcomes, three featured measures of immediate delayed outcomes, and two assessed intermediate outcomes. Two of the studies involved single cases, one involved eight cases, and the other four involved at least 20 cases. Given the small number of studies, we could not conduct a meta-analysis. Instead, we used box scores (our judgment based on the evidence of the outcomes) to aggregate the effects of ASR across studies.

Researchers used a variety of terms in their studies: DG, recommendations, directives, or advice. In examining the studies, however, we determined that the treatments in these seven studies were more psychodynamic and humanistic rather than CBT, and that the skills assessed seemed to be more on the indirect end of the continuum of DG. Hence, we included all of the studies that seemed to include ASR skills. Below, in reviewing our research analysis, we employ the respective terms that the authors used in their original publications.

Outcome Measures

The specific *immediate in-session* outcomes used in the analyzed studies (see Table 9.1) included judge-rated client collaboration (similar to estimates of moment-by-moment

Table 9.1 Studies of Immediate and Intermediate Outcomes of Therapist Advice, Suggestions, and Recommendations[a]

Study	Sample	Measures of ASR, Outcomes, and Moderators	Results
Duan et al. (2012)	96 clients (70 female, 26 male; age: $M = 21.52$ years, $SD = 2.20$) nested within 43 humanistic therapists (9 male, 34 female; across a range of experience from practicum students to staff psychologists) in a Chinese counseling center. Study used data collected before and after each session until the 6th session.	Measure of directives: Defined as verbal communication to client from therapist that directly or indirectly encourages client to feel, think, or behave in a new way outside of therapy sessions. Immediately after each session, clients wrote all the directives from the counselor and indicated the primary one. Measure of intermediate outcome: Implementation Rating Scale is rated by client using a 6-point scale (1 = strongly disagree, 6 = strongly agree) immediately before next session. Measure of moderators: (a) RRS (Scheel et al., 1999) assesses fit, difficulty, and therapist influence for the primary directive; (b) types of directive in content (emotional, cognitive, and behavioral), focus (on self, on others, and on self and others), and presenting problem (medical, interpersonal, academic, counseling-related, and intrapersonal).	Intermediate outcomes: Clients reported that they implemented the primary directive an average of 4.52 ($SD = 0.95$) on a 6-point scale (6 = high). No therapist effects. (+ box score) Clients implemented more counseling-related directives than those related to interpersonal or intrapersonal concerns. For primary directive from session 1, implementation as reported before session 2 was higher if recommendations were not difficult (although fit and influence did not matter). Across all 6 sessions, the difficulty, fit, and influence of directives were not significantly related to implementation.
Fitzpatrick et al. (2001)	21 archival sessions with 10 female and 11 male clients, and 7 RET, 6 client-centered, 3 CBT, 3 psychodynamic, and 2 Gestalt therapists, all apparently from the United States.	Measure of DG: Category in HCVRMCS (Hill, 1978; Hill et al., 1981) as coded by trained judges from audiotapes and transcripts. Measure of immediate outcome: Category System of Client Good Moments (revised by Stalikas et al., 1997) has 4 categories: provision of significant material, exploratory, expressive, and expression of strong feelings toward therapist (all of these would be evidence of positive effects). Measure of moderator: Working Alliance Inventory–Observer Form (Tichenor & Hill, 1989).	Immediate in-session outcomes with moderator effects: When working alliance was moderate ($n = 9$), therapist DG was associated with client provision of significant information more often than expected by chance (+ box score); nonsignificant for exploratory (= box score); nonsignificant for expressive (= box score); nonsignificant for expression of strong feelings toward therapist (= box score). When working alliance was high ($n = 5$), there was no association between DG and good moments (= box score for 4 outcomes). When working alliance was low ($n = 7$), there was no association between DG and good moments (= box score for 4 outcomes).

Hill et al. (1983)	Case study in United States of 12 sessions with a 20-year-old White female undergraduate client and an experienced 31-year-old White female relationally and insight-oriented PhD-level therapist.	Measure of DG: Category in HCVRMCS (Hill, 1978; Hill et al., 1981) as coded by trained judges from transcripts. Measures of immediate in-session outcome: CVRS (Hill et al., 1981), using categories of description, experiencing, and insight, as coded by trained judges from transcripts (description would be a neutral effect; experiencing and insight would be a positive effect). Measure of immediate delayed outcome: Post-session questionnaire in which both client and therapist listed the positive and negative events in the session. Measure of moderators: None.	Immediate in-session outcomes: Client description occurred less likely than would be expected by chance after DG (+ box score). Nonsignificant findings for client experiencing (= box score). Nonsignificant findings for client insight (= box score). Immediate delayed outcomes: Client indicated not getting immediate answers for how to cope with problems (DG) as a negative event (– box score). Therapist did not list DG for any positive or negative events (= box score).
Hill et al. (1988)	8 case studies of 12-session courses of psychotherapy in the United States. The 8 clients were adult and female and were depressed, anxious, and had self-esteem and relationship problems. The experienced therapists (4 male, 4 female; all White) came from a range of theoretical orientations.	Measure of DG: Category in HCVRCS (Hill, 1978; Hill et al., 1981) as coded by trained judges from transcripts. Measure of immediate in-session outcome: Client Experiencing scale (Klein et al., 1970, 1986) rated by trained judges using a 7-point scale (1 = impersonal, superficial; 7 = feelings are explored and experiencing serves as reference for problem resolution and self-understanding). Measures of immediate delayed outcome: (a) Helpfulness was rated by therapists and clients on a 9-point scale (1 = extremely hindering, 9 = extremely helpful) during a video review after sessions; (b) clients indicated their reactions to each therapist speaking turn during a video review after sessions using the Client Reactions System (Hill, 1988), which has 5 major clusters—supported, therapeutic work, challenged, negative reactions, and no reaction—coded by clients (supported and therapeutic work would be considered positive, challenged and negative would be considered negative, and no reaction would be considered neutral). Measure of moderators: None.	Immediate in-session outcomes: Ratings of client experiencing following speaking turns that included DG averaged 2.24 (*SD* = 0.54) on a 7-point scale (7 = high) (– box score). Immediate delayed outcomes: DG was rated 6.42 (*SD* = 1.26) on a 9-point scale (9 = high) or neutral by therapists (= box score). DG was rated 6.28 (*SD* = 1.54) on a 9-point scale (9 = high) or neutral by clients (= box score). Clients did not indicate supported, therapeutic work, challenged, negative reactions, or no reactions more or less often than expected by chance for DG (= box score for 5 outcomes).

(*continued*)

Table 9.1 Continued

Study	Sample	Measures of ASR, Outcomes, and Moderators	Results
O'Farrell Et al. (1986)	Case study in United States of 20 sessions with 20-year-old White female client and an experienced 34-year-old White female relationally and insight-oriented PhD-level therapist (same therapist as in Hill et al., 1983).	Measure of DG: Category in HCVRMCS (Hill, 1978; Hill et al., 1981) as coded by trained judges from transcripts. Measure of immediate in-session outcome: CVRS (Hill et al., 1981), using categories of description, experiencing, and insight (description would be a neutral effect; experiencing and insight would be a positive effect). Measure of immediate delayed outcome: Post-session questionnaire in which both client and therapist listed the positive and negative events in the session. Measure of moderators: None.	Immediate in-session outcomes: Nonsignificant findings for client description (= box score). Nonsignificant findings for client experiencing (= box score). Nonsignificant findings for client insight (= box score). Immediate delayed outcomes: DG was not mentioned as a positive or negative event by client (= box score). DG was not mentioned as a positive or negative event by therapist (= box score).
Prass et al. (2021)	First advice event in the initial 20 sessions of psychodynamic psychotherapy for 98 (62 female, 36 male; 61 White, 37 POC) adult community clients nested within 30 (21 female, 9 male; 17 White, 13 POC) doctoral student therapists in the United States.	Measure of advice: Defined as therapist giving the client suggestions or recommendations about what to do, think, or feel in response to a problem or need, as coded by trained judges from videotapes and transcripts. Measure of immediate outcome: Client Collaboration rated by trained judges from videotapes with the Use of Therapist Interventions Scale (Allen et al., 1996), a 5-point scale (1 = counterproductive use, 5 = optimal use). Measure of moderators: Whether advice was related to the therapy process (i.e., therapy-related) or to concerns outside of therapy.	Immediate in-session outcomes: For solicited out-of-therapy advice for 25 clients, pre ($M = 3.34$, $SD = 0.55$) vs. post ($M = 3.12$, $SD = 0.70$), $d = .35$ (– box score). For solicited therapy-related advice for 3 clients, pre ($M = 3.50$, $SD = 0.50$) vs. post ($M = 3.00$, $SD = 0.87$), $d = .70$ (– box score). For unsolicited advice for 61 clients, pre ($M = 3.20$, $SD = 0.77$) vs. post ($M = 2.90$, $SD = 0.90$), $d = .36$ (– box score). Moderators of immediate in-session outcomes: For solicited advice events, subsequent client collaboration (controlling for antecedent collaboration and session number) was lower when clients sought therapy-related advice (vs. outside therapy advice) and when therapists gave advice (vs. did not give advice).

Scheel et al. (1999)	102 (70 female, 32 male; 90 White, 12 POC; age: $M = 23.73$ years, $SD = 4.24$) clients in U.S. counseling center worked with 27 (15 female, 13 male; 25 White, 2 POC; 8 staff psychologists, 8 interns, 11 practicum students across theoretical orientations) therapists.	Measure of recommendations: Defined as anything therapist suggests a client do or think between sessions. After session, therapists made list of recommendations they offered in session and identified one as the primary recommendation. Measure of intermediate outcome: Implementation Rating Scale is rated by client using a 6-point scale (1 = strongly disagree, 6 = strongly agree) immediately before next session. Measures of moderators: (a) RRS (Scheel et al., 1999) assesses fit, difficulty, and influence; (b) types of recommendations: social interactions, stress management, promotion of self-esteem, validation of internal experiences, reframing meaning, referral, decision-making, request for action.	Intermediate outcomes: Clients reported that they implemented the primary recommendation an average of 4.67 ($SD = 1.03$) on a 6-point scale (6 = high) (+ box score). No significant differences in implementation for different types of recommendations, and no significant therapist effects. Difficulty and Therapist Influence subscales of the RSS were significant unique predictors of implementation, with higher implementation associated with lower difficulty level and higher therapist influence (fit of recommendation overlapped too much with therapist influence to be a unique predictor, but was also highly correlated with implementation).

[a]HCVRMCS (Hill, 1978; Hill et al., 1981) includes a category of direct guidance (i.e., suggestions, directives, instructions, or advice about what the client should do). Box scores are for ASR outcomes: Positive denotes positive effect, neutral denotes neutral/no effect, and negative denotes negative effect.

ASR, advice, suggestions, recommendations; CBT, cognitive–behavioral therapy; CVRS, Client Verbal Response Modes Category System; DG, direct guidance; HCVRMCS, Hill Counselor Verbal Response Mode Category System; POC, people of color; RET; RRS, Recommendation Rating Scale.

working alliance in sessions) and codings by judges of client behaviors (e.g., storytelling, experiencing, insight, provision of significant material, exploratory, expressive, expression of strong feelings toward therapist). These immediate outcomes were typically assessed in the subsequent first or second sentence, first speaking turn, or a 3-minute window after the ASR was given. *Immediate delayed* outcomes (see Table 9.1) included judgments of verbalized intent to act assessed later in sessions, and measures based on post-session reports or reviews of videotapes of sessions (video was stopped after each therapist speaking turn so that the therapist and client could rate the helpfulness of the entire speaking turn and the client could indicate their reactions to the speaking turn). An *intermediate* outcome assessed at the beginning of subsequent sessions was client-reported implementation of recommendations.

Coding Procedures

Table 9.1 contains the coded results of the seven studies. For all outcomes (but not for the potential moderators), the three authors read each study and consensually arrived at a box score for each outcome: + denotes a positive effect, 0 denotes a neutral/no effect, and – denotes a negative effect. To determine an overall box score for each outcome across samples, we assigned +1 to a positive box score, 0 to a neutral box score, and −1 to a negative box score.

Immediate Outcomes of ASR

Immediate In-Session Outcomes

Ratings of Client Collaboration

Client collaboration, using a 5-point scale ranging from 1 (*counterproductive*) to 5 (*optimal use*), was employed in one study (Prass et al., 2021) with three overlapping subsamples (solicited out-of-session advice, n = 25; solicited therapy-related advice, n = 3; and unsolicited advice, n = 61). The box score for all three samples was negative. Furthermore, in the two Prass et al. subsamples of solicited advice, client collaboration increased when therapists did *not* give advice.

Ratings of Client Experiencing

Direct guidance was associated with the lowest level of client experiencing in comparison with other therapist responses (one negative box score) in the Hill et al. (1988) study with eight clients.

Judgments of Productive Client Behaviors

Client verbal behaviors following DG were assessed in three studies. Fitzpatrick et al. (2001) coded four types of what they called client "good moments" (provision of significant information, exploratory, expressive, and expression of strong feelings toward therapist). Hill et al. (1983) and O'Farrell et al. (1986) coded client description, experiencing, and insight (the lack of the first and presence of the two latter behaviors could be considered good moments).

In the study by Fitzpatrick et al. (2001) with 21 clients, the good moment subtype of provision of significant information was associated with ASR for nine clients who had a moderate working alliance (WA), although none of the other three types of good moments (exploratory, expressive, and expression of strong feelings toward therapist) were related to DG (one positive and three neutral box scores). None of the four types of good moments were associated with DG for five clients with high WA (four neutral box scores) or for seven clients with low WA (four neutral box scores). Thus, overall, there were one positive and 11 neutral box scores. In the Hill et al. (1983) case study, client description (i.e., unnecessary storytelling) was less likely than chance to occur after therapist DG, to which we assigned a positive box score, given that description is not considered therapeutic. In contrast, client experiencing and insight were not associated with DG, leading to two neutral box scores. In the O'Farrell et al. (1986) case study, none of the three client behaviors (description, experiencing, insight) were more or less likely to occur than chance (thus three neutral box scores) after therapist DG. In sum, there were two positive and 14 neutral box scores for productive client behaviors.

Moderators of Immediate Outcomes

The quality of the WA moderated the association between therapist DG and the client provision of significant information (one of four types of good moments in Fitzpatrick et al., 2001). When the WA was moderate, DG was associated with the client provision of significant information more often than would be expected by chance, but this effect was not found when the WA was judged as high or low. None of the other three types of good moments (exploratory, expressive, and expression of strong feelings toward therapist) were associated with DG.

Antecedent client collaboration was related to the immediate outcome of the advice for solicited advice in Prass et al. (2021). That result suggested that clients responded better to the advice if they were initially collaborating well with the therapist.

The content of the advice was investigated in one study. In Prass et al. (2021), therapy-related advice was associated with poorer outcomes in terms of client collaboration than was outside-of-therapy advice.

Finally, it is possible that attachment style moderated the immediate outcomes of advice. In the study by Prass et al. (2021), when advice was solicited, therapists gave more advice when they were similar in terms of anxious attachment style, whereas therapists gave less advice if either they or the client was avoidantly attached. For unsolicited advice, therapists who were avoidantly attached were less likely to give advice to clients who were anxiously attached. The moderating effect of attachment style on the immediate outcomes was not investigated, but client collaboration was generally lower after advice, so it may be that attachment style is implicated.

Immediate Delayed Outcomes

The immediate delayed effects of DG and advice (terms used by the researchers) were assessed in four studies with 50 clients. Immediate delayed means that the outcomes of specific ASR events were assessed immediately after sessions (reports of positive and negative events, ratings of helpfulness, client reactions).

Ratings Based on Videotape Reviews

Therapist- and client-rated helpfulness and client-rated reactions were assessed during videotape review immediately after sessions for DG in the Hill et al. (1988) study. Both therapists and clients rated DG as neutral in terms of helpfulness (two neutral box scores). None of the five clusters of client reactions (supported, therapeutic work, challenged, negative reactions, no reaction) occurred more or less often than might be expected by chance for DG in Hill et al. (1988) (five neutral box scores).

Post-Session Reports

In one case (Hill et al., 1983), the client reported that not getting immediate answers was negative, but this was not replicated in the other case study (O'Farrell et al., 1986), yielding one neutral and one negative box score. Nothing positive or negative was mentioned by the therapist related to DG/ASR in either case (two neutral box scores). Hence, there were 10 neutral and one negative box scores.

Summary for Immediate Outcomes

Across three types of immediate in-session outcomes, there were two positive, 14 neutral, and four negative box scores. There was also some evidence of moderating effects for WA, client collaboration prior to the ASR, and client and therapist attachment styles (although these were found in one study each). Across the immediate delayed outcomes, there were 10 neutral and one negative box scores with moderators not having been studied. Thus, the immediate outcomes were mostly neutral.

Intermediate Outcomes of ASR

Client-rated implementation of recommendations or directives (the terms used by the respective researchers) was reported in two studies with a total of 198 clients. These two studies used a different method than the other six studies. Rather than studying all the available clients as in the other six studies, Scheel et al. (1999) relied on research assistants making a clinical judgment of whether clients sitting in a waiting room at a counseling center could tolerate being invited to participate, and Duan et al. (2012) allowed clients already being seen in a counseling center to self-select into whether they wanted to participate in a research study. Furthermore, rather than having trained judges assess the occurrence of the ASR and the outcomes of all ASR that occurred in sessions, as was done in other studies (excluding Fitzpatrick et al., 2001), Scheel et al. asked therapists to indicate the primary recommendation they gave in the target session and then provided that recommendation to clients to use in evaluating the recommendation. Duan et al. asked both therapists and clients to write all the recommendations that had been given and then evaluate them. In both studies, these recommendations were the ones that clients used at the beginning of subsequent sessions to rate their implementation. Thus, it may be that only those recommendations that stood out were remembered and reported, and that the very act of responding to the written recommendation after the session emphasized it for the client.

In sum, the box scores for both Duan et al. (2012) and Scheel et al. (1999) were positive. Thus, there was a positive association between directives and implementation as rated by clients at the beginning of a subsequent session.

In terms of moderators, in Scheel et al.'s (1999) study, client-rated implementation did not differ based on types of therapist recommendations (social interactions, stress management, promotion of self-esteem, validation of internal experience, reframing meaning, referral, decision-making, request for action). In contrast, in the study by Duan et al. (2012), the Chinese clients reported that they had implemented more counseling-related directives than those related to interpersonal or intrapersonal concerns. In addition, Scheel et al. reported higher implementation when the recommendation was not difficult and there was a higher level of therapist influence (i.e., the therapist was rated as expert, attractive, and trustworthy). In the study by Duan et al. (2012), client-reported implementation at the beginning of Session 2 was higher when the primary directive they received in Session 1 was lower in difficulty, although implementation was not moderated by fit or therapist influence. When the data were examined across the six sessions, however, the rated fit, difficulty level, and therapist influence of the directives were not consistently related to client implementation. Thus, results were not replicated across Scheel et al. (1999) and Duan et al. (2012).

Duan et al. (2012) observed that therapist directives in China may benefit clients through a different mechanism than found in Scheel et al. (1999). In Duan et al., the quantity of therapist directives was related to WA, which mediated a positive relationship with client symptom reduction. Perhaps receiving therapist directives made clients feel better (their expectations were met) about the relationship with the therapist and that, in turn, led to positive client change. Thus, there may be cultural differences in expectations for and outcomes of ASR.

Summary of ASR Outcomes

Immediate outcomes of ASR were overall neutral (although client collaboration significantly decreased), whereas the intermediate outcomes were positive. Although the operational definitions of ASR were not completely clear, and skills from across the continuum of directiveness were probably included in every investigation, these studies varied in ways that may explain the discrepant results. We suspect, for example, that the skills differed across studies in terms of directiveness. In four studies (Hill et al., 1983, 1988; O'Farrell et al., 1986; Prass et al., 2021), it appeared, given the examples provided and because therapists were generally more psychodynamic, that the skills were more in the range of advice and suggestions. The study by Fitzpatrick et al. (2001), by contrast, included therapists from across the range of orientations, and thus more likely represented skills along the whole continuum of DG. At the other end of the continuum, Scheel et al. (1999) specifically asked for recommendations, and Duan et al. (2012) asked for directives, and thus the skills they examined might have been more directive and persuasive than those explored in other studies.

Possible Negative Effects and Harm

Based on the results of our research review, it appears that in one study, ASR on average lowered client collaboration immediately following ASR (Prass et al., 2021). Perhaps clients start to expect that therapists will solve their problems, and thus become passive rather than active agents in their healing. They may come to believe that therapists are the experts and know more about them than they do about themselves. Sessions may then become stilted and less productive, as clients become inactive and wait for the therapist to take charge. In none of the studies, however, did authors report any clients being harmed by ASR.

Although not examined in studies included in this review, one potential situation in which harm may occur for ASR on the directive end of the continuum is when client reactance is high. As noted above, highly reactant clients often drop out of psychotherapy or become resistant when given high levels of directiveness (Edwards et al., 2019).

Diversity Considerations

The first author (CEH) heard the following story while visiting China with the third author (CD): Once upon a time in China, before much Western influence, there was a wise political counselor who was renowned for her sage advice. People waited in line patiently, bearing gifts, to hear her advice about major life problems. Then, as the Western influence came in, she was told that she should not give advice but, rather, should listen empathically. She thus began to not give advice but, rather, to listen empathically. Interestingly, people stopped coming to see her. Frustrated, she finally returned to her natural style of giving advice, and people once again sought her out for her wisdom. This example speaks to the need to be responsive to cultural expectations in advice-giving.

In our set of reviewed studies, there was only one quantitative study in which outcomes of ASR were investigated outside of the United States (Duan et al., 2012). We thus focus on a few non-outcome studies to shed light on the possible influence of culture on the effects of therapist ASR.

Duan and colleagues (2015) studied Chinese counselors' perspectives about using directives in psychotherapy. They found that counselors generally viewed directives as being appropriate and necessary. Counselors asserted, however, that they should focus on the factors that ensure the effectiveness of directives, including the content fitting the client, delivering the directives via indirect and implicit communication, and the consideration of both immediate and prolonged impacts.

Duan et al. (2022) then studied Chinese clients' perspectives about advice in psychotherapy. Most clients expected counselors to give directives, reported having received directives and feeling good afterwards, and indicated that they had felt discontented when they did not receive as many directives as they wanted or when they received directives that did not fit their needs. In addition, some clients perceived nondirective counselor skills as being directive (e.g., asking about feelings implies that the client should explore their feelings). Furthermore, clients indicated that they would implement only those directives that they anticipated would have a clear benefit, and they would not implement those that seemed difficult to do.

In another study, Joo and colleagues (2019) interviewed students who had taken a helping skills course in Korea and asked how they had modified their skills to meet the needs of their Korean clients. Participants typically indicated being worried or hesitant about using action-stage skills, including ASR, with South Korean clients, even when clients requested them. Some feared increasing client dependency or clients reacting negatively toward action skills. One counselor shared that

> when I was a beginning counselor, I used to tell my clients what to do and what they can try to do outside of the sessions, but I came to realize that it does not work when clients do not have a clear understanding about it, regardless of what I said to them.

In addition, participants typically indicated that they used information-giving skills as opposed to ASR because it seemed more appropriate for South Korean clients. Joo et al. recommended that rather than immediately providing advice or recommendations, therapists should try to discern what clients were implicitly asking for when requesting directives (e.g., validation), given that providing too many directives could reduce client autonomy.

Of course, there is probably more variation within than across groups, so it is important not to generalize results to all persons within a culture. In addition, therapists sometimes misunderstand the experiences of diverse clients (Sue et al., 2019), which makes cultural competence imperative for effective use of ASR. Therapists working with clients from non-Western cultures must consider the role of local culture, including values and customs, in determining whether, or how, to use ASR. As noted by MacGeorge and Van Swol (2018, p. 15), "culture shapes what we recognize as [ASR] and how we are expected to respond to it."

Limitations of the Research

There is some progress in ASR research. In contrast to early research in which ASR was broadly defined and its frequency was correlated with session and treatment outcome, researchers have begun to examine the immediate in-session outcomes of the more narrowly defined ASR controlling for antecedent client behaviors (e.g., Prass et al., 2021). In addition, researchers are more often studying naturally occurring psychotherapy, using multiple judges and consensus among judges, and examining potential moderators (e.g., Prass et al., 2021) rather than relying on analogue or quasi-naturalistic methods. Greater attention is also now focused on the outcomes of ASR with culturally diverse clients (e.g., Duan et al., 2012).

Despite these promising developments, the major limitation of the research is the paucity of studies. Even within the seven studies included in this review, there was an immense diversity of participants and methods (see Table 9.1), making it difficult to aggregate results and generalize them to other populations and settings. We suspect that there are so few studies of the immediate outcomes of ASR because conducting such studies is both time-consuming and labor-intensive, as well as more complex than administering self-report measures after sessions.

The studies also varied in terms of how the skills were selected and investigated. In five studies, all ASR that occurred within sessions were coded by trained judges based on observing sessions. Thus, we have no evidence that clients heard or paid attention to the ASR. In contrast, Scheel et al. (1999) and Duan et al. (2012) asked therapists and clients to record all the remembered recommendations/directives and then designate the primary one and rate its fit, difficulty, and level of therapist influence; at the beginning of the subsequent session, clients rated whether they had implemented the recommendations/directives. Thus, only the recommendations/directives that were salient and written were studied. Clients may well have remembered only the salient ones and may have felt some pressure to implement the recommendations/directives because they were asked about them.

Given that not all outcomes reviewed were included in all the studies, we cannot know if outcomes were initially negative, then neutral, and later became positive across ASR. But based on the differences across studies, it seems most likely that the average ASR in session was relatively nondirective mild and lowered client immediate collaboration, but if recorded and emphasized, it may have had a positive outcome in terms of implementation. Similarly, Meichenbaum and Turk (1987) discussed how directives provided by health care professionals are more likely to be adhered to (i.e., implemented) if written and a small number of them are given.

Researchers have also begun to attend to moderating variables, but the only attempted replication study was conducted by Duan et al. (2012), who sought to replicate Scheel et al.'s (1999) findings about the effects of difficulty, fit, and therapist influence as moderators of implementation of recommendations. Notably, the results did not replicate across the two studies, perhaps due to between-study differences in client recruitment, sample composition, sessions sampled, and cultural differences.

Overall, our review suggests that researchers need to continue to analyze process data to examine immediate and intermediate outcomes of ASR. More research is also needed on the markers of when clients are likely to be receptive to ASR, moderators of outcomes (e.g., attachment styles, cultural diversity, personality traits, and defensive structure of therapists and clients who respond well or poorly to ASR), and types of ASR outcomes. Special attention needs to be paid to changes in how clients respond to ASR over time. Interviews with therapists and clients, perhaps using videotape-assisted recall methods about specific instances of ASR, could provide valuable information about the experiences of giving and receiving ASR. Conversation analysis (Hepburn & Potter, 2021) might also be a beneficial method for examining more of the nuances and contexts of when and how advice is given and received. Finally, researchers could study the effects of receiving or not receiving ASR for those clients who request it.

Training Implications

We know of no literature on training students in ASR (Knox & Hill, 2021). From our experiences with training (Hill, 2020), the greatest difficulty that beginning trainees encounter involves a shift from liberally giving ASR and feeling invested in the clients adhering to their advice to using it in a more restrained and intentional manner and observing the effects on clients. Relatedly, trainers might focus on helping students learn the skill with moderate explicitness and directiveness.

We suspect that, as with learning psychotherapy skills in general (see Hill et al., 2014), instruction, modeling, practice, and feedback are all important components of ASR training, with practice plus feedback probably being the most influential. Practicing how to respond in salient scenarios, such as when clients demand advice or when therapists feel pulled to provide advice because clients are suicidal or feeling helpless, as is done in deliberate practice (e.g., Rousmaniere, 2016), might prove helpful. Trainees can also learn to observe client responses to ASR (e.g., they say "Yes, but . . .," comply passively, or eagerly talk about how they could implement the ASR). We also suspect that training students to be aware of their personal experiences, reactions, and countertransference related to ASR, and to be culturally sensitive to client values and experiences, would prove helpful.

Therapeutic Practices

Although the immediate in-session effects of advice are neutral, the practice recommendations are more positive. There are clearly times when the most responsive skill to use with clients is ASR. Thus, rather than saying that therapists should never use ASR (as I, CEH, was taught in my training), we recommend that psychotherapists selectively and intentionally use ASR in response to client needs. We thus offer the following evidence-based practices:

- Decide what kind of psychotherapist you want to be (e.g., expert, friend, cheerleader, problem-solver, sounding board, analyst) and how comfortable you feel giving ASR.
- Be aware of your cultural identities and social positions in relation to clients and consider those when deciding if, when, and how to use ARS.
- Consider providing ASR to clients who are low in reactance level but not to those who are high in reactance level.
- When feeling a "pull" to give advice, reflect about what you are intending to accomplish and what the best response would be.
- Consider, when tempted or asked to give ASR, if it would prove more effective for the client to develop their own solution.
- Be clear and not too directive when giving advice.
- When you provide ASR, observe the clinical effects on client collaboration, the therapeutic relationship, ruptures, eventual acceptance and implementation, and client reactions (e.g., gratitude, anger).
- When you choose not to provide ASR after feeling a "pull" to provide it, observe the clinical effects on client collaboration, the therapeutic relationship, and client reactions.
- Consider asking about clients' feelings, what they have tried before, and what has worked instead of quickly offering ASRs.

References

* Studies included in the research review.

Abraham, K. (1955). Psychoanalytic notes on Cove's system of self-mastery. In H. Abraham (Ed.), *Clinical papers and essays on psycho-analysis* (H. Abraham & D. R. Ellison, Trans.; pp. 306–327). Basic Books. (Original work published 1925)

Allen, J. G., Coyne, L., Colson, D. B., Horwitz, L., Gabbard, G. O., Frieswyk, S. H., & Newson, G. (1996). Pattern of therapist interventions associated with patient collaboration. *Psychotherapy: Theory, Research, Practice, Training, 33*(2), 254–261. https://doi.org/10.1037/0033-3204.33.2.254

Bohart, A. C., & Tallman, K. (1999). *How clients make therapy work: The process of active self-healing*. American Psychological Association.

Brodley, B. T. (2006). Client-initiated homework in client-centered therapy. *Journal of Psychotherapy Intervention, 16*, 140–161. https://doi.org/10.1037/1053-0479.16.2.140

Brown-Standridge, M. D. (1989). A paradigm for constructing of family therapy tasks. *Family Process, 28*(4), 471–489. https://doi.org/10.1111/j.1545-5300.1989.00471.x

Clark, G. I., & Egan, S. J. (2015). The Socratic method in cognitive behavioral therapy: A narrative review. *Cognitive Therapy and Research, 39*, 863–879. https://doi.org/10.1007/s10608-015-9707-3

*Duan, C., Hill, C., Jiang, G., Hu, B., Chui, H., Hui, K., & Liu, J. (2012). Therapist directives: Use and outcomes in China. *Psychotherapy Research, 22*, 442–457.https://doi.org/10.1080/10503307.2012.664292

Duan, C., Hill, C., Jiang, G., Hu, B., Lei, Y., Chen, J., & Yu, L. (2015). The counselor perspective on the use of directives in counseling in China: Are directives different in China as in the United Sates. *Counseling Psychology Quarterly, 28*(1), 57–77.https://doi.org/10.1080/0965070.2014.965659

Duan, C., Hill, C., Jiang, G., Li, S., Duan, X., Li, F., Hu, B., Yu, L. & Du, M. (2022). Client views of counselor directives (指导): A qualitative study in China. *Counselling Psychology Quarterly, 35*(2), 303–323. https://doi.org/10.1080/09515070.2020.1768049

Duan, C., Knox, S., & Hill, C. E. (2018). Advice-giving in psychotherapy. In E. MacGeorge & L. Van Swol (Eds.), *Oxford handbook of advice* (pp. 175–198). Oxford University Press.

Edwards, C. J., Beutler, L. E., & Someach, K. (2019). Reactance level. In J. C. Norcross & B. E. Wampold (Eds.), *Psychotherapy relationships that work: Volume 2. Evidence-based therapist responsiveness* (pp. 188–211). Oxford University Press.

Egan, G. (1994). *The skilled helper* (5th ed.). Brooks/Cole.

Elliott, R. (1985). Helpful and nonhelpful events in brief counseling interviews: An empirical taxonomy. *Journal of Counseling Psychology, 32*, 307–322. https://doi.org/10.1037/0022-0167.32.3.307

Elliott. R., Hill, C. E., Stiles, W. B., Friedlander, M. L., Mahrer, A. R., & Margison, F. R. (1987). Primary therapist response modes: Comparison of six rating systems. *Journal of Consulting and Clinical Psychology, 55*, 218–223. https://doi.org/10.1037/0022-006X.55.2.218

*Fitzpatrick, M. R., Stalikas, A., & Iwakabe, S. (2001). Examining counselor interventions and client progress in the context of the therapeutic alliance. *Psychotherapy, 38*(2), 160–1170. https://doi.org/10.1037/0033-3204.38.2.160

Friedlander, M. L. (1982). Counseling discourse as a speech event: Revision and extension of the Hill Counselor Verbal Response Category System. *Journal of Counseling Psychology, 29*, 425–429. https://doi.org/10.1037/0022-0167.29.4.425

Gaylin, W. (2000). Nondirective counseling or advice? Therapy as value laden. *The Hastings Center Report, 30*, 31–33.

Hepburn, A., & Potter, J. (2021). *Essentials of conversation analysis*. American Psychological Association.

Hill, C. E. (1978). Development of a counselor verbal response category system. *Journal of Counseling Psychology, 25*(5), 461–468. https://doi.org/10.1037/0022-0167.25.5.461

Hill, C. E. (2020). *Helping skills: Facilitating exploration, insight, and action* (5th ed.). American Psychological Association.

Hill, C. E., & Kellems, I. S. (2002). Development and use of the Helping Skills Measure to assess client perceptions of the effects of training and of helping skills in sessions. *Journal of Counseling Psychology, 49*(2), 264–272. doi.org/10.1037/0022-0167.49.2.264

*Hill, C. E., Carter, J. A., & O'Farrell, M. K. (1983). A case study of the process and outcome of time-limited counseling. *Journal of Counseling Psychology, 30*(1), 3–18. https://doi.org/10.1037/0022-0167.30.1.3

*Hill, C. E., Helms, J. E., Tichenor, V., Spiegel, S. B., O'Grady, K. E., & Perry, E. S. (1988). Effects of therapist response modes in brief psychotherapy. *Journal of Counseling Psychology, 35*(3), 222–233. https://doi.org/10.1037/0022-0167.35.3.222

Hill, C. E., Spangler, P. T., Jackson, J., & Chui, H. (2014). Training undergraduate students to use insight skills: Integrating the results of three studies. *The Counseling Psychologist, 42*(6), 800–820. https://doi.org/10.1177/0011000014542602

Hill, C. E., Thames, T. B., & Rardin, D. (1979). A comparison of Rogers, Perls, and Ellis on the Hill Counselor Verbal Response Category System. *Journal of Counseling Psychology, 26*(3), 198–203. https://doi.org/10.1037/0022-0167.26.3.198

Hilsenroth, M. J., Blagys, M. D., Ackerman, S. J., Bonge, D. R., & Blais, M. A. (2005). Measuring psychodynamic–interpersonal and cognitive–behavioral techniques: Development of the Comparative Psychotherapy Process Scale. *Psychotherapy: Theory, Research, Practice, Training, 42*(3), 340–356. https://doi.org/10.1037/0033-3204.42.3.340

Joo, E. S., Hill, C. E., & Kim, Y. H. (2019). Using helping skills with Korean clients: The perspectives of Korean counselors. *Psychotherapy Research, 29*, 812–823. https://dx.doi.org/10.1080/10503307.2017.1397795

Knox, S., & Hill, C. E. (2021). Training and supervision in psychotherapy: What we know and what we need to know. In M. Barkham, W. Lutz, & L. G. Castonguay (Eds.), *Bergin and Garfield's handbook of psychotherapy and behavior change* (50th anniversary ed., pp. 327–349). Wiley.

Lazarus, A. A. (1996). Some reflections after 40 years of trying to be an effective psychotherapist. *Psychotherapy, 33*(1), 142–145. https://dx.doi.org/10.1037/0033-3204.33.1.142

MacGeorge, E., & Von Swol, L. (Eds.). (2018). *Oxford handbook of advice*. Oxford University Press.

Meichenbaum, D., & Turk, D. C. (1987). *Facilitating treatment adherence: A practitioner's guidebook*. Plenum.

Murphy, P. M., Cramer, D., & Lillie, F. J. (1984). The relationship between curative factors perceived by patients in their psychotherapy and treatment outcome: An exploratory study. *British Journal of Medical Psychology, 57*(2), 187–192. https://doi.org/10.1111/j.2044-8341.1984.tb01599.x

Nichols, M. P., & Paolino, T. J. (1986). *Basic technique of psychodynamic psychotherapy: Foundation of clinical practice*. Gardner Press.

*O'Farrell, M. K., Hill, C. E., & Patton, S. (1986). Comparison of two cases of counseling with the same counselor. *Journal of Counseling and Development, 65*(3), 141–145.https://dx.doi.org/10.1002/j.1556-6676.1986.tb01261.x

*Prass, M., Ewell, A., Hill, C. E., & Kivlighan, D. M., Jr. (2021). Solicited and unsolicited advice-giving in psychotherapy: Is it advised? *Counselling Psychology Quarterly, 34*(2), 253–274. https://doi.org/10.1080/09515070.2020.1723492

Prochaska, J. O., DiClemente, C. C., & Norcross, J. C. (1992). In search of how people change: Applications to addictive behaviors. *American Psychologist, 47*(9), 1102–1114. https://dx.doi.org/10.1037/0003-066X.47.9.1102

Rice, L. N., & Greenberg, L. S. (1984). *Patterns of change*. Guilford.

Rita, S. F., & John, S. F. (1999). *Clinical interviewing*. China Light.

Rogers, C. R. (1980). *A way of being*. Houghton Mifflin.

Rousmaniere, T. (2016). *Deliberate practice for psychotherapists: A guide to improving clinical effectiveness*. Routledge. http://dx.doi.org/10.4324/9781315472256

Scheel, M. J., Hanson, W. E., & Razzhavaikina, T. I. (2004). The process of recommending homework in psychotherapy: A review of therapist delivery methods, client acceptability, and factors that affect compliance. *Psychotherapy: Theory, Research, Practice, Training, 41*(1), 38–55. https://doi.org/10.1037/0033-3204.41.1.38

*Scheel, M. J., Seaman, S., Roach, K., Mullin, T., & Mahoney, K. B. (1999). Client implementation of therapist recommendations predicted by client perception of fit, difficulty of implementation, and therapist influence. *Journal of Counseling Psychology, 46*(3), 308–316. https://doi.org/10.1037/10412-000

Silverman, W. (1999). Editorial: If it's Tuesday with depressive symptoms it must be cognitive–behavioral therapy. *Psychotherapy: Theory, Research, Practice, Training, 36*(4), 317–319. https://doi.org/10.1037/h0092419

Stiles, W. B., Shapiro, D. A., & Firth-Cozens, J. A. (1988). Verbal response modes use in contrasting psychotherapies: A within-subjects comparison. *Journal of Consulting and Clinical Psychology, 56*(5), 727–733. https://doi.org/10.1037/0022-006X.56.5.727

Stricker, G. (2006). Using homework in psychodynamic psychotherapy. *Journal of Psychotherapy Integration, 16*, 219–237. https://doi.org/10.1037/1053-0479.16.2.219

Sue, D. W., Sue, D., Neville, H. A., & Smith, L. (2019). *Counseling the culturally diverse: Theory and practice*. Wiley.

Walborn, F. S. (1996). *Process variables: Four common elements of counseling and psychotherapy* (pp. 219–244, 270–271). Brooks/Cole.

10

Integrating Between-Session Homework

Truls Ryum, Mia Bennion, and Nikolaos Kazantzis

Authors' Note: Nikolaos Kazantzis disclosed his royalties from Guilford, Routledge, and Springer Nature publishers. Other authors declare no conflict of interest.

A common goal across all psychotherapies is to help clients extend and integrate the benefits from in-session activities into their daily lives. Clients spend most of their time outside of the consulting room, so it makes intuitive sense for therapists to encourage clients to make use of the time between sessions for therapeutic work and to advance progress toward ultimate treatment goals. Indeed, *homework*, or between-session therapeutic activity, has been identified as a common process across theoretical orientations (Kazantzis & Ronan, 2006). Although there are divergent opinions as to what constitutes homework, and how explicitly between-session activities should be integrated into treatment (Nelson et al., 2007), the use of between-session homework (BSH) may nonetheless be considered a common factor (Garfield, 1997; Kazantzis & Ronan, 2006).

It may be surprising to some that homework in psychotherapy may be traced to the writings of Sigmund Freud (1952), who encouraged phobic clients to face their fears and enact different relationships outside of the therapeutic relationship, once unconscious conflicts and drives had been resolved in psychoanalysis. More systematic attempts to integrate between-session activities into psychotherapy were later proposed from multiple theoretical orientations, but most notably from the behavioral and cognitive–behavioral therapies (CBTs; Shelton & Ackerman, 1974; Shelton & Levy, 1981). For example, Aaron T. Beck and colleagues emphasized homework as a crucial vehicle of change in their seminal manual of cognitive therapy for depression (Beck et al., 1979). Since then, a steadily increasing body of research has underpinned the role of homework as a central component in psychotherapy in general, and in CBTs specifically.

After defining and illustrating BSH, we examine the immediate (in-session) effects, as well as the potential for intermediate (session-to-session) effects of therapists' use of BSH in adult psychotherapy. We show that previous reviews have centered on homework adherence (or compliance), whereas the present focus centers on the behaviors of the therapist when using BSH. We also discuss possible harm, diversity factors, training implications, as well as therapeutic practices.

Definitions

Various terms have been proposed to capture the essence of BSH (Kazantzis, 2000; Kazantzis & Ronan, 2006): extratherapy assignments, extra-treatment practice

Truls Ryum, Mia Bennion, and Nikolaos Kazantzis, *Integrating Between-Session Homework* In: *Psychotherapy Skills and Methods That Work*. Edited by: Clara E. Hill and John C. Norcross, Oxford University Press. © Clara E. Hill and John C. Norcross 2023.
DOI: 10.1093/oso/9780197611012.003.0010

assignments, in vivo behavioral practice assignments, and home practice activities, to name a few. In general, authors from integrative approaches have favored the term *between-session assignments* (Nelson et al., 2007), whereas cognitive–behavioral writers have traditionally relied more on *homework*. Recently, the alternative term *action plans* has been proposed (Kazantzis & Miller, 2022). Each term may evoke different reactions from both therapists and clients, clearly because *homework* has an association with the educational model and will, for some clients, elicit a certain amount of fear associated with evaluation, control, or failure (Fehm & Kazantzis, 2004; Kazantzis, Arntz, et al., 2010). Consequently, the word *homework* is not recommended for use in practice with clients (Kazantzis, MacEwan, & Dattilio, 2005), but in this chapter, we use BSH as a unifying term, acknowledging that there is no universally agreed-upon term.

A common rationale for engaging clients in BSH is to foster learning in some form (Kazantzis & L'Abate, 2007b), but there is diversity in what constitutes between-session activities across treatment approaches. To illustrate, BSH may comprise such diverse methods as bibliotherapy, promoting emotional awareness, reflection, relaxation exercises, self-monitoring to understand the connection between daily activities and mood, recording one's automatic thoughts and developing alternative responses, exposure to feared stimuli (in vivo, imaginal, or interoceptive), as well as scheduling and engaging in activities to promote a sense of accomplishment or pleasure, just to name a few. Offering a unifying definition of BSH is thus not easy, but here we define *BSH* generically as activities that enable the client to gather information and generalize new learning from the therapeutic setting to the everyday life situations in which their problems occur. We emphasize that BSH should be viewed not only as a task undertaken by the client but also as an interpersonal *process* that unfolds between the therapist and client, both within and between sessions.

Another point of differing opinions is to what extent BSH should primarily be initiated, suggested, or even *prescribed* by the therapist (e.g., Ellis, 1962); self-initiated by the client (Brodley, 2006); or collaboratively negotiated between therapist and client (Kazantzis et al., 2013). In most cognitive and behavioral therapies, the process of designing, planning, and reviewing BSH is explicitly on each session agenda, although negotiated between therapist and client and undertaken with collaborative empiricism (Kazantzis et al., 2017). BSH tasks are ideally tailored to the client based on the evidence for therapeutic methods and strategies for their presenting problem and context.

The use of BSH is not emphasized in traditional psychoanalysis or psychoanalytic psychotherapy, but it has been advocated for (Stricker, 2006) and reported being used in large practice surveys of psychodynamic therapists (Fehm & Kazantzis, 2004; Kazantzis, Lampropoulos, et al., 2005). At the same time, the use of BSH has typically been found to differentiate psychodynamic therapy (PDT) from CBT in clinical trials (e.g., Goldfried et al., 1997; Goldfried & Raue, 1998; Svartberg et al., 2004) and is usually not included within psychodynamic treatment manuals. Compared to CBT, more emphasis is usually given to a nondirective therapeutic stance, which centers on the client–therapist relationship, and analysis of transference as more important for therapeutic change compared to outside-session behavior. BSH may therefore be offered as a possibility by the therapist to help illuminate the client's intra- or interpersonal dynamics (insight). For example, BSH may consist of the therapist asking the client to write their dreams, to attend to emotional reactions or interpersonal dynamics during the week, or more directly to ask the client to try new and specific behaviors in relational contexts (see

Chapter 9, this volume, related to advice, suggestions, and recommendations). Explicit suggestions or negotiating of BSH are usually avoided but may be given in a more indirect fashion, such as "I wonder what would have happened if you had . . ." (Stricker, 2006).

Psychotherapists adhering to a humanistic and experiential theories (HET) approach may include BSH in their clinical work, tailored to fit the client and circumstances. Overt planning of BSH is usually seen as incompatible with the basic tenets of classical humanistic theory (Rogers, 1961), but client-initiated BSH is welcomed (Brodley, 2006), typically suggested as "Try this if you find it helpful . . ." rather than as required or expected between-session activities. The rationale for including BSH in HET is to help clients practice new ways of processing and making sense of their emotional experience (i.e., awareness, regulation, and transformation of emotion), in order to consolidate and reinforce in-session changes through extra-sessional practice (Greenberg & Warwar, 2006).

Notwithstanding different vocabularies, the field appears to be moving toward a formulation of BSH characterized by assimilation and integration (see Ronan & Kazantzis, 2006; special issue of *Journal of Psychotherapy Integration*). For example, across a range of psychotherapies, BSH can include having the client pay attention to emotions not fully in awareness, focusing on experiences that are actively avoided or unacknowledged, becoming more aware of self-criticism, and fostering self-compassion and acceptance (Hayes, 2022). For this chapter, we have deliberately selected the term "integrating" in the title to convey the view that BSH should ideally not be viewed as an isolated "add-on" but, rather, as an in-session process that draws upon all aspects of the therapeutic relationship, and it should be integrated through the early, middle, and late phases of the session (Kazantzis & Miller, 2022).

Clinical Description and Indications

If, when, and how BSH is integrated in psychotherapy depend on a variety of factors, such as the clients' specific needs and the rationale of the treatment approach, and the therapist needs to be responsive to both the client's needs and the emerging therapeutic context (Stiles et al., 1998; Watson & Wiseman, 2021). In general, BSH may be utilized in all treatment phases (early, middle, and late), and there is no fixed indication. BSH may target symptoms and behaviors tied to locations outside the consulting room, such as with obsessive–compulsive disorder (OCD) or interpersonal relationships. The nature of BSH may change as treatment progresses, depending on the client's stage of change (e.g., precontemplation, contemplation, preparation, action, maintenance; Prochaska & Norcross, 2018). A BSH task in the early treatment phase of CBT may consist of helping the client become more aware of negative automatic thoughts using the situation–thoughts–emotions–behavior present during schema activation, and in a later treatment phase consist in jointly developing a relapse-prevention plan.

Therapist Behaviors

Early guides for integrating BSH into psychotherapy were presented in practice guides for behavior therapy (Shelton & Ackerman, 1974) and cognitive therapy (Beck et al.,

1979), and a comprehensive protocol exists (Kazantzis, MacEwan, et al., 2005). The behavioral models centered on a specific plan for the BSH, in terms of when, where, how often, and how long the task should take (Shelton & Levy, 1981), but practitioner surveys have suggested these steps are not frequently implemented (Kazantzis & Deane, 1999), even though BSH is reported as frequently incorporated into PDT and CBT (Kazantzis, Lampropoulos et al., 2005).

In these guides, the in-session process has been defined as selecting, planning, and reviewing BSH early at the outset of the session. Kazantzis, MacEwan, et al. (2005) advocate for a 10/40/10 split of the consultation hour, where the collaborative design of BSH is integrated into the main portion of the session, the negotiation of the specific plan for BSH practice is part of the blended summary and feedback process within the last 10 minutes of the session, and the review and feedback on the process of engagement is nested within the establishment of the agenda within the first 10 minutes of the subsequent session. As with all structural aspects of the therapy, the extent to which the integration of BSH is overly "signposted" or even allocated a specific amount time will depend on the therapist's style and the therapeutic needs of the client. For example, a client with a highly activated negative belief about being controlled by others, and therefore possibly by the therapist, may benefit from an embedded structure in which verbal communication is fluid and there is less specificity in the transition between different aspects of BSH. By contrast, a different client favoring time-efficient consultation sessions may value overt statements regarding time allocation to review and planning of BSH.

As intimated above, it is important to note that all therapist behaviors regarding BSH exist within a context of the therapeutic relationship (Kazantzis, 2018). Accordingly, all the usual relational skills that would be expected in psychotherapy, such as both emotion-focused and perspective-taking empathy, are important, particularly when anticipating practical obstacles to BSH engagement and when acknowledging difficulties encountered as part of the BSH review. Therefore, therapist BSH behaviors are ideally nested within a strong therapeutic bond, with clear agreement on the goals and tasks for the BSH as a natural extension of the in-session work. Furthermore, collaboration is indicated in shared input, responsiveness to those decisions, and shared decision-making in the selection and planning of BSH. Any given task also has the potential to be an experimental test of the client's assumptions about their problems or ways of coping, which themselves can be elucidated as part of the in-session design of BSH using Socratic dialogue (Kazantzis & Stuckey, 2018). The culmination of these therapist efforts is an increased probability of engagement with the BSH, although client engagement cannot simply be taken as a measure of therapist skill or competence because each BSH is different, and each client will have unique experiences when engaging with BSH. In the following, we address some core therapist behaviors associated with the cycle of designing, planning, and reviewing BSH.

Designing BSH

The process of selecting an appropriate BSH usually follows from the in-session work (Jensen et al., 2020), based on evidence-based therapeutic techniques and strategies. By adopting a collaborative approach, within a working alliance of agreement on the task and its alignment with the client's personal goals, there is utility in soliciting feedback on whether the client understands the BSH task and its rationale. A range of health belief models, including the stages of change, self-determination theory, and motivational interviewing, are relevant to the design of BSH (Kazantzis & L'Abate, 2007a). Equal attention can be given to the situational antecedents or triggers to the implementation of the BSH, and its likely consequences. Clearly, both classical and operant learning processes are relevant in understanding the extent to which BSH is relevant, effective, and helps generalize and maintain clients' sustained coping and enriched quality of life (e.g., increase of positive emotions, reduction of distress).

Planning BSH

Adopting the frame that the client is the "expert on their life" can be useful when negotiating the specifics of when, where, how often, and how long the task should take. Comprehensive guides for the integration of BSH (Kazantzis, MacEwan, et al., 2005) advocate for a summary of the component parts followed by client feedback on the perceived importance, readiness, and confidence to engage with the "whole" BSH. Of course, the type of BSH can determine how the specificity is applied, given that some are to be applied based on emotions arising in a specific situation, others when relational strain occurs, and often when time and privacy permit.

Reviewing BSH

Conceptualizing client engagement with BSH as merely "adherence" or "compliance" does not capture the collaboration expected when integrating BSH in psychotherapy, and clients' appraisals of a task are often elicited when attempting BSH (Kazantzis & Miller, 2022). For example, clients may experience BSH as being "too difficult" or "not useful," or an assigned task that did not go as planned may activate negative beliefs about personal value ("I am inadequate") or the therapy process ("The therapist is going to judge me"). An important task for the therapist when integrating BSH is therefore to enquire about the client's beliefs about the benefits of the BSH, possible enjoyment and perceived contribution to progress and mastery, their perceived skill acquisition, and any encountered obstacles or difficulties.

Assessment

Assessment of the Integration of BSH

In contrast to the extensive literature on the assessment of client adherence or compliance with BSH (see the Research Review section), a relative minority of studies have assessed *therapist behaviors* associated with the integration of BSH in treatment. Whereas some studies have utilized qualitative methods (e.g., interviews) to examine clients' experiences with engaging with BSH, most studies have relied on quantitative measures when examining therapist behaviors and client compliance with BSH. The most frequently adopted method has been independent assessments of recorded treatment sessions by trained raters, but with measures that were often not designed to provide a *comprehensive* evaluation of therapist behaviors associated with BSH. For example, a number of studies have used a behavioral methods/homework subscale from the Collaborative Study Psychotherapeutic Rating Scale (CSPRS; Hollon et al., 1988), which was originally developed to distinguish therapist behaviors in CT, interpersonal therapy, and clinical management of pharmacotherapy. The subscale positions BSH as "behavioral methods" due to BSH involving a very concrete feature of the process of sessions, but in doing so has omitted cognitive-focused BSH (e.g., Sasso et al., 2016). Similarly, the Cognitive Therapy Scale (CTS; Young & Beck, 1980), which was originally developed to assess therapist behaviors in the delivery of the overall therapy, has been repurposed and reformatted (e.g., Bryant et al., 1999), with only the "homework" items presented in associations with outcome (e.g., Ryum et al., 2010).

Few studies have assessed therapist behaviors with measures from the perspective of the client or therapist, with some exceptions; for example, the Comparative Psychotherapy Process Scale (CPPS; Hilsenroth et al., 2005) has been used as a client self-report measure, and the Session Assignment and Feedback Form (SAFF; Hong et al., 2012) has been used by both clients and therapists. The CPPS contains two subscales assessing therapists' use of cognitive–behavioral and psychodynamic–interpersonal techniques, but with only two items tapping into homework and outside of session activity. The SAFF contains two sections—one that records the specific BSH assigned in the session and the extent of completion the following week, and a second section asking the client to write down one or two things they want to remember from the session.

One of the most comprehensive observer-based measures of therapist behaviors in the use of BSH is the Homework Adherence and Competence Scale (HAACS; Kazantzis, Wedge, et al., 2005), which assesses not only therapist adherence but also therapist *competence* in the use of BSH. This 19-item measure comprises three subscales related to designing (e.g., "How well did the therapist present a rationale for homework?"), assigning (e.g., "How well did the therapist collaborate with the client to specify how the homework would be practically integrated into the client's life?"), and reviewing (e.g., "How well did the therapist attempt to problem solve practical obstacles to homework?") BSH. The Homework-Specific Therapist Behaviors Scales (HSTBS; Conklin et al., 2018) is another example of a comprehensive measure, comprising 16 items assessing therapist behaviors related to assigning, reviewing, and overcoming obstacles to the client's completion of BSH. The psychometric properties of both HAACS and HSTBS have been found to be good in previous research (e.g., Conklin et al., 2018; Yew et al., 2021).

Assessment of Outcomes of BSH

In accordance with the focus of this volume, we distinguished *immediate in-session* outcome from *intermediate outcome*, with the latter term reserved for BSH effect on session-to-session changes. In principle, though, both immediate and intermediate outcomes could be assessed in similar ways with quantitative (e.g., observer and/or self-report measures) or qualitative (e.g., interviews) methods. Outcomes may either be direct changes in psychological health (symptoms, distress, etc.) or, more indirectly, change in an intermediate variable such as compliance or engagement with BSH. For example, some studies have assessed outcome with the Beck Depression Inventory as a measure of symptom change (e.g., Strunk, Brotman, DeRubeis, et al., 2010), but this approach could also pertain to the extent mechanisms of psychopathology have been successfully addressed. It would thus be possible to examine if therapist behaviors in BSH integration led to meaningful change in clients' skill in the identification of and coping with emotions within behavioral activation therapy, or in the acquisition of skill in identifying and reappraising problematic cognitions in CBT for depression. Other studies have employed qualitative methods with interviews to examine clients' experiences with the use of BSH, including benefits and challenges (e.g., Berg et al., 2008; Finning et al., 2017).

A number of studies have assessed client *compliance* with BSH as a proxy measure of outcome, which may include the client's engagement with the task, the experience in completing the task (perceived mastery, progress toward therapy goals, etc.), or theoretically meaningful determinants of engagement during the session (e.g., perceived understanding of the rationale or collaboration, credibility/expectancy, specificity, or match with therapy goals). Several measures have been designed to measure effects of BSH, such as the observer-based Homework Rating Scale–Revised (HRS-II; Kazantzis, Deane, et al., 2005) with psychometric support from multiple research teams (e.g., Yew et al., 2021). This 12-item scale measures the client's engagement (i.e., quantity ["the client was able to do the activity"], quality ["the client was able to do the activity well"], as well difficulties and obstacles experienced), homework beliefs (comprehension, rationale, collaboration, and specificity), and perceived consequences of doing homework (pleasure, mastery, and progress). This operationalization takes into account that compliance or adherence with BSH may be less important than the extent of skill acquisition (Kazantzis et al., 2004, 2017) or the *quality* of BSH compliance (e.g., Neimeyer & Feixas, 1990). Specifically, the quality of BSH compliance takes into account how invested or skillfully the client engages with a particular BSH task, and not just the time spent or number of BSH practices undertaken.

Therapist behavior has primarily been studied in relation to BSH adherence or compliance, and it is important to consider that therapist behaviors regarding BSH may have other unmeasured impacts (Kazantzis & Miller, 2022). Crucially, for BSH, if the therapist has less than optimally selected and planned the task with the client, there is potential for negative views of the task, or negative interpretations of the process for the BSH, all of which will then impact on the completion (see the theoretical model in Kazantzis & Miller, 2022).

Clinical Examples

There is a large diversity in the use of BSH. We emphasize that the use of any between-session task should remain flexible, both within and across treatment approaches. In Boxes 10.1 and 10.2, we offer illustrative examples of BSH in CBT, PDT, and HET, classified into two broad categories (insight and behavior change) that have received support as transtheoretical change categories (e.g., McCullough et al., 2003; Ryum et al., 2014; Valen et al., 2011).

Box 10.1 Examples of Action-Oriented Between-Session Homework in Psychotherapy

Behavioral activation in the treatment of depression, such as scheduling of periods of exercise or participation in formerly pleasurable activities to avoid inactivity (and rumination) and increase the likelihood of access to positive reinforcement (CBT).

Safe place homework for clients who have experienced abuse and report feeling scared about attending to and experiencing their feelings in therapy. Examples of a safe place include a favorite room, a mountaintop, or an imaginary cabin in the forest (HET).

Taking risks, such as recognizing opportunities to try new ways of being with others (e.g., allowing oneself to be more open, asserting needs), and noting how this impacts others' responses as well as own feelings about the interaction (PDT).

Exposure exercises (in vivo, interoceptive, imaginative) with response prevention, which may help the client learn that anxiety will eventually subside without engaging safety behaviors or rituals (CBT).

Letting go of past relationships, such as the death of a loved one or divorce. Instructing the client to write a letter in the first-person saying goodbye to the person they have lost, to move forward, may help them deal with a painful loss that remains unacknowledged (HET).

Promoting self-empathy through asking the client to imagine the part of themselves that is in pain as a vulnerable child and to sooth the child (HET).

Relaxation training, such as in progressive muscle relaxation or biofeedback (CBT).

Regulated breathing for clients who are emotionally under- and overregulated, which may consist of having the client notice the present breathing pattern and to use the breathing instructions in the safe place exercise to regulate their breathing (HET).

CBT, cognitive-behavioral therapy; HET, humanistic and experiential therapies; PDT, psychodynamic therapy.

Landmark Studies and Previous Reviews

A challenge for the reader concerns the variety of research questions and the associated diversity in research methods that have been adopted to study BSH in psychotherapy. We present in Figure 10.1 a diagrammatic illustration of study designs involving pre-post evaluations of therapy involving BSH, where effects of BSH were assumed (type I studies); treatments have been compared according to whether they include BSH or not (type II studies); BSH adherence/compliance has been associated with a distal outcome (type III studies); and, most recently, the effects of BSH have been examined as a mediator of process–outcome relations (type IV studies). The focus of this chapter's

Box 10.2 Examples of Insight-Oriented Between-Session Homework in Psychotherapy

Suggest to the client to take a few minutes every day to *pay attention to what they feel, without judging their emotion* (HET).

Unravel cognitive distortions by identifying and challenging automatic thoughts using dysfunctional thought record (CBT).

Behavioral experiments to test beliefs. For example, "If I criticize myself, I will work harder" versus "If I am kind to myself, I will be motivated to work harder" (CBT).

Suggest to the client to remember or write down *dreams* (PDT).

Raising awareness, such as how interpersonal dynamics impact the client's feelings, how wishes and fears may impact interpersonal relationships, or how ways the client protects themself interfere with meeting own needs (PDT).

Keep an *emotion diary (*HET) or use other self-monitoring strategies through worksheets to reveal the relations between thoughts, emotions, and behaviors, as well as fluctuation in mood, symptoms, and activity (CBT).

Reflection on a session (HET, PDT, CBT).

Mindfulness meditation in various forms to facilitate awareness and acceptance (CBT, HET).

Bibliotherapy in multiple forms, for example, to promote knowledge about a psychological disorder and useful coping strategies (CBT).

CBT, cognitive–behavioral therapy; HET, humanistic and experiential therapies; PDT, psychodynamic therapy.

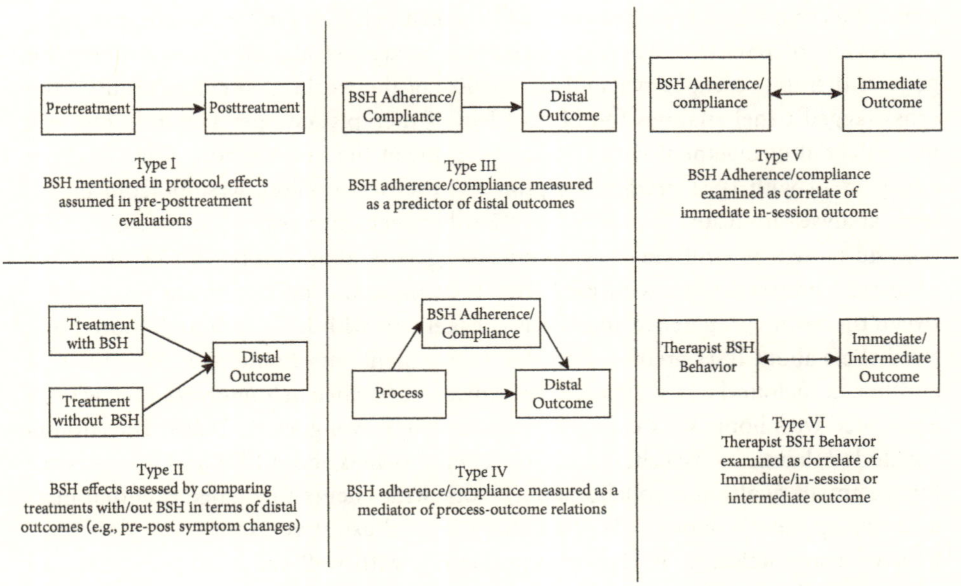

Figure 10.1 Examples of research studies on between-session homework in psychotherapy. BSH, between-session homework.

review, however, after presenting landmark studies and previous reviews and meta-analyses, is on the immediate in-session outcome of BSH adherence/compliance (type V studies) and therapist behaviors associated with the integration of BSH in treatment (type VI studies).

Landmark Studies

Sasso et al. (2016) examined therapist adherence to CT techniques in relation to symptom change in early sessions of CT for depression, disaggregating within-client and between-client variation in therapist adherence and the therapeutic alliance. The sample consisted of 57 clients participating in a two-site, randomized controlled trial (CT vs. pharmacotherapy vs. placebo). Adherence to three cognitive methods was examined using the CSPRS (Hollon et al., 1988): (a) cognitive methods, (b) negotiating/structuring sessions, and (c) behavioral methods/homework. Results suggested that between clients, variability in adherence to cognitive methods and negotiating/structuring sessions predicted symptom change in the next session, indicating effects due to stable client characteristics. Within clients, however, only variability in ratings of adherence to cognitive methods predicted next session change, and neither between-client nor within-client adherence to behavioral methods/homework predicted symptom change. The authors concluded that only cognitive methods emerged as a within-client predictor of next-session symptom change, with no support for the use of BSH, but the study illustrates an innovative approach to examining BSH.

Yew et al. (2021) examined mediators and moderators of the homework–outcome relation in CBT for depression. Clients (N = 50) were taken from an experimental study, comparing the effects of various components in CT. The study notably incorporated a comprehensive assessment of therapist behaviors in the design, planning, and review of BSH (i.e., HAACS; Kazantzis, Wedge, et al., 2005). Controlling for general therapist competence and the quality of the working alliance, results from cross-lagged panel analyses found no effect of therapist competence in homework use on client engagement with BSH or outcome at the next session. Nor did client engagement with BSH predict symptoms at the nest session. Results from multilevel analyses indicated a positive relation between therapist competence in BSH use and patient magnitude of symptoms, suggesting that clients with higher levels of distress engaged more with BSH. However, there was no significant relation between therapist competence and client engagement with BSH, although more positive beliefs about BSH predicted greater engagement with homework. We note that another study found direct effects of therapist competence in homework review to be associated with homework engagement (Zelencich, Wong, et al., 2020). The authors concluded that therapists should explore clients' beliefs about BSH and its relevance for treatment goals, and collaboratively work with clients to change eventual maladaptive appraisals about BSH. This study is an illustrative example of a comprehensive examination of BSH in psychotherapy, with well-validated measures and rigorous methodology.

Previous Meta-Analyses and Reviews

Empirical research examining BSH commenced in the 1980s, but few studies have examined therapist behaviors that facilitate or hamper clients' engagement with BSH, with some notable exceptions (i.e., type VI studies in Figure 10.1). For example, therapist competence in reviewing (Bryant et al., 1999; Weck et al., 2013) or selecting and planning of BSH (Conklin et al., 2018; Jungbluth & Shirk, 2013; Ryum et al., 2010, 2022; Shaw et al., 1999) has been related to positive treatment outcomes (but for negative results, see Yew et al., 2021). This finding suggests that therapists may play a prominent role in engaging clients with BSH, by collaboratively discussing its purpose, planning and reviewing BSH, and addressing potential barriers to its completion.

Previous meta-analyses and reviews have focused on (a) *the causal* (comparing treatment in terms of distal outcomes with and without BSH; type II studies in Figure 10.1) and (b) *the correlational* relation between BSH compliance and distal outcomes (type III studies in Figure 10.1). Kazantzis and colleagues (2010) extended their previous review (Kazantzis et al., 2000) and meta-analyzed 14 studies (477 clients) of only direct comparisons (i.e., comparing therapy with and without BSH) with distal treatment outcomes published between 1980 and 2007. All studies were based on CBT for anxiety, depression, or mixed diagnosis, and the causal effect of adding BSH to therapy was found to be significant, with a medium effect size over and above the effect of the treatment ($d = 0.53$, 95% confidence interval [CI] = 0.35–0.72, $p < .0001$). Mausbach and colleagues (2010) meta-analyzed 23 uncontrolled studies on CBT published between 2000 and 2008, comprising client samples with anxiety, depression, or mixed diagnoses. The linear (correlational) association between BSH compliance and outcome was found to be medium ($r = 0.26$, 95% CI = 0.19–0.33), which implies that greater compliance (i.e., quantity) of BSH was associated with improved outcomes (see also Kazantzis et al., 2000; Kazantzis, Whittington, et al., 2010).

Kazantzis and colleagues (2016) examined the relation between quantity (15 studies, 1,537 clients) as well as quality (three studies, 417 clients) of client BSH compliance and distal outcomes (type III studies in Figure 10.1) in a meta-analysis of CBT studies published between 2008 and 2015. Clients presented with various diagnoses, such as OCD, depression, obesity, and generalized anxiety disorder. Both quantity and quality of BSH compliance were related to outcome, with mostly medium to large effect sizes that remained relatively stable at follow-up (1–12 months later). Despite previous calls for more sophisticated assessment of immediate BSH effects (e.g., Dozois, 2010; Kazantzis, Whittington, et al., 2010), the meta-analysis identified only three studies that assessed BSH quality in relation to outcome (see also Wheaton & Chen, 2021).

In summary, the evidence demonstrates that the addition of BSH to CBT enhances its effectiveness and that clients who engage regularly with BSH have better distal outcomes compared to patients who engage less with BSH (e.g., Kazantzis et al., 2016; Mausbach et al., 2010). To what extent the findings generalize to other psychotherapy approaches is, however, uncertain. Also, to the best of our knowledge, there are no published systematic reviews or meta-analyses examining the immediate and intermediate effects of therapist behaviors associated with the integration of BSH in psychotherapy (type V and VI studies in Figure 10.1).

Research Review

Search Strategy and Inclusion Criteria

For the present systematic review, we included studies on individual psychotherapy with adult clients (previous meta-analyses have included both children and group psychotherapy). We conducted a search of the PubMed database from January 1980 to June 2022 with a sensitive strategy involving combinations of "homework" (homework, homeworks, extra treatment*, extra therap*, home practic*, behavioral practic*, behavioural practic*, self help assignment*, between session [using terminology identified in previous review by Kazantzis (2000)]) and compliance (compliance, compliances, patient compliance, treatment compliance) or adherence (adhere, adhered, adherence, adherences, adherent, adherents, adherer, adherers, adheres, adhering) or engagement (engage, engaged, engagement, engagement s, engagements, engages, engaging) or social participation (social, participation, social participation) of subject headings and text word searches to maximize identification of relevant studies.

This search strategy identified an initial sample of 1,098 papers for screening, of which 25 were included in the present review representing studies of immediate (in-session) or intermediate (session-to-session) outcomes (see Preferred Reporting Items for Systematic Reviews and Meta-Analyses [PRISMA] flowchart in Figure 10.2); two of these studies were added based on authors' knowledge of their relevance. We excluded studies involving stand-alone technology treatments without therapist interaction (e.g., stress-reduction strategies delivered by technology platforms, interventions not psychotherapeutic in nature); studies centered on BSH adherence/compliance as correlates of distal outcomes; studies that were not focused on BSH; reviews; editorials; protocol descriptions; assessment or psychometric papers; studies on child/adolescent samples; studies on group therapy; and papers examining technology augmentation delivery. We reviewed a random 20% sample of the excluded studies to ensure that none of these studies were wrongly excluded (e.g., false negatives).

Coding Procedures

Table 10.1 contains the coded results of the 25 studies. Given the relatively small number of studies, with different methods, research questions, and diverse client and therapist samples, we did not perform a meta-analysis. Rather, we conducted box scores (our judgment based on the evidence of the outcomes) to aggregate the effects of therapist behaviors on immediate and intermediate outcomes across studies. These 25 studies encompassed in total 1,304 clients and 118 therapists, although these numbers are not independent because some data sets/samples were analyzed multiple times in independent publications. We were also unable to determine the number of therapists in 10 studies. We assigned + to denote a positive effect, = to denote a neutral/no effect, and – to denote a negative effect in each study. To determine an overall box score across samples, we assigned a +1 to a positive box score, 0 to a neutral box score, and –1 to a negative box score. To account or adjust for sample size, we then multiplied the box score by the sample size for the finding, summed across the samples, and divided by the

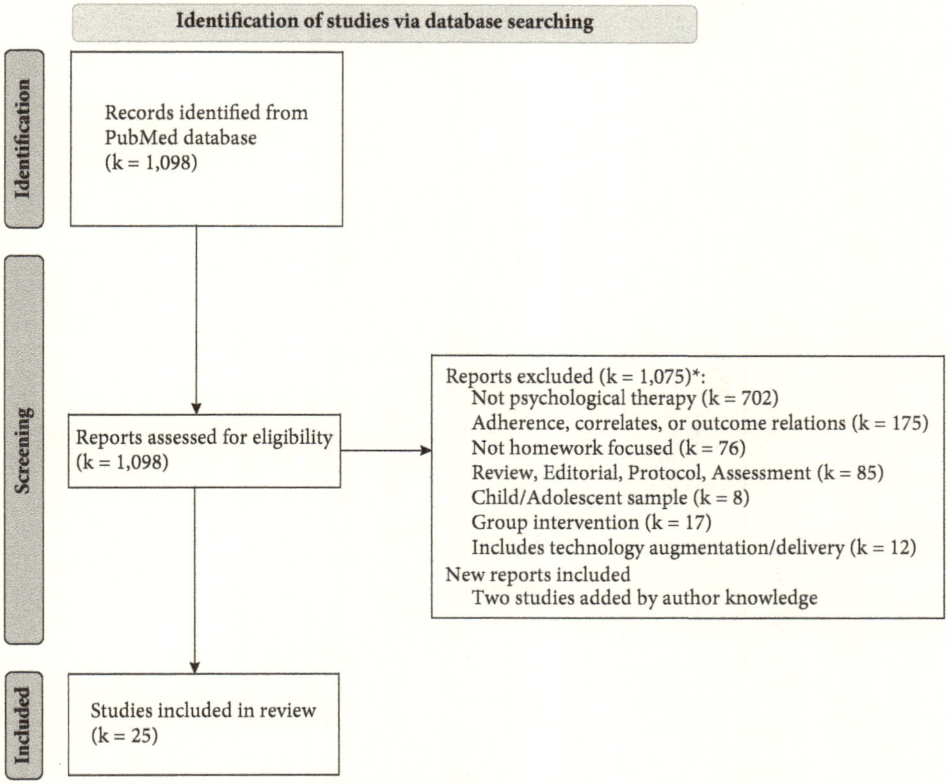

*Reported exclusion reasons are not mutually exclusive.

Figure 10.2 PRISMA flowchart for the identification of the 25 studies of therapist behavior in the integration of between-session homework in psychotherapy.

total sample size to get a weighted box score for each outcome. Eventual disagreements in the coding process were resolved by discussion among the three authors.

Immediate In-Session Outcomes

Nine studies with a total of 322 clients examined therapist behaviors associated with BSH on immediate in-session outcomes. We had the most data from qualitative studies (six studies with a total of 94 clients) that sought client feedback from interviews on the experience of being asked to engage in BSH, as well as the perspectives of the therapists, although with the use of different methods and research questions. Three quantitative studies reported on immediate, in-session symptom change (228 clients in total).

Qualitative Studies

Four studies that sought client feedback from interviews reported clients' experiences and compliance with BSH as mixed (Berg et al., 2008; Finning et al., 2017), poor (Ayers et al., 2012), or even as the biggest challenge among clients who had either withdrawn or

Table 10.1 Studies Examining Immediate and Intermediate Outcomes of Between-Session Homework

						BSH				
Source	No. of Clients	No. of Therapists	Diagnosis	Treatment	Time of Outcome	Moderators Examined	Design	Therapist Behaviors	Adherence Measures	Effect
Abramowitz et al. (2002)	28		OCD	ERP	Intermediate	Symptom severity, comorbidity, medication, treatment schedule	Quantitative	n.a.	HCS (T)	+
Adshead et al. (1988)	1		OCD	PI	Intermediate		Qualitative	n.a.	n.a.	+
Ayers et al. (2012)	12	1	Hoarding	CBT	Immediate	Executive functioning	Qualitative	n.a.	n.s.	–
Barnes et al. (2013)	26		Treatment-resistant depression	CBT	Immediate	Fear of failure, avoidance, support, motivation	Qualitative	n.a.	n.a.	–
Berg et al. (2008)	14		Depression, medical adherence	CBT	Immediate	Feeling ill (due to HIV)	Qualitative	n.a.	n.a.	–

Bluett et al. (2016)	96		Social anxiety	ET	Immediate	Rationale	Quantitative	n.a.	CES (C)	0
Conklin et al. (2018)	66	4	Depression	CT	Intermediate		Quantitative	HSTBS (O)	HES-G (O), HES-CT (O)	+
Cooper et al. (2016)	176	14	Recurrent/ chronic depression	CT	Intermediate	Early symptom change, demo-graphics, therapeutic alliance	Quantitative	CSPRS (O)	n.a.	+
Don et al. (2019)	2	1	Depression	CBT	Immediate	Practical problems, comorbid symptoms	Qualitative	Likert scale (T)	n.a.	0
Fehm & Mrose (2008)	80		Mixed anxiety/ depression	CBT	Intermediate	Commitment, chal-lenge, concreteness, relation to therapy, attitudes toward BSH	Quantitative	Likert Scale (C)	Likert scale (T)	–
Finning et al. (2017)	36		Depression	BA vs. CBT	Immediate		Qualitative	n.a.	n.a.	0
Fracalanza et al. (2014)	57		GAD	WIM	Immediate	Type of exposure	Quantitative	n.s.	LIWC (S)	+

(*continued*)

Table 10.1 Continued

Source	No. of Clients	No. of Therapists	Diagnosis	Treatment	Time of Outcome	BSH				
						Moderators Examined	Design	Therapist Behaviors	Adherence Measures	Effect
Jensen et al. (2020)	41	6	Anxiety/ depression	CBT/ACT/ DBT	Intermediate	Congruence; diagnosis, demographics, session number	Quantitative	SAFF (T/C)	SAFF (O)	+
Mathes et al. (2020)	41		OCD	ERP	Intermediate		Quantitative	n.a.	n.a.	+
Ohaeri (1997)	4	1	Mixed	CBT	Immediate	Symptom severity	Qualitative	n.a.	n.a.	+
Owen et al. (2012)	75	25	Mixed	IT	Immediate	Number of sessions, alliance	Quantitative	CPPS (C)	IEQ (C)	+
Sasso et al. (2015)	57	6	Depression	CT	Intermediate	Anxiety, number of depressive episodes	Quantitative	CSPRS (O)	n.a.	+
Sasso et al. (2016)	57	6	Depression	CT	Intermediate		Quantitative	CSPRS (O)	n.a.	0
Sijercic et al. (2016)	37	4	GAD	CBT	Intermediate	Interpersonal context, baseline symptoms	Quantitative	n.a.	HCS (T/C)	–
Strunk, Brotman, & DeRubeis (2010)	60	6	Depression	CT	Intermediate	Early symptom change	Quantitative	CSPRS (O)	n.a.	–

Strunk et al. (2012)	176	14	Recurrent/ chronic depression	CT	Intermediate	Early symptom change, pharmacotherapy, client expectation, alliance	Quantitative	CSPRS (O)	n.a	+
Weck et al. (2013)	54	20	Recurrent depression in remission	MCT	Intermediate	Demographics, number of previous depressive episodes, education, previous psychotherapy, comorbidity	Quantitative	CTS (O)	HCS (O)	+
Willner-Reid et al. (2016)	27		Opioid addiction	CBT	Intermediate	Simplified vs. standard homework, verbal ability, demographics	Quantitative	n.a.	n.s	–
Yew et al. (2021)	50	4	Depression	CBT	Intermediate	Education, marital status, baseline symptoms, homework beliefs	Quantitative	HAACS (O)	HRS-II (O)	0
Zelencich, Wong, et al. (2020)	31	6	Traumatic brain injury + anxiety/ depression	CBT	Intermediate	Age, length of recovery, executive functioning	Quantitative	HAACS (O)	HRS-II (O)	+

ACT, acceptance and commitment therapy; BA, behavioral activation; BSH, between-session homework; C, client ratings; CBT, cognitive–behavioral therapy; CES, Credibility/ Expectancy Scale; CPPS, Comparative Psychotherapy Process Scale; CSPRS, Collaborative Study Psychotherapeutic Rating Scale (Cognitive Behavioral Subscale); CT; cognitive therapy; CTS, Cognitive Therapy Scale; DBT, dialectical behavior therapy; ERP, exposure and response prevention; ET, exposure therapy; GAD, generalized anxiety disorder; HAACS, Homework Adherence and Competence Scale; HCS, Homework Compliance Scale; HRS-II, Homework Rating Scale–Revised; HSTBS, Homework-Specific Therapist Behavior Scales; IEQ, Intersession Experience Questionnaire; IT, integrative therapy; LIWC, Linguistic Inquiry and Word Count; MCT, maintenance cognitive therapy; n.a., not assessed; n.s., not specified; O, observer ratings; OCD, obsessive–compulsive disorder; PI, paradoxical instructions; S, software; SAFF, Session Assignment and Feedback Form; T, therapist ratings; WIM, written imaginal exposure; +, –, and 0 denote positive, negative, and neutral box scores, respectively.

were discharged from treatment due to nonadherence (Barnes et al., 2013). Commonly reported barriers to engagement with BSH included the time and effort required to complete BSH due to feeling ill and not understanding BSH or the nature of therapy more broadly (Berg et al., 2008); forgetfulness, the level of difficulty, and other competing demands (Ayers et al., 2012); negative associations with school homework experiences and fear of failure and being judged, difficulties with having to work alone between sessions, and low motivation due to depression and challenging homework (e.g., worksheets to be completed throughout the day) (Barnes et al., 2013); and the experience of bringing therapy into everyday life with the potential of worsening mood, as well as pressure to complete BSH (Finning et al., 2017).

Therapist behaviors that might promote client engagement with BSH included addressing clients' concerns and expectations at the beginning of treatment (Berg et al., 2008); talking to clients about the challenges of treatment and exploring possible barriers to treatment engagement and completion (Barnes et al., 2013); providing instructions and rationale for BSH clearly (Ayers et al., 2012; Berg et al., 2008); helping clients review and process homework and considering client feedback (Berg et al., 2008); addressing avoidance behaviors, highlighting previous success, problem-solving skills, and home visits (Ayers et al., 2012); as well as offering reassurance, being open, discussing difficulties experienced, and adapting treatment to individual clients' needs (Finning et al., 2017).

Two case studies reported either neutral (Don et al., 2019) or positive effects (Ohaeri, 1997) of therapist behaviors in relation to BSH. Don et al. (2019) noted a need for therapists to be flexible and deviate from the treatment manual (e.g., use of BSH) in the context of urgent practical challenges, requiring cognitive interventions and problem-solving strategies. Ohaeri (1997) emphasized therapist-initiated BSH for treatment outcome, such as diary to monitor responses to stimuli and self-instructions in the form of reciting information highlighted in the previous session. Compliance might be enhanced if diaries for the subsequent days (before the next appointment) were drawn up jointly during the preceding session.

Quantitative Studies

Two studies reported results from brief interventions (experimental studies) on anxiety (Bluett et al., 2016; Fracalanza et al., 2014), whereas a third study reported from an outcome study (Owen et al., 2012). In Bluett et al. (2016), presenting a credible rationale for exposure and BSH led to strong engagement with BSH and initial engagement with in-session exposure, with most outcomes improving more compared to a control condition, although with no group difference in engagement with BSH. Similarly, adherence to written instructions in exposure treatment was associated with greater improvement in worry in another study (Fracalanza et al., 2014). Finally, clients' ratings of therapists' use of psychodynamic–interpersonal techniques predicted more general intersession thoughts, after controlling for other predictors, whereas clients' ratings of cognitive–behavioral techniques (e.g., assigning BSH) were not associated with intersession activity. The most consistent finding, however, was that the working alliance was associated with general thoughts about therapy, intersession activity, and emotional reactions when thinking about therapy, indicating that clients who were in collaborative and purposeful work with their therapist were more likely to think about therapy between sessions (Owen et al., 2012).

Summary for Immediate Outcomes

The weighted box score across the six qualitative studies by sample size was negative (–48/94 = –.51), whereas for the three quantitative studies, the weighted box score by sample size was positive (132/228 = .58). When we weighted both qualitative and quantitative studies on immediate outcomes by the sample size (nine studies), we found an overall neutral box score (84/322 = .26). The results suggest that immediate outcomes of BSH may be both positive and negative, which probably at least partly reflect the heterogeneous nature of the included studies with different research questions, methods applied, and client samples, making comparisons challenging.

Moderators of Immediate Outcomes

Eight of the nine studies examined moderators (correlates) of outcomes, but with only two experimental studies. As already noted, Bluett et al. (2016) found that the presentation of a credible rationale for exposure resulted in higher immediate symptom reduction (but not homework completion) in comparison to a control group, and greater adherence to writing instructions was associated with greater improvement in worry compared to a control condition in another study (Fracalanza et al., 2014). The remaining studies examined moderators post hoc. Difficulty with engaging in BSH was associated with physical health among HIV-infected clients (Berg et al., 2008) and cognitive deficits among older adults (Ayers et al., 2012), and the need for more sessions and flexibility in scheduling appointments, as well as the use of problem-solving therapy, modules from traditional cognitive rehabilitation, and simplified BSH, were proposed as helpful strategies, respectively. Other studies have suggested that clients' engagement with BSH may be moderated by symptom severity (Ohaeri, 1997), the exploration of possible barriers to treatment engagement and completion (e.g., fear of failure, avoidance, low motivation) (Barnes et al., 2013), flexibility in therapists' adherence to the treatment manual taking into account practical problems or acute crisis (Don et al., 2019), or the treatment phase and the need for clients to work through affective reactions and relational patterns before trying out new ways of relating between sessions (Owen et al., 2012).

In summary, the results for studies examining moderators of immediate in-session outcomes suggest that therapist flexibility, the presentation of a rationale for BSH, discussing barriers to homework completion, and designing tasks that take into account clients' presenting difficulties (e.g., cognitive deficits or other health concerns) are some therapist behaviors that may facilitate a successful integration of BSH in treatment.

Intermediate Outcomes

Sixteen studies with a total of 982 clients examined therapist behaviors associated with intermediate (session-to-session) outcomes. Fifteen studies were quantitative in design, whereas one study was qualitative. Nine studies examined therapist behaviors associated with BSH and symptom change or treatment dropout, whereas the remaining studies examined therapist behaviors associated with client engagement with BSH.

Symptom Change and Dropout

Five studies examined therapist adherence to (a) cognitive structuring, (b) negotiating/structuring sessions, and (c) behavioral methods/homework in relation to early session-to-session symptom change. Three of these studies (Sasso et al., 2015, 2016; Strunk, Brotman, & DeRubeis, 2010) utilized the same client sample, and the remaining two studies used a second sample (Cooper et al., 2016; Strunk et al., 2012). Adherence to cognitive methods and negotiating/structuring sessions, but not to behavioral methods/homework, was associated with symptom change in one study (Strunk, Brotman, & DeRubeis, 2010), but divergent results were reported by Strunk et al. (2012), who found adherence to behavioral methods/homework (but not cognitive strategies) to predict symptom improvement.

Examining within- and between-client effects (Sasso et al., 2016), variability in therapists' adherence to cognitive methods and negotiating/structuring sessions predicted symptom change in the next session between clients, indicating effects due to stable client characteristics. Within clients, only variability in adherence to cognitive methods predicted next session change, and neither between- nor within-client adherence to behavioral methods/homework predicted symptom change. In a follow-up study (Sasso et al., 2015), greater adherence to behavioral methods/homework nonetheless predicted symptom improvement more strongly among clients high in pretreatment anxiety and clients with relatively few prior depressive episodes. Last, therapist adherence to behavioral methods/homework (as well as the quality of the therapeutic alliance) predicted reduced odds of dropout, whereas therapist adherence to negotiating/structuring sessions predicted greater odds of dropout (Cooper et al., 2016). The latter effect was only significant when behavioral methods/homework was included in the model, suggesting that clients with greater interpersonal difficulties may elicit more explicit efforts on the part of the therapists to engage in a process of negotiating therapeutic topics and structuring sessions, placing them at higher risk of dropout.

Mathes et al. (2020) examined within- and between-session trajectories of change of fear, disgust, and urge to wash as predictors of outcome in brief exposure therapy with OCD. Only within-session fear predicted post-treatment outcome; urge to wash reduced significantly slower than fear and disgust within each session, and it did not predict outcome over and above fear and disgust responses. The authors advised therapists to design exposure tasks that maximize within-session exposure while being mindful that urges to engage in compulsive behaviors reduce at a slower rate. In another study, higher levels of client engagement with homework were associated with greater improvement in symptoms of anxiety and depression, whereas higher levels of therapist competence in reviewing homework were only associated with greater improvement in anxiety symptoms (Zelencich, Wong, et al., 2020). The authors highlighted the importance of therapists facilitating clients' engagement with homework, while attending to executive deficits among clients with traumatic brain injury. Last, Sijercic et al. (2016) found that client counterchange talk (CCT) expressed in the presence of resistance (opposition to the therapist or therapy) predicted poorer homework compliance and outcome up to 1-year post-treatment, controlling for symptom severity.

Engagement with BSH

Eight studies examined therapist behaviors promoting client engagement with BSH. Therapist adherence to assigning homework (Conklin et al., 2018), as well as therapist competence in reviewing homework (Weck et al., 2013), was found to predict client engagement and compliance with homework. A third study, however, found no association between therapist competence in the use of homework and client engagement with BSH, controlling for general therapist competence and the quality of the working alliance (Yew et al., 2021). Similarly, Weck et al. (2013) found no support for the role of general therapist competence in relation to client engagement with BSH. However, more positive beliefs about homework (Yew et al., 2021), task concreteness (Fehm & Mrose, 2008), and the level of congruence between homework assignment content and clients' takeaways from the session (Jensen et al., 2020) were all found to predict engagement or compliance with BSH, suggesting that therapists should solicit feedback about what the client found important in the session and use this to discuss and assign homework consistent with this information, explore clients' beliefs about BSH and its relevance for treatment goals, and ensure that clients know what to do.

One study found that greater compliance with in-session exposure was associated with compliance with BSH, clients who understood the treatment rationale were more compliant with in-session exposure, and both understanding the treatment rationale and compliance with in-session and between-session homework predicted reduced symptoms post-treatment (Abramowitz et al., 2002).

In an experimental study, Willner-Reid et al. (2016) found no effects of simplified homework or electronic reminders on engagement or completion of homework, but standard homework buffered against craving following environmental exposure to drug cues. The authors concluded that a simplification of homework assignments was mostly ineffective, or even counterproductive in this sample, perhaps because they did not engage sufficient depth or processing or were perceived as too simplistic by the participants.

Sijercic et al. (2016) found that client CCT expressed in the presence of resistance (opposition to the therapist or therapy) predicted lower homework compliance, controlling for symptom severity, suggesting that therapists should be alert to the interpersonal context when asking clients for agreement or assent, such as in engagement with BSH. Similarly, Fehm and Mrose (2008) highlighted an apparent gap between recommendations for assigning homework and actual therapist behaviors, with clients reporting high levels of anticipatory anxiety, not being involved in designing tasks in 37% of all cases, being ambiguous about their ability to complete the tasks, and only rarely provided with written material to enhance recollection of the tasks and increase compliance.

One qualitative study (Adshead et al., 1988) presented a case report of a woman with persistent obsessive–compulsive rituals who, after a relapse, demonstrated marked self-exposure with response prevention, as well as symptom improvement, after being advised to increase her rituals and abstain from exposure (paradoxical instructions). The authors suggested that some clients may benefit from paradoxical strategies to promote compliance with treatment and BSH, despite practical and ethical challenges.

Summary of Intermediate Outcomes

Box scores were positive for 10 studies, neutral for two studies, and negative for four studies. The weighted box score by sample size for all studies examining intermediate outcomes was .53 (671 – 204/875). Hence, we conclude that there is more and stronger support for the role of BSH in association with intermediate outcomes compared to that with immediate outcomes.

Moderators of Intermediate Outcomes

Thirteen of the 16 studies examined moderators of intermediate outcomes, mostly in post hoc assessments. Greater therapist adherence to behavioral methods/homework predicted symptom improvement more strongly for clients high in pretreatment anxiety and with relatively few prior depressive episodes (Sasso et al., 2015). Therapist adherence to cognitive techniques, however, was not associated with prior symptom improvement (Strunk, Brotman, & DeRubeis, 2010), and the positive association between adherence to behavioral activation/homework and symptom improvement was significant even when considering the quality of the alliance, prior symptom change, concurrent pharmacotherapy, and client's expectations for therapeutic improvement (Strunk et al., 2012). Yew et al. (2021) found no moderating effects of education level and marital status on the engagement–outcome relation, but higher baseline levels of depressive symptoms predicted a stronger engagement–outcome relationship. Sijeric et al. (2016) found that the presence of early counterchange statements uttered in order to oppose the therapist/therapy should serve as a critical process marker in therapy and alert therapists to the interpersonal context and client opposition when giving advice or other demands that involve asking clients for agreement or assent, such as engagement with homework.

Simplified homework did not differentially increase homework-completion rates or quality/enthusiasm/understanding ratings as a function of clients' verbal ability in an experimental study (Willner-Reid et al., 2016), but the level of homework task concreteness was associated with homework completion in another study (Fehm & Mrose, 2008), suggesting that the more clearly clients knew what to do and the steps to be taken, the better the completion rate. Demographic factors (Jensen et al., 2020; Weck et al., 2013; Willner-Reid et al., 2016), baseline level of symptom severity (Abramowitz et al., 2002; Sijercic et al., 2016), diagnosis (Jensen et al., 2020), session number/treatment schedule (Abramowitz et al., 2002; Jensen et al., 2020), antidepressant medication use (Abramowitz et al., 2002; Weck et al., 2013), and comorbidity (Abramowitz et al., 2002; Weck et al., 2013) have not been found to be associated with homework compliance. Likewise, early symptom change, differences in clients' use of antidepressants, and demographic factors did not account for the relations between therapist behaviors and odds of dropout, but both the working alliance and age correlated positively with behavioral methods/homework (Cooper et al., 2016). Zelencich et al. (2020) found the working alliance to be associated with higher levels of homework engagement, but when controlling for confounding variables, including executive functioning, only homework engagement remained significantly associated with change in depressive symptoms.

In summary, although multiple variables have been examined as moderators of intermediate outcomes, across client populations and treatments, the most consistent finding is the mostly negligible effects of the examined moderators. Symptom severity/comorbidity as well as client demographics appear to have mostly negligible effects on client engagement with BSH, in accordance with null findings indicating no moderating effects of examined variables on symptom improvement. There is, however, some evidence that the concreteness of a task, the degree of congruence between session takeaway and BSH, and more positive beliefs about homework may positively influence client engagement with BSH.

Summary for Immediate and Intermediate Outcomes

Overall, there was most research supporting a beneficial effect of therapist behaviors on intermediate effects of BSH, whereas the effects on immediate outcomes were more mixed and overall neutral. Nevertheless, the results suggest that certain therapist behaviors associated with integrating BSH in psychotherapy may help clients achieve realistic and clear expectations about BSH, facilitate engagement, and promote symptom improvement. Specifically, therapist behaviors that appear to be important include (a) collaboratively designing, planning, and reviewing BSH in accordance with the clients' goals and values; (b) aligning BSH with the takeaways from the session; (c) explaining and presenting a convincing rationale for the homework; (d) discussing potential difficulties and barriers to engaging with specific tasks; (e) providing a written summary (including instructions and rationale); (f) considering client feedback; and (g) being responsive to the client's need and emerging context. We also note that the results suggest BSH may prove challenging for some clients, for both practical and emotional reasons, and may require substantial support and guidance from a therapist to be helpful. Negative beliefs about fear of failure and being judged are common among clients, and therapists should anticipate obstacles and being open to client feedback in the cycle of selecting, planning, and reviewing BSH.

Overall, we find the results from the present review on immediate and intermediate outcomes associated with integrating BSH in treatment (type V and VI studies in Figure 10.1) to be in accordance with prior research demonstrating beneficial effects of BSH on distal outcomes.

Possible Negative Effects and Harm

The present review highlights some potential challenges when engaging clients with BSH, as noted in several of the reviewed studies, and reviews from practice settings have also reported client engagement with BSH as lower than expected or desired (Kazantzis, Lampropoulos, et al., 2005). A significant percentage of clients are reluctant to engage with BSH for both practical and emotional reasons, which may result in limited improvement or even premature dropout. Although we are not aware of research that has specifically assessed eventual rates of possible negative effects associated with the use of BSH, several studies have reported adverse effects. Notably, BSH may create pressure, anxiety, and fear of failure on the part of the client (e.g., Barnes et al., 2013; Fehm & Mrose, 2008; Finning et al., 2017); bring therapy into everyday life with the potential to worsening mood (Callan et al., 2012; Finning et al., 2017); and has even been reported as the biggest challenge in treatment and a possibly painful process (Barnes et al., 2013). Persistent non-engagement with BSH may also be a way for the client to oppose treatment or the therapist (Okamoto & Kazantzis, 2021; Safran et al., 2011; Sijercic et al., 2016) and may indicate a rupture in the therapeutic alliance (Safran & Muran, 2000).

Because there is scant research, caution is warranted when discussing negative effects pertaining to specific types of homework that may generate negative effects. Structured worksheets to be completed throughout the day (e.g., thought and activity diaries) have, however, been reported as particularly difficult among depressed clients (Barnes et al., 2013). Even more tentative, Gasman (1992) noted that severe negative effects, including suicide, had been reported among clients watching recorded videotapes at home of their own treatment sessions as part of exposure homework, and cautioned against using this method with severely distressed clients. But again, research in this area is very limited, and there is clearly a need for more studies in order to draw any firm conclusions. Generally, we advocate for increased responsibility on the part of therapists in accounting for clients' non-engagement with BSH, and we emphasize the importance of fostering a collaborative relationship in which engagement with BSH should be discussed through Socratic dialogue and improved by soliciting feedback about what the client found important about the session.

Diversity Considerations

Results from the present review suggest that the impact of client characteristics (i.e., demographics, symptoms, education level, gender, age, etc.) on BSH is mostly negligible, which is consistent with previous studies reporting no significant effects from gender, ethnicity, or socioeconomic status on clients' engagement with BSH (Sachsenweger et al., 2015; Stirman et al., 2018; Woods et al., 2002). This would be expected to the extent therapists are responsive to clients' needs and the emergent context in planning, designing, and reviewing BSH. Notably, although the impact of marital status on BSH has been explored previously (Yew et al., 2021), less attention has been paid to the possible effects of sexual orientation. There is thus a need for further research examining moderators in relation to BSH; to date, only a few experimental studies in this area of research have been performed.

Concerningly, studies have mostly included Western clients, and studies addressing the role of ethnicity in BSH are limited. For example, recommendations for integrating BSH in work with Chinese clients have been presented elsewhere, pertaining to cultural values and practices, problem-solving strategies, and other traditional beliefs, such as working hard, investing in self-improvement, moderation, and respect for authority (Foo & Kazantzis, 2007). Aguilera et al. (2018) investigated BSH within a low-income Latino population, with findings emphasizing the importance of therapist review of BSH in relation to improved treatment outcomes. Cultural beliefs may particularly have a notable impact on clients' beliefs about their problem, coping styles, or specific BSH tasks (Asnaani & Hofmann, 2012), but more research on the impacts of diversity and BSH is clearly warranted.

Limitations of the Research

There have been several calls for more sophisticated research designs examining the efficacy of BSH in psychotherapy (e.g., Kazantzis et al., 2016; Kazantzis, Whittington, et al., 2010; Neimeyer & Feixas, 1990), but progress during the past three decades has been slow. In particular, the largely one-sided emphasis on client engagement has been unfortunate because therapist behaviors and attitudes are likely to facilitate or hamper clients' engagement with BSH (e.g., Bunnell et al., 2021; Haarhoff & Kazantzis, 2007). To the best of our knowledge, this review is the first attempt to systematically synthetize research on therapist behaviors associated with immediate and intermediate outcomes in relation to BSH.

Support for the role of therapist behaviors associated with BSH that promote immediate and intermediate outcomes has mostly come from studies on behavioral and cognitive–behavioral therapies, in controlled trials with therapists trained and monitored for adherence, and with the majority of clients presenting with depression or anxiety-related disorders. To what extent the results may generalize to other therapeutic approaches (HET, PDT), therapists, problems (e.g., personality disorders, eating disorders), or naturalistic treatment settings is uncertain. There are obviously both theoretical and practical challenges associated with adapting the CBT framework of BSH (and its related measures of therapist competence and client compliance) to other treatment approaches, but we encourage researchers to conceive of ways of examining the use and integration of BSH in other treatment approaches as well.

There are limitations as to how engagement with BSH has been assessed in previous research. As shown (see Table 10.1), approximately half of the reviewed studies did not include a measure (scale) of therapist behaviors or client engagement (n.a.), or the measure was not specified (n.s.). For the remaining studies, diversity is vast pertaining to the measures employed. Only two scales assessing therapist behaviors (CSPRS, HAACS) and client compliance (HCS, HRS-II) have been used in more than one study, which makes it difficult to compare results across studies. Several scales (e.g., CSPRS, CTS) were originally developed to assess a broader range of therapist behaviors, and only HAACS and HSTBS were specifically designed to provide a comprehensive assessment of therapist behaviors associated with integrating homework in psychotherapy.

Most of the reviewed studies are correlational, which prohibits definite conclusions regarding causality (third variable problem, such as clients' level of self-efficacy, motivation, or other qualities that may have an impact on therapeutic outcome). Some studies (e.g., Sasso et al., 2016) have disaggregated between-client and within-client effects, which rules out stable client characteristics as a confounding variable, but few have been experimental (e.g., Bluett et al., 2016; Fracalanza et al., 2014; Willner-Reid et al., 2016). Some studies have reported modeling therapist effects (e.g., Jensen et al., 2020; Owen et al., 2012; Sasso et al., 2015; Strunk, Brotman, & DeRubeis, 2010; Strunk et al., 2012; Weck et al., 2013), but effects pertaining specifically to the integration of BSH have rarely been reported (but see, e.g., Jensen et al., 2020; Owen et al., 2012), and sample sizes have mostly been inadequate to address this question properly (i.e., an adequate number of clients nested within an adequate number of therapists to model reliable estimates). Currently, we can only speculate as to whether there are therapist effects pertaining to integrating BSH in treatment, as has been demonstrated in outcome research in general (e.g., Johns et al., 2019) and for the alliance–outcome relation specifically (Del Re et al., 2021).

As noted, the integration of BSH into psychotherapy is not always easy and straightforward, and it would be particularly important to learn more about what happens when BSH is unsuccessful or goes awry. Using in-depth and qualitative analyses of case examples, from both clients' and therapists' perspectives, would prove helpful. For example, how does an unsuccessful or bad experience with BSH impact the therapeutic relationship, and how does such an experience influence the client's future attempts? How does the client's experience of shame after not doing BSH influence the therapeutic relationship, and how may such an experience be improved? Is the client's self-efficacy negatively affected when a method that worked in the session does not work outside, such as at home, work, or school (Lambert et al., 2007)?

We note that none of the included studies have addressed client-initiated BSH, which of course is not expected in a volume devoted to therapist behaviors and methods. However, self-initiated homework may play a prominent role in generalizing the work from the consulting room to the client's daily life.

Training Implications

We are not aware of empirical research on how clinical training and supervision may facilitate the acquisition and effective use of BSH among psychotherapists. Nor are we aware of any research-supported training programs on the teaching of BSH specifically. Of course, reading material (e.g., treatment manuals and guides on how to integrate BSH in treatment) and didactic courses are important for psychotherapists in training to develop a sophisticated understanding of how to facilitate the integration of BSH in treatment, but we believe that hands-on, in vivo experiences with practical use of BSH are even more essential for beginning therapists (and perhaps even more seasoned therapists). Supervision, based on videotaped sessions with actual clients, is probably the best way for therapists to receive specific feedback on their performance and use of BSH in therapy, which in most instances is needed to improve clinical practice.

To maximize learning and practical takeaways for trainees, we suggest adopting a theoretical framework and assessing therapist behaviors associated with BSH with a well-validated measure, such as the Homework Adherence and Competence Scale. This will probably help beginning therapists select and target specific skills that need improvement pertaining to the process of selecting, planning, reviewing, and overcoming obstacles in the integration of BSH in psychotherapy (Conklin et al., 2018; Kazantzis, Deane, et al., 2005; Kazantzis & L'Abate, 2007a). This practice could of course be complemented with an assessment of the client's engagement with BSH, again preferably assessed with a well-validated measure such as HRS-II. Other avenues to practical training in the use of BSH could include role-plays with colleagues and deliberate practice.

In addition, we advise psychotherapists in training (as well as more experienced therapists) to examine their assumptions and attitudes about BSH that may have a negative impact on its integration into treatment (Bunnell et al., 2021). Common negative attitudes among therapists are "Homework tasks will make the client overstructured and controlled," "Homework will increase the client's sense of vulnerability," and "Homework assignments are overwhelmingly for clients who are distressed" (Haarhoff & Kazantzis, 2007). Relatedly, therapists' core schemas, such as "demanding standards" (obsessive, perfectionistic, controlling) and "excessive self-sacrifice" (overemphasizing the relationship, fear abandonment), may also hamper effective integration of BSH into treatment. Therapists should understand that the use of BSH is an important part of clinical training and practice and that specific therapist behaviors and attitudes may facilitate or hamper clients' engagement with BSH.

Therapeutic Practices

Here, we provide some takeaways for clinicians who want to integrate BSH in their clinical practice. These recommendations are primarily distilled from the present research review but are also in accordance with therapist guidelines (Kazantzis, MacEwan, et al., 2005). We emphasize that empirical support for the recommendations may be found in studies using HAACS to assess therapist adherence and competence in the use of BSH, which was specifically designed to measure the model for practice our recommendations rests upon. For example, when HAACS has been included in studies of CBT, therapist competence in reviewing homework has shown direct associations with client engagement (Zelencich, Kazantzis, et al., 2020), and the scale has been shown to generate high levels of interrater reliability estimates (Yew et al., 2021). Results utilizing HSTBS (Conklin et al., 2018), which is based on the same literature and has significant content overlap with HAACS, adds support to our recommendations. Specifically, we suggest the following:

- Consider client's engagement with between-sessions activities as potentially beneficial, whatever the specific tasks may be.
- Engage the client in a collaborative discussion of the potential benefits of BSH.
- Try to instill positive expectations and hope.
- Assign BSH aligned with the session content and relevant to the client's problem, goals, and values.
- Provide a brief, clear, and convincing rationale to the client for engaging in BSH.
- Ensure that you have adequately explored the client's understanding of BSH, including potential benefits and barriers, and that there is a mutual understanding of the task.
- Assess the client's immediate and delayed outcomes associated with BSH, including in-session reactions and engagement (or lack of thereof).
- Ensure that the client has the resources available for conducting the task.
- Tailor BSH to the client's cultural expectations and preferences.
- Explore the client's attribution of meaning to BSH when there is resistance, avoidance, or other variants of noncompliance.

- Evaluate BSH by effort and process rather than outcome. BSH is optimally an evolving learning process, in which finding out what does not work also proves useful.
- Avoid blaming the client for BSH not completed; maybe it was too difficult, the client did not have the necessary resources, or the rationale was not clearly communicated.
- Use strategies to enhance BSH, such as writing down tasks (and rationale) and asking for feedback from the client.
- Devote sufficient time to integrate BSH in treatment.
- Remember that clients are more likely to complete BSH congruent with the content they want to remember from a session.
- Remind the client that BSH is an opportunity to learn something new—even if the task does not go exactly as planned.

References

* Studies included in the research review.

*Abramowitz, J. S., Franklin, M. E., Zoellner, L. A., & DiBernardo, C. L. (2002). Treatment compliance and outcome in obsessive–compulsive disorder. *Behavior Modification*, *26*(4), 447–463. https://doi.org/10.1177/0145445502026004001

*Adshead, G., Drummond, L. M., & Mercer, S. (1988). Paradoxical intention and anti-exposure in a non-compliant, obsessive–compulsive ritualiser. *British Journal of Psychiatry*, *153*, 821–823. https://doi.org/10.1192/bjp.153.6.821

Aguilera, A., Ramos, Z., Sistiva, D., Wang, Y., & Alegria, M. (2018). Homework completion via telephone and in-person cognitive behavioral therapy among Latinos. *Cognition Therapy and Research*, *42*(3), 340–347. https://www.ncbi.nlm.nih.gov/pmc/articles/PMC5927598/pdf/nihms932880.pdf

Asnaani, A., & Hofmann, S. G. (2012). Collaboration in multicultural therapy: Establishing a strong therapeutic alliance across cultural lines. *Journal of Clinical Psychology*, *68*, 187–197.

*Ayers, C. R., Bratiotis, C., Saxena, S., & Wetherell, J. L. (2012). Therapist and patient perspectives on cognitive–behavioral therapy for older adults with hoarding disorder: A collective case study. *Aging & Mental Health*, *16*(7), 915–921. https://doi.org/10.1080/13607863.2012.678480

*Barnes, M., Sherlock, S., Thomas, L., Kessler, D., Kuyken, W., Owen-Smith, A., Lewis, G., Wiles, N., & Turner, K. (2013). No pain, no gain: Depressed clients' experiences of cognitive behavioural therapy. *British Journal of Clinical Psychology*, *52*(4), 347–364. https://doi.org/10.1111/bjc.12021

Beck, A. T., Rush, J., Shaw, B., & Emery, G. (1979). *Cognitive therapy of depression*. Guilford.

*Berg, C., Raminani, S., Greer, J., Harwood, M., & Safren, S. (2008). Participants' perspectives on cognitive–behavioral therapy for adherence and depression in HIV. *Psychotherapy Research*, *18*(3), 271–280. https://doi.org/10.1080/10503300701561537

*Bluett, E. J., Landy, L. L., Twohig, M. P., & Arch, J. J. (2016). Does the theoretical perspective of exposure framing matter? Acceptance, fear reduction/cognitive reappraisal, and values-framing of exposure for social anxiety. *Journal of Cognitive Psychotherapy*, *30*(2), 77–93. https://doi.org/10.1891/0889-8391.30.2.77

Brodley, B. (2006). Client-initiated homework in client-centered therapy. *Journal of Psychotherapy Integration*, *16*(2), 140–161.

Bryant, M. J., Simons, A. D., & Thase, M. E. (1999). Therapist skill and patient variables in homework compliance: Controlling a uncontrolled variable in cognitive therapy outcome research. *Cognitive Therapy and Research, 23*, 381–399. https://doi.org/10.1023/A:1018703901116

Bunnell, B. E., Nemeth, L. S., Lenert, L. A., Kazantzis, N., Deblinger, E., Higgins, K. A., & Ruggiero, K. J. (2021). Barriers associated with the implementation of homework in youth mental health treatment and potential mobile health solutions. *Cognitive Therapy and Research, 45*(2), 272–286.

Callan, J. A., Dunbar-Jacob, J., Sereika, S. M., Stone, C., Fasiczka, A., Jarrett, R. B., & Thase, M. E. (2012). Barriers to Cognitive Behavioral Therapy Homework Completion Scale–Depression version: Development and psychometric evaluation. *International Journal of Cognitive Therapy, 5*(2), 219–235. https://doi.org/10.1521/ijct.2012.5.2.219

*Conklin, L. R., Strunk, D. R., & Cooper, A. A. (2018). Therapist behaviors as predictors of immediate homework engagement in cognitive therapy for depression. *Cognitive Therapy and Research, 42*(1), 16–23. https://doi.org/10.1007/s10608-017-9873-6

*Cooper, A. A., Strunk, D. R., Ryan, E. T., DeRubeis, R. J., Hollon, S. D., & Gallop, R. (2016). The therapeutic alliance and therapist adherence as predictors of dropout from cognitive therapy for depression when combined with antidepressant medication. *Journal of Behavior Therapy and Experimental Psychiatry, 50*, 113–119. https://doi.org/10.1016/j.jbtep.2015.06.005

Del Re, A. C., Flückiger, C., Horvath, A. O., & Wampold, B. E. (2021). Examining therapist effects in the alliance–outcome relationship: A multilevel meta-analysis. *Journal of Consulting and Clinical Psychology, 89*(5), 371–378.

*Don, F. J., Driessen, E., Molenaar, P. J., Spijker, J., & Dekker, J. J. M. (2019). Early interventions in cognitive behavioral therapy for depression: A study contrasting a low-adherent and a highly adherent case. *Psychotherapy, 56*(1), 48–54. https://doi.org/10.1037/pst0000219

Dozois, D. (2010). Understanding and enhancing the effects of homework in cognitive–behavioral therapy: Introduction to a special section. *Clinical Psychology: Science and Practice, 17*, 157–161.

Ellis, A. (1962). *Reason and emotion in psychotherapy*. Lyle Stuart.

Fehm, L., & Kazantzis, N. (2004). Attitudes and use of homework assignments in therapy: A survey of German psychotherapists. *Clinical Psychology & Psychotherapy, 11*(5), 332–343. https://doi.org/10.1002/cpp.419

*Fehm, L., & Mrose, J. (2008). Patients' perspective on homework assignments in cognitive–behavioural therapy. *Clinical Psychology & Psychotherapy, 15*(5), 320–328. https://doi.org/10.1002/cpp.592

*Finning, K., Richards, D. A., Moore, L., Ekers, D., McMillan, D., Farrand, P. A., O'Mahen, H. A., Watkins, E. R., Wright, K. A., Fletcher, E., Rhodes, S., Woodhouse, R., & Wray, F. (2017). Cost and outcome of behavioural activation versus cognitive behavioural therapy for depression (COBRA): A qualitative process evaluation. *BMJ Open, 7*(4), e014161. https://doi.org/10.1136/bmjopen-2016-014161

Foo, K. H., & Kazantzis, N. (2007). Integrating homework assignments based on culture: Working with Chinese patients. *Cognitive and Behavioral Practice, 14*, 333–340.

*Fracalanza, K., Koerner, N., & Antony, M. M. (2014). Testing a procedural variant of written imaginal exposure for generalized anxiety disorder. *Journal of Anxiety Disorders, 28*(6), 559–569. https://doi.org/10.1016/j.janxdis.2014.05.011

Freud, S. (1952). Inhibitions, symptoms, and anxiety. In R. M. Hutchins (Ed.), *Great books of the western world* (pp. 718–754). Encyclopedia Britannica.

Garfield, S. L. (1997). Brief psychotherapy: The role of common and specific factors. *Clinical Psychology & Psychotherapy, 4*(4), 217–225. https://doi.org/10.1002/(Sici)1099-0879(199712)4:4<217::Aid-Cpp134>3.0.Co;2-Y

Gasman, D. H. (1992). Double-exposure therapy: Videotape homework as a psychotherapeutic adjunct. *American Journal of Psychotherapy, 46*(1), 91–101. https://doi.org/10.1176/appi.psychotherapy.1992

Goldfried, M. R., Castonguay, L. G., Hayes, A. M., Drozd, J. F., & Shapiro, D. A. (1997). A comparative analysis of the therapeutic focus in cognitive-behavioral and psychodynamic–interpersonal sessions. *Journal of Consulting and Clinical Psychology*, *65*(5), 740–748. https://doi.org/10.1037/0022-006x.65.5.740

Goldfried, M. R., & Raue, P. J. (1998). The therapeutic focus in significant sessions of master therapists: A comparison of cognitive–behavioral and psychodynamic–interpersonal interventions. *Journal of Consulting and Clinical Psychology*, *66*(5), 803–810. https://doi.org/10.1037/0022-006X.66.5.803

Greenberg, L. S., & Warwar, S. H. (2006). Homework in an emotion-focused approach to experiential therapy. *Journal of Psychotherapy Integration*, *16*(2), 178–200.

Haarhoff, B. A., & Kazantzis, N. (2007). How to supervise the use of homework in cognitive–behavior therapy: The role of trainee therapist beliefs. *Cognitive and Behavioral Practice*, *14*, 325–332.

Hayes, S. C. (2022). Acceptance and defusion. *Cognitive and Behavioral Practice*, *29*(3), 571–574.

Hilsenroth, M. J., Blagys, M. D., Ackerman, S. J., Bonge, D. R., & Blais, M. A. (2005). Measuring psychodynamic–interpersonal and cognitive–behavioral technique: Development of the Comparative Psychotherapy Process Scale. *Psychotherapy: Theory, Research, Practice, Training*, *42*, 340–356.

Hollon, S. D., Evans, M. D., Auerbach, A., DeRubeis, R. J., Elkin, I., Lowrey, A., & Piasecki, J. M. (1988). Development of a system for rating therapies for depression: Differentiating cognitive therapy, inter-personal psychotherapy and a clinical management pharmacotherapy [Unpublished manuscript]. Nashville, TN: Vanderbilt University.

Hong, J. J., Beckner, V., Persons, J. B., Ling, A., Liu, H., & Owen, D. J. (2012). Session Assignment and Feedback Form—v.12 (SAFF). https://static1.squarespace.com/static/5934abbb1b631ba4718d4c2d/t/5b5252ee2b6a28997c74dbc8/1532121913450/SAFF

*Jensen, A., Fee, C., Miles, A. L., Beckner, V. L., Owen, A., & Persons, J. B. (2020). Congruence of patient takeaways and homework assignment content predicts homework compliance in psychotherapy. *Behavior Therapy*, *51*, 424–433.

Johns, R. G., Barkham, M., Kellett, S., & Saxon, D. (2019). A systematic review of therapist effects: A critical narrative update and refinement to Baldwin and Imel's (2013) review. *Clinical Psychology Review*, *67*, 78–93.

Jungbluth, N. J., & Shirk, S. R. (2013). Promoting homework adherence in cognitive–behavioral therapy for adolescent depression. *Journal of Clinical Child and Adolescent Psychology*, *42*(4), 545–553. https://doi.org/10.1080/15374416.2012.743105

Kazantzis, N. (2018). Introduction to the special issue on processes of cognitive behavioral therapy: Does "Necessary, but not sufficient" still capture it? *Cognitive Therapy & Research*, *42*, 115–120. https://doi.org/10.1007/s10608-018-9891-z

Kazantzis, N. (2000). Power to detect homework effects in psychotherapy outcome research. *Journal of Consulting and Clinical Psychology*, *68*, 166–170.Kazantzis, N., Arntz, A. R., Borkovec, T., Holmes, E. A., & Wade, T. (2010). Unresolved issues regarding homework assignments in cognitive and behavioural therapies: An expert panel discussion at AACBT. *Behaviour Change*, *27*(3), 119–129. https://doi.org/10.1375/bech.27.3.119

Kazantzis, N., Brownfield, N. R., Mosely, L., Usatoff, A. S., & Flighty, A. J. (2017). Homework in cognitive behavioral therapy: A systematic review of adherence assessment in anxiety and depression (2011–2016). *Psychiatric Clinics of North America*, *40*(4), 625–639. https://doi.org/10.1016/j.psc.2017.08.001

Kazantzis, N., Dattilio, F. M., Cummins, A., & Clayton, X. (2013). Homework assignments and self-monitoring. In S. G. Hofman, D. J. A. Dozois, W. Rief, & J. Smits (Eds.), *The Wiley handbook of cognitive behavioral therapy* (Vol. 1, pp. 311–330). Wiley.

Kazantzis, N., & Deane, F. P. (1999). Psychologists' use of homework assignments in clinical practice. *Professional Psychology: Research and Practice*, *30*, 581–585.

Kazantzis, N., Deane, F. P., & Ronan, K. R. (2000). Homework assignments in cognitive and behavioral therapy: A meta-analysis. *Clinical Psychology: Science and Practice*, *7*(2), 189–202. https://doi.org/10.1093/clipsy/7.2.189

Kazantzis, N., Deane, F., & Ronan, K. R. (2004). Assessing compliance with homework assignments: Review and recommendations for clinical practice. *Journal of Clinical Psychology*, *60*(6), 627–641.

Kazantzis, N., Deane, F. P., Ronan, K. R., & L'Abate, L. (2005). *Using homework assignments in cognitive behavior therapy*. Routledge.

Kazantzis, N., & L'Abate, L. (2007a). *Handbook of homework assignments in psychotherapy: Research, practice, prevention*. Springer.

Kazantzis, N., & L'Abate, L. (2007b). Introduction and historical overview. In N. Kazantzis & L. L'Abate (Eds.), *Handbook of homework assignments in psychotherapy* (pp. 1–16). Springer.

Kazantzis, N., Lampropoulos, G. L., & Deane, F. P. (2005). A national survey of practicing psychologists' use and attitudes towards homework in psychotherapy. *Journal of Consulting and Clinical Psychology*, *73*, 742–748.

Kazantzis, N., MacEwan, J., & Dattilio, F. M. (2005). A guiding model for practice. In N. Kazantzis, F. P. Deane, K. R. Ronan, & L. L'Abate (Eds.), *Using homework assignments in cognitive behavior therapy* (pp. 359–407). New York: Routledge.

Kazantzis, N., & Miller, A. R. (2022). A comprehensive model of homework in cognitive behavior therapy. *Cognitive Therapy and Research*, *46*(1), 247–257. https://doi.org/10.1007/s10608-021-10247-z

Kazantzis, N., & Ronan, K. R. (2006). Can between-session (homework) activities be considered a common factor in psychotherapy? *Journal of Psychotherapy Integration*, *16*(2), 115–127.

Kazantzis, N., & Stuckey, M. E. (2018). Inception of a discovery: Re-Defining the use of Socratic dialogue in cognitive behavioral therapy. *International Journal of Cognitive Therapy*, *11*(2), 117–123. https://doi.org/10.1007/ s41811-018-0015-z

Kazantzis, N., Wedge, P., & Dobson, K. S. (2005). Homework Adherence and Competence Scale (HAACS). Massey University.

Kazantzis, N., Whittington, C., & Dattilio, F. (2010). Meta-analysis of homework effects in cognitive and behavioral therapy: A replication and extension. *Clinical Psychology: Science and Practice*, *17*(2), 144–156. https://doi.org/10.1111/j.1468-2850.2010.01204.x

Kazantzis, N., Whittington, C., Zelencich, L., Kyrios, M., Norton, P. J., & Hofmann, S. G. (2016). Quantity and quality of homework compliance: A meta-analysis of relations with outcome in cognitive behavior therapy. *Behavior Therapy*, *47*(5), 755–772. https://doi.org/10.1016/j.beth.2016.05.002

Lambert, M. J., Harmon, S. C., & Slade, K. (2007). Directions for research on homework. In N. Kazantzis & L. L'Abate (Eds.), *Handbook of homework assignments in psychotherapy: Research, practice, and prevention* (pp. 407–423). Springer. https://doi.org/10.1007/978-0-387-29681-4_24

*Mathes, B. M., Day, T. N., Wilver, N. L., Redden, S. A., & Cougle, J. R. (2020). Indices of change in exposure and response prevention for contamination-based OCD. *Behaviour Research and Therapy*, *133*, 103707. https://doi.org/10.1016/j.brat.2020.103707

Mausbach, B. T., Moore, R., Roesch, S., Cardenas, V., & Patterson, T. L. (2010). The relationship between homework compliance and therapy outcomes: An updated meta-analysis. *Cognitive Therapy and Research*, *34*(5), 429–438. https://doi.org/10.1007/s10608-010-9297-z

McCullough, L., Larsen, A. E., Schanche, E., Andrews, S., Kuhn, N., Hurley, C. L., Carley, M., & Francis-Ranier, E. (2003). *Achievement of Therapeutic Objectives Scale: ATOS scale* [Unpublished manuscript]. Short-Term Psychotherapy Research Program at Harvard Medical School.

Neimeyer, R. A., & Feixas, G. (1990). The role of homework and skill acquisition in the outcome of group cognitive therapy for depression. *Behavior Therapy*, *21*(3), 281–292. https://doi.org/10.1016/S0005-7894(05)80331-4

Nelson, D. L., Castonguay, L. G., & Barwick, F. (2007). Directions for the integration of homework in practice. In N. Kazantzis & L. L'Abate (Eds.), *Handbook of homework assignments in psychotherapy: Research, practice, prevention* (pp. 425–444). Springer.

*Ohaeri, J. U. (1997). Experience of cognitive behaviour therapy in psychiatric practice in Nigeria: II. Illustrative case histories. *African Journal of Medicine and Medical Sciences, 26*(3–4), 197–201.

Okamoto, A., & Kazantzis, N. (2021). Alliance ruptures in cognitive–behavioral therapy: A cognitive conceptualization. *Journal of Clinical Psychology, 77*, 384–397.

*Owen, J., Quirk, K., Hilsenroth, M. J., & Rodolfa, E. (2012). Working through: In-session processes that promote between-session thoughts and activities. *Journal of Counseling Psychology, 59*(1), 161–167. https://doi.org/10.1037/a0023616

Prochaska, J. O., & Norcross, J. C. (2018). *Systems of psychotherapy: A transtheoretical analysis* (9th ed.). Oxford University Press.

Rogers, C. R. (1961). *On becoming a person: A therapist's view of psychotherapy*. Constable.

Ryum, T., Stiles, T. C., Svartberg, M., & McCullough, L. (2010). The effects of therapist competence in assigning homework in cognitive therapy with cluster C personality disorders: Results from a randomized controlled trial. *Cognitive and Behavioral Practice, 17*(3), 283–289. https://doi.org/10.1016/j.cbpra.2009.10.005

Ryum, T., Store-Valen, J., Svartberg, M., Stiles, T. C., & McCullough, L. (2014). Factor analysis of the Achievement of Therapeutic Objectives Scale (ATOS) in short-term dynamic psychotherapy and cognitive therapy. *Psychological Assessment, 26*(3), 925–934. https://doi.org/10.1037/a0036570

Ryum, T., Svartberg, M., & Stiles, T. C. (2022). Homework assignments, agenda setting and the therapeutic alliance in cognitive therapy with cluster C personality disorders: Synergetic or antagonistic ingredients? *Cognitive Therapy and Research, 46*, 448–455. https://doi.org/10.1007/s10608-021-10268-8

Sachsenweger, M. A., Fletcher, R. B., & Clarke, D. (2015). Pessimism and homework in CBT for depression. *Journal of Clinical Psychology, 71*(12), 1153–1172. https://doi.org/10.1002/jclp.22227

Safran, J. D., & Muran, J. C. (2000). *Negotiating the therapeutic alliance: A relational treatment guide*. Guilford.

Safran, J. D., Muran, J. C., & Eubanks-Carter, C. (2011). Repairing alliance ruptures. *Psychotherapy, 48*, 80–87.

*Sasso, K. E., Strunk, D. R., Braun, J. D., DeRubeis, R. J., & Brotman, M. A. (2015). Identifying moderators of the adherence–outcome relation in cognitive therapy for depression. *Journal of Consulting and Clinical Psychology, 83*(5), 976–984. https://doi.org/10.1037/ccp0000045

*Sasso, K. E., Strunk, D. R., Braun, J. D., DeRubeis, R. J., & Brotman, M. A. (2016). A re-examination of process–outcome relations in cognitive therapy for depression: Disaggregating within-patient and between-patient effects. *Psychotherapy Research, 26*(4), 387–398. https://doi.org/10.1080/10503307.2015.1026423

Shaw, B. F., Elkin, I., Yamaguchi, J., Olmsted, M., Vallis, T. M., Dobson, K. S., Lowery, A., Sotsky, S. M., Watkins, J. T., & Imber, S. D. (1999). Therapist competence ratings in relation to clinical outcome in cognitive therapy of depression. *Journal of Consulting and Clinical Psychology, 67*(6), 837–846. https://doi.org/10.1037//0022-006x.67.6.837

Shelton, J. L., & Ackerman, J. M. (1974). *Homework in counseling and psychotherapy: Examples of systematic assignments for therapeutic use by mental health professionals*. Thomas.

Shelton, J. L., & Levy, R. L. (1981). A survey of the reported use of assigned homework activities in contemporary behavior therapy literature. *The Behavior Therapist, 4*, 13–14.

*Sijercic, I., Button, M. L., Westra, H. A., & Hara, K. M. (2016). The interpersonal context of client motivational language in cognitive-behavioral therapy. *Psychotherapy*, *53*(1), 13–21. https://doi.org/10.1037/pst0000017

Stiles, W. B., Honos-Webb, L., & Surko, M. (1998). Responsiveness in psychotherapy. *Clinical Psychology: Science and Practice*, *5*(4), 439–458. https://doi.org/10.1111/j.1468-2850.1998.tb00166.x

Stirman, S. W., Gutner, C. A., Suvak, M. K., Adler, A., Calloway, A., & Resick, P. (2018). Homework completion, patient characteristics, and symptom change in cognitive processing therapy for PTSD. *Behavior Therapy*, *49*(5), 741–755. https://doi.org/10.1016/j.beth.2017.12.001

Stricker, G. (2006). Using homework in psychodynamic psychotherapy. *Journal of Psychotherapy Integration*, *16*(2), 219–237.

*Strunk, D. R., Brotman, M. A., & DeRubeis, R. J. (2010). The process of change in cognitive therapy for depression: Predictors of early inter-session symptom gains. *Behaviour Research and Therapy*, *48*(7), 599–606. https://doi.org/10.1016/j.brat.2010.03.011

Strunk, D. R., Brotman, M. A., DeRubeis, R. J., & Hollon, S. D. (2010). Therapist competence in cognitive therapy for depression: Predicting subsequent symptom change. *Journal of Consulting and Clinical Psychology*, *78*(3), 429–437. https://doi.org/10.1037/a0019631

*Strunk, D. R., Cooper, A. A., Ryan, E. T., DeRubeis, R. J., & Hollon, S. D. (2012). The process of change in cognitive therapy for depression when combined with antidepressant medication: Predictors of early intersession symptom gains. *Journal of Consulting and Clinical Psychology*, *80*(5), 730–738. https://doi.org/10.1037/a0029281

Svartberg, M., Stiles, T. C., & Seltzer, M. H. (2004). Randomized, controlled trial of the effectiveness of short-term dynamic psychotherapy and cognitive therapy for cluster C personality disorders. *American Journal of Psychiatry*, *161*(5), 810–817. https://doi.org/10.1176/appi.ajp.161.5.810

Valen, J., Ryum, T., Svartberg, M., Stiles, T. C., & McCullough, L. (2011). The Achievement of Therapeutic Objectives Scale: Interrater reliability and sensitivity to change in short-term dynamic psychotherapy and cognitive therapy. *Psychological Assessment*, *23*(4), 848–855. https://doi.org/10.1037/a0023649

Watson, J. C., & Wiseman, H. (2021). *The responsive psychotherapist: Attuning to clients in the moment*. American Psychological Association.

*Weck, F., Richtberg, S., Esch, S., Höfling, V., & Stangier, U. (2013). The relationship between therapist competence and homework compliance in maintenance cognitive therapy for recurrent depression: Secondary analysis of a randomized controlled trial. *Behavior Therapy*, *44*, 162–172.

*Willner-Reid, J., Whitaker, D., Epstein, D. H., Phillips, K. A., Pulaski, A. R., Preston, K. L., & Willner, P. (2016). Cognitive-behavioural therapy for heroin and cocaine use: Ecological momentary assessment of homework simplification and compliance. *Psychology and Psychotherapy*, *89*(3), 276–293. https://doi.org/10.1111/papt.12080

Woods, C. M., Chambless, D. L., & Steketee, G. (2002). Homework compliance and behavior therapy outcome for panic with agoraphobia and obsessive compulsive disorder. *Cognitive Behavior Therapy*, *31*(2), 88–95.

*Yew, R. Y., Dobson, K. S., Zyphur, M., & Kazantzis, N. (2021). Mediators and moderators of homework–outcome relations in CBT for depression: A study of engagement, therapist skill, and client factors. *Cognitive Therapy and Research*, *45*(2), 209–223. https://doi.org/10.1007/s10608-019-10059-2

Young, J., & Beck, A. T. (1980). *Cognitive Therapy Scale: Rating manual* [Unpublished manuscript]. University of Pennsylvania, psychotherapy Research Unit, Philadeplhia, PA.

Zelencich, L. M., Kazantzis, N., Wong, D. N., McKenzie, D. P., Downing, M., & Ponsford, J. L. (2020). Predictors of homework engagement in CBT adapted for traumatic brain injury: Pre/post-injury and therapy process factors. *Cognitive Therapy and Research*, *44*(1), 40–51. https://doi.org/10.1007/s10608-019-10036-9

*Zelencich, L. M., Wong, D., Kazantzis, N., McKenzie, D. P., Downing, M., & Ponsford, J. L. (2020). Predictors of anxiety and depression symptom improvement in CBT adapted for traumatic brain injury: Pre/post-injury and therapy process factors. *Journal of the International Neuropsychology Society*, *26*(1), 97–107. https://doi.org/10.1017/s1355617719000791

11
Silence

Heidi M. Levitt and Zenobia Morrill

The topic of silence in psychotherapy has long been seen as compelling (e.g., Freud, 1912) but as enigmatic. Because silences are, by definition, a lapse in verbal communication between speakers, they may be experienced as impenetrable and so pose particular problems for psychotherapists. The use and toleration of silences has been described as the experience in therapy that is most challenging for new therapists because of the anxiety caused by this uncertainty (Benjamin, 1981). In this chapter, we review and synthesize the research that is critical for therapists who desire to skillfully use silences in their sessions.

In order to make clear why this skill is essential, we first describe silent processes that have established links with a variety of outcomes, based on both quantitative and qualitative research. We describe findings that show that therapists differentiate among silences and actively seek to both initiate and respond to clients' silences in a productive manner. Because the key to the skillful use of silences appears to depend on therapists' ability to differentiate these silent processes, we conduct an original review of the research on clients' and therapists' experiences of silences that makes evident the varied processes associated with good versus poor outcomes. We conduct an integrative meta-analytic review of the research on silences that occur within the flow of therapeutic dialogue as well as a qualitative analysis of the research on silences that halt dialogue—sometimes going on for multiple sessions. We conclude with limitations of this research evidence, diversity considerations, training implications, and—based on our research findings—therapeutic practices about silences.

Definitions

Silences are most often defined as moments within the therapy session in which dialogue is halted. During these silent moments, the clinician is deliberately not speaking or interjecting. Nor is the client. Silence is a deeply interactional process in psychotherapy. Unlike many other therapy interventions, clients and therapists both have to engage in it—typically without any discussion beforehand. In this chapter, although we view silences as co-constructed, we consider the therapists' work in silences as the ability to differentiate types of silences and then respond skillfully to silences that are associated with good and poor outcomes, defined broadly.

Across time, research studies have used varying metrics to determine the duration of time that constitutes a silence. Some case studies examined psychotherapy treatments in which most sessions passed almost wordlessly—sometimes for multiple years (Fuller

Heidi M. Levitt and Zenobia Morrill, *Silence* In: *Psychotherapy Skills and Methods That Work*. Edited by: Clara E. Hill and John C. Norcross, Oxford University Press. © Clara E. Hill and John C. Norcross 2023. DOI: 10.1093/oso/9780197611012.003.0011

& Crowther, 1998). Most of this literature on *extended silences* in psychotherapy, which was the initial focus of psychotherapy researchers, comes from psychodynamic perspectives. These were mostly theoretical pieces and case descriptions that explored possible client motivations underlying silences, such as therapeutic resistance (Freud, 1912; Reik, 1926), regression (Winnicott, 1965), rage (Zeligs, 1961), intimacy and trust (Trad, 1993), and the communication of transferential struggle (Fliess, 1949; Sabbadini, 1991). These descriptions drew attention to silence as a process worthy of contemplation and study.

Research on silence gradually extended to humanistic therapists who considered silence to be important for emotional attunement (e.g., Gendlin, 1969), although they tended to study briefer silences that occurred within the flow or structure of an exchange. Then silences were studied by cognitive therapists (e.g., Perfetti & Bertuccelli-Papi, 1985), who also tended to study silences within dialogue but saw them as reflective of cognitive processing. Recently, a wave of psychoanalytic conversation analysts have examined silences that are very brief, even less than a second long (e.g., Buchholtz, 2021).

The duration of time that has been used to define a silence has been inconsistent across studies (e.g., 5 seconds [Hill et al., 2019], 3 seconds [Levitt, 2001a], a tenth of a second [Carr & Smith, 2014]). In other research, the duration of silence was defined by the part of the session that did not include speech (e.g., a 45-minute silent session with only a few sentences spoken; Ronningstam, 2006) or the number of sessions characterized by almost total silence. These differences in the duration of silences have complicated the study of how these silences function in psychotherapy because *extended silences* that engulf a good proportion of the session (e.g., 10 minutes or longer) appear to indicate disparate phenomena from *in-dialogue* silences that occur more routinely in the flow of therapy. As a result, our research review examines brief and extended silences separately.

A second definitional issue is that there are (at least) two people in a psychotherapy relationship and so silences are always co-created by the therapist and the client. (If the therapist does not talk but the client keeps talking or vice versa, there is no silence.) Thus, silences are not solely implemented by therapists or clients alone. Therapists may model or engage in specific silent processes with clients in hopes of sustaining or fostering that process for the client. Sometimes therapists direct clients to contemplate an issue quietly or use silences themselves to consider what they would like to say next, but at other times their activity is to respond to their clients' silent process or to engage in a mutual silence. In any case, their goal is to ensure that a silent process leads to a productive outcome.

Although they are comparatively easy to identify on a superficial level, because of the absence of speech, the meaning of silences is not as easy to ascertain, and they entail distinctive client and therapist processes. At their zenith, they can indicate moments when clients are deeply attuned to internal experiences or in a space of reflective communion with their therapists. At their nadir, they may indicate internal disconnection and withdrawal of the client or therapist, during which the alliance is threatened by disintegration. Silences associated with good and poor outcomes require differentiation.

A final definitional note is that silence is best understood as a temporal process. Therefore, therapist skills may relate to initiating, sustaining, and responding to types of silences, as well as interpreting underlying causes of extended silences. Unlike some skills, silences do not necessitate a singular period or form of intervention, and they often only become therapeutic because they are contextualized by other processes—such as those that led to, or facilitated recovery from, the silence. Although therapists might suggest that a client engage in a type of silence (e.g., "take a moment to reflect on your feelings"), the client must know how, and be willing, to engage in that reflection in order for that silence to occur. Many clients cannot sustain introspective silences when entering psychotherapy, and part of therapists' work may be to help clients learn skills for entering, holding, or moving on from distinctive forms of silence.

Given that silences contain distinctive processes and are intrinsically relational and temporal processes, researchers have refrained from studying silent processes experimentally. Silence, as a joint lapse of speech, cannot be introduced independently by therapists (unlike many other interventions), and therapists forcing silence would be contrived. Indeed, there are ethical concerns about experimentally or randomly requiring silences in psychotherapy sessions. Although research has shown that therapists deliberate about their engagement in silences in therapy (e.g., Hill et al., 2003), experimental research has not been conducted in which therapists have intentionally used or avoided specific types of silences—in part due to the ethical considerations that this behavior would pose.

There are many therapeutic traditions that formally structure silent processing. These include hypnosis (Wall, 2018), focusing (Gendlin, 1969), mentalization (Bateman & Fonagy, 2013), mindfulness meditation (Heppner & Shirk, 2018), and arts- and movement-based therapies (Serlin, 2015). This review does not examine these sorts of practices that structure prolonged silence; rather, it focuses on moments of silence that occur in routine individual psychotherapy.

Clinical Descriptions and Indicators

As we describe in our research review, there are silent processes associated with productive outcomes as well as poor outcomes. Learning to differentiate types of silent processes appears to be the first step in skillful use of and responding to silences.

Ideally, silent moments in psychotherapy occur when clients are deeply tuned in with themselves and novel experiences and insights unfold. They can be moments when therapists are guiding and supporting, communing with clients, and gaining insights into clients' internal worlds and needs. Their structuring may support clients' ability to become comfortable with self-examination, to enhance exploration, and to embrace a sense of agency and self-direction (e.g., Levitt & Whelton, 2022).

At the same time, these moments can be associated with anxiety, negative transference, and resistance for clients. Clients may feel paralyzed and uncertain how to respond when threatening issues arise. They may not feel comfortable telling the therapist when they do not understand or ardently disagree with a perspective that has been shared. And these more challenging silences can leave therapists baffled on how best to respond (e.g., Daniel et al., 2018). Silence processes typically emerge organically in session rather than being prescribed by therapists, and so the idea of contraindications for their use is incommensurate with the nature of silences. (For instance, it would not be possible or desirable for therapists to stop clients from pausing when they feel threatened by a topic that has arisen.) However, once a problematic silence emerges, clients have reported appreciating when therapist intervene skillfully to process their experience or engage in repair (e.g., Levitt, 2001b). Because of the multiple ways that therapists can use silences and their varied outcomes, assessing the processes within silences is key.

Assessment

Attention to the study of silence (or pauses; the terms have been used interchangeably) grew in the 1970s and 1980s following the development of measures used to categorize therapists' verbal responses (see Elliott et al., 2001). Some of these measures considered silence to be a response mode (notably, Hill's [1986] Verbal Response Category System), which led to studies that examined therapists' use of silences in therapy. However, in these programs, silences were examined as a homogeneous variable, which may have been why these studies did not result in consistent findings. Then in the early 2000s, researchers studying silences began to differentiate processes within silences—from clients' perspectives and from therapists' perspectives. They advanced research on silence by viewing it as a heterogeneous factor, rather than by collapsing all silences into one category. This approach increased the research sensitivity and led to newer measures. This more nuanced analysis permitted greater fidelity in the study of silences.

Assessment of Silences

The assessment typology most often used to distinguish forms of clients' experiences of silences in psychotherapy is the Pausing Inventory Categorization System (PICS; Levitt, 2001a). This measure was developed from a qualitative analysis of interviews with clients about their experiences of in-dialogue silences. In the PICS, silences in psychotherapy are organized into three overarching categories that contain seven silence processes (duration of pause indicated in seconds within the parenthetic examples). First, there are three *productive silences,* which include *emotional silences* that give clients time to access and contact feelings (e.g., "I feel so sad [p: 05] like everything feels [p: 03] hopeless"); *expressive silences,* during which clients symbolize and find language for their internal experience (e.g., "It is like being in a candy store but everything is behind glass [p: 03] or like it is locked and I'm outside looking in"); and *reflective silences,* in which clients arrive at new insights, make connections, and contemplate issues. Sometimes this latter category has been divided into *high reflective* silences that occur in relation to personally important issues (e.g., "It is confusing but [p: 06] I think maybe this means my mother did love me") and *low reflective* silences in which clients consider superficial issues (e.g., "Hmmm [p: 03] I'm not sure what I want to eat for lunch?"; Levitt & Frankel, 2004). Second, there are two forms of obstructive silences: *disengaged silences* that occur when an issue that raises anxiety leads clients to withdraw or stop processing (e.g., "I don't want to talk about that [p: 08] but maybe we can talk instead about my sister"); and *interactive silences,* during which clients shift from considering their own experiences to thinking about the therapist, usually because they feel confused about what the therapist wants or means, feel judged, or are engaging in impression management (e.g., "I don't agree with you [p:10] I just don't think that you understand"). Finally, there are two neutral silence processes: *mnemonic silences*, during which clients attempt to remember an event or experience, and *associational pauses*, which occur in the process of switching topics.

The PICS has high interrater reliability across a number of studies, as well as client-rater reliability in which clients' descriptions of silences were compared to raters' coding (Levitt & Morrill, 2021). In addition, it has been translated and used across many languages (Levitt & Morrill, 2021) and subject to cross-cultural validation (with categories of silences being affirmed in Spanish qualitative research on therapy in Chile; Guzmán et al., 2018), and it has content validity from its grounding in qualitative analysis.

In addition to this cross-cultural validation of its productive and obstructive categories, and analyses by the authors of the PICS (e.g., Levitt, 2001a, 2001b, 2002; Frankel et al., 2006; Stringer et al., 2010), other researchers have found evidence of the occurrence of expressive processes (Bravesmith, 2012; Tindall & Robinson, 1947), emotional processes (Tindall & Robinson, 1947), reflexive processes (Tindall & Robinson, 1947), obstructive processes (Acheson et al., 2020), disengaged processes (Bravesmith, 2012; Martyres, 1995; Tindall & Robinson, 1947; Wilmer, 1995), and interactional processes (Blos, 1972; Bravesmith, 2012; Tindall & Robinson, 1947). These findings increase the confidence in the typology proposed by the PICS measure to understand silent processes.

The assessment tool used most often by researchers to assess therapists' behaviors during silences is Bartels et al.'s (2016) Strength of Connection Scale (SCS). The SCS has four categories: *connectional* (seeking emotional attunement with clients), *invitational* (inviting clients' self-reflection), *neutral* (waiting and listening), and *disengaged* (disconnecting from clients) processes. A fifth category of *reflective* activity has since been added (Cuttler et al., 2019; Hill et al., 2019).

Similarly, other studies have found evidence of connectional processes (Carr & Smith, 2014; Ladany et al., 2004), invitational processes (Hill et al., 2003; Ladany et al., 2004; Tindall & Robinson, 1947), neutral processes (Tindall & Robinson, 1947), disengaged processes (Ladany et al., 2004), and reflective processes (Hill et al., 2003, 2019; Tindall & Robinson, 1947). The SCS has validity from qualitative research and has good interrater reliability (Cuttler et al., 2019).

Assessment of Outcomes

There are three ways in which outcomes are conceptualized in this review: (1) outcome measured in the same session (i.e., proximal outcome); (2) outcomes measured at the end of therapy (i.e., distal outcome); and (3) immediate in-session outcomes of pauses that report the consequences of silences as described by clients and therapists in qualitative research.

Most (25) of the 33 studies reviewed examined immediate in-session outcomes. Positive immediate outcomes often included insight, greater attunement to emotional experience, and increased capacity to symbolize or verbalize internal experience. Negative immediate outcomes often included dissociation, resistance, confusion, or withdrawal from engagement in therapy.

Similarly, most studies examined proximal and/or distal quantitative outcome variables (23 studies). Of these outcomes, most typically (in 9 of the 33 studies) the outcomes assessed were symptoms of psychological distress, with the most common measures being the Beck Depression Scale (Beck et al., 1961), Symptom Checklist (Deogratis et al., 1976), and the Therapist Perception Questionnaire (Strupp et al., 1964). The second most common quantitative outcome (in 4 studies) was interpersonal problems, with the most common measures being the Inventory of Interpersonal Problems (Horwitz et al., 2000) and the Outcome Questionnaire-45 (Lambert et al., 1966).

Clinical Examples

In this section, we provide a portion of a hypothetical transcript of an individual psychotherapy session to illustrate different kinds of in-dialogue silences. In parentheses after each silence, we provide the length of the pause, the coding of client (C experiences) behaviors using the PICS, and the coding of therapist (T) behaviors using the SCS.

T: What seems to be the most important thing for you to focus on today?

C: I have been thinking a lot about my relationship with my daughter (p: 05; client reflective, therapist neutral). What is worrying me is that I think I am setting a bad role model for her, and I think she is just the most precious thing in my world but I don't know how to change it.

T: It is hard (p: 03; client reflective, therapist connectional). What do you think you are doing to be a bad role model? (p: 03; client reflective, therapist invitational)

C: I feel like it's sort of like, I'm just too (p: 04; client expressive, therapist neutral) too strong (p: 03; client expressive, therapist neutral), not quite perfectionistic but like I push myself to do way too much. More than I should. Sometimes I just am exhausted (p: 03; client emotional, therapist connectional) and I desperately want to sleep. I don't have the luxury to stop though without letting people down or giving up on the causes that are important to me and so I push on (p: 03; client reflective, therapist reflective). This is what I am seeing in her now, but she is only a kid still and shouldn't have so much pressure.

T: Maybe you should stop putting all this pressure on yourself. It is too much.

C: How can I? I've been working so hard to accomplish these goals and I don't think giving up would be a good role model either. When you say this, I just feel (p: 06; client interactional, therapist neutral), I feel like you don't understand me at all (p: 05; interactional client pause, reflective therapist pause). I've told you how I am on the verge of getting my business really recognized by the people who matter.

T: What would it feel like if you let go of the pressure? I don't know what it would be like (p: 03; client reflective, therapist disengaged) if you just said, "It will take me a lot longer but I'll get there at a better pace?"

C: (p: 07; client disengaged, therapist reflective) I just want my daughter to find a healthier way to be while she is a kid and doesn't have all the life pressure of adults. I want to help her.

T: You really want to help her, but it is hard to think about how you could change the model that you provide for her. That is really difficult. You don't want to go there. There is a block.

C: Yeah. That is true (p: 04; client reflective, therapist connectional). I feel like my own pressure is inescapable and insurmountable. I can't give myself a break.

This excerpt provides a sense of how in-dialogue pauses might sound in the flow of a session. It also provides an example of how, by identifying what is happening in an obstructive pause, the therapist acknowledges how this moment is challenging for the client (it "is really difficult" to think about this topic). The empathic reflection ("You don't want to go there. There is a block") helps the client notice the block and shift to focus on the underlying issue ("My own pressure is inescapable").

Landmark Studies and Previous Reviews

The only prior review of the silence research that we located was a narrative review of psychotherapy research findings generated from the PICS (Levitt & Morrill, 2021). This review described the development of the PICS, which has been used in psychotherapy research in nine countries. Findings were grouped into the following categories: (a) intensive case studies of psychodynamic therapy, finding that reflective silences increased across therapy of approximately 1 year (Gindi, 2002; Guzmán et al., 2018); (b) comparisons of good and poor therapies in clinical trials, which focused on the York Depression Project (Frankel et al., 2006) and the Munich psychotherapy study (Schlotheuber, 2018); (c) comparisons across psychotherapy orientations (Daniel et al., 2018; Holtmann et al., 2018); and (d) examinations of PICS silent process with other processes, such as a computer textual analysis of emotional tone and abstraction level (Mergenthaler & Levitt, 2005), an analysis of adolescents in psychoanalytic therapy and therapist interventions (Acheson et al., 2020), and an effectiveness study of silences that signified clients' in-session disengagement (Stringer et al., 2010). Because we include most of these studies in our meta-analyses, we do not go into greater detail here.

A recent landmark publication is a book that contains theoretical considerations of silence as well as conversation analyses on silence in psychoanalysis (Dimitrijević & Buchholtz, 2021). The valuable studies described in this book consider not only the functions of and experiences that occur during pauses in psychoanalytic therapy but also the outcomes that might ensue from them. For instance, one chapter described how therapists used silences to examine patients' internal thought processes and together produced shared images (Dreyer & Franzen, 2021). Another study showed that pausing following therapists' mistakes (e.g., when a therapist misremembered an important detail of a client's life) created the possibility for therapists to save face in the moment but, if not handled adequately, also could lead to the dissolution of the patients' faith in the therapy over the long term (Buchholz, 2021). This book extends the historical inquiry into the motives for therapeutic silence using a psychoanalytic perspective.

Research Review

We examined studies in the published peer-reviewed English-language research on silences within adult individual psychotherapy. Exclusion criteria were thus unpublished studies, research appearing in other languages than English, and studies on modalities other than individual therapy.

Search Strategy and Studies

We used the PsycInfo database to locate primary research, by searching for articles that used the terms "silenc*" or "paus*" in the title and contained the terms "psychotherapy or therapy or counseling or counselling or therapist or client or session" in any field. Following the recommendation of Timulak (2009) for conducting qualitative meta-analyses, we included only published peer-reviewed research in this study as a form of quality control. Also, we excluded studies that collapsed all silences in a session or therapy together (e.g., just examined the total amount of silence within a session), because repeated evidence has indicated that there are distinctive processes occurring within different types of silences (e.g., Hill et al., 2003; Ladany et al., 2004; Levitt, 2001a).

Initially, we identified 597 possible articles (see Figure 11.1 for flow diagram). We identified terms that counterindicated the relevance of articles for this psychotherapy study (e.g., nursing, mutism, neurology) to assist us in locating articles outside the scope of our research review based on their title (if unsure, we consulted the abstract or referred the article to full text reading), leading us to reduce the number of articles to 233. Articles excluded focused on people who are silenced by others (e.g., refugees; 35), conditions that led to silence (e.g., brain damage, cancer, schizophrenia; 118), topics about which people are often silent (e.g., the holocaust or menstruation; 123), therapy formats that were not individual therapy (e.g., group therapy; 33), non-English-language articles (52), and duplicate articles (3).

Following this, we independently read the remaining articles' titles and abstracts. Through this process, we removed 190 articles for the following reasons: nonempirical articles (31); articles related to topics about which people tend to be silent (41); biological disorders that lead to silence (49); therapy formats other than non-individual therapy that had not been identified earlier (37); non-peer-reviewed literature, such as dissertations (22); and articles that aggregated all forms of silence together (10). Then, we independently read the full text of the remaining 43 articles. There were a further 12 articles removed for the following reasons: nonempirical articles (3); articles featuring topics about which people are silent (1); therapy formats other than individual therapy (1); non-peer-reviewed literature (2); articles that collapsed all forms of silence (3); and non-English articles (2).

Thus, we came to consensus that 30 articles should be admitted into the meta-analysis. In addition, because of a prior review we had conducted (Levitt & Morrill, 2021), we knew of an additional three articles that had not been located in this search process and added them to the tally. In total, 33 articles were reviewed, including 17 studies on

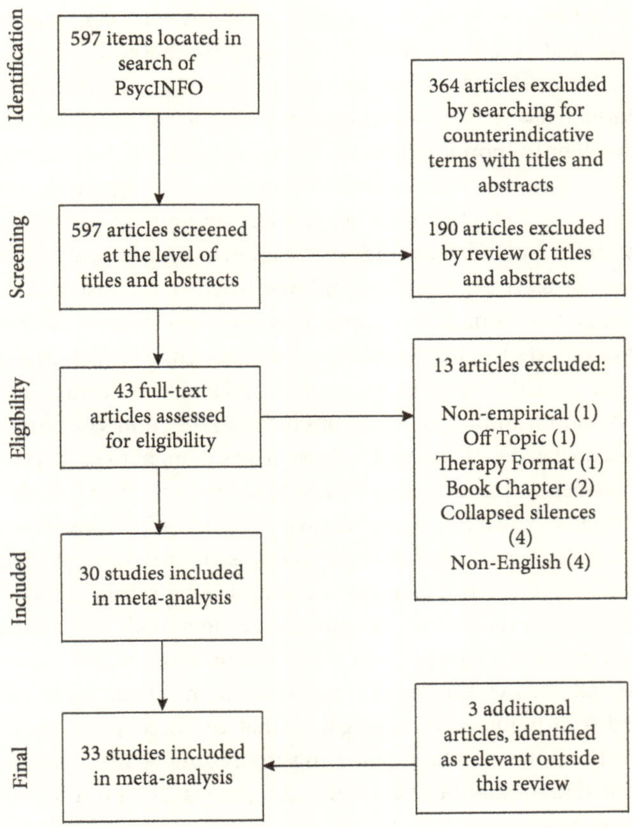

Figure 11.1 Article selection flow diagram.

in-dialogue silences that examined the silences of 276 clients and 192 therapists and 16 studies focused on the extended silences of 33 clients and 17 therapists. Timulak (2009) estimated that 12 is the average number of studies for qualitative meta-analyses, and 100 studies has been recommended as a maximum (Paterson et al., 2001). Our analysis falls within this recommended range.

Integrative and Qualitative Meta-Analysis

The meta-analyses presented in this chapter were informed by a critical–constructivist grounded theory approach (Levitt, 2021) and situated within critical and constructivist epistemological perspectives. Thus, we were interested in how silent processes were constructed, how they functioned in the sessions, and how these functions might differ in relation to the participants' cultural and societal situations and in-therapy power relations. As well, we synthesize the research on cues that can aid therapists in skillfully differentiating and responding to silent processes associated with good and poor outcomes.

The studies in our review used a range of methods (process measure, qualitative, survey designs), and so an integrative meta-analytic method was used to integrate findings across these methods (for methodological details, see Wu & Levitt, 2022). This process was inductively driven, meaning that we reviewed the findings from each of these studies to identify common themes. Then, we organized the findings in tables (see Tables 11.1–11.9). Findings from across methods were brought to bear when considering each concern, and a higher order or summary finding was created that synthesized the primary findings and indicated their association to process and outcome.

In the tables, we used box scores to indicate whether the responses to the silences enhanced (+), impeded (–), or did not appear to affect (=) the therapy outcomes to summarize the effects of varied silent processes. These designations were determined by assessing if silent processes were described by clients to be related to outcomes that were helpful, hindering, or as neutral and/or if correlations between the counts or proportions of silent processes were associated with measures of constructs thought to be helpful, hindering, or neutral. When evidence was mixed, we looked to see if there was a preponderance of evidence in one direction, and if not, we indicated the relationship to outcome as neutral.

In contrast to the research on in-dialogue silences, the articles identified as pertaining to extended silences all used a qualitative method. As a result, we used a qualitative meta-analytic approach rather than the integrative meta-analysis just described. In this approach, the findings from the primary studies were recorded and then organized into categories that reflected commonalities between them. Then, these initial categories were organized into higher order categories that captured patterns in the findings. Saturation—or the point at which analyzing the results of the remaining studies no longer contributed to the addition of novel findings—was achieved at the 10th study out of 16 total articles about extended silences.

Methodological Integrity Checks

We used several procedures to strengthen the methodological integrity of our research review. In identifying articles for inclusion, we used a process of consensus in both the reviews of the titles/abstracts and the reviews of the full articles. Consensus processes can be helpful for both critical and constructivist qualitative researchers because they encourage researchers to be more comprehensive in considering a topic with a broader diversity of meanings and perspectives in mind (Levitt, 2021). As well, we discussed the development of findings and the development of principles together to maximize our sensitivity to possible interpretations. The authors recorded memos, which are notes intended to assist researchers in their reflection on their assumptions and the procedures used throughout qualitative analyses.

Description of Articles

Of the 33 articles included in the research review, 17 focused on silences within dialogue; eight of these focused on therapists' experiences, 14 on clients' experiences, and four articles focused on silences of both parties. Another 16 articles focused on extended silences. These latter articles were all qualitative psychoanalytic or psychodynamic studies that focused on the interchange between clients and therapists rather than on either perspective in isolation. (The sum of these latter numbers surpassed the total number of articles because some studies included multiple foci of analyses.) The studies heralded from seven countries (the United States, United Kingdom, Norway, Greece, Canada, Denmark, and Australia). Clients were seen within a variety of health care settings, including community health care centers, private practices, hospitals, research clinics, and university clinics. It was striking that the research on extended silences was exclusively conducted within psychoanalytic therapies (conducted by psychoanalysts, Jungian therapists, and Kleinians), whereas the research on in-dialogue silences was conducted on a variety of psychotherapy orientations, including psychodynamic therapy (14), humanistic therapy (8), cognitive–behavioral therapy (CBT; 8), feminist–multicultural therapy (1), and integrative therapy (1). Of the 17 studies that examined in-dialogue silences, 10 studies reported counts of silences, and together these added up to 11,793 silences. Silences were not tallied in the extended silence qualitative studies.

In the following sections (see Tables 11.1–11.9), we summarize the findings related to in-dialogue silent processes and the processes and cues that appear useful for the development of therapists' skill. In Table 11.10, we summarize findings that provide evidence of how the meanings of extended silences guide therapists' formulations and interventions that influence outcome.

In-Dialogue Silences and Their Association with Outcome

In the following sections, the research on clients' and therapists' experiences of pausing within session dialogue is examined in turn. The tables group the results into categories based on similar questions. Each table presents the central findings from each study, and in the final column, we summarize the integrated meta-analytic finding and its relation to a productive or poor process or outcome. When findings appeared to contradict each other, we identified distinguishing features of articles within the tables to highlight possible bases for those differences. The research designs of the primary articles are described (e.g., process measure study, qualitative study, quantitative survey study). Although the integrative findings describe the nature of the findings with greater fidelity, box scores are presented in the tables as a heuristic to help readers quickly observe whether general patterns described in our findings relate to good or poor immediate, proximal, or distal outcomes.

Client Experiences of In-Dialogue Silences

In this section, we first review the research that establishes a link between silent processes that clients' experience and psychotherapy outcomes. Then, we summarize the research that presents cues that differentiate these processes so that therapists can distinguish and respond skillfully to silences associated with productive or obstructive outcomes.

Table 11.1 Client Pausing Processes That Influence Immediate Psychotherapy Outcomes

Findings Organized in Categories	Study	Study Details	Linking the Silent Processes to Therapist Responses and Outcomes (Box Scores +, −, or =)
Expressive pauses: These silences led clients to improved symbolizations of their experience.	Levitt (2001a), QL	Clients described engaging in expressive pauses and described the process and outcome entailed in these moments. (+)	Expressive pauses are productive pauses associated with good micro-outcomes for clients across multiple studies. It appeared helpful for therapists to permit, sustain, or encourage to support clients in these silences to develop new symbolization for their experiences. (+)
	Levitt (2002), QL	Clients described engaging in expressive pauses and described in detail the process and outcome entailed in these moments. (+)	
	Tindall & Robinson (1947), PM	A process measure was developed that independently included an expressive pausing process associated with similar immediate in-session processes as in the Levitt (2001) study. (+)	
	Bravesmith (2007), QL	In this multiple case study, clients' experiences of pauses in Jungian therapy were examined. (+)	
Emotional pauses: These silences led clients to better attunement to and differentiation of emotions.	Levitt (2001a), QL	Clients described engaging in emotional pauses and described the process and outcome entailed in these moments. (+)	Emotional pauses are productive pauses associated with good micro-outcomes for clients across multiple studies. Clients described it as helpful when therapists allowed, continued, or invited these moments to allow clients to deeply contact emotion, explore feelings, and differentiate distinct feelings from within global distress. (+)
	Levitt (2002), QL	Clients described engaging in emotional pauses and described in detail the process and outcome entailed in these moments. (+)	
	Tindall & Robinson (1947), PM	A process measure was developed that independently included an emotional pausing process associated with similar micro-outcome processes as in the Levitt (2001) study. (+)	
Reflective pauses: These silences led clients to develop insights, make connections, and increase self-awareness.	Frankel et al. (2006), PM	A process measure was adjusted to differentiate between types of reflective silence processes. (+)	Reflective silences are productive pauses associated with good micro-outcomes for clients. It was found to be helpful when therapists invited, held, or permitted these silences because it allowed clients to shape meaning, develop new insights, and notice patterns. (+)

	Levitt (2001a), QL	Clients described engaging in reflective pauses and described the process and outcome entailed in these moments. (+)	
	Levitt (2002), QL	Clients described engaging in reflective pauses and described in detail the process and outcome entailed in these moments. (+)	
	Tindall & Robinson (1947), PM	A process measure was developed that independently included a reflective pausing process associated with similar micro-outcome processes as in the Levitt (2001) study. (+)	
Disengaged pauses: These silences led to clients' withdrawal or shutting down in therapy. When examined in therapy, they may lead to insight into defenses and an increased capacity to process threatening issues.	Levitt (2001a), QL	Clients described engaging in disengaged pauses and described the process and outcome entailed in these moments. (–/+)	Disengaged silences are obstructive pauses typically associated with poor micro-outcomes for clients. (–) Although it is less routine, when explored therapeutically, disengaged silences may lead to positive outcomes such as insight, new awareness of defenses, and capacity to engage in therapy. It was described as helpful when therapists would directly talk with clients about their experiences during these pauses in order to examine how they responded to threatening material and themes. (+)
	Levitt (2001b), QL	Clients described engaging in disengaged pauses and described in detail the process and outcome entailed in these moments. (–/+)	
	Tindall & Robinson (1947), PM	A process measure was developed that independently described a disengaged pausing process associated with similar micro-outcome processes as in the Levitt (2001) study. (–)	
	Wilmer (1995), QL	A psychoanalyst asked patients about their experiences of silence and analyzed their responses; silence was seen as separation from others in the face of threat. (–/+)	
	Martyres (1995), QL	This was a qualitative psychoanalytic multiple case study of a client that described silence as a "blanket" that distanced him from threatening emotions. (–/+)	
	Bravesmith (2007), QL	In this multiple case study, clients experiences of pauses in Jungian therapy were examined. (–/+)	

(*continued*)

Table 11.1 Continued

Findings Organized in Categories	Study	Study Details	Linking the Silent Processes to Therapist Responses and Outcomes (Box Scores +, −, or =)
Interactional pauses: These silences resulted in confusion or a rift in the therapy relationship. When examined in therapy, they may strengthen the therapeutic connection, resolve potential rifts, and make possible new work in therapy.	Blos (1972), QL	This was a qualitative case study that described interactional processes for a client in psychoanalysis. (−/+)	Interactional silences are obstructive pauses typically associated with poor micro-outcomes for clients. (−) Although it is less routine, when explored therapeutically, interactional silences may lead to positive outcomes such as the resolution of rifts, the strengthening of the therapeutic relationship, or disclosure of new issues. Clients found it helpful when therapists invited clients to process these moments and examined relational and transferential processes that were unfolding. (+)
	Levitt (2001a), QL	Clients described engaging in interactional pauses and described the process and outcome entailed in these moments. (−/+)	
	Levitt (2001b), QL	Clients described engaging in interactional pauses and described in detail the process and outcome entailed in these moments. (−/+)	
	Tindall & Robinson (1947), PM	A process measure was developed that independently described an interactional pausing process associated with similar micro-outcome processes as in the Levitt (2001) study. (−)	
	Bravesmith (2007), QL	In this multiple case study, clients' experiences of pauses in Jungian therapy were examined. (−/+)	

PM, process measure study; QL, qualitative study.

Table 11.2 Client Pausing Processes That Influence Psychotherapy Outcomes

Findings Organized in Categories	Study	Study Details	Linking the Silent Processes to Therapist Responses and Outcomes (+, –, or =)
Productive silences grouped together: Good outcome therapies appear to have more productive silences than poor outcome therapies.	Frankel et al. (2006), PM	Adjusting for number of EFT sessions and total silences, the productive silences approached significance, all in the hypothesized direction with good outcome depressed clients when compared to poor outcome clients, using a composite symptom-change score to differentiate outcomes. (+)	(+) Findings leaned toward good outcome therapies being more likely to have more productive silences and fewer obstructive silences than poor outcome therapies. These findings support the Table 11.1 qualitative findings that it is helpful when therapists sustain, invite, or encourage productive silences in sessions.
	Daniel et al. (2018), PM	Good outcome dyads had more emotional, expressive, and high reflective silences than the poor-outcome PDT dyads—both for eating disordered clients. (+)	
Obstructive silences grouped together: Good outcome therapies appear to have fewer obstructive silences than poor outcome therapies.	Frankel et al. (2006), PM	Adjusting for number of EFT sessions and total silences, the obstructive silences approached significance, all in the hypothesized direction with depressed clients. (–)	(–) Findings leaned toward good outcome therapies being more likely to have fewer obstructive silences than poor outcome therapies. These findings support the Table 11.1 qualitative findings that it is helpful for therapists to interrupt and process what is happening for clients in obstructive silences, rather than to allow them to continue.
	Daniel et al. (2018), PM	Good outcome dyads had fewer disengaged and interactional silences than the poor outcome PDT dyads—both for eating disordered clients. (–)	
Disengaged silences: Disengaged silences are negatively related to outcome, especially to negative self-appraisal.	Frankel et al. (2006), PM	Disengaged silences were found to be significantly higher in poor outcome EFT therapy than good outcome. (–)	(–) Because disengaged silences appear to be correlated with poorer outcome on symptom measures, especially self-appraisal, being able to detect disengaged silences can help therapists ask about clients' self-esteem and belief in their ability to face negative emotions, supporting the qualitative findings in Table 11.1.
	Stringer et al. (2010), PM	Disengaged silences were found to be significantly higher in the third or fourth session of poor outcome therapies, inclusive of CBT, humanistic, feminist–multicultural, and integrative approaches, both immediately after that session and at the end of therapy. Disengaged pauses were found to be correlated with negative emotions and especially predictive of negative self-appraisals on the Beck Depression Scale (Beck et al., 1997)—even when the effects of the alliance were controlled. (–)	

(*continued*)

Table 11.2 Continued

Findings Organized in Categories	Study	Study Details	Linking the Silent Processes to Therapist Responses and Outcomes (+, −, or =)
Interactional silences: Interactional silences do not appear to be related to outcome.	Frankel et al. (2006), PM	Interactional silences were not found to be significantly higher in poor outcome EFT than good outcome. (=)	(=) Interactional silences do not seem to be significantly higher in poor outcome therapies. Authors hypothesize that this may be because therapists in EFT are very sensitive to gaps between therapists' and clients' understanding and tend to intervene when these silences occur to reduce the occurrence of rifts.
Productive silences grouped together, collaboration: Client collaboration before a pause does not predict if it is a productive pause, but productive pauses lead to greater client collaboration, especially for clients with higher attachment anxiety.	Cuttler et al. (2019), PM	Client collaboration before silence did not predict whether clients were productive or obstructive during silences that followed. (=)	(+) Structuring productive pauses (e.g., inviting moments to reflect on emotions, symbolization, or reflection) is associated with greater client collaboration in therapy, especially for clients with higher attachment anxiety. Learning to identify and foster productive silences may be especially helpful for these clients.
	Hill et al. (2019), PM	Increases in subsequent client collaboration were found after productive silences in a case study (looking at reflective and emotional silences together). (+)	
	Cuttler et al. (2019), PM	Client collaboration was higher when productive client silences occurred for clients who were higher (vs. lower) in attachment anxiety. (+)	
Emotional silences, collaboration: Emotional silences may lead to increased client collaboration.	Cuttler et al. (2019), PM	Emotional silences were related to increase in client collaboration in this multi-case analysis. (+)	(+) Further research is needed on permitting and encouraging emotional silences (e.g., by reassuring clients that it is ok to stay focused on their emotions or encouraging them to take a moment to notice their feelings) and its ability to increase clients' engagement in psychotherapy.
	Hill et al. (2019), PM	Emotional silences were not directly related to increased client collaboration. Researchers described that a reason for the finding may be because collaboration at the end of therapy was high for this single case study and this is where most of the emotional silences occurred and there was little variation to account for. (=)	

Expressive silences, collaboration: Expressive silences led to increased client collaboration.	Cuttler et al. (2019), (PM	Expressive silences were related to increase in client collaboration.	(+) Asking clients to take time to find language that accurately captured their experiences may increase clients' engagement. Therapists may wish to encourage these types of silences.
Reflective silences, collaboration: Reflective silences are less unlikely to be related to increased post-silence collaboration when levels of reflective silences are grouped together.	Hill et al. (2019), PM	Reflective silences were related to increase in client collaboration in a single case study. (+)	(=) Reflective silences do not appear to be related to increased client collaboration after silences. Future research may examine reflective silences further by distinguishing "high" (insights, meaning making, and connections related to therapeutic issues) and "low" reflective processes (those associated with more routine-level decisions and processing).
	Cuttler et al. (2019), PM	Reflective silences were not related to increase in client collaboration in a multi-case study. (=)	

CBT, cognitive–behavioral therapy; ETF, emotion-focused therapy; PDT, psychodynamic therapy; PM, process measure study; QL, qualitative study.

Table 11.3 Research Differentiating Pauses on Client Development, Attachment, and Alliance

Findings Organized in Categories	Study	Study Details	Linking the Silent Processes to Therapist Responses and Outcomes (+, –, or =)
Client developmental stage: Adolescents may experience a need for distance from therapist and demonstrate this using increasing obstructive pauses.	Acheson et al. (2020), PM	Case 3 adolescent with depression in psychoanalytic therapy: Obstructive silences increased but productive stayed stable, as they wanted insight but worried about being judged and wanted to keep a distance from therapist. Most of this obstructive silence related to adolescents' conflict, perhaps due to their developmental stage or depression. (–)	(–) Adolescents may seek independence and engage in obstructive pauses that increase. It can be helpful to ask about the content of these pauses and inquire about the feeling of judgment in therapy.
Obstructive silences grouped together, alliance: More frequentobstructive pauses were associated with poorer alliances.	Daniel et al. (2018), PM	More frequent obstructive pauses were associated with poorer alliance. (–)	(–) Therapists will want to attend carefully to obstructive pauses' effect on alliance, especially if they are frequent in sessions. They can ask clients about experiences in these moments and about their feelings about the therapy relationship.
Obstructive silences grouped together, attachment: The percentage of obstructive pauses per session may differ in relation to client attachment style in CBT, but not PAT or PDT.	Daniel et al. (2018), PM Cuttler et al. (2019), PM	More obstructive pauses occurred for dismissing than secure or preoccupied clients, but when examining therapies separately, these were not significantly different in psychoanalytic, only in CBT. (–) No relationship was found between pausing processes and client attachment anxiety, when looking at the first silence in each psychodynamic case. No interaction was found either between collaboration and attachment when examining obstructive silences. (=)	(–/=) Different findings on the relationship in attachment and obstructive pauses suggest that an association between these processes may be more likely with clients with an eating disorder or may be more likely when looking beyond the initial silent moment in a case. In PDT, it appears that clients of any attachment style can engage in productive or obstructive silences, suggesting that the pausing dynamic may be more dependent on therapists' guidance than client predisposition.

CBT, cognitive–behavioral therapy; PAT, psychoanalytic therapy; PDT, psychodynamic therapy; PM, process measure study; QL, qualitative study.

Clients' Pausing Processes and Immediate In-Session Outcomes

Across both qualitative and process measure research, silent processes have been associated with *immediate psychotherapy outcomes*—that is, small gains or setbacks that emerge in the course of the therapy dialogue (see Table 11.1). Productive silences were found to lead to positive immediate outcomes by clients across studies. Expressive pauses led to the symbolization of experience; emotional pauses to greater attunement to emotion; and reflective pauses to outcomes such as insight, connection-making, and greater awareness. Encouraging these moments was helpful.

In contrast, obstructive silences mostly led to poor immediate outcomes. They included disengaged pauses, which led to clients' withdrawal or shutting down, and interactional pauses, which led to rifts in clients' sense of security in therapy or confusion. However, clients also reported across studies that therapists' inquiry into these moments allowed them to recognize defenses or relational barriers and to strengthen the therapeutic connection and permit transformative moments of insight. These findings demonstrated that pausing processes can lead to both positive and negative immediate outcomes, and so responding differentially to these process matters (see Table 11.1 below for further guidance on therapists' responses).

Clients' Pausing Processes and Proximal and Distal Psychotherapy Outcomes: Symptom Change and Collaboration

Clients' pauses were associated with both positive and negative therapy outcomes (see Table 11.2). Across three studies, process measure research suggested that good outcome therapies have more productive silences and fewer obstructive silences than poor outcome therapies. These associations with outcome were found in therapies with diverse diagnostic groups, including depressed (Frankel et al., 2006), eating disorder presentations (Daniel et al., 2018), and a mixed group (Stringer et al., 2010).

In particular, disengaged pauses were significantly more frequent in poor outcome (vs. good outcome) emotion-focused therapy (EFT; Frankel et al., 2006), as well as in a study of varied orientations (Stringer et al., 2010). Disengaged pauses appeared to be particularly predictive of negative emotions and poor self-appraisal—a relationship that persisted even when the alliance was controlled (Stringer et al., 2010). In contrast, interactional pauses were not found to be more frequent in poor outcome EFT (Frankel et al., 2006). The authors argued that this was because EFT therapists were trained to resolve rifts associated with these pauses.

Two studies examined the relationship between productive pauses and client collaboration. Clients' collaboration (i.e., their level of engagement in the change process) before a pause (Cuttler et al., 2019) was not found to predict if an upcoming pause would be productive, although productive pauses were associated with increases in later collaboration (Cuttler et al., 2019; Hill et al., 2019), especially for clients with higher levels of attachment anxiety (Cuttler et al., 2019). These findings suggested that collaboration may be seen as an outcome of productive silences. When examined separately, emotional silences and expressive silences were associated with higher client collaboration in one multi-case study (Cuttler et al., 2019), but in a case study, the authors explained that because emotional pauses mostly occurred

Table 11.4 Research Differentiating Pauses on Proportions and Durations of Pauses

Findings Organized in Categories	Study	Study Details	Linking the Silent Processes to Therapist Responses and Outcomes (+, –, or =)
Productive silences grouped together: The percentage of productive pauses is high.	Frankel et al. (2006), PM	Percentage of productive pauses in EFT of adults with depression was 71.1% and approached significance for being larger in the good outcome cases than the poor outcome ones. (+)	(+) Most silences conducted in psychotherapy appear to be pauses that clients have described as productive (see Table 11.1). This finding suggests that therapists often will want to support clients to use silence to engage in reflecting, emotional processing, and symbolization of experience.
	Hill et al. (2019), PM	Percentage of productive pauses in a psychodynamic treatment of depression was 86% (reflective 41%; emotional 39%; expressive 6%). (+)	
	Tindall & Robinson (1947), PM	Percentage of client productive pauses in client-centered therapy appeared high. These included "organizational pauses" (like reflective pauses; 35.4%) and "normal" pauses, which were emotionally neutral and occurred at the end of topics (38.2%), appearing to entail reflective or associational pauses. (+)	
Obstructive silences grouped together: The proportion of obstructive silences varies across psychotherapies.	Levitt (2001b), QL	Percentage of obstructive pauses for adults with different issues from across humanistic, CBT, and interpersonal therapies was 41.1%. (+)	(+, –) The proportion of obstructive pauses appears to vary. Therapy with adolescents appears especially high in obstructive silences. Therapists using PAT also appear to tolerate more obstructive silences than other therapists.
	Hill et al. (2019), PM	Percentage of obstructive pauses in psychodynamic treatment of adults with depression was 12% (disengaged 10%, interactional 2%). (–)	
	Frankel et al. (2006), PM	Percentage of obstructive pauses in EFT of adults with depression was 11.2%. (–)	

	Tindall & Robinson (1947), PM	Percentage of obstructive pauses in client-centered therapy was 26.3% (indecisional pauses, like disengaged pauses, 16.8%; solicitation, like interactional pauses, 9.5%) (–)	
	Acheson et al. (2020), PM	Percentage of obstructive pauses in PAT of adolescents with depression was 69.1%. (+)	
Duration of pauses: Type of silent process was not associated with differences in pausing duration, with the exception of clients' obstructive pauses.	Cuttler et al. (2019), PM; Hill et al. (2019), PM	Client pausing processes were not associated with duration of the silences. (=)	(+/–) Duration of silence is not a reliable cue to distinguish most silent processes; however, research suggests that lengthier silences may be markers of obstructive (especially interactional) client processes, so therapists may wish to intervene in these moments.
	Levitt (2001b), QL	The mean duration of interactional pauses was significantly longer than other silences (+), but There were no significant differences between the durations of other client pause type. (=)	
	Daniel et al. (2018), PM	Obstructive client silences were longer compared to neutral silences. (+)	

CBT, cognitive–behavioral therapy; EFT, emotion-focused therapy; PAT, psychoanalytic treatment; PM, process measure study; QL, qualitative study.

Table 11.5 Research Differentiating Pauses by Speaker Turns

Findings Organized in Categories	Study	Study Details	Linking the Silent Processes to Therapist Responses and Outcomes (+, –, or =)
Productive silences grouped together: Most productive silences occur within client speech.	Daniel et al. (2018), PM	The majority of productive silences occur between two clients speaking turns. (+)	(+) It appears that therapists tend not to interrupt clients when they are engaged in the productive work that clients describe that these silent processes entail. It is skillful to allow these pauses.
Obstructive silences grouped together: Most obstructive silences occur within therapist speech or between switching speakers.	Daniel et al. (2018), PM	Unlike productive pauses, which are more likely to occur within client speech, obstructive pauses tend to occur within therapist speech or at moments between speakers switching. (–)	(–) Obstructive pauses have been described as impeding positive process. See findings for speaker turn for disengaged and interactional pauses for more specificity.
Disengaged silences: Disengaged pauses were typically between client and therapist speech.	Levitt (2001b), QL	"Typically, disengaged pauses (40%) were found to fall between client and therapist speech turns (with another 26% between therapist–client speech, 26% within therapist speech and 9% within client speech turns)" (p. 231). (–)	(–) Disengaged pauses appear to typically occur following the client saying something that has increased their anxiety and then the client stops. Awareness of this pattern can help therapists detect these processes so they can intervene.
Interactional silences: Interactional pauses typically follow therapist speech	Levitt (2001b), QL	"These pauses usually followed therapist speech (76%), and dialogue was more often reinitiated by the therapist (50%) than by the client (26%; the remaining 24% followed the clients' speech)" (p. 235). (–)	(–) Interactional pauses appear to occur most often within therapist speaking turns, likely because the therapist says something that the client finds problematic or confusing and then the therapist tries to clarify or repair.

PM, process measure study; QL, qualitative study.

Table 11.6 Research Differentiating Pauses by Trajectory of Clients' Silences

Findings Organized in Categories	Study	Study Details	Linking the Silent Processes to Therapist Responses and Outcomes (+, −, or =)
Client silent processes: Good and poor outcomes generally did not show linear changes in most silences across sessions, although emotional silences and disengaged silences both may increase over time in poor outcomes.	Frankel et al. (2006), PM	No significant linear changes were found in frequency of obstructive silence across good and poor EFT sessions across the course of therapy (=), but a significant interaction between session number and outcome was found for emotional pauses, in which the good outcome group showed more emotional pauses at the beginning (+), and the poor outcome group showed more at the end. (−)	(=) Further study of the trajectory of silences is needed. Structuring silent moments early in therapy where clients access and connect with and contact with emotions may help clients progress in therapy and improve from depression. It may take more sessions for clients in poor outcome therapy to connect with emotions nondefensively. The greater emotion at end for poor clients might tie to greater defensiveness as well. This pattern may function differently for long-term clients.
	Acheson et al. (2020), PM	Case 1 adolescent with depression in PAT (who remained the most depressed of the cases examined): decreasing obstructive silences and small increase in productive silence—interpreted as a more gradually lowering of defenses than the more recovered cases. (−)	
	Daniel et al. (2018), PM	Two significant outcome group and treatment phase interactions were found in which (a) the relative frequency of productive pauses was greater with good outcome clients in the early and especially the middle phase of PDT (+), whereas poor outcome clients surpassed the good outcome clients in these pauses within the end phase of treatment; and (b) the proportion of obstructive pauses was higher in early, mid, and especially the ending phase of poor outcome therapy than in the good outcome cases.	
	Hill et al. (2019), PM	Good outcome PDT long-term client was equally reflective (=), less disengaged (−), and more emotional in silences in last 5 sessions than in the first 5 sessions.	
Termination: Obstructive silences appear to increase when clients are more ambivalent about termination.	Acheson et al. (2020), PM	Case 2 adolescent with depression in PAT: Increasing obstructive and decreasing productive silences at the end phase appeared associated with ambivalence and withdrawal from attachment at termination. (−)	(−) A new pattern of longer silences near termination may indicate concerns about termination, and it can be helpful to ask about the content of these pauses or inquire about clients' feelings around termination.

EFT, emotion-focused therapy; PAT, psychoanalytic therapy; PDT, psychodynamic therapy; PM, process measure study; QL, qualitative study.

Table 11.7 Therapists' Observation of Processes in Pauses That Influence Immediate Outcomes

Findings Organized in Categories	Study	Study Details	Linking the Silent Processes to Therapist Responses and Outcomes (+, –, or =)
Relational immediate outcomes of pauses	Hill et al. (2003), QTS	Licensed therapists (81) with varied orientations indicated their agreement with reasons for pauses, suggesting that pauses supported the relationship. (+)	Therapists reported that they used silences to create client perceptions of empathy, respect, and support in order to facilitate immediate gains (e.g., nurturance, acceptance) and the conditions tied to positive outcomes generally. (+)
	Ladany et al. (2004), QL	Therapists (12) with varied orientations in this study led to the finding that enhancement of the relationship was a reason for using or breaking silence and its influence on therapy. (+)	
Clients' reflection immediate outcomes	Hill et al. (2003), QTS	Licensed therapists with varied orientations indicated that pauses supported client reflection. (+)	Therapists reported that they engaged in silences to increase client reflection in order to generate immediate gains (e.g., insight) and promote positive outcomes. (+)
	Ladany et al. (2004), QL	Therapists with varied orientations reported that client reflection was a reason for using or breaking silence and its influence on therapy. (+)	
Immediate outcomes regarding clients' engagement	Hill et al. (2003), QTS	Licensed therapists with varied orientations indicated that client engagement was supported by the use of pauses. (+)	Therapists reported that they used silent processes to increase client responsibility and engagement in the therapeutic process, in order to facilitate immediate outcomes (e.g., responsibility for self) and generally positive outcomes. (+)
	Ladany et al. (2004), QL	Therapists with varied orientations reported that client engagement was a reason for using or breaking silence and its influence on therapy. (+)	
Immediate outcomes regarding clients' emotionality	Hill et al. (2003), QTS	Licensed therapists with varied orientations indicated that pauses supported client emotional experience. (+)	Therapists reported that they supported silences to help clients contact and explore emotions, in an effort to reach immediate positive outcomes (identification of emotion) as well as positive outcome. (+)
	Ladany et al. (2004), QL	Therapists with varied orientations indicated that gains in emotionality were a reason for using or breaking silence and its influence on therapy. (+)	

Immediate outcomes regarding clients' disengagement or withdrawal	Hill et al. (2003), QTS	Licensed therapists with varied orientations indicated that pauses can occur due to client disengagement. (–)	Therapists reported that they used silences to help clients face avoided issues, in an effort to reduce immediate negative outcomes (e.g., stopping avoidance) as well as to further positive outcome. (–)
	Ladany et al. (2004), QL	Therapists with varied orientations reported that client disengagement was a reason why silence occurs in therapy. (–)	
Immediate outcomes regarding therapists' capacity to assess clients and form interventions	Hill et al. (2003), QTS	Licensed therapists with varied orientations indicated that pauses allowed them time for forming interventions and for assessing clients' state. (+)	Therapists reported that they engaged in silences to formulate responses or assessments of clients, which they thought would provide the immediate gain of better understanding the process and support good outcome generally. (+)
	Ladany et al. (2004), QL	Therapists with varied orientations reported that pauses allowed them time for forming interventions tailored for clients. (+)	
Immediate outcomes regarding unproductive silences	Hill et al. (2003), QTS	Licensed therapists with varied orientations agreed that silences can engage negative processes. (–)	Therapists reported that unproductive silences should be interrupted or they can lead to negative outcomes. (–)
	Ladany et al. (2004), QL	Therapists with varied orientations reported that silences can have a negative influence on therapy. (–)	

QL, qualitative study; QTS, quantitative survey study.

Table 11.8 Therapists' Activity During Pauses That Influences Clients' Pausing Processes and Psychotherapy Immediate Outcomes

Findings Organized in Categories	Study	Study Details	Linking the Silent Processes to Therapist Responses and Outcomes (+, –, or =)
Emotional silences: Emotional client silences can be predicted by therapists' activity.	Hill et al. (2019), PM	Emotional silences more likely following therapists' connectional behavior but less after invitational behavior. (+)	(+) To stimulate emotional connection, therapists appeared to use empathic reflections and paraphrases rather than direct questioning, and rather than cognitive processing.
Reflective silences: Reflective client silences can be predicted by therapists' activity.	Hill et al. (2019), PM	Reflective silences more likely following therapists' invitational behavior but less after connectional behavior. (+)	(+) This is the reverse of the earlier finding about emotional pauses. Therapists stimulated cognitive processing, rather than emotional connection, by using invitations or questions to examine an issue.
Disengaged silences: Disengaged client silences may be predicted by therapists' invitational activity.	Hill et al. (2019), PM	Disengaged silences more likely following therapists' invitational behavior but less after connectional behavior. (–)	(–) To avoid disengagement, therapists appeared to use more empathic reflections and paraphrases that facilitate connection with clients rather than direct questioning.
Proportion of therapists' silence activities: Therapists' activity (four codes based on Bartels et al.'s [2016] strength of connection scale: connectional, invitational, neutral, or disengaged) was mostly invitational and then connectional.	Hill et al. (2019), PM	"The psychodynamic therapist's behavior during silence events was invitational 68%, connectional 21%, reflective 5%, neutral 4%, and disengaged 1% of the time" (p. 582).	(+) Therapists' silences appear to be used for productive purposes much more often than they occur for unproductive purposes. Invitational pauses were common across the therapies. The use of neutral pauses and reflective pauses may benefit from more research. Developing an awareness of these processes can allow therapists to self-reflect on their own pausing processes.
	Cuttler et al. (2019), PM	The psychodynamic therapists' behaviors during silence events were productive 66.3% of the time (connectional 6.8% and invitational 60.5%) and unproductive 33.7% of the time (neutral 20.9%, reflective 10.5%, disengaged 2.3%).	
	Tindall & Robinson (1947), PM	In client-centered transcripts, therapists' pauses were distributed as: deliberate (like invitational) 29.6%, organizational (like reflective) 53.1%, and normal (these appear to combine reflective and neutral associational pauses) 17.3%.	

PM, process measure study.

Table 11.9 Therapists' Activity at Pauses That Influences Client Collaboration

Findings Organized in Categories	Study	Study Details	Linking the Silent Processes to Therapist Responses and Outcomes (+, −, or =)
Client collaboration: Productive therapist activity (invitational or connectional) was associated with greater client collaboration.	Hill et al. (2019), PM	At the silence level and session level, there was higher client collaboration after pauses when therapists were more likely than typical to be either invitational or connectional. (+)	(+) Seeing that therapists are attentive and inquiring during silences appears related to greater engagement from clients' post-silence, making a difference especially with secure clients.
	Cuttler et al. (2019), PM	Productive therapist activity (mostly invitational) during silences was associated with greater client collaboration after the silences, especially for clients who had less attachment anxiety (vs. more). (+)	

PM, process measure study.

at the end of sessions when collaboration was highest, this finding might have been obscured (Hill et al., 2019). Reflective silences were associated with increased collaboration in a case study (Hill et al., 2019), but this was not replicated in a multi-case study (Cuttler et al., 2019).

Together with the findings in the prior section, this research has demonstrated that there are pausing processes that clients experience that are associated with varied psychotherapy outcomes. Productive pauses are associated with good micro-outcomes (e.g., increased expressive capacity, emotional attunement, insight), as well as positive therapy outcomes (e.g., fewer depressive symptoms, collaboration), and obstructive pauses are associated with poor micro-outcomes (e.g., withdrawal, relational rifts, confusion) and therapy outcomes (e.g., more depressive symptoms, negative emotions, negative self-appraisal). Given this finding, it behooves therapists to learn to differentiate types of pauses so that they can engage responsively with clients by supporting the occurrence of productive pauses and by intervening to disrupt and examine obstructive pauses. And indeed, research suggests that therapists are seeking to differentiate silences (see Table 11.7). Research on these cues to differentiate types of silences is the focus of the next sections.

Cues to Differentiating Productive Pauses from Obstructive Pauses

Alliance, and Sometimes Attachment This section reviews the research examining the relationship between clients' silent processes with client attachment style and alliance

Table 11.10 Hierarchy of Findings for Extended Silences

Cluster Title and No. of Studies That Contributed (of 16)	Category Title	No. of Studies That Contributed (of 16)
Cluster 1: Silence as a Cocoon: Clients enter prolonged silence to conjure a sense of safety and coherence amid reenactment of relational pain (16).	Category 1.1: Silence as a shield that serves as a guardian of the self and protects against trauma repetition in the therapy relationship.	14
	Category 1.2: Clients resorted to extended silence when they did not experience the resources or relational modeling to make their experiences intelligible to another.	9
Cluster 2: Beyond Words: Extended silences communicate clients' wishes, needs, and experiences in need of integration and acceptance (16).	Category 2.1: Extended silence as signifying desire for communion and containment of intolerable experiences.	11
	Category 2.2: Extended silence as invoking reverie and conveying experiences that escape words.	11
	Category 2.3: Silence as reexperiencing aggression and contempt about authority figures, from the client's life, with the therapist.	11
Cluster 3: Exiting the silent period occurred successfully when therapists affirmed and supported clients' integration of previously indescribable experiences (13).	Category 3.1: Extended silence ended when trust and connection are established, and the therapist's motive is understood as empowering clients' self-understanding.	7
	Category 3.2: Silence may be used to resolve clients' reexperiencing when pain is reworked toward healthy autonomy and self-organization, but if the client's process goes unsupported, stagnation may result.	12

Core Category: The "Silent Cure": Extended silences as generative of healing transformation (16)

(see Table 11.3). Issues with attachment appeared related to obstructive pauses. More obstructive pauses occurred for clients with dismissing attachment styles compared to secure or preoccupied clients in CBT. However, this finding did not hold when examining psychoanalytic or psychodynamic approaches to therapy (Cuttler et al., 2019; Daniel et al., 2018), perhaps because securely attached clients in CBT paused less often. This finding may be because psychoeducation and learning strategies may be used more routinely in CBT than experiential and introspective exploratory processes (Levitt & Williams, 2010), making it more difficult for these therapists to process silent obstructive dynamics. Also, obstructive silences have been interpreted as reflecting the dynamics of therapy with adolescents, who may be in a transitional stage of negotiating attachment, and as reflecting ambivalence about termination (Acheson et al., 2020). In another study, the frequency of obstructive pauses explained part of the association between insecure attachment and the therapeutic alliance in psychoanalytic therapy; it was unclear if this relationship held for CBT because the model did not converge (Daniel et al., 2018). Understanding these dynamics can allow therapists to better differentiate when obstructive silences are occurring in their therapies so as to skillfully intervene to address alliance and attachment issues (as described in Levitt, 2001b).

Proportions and Durations of Pauses Noticing patterns in the proportion and duration of pauses can support therapists in identifying types of silences and responding skillfully (see Table 11.4). The meta-analytic findings suggested that most silences tend to be productive. However, the proportion of obstructive silences varied considerably (from 11.2% to 69.1%) and was markedly higher in a study of psychoanalytic therapy with adolescents than that of neutral pauses (Daniel et al., 2018).

Although two studies did not find that the duration of pauses differed in relation to the pausing processes experienced by clients (Cuttler et al., 2019; Hill et al., 2019), two found that obstructive (especially interactional) pauses were lengthier (Daniel et al., 2018; Levitt, 2001b). Therefore, it appears that duration is not a cue that is useful to distinguish most pauses, but it may be a useful cue for interactive pauses (i.e., when clients stop because they are confused by therapists or worried about being judged). Distinguishing clients' silent processes can allow therapists to inquire into and process the contents of these pauses, a process that qualitative research has associated with transforming negative outcomes of these pauses (confusion, relational rift) to positive outcomes (e.g., insight, relational trust; e.g., Levitt, 2001b). In contrast, therapists' activities during silences (using the SCS) did not appear to be associated with the duration of silences (Cuttler et al., 2019; Hill et al., 2019).

Placement of Pauses Between Speaker Turns Speech turn patterns also can aid therapists in the method of distinguishing types of silences (see Table 11.5). Most productive silences occurred within client speech turns (rather than between speakers or during therapists' speech), which suggests that clients were using the silences to further their exploration rather than to be obstructive or resistant (Daniel et al., 2018). Disengaged pauses tended to occur between client and therapist speech turns, suggesting that clients stopped after approaching a threatening topic, after which the therapist intervened to provide support. This dynamic is supported by research on therapists' experiences of pauses; this research suggested that therapists will interrupt pauses when they see the process as unproductive (Ladany et al., 2004). In contrast, interactional pauses were most likely to occur following therapists' speech, perhaps indicating that the therapists' communication was interpreted by clients as confusing or upsetting, which led to a pause.

Therapists have been found to use pauses to formulate or reformulate their interventions (Ladany et al., 2004), and this may be especially likely when a silence is recognized as an interactional pause in order to avoid a relational rupture. An ability to differentiate these types of silences can increase therapists' sensitivity to types of silences and may help them respond in a manner to support clients to sustain productive silent moments and to intervene during obstructive ones (evidence that they actively do this is presented in Table 11.7).

Trajectory of Clients' Silences As therapists seek to differentiate silent processes to improve their therapy, cues about the trajectory of silences may assist them (see Table 11.6). Emotional pauses were found to be higher at the beginning of good outcome emotion-focused therapy (EFTcompared to poor outcome EFT (Frankel et al., 2006). In varied poor outcome therapies, emotional pauses were found to be higher at the end (compared to good outcome therapies: Daniel et al., 2018; Frankel et al., 2006; Hill et al., 2019). This strong finding, replicated in three process measure studies, appeared to demonstrate that the poor outcome clients may take longer to develop emotional processing skills that good outcome clients already had at the beginning of treatment. In contrast, in psychoanalytic therapy, the proportion of obstructive pauses was higher in the early, mid, and especially the ending phase of poor outcome therapy than in the good outcome cases (Daniel et al., 2018). Understanding these patterns can lead to stronger identification of pausing processes.

Therapists' Experiences of In-Dialogue Silences

Based on the research presented in the prior section on clients' experiences of silences, it appears that there are specific types of silence that are differentially associated with immediate, proximal, and distal therapy outcomes and that clients provide evidence that therapists attuned interventions facilitate good outcome. This section reviews research evidence that therapists are not only actively differentiating types of pausing experiences but also agree that these moments facilitate varied forms of productive micro-outcomes. Whereas most clients' pauses signified either the processing of their own experience or an obstacle to processing, most therapists' pauses appear to be intentional and meant to guide or influence the client's process and outcome or to strengthen the relationship (Hill et al., 2003).

Therapists' Observations of Pausing Processes and Immediate Outcomes

Table 11.7 presents findings from a survey and a qualitative study (Hill et al., 2003; Ladany et al., 2004), both of which asked therapists about their experiences of silences and the influence of silences. These studies provide information on how silence influences outcome that is grounded in therapist expertise as a valuable source of information about outcome and as a confirming perspective on the evidence based on clients' reports of how outcome and silent processes are linked. These studies demonstrated that therapists thoughtfully observed how silences influenced their clients and that they used silences to either improve clients' immediate outcomes or provide time for themselves to assess clients or shape interventions. They engaged silences in this manner because their experience indicated that it would provide "conditions that would facilitate the therapeutic work" (Ladany et al., 2004, p. 83)—in other words, they engaged in these silent processes because their clinical expertise indicated that they contributed toward good outcomes. Future research can continue to explore these links.

In the qualitative analysis (Ladany et al., 2004), pauses were most often described by therapists as a way to convey empathy, respect, and support or to facilitate clients' expression of feelings. In order to prevent misinterpretations of silence, therapists reported educating clients about silences in therapy in order to normalize pausing so that clients would increase their introspection and positive gains. Also, therapists described using silence less often with clients who might interpret silence critically, such as with clients who were dangerous to themselves, overwhelmed, had a distorted sense of reality, or who were from families who weaponized silence because, presumably, they thought they would be less effective or hinder positive outcome. In this research, therapists reported that if they were unsure of how a silence was being experienced or thought it was unproductive, they tended to break the silence to inquire with the client about their experience. This research suggests the utility of providing cues to differentiate silent processes to support therapists' ability to respond skillfully.

Therapists' Activity During Pauses and Psychotherapy Immediate Outcomes via Productive and Obstructive Client Processes

This section reviews research using the SCS measure that examined therapists' activities at silent moments and their relation with the productive and obstructive pauses identified in the PICS (which were shown to be tied to both outcomes and immediate outcomes earlier in this chapter as well). It provides evidence that therapists engage in behaviors that influence clients' pausing processes and whether they are associated with good or poor outcomes. Clients' emotional silences were found to be more likely to follow therapists' connectional behavior and less likely to follow invitational behavior (Hill et al., 2019), suggesting that empathic reflection, rather than questioning, was more likely to lead to emotional processing (see Table 11.8). The reverse was found with reflective and disengaged silences, which were more likely to follow questioning. These findings suggest that disengaged silences might follow after clients were invited (i.e., therapists' invitational behavior) to consider threatening issues, so clients were less likely to engage in emotional processing at these times. Although this is only one study, it makes an important contribution by indicating how therapists' activities facilitate client's productive or obstructive pausing processes.

These findings can be especially insightful when considering that across three studies examining the proportion of therapists' activities during pauses, therapists' invitational activities were commonly used (Cuttler et al., 2019; Hill et al., 2019; Tindall & Robinson, 1947), suggesting that therapists are often using pauses to stimulate reflective behavior and insight, although disengagement might sometimes result.

Therapists' Activity at Pauses and Psychotherapy Outcomes: Client Collaboration

Productive therapist activity (both invitational and connectional silences) was associated with greater client collaboration (Cuttler et al., 2019; Hill et al., 2019). This pattern suggested that therapists' deliberate use of pauses was effective in engaging clients in the change process (see Table 11.9). Clients' attachment style, however, was not associated with therapists' pausing activity (Cuttler et al., 2019), indicating that therapists' pausing strategies were used similarly across a range of clients with varied relational histories.

Review of Extended Silences and Their Association with Immediate Outcomes

In this section, we review the qualitative findings on extended silences in therapy. Sixteen of the research studies featured periods or entire sessions of therapy characterized by prolonged silence, sometimes spanning months or years. The phenomenon of extended silence is one of the most perplexing and unsettling experiences for therapists (e.g., Brown, 1987; Lane et al., 2002). One therapist described it (Brown, 1987):

> If only she [client] would speak! Why is she doing this to me? Why is she angry at me? . . . Is it possible that only twenty-four minutes have elapsed since we entered into this excruciatingly loud silence? . . . Who's in the hot seat, anyway? . . . I find myself wishing for a fire drill, or maybe just a fire. . . . How can she torture me like this? (pp. 126–127)

These extended silences are related to in-dialogue pauses in that they contain important and meaningful processes, yet they are distinct in that they are not categorizable by the same measures and in-session contextual cues. As such, they required a separate qualitative meta-analysis.

It is vital that clinicians develop the skills to understand and respond to the underlying messages of enduring silences, particularly given they sometimes comprised the bulk of what occurred in session. Indeed, our findings demonstrated that it would be a mistake to assume that sessions shrouded by silence indicate that the client has nothing to express. To the contrary, we found that extended silences contained distinct meanings relevant to clients' capacity to express pain, engage in relationship (including the therapy relationship), enact unresolved grief, and work through trauma. The cases consistently suggest that developing the skills to identify and respond to the processes underlying prolonged silences is vital to resolving the silence itself and to enhancing therapy outcomes.

Approximately half (16) of the articles identified in our research review (see Figure 11.1) explored prolonged silence in psychotherapy. All 16 studies utilized a case study method to examine silence in a psychoanalytic psychotherapy. Given this, the therapies included in this analysis mostly were scheduled twice weekly and occurred over a multiyear treatment course. In most cases, the silent period resolved within a year but in at least three cases (9%), the therapy was marked by a year or more of little or no speech. A sizable proportion of the studies on prolonged silences (8; 24%) featured adolescent clients. All studies were written from the clinician's psychoanalytic and first-person perspective.

We have used separate terms to differentiate the levels of our hierarchical analysis. Extended silences were captured across these studies by three *clusters*, which contained seven *categories*. Table 11.10 presents the hierarchy organization of findings. Each category is accompanied by a description of attendant therapeutic skills used to understand and address prolonged silences.

Results of this qualitative meta-analysis demonstrated that therapists typically sought to conceptualize the function and meaning of these silences to effectively respond and enhance outcomes. Our findings underscored that silence functioned as part of how clients experienced and worked through unresolved pain and arrested development toward healthy integration and growth. Crucial to the successful resolution of extended silences (see Cluster 3) were therapists' skills in recognizing, understanding, and identifying clients' experiences that triggered and sustained the enduring silence (see Clusters 1 and 2).

Cluster 1: Silence as a Cocoon

The first cluster described the skill of conceptualizing prolonged silence alongside clients' histories of unresolved loss, relational pain, or trauma. In all (16) studies, therapists identified that extended silence in therapy arose with clients who experienced painful relational events, particularly with primary attachment figures (e.g., death of a parent, experiences of physical or emotional abandonment, sexual trauma, or harsh messages about their inadequacy). Thus, therapists worked to conceptualize silence as their clients' return to a critical developmental-stage conflict to address and integrate unresolved loss and emotional pain. The two categories within this section describe how therapists used this understanding of extended silence as a regression toward enhancing a specific therapy outcome: building a healthier self and relational capacity. Although some clients entered therapy for reasons related to their silence and withdrawal in external relationships (e.g., Cristy, 1993; Gensler, 2015; Hadda, 1991), many fell silent some time into the therapy process. Therapists identified how silence was prompted by recent life events (e.g., career demotion; see, e.g., Ronningstam, 2006) that provoked or triggered past experiences of loss and inadequacy.

Category 1.1: Silence as a Shield That Serves as a Guardian of the Self and Protects Against Trauma Repetition in the Therapy Relationship

Findings from almost all (14) of the studies described how some clients entered into prolonged silence as a way to protect themselves, contextualized by clients' histories of unresolved emotional pain. One function of prolonged silence that therapists identified was as the client's attempts to install a buffer against intolerable fears of abandonment, fragmentation, rejection pain, and being hurt. Understanding clients' retreat away from expressing unmet needs, feelings, or desires when they arose in therapy guided therapists in responding to clients' experiences rather than reenacting their being stifled.

Silence was conceptualized as a guardian of the client's self (Ronningstam, 2006), deployed to protect their inner space, integrity, and self-processing. Prolonged silence was a way for clients to exercise control or agency in relationship, which sometimes involved denying or delaying experiences and emotions that did yet feel amenable to integration (Weisman, 1955). Analyst scholars interpreted clients' movement into silence and withdrawal as a potent tool "to redress the problem that if speaking has led to faulty assumptions about being known, then speaking is not safe. Speaking is also sometimes unconsciously equated with aggressive action" (Cooper, 2012, p. 913). Cristy (1993) articulated a similar interpretation to explain a client's entry into silence: "I imagined that she was afraid she would devour me if she talked (e.g., if she opened her mouth). Or that she was afraid I might devour her if she did not keep some distance with her silence" (p. 189). However, Leira (1995) referenced Winnicott (1956) who said, "The early building up of the ego is (therefore) silent" (p. 304) to express that extended silence might naturally be generative for ego development toward healthier relating.

Understanding extended silence as a way for clients to protect their agency could assist therapists in employing interventions that identify, respect, and honor clients' autonomy while also increasing clients' awareness of their discomfort, painful loss, or unresolved affect related to the extended silence. However, it was difficult for therapists to be skillful when helplessness and hostility were projected onto them or evoked within them in response to clients' prolonged silence. Less constructive outcomes appeared to result when the analyst felt like the helpless child and the patient assumed the role of withholding or abandoning other (Khan & Masud, 1963). It was important for therapists to recognize this impasse and avoid succumbing to it. For instance, rather than foregoing an opportunity to understand the meaning of the prolonged silence within clients' relational history, some therapists responded by demonstrating empathic attunement (Hadda, 1991) and worked to instill trust within the relationship through self-disclosure and meta-communication interventions (Gensler, 2015).

Category 1.2: Clients Resorted to Extended Silence When They Did Not Have the Resources Nor the Relational Modeling to Make Their Experiences Intelligible to Another

Another cause of entry into extended silences was that clients simply did not know what to say or how to express their experiences. Just over half (nine) of the studies contributed to this category. Numerous cases with adults (Kurtz, 1984; Ronningstam, 2006; Serani, 2000; Weisman, 1955) detailed clients' inability or unwillingness to express themselves verbally when respectful reciprocal relationships had not been experienced nor modeled in their lives. Clients may have felt overshadowed, stifled, or subsumed by the needs of a dominant other (Hadda, 1991).

Indeed, entry into an extended silence as a reenactment of prior oppression might also reveal areas of needed support. Kurtz (1984) recounted the loneliness that accompanied this same client's prolonged silence, sharing that she had once uttered, "Sometimes I am silent because I am completely alone, like a prisoner on the moon" (p. 235). In addition, clients' histories sometimes featured silence as a form of expression that contained a multitude of meanings, such as both aggression and comfort, in the case of a client who was raised by a mother who was deaf and for whom silence was familiar (Serani, 2000; Ronningstam, 2006).

Therapists worked to recognize when and how clients needed support around understanding and verbalizing their experiences, particularly those of disempowerment, abandonment, and the risk entailed in connection. They modeled openness and vulnerability by expressing their own needs for help and wishes to connect with the patient amid the silence. Therapists sometimes empathically interpreted the silence, which enabled patients to then verbalize their affect and experiences contained within the silence (e.g., Greene, 1982). Modeling and making intelligible clients' experiences nonjudgmentally aided them in the ultimate resolution of the extended silence when clients' feelings and experiences became comprehensible, reassured, and less threatening.

Cluster 2: Beyond Words: Extended Silences Communicate Clients' Wishes, Needs, and Experiences in Need of Integration and Acceptance

This second cluster highlighted how therapists conceptualized the enduring function of the "silent period" (Anagnostaki, 2013, p. 156). Determining the function of the silent period was key to understanding why it was sustained and how it could be addressed and resolved. Results from all 16 studies contributed to this cluster. The length of the silent periods and the amount of speech interspersed throughout them varied widely (e.g., in the most extreme case, complete silence lasted approximately 3 years in four-times-weekly analysis with a preadolescent client; see Anagnostaki, 2013).

Category 2.1: Extended Silence as Signifying Desire for Communion and Containment of Intolerable Experiences

Of the 16 studies about extended silence, 11 included therapists' views that silence provided clues about clients' desires and fantasies, such as wishes to be mirrored (Hadda, 1991) and accepted. Silence, although an attempt to protect against the traumatic dissolution of the self (Category 1.1), also signified clients' wishes to experience safety in relationship. Therapists sometimes conceptualized the silence as an experience of merging subject–object duality. For instance, they referred to a "therapeutic symbiosis" (Cristy, 1993, p. 186), "primordial unity" (Serani, 2000, p. 517), "fusion" (Pugh, 1997, p. 283), and to Winnicott's (1965) concept of "being alone in the presence of the mother" (Pugh, 1997, p. 287). Winnicott's concept was invoked to understand the paradox of how silence could function as the clients' attempt at being alone while in the presence of another. Clients sought to discover and clarify their unique experiences after not being able to do so in past relationships.

Prolonged silence functioned to preserve the possibility of being loved when clients felt speech to be too risky or futile (Kurtz, 1984). Indeed, silences revealed clients' hope. In them, clients attempted to create a more safe and loving connection in the face of their fears (e.g., inadequacy, abandonment; see Category 1.1). Upon conceptualizing prolonged silence in this way, therapists could accept, respond, and provide clients' underlying needs for safety in the therapeutic relationship. Therefore, therapists attempted to provide such a holding environment, using mirroring interventions meant to support the client's need for healthy individuation. As Hadda (1991) articulated about her client,

> She was able to be silent with me because she had learned that I would be accepting of the silence and of her. Moreover, she could rely on the fact that I would not punish her for her autonomous adventures by abandoning her. (p. 122)

Hadda saw silence as "an indicator of the need for a calm, accepting environment, free from demands that she [as in, the client] fulfil a requirement on my part that she speak" (p. 127).

However, although silence may have preserved the hope of safe communion, it sometimes obstructed it from occurring when the early object loss was reenacted (Greene, 1982; Zeligs, 1960). To avoid re-creating the painful loss, therapists had to skillfully discern if the silence represented clients' rejection of the analyst to avoid incurring pain and to temper destructive fantasies. In these cases, silence functioned to deny clients the chance to experience reconciliation, obstructing successful outcomes (Ronningstam, 2006). Therapists analyzed contextual clues, such as triggers of the silence and clients' nonverbal behavior, to identify whether clients were withdrawing from relationship or exercising their agency with creative attempts at safe communion.

Category 2.2: Extended Silence as Invoking Reverie to Convey Experiences That Escape Words

Findings articulated that silence sometimes was maintained because clients were unable to verbalize experiences (e.g., pain, loss; see Greene, 1982) that eluded symbolization through speech. Therapists from 11 studies observed clients attempting to express their experiences, even when they were not amenable to symbolization through speech. As Fuller and Crowther (1998) summarized, "Our patients made pre-symbolic use of us which speech would have disturbed" (p. 540). For example, therapists observed other ways that clients communicated, such as by drawing (Pugh, 1997), using nonverbal signs or gestures (Serani, 2000; Zeligs, 1960), positioning their body and their location in the space (Anagnostaki, 2013), posture (Khan & Masud, 1963), and play (Cristy, 1993; Leira, 1995). By conceptualizing what clients were attempting to symbolize, therapists could convey interest in the clients' lived experiences and foster understanding in the relationship.

Toward resolving prolonged silence, therapists sought to identify their own experiences within the transference–countertransference dynamic. They drew from psychoanalytic theory to interpret silence as containing possible projective experiences. For example, Ronningstam (2006) wrote the following:

> Susan's silence was more profound and existential and, to my surprise, I noticed that I continued to feel present, curious and creative. That contrasted to my experiences of silence with some of my other patients with whom I could feel empty, constricted, numb, or dreadfully bored. (p. 1286)

Therapists attended to experiences of reverie and images to unveil how silence could be communicating clients' mood and affect experientially and intersubjectively. Sometimes, clients and therapists were able to identify what was occurring in the silent period, such as when Leira (1995) shared,

> I asked him once at the beginning of this period how it felt to be sitting there without saying a word. He said it felt very important and that a lot was happening inside him for which he did not have words. It felt good just not to say anything even though he felt awful. He said the sessions were very important. So we continued sitting there, in silence. (p. 50)

The understanding of prolonged silence in psychotherapy was described as a vehicle for connection and as contributive to therapeutic growth enabled therapists to manage frustrations when they could not easily identify what clients wished to symbolize. Protracted silence functioned to provide a sanctuary for retreat, during which clients grappled with expressing themselves. This understanding enabled therapists to convey interest and determination to understanding and accepting clients, which they reported deepened the therapy process and accelerated good outcome (Hadda, 1991).

Category 2.3: Silence as Reexperiencing Aggression and Contempt About Authority Figures from the Client's Life with the Therapist

Eleven studies depicted cases in which prolonged silence included anger and aggression directed toward the therapist. Therapists interpreted these contemptuous feelings as connected to other relationships in the client's life because it highlighted how the function of silence was related to clients' unresolved pain experience. For example, therapists viewed clients to resort to silence when they feared regressing into verbalizing feelings of hostility, which risked inducing subsequent abandonment and guilt feelings.

On the one hand, clients' use of extended silence might instead re-create their sense of shame, powerlessness, and inadequacy. On the other hand, clients might wield sadness to exercise agency and identify with the aggressor to protect oneself from injury. As one therapist described, "Little by little, I understood that he was repeating the transference, thorough the reversal of roles . . . with a mother who, for many reasons, had been inaccessible to him and whom he had experienced as remote and indifferent" (Leira, 1995, p. 58). In these cases, clients withdrew from the encounter through silence rather than being rejected and hurt by another's withdrawal. This understanding of silence informed therapists' attunement to clients' aggression, enabling them to effectively engage in identifying and holding the feelings that clients had deemed intolerable to them or threatening to the relationship. This enhanced successful resolution of the silence by addressing the unresolved conflicts that catalyzed it. Clients' fears of abandonment, judgment, or rejection were mitigated by therapists' responses.

Cluster 3: Exiting the Silent Period Occurred Successfully When Therapists Affirmed and Supported Clients' Integration of Previously Indescribable Experiences

The final cluster illustrated the potential contributive outcomes of prolonged silence, particularly when therapists could identify their function in therapy and address clients' needs. It detailed how therapists supported clients to clarify their experiences through speech. First, therapists had to be attuned to clients' ineffable and intolerable experiences in order to cultivate safety within the therapy relationship and guide clients' expression. This cluster included 13 studies, some of which described how therapists used silence as an intervention in response.

Category 3.1: Extended Silence Resolved When Trust and Connection Were Established, and the Therapist's Motive Was Understood as Empowering Clients' Self-Understanding

Almost half (seven) of the studies discussed therapists' responses to prolonged silence and the importance of allowing time for clients to understand that their agency and need for silence would be respected. Therapists aimed to convey interest and attunement to clients' unique processes. Some used silence or reflection interventions to support clients in identify, making meaning, and symbolizing their own processes effectively. In particular, when clients' prolonged silences were experienced as generative, therapists' silence could express solidarity and support. At other times, therapists' silence in response to clients' silence could appear retaliatory if clients perceived the therapist as being hostile. Therefore, interspersing observational and reflective comments in the shared silence could convey to clients that the therapist was participating, yet supportive of clients' wish to maintain separateness. Alternatively, therapists identified that uncovering interpretation interventions risked being experienced as reproachful to clients.

Indeed, therapists were tasked with responding to clients' paradoxical desires to be in communion and yet affirm clients' self and experiences. Kurtz (1984) presented case material that depicted one client's experience of their analyst's silence:

> After two and a half years Melissa said, "When you say nothing, I feel terribly alone and I begin to withdraw into myself. But when you speak, I feel controlled and angry,

> especially if I think you're not understanding me and are just pleasing yourself. But I have another way of feeling now which is newer and more tentative where I'm neither abandoned nor overwhelmed—just with you. You're silent but you're there, or you're speaking and I'm not overpowered. I would like to be there more but I can't be sure of it yet." (p. 230)

Therapists' silences across these seven studies varied, but each case represented an attempt by the therapist to respond to the client's unique wishes and needs. Therapists aimed to affirm to the client that they could safely engage in reworking pain and self-understanding in the presence of another. This process was in service of the outcome of a healthier and relational self who is capable of effectively symbolizing experiences in relationship.

Category 3.2: Silence May Be Resolved When Pain Is Reworked Toward Healthy Autonomy and Self-Organization, but if the Clients' Silent Process Goes Unsupported, Stagnation May Result

Most (12) studies described a process of exiting from enduring periods of silence. Some therapists articulated that this resolution was marked by the analyst's support of clients' psychosocial developmental process and its reenactment through silence. This outcome was accomplished in therapy when the relational dynamic affirmed and supported clients' integration of experiences without overpromising fusion in the therapy relationship. Exiting the extended silence was achieved when the client developed a capacity to express their experiences, as in the following case detailed by Ronningstam (2006):

> In the end of what I defined as the "silent phase," Susan was able to identify an inner experience and accompanying feelings and convey this in her verbal interaction and relationship to me. She had begun to feel, tolerate and process her affects and to process inner psychological conflicts, and she was on her way to becoming the owner of her own feelings. (p. 1291)

This metamorphosis was contingent upon whether clients' extended silence in the encounter ultimately functioned within the therapy dyad to express or guard a healthy developmental progression of increased self-awareness. Indeed, if therapists allowed silence to shield the client indefinitely, or merged with the clients' beliefs and wishes, then the therapy process could remain stagnant, maintaining client's undifferentiated emotions and unresolved emotional pain.

Core Category: The "Silent Cure": Extended Silences as Generative of Healing Transformation

All 16 studies about extended silence contributed to the core finding of this qualitative meta-analysis. Although prolonged silence in psychotherapy was particularly difficult and distressing for therapists, these findings demonstrated that there were ways to understand the function of extended silence (Clusters 1 and 2) such that it could inform the course of therapy and its successful outcome (Cluster 3). Silence was found to contain within it underlying processes that represented clients' blocked needs (Cluster 2). Understanding extended silence as a creative form of client expression enabled therapists to empathically tailor the process to address these blocks while respecting clients' capacities, agency, and growth edges (Clusters 1, 2, and 3, respectively).

Possible Negative Effects and Harm

Obstructive silences are moments in which clients withdraw from the relationship, avoid pressing issues, become confused, or disengage from therapeutic tasks. They have been associated with poor outcomes (Daniel et al., 2018; Frankel et al., 2006; Stringer et al., 2010) and with poorer alliances (Daniel et al., 2018). Clients report that these obstructive pauses can be tense, awkward, or overwhelming (e.g., Acheson et al., 2020; Stringer et al., 2010; Tindall & Robinson, 1947). Clients have reported, however, that even though these moments halt the therapeutic process, their close examination may allow the psychotherapy to move deeper and eventually reach positive outcomes (e.g., Blos, 1972; Bravesmith, 2012; Leira, 1995; Levitt, 2001a).

Research has indicated that therapists are more apprehensive about permitting long or frequent silences when working with clients who may interpret silences as judgmental. These clients include those with histories of feeling criticized, rejected, paranoid, psychotic, highly disturbed, or those with personality disorders (Hill et al., 2003). Silences in these cases were thought to interfere with the development of a strong therapeutic relationship.

Limitations of the Research

The current meta-analytic review has advanced the previous narrative review (Levitt & Morrill, 2021) by examining extended silences and including more recent studies, although it did not admit unpublished results or non-English literature. Limitations include that some silent processes have only been examined in a few studies. As a result, future researchers may wish to reexamine the questions assessed here to assess the robustness of findings. A pressing question is how to assess silences within the therapy dialogue and understand them in relation to what clients and therapists experience as change processes and therapy outcomes.

Other prominent limitations include that there are relatively few research studies examining the relation between therapist skill in dealing with silences and treatment outcomes (immediate, proximal, and distal). Although there is strong qualitative evidence on clients' and therapists' processes during in-dialogue silences and what clients and therapists have judged to be helpful in relation to these, quantitative studies are needed to examined how training in silence processes and therapists' skill may influence these complex, dynamic processes.

When examining extended silences, researchers have often converged on the same questions (namely what motivates, sustains, and resolves these silences), which has led to a stronger basis for interpretations of silent processes, but this work has been conducted exclusively from a psychodynamic perspective. It can be interesting to consider why this is, and to examine distinctions in how client silent processes are managed in varied orientations that make extended silences almost nonexistent in other approaches or prevent their analyses. In-session experiences that might be labeled by an analyst in one manner (e.g., resistant silences) might be understood differently in other approaches. Research indicates that from clients' perspectives, these moments often are experienced as self-protection, relationship management, self-discovery, or as preparation to engage in threatening exploration (Frankel & Levitt, 2009). Continued research on the influence of training therapists to become skillful in their use of silence is needed for extended silences as well.

Diversity Considerations

More empirical research is needed on silence and diversity. Most studies reviewed herein did not directly address cultural dimensions of silence. In only a few instances was silence discussed as a function of cultural context (Knutson & Kristiansen, 2015; Ronningstam, 2006). At the same time, our findings underscored that the context of silence is key to discerning its meaning. Clients' and therapists' identities and social location probably shape what each party understands silence to be communicating and how it was used. For example, Hill et al. (2003) found that male therapists and clients were significantly more likely than their female counterparts to use silence as a "shield" that established a boundary between self and other in therapy. This finding demonstrates how social identities, in this case gender, could influence the function of silence in therapy. In another example, a therapist described her Swedish cultural background as a possible contributive factor that bolstered her tolerance for silence (Ronningstam, 2006) and perhaps facilitated her ability to empathically connect when silence functioned as protective for clients.

Moreover, because silence serves different functions across social identity dimensions (e.g., gender, race, class, ability), its meaning could be lost in translation or misinterpreted within the therapy dyad. Knutson and Kristiansen (2015) reviewed myriad meanings of silence that could vary as a function of cultural background. For instance, in some ethnicities and geographic locations, silence could represent politeness and the socially sanctioned avoidance of conflict to save face. In stark contrast, other cultures may interpret silences as clear signifiers of hostility and disagreement. As another example, religious and spiritual lenses potentially impact the usage and interpretation of silence (Weisman, 1955). Just as cultural phenomena shape nonverbal communication patterns such as touch and physical proximity, they also impact how silence is employed, the nuance of which may go undetected in psychotherapy—as in the case of the client who found interpersonal silence reassuring after being raised in a Deaf household.

One study in our review (Blos, 1972) referenced literature that explored the influence of socioeconomic background on the use of silence in therapy. Clients from lower socioeconomic status background were found more likely to use silence because they were unfamiliar with the procedures in therapy and believed their role was to respond to questions or to speak when addressed. In this example, silence represented a discrepancy about expectations in therapy procedures rather than an unconscious repression or expression of hostility. Five studies (Bravesmith, 2012; Fuller & Crowther, 1998; Knutson & Kristiansen, 2015; Serani, 2000; Weisman, 1955) presented case material in which women clients' experiences of sexual assault and infertility were interpreted by therapists as possibly informing their usage of silence to exercise agency and preserve bodily integrity in therapy.

Discerning the meaning of silence in psychotherapy may entail examining the cultural assumptions of psychotherapy more broadly. Notably, although the sociocultural aspects of silence were explored in the research reviews, few studies in our analysis overtly analyzed the meanings of silences as shaped by cultural context and positionality. Across the case studies reviewed, clients' and therapists' social identities were rarely mentioned explicitly, and only once were these characteristics included within the formal analysis (Hill et al., 2003). We recommend that future research attend to cultural aspects that shape the use and meaning of silence in therapy, examining both cultural and professional power dynamics through an intersectional lens.

Training Implications

Although we found no research on how to train therapists to recognize and work with client silences, in my experience supervising and training novice therapists to use and respond to silences in therapy during the past two decades (HL), I have found that they can learn to distinguish productive and obstructive pauses once they are alerted to their processes. I also have seen that sensitivity lead them to become more deliberate in encouraging productive pausing processes and in intervening when obstructive ones occur.

In accordance with our training experiences, research has suggested that therapists seek to conceptualize their client processes in therapeutic silences and to engage in helpful activities (see Tables 11.7–11.9) but can be baffled by or anxious about working with silences (e.g., Daniel et al., 2018; Ladany et al., 2004). For all these reasons, explicit training seems warranted. We recommend that psychotherapy training features a central component focused on developing skills in relational and common processes, inclusive of silence training. Our meta-analysis revealed that productive and obstructive silences are regularly associated with good and poor immediate outcomes (see Tables 11.1 and 11.2). These findings are alongside of clients' reports and case studies demonstrating that therapist intervention in silences can be transformative (see Tables 11.1 and 11.10). These results suggest that the development of skills is central to working responsively with silences in therapy toward productive outcomes. Valuable training goals for trainees include (a) learn to distinguish types of in-dialogue client pauses, (b) identify both client and therapist pausing processes, (c) practice supporting and encouraging productive pauses, (d) become adept at inquiring about clients' experiences in moments when pauses are obstructive so as to reach an understanding of the processes therein, and (e) learn how to interpret and respond to extended silences.

We also recommend training in the delivery of silent processes (e.g., considering their placement between or within speech clauses, duration of silence; see Carr & Smith, 2014). These can bolster both the impact of silences and therapist confidence when engaging in these moments with clients. In our clinical training, we find often that therapists think that they are pausing for a length of time, and supporting clients to have time to process or become in tune with their emotions, when their pace is actually quite rapid. Deliberate practice in modeling and permitting productive pauses (e.g., Rousmaniere, 2017) may benefit therapist training.

Therapeutic Practices

Although research on the following recommendations is limited, these practices are supported by the research we have reviewed and our clinical and teaching experiences:

- Support or encourage clients' productive pausing processes by, for example, connecting with emotions, forming expressions, engaging reflections, and meaning making (see Table 11.1).
- Consider reassuring clients that they are welcome to sustain introspective silence and to take their time in these moments. Clients sometimes cut short productive silence processes because they are worried about their therapist waiting for them, so reassurance that it is good to take time to reflect and feel can be useful (e.g., Levitt, 2002).
- Offer connecting or invitational silences, which predict productive pauses and appear especially helpful for clients with high attachment anxiety (Cuttler et al., 2019).
- Provide guidance and structure for clients to engage in productive pauses, especially if they have not had experience in silence with caring others. You might ask clients to sit back and "take a few moments" to silently contact an emotion, find a word, or reflect; clients report that these processes are typically helpful (see Table 11.1).
- Inquire into obstructive pauses (or suspected obstructive pauses) by asking about clients' experiences and thoughts during those moments ("What is happening for you during this silence?"). These include inquiring about the silence, talking directly about silences, and inviting clients to share when therapists make errors; clients have reported that these interventions can transform obstructive pauses into moments of insight, trust, and therapeutic gains (see Table 11.1).
- Maintain an empathic presence when an extended silence is obstructive by providing judicious comments or inferences meant to mirror the client (e.g., "This is really difficult"), without overzealous interpretation that may be perceived as reproachful (see Table 11.10).
- Be especially careful with clients who may interpret silences as judgmental (e.g., histories of feeling criticized, paranoid, psychotic, or personality disorders; Hill et al., 2003).
- Interpret extended pauses in light of clients' interpersonal history of intimacy, trauma, and cultural identities; view silence as a form of communication (e.g., of anger, unity, withdrawal; see Table 11.10).
- Be mindful that clients' silence can generate feelings in you (e.g., feeling punished, connected, abandoned) that can give you a deeper understanding of clients' internal world. Examining these countertransferential reactions can increase your empathic capacity and help you develop responsive interventions that lead to productive therapy (see Table 11.10).

References

* Studies included in the meta-analysis.

*Acheson, R., Verdenhalven, N., Avdi, E., & Midgley, N. (2020). Exploring silence in short-term psychoanalytic psychotherapy with adolescents with depression. *Journal of Child Psychotherapy*, *46*(2), 224–240.

*Anagnostaki, L. (2013). Beyond silence: Working with Phoebe. *Journal of Child Psychotherapy*, *39*, 156–170. https://doi.org/10.1080/0075417X.2013.806053

Bartels, J., Rodenbach, R., Ciesinski, K., Gramling, R., Fiscella, K., & Epstein, R. (2016). Eloquent silences: A musical and lexical analysis of conversation between oncologists and their patients. *Patient Education and Counseling*, *99*, 1584–1594. https://doi.org/10.1016/j.pec.2016.04.009

Bateman, A., & Fonagy, P. (2013). Mentalization-based treatment. *Psychoanalytic Inquiry*, *33*, 595–613.

Beck, A. T., Ward, C. H., Mendelson, M., Mock, J., & Erbaugh, J. (1961). An inventory for measuring depression. *Archives of General Psychiatry*, *4*, 561–571.

Benjamin, A. (1981). *The helping interview* (3rd ed.). Houghton Mifflin.

*Blos, P. J. (1972). Silence: A clinical exploration. *Psychoanalytic Quarterly*, *41*, 348–363.

*Bravesmith, A. (2012). Silence lends integrity to speech: Transcending the opposites of speech and silence in the analytic dialogue. *British Journal of Psychotherapy*, *28*(1), 21–34.

*Brown, G. R. (1987). Therapeutic effect of silence: Application to a case of borderline personality. *Current Issues in Psychoanalytic Practice*, *4*(3–4), 123–130.

Buchholtz, M. B. (2021). Pauses are conversations: What they tell us when we listen. In A. Dimitrijević & M. B. Buchholtz (Eds.), *Silence and silencing in psychoanalysis: Cultural, clinical, and research perspectives* (pp. 251–274). Routledge.

*Carr, E. S., & Smith, Y. (2014). The poetics of therapeutic practice: Motivational interviewing and the powers of pause. *Culture, Medicine, and Psychiatry*, *38*, 83–114. https://doi.org/10.1007/s11013-013-9352-9

Cooper, S. (2012). Exploring a patient's shift from relative silence to, verbal expressiveness: Observations on an element of the analyst's participation. *The International Journal of Psychoanalysis*, *93*, 897–916.

*Cristy, B. L. (1993). Beyond words: The psychodynamics of a therapy in silence with a twelve-year-old girl. *Clinical Social Work Journal*, *21*, 179–193. https://doi.org/10.1007/BF00754533

*Cuttler, E., Hill, C. E., King, S., & Kivlighan, D. M. J. (2019). Productive silence is golden: Predicting changes in client collaboration from process during silence and client attachment style in psychodynamic psychotherapy. *Psychotherapy*, *56*, 568–576. https://doi.org/10.1037/pst0000260

*Daniel, S. F., Folke, S., Lunn, S., Gondan, M., & Poulsen, S. (2018). Mind the gap: In-session silences are associated with client attachment insecurity, therapeutic alliance, and treatment outcome. *Psychotherapy Research*, *28*, 203–216. https://doi.org/10.1080/10503307.2016.1177673

Derogatis, L. R., & Savitz, K. L. (1999). The SCL-90-R, Brief Symptom Inventory, and matching clinical rating scales. In M. E. Maruish (Ed.), *The use of psychological testing for treatment planning and outcome assessment* (2nd ed., pp. 679–724). Erlbaum.

Dimitrijević, A., & Buchholtz, M. B. (2021). *Silence and silencing in psychoanalysis: Cultural, clinical, and research perspectives*. Routledge.

Dreyer, F., & Franzen, M. M. (2021). How to move on after silences. In A. Dimitrijević & M. B. Buchholtz (Eds.), *Silence and silencing in psychoanalysis: Cultural, clinical, and research perspectives* (pp. 251–274). Routledge.

Elliott, R., Hill, C. E., Stiles, W. B., Friedlander, M. L., Mahrer, A. R., & Margison, F. R. (2001). Primary therapist response modes: Comparison of six rating systems. In C. E. Hill (Ed.), *Helping skills: The empirical foundation* (pp. 9–19). American Psychological Association.

Fliess, R. (1949). Silence and verbalization: A supplement to the theory of the analytic rule. *International Journal of Psychoanalysis*, *30*, 21–30.

Frankel, Z., & Levitt, H. M. (2009). Clients' experiences of disengaged moments in psychotherapy: A grounded theory analysis. *Journal of Contemporary Psychotherapy*, *39*(3), 171–186. https://doi.org/10.1007/s10879-008-9087-z

*Frankel, Z. F., Levitt, H. M., Murray, D. M., Greenberg, L. S., & Angus, L. E. (2006). Assessing psychotherapy silences: An empirically derived categorization system and sampling strategy. *Psychotherapy Research, 16*, 627–638. https://doi.org/10.1080/10503300600591635

Freud, S. (1912). *The dynamics of transference. The standard edition of the complete psychological works of Sigmund Freud.*

*Fuller, V. G., & Crowther, C. (1998). A dark talent: Silence in analysis. *Journal of Analytical Psychology, 43*, 523–543. https://doi.org/10.1111/1465-5922.00051

Gendlin, E. T. (1969). Focusing. *Psychotherapy: Theory, Research & Practice, 6*, 4–15. https://doi.org/10.1037/h0088716

*Gensler, D. (2015). Silence in adolescent psychotherapy. *Journal of Infant, Child & Adolescent Psychotherapy, 14*, 188–195. https://doi.org/10.1080/15289168.2015.1032635

Gindi, S. (2002). *Patterns of silences: A case study of a young adult with learning disabilities* [Unpublished master's thesis]. University of Toronto.

*Greene, M. (1982). On the silence of the therapist and object loss. *International Journal of Psychoanalytic Psychotherapy, 9*, 183–200.

Guzmán, M., Vidal, J., Soto, M., Jaime, D., Tomicic, A., Martínez, C., & Levitt, H. M. (2018). *Coding System of Silences for Therapists and Patients (PICS-TP): A manual for training and coding silences of therapists and patients in psychotherapy for a Spanish-speaking context.* University of Chile.

*Hadda, J. (1991). The ontogeny of silence in an analytic case. *International Journal of Psychoanalysis, 72*, 117–130.

Heppner, W. L., & Shirk, S. D. (2018). Mindful moments: A review of brief, low-intensity mindfulness meditation and induced mindful states. *Social and Personality Psychology Compass, 12*, e124214.

Hill, C. E. (1986). An overview of the Hill Counselor and Client Verbal Response Modes Category Systems. In L. S. Greenberg & W. M. Pinsof (Eds.), *The psychotherapeutic process: A research handbook* (pp. 131–159). Guilford.

*Hill, C. E., Kline, K. V., O'Connor, S., Morales, K., Li, X., Kivlighan, D. M. J., & Hillman, J. (2019). Silence is golden: A mixed methods investigation of silence in one case of psychodynamic psychotherapy. *Psychotherapy, 56*, 577–587. https://doi.org/10.1037/pst0000196

Hill, C. E., & Thompson, B. J., & Ladany, N. (2003). Therapist use of silence in therapy: A survey. *Journal of Clinical Psychology, 59*, 513–524. http://dx.doi.org/10.1002/jclp.10155

Holtmann, K. C., Seybert, C., & Huber, D. (2018). *Sprachliche Charakteristika der Depression. Eine vergleichende Empirische Studie zu Sprechverhalten und Sprechpausen in Psychotherapie* [Verbal characteristics and speech-pause behavior in depressed patients: A compared process-analysis of psychoanalytic, psychodynamic and cognitive–behavioral therapy]. International Psychoanalytic University.

Horowitz, L. M., Rosenberg, S. E., Baer, B. A., Ureño, G., & Villaseñor, V. S. (1988). Inventory of Interpersonal Problems: Psychometric properties and clinical application. *Journal of Consulting and Clinical Psychology, 56*, 885–892.

*Khan, M., & Masud, R. (1963). Silence as communication. *Bulletin of the Menninger Clinic, 27*, 300–317.

*Knutson, H. V., & Kristiansen, A. (2015). Varieties of silence: Under-standing different forms and functions of silence in a psychotherapeutic setting. *Contemporary Psychoanalysis, 51*(1), 1–30.

*Kurtz, S. A. (1984). On silence. *Psychoanalytic Review, 71*, 227–245.

*Ladany, N., Hill, C. E., Thompson, B. J., & O'Brien, K. M. (2004). Therapist perspectives on using silence in therapy: A qualitative study. *Counselling and Psychotherapy Research, 4*, 80–89. http://dx.doi.org/10.1080/14733140412331384088

Lambert, M. J., Hansen, N. B., Umpress, V., Lunnen, K., Okiishi, J., Burlingame, G. M., et al. (1996). *Administration and scoring manual for the OQ-45.2.* American Professional Credentialing Services.

*Lane, R. C., Koetting, M. G., & Bishop, J. (2002). Silence as communication in psychodynamic psychotherapy. *Clinical Psychology Review, 22*(7), 1091–1104.

*Leira, T. (1995). Silence and communication: Nonverbal dialogue and therapeutic action. *Scandinavian Psychoanalytic Review, 18*, 41–65. https://doi.org/10.1080/01062301.1995.10592330

*Levitt, H. M. (2001a). The sounds of silence in psychotherapy: The categorization of clients' pauses. *Psychotherapy Research, 11*, 295–309. https://doi.org/10.1080/713663985

*Levitt, H. M. (2001b). Clients' experiences of obstructive silence: Integrating conscious reports and analytic theories. *Journal of Contemporary Psychotherapy, 31*, 221–244. https://doi.org/10.1023/A:1015307311143

*Levitt, H. M. (2002). The unsaid in the psychotherapy narrative: Voicing the unvoiced. *Journal of Counseling Psychology Quarterly, 15*, 333-350. https://doi.org/10.1080/0951507021000029667

Levitt, H. M. (2021). *Essentials of critical-constructivist grounded theory*. American Psychological Association.

Levitt, H. M., Butler, M., & Hill, T. (2006). What clients find helpful in psychotherapy: Developing principles for facilitating moment-to-moment change. *Journal of Counseling Psychology, 53*, 314–324.

Levitt, H. M., & Frankel, Z. (2004). Pausing Inventory Classification System (PICS) manual, 2nd Revision [Unpublished manuscript]. University of Memphis.

Levitt, H. M., & Morrill, Z. (2021). Measuring silence: The Pausing Inventory Categorization System and a review of findings. In M. Buchholz & A. Dimitrijevic (Eds.), *Silence and silencing in psychoanalysis: Cultural, clinical and research perspectives* (pp. 233–250). Routledge.

Levitt, H. M., Neimeyer, R. A., & Williams, D. C. (2005). Rules versus principles in psychotherapy: Implications of the quest for universal guidelines in the movement for empirically supported treatments. *Journal of Contemporary Psychotherapy, 35*, 117–129. https://doi.org/10.1007/s10879-005-0807-3

Levitt, H. M., & Whelton, W. (2022). *Power and liberation in psychotherapy: An integration of feminist–multicultural and humanistic psychotherapies* [Unpublished manuscript]. University of Massachusetts.

Levitt, H. M., & Williams, D. C. (2010). Facilitating client change: Principles based upon the experience of eminent psychotherapists. *Psychotherapy Research, 20*, 337–352.

Martyres, G. (1995). On silence: A language for emotional experience. *Australian and New Zealand Journal of Psychiatry, 29*(1), 118–123.

Mergenthaler, E., & Levitt, H. M. (2005, June 24). Pausing experiences and the therapeutic cycles model [Paper presentation]. In *Micro-processes in therapeutic dialogue: How do patient and therapist do the work of therapy?* Conference conducted at the 36th International Meeting of the Society for Psychotherapy Research, Montreal, Canada.

Paterson, B. L., Thorne, S. E., Canam, C., & Jillings, C. (2001). *Meta-study of qualitative health research: A practical guide to meta-analysis and meta-synthesis*. SAGE.

Perfetti, C. C., & Bertuccelli-Papi, M. (1985). Towards a cognitive typology of pause phenomena. *Communication & Cognition, 18*, 339–351.

*Pugh, D. (1997). Silence as a form of analytic communication at the level of the basic fault. *Psychodynamic Counselling, 3*, 279–289. https://doi.org/10.1080/13533339708402493

Reik, T. (1926). The psychological meaning of silence. *Psychoanalytic Review, 55*, 172–186.

*Ronningstam, E. (2006). Silence: Cultural function and psychological transformation in psychoanalysis and psychoanalytic psychotherapy. *International Journal of Psychoanalysis, 87*, 1277–1295. https://doi.org/10.1516/D6W0-3E0N-MR79-J7JA

Rousmaniere, T. (2017). *Deliberate practice for psychotherapists: A guide to improving clinical effectiveness*. Routledge.

Sabbadini, A. (1991). Listening to silence. *British Journal of Psychotherapy, 7*, 406–415. https://doi.org/10.1111/j.1752-0118.1991.tb01145.x

Schlotheuber, R. E. (2018). Pausing processes in psychoanalytic therapies [Unpublished master's thesis]. University of Witten.

*Serani, D. (2000). Silence in the analytic space, resistance or reverie? A perspective from Loewald's theory of primordial unity. *Contemporary Psychoanalysis, 36*, 505–519. https://doi.org/10.1080/00107530.2000.10747059

Serlin, I. (2015). Dance, creative arts, and somatic therapies in the healing of trauma. *PsycCRITIQUES*, 60, Article 9. https://doi.org/10.1037/a0039374

*Stringer, J. V., Levitt, H. M., Berman, J. S., & Mathews, S. S. (2010). A study of silent disengagement and distressing emotion in psychotherapy. *Psychotherapy Research*, *20*, 495-510. https://doi.org/10.1080/10503301003754515

Strupp, H. H., Wallach, M. S., & Wogan, M. (1964). Psychotherapy experience in retrospect: Questionnaire survey of former patients and their therapists. *Psychological Monographs*, *78*, 1–45.

Timulak, L. (2009). Meta-analysis of qualitative studies: A tool for reviewing qualitative research findings in psychotherapy. *Psychotherapy Research*, *19*, 591–600. https://doi.org/10.1080/10503300802477989

*Tindall, R. H., & Robinson, F. P. (1947). The use of silence as a technique in counseling. *Journal of Clinical Psychology*, *3*, 136–141. https://doi.org/10.1002/1097-4679(194704)3:2<136::AID-JCLP2270030205>3.0.CO;2-E

Trad, P. V. (1993). Silence: The resounding experience. *American Journal of Psychotherapy*, *47*, 167–170.

Wall, T. W. (2018). Hypnosis: A psychodynamic perspective. *American Journal of Clinical Hypnosis*, *60*, 218–238.

*Weisman, A. D. (1955). Silence and psychotherapy. *Psychiatry*, *18*, 241–260.

*Wilmer, H. A. (1995). Silence: Something we rarely hear, which does not exist. *Journal of the American Academy of Psychoanalysis*, *23*, 723–730.

Winnicott, D. W. (1948). Children's hostels in war and peace. *British Journal of Medical Psychiatry*, *21*, 175–180. https://doi.org/10.1111/j.2044-8341.1948.tb01168.x

Winnicott, D. W. (1956). Primary maternal preoccupation. In: *Through pediatrics to psychoanalysis*. London: Hogarth Press, 1975: 300–305.

Winnicott, D. W. (1965). *The maturational process and the facilitating environment*. Hogarth.

Wu, M. B., & Levitt, H. M. (2022). How to become a responsive therapist: A study of experiences of developing therapists. *Psychotherapy Research*, *32*, 763–777. https://doi.org/10.1080/10503307.2021.2009929

*Zeligs, M. A. (1960). The role of silence in transference, countertransference, and the psychoanalytic process. *International Journal of Psychoanalysis*, *41*, 407–412.

Zeligs, M. A. (1961). The psychology of silence. *Journal of the American Psychoanalytic Association*, *9*, 7–43.

12

Facilitating Dyadic Synchrony

Dana Atzil-Slonim, Christina S. Soma, Xinyao Zhang, Adar Paz, and Zac E. Imel

Psychotherapy is more than a verbal practice, since much of a therapist's skill set is also nonverbal (Ramseyer & Tschacher, 2011; J. Schore & Schore, 2014). Clients communicate their internal states not only verbally but also through facial expressions, vocal tones, and body movements. Therapists' ability to identify and express nonverbal communication, their sensitivity to slight changes in clients' behavior and emotions, their awareness of their own bodily sensations and expressions, and their ability to regulate affect together with clients are all crucial clinical skills that underlie many verbal therapeutic methods. The core of these abilities is the facilitation of *dyadic synchrony*, or enabling the coordination of physiological and behavioral signals between client and therapist.

When people interact, they tend to spontaneously coordinate their behavior and physiology over time (Feldman, 2012). For example, when people are engaged in a naturally flowing conversation, their vocal tones tend to become aligned, and their bodies tend to start moving in the same cadence (Delaherche et al., 2012). Synchrony appears to play a central role in building rapport between individuals, in co-regulating emotional states, and in improving social learning (Delaherche et al., 2012; Feldman, 2021).

From an evolutionary perspective, synchrony is thought to be an ancient survival mechanism that elicited coordinated actions. Human infants are dependent on their caregivers to regulate their physiology and behavior, so their survival depends on social bonds (Feldman, 2021). Face-to-face synchronous interactions between infants and caregivers based on familiarity, matching, and attunement accelerate the maturation of infants' relational skills and provide essential environmental input for the development of self-regulation capabilities. Through dyadic synchrony, children learn social skills that help them thrive in their community. Individuals gradually develop more productive self-regulation abilities and better interpersonal skills, which in turn lead to enhanced well-being (Beebe & Lachmann, 1988; A. Schore, 2015).

Despite the gradual development from complete dependence to more independence in the ability to regulate oneself, adults' physiology and behavior are continuously open to regulation by others through dyadic synchrony (Feldman, 2012). Especially in close relationships, synchrony occurs from birth throughout the entire life span. Its benefits have been demonstrated across various individual and social outcomes (Feldman, 2012). For example, higher synchrony between romantic couples is associated with greater relationship satisfaction and well-being (e.g., Butler, 2015). Given that psychotherapy is a special type of close relationship, there are good reasons to assume that synchrony plays an important role in psychotherapy as well.

Dana Atzil-Slonim, Christina S. Soma, Xinyao Zhang, Adar Paz, and Zac E. Imel, *Facilitating Dyadic Synchrony*
In: *Psychotherapy Skills and Methods That Work*. Edited by: Clara E. Hill and John C. Norcross, Oxford University Press.
 DOI: 10.1093/oso/9780197611012.003.0012

Many psychotherapy theories highlight the importance of synchrony between clients and therapists (Aron & Harris, 2014; Fosha, 2001; McCullough, 2003; Winnicott, 1971). According to these theories, psychotherapy seeks to provide clients whose development lacked early synchrony with an emotionally attuned other a corrective emotional experience that replicates more optimal development (Fosha, 2001). Therapists' ability to attune their behavior and physiology to clients' nonverbal communication and accelerate or decelerate their own arousal in response to clients' signals may allow clients to expand their emotion regulation capacities, leading to better therapeutic outcomes (J. Schore & Schore, 2014).

In this chapter, the facilitation of dyadic synchrony is discussed as a core therapist skill. We define dyadic synchrony, differentiate it from similar constructs, and provide a clinical example. We review the literature on the ways in which different forms of dyadic synchrony are assessed and their associations with psychotherapy outcomes. We then provide a meta-analysis that depicts the differences between synchrony and pseudo-synchrony in psychotherapy studies. We also describe situations in which synchrony may not be beneficial, and we address how dimensions of diversity complicate and inform work on synchrony. Finally, we present training implications and therapeutic practices based on the research evidence.

Definitions

Numerous terms have been used in the literature to describe interdependence in dyadic processes (e.g., synchrony, congruence, convergence, mimicry, coordination, matching, reciprocity). This breadth of usage may blur important distinctions and make these dyadic processes difficult to apprehend. We define therapist facilitation of *dyadic synchrony* in psychotherapy as the therapist's ability to become coordinated with the client's behavioral and physiological dynamics as they temporally change within sessions.

One important feature of this definition is therapists' ability to *become* coordinated with their clients' nonverbal cues. Dyadic synchrony exists on a continuum, ranging from intuitive synchrony that occurs spontaneously when therapists and clients are affected by the presence of each other to more deliberate synchrony that may occur when therapists increase their awareness of nonverbal signals in the clients' and their own behavior. Somewhat similar to skillful dancing, facilitating dyadic synchrony requires therapists to move along this continuum between allowing themselves to spontaneously echo the moment-to-moment rhythmic structures of their clients' nonverbal behavior and more deliberately identifying the intensity and direction of their clients' affective charge and modifying their own behavior to synchronize with their clients and lead them to a more adaptive emotional state.

A second feature of this definition is the therapist's ability to be sensitive to the *temporal qualities* of the client's behavioral and physiological cues as they change dynamically over time. Unlike congruence or matching, which refer to the correspondence between dyad members in a more static state, synchrony is a dynamic phenomenon that is more accurately described as continuous interpersonal coordination (Wiltshire et al., 2020). Therapists' coordination with their clients may occur at various times spans, from milliseconds, through the session level, to the treatment level. Here, we focus on the time-intensive dynamic covariation of the client's and the therapist's physiology and behavior within sessions. For each behavior or physiological index measured for one member of the dyad, there is a limited window of time for the other member to produce a coordinated response (Delaherche et al., 2012). For example, synchrony can be estimated as the extent to which client's and therapist's moment-to-moment physiology or vocal tone rise and fall in unison, within a session. By contrast, if there is an association between client's and therapist's emotions as self-reported by each at the end of a therapy session, this would not be viewed as evidence for synchrony but, rather, as congruence (e.g., Atzil-Slonim et al., 2018).

A third feature of the definition is that the coordination between the therapist's and the client's behavior or physiology must be nonrandom. Given that many intrapersonal affective measures have an oscillatory pattern, this may produce an autocorrelation within the signal, which can lead to spurious interpersonal correlations (Dean & Dunsmuir, 2016). Essentially, there may be an apparent correlation in a given behavior over time because simply being in a conversation creates certain conditions that are common to both members of the dyad but cannot be ascribed to some underlying process of mutual influence. To rule out the possibility of an association occurring by chance, researchers have suggested comparing synchrony to *pseudo-synchrony.* Pseudo-synchrony is typically estimated by comparing synchrony in shuffled pairs (e.g., by randomly matching audio from two people who did not actually speak or shuffling dialogue within a session) to genuine interactions to estimate the strength of the phenomenon of synchrony (Ramseyer & Tschacher, 2010).

Finally, synchrony is a complex phenomenon, and it is important to define its association with related concepts. One central aspect of dyadic synchrony is the co-regulation of emotional processes (Delaherche et al., 2012). Whereas synchrony refers to how members of a dyad change together over time, *co-regulation* refers to the ways in which the presence of one member of the dyad promotes affective homeostasis in the other member (Butler & Randall, 2013). Other similar concepts, such as emotional contagion, mimicry, or the "chameleon effect," refer to imitation within a social interaction (Hatfield et al., 1993). *Convergence* is the gradual minimization of differences between conversational partners over time (Delaherche et al., 2012).

Although these processes differ from synchrony, they are not fully independent (Butler, 2015). For example, the client's and therapist's vocal arousal may rise and fall in unison (synchrony), while at the same time the therapist is drawing the client down into a more stable arousal level (co-regulation; e.g., Paz et al., 2021; Soma et al, 2020). Alternatively, if the therapist consciously or unconsciously crosses their legs after the client crossed their legs (mimicry or chameleon effect), this can become synchrony if they continue to cross and uncross their legs throughout the session. It is also possible that over time and repeated experience, synchronous interactions between this therapeutic dyad can result in greater dyadic similarity (convergence).

Clinical Description and Indications

The biobehavioral signature of therapists' facilitation of dyadic synchrony can take several forms depending on the communication modality and the time resolution.

Specifically, dyadic synchrony can be manifested in physiological measures such as electrodermal activity (EDA) or heart rate variability, vocal measures (e.g., vocal pitch, intensity, speech rate), and visual (facial expression, motion energy analysis) or linguistic (e.g., language style) cues. Synchrony processes can operate on the millisecond to minute timescale. For example, when the client and the therapist are talking to each other, their breathing patterns may become synchronized, which in turn may synchronize their heart rate. This can also occur when their movements, tone of voice, and gaze become aligned. Synchrony can also operate at a longer timescale—for example, when the client's and the therapist's language style become similar over an entire session.

Although synchrony tends to occur when two people interact, there are several steps the therapist can take to make synchrony beneficial for the client. A skilled therapist is aware of small shifts in the client's affective and bodily states, tracks the intensity and direction of the client's affective charge, and helps the client regulate more intense emotions. Therapists' ability to be attuned to the nonverbal moment-to-moment rhythmic structures of clients' internal states and to modify their own behavior to synchronize with that structure is a crucial clinical skill. When these synchronous interactions are repeated many times, clients may gradually expand their ability to sustain, tolerate, and regulate affective states by drawing on the combined resources of the dyad, which are frequently internalized (J. Schore & Schore, 2014).

A skilled therapist can flexibly move between more and less synchronized states. Humans tend to dynamically move in and out of synchrony (Gelo & Salvatore, 2016; Mayo & Gordon, 2020), and theories suggest that this pattern is more adequate than either too many or too few levels of synchrony (Feldman, 2007). Several client and situational characteristics have been suggested as probable indications and contraindications for dyadic synchrony (Ramseyer, 2020). For example, synchronizing with depressed clients who tend to experience blunted emotions may not be beneficial. With such clients, therapists may need to maintain a delicate balance between synchrony and upregulation of adaptive emotions. Similarly, if therapists become highly synchronized with clients who experience intense anxiety, this may lead to escalating negative emotionality. To better help clients in such situations, therapists may need to downregulate their own affect that arises in response to the clients' affect.

Thus, effective synchrony may depend on the therapist's ability to dynamically move towards and away from the clients' physiology and behavior. Therapists can be attuned to the clients' nonverbal behavior and allow themselves to be influenced by it. At the same time, it is important for therapists to regulate their own affective and bodily states, which can change in response to the clients' experiences, to help the clients regulate their emotions.

Figure 12.1 presents the dyadic signals extracted from 15 minutes of a successful psychotherapy session, taken from a good outcome case (for more details, see Atzil-Slonim et al., 2022). Four types of signals are presented: the EDA (Figure 12.1A), the respiratory sinus arrhythmia (RSA; Figure 12.1B), the affective valence extracted from facial expression (Figure 12.1C), and the affective arousal extracted from vocal features (Figure 12.1D). The physiological channels (Figures 12.1A and 12.1B) indicate that the dyad had moments of relative synchrony; however, these moments also present a time lag between signals, indicating the therapist's effort to emotionally attune to the client, and the dyad's dynamic movement in and out of synchrony. The facial expression channel (Figure

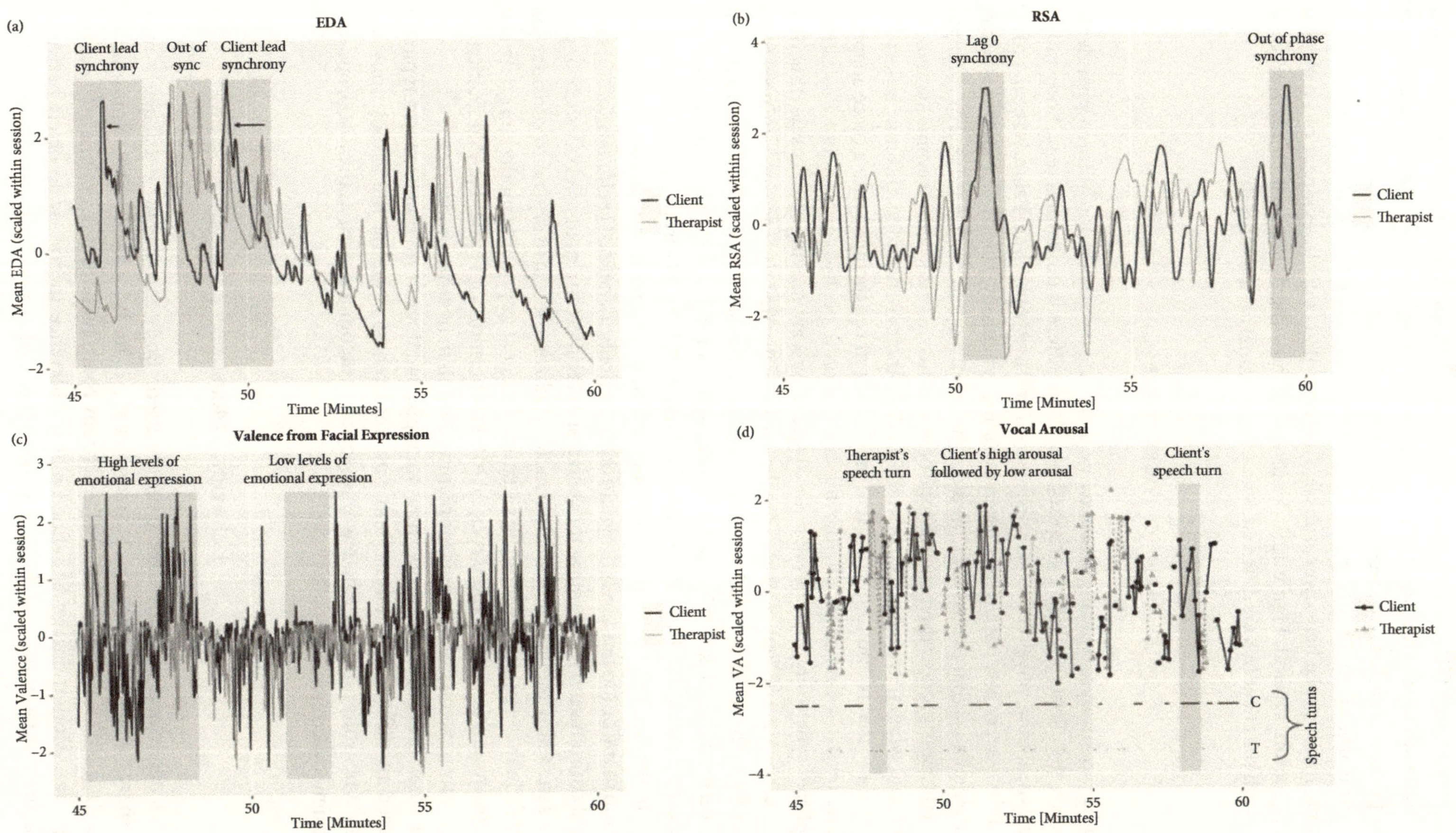

Figure 12.1 Example of therapist's facilitation of dyadic synchrony. EDA, electrodermal activity; RSA, respiratory sinus arrhythmia.

12.1C) shows that the session began with the client's negative emotional expressions that were met with relatively neutral affect by the therapist. Subsequently, the client expressed more positive emotions that were met with stronger positive expressions by the therapist. The vocal arousal channel (Figure 12.1D) shows that when the client experienced high arousal, the therapist had lower arousal, a dynamic that could be evidence of a pattern of co-regulation. Overall, Figure 12.1 demonstrates how the therapist skillfully worked in sync with the client in four different nonverbal channels at the same time.

Assessment

Dyadic synchrony is typically assessed by calculating the association or interdependence between the clients' and the therapists' signals in different modalities (e.g., body movement, vocal tone, physiology, facial expression and text) over time. Palumbo et al. (2017) identified several key parameters when assessing synchrony. *Direction* indicates whether the therapist's signal precedes or predicts the client's signal or vice versa. For example, when therapists follow their clients' tone of voice, this may reflect their attunement to the client, and when therapists' tone of voice predicts their clients' tone, this may reflect co-regulation—that is, "pulling" the client on the part of the therapist into a more adaptive arousal level. *Sign* refers to whether the correlation is positive or negative. Positive or "in phase" synchrony indicates that the dyad's signals are moving in the same direction, whereas negative or "out of phase" synchrony indicates that they are moving away from each other. The ideal interaction is not necessarily made up of absolute synchrony and coordination (Tronick, 2007). Rather, a successful coordination requires therapists to dynamically move toward and away from their clients (Mayo & Gordon, 2020). *Magnitude* refers to the strength of the association between the dyad members' signals. Because either too many or too few levels of synchrony may not be beneficial (Feldman, 2007), successful coordination may require the therapist to facilitate the right level of synchrony.

To assess how therapists facilitate dyadic synchrony, it is also crucial to consider the clients' characteristics as well as the situational context as possible moderators between synchrony and outcome (Ramseyer, 2020). Furthermore, it is possible that facilitating synchrony in some modalities is more important than in other modalities.

In what follows, we describe how therapist facilitation of synchrony is typically assessed in different modalities and how researchers examine the associations between synchrony and immediate within-session outcomes as well as the distal, end-of-treatment outcomes.

Behavioral Measures

Several behavioral measures are typically used. Body movement, particularly motion energy analysis (MEA; e.g., Altmann et al., 2020; Prinz et al., 2021; Ramseyer & Tschacher, 2011), assesses nonverbal synchrony based on body movements using video recordings. Motion energy is defined as the difference in gray-scale pixels between consecutive video frames (Ramseyer & Tschacher, 2011). Synchrony can be quantified by the cross-correlation or cross-lagged correlation between two people's Fisher's z

transformed motion energy values (for a comparison and categorization of 10 MEA-based synchrony metrics, see Schoenherr and colleagues 2019). To examine whether client–therapist movement synchrony occurs at a higher level than chance, researchers usually compare real synchrony to pseudo-synchrony (described above).

Speakers' vocal pitch has also been shown to be associated with their emotional states (Bachorowski, 1999; Hammerschmidt & Jürgens, 2007; Russell et al., 2003) and is commonly measured by the mean fundamental frequency (mean f_0). The mean f_0 refers to the lowest voice frequency a speaker can produce. Vocal synchrony is often calculated as the correlation between two people's mean f_0 over a period of time, which is presumed to imply the co-fluctuation of these two people's emotional states (Bryan et al., 2018; Gaume et al., 2019; Imel et al., 2014).

Researchers have also quantified the emotional facial expression synchrony between clients and therapists (Altmann et al., 2021). Novel technologies such the FaceReader (Lewinski et al., 2014) and OpenFace (Baltrušaitis et al., 2016) allow for moment-by-moment automatic emotion recognition.

Physiological Measures

Physiological indices can also assess the subtle synchrony of psychological states. Skin conductance (SC) or EDA is considered an indicator of sympathetic responses and affect (Lidberg & Gunnar Wallin, 1981). Sympathetic responses lead to the innervation of sweat glands, which causes a change in SC (Edelberg, 1993). Synchrony of EDA suggests a simultaneous change in two people's affects. Synchrony can be quantified as the correlation of two people's EDA (Robinson et al., 1982). It can also be represented by the concordance index (Marci et al., 2007), which is calculated as the log odds of the overall positive over negative correlations of two people's EDA change rates. The common metrics used in MEA can also be applied to EDA time-series data, such as windowed cross-lagged correlation (Bar-Kalifa et al., 2019; Prinz et al., 2022).

Respiratory rate and heart rate are influenced by the autonomic nervous system and may also be indicators of sympathetic responses and affect (Tschacher & Meier, 2020). Other indicators such as heart rate variability or electrocardiograms (ECGs) can also be tracked. In the only study that assessed the feasibility of using these indicators (Tschacher & Meier, 2020), both the concordance index and the windowed cross-lagged correlation were applied to each of these time series to quantify synchrony. In Robinson and colleagues' (1982) early study on SC synchrony, finger skin temperature was also assessed, and synchrony was quantified by Pearson's correlations of the finger skin temperature time series.

Respiratory sinus arrhythmia reflects the extent to which successive heartbeats vary within the breathing frequency band (Berntson et al., 1997). RSA is a common index of cardiac vagal control because it is linked to the extent to which the myelinated vagal nerve modulates cardiac activity (Porges, 2003), thus making RSA a well-established biomarker of the parasympathetic nervous system. Ample research has documented the association between RSA and favorable emotional regulatory processes (for a review, see Balzarotti et al., 2017). To the best of our knowledge, client–therapist RSA synchrony has yet to be examined. However, studies investigating RSA synchrony in other relational contexts have found it to be related to relational outcomes (Helm et al., 2014).

Verbal Measures

Verbally based measures focus mainly on the conversations between clients and therapists. Therapists' linguistic synchrony with their clients may reflect their ability to attune to their clients' idiosyncratic language (Shapira et al., 2022). One way to assess linguistic synchrony is language style matching (LSM; Aafjes-van Doorn et al., 2020; Doorn & Müller-Frommeyer, 2020; Lord et al., 2015)—that is, the extent to which two people produce similar rates of syntactically important function words such as articles and pronouns, which are known to be associated with speakers' social–psychological states (Chung & Pennebaker, 2007). The match between two people's rates of using function words is considered to indicate synchrony (Aafjes-van Doorn et al., 2020). LSM is calculated as the proportion of function words in nine categories: auxiliary verbs, articles, adverbs, personal pronouns, indefinite pronouns, prepositions, negations, conjunctions, and quantifiers. The overall LSM is the average (Gonzales et al., 2010).

Overall, measures of synchrony vary considerably in terms of modality and the algorithms needed to calculate synchrony. For example, even within the same modality (e.g., MEA), changing the parameter settings and algorithms can alter the results drastically (Schoenherr, Paulick, Worrack, et al., 2019). Whereas dyadic synchrony is typically measured by assessing the interdependence or association between the clients' and the therapists' signals, to assess whether therapists facilitate dyadic synchrony in a beneficial way, several additional parameters (e.g., the direction, sign, and magnitude of synchrony), as well as possible moderators (e.g., trait-like and state-like characteristics and the modality of synchrony), need to be considered. In addition, to estimate the strength of synchrony, many studies have demonstrated that synchrony occurs above chance level by comparing pseudo-synchrony to real synchrony (Ramseyer & Tschacher, 2010). Finally, many studies take the multilevel structure of the data (sessions nested within clients nested within therapists) into account to examine the associations between synchrony and session-level or treatment-level outcome (e.g., Prinz et al., 2021).

Clinical Example

The following clinical illustration was taken from a study of clients in short-term psychodynamic psychotherapy (Atzil-Slonim et al., 2022). The session was rated by clinical judges as evidencing high behavioral synchrony according to the Coding Interactive Behavior manual (Feldman, 1998). The client, a woman in her 40s, was diagnosed with major depressive disorder (some characteristics have been changed to protect the identity of the client). Her primary distress was related to her relationship with her husband; she felt that she could not share her experiences with him.

The moment the therapist opened the door and looked at the client's facial expression, she realized that the client was extremely upset. They both sat and stared at each other. Even before words were uttered, the therapist (T) felt tension in her own body. The therapist's tone of voice was a little high and trembling when she asked the client how she felt. The client (C) began to answer in a hushed tone which suggested that she was nervous and not quite comfortable.

C: My nephew has been diagnosed with a medical condition. His mother told me.

T: Can you say more about what you found out?

C: Yes. He is a great guy, just about to start college. And I don't know what will happen now. It made me wonder if I also have this condition, maybe my kids. Because it may be genetic.

T: You say you are afraid. Can you elaborate?

The client's nonverbal behavior indicates high arousal. Her vocal pitch is high, and she is restless. The therapist seems curious about the client's experience. In contrast to the client, the therapist's vocal tone and nonverbal behavior indicates calm.

C: What do you mean? Of course I'm afraid, wouldn't you be? This is a serious condition. I tried to talk with my husband about it, but you know what it's like talking to him, he can say things that may sound like he is listening but I know he is not. I don't know if he really cares.

The client is expressing her frustration that the therapist is not in sync with her. The client's vocal tone becomes even more strident and her facial expression indicates anger. She turns away from the therapist.

T: You feel that I didn't really listen to you . . .

The therapist's arousal increases, and her vocal tone becomes higher. The client crosses her legs and leans to the right. Without either noticing, the therapist also crosses her legs and leans in the same direction. Synchrony is high at that point, but it includes high levels of negative emotions.

[50 seconds of silence]

T: I realize now how stressful this experience may be for you. It is so scary what might happen to your nephew, and that it might affect you and your children. It is so frustrating that you are sharing this stressful experience and you feel like nobody really cares.

The therapist gradually downregulates her own emotions. Her vocal arousal decreases from sentence to sentence. She leans back, while maintaining good eye contact with the client.

C: I'm so worried about him and about us . . .

The client is in tears; her voice is quiet.

T: You look sad.

C: (crying quietly) I am so sad . . . he is so young . . .

T: It is so sad.

Both the client's and the therapist's facial expressions are very sad. The client is crying. The situation reflects high intimacy and high synchrony.

This vignette illustrates how the therapist worked skillfully to synchronize with the client where the goal was to co-regulate stressful and overwhelming emotions. The therapist was aware of the client's nonverbal behavior from the beginning and noticed that the client was upset. The nonverbal synchrony between the client and the therapist increased, but in a way that reflected an escalation of stressful emotions. The therapist tracked this escalation and downregulated the distress by modulating her own emotional state. The client followed, and her arousal level returned to a more homoeostatic level. Then, after a short silence, the therapist noticed the tears in her client's eyes, and synchronously her facial expression became sad. She upregulated the grief and emotional pain and shared these emotions with her client. The high nonverbal synchrony that was evident at that point seemed to allow the client to express her emotions and to feel less alone in her painful experience.

Landmark Studies and Previous Reviews

The past decade has seen a surge of research into the effects of client–therapist synchrony in psychotherapy. Most of these studies have focused on examining the existence of synchrony and its associations with outcome. However, currently there is minimal research examining how, when, and with whom therapists can facilitate synchrony in a beneficial way.

One of the earliest landmark studies on synchrony in psychotherapy was conducted by Ramseyer and Tschacher (2011). They used MEA to analyze 104 videotaped sessions of 70 client–therapist dyads and found that movement synchrony between clients and therapists was significantly higher than chance. Movement synchrony was also a longitudinal predictor of symptom reduction or better functioning at the end of psychotherapy, ranging from small to medium effect sizes. In a follow-up study using the same sample and a similar method, client–therapist synchrony occurred for movement of the head and the rest of the body (Ramseyer & Tschacher, 2014). They also demonstrated how synchrony in different facets of the nonverbal client–therapist interaction was differently related to psychotherapy outcomes. Head synchrony, unlike body synchrony, predicted the global outcome of therapy. Conversely, body but not head synchrony predicted session outcome.

In one of the few studies to have addressed physiological synchrony in real psychotherapy sessions, Tschacher and Meier (2020) systematically examined physiological synchrony in respiration, ECG, heart rate, and heart rate variability. Specifically, they examined the association between physiological synchrony and post-session outcome in 55 sessions from four clients treated by one psychotherapist. Physiological synchrony was assessed by examining the coupling of respiratory behavior, heart rate, and heart rate variability by windowed cross-correlation and correlation of local slopes. Both methods included surrogate controls using segment-wise shuffling. Physiological synchrony was significantly present, suggesting sympathetic and parasympathetic coupling of therapist and client, and was positively associated with session outcomes with small to moderate effect sizes.

Researchers have only recently started to assess how and for whom therapists can facilitate synchrony in a beneficial way. One such study by Paulick, Rubel, et al. (2018) examined whether the amount of synchrony, dyad types (same- vs. opposite-sex dyads), and levels of client symptom severity would moderate the association between movement synchrony and outcome in a sample of 143 clients treated by 27 therapists. They found a small effect link between the amount of synchrony and therapeutic success, indicating that medium levels of synchrony were associated with better treatment results.

Another study assessed how therapists facilitate synchrony in an adaptive way by focusing on co-regulation in 21,133 vocal arousal observations from 279 sessions in a sample of 30 clients treated by 24 therapists (Paz et al., 2021). Specifically, co-regulation was examined by assessing whether the changes in clients' vocal arousal levels from one speech turn to the next are predicted by the therapists' vocal arousal levels at the previous speech turn. They found that better outcomes were achieved in sessions in which clients' vocal arousal was "pulled" by their therapists toward the clients' baseline vocal arousal levels.

Koole and Tschacher (2016) were the first to review the literature on synchrony in psychotherapy. They noted that although there is a growing body of literature examining the existence of synchrony in psychotherapy, the ways in which synchrony leads to beneficial treatment outcome remain unclear.

To the best of our knowledge, the only previous systematic review of this nascent research literature was conducted by Wiltshire and colleagues (2020). They reviewed 15 published studies in English that assessed the correlations between client–therapist coordination in different modalities (e.g., body movements, voice, and physiology) and treatment outcome (e.g., symptomatology and dropouts) in samples ranging from two to 101 dyads (M = 36 dyads). A variety of disorders were investigated in the studies. Most of the studies reported that stronger coordination was associated with better end-of-treatment outcomes, such as goal attainment. Movement coordination was the most highly associated with distal outcomes. Studies on vocal measures were mixed. One study found that vocal coordination was associated with better treatment outcomes (Rocco et al., 2017), whereas another indicated that vocal coordination was associated with an increase in clients' symptoms (Reich et al., 2014).

Research Review

Researchers have primarily examined the existence of dyadic synchrony and its association with treatment outcomes. Very few studies to date include other parameters of synchrony (e.g., direction, pattern, and magnitude) or the ways in which therapists facilitate synchrony in a beneficial way. Here, we conducted a systematic review of studies that examined synchrony between clients and therapists in different modalities (e.g., movement, voice, physiology, and linguistic) and its association with proximal (in-session) or distal (treatment-end) outcome in psychotherapy. In addition, we conducted a meta-analysis on studies that compared synchrony to pseudo-synchrony in psychotherapy, with the aim of estimating the strength of synchrony in psychotherapy.

Methods

Literature Search and Retrieval

Three doctoral students conducted a literature search according to Preferred Reporting Items for Systematic Reviews and Meta-Analyses (PRISMA) guidelines for meta-analyses (Moher et al., 2010; Figure 12.2). To identify studies of synchrony in psychotherapy, the literature search included the following databases: PubMed, Academic

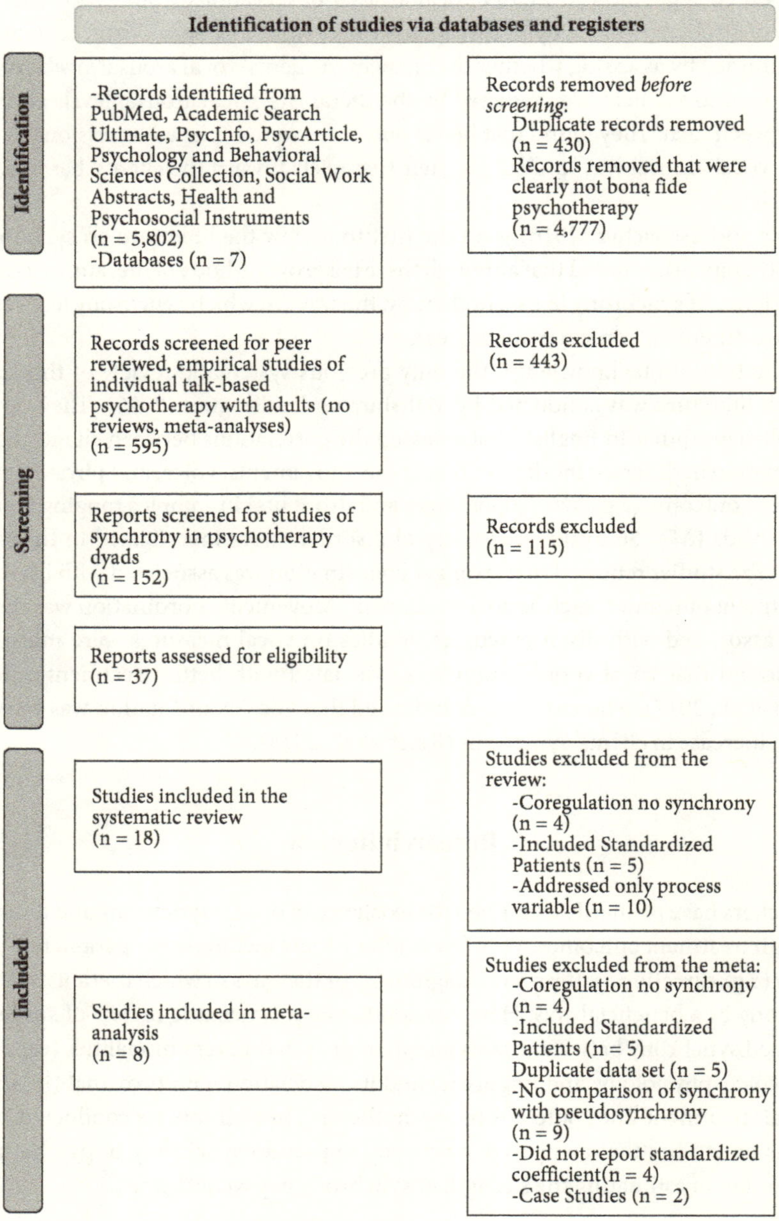

Figure 12.2 PRISMA description of literature search.

Search Ultimate, PsycInfo, PsycArticle, Psychology and Behavioral Sciences Collection, Social Work Abstracts, and Health and Psychosocial Instruments. They used the search terms ("synchrony" AND "psychotherapy" OR "therapy" OR "counseling"; "mutual influence" AND "psychotherapy" OR "therapy" OR "counseling"; "coregulation" AND "psychotherapy" OR "therapy" OR "counseling"; "communication accommodation" AND "psychotherapy" OR "therapy" OR "counseling"). The initial search yielded 5,802 articles. After removing duplicates (n = 430) and titles that were obviously not related to psychotherapy (n = 4,777), the number of articles was 595. After implementing the inclusion and exclusion criteria, as described below, the results of the searches were merged and the abstracts were obtained and reviewed independently, and then each full text was jointly evaluated by the three raters.

Eligibility Criteria

Studies were eligible if they examined adult individual psychotherapy dyads with real clients (i.e., not standardized patients or hired actors). Hence, articles on couple therapy or romantic relationships, group therapy, inpatient treatment, and child and adolescent treatment were all excluded (n = 443). In addition, reviews, meta-analyses, and dissertations were excluded. We limited the articles to those written in English, journal articles, and books. We included studies that measured correlations between independent characteristics of two dyad members engaging in psychotherapy, such as skin conductance, lexical features, word use, tone of voice, or facial and body expressions, and where synchrony was defined as a within-session phenomenon.

The remaining 152 articles were then examined for their inclusion of synchrony in the title or after examining the abstract. We included articles in which the client and therapist were independently assessed for their internal state and not their partner's experience. We excluded studies that examined the correlation between two independent raters on presumably the same underlying phenomenon, such as the assessment of the correlation of client-rated and therapist-rated alliances, or the correlation of therapist-rated client emotions and clients' rating of their own emotions. Studies that rated session-level observations, as opposed to within-session observations, were also excluded.

For the systematic review, we further excluded studies that only assessed process variables (Bryan et al., 2018; Cohen et al., 2021; Deres-Cohen et al., 2021; Gaume et al., 2019; Marci et al., 2007; Bar-Kalifa et al., 2019; Ramseyer et al., 2020; Ramseyer & Tschacher, 2010; Robinson et al., 1982; Rocco et al., 2018; Soma et al., 2020; Wieder & Wiltshire, 2020) and one study that assessed co-regulation (Paz et al., 2021). A total of 135 studies were excluded.

For the meta-analysis, we further excluded articles in which the data had been utilized in a previous study (Bar-Sella et al., 2022; Cohen et al., 2021; Lutz et al., 2020; Ramseyer & Tschacher, 2014; Schoenherr, Straus, Paulick, et al., 2021). Studies that did not include a direct comparison of synchrony and pseudo-synchrony were excluded from meta-analysis but included in the systematic review (Aafjes-van Doorn et al., 2020; Altmann et al., 2020; Reich et al., 2014), as were studies that did not report the pseudo-synchrony estimate (Schoenherr, Paulick, Strauss, et al., 2019). Single-case studies were excluded (Andreas et al., 2023; Ramseyer & Tschacher, 2006) from the meta-analysis but included in the systematic review. A total of 144 studies were excluded.

The final database was composed of 17 studies for the systematic review and eight for the meta-analysis (Tables 12.1–12.4). The 17 studies featured 792 clients and 285 psychotherapists; the eight studies included 558 clients and 174 therapists in total. One study in the meta-analysis did not report therapist sample size (Ramseyer et al., 2020) and was not counted in the total therapist sample size.

Systematic Review

Unfortunately, none of the 17 studies identified in our literature search focused on therapist behaviors that facilitates dyadic synchrony. Hence, we could not review what therapists do to enable dyad to be synchronous or how therapists work to develop an optimal level of synchrony in dyads. Instead, in the studies included here, we briefly review the relation between synchrony and a number of distal and proximal outcomes. We could not synthesize the results into a full meta-analysis because some studies did not report effect sizes. Instead, we used box score analyses to aggregate the effect of synchrony across all studies (following the procedure of Hill et al., 2023).

A weighted box score analysis was conducted for proximal and distal outcomes separately as follows. Each outcome finding was evaluated. If there was a positive effect (e.g., lower symptom, higher efficacy, better relationship quality), then the outcome was assigned a box score of +1; if there was a negative effect, the outcome was assigned −1; if there was no effect, or the effect did not reach significance, it was assigned 0. For a study with multiple outcome findings, we averaged the box scores of the findings to represent the box score of that study. We calculated the overall effect by averaging the box scores across studies, weighted by the sample size of each study. Moderators were not included in the box score analysis.

Because one therapist often had multiple clients but not vice versa, we used client sample size as the sample size of a study. For example, if a study with a box score of + 1 had 40 clients, and another study with a box score of −1 had 60 clients, the overall effect is

$$\frac{(+1)\times 40+(-1)\times 60}{40+60}=-2$$

An overall score between −1.00 and −0.50 represents a negative overall effect (i.e., higher synchrony is associated with worse outcomes), whereas an overall score between −0.49 and +0.49 is considered neutral, and that between 0.50 and 1.00 is considered to be positive.

There were studies in which the results of individual measures and the combined results were reported. In this case, only individual measures were considered in the box score analysis. If only the combined results were reported, they were used in the box score analysis. In cases in which the same hypothesis was estimated on the same measures, but with several different methods (e.g., the relationship between synchrony and therapist-rated progress, measured by particular scales, was estimated by mixed model

Table 12.1 Empirical Studies on Synchrony and Proximal Outcomes: Basic Information and Settings ($N = 8$)

Study	Year	Client *N*	Therapist *N*	Synchrony Type	Outcome Measures	Method of Analysis	Time Resolution
Andreas et al.	2023	1	1	Body movement (MEA)	SCL-K-9	Synchrony: WCLC Outcome: Pearson's *r*	Window size: 10 s Max time lag: ±5 s
Prinz et al.	2021	175	57	Body movement (MEA)	HSCL	Synchrony: WCLC (peak) Outcome: Multilevel model	Window size: 5 s Max time lag: ±5 s Step size: 1 s
Prinz et al.	2022	60	6	Skin conductance	ORS	Synchrony: WCLC (peak) Outcome: Multilevel model	Window size: 2 min Max time lag: ±10 s
Ramseyer & Tschacher	2011	70	42	Body movement (MEA)	BPSR	Synchrony: WCLC Outcome: Multilevel model, Pearson's *r*	Window size: 1 min Max time lag: ±5 s Step size: 0.1 s
Ramseyer & Tschacher	2014	70	-	Body and head movements (MEA)	BPSR	Synchrony: WCLC Outcome: Pearson's *r*, partial Pearson's *r*	Window size: 1 min Max time lag: ±5 s
Ramseyer & Tschacher	2016	1	1	Hand movement (MEA)	BPSR	Synchrony: WCLC Outcome: Pearson's *r*, backward stepwise regression	Window size: 1 min Max time lag: ±5 s Step size: 0.04 s
Ramseyer	2020	12	10	Body movement (MEA)	BPSR, SCL-K-9	Synchrony: WCLC Outcome: Multilevel model, QUIPA	Window size: 1 min Max time lag: ±5 s Step size: 1 min

(*continued*)

Table 12.1 Continued

Study	Year	Client *N*	Therapist *N*	Synchrony Type	Outcome Measures	Method of Analysis	Time Resolution
Tschacher & Meier	2020	4	1	Respiration, electrocardiogram, heart rate, heart rate variability	Session report questionnaire (precursor of BPSR)	Synchrony: WCLC, CO Outcome: Multivariate multilevel regression, multivariate ordinary regression, multivariate stepwise regression	Respiration WCLC Window size: 30 s Max time lag: ±1–5 s CO Segment size: 30 s Window size: 3 s Step size: 1 s Electrocardiogram WCLC Window size: 1 min Max time lag: ±1 s CO Segment size: 1 min Window size: 0.25–0.5 s Step size: 0.25–0.5 s Heart rate and variability WCLC Window size: 4 min Max time lag: ±0.5–2 min CO Segment size: 4–8 min Window size: 1 min Step size: 1 min

Abbreviated measures: BPSR, Bern Post-Session Report; HSCL, Hopkins Symptoms Checklist; ORS, Outcome Rating Scale; SCL-K-9, Symptom Checklist K-9.

Abbreviated methods: CO, concordance; QUIPA, quantitative idiographic process analysis; WCLC, windowed cross-lagged correlation; WCLC (peak), windowed cross-lagged correlation with a peak-picking algorithm.

MEA, motion energy analysis.

and ordinary regression separately), the findings were first averaged across methods within this hypothesis and then averaged with other findings in the same study.

Synchrony and Proximal Treatment Outcomes

Eight studies examined the association between synchrony and session-level outcomes, involving 323 clients and 118 therapists (Tables 12.1 and 12.2). Most studies used MEA as the measure of synchrony and used the Bern Post-Session Report or Symptom Checklist K-9 as the outcome measure. The associations were assessed either in the same session or one session apart. Weighted box score analysis revealed that the overall association of synchrony and proximal outcomes was neutral to mildly positive (weighted box score = .257).

Movement Synchrony

Findings from the six MEA studies, which involved 259 clients and 111 therapists, were mixed. The weighted box score was .214, showing a neutral to mildly positive association of movement synchrony and proximal outcomes. Four studies reported positive associations between body synchrony and outcomes, such as lower symptom levels (Andreas et al., 2023; Ramseyer, 2020) and higher clients' self-efficacy (Ramseyer & Tschacher, 2011, 2014). Body synchrony was not associated with client-rated well-being (Ramseyer & Tschacher, 2006). A negative association was found with therapist-rated progress (Ramseyer, 2020), whereas another study could not replicate this finding (Ramseyer & Tschacher, 2006).

Two studies examined the associations between synchrony and the outcomes of the following session (Prinz et al., 2021; Ramseyer, 2020). They reported nonsignificant associations between synchrony and symptom levels in the next session, although Ramseyer (2020) noted a medium effect size and marginal significance.

Moderators were assessed in some studies. Andreas et al. (2023) found that the association between synchrony and symptom was only significant in a telehealth setting but not in an in-person setting. Ramseyer and Tschacher (2014) found that the association between synchrony and client self-efficacy only appeared with body synchrony but not head synchrony.

Physiological Synchrony

The weighted box score for physiological synchrony was .479, implying a positive association with proximal outcomes. However, only two studies were found for this analysis, including 64 clients and seven therapists. The result may be limited by low statistical power. In the only study that used SC as the measure of synchrony (Prinz et al., 2022), higher synchrony predicted better outcomes in the next session (Outcome Rating Scale), which was moderated by the interventions used (imagery rescripting vs. cognitive–behavioral). In particular, imagery rescripting segments showed such association, but not in the segments with cognitive–behavioral interventions.

In another study that assessed respiratory, ECG, and heart rate synchronies (Tschacher & Meier, 2020), respiratory synchrony was positively associated with therapist-rated progress in the same session. Higher heart rate synchrony was associated with higher therapist-rated progress and client-rated well-being, but lower client-rated progress in the same session.

Table 12.2 Empirical Studies on Synchrony and Proximal Outcomes: Results and Evaluations

Study	Year	Pseudo-Synchrony	Moderator/ Mediator	Therapist Effect	Client Effect	Included in Meta-Analysis	Results
Andreas et al.	2023	✔	✔	✖	✖	✖	Significant synchrony in face-to-face, $ES = 11.11^{**}$; and video-based settings, $ES = 4.48^{**}$. Moderate and negative correlation between synchrony and client symptom level in the same session in video-based setting, $r = -.38^{*}$ (+1 bs), but not in face-to-face setting, $r = .04$, NS (0 bs).
Prinz et al.	2021	✔	✔	✔	✔	✔	Medium to large effect synchrony over pseudo-synchrony, $d = .72$. Synchrony did not predict client symptoms in the next session, $Bs = [-.06, -.08]$, NS (0×2 bs).
Prinz et al.	2022	✔	✔	✔	✔	✓	Therapist ICC = .10 for synchrony. Higher synchrony in imagery rescripting segments predicted better outcome in the next session, $\beta = .22$, CI [.02, .41] (+1 bs); but not with cognitive–behavioral segments, $\beta = .08$, CI [–.16, .33] (0 bs).
Ramseyer & Tschacher	2011	✔	✖	✔	✔	✔	Medium effect synchrony over pseudo-synchrony, $ds = [.50, .59]^{***}$; therapist ICC = .08. Higher synchrony was associated with higher client-rated self-efficacy in the initial sessions, $r = .35^{*}$ (+1 bs); and these two were marginally associated in the final third, $r = .26^{+}$ (0 bs).
Ramseyer & Tschacher	2014	✔	✔	✖	✖	✖	Medium to large effect synchrony over pseudo-synchrony in head movement, $d = .74^{***}$; small effect synchrony in body movement, $d = .20^{*}$. Body synchrony positively associated with client-rated self-efficacy in the same session, $r = .304^{*}$ (+1 bs), after controlling for head synchrony. Body and head combined synchrony positively associated with clients' self-efficacy in the same session, $r = .388^{***}$. No association between head synchrony and clients' self-efficacy with body synchrony controlled, $r = .164$, NS (0 bs).

Ramseyer & Tschacher	2016	✔	✖	✖	✖	✖	Small to medium effect size between synchrony and pseudo-synchrony, $d = .48^{*}$. Synchrony was not associated with therapist- or client-rated progress in the same session, $rs = [.05, .20]$, NS (0 × 2 bs). Synchrony was not associated with client-rated well-being, $r = .24$, NS (0 bs).
Ramseyer	2020	✔	✖	✖	✔	✔	Medium to large effect size between synchrony and pseudo-synchrony, $d = .76$. Dyad ICC = .123. Higher synchrony marginally predicted higher symptoms in the next session, SCL-K-9 $T = .51^{+}$, $d = .59$ (0 bs). Less therapist-rated progress associated with higher synchrony in the same session, BPSR $t(145.7) = -2.11^{*}$ (−1 bs). Higher symptoms associated with lower synchrony in the same session, SCL-K-9 $t(99.5) = -1.70^{**}$ (+1 bs).
Tschacher & Meier	2020	✔	✖	✖	✔	✖	Significant in-phase respiratory synchrony, WCLC $ES = .85^{*}$, dyad ICC = .09. Significant anti-phase heart rate synchrony, WCLC $ES = -1.53^{*}$. In-phase and anti-phase synchrony canceled each other out with heart rate variability, WCLC $ES = -.06$, NS. Higher respiratory synchrony was predicted by therapist-rated progress in the same session by some methods, WCLC $ts = [1.71, 2.38^{*}]$ (ave. +.5 bs); CO $ts = [-.52, -.49]$, NS (ave. 0 bs). Higher heart rate synchrony was predicted by (a) higher client-rated well-being, CO $ts = [2.63, 5.73]^{*}$ (ave. +1 bs); WCLC $t = .03$, NS (0 bs); (b) higher therapist-rated progress, WCLC $ts = [3.15, 3.42]^{**}$ (ave. +1 bs); CO $ts = [.63, .98]$, NS (ave. 0 bs); and (c) lower client-rated progress in the same session, CO $ts = [-2.09^{*}, -1.46]$ (ave. −.25 bs); WCLC $ts = [-1.63, -1.60]$, NS (ave. 0 bs). Heart rate variability synchrony was not associated with any outcome, $ts = [-.87, .87]$, NS (0 × 6 bs).

Notes. For estimates reported in a range with an overall significance level, the highest p value was picked. If different measures were involved in these estimates, box scores were counted separately and the total counts were reported (e.g., +1 × 2 bs). If different methods were used but on the same measures regarding the same hypotheses, the average box scores were reported (e.g., ave. −.25 bs).

Abbreviated measures: BPSR, Bern Post-Session Report; SCL-K-9, Symptom Checklist K-9.

Abbreviated methods: CO, concordance; WCLC, windowed cross-lagged correlation.

bs, box score; ICC, intraclass correlation; NS, not significant.

$^{+}p < .10$. $^{*}p < .05$. $^{**}p < .01$. $^{***}p < .001$.

Table 12.3 Empirical Studies on Synchrony and Distal Outcomes: Basic Information and Settings ($N = 14$)

Study	Year	Client *N*	Therapist *N*	Synchrony Type	Outcome Measures	Method of Analysis	Time Resolution
Aafjes-van Doorn et al.	2020	7	5	Use of function words (LSM)	PHI, GAF	Synchrony: rLSM Outcome: Pearson's *r*	Talk turn
Altmann et al.	2020	267	119	Body movement (MEA)	BDI, IIP	Synchrony: WCLC (peak) Outcome: Multilevel model, multigroup analysis	Window size: 5 s Max time lag: ±5 s
Paulick, Deisenhofer et al.	2018	143	27	Body movement (MEA)	BSI, IIP, OQ-30, dropout	Synchrony: WCLC Outcome: Multilevel model, *t*-test	Window size: 1 min Max time lag: ±5 s Step size: 0.1 s
Paulick, Rubel, et al.	2018	93	23	Body movement (MEA)	BSI	Synchrony: WCLC Outcome: Multilevel model, *t*-test	Window size: 1 min Max time lag: ±5 s Step size: 0.1 s
Prinz et al.	2021	175	57	Body movement (MEA)	OQ-30	Synchrony: WCLC (peak) Outcome: Multilevel model	Window size: 5 s Max time lag: ±5 s Step size: 1 s
Prinz et al.	2022	60	6	Skin conductance	TAI	Synchrony: WCLC (peak) Outcome: Multilevel model	Window size: 2 min Max time lag: ±10 s
Ramseyer & Tschacher	2011	70	42	Body movement (MEA)	GAS, VEV, BSI, IIP, GSE, MAQ	Synchrony: WCLC Outcome: Multilevel model, Pearson's *r*	Window size: 1 min Max time lag: ±5 s Step size: 0.1 s
Ramseyer & Tschacher	2014	70	—	Body movement (MEA)	GAS, VEV	Synchrony: WCLC Outcome: Partial Pearson's *r*	Window size: 1 min Max time lag: ±5 s
Ramseyer	2020	12	10	Body movement (MEA)	BSI, IIP	Synchrony: WCLC *Outcome:* Multilevel model, QUIPA	Window size: 1 min Max time lag: ±5 s Step size: 1 min
Reich et al.	2014	52	16	Vocal pitch (f_0)	HSCL, BDI, OQ-45.2	Pearson's *r*	Talk turn

Schoenherr, Paulick, Strauss, et al.	2019	267	119	Body movement (MEA)	Dropout (binary, categorical, continuous)	Synchrony: WCLC (peak) Outcome: Point–biserial correlation, logistic regression, multinomial regression, multilevel Cox regression	Window size: 5 s Max time lag: ±5 s Step size: 0.04 s
Schoenherr, Paulick, Worrack, et al.	2019	84	—	Body movement (MEA)	IIP	Synchrony: CLC, CLR, WCC, WCLC, WCLC (peak), WCLR, CRQ Outcome: Partial Pearson's *r*	CLC & CLR Step size: 0.04 s WCC Window size: 10 s Step size: 1 s WCLC Window size: 1 min WCLC (peak) Window size: 5 s Step size: 0.04 s WCLR Window size: 5 s Step size: 0.04 s
Schoenherr, Strauss, Paulick, et al. ()	2021	100	38	Body movement (MEA)	ECR, LSAS	Synchrony: WCLC (peak) Outcome: Pearson's *r*, multilevel backward stepwise regression, multigroup analysis	Window size: 5 s Max time lag: ±5 s Step size: 0.04 s
Schoenherr, Strauss, Stangier, et al.	2021	64	31	Vocal pitch (f_0), range of vocal frequency, body movement (MEA)	ECR, LSAS, IIP	Synchrony: WCLC (peak) Outcome: Forward stepwise regression, multilevel model	Vocal: Interpausal unit (talk turn) Body Window size: 5 s Max time lag: ±5 s Step size: 0.04 s

Abbreviated measures: BDI, Beck Depression Inventory; BSI, Brief Symptom Inventory; ECR, Experiences in Close Relationship Scale; GAF, Global Assessment of Functioning; GAS, Goal Attainment Scaling; GSE, General Self-Efficacy Scale; HSCL, Hopkins Symptom Checklist; IIP, Inventory of Interpersonal Problems; LSAS, Liebowitz Social Anxiety Scale; MAQ, Measure of Attachment Quality; OQ-30, Outcome Questionnaire–30; OQ-45.2, Outcome Questionnaire—Interpersonal Relationship subscale; PHI, Personality Health Index; TAI, Test Anxiety Inventory; VEV, Questionnaire to Assess Changes in Experiencing and Behavior.

Abbreviated methods: CO, concordance; CLC, cross-lagged correlation; CLR, cross-lagged regression; CRQ, cross-recurrence quantification; QUIPA, quantitative idiographic process analysis; rLSM, reciprocal LSM; WCC, windowed cross-correlation; WCLC, windowed cross-lagged correlation; WCLC (peak), windowed cross-lagged correlation with a peak-picking algorithm; WCLR, windowed cross-lagged regression.

LSM, language style matching; MEA, motion energy analysis.

Summary

Studies on session-level outcomes yielded mixed results. The neutral to mildly positive overall box score could mean that synchrony might associate with positive outcomes, but there is not enough evidence to support this. This finding could also mean that the relations between synchrony and outcomes are complex and are moderated by many factors. This is evidenced by several significant moderators found in these studies (e.g., types of methods used, interviewing settings, or body parts of movement synchrony). If these moderators were not considered, the cumulative evidence could show spurious insignificance.

Synchrony and Distal Treatment Outcomes

A total of 14 studies examined how synchrony relates to the distal, end-of-treatment outcomes of therapy (see Table 12.3 and 12.4), covering 786 clients and 282 therapists in total, spanning the United States and Europe. Some studies drew samples from the same databases. To avoid duplicates, the study with the largest sample size was used to represent the other studies. Synchrony was assessed in four ways: MEA, voice, SC, and LSM. Similar to proximal outcomes, a weighted score analysis revealed that the overall association of synchrony and distal outcomes was neutral to mildly positive (weighted box score = .343).

Movement Synchrony

Ten studies employed MEA, involving 667 clients and 255 therapists. The weighted box score of this modality was .389, showing a neutral but mildly positive association of movement synchrony and distal outcomes. The findings were mixed. For example, four studies found that more movement synchrony was associated with less post-treatment interpersonal dysfunction (Altmann et al., 2020; Ramseyer & Tschacher, 2011; Schoenherr, Paulick, Worrack, et al., 2019; Schoenherr, Strauss, Stangier, et al., 2021), including a large study that involved 267 clients (Altmann et al., 2020). However, another large study with 143 clients could not replicate this result (Paulick, Deisenhofer, et al., 2018).

Moderators were important in determining where the association between synchrony and distal outcomes occurred. For example, Paulick, Rubel, et al. (2018) found that the positive association between body synchrony and clients' post-treatment distress only appeared in clients with depression, but not anxiety (no comorbidity). Another study found that head movement synchrony was associated with clients' better well-being, but not with body movement synchrony (Ramseyer & Tschacher, 2014). Two other studies showed significant moderating effects of therapeutic approaches in the synchrony–outcome relation (Altmann et al., 2020; Schoenherr, Strauss, Paulick, et al., 2021).

Therefore, the mildly positive box score in this modality implies that there might be a positive association between movement synchrony and distal outcomes, but this association could have been heavily masked by many moderators.

Vocal Synchrony

In two studies using vocal pitch (Reich et al., 2014; Schoenherr, Strauss, Stangier, et al., 2021), we found a neutral but mildly negative association between synchrony and distal

Table 12.4 Empirical Studies on Synchrony and Distal Outcomes: Results and Evaluations

Study	Year	Pseudo-synchrony	Moderator/ Mediator	Therapist Effect	Client Effect	Included in Meta-Analysis	Results
Aafjes-van Doorn et al.	2020	✖	✖	✖	✖	✖	No significant correlation between talk-turn level synchrony and change in either measure of functioning, PHI $r = .21$, NS (0 bs); GAF $r = -.02$, Ns (0 bs).
Altmann et al.	2020	✖	✔	✔	✖	✖	Higher synchrony predicted lower interpersonal problem, IIP βs = [−.16, −.20]** (+1 × 2 bs); but not depression, BDI βs = [−.10, .02] (0 × 2 bs). The association between synchrony and interpersonal problem was stronger in manualized PDT group than manualized CBT group, $\Delta B = .03^{*}$. No other comparisons of therapeutic approaches reached significance.
Paulick, Deisenhofer, et al.	2018	✔	✖	✔	✖	✔	Large effect synchrony over pseudo-synchrony, $t(141) = 15.27^{***}$, $d = 1.67$. Therapist ICC = .14. Synchrony was not a significant predictor of outcomes: OQ-30 β = −.02, NS; BSI β = −.02, NS; IIP β = .01, NS (0 × 3 bs). Synchrony predicted dropout with marginal significance, β = −.02^{+} (0 bs). Compared to non-improvement and consensual termination group, synchrony was lower in non-improvement and dropout group, OQ-30 $M = -2.14^{*}$; BSI $M = -1.46^{+}$; IIP $M = -1.58^{*}$ (+1 × 2 + 0 bs); and was slightly lower in improvement group, OQ-30 $M = -1.79^{**}$; BSI $M = -.69$; IIP $M = -.21$ (−1 + 0 × 2 bs).

(*continued*)

Table 12.4 Continued

Study	Year	Pseudo-synchrony	Moderator/ Mediator	Therapist Effect	Client Effect	Included in Meta-Analysis	Results
Paulick, Rubel, et al.	2018	✔	✔	✔	✖	✖	Medium effect synchrony over pseudo-synchrony across diagnostic types and time of assessment, *ds* = [.33, .57]. Therapist ICC = .02. Synchrony was significantly lower in clients with depression than anxiety, $B = -3.46^{**}$. Synchrony increased over time in depressed clients but decreased in anxious clients, interaction $B = 2.19^{**}$. Synchrony positively predicted symptom reduction in clients with depression, $B = .13^{*}$ (+1 bs); but not in clients with anxiety, $B = -.06$, NS (0 bs).
Prinz et al.	2021	✔	✖	✔	✔	✔	Medium to large effect synchrony over pseudo-synchrony, $d = .72$. No association between synchrony and outcome, $F(2, 130) = 21.34$, NS (0 bs).
Prinz et al.	2022	✖	✔	✔	✔	✖	Therapist ICC = .10 for synchrony. Higher synchrony in imagery rescripting segments predicted lower post-treatment test anxiety, $\beta = -.25$, CI [−.50, −.01] (+1 bs); but not in cognitive–behavioral segments, $\beta = -.09$, CI [−.34, .16] (0 bs).

Ramseyer & Tschacher	2011	✔	✖	✔	✔	✔	Moderate effect synchrony over pseudo-synchrony, *ds* = [.50, .59]***. Therapist ICC = .08. Positive correlations between synchrony in the initial third of treatment and some outcome changes (by Cohen's *d*): IIP $r = .35^{*}$ (+1 bs); BSI $r = .35^{*}$ (+1 bs); GSE $r = .27^{+}$ (0 bs); MAQ $r = .25^{+}$ (0 bs); overall $r = .45^{**}$. Positive correlations between synchrony in the final third and some outcome changes, IIP $r = .24^{+}$ (0 bs); BSI $r = -.03$ (0 bs); GSE $r = .27^{*}$ (+1 bs); MAQ $r = .16$ (0 bs); overall $r = .24^{+}$. Positive correlations between synchrony in the initial third of treatment and overall retrospective outcome, VEV + GAS $r = .32^{*}$ (+1 bs). No significant correlations in the final third, $r = .20$, NS (0 bs).
Ramseyer & Tschacher	2014	✔	✔	✖	✖	✖	Medium to large effect synchrony over pseudo-synchrony in head movement, $d = .74^{***}$; small effect size in synchrony of body movement, $d = .20^{*}$. Head synchrony was positively associated with clients' goal attainment, GAS $r = .30^{*}$ (+1 bs); and marginally with changes in experiencing and behavior, VEV $r = .22^{+}$ (0 bs). No significant correlations between outcomes and body synchrony *rs* = [.01, .04], NS (0 × 2 bs).

Table 12.4 Continued

Study	Year	Pseudo-synchrony	Moderator/Mediator	Therapist Effect	Client Effect	Included in Meta-Analysis	Results
Ramseyer	2020	✔	✖	✖	✔	✔	Medium to large effect synchrony over pseudo-synchrony, $d = .76$. Dyad ICC = .12. Pre to post improvement in interpersonal problems marginally and negatively associated with synchrony, IIP $t(54.9) = -1.78^{+}$ (0 bs). No significant association between pre–post symptom change and synchrony, BSI NS (0 bs).
Reich et al.	2014	✖	✖	✔	✖	✖	Small effect overall synchrony, $r = .12^{**}$. Therapist ICC = .78. No significant difference between therapist-led synchrony ($r = .15$, therapist ICC = .70) and therapist-followed synchrony ($r = .09$, therapist ICC = .52), $t(15) = 1.33$, NS. Moderate and positive correlation between client-led synchrony and depression, $r = .69^{*}$ (−1 bs). No significant correlations between synchrony and other outcomes, $rs = [.03, .41]$, NS (0 × 5 bs).
Schoenherr, Paulick, Strauss, et al.	2019	✔	✔	✔	✖	✖	Marginally significant correlation between synchrony (session 3) and dropout, $r = -.18^{+}$ (0 bs). Higher synchrony predicted lower risk of dropout, Cox regression $B = -.05^{*}$, OR = .95 (+1 bs); logistic regression $B = -.06^{*}$, OR = .94 (+1 bs); multinomial regression $B = -.22^{***}$, OR = .80 (+1 bs).

							Treatment type marginally moderated the relationship between synchrony and risk of dropout, integrative CBT: OR = .97, NS; manualized CBT OR = 1.02, NS; manualized PDT OR = .91⁺. Gender match of client and therapist moderated this effect, mixed-sex dyad OR = .94*; same-sex dyad OR = .97, NS.
Schoenherr, Paulick, Worrack, et al.	2019	✖	✖	✖	✖	✖	Varied synchrony strengths measured by different methods, *r*s = [.036, .115]. R^2s = [.005, .269]. Exploratory factor analysis revealed three different types of synchrony measure: Frequency of synchrony, strength of synchrony within identified synchronization intervals, and strength of synchrony of total dyadic interaction. Second-order confirmatory factor analysis revealed a single synchrony factor loaded on the three types of synchrony measures, βs = [.67, .88]. Only 3 out of 7 metrics significantly correlated with interpersonal problem: windowed cross-correlation by average $r = -.27^*$ (+1 bs); windowed cross-lagged correlation (peak) by ratio $r = -.26^*$ (+1 bs); windowed cross-lagged regression by ratio $r = -.28^*$ (+1 bs). Others were insignificant, *r*s = [−.20, .08], NS (0 × 4 bs).

Table 12.4 Continued

Study	Year	Pseudo-synchrony	Moderator/Mediator	Therapist Effect	Client Effect	Included in Meta-Analysis	Results
Schoenherr, Strauss, Paulick, et al.	2021	✖	✔	✔	✖	✖	On average, synchrony interval made up 20.77% of the total time being assessed. Therapist ICC = .40 for CBT group, and .07 for PDT group. Overall synchrony negatively correlated with attachment anxiety, $r = -.21^{*}$. Therapist-led synchrony negatively correlated with attachment anxiety, $r = -.25^{*}$ (+1 bs). Client-led synchrony was not associated with attachment anxiety, $r = -.16$, NS (0 bs). No synchronies were associated with attachment avoidance, social anxiety, or social avoidance $rs = [-.10, .12]$, NS (0 × 6 bs). Higher synchrony in session 8 predicted lower attachment anxiety, overall $\beta = -.66^{*}$, therapist-led $\beta = -.75^{**}$ (+1 bs). Therapeutic approach moderated the relationship between synchrony and attachment anxiety, overall $\beta = .53^{*}$, therapist-led $\beta = .58^{**}$.

Schoenherr, Strauss, Stangier, et al.	2021	✔	✖	✔	✖	✖	Medium to large effect therapist-led vocal synchrony over pseudo-synchrony (so as below), average $d = .72^{***}$; large effect client-led vocal synchrony, average $d = 1.39^{***}$; large effect therapist-led vocal range synchrony, average $d = 1.17^{***}$; large effect client-led vocal range synchrony, average $d = 1.68^{***}$. Higher therapist-led vocal synchrony predicted higher interpersonal problem, $\beta = .37^{*}$ (−1 bs); and lower attachment anxiety, $\beta = -.27^{*}$ (+1 bs); but was not associated with social anxiety, $\beta s = [.12, .26]$, NS (0 × 2 bs). Higher therapist-led vocal range synchrony predicted higher attachment avoidance, $\beta = .28^{*}$ (−1 bs); and attachment anxiety, $\beta = .32^{*}$ (−1 bs). Higher client-led vocal synchrony predicted greater social anxiety and avoidance, $\beta s = [.24, .34]^{*}$ (−1 × 3 bs); and greater attachment avoidance, $\beta = .25^{*}$ (−1 bs); but was not associated with other outcomes, $\beta s = [.16, .23]$, NS (0 × 3 bs). Higher client-led vocal range synchrony predicted lower social avoidance, $\beta = -.29^{*}$ (+1 bs). Higher client-led body movement synchrony predicted lower interpersonal problem, $\beta = -.29^{*}$ (+1 bs).

Notes. For estimates reported in a range with an overall significance level, the highest *p* value was picked. If different measures were involved in these estimates, box scores were counted separately and the total counts were reported (e.g., +1 × 2 bs). If different methods were used but on the same measures regarding the same hypotheses, the average box scores were reported (e.g., ave. −.25 bs).

Abbreviated measures: BDI, Beck Depression Inventory; BSI, Brief Symptom Inventory; GAF, Global Assessment of Functioning; GAS, Goal Attainment Scaling; GSE, General Self-Efficacy Scale; IIP, Inventory of Interpersonal Problems; MAQ, Measure of Attachment Quality; OQ-30, Outcome Questionnaire–30; PHI, Personality Health Index; VEV, Questionnaire to Assess Changes in Experiencing and Behavior.

Abbreviated method: QUIPA, quantitative idiographic process analysis.

bs, box score; CBT, cognitive–behavioral therapy; ICC, intraclass correlation; NS, not significant; PDT, psychodynamic therapy.

$^{+}p < .10$. $^{*}p < .05$. $^{**}p < .01$. $^{***}p < .001$.

outcomes (weighted box score = –.222). The two studies featured 116 clients and 47 therapists. This result implies that more vocal synchrony may be detrimental to distal outcomes.

Mixed associations were found based on the way that pitch was estimated (e.g., fundamental frequency vs. the range of fundamental frequency), how outcomes were assessed, and who led the synchrony. For example, therapist-led pitch synchrony was found to predict higher post-treatment interpersonal dysfunction but lower attachment anxiety (Schoenherr, Strauss, Paulick, et al., 2021). Client-led pitch synchrony was found to predict higher post-treatment social anxiety and avoidance, attachment avoidance (Schoenherr, Strauss, Paulick, et al., 2021), and depression (Reich et al., 2014), but it had no association with interpersonal dysfunction (Reich et al., 2014). In the only study with pitch range synchrony (Schoenherr, Strauss, Paulick, et al., 2021), therapist-led pitch range synchrony predicted higher post-treatment attachment avoidance and anxiety, but client-led pitch range synchrony predicted lower post-treatment social avoidance.

Physiological Synchrony

Prinz et al., (2022) tested the associations between SC and outcomes. The Test Anxiety Inventory was used to assess the test anxiety level of clients. The results showed that higher synchrony during image rescripting interventions predicted lower post-treatment test anxiety, but there was no significant association between synchrony during cognitive–behavioral interventions and post-treatment test anxiety. Hence, a + .5 box score was assigned to this modality.

Linguistic Synchrony

In the only study that involved LSM (Aafjes-van Doorn et al., 2020), Personality Health Index and Global Assessment of Functioning were used as indicators of outcomes, and the overall synchrony was quantified by the average synchrony aggregated across talk turns. There were no significant correlations between LSM and outcomes, giving a 0 box score to this modality.

Summary

The number of studies involved in this area allowed for a more comprehensive synthesis of the findings. This overall pattern may mask differences based on the measure of synchrony and the outcome measures used. For example, the overall association between synchrony and distal outcomes was neutral to mildly positive. When looking at individual modalities, movement synchrony showed a similar neutral to mildly positive association with outcomes. But vocal synchrony came with a neutral to mildly negative association with outcomes. Similar to studies with proximal outcome, it is possible that the results were masked by many moderators (e.g., the measuring modalities and outcomes used) that need to be differentiated.

Meta-Analysis of Synchrony Versus Pseudo-Synchrony

Eight studies compared the synchrony between therapist and client dyads and simulated pairings of random dyads (i.e., synchrony vs. pseudo-synchrony; see Table 12.1–12.4).

The means, standard deviations, and effect sizes (Cohen's *d*) were extracted. For studies in which the mean and standard deviation of the sample were missing, *d* reported in the primary study and sample size were utilized to compute the effect size variance. All analyses were conducted in R (R Development Core Team, 2016) using the MAd package (Del Re & Hoyt, 2014).

Across the eight studies, the total number of clients was 557 ($M = 69.63$; $SD = 60.10$; range, 12–175) and the total number of therapists was 174 ($M = 24.86$; $SD = 18.62$; range 8 to 57; one study did not report the number of therapists). The total number of sessions included in the meta-analysis was 1,162 ($M = 179$; $SD = 155.87$; median = 132), with the number ranging from 10 to 423 sessions.

As predicted, there was a significant difference between the effect size of synchrony and pseudo-synchrony ($d = 1.01$, 95% confidence interval (CI) [0.56, 1.47], $p < .001$). This large effect size indicated a higher level of synchrony in real dyads versus simulated dyads.

The effect sizes of each study are listed in the forest plot shown in Figure 12.3. As seen in Figure 12.3, the effect size in Marci et al. (2007) was quite substantial. We removed this effect size from the analysis and found that the effect synchrony compared to pseudo-synchrony remained significant ($d = 0.86$, 95% CI [0.60, 1.11], $p < .001$).

We tested for publication bias and found that the sample would require 135 nonsignificant studies to render the result null.

Across this set of studies, authentic client and psychotherapist dyad pairs exhibited synchronized behavioral patterns to a much greater extent than shuffled pairs. This provides evidence for the presence of synchrony in psychotherapy interactions.

Possible Negative Effects and Harm

Synchrony in itself may not always be beneficial (e.g., Ramseyer, 2020). It has been suggested that the context in which synchrony occurs is crucial to understanding when synchrony leads to positive outcomes and when it does not (Shamay-Tsoory et al.,

Study	**Cohen's *d***	**Variance**
Bar-Kalifa et al, 2019	1.59	0.01
Deres-Cohen 2021	0.73	0.004
Marci 2007	2.36	0.139
Paulick 2018	1.56	0.022
Prinz 2020	0.6	0.003
Ramseyer 2020	0.76	0.018
Ramseyer et al, 2020	0.27	0.015
Ramseyer & Tschacher 2010/2011	0.49	0.078
Summary	**1.04**	**0.036**

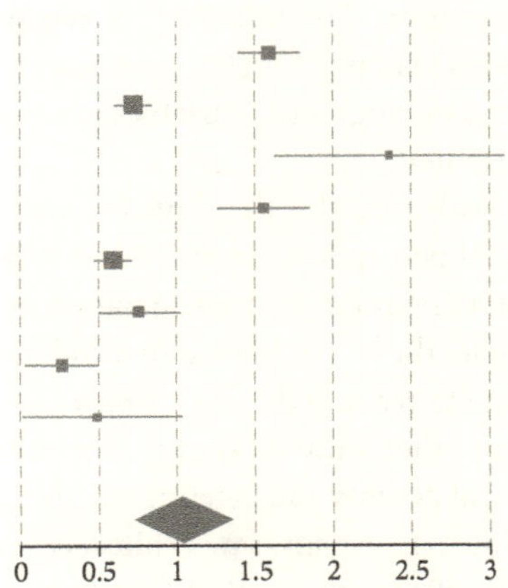

Figure 12.3 Forest plot of the included studies, effect sizes, and variances.

2019). For example, during alliance ruptures, there may be an increased correlation in biobehavioral signals. However, this synchrony is not likely to be evidence of a mutual understanding but, rather, an escalation of negative emotions. Similarly, when clients share depressive thoughts and therapists start to feel anxious about their ability to help the clients, both the clients' and the therapists' vocal or physiological arousal are synchronously elevated. However, this interaction may not help clients regulate their emotions and may not result in a positive session outcome. These directions have yet to be studied.

Diversity Considerations

There are well-documented disparities in the mental health care of minoritized and historically oppressed populations throughout the mental health system (e.g., Committee on Understanding and Eliminating Racial and Ethnic Disparities in Health Care et al., 2004; Maura & Weisman de Mamani, 2017; Merced et al., 2020; Miranda et al., 2008; Satcher, 2001). However, little is known about the micro processes occurring during multicultural interactions. Synchrony may be one of the processes impacted by differences in cultural and identity differences within dyads, and it may differ as a function of identity factors such as gender, race/ethnicity, immigration status, body size, ability status, and other lived experiences. For example, researchers have posited that the gender of the therapist and client may impact synchrony (Ramseyer & Tschacher, 2011). However, there has been little empirical exploration to date on the possible ways in which cultural and identity variables impact the synchrony in psychotherapy.

The articles reviewed in this chapter broadly included participants from university populations, those with access to university-funded mental health clinics, and often utilized the same data sample, thus limiting the number and types of people represented in the review, meta-analysis, and the broader synchrony literature. Although there appeared to be some geographic diversity in samples (e.g., Switzerland, Germany, Israel, United States), these samples did not represent a global population that would include a greater diversity of races, ethnicities, and nationalities. In addition, the samples were restricted to the gender binary (i.e., male and female), and many did not include sexual orientation. For research on synchrony to be generalized to a broader population, researchers must include participants from diverse backgrounds and collect more detailed demographic variables to understand where some variance of synchrony can be attributed.

Studies outside the clinical domain have shown that diversity issues can impact emotional perception, empathy, and outcomes (e.g., Grammer et al., 1998), which may be a starting point to understanding how cultural factors may impact synchrony. For example, there is evidence that individuals from different cultural backgrounds are less likely to react to the emotional experiences of individuals whom they identify as being from other cultural groups (Avenanti et al., 2010; Forgiarini et al., 2011). Measures of neural activity indicated the activation of pain centers of the brain to be faster when White participants saw White faces rather than Black faces experiencing pain (Azevedo et al., 2013; Sessa et al., 2014). In other words, the physiological perception of pain may be faster and more intense within same-race dyads.

There is also evidence that increased contact with members of the other group can reduce other-race differences in physiological responses to another's pain (Cao et al., 2015). Studies in the health care field have reported treatment disparities for racial/ethnic minority (REM) clients that may be due to the ways in which clinicians perceive the experience of REM clients. For instance, compared to White clients, REM clients are often prescribed significantly fewer pain medications by White clinicians. This could potentially be due to clinicians' differences in the perception and empathy for the pain experienced by REM clients (e.g., Burgess et al., 2010). Findings also indicate that mixed-gender pairs are less likely to be synchronous than same-gender pairs during emotionally intimate conversations (Grammer et al., 1998).

Researchers might expand these health care investigations to determine whether, and to what extent, cultural and identity variables affect psychotherapists' ability to synchronize with their clients. There may be differences in synchrony based on how therapists and clients perceive and express nonverbal behavior such as tone of voice, body movements, and facial expression, based on cultural factors. Future studies should address how these dimensions of diversity affect synchrony in psychotherapy and moderate its association with treatment outcome.

Limitations of Research

As psychotherapy studies examining synchrony have started to amass, it has become clear that synchrony is not always associated with favorable therapy outcomes (e.g., Reich et al., 2014; Schoenherr, Strauss, Paulick, et al., 2021). Unfortunately, there are currently very few studies examining how therapists facilitate dyadic synchrony in ways that lead to beneficial outcomes. There is an obvious need for more studies that consider how therapists successfully facilitate synchrony, as well as studies that include client, therapist, and/or situational moderators in which synchrony leads to better (or worse) therapeutic outcomes.

Our systematic review and meta-analyses point to the need for standardization in the research. As indicated in previous studies (Kleinbub, 2017; Koole et al., 2020; Palumbo et al., 2017; Wiltshire et al., 2020), the lack of consensus in the synchrony literature with respect to terminology and methodology impedes cross-study comparisons and makes it difficult to derive robust conclusions as to the associations between synchrony and outcomes. The research community should aim for a consensus on common terminologies and practices.

Another issue that may have contributed to the inconclusive results is the heterogeneity of settings to assess synchrony and the small number of studies within each setting, as shown in Tables 12.1 and 12.2. In addition, the ways the results are presented limited our ability to synthesize the findings into a full meta-analysis on the association between synchrony and outcomes. Because the synchrony literature addresses complex questions of mutual influence over time, complex models should be standard in most studies. At the same time, it is important to report the basic descriptive statistics such as effect sizes, the correlation between the clients' and the therapists' signals, and the associations with outcome variables. Synchrony studies should also include a clearer report of the estimates of synchrony versus pseudo-synchrony.

In addition, few studies specified when and for whom synchrony leads to positive results. Of the 25 studies included in our review, only five studies had some form of moderators (20%) and none included mediators. Furthermore, the studies reviewed here lacked client and therapist diversity in terms of cultural identities, and no study examined cultural and identity variables that may impact therapist facilitation of synchrony.

Several directions could contribute to a better understanding of the role of synchrony in psychotherapy. Effective synchrony may depend on the therapists' ability to induce co-regulation patterns and reduce morphogenic processes, perhaps through their capacity to self-regulate their own emotions in the session (Paz et al., 2021; Soma et al., 2020). Future studies can account for emotional context as a possible state-like moderator and examine, for example, whether in situations of intrapersonal or interpersonal distress, synchrony leads to poorer results, whereas in situations of emotional pain or positive emotions, synchrony leads to beneficial results. Future studies can also consider examining whether clients' traits (e.g., diagnosis) or therapists' traits (e.g., emotion regulation capabilities) moderate the association between synchrony and outcome.

Differences in patterns of synchrony can also be considered (Butler, 2015). Synchrony is commonly examined as a positive association between two persons' stream of biobehavioral signals. One disadvantage of this approach is that it overlooks the fact that successful interpersonal coordination requires partners to dynamically move toward and away from each other (Mayo & Gordon, 2020). Recent models of synchrony suggest that people tend to move in and out of synchrony while they interact, and that these interpersonal dynamics are complementary and adaptive (Feldman, 2021; Mayo & Gordon, 2020). Future studies should examine whether flexible movement between synchronized and unsynchronized states is associated with beneficial outcomes.

Finally, most research on client–therapist synchrony has focused on one modality of synchrony (e.g., movement, vocal, physiological) and has measured synchrony on a single-session or pooled sampled session basis. However, assessment of a client's broader biopsychosocial context at multiple time points during treatment could better capture the complexity of the therapeutic process. It is crucial to include a multimethod assessment of synchrony that takes different behavioral and biological processes into account.

Training Implications

Our clinical experience and the research literature to date have several implications for training. Supervisors and educators can help trainees pay more attention to what occurs at the nonverbal level between their clients and themselves (Ogden et al., 2006) and teach them to identify moments of synchrony, mys-synchrony, and avoidance in their responses (Feldman, 2012). The maturation of innovative technologies for monitoring the therapeutic process, along with the development of advanced feedback systems, may allow therapists and their supervisors to detect moments of increased or decreased synchrony and to explore the context in which these dynamics occurred and their consequences (Paulick, Rubel, et al., 2018). Supervisors can encourage trainee therapists to utilize their own emotional arousal cues that arise in response to the clients' signals (e.g., Knox & Hill, 2003). Therapists can be trained to identify moments in a session in which they unintentionally synchronized with their clients in a way that amplified or escalated ineffective regulatory process.

With the help of their supervisors, they can learn to strengthen their ability to downregulate unproductive emotional processes and to upregulate productive emotional processes (Geller, 2009). For example, a therapist and a supervisor could explore the segment of a video in which the client and the therapist were vocally synchronized in a moment of distress, which, based on the client's self-reports at the end of the session, led to more distress in the client. This exploration may lead to a better understanding of when it is important for the therapist to let themself be touched by the client's emotions and how at the same time the therapist can downregulate themself to help the client tolerate their own emotions and eventually achieve better well-being.

We encourage future training programs to use automatically measured synchrony in multiple modalities (text, audio, video, physiology, etc.) along with psychometric feedback. These will help therapists to be more aware of their own verbal and nonverbal behavior in contacts with their clients.

Therapeutic Practices

- Attend to what occurs at the nonverbal level between clients and yourself because this vehicle provides important information about the clients' mental states, thoughts, and feelings.
- Notice changes in the client's nonverbal signals in different channels, such as breathing patterns, body movement, tone of voice, linguistic style, and facial expression.
- Observe and perhaps be influenced by the client's nonverbal behavior. Be aware of your own affective and bodily states that change in response to the client's nonverbal behavior.
- Allow yourself to move flexibly in and out of synchrony, knowing that flexible dynamic movements between synchronization and separation may prove adaptive.
- Consider the emotional context in which synchrony occurs. Some contexts probably call for high synchrony (e.g., when clients experience adaptive emotions), whereas other contexts probably call for relatively low levels of synchrony (e.g., when clients experience maladaptive emotions).
- Consider the client's culture and identity, and how these might impact your interpretations or assumptions about the therapeutic interaction and synchrony.
- Aim to detect the intensity and the direction of the dyadic emotional dynamic by upregulating adaptive emotions and downregulating maladaptive emotions.

References

* Studies included in the research review.

*Aafjes-van Doorn, K., Porcerelli, J., & Müller-Frommeyer, L. C. (2020). Language style matching in psychotherapy: An implicit aspect of alliance. *Journal of Counseling Psychology, 67*(4), 509–522.

*Altmann, U., Brümmel, M., Meier, J., & Strauss, B. (2021). Movement synchrony and facial synchrony as diagnostic features of depression. Journal of Nervous & Mental Disease, *209*(2), 128–136). https://doi.org/10.1097/nmd.0000000000001268

*Altmann, U., Schoenherr, D., Paulick, J., Deisenhofer, A.-K., Schwartz, B., Rubel, J. A., Stangier, U., Lutz, W., & Strauss, B. (2020). Associations between movement synchrony and outcome in patients with social anxiety disorder: Evidence for treatment specific effects. *Psychotherapy Research, 30*(5), 574–590.

*Andreas, S., Gablonski, T. C., Tschacher, W., Gebhardt, A., Rabung, S., Schulz, H., & Kadur, J. (2023). Long-term psychodynamic psychotherapy in a face-to-face versus videoconferencing setting: A single case study. *Journal of Clinical Psychology, 79*(2), 277–295.

Aron, L., & Harris, A. (2014). *Relational psychoanalysis: Volume 5. Evolution of process*. Routledge.

Atzil-Slonim, D., Bar-Kalifa, E., Fisher, H., Peri, T., Lutz, W., Rubel, J., & Rafaeli, E. (2018). Emotional congruence between clients and therapists and its effect on treatment outcome. *Journal of Counseling Psychology, 65*(1), 51–64.

Atzil-Slonim, D., Stolowicz-Melman, D., Bar-Kalifa, E., Gilboa-Schechtman, E., Paz, A., Wolff, M., Rotter, I., Zagoory, O., & Feldman, R. (2022). Oxytocin reactivity to the therapeutic encounter as a biomarker of change in the treatment of depression. *Journal of Counseling Psychology, 69*(5), 755–776.

Avenanti, A., Sirigu, A., & Aglioti, S. M. (2010). Racial bias reduces empathic sensorimotor resonance with other-race pain. *Current Biology, 20*(11), 1018–1022.

Azevedo, R. T., Macaluso, E., Avenanti, A., Santangelo, V., Cazzato, V., & Aglioti, S. M. (2013). Their pain is not our pain: Brain and autonomic correlates of empathic resonance with the pain of same and different race individuals. *Human Brain Mapping, 34*(12), 3168–3181.

Bachorowski, J.-A. (1999). Vocal expression and perception of emotion. *Current Directions in Psychological Science, 8*(2), 53–57.

Baltrušaitis, T., Robinson, P., & Morency, L.-P. (2016). OpenFace: An open source facial behavior analysis toolkit. In 2016 IEEE Winter Conference on Applications of Computer Vision (WACV) (pp. 1–10). IEEE.

Balzarotti, S., Biassoni, F., Colombo, B., & Ciceri, M. R. (2017). Cardiac vagal control as a marker of emotion regulation in healthy adults: A review. *Biological Psychology, 130*, 54–66.

Bar-Kalifa, E., Prinz, J. N., Atzil-Slonim, D., Rubel, J. A., Lutz, W., & Rafaeli, E. (2019). Physiological synchrony and therapeutic alliance in an imagery-based treatment. *Journal of Counseling Psychology, 66*(4), 508–517.

Bar-Sella, A., Randall, A. K., & Zilcha-Mano, S. (2022). Understanding interdependence of patients' and therapists' affect experiencing: Examination at sample and individual difference levels. *Journal of Counseling Psychology, 69*(2), 188–198.

Beebe, B., & Lachmann, F. M. (1988). The contribution of mother–infant mutual influence to the origins of self- and object representations. *Psychoanalytic Psychology, 5*(4), 305–337.

Berntson, G. G., Bigger, J. T., Jr., Eckberg, D. L., Grossman, P., Kaufmann, P. G., Malik, M., Nagaraja, H. N., Porges, S. W., Saul, J. P., Stone, P. H., & van der Molen, M. W. (1997). Heart rate variability: Origins, methods, and interpretive caveats. *Psychophysiology, 34*(6), 623–648.

Bryan, C. J., Baucom, B. R., Crenshaw, A. O., Imel, Z., Atkins, D. C., Clemans, T. A., Leeson, B., Burch, T. S., Mintz, J., & Rudd, M. D. (2018). Associations of patient-rated emotional bond and vocally encoded emotional arousal among clinicians and acutely suicidal military personnel. *Journal of Consulting and Clinical Psychology, 86*(4), 372–383.

Burgess, D. J., Warren, J., Phelan, S., Dovidio, J., & van Ryn, M. (2010). Stereotype threat and health disparities: What medical educators and future physicians need to know. *Journal of General Internal Medicine, 25*(Suppl. 2), S169–S177.

Butler, E. A. (2015). Interpersonal affect dynamics: It takes two (and time) to tango. *Emotion Review*, *7*(4), 336–341.

Butner, J. E., Berg, C. A., Baucom, B. R., & Wiebe, D. J. (2014). Modeling coordination in multiple simultaneous latent change scores. *Multivariate Behavioral Research*, *49*(6), 554–570.

Cao, Y., Contreras-Huerta, L. S., McFadyen, J., & Cunnington, R. (2015). Racial bias in neural response to others' pain is reduced with other-race contact. *Cortex*, *70*, 68–78.

Chung, C., & Pennebaker, J. (2007). The psychological functions of function words. In K. Fiedler (Ed.), Social *communication* (Vol. 1, pp. 343–359). Psychology Press. https://books.google.com/books?hl=en&lr=&id=zzW5dqN8NiUC&oi=fnd&pg=PA343&dq=Chung+C+Pennebaker+J+W+(2007)+The+psychological+functions+of+function+words+Social+communication+1+343-359&ots=fzQifqHy9h&sig=sFDTlCJqW1FhWLws6d8P7CDrFXs

Cohen, K., Ramseyer, F. T., Tal, S., & Zilcha-Mano, S. (2021). Nonverbal synchrony and the alliance in psychotherapy for major depression: Disentangling state-like and trait-like effects. *Clinical Psychological Science*, *9*(4), 634–648.

Committee on Understanding and Eliminating Racial and Ethnic Disparities in Health Care, Board on Health Sciences Policy, & Institute of Medicine. (2004). *Unequal treatment: Confronting racial and ethnic disparities in health care*. National Academies Press.

Dean, R. T., & Dunsmuir, W. T. M. (2016). Dangers and uses of cross-correlation in analyzing time series in perception, performance, movement, and neuroscience: The importance of constructing transfer function autoregressive models. *Behavior Research Methods*, *48*(2), 783–802.

Delaherche, E., Chetouani, M., Mahdhaoui, A., Saint-Georges, C., Viaux, S., & Cohen, D. (2012). Interpersonal synchrony: A survey of evaluation methods across disciplines. *IEEE Transactions on Affective Computing*, *3*(3), 349–365.

Del Re, A. C., & Hoyt, W. T. (2014). MAd: Meta-analysis with mean differences. *R package version 0.8-2*.

Deres-Cohen, K., Dolev-Amit, T., Peysachov, G., Ramseyer, F. T., & Zilcha-Mano, S. (2021). Nonverbal synchrony as a marker of alliance ruptures. *Psychotherapy*, *58*(4), 499–509.

Doorn, K. A., & Müller-Frommeyer, L. (2020). Reciprocal language style matching in psychotherapy research. *Counselling and Psychotherapy Research*, *20*(3), 449–455. https://doi.org/10.1002/capr.12298

Edelberg, R. (1993). Electrodermal mechanisms: A critique of the two-effector hypothesis and a proposed replacement. In J. Roy, W. Boucsein, D. Fowles, & J. Gruzelier (Eds.), Progress in *electrodermal research* (pp. 7–29). Springer. https://doi.org/10.1007/978-1-4615-2864-7_2

Feldman, R. (1998). *Coding interactive behavior (CIB)* [Unpublished manual]. Department of Psychology, Bar-Ilan University.

Feldman, R. (2007). Parent–infant synchrony and the construction of shared timing; physiological precursors, developmental outcomes, and risk conditions. *Journal of Child Psychology and Psychiatry, and Allied Disciplines*, *48*(3–4), 329–354.

Feldman, R. (2012). Bio-behavioral synchrony: A model for integrating biological and microsocial behavioral processes in the study of parenting. *Parenting*, *12*(2–3), 154–164. https://doi.org/10.1080/15295192.2012.683342

Feldman, R. (2021). Social behavior as a transdiagnostic marker of resilience. *Annual Review of Clinical Psychology*, 17(1), 153–180. https://doi.org/10.1146/annurev-clinpsy-081219-102046

Forgiarini, M., Gallucci, M., & Maravita, A. (2011). Racism and the empathy for pain on our skin. *Frontiers in Psychology*, *2*. https://doi.org/10.3389/fpsyg.2011.00108

Fosha, D. (2001). The dyadic regulation of affect. *Journal of Clinical Psychology*, *57*(2), 227–242.

Gaume, J., Hallgren, K. A., Clair, C., Schmid Mast, M., Carrard, V., & Atkins, D. C. (2019). Modeling empathy as synchrony in clinician and patient vocally encoded emotional arousal: A failure to replicate. *Journal of Counseling Psychology*, *66*(3), 341–350.

Geller, S. (2009). Cultivation of therapeutic presence: Therapeutic drumming and mindfulness practices. *Journal for Client-Centered Psychotherapy*, *47*(4), 273–287

Gelo, O. C. G., & Salvatore, S. (2016). A dynamic systems approach to psychotherapy: A metatheoretical framework for explaining psychotherapy change processes. *Journal of Counseling Psychology*, *63*(4), 379–395.

Gonzales, A. L., Hancock, J. T., & Pennebaker, J. W. (2010). Language style matching as a predictor of social dynamics in small groups. *Communication Research, 37*(1), 3–19.

Grammer, K., Kruck, K. B., & Magnusson, M. S. (1998). The courtship dance: Patterns of nonverbal synchronization in opposite-sex encounters. *Journal of Nonverbal Behavior, 22*(1), 3–29.

Hammerschmidt, K., & Jürgens, U. (2007). Acoustical correlates of affective prosody. *Journal of Voice, 21*(5), 531–540.

Hatfield, E., Cacioppo, J. T., & Rapson, R. L. (1993). Emotional contagion. *Current Directions in Psychological Science, 2*(3), 96–100.

Helm, J. L., Sbarra, D. A., & Ferrer, E. (2014). Coregulation of respiratory sinus arrhythmia in adult romantic partners. *Emotion, 14*(3), 522–531.

Imel, Z. E., Barco, J. S., Brown, H. J., Baucom, B. R., Baer, J. S., Kircher, J. C., & Atkins, D. C. (2014). The association of therapist empathy and synchrony in vocally encoded arousal. *Journal of Counseling Psychology, 61*(1), 146–153. https://doi.org/10.1037/a0034943

Kleinbub, J. R. (2017). State of the art of interpersonal physiology in psychotherapy: A systematic review. *Frontiers in Psychology, 8*, 2053.

Knox, S., & Hill, C. E. (2003). Therapist self-disclosure: Research-based suggestions for practitioners. *Journal of Clinical Psychology, 59*(5), 529–539.

Koole, S. L., Atzil-Slonim, D., Butler, E., Dikker, S., Tschacher, W., & Wilderjans, T. (2020). Insync with your shrink. In J. Forgas, W. Crano, & K. Fiedler (Eds.), *Applications of social psychology* (pp. 161–184). Routledge.

Koole, S. L., & Tschacher, W. (2016). Synchrony in psychotherapy: A review and an integrative framework for the therapeutic alliance. *Frontiers in Psychology, 7*, 862.

Lewinski, P., den Uyl, T. M., & Butler, C. (2014). Automated facial coding: Validation of basic emotions and FACS AUs in FaceReader. *Journal of Neuroscience, Psychology, and Economics, 7*(4), 227–236.

Lidberg, L., & Gunnar Wallin, B. (1981). Sympathetic skin nerve discharges in relation to amplitude of skin resistance responses. *Psychophysiology, 18*(3), 268–270. https://doi.org/10.1111/j.1469-8986.1981.tb03033.x

Lord, S. P., Sheng, E., Imel, Z. E., Baer, J., & Atkins, D. C. (2015). More than reflections: Empathy in motivational interviewing includes language style synchrony between therapist and client. *Behavior Therapy, 46*(3), 296–303.

Lutz, W., Prinz, J. N., Schwartz, B., Paulick, J., Schoenherr, D., Deisenhofer, A.-K., Terhürne, P., Boyle, K., Altmann, U., Strauß, B., Rafaeli, E., Atzil-Slonim, D., Bar-Kalifa, E., & Rubel, J. (2020). Patterns of early change in interpersonal problems and their relationship to nonverbal synchrony and multidimensional outcome. *Journal of Counseling Psychology, 67*(4), 449–461.

Marci, C. D., Ham, J., Moran, E., & Orr, S. P. (2007). Physiologic correlates of perceived therapist empathy and social–emotional process during psychotherapy. *Journal of Nervous and Mental Disease, 195*(2), 103–111.

Maura, J., & Weisman de Mamani, A. (2017). Mental health disparities, treatment engagement, and attrition among racial/ethnic minorities with severe mental illness: A review. *Journal of Clinical Psychology in Medical Settings, 24*(3–4), 187–210.

Mayo, O., & Gordon, I. (2020). In and out of synchrony—Behavioral and physiological dynamics of dyadic interpersonal coordination. *Psychophysiology, 57*(6), e13574. https://doi.org/10.1111/psyp.13574

McCullough, L. (2003). *Treating affect phobia: A manual for short-term dynamic psychotherapy*. Guilford.

Merced, K., Imel, Z. E., Baldwin, S. A., Fischer, H., Yoon, T., Stewart, C., Simon, G., Ahmedani, B., Beck, A., Daida, Y., Hubley, S., Rossom, R., Waitzfelder, B., Zeber, J. E., & Coleman, K. J. (2020). Provider contributions to disparities in mental health care. *Psychiatric Services, 71*(8), 765–771.

Miranda, J., McGuire, T. G., Williams, D. R., & Wang, P. (2008). Mental health in the context of health disparities. *American Journal of Psychiatry, 165*(9), 1102–1108.

Moher, D., Liberati, A., Tetzlaff, J., Altman, D. G., & PRISMA Group. (2010). Preferred Reporting Items for Systematic Reviews and Meta-Analyses: The PRISMA statement. *International Journal of Surgery, 8*(5), 336–341.

Ogden, P., Pain, C., & Fisher, J. (2006). A sensorimotor approach to the treatment of trauma and dissociation. *Psychiatric Clinics*, *29*(1), 263–279.

Palumbo, R. V., Marraccini, M. E., Weyandt, L. L., Wilder-Smith, O., McGee, H. A., Liu, S., & Goodwin, M. S. (2017). Interpersonal autonomic physiology: A systematic review of the literature. *Personality and Social Psychology Review*, *21*(2), 99–141.

*Paulick, J., Deisenhofer, A.-K., Ramseyer, F. T., Tschacher, W., Boyle, K., Rubel, J., & Lutz, W. (2018). Nonverbal synchrony: A new approach to better understand psychotherapeutic processes and drop-out. *Journal of Psychotherapy Integration*, *28*(3), 367–384.

*Paulick, J., Rubel, J. A., Deisenhofer, A.-K., Schwartz, B., Thielemann, D., Altmann, U., Boyle, K., Strauß, B., & Lutz, W. (2018). Diagnostic features of nonverbal synchrony in psychotherapy: Comparing depression and anxiety. *Cognitive Therapy and Research*, *42*(5), 539–551.

Paz, A., Rafaeli, E., Bar-Kalifa, E., Gilboa-Schectman, E., Gannot, S., Laufer-Goldshtein, B., Narayanan, S., Keshet, J., & Atzil-Slonim, D. (2021). Intrapersonal and interpersonal vocal affect dynamics during psychotherapy. *Journal of Consulting and Clinical Psychology*, *89*(3), 227–239.

Porges, S. W. (2003). The polyvagal theory: Phylogenetic contributions to social behavior. *Physiology & Behavior*, *79*(3), 503–513.

*Prinz, J., Boyle, K., Ramseyer, F. T., Kabus, W., Bar-Kalifa, E., & Lutz, W. (2021). Within and between associations of nonverbal synchrony in relation to Grawe's general mechanisms of change. *Clinical Psychology & Psychotherapy*, *28*(1), 159–168.

*Prinz, J., Rafaeli, E., Reuter, J. K., Bar-Kalifa, E., & Lutz, W. (2022). Physiological activation and co-activation in an imagery-based treatment for test anxiety. *Psychotherapy Research*, *32*(2), 238–248.

*Ramseyer, F. T. (2020). Exploring the evolution of nonverbal synchrony in psychotherapy: The idiographic perspective provides a different picture. *Psychotherapy Research*, *30*(5), 622–634.

Ramseyer, F. T., Ebert, A., Roser, P., Edel, M.-A., Tschacher, W., & Brüne, M. (2020). Exploring nonverbal synchrony in borderline personality disorder: A double-blind placebo-controlled study using oxytocin. *British Journal of Clinical Psychology*, *59*(2), 186–207.

Ramseyer, F. T., & Tschacher, W. (2006). Synchrony: A core concept for a constructivist approach to psychotherapy. *Constructivism in the Human Sciences*, *11*(1–2), 150–171.

Ramseyer, F. T., & Tschacher, W. (2010). Nonverbal synchrony or random coincidence? How to tell the difference. In A. Esposito, N. Campbell, C. Vogel, A. Hussain, & A. Nijholt (Eds.), *Development of multimodal interfaces: Active listening and synchrony: Second COST 2102 International Training School, Dublin, Ireland, March 23–27, 2009, Revised Selected Papers* (pp. 182–196). Springer.

*Ramseyer, F. T., & Tschacher, W. (2011). Nonverbal synchrony in psychotherapy: Coordinated body movement reflects relationship quality and outcome. *Journal of Consulting and Clinical Psychology*, *79*(3), 284–295.

*Ramseyer, F. T., & Tschacher, W. (2014). Nonverbal synchrony of head- and body-movement in psychotherapy: Different signals have different associations with outcome. *Frontiers in Psychology*, 5, 979.

R Development Core Team. (2016). R: A lang*uage and* environ*ment for* stat*istical computing*. R Foundation for Statistical Computing. https://www.R-project.org

*Reich, C. M., Berman, J. S., Dale, R., & Levitt, H. M. (2014). Vocal synchrony in psychotherapy. *Journal of Social and Clinical Psychology*, *33*(5), 481–494. https://doi.org/10.1521/jscp.2014.33.5.481

Robinson, J. W., Herman, A., & Kaplan, B. J. (1982). Autonomic responses correlate with counselor–client empathy. *Journal of Counseling Psychology*, *29*(2), 195–198.

Rocco, D., Gennaro, A., Salvatore, S., Stoycheva, V., & Bucci, W. (2017). Clinical mutual attunement and the development of therapeutic process: A preliminary study. *Journal of Constructivist Psychology*, *30*(4), 371–387.

Rocco, D., Pastore, M., Gennaro, A., Salvatore, S., Cozzolino, M., & Scorza, M. (2018). Beyond verbal behavior: An empirical analysis of speech rates in psychotherapy sessions. *Frontiers in Psychology*, *9*, 978.

Russell, J. A., Bachorowski, J.-A., & Fernandez-Dols, J.-M. (2003). Facial and vocal expressions of emotion. *Annual Review of Psychology, 54*, 329–349.

Satcher, D. (2001). Mental health: Culture, race, and ethnicity—A supplement to Mental Health: A report of the Surgeon General. U.S. Department of Health and Human Services. https://doi.org/10.13016/JELA-CKXW

*Schoenherr, D., Paulick, J., Strauss, B. M., Deisenhofer, A.-K., Schwartz, B., Rubel, J. A., Lutz, W., Stangier, U., & Altmann, U. (2019). Nonverbal synchrony predicts premature termination of psychotherapy for social anxiety disorder. *Psychotherapy, 56*(4), 503–513.

*Schoenherr, D., Paulick, J., Worrack, S., Strauss, B. M., Rubel, J. A., Schwartz, B., Deisenhofer, A.-K., Lutz, W., Stangier, U., & Altmann, U. (2019). Quantification of nonverbal synchrony using linear time series analysis methods: Lack of convergent validity and evidence for facets of synchrony. *Behavior Research Methods, 51*(1), 361–383.

*Schoenherr, D., Strauss, B., Paulick, J., Deisenhofer, A.-K., Schwartz, B., Rubel, J. A., Boyle, K., Lutz, W., Stangier, U., & Altmann, U. (2021). Movement synchrony and attachment related anxiety and avoidance in social anxiety disorder. *Journal of Psychotherapy Integration, 31*(2), 163–179. https://doi.org/10.1037/int0000187

*Schoenherr, D., Strauss, B., Stangier, U., & Altmann, U. (2021). The influence of vocal synchrony on outcome and attachment anxiety/avoidance in treatments of social anxiety disorder. *Psychotherapy, 58*(4), 510–522.

Schore, A. N. (2015). *Affect regulation and the origin of the self: The neurobiology of emotional development*. Routledge.

Schore, J. R., & Schore, A. N. (2014). Regulation theory and affect regulation psychotherapy: A clinical primer. *Smith College Studies in Social Work, 84*(2–3), 178–195.

Sessa, P., Meconi, F., Castelli, L., & Dell'Acqua, R. (2014). Taking one's time in feeling other-race pain: An event-related potential investigation on the time-course of cross-racial empathy. *Social Cognitive and Affective Neuroscience, 9*(4), 454–463.

Shamay-Tsoory, S. G., Saporta, N., Marton-Alper, I. Z., & Gvirts, H. Z. (2019). Herding brains: A core neural mechanism for social alignment. *Trends in Cognitive Sciences, 23*(3), 174–186.

Shapira, N., Atzil-Slonim, D., Tuval-Mashiach, R., & Shapira, O. (2022, July). Measuring linguistic synchrony in psychotherapy. In Proceedings of the *Eighth Workshop* on *Computational* Linguistics and Clinical Psychology (pp. 158–176). Association for Computational Linguistics.

Soma, C. S., Baucom, B. R. W., Xiao, B., Butner, J. E., Hilpert, P., Narayanan, S., Atkins, D. C., & Imel, Z. E. (2020). Coregulation of therapist and client emotion during psychotherapy. *Psychotherapy Research, 30*(5), 591–603.

Tronick, E. (2007). *The neurobehavioral and social–emotional development of infants and children*. Norton.

*Tschacher, W., & Meier, D. (2020). Physiological synchrony in psychotherapy sessions. Psychotherapy Research, *30*(5), 558–573. https://doi.org/10.1080/10503307.2019.1612114

Wieder, G., & Wiltshire, T. J. (2020). Investigating coregulation of emotional arousal during exposure-based CBT using vocal encoding and actor–partner interdependence models. *Journal of Counseling Psychology, 67*(3), 337–348.

Wiltshire, T. J., Philipsen, J. S., Trasmundi, S. B., Jensen, T. W., & Steffensen, S. V. (2020). Interpersonal coordination dynamics in psychotherapy: A systematic review. *Cognitive Therapy and Research, 44*(4), 752–773.

Winnicott, D. W. (1971). The use of an object and relating through identifications. *Playing and Reality*. https://ci.nii.ac.jp/naid/20000542188

13
Role Induction

Joshua K. Swift, Elizabeth A. Penix, and Ailun Li

Beginning psychotherapy can be difficult for many patients. For some patients, the difficulty lies in facing the unknown. For example, novice patients may experience worry or anxiety because they do not know what will be expected of them, but they want to make sure they behave in the "right" way. Experienced patients may have a general idea about the nature of psychotherapy, but they still frequently worry about meeting a new therapist for the first time. Even when an initial worry may not be present, many new patients find the initial phase challenging when they do not possess the knowledge about psychotherapy to effectively engage in it. After all, the psychotherapy relationship is different from most other relationships, and the nature of the treatment often looks different from other health care.

For many beginning patients, the difficulty lies in holding expectations that are either unrealistic or cannot be met. A novice patient may hold inaccurate beliefs about what psychotherapy is supposed to be like based on extreme, sensationalistic, or unethical portrayals of psychotherapy that they have seen in the movies or on television. Experienced patients may hold beliefs about the "correct" behaviors for psychotherapy based on their experiences with a past mental health professional, but those expectations may not fit the approach of their new psychotherapist. In order to increase the likelihood of success in psychotherapy, it is important for patients to know, from the beginning, how to effectively engage with their psychotherapist in treatment.

The focus of this chapter is on role induction, which is one method to prepare patients for psychotherapy. In this chapter, we provide a definition and description of role induction, provide clinical examples of its use, and discuss diversity considerations. We then present results of a meta-analysis examining the immediate and outcome effects of providing patients with role induction. We then identify the limitations of the existing research and finish with training implications and practice recommendations.

Definitions

Role induction is the process of providing patients with education designed to prepare them for psychotherapy and help them build accurate expectations regarding the roles and behaviors that may occur within that relationship (Orne & Wender, 1968). Although the exact information that is presented during role induction may vary depending on the individual client, the setting, or the specific treatment that will be used, the process of doing role induction is a pantheoretical method that prepares patients for psychotherapy, regardless of theoretical orientation.

Joshua K. Swift, Elizabeth A. Penix, and Ailun Li, *Role Induction* In: *Psychotherapy Skills and Methods That Work*.
Edited by: Clara E. Hill and John C. Norcross, Oxford University Press. © Clara E. Hill and John C. Norcross 2023.
DOI: 10.1093/oso/9780197611012.003.0013

The literature has utilized alternative terms to describe this process, including anticipatory socialization, pre-therapy education, pre-therapy training, and providing patients with a treatment rationale. Most often, role induction has referred to teaching patients about appropriate psychotherapy roles or expected behaviors for both the therapist and the patient, but it can also include education about the treatment methods, treatment duration, and expected outcomes (Oldham et al., 2012; Orne & Wender, 1968; Swift & Greenberg, 2015). Thus, role induction can address several types of expectations that patients hold, including role, therapist, treatment, and outcome expectations.

Role induction can be distinguished from other early treatment methods, including those that accommodate patient preferences and build patient hope. Methods designed to address patient preferences, such as shared decision-making and collaboration, typically involve patients sharing their personal beliefs, experiences, and information with their therapists regarding what they believe would be most helpful for them in treatment (Swift et al., 2018, 2021; Trusty et al., 2019). In contrast, role induction primarily involves therapists sharing information that patients may need in order to succeed in psychotherapy. This therapist-to-patient information sharing can often occur before, in conjunction with, or immediately after a shared treatment decision-making process.

Role induction is also distinguishable from methods designed to build patient hope in psychotherapy. Those methods include having a therapist share their education and experience, highlighting strengths of a treatment, providing the patient with support, sharing about successfully treated cases, and expressing confidence in psychotherapy and the patient (Constantino et al., 2018). Although hope-building statements can be integrated into role induction, with role induction the focus is on building accurate and realistic expectations for treatment. For example, many patients believe that it will only take two or three sessions of psychotherapy to solve their presenting concerns. This is an overly optimistic or hopeful outcome expectation. Role induction can help patients build more realistic beliefs about duration (Swift & Callahan, 2008, 2011).

Clinical Description and Indications

The topics and format of role induction in psychotherapy vary widely. In the seminal paper on role induction (Orne & Wender, 1968), four main elements were identified: (a) establishing rapport, (b) providing an explanation of psychotherapy, (c) describing the roles of the participants, and (d) anticipating the patient's challenges to completing psychotherapy. Establishing empathic rapport and a bond in psychotherapy has been written on extensively by others (Elliott et al., 2018; Fluckiger et al., 2018), and we do not believe it is a goal exclusive to role induction, so we do not elaborate on it further here.

Regarding educating patients, general information can include a discussion about why talk-based treatments can be effective, goals that might be appropriate for treatment, how often sessions will be held and how long they will typically last, change patterns that might be observed over the course of psychotherapy (e.g., potential for setbacks or deterioration), how long treatment might last (with the goal to build more accurate duration expectations), and how to go about ending treatment. Specific information can include a discussion about how particular treatment strategies will be tailored to the patient's presenting problems. This discussion can include a description of the specific theory (e.g., client-centered therapy, cognitive–behavioral therapy, psychodynamic psychotherapy) and the unique methods associated with it. Research support and past experiences with successful cases can prove helpful.

A discussion of the appropriate patient and therapist roles can include an encouragement for patients to be open and honest with what they share, even if it is painful or embarrassing. Therapists can describe whether they will take a lead role in structuring sessions or if that will be dependent on the patient. Information on the best topics for discussion, whether the therapist will give advice or teach the patient new skills, and the ways the therapist will share ideas can be helpful. If homework or unique session activities (e.g., in-session exposures, mindfulness exercises, two-chair activities) will be employed, those could also be described here.

Last, a discussion of potential problems in psychotherapy can prove helpful. Patients can be warned that treatment can be difficult at times and they may periodically have thoughts of dropping out. It is advisable that the blame for these thoughts and feelings not be solely placed on the patient. Instead, patients can be informed by therapists that they will likely make mistakes and may unintentionally say something that hurts the patients' feelings. Warning patients of this possibility helps them see the psychotherapist as a fallible human and recognize that mistakes do not automatically mean ill intent. In addition, therapists can tell patients that engaging in psychotherapy can be difficult, especially given the logistical (e.g., time, transportation) and emotional resources required to participate. Bringing up these topics early can lead to further discussion and negotiation if they present a challenge for patients later in treatment.

Role induction usually occurs early in treatment. In fact, some role induction can occur prior to patients even starting psychotherapy. After patients schedule an initial appointment, an informational packet with role induction information can be mailed to them, and they can be asked to review it prior to their first session. Alternatively, role induction information can be included as a page on a clinic or practice website.

One of the most frequently tested role induction formats is a video presentation. Simple videos of therapists describing their practice and providing a tour of their office space provide information in an engaging manner. Such videos can also be posted to websites or played for patients in a waiting room while they complete other online paperwork.

Even when informational pamphlets, websites, or videos are used, some role induction is ideally provided in person during the first appointment. Therapists can give an overview of what will happen during the initial sessions, share information about psychotherapy and roles, and answer any questions that patients may have. At the end of the initial interview(s), therapists can then provide more detailed information based on the individual patient's needs and the treatment approach that will be used.

Psychotherapists will also likely need to provide some education throughout the treatment process. This information can be provided when patients reach a stuck point and need a reminder about what comes next or recommended roles. It can also occur when a change in the course of psychotherapy is needed, a new technique is introduced, or termination is anticipated.

Assessment

Specific measures assessing the presence of role induction have yet to be developed. This may be due to the fact that past role induction research has relied on experimental designs (the content and presence of role induction were predetermined by the study methodology). In these designs, role induction is present for the experimental group and not present for the control group. Foreseeably, one could develop a role induction measure that assesses whether therapists provided role induction (and the specific types of information that were or were not provided) prior to or at the start of treatment. Such a measure could be completed by clients, therapists, or researchers at some point during the psychotherapy process.

The impact of role induction can be assessed at different levels, including the impact on psychotherapy beliefs and knowledge, in-session behaviors, therapeutic alliance, and distal treatment outcomes. At the most basic level, client opinions about role induction procedures can be assessed. For example, Delgadillo and Groom (2017) designed an acceptability questionnaire for clients to complete after having received the role induction. On this measure, clients were asked to complete three Likert-type items (ranging from 0 [low] to 10 [high]) assessing the relevance of the role induction, the quality of the presentation, and the quality of the role induction materials. As another example, Johansen and colleagues (2011) created an attitudes toward role induction measure that included two Likert-type items (ranging from 1 [strongly disagree] to 7 [strongly agree]) assessing understandability and the likelihood of recommending it to others seeking psychotherapy. Because these measures/assessment items were created primarily for descriptive purposes within their individual studies, psychometric properties have yet to be tested.

At the next level, the effectiveness of role induction can be determined by testing whether patients who receive pre-therapy education possess more accurate knowledge and beliefs about psychotherapy compared to patients who do not receive it. This is often assessed immediately after the administration of the role induction. For example, Deane and colleagues (1992) and Zwick and Attkisson (1985) used the Psychotherapy Questionnaire (PQ; Zwick & Attkisson, 1984), a 17-item, true or false measure, where patients are asked to indicate which items are or are not applicable to psychotherapy. They report an adequate level of internal consistency for the PQ. A similar but shorter (14 items) measure was created and used by Childress and Gillis (1977); however, psychometric properties for their measure were not reported. As another example, using a single item with an open response format, Swift and Callahan (2011) tested whether patients who received role induction believed that their treatment duration would more closely match typical treatment durations that are associated with recovery based on the dose–effect literature.

At the level of immediate or in-session outcomes, the effectiveness of role induction can be assessed by measuring in-session behaviors, such as speaking turns, voice quality, and time spent on productive content. As an example, in one early role induction study, Hoehn-Saric and colleagues (1964) had judges rate client behaviors using the Kirtner–Cartwright In-therapy Behavior Scale (Kirtner & Cartwright, 1958) and the Therapy Behavior Scale, which was created for their study. For both scales, trained judges watched several segments of sessions and then reported whether the client engaged in any of several (five for the Kirtner–Cartwright Scale, 31 for the Therapy Behavior Scale) desirable and undesirable psychotherapy behaviors. Similarly, Warren and Rice (1972) used the Rice–Wagstaff–Butler client process classification system (Rice & Wagstaff, 1967), which focuses on voice quality and expressive stance dimensions. Successful role induction is thought to induce not only more positive general patient behaviors (e.g., openness) but also the behaviors that the specific role induction discusses in detail (e.g., a cognitive–behavioral therapy role induction might lead to increased identification of maladaptive thoughts by patients, whereas an emotion-focused therapy role induction might lead to a greater expression of emotions).

In addition, the effects of role induction on patient dropout have frequently been tested in the literature. This is important because research has shown that patients who complete psychotherapy show more positive short-term and long-term treatment outcomes compared to patients who choose to drop out (Swift & Greenberg, 2015). A discussion of methods for operationalizing dropout can be found elsewhere (Swift et al., 2009; Swift & Greenberg, 2015).

Research has also tested the effectiveness of role induction on the therapeutic alliance. Appropriate role expectations can facilitate a consensus and agreement between the patient and therapist on appropriate tasks and goals of treatment—two of the three elements from Bordin's (1979) conceptualization of the alliance. Although much of the research on the impact of role induction on the alliance has used patient report measures of the global alliance (Johansen et al., 2011; Strassle et al., 2011), some studies have assessed patients' or therapists' perceptions of behaviors that facilitate the alliance (e.g., warmth; Childress & Gillis, 1977), and others have assessed therapists' perceptions of the alliance (Johansen et al., 2011; Strassle et al., 2011).

At the final level, the effectiveness of role induction has been evaluated by comparing distal treatment outcomes between those who have received role induction and those who have not. Some studies have asked patients and therapists to evaluate patient change or improvement (Hoehn-Saric et al., 1964; Jacobs et al., 1972; Zwick & Attkisson, 1985). Others have tested for change on established measures of symptoms, functioning, or global distress (Lambert & Lambert, 1984; Larsen et al., 1983; Strassle et al., 2011; Wilson, 1985). Several studies have assessed for the impact of role induction on patient satisfaction with treatment (Deane et al., 1992; Zwick & Attkisson, 1985). Although most studies have assessed outcomes post-treatment, several studies have also examined them mid-treatment—often after one, two, three, or four sessions.

Clinical Examples

Case Example 1

The first case example demonstrates how role induction can be incorporated into the initial intake. "Zoe" was 21 years old and identified as a White, cisgender female, bisexual, and agnostic (name and some identifying information have been changed in order to protect the patient's identity). She sought psychotherapy at a community mental health clinic to help navigate anxiety (e.g., feeling "on edge") and depression symptoms (e.g., low mood), as well as ongoing interpersonal conflict after her boyfriend cheated on her.

In their intake session, Zoe and her therapist worked on developing mutual psychotherapy goals related to navigating her depression symptoms and relationship difficulties. Zoe's therapist, who primarily utilized cognitive–behavioral methods, initiated a conversation about role induction immediately after completing a psychosocial interview and establishing the treatment goals:

T: I remember from earlier that you mentioned you hadn't been in therapy before.

C: Yeah, this is my first time trying therapy out. Since I work at a clinic, I figure that it's worth a shot, but I don't really know what it's like.

T: Sounds like you have some idea about what therapy is all about from your undergrad and work experiences, but the actual process is still, uh, fuzzy to you.

C: Exactly.

T: Cool. Let's walk through that process together and hopefully de-mystify therapy a bit.

C: Yeah . . . sounds good to me.

T: Great. Unlike other health professionals you might've worked with, therapy is more of a collaborative effort where we work together on things that are important to you. This really hinges on you being the expert on you, and I add in my expertise on what therapy can look like and what might be effective skills for addressing concerns you'd like to work on. So for example, each week we'll touch base about what we'd like to focus on for that session. For some folks, they find it helpful to jot notes down on paper or their phone to help jog their memory.

C: I definitely space sometimes, so writing it down is probably a good idea [laughs].

T: Jotting things down sounds great to me, and we can definitely see how that goes and go from there. Um . . . another thing that we might work on together is figuring out what skills you might like to practice between sessions. We think about therapy as kind of like a sport, where the more we practice things that might be helpful to you, the more effective and easier it is to do those things when you really need them.

C: Oh okay, that makes sense [shuffles feet]. I think my only question about that is that sometimes I really do get swamped at work, and I don't know if I always . . . have a lot of time.

T: That's a great point, and I appreciate you highlighting that for me. I totally get that life happens sometimes and that you're at a busy spot with work. One of the ways that we can navigate that is by working together to figure out reasonable goals for practicing that meet whatever demands you have that week. So that might be an option. What are your thoughts about other ways we could navigate that?

C: Hmm . . . yeah I think just making sure we keep an eye on how busy I am sounds good to me.

T: Good deal. So, you might be wondering at this point what kinds of things we might actually do to start targeting the things we would like to work on together, like navigating your relationship and feeling down lately. Based on what we talked about today, I am thinking there might be a couple of options that could be a good fit. So, the first option is an approach that we call cognitive behavioral therapy. This approach, which we call "CBT" for short, is really focused on going over the way that we think about things, the emotions that we experience, and what we do in response. We know that going after these pieces can really help us navigate stressful situations and improve depression symptoms. What questions do you have about this first option?

C: Um, I can't think of any right now.

T: Sounds good. The second approach is a flavor of CBT so to speak, but has a few important differences. It's called acceptance and commitment therapy or "ACT" for short. Although there are some similarities with CBT, like a focus on emotions and what we do in response, this approach really emphasizes the importance of living life in a way that is meaningful and in line with what you value. ACT also emphasizes getting in touch with what we're experiencing in the present moment and getting "unhooked" from thoughts that aren't very helpful for us in the long run. So, the two major ones are CBT and ACT, and both have a lot of research evidence that suggests that they both can help with the things that we agreed we want to work on. I realize, though, that I just threw a lot of information at you, and am curious what your thoughts, reactions, and questions might be at this point.

C: Yeah, I follow that. I think I remember CBT getting mentioned in my classes, but the ACT one sounds new. I really like what you were saying about thinking about what is meaningful to me, though. So maybe ACT?

T: Yeah, it sounds like the piece about values and meaning resonated with you in particular.

C: Mhmm.

T: Sounds good—let's go with ACT then. There's some research that suggests that we should be seeing some significant improvements with this approach in 12–16 weeks. But, of course, everyone's trajectory is a little different and that time frame can vary person to person. So, one of the things we will do each week is have you fill out the measures we talked about earlier to serve as a sort of "thermometer" to evaluate whether we're seeing the improvements we'd expect to see.

C: Oh okay, that sounds good.

T: Great. One more thing on that. It matters a lot to me that you feel like your therapist is connecting with you and what we work on together. So, periodically we will check in to see what your thoughts are about how you feel about our connection, what seems to be helpful and going well, and what things we can mix up in the future to make therapy even more effective for you. What questions do you have about the measures or those check-ins so far?

C: Um . . . I can't think of anything right now. I appreciate the check-ins though.

T: Of course. I realize that we've only known each other for a day so far, but I was thinking we could even check in on how you feel about our connection and our first session today. What do you think?

C: Sure, we can do that.

In this case example, the therapist provided role induction for a number of therapy components, including (a) patient and therapist roles in therapy, (b) treatment rationale, and (c) treatment duration. For Zoe, reviewing the ways in which both she and her therapist could contribute to reaching her goals helped her feel more comfortable and knowledgeable about navigating the previously unfamiliar therapy process. She noted that this review alleviated her initial concerns that their work together would look like "therapy in the movies" or "going back to school." In addition, she described how preemptively establishing expectations for assigning homework in a collaborative manner allowed her to engage in assignments while feeling like her therapist would work with her to ensure that homework goals were appropriate and helpful to her. She later reported that setting expectations for a collaborative therapy process and discussing the alliance helped her feel even more confident in sharing feedback about therapy activities, her progress, and her relationship with the therapist. Furthermore, she discussed how the therapist explaining how ACT aligned with her treatment goals as well as the time frame that it could take to reach her goals helped her remain engaged in therapy when she experienced a "flare-up" of her depression symptoms later in treatment.

Case Example 2

The following case example focuses on how role induction can be incorporated into an intake appointment with a patient who has previous psychotherapy experience. "Manuel" was in his early 30s and identified as cisgender male, gay, biracial (Latino and Native American), and a "nonpracticing Catholic." Manuel's primary care provider referred him to therapy after he endorsed significant mood symptoms (e.g., feeling "in the dumps," low motivation, hypervigilance, intrusive symptoms) linked with his complex trauma history (e.g., repeated childhood sexual assault, repeated bullying, deaths of his boyfriend and best friend).

During the intake, the therapist provided psychoeducation about the link among trauma events, post-traumatic stress disorder (PTSD), and depression. They reviewed potential treatment goals, and Manuel requested that they first focus on targeting his difficulties regulating his emotions and then processing his trauma experiences. The therapist initiated a review of past psychotherapy experiences to assess Manuel's familiarity with both psychotherapy and potential PTSD treatments. Manuel noted that he had tried therapy before with his high school counselor.

T: Tell me about your experiences with them.

C: Well, I didn't feel like it was a good, like, vibe for me. We mostly just talked. He kept focusing on my sexual orientation, even though I have been out since the beginning of high school.

T: Ah, so your counselor didn't really focus on what you wanted to work on, and instead focused on your orientation even though that wasn't driving the concerns that you had. That sounds really frustrating to have him not really hear you.

C: Yes absolutely. It wasn't a very good experience.

T: Yeah, I'm sorry to hear that, and I realize that you being here to try therapy again is a risk you're taking. In our work together, it is important to me that you feel safe in working through topics and skills that really go after what you'd like to work on in therapy. How would you feel about checking in about your thoughts about whether our work is matching what you want to work on?

C: Yeah that, like, makes a lot of sense to me.

T: Sounds good. I am reflecting on how you mentioned that, by the time you worked with your counselor, you had gone through a number of stressful experiences related to bullying and sexual abuse. Did you ever specifically target those experiences in your work with your previous counselor at all?

C: Umm . . . no I don't think so, not that I can remember. Yeah.

T: So you probably didn't really delve into your trauma history or focus on that.

C: [Patient shakes his head.]

T: In reflecting on how processing your past experiences is a major goal for our work together, I was thinking it would be good to go over some options for targeting that.

C: Yes, please.

T: Great. So one option is called Skills Training in Affective and Interpersonal Regulation, or STAIR for short. The three important components of STAIR are helping manage strong emotions, processing the impact of your experiences on you and your relationships, and explicitly going through your trauma memories in a structured way that helps you organize those memories in your brain. There's a lot of evidence that going after these topics is really helpful for folks who have survived a lot of trauma experiences, particularly childhood sexual abuse.

C: So exactly like what I've gone through.

T: Yes, definitely. The other approach is called cognitive processing therapy. This one does also have components that target emotions and focuses on processing your trauma memories. But, this approach differs in that it really focuses on the impact of trauma experiences on how you think about yourself, others, the world, the future, etcetera. We especially go after what we call "stuck points." Those are beliefs that make it difficult for us to fully process those experiences and may not be very helpful to us in the long run. There is also a lot of research evidence backing the usefulness of reframing these stuck points, too. What are your questions so far about STAIR and cognitive processing therapy?

C: Um . . . [pauses]. I can't think of any questions right now. I think that I really want to get some, uh, help with my emotions and just get my experiences off my chest. Going through how trauma has impacted my relationships, especially with my boyfriend and my family, would be good too.

T: So maybe leaning towards STAIR then.

C: Yeah, I think so.

T: Great. I think that approach will be a great fit too. I also wanted to go over what that might look like for us in our work together, since that will probably feel very different from your work with your previous counselor.

C: How's that?

T: Yeah, with STAIR, things will be really targeting emotions, relationships, etcetera that are associated with your trauma experiences. We'll also incorporate some worksheets that help us work through new skills we go over, and there will be some opportunities for you to practice what we talk about outside of therapy. So, it might feel a little more targeted or structured than your previous therapy experiences.

C: That sounds good. I really just want to move on, so I'll try, like, anything.

T: I can definitely hear that you're ready and motivated, and we know that this is a really effective approach. There's some variability in how long the approach will take to see marked improvements in PTSD symptoms, but we expect maybe around 16 weeks when meeting on a weekly basis. Most folks experience improvements in the trauma symptoms we've talked about within the first month or two though. We'll make sure to check in to see how your symptoms are changing and how effective you think STAIR is over time. If we feel like there isn't movement in the right direction or that you're feeling stuck, we can also put other approaches back on the table.

C: Cool, cool.

In this example, the therapist targeted role induction for several psychotherapy components, including (a) how topics are selected in session, (b) treatment rationale, (c) treatment duration, and (d) patient and therapist roles. After completing several therapy sessions, Manuel verbally described to his therapist during an alliance review how it felt empowering to have this therapist listen to his past experiences in therapy and establish their sessions as a space to work on topics and treatment goals that were meaningful to him. He noted that although he was still anxious to talk more about his trauma experiences, this discussion helped him feel more open to potentially doing so in the future. Furthermore, he reported that initially reviewing treatment options and how they were related to his treatment goals helped ease his concerns about whether therapy could work for him. He described appreciation for how, even during their first session together, the therapist established a collaborative space where he could share feedback on the treatment approach used. During a mid-treatment alliance review in which Manuel requested transitioning to a different treatment approach, Manuel discussed how this collaborative framework helped him provide feedback that he did not feel like the original approach was working for him. He noted that this framework also helped him feel more confident in reviewing alternative treatment options with the therapist instead of avoiding that conversation and dropping out of therapy.

Landmark Studies and Previous Reviews

The earliest empirical study of role induction that we identified was published in 1964 (Hoehn-Saric et al., 1964). In this study, 40 adult psychotherapy outpatients with no psychotherapy experience were randomly assigned to a role induction or control condition. Those assigned to role induction received a role induction interview, which

> covered four main components: (1) a general exposition of psychotherapy; (2) a description and explanation of the expected behavior of a patient and of a therapist; (3) a preparation for certain typical phenomena in the course of therapy (e.g., resistance); and (4) the induction of a realistic expectation for improvement within four months of treatment. (p. 270)

The interview was conducted in a discussion format, with specific examples from each patient's own history being used and the patients being encouraged to interrupt and ask questions. Patients assigned to the control condition met with the same researcher only to receive the timing of their first appointment. Patients in both conditions were then randomly assigned to meet with a psychiatry resident for 4 months of weekly individual psychotherapy. The residents were unaware of the experimental condition of their patients. Overall, patients who received the role induction attended more sessions, were less likely to drop out, and were rated by their therapists more positively on the therapeutic relationship and as having made significantly more improvement compared to patients in the control condition. Interestingly, no differences were observed in their self-ratings of overall improvement by the end of psychotherapy. Limitations with this study can be seen in the exclusion of clients with previous psychotherapy experience, the use of a single senior research psychiatrist to provide the role induction, and unequal attention between the role induction and control group participants, all of which may have biased the results in favor of the role induction condition.

Throughout the years, several reviews of the topic with recommendations for implementing role induction have also been provided (e.g., Bedics, 2019; Orlinsky et al., 1994; Orlinsky & Howard, 1986; Swift & Greenberg, 2015; Walitzer et al., 1999). However, only two reviews have used meta-analytic techniques to synthesize the results from the literature.

The first meta-analysis conducted on role induction was an unpublished dissertation (Monks, 1995). Through use of a database search, 28 studies were identified for inclusion in that meta-analysis. The results from those 28 studies indicated that role induction had small but significant positive impacts on treatment outcomes ($d = 0.34$), attendance ($d = 0.31$), dropout ($d = 0.23$), and in treatment behavior ($d = 0.20$). Note that Monks' dissertation included both individual and group treatments and both child and adult patients.

More recently, a second meta-analysis was conducted in which the efficacy of role induction was evaluated along with other methods designed to improve psychotherapy attendance (Oldham et al., 2012). Both keyword and root and branch searches were used to identify eligible studies. A total of 14 role induction studies were identified for inclusion. The results from this meta-analysis indicated a moderate size effect ($d = 0.50$) in favor of role induction improving attendance in psychotherapy. Role induction was observed to be just as effective as preference accommodation and motivational interviewing, and more effective than telephone/postal reminders, case management, and implementation intentions. The larger effect size seen in this meta-analysis compared to the previous one may be due to stricter inclusion criteria regarding study methodology (i.e., randomized controlled trials only). In contrast to Monks' dissertation, Oldham and colleagues' meta-analysis was exclusive to adult patients, but it still included both group and individual therapies.

Research Review

The purpose of the current meta-analysis was to examine whether including role induction in individual psychotherapy leads to fewer treatment dropouts, more positive in-session client impacts, and more positive mid-treatment and post-treatment outcomes. The existing research on role induction has used experimental designs, with patients being randomized to role induction or control conditions. Thus, the results of the meta-analysis provide a causal link between the role induction and immediate and distal outcomes.

Inclusion Criteria

To be included in the meta-analysis, studies had to experimentally test the impact of role induction on treatment dropout, immediate in-session client impacts, and/or mid- or post-treatment outcomes. Thus, studies had to include a direct comparison between patients who were provided role induction and patients who were not. Studies were excluded if they used a nonclinical sample (e.g., analogue studies with undergraduate studies who were not seeking psychotherapy), group psychotherapy, couple or family therapy, or treatment for children and adolescents. Last, given the language abilities of the authors, studies had to be published in English.

Search Strategy

Three search strategies identified studies for inclusion in the meta-analysis: a database search, a root (reference lists) and branch (citing articles) search of included studies, and a root and branch search of previous reviews of the topic. Initially, potential articles were reviewed at the title and abstract level by the first author. Articles that seemed like they could meet inclusion criteria at that level of review were then reviewed at the full-text level, also by the first author. Figure 13.1 presents a flowchart of the search results.

On September 2, 2021, a database search was conducted in PsycInfo using the keywords psychotherapy OR therapy OR counseling OR intervention OR treatment AND role induction OR pre-therapy training OR anticipatory socialization OR patient preparation OR role preparation OR treatment rationale OR pre-therapy education. This resulted in 1,508 non-duplicate results. Of these studies 1,128 were removed because they were deemed to not be about psychotherapy, 292 were not relevant to the topic of role induction, 41 were not experimental studies testing the effect of role induction (e.g., reviews of the topic), 20 were analogue studies with a nonclinical sample, and 10 were of group/family/child treatments. This left 17 studies to be reviewed at the full-text level.

Five previous systematic reviews of the topic were identified in the literature (Monks, 1995; Oldham et al., 2012; Orlinsky et al., 1994; Orlinsky & Howard, 1986; Walitzer et al., 1999). For each of these, we performed a root and branch search by reviewing each study that was included in their review as well as each study that had cited one of the reviews. This resulted in 261 articles that were reviewed for possible inclusion. Of these studies, 84 were duplicates or had already been reviewed at the keyword stage, 17 were not about psychotherapy, 116 were not relevant to the topic of role induction, nine were not experimental studies testing the effect of role induction (e.g., review papers), three were analogue studies with a nonclinical sample, 16 were of group/family/child treatments, and three were unpublished dissertations. This left 13 new studies to be reviewed at the full-text level; however, the full text for one was not obtainable even through a request to the corresponding author.

Last, we searched the roots (reference lists) and branches (citing articles) for each article that was identified as meeting all inclusion criteria. This resulted in 362 potential studies that were reviewed. Of these studies, 23 were duplicates or had already been

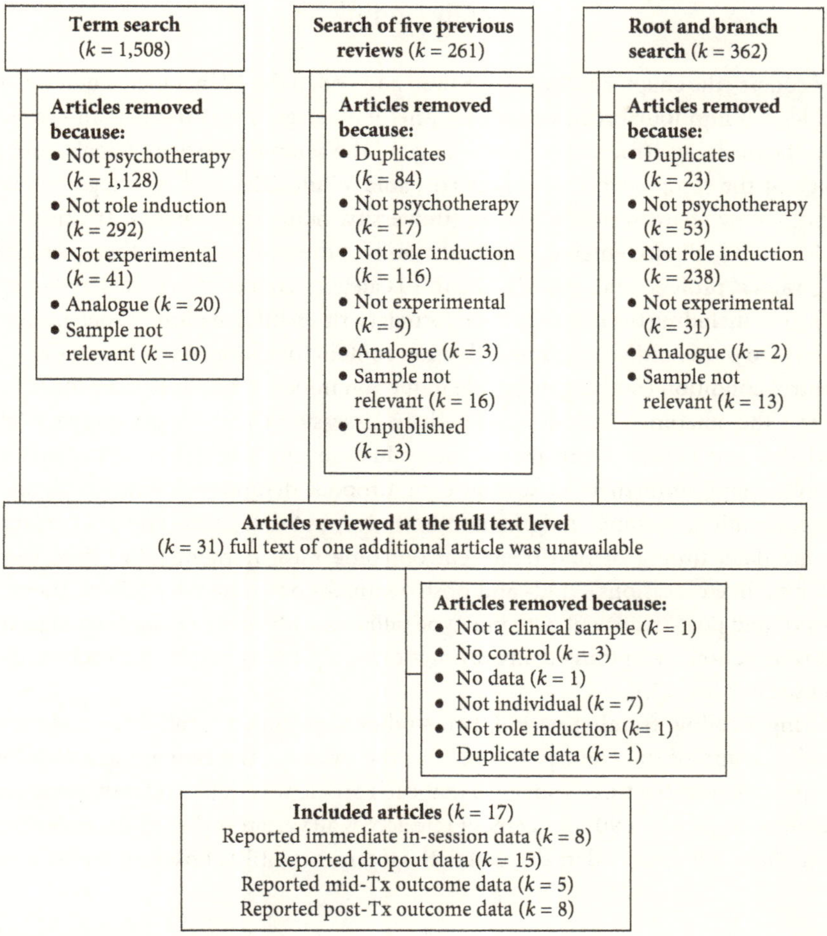

Figure 13.1 Flowchart of the search.

reviewed at a previous stage, 53 were not about psychotherapy, 238 were not relevant to the topic of role induction, 31 were not experimental studies testing the effect of role induction, two were analogue studies with nonclinical samples, and 13 were of group/family/child treatments. Thus, two new studies to be reviewed at the full-text level were identified through this search strategy.

A full-text review was performed on 31 articles that were identified as potentially relevant through these three search strategies. A total of 14 articles were removed at the full-text review stage—one because it did not include a clinical sample, three because they did not include an experimental control group, one because it did not include any relevant data, seven because the treatment was not individual psychotherapy, one because role induction was not provided, and one because it described data that were also from an already included study. The full-text review resulted in 17 studies that met all inclusion criteria and were thus included in the meta-analysis. These 17 studies included data from 1,555 clients (842 who received role induction and 713 who served as controls).

Study Coding

Three coders (the chapter authors) reviewed and coded the 17 included studies. Coded variables fell into four broad categories. The first category was the patient characteristics: diagnosis, age (mean age), percentage of the sample who were female, and percentage of the sample who were non-Hispanic White. The second category was the psychotherapy characteristics: setting (university, outpatient, mixed), treatment orientation (CBT, client-centered, psychodynamic, other, mixed), and therapist experience (trainee, professional, mixed). The third category concerned characteristics of the conditions: including the role induction format (written information, verbal discussion, audio/video presentation), the role induction content (duration, roles, mixed), and type of control condition (nothing, non-role induction information, wait). The fourth category was the outcomes: including immediate in-session client impact category (client knowledge and beliefs, client mood, an evaluation of client behavior/suitability for psychotherapy), immediate in-session data, dropout definition (clinically significant change, duration, therapist judgment, other), dropout data, mid- and post-treatment outcome data, timing of mid-treatment outcome measurement (after first, second, third, fourth, etc. sessions), mid- and post-treatment outcome rater (client, therapist), and mid- and post-treatment outcome type (alliance, subjective rating of change, treatment satisfaction, symptoms/distress/functioning). Coding results for each study are presented in Table 13.1.

During a coding training period, two studies were coded by all three coders, with open discussion of the codings throughout the process. The remaining articles were then split between the three coders so that each article was independently reviewed by two coders. There was a 90% agreement rate across all variables during the independent coding phase. All three coders discussed disagreement until a consensus was reached.

Methodological Decisions

The effects of role induction were tested in four meta-analyses comparing immediate in-session client impacts, dropout rates, mid-treatment outcomes, and post-treatment outcomes between patients in role induction and control conditions. Between-condition effect sizes were first calculated for each study. For the dropout data, an odds ratio (*OR*) was calculated representing the likelihood of a control patient dropping out compared to the likelihood of a role induction patient dropping out. In these calculations, an *OR* greater than 1 indicates that control patients were more likely to drop out prematurely, an *OR* less than 1 indicates that role induction patients were more likely to drop out prematurely, and an *OR* of 1 indicates that patients in both conditions were equally likely to drop out. For the in-session client impacts, mid-treatment outcome, and post-treatment outcome data, a Cohen's *d* was calculated representing the degree of difference in outcome scores between role induction and control conditions. Several studies included data for more than one mid- and post-treatment outcome variable. In these cases, an average *d* was calculated using a fixed effects model based on all of the outcome data that were reported.

Table 13.1 Characteristics of the Studies Included in the Meta-Analysis

Study	Client Diagnosis	Client Age, Years (*M*)	Client % Female	Client % White	Setting Type	Tx Orient	Therapist Experience	RI Format	RI Content	Control Type	Outcomes
Callahan et al. (2014)	Mixed	29.55	63.30	74.70	Univ.	Mixed	Trainee	Info.	Duration	Nothing	In-session k & b Dropout Post-change
Childress & Gillis (1977)	Mixed	30.80	70.59	—	Out.	CC	Pro.	Verbal	Mixed	Nothing	Mid-change
Deane et al. (1992)	Mixed	33.00	61.00	93.00	Out.	Other	Pro.	A/V	Mixed	Wait	In-session k & b Post-satisfaction Post-change
Delgadillo et al. (2015)	Mixed	40.58	58.70	83.20	Out.	CBT	—	Info.	Mixed	Nothing	Dropout
Delgadillo & Groom (2017)	Mixed	37.00	59.20	91.80	Out.	CBT	Pro.	Verbal	Mixed	Nothing	Dropout Post-change
Hoehn-Saric et al. (1964)	Mixed	30.00	57.50	87.50	Out.	—	Trainee	Verbal	Mixed	Nothing	In-session behavior Dropout
Jacobs et al. (1972)	—	—	68.33	72.00	Out.	—	Trainee	Verbal	Mixed	Nothing	Dropout Post-change
Johansen et al. (2011)	Mixed	25.87	77.00	58.00	Univ.	Mixed	Mixed	A/V	Mixed	Non-RI info.	In-session mood Dropout Mid-alliance
Lambert & Lambert (1984)	—	—	53.33	—	Out.	Mixed	Pro.	A/V	Roles	Non-RI info.	In-session k & b Dropout Post-satisfaction Post-change

(*continued*)

Table 13.1 Continued

Study	Client Diagnosis	Client Age, Years (*M*)	Client % Female	Client % White	Setting Type	Tx Orient	Therapist Experience	RI Format	RI Content	Control Type	Outcomes
Larsen et al. (1983)	—	—	—	—	Out.	—	—	Verbal	Mixed	Nothing	In-session behavior Dropout Mid-change Post-change
Reis & Brown (2006)	Mixed	39.3	66.40	80.80	Out.	Mixed	Pro.	A/V	Roles	Non-RI info.	Dropout
Sloane et al. (1970)	Mixed	25.00	52.78	86.11	Out.	—	Trainee	Verbal	Mixed	Nothing	Dropout
Strassle et al. (2011)	—	30.46	60.71	—	Univ.	—	Trainee	A/V	Mixed	Nothing	Dropout Mid-alliance Mid-change Post-change
Swift & Callahan (2011)	Mixed	28.68	62.00	78.00	Univ.	CBT	Trainee	Info.	Duration	Nothing	In-session k & b Dropout
Warren & Rice (1972)	—	28.90	43.64	—	Univ.	CC	Pro.	Verbal	Mixed	Nothing	Dropout Post-change
Wilson (1985)	—	26.30	64.00	92.00	Mixed	—	—	A/V	Mixed	Nothing	Dropout
Zwick & Attkisson (1985)	Mixed	29.00	60.00	50.00	Out.	PD	Mixed	A/V	Mixed	Nothing	In-session k & b In-session behavior Dropout Mid-satisfaction Mid-change

A/V, audio/visual; CBT, cognitive–behavioral therapy; CC, client-centered psychotherapy; Info, information; k & b, knowledge and beliefs; orient., orientation; Out., outpatient; PD, psychodynamic psychotherapy; Pro, professional; RI, role induction; Tx, treatment; Univ., university

After calculating individual study effect sizes, an overall weighted *OR* and overall weighted immediate in-session impact, mid-treatment, and post-treatment outcome *d* values were calculated averaging across all studies using a random effects model. An effect size *r* is also reported for the outcome findings, representing the association between receiving role induction and displaying more positive behaviors and change compared to those in the control conditions. A one-study-removed analysis was conducted to examine whether individual studies were having a large impact on the overall findings. A *Q*-statistics was used to test for heterogeneity, and I^2 values were calculated to represent the degree of heterogeneity in study effect sizes. Last, a fail-safe *N* was calculated to examine the robustness of the overall results against missing studies.

The patient, psychotherapy, condition, and outcome variables were then tested as potential moderators and covariates of the dropout, mid-treatment, and post-treatment outcome effects. Categorical moderators were tested using a *Q*-statistic and mixed effects models. With this type of moderator analysis, a significant between-group *Q*-statistic indicates a higher than chance level of between-group differences in effect sizes. Continuous moderators were tested using meta-regression techniques and random effects models. For these analyses, a regression coefficient was calculated representing the linear relationship between the continuous moderator and the study effect size.

Client Experiences of Role Induction

An initial evaluation of role induction can be made by assessing client opinions about the role induction itself. A meta-analysis was not conducted on these three studies given that ratings in this area are not applicable to control conditions and very few studies reported this type of data. However, a narrative review and box score analysis of the results can be provided from three studies that reported data on acceptability.

Delgadillo and Groom (2017) asked clients (n = 49) in their role induction group to rate the relevance and quality of the role induction. Based on the positive ratings in all categories, Delgadillo and Groom concluded that their role induction was deemed highly acceptable. Johansen et al. (2011) asked patients (n = 70) to rate whether their role induction was understandable and whether patients would recommend it to others seeking psychotherapy. Positive ratings were observed in both areas. Interestingly, they also had control group clients rate the control video (a portion of a documentary about waterfowl fishing and swimming) with the same two items. Although control group clients rated their video as equally understandable as role induction clients, the control group clients were significantly less likely to recommend their video to those who are seeking psychotherapy. A third study (Alvidrez et al., 2005), which did not meet criteria to be included in our meta-analyses due to a lack of measurement of outcomes, asked older African American adult clients (n = 32) to qualitatively evaluate culturally tailored role induction materials provided prior to the start of treatment. In follow-up interviews, the clients in this study described positive experiences with the role induction materials. Although the results of these studies are specific to the role induction procedures that were tested in each, they do suggest that clients, in general, perceive the use of role induction favorably. In fact, in a box score analysis (one per study), the results of these three studies are uniformly positive.

Immediate In-Session Impacts

Ten studies provided data on immediate in-session impacts on client knowledge and beliefs, behaviors, and mood between role induction and control groups. However, two of these studies did not provide enough data to calculate an effect size between conditions. In one of these studies (Sloane et al., 1970), the authors stated that the results indicated that control group clients were evaluated as more suitable for treatment; whereas in the other study (Warren & Rice, 1972), the authors concluded that role induction clients were evaluated as more suitable for treatment. Thus, the following results are based on data from eight studies and 651 clients. The data from these eight studies include eight effect sizes of immediate impacts on clients' knowledge and beliefs, five effect sizes of therapist or researcher evaluations of client in-session behavior, and two effect sizes of client in-session mood.

A plot of the immediate in-session effects sizes for each study and their weighted average effect size is presented in Figure 13.2. The overall effect of role induction on immediate in-session impacts was significant, $d = 0.64$, 95% confidence interval (CI) [0.25, 1.03], $p < .01$, $r = .31$. This finding indicates that patients who received role induction showed more positive in-session knowledge and behaviors compared to patients who did not receive role induction. The one-study-removed analyses (conducting the meta-analysis repeatedly while removing a different study each time) resulted in *d*s ranging from 0.47 to 0.76. Calculation of the fail-safe *N* indicated that 135 unpublished studies with nonsignificant results would be necessary to reduce dropout effect to a nonsignificant level. Significant heterogeneity in the outcome effect sizes between studies was found, $Q(7) = 62.50$, $p < .01$, $I^2 = 88.80$, suggesting a large amount of variability between studies in the effect of role induction on mid-treatment outcomes.

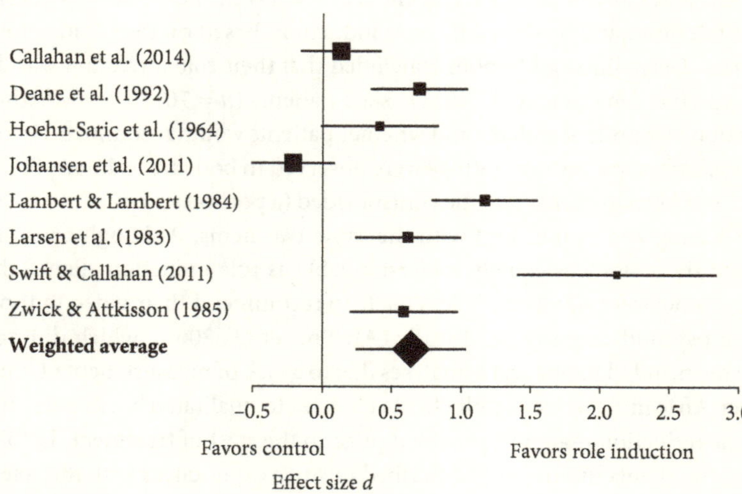

Figure 13.2 Forest plot of immediate in-session impact effect sizes.

Effect on Dropout

Fifteen of the 17 included studies (1,307 clients) reported data on treatment dropout, as defined by the individual study authors. A plot of the *OR* effect sizes for each study and the weighted average effect size is provided in Figure 13.3. The overall effect of role induction on psychotherapy dropout was significant, *OR* = 1.64, 95% CI [1.06, 2.53], $p = .03$. This finding indicates that patients who received role induction at the start of their treatment were 1.64 times less likely to prematurely terminate than patients who did not receive role induction. The one-study-removed analyses resulted in *OR*s ranging from 1.42 to 1.80, indicating that the results were not highly influenced by any single study. Calculation of the fail-safe *N* indicated that 27 unpublished studies with nonsignificant results would be necessary to reduce dropout effect to a nonsignificant level. Significant heterogeneity in the study *OR*s was found, $Q(14) = 32.10$, $p < .01$, $I^2 = 56.39$, suggesting a moderate amount of variability in the effect of role induction on dropout across studies.

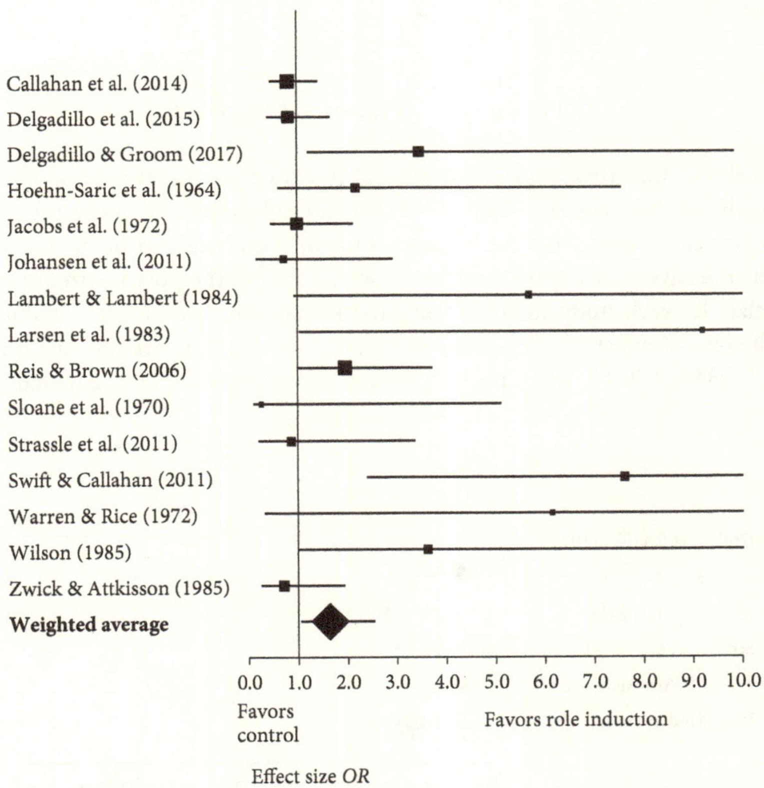

Figure 13.3 Forest plot of dropout effect sizes.

Effect on Mid-Treatment Outcomes

Only five of the 17 included studies (288 clients) provided mid-treatment outcome data. These five studies included four effect sizes for subjective reports of client change, four effect sizes for objective measurements of symptoms, four effect sizes for ratings of the alliance, and one effect size for client satisfaction with treatment. A plot of the mid-treatment outcome effects sizes for each study and their weighted average effect size is presented in Figure 13.4. The overall effect of role induction on mid-treatment outcomes was not significant, $d = 0.26$, 95% CI [−0.23, 0.75], $p = .30$, $r = .19$. This finding indicates that patients who received role induction did not show more positive outcomes when measured during treatment (ranging from after the first session to after the fourth session of treatment) compared to patients who did not receive role induction. The one-study-removed analyses resulted in *d*s ranging from 0.05 to 0.45. The effect on mid-treatment outcomes seemed to be most largely influenced by one study (Childress & Gillis, 1977) in a positive direction and two studies (Johansen et al., 2011; Strassle et al., 2011) in a negative direction. Significant heterogeneity in the outcome effect sizes between studies was found, $Q(4) = 13.81$, $p < .01$, $I^2 = 71.03$, suggesting a large amount of variability between studies in the effect of role induction on mid-treatment outcomes.

Effect on Post-Treatment Outcomes

Eight of the 17 included studies (662 clients) provided post-treatment outcome data. These eight studies included four effect sizes for subjective measurements of client change, five effect sizes for patient-reported satisfaction with treatment, and 16 effect sizes for objective measurements of symptoms. A plot of the post-treatment outcome effects sizes for each study and their weighted average effect size is presented in Figure 13.5. The overall effect of role induction on post-treatment outcomes was significant, $d = 0.33$, 95% CI [0.11, 0.55], $p < .01$, $r = .16$. This effect size indicates that patients

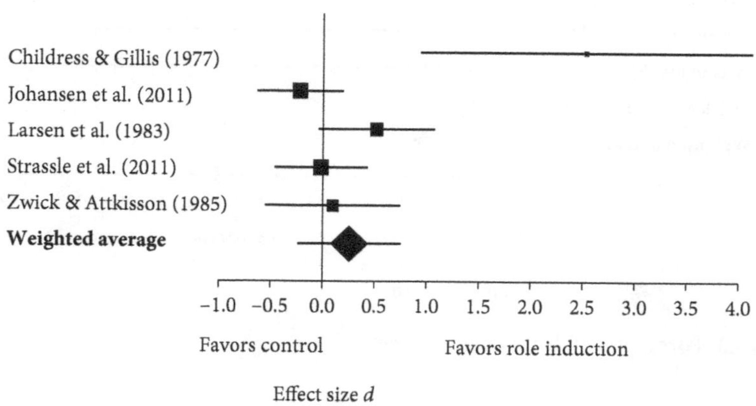

Figure 13.4 Forest plot of mid-treatment outcome effect sizes.

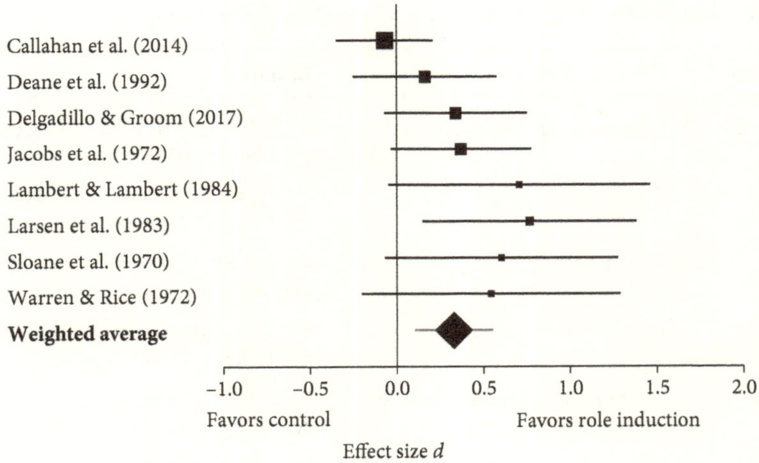

Figure 13.5 Forest plot of post-treatment outcome effect sizes.

who received role induction experienced more positive outcomes by the end of treatment compared to patients who did not receive role induction. The one-study-removed analyses resulted in *d*s ranging from 0.27 to 0.41, indicating that the outcome results were not highly influenced by any single study. Calculation of the fail-safe *N* indicated that 26 unpublished studies with nonsignificant results would be necessary to reduce the outcome effect size to a nonsignificant level. Significant heterogeneity in the outcome effect sizes between studies was found, $Q(7) = 11.65, p = .11, I^2 = 39.89$, suggesting a moderately small amount of variability between studies in the effect of role induction on post-treatment outcomes.

Patient Moderators of the Role Induction Effects

Results of the statistical tests examining the patient moderators of age, the percentage of the sample that identified as female, and the percentage of the sample that identified as non-Hispanic White are provided in Table 13.2. In summary, age was a significant moderator of the effect of role induction on immediate in-session impacts (role induction was more effective for older clients), but it was not a significant moderator of role induction's effects on dropout, mid-treatment outcomes, or post-treatment outcomes. Similarly, the percentage of the sample that identified as female was a significant moderator of the effect of role induction on immediate in-session impacts (role induction was more effective when there were fewer females in the sample), but it was not a significant moderator of the effects on dropout, mid-treatment outcomes, or post-treatment outcomes. Last, the percentage of the sample that identified as non-Hispanic White was a significant moderator of role induction's effects on both immediate in-session impacts and dropout (role induction was more effective and led to fewer dropouts when a larger portion of the sample identified as non-Hispanic White), but it was not a significant moderator of post-treatment outcomes.

Table 13.2 Results from the Tests of Client Moderators of Role Induction Effects

Moderator	Outcome Domain	Results
Average age	**Immediate in-session impacts**	**$k = 6, B = 0.11$, 95% CI [−0.05, 0.18], $z = 3.66, p < .01, R^2_{analog} = .30$**
	Dropout	$k = 12, B = 0.01$, 95% CI [−0.04, 0.06], $z = 0.28, p = .78, R^2_{analog} = .00$
	Mid-treatment outcomes	$k = 4, B = 0.09$, 95% CI [-0.04, 0.22], $z = 1.40, p = .16, R^2_{analog} = .18$
	Post-treatment outcomes	$k = 5, B = 0.01$, 95% CI [−0.04, 0.06], $z = 0.38, p = .71, R^2_{analog} = .02$
% female	**Immediate in-session impacts**	**$k = 7, B = -0.05$, 95% CI [−0.07, −0.03], $z = 5.77, p < .01, R^2_{analog} = .54$**
	Dropout	$k = 14, B = -0.03$, 95% CI [−0.08, 0.03], $z = 1.00, p = .32, R^2_{analog} = .03$
	Mid-treatment outcomes	$k = 4, B = -0.01$, 95% CI [−0.04, 0.02], $z = 0.69, p = .49, R^2_{analog} = .04$
	Post-treatment outcomes	$k = 7, B = -0.02$, 95% CI [−0.05, 0.01], $z = 1.51, p = .13, R^2_{analog} = .26$
% non-Hispanic White	**Immediate in-session impacts**	**$k = 6, B = 0.01$, 95% CI [0.00, 0.02], $z = 2.56, p = .01, R^2_{analog} = .14$**
	Dropout	**$k = 11, B = 0.03$, 95% CI [0.01, 0.06], $z = 2.62, p < .01, R^2_{analog} = .27$**
	Mid-treatment outcomes	Not enough data available to test this effect
	Post-treatment outcomes	$k = 5, B = 0.01$, 95% CI [−0.01, 0.03], $z = 0.92, p = .36, R^2_{analog} = .14$

Note. Significant results are bolded.

Psychotherapy Moderators of the Role Induction Effects

Results of the statistical tests examining the psychotherapy moderators of setting, treatment orientation, and therapist level are provided in Table 13.3. The included role induction studies were either conducted in university clinic ($k = 5$) or outpatient ($k = 11$) settings (one study was conducted in both outpatient and university clinics). The setting in which the study took place was not a significant moderator of immediate in-session impacts, dropout, mid-treatment outcomes, or post-treatment outcomes. Several treatment orientations were identified in the meta-analyzed studies, including CBT ($k = 3$), patient-centered psychotherapy ($k = 2$), psychodynamic psychotherapy ($k = 1$), other ($k = 1$), and studies in which multiple orientations were used ($k = 4$). An additional six studies did not report a treatment orientation. Based on the available data, treatment orientation was only tested as a moderator of the dropout effect. Results from this analysis indicated that role induction had a similar effect in reducing dropout when comparing cognitive–behavioral to other types of treatments.

Table 13.3 Results from the Tests of Psychotherapy Moderators of Role Induction Effects

Moderator	Outcome Domain	Results
Setting (university vs. outpatient clinics)	Immediate in-session impacts	$Q_B(1) = 0.04, p = .84$
	Dropout	$Q_B(1) = 0.00, p = .97$
	Mid-treatment outcomes	$Q_B(1) = 3.18, p = .07$
	Post-treatment outcomes	$Q_B(1) = 0.75, p = .39$
Treatment orientation (CBT vs. other)	Immediate in-session impacts	Not enough data available to test this effect
	Dropout	$Q_B(1) = 0.93, p = .34$
	Mid-treatment outcomes	Not enough data available to test this effect
	Post-treatment outcomes	Not enough data available to test this effect
Therapist level (professional vs. trainee vs. mixed)	Immediate in-session impacts	$Q_B(2) = 2.63, p = .27$
	Dropout	**$Q_B(2) = 7.01, p = .03$**
	Mid-treatment outcomes	**$Q_B(2) = 10.28, p < .01$**
	Post-treatment outcomes	$Q_B(1) = 0.21, p = .65$

Note. Significant results are bolded.
CBT, cognitive–behavioral therapy.

In terms of the therapists, six of the studies had trainees, six had professionals, two had both trainees and professionals, and three did not report the experience level of the therapists. Role induction effects did not differ between therapist groups on immediate in-session impacts or post-treatment outcomes. However, role induction clients were significantly less likely to drop out than control clients when their therapist was a professional ($k = 4$, $OR = 1.39$) compared to trainee ($k = 6$, $OR = 1.39$) or a mixed therapist sample ($k = 2$, $OR = 0.71$). Similar differences were also observed for mid-treatment outcomes, with larger effect sizes observed with professionals ($k = 1$, $d = 2.53$) compared to trainee ($k = 1$, $d = -0.02$) and mixed ($k = 2$, $d = -0.13$) samples.

Condition Moderators of the Role Induction Effects

Results of the statistical tests examining the condition moderators of role induction type, content, and control type are provided in in Table 13.4. Role induction was presented to participating patients through written information (paper or electronic, $k = 3$), a verbal discussion ($k = 7$), or an audio/visual presentation ($k = 7$). These three formats were similarly effective at having immediate in-session impacts, reducing dropout, and improving mid-treatment outcomes. However, by the end of treatment, role induction appeared to have the largest impact when provided through a verbal discussion ($k = 5$,

Table 13.4 Results from the Tests of Condition Moderators of Role Induction Effects

Moderator	Outcome Domain	Results
RI format (verbal vs. audio/visual vs. written information)	Immediate in-session impacts	$Q_B(2) = 0.33, p = .85$
	Dropout	$Q_B(2) = 0.41, p = .81$
	Mid-treatment outcomes	$Q_B(1) = 2.12, p = .15$
	Post-treatment outcomes	$\mathbf{Q_B(2) = 8.48, p = .01}$
RI content (roles only vs. duration only vs. mixed)	**Immediate in-session impacts**	$\mathbf{Q_B(2) = 7.99, p = .02}$
	Dropout	$Q_B(2) = 1.37, p = .50$
	Mid-treatment outcomes	Not enough data available to test this effect
	Post-treatment outcomes	$\mathbf{Q_B(2) = 8.42, p = .02}$
Control type (nothing vs. wait vs. non-RI information)	Immediate in-session impacts	$Q_B(2) = 0.10, p = .95$
	Dropout	$Q_B(1) = 0.06, p = .81$
	Mid-treatment outcomes	$Q_B(1) = 3.13, p = .08$
	Post-treatment outcomes	$Q_B(2) = 1.60, p = .45$

Note. Significant results are bolded.
RI, role induction.

$d = 0.46$), followed by an audio/visual presentation ($k = 2$, $d = 0.34$), with a slightly negative effect when provided through written information ($k = 1$, $d = -0.07$).

The content of the role induction likewise differed across studies. Most ($k = 13$) provided patients with a mix of information on the expected roles, treatment duration, and treatment rationale; however, two studies provided information on expected treatment duration only, and two provided information on expected roles only. The type of information provided did have a significant impact on immediate in-session impacts. Specifically, the largest effects were observed when the role induction focused on expected roles ($k = 1$, $d = 1.17$), followed by duration ($k = 2$, $d = 1.10$), followed last by a mix of information ($k = 5$, $d = 0.41$). However, the content of the role induction did not significantly moderate the dropout effect, and not enough data were available to test content as a moderator of the mid-treatment outcome effect. The content of the role induction did have a significant impact on the post-treatment outcome effect. Specifically, the largest effects were observed when the role induction focused on expected roles ($k = 1$, $d = 0.71$), followed by a mix of information ($k = 6$, $d = 0.39$), with slightly negative effects when only expected duration was discussed ($k = 1$, $d = -0.07$).

The type of control condition differed between studies, with the majority of studies ($k = 13$) having control groups that simply lacked the role induction information, three studies providing patients with information that was not relevant to psychotherapy (e.g., a video about a large insurance provider), and one study asking control patients to wait for a similar amount of time. The type of control that was used did not significantly moderate the effect of role induction on immediate in-session impacts, dropout, mid-treatment outcomes, or post-treatment outcomes.

Measurement Moderators of the Role Induction Effects

Results of the statistical tests examining the measurement moderators are provided in Table 13.5. A meta-regression analysis suggested that timing of the mid-treatment outcome measurement (after one, two, or four sessions) was not a significant predictor of the effect sizes. For immediate in-session impacts, role induction did have larger or smaller impacts depending on the type of variable that was being measured. Role induction had the largest immediate in-session impact on improving clients' knowledge and beliefs about psychotherapy ($k = 8$, $d = 1.06$), followed by in-session evaluations of client behavior ($k = 5$, $d = 0.43$). However, in one study (Johansen et al., 2011) with two measurements, clients who received role induction reported more negative in-session moods compared to clients in the control group ($k = 2$, $d = -0.22$). In terms of mid-treatment outcomes, whereas role induction had positive effects on subjective reporting of change ($k = 4$, $d = 1.08$) and symptoms ($k = 4$, $d = 0.15$), it had negative effects for mid-treatment ratings of the alliance ($k = 4$, $d = -0.16$) and satisfaction ($k = 1$, $d = -0.43$). At post-treatment, nonsignificant differences in the effectiveness or role induction were observed between outcome types: subjective measurements of change ($k = 4$, $d = 0.79$), patient reported satisfaction ($k = 5$, $d = 0.33$), or objective measurements of symptoms ($k = 16$, $OR = 0.23$). Last, we tested whether the role induction effects on mid-treatment and post-treatment outcomes differed depending on whether the outcome was therapist-rated or patient-rated. No significant differences in effect sizes between the raters were found at either time point.

Summary of Results

Providing patients with role induction at the start of psychotherapy appears to be an effective treatment method. Specifically, three studies reported positive client attitudes and experiences with role induction, including high ratings of role induction quality, relevance, favorability, understandability, and utility. Patients who received role induction also showed more positive immediate in-session behaviors, knowledge, and beliefs compared to patients who did not receive role induction ($d = 0.64$). In addition, they were 1.64 times less likely to drop out of treatment prematurely compared to control patients. Furthermore, patients who received role induction showed more positive post-treatment outcomes ($d = 0.33$) compared to those who did not. Interestingly, mid-treatment outcomes were not statistically significant; however, the obtained effect size ($d = 0.26$) is considered a small but meaningful clinical effect. The lack of statistical significance was probably due to the small number of studies in the mid-treatment outcome analyses.

Table 13.5 Results from the Tests of Measurement Moderators of Role Induction Effects

Moderator	Results
Timing of mid-treatment DV measurement	$k = 5, B = 0.15$, 95% CI [−0.02, 0.33], $z = 1.77, p = .08, R^2_{analog} = .23$
Immediate DV domain (knowledge and beliefs vs. evaluation of client behavior vs. client mood)	$Q_B(2) = 16.36, p < .01$
Mid-treatment DV domain (alliance vs. subjective rating of change vs. satisfaction vs. symptoms/distress)	$Q_B(3) = 9.37, p = .03$
Post-treatment DV domain (subjective rating of change vs. satisfaction vs. symptoms/distress)	$Q_B(2) = 4.62, p = .10$
Mid-treatment DV rater (therapist vs. client)	$Q_B(1) = 0.68, p = .41$
Post-treatment DV rater (therapist vs. client)	$Q_B(1) = 2.00, p = .16$

Note. Significant results are bolded.
DV, dependent variable; RI, role induction.

Across the board, most of the moderators that were tested produced nonsignificant results, suggesting that the effects of role induction tend to be pretty stable. However, a few notable exceptions were observed. Role induction seemed to be more effective in studies that included a greater number of non-Hispanic White patients. This brings into question whether existing role induction methods are adequately suited to Black, Indigenous, and people of color (BIPOC) individuals. The role induction effects were also most pronounced for dropout and mid-treatment outcomes when patients were working with professional therapists rather than trainees. These effects were not present for the immediate in-session impacts, however, and they disappeared by the post-treatment outcome measurement.

At post-treatment, two interesting significant findings were observed. First, role induction had the largest effect when delivered through a verbal conversation with patients. Second, role induction had large impacts on both immediate in-session client behaviors and post-treatment outcomes when the focus of the discussion was on expected psychotherapy roles (as contrasted with expected duration or a mix of information on both roles and duration).

Possible Negative Effects and Harm

Findings from our meta-analysis suggest that providing role induction is beneficial for optimizing treatment retention and post-treatment outcomes. No specific negative effects or harms from role induction were identified in the published research. Still, harms may be possible if role induction is not tailored to meet individual patients' needs. For example, patients who have past experiences with psychotherapy may become bored or uninterested if therapists spend a significant amount of time on role induction topics that overlap with their existing knowledge of the process.

Diversity Considerations

Previous meta-analyses have found that psychotherapy personalized to the needs of patients with diverse identities is even more effective than non-tailored treatments (e.g., latest and largest is Soto et al., 2018; see also Benish et al., 2011; Hall et al., 2016; Huey & Tilley, 2018). The importance of accounting for diverse patient identities in psychotherapy was also evident in our meta-analysis. Role induction was more effective in promoting treatment retention and immediate in-session impacts in samples that had a greater percentage of non-Hispanic White patients compared to patients with diverse racial and ethnic identities. It is unclear why this was the case. One possibility is that many role induction methods were specifically developed by White researchers with White patients in mind.

This limitation may prove clinically important because previous research suggests that it is particularly meaningful for potential patients who identify as Black to read pre-therapy materials that are tailored to discuss Black patients' experiences in therapy (Alvidrez et al., 2005, 2010). Some of the cultural alterations suggested from these studies included targeting concerns about involuntary hospitalization, discussing how therapists with different racial/ethnic identities could still be helpful, and mentioning therapist receptivity to discussing religious and spiritual beliefs in therapy (Alvidrez et al., 2005). Efforts to optimize role induction to meet the needs of patients with diverse racial and ethnic identities are an important direction for practice and future research.

Research on the utility of role induction for other diverse identities is also limited. Some role induction methods have been tested in diverse patient populations, such as immigrants in Hawaii (Lambert & Lambert, 1984), a role induction video in Spanish for Puerto Rican patients (Schwarz, 1990), materials tailored for older adults (Alvidrez et al., 2005; Latour & Cappeliez, 1994), and with patients with lower socioeconomic status (Heitler, 1973; Jacobs et al., 1972). To our knowledge, however, no studies have directly compared the effectiveness of tailored and non-tailored role induction materials for diverse patient identities. Similarly, no studies have examined whether specific patient characteristics may moderate the effectiveness of role induction methods.

Limitations of the Research

Although the role induction literature does have a long history, there are still a number of limitations. First, much of the research on role induction is older, with the majority of studies being conducted more than two decades ago. It may be that given the positive results from early studies and reviews on role induction, its efficacy is taken as a given and researchers have become less interested in studying the topic. In addition, many current treatment packages include role induction as part of the first or second session. The efficacy of these treatment packages is often studied as a whole rather than examining the individual nonspecific components separately. But, identifying the efficacy of the specific components is essential in order to identify what methods actually cause change in psychotherapy. We believe that a renewed interest in this area of research is needed. It is uncertain whether previous models for role induction and the education that was provided to patients in those early studies remain applicable to contemporary treatments.

Future work should investigate the contexts under which role induction is most effective. The majority of previous studies focused on group psychotherapy and were not included in the current meta-analysis, which focused exclusively on individual psychotherapy with adults. Additional research examining the efficacy of role induction as a preparatory method for individual treatments is needed. In addition, most of the included studies were not exclusive to one form of psychotherapy. Based on this, treatment orientation was only tested as a moderator for psychotherapy dropout (specifically comparing CBT approaches to other specified approaches). No differences in the effectiveness of role indication between the orientations were found. However, future research comparing the value of role induction and the ease at which one can be oriented between different theoretical orientations and treatment approaches is needed.

Most of the existing research on role induction, the effects of which are now well-established, has focused solely on testing its effectiveness against control conditions. Research is now needed to examine differing types of role induction to test their relative efficacy. For example, role induction can focus on psychotherapy outcomes and duration, patient and therapist roles and behaviors, the treatment rationale, or all of these. In addition, the development of psychometrically sound measures of role induction would allow for additional research using naturalistic and non-experimental designs.

Studies are needed to directly compare which types of information and which formats are most effective when preparing patients to begin psychotherapy. Although some of these components were tested in the meta-analysis, the effects were based on cross-study comparisons. Direct within-study comparisons of different styles and formats of role induction are needed.

Although role induction was introduced as a method designed to help low-income patients (Orne & Weidner, 1968), no research has tested whether it is more or less effective for certain groups of patients. Patients of all income levels may know little about the nature of psychotherapy and could benefit from pre-therapy education. Indeed, most of the research has been conducted with primarily White samples, and the presenting concerns in these samples have been mixed. Research focusing on BIPOC patients is urgently warranted.

Training Implications

Currently, there are no empirical studies examining the efficacy of training in role induction methods; however, some training recommendations seem warranted given the causal link between the method and enhanced psychotherapy retention and treatment outcomes. Role induction training can include a didactic component where its research is discussed in classes on treatment methods. Students can role-play role induction procedures with supervisors and other students. These role-plays can focus on specific cases, problems, or treatment packages used in the clinical setting. Although specific training websites for role induction are not currently available, we suggest that training be modeled after the role induction techniques that have been shown to produce positive results in the empirical literature (e.g., Orne & Wender, 1968).

Furthermore, supervisors can demonstrate psychotherapy role induction by beginning supervision with role induction for the supervisory relationship. Discussions on roles and expectations in supervision may serve as a good model for trainee therapists to discuss roles and expectations with their psychotherapy clients. We also suggest that educators and supervisors integrate role induction training with other psychotherapy processes that facilitate treatment outcomes, such as building outcome expectations and accommodating client preferences.

It may prove helpful for educators and supervisors to highlight when role induction may be indicated for critical topics, such as concerns about confidentiality or involuntary hospitalization, navigating patient concerns about how therapists' identities (e.g., gender identity, race, age) may impact treatment, and how patients may provide feedback. We also recommend that trainees gain experience with providing role induction to patients with a variety of diverse identities, presenting concerns, and potential psychotherapy approaches. In developing these "meta-skills," trainees may benefit from prompts to reflect on how their and their patients' identities, beliefs, and experiences may contribute to similar or dissimilar conceptualizations of the psychotherapy process.

Therapeutic Practices

The results from our meta-analysis suggest that role induction results in enhanced treatment retention and outcomes. The following recommendations for practice are therefore offered (the first five are based on direct evidence from the meta-analytic findings on role induction, and the rest are based on other research and clinical experience):

- Assess patients' knowledge of psychotherapy, including knowledge of patient and therapist roles, selection of session topics, treatment rationale, and therapy duration.
- Use this information to shape the extent and content of role induction for those particular patients.
- Provide role induction prior to or during the intake session when possible.
- Discuss, as indicated, patient roles, therapist roles, session topics, and treatment rationale; research evidence indicates that discussion of respective roles produced the greatest impact.
- Consider utilizing a verbal discussion to deliver role induction information (because it exerts the most impact, on average).
- Personalize the role induction to the individual client, on such characteristics as their strong preferences, presenting concerns, readiness/stage of change, and past treatment experiences (Norcross & Wampold, 2018).
- Adapt role induction to patients' diverse cultural identifies; examples include monitoring cultural or family beliefs, addressing concerns about therapists' identities (e.g., gender identity, race/ethnicity, age), and processing negative experiences in psychotherapy (e.g., microaggressions, past therapist comments; Soto et al., 2019).
- Integrate other psychotherapy methods linked with enhanced outcomes when providing role induction. Examples include establishing a collaborative relationship,

assessing patient preferences when reviewing treatment rationales and session topics, and setting optimistic but still appropriate outcome expectations when reviewing treatment rationales (Norcross & Lambert, 2018).

- Monitor the need to revisit role induction (e.g., addressing topics not addressed during intake, providing clarification on role induction-related topics) throughout the treatment process.

References

* Studies included in the research review.

Alvidrez, J., Areán, P. A., & Stewart, A. L. (2005). Psychoeducation to increase psychotherapy entry for older African Americans. *American Journal of Geriatric Psychiatry, 13*(7), 554–561. https://doi.org/10.1097/00019442-200507000-00003

Alvidrez, J., Snowden, L. R., & Kaiser, D. M. (2010). Involving consumers in the development of a psychoeducational booklet about stigma for Black mental health clients. *Health Promotion Practice, 11*(2), 249–258. https://doi.org/10.1177/1524839908318286

Bedics, J. D. (2019). Initiating the therapeutic encounter. *Psychotherapy, 56*(1), 5–6. https://doi.org/10.1037/pst0000223

Benish, S., Quintana, S., & Wampold, B. (2011). Culturally adapted psychotherapy and the legitimacy of myth: A direct-comparison meta-analysis. *Journal of Counseling Psychology, 58*(3), 279–289. https://doi.org/10.1037/a0023626

Bordin, E. S. (1979). The generalizability of the psychoanalytic concept of the working alliance. *Psychotherapy, 16*(3), 252–260. https://doi.org/10.1037/h0085885

*Callahan, J. L., Gustafson, S. A., Misner, J. B., Paprocki, C. M., Sauer, E. M., Saules, K. K., Schwartz, J. L., Swift, J. K., Whiteside, D. M., Wierda, K. E., & Wise, E. H. (2014). Introducing the Association of Psychology Training Clinics' collaborative research network: A study on client expectancies. *Training and Education in Professional Psychology, 8*(2), 95–104. https://doi.org/10.1037/tep0000047

*Childress, R., & Gillis, J. S. (1977). A study of pretherapy role induction as an influence process. *Journal of Clinical Psychology, 33*(2), 540–544. https://doi.org/10.1002/1097-4679(197704)33:2<540::AID-JCLP2270330244>3.0.CO;2-L

Constantino, M. J., Visla, A., Coyne, A. E., & Boswell, J. F. (2018). A meta-analysis of the association between patients' early treatment outcome expectation and their posttreatment outcomes. *Psychotherapy, 55*(4), 473–485. https://doi.org/10.1037/pst0000169

*Deane, F. P., Spicer, J., & Leathem, J. (1992). Effects of videotaped preparatory information on expectations, anxiety, and psychotherapy outcome. *Journal of Consulting and Clinical Psychology, 60*(6), 980–984. https://doi.org/10.1037/0022-006X.60.6.980

*Delgadillo, J., & Groom, M. (2017). Using psychoeducation and role induction to improve completion rates in cognitive behavioural therapy. *Behavioural and Cognitive Psychotherapy, 45*, 170–184. https://doi.org/10.1017/S1352465816000643

*Delgadillo, J., Moreea, O., Murphy, E., Ali, S., & Swift, J. K. (2015). Can low-cost strategies improve attendance rates in brief psychological therapy? Double-blind randomized controlled trial. *Journal of Clinical Psychology, 71*(12), 1139–1152. https://doi.org/10.1002/jclp.22228

Elliott, R., Bohart, A. C., Watson, J. C., & Murphy, D. (2018). Therapist empathy and client outcome: An updated meta-analysis. *Psychotherapy, 55*(4), 399–410. https://doi.org/10.1037/pst0000175

Fluckiger, C., Del Re, A. C., Wampold, B. E., & Horvath, A. O. (2018). The alliance in adult psychotherapy: A meta-analytic synthesis. *Psychotherapy, 55*(4), 316–340. https://doi.org/10.1037/pst0000172

Hall, G. C. N., Ibaraki, A. Y., Huang, E. R., Marti, C. N., & Stice, E. (2016). A meta-analysis of cultural adaptations of psychological interventions. *Behavior Therapy, 47*(6), 993–1014. https://doi.org/10.1016/j.beth.2016.09.005

Heitler, J. B. (1973). Preparation of lower-class patients for expressive group psychotherapy. *Journal of Consulting and Clinical Psychology, 41*(2), 251–260. https://doi.org/10.1037/h0035173

*Hoehn-Saric, R., Frank, J. D., Imber, S. D., Nash, E. H., Stone, A. R., & Battle, C. C. (1964). Systematic preparation of patients for psychotherapy: I. Effects on therapy behavior and outcome. *Journal of Psychiatric Research, 2*(4), 267-281. https://doi.org/10.1016/0022-3956(64)90013-5

Huey, S. J., & Tilley, J. L. (2018). Effects of mental health interventions with Asian Americans: A review and meta-analysis. *Journal of Consulting and Clinical Psychology, 86*(11), 915–930. https://doi.org/10.1037/ccp0000346

*Jacobs, D., Charles, E., Jacobs, T., Weinstein, H., & Mann, D. (1972). Preparation for treatment of the disadvantaged patient: Effects on disposition and outcome. *American Journal of Orthopsychiatry, 42*(4), 666–674. https://doi.org/10.1111/j.1939-0025.1972.tb02533.x

*Johansen, A. B., Lumley, M., & Cano, A. (2011). Effects of video-based therapy preparation targeting experiential acceptance or the therapeutic alliance. *Psychotherapy, 48*(2), 163–169. https://doi.org/10.1037/a0022422

Kirtner, W. L., & Cartwright, D. S. (1958). Success and failure in client-centered therapy as a function of initial in-therapy behavior. *Journal of Consulting Psychology, 22*(5), 329–333. https://doi.org/10.1037/h0042982

*Lambert, R. G., & Lambert, M. J. (1984). The effects of role preparation for psychotherapy on immigrant clients seeking mental health services in Hawaii. *Journal of Community Psychology, 12*(3), 263–275. https://doi.org/10.1002/1520-6629(198407)12:3<263::AID-JCOP2290120310>3.0.CO;2-J

*Larsen, D. L., Nguyen, T. D., Green, R. S., & Attkisson, C. C. (1983). Enhancing the utilization of outpatient mental health services. *Community Mental Health Journal, 19*(4), 305–320. https://doi.org/10.1007/BF00755411

Latour, D., & Cappeliez, P. (1994). Pretherapy training for group cognitive therapy with depressed older adults. *Canadian Journal on Aging, 13*(2), 221–235. https://doi.org/10.1017/S0714980800006036

Monks, G. (1995). *A meta-analysis of role induction studies* [Unpublished doctoral dissertation]. University of Hartford.

Norcross, J. C., & Lambert, M. J. (2018). Psychotherapy relationships that work III. *Psychotherapy, 55*(4), 303–315. https://doi.org/10.1037/pst0000193

Norcross, J. C., & Wampold, B. E. (2018). A new therapy for each patient: Evidence-based relationships and responsiveness. *Journal of Clinical Psychology, 74*(11), 1889–1906. https://doi.org/10.1002/jclp.22678

Oldham, M., Kellett, S., Miles, E., & Sheeran, P. (2012). Interventions to increase attendance at psychotherapy: A meta-analysis of randomized controlled trials. *Journal of Consulting and Clinical Psychology, 80*(5), 928–939. https://doi.org/10.1037/a0029630

Orlinsky, D. E., Grawe, K., & Parks, B. K. (1994). *Process and outcome in psychotherapy: Noch einmal.* In A. E. Bergin & S. L. Garfield (Eds.), *Handbook of psychotherapy and behavior change* (pp. 270–376). Wiley.

Orlinsky, D. E., & Howard, K. I. (1986). Process and outcome in psychotherapy. In S. Garfield & A. Bergin (Eds.), *Handbook of psychotherapy and behavior change* (3rd ed., pp. 311–381). Wiley.

Orne, M. T., & Wender, P. H. (1968). Anticipatory socialization for psychotherapy: Method and rationale. *American Journal of Psychiatry, 124*(9), 1202–1212. https://doi.org/10.1176/ajp.124.9.1202

*Reis, B. F., & Brown, L. G. (2006). Preventing therapy dropout in the real world: The clinical utility of videotape preparation and client estimate of treatment duration. *Professional Psychology: Research and Practice, 37*(3), 311–316. https://doi.org/10.1037/0735-7028.37.3.311

Rice, L. N., & Wagstaff, A. K. (1967). Client voice quality and expressive style as indexes of productive psychotherapy. *Journal of Consulting Psychology, 31*(6), 557–563. https://doi.org/10.1037/h0025164

Schwarz, D. A. (1990). *The effect of a Spanish pre-therapy orientation videotape on Puerto Rican clients' knowledge about psychotherapy, improvement in therapy, attendance patterns and satisfaction with services* [Doctoral dissertation, Temple University]. ProQuest Dissertations and Theses Global.

*Sloane, R. B., Cristol, A. H., Pepernik, M. C., & Staples, F. R. (1970). Role preparation and expectation of improvement in psychotherapy. *Journal of Nervous and Mental Disease, 150*(1), 18–26. https://doi.org/10.1097/00005053-197001000-00003

Soto, A., Smith, T. B., Griner, D., Domenech Rodriguez, M., & Bernal, G. (2018). Cultural adaptations and therapist multicultural competence: Two meta-analytic reviews. *Journal of Clinical Psychology, 74*(11), 1907–1923. https://doi.org/10.1002/jclp.22679

*Strassle, C. G., Borckardt, J. J., Handler, L., & Nash, M. (2011). Video-tape role induction for psychotherapy: Moving forward. *Psychotherapy, 48*(2), 170–178. https://doi.org/10.1037/a0022702

Swift, J. K., & Callahan, J. L. (2008). A delay discounting measure of great expectations and the effectiveness of psychotherapy. *Professional Psychology: Research and Practice, 39*(6), 581–588.

*Swift, J. K., & Callahan, J. L. (2011). Decreasing treatment dropout by addressing expectations for treatment length. *Psychotherapy Research, 21*(2), 193–200. https://doi.org/10.1080/10503307.2010.541294

Swift, J. K., Callahan, J. L., Cooper, M., Parkin, S. R. (2018). The impact of accommodating client preference in psychotherapy: A meta-analysis. *Journal of Clinical Psychology, 74*(11), 1924–1937. https://doi.org/10.1002/jclp.22680

Swift, J. K., Callahan, J. L., & Levine, J. C. (2009). Using clinically significant change to identify premature termination. *Psychotherapy, 46*(3), 328–335. https://doi.org/10.1037/a0017003

Swift, J. K., & Greenberg, R. P. (2015). *Premature termination in psychotherapy: Strategies for engaging clients and improving outcomes*. American Psychological Association.

Swift, J. K., Mullins, R. H., Penix, E. A., Roth, K. L., & Trusty, W. T. (2021). The importance of listening to patient preferences when making mental health care decisions. *World Psychiatry, 20*(3), 316–317. https://doi.org/10.1002/wps.20912

Trusty, W. T., Penix, E. A., Dimmick, A. A., & Swift, J. K. (2019). Shared decision-making in mental and behavioural health interventions. *Journal of Evaluation in Clinical Practice, 25*(6), 1210–1216. https://doi.org/10.1111/jep.13255

Walitzer, K. S., Dermen, K. H., & Connors, G. J. (1999). Strategies for preparing clients for treatment: A review. *Behavior Modification, 23*(1), 129–151. https://doi.org/10.1177/0145445599231006

*Warren, N. C., & Rice, L. N. (1972). Structuring and stabilizing of psychotherapy for low-prognosis clients. *Journal of Consulting and Clinical Psychology, 39*(2), 173–181. https://doi.org/10.1037/h0033430

*Wilson, D. O. (1985). The effects of systematic client preparation, severity, and treatment setting on dropout rate in short-term psychotherapy. *Journal of Social and Clinical Psychology, 3*(1), 62–70. https://doi.org/10.1521/jscp.1985.3.1.62

Zwick, R., & Attkisson, C. C. (1984). The use of reception checks in client pretherapy orientation research. *Journal of Clinical Psychology, 40*(2), 446–452. https://doi.org/10.1002/1097-4679(198403)40:2<446::AID-JCLP2270400210>3.0.CO;2-1

*Zwick, R., & Attkisson, C. C. (1985). Effectiveness of a client pretherapy orientation videotape. *Journal of Counseling Psychology, 32*(4), 514–524. https://doi.org/10.1037/0022-0167.32.4.514

14

Collaborative Assessment Methods

Filippo Aschieri, Arnold A. P. van Emmerik, Carlijn J. M. Wibbelink, and Jan H. Kamphuis

Collaborative assessment methods (CAMs)—working with clients during all phases and aspects of psychological assessment and testing—have a history dating back to the second half of the previous century (Fantini et al., 2022). As early as 1953, Luborsky asked his clients to engage in the interpretations of their testing results. Three years later, Harrower (1956) provided the first documented example of how to engage clients in interpreting their testing responses. For example, she would enlist clients in reflecting on their specific Rorschach responses and relate these to their presenting problems. Baker (1964) pioneered a description of how to provide sensitive and helpful feedback procedures to clients. For example, she stressed the importance of avoiding jargon; tailoring and framing test interpretations in an understandable, usable way for clients; and emphasizing the clients' self-observation skills during the discussion of test results. Approximately 10 years later, Craddick (1975) argued that clinicians should always ask clients at the earliest possible occasion about their goals for testing and frame clients' goals as "assessment questions." A hallmark event was Constance Fischer's (1985/1994) book *Individualizing Psychological Assessment*, which provided the first comprehensive summary of how to use assessment procedures collaboratively. The procedural description of CAMs in books (Fischer, 1985/1994) and manuals (Finn, 1996) has paved the way for subsequent applications and empirical testing of their clinical benefits.

In this chapter, we provide a definition and description of CAMs, illustrate their clinical use by providing excerpts from a case, describe landmark studies and earlier reviews, and present a meta-analytic and qualitative research review on the distal and immediate outcomes of CAMs to the extent that these are available in the literature. We also discuss possible negative effects and harm; diversity considerations; and limitations of the extant research, such as the need for studies of the immediate outcomes of CAMs. We close with training implications and therapeutic practices based on the research evidence.

Definitions

Psychological assessment can be defined broadly as the process of completing formal psychological tests or measures and receiving feedback on the results. CAMs represent a distinct area of psychological expertise that centers around actively involving the client in the meaning-making of the assessment findings and turning the process into a collaborative experience. The meaning-making activities range from clients' involvement

Filippo Aschieri, Arnold A. P. van Emmerik, Carlijn J. M. Wibbelink, and Jan H. Kamphuis, *Collaborative Assessment Methods*
In: *Psychotherapy Skills and Methods That Work*. Edited by: Clara E. Hill and John C. Norcross, Oxford University Press.
 DOI: 10.1093/oso/9780197611012.003.0014

in formulating the goals of the testing to expanding the understanding of their results and articulating new ways of understanding their presenting problems based on a shared understanding of their testing results. CAMs research includes studies on the "bare bones" of assessment (e.g., testing and some form of test feedback with therapeutic intent) as well as studies that examine the efficacy of a full model of assessment based on CAMs.

Applications of CAMs include both structured and semistructured models. Probably best known and researched are Therapeutic Assessment (Fantini et al., 2022), Collaborative Assessment (Aschieri & Vetere, 2020), and Collaborative Assessment and Management of Suicidality (Comtois et al., 2011; Jobes, 2012). CAMs in Therapeutic Assessment are framed within a model of change that integrates emotion-focused methods (Fosha, 2004), a post-modern and narrative approach to the client's identity (Aschieri, 2012), and a psychodynamic (Kamphuis & Finn, 2018) and neurobiological understanding (Finn, 2012) of how therapists and clients co-regulate their emotions during sessions and how this translates to changes in a client's life. CAMs in Collaborative Assessment include more broadly all applications of collaborative principles and methods in the use of testing.

CAMs in Collaborative Assessment and Management of Suicidality have a much more specific and explicit focus: They are designed to engage clients at risk for suicide to identify and to understand and resolve the "drivers" of suicidal ideation as continually assessed by the Suicide Status Form (Jobes et al., 1997). Hence, CAMs as seen in Therapeutic Assessment, Collaborative Assessment, and Collaborative Assessment and Management of Suicidality differ from the traditional information-gathering model of assessment (Finn & Tonsager, 1997), which is more descriptive and prescriptive and is typically unilaterally managed by the assessor.

This chapter, and the focus of our meta-analytic review, is limited to Collaborative Assessment and Therapeutic Assessment because these methods typically involve a limited number of sessions (typically two to five). Collaborative Assessment and Management of Suicidality, on the other hand, as described in several protocols, may take up to 16 weeks of intensive working through. We deem such a lengthy treatment outside the scope of the present chapter. The interested reader is referred to a recent meta-analysis on Collaborative Assessment and Management of Suicidality (Swift et al., 2021).

CAMs are rooted in humanistic and phenomenological psychology principles (Fischer, 2000). Key elements of the method are to collaborate with clients and to emphasize the understanding of how their psychological features interplay with their "lively flux" of experiences (p. 4), with the goal of "not just to describe or classify the person's present state but to identify viable options to problematic comportment" (p. 5). Moreover, CAMs are consistent with a social constructionist approach to therapy in acknowledging the clients as the expert on their own lives (Anderson & Goolishian, 1992). Systemic thinking is also integral to CAMs because the testing aims to understand how clients' problems are adaptations to less-than-optimal contexts of living (Fantini et al., 2013).

The main methods are (a) involving clients in setting their goals for the assessment, (b) engaging clients in discussing how their experiences during the testing phase and the contents of their tests responses reflect their real-life dilemmas, and (c) jointly understanding how test results and experiences relate to their goals for the assessment and their next steps in life. When clinicians help clients formulate their goals in terms of questions they have about themselves, or about their lives, and about what they wish to learn from the testing, they aim to stimulate the clients' exploratory system and regulate their attachment system. In fact, attachment researchers have explained how the attachment system and the exploration system (i.e., the inborn system that guides novelty-seeking and learning) are reciprocally activated (Mikulincer & Shaver, 2007). Engaging clients in interpreting their testing results can be seen as a social constructivist process to building new knowledge and understanding as a result of the joint efforts of clients (who participate as experts in their lives) and clinicians (who participate as experts in psychological theories and tests). Providing clients with comprehensive feedback on their assessment results can be seen as an example of narrative therapy.

Clinical Description and Indications

Clinicians using CAMs seek to advance the treatment utility of psychological assessment (Kamphuis et al., 2021). Collaborative assessors aim to provide a secure attachment environment by means of collaborative communication, emotional attunement, and repair of disruptions, while engaging clients in becoming curious about themselves and their presenting problems. Collaborative assessors emphasize empathy and stimulate curiosity and openness. Clinicians using CAMs attempt to build epistemic trust (Fonagy & Allison 2014; Kamphuis & Finn, 2018)—an individual's willingness to consider new knowledge coming from others as reliable and relevant, and therefore worth integrating into their lives.

In line with the spirit of collaborative assessment, clinicians monitor clients' reactions during the testing and solicit their views about the course of the testing process. They involve clients in the assessment and enlist them in developing the focus of the assessment in the form of individualized assessment questions. Identifying personal and specific goals for the assessment typically serves to lower anxiety in clients and, conversely, to increase motivation to participate in the sessions.

During the testing phase, collaborative assessors explain the purpose of each test vis-à-vis the client's assessment questions and jointly explore the meaning of the test findings in the context of those questions. Assessors offer emotional and cognitive support to clients while they process new understandings obtained through the collaborative discussion of their results. Such increased understanding can be accompanied by positive emotions (due to a better understanding of unclear issues; Aschieri & Smith, 2012) as well as negative emotions (due to an increased awareness of the problems; Durosini et al., 2017). Fischer (1985/1994) also emphasized using testing sessions to help clients try out and practice "new behaviors" that "branch off" from their usual ways of being. In this way, clients and assessors identify viable next steps that will help them meet their life goals after the assessment is completed.

At the end of the assessment, assessors provide collaborative feedback to support clients in better understanding the origins of their presenting problems. Feedback typically involves connecting test findings to the goals for the assessment and discussing implications for clients' lives. The immediate outcomes of understanding clients' problems through the lenses of the test results may include more self-compassion, increased coherence of self-understanding, and less shame about problem behaviors.

Unfortunately, to date, there is no specific research that addresses the important question of for whom CAMs work well versus for whom they are less suitable or even contraindicated. Kamphuis and Finn (2018) speculated that contraindications are most likely not well specified by diagnostic categories but proposed instead that the critical variable is transdiagnostic in nature—that is, the client's potential to hold a minimum level of epistemic trust (Kamphuis & Finn, 2018). Typically, this is particularly challenging in patients in (involuntary) forensic practice or with strong paranoid tendencies.

Assessment

Assessment of Collaborative Assessment Methods

Unfortunately, no standardized measures have been developed to systematically assess the presence of CAMs or their ingredients. Such measures are much needed, however, to better assess the immediate outcomes of CAMs and their ingredients. Future research could, for example, operationalize CAMs methods based on Therapeutic Assessment manuals for adult clients (Fantini et al., 2022) and for families with children (Tharinger et al., 2008), and subsequently have trained observers rating the presence and quality of CAMs and their ingredients.

Outcome Assessment

Following Durosini and Aschieri (2021), the measures used to index the immediate and distal outcomes of CAMs can be grouped into three domains: treatment process, symptom reduction, and personal growth.

Treatment process scales include all measures that refer to therapeutic alliance, such as the Alliance scale of the Client Satisfaction Questionnaire–8 (Attkisson & Zwick, 1982) or the Treatment Satisfaction Questionnaire (Pegg et al., 2001). The Assessment Questionnaire (AQ; Finn et al., 1995) includes three scales related to client satisfaction with the assessment process: positive mirroring (12 items; e.g., *The assessment captured the "real" me*), positive relationship with the assessor (12 items; e.g., *The assessor was interested in what I had to say*), and (lack of) negative feelings for the assessment (11 items; e.g., *The assessment made me feel that my life is nothing but problems*).

Symptoms have been measured by scales such as the Symptom Checklist–90-Revised (Derogatis, 1983) and the Demoralization scale of the Minnesota Multiphasic Personality Inventory–2-Restructured Form (MMPI-2-RF, Tellegen & Ben-Porath, 2008/2011). These measures are widely used and well validated, and they typically assess distal outcome.

The AQ (Finn et al., 1995) also includes one scale related to client personal growth: New Self-Awareness (13 items; e.g., *I gained a new understanding of myself*). The

New Self-Awareness scale of the AQ has been used in empirical research on personal growth, and the Self-Esteem Questionnaire has also served this purpose (Cheek & Buss, 1981). The four scales of the AQ constitute a higher order factor, namely how positive the assessment experience was for clients. Reliability was satisfactory (α coefficients in three groups of college students, inpatients, and outpatients were between .79 and .93), and test–retest coefficients varied between .75 and .84. The AQ total score and its scales were not correlated to measures of social desirability, suggesting that its outcomes are not strongly influenced by positive response bias.

Clinical Examples

We report excerpts from the video-recorded assessment of "Ain," a 28-year-old Caucasian cisgender male identifying as heterosexual, who was assessed in Italy. Ain sought assessment following the breakup with his girlfriend, Sabine (Ain and Sabine are pseudonyms).

The first session started with a warm welcome by the clinician (F) and then focused on collaboratively defining Ain's (A) goals for his assessment.

F: So, what goals and questions do you have for this assessment?

A: I don't know really. . . . I just think that after I broke up with Sabine I keep feeling there was something wrong with me.

F: I see, that must be painful.

A: Yes, and I blame myself because it's also my fault that she broke up with me.

F: Mmm, can you say more?

A: You know, I feel somehow bad about this . . . and it's hard to talk about it.

F: Uhm, is there any shame about what you are thinking about?

A: Yes! I feel shame because it's not easy to admit that you have a sexual problem. . . . I have this problem with ejaculation, and lately with Sabine it became almost impossible to make love . . . since I could not hold back for more than a few seconds!

F: Oh yes, and in our culture this problem is really loaded with shame, while, actually, it's a pretty common problem for many male clients I have spoken to.

The assessor immediately tries to enlist the client as an active participant in the assessment. The assessor asks the client to set the goals for the process and works with him to make them more specific. In addition, emotional support, counteracting shame, and mirroring help clients deepen and focus their goals.

F: So, when did this problem with premature ejaculation begin?

A: Hard to say. I always felt a bit clumsy in intimacy with my partners, but it got worse when I decided to leave home and move in with Sabine. Before then our sex life was much better, we had fewer occasions to meet, but they were much more exciting.

Initial clients' goals are fine-tuned through circular questioning (Brown, 1997). This questioning helps transform clients' presenting problems (e.g., "I suffer from premature ejaculation and I need psychological therapy") into contextualized, specific questions about themselves and their relationships with the world (e.g., "Why did I develop this problem since I left home to live with Sabine?")

In the central part of the assessment, the clinician typically administers psychological testing. The choice of tests reflects the clients' goals for the assessment. Clients are actively engaged in "building connections" between their test responses, their real-life experiences, and their assessment goals (Fantini et al., 2022). For example, clients can discuss and deepen their answers to specific self-report items, or by associating images, thoughts, and emotions to their responses to projective or narrative tests. The assessor uses open-ended questions to explore items from self-report questionnaires and follows up on clients' answers to connect their observations to their assessment questions and real-life experiences. This process usually occurs directly after the completion of a test, to capture the immediate emotional reactions and thoughts of clients during the testing session.

In the case of Ain, his MMPI-2-RF results included—among critical items—"*My sex life is satisfactory* (False)" and elevations on the internalizing psychopathology scales, which pointed to anxiety and depressive symptomatology.

The assessor started expanding Ain's experience related to the item about Ain's sex life:

F: So, you replied false to "My sex life is satisfactory." Could you tell me more about it?

A: Yes, actually I realize that the more I felt pressured to maintain an adult relationship, the more I felt my sex life was unsatisfactory.

F: That must be confusing. And do you have a sense of how this relates to your mood?

A: I never thought about it. Maybe I am more worried than otherwise?

F: This seems to be true from your test results. As you see, these dots indicate your scores on the test. Each dot corresponds to a feature of your psychological functioning. The higher the scores are, the more likely the corresponding psychological features are relevant for you. Is that clear?

A: Yes. What do these elevations mean?

F: These suggest that you have been harboring a lot of anxiety. Does that fit with your experience?

A: Oh yes! Every time Sabine and I were about to make love I felt so much anxiety! And that makes things worse!

F: Of course, how difficult it must have been to approach sex in such an emotional state!

A: Indeed. . . .

F: And let me try to connect this with the sexual problem: Is it possible that this anxiety when you are faced with the sexual problem turns into some type of demoralization or hopelessness?

A: It does. That's exactly how I feel, I have started to think about myself like a failure (Ain cries).

F: I am sorry to hear that. How does it feel to talk about these things with me now?

A: It's painful, really, but it's also the first time I feel I can open up, and I don't feel judged. When I was a child, in my family, whenever I had a problem I felt I had to simply move on as soon as I could, otherwise, my mother would have scolded me.

F: Really? Can you tell me more about that?

A: Yes, since my father passed away, when I was 4 or 5, my mother raised me as a single mother. I have so much gratitude for her for doing it. She made it so I never lacked for anything (Ain keeps describing the sacrifices his mother made to allow him to study and have a nice life).

F: And I wonder if you tried to make things easier for her by keeping your problems to yourself.

A: Yes, also because she never liked to comfort me when I was sad, she told me, "Come on! Do not allow this problem to get you down" . . . she was probably telling me what she was telling herself after my father passed away.

F: That makes sense. But these scores suggest that over the years, you piled up so many negative emotions that you could not process with your mother, and now, these negative emotions can create a vicious cycle with your sex life: The more you feel unsatisfied about your sex life, the more you feel down and blue. And on the other hand, the more you harbor anxiety and hopelessness, the harder it is for you to enjoy intimacy with Sabine.

After scoring the tests, assessors offer their expertise about the meaning of a particular test score, and clients bring their expertise in how that test variable shows up in their lives. For example, Ain's Rorschach was administered and scored according to the Rorschach Performance Assessment System (Meyer et al., 2011), and it revealed an elevation in one area: Oral-Dependent Language (ODL%, indicative of clients "implicitly motivated by dependent needs, related to an underlying dependent trait or a state"; Mihura & Meyer, 2018, p. 7). After the assessor globally explained how the Rorschach is scored, he engaged Ain in discussing the interpretation of ODL%.

F: Now, I would like to tell you about this variable, called Oral-Dependent Language, which is coded whenever you use terms and images that suggest themes of nurturance, needing support or help, oral activity, food, and eating, or birth and fragility . . .

A: (Interrupts the assessor) Oh, I remember, all the "mouths" and the food that I saw in the cards!

F: Yes, believe it or not (smiles) there is a lot of research that connects this variable to people who feel they need more support, more nurturance from their environment, and may not receive it. I wonder if this might be true also for you?

A: Well, it depends, I am a very independent person. (Ain describes his profession and how independent he is in that role) . . . but as we said last time talking about my mother, I realized that during much of my growing up the only person who supported me was my mother.

F: Yes, I remember that too. And I wonder to what extent you felt that Sabine was available for you . . . emotionally.

A: Good question! Initially, it was good because we talked a lot about things, our lives, our problems . . . then she lost her mother, and since then I started to take care of her a lot, particularly early on after we moved in together.

F: Interesting, so it seems that starting to live together made you closer physically, but at the same time, you felt you lost the relationship with your mother and started to feel that Sabine was less available for you emotionally. Am I right?

The assessor and Ain continued to discuss the role of the lack of support that Ain experienced from Sabine in relation to the sexual problem, connecting it to the extent to which he felt alone in the couple and his depression.

At the end of the assessment, CAMs are used to discuss and summarize the assessment findings to provide clients with a clear, accurate, coherent, and compassionate understanding of their initial questions for the assessment. For example,

> Initially you asked me, "Why did I develop this problem since I left home to live with Sabine?" Results from the testing showed that you harbor a lot of painful feelings, which you tried to avoid either by "pushing through" life, and by enjoying the relationship with your mother. Initially, you experienced Sabine as a good partner also because you felt you could rely on her for emotional comfort and support. However, with the decision live together you realized you missed the emotional support you had from your mother, and at the same time you felt that Sabine could not tolerate talking about your problems after the loss of her own mother. So, when you had physical intimacy with Sabine, the negative emotions that you were able to ignore and keep at bay in your everyday life were stirred up, and manifested themselves in the form of the sexual problem. Hence, you found yourself in a vicious cycle of depression, that created problems in your relationship, that increased depression, that in turn made it very hard to have a fulfilling sex life. Does this fit with your experience?"

In the final summary and discussion session that is intended to answer the client's questions, tests results and shared observations are integrated into a case formulation that aims to provide a comprehensive and coherent account—which is still open to change, especially if resulting from the client's input—of the client's struggles and resources (Eells, 2022). In the feedback phase, clinicians using CAMs seek to actively enlist clients to agree, modify, or disagree with the interpretation and integration of their assessment findings. Therapeutic Assessment also includes a careful decision about which parts of the assessment results are important to be shared with the clients and how such sharing should proceed (Finn, 1996). Depending on clients' availability and capacity to integrate new and potentially unsettling information, assessors gradually present a more complete story that constitutes the answer to clients' initial questions.

In the case of Ain, after the assessment ended, he decided to keep working on the long-term effects of his father's loss in further psychotherapy with the same assessor. This is a frequent outcome when clients feel the need for more work and assessors can provide the treatment that the assessment indicated would be useful for clients.

Landmark Studies and Previous Reviews

Finn and Tonsager (1992) conducted a randomized controlled trial in a university counseling center comparing a short version of Therapeutic Assessment (i.e., collection of assessment questions, administration of the MMPI-2, and feedback) to three sessions of examiner attention/supportive psychotherapy (i.e., initial session to talk about presenting problems, one information session on the MMPI-2, and another session to talk about presenting problems or reactions to the study). Participants in the collaborative test feedback group were provided with MMPI-2–based feedback. A significant and large reduction in self-reported symptomatology (*d* = .85) and increase in self-esteem (*d* = .45) were observed for the Therapeutic Assessment group compared to the control condition.

Newman and Greenway (1997) replicated this study and improved it by having the control group also complete the MMPI-2, thus providing a more stringent comparison. Again, the MMPI-2 collaborative feedback group demonstrated a significant reduction of self-reported symptoms and distress at a 2-week follow-up compared to the clients included in the control group (who received delayed feedback; *d* = .44). Also, clients who received collaborative feedback reported a significant increase in self-esteem immediately following the feedback session compared to the control group (*d* = .27).

De Saeger and colleagues (2014) compared Therapeutic Assessment with a goal-focused approach specifically designed to motivate clients with severe personality disorders to attend subsequent treatment. Participants receiving Therapeutic Assessment had higher expectations that the treatment they were about to receive would be helpful. These clients also showed higher satisfaction with Therapeutic Assessment and a stronger therapeutic alliance with the Therapeutic Assessment clinician compared to the control condition. Importantly, in this population, Therapeutic Assessment did not lead to reduced symptom severity.

Several meta-analyses on CAMs have been published that partly but not completely overlap with the present research review. Poston and Hanson (2010) and Hanson and Poston (2011) summarized the effect of providing clients with individualized feedback on their testing. In their 2010 article, the authors analyzed effect sizes from 17 studies including a total of 1,496 participants. The effects of providing individualized feedback resulted in better outcomes (*d* = 0.42) than control conditions (e.g., no feedback or delayed feedback).

Durosini and Aschieri (2021) subsequently performed a meta-analysis that examined exclusively the efficacy of well-defined Therapeutic Assessment with adult clients from clinical settings and included nine studies with a total of 491 participants. The results revealed statistically significant effects of Therapeutic Assessment compared to active control groups on measures of treatment process (*g* = .46), clients' symptoms (*g* = .34), and clients' self-enhancement (*g* = .37). Of note, these effects were obtained in only two or three Therapeutic Assessment sessions. Moreover, moderator analyses showed that the presence of supervision and longer and more complete Therapeutic Assessment did not substantially impact these outcomes. The authors concluded that the most important aspect of Therapeutic Assessment may be its use of respect, collaboration, and empathic understanding of clients, and not so much the exact way in which the assessment is implemented.

Research Review

Like Poston and Hanson's (2010) meta-analytic review, we review studies on Therapeutic Assessment and Collaborative Assessment but extend the search to 2021 and include only studies that involve adult clients in clinical settings (leaving out analogue studies and studies conducted in educational or workplace settings). Our study differs from the Durosini and Aschieri (2021) review by also including studies on Collaborative Assessment. We include a meta-analytic review and a qualitative review, each separately addressing both the distal and immediate outcomes of CAMs to the extent that these are available in the literature.

Search Strategy and Inclusion Criteria

Assessment utility, *therapeutic assessment*, *collaborative assessment*, *test feedback*, *assessment feedback*, and *test interpretation* were entered as search terms in title or abstract in the PsycInfo, Web of Science, and PubMed databases in May 2021. This electronic search was limited to studies including adults and to publications in languages that at least two authors understood (English, French, Dutch, Italian). We also conducted an informal search using suggestions by selected scholars from Therapeutic Assessment Institute faculty (k = 16 entries) and studies included in the previous meta-analyses from Poston and Hanson (2010; 16 entries) and Durosini and Aschieri (2021; nine entries).

To be included in the meta-analytic review, studies were required to meet the following criteria:

1. Evaluate CAMs with adult clients: Articles involving children and adolescents (e.g., Tharinger et al., 2009) were excluded from the meta-analytic review.
2. Evaluate a form of psychological CAMs: For example, articles on therapeutic assessment in somatic (e.g., Bouche et al., 2020) and neuropsychological (Gruters et al., 2021) settings were excluded.
3. Publication in a peer-reviewed journal: Dissertations, conference presentations, and book chapters were excluded because it was difficult to retrieve them and determine their eligibility.
4. Utilize a between-group design suitable for calculating one or more Cohen's d effect sizes: Studies without a control or comparison group were excluded from the meta-analytic review.
5. Measure some aspect of therapeutic benefit or outcome in a clinical sample: For example, studies conducted with healthy students were excluded from the meta-analytic review (e.g., Luzzo & Day, 1999).
6. Utilize authentic test data (i.e., based on actual test interpretation, not pre-canned Barnum-type statements).

Because studies excluded from the meta-analysis could have included something about immediate in-session outcomes that would illuminate the process, we re-examined all studies that were excluded from the meta-analytic review for this possibility, the result of which is described in the Qualitative Research Review section below.

Figure 14.1 summarizes the screening and inclusion process of the meta-analytic review. After removing duplicates, we first screened records by reading the respective titles and abstracts. Two authors (FA and AvE) independently screened all records using Rayyan software (Ouzzani et al., 2016), yielding a 96% agreement (Cohen's k = .70, substantial agreement). All records considered by at least one of the two raters as potentially

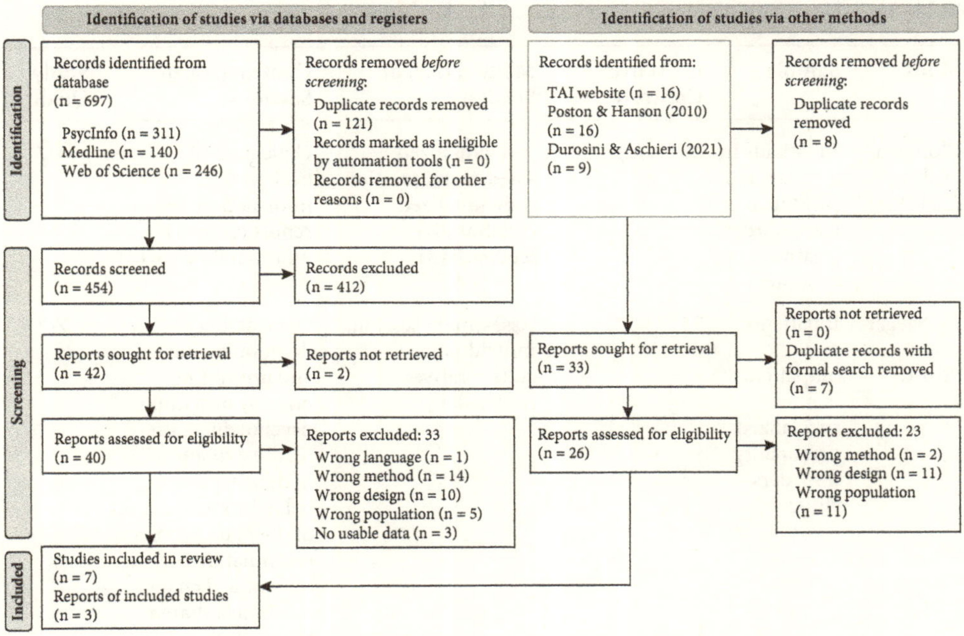

Figure 14.1 Flowchart of study identification, screening, and inclusion.

relevant for the meta-analysis were included in the subsequent full-text screening. The 42 records assessed for full-text screening from the formal literature search and the 33 entries collected through the informal search included seven overlapping articles. After excluding double entries and irretrievable articles, we ended up with a total of 66 articles for full-text screening.

Two of three authors (AvE, JHK, and FA) independently assessed the 66 full-text papers for eligibility, yielding an overall 84% agreement (Cohen's $k = .56$, moderate agreement). The nine disagreements were resolved by discussion among the raters. Thirty-three papers from the formal search and 23 papers from the informal search did not meet one or more of the eligibility criteria and were excluded, resulting in the initial inclusion of 10 papers. Post hoc discussions led to the further exclusion of one study which investigated a method that was not collaborative (Wild et al., 2007) and to the inclusion of one additional study that met all the inclusion criteria (Pegg et al., 2005).

The final set of included studies thus consisted of 10 records that were used to extract effect sizes (Table 14.1). The quality of the included studies was evaluated using the same criteria used by Durosini and Aschieri (2021), and these ratings are summarized in Table 14.2.

Statistical Analyses

A standardized mean difference (Cohen's *d*) was calculated to quantify the effect of CAMs compared to a control or comparison condition. We focused on between-group differences on all available outcome points. Cohen's *d* was calculated by using means

Table 14.1 Description of Studies Included in the Analyses

Study	Sample	*N* (Active/ Control)	Method (No. of Sessions)	Control (No. of Sessions)	Study Quality
Blonigen et al. (2015)	Inpatients in a residential substance use disorder treatment program	26 (17/9)	Individualized assessment questions; individualized collaborative feedback (3)	Collection of background information; self-report testing; 1-month follow-up (2)	4/7
De Saeger et al. (2014)	Inpatients and outpatients in a specialized personality disorders clinic	74 (37/37)	Assessment session; individualized collaborative feedback (4)	Contrasting demoralization and promoting hope by providing psychoeducation on the dynamics of maladaptive behaviors; discussion of the main problem; examination of dilemma of change; reaching a shared reappraisal of the problems; future goal setting (4)	7/7
Essig & Kelly (2013)	Outpatients seeking career counseling in a university counseling center	23 (11/12)	Individualized collaborative feedback (2)	Completion of a career counseling self-report test; gathering information about career indecision; standardized feedback according to the test manual (2)	3/7
L. Miller et al. (2013)	Outpatients with chronic pain seeking counseling with their partners in a university laboratory	47 couples (24/ 23)	Provision of individualized collaborative assessment and feedback on couples' communication processes around pain (2)	Collection of information on the couple's relationship and pain coping strategies; psychoeducation on chronic pain; 1-month follow-up (2)	5/7
W. Miller et al. (1993)	Drinkers applying for a check-up to find out if their alcohol use is harming them	42 (14/14;14)	2-hour testing session including a range of biomedical, neuropsychological, and alcohol consumption measures; individualized feedback using client-centered feedback style (2); wait list (0)	2-hour testing session including a range of biomedical, neuropsychological, and alcohol consumption measures; individualized feedback using directive feedback style (2)	4/7

Table 14.1 Continued

Study	Sample	*N* (Active/ Control)	Method (No. of Sessions)	Control (No. of Sessions)	Study Quality
Finn & Tonsager (1992)	Outpatients seeking treatment for various disorders in a university-based service	60 (32/28)	Individualized collaborative feedback (3)	Discussion of client's concerns and reactions to the study; 2-week follow-up (3)	5/7
Hilsenroth et al. (2002)	Outpatients seeking treatment at two university-based community clinics	68 (34/34)	Performance-based tests; individualized collaborative feedback (4)	Semistructured clinical interview; self-report testing; administration of performance-based or cognitive tests (3)	6/7
Morey et al. (2010)	Outpatients with borderline personality disorder and suicidal ideation seeking treatment in a university clinic	16 (8/8)	Individualized collaborative feedback incorporated into first two sessions of manual-assisted cognitive–behavior therapy (2)	First two sessions of manual-assisted cognitive–behavior therapy as usual (2)	4/7
Newman & Greenway (1997)	Outpatient students in a university counseling service	60 (30/30)	Collection of individualized questions and testing; individualized collaborative feedback (2)	Semistructured interview about client's presenting problems; collection of individualized questions and testing; delayed individualized collaborative feedback (3)	4/7
Pegg et al. (2005)	Active and veteran military personnel admitted to a traumatic brain injury unit	28 (14/14)	Personalized information-provision sessions discussing neuropsychological evaluation and treatment progress, superimposed on care as usual (3)	General information sessions designed as an attention-placebo condition, superimposed on care as usual (3)	3/7

Table 14.2 Quality Assessment of Studies Included in the Analyses

Study	Detailed Description of Method	Clinicians Received Training in Method	Supervision of Clinicians Providing Method	Sufficient Statistical Power to Find Significant Effects of the Method (≥50 Persons in the Comparison Between Experimental and Control Groups)	Intention-to-Treat Analyses	Randomization Performed by Independent (Third) Party	Assessors Were Blinded to Study Condition (for Self-Reported Outcomes, It Was Assumed That This Criterion Was Met)
Blonigen et al. (2015)	Yes	Yes	No	No	No	Yes	Yes
De Saeger et al. (2014)	Yes	Yes	Yes	Yes	Yes	Yes	Yes
Essig & Kelly (2013)	Yes	Yes	No	No	No	No	Yes
L. Miller et al. (2013)	Yes	Yes	No	No	Yes	Yes	Yes
W. Miller et al. (1993)	Yes	Yes	No	No	Yes	No	Yes
Finn & Tonsager (1992)	Yes	Yes	Yes	Yes	No	No	Yes
Hilsenroth et al. (2002)	Yes	Yes	Yes	Yes	Yes	No	Yes

and standard deviations or by transforming a test statistic (t-value) or effect size (partial η^2). For one study, two effect sizes were coded as zero because the effects were described as nonsignificant without any statistical information. A positive Cohen's d indicated a more positive treatment process, fewer symptoms, or more personal growth in CAMs compared to the control condition.

Most studies reported on more than one effect; therefore, we applied a three-level random-effects model to account for the dependency between effect sizes (Assink & Wibbelink, 2016; Cheung, 2014; Van den Noortgate et al., 2013). A three-level random-effects model takes three sources of variance into account: sampling variance (level 1), the variance between effect sizes from the same study (level 2), and variance between studies (level 3). The overall effect for each outcome type (i.e., treatment process, symptom reduction, and personal growth) was estimated in separate intercept-only models. Next, one-tailed log-likelihood ratio tests were conducted to determine whether significant variation was present at level 2 or level 3. In case there was evidence for heterogeneity in effect sizes, moderator analyses were conducted by extending the model with the potential moderators (i.e., age, gender, ethnicity, sample type, number of sessions, method type, control condition, quality of the study, and time between the method application and assessment). Before conducting the analyses, we checked for outliers ($z < -3.29$ or $z > 3.29$; Tabachnick & Fidell, 2013). No outliers were identified. Furthermore, categorical moderator variables were converted to dummy variables, and continuous variables were centered.

After the overall effects were estimated and moderator analyses were conducted, we tested for possible publication bias by using the trim-and-fill procedure (Duval & Tweedie, 2000a, 2000b). For each outcome type, the symmetry of a funnel plot (a scatter plot of the distribution of each effect size on the x-axis against the standard error) was examined. An asymmetric funnel plot, manifested in missing effect sizes on the left side of the plot, indicates possible publication bias. In the case of an asymmetric funnel plot, "missing" effect sizes are imputed to restore the symmetry and an adjusted overall effect size is estimated.

The analyses were performed in R (version 4.0.5; R Development Core Team, 2015), using the "rma.mv" function of the "metaphor" package (Viechtbauer, 2010) and based on guidelines formulated by Assink and Wibbelink (2016). To estimate model parameters, the restricted maximum likelihood procedure was used. In addition, the Knapp and Hartung adjustment (2003) was applied to control for Type I error rates. In all analyses, a p value of $< .05$ was considered statistically significant.

The 10 studies included in the meta-analytic review reported 70 effect sizes and a total sample size of 444 patients (seven studies, 27 effect sizes, $n = 320$ for treatment process; seven studies, 32 effect sizes, $n = 332$ for symptoms; and five studies, 11 effect sizes, $n = 264$ for personal growth), of whom 221 participated in the CAMs and 223 participated in a control or comparison group (the included studies did not systematically report the number of therapists involved).

Outcomes of CAMs

Table 14.3 presents the results for the overall *distal* effect of CAMs on treatment process, symptom reduction, and personal growth. First, a significant medium effect was found for treatment process ($d = 0.59$, $p = .021$), indicating that CAMs were related to a more positive treatment process (assessed by client-reported post-session measures) compared to the control condition. Second, a significant small effect was found for symptoms ($d = 0.19$, $p = .036$), suggesting that CAMs were related to reduced symptoms compared to the control condition. Finally, a significant small to medium effect was found for personal growth ($d = 0.42$, $p = .017$), suggesting that it enhanced personal growth compared to the control condition.

The three-level meta-analytic approach allowed assessing heterogeneity between effect sizes from the same study (i.e., level 2 variance), as well as heterogeneity between studies (i.e., level 3 variance). For symptoms and personal growth, no significant variation was found on either level (see Table 14.3). For treatment process, no significant variation was found on the second level, whereas significant variation was found on the third level ($\chi^2(1) = 21.70$, $p < .001$). Consequently, moderator analyses were conducted only on treatment processes to examine whether characteristics related to the patient, method, and study could explain the variation between effect sizes.

Table 14.4 presents the results of these moderator analyses. Only method type moderated the effect of CAMs on treatment process, $F(1, 25) = 24.32$, $p < .001$. The effect size for Therapeutic Assessment was significantly smaller than the effect size for Collaborative Assessment ($\Delta d = -1.46$), although both effect sizes were significant ($d = 1.89$, $p < .001$ vs. $d = .43$, $p < .001$). Other variables (i.e., age, gender, ethnicity, sample type, number of sessions, quality of the study, and time between CAMs and assessment) did not moderate the effect of CAMs on treatment process.

We examined the possible publication bias for each outcome. Ideally, unpublished materials would have been included in our search; however, it was difficult to retrieve them. The risk of a biased estimate of the overall effect would decrease when unpublished materials are included in a meta-analysis. Therefore, testing for potential publication bias is especially important when only published studies are included. The trim-and-fill procedure is based on the assumption that publication bias produces asymmetric funnel plots with missing effect sizes in the (bottom) left-hand corner. These effects are missing (i.e., not published and, therefore, not included in the meta-analysis) because they were small, nonsignificant, or perhaps reversed effects (Duval & Tweedie, 2000b). By using the trim-and-fill procedure, the degree of asymmetry of the funnel plot is examined and, in case of an asymmetric funnel plot, missing effect sizes are estimated. Figure 14.2 shows that no missing effect sizes were estimated, suggesting the absence of publication bias.

Unfortunately, the studies included in the meta-analytic review only reported distal outcomes and did not provide data on *immediate* outcomes of CAMs.

Summary of Meta-Analytic Review

Based on the current meta-analytic review, CAMs, consisting of on average 2.7 sessions (range from one to four sessions), exert significant positive distal effects on treatment process, patient symptoms, and personal growth compared to a control condition. Method type moderated the distal effects on treatment process outcomes, with smaller effects for Therapeutic Assessment than for Collaborative Assessment. Of note, only

Table 14.3 Overall Effect of Collaborative Assessment Methods on Symptoms, Treatment Process, and Personal Growth Outcomes

Outcome	No. of Independent Studies	No. of ES	Cohen's *d*	95% CI	*p* Value	% Variance Level 1[a]	Variance Level 2[b]	% Variance Level 2[b]	Variance Level 3[c]	% Variance Level 3[c]
Treatment process	7	27	0.591 (0.239)	0.098; 1.083	.021*	19.15	0.000	0.000	0.358***	80.85
Symptoms	7	32	0.186 (0.085)	0.013; 0.360	.036*	84.74	0.000	0.000	0.021	15.26
Personal growth	5	11	0.422 (0.148)	0.092; 0.752	.017*	56.78	0.000	0.000	0.066	43.22

[a]Sampling variance.

[b]Variance between the effect sizes from the same study.

[c]Variance between studies.

CI, confidence interval; ES, effect sizes.

$^{*}p < .05$. $^{***}p < .001$.

Table 14.4 Results of the Moderator Analyses for Treatment Process Outcomes

Moderator Variables	No. of Independent Studies	No. of ES	Intercept/Mean *d* (95% CI)	β_1 (95% CI)	$F(df1, df2)$	*p* Value
Patient characteristics						
Age	7	27	0.605 (0.059, 1.151)*	0.011 (−0.050, 0.073)	0.146 (1, 25)	.706
Gender (% male)	7	27	0.608 (0.155, 1.062)*	0.011 (−0.006, 0.028)	1.746 (1, 25)	.198
Ethnicity (% Caucasian)	4	16	0.791 (0.032, 1.549)*	−0.025 (−0.062, 0.011)	2.203 (1, 14)	.160
Sample type						
Outpatient (RC)	4	12	0.270 (−0.285, 0.825)		2.361 (2, 24)	.116
Inpatient	2	9	1.274 (0.496, 2.052)**	1.004 (0.048, 1.959)*		
Mixed	1	6	0.533 (−0.497, 1.563)	0.263 (−0.907, 1.433)		
Method						
No. of sessions	7	27	0.611 (0.049, 1.173)*	0.132 (−0.746, 1.010)	0.096 (1, 25)	.759
Method type					24.324 (1, 25)	<.001***
CA (RC)	1	5	1.890 (1.317, 2.463)***			
TA	6	22	0.428 (0.219, 0.638)***	−1.462 (−2.072, −0.851)***		
Study characteristics						
Quality rating	7	27	0.563 (0.024, 1.101)*	−0.088 (−0.464, 0.288)	0.232 (1, 25)	.634
Time until assessment	7	27	0.503 (−0.027, 1.033)+	0.014 (−0.016, 0.045)	0.952 (1, 25)	.339

Note. Control condition (active vs. non-active) could not be included as a moderator because no studies with a non-active control condition included outcomes related to the treatment process.

CI, confidence interval; *df*, degrees of freedom; ES, effect sizes; β_1, estimated regression coefficient; TA, Therapeutic Assessment; CA, Collaborative Assessment; RC, Reference Category.

$^{+}p < .10$. $^{*}p < .05$. $^{**}p < .01$. $^{***}p < .001$.

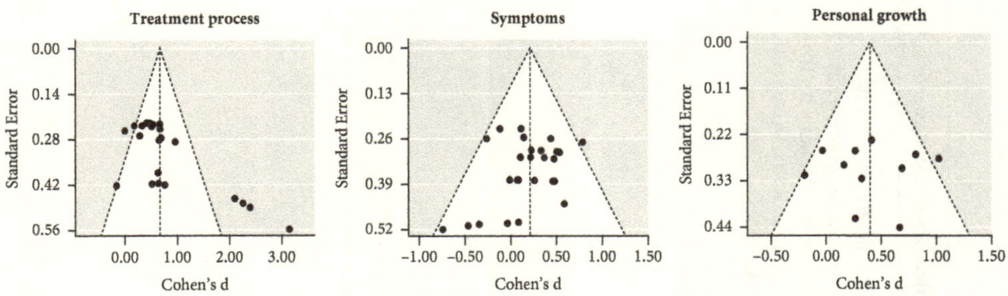

Figure 14.2 Funnel plots for treatment process, symptoms, and personal growth outcomes.

two studies examined Collaborative Assessment, whereas eight studies evaluated Therapeutic Assessment, suggesting that the effect size estimate for Collaborative Assessment may lack precision. In addition, it is possible that the different effect sizes of these methods are better explained by differences between the study populations or other study characteristics than by differences between the methods.

Qualitative Research Review

As noted above, studies that did not meet the inclusion criteria of our meta-analytic research review were re-examined for their relevance to a qualitative research review of the distal and immediate outcomes of CAMs. Table 14.5 summarizes six studies that reported distal and/or immediate outcomes of CAMs but were excluded from the meta-analytic review. This qualitative research review also includes a study that aggregated multiple daily repeated-measures single-case studies of CAMs (Smith et al., 2015). Overall, all six cases had a positive outcome, and none of the clients involved showed negative effects from the interventions.

As can be seen in Table 14.5, CAMs were associated with positive effects on a diverse range of *distal* outcomes that reflect the diversity of the clients' presenting problems and assessment goals. The effect sizes of CAMs in the single-case studies described in Table 14.5 were comparable to an aggregated analysis of nine single-case studies of Therapeutic Assessment as a consultation during ongoing treatment (Smith et al., 2015). This aggregate analysis suggested a moderate effect of CAMs in reducing symptomatic distress ($d = -.50$) between the baseline phase and the combined intervention and follow-up phases.

Our re-examination of the studies that were excluded from the meta-analytic review did not identify studies that reported on the *immediate* outcomes of specific CAMs ingredients. Three studies (Aschieri & Smith, 2012; Durosini et al., 2017; Fantini & Smith, 2018), however, reported on the trajectory of change that was observed in the clients (see Table 14.5). Although this at best only roughly approximates the concept of immediate outcomes and points to the need for future studies of such outcomes of CAMs (see Limitations of the Research), it gives us an initial glimpse of how outcomes may be associated with specific CAMs ingredients.

Table 14.5 Summary of Repeated-Measures Single-Case Studies

Study	Description of the Client	CAMs Ingredients	Main Distal Outcomes	Trajectory of Change
Aschieri & Smith (2012)	A 21-year-old female with academic problems, low self-esteem, and loneliness.	A formal Therapeutic Assessment that included the definition of assessment goals in the form of individualized questions, and collaborative discussion of the assessment experience and results of the MMPI-2, RIM, and EMP.	Comparing pre-intervention and intervention, the results showed a statistically significant decrease of a composite measure of daily self-reported anxiety, loneliness, love for self and others, and degree to which the client was hard on herself ($r = -.55$).	A statistically significant improvement of symptoms over time that began with the first session of the Therapeutic Assessment ($r = .58$).
Smith & George (2012)	A 52-year-old female cancer survivor (stage IV melanoma) with anxiety, depressive symptoms, and emotional volatility, who complained about losing the emotional sturdiness she had felt before the cancer.	A formal Therapeutic Assessment that partially overlapped with long-term psychotherapy. CAMs included definition of assessment goals in the form of individualized questions; collaborative discussion of the assessment experience and results of the EMP and AAP; and a personalized set of personalized sentence stems to be completed by the client.	Comparing pre-intervention and intervention, the results showed a statistically significant decrease of a composite measure of daily self-reported tearfulness, self-efficacy, level of inactivity, and illness fear/anxiety ($r = -.61$).	Not reported.
Tarocchi et al. (2013)	A 37-year-old female diagnosed with complex post-traumatic stress disorder, who felt desperate, fatigued, powerless, and like a failure. The client experienced a very disruptive and traumatizing family, and abusive couple relationships.	A formal Therapeutic Assessment that included the definition of assessment goals in the form of individualized questions, and collaborative discussion of the assessment experience and results of the AAP and RIM.	Comparing pre-intervention and intervention, the results showed a statistically significant decrease of a composite measure of daily self-reported loneliness, despair, and anxiety ($r = -.64$).	Not reported.

Durosini et al. (2017)	A 52-year-old male diagnosed with persistent complicated bereavement disorder, major depressive disorder, and post-traumatic stress disorder. Psychological problems emerged after the death of both parents, after which he withdrew from his family and numbed his feelings.	A formal Therapeutic Assessment that included the definition of assessment goals in the form of individualized questions, and collaborative discussion of the assessment experience and results of the MMPI-2-RF, EMP, and storytelling to non-standardized images.	Comparing the intervention and the follow-up, results showed a statistically significant decrease of a composite measure of daily self-reported loneliness, suffering, longing for deceased parents, emotional numbing, and sense of failure ($r = -.49$).	An inverted "U"-shape trajectory, in which a transient period of worsening at the onset of the intervention was followed by a significant improvement ($r = .51$).
Fantini & Smith (2018)	A 22-year-old female university student who suffered from angry outbursts, lack of motivation, feeling distant from others, and being detached from her emotions. The client had witnessed a family secret, which eventually led to the separation of her parents.	A formal Therapeutic Assessment that included the definition of assessment goals in the form of individualized questions, and collaborative discussion of the assessment experience and results of the MMPI-2-RF, RIM, and EMP.	A composite measure of daily self-reported anxiety and fear of losing someone significantly increased after the discussion of the RIM ($r = .80$) and decreased after the last session of the assessment ($r = -.73$)	An inverted "U"-shape trajectory, in which a transient period of worsening at the onset of the intervention was followed by a significant improvement ($r = .73$).
David et al. (2022)	A mid-20s client, born biologically female, who identified as trans-masculine nonbinary, and was assessed midway an ongoing therapy for depression and problematic relationships.	A formal Therapeutic Assessment that included the definition of assessment goals in the form of individualized questions, and collaborative discussion of the experience and results of the AAP, MCMI-IV, CWS, BDI-II, BAI, EMP, and PFS.	The client reported stably high levels of satisfaction, alliance, presence during the course of the sessions, and high satisfaction and new understandings at the end.	Not reported.

AAP, Adult Attachment Projective System (George & West, 2012); BAI, Beck Anxiety Inventory (Beck et al., 1993); BDI-II, Beck Depression Inventory Second Edition (Beck et al., 1996); CAMs, collaborative assessment methods; CWS, Crisi Wartegg System (Crisi & Palm, 2018); EMP, Early Memories Procedure (Bruhn, 1992a, 1992b); MCMI-IV, Millon Clinical Multiaxial Inventory Fourth Edition (Millon et al., 2015); MMPI-2, Minnesota Multiphasic Inventory Second Edition (Butcher et al., 2001); MMPI-2-RF, Minnesota Multiphasic Inventory–2 Revised Form (Tellegen & Ben-Porath, 2008/2011); PFS, Picture Frustration Study (Rosenzweig, 1978); RIM, Rorschach Inkblot Method (Rorschach, 1921).

Two types of change trajectories can be identified. First, Aschieri and Smith (2012) reported a continuous and linear improvement of the client's problems starting after the first session (the definition of assessment goals in the form of individualized questions) and ending in the final session (the final collaborative discussion of the assessment experience and test results), suggesting an incremental effect of successive CAMs ingredients. Second, Durosini et al. (2017) and Fantini and Smith (2018) reported an inverted U-shaped trajectory, in which the client's problems seem to increase during initial CAMs ingredients, to subsequently improve as further CAMs ingredients follow.

The presence of a linear decrease in clients' distress is also suggested by the aggregated analysis of Smith et al. (2015) discussed above. The trajectory of change across participants suggested that Therapeutic Assessment decreased symptoms and distress from baseline onwards, and that the rate of change slowed with time during the follow-up period.

Summary of Qualitative Review

Although the few available repeated-measures single-case studies of CAMs need to be interpreted cautiously, their qualitative review seems to underscore the positive distal effects of CAMs that were observed in the meta-analytic review. Perhaps most important, they point to a clear and urgent need for studies of the immediate outcomes of specific CAMs ingredients.

Possible Negative Effects and Harm

Unfortunately, possible negative effects of CAMs have not been studied to date. Implicit or explicit signs of client discomfort as well as micro-ruptures of the assessor–client relation are possible negative effects of CAMs. However, clinical experience suggests that negative outcomes are rare, although disappointing and even negative outcomes in individual cases have been documented. Some of these outcomes can be attributed to a distorted use of transference–countertransference dynamics between clients and clinicians (Aschieri, 2016), which typically can be addressed through supervision (Smith, 2017). For example, the assessor's identification with the rescuer position (Karpman, 1968) contributed to the failure of a couple's assessment (Finn, 2007).

Open to empirical testing, we hypothesize that CAMs require that clients relax any epistemic hypervigilance and restore epistemic trust. Clients who remain in a state of epistemic hypervigilance will probably not derive personal self-awareness. In contrast, those who adopt an epistemic hypovigilant stance may too readily accept new "insights" that do not really fit them.

CAMs are challenging in settings in which the reasons for the assessment are extrinsic to the clients, such as in forensic and mandatory assessments. Whereas some of these methods (e.g., discussing the informed consent, discussing emotional reactions to testing, providing feedback about the assessment results) have been advocated by some authors to be used also in these contexts (Evans, 2012; Fischer, 1985/1994; Goldenson et al., 2022), other methods are more problematic. For example, routinely engaging clients in interpreting their testing results could be seen as unreliable because patients may deliberately manipulate these interpretations.

Diversity Considerations

The utility of CAMs has been documented with a wide diversity of clients. These include different genders (including LGBT+ populations; Finn, 2011), age groups (children [Tharinger et al., 2008], adolescents [Smith et al., 2010], and older adults [Durosini et al., 2017]), cultural identities (Fantini, 2016), and nationalities (e.g., United States [Finn & Tonsager, 1992], Dutch [De Saeger, 2014], and Italian [Aschieri & Smith, 2012]). CAMs have also been employed in a variety of clinical settings, including inpatient (Aschieri & Vetere, 2020), outpatient (Finn, 2011), and correctional facilities (Chudzik, 2016).

In 2016, a special section of the *Journal of Personality Assessment* focused on the role of culture in the use of CAMs. In the introduction to the section, Bruce Smith (2016) argued that its flexibility with regard to the selection of assessment procedures (including culturally sensitive tests), along with "assessors constantly ask[ing] clients to help them understand their background and traditions [allows] that culturally situated behaviors and attitudes are not misunderstood or pathologized" (p. 564). Others have speculated that a crucial element of CAMs' suitability for culturally diverse clients is their emphasis on the context for constructing clients' case conceptualizations, integrating "clients' characteristics such as gender, gender identity, sexual orientation, ethnicity, religion, immigrant status, economic background, physical challenges, as well as the relationship between these variables and the client's life context" (Fantini et al., 2022, p. 160). Also, the collaborative nature of CAMs may be refreshing and empowering for some diverse, underprivileged clients, providing them a sense of respect and self-efficacy (Martin, 2018).

There is still a lack of empirical research on the effect of CAMs with diverse populations. At the same time, assessors using CAMs to provide culturally tailored conceptualizations may avoid the risk of stereotypical, erroneous, incomplete, or potentially damaging understandings of clients (Clauss-Ehlers et al., 2019; Finn, 2011; Guerrero et al., 2011; Haydel et al. 2011; Martin, 2018; Mercer, 2011).

Limitations of the Research

Controlled outcome research on CAMs remains relatively scarce and is almost exclusively focused on direct distal outcomes. Of note, only 10 studies and 70 effect sizes were included in this meta-analysis, which warrants some caution in interpreting the results. Hence, more research is needed in this field.

Studies are needed that also investigate the indirect effects of assessment—that is, benefits that may occur from superior treatment selection and treatment planning that were derived from the assessment findings and feedback (Kamphuis et al., 2021). Such research is complex to conduct, although more than three decades ago Hayes and colleagues (1987) suggested powerful research designs to address these challenges.

However, to our knowledge, no study has ever fully employed a manipulated assessment design, in which the effects of one method of assessment (e.g., Therapeutic Assessment) are compared to those of another method (e.g., assessment as usual) in an randomized controlled trial that assesses outcome immediately as well as after subsequent treatment. Another priority for future research is to test putative theoretical mechanisms that explain the treatment utility of CAMs while controlling for the assessors' expectations about the effect of these methods.

Research is also missing on the specific methods used in CAMs and, specifically, in Therapeutic Assessment. Tharinger and Pilgrim (2012) showed the effectiveness of using fables as a means to provide Therapeutic Assessment results to families with children. Future studies should focus on the immediate effect of CAM components with adult clients, such as gathering assessment questions, extended inquiry of test responses, or providing them with written letters containing the results of their individualized assessment. To do such research, it will be important to develop standardized and psychometrically sound measures that assess the quality of the delivery of CAMs and their ingredients.

Finally, another potentially interesting line of research would assess the immediate in-session outcomes and trajectories of change of CAMs. This line of research would build on the published single-case repeated-measures quasi-experiments involving adult clients with a variety of diagnoses that we described above (Aschieri & Smith, 2011; Smith et al., 2015; Tarocchi et al., 2013). Such studies could elucidate how clients change during, and possibly after, CAMs.

Training Implications

Clinicians interested in using CAMs can acquire two distinct sets of skills. First, CAMs rely on a firm knowledge of psychological testing (knowing how to administer and interpret tests). Second, CAMs require clinical skills and relational sensitivity to make test interpretation useful and tailored to clients' needs.

Fantini and colleagues (2022) have detailed the main steps in learning Therapeutic Assessment. Tests are generally taught in undergraduate programs. Further training on tests can be found through test publishers and conferences of professional organizations, such as the Society for Personality Assessment (https://www.personality.org) and the International Society of Rorschach and Projective Methods (https://internationalrorschachsociety.com).

Clinical skills are often acquired in graduate and through post-graduate training. The University of Denver School of Professional Psychology PsyD program offers an emphasis on CAMs, and in Italy the Scuola di Specializzazione in Psicoterapia Integrata-Sanicare (School of Specialization in Integrated Psychotherapy-Sanicare) is teaching CAMs. More short-term training is routinely offered by the Therapeutic Assessment Institute (http://www.therapeuticassessment.com), the European Center for Therapeutic Assessment (Milan, Italy), the Asian-Pacific Center for Therapeutic Assessment (Tokyo, Japan), and the Viersprong Institute for Personality Disorders (Bergen op Zoom, the Netherlands).

Therapeutic Practices

- Choose CAMs when conducting a psychological or psychosocial assessment because they exert, in an average of 2.7 sessions, positive effects on distal treatment processes and outcomes.
- Invite clients to articulate personal questions for their assessment and to tailor it toward their goals.
- Enlist patients in interpreting the assessment findings and provide collaborative feedback.
- Be aware that the respect, collaboration, and empathic understanding of clients may be the primary mechanism of CAMs' effectiveness, not so much the exact way in which CAMs are implemented.
- Use test results collaboratively to help clients develop a different view of themselves, especially one that is more accurate, compassionate, and useful.

References

*** Studies included in the meta-analysis.**

Anderson, H., & Goolishian, H. (1992). The client is the expert: A not-knowing approach to therapy. *Therapy as Social Construction*, *25*, 25–39.

Aschieri, F. (2012). Epistemological and ethical challenges in standardized testing and collaborative assessment. *Journal of Humanistic Psychology*, *52*(3), 350–368.

Aschieri, F. (2016). Shame as a cultural artifact: A call for self-awareness and reflexivity in personality assessment. *Journal of Personality Assessment*, *98*(6), 567–575.

Aschieri, F., & Smith, J. D. (2011). Il test di Rorschach come intervento terapeutico. Risultati di un caso singolo a misure ripetute. In *XIII Congresso Nazionale della Sezione di Clinica e Dinamica* (pp. 176–176). Espress Edizioni.

Aschieri, F., & Smith, J. D. (2012). The effectiveness of therapeutic assessment with an adult client: A single-case study using a time-series design. *Journal of Personality Assessment*, *94*(1), 1–11.

Aschieri, F., & Vetere, C. (2020). Using the Rorschach as a group intervention to promote the understanding of adolescents by staff members in inpatient residential programs. *Rorschachiana*, *41*(2), 120–143. https://doi.org/10.1027/1192-5604/a000127

Assink, M., & Wibbelink, C. J. M. (2016). Fitting three-level meta-analytic models in R: A step-by-step tutorial. *Quantitative Methods for Psychology*, *12*, 154–174. https://doi.org/10.20982/tqmp.12.3.p154

Attkisson, C. C., & Zwick, R. (1982). The Client Satisfaction Questionnaire: Psychometric properties and correlations with service utilization and psychotherapy outcome. *Evaluation and Program Planning*, 5(3), 233–237. https://doi.org/10.1016/0149-7189(82)90074-x

Baker, G. (1964). A therapeutic application of psychodiagnostic test results. *Journal of Projective Techniques & Personality Assessment*, *28*(1), 3–8.

Beck, A. T., Epstein, N., Brown, G., & Steer, R. (1988). Beck Anxiety Inventory. *Journal of Consulting and Clinical Psychology*, *56*, 893–897.

Beck, A. T., Steer, R. A., & Brown, G. K. (1996). *Beck Depression Inventory (BDI-II)* (Vol. 10, No. 3). Pearson.

*Blonigen, D. M., Timko, C., Jacob, T., & Moos, R. H. (2015). Patient-centered feedback on the results of personality testing increases early engagement in residential substance use disorder treatment: A pilot randomized controlled trial. *Addiction Science & Clinical Practice*, *10*(1), 9. https://doi.org/10.1186/s13722-015-0030-9

Bouche, C., Gomes David, M., Salleron, J., Rauch, P., Leufflen, L., Buhler, J., & Marchal, F. (2020). Evaluation of pre-therapeutic assessment in endometrial cancer staging. *Diagnostics*, *10*(12), 1045.

Brown, J. (1997). Circular questioning: An introductory guide. *Australian and New Zealand Journal of Family Therapy*, *18*(2), 109–114. https://doi.org/10.1002/j.1467-8438.1997.tb00276.x

Bruhn, A. R. (1992a). The early memories procedure: A projective test of autobiographical memory (Part I). *Journal of Personality Assessment*, *58*, 1–15.

Bruhn, A. R. (1992b). The early memories procedure: A projective test of autobiographical memory (Part II). *Journal of Personality Assessment*, 58, 326–346.

Butcher, J., Graham, J., Tellegen, A., Dahlstrom, W., & Kaemmer, B. (2001). *Minnesota Multiphasic Personality Inventory–2 (MMPI-2): Manual for administration, scoring, and interpretation* (Rev. ed.). University of Minnesota Press.

Cheek, J. M., & Buss, A. H. (1981). Shyness and sociability. *Journal of Personality and Social Psychology*, *41*, 330–339.

Cheung, M. W. L. (2014). Modeling dependent effect sizes with three-level meta-analyses: A structural equation modeling approach. *Psychological Methods*, *19*, 211–229. https://doi.org/10.1037/a0032968

Chudzik, L. (2016). Therapeutic assessment of a violent criminal offender: Managing the cultural narrative of evil. *Journal of Personality Assessment*, *98*(6), 585–589.

Clauss-Ehlers, C. S., Chiriboga, D. A., Hunter, S. J., Roysircar, G., & Tummala-Narra, P. (2019). APA multicultural guidelines executive summary: Ecological approach to context, identity, and intersectionality. *American Psychologist*, *74*(2), 232–244. https://doi.org/10.1037/amp0000382

Comtois, K. A., Jobes, D. A., O'Connor, S., Atkins, D. C., Janis, K., E. Chessen, C., Landes, S. J., Holen, A., & Yuodelis-Flores, C. (2011). Collaborative Assessment and Management of Suicidality (CAMS): Feasibility trial for next-day appointment services. *Depression and Anxiety*, *28*(11), 963–972.

Craddick, R. A. (1975). Sharing oneself in the assessment procedure. *Professional Psychology*, *6*(3), 279–282. https://doi.org/10.1037/0735-7028.6.3.279

Crisi, A., & Palm, J. A. (2018). *The Crisi Wartegg System (CWS): Manual for administration, scoring, and interpretation*. Routledge

David, R. M., Carroll, A. J., & Smith, J. D. (2022). Virtual delivery of therapeutic assessment: An empirical case study. *Journal of Personality Assessment*, *104*(3), 417–427.

Derogatis, L. R. (1983). *SCL-90-R, administration, scoring, and procedure manual–II for the R(evised) version and other instruments of the psychopathology rating scale series*. Clinical Psychometric Research.

*De Saeger, H., Kamphuis, J. H., Finn, S. E., Smith, J. D., Verheul, R., van Busschbach, J. J., Feenstra, D. J., & Horn, E. K. (2014). Therapeutic assessment promotes treatment readiness but does not affect symptom change in patients with personality disorders: Findings from a randomized clinical trial. *Psychological Assessment*, *26*, 474–483. doi:10.1037/a0035667

Durosini, I., & Aschieri, F. (2021). Therapeutic assessment efficacy: A meta-analysis. *Psychological Assessment*, *33*(10), 962–972. https://doi.org/10.1037/pas0001038

Durosini, I., Tarocchi, A., & Aschieri, F. (2017). Therapeutic assessment with a client with persistent complex bereavement disorder: A single-case time-series design. *Clinical Case Studies*, *16*(4), 295–312.

Duval, S., & Tweedie, R. (2000a). A nonparametric "trim and fill" method of accounting for publication bias in meta-analysis. *Journal of the American Statistical Association*, *95*, 89–99. https://doi.org/10.1080/01621459.2000.10473905

Duval, S., & Tweedie, R. (2000b). Trim and fill: A simple funnel plot-based method of testing and adjusting for publication bias in meta-analysis. *Biometrics*, *56*, 455–463. https://doi.org/10.1111/j.0006-341X.2000.00455.x

Eells, T. D. (Ed.). (2022). *Handbook of psychotherapy case formulation*. Guilford.

*Essig, G. N., & Kelly, K. R. (2013). Comparison of the effectiveness of two assessment feedback models in reducing career indecision. *Journal of Career Assessment, 21*(4), 519–536. https://doi.org/10.1177/1069072712475283

Evans, F. B. (2012). Therapeutic assessment alternative to custody evaluations: An adolescent whose parents could not stop fighting. In S. E. Finn, C. T. Fischer, & L. Handler (Eds.), *Collaborative/Therapeutic Assessment: A casebook and guide* (pp. 357–378). Wiley.

Fantini, F. (2016). Family traditions, cultural values, and the clinician's countertransference: Therapeutic Assessment of a young Sicilian woman. *Journal of Personality Assessment, 98*(6), 576–584.

Fantini, F., Aschieri, F., & Bertrando, P. (2013). "Is our daughter crazy or bad?" A case study of Therapeutic Assessment with children. *Contemporary Family Therapy, 35*(4), 731–744.

Fantini, F., Aschieri, F., David, R. M., Martin, H., & Finn, S. E. (2022). *Therapeutic Assessment with adults: Using psychological testing to help clients change.* Routledge.

Fantini, F., & Smith, J. D. (2018). Using R-PAS in the therapeutic assessment of a university student with emotional disconnection. In J. Mihura & G. Meyer (Eds.), Using the Rorschach Performance Assessment System (R-PAS) (pp. 138–157). Guilford.

Finn, S. E. (1996). *Manual for using the MMPI-2 as a therapeutic intervention.* University of Minnesota Press.

Finn, S. E. (2007). *In our clients' shoes: Theory and techniques of Therapeutic Assessment.* Erlbaum.

Finn, S. E. (2011). Therapeutic Assessment "on the front lines": Comment on articles from West Coast Children's Clinic. *Journal of Personality Assessment, 93*(1), 23–25. https://doi.org/10.1080/00223891.2011.529007

Finn, S. E. (2012). Implications of recent research in neurobiology for psychological assessment. *Journal of Personality Assessment, 94*(5), 440–449.

Finn, S. E., Schroeder, D. G., & Tonsager, M. E. (1995). *The Assessment Questionnaire-2 (AQ-2): A measure of clients' experiences with psychological assessment* [Unpublished manuscript]. Center for Therapeutic Assessment.

*Finn, S. E., & Tonsager, M. E. (1992). Therapeutic effects of providing MMPI-2 test feedback to college students awaiting psychotherapy. *Psychological Assessment, 4*, 278–287. doi:10.1037/1040-3590.4.3.278

*Finn, S. E., & Tonsager, M. E. (1997). Information-gathering and therapeutic models of assessment: Complementary paradigms. *Psychological Assessment, 9*(4), 374–385.

Fischer, C. T. (1994). *Individualizing psychological assessment.* Routledge. (Original work published 1985)

Fischer, C. T. (2000). Collaborative, individualized assessment. *Journal of Personality Assessment, 74*(1), 2–14.

Fonagy, P., & Allison, E. (2014). The role of mentalizing and epistemic trust in the therapeutic relationship. *Psychotherapy, 51*(3), 372–380.

Fosha, D. (2004). "Nothing that feels bad is ever the last step": The role of positive emotions in experiential work with difficult emotional experiences. *Clinical Psychology & Psychotherapy, 11*(1), 30–43.

George, C., & West, M. (2012). *The Adult Attachment Projective Picture System.* Guilford.

Goldenson, J., Brodsky, S. L., & Perlin, M. L. (2022). Trauma-informed forensic mental health assessment: Practical implications, ethical tensions, and alignment with therapeutic jurisprudence principles. *Psychology, Public Policy, and Law, 28*(2), 226–239. https://doi.org/10.1037/law0000339

Gruters, A. A., Christie, H. L., Ramakers, I. H., Verhey, F. R., Kessels, R. P., & de Vugt, M. E. (2021). Neuropsychological assessment and diagnostic disclosure at a memory clinic: A qualitative study of the experiences of patients and their family members. *The Clinical Neuropsychologist, 35*(8), 1398–1414.

Guerrero, B., Lipkind, J., & Rosenberg, A. (2011). Why did she put nail polish in my drink? Applying the Therapeutic Assessment model with an African American foster child in a community mental health setting. *Journal of Personality Assessment, 93*(1), 7–15. https://doi.org/10.1080/00223891.2011.529002

Hanson, W. E., & Poston, J. M. (2011). Building confidence in psychological assessment as a therapeutic intervention: An empirically based reply to Lilienfeld, Garb, and Wood (2011). *Psychological Assessment*, *23*(4), 1056–1062.

Harrower, M. (1956). Projective counseling—A psychotherapeutic technique. *American Journal of Psychotherapy*, *10*, 74–86.

Haydel, M. E., Mercer, B. L., & Rosenblatt, E. (2011). Training assessors in Therapeutic Assessment. *Journal of Personality Assessment*, *93*(1), 16–22. https://doi.org/10.1080/00223891.2011.529004

Hayes, S. C., Nelson, R. O., & Jarrett, R. B. (1987). The treatment utility of assessment: A functional approach to evaluating assessment quality. *American Psychologist*, *42*(11), 963.

*Hilsenroth, M. J., Ackerman, S. J., Clemence, A. J., Strassle, C. G., & Handler, L. (2002). Effects of structured clinician training on patient and therapist perspectives of alliance early in psychotherapy. *Psychotherapy: Theory, Research, Practice, Training*, *39*(4), 309–323. https://doi.org/10.1037/0033-3204.39.4.309

Jobes, D. A. (2012). The Collaborative Assessment and Management of Suicidality (CAMS): An evolving evidence-based clinical approach to suicidal risk. *Suicide and Life-Threatening Behavior*, *42*(6), 640–653.

Jobes, D. A., Jacoby, A. M., Cimbolic, P., & Hustead, L. A. T. (1997). Assessment and treatment of suicidal clients in a university counseling center. *Journal of Counseling Psychology*, *44*(4), 368–377.

Kamphuis, J. H., & Finn, S. E. (2018). Therapeutic assessment in personality disorders: Toward the restoration of epistemic trust. *Journal of Personality Assessment*, *101*(6), 662–674. doi:10.1080/00223891.2018.1476360

Kamphuis, J. H., Noordhof, A., & Hopwood, C. J. (2021). When and how assessment matters: An update on the Treatment Utility of Clinical Assessment (TUCA). *Psychological Assessment*, *33*(2), 122–132. https://doi.org/10.1037/pas0000966

Karpman, S. (1968). Fairy tales and script drama analysis. *Transactional Analysis Bulletin*, *7*(26), 39–43.

Knapp, G., & Hartung, J. (2003). Improved tests for a random effects meta-regression with a single covariate. *Statistics in Medicine*, *22*, 2693–2710. https://doi.org/10.1002/sim.1482

Luborsky, L. (1953). Self-interpretation of the TAT as a clinical technique. *Journal of Projective Techniques*, *17*, 217–223.

Luzzo, D. A., & Day, M. A. (1999). Effects of Strong Interest Inventory feedback on career decision-making self-efficacy and social cognitive career beliefs. *Journal of Career Assessment*, *7*(1), 1–17. https://doi.org/10.1177/106907279900700101

Martin, H. (2018). Collaborative/Therapeutic Assessment and diversity: The complexity of being human. In S. R. Smith & R. Krishnamurthy (Eds.), *Diversity-sensitive personality assessment* (pp. 278–293). Routledge.

Mercer, B. L. (2011). Psychological assessment of children in a community mental health clinic. *Journal of Personality Assessment*, *93*(1), 1–6. https://doi.org/10.1080/00223891.2011.528741

Meyer, G. J., Viglione, D. J., Mihura, J. L, Erard, R. E., & Erdberg, P. (2011). *Rorschach Performance Assessment System: Administration, coding, interpretation, and technical manual.* Rorschach Performance Assessment System.

Mihura, J. L., & Meyer, G. J. (2018). Introduction to R-PAS. In J. L. Mihura & G. J. Meyer (Eds.), *Using the Rorschach Performance Assessment System (R-PAS)* (pp. 3–22). Guilford.

Mikulincer, M., & Shaver, P. R. (2007). Boosting attachment security to promote mental health, prosocial values, and inter-group tolerance. *Psychological Inquiry*, *18*(3), 139–156.

*Miller, L. R., Cano, A., & Wurm, L. H. (2013). A motivational therapeutic assessment improves pain, mood, and relationship satisfaction in couples with chronic pain. *Journal of Pain*, *14*(5), 525–537. https://doi.org/10.1016/j.jpain.2013.01.006

*Miller, W. R., Benefield, R. G., & Tonigan, J. S. (1993). Enhancing motivation for change in problem drinking: A controlled comparison of two therapist styles. *Journal of Consulting and Clinical Psychology*, *61*(3), 455–461. https://doi.org/10.1037//0022-006x.61.3.455

Millon, T., Grossman, S., & Millon, C. (2015). *Millon Clinical Multiaxial Inventory–IV (MCMI-IV)*. Pearson.

*Morey, L. C., Lowmaster, S. E., & Hopwood, C. J. (2010). A pilot study of manual-assisted cognitive therapy with a therapeutic assessment augmentation for borderline personality disorder. *Psychiatry Research, 178*, 531–535. doi:10.1016/j.psychres.2010.04.055

*Newman, M. L., & Greenway, P. (1997). Therapeutic effects of providing MMPI-2 test feedback to clients at a university counseling service: A collaborative approach. *Psychological Assessment, 9*(2), 122–131.

Ouzzani, M., Hammady, H., Fedorowicz, Z., & Elmagarmid, A. (2016). Rayyan—a web and mobile app for systematic reviews. *Systematic Reviews, 5*(1), 1–10.

Pegg, P. O., Seel, R. T., & Auerbach, S. M. (2001). *Treatment Satisfaction Questionnaire*. Virginia Commonwealth University.

*Pegg, P. O., Jr., Auerbach, S. M., Seel, R. T., Buenaver, L. F., Kiesler, D. J., & Plybon, L. E. (2005). The impact of patient-centered information on patients' treatment satisfaction and outcomes in traumatic brain injury rehabilitation. *Rehabilitation Psychology, 50*(4), 366–374.

Poston, J. M., & Hanson, W. M. (2010). Meta-analysis of psychological assessment as a therapeutic intervention. *Psychological Assessment, 22*, 203–212. doi:10.1037/a0018679

R Development Core Team. (2016). *R: A language and environment for statistical computing*. R Foundation for Statistical Computing. https://www.R-project.org

Rorschach, H. (1921). *Psychodiagnostik: Methodik und ergebnisse eines warhrnehmungsdiagnostischen Experiments (deutenlassen von zufallsformen)* (Vol. 2). Bircher.

Rosenzweig, S. (1978). *The Rosenzweig Picture-Frustration (PF) study: Basic manual*. Psychological Assessment Resources.

Smith, J. D. (2016). Introduction to the special section on cultural considerations in Collaborative and Therapeutic Assessment. *Journal of Personality Assessment, 98*(6), 563–566. https://doi.org/10.1080/00223891.2016.1196455

Smith, J. D. (2017). Introduction to the special section on teaching, training, and supervision in personality and psychological assessment. *Journal of Personality Assessment, 99*(2), 113–116. https://doi.org/10.1080/00223891.2016.1217873

Smith, J. D., Eichler, W. C., Norman, K. R., & Smith, S. R. (2015). The effectiveness of collaborative/therapeutic assessment for psychotherapy consultation: A pragmatic replicated single-case study. *Journal of Personality Assessment, 97*(3), 261–270.

Smith, J. D., & George, C. (2012). Therapeutic Assessment case study: Treatment of a woman diagnosed with metastatic cancer and attachment trauma. *Journal of Personality Assessment, 94*(4), 331–344.

Smith, J. D., Handler, L., & Nash, M. R. (2010). Therapeutic Assessment for preadolescent boys with oppositional-defiant disorder: A replicated single-case time-series design. *Psychological Assessment, 22*(3), 593–602. https://doi.org/10.1037/a0019697

Swift, J. K., Trusty, W. T., & Penix, E. A. (2021). The effectiveness of the Collaborative Assessment and Management of Suicidality (CAMS) compared to alternative treatment conditions: A meta-analysis. *Suicide and Life-Threatening Behavior, 51*(5), 882–896.

Tabachnick, B. G., & Fidell, L. S. (2013). *Using multivariate statistics* (6th ed.). Allyn & Bacon.

Tarocchi, A., Aschieri, F., Fantini, F., & Smith, J. D. (2013). Therapeutic assessment of complex trauma: A single-case time-series study. *Clinical Case Studies, 12*(3), 228–245.

Tellegen, A., & Ben-Porath, Y. S. (2011). *Minnesota Multiphasic Personality Inventory–2 Restructured Form: Technical manual*. University of Minnesota Press. (Original work published 2008)

Tharinger, D. J., Finn, S. E., Austin, C. A., Gentry, L. B., Bailey, K. E., Parton, V. T., & Fisher, M. E. (2008). Family sessions in psychological assessment with children: Goals, techniques, and clinical utility. *Journal of Personality Assessment, 90*(6), 547–558. https://doi.org/10.1080/00223890802388400

Tharinger, D. J., Finn, S. E., Gentry, L., Hamilton, A., Fowler, J., Matson, M., Krumholz, L., & Walkowiak, J. (2009). Therapeutic Assessment with children: A pilot study of treatment acceptability and outcome. *Journal of Personality Assessment, 91*, 238–244.

Tharinger, D. J., & Pilgrim, S. (2012). Parent and child experiences of neuropsychological assessment as a function of child feedback by individualized fable. *Child Neuropsychology, 18*(3), 228–241.

Van den Noortgate, W., López-López, J. A., Marín-Martínez, F., & Sánchez-Meca, J. (2013). Three-level meta-analysis of dependent effect sizes. *Behavior Research Methods, 45*, 576–594. https://doi.org/10.3758/s13428-012-0261-6

Viechtbauer, W. (2010). Conducting meta-analyses in R with the Metafor package. *Journal of Statistical Software, 36*, 1–48. https://doi.org/10.18637/jss.v036.i03

Wild, T. C., Cunningham, J. A., & Roberts, A. B. (2007). Controlled study of brief personalized assessment-feedback for drinkers interested in self-help. *Addiction, 102*(2), 241–250.

15
Routine Outcome Monitoring

Michael Barkham, Kim de Jong, Jaime Delgadillo, and Wolfgang Lutz

In this chapter, we summarize the research evidence on conducting routine outcome monitoring (ROM) in individual adult psychological therapies. A previous account of this topic (Lambert et al., 2019) focused on two specific ROM systems: the OQ-45 measure and feedback system (Lambert et al., 2013) and the Partners in Change Outcome System (PCOMS; Duncan & Reese, 2015). By contrast, we adopt a structural perspective, focusing on the process of ROM, recognizing that multiple measures and constructs can lend themselves to this process. We summarize the research evidence and include an abridged version of the most comprehensive meta-analysis published on this topic, comprising 58 studies drawn from 49 randomized controlled trials (RCTs) and nine practice-based studies using a wide array of ROM measures and feedback systems (see De Jong et al., 2021). Prior to setting out the main sections of the chapter, we provide a brief background on the context of ROM.

Since the mid-1900s, it has been noted that statistical (i.e., actuarial) models are more accurate than clinical judgments (Meehl, 1954), and research has provided strong evidence to question the empirical accuracy and clinical effectiveness of traditional forms of clinical judgment and intuition (Ægisdóttir et al., 2006). Psychotherapists have been found to be overconfident in evaluating their own effectiveness, with one survey of U.S. practitioners in private practice reporting the belief that 85% of their patients benefitted from therapy (Walfish et al., 2012). However, the return rate of that survey was 26%, and respondents were more likely to be practitioners who thought they had good outcomes. A partial UK-based replication (with a 15% return rate) found broadly similar findings but not so pronounced (i.e., 65% of patients benefitting), suggesting some possible personality and/or cultural differences (Parker & Waller, 2015). This issue is especially critical when it potentially blinds a therapist to a patient's evolving worsening outcomes. Given this context, enhancing the validity of in-session therapist behaviors and client outcomes calls for a measurement-based approach to psychological therapies informed by data and using feedback as a central therapeutic process (Lutz, Schwartz, et al., 2022).

A specific subgroup of patients of concern are those who deteriorate. In an often-cited study, 40 therapists (20 experienced and 20 trainees) were asked to predict their patients who might deteriorate by the end of therapy, having been informed that the overall expected deterioration rate would be in the region of 8% (Hannan et al., 2005). Of the 550 clients (at a university counseling center), 40 actually deteriorated by the end of therapy, but only three were predicted by therapists as likely to deteriorate, and of these, only one was correct. By contrast, actuarial methods correctly identified 36 of the 40 (90%) clients who deteriorated. These collective findings broadly attest to biases

Michael Barkham, Kim de Jong, Jaime Delgadillo, and Wolfgang Lutz, *Routine Outcome Monitoring* In: *Psychotherapy Skills and Methods That Work.* Edited by: Clara E. Hill and John C. Norcross, Oxford University Press. © Clara E. Hill and John C. Norcross 2023.
DOI: 10.1093/oso/9780197611012.003.0015

in clinicians' judgments and support the adoption of data-informed approaches to psychotherapy using ROM.

Routine outcome measurement and feedback have their roots in the paradigm of practice-based evidence and specifically that of *patient-focused research* (Howard et al., 1996). Such an approach encompasses findings from early reviews in the literature (e.g., Bergin, 1963) and subsequent texts (e.g., Lambert, 2010) attesting to the fact that not all patients improve and a proportion of them deteriorate. In such cases, administering outcome measures—either continuously or at regular intervals as a means of checking progress and informing treatment decision-making processes—can yield an *additive* effect over and above the effects of the standard delivery of psychotherapy (De Jong et al., 2021; Lutz et al., 2021).

Hence, it is a method that has the potential to enhance existing therapy outcomes for some patients at a relatively small additional cost (Delgadillo et al., 2021). Developments in information technology and software packages have likely made the adoption of repeated session-by-session outcome measures less onerous for individual practitioners and contributed to standardization in the production of progress graphs (Ogles et al., 2022). The role of software packages is important, with ROM systems using increasingly advanced statistical procedures that identify whether a patient's progress is *not on track* (NOT) compared with historical data from patients presenting with similar clinical profiles (Drapeau, 2012). Notwithstanding these developments, however, the single area of major concern and focus for action relates to implementation (Bovendeerd et al., 2022; Lutz, Rubel, et al., 2022).

Definitions

Routine outcome monitoring has been referred to by various terms, including the following: outcome feedback, progress monitoring, routine outcome monitoring and feedback, measurement-based care, continuous outcome measurement, and feedback informed treatment. Notwithstanding some technical distinctions among these terms, they all contain common features that can be grouped into three distinct phases: (a) collecting patient data on a regular basis; (b) feeding back these data to the therapist and, on many occasions, also to the patient; and (c) when appropriate, adapting the process or focus of therapy in light of the feedback. These three phases have been presented in the literature as a transtheoretical model of measurement-based care, named Collect, Share, Act (Barber & Resnick, 2022).

An inclusive definition of ROM that captures these three phases describes it as involving "the implementation of standardized measures, usually on a session-to-session basis, to guide clinical decision-making, monitor treatment progress, and indicate when treatment adjustment is needed" (Pinner & Kivlighan, 2018, p. 248). ROM has been described as a "relatively straightforward evidence-based practice . . . that the clinician can add to any type of psychotherapy . . . without requiring changes in that psychotherapy" (Persons et al., 2016, p. 25).

ROM data are drawn from patient-reported outcome measures (PROMs), which are psychometric tools providing the foundation and content base for the related practices of ROM and, crucially, progress feedback and adjustment. The extent to which all three features (data collecting, feeding back, and adapting therapy) are implemented ranges from no use of feedback, to feedback results being available only to the therapist, to the results being fed back to the therapist and patient resulting in a discussion of PROMs that can affect subsequent treatment (Krägeloh et al., 2015). The latter approach, in which regular feedback based on PROMs is integrated into psychotherapy, is the preferred and probably most effective method. This provides a signal, flag, or alert for the therapist that a patient's treatment response is NOT and that some adaptation to the treatment plan is indicated.

Determining the necessary treatment adaptations is a therapeutic method termed *clinical troubleshooting*, using a combination of clinical and research evidence (De Jong et al., 2023). A similar process occurs via the application of *statistical prediction models* and, in some cases, the provision of clinical decision suggestions in areas of therapeutic work that a therapist could address. This is particularly the case for what have been termed *clinical support tools* (CSTs), which are designed to identify and address problems that might be interfering with treatment progress (e.g., Harmon et al., 2007; Lambert, 2010; Lucock et al., 2015).

The American Psychological Association (APA) has long recommended the use of ROM and feedback methodology in routine care (APA, 2006) along with the centrality of outcome measurement to measurement-based care (Wright et al., 2017, 2020). An APA governance-appointed Advisory Committee for Measurement-Based Care and the Mental and Behavioral Health Registry has argued for a professional practice guideline focusing on measurement-based care. The committee proposes the draft statement: "Psychologists aim to routinely assess treatment process and outcomes and integrate that information in ongoing collaboration with their patients" (Boswell et al., 2023, p. 9).

The Joint Commission (2018), a U.S.-based organization focused on quality improvement of health care, while always promoting the assessment of outcomes, now requires organizations

> to accomplish this [assessment of outcomes] through the use of a standardized tool or instrument. Feedback derived through these standardized instruments may be used to inform goals and objectives, monitor individual progress, and inform decisions related to individual plans for care, treatment, or services. (p. 1)

The Roadmap for Mental Health Research in Europe has adopted a similar position (Emmelkamp et al., 2014).

Aside from recommendations of various organizations, national policymakers and regulatory bodies in some countries have made measuring treatment outcomes a requirement, such as in Australia (Burgess et al., 2015), Canada (Tasca et al., 2019), England (Clark, 2018), and Norway (Knapstad et al., 2018). In other countries, national (e.g., the Netherlands; Delespaul, 2015) and local (e.g., Israel; Tzur Bitan et al., 2018) efforts to implement ROM have proved challenging.

ROM has been widely espoused in multiple adult therapeutic modalities—for example, psychodynamic therapy (Winkeljohn Black et al., 2017), couple therapy (Anker et al., 2009), and group therapy (Slone et al., 2015)—as well as with specific presenting problems, such as substance abuse (Crits-Christoph et al., 2012), and in youth settings (Bickman, 2008). It is pan-theoretical and, as a therapeutic method, combines elements of supervision, continuous assessment, and overall quality assurance. However, in the absence of policy or clinical directives to implement ROM, the willingness to adopt and use this method is likely to be a function of the openness of individual therapists (e.g., Rye et al., 2019).

Clinical Description and Indications

Routine outcome monitoring presents three sequential phases: collection of data, feeding back data, and adapting therapy (Collect, Share, Act [Barber & Resnick, 2022]). Importantly, each phase builds on and is dependent on the preceding phase.

Collecting Patient Data on a Regular Basis

The first phase of ROM comprises consideration and selection of a standardized outcome measure, with the two most frequently researched feedback systems being the OQ-45 System comprising the OQ-45 measures and Analyst software (Lambert et al., 2013) and the PCOMS (Duncan & Reese, 2015), with the latter often referred to by its two separate components—the Outcome Rating Scale (ORS; Miller et al., 2003) and the Session Rating Scale (Duncan et al., 2003). There are also other outcome measures that have been used for ROM (for reviews, see Drapeau, 2012; see also Barkham et al., 2015; Boswell, Kraus, Castonguay, et al., 2015; Brown et al., 2015; Kopta et al., 2015; Miller et al., 2015; Youn et al., 2015).

More recently, newly developed ROM systems incorporate sophisticated prediction and decision-making tools. For example, the Trier Treatment Navigator (TTN; Lutz et al., 2019; Lutz, Deisenhofer, et al., 2022) includes a clinical support tool that provides treatment recommendations at the beginning of treatment as well as adjustments later in therapy in response to NOT signals. Another hallmark of more recent ROM systems is their iterative development in which a system is continually adapted to the needs of practice (e.g., NORSE Feedback System; McAleavey et al., 2021; Moltu et al., 2021).

Whichever measurement tool is adopted, consideration needs to be given to a range of factors, including suitability (i.e., fit) with the patient population, clinical utility (i.e., being clinically meaningful to practitioners), having psychometrically sound measurement properties (i.e., being valid and reliable), being financially viable in terms of resources needed to support implementation, and of minimal burden to patients in light of the need for repeated administration. The selection of the measure will likely have greater subsequent success if the decision on which measure or system to adopt is made collectively within the clinical team. Once a decision has been made, a priority is for all practitioners to be trained in the administration, use, and interpretation of the measure.

Practitioners need a thorough knowledge base of the measure in order for them to introduce ROM at the start of a course of therapy. Crucially, they need to communicate to patients the rationale for completing the outcome measure and explain its role in therapy. ROM will likely have greater utility if introduced and explained at the earliest stage of individual therapy, and it is important to orient patients to the purpose, structure, and use of ROM as part of the routine process of therapy. In particular, therapists need to explain how the questionnaire is interpreted and how it might inform the treatment process. Explaining the interpretation of questionnaires can enable a transparent and collaborative conversational approach to the process of ROM.

The introduction of ROM by the therapist to a patient will likely reflect a blend of standard and personalized responses based on clinical principles (De Jong et al., 2023). These include offering explanation ("*We're using the measure to track progress . . .*"), personalizing ("*Completing items is an extension of your voice—it says something about you*"), and using language that acts as a bridge between ROM and everyday life ("*So ROM is like a thermometer . . .*"). In addition, regular checking with the patient ("*Does that make sense to you?*"), setting expectations ("*So, filling in that questionnaire is something you'll be doing every session . . .*"), and sharing information about ROM ("*So, when I look at the scores you have given, what I see is . . .*") provide the basis for integrating ROM into routine practice.

ROM can be collected session-by-session or less frequently but at regular intervals (e.g., monthly). The former is likely to occur in contexts that are more resource rich (e.g., research clinics) or where it is nationally mandated (e.g., the English NHS Talking Therapies for Anxiety and Depression program, previously known as the Improving Access to Psychological Therapies program; Clark, 2018). It is likely that session-by-session ROM data collection is more important for shorter term treatments, whereas more intermittent but regular administration of measures fits with longer term treatments. Regardless of the regularity of data collection, it probably works best to review ROM data early in the session in order to leave available time to respond to the most recent data as they may provide a focus for the current session. But it is important for reviewing data not to override any immediate clinical concerns expressed by the patient at the outset of a session.

Some final considerations in relation to data collection. First, the focus need not be totally on symptoms. A patient's quality of life and interpersonal relations are equally as important, and measures tapping these aspects of life might be considered within a ROM system (e.g., Keetharuth et al., 2018). ROM can also include measures of within-session processes (e.g., the therapeutic relationship). Second, almost all ROM measures are nomothetic, and there are increasing calls for idiographic measures to be included (e.g., PSYCLOPS [Ashworth et al., 2004]; see also Sales et al., 2023). Third, as with using any outcome measure, nomothetic or idiographic, consideration should be given to any cultural adaptations that would increase the accessibility of ROM for patients from culturally diverse and ethnic minority populations (e.g., Koslofsky & Rodíguez, 2017).

Overall, the aim of this initial phase is for practitioners to give patients the rationale and appropriate information for them to understand the measure(s) they are routinely completing and the role ROM plays in the therapy process. This initial work creates the most favorable context for patients to engage in and value ROM such that they complete the outcome measure(s) on a regular basis as agreed with their therapist.

Feeding Back Data to Participants

The second phase comprises the therapist obtaining outcomes information directly from the patient or the feedback system and then sharing this information with the patient. This is best achieved by the therapist reviewing outcome measures with the patient either proactively (i.e., routinely) or in response to an alert generated by a monitoring system. Data need to be reviewed in the form of a conversation rather than simply being told the numbers. Hence, rather than "*The data shows you to be severely depressed this week*," it is probably better to frame as a proposition that allows the patient to confirm, question, or qualify the response: "*The data places you in the severe range this week; does that match with how you have been feeling?*"

The timing of feedback is important, and a balance needs to be taken between following an overly protocolized agenda (e.g., "*We always check on ROM scores at the beginning of a session*") and being responsive to the current state of the patient and their need to talk about a specific clinical issue (Drew et al., 2021). Regardless of when ROM is reviewed, the aim is to ensure not only the continuous reinforcement of outcome monitoring as a shared task but also that potential problems (e.g., symptomatic deterioration) can be prioritized and dealt with as part of the session. If use of the data is to be actionable, then there needs to be sufficient time remaining in the session to respond to the data and their implications.

In most cases, measures will indicate that the patient is progressing as expected, in which case the therapist can offer this interpretation and check the patient's perspective about this interpretation. In addition, a therapist can track responses to individual items within any measure—for instance, noticing which items have changed more substantially than others since the last measurement (Cross et al., 2015). In this way, marked change in individual items, showing either improvement or deterioration, can provide a clinical focus and thereby act as a clinical process tool for therapeutic discussions (Faija et al., 2022). Such practice integrates the outcome measure and its individual items into the therapy session and conversation.

Two main methods are used to generate feedback: rational and empirical. *Rational* methods determine a cutoff point for considering a patient to have worsened based on rational thinking combined with a priori clinical judgment based on clinical rule of thumb, distribution-based rule, or psychometric rule. The clinical rule of thumb adopts a criterion related to the performance on the outcome measure based on clinical impressions, whereas the use a distribution-based rule is usually based on the population norms for an instrument. However, this latter method does not take change into account. Psychometric rules use certain statistical characteristics of the outcome instrument as a criterion, with the Reliable Change Index (RCI) being the most commonly used (Jacobson & Truax, 1991). This method is determined by the specific psychometric properties of a given measure. A more sensitive index for deterioration might be the use of the raw measurement error of the instrument, typically smaller than the RCI (Nugter et al., 2013).

Empirical methods use data from historical cases to generate expected recovery curves (Finch et al., 2001) or expected treatment response models (Lutz et al., 1999). These procedures predict how new patients will progress in therapy compared with patients from the archived data set who presented with similar characteristics (i.e., patients who are, clinically, nearest neighbors; Lutz et al., 2005). During treatment, a patient's actual progress is compared with the prediction, and when a patient deviates by a predetermined amount from the predicted course, a warning signal is given to the therapist that the patient is NOT as opposed to being on track (OT).

In addition to feeding back information derived from visual analyses of outcome measures and numerical data, therapists can use CSTs (Lambert et al., 2015; Slade et al.,

2008), also referred to as *clinical problem-solving tools* (Lutz et al., 2021). Examples of CSTs can be seen in the OQ-System (Lambert et al., 2013) and the TTN (Lutz et al., 2019). The main component of CST feedback within the OQ-System is the Assessment for Signal Clients (ASC; Lambert et al., 2015), a 40-item self-report questionnaire that is completed by patients who are deemed at risk of deterioration and focuses on four domains: (a) therapeutic alliance, (b) motivation, (c) social support, and (d) coping with problematic life events. With domain scores benchmarked against norms, the ASC helps the therapist identify specific areas that may be contributing to a patient's deterioration, with the aim of utilizing this information in clinical decision-making.

The ASC has also been used as a central component in the TTN, but supplemented with the Affective Style Questionnaire (Hofmann & Kashdan, 2010), a 20-item self-report measure assessing emotional regulation. Both measures are administered at every fifth session. Figure 15.1 displays the output from the TTN showing routinely collected data [A] as against the expected treatment response curve [C] based on a nearest neighbor

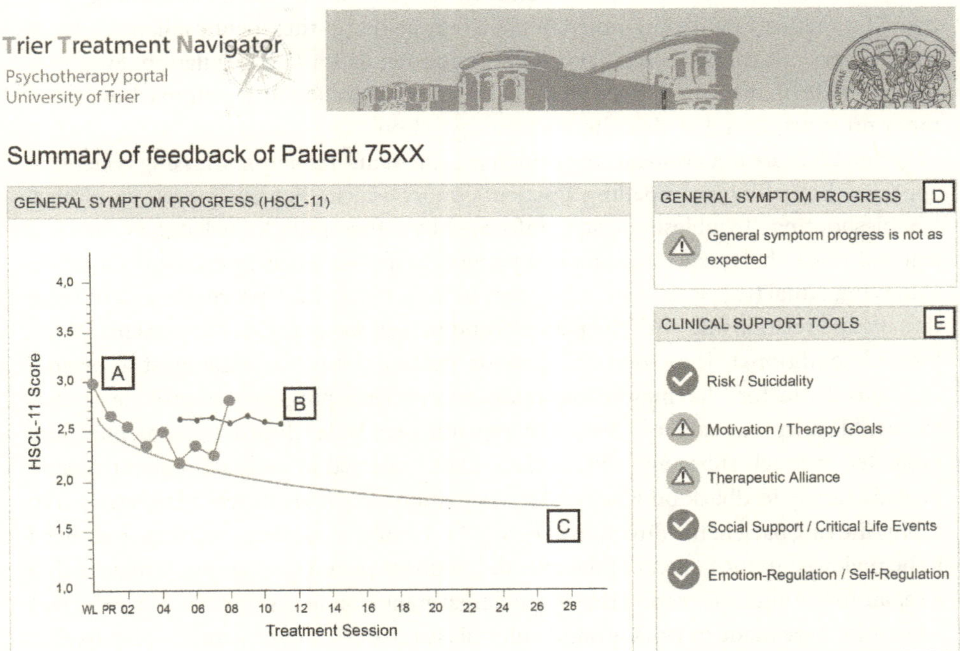

Figure 15.1 Example of feedback graph with clinical support tools. The screenshot shows the symptomatic progress of a patient measured with the Hopkins Symptom Checklist–11 (HSCL-11) within the clinical navigation system by Lutz et al. (2019). A: Individual measurement points for the patient measured at the beginning of each session; B: Dynamic failure boundary; C: Expected treatment response curve; D: As soon as the patient's HSCL-11 score exceeds the failure boundary (marked in the graph with an arrow), the therapist receives a warning signal (top right corner) and more detailed information is provided by the clinical problem-solving tools (CSTs) below; E: CSTs are divided into five domains. The exclamation mark indicates the domains in which the patient has specific problems. The therapist is able to click on these icons to gain access to the activated tools. The check mark signals that the patient has few or no problems in the respective domain.

approach—that is, based on a defined number of patients from a data archive who most closely resemble the specific patient. The crucial flag occurs at session 9 when the outcome measure exceeds the dynamic failure boundary [B], producing a warning flag [D]. Completion of the clinical support tools [E] shows that the patient is experiencing difficulties regarding motivation/therapy goals and the therapeutic alliance, which then provide a refocusing of therapy to address these domains in the third phase of ROM.

Adapting the Process or Focus of Therapy in Light of Feedback

The third phase comprises, when necessary, adapting or reorienting the focus of psychotherapy in light of feedback. This phase is a clinical process that determines the decisions and actions of the therapist in response to the available feedback data. Hence, as in Figure 15.1, with the aid of clinical support tools, the TTN includes adaptive recommendations during treatment based, in this example, on data from five patient domains of experience, which are identified for patients at risk for becoming NOT cases: (a) risk/suicidality, (b) motivation/therapy goals, (c) therapeutic alliance, (d) social support/critical life events, and (e) emotion regulation/self-regulation. Such systems provide predictions derived from the use of computational algorithms drawing on many previous cases that yield therapeutic suggestions.

When CSTs are not available, the principle is the same, namely addressing issues that appear to be stalling or impeding a patient's improvement, but is achieved via clinical troubleshooting. Troubleshooting is informed by a therapist's knowledge of the clinical and research evidence relating to a patient's response to treatment. This might include contextual (e.g., lack of social support in the patient's life), process (e.g., a difficult therapeutic relationship with the patient), and patient factors (e.g., the presence of comorbid conditions). These domains provide starting points for a therapist to explore and consider factors that may be impinging on a patient's progress and provide clues as to possible adaptations. From here, a therapeutic plan is developed, implemented, and evaluated through subsequent ROM data. Data collected at each subsequent session provide timely feedback on whether the adaptations to the treatment plan have led to scores moving back in the direction of being OT. Finally, the actions and responses need to be reviewed in the context of the overall treatment plan. For example, it may be that a repair to the alliance enables the original treatment plan to resume. Or it may be that adaptations are made to work around cultural issues, or that the treatment plan itself is altered in order to change the focus of therapeutic work.

Assessment

During the Course of Therapy

Assessment of ROM considers both adherence and competence. Adherence refers to the completion of outcome or session measures, involving patients, therapists, and the supporting administrative system. Competence focuses on active use of the feedback by the therapist in adapting the focus or direction of therapy.

The simplest index of adherence regarding data collection is the proportion of completed outcome measures: The actual number will depend on the agreed frequency of completion. This adherence index can also be enhanced by an index of the quality of data completion; for example, a higher rate of missing items will make the data less robust but may also indicate a clinical concern for a patient, highlighting the value of missing data—or be indicative of an issue with the measure itself (e.g., a poor cultural fit regarding an item for certain patients).

In terms of sharing feedback data, several key therapist factors can be assessed. One factor is the therapist's use of externally sourced information, which can be measured by the Internal and External Feedback Propensity Scales (Herold et al., 1996). These scales tap aspects of internal propensity (e.g., "As long as I think I have done something well, I am not too concerned about how other people think I have done") and external propensity (e.g., "I like getting frequent feedback from others regarding my performance"; Herold et al., 1997). Commitment to providing feedback has also been measured using an adapted version of the Goal Commitment Scale (Hollenbeck & Klein, 1987), in which, for example, the item "It's hard to take this goal seriously" was adapted to read "It is hard to take [the idea of using these measures in my clinical practice] seriously."

The assessment of competence in terms of adapting the focus or direction of therapy is more difficult to assess and is largely in the sphere of clinical supervision. The outcome of any adaptations should yield session outcome data moving back below the failure boundary (recall Figure 15.1) or where the direction of change is generally positive.

Distal Treatment Outcomes

Two key distal outcomes of ROM relate to end-state and rate of change. The end-state is indexed by the proportion of patients deteriorating in the feedback condition as contrasted with the comparison group. In effect, this is the main index for determining the effectiveness of ROM and will mean a patient's scores at the end of psychotherapy being within the boundaries of the expected treatment response curve. Additional criteria to assess impact are determining whether the first to last change score exceeds the RCI and whether the end score identifies the patient as being both reliably and clinically significantly improved (Jacobson & Truax, 1991). In addition to the end-state assessment, the rate of change is a further index of change that considers the number of sessions attended to achieve an outcome (Lambert et al., 2001). Another index is a reduction in dropout rates (De Jong et al., 2021). Evidence from meta-analyses has usually reported outcomes based either on all patients (i.e., OT and NOT) combined or separately. For example, the PCOMS has generally considered all cases, whereas the OQ-45 has more often considered the subgroup of NOT cases.

The adoption of the criteria of reliable and clinically significant change in determining the effectiveness of ROM in routine practice has been challenged. This challenge largely rests on the basis of an absence of any counterfactual—that is, what the outcome would have been had feedback *not* been provided (Langkaas et al., 2018). It is argued that although adopting methods of reliable and clinical significance captures change, these methods do not determine *induced difference*—that is, the effect induced specifically by the actions comprising the ROM procedure.

Clinical Example

The clinical example presented here provides an account of the three distinct phases: introducing ROM, feeding the results back to the patient, and adapting therapy in light of feedback information, informed by clinical troubleshooting. This case is based on a real patient who gave permission for it to be used for teaching purposes. The transcript is based on clinical case notes, and some elements of the case have been changed. A fictitious name is used for the patient.

Samira was a 22-year-old woman of color, unemployed, in substantial financial debt, and sharing a house with her partner and his brother. Samira sought psychotherapy after being the victim of an armed violent attack in her house by criminal debt collectors. She was pregnant at the time, and the attack led to a miscarriage that was accompanied by substantial blood loss, which stained the carpet in her house. After the traumatic event, Samira developed obsessive cleaning behavior and disinfecting rituals. She met criteria for post-traumatic stress disorder (PTSD) and contamination-focused obsessive–compulsive disorder (OCD) at the start of treatment. In collaboration with Samira, it was decided that the PTSD symptoms were the most debilitating and would be the primary focus of treatment. Samira wanted to feel like she could speak to people again, and leave the house by herself and eventually get a job and make friends. The recommended treatment was cognitive–behavioral therapy with imagery exposure for PTSD.

Introducing ROM: Early Sessions

Samira (S) was asked by the therapist (T) to complete the Generalized Anxiety Disorder–7 (GAD-7) questionnaire prior to each session through an electronic form. During the first session, Samira was introduced to working with ROM:

T: An important part of the treatment involves keeping track of your anxiety over time, so that we can get an idea of whether the treatment is working and helping you feel better or not. We use a brief questionnaire to do this. Were you able to complete the questionnaire before this appointment?

S: Yes, here it is.

T: Great, thanks. Based on your answers, I can work out a score that tells us how intense the anxiety has been recently. You can think of it as a sort of thermometer of distress. Like your temperature, which fluctuates from day to day, your anxiety symptoms also go up and down, and this measure helps us to track these changes during treatment. Does that make sense?

S: Yes, true. I have good days and bad days.

T: Exactly. If we can keep track of these ups and downs, it can help us to learn about the things that make your anxiety worse and the coping strategies that might help to make things better for you. If therapy helps, we might expect to see these measures going down over time.

S: OK, I hope so. I find that the anxiety is overwhelming lately . . .

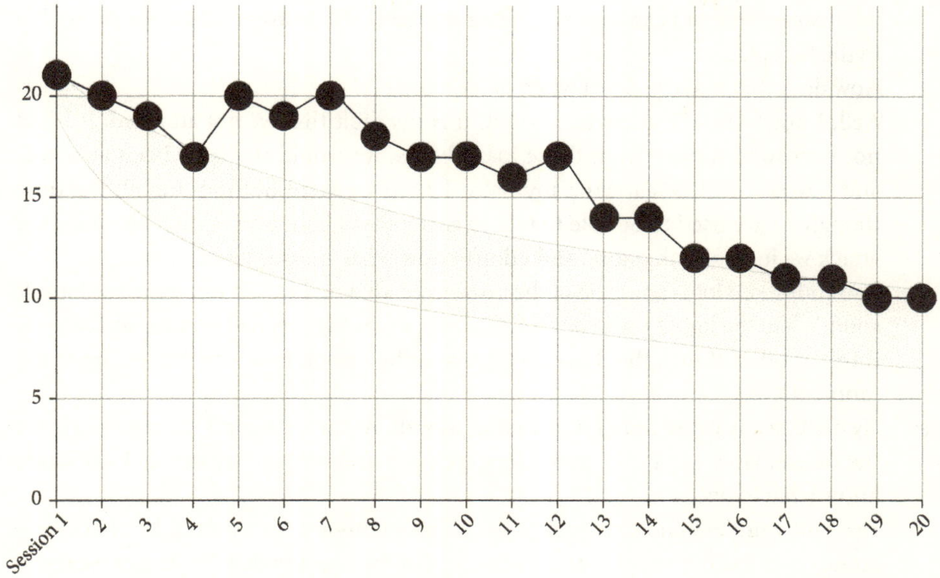

Figure 15.2 Symptoms per session on the Generalized Anxiety Disorder–7 questionnaire.

During the first session, Samira received an explanation about the interpretation of the scores and was informed that the therapist would discuss her progress with her briefly at the start of each session. At the next session, Samira had had more interchanges with her partner over her cleaning behaviors, and she asked the therapist for advice on how to navigate the irritation that her cleaning behavior caused her boyfriend, resulting in frequent arguments. Samira and her therapist spent more than half the session on problem-solving this matter. At the following session, this seemed to have paid off, and her anxiety score had reduced a little.

Feeding Back in Response to an Alert Signal: Sessions 5–7

The ROM system calculated an expected treatment recovery (ETR) curve, which provided an alert to the therapist at session 5 denoting that Samira was NOT as her score clearly exceeded the failure boundary (upper green/gray line in Figure 15.2). There was a substantial increase in anxiety symptoms, and it was evident to the therapist that the treatment was going in the wrong direction and the patient was at risk of ending therapy. So, the therapist discussed potential reasons for Samira's increase in anxious symptoms with her:

T: Shall we have a look at your progress chart? Although the scores in the initial sessions showed improvement, the scores now show your anxiety is going up again this week, and this time quite a bit more than in your second and third session. Does that fit with how you have been feeling in the past week?

S: Um . . . yes. I find it so hard to get through each day. My boyfriend is very annoyed with me about the amount of time cleaning. He says that I should focus on getting a job instead, so that I can start paying off my debts. These are what got me in trouble in the first place.

T: How does that make you feel when he says that?

S: Well, I don't know. I guess he is right. It is my fault that we got attacked. If I had not borrowed money from those loan sharks, we would not have been attacked, and I would still be carrying my baby. I wish we were not fighting all the time though . . . we used to be able to talk to each other about everything, but since the attack we just can't anymore, and I don't know what to do anymore.

T: It sounds like a lot is going on at the same time, that makes you feel quite anxious. It sounds like the fights with your boyfriend are making you feel very tense. Can you think of other things that have a negative influence on how you are feeling at the moment?

S: My debts really cause me a lot of anxiety as well. At the moment I cannot even leave the house. How am I ever going to start a job and resolve my debts? I just don't know what to do.

T: Yes, I fully understand that your financial problems are very stressful. What else is going on at the moment? Is there anything in the therapy that might not work for you, perhaps?

Samira engaged in a conversation with the therapist and together they noticed that the comorbid OCD symptoms were a source of conflict in her intimate relationship, and this caused Samira to bring it up in treatment a lot.

In the next few sessions, Samira and her therapist tried to get a fuller assessment of whether the trauma was still the appropriate focus and how the OCD symptoms should be discussed in treatment. Through a functional analysis, Samira and her therapist concluded that Samira was using the cleaning as a way of preventing engagement with the traumatic memory. Bringing the OCD symptoms up in session prevented her from having to work on the trauma, and it gave her short-term relief in terms of discussing strategies of dealing with the discourse in her relationship. The behavior itself also made her feel less dirty, and she would feel more relaxed after cleaning.

Making Adaptations to Therapy: Sessions 8–12

In order to disrupt the maintenance cycle of OCD and PTSD, the following adapted treatment plan was agreed between the therapist and patient: (a) Reduce cleaning time (exposure and response prevention), replace the cleaning time with (b) writing and reading a trauma account, (c) a problem-solving window using a structured worksheet, and (d) relaxing activities outside of the house (e.g., walking, drawing, photography). The rationale was that the first strategy would disrupt her OCD and open the possibility of approaching (rather than avoiding) exposure to the trauma memories. The second strategy enabled Samira to start to become exposed to trauma memories in a contained, structured, gradual, and tolerable way. The third strategy enabled her to map out possible solutions to pressing problems that she found stressful and demoralizing (financial problems, relationship problems). The fourth strategy enabled her to gain some sense of relief and relaxation, which she was previously attempting to achieve (ineffectively) through compulsive cleaning. These strategies were integrated into her routine slowly over several weeks (sessions 8–12).

Therapeutic Impact of Adaptations: Sessions 13–20

Samira's anxiety began to go down slowly as assessed by the patient-completed GAD-7. The improvement in symptoms helped Samira become more engaged with the therapy starting at session 13, and her symptoms continued to improve. By session 16, Samira started searching for a job, and her scores began to fall within the boundaries of the ETR curve. It was agreed to bring the therapy to a close at session 20. At that point, Samira scored 10 on the GAD-7, indicating reliable improvement and within the boundaries of the ETR curve.

Overall, this case illustrates the need to personalize the treatment plan by identifying, formulating, and working with/around complicating factors, until the point when an evidence-based treatment can be resumed (e.g., when the obstacles have been dealt with, at least partly). In this way, feedback-informed treatment balances both evidence-based practice (e.g., applying empirically supported treatment methods) and the flexible personalization of the treatment plans—specifically to address obstacles to improvement. Other detailed clinical case studies documenting the role of ROM in adapting treatment plans have been reported in the literature (for a sample of clinical cases, see De Jong & Aafjes-van Doorn [2022] and associated special issue in *Journal of Clinical Psychology* [2022]).

Landmark Studies and Previous Reviews

Landmark Studies

The original investigation of patient feedback was conducted by Lambert and colleagues (2001), noteworthy for its experimental design and replication (Lambert et al., 2002). A previous review of this topic (Lambert et al., 2019) identified four landmark studies, two of which utilized the OQ-45 (Harmon et al., 2007; Simon et al., 2013) and two the PCOMS (Anker et al., 2009; Schuman et al., 2015). We take a complementary approach by prioritizing methodological rigor (reduced risk of bias in studies) as well as methodological advances drawn from the most recent substantive meta-analysis (De Jong et al., 2021), in which only four of 58 studies met the highest threshold for addressing risk of bias. Chronologically, these studies (and nation) were Berking et al. (2006; Switzerland), Davidsen et al. (2017; Denmark), Errázuriz and Zilcha-Mano (2018; Chile), and Bovendeerd et al. (2022; the Netherlands). Here, we consider the three most recent studies, all of which used components of the OQ and/or PCOMS systems, and none were carried out by the measure developers, thereby minimizing any effects of system developer allegiance.

Davidsen et al. (2017) conducted an RCT to determine the effect of client feedback in group psychotherapy for patients diagnosed with eating disorders (bulimia nervosa, binge eating disorder, or eating disorder not otherwise specified). Attendance and treatment outcomes were the main foci. Randomization was stratified for treatment type and diagnosis, with treatment allocation concealed from the investigators. Eighty participants were allocated to the experimental group, in which participants gave and received feedback about therapy progress and alliance, measured before and after each session using the ORS and Group Session Rating Scale. Seventy-nine participants were assigned to the control condition (no feedback), with both groups receiving 20–25 weekly group psychotherapy sessions. Rate of attendance at treatment sessions was the primary outcome, and severity of eating disorder symptoms measured with the Eating Disorder Examination interview was the secondary outcome. Patient outcome measures were the Symptom Checklist–90-R and the ORS (psychological distress), the Sheehan Disability Scale (social functioning), and the Self-Harm Inventory (episodes of self-harm and suicide).

Results showed feedback compared with control did not affect the rate of attendance, the severity of symptoms, or any of the exploratory outcomes (all *p* values ranged from .06 to .67). Davidsen et al. (2017) concluded that feedback neither increased attendance nor improved outcomes for outpatients in group psychotherapy for eating disorders. Crucially, however, it appeared that although therapists had previously endorsed the feedback procedures and looked at the PCOMS scores, they rarely acted on the information to adapt the course of or length of treatment.

Errázuriz and Zilcha-Mano (2018), in one of the few non-Western studies in the field, used three outcome indices—symptomatology, the working alliance, and both combined—to evaluate a low-cost form of feedback compared with the OQ-45 progress feedback report, thereby yielding four active feedback conditions plus a no feedback condition. They also investigated a range of moderators, including patient, therapist, and process factors, and employed multilevel modeling as well as conducting follow-up interviews with therapists. The sample comprised a total of 547 patients, with each condition comprising between 104 and 116 patients. The total sample was 75% female, average age 41 years, with 95% of the sample being Latino and treated in an outpatient individual psychotherapy setting in Chile.

Results showed that feedback had no effect on outcome, session attendance, or alliance for any of the cases, including NOT cases. Because therapists could decide whether or not to share the feedback they had received with the patient, ascertaining the extent to which feedback was shared with patients was important. Follow-up interviews identified that 64.7% of therapists used feedback sometimes or always, and when only this sample was analyzed, the results were the same. That is, there was no main effect for feedback based on the whole sample, on just the NOT cases, or for therapists who did report using the feedback.

However, Errázuriz and Zilcha-Mano (2018) did find that in NOT cases, baseline severity moderated feedback effects and that patients with a low baseline severity benefited more in most of the feedback conditions. Furthermore, for highly severe patients, the outcomes in the control group and the group receiving feedback on the alliance were superior to outcomes for patients receiving feedback regarding their symptoms. This effect was largely due to there being adverse effects for this specific patient group (i.e., more severe). Crucially, however, because the study was focusing on evaluating a low-cost implementation of feedback, clinical support tools were not included in the study. The authors concluded that providing feedback to therapists without offering them tools to improve treatment may be ineffective and even detrimental. Therapists receiving negative feedback in relation to patients with more severe disorders may be placed at a disadvantage without access to the clinical support tools that appear to play a crucial role in delivering effective feedback.

A significant portion of the literature has been characterized by biases arising from researcher allegiance and from a lack of independent outcome measures (i.e., independent of the feedback measure). Bovendeerd et al. (2022) addressed these two key issues in a cluster randomized trial of systematic client feedback (SCF) in which feedback using an adapted form of the PCOMS was compared with treatment-as-usual (TAU). The independent outcome measure was the OQ-45. Patients were drawn from four treatment centers, and power calculations were based on assumptions of a small effect, resulting in a minimum of 208 patients per center and 16 patients per therapist. A total of 1,933 patients were recruited into the trial, but 200 patients did not attend therapy, yielding an analyzed sample of 1,733 patients. Patient presentation was mild to moderate depression and anxiety (OQ-45 baseline scores for SCF and TAU conditions were 76.12 and 73.89, respectively).

Two analyses were conducted—intent-to-treat (ITT) and per protocol (PP)—and a three-level model was used (patient, therapist, center). For the ITT analysis, the gains in the feedback condition exceeded those for the TAU condition at all assessment points. At 1 year, the gains were more than 25% greater for the feedback condition on the OQ-45 compared with the TAU condition, representing an additional gain of 5.25 OQ-45 points (24.88 vs. 19.63). Although patients in both conditions made the majority of their gains within the initial 3 months, the key finding was the additional gains made across 12 months in the feedback condition compared with TAU. A virtually similar result was obtained in the PP analysis. No significant effects were found on the other outcome variables.

These three high-quality studies provide a representative summary of the range of outcomes for ROM. The null findings from group (Davidsen et al., 2017) and individual therapy (Errázuriz and Zilcha-Mano, 2018) indicate that ROM is not a panacea for all patients under all conditions. The former may be a result of applying feedback within highly structured therapies in which therapist flexibility in individually adapting therapy is limited. It may be that when applied to more intensive treatments, there is a ceiling effect that mitigates against additional gains from ROM.

In terms of the Errázuriz and Zilcha-Mano (2018) study, the result clearly identifies the importance of moderators, in particular patient severity, with the salutary finding that negative feedback can have an aversive effect. What is unknown from the study is whether the inclusion of CSTs, which are associated with the largest feedback effects, would have obviated the aversive impact. Although the attempt to test low-cost variants of feedback in a routine non-Western clinical setting is one of the most real-world controlled designs in the field, it may be that the exclusion of a key component in effective feedback compromised its impact. However, it showed the potential role of moderators, albeit in the context of an overall null finding. The study confirmed the importance of determining under what specific conditions feedback is effective, which may allow for more targeted efforts.

The positive findings using samples from national health care settings with an independent outcome measure (Bovendeerd et al., 2022) endorse findings, for example, from the English national NHS Talking Therapies for Anxiety and Depression program comprising a large analyzed sample (1,733 patients) in which, after controlling for therapist effects, patients classified as NOT had less severe symptoms ($d = 0.22$) after treatment as measured by an independent outcome measure when they received feedback compared with those in the control group. The study showed that supplementing psychological therapy with low-cost outcome feedback improved outcomes for patients who were at risk of poor response to treatment (see Delgadillo et al., 2018).

Meta-Analytic Reviews

At least 50 controlled, quasi-experimental, observational, and implementation studies have investigated the effectiveness of ROM feedback systems applied in several countries during the past 20 years. These studies have been synthesized across numerous systematic reviews (e.g., Carlier et al., 2012; Davidson et al., 2014; Gondek et al., 2016; Krägeloh et al., 2015; Mackrill & Sørensen, 2020) and at least 11 meta-analyses (Bergman et al., 2018; De Jong et al., 2021; Kendrick et al., 2016; Knaup et al., 2009; Lambert et al., 2003, 2018; Østergård et al., 2020; Pejtersen et al., 2020; Rognstad et al., 2023; Shimokawa et al., 2010; Tam & Ronan, 2017).

Early meta-analyses suggested that ROM feedback improves distal treatment outcomes relative to usual psychological care. However, trials published at that time (approximately a dozen) were predominantly from the United States and located in university counseling settings (Knaup et al., 2009; Lambert et al., 2003; Shimokawa et al., 2010). A seminal meta-analysis reported a pooled (intention-to-treat) effect size of $g = 0.28$ ($p = .003$) favoring feedback-informed treatment relative to usual care in cases classed as NOT using the OQ-45 measure (Shimokawa et al., 2010). The pooled (intention-to-treat) effect size was larger when examining data from studies that supplemented feedback with clinical support tools ($g = 0.44$). These promising results motivated feedback studies in other countries, treatment settings, age groups, and outcome measures.

Recent meta-analyses have examined the effects of feedback with specific measures, principally the OQ-45 and PCOMS (Lambert et al., 2018; Østergård et al., 2020; Pejtersen et al., 2020), and on specific populations such as children and young people (Bergman et al., 2018; Tam & Ronan, 2017) and presenting conditions (e.g., common mental health disorders; Rognstad et al., 2023). As the literature from trials accumulated, meta-analyses of ROM with heterogeneous populations and outcome measures emerged. Such broad meta-analyses reported discrepant findings. For example, one review reported a pooled effect size of $g = 0.10$ favoring feedback in short-term therapies but no significant effect in long-term therapies (Knaup et al., 2009), whereas another review reported no significant overall effect of feedback but reported a significant effect size of $g = 0.22$ favoring feedback in NOT cases (Kendrick et al., 2016). The most comprehensive meta-analysis to date, including an examination of potential moderators, is reported in the next section (De Jong et al., 2021). A further recent meta-analysis of only RCTs reported a virtually identical effect size reported by De Jong et al. (2021) of 0.14 for a total sample and slightly larger effect size of 0.29 for NOT cases (Rognstad et al., 2023).

Overall, the additive effect sizes from these meta-analyses of psychological therapy with feedback compared to psychological therapy without feedback can be summarized as ranging from small ($g = 0.14$; Lambert et al., 2018; Rognstad et al., 2023) when based on all cases, to medium ($g = 0.33$; e.g., Lambert et al., 2018) when based on NOT cases, and increasing to 0.49 when CST feedback was used (Lambert et al., 2018). These mixed findings seem to be a function of the analyzed samples and their heterogeneity, which requires a comprehensive examination of potential moderators of effects sizes across studies.

Research Review

In this section, we provide an abridged version of the largest meta-analysis conducted to date on ROM (De Jong et al., 2021). Readers are directed to the original source for the full details, which is available under Creative Commons License. Given that the search was carried out in September 2020, within the preparation time frame of this chapter, together with the extensive inclusion criteria of the study, we considered this review to be sufficiently up-to-date so as not to warrant a new search and meta-analysis. It comprised both RCTs and practice-based studies, did not limit the focus to selected feedback systems, included studies in several languages, and was not conducted by a developer of a feedback system.

Search Strategy and Inclusion Criteria

The starting search date was set at 2001 (this marked the introduction of progress feedback) and included literature to September 30, 2020. The sources for the searches comprised PsycInfo, PubMed, and Web of Science, with additional searches of the Current Controlled Register Trials Register and Google Scholar. Indicative search terms for PsycInfo included the terms "feedback" OR "outcome monitoring" OR "routine outcome measurement" OR "progress monitoring" within the context of psychotherapy, counseling, and mental health care. Exclusion terms included NOT education NOT (video-feedback OR video feedback) NOT (bio-feedback OR biofeedback OR "EEG feedback" OR brain) NOT (schizophrenia OR psychosis) NOT motor. Full search terms for all databases are available as supplemental material linked to the original publication. In addition, existing meta-analyses were screened for relevant publications as well as calls using the listserv of the Society for Psychotherapy Research and emails to known researchers in the field seeking unpublished studies. Inclusion criteria were published and unpublished studies that (a) examined effects of feedback on patient outcome; (b) compared one or more feedback groups and a no feedback control group or cohort; (c) focused on psychological interventions in a psychological therapy, psychiatry, or counseling setting; (d) treated patients with mental health or substance abuse problems; (e) assessed end-of-treatment outcomes; and (f) in which therapists received ROM information about their patients on at least three occasions during treatment. Documents in English, German, and Dutch were included, a feature that enhanced the inclusivity of the meta-analysis in comparison with previous meta-analytic reviews.

Progress feedback was defined as "providing information on treatment progress from standardized measures to a clinician and/or patient on a regular basis throughout the course of treatment." Studies were coded for a range of feedback characteristics (e.g., instrument, type of feedback) and study characteristics (e.g., treatment duration, setting). Of 40 authors approached by the team for additional information about their data, 31 provided it.

Primary and Secondary Outcomes

The primary outcome was the difference in post-therapy symptom reduction on a standardized outcome measure between patients in the feedback group and patients in the treatment as usual/without feedback group. For cohort studies, the standardized mean difference in change score was taken as the effect size measure (i.e., accounting for the pretreatment scores). To meet criteria for inclusion at follow-up, data were required to be at least 1 month following the end of treatment or study and represent a standardized mean difference in change score from pre-treatment.

Secondary outcomes were post-treatment differences between the feedback and control groups in dropout rate, deteriorated cases, and treatment duration. Dropout included treatment dropouts and study dropouts as well as cases with only one or two sessions. Reliable deterioration was defined according to standard criteria (Jacobson & Truax, 1991), and treatment duration was defined by the number of sessions received.

Study Quality

The quality of RCTs was assessed using the Risk of Bias (Higgins et al., 2020), and the cohort studies were rated using the Risk of Bias in Non-randomized Studies of Interventions template (Sterne et al., 2016). In addition, the potential for allegiance bias was coded in the affirmative if the developer of the feedback system was a co-author on the study.

Moderating Variables

Multiple moderating variables were investigated. These included voluntary versus mandatory participation, treatment intensity, adult versus youth, therapy modality (individual, group), and length (fixed vs. open). Outcome assessment was differentiated according to whether it was independent or not of the measure used to provide feedback. Type of feedback was coded (raw data, ERT, or CSTs), including additional information on aspects of therapy (e.g., alliance). Particular features of feedback were distinguished according to timing (before or within session vs. delayed) and frequency (continuous vs. intermittent). Data were coded whether patients had direct access to feedback or not. Studies were distinguished between those in which therapists received training in the feedback tool versus not.

Meta-Analytic Approach

A three-level meta-analysis was conducted, thereby taking account of three levels of variability in effect sizes (Cheung, 2014): (a) the sampling variance of the individual extracted effect sizes (level 1), (b) the variance between effect sizes extracted from the same study (level 2), and (c) the variance between effect sizes extracted from different studies (level 3). The overall effect size and variance estimates were derived from a random effects three-level model. The likelihood ratio tests determined whether the within and between effect size estimates were significantly different from zero.

The three-level random effects analyses were conducted twice: first for full samples (both NOT and OT cases) using data from all studies, and second for only a subsample of studies providing data for NOT cases. The I^2 statistic was used as a standardized measure of heterogeneity (Nakagawa & Santos, 2012). Because the secondary outcomes (dropout, percentage of deteriorated cases, treatment duration) did not have nested data, standard random and mixed effects meta-analysis models were conducted. Moderation analyses were conducted using the same moderators used in the models as the primary outcome variables.

Egger's regression test of funnel plot asymmetry (Egger et al., 1997) was used to evaluate publication bias for the results of the standard random effect models. An adapted version of Egger's regression test was used to assess publication bias in the three-level random effect models.

For the overall effect of feedback, the fail-safe *N* was estimated. The fail-safe *N* refers to the number of potentially missing studies with a *z* value of 0 that would need to be added in order to make the overall effect size statistically insignificant.

Sample

The final sample comprised 58 studies, 21,699 patients (41.9% controls; 58.1% feedback), and 110 effect sizes. The vast majority of studies were conducted in counseling or outpatient settings (84%), with adults (91%), in individual or couple therapies (71%). A total of 97% of the studies were accounted for by Europe and the United States (52% and 45%, respectively), with the OQ System and PCOMS being the most frequently used feedback systems (38% and 36%, respectively). Use of ETRs as the means for providing feedback was the most common (45%), followed by use of raw scores (38%); ETRs together with CSTs accounted for the least (17%). Feedback was provided immediately (59%) more often than delayed (41%), with 88% of the studies providing session-by-session feedback.

Study Quality

The overall risk of bias was high for 31% of RCTs and 100% for all cohort studies due to the high risk of confounding arising from the absence of randomization. Anticipating the moderator analyses (below), larger effects were obtained in studies in which the developer of the feedback system was a co-author ($d = 0.21$, 95% confidence interval [CI]

[0.12, 0.31]) than not ($d = 0.12$, 95% CI [0.06, 0.19]). That suggests the possibility of researcher allegiance.

Results for Full Sample

The average sample for the 58 studies was 321.4 ($SD = 433.6$; median = 184) per study, and using an average of 2.04 ($SD = 1.73$) outcome measures per study. The overall effect size was $d = 0.15$, 95% CI [0.10, 0.20] (Figure 15.3). The between-study heterogeneity was 72.6%, and the within-study variance was 0.

Five moderator variables had a significant impact on outcomes. Larger effects were found for the following: (a) the ORS ($d = 0.34$) compared with the OQ-45 ($d = 0.11$) or other outcome instruments ($d = 0.12$); (b) the PCOMS feedback system ($d = 0.24$) in contrast to the OQ System ($d = 0.13$) or other feedback systems ($d = 0.07$); (c) studies conducted in the United States ($d = 0.23$) compared with those conducted elsewhere ($d = 0.11$); (d) use of the feedback instrument as the outcome measure ($d = 0.19$) compared with use of an independent measure ($d = 0.08$); and (e) an effect of publication date, with later studies yielding an effect size of 0.02 lower per year since the initial study in 2001. Larger effects were also obtained in studies in which the developer of the feedback system was a co-author ($d = 0.21$, 95% CI [0.12, 0.31]) than not ($d = 0.12$, 95% CI [0.06, 0.19]).

Ten effect sizes were derived from four studies providing follow-up data. The three-level random effects model yielded an overall effect size of feedback of 0.18 (95% CI [0.03, 0.39]) compared to no-feedback control groups. Due to the small number of studies, this was not statistically significant. Moreover, a sensitivity analysis excluding one study (Anker et al., 2009) substantially reduced the pooled effect size ($d = 0.09$, 95% CI [0.13, 0.32]).

Results for Not on Track Cases

The NOT subgroup comprised 27 studies, 15,146 patients (40.1% controls; 59.9% feedback), and 43 effects. The analysis yielded an overall effect size of $d = 0.17$ (95% CI [0.09, 0.25]; Figure 15.4). The effect size increased slightly as a result of sensitivity analyses excluding non-RCTs ($d = 0.20$, 95% CI [0.11, 0.28]), as well as excluding studies using a control group adopting some form of outcome monitoring ($d = 0.20$, 95% CI [0.12, 0.27]). The between-group heterogeneity was 28%, and it was 36% for the within-study variance. In the NOT sample, feedback type was a significant moderator. Specifically, studies utilizing CSTs ($d = 0.36$) were more effective than feedback systems using raw scores ($d = 0.04$) or ETRs ($d = 0.12$): $F(2, 40) = 5.08, p = .01$.

Results for Secondary Outcomes

Information on dropout was available for 39 studies, comprising 14,369 patients (48.9% controls; 51.1% feedback). Analyses showed differential dropout rates for feedback

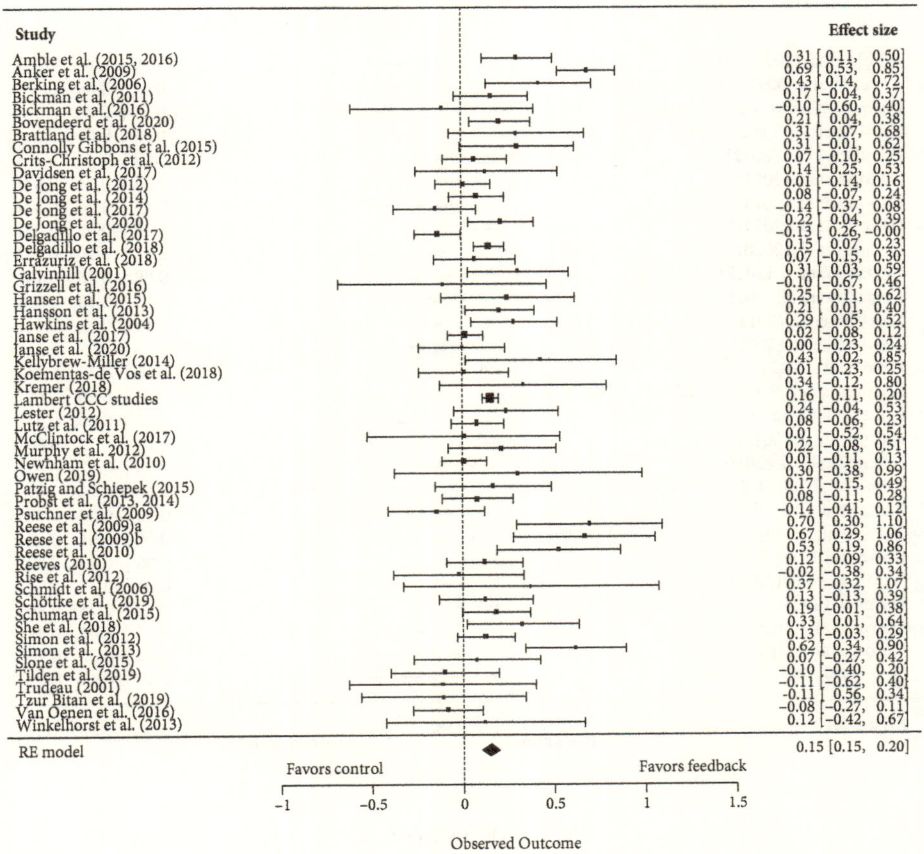

Figure 15.3 Effects of feedback in full sample (on-track and not-on-track combined). One extreme effect size was excluded from the analyses. Some studies by Lambert and colleagues used the same outcome data as an archival control group (Harmon et al., 2007; Lambert et al., 2001, 2002; Slade et al., 2008; Whipple et al., 2003). Therefore, the studies conducted in the Brigham Young University college counseling center were combined into one effect size, referred to as *Lambert CCC studies*.

groups of 20.9% compared to 24.5% for control groups, amounting to an approximately 20% greater chance of dropout in the absence of feedback (odds ratio [*OR*] = 1.19, 95% CI [1.03, 1.38], $p < .01$). Heterogeneity across studies was 47.8%. The effect was moderated by feedback instrument, with studies using the PCOMS (*OR* = 1.48) yielding significantly higher effects of feedback on reducing dropout than for the OQ System (*OR* = 1.21) and for studies using other feedback systems (*OR* = 1.08). Effect sizes were also larger for studies carried out in the United States (*OR* = 1.77) compared with outside the United States (*OR* = 1.07): $Q_M(1) = 8.99, p = .003$.

Data on the percentage of deteriorated cases was available for 26 studies, comprising 10,413 patients (46.4% control; 53.6% feedback), and analyses showed no significant differences between feedback and control conditions. The heterogeneity across studies was 7.1%. Moderating effects were found for training and type of feedback. Studies in

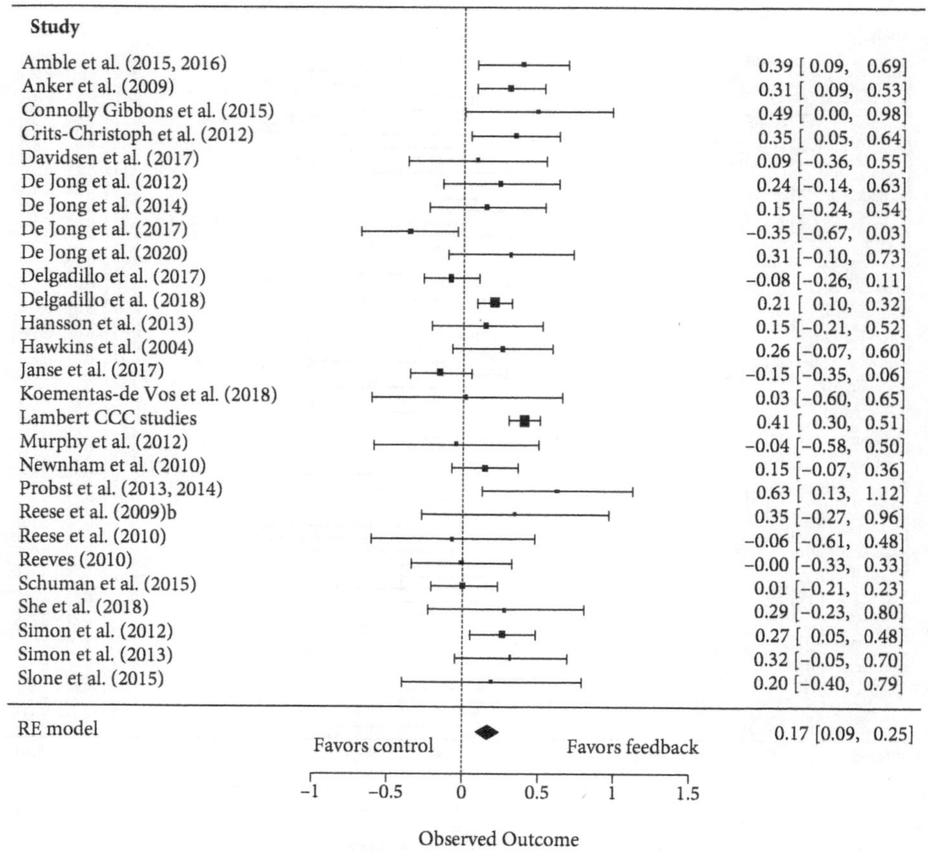

Figure 15.4 Effect of feedback in not-on-track subgroup.

which therapists received training in feedback yielded larger effects (*OR* = 1.28) than when no training was available (*OR* = 0.81), $Q_M = 5.45$, $p = .02$. Studies using ETRs in the feedback resulted in larger effects (*OR* = 1.36) than studies using CSTs (*OR* = 1.29) or raw scores (*OR* = 0.81), $Q_M = 6.70$, $p = .04$.

Feedback had no overall effect on the number of sessions conducted ($d = 0.04$, 95% CI [−0.06, 0.15]), a finding associated with high heterogeneity across studies (86.3%). No significant moderators of the effect of feedback on treatment duration were found.

Publication Bias

The results suggest that there was no publication bias regarding the results for the meta-analytic models. The *p* values were .55 (full sample) and .58 (NOT sample). In addition, the fail-safe *N* for the effect of feedback in the full sample was 3,695, meaning that an additional 3,695 studies would be required to overturn this result, suggesting that the effect of feedback is robust.

Different Feedback Systems

There were clear outcome differences between the two main feedback systems (OQ System and PCOMS) in the full sample. PCOMS yielded larger effect sizes in the full sample, but it had little effect in the NOT subgroup. By contrast, the OQ System seemed more effective with NOT cases, particularly in combination with CSTs. Because PCOMS did not show a differential effect benefitting NOT cases, it can be viewed as a more generic feedback system useful in OT cases, whereas the OQ System is more effective in NOT cases.

Such a result is consistent with the developmental rationale for each system. Namely, the PCOMS was constructed to be completed and discussed in session, thereby promoting better communication between patient and therapist. By contrast, the OQ System was premised on the basis of targeting patients who were at risk of failing in treatment. The PCOMS and its component outcome measure, the ORS, yielded larger effects, likely due to the latter being more sensitive to change than other outcome measures. Overall, the most parsimonious conclusion is that ROM was modestly helpful in general but not with all patients.

Cumulative and Causal Evidence

Locating the results of this meta-analysis in the broader evidence base provides some clarity on the impact of feedback. The effect sizes of psychological therapy with client feedback compared to psychological therapy without client feedback confirm the lower estimate ($g = 0.15$; De Jong et al., 2021) as previously reported in the literature ($g = 0.14$; Lambert et al., 2018). The largest effect obtained in the NOT sample for feedback enhanced by CSTs ($g = 0.36$; De Jong et al., 2021), an effect slightly lower than previously reported for NOT with CSTs ($g = 0.49$; Lambert et al., 2018), but similar to both the effect of PCOMS for all samples ($g = 0.40$) and NOT samples using the OQ-45 ($g = 0.33$; Lambert et al., 2018). These effects, we should remember, are *additive* to the effects of standard treatment (i.e., when there is no feedback).

Effect sizes regarding improvement for NOT patients with feedback versus TAU have been reported in seven meta-analyses (De Jong et al., 2021; Kendrick et al., 2016; Lambert et al., 2003, 2018; Østergård et al., 2020; Rognstad et al., 2022; Shimokawa et al., 2010). The effects range between $g = 0.17$ (De Jong et al., 2021) and $g = 0.53$ (Shimokawa et al., 2010). Three meta-analyses have assessed the effects of feedback with CSTs compared to no-feedback controls in NOT cases and have found effect sizes ranging from $g = 0.36$ to $g = 0.53$ (De Jong et al., 2021; Lambert et al., 2018; Shimokawa et al., 2010).

In addition to the effects of feedback on symptom reduction, meta-analyses have assessed the effects of feedback on the odds of treatment success, treatment duration, and the odds of dropout. Feedback increased the rate of improvement in NOT cases when CSTs were included ($OR = 2.40$ vs. $OR = 1.89$ without CSTs; Lambert et al., 2018). In terms of the effect of feedback on treatment duration, contrary to the findings of the present meta-analysis, differential effects have been reported between OT and NOT cases. OT cases have been reported to receive on average 0.69 sessions fewer when feedback was provided, whereas NOT cases receive 0.73 sessions more when feedback was provided (Kendrick et al., 2016). Although these results concur with earlier findings (e.g., Lambert et al., 2003), results need further investigation. And regarding dropout, one salient finding from the meta-analysis of De Jong et al. (2021) is the effect of feedback on reducing dropout (recall by approximately 20%). Reducing dropout rates needs to be a major focus of effort for clinics and services.

Recall that these effects are *additive* to the effects of standard treatment with no feedback. The average effect size of feedback ($g = 0.15$) corresponds to a success rate difference (SRD; Furukawa & Leucht, 2011) of 8.45%. This effect size increases when clinical support tools for NOT cases are used to $g \approx 0.36$–0.53, which corresponds to an SRD between 20.09% and 29.22%.

Interpretation of effect sizes is crucial, particularly when between-group effect sizes (as cited in this chapter) are compared with effect sizes from correlational studies (Kraft, 2020). Between-group effect sizes reflect causal effects, whereas effects from correlational studies represent only descriptive relations between two variables. Correlational designs and deducted effect sizes are, on average, substantially larger than those from between-group designs and their respective effects sizes (Kraft, 2020).

In summary, patient feedback is a relatively simple method provided in addition to psychological treatment, where the effects compared to a range of control conditions are moderate to large (e.g., Barkham & Lambert, 2021). In other words, feedback offers value above and beyond the general effectiveness of psychotherapy. Overall, client feedback is effective in many settings, primarily with patients at risk of deterioration and with the use of CSTs. However, effect sizes depend on the comparison group and the feedback method used.

Research Review on Components of ROM

We have complemented the meta-analysis with evidence drawn from a selective narrative review of studies addressing components in each of the three ROM phases. Evidence relating to the first phase of ROM (data collection) indicates that patients generally support monitoring outcomes during therapy (see reanalysis of data from Lutz et al. [2011] as reported in Castonguay et al. [2013]). Reports show that patients prefer using a short measure to monitor progress if the therapist believes it to be useful (Thew et al., 2015; Zimmerman & McGlinchey, 2008). Yet, qualitative data have also revealed patients' doubts about completing measures when their providers either did not look at or did not make use of the information (Talib et al., 2018).

A systematic review comprising 26 studies noted four meta-themes identified by patients (Solstad et al., 2019): concern about motives for adopting ROM (i.e., suspicion that ROM was being used to determine service effectiveness rather than used for patients' benefit); dominance of symptom focus (i.e., the need to broaden out to include other domains of experience such as social functioning that better reflect the complexity of patients' lives); the need to provide a rationale, engaging with patients, and explaining how the data will be used (Börjesson & Boström, 2020); and developing a collaborative practice in which ROM becomes a clinical process tool to direct and deepen the therapeutic dialogue (Faija et al., 2022). Detailed analysis of a small sample of patients using the NORSE feedback system has shown that although ROM enhances their awareness of emotions and experiences (see also Greenhalgh et al., 2018), patients can also be uncertain about whether the assignment of a specific rating on a scale actually captures their felt experience (Solstad et al., 2021). However, there was an overall view that the use of ROM was an enabling process that helped direct the focus of therapeutic dialogue.

Research into the frequency of data completion suggests no significant difference between continuous feedback (i.e., every session) and less frequent feedback (De Jong et al., 2021). A comparison between a basic (e.g., every fifth session) and a high-intensive (every session) delivery of feedback showed no difference in outcomes, but the latter resulted in fewer therapy sessions and a lower patient dropout rate (Janse et al., 2020). Prediction modeling of patient outcomes and dropout have been used on basic ROM data collected at intervals of between five and 15 sessions to show that the use of more sophisticated analyses is not dependent on session-by-session data (Mütze et al., 2022). Although such a result provides support for a less intense program of obtaining ROM data, securing useful data on the course of treatment was only viable due to the longer term duration of treatments, in which the mean number of sessions was 39 (range: 5–95). Continuous data collection also facilitates clinical decision-making, by increasing the odds of identifying early that a patient is not progressing well.

Obtaining baseline data is crucial therapeutically but also because most computerized feedback systems generate interpretation rules, such as expected treatment response curves or early response signals, based on the pretreatment baseline measure (Lutz et al., 2002). The limitations of relying on fixed predictions based solely on an initial assessment are being addressed by moves toward more dynamic modeling in which predictions are continually updated and have been shown to exceed the performance of previous methods (e.g., Bone et al., 2021).

Research focusing on the second phase (feeding back data) has found that although completion of self-report measures can result in greater self-learning by some patients, the impact on outcomes and treatment likely depends on how the information is subsequently shared and used in therapy (Greenhalgh et al., 2018). Data need to be reviewed in the form of a conversation rather than simply being told the numbers that can be viewed within the context of shared decision-making. An RCT showed no evidence that ROM enhanced shared decision-making overall across a range of patient presenting problems (Metz et al., 2019). However, it was associated with better outcomes for patients experiencing mood disorders, with the suggestion that the feedback was not sufficiently targeted to the other presenting conditions.

There is greater benefit in viewing ROM data collaboratively between patient and therapist (Hepner et al., 2019) rather than feeding back directly to patients (e.g., Slade et al., 2008). Research suggests both patients and therapists have similar preferences for how feedback is presented, preferring greater specificity in relation to the nature of predictors as well as of advice (Hilhorst et al., 2022). Both have preferences for feedback to be presented as either a continuous outcome or an outcome that is expressed in terms of a probability, with the feedback representation comprising both text and images. More generally, in terms of technical support to aid ROM and feedback, evidence from a systematic review shows the use of communication technologies (e.g., smartphones, tablets) to be practical and feasible in psychological therapies (Gual-Montolio et al., 2020).

Evidence supports the use of CSTs to augment feedback. In studies focusing on NOT patients in which a feedback arm was compared with one accessing CSTs, results have consistently favored CSTs ($d = 0.36$) compared with expected treatment response ($d = 0.12$) or use of raw scores ($d = 0.04$; De Jong et al., 2021). Results from other meta-analyses have yielded slightly larger effects for CSTs (e.g., 0.49; Lambert et al., 2018).

One key CST is the ASC (Lambert et al., 2015). In a study of 107 off-track outpatients, 58% had sufficient problems detected by one of the ASC scales to trigger an alarm, with 29% of all NOT patients meeting the criterion level for an alarm in the area of (lack of) social support (White et al., 2015). Lack of social support was more often identified as a flag for deterioration than were problems in the therapeutic alliance. Indeed, the dearth of social support as the single best predictor of patient deterioration has been replicated (Probst et al., 2020). In contrast to the prominence of external factors to therapy, scales relating to internal therapy processes (therapeutic alliance) either did not predict deterioration or, for the motivation scale, did so but inconsistently. In another study, an analysis comparing 273 OT and 143 NOT cases showed suicidality, motivation, and life events to be better predictors of subsequent deterioration in NOT cases (Schilling et al., 2021). These findings relating to the role of life events and the lack of social support in the lives of patients are a salutary reminder of the importance of the social and interpersonal world of patients outside of therapy and contrast with the considerable attention paid to in-session concepts, such as the therapeutic alliance.

In the third phase (adapting), evidence of adapting the focus or direction of therapy has been shown from analyses of patient–therapist dyads, with specific examples within the course of therapy and across services (Brooks Holliday et al., 2021). The within-session adjustments included the following: setting and monitoring treatment goals; determining the most appropriate therapeutic approach for a given patient; adjusting the pace of therapy; focusing the nature of the discussion during a given session and/or assigning treatment "homework"; or adjusting therapeutic modalities. Adjustments focusing on specific service parameters included making referrals to additional forms of care; making transition, terminations, or discharge decisions; facilitating communication with other clinicians and joint decision-making; and initiating/adjusting medication. Overall, a set of best practices for discussing feedback proposed providing a strong rationale for ROM, discussing ROM every time measures are administered; actively engaging patients in the discussion of ROM; and using a graph to show progress to patients.

Moderators

A number of potential moderators of ROM's effects have been investigated, but with little consistency across studies, and with many studies being underpowered, the research yield has been limited. However, the use of clinical support tools enhances the impact of feedback (Lutz, Deisenhofer, et al., 2022), particularly in NOT cases (De Jong et al., 2021). A number of studies have also shown therapist effects to moderate feedback effects (e.g., Bovendeerd et al., 2022; Janse et al., 2020). A reanalysis of six earlier

ROM studies using the OQ-45 found that the provision of feedback reduced the size of the therapist effect, thereby leveling the variability between more and less effective therapists (Delgadillo et al., 2022). Therapist positive attitude to feedback and using specific modifications in light of feedback have been found to be associated with enhanced effects (Lutz et al., 2015), whereas therapist-rated usefulness of feedback has been found to be a significant moderator of feedback outcome associations (Lutz, Deisenhofer, et al., 2022).

The direct study of therapist effects and ROM has found female therapists and those with a greater commitment to feedback to show higher probability of using the information provided by a feedback system and therapists who used the feedback system also to be more effective for NOT patients (De Jong et al., 2012). Specifically, therapists with a low internal feedback propensity who were more committed to using the feedback at the beginning of the study saw patients who improved more quickly. By contrast, therapists with a high internal feedback propensity (i.e., were more likely to trust their own opinion than that of feedback from external sources) saw patients with a slower rate of change (De Jong et al., 2012).

Implementation has been shown to impact ROM effects (Bovendeerd et al., 2022; Simon et al., 2013; van Sonsbeek et al., 2021). Several multicenter studies found differential effects of feedback within their trial, with some locations showing medium effects and other locations showing no effect at all (e.g., Bovendeerd et al., 2022). The effects of ROM have been found to increase over time, with one study showing post-treatment scores for patients recruited at the end of a study to have an effect size 0.467 greater than the post-treatment score of patients who started treatment at the commencement of the trial (Brattland et al., 2018). Although no specific factors were investigated to account for the improvement, monthly ROM meetings and biannual 1-day workshops were a feature of the implementation. Such a finding underscores the centrality of investing in resources to support high-quality ROM implementation.

Implementation Science

Although the literature on the benefits of ROM has yielded both positive and null findings, it is almost unanimous in identifying implementation as the main barrier for successful ROM. Obstacles to implementation of outcome measurement in routine practice have long been documented in the literature (e.g., Marks, 1998). These barriers can be grouped into three main categories: (a) the people (i.e., patient or therapist), (b) organizational aspects, and (c) systems (Lewis et al., 2019; Van Wert et al., 2021). Unlike many, or most, therapeutic methods, effective use of ROM is dependent on a climate of organizational support. Indeed, the aspiration has been referred to as developing a "culture for feedback" (Bertolino & Miller, 2012). In addition, a distinction has been made between practice issues and attitudinal issues, with cultural and philosophical issues being potentially greater obstacles than practical issues to successful implementation (Boswell, Kraus, Miller, et al., 2015; Boyce et al., 2014).

Commonly reported barriers include ease of accessing and using ROM systems, guidance on selecting outcome measures, and organizational accountability (Van Wert et al., 2021). A systematic review of ROM implementation identified a wide range of factors comprising leadership, interorganizational factors, feedback culture, implementation team, coordinators and champions, supervision, training, measures, and generating a language for ROM use in clinical practice (Mackrill & Sørensen, 2020).

Attitudinal barriers to ROM have been explicitly investigated using the Evidence-based Practice Attitude Scale–Routine Outcome Monitoring (Rye et al., 2019). These studies showed that holding more positive attitudes regarding the adoption of ROM predicted greater use of standardized instruments. Limitations centered on ROM being seen as too narrowly focused, not suitable for patients presenting with multiple problems, and hindering the relationship between patient and therapist. Such concerns predicted poorer uptake of standardized measures (Rye et al., 2019). Therapists with a higher commitment to client feedback also had a higher probability to make use of the psychometric feedback system, and those therapists were more effective for NOT patients (De Jong et al., 2021). Similarly, therapists' satisfaction with the ROM system and the use of the feedback information tend to predict the magnitude of feedback effects (Lutz et al., 2015).

Strategies for improving implementation have been described by many authors (e.g., Bear et al., 2022; Lewis et al., 2019; Lutz et al., 2021; Mellor-Clark et al., 2016; Nilsen, 2015; Nilsen & Birken, 2020). Drawing from these sources and case examples, psychotherapists and organizations that plan to adopt ROM can consider the following actions: Nominate an implementation leader, supported by an implementation team; secure a costed plan for implementation, including technology, resources, and clinical time necessary to train therapists; share good practices in monitoring and feedback; automate the collection of data; and adopt an available feedback system that uses signaling technologies.

Possible Negative Effects and Harm

Evidence suggests two groups of patients might experience negative effects of ROM: patients with severe psychopathology and those experiencing cluster B personality disorders. As reported previously, patients experiencing greater severity experienced an aversive effect when in receipt of negative feedback in which clinical support tools were not available (Errázuriz & Zilcha-Mano, 2018). In this instance, the absence of CSTs may have been crucial, such that it is not severe psychopathology per se that is the issue but, rather, this factor combined with the absence of resources to support therapists with this specific patient group.

Adverse effects have also been reported both for NOT patients and for those presenting with cluster B personality disorders and also personality disorders not otherwise specified (De Jong et al., 2018). The patient sample comprised day patients and inpatients aged between 17 and 36 years, all diagnosed with severe personality disorders and receiving a long-term intensive psychotherapeutic program. The study compared a no-feedback control group with a group in which the therapist team received feedback and a group in which both the therapist team and the client received feedback. There was a significant difference in treatment course in the first 6 months of treatment, with the group in which patients and therapists received feedback showing higher levels of symptom distress than the other two groups. Crucially, this result seemed to be a function of NOT patients who met criteria for a cluster B personality disorder or PD-NOS, but it did not apply to patients presenting with cluster C personality disorder. However, after this initial increase, the symptoms in this group decreased and were no longer significantly different from the other two groups by 39 weeks.

These collective findings confirm that feedback arising from ROM is not a panacea for enhancing treatment and may not be best suited to people who are more vulnerable psychologically. It may be the combination of discouraging feedback and greater severity or vulnerability makes negative feedback an unwelcome component, particularly in situations in which there are not the resources to support delivery of CSTs or where the flexibility of the therapist may be limited (e.g., in inpatient settings). Notwithstanding these cautionary notes, we are not aware of any reports documenting data on patients being harmed by ROM.

Diversity Considerations

Diversity, and in particular an intersectional approach, has been poorly covered in ROM and feedback literature. Diverse populations tend to be underrepresented in studies, and the reporting of socioeconomic and ethnic minority variables is rare. In addition, only two studies have been conducted in non-Western countries (Errázuriz & Zilcha-Mano, 2018 [Chile]; She et al, 2018 [China]). The study in Chile was presented earlier (see the section on Landmark Studies). In a study carried out in a Chinese college counseling center ($N = 157$), feedback based on the PCOMS was found to have a significant positive effect on treatment outcomes both in the full sample and in the NOT students. The latter group had six times the rate of reliable change in the feedback group than in the no-feedback condition (She et al., 2018). Importantly, the administration and use of the PCOMS was culturally adapted such that counselors did not administer the measure and did not have to make use of it in the session (Sun et al., 2021).

Limitations of the Research

In addition to the predominantly Western samples and minimal research extending beyond that cultural space, the major limitations concern poor implementation and lack of statistical power. Null findings highlight research dilemmas in these two specific areas (e.g., van Sonsbeek et al., 2021), along with complex designs (e.g., Errázuriz & Zilcha-Mano, 2018), mismatch between feedback system and the patient population (e.g., van Oenen et al., 2016), and infrequent application of feedback (e.g., Schöttke et al., 2020).

Regarding statistical power, only 20% of the studies in the main meta-analysis reported here (De Jong et al., 2021) comprised a total patient sample greater than 500. Power calculations consistently fail to account for therapists despite evidence attesting to their effect in routine practice (Baldwin & Imel, 2013; Johns et al., 2019). Adequate power is also essential to advance our understanding of potential moderators, which, along with a greater focus of mechanisms and theoretical models (e.g., Sapyta et al., 2005), is urgently needed.

A portion of research is closely aligned (e.g., via co-authorship) with measure developers. Reliance on highly selected samples of committed practitioners, sometimes with leading international experts as advisors, lessens the generalizability of such studies. Independence of authorship and ROM systems as well as adequately powered studies of clinical as opposed to student populations are required together with follow-up data. In the reported meta-analysis, only four studies included follow-up data greater than 1 month, and the maximum was at 6 months (De Jong et al., 2021). There is a need for follow-up data to be collected at upwards of 12 months and preferably longer. However, practical and possible ethical issues of clinical responsibility arise when extending the concept of routine monitoring beyond the time at which direct care is provided.

All the routine outcome measures reported in the current review are based on nomothetic principles. Some practitioners would prefer using idiographic outcome measures (Jensen-Doss et al., 2018) accompanied by a growing evidence base regarding the psychometric standing of idiographic measures, which can be either problem focused or goal focused (Cooper & Xu, 2023; Sales et al., 2023). However, adopting an experimental design to determine preferences between idiographic and nomothetic approaches found no difference (Bugatti & Boswell, 2022). A balance between standardization and personalization in ROM may yield better rates of adoption by practitioners (Bjaastad et al., 2019).

Finally, outcome measures used in ROM assume structural invariance over time; that is, the interpretation of items remains the same over time. Analyses of several outcome measures have yielded differing results, with longitudinal invariance being found in some measures and not in others (e.g., Coleman et al., 2022; Rosenström et al., 2022).

Training Implications

Training in ROM has been examined as a potential moderator but has not been found to significantly impact feedback effects on symptom reduction or dropout, although it has resulted in decreasing the percentage of deteriorated cases (De Jong et al., 2021). However, training in feedback was highly varied between studies, ranging from a 2-hour introduction to a full day of training with added booster sessions and monthly supervision. In other studies, results have shown that positive attitudes toward ROM (Edbrooke-Childs et al., 2016) and rates of ROM adoption (Persons et al., 2016) can be both enhanced following planful and well-designed training. A notable finding of the latter study was that at 12-month follow-up, practitioners were still adhering to using ROM in 57% of sessions as compared with 40% initially. But, importantly, these data related to the use of any progress monitoring measure, thereby generalizing from the specific measure used in the training program.

Findings from a survey of U.S. psychology training clinics found the top two ranked reasons for using ROM were to help trainees determine when there was a need to adapt treatment and to help them make better treatment decisions (Peterson & Fagan, 2017). And the two top-ranked reasons why ROM was not adopted in training clinics were lack of resources (e.g., personnel, money) and hesitancy by supervisors to adopt measures with which they were unfamiliar.

In terms of learning ROM, whereas passive learning (e.g., reading, workshops) increases knowledge, strategies that include behavioral rehearsal and modeling of practical actions are likely to enhance the delivery of ROM (Beidas et al., 2014). These include components that are primarily interactions with patients (e.g., explaining the rationale, responding to patients' reactions to data, and addressing adaptations to treatment). The adoption of deliberate practice is likely to support a more active and method-based approach to learning key components of ROM (Rousmaniere, 2017).

In addition, actions for improving the adoption of ROM include training the trainers as well as trainees. ROM as a tool in supervision has been espoused, essentially emphasizing the view that supervisors and the supervision process are integral to securing the adoption of ROM by trainees (Swift et al., 2015). Accounts of differing training programs premised on ROM have been reported in the literature—for example, in the United States (e.g., Cooper et al., 2021) and Germany (e.g., Lutz et al., 2023).

To achieve successful implementation requires collaborative leadership and time (Goldberg et al., 2016). The time taken to successfully implement ROM depends on the target by which it is being evaluated and the level of resource available. And once achieved, it is about maintaining and sustaining the practice. Some ROM activities can be achieved in months, whereas others may take longer (e.g., Cooper et al., 2021; see also De Jong et al., 2023).

Therapeutic Practices

- Consider adopting ROM as an evidence-based addition to psychotherapy, regardless of theoretical orientation. It provides transparency regarding patient outcomes; is viewed favorably by patients; and acts as a complement to clinician judgments of patient outcomes, particularly of deterioration.
- Remember that although the effect of ROM for all patients, on average, is small, it is additive to the general effectiveness of psychological therapies and slightly greater for patients who are NOT.
- Develop a positive attitude toward ROM because attitude is a significant factor in the success of ROM and cultivates a community of ROM champions. This supports a positive learning and implementation environment.
- Ensure that the outcome measure is both psychometrically sound and clinically practical. Therapists need to be familiar with the measure and its interpretation so that patients understand how a measure is scored, what it means, and how that information can be used to help them progress in therapy.
- Introduce ROM together with a clear rationale for its use to each patient early in the course of therapy, preferably in the first session so that the expectations are set out clearly and ROM is presented as an integral part of therapy and not an add-on.
- Engage patients in discussions about ROM with a particular emphasis on the data using teach-back methods to facilitate dialogue about the match or mismatches between the data and their psychological health.
- Take account of the clinical population and setting because ROM is not a panacea. Patients presenting with high levels of severity or cluster B personality disorders may not benefit due to the impact of repeated negative feedback. Certain clinical

settings may also limit the benefits of ROM where there is insufficient flexibility for the therapist to adapt the focus or direction of treatment.

- Administer outcome measures frequently. Although it is not essential to capture data at every session, there needs to be sufficient data density to recognize patterns of deterioration at the earliest opportunity so that treatment adaptations can be considered. Hence, if planned treatment durations are likely to be shorter, then more frequent administration of ROM is advisable (e.g., at each session).
- Frame ROM in-session activity in terms of three actionable phases: administering measures, feeding back results, and adapting therapy (where indicated). The first and second phases can apply to all patients, but the third applies only to those who are identified as NOT and when there is evidence of deterioration.
- Use a graph to show progress to patients because visualization enables them to have a better understanding of the overall concept of ROM as well as connect data with possible treatment options. Use a computer program that will generate expected treatment curves if available; if not, using graphs generated by Excel can be informative. The use of expected treatment curves also results in lower deterioration rates.
- Use ROM to adjust treatment when patients are NOT in terms of their predicted outcomes or when outcome measures are showing patient deterioration.
- Supplement ROM with clinical support tools, particularly for NOT patients, because these have consistently yielded the largest effects in research on ROM. These provide therapists with a clinical focus to address potential reasons for a lack of progress or deterioration.
- Implement training in ROM for therapists because this enhances reduction in patient deterioration rates. Active models of training involving role-plays and deliberate practice are likely to enhance the interactive components of ROM above and beyond passive knowledge acquisition. Provision of ROM training for the trainers (i.e., supervisors) is an important component.
- Provide sufficient time and resources to support the adoption of ROM. The time taken to implement ROM will depend on the specific stated aims of the project, the resources available to support it, and the compliance of all stakeholders involved.
- Consider culturally appropriate adaptations to the content or processes of ROM to ensure that it does not disadvantage culturally diverse populations.
- Identify and address obstacles to successful implementation of ROM before attempting to initiate it.

References

Ægisdóttir, S., White, M. J., Spengler, P. M., Maugherman, A. S., Anderson, L. A., Cook, R. S., Nichols, C. N., Lampropoulos, G. K., Walker, B. S., Cohen, G., & Rush, J. D. (2006). The Meta-Analysis of Clinical Judgment Project: Fifty-six years of accumulated research on clinical versus statistical prediction. *The Counseling Psychologist*, *34*(3), 341–382. https://doi.org/10.1177%2F0011000005285875

American Psychological Association, Presidential Task Force on Evidence-Based Practice. (2006). Evidence-based practice in psychology. *American Psychologist*, *61*(4), 271–285. https://doi.org/10.1037/0003-066X.61.4.271

Anker, M. G., Duncan, B. L., & Sparks, J. A. (2009). Using client feedback to improve couple therapy outcomes: A randomized clinical trial in a naturalistic setting. *Journal of Consulting and Clinical Psychology*, *77*(4), 693–704. https://doi.org/10.1037/a0016062

Ashworth, M., Shepherd, M., Christey, J., Matthews, V., Wright, K., Parmentier, H., Robinson, S., & Godfrey, E. (2004). A client-generated psychometric instrument: The development of "PSYCHLOPS." *Counselling & Psychotherapy Research*, *4*(2), 27–31. https://doi.org/10.1080/14733140412331383913

Baldwin, S. A., & Imel, Z. (2013). Therapist effects: Findings and methods. In M. J. Lambert (Ed.), *Bergin and Garfield's handbook of psychotherapy and behavior change* (6th ed., pp. 258–296). Wiley.

Barber, J., & Resnick, S. G. (2022). Collect, Share, Act: A transtheoretical clinical model for doing measurement-based care in mental health treatment. *Psychological Services*. Advance online publication. https://doi.org/10.1037/ser0000629

Barkham, M., & Lambert, M. J. (2021). The efficacy and effectiveness of psychological therapies. In M. Barkham, W. Lutz, & L. G. Castonguay (Eds.), *Bergin and Garfield's handbook of psychotherapy and behavior change* (7th ed., pp. 135–189). Wiley.

Barkham, M., Mellor-Clark, J., & Stiles, W. B. (2015). A CORE approach to progress monitoring and feedback: Enhancing evidence and improving practice. *Psychotherapy*, *52*(4), 402–411. https://doi.org/10.1037/pst0000030

Bear, H. A., Dalzell, K., Edbrooke-Childs, J., & Wolpert, M. (2022). Applying behaviour change theory to understand the barriers to implementing routine outcome monitoring. *British Journal of Clinical Psychology*, *61*(3), 557–578. https://doi.org/10.1111/bjc.12322

Beidas, R. S., Cross, W., & Dorsey, S. (2014). Show me, don't tell me: Behavioral rehearsal as a training and analogue fidelity tool. *Cognitive and Behavioral Practice*, *21*, 1–11. http://dx.doi.org/10.1016/j.cbpra.2013.04.002

Bergin, A. E. (1963). The effects of psychotherapy: Negative results revisited. *Journal of Counseling Psychology*, *10*, 224–250.

Bergman, H., Kornør, H., Nikolakopoulou, A., Hanssen-Bauer, K., Soares-Weiser, K., Tollefsen, T. K., & Bjørndal, A. (2018). Client feedback in psychological therapy for children and adolescents with mental health problems. *Cochrane Database of Systematic Reviews*, *8*, CD011729. https://doi.org/10.1002/14651858.CD011729.pub2

Berking, M., Orth, U., & Lutz, W. (2006). How effective is systematic feedback of treatment progress to the therapist? An empirical study in a cognitive–behavioural-oriented inpatient setting. *Zeitschrift fur Klinische Psychologie und Psychotherapie*, *35*, 21–29. https://doi.org/10.1026/1616-3443.35.1.21

Bertolino, B., & Miller, S. D. (2012). *ICCE manuals on feedback-informed treatment* (Vols. 1–6). ICCE Press.

Bickman, L. (2008). A measurement feedback system (MFS) is necessary to improve mental health outcomes. *Journal of the American Academy of Child and Adolescent Psychiatry*, *47*(10), 1114–1119. https://doi.org/10.1097/CHI.0b013e3181825af8

Bjaastad, J. F., Jensen-Doss, A., Moltu, C., Jakobsen, P., Hagenberg, H., & Joa, I. (2019). Attitudes toward standardized assessment tools and their use among clinicians in a public mental health service. *Nordic Journal of Psychiatry*, *73*(7), 387–396. https://doi.org/10.1080/08039488.2019.1642383

Bone, C., Simmonds-Buckley, M., Thwaites, R., Sandford, D., Merzhvynska, M., Rubel, J., Deisenhofer, A. K., Lutz, W., & Delgadillo, J. (2021). Dynamic prediction of psychological treatment outcomes: Development and validation of a prediction model using routinely collected symptom data. *Lancet Digital Health*, *3*(4), e231–e240. https://doi.org/10.1016/S2589-7500(21)00018-2

Börjesson, S., & Boström, P. K. (2020). "I want to know what it is used for": Clients' perspectives on completing a routine outcome measure (ROM) while undergoing psychotherapy. *Psychotherapy Research*, *30*(3), 337–347. https://doi.org/10.1080/10503307.2019.1630780

Boswell, J. F., Hepner, K. A., Lysell, K., Rothrock, N. E., Bott, N., Childs, A. W., Douglas, S., Owings-Fonner, N., Wright, C. V., Stephens, K. A., Bard, D. E., Aajmain, S., & Bobbitt, B. L.

(2023). The need for a measurement-based care professional practice guideline. *Psychotherapy, 60*(1), 1–16. https://doi.org/10.1037/pst0000439

Boswell, J. F., Kraus, D. R., Castonguay, L. G., & Youn, S. J. (2015). Treatment Outcome Package: Measuring and facilitating multidimensional change. *Psychotherapy, 52*(4), 422–431. https://doi.org/10.1037/pst0000028

Boswell, J. F., Kraus, D. R., Miller, S. D., & Lambert, M. J. (2015). Implementing routine outcome monitoring in clinical practice: Benefits, challenges, and solutions. *Psychotherapy Research, 25*(1), 6–19. https://doi.org/10.1080/10503307.2013.817696

Bovendeerd, B., De Jong, K., de Groot, E., Moerbeek, M., & de Keijser, J. (2022). Enhancing the effect of psychotherapy through systematic client feedback in outpatient mental health-care: A cluster randomized trial. *Psychotherapy Research, 32*(6), 710–722. https://doi.org/10.1080/10503307.2021.2015637

Boyce, M. B., Browne, J. P., & Greenhalgh, J. (2014). The experiences of professionals with using information from patient-reported outcome measures to improve the quality of healthcare: A systematic review of qualitative research. *BMJ Quality and Safety, 23*(6), 508–518. https://doi.org/10.1136/bmjqs-2013-002524

Brattland, H., Koksvik, J. M., Burkeland, O., Gråwe, R. W., Klöckner, C., Linaker, O. M., Ryum, T., Wampold, B., Lara-Cabrera, M. L., & Iversen, V. C. (2018). The effects of routine outcome monitoring (ROM) on therapy outcomes in the course of an implementation process: A randomized clinical trial. *Journal of Counseling Psychology, 65*(5), 641–652. https://doi.org/10.1037/cou0000286

Brooks Holliday, S., Hepner, K. A., Farmer, C. M., Mahmud, A., Kimerling, R., Smith, B. N., & Rosen, C. (2021). Discussing measurement-based care with patients: An analysis of clinician–patient dyads. *Psychotherapy Research, 31*(2), 211–223. https://doi.org/10.1080/10503307.2020.1776413

Brown, G. S., Simon, A., Cameron, J., & Minami, T. (2015). A collaborative outcome resource network (ACORN): Tools for increasing the value of psychotherapy. *Psychotherapy, 52*(4), 412–421. https://doi.org/10.1037/pst0000033

Bugatti, M., & Boswell, J. F. (2022). Clinician perceptions of nomothetic and individualized patient-reported outcome measures in measurement-based care. *Psychotherapy Research, 32*(7), 898–909. https://doi.org/10.1080/10503307.2022.2030497

Burgess, P., Pirkis, J., & Coombs T. (2015). Routine outcome measurement in Australia. *International Review of Psychiatry, 27*(4), 264–275. https://doi.org/10.3109/09540261.2014.977234

Carlier, I. V., Meuldijk, D., Van Vliet, I. M., Van Fenema, E., Van der Wee, N. J., & Zitman, F. G. (2012). Routine outcome monitoring and feedback on physical or mental health status: Evidence and theory. *Journal of Evaluation in Clinical Practice, 18*, 104–110. https://doi.org/10.1111/j.1365-2753.2010.01543.x

Castonguay, L. G., Barkham, M., Lutz, W., & McAleavy, A. (2013). Practice oriented research: Approaches and applications. In M. J. Lambert (Ed.), *Bergin and Garfield's handbook of psychotherapy and behavior change* (6th ed., pp. 85–133). Wiley.

Cheung, M. W.-L. (2014). Modeling dependent effect sizes with three-level meta-analyses: A structural equation modeling approach. *Psychological Methods, 19*(2), 211–229. https://doi.org/10.1037/a0032968

Clark, D. M. (2018). Realizing the mass public benefit of evidence-based psychological therapies: The IAPT program. *Annual Review of Clinical Psychology, 14*, 159–183. https://doi.org/10.1146/annurev-clinpsy-050817-084833

Coleman, J. J., Dong, Y., Dumas, D., Owen, J., & Kopta, M. (2022). Longitudinal measurement invariance of the Behavioral Health Measure in a clinical sample. *Journal of Counseling Psychology, 69*(1), 100–110. https://doi.org/10.1037/cou0000524

Cooper, L. D., Murphy, H. G., Delk, L. A., Fraire, M. G., Van Kirk, N., Sullivan, C. P., Waldron, J. C., Halliburton, A. E., Schiefelbein, F., & Gatto, A. (2021). Implementing routine outcome monitoring in a psychology training clinic: A case study of a process model. *Training and Education in Professional Psychology, 15*(2), 87–96. https://doi.org/10.1037/tep0000298

Cooper, M., & Xu, D. (2023). Goals Form: Reliability, validity, and clinical utility of an idiographic goal-focused measure for routine outcome monitoring in psychotherapy. *Journal of Clinical Psychology*, *79*(3), 641–666. https://doi.org/10.1002/jclp.23344

Crits-Christoph, P., Ring-Kurtz, S., Hamilton, J. L., Lambert, M. J., Gallop, R., McClure, B., Kulaga, A., & Rotrosen, J. (2012). A preliminary study of the effects of individual patient-level feedback in outpatient substance abuse treatment programs. *Journal of Substance Abuse Treatment*, *42*(3), 301–309. https://doi.org/10.1016/j.jsat.2011.09.003

Cross, S., Mellor-Clark, J., & Macdonald, J. (2015). Tracking responses to items in measures as a means of increasing therapeutic engagement in clients: A complementary clinical approach to tracking outcomes. *Clinical Psychology & Psychotherapy*, *22*(6), 698–707. https://doi.org/10.1002/cpp.1929

Davidsen, A. H., Poulsen, S., Lindschou, J., Winkel, P., Tróndarson, M. F., Waaddegaard, M., & Lau, M. (2017). Feedback in group psychotherapy for eating disorders: A randomized clinical trial. *Journal of Consulting and Clinical Psychology*, *85*(5), 484–494. https://doi.org/10.1037/ccp0000173

Davidson, K., Perry, A., & Bell, L. (2014). Would continuous feedback of patient's clinical outcomes to practitioners improve NHS psychological therapy services? Critical analysis and assessment of quality of existing studies. *Psychology and Psychotherapy: Theory, Research and Practice*, *88*(1), 21–37. https://doi.org/10.1111/papt.12032

De Jong, K., & Aafjes-van Doorn, K. (2022). Routine outcome monitoring: The need for case examples. *Journal of Clinical Psychology*, *78*(10), 1963–1972. https://doi.org/10.1002/jclp.23441

De Jong, K., Conijn, J. M., Gallagher, R., Reshetnikova, A. S., Heij, M., & Lutz, M. C. (2021). Using progress feedback to improve outcomes and reduce drop-out, treatment duration, and deterioration: A multilevel meta-analysis. *Clinical Psychology Review*, *85*, 102002. https://doi.org/10.1016/j.cpr.2021.102002

De Jong, K., Delgadillo, J., & Barkham, M. (2023). *Routine outcome monitoring and feedback in psychological therapies*. Open University Press.

De Jong, K., Segaar, J., Ingenhoven, T., van Busschbach, J., & Timman, R. (2018). Adverse effects of outcome monitoring feedback in patients with personality disorders: A randomized controlled trial in day treatment and inpatient settings. *Journal of Personality Disorders*, *32*(3). https://doi.org/10.1521/pedi_2017_31_297

De Jong, K., van Sluis, P., Nugter, M. A., Heiser, W. J., & Spinhoven, P. (2012). Understanding the differential impact of outcome monitoring: Therapist variables that moderate feedback effects in a randomized clinical trial. *Psychotherapy Research*, *22*(4), 464–474. https://doi.org/10.1080/10503307.2012.673023

Delespaul, P. A. E. G. (2015). Routine outcome measurement in the Netherlands—A focus on benchmarking. *International Review of Psychiatry*, *27*(4), 320–328. https://doi.org/10.3109/09540261.2015.1045408

Delgadillo, J., Deisenhofer, A. K., Probst, T., Shimokawa, K., Lambert, M. J., & Kleinstäuber, M. (2022). Progress feedback narrows the gap between more and less effective therapists: A therapist effects meta-analysis of clinical trials. *Journal of Consulting and Clinical Psychology*, *90*(7), 559–567. https://doi.org/10.1037/ccp0000747

Delgadillo, J., De Jong, K., Lucock, M., Lutz, W., Rubel, J., Gilbody, S., Ali, S., Aguirre, E., Appleton, M., Nevin, J., O'Hayon, H., Patel, U., Sainty, A., Spencer, P., & McMillan, D. (2018). Feedback-informed treatment versus usual psychological treatment for depression and anxiety: A multisite, open-label, cluster randomised controlled trial. *Lancet Psychiatry*, *5*(7), 564–572. https://doi.org/10.1016/S2215-0366(18)30162-7

Delgadillo, J., McMillan, D., Gilbody, S., De Jong, K., Lucock, M., Lutz, W., Rubel, J., Aguirre, E., & Ali, S. (2021). Cost-effectiveness of feedback-informed psychological treatment: Evidence from the IAPT-FIT trial. *Behaviour Research and Therapy*, *142*, 103873. https://doi.org/10.1016/j.brat.2021.103873

Drapeau, M. (2012). Ten tools for progress monitoring in psychotherapy. *Integrating Science and Practice*, *2*, 1–45. https://www.mcgill.ca/psy/files/psy/10_tools_pdf_final.pdf

Drew, P., Irvine, A., Barkham, M., Faija, C., Gellatly, J., Ardern, K., Armitage, J. C., Brooks, H., Rushton, K., Welsh, C., Bower, P., & Bee, P. (2021). Telephone delivery of psychological interventions: Balancing protocol with patient-centred care. *Social Science & Medicine, 277*, 113818. https://doi.org/10.1016/j.socscimed.2021.113818

Duncan, B. L., Miller, S. D., Sparks, J., Claud, D., Reynolds, L., Brown, J., & Johnson, L. (2003). The Session Rating Scale: Preliminary psychometric properties of a "working" alliance measure. *Journal of Brief Therapy, 3*(1), 3–12.

Duncan, B. L., & Reese, R. J. (2015). The Partners for Change Outcome Management System (PCOMS): Revisiting the client's frame of reference. *Psychotherapy, 52*, 391–401. https://doi.org/10.1037/pst0000026

Edbrooke-Childs, J., Wolpert, M., & Deighton, J. (2016). Using Patient Reported Outcome Measures to Improve Service Effectiveness (UPROMISE): Training clinicians to use outcome measures in child mental health. *Administration and Policy in Mental Health, 43*(3), 302–308. https://doi.org/10.1007/s10488-014-0600-2

Egger, M., Smith, G. D., Schneider, M., & Minder, C. (1997). Bias in meta-analysis detected by a simple, graphical test. *BMJ, 315*(7109), 629–634. https://doi.org/10.1136/bmj.315.7109.629

Emmelkamp, P. M., David, D., Beckers, T., Muris, P., Cuijpers, P., Lutz, W., Andersson, G., Araya, R., Banos Rivera, R. M., Barkham, M., Berking, M., Berger, T., Botella, C., Carlbring, P., Colom, F., Essau, C., Hermans, D., Hofmann, S. G., Knappe, S., . . . Vervliet, B. (2014). Advancing psychotherapy and evidence-based psychological interventions. *International Journal of Methods in Psychiatric Research, 23*(Suppl. 1), 58–91. https://doi.org/10.1002/mpr.1411

Errázuriz, P., & Zilcha-Mano, S. (2018). In psychotherapy with severe patients discouraging news may be worse than no news: The impact of providing feedback to therapists on psychotherapy outcome, session attendance, and the alliance. *Journal of Consulting and Clinical Psychology, 86*(2), 125–139. https://doi.org/10.1037/ccp0000277

Faija, C. L., Bee, P., Lovell, K., Lidbetter, N., Gellatly, J., Ardern, K., Rushton, K., Brooks, H., McMillan, D., Armitage, C. J., Woodhouse, R., & Barkham, M. (2022). Using routine outcome measures as clinical process tools: Maximising the therapeutic yield in the IAPT programme when working remotely. *Psychology and Psychotherapy: Theory, Research and Practice, 95*(3), 820–837. https://doi.org/10.1111/papt.12400

Finch, A. E., Lambert, M. J., & Schaalje, B. G. (2001). Psychotherapy quality control: The statistical generation of expected recovery curves for integration into an early warning system. *Clinical Psychology and Psychotherapy, 52*, 391–401. https://doi.org/10.1037/pst0000026

Furukawa, T. A., & Leucht, S. (2011). How to obtain NNT from Cohen's d: Comparison of two methods. *PLoS ONE, 6*(4), e19070. https://doi.org/10.1371/journal.pone.0019070

Goldberg, S. B., Rousmaniere, T., Miller, S. D., Whipple, J., Nielsen, S. L., Hoyt, W. T., & Wampold, B. E. (2016). Do psychotherapists improve with time and experience? A longitudinal analysis of outcomes in a clinical setting. *Journal of Counseling Psychology, 63*(1), 1–11. https://doi.org/10.1037/cou0000131

Gondek, D., Edbrooke-Childs, J., Fink, E., Deighton, J., & Wolpert, M. (2016). Feedback from outcome measures and treatment effectiveness, treatment efficiency, and collaborative practice: A systematic review. *Administration and Policy in Mental Health and Mental Health Services Research, 43*(3), 325–343. https://doi.org/10.1007/s10488-015-0710-5

Greenhalgh, J., Gooding, K., Gibbons, E., Dalkin, S., Wright, J., Valderas, J., & Black, N. (2018). How do patient reported outcome measures (PROMs) support clinician–patient communication and patient care? A realist synthesis. *Journal of Patient-Reported Outcomes, 2*, Article 42. https://doi.org/10.1186/s41687-018-0061-6

Gual-Montolio, P., Martínez-Borba, V., Bretón-López, J. M., Osma, J., & Suso-Ribera, C. (2020). How are information and communication technologies supporting routine outcome monitoring and measurement-based care in psychotherapy? A systematic review. *International Journal of Environmental Research and Public Health, 17*(9), 3170. https://doi.org/10.3390/ijerph17093170

Hannan, C., Lambert, M. J., Harmon, C., Nielsen, S. L., Smart, D. W., Shimokawa, K., & Sutton, S. W. (2005). A lab test and algorithms for identifying clients at risk for treatment failure. *Journal of Clinical Psychology, 61*, 155–163. https://doi.org/10.1002/jclp.20108

Harmon, C. S., Lambert, M. J., Smart, D. M., Hawkins, E., Nielsen, S. L., Slade, K., & Lutz, W. (2007). Enhancing outcome for potential treatment failures: Therapist–client feedback and clinical support tools. *Psychotherapy Research, 17*(4), 379–392. https://doi.org/10.1080/10503300600702331

Hepner, K. A., Farmer, C. M., Brooks Holliday, S., Bharil, S., Kimerling, R. E., McGee-Vincent, P., McCaslin, S. E., & Rosen, C. (2019). *Displaying behavioral health measurement-based care data: Identifying key features from clinician and patient perspectives.* RAND. https://www.rand.org/pubs/research_reports/RR3078.html

Herold, D. M., Parsons, C. K., & Fedor, D. B. (1997). *Individual feedback propensities and their effects on motivation, training success and performance.* U.S. Army Research Institute for the Behavioral and Social Sciences.

Herold, D. M., Parsons, C. K., & Rensvold, R. B. (1996). Individual differences in the generation and processing of performance feedback. *Educational and Psychological Measurement, 56*(1), 5–25.

Higgins, J. P. T., Savović, J., Page, M. J., Elbers, R. G., & Sterne, J. A. C. (2020). Assessing risk of bias in a randomized trial. In J. P. T. Higgins, J. Thomas, J. Chandler, M. Cumpston, T. Li, M. J. Page, & V. A. Welch (Eds.), *Cochrane handbook for systematic reviews of interventions* (version 6.1, updated September 2020). Cochrane. https://training.cochrane.org/handbook

Hilhorst, L., Stappen, J. V., Lokkerbol, J., Hiligsmann, M., Risseeuw, A. H., & Tiemens, B. G. (2022). Patients' and psychologists' preferences for feedback reports on expected mental health treatment outcomes: A discrete-choice experiment. *Administration and Policy in Mental Health, 49*, 707–721. https://doi.org/10.1007/s10488-022-01194-2

Hofmann, S. G., & Kashdan, T. B. (2010). The Affective Style Questionnaire: Development and psychometric properties. *Journal of Psychopathology and Behavioral Assessment, 32*(2), 255–263. https://doi.org/10.1007/s10862-009-9142-4

Hollenbeck, J. R., & Klein, H. J. (1987). Goal commitment and the goal-setting process: Problems, prospects, and proposals for future research. *Journal of Applied Psychology, 72*, 212–220.

Howard, K. I., Moras, K., Brill, P. L., Martinovich, Z., & Lutz, W. (1996). Evaluation of psychotherapy: Efficacy, effectiveness, and patient progress. *American Psychologist, 51*(10), 1059–1064. https://doi.org/10.1037//0003-066x.51.10.1059

Jacobson, N. S., & Truax, P. (1991). Clinical significance: A statistical approach to defining meaningful change in psychotherapy research. *Journal of Consulting and Clinical Psychology, 59*, 12–19. https://doi.org/10.1037/0022-006X.59.1.12

Janse, P. D., De Jong, K., Veerkamp, C., van Dijk, M. K., Hutschemaekers, G., & Verbraak, M. (2020). The effect of feedback-informed cognitive behavioral therapy on treatment outcome: A randomized controlled trial. *Journal of Consulting and Clinical Psychology, 88*(9), 818–828. https://doi.org/10.1037/ccp0000549

Jensen-Doss, A., Haimes, E. M. B., Smith, A. M., Lyon, A. R., Lewis, C. C., Stanick, C. F., & Hawley, K. M. (2018). Monitoring treatment progress and providing feedback is viewed favorably but rarely used in practice. *Administration and Policy in Mental Health and Mental Health Services Research, 45*(1), 48–61. https://doi.org/10.1007/s10488-016-0763-0

Johns, R. G., Barkham, M., Kellett, S., & Saxon, D. (2019). A systematic review of therapist effects: A critical narrative update and refinement to review. *Clinical Psychology Review, 67*, 78–93. https://doi.org/10.1016/j.cpr.2018.08.004

Keetharuth, A. D., Brazier, J, Connell, J., Bjorner, J. B., Carlton, J., Taylor Buck, E., Ricketts, T., McKendrick, K., Browne, J., Croudace, T., & Barkham, M., on behalf of the ReQoL Scientific Group. (2018). Recovering Quality of Life (ReQoL): A new generic self-reported outcome measure for use with people experiencing mental health difficulties. *British Journal of Psychiatry, 212*, 42–49.

Kendrick, T., El-Gohary, M., Stuart, B., Gilbody, S., Churchill, R., Aiken, L., Bhattacharya, A., Gimson, A., Brütt, A. L., De Jong, K., & Moore, M. (2016). Routine use of patient reported outcome measures (PROMs) for improving treatment of common mental health disorders in adults. *Cochrane Database of Systematic Reviews, 7*(7), CD011119. https://doi.org/10.1002/14651858.CD011119.pub2

Knapstad, M., Nordgreen, T., & Smith, O. R. (2018). Prompt mental health care, the Norwegian version of IAPT: Clinical outcomes and predictors of change in a multicenter cohort study. *BMC Psychiatry*, *18*(1), 1–16. https://doi.org/10.1186/s12888-018-1838-0

Knaup, C., Koesters, M., Schoefer, D., Becker, T., & Puschner, B. (2009). Effect of feedback of treatment outcome in specialist mental healthcare: Meta-analysis. *British Journal of Psychiatry*, *195*, 15–22. https://doi.org/10.1192/bjp.bp.108.053967

Kopta, M., Owen, J., & Budge, S. (2015). Measuring psychotherapy outcomes with the Behavioral Health Measure–20: Efficient and comprehensive. *Psychotherapy*, *52*(4), 442–448. https://doi.org/10.1037/pst0000035

Koslofsky, S., & Rodíguez, M. M. D. (2017). Cultural adaptations to psychotherapy: Real-world applications. *Clinical Case Studies*, *16*(1), 3–8. https://doi.org/10.1177/1534650116668273

Kraft, M. A. (2020). Interpreting effect sizes of education interventions. *Educational Researcher*, *49*(4), 241–253. htttps://doi.org/10.3102/0013189X20912798

Krägeloh, C. U., Czuba, K. J., Billington, D. R., Kersten, P., & Siegert, R. J. (2015). Using feedback from patient-reported outcome measures in mental health services: A scoping study and typology. *Psychiatric Services*, *66*(3), 224–241. https://doi.org/10.1176/appi.ps.201400141

Lambert, M. J. (2010). *Prevention of treatment failure: The use of measuring, monitoring, & feedback in clinical practice*. American Psychological Association Press.

Lambert, M. J., Bailey, R. J., White, M., Tingey, K. M., & Stevens, E. (2015). *Clinical support tool manual (Brief Version–40)*. OQMeasures.

Lambert, M. J., Kahler, M., Harmon, C., Burlingame, G. M. Shimokawa K., & White, M. M. (2013). *Administration and scoring manual: Outcome Questionnaire OQ-45.2*. OQMeasures.

Lambert, M. J., Whipple, J. L., Hawkins, E. J., Vermeersch, D. A., Nielsen, S. L., & Smart, D. W. (2003). Is it time for clinicians to routinely track patient outcome? A meta-analysis. *Clinical Psychology: Science and Practice*, *10*(3), 288–301. https://psycnet.apa.org/doi/10.1093/clipsy.bpg025

Lambert, M. J., Whipple, J. L., & Kleinstäuber, M. (2018). Collecting and delivering progress feedback: A meta-analysis of routine outcome monitoring. *Psychotherapy*, *55*(4), 520–537. https://doi.org/10.1037/pst0000167

Lambert, M. J., Whipple, J. L., & Kleinstäuber, M. (2019). Collecting and delivering client feedback. In J. C. Norcross & M. J. Lambert (Eds.), *Relationships that work* (3rd ed., pp. 580–630). Oxford University Press.

Lambert, M. J., Whipple, J. L., Smart, D. W., Vermeersch, D. A., Nielsen, S. L., & Hawkins, E. J. (2001). The effects of providing therapists with feedback on client progress during psychotherapy: Are outcomes enhanced? *Psychotherapy Research*, *11*, 49–68. https://doi.org/10.1093/ptr/11.1.49

Lambert, M. J., Whipple, J. L., Vermeersch, D. A., Smart, D. W., Hawkins, E. J., Nielsen, S. L., & Goates, M. (2002). Enhancing psychotherapy outcomes via providing feedback on client progress: A replication. *Clinical Psychology & Psychotherapy*, *9*(2), 91–103. https://doi.org/10.1002/cpp.324

Langkaas, T. F., Wampold, B. E., & Hoffart, A. (2018). Five types of clinical difference to monitor in practice. *Psychotherapy*, *55*(3), 241–254. https://doi.org/10.1037/pst0000194

Lewis, C. C., Boyd, M., Puspitasari, A., Navarro, E., Howard, J., Kassab, H., Hoffman, M., Scott, K., Lyon, A., Douglas, S., Simon, G., & Kroenke, K. (2019). Implementing measurement-based care in behavioral health: A review. *JAMA Psychiatry*, *76*(3), 324–335. https://doi.org/10.1001/jamapsychiatry.2018.3329

Lucock, M., Halstead, J., Leach, C., Barkham, M., Tucker, S., Randall, C., Lloyd, J., Khan, W., Catlow, H., Waters, E., & Saxon, D. (2015). A mixed method investigation of patient monitoring and feedback in routine practice: Barriers and facilitators. *Psychotherapy Research*, *25*(6), 633–646. https://doi.org/10.1080/10503307.2015.1051163

Lutz, W., Böhnke, J. R., & Köck, K. (2011). Lending an ear to feedback systems: Evaluation of recovery and non-response in psychotherapy in a German outpatient setting. *Community Mental Health Journal*, *47*(3), 311–317. https://doi.org/10.1007/s10597-010-9307-3

Lutz, W., Deisenhofer, A.-K., Rubel, J., Bennemann, B., Giesemann, J., Poster, K., & Schwartz, B. (2022). Prospective evaluation of a clinical decision support system in psychological therapy. *Journal of Consulting and Clinical Psychology, 90*(1), 90–106. https://doi.org/10.1037/ccp0000642

Lutz, W., Deisenhofer, A.-K., Weinmann-Lutz, B., & Barkham, M. (2023). Data and feedback-informed clinical training and practice. In L. G. Castonguay & C. E. Hill (Eds.), *Becoming better therapists: Advancing training and supervision in psychotherapy*. American Psychological Association.

Lutz, W., De Jong, K., Rubel, J. A., & Delgadillo, J. (2021). Measuring, predicting, and tracking change in psychotherapy. In M. Barkham, W. Lutz, & L. G. Castonguay (Eds.), *Bergin and Garfield's handbook of psychotherapy and behavior change* (7th ed., pp. 89–133). Wiley.

Lutz, W., Leach, C., Barkham, M, Lucock, M., Stiles, W. B., Evans, C., Noble, R., & Iveson, S. (2005). Predicting change for individual psycho therapy clients on the basis of nearest neighbors. *Journal of Consulting and Clinical Psychology, 73*(5), 904–913. https://doi.org/10/1037/0022-006X.73.5.904

Lutz, W., Martinovich, Z., & Howard, K. I. (1999). Patient profiling: An application of random coefficient regression models to depicting the response of a patient to outpatient psychotherapy. *Journal of Consulting and Clinical Psychology, 67*(4), 571–577. https://doi.org/10.1037//0022-006x.67.4.571

Lutz, W., Martinovich, Z., Howard, K. I., & Leon, S. C. (2002). Outcomes management, expected treatment response, and severity-adjusted provider profiling in outpatient psychotherapy. *Journal of Clinical Psychology, 58*(10), 1291–1304. https://doi.org/10.1002/jclp.10070

Lutz, W., Rubel, J., Deisenhofer, A. K., & Moggia, D. (2022). Continuous outcome measurement in modern data-informed psychotherapies. *World Psychiatry, 21*(2), 215–216. https://doi.org/10.1002/wps.20988

Lutz, W., Rubel, J., Schiefele, A. K., Zimmermann, D., Böhnke, J. R., & Wittmann, W. W. (2015). Feedback and therapist effects in the context of treatment outcome and treatment length. *Psychotherapy Research, 25*(6), 647–660. https://doi.org/10.1080/10503307.2015.1053553

Lutz, W., Rubel, J. A., Schwartz, B., Schilling, V., & Deisenhofer, A.-K. (2019). Towards integrating personalized feedback research into clinical practice: Development of the Trier Treatment Navigator (TTN). *Behaviour Research and Therapy, 120*, 103438. https://doi.org/10.1016/j.brat.2019.103438

Lutz, W., Schwartz, B., & Delgadillo, J. (2022). Measurement-based and data-informed psychological therapy. *Annual Review of Clinical Psychology, 18*, 71–98. https://doi.org/10.1146/annurev-clinpsy-071720-014821

Mackrill, T., & Sørensen, K. M. (2020) Implementing routine outcome measurement in psychosocial interventions—A systematic review. *European Journal of Social Work, 23*(5), 790–808. https://doi.org/10.1080/13691457.2019.1602029

Marks, I. (1998). Overcoming obstacles to routine outcome measurement: The nuts and bolts of implementing clinical audit. *British Journal of Psychiatry, 173*, 281–286. https://doi.org/10.1192/bjp.173.4.281

McAleavey, A. A., Nordberg, S. S., & Moltu, C. (2021). Initial quantitative development of the Norse Feedback system: A novel clinical feedback system for routine mental healthcare. *Quality of Life Research, 30*(11), 3097–3115. https://doi.org/10.1007/s11136-021-02825-1

Meehl, P. E. (1954). *Clinical versus statistical prediction: A theoretical analysis and a review of the evidence*. University of Minnesota Press.

Mellor-Clark, J., Cross, S., Macdonald, J., & Skjulsvik, T. (2016). Leading horses to water: Lessons from a decade of helping psychological therapy services use routine outcome measurement to improve practice. *Administration and Policy in Mental Health, 43*(3), 279–285. https://doi.org/10.1007/s10488-014-0587-8

Metz, M. J., Veerbeek, M. A., Twisk, J. W. R., van der Feltz-Cornelis, C. M., de Beurs, E., & Beekman, A. T. F. (2019). Shared decision-making in mental health care using routine outcome monitoring: Results of a cluster randomised-controlled trial. *Social Psychiatry and Psychiatric Epidemiology, 54*(2), 209–219. https://doi.org/10.1007/s00127-018-1589-8

Miller, S. D., Duncan, B. L., Brown, J., Sparks, J., & Claud, D. (2003). The Outcome Rating Scale: A preliminary study of the reliability, validity, and feasibility of a brief visual analog measure. *Journal of Brief Therapy, 2*, 91–100.

Miller, S. D., Hubble, M. A., Chow, D., & Seidel, J. (2015). Beyond measures and monitoring: Realizing the potential of feedback-informed treatment. *Psychotherapy, 52*(4), 449–457. https://doi.org/10.1037/pst0000031

Moltu, C., McAleavey, A. A., Helleseth, M. M., Møller, G. H., & Nordberg, S. S. (2021). How therapists and patients need to develop a clinical feedback system after 18 months of use in a practice–research network: A qualitative study. *International Journal of Mental Health Systems, 15*(1), Article 43. https://doi.org/10.1186/s13033-021-00465-z

Mütze, K., Witthöft, M., Lutz, W., & Bräscher, A. K. (2022). Matching research and practice: Prediction of individual patient progress and dropout risk for basic routine outcome monitoring. *Psychotherapy Research, 32*(3), 358–371. https://doi.org/10.1080/10503307.2021.1930244

Nakagawa, S., & Santos, E. S. A. (2012). Methodological issues and advances in biological meta-analysis. *Evolutionary Ecology, 26*(5), 1253–1274.

Nilsen, P. (2015). Making sense of implementation theories, models and frameworks. *Implementation Science, 10*, Article 53. https://doi.org/10.1186/s13012-015-0242-0

Nilsen, P., & Birken, S. A. (Eds.). (2020). *Handbook on implementation science*. Elgar.

Nugter, M. A., De Jong, K., & Kortrijk, H. E. (2013). Meten van veranderingen bij patiënten. In V. J. A. Buwalda, M. A. Nugter, W. van Tilburg, & A. T. F. Beekman (Eds.), *Praktijkboek ROM in de ggz II: Implementatie en gebruik bij verschillende doelgroepen* (pp. 149–164). De Tijdstroom.

Ogles, B. M., Goates-Jones, M. K., & Erekson, D. M. (2022). Treatment success or failure? Using a narrative interview to supplement ROM. *Journal of Clinical Psychology, 78*(10), 1986–2001. https://doi.org/10.1002/jclp.23345

Østergård, O. K., Randa, H., & Hougaard, E. (2020). The effect of using the Partners for Change Outcome Management System as feedback tool in psychotherapy—A systematic review and meta-analysis. *Psychotherapy Research, 30*(2), 195–212. https://doi.org/10.1080/10503307.2018.1517949

Parker, Z. J., & Waller, G. (2015). Factors related to psychotherapists' self-assessment when treating anxiety and other disorders. *Behaviour Research and Therapy, 66*, 1–7. https://doi.org/10.1016/j.brat.2014.12.010

Pejtersen, J. H., Viinholt, B. C. A., & Hansen, H. (2020). Feedback-informed treatment: A systematic review and meta-analysis of the Partners for Change Outcome Management System. *Journal of Counseling Psychology, 67*(6), 723–735. https://doi.org/10.1037/cou0000420

Persons, J. B., Koerner, K., Eidelman, P., Thomas, C., & Liu, H. (2016). Increasing psychotherapists' adoption and implementation of the evidence-based practice of progress monitoring. *Behaviour Research and Therapy, 76*, 24–31. https://doi.org/10.1016/j.brat.2015.11.004

Peterson, A. P., & Fagan, C. (2017). Training the next generation in routine outcome monitoring: Current practices in psychology training clinics. *Training and Education in Professional Psychology, 11*(3), 182–189. https://doi.org/10.1037/tep0000148

Pinner, D. H., & Kivlighan, D. M., III. (2018). The ethical implications and utility of routine outcome monitoring in determining boundaries of competence in practice. *Professional Psychology: Research and Practice, 49*(4), 247–254. https://doi.org/10.1037/pro0000203

Probst, T., Kleinstäuber, M., Lambert, M. J., Tritt, K., Pieh, C., Loew, T. H., Dahlbender, R. W., & Delgadillo, J. (2020). Why are some cases not on track? An item analysis of the Assessment for Signal Cases during inpatient psychotherapy. *Clinical Psychology & Psychotherapy, 27*(4), 559–566. https://doi.org/10.1002/cpp.2441

Rognstad, K., Wentzel-Larsen, T., Neumer, P.-S., & Kjøbli, J. (2023). A systematic review and meta-analysis of measurement feedback systems in treatment for common mental health disorders. *Administration and Policy in Mental Health and Mental Health Services Research, 50*, 269–282. https://doi.org/10.1007/s10488-022-01236-9

Rosenström, T. H., Mylläri, S., Malkki, V., & Saarni, S. E. (2022). Feasibility of generic, short, and easy-to-use assessment of psychological distress during psychotherapy: Longitudinal measurement invariance of CORE-10 and -OM. *Psychotherapy Research, 32*(8), 1090–1099. https://doi.org/10.1080/10503307.2022.2074807

Rousmaniere, T. (2017). *Deliberate practice for psychotherapists: A guide to improving clinical effectiveness*. Routledge.

Rye, M., Rognmo, K, Aarons, G. A., & Skre, I. (2019). Attitudes towards the use of routine outcome monitoring of psychological therapies among mental health providers: The EBPAS-ROM. *Administration and Policy in Mental Health, 46*(6), 833–846. https://doi.org/10.1007/s10488-019-00968-5

Sales, C., Ashworth, M., Ayis, S., Barkham, M., Edbrooke-Childs, J., Faísca, L., Jacob, J., Xu, D., & Cooper, M. (2023). Idiographic patient reported outcome measures (I-PROMs) for routine outcome monitoring in psychological therapies: Position paper. *Journal of Clinical Psychology, 79*(3), 596–621. https://doi.org/10.1002/jclp.23319

Sapyta, J., Riemer, M., & Bickman, L. (2005). Feedback to clinicians: Theory, research, and practice. *Journal of Clinical Psychology, 61*(2), 145–153. https://doi.org/10.1002/jclp.20107

Schilling, V. N. L. S., Zimmermann, D., Rubel, J. A., Boyle, K. S., & Lutz, W. (2021). Why do patients go off track? Examining potential influencing factors for being at risk of psychotherapy treatment failure. *Quality of Life Research, 30*, 3287–3298. https://doi.org/10.1007/s11136-020-02664-6

Schöttke, H., Unrath, M., & Uhlmann, C. (2020). The effect of patient progress feedback on psychotherapy outcome. *Verhaltenstherapie, 30*(3). https://doi.org/10.1159/000503765

Schuman, D. L., Slone, N. C., Reese, R. J., & Duncan, B. (2015). Efficacy of client feedback in group psychotherapy with soldiers referred for substance abuse treatment. *Psychotherapy Research, 25*(4), 396–407. https://doi.org/10.1080/10503307.2014.900875

She, Z., Duncan, B. L., Reese, R. J., Sun, Q., Shi, Y., Jiang, G., Wu, C., & Clements, A. L. (2018). Client feedback in China: A randomized clinical trial in a college counseling center. *Journal of Counseling Psychology, 65*(6), 727–737. https://doi.org/10.1037/cou0000300

Shimokawa, K., Lambert, M. J., & Smart, D. W. (2010). Enhancing treatment outcome of patients at risk of treatment failure: Meta-analytic and mega-analytic review of a psychotherapy quality assurance system. *Journal of Consulting and Clinical Psychology, 78*, 298–311. https://doi.org/10.1037/a0019247

Simon, W., Lambert, M. J., Busath, G., Vazquez, A., Berkeljon, A., Hyer, K., Granley, M., & Berrett, M. (2013). Effects of providing patient progress feedback and clinical support tools to psychotherapists in an inpatient eating disorders treatment program: A randomized controlled study. *Psychotherapy Research, 23*(3), 287–300. https://doi.org/10.1080/10503307.2013.787497

Slade, K., Lambert, M. J., Harmon, S. C., Smart, D. W., & Bailey, R. (2008). Improving psychotherapy outcome: The use of immediate electronic feedback and revised clinical support tools. *Clinical Psychology & Psychotherapy, 15*(5), 287–303. https://doi.org/10.1002/cpp.594

Slone, N. C., Reese, R. J., Mathews-Duvall, S., & Kodet, J. (2015). Evaluating the efficacy of client feedback in group psychotherapy. *Group Dynamics, 19*, 122–136. https://doi.org/10.1037/gdn0000026

Solstad, S. M., Castonguay, L. G., & Moltu, C. (2019). Patients' experiences with routine outcome monitoring and clinical feedback systems: A systematic review and synthesis of qualitative empirical literature. *Psychotherapy Research, 29*(2), 157–170. https://doi.org/10.1080/10503307.2017.1326645

Solstad, S. M., Kleiven, G. S., & Moltu, C. (2021). Complexity and potentials of clinical feedback in mental health: An in-depth study of patient processes. *Quality of Life Research, 30*(11), 3117–3125. https://doi.org/10.1007/s11136-020-02550-1

Sterne, J. A., Hernán, M. A., Reeves, B. C., Savović, J., Berkman, N. D., Viswanathan, M., Henry, D., Altman, D. G., Ansari, M. T., Boutron, I., Carpenter, J. R., Chan, A. W., Churchill, R., Deeks, J. J., Hróbjartsson, A., Kirkham, J., Jüni, P., Loke, Y. K., Pigott, T. D., . . . Higgins, J. P. (2016). ROBINS-I: A tool for assessing risk of bias in non-randomised studies of interventions. *BMJ, 355*, i4919. https://doi.org/10.1136/bmj.i4919

Sun, Q., Wu, C., Wang, C., Yu, L., She, Z., & Falkenström, F. (2021). Alliance–outcome relation and progress feedback: Secondary data analyses of a randomized clinical trial study in China. *Psychotherapy Research, 31*(2), 145–156. https://doi.org/10.1080/10503307.2020.1772517

Swift, J. K., Callahan, J. L., Rousmaniere, T. G., Whipple, J. L., Dexter, K., & Wrape, E. R. (2015). Using client outcome monitoring as a tool for supervision. *Psychotherapy, 52*(2), 180–184. https://doi.org/10.1037/a0037659

Talib, T. L., DeChant, P., Kean, J., Monahan, P. O., Haggstrom, D. A., Stout, M. E., & Kroenke, K. (2018). A qualitative study of patients' perceptions of the utility of patient-reported outcome measures of symptoms in primary care clinics. *Quality of Life Research, 27*(12), 3157–3166. https://doi.org/10.1007/s11136-018-1968-3

Tam, H. E., & Ronan, K. (2017). The application of a feedback-informed approach in psychological service with youth: Systematic review and meta-analysis. *Clinical Psychology Review, 55*, 41–55. https://doi.org/10.1016/j.cpr.2017.04.005

Tasca, G. A., Angus, L., Bonli, R., Drapeau, M., Fitzpatrick, M., Hunsley, J., & Knoll, M. (2019). Outcome and progress monitoring in psychotherapy: Report of a Canadian Psychological Association task force. *Canadian Psychology, 60*(3), 165–177. https://doi.org/10.1037/0022-006X.73.5.904

The Joint Commission. (2018, February 6). *R_3 report: Requirement, rationale, reference.* https://www.jointcommission.org/-/media/tjc/documents/standards/r3-reports/r3_13_outcome_measures_1_30_18_final.pdf

Thew, G., Fountain, L., & Salkovskis, P. (2015). Service user and clinician perspectives on the use of outcome measures in psychological therapy. *The Cognitive Behaviour Therapist, 8*, e23. https://doi.org/10.1017/S1754470X15000598

Tzur Bitan, D., Ganor, O., Biran, L., & Bloch, Y. (2018). Implementing routine outcome monitoring in public mental health services in Israel: Shared and unique challenges. *Journal of Evaluation in Clinical Practice, 24*, 323–330. https://doi.org/10.1111/jep.12839

van Oenen, F. J., Schipper, S., Van, R., Schoevers, R., Visch, I., Peen, J., & Dekker, J. (2016). Feedback-informed treatment in emergency psychiatry: A randomised controlled trial. *BMC Psychiatry, 16*(1), Article 110. https://doi.org/10.1186/s12888-016-0811-z

van Sonsbeek, M. A. M. S., Hutschemaekers, G. J. M., Veerman, J. W., Vermulst, A., Kleinjan, M., & Tiemens, B. G. (2021). Challenges in investigating the effective components of feedback from routine outcome monitoring (ROM) in youth mental health care. *Child & Youth Care Forum, 50*(2), 307–332. https://doi.org/10.1007/s10566-020-09574-1

Van Wert, M. J., Malik, M., Memel, B., Moore, R., Buccino, D., Hackerman, F., Kumari, S., Everett, A., & Narrow W. (2021). Provider perceived barriers and facilitators to integrating routine outcome monitoring into practice in an urban community psychiatry clinic: A mixed-methods quality improvement project. *Journal of Evaluation and Clinical Practice, 27*(4), 767–775. https://doi.org/10.1111/jep.13457

Walfish, S., McAlister, B., O'Donnell, P., & Lambert, M. J. (2012). An investigation of self-assessment bias in mental health providers. *Psychological Reports, 110*(2), 639–644. https://doi.org/10.2466/02.07.17.PR0.110.2.639-644

Whipple, J. L., Lambert, M. J., Vermeersch, D. A., Smart, D. W., Nielsen, S. L., & Hawkins, E. J. (2003). Improving the effects of psychotherapy: The use of early identification of treatment and problem-solving strategies in routine practice. *Journal of Counseling Psychology, 50*(1), 59–68. https://doi.org/10.1037/0022-0167.50.1.59

White, M. M., Lambert, M. J., Ogles, B. M., Mclaughlin, S. B., Bailey, R. J., & Tingey, K. M. (2015). Using the Assessment for Signal Clients as a feedback tool for reducing treatment failure. *Psychotherapy Research, 25*(6), 724–734. https://doi.org/10.1080/10503307.2015.1009862

Winkeljohn Black, S., Owen, J., Chapman, N., Lavin, K., Drinane, J. M., & Kuo, P. (2017). Feedback informed treatment: An empirically supported case study of psychodynamic treatment. *Journal of Clinical Psychology, 73*(11), 1499–1509. https://doi.org/10.1002/jclp.22529

Wright, C. V., Beattie, S. G., Galper, D. I., Church, A. S., Bufka, L. F., Brabender, V. M., & Smith, B. L. (2017). Assessment practices of professional psychologists: Results of a national survey. *Professional Psychology: Research and Practice, 48*(2), 73–78. https://doi.org/10.1037/pro0000086

Wright, C. V., Goodheart, C., Bard, D., Bobbitt, B. L., Butt, Z., Lysell, K., McKay, D., & Stephens, K. (2020). Promoting measurement-based care and quality measure development: The APA mental and behavioral health registry initiative. *Psychological Services*, *17*(3), 262–270. https://doi.org/10.1037/ser0000347

Youn, S. J., Castonguay, L. G., Xiao, H., Janis, R., McAleavey, A. A., Lockard, A. J., Locke, B. D., & Hayes, J. A. (2015). The Counseling Center Assessment of Psychological Symptoms (CCAPS): Merging clinical practice, training, and research. *Psychotherapy*, *52*(4) 432–441. https://doi.org/10.1037/pst0000029

Zimmerman, M., & McGlinchey, J. B. (2008). Depressed patients' acceptability of the use of self-administered scales to measure outcome in clinical practice. *Annals of Clinical Psychiatry*, *20*(3), 125–129. https://doi.org/10.1080/10401230802177680

16

Strength-Based Methods

Christoph Flückiger, Thomas Munder, A. C. Del Re, and Nili Solomonov

Authors' Note: We thank Alan-David Mardi, Ladina Hummel, and Christophe Luder for their contributions to this meta-analysis, which was supported by grants PP00P1_1163702 and PP00P1_190083 from the Swiss Science National Foundation.

In treatments for specific disorders, the emphasis on methods to reduce symptomatology (compensation) often comes at the expense of enhancing patients' strengths, adaptive skills, and resilience (capitalization). Clients may be struggling in one domain (e.g., social withdrawal) while functioning adaptively in other domains (e.g., professional career). A skillful balance between capitalization and compensation strategies within a collaborative therapeutic relationship probably leads to optimal treatment outcomes (e.g., Cronbach & Snow, 1977; Gelso & Woodhouse, 2003). For therapists, a first step in capitalization is to systematically perceive patients' existing strengths and form hypotheses about how patients' strengths can be used in therapy. During therapy, the therapists may learn to respond to the strengths of the patients and use them as a catalyst for change.

In this chapter, we begin with the definitions of strength- and resilience-based methods in psychotherapy, its measures, existing meta-analytic evidence, and clinical examples. We provide a systematic overview of process–outcome studies that investigate in-session strength-based methods and its relation to intermediate outcomes. Furthermore, we conduct a meta-analysis to determine whether strength-based methods maximize or minimize psychotherapy efficacy under bona fide (intended to be fully therapeutic) conditions. Based on the research evidence, we conclude with potential harmful effects, diversity considerations, research limitations, training implications, and therapeutic practices.

Definitions

Strength-based methods (SBM) represent efforts to respond sensitively to the patient's strengths in psychotherapy without neglecting their sufferings. The term *strength-based methods* (also called *resilience-based*, *resource-oriented*, or *positive interventions*) refers to therapist behaviors designed to acknowledge, validate, and foster the client's strengths, capabilities, and motivational readiness for psychotherapy change. SBM are based on the premise that working with patient strengths is key to psychotherapeutic change. Attention to an individual's strengths acknowledges the richness and diversity of life. The unpleasant, unsatisfying, and disturbing parts as well as the pleasant, satisfying, functional parts of behavior are integrated into a fuller picture of mental health.

Christoph Flückiger, Thomas Munder, A. C. Del Re, and Nili Solomonov, *Strength-Based Methods* In: *Psychotherapy Skills and Methods That Work.* Edited by: Clara E. Hill and John C. Norcross, Oxford University Press. © Clara E. Hill and John C. Norcross 2023. DOI: 10.1093/oso/9780197611012.003.0016

An example of a strength is *resilience*—that is, the capacity to cope adaptively with adversity with minimal psychological suffering (e.g., Bonanno, 2021; Lee et al., 2013). Other examples of human strengths include well-being (e.g., Jepp et al., 2020; Kahneman et al., 1999; Tay & Diener, 2011), self-efficacy (Scholz et al., 2002), human agency (Bandura, 2006), resources (Hobfoll, 1989), and happiness (Helliwell et al., 2021).

Whereas mental health is often seen as a unidimensional dichotomy or continuum of psychological suffering (e.g., depression yes/no; mild, moderate, severe major depressive episode; 0–100 global assessment of functioning), a bidimensional conceptualization considers psychological strengths in addition to problems and suffering (e.g., Cacioppo et al., 2012). In this chapter, we use a bidimensional working definition of *mental health* as actively and intentionally engaging fully in life as a mainly independent quality that is not exclusively due to the absence of suffering or the absence of a mental disorder (e.g., Jankowski et al., 2020).

The broaden and build theory (Catalino & Fredrickson, 2011; Fredrickson, 2001) postulates a self-directed process of competence acquisition related to mental health. Immediate positive affect expands attention and information processing, triggering a positive feedback process through more versatile problem-solving attempts ("broaden"). In turn, physical, intellectual, and social abilities are practiced, which can lead to further competence acquisition at a later point in time ("build"). This results in a reciprocal triggering and building process between positive affect and competence building.

Neurobiological research has shown that the utilization of skills and engagement in pleasurable activities during psychotherapy may facilitate activation of the key reward regions of the brain (e.g., Solomonov et al., 2020). These regions are involved in anticipation and consumption of rewards and contribute to the experience of positive affect. Mental health conditions, such as major depression, are associated with deficits in the reward system, which in turn lead to exacerbation in psychological suffering (Ng et al., 2019). For psychotherapy, it is assumed that cumulative positive experiences reduce mood symptoms and contribute to long-term therapeutic benefits (e.g., Jankowski et al., 2020).

Strength-based psychotherapy refers to multiple treatment approaches, including positive psychotherapy (Conoley & Scheel, 2018; Parks & Schueller, 2014; Rashid & Seligman, 2019), strength-based and/or resilience-focused cognitive–behavioral therapy (CBT; e.g., Cheavens et al., 2012; Padesky & Mooney, 2012; Willutzki et al., 2004), and psychotherapy integration (e.g., Flückiger et al., 2010, 2018; Gelso & Woodhouse, 2003; Grawe, 1997; Scheel et al., 2013).

More generally, there is probably no major psychotherapy orientation in which SBM are not emphasized in some way. In CBT, some methods are designed to promote and maintain pleasant states and to elaborate on adequate therapy goals (e.g., Fava, 2016; Padesky & Mooney 2012). There are versions of psychodynamic therapy that focus on strengths, insight, meaning-making (Phillips, 2015), and thriving in relationships (Tolpin, 2002). SBM are identified as a basic identity factor in counseling psychology and humanistic psychotherapy (e.g., Gelso & Woodhouse, 2003; Satir et al., 1991; Scheel et al., 2013). In a broader context, related concepts for the integration of capitalization methods into mental health services include empowerment (e.g., Werbrouck et al., 2018), recovery (Leendertse et al., 2021), salutogenesis (Mittelmark et al., 2017), and meaning of life (e.g., Hill, 2018). The emphasis on strengths is in fortuitous synchrony with the emergence of patient-centered care (Rathert et al., 2013).

Clinical Description and Indications

Strength-based methods demonstrate how patients' strengths can be used for therapeutic change. That is, all SBM make use of patient strength, but they vary in their specific clinical context. Here, we provide an overview of different ways in which SBM are conceptualized in practice:

- *Therapist responsiveness to the patient self-directed strength and/or therapist strength-based instructions*: SBM exist in transaction (at least a dyadic construct)—that is, patients proactively contribute to their therapy (e.g., Bohart, 2007; Macdonald & Muran, 2021; Ryan & Deci, 2008). Some psychotherapies emphasize the therapist's strength-based responsiveness to the patient's self-directed abilities and motivational readiness (Flückiger et al., 2013, 2021), whereas others highlight the therapist's strength-based instructions and patient compliance with those instructions (Suhr et al., 2017). It is difficult to separate these two strength-based aspects in sessions because patients, as part of their patient role, often are guided by therapists to emphasize positively valued aspects during sessions.
- *Disorder-specific and/or general strength-based methods*: Whereas several clinician's guides propose disorder-specific SBM (e.g., positive psychotherapy for psychosis; Riches et al., 2016), others highlight more generic SBM that include working on, for example, well-being and personal engagement (e.g., strength-based CBT to build on resilience; Padesky & Mooney, 2012).
- *Trait and/or state strengths*: Some SBM build on individual traits (e.g., character strengths; Niemiec, 2018), whereas others focus on the situational strengths in a particular therapeutic action/moment (Gonçalves et al., 2014).
- *Capitalizing on preexisting strengths and/or building new strengths*: Some SBM enhance preexisting abilities (e.g., proposing actions that correspond with the patients' preexisting skills; Cheavens et al., 2012). Other methods highlight the installation of new skills (e.g., building pleasure; Rashid & Seligman, 2019).
- *Building patients' individual strengths and/or building social and community strengths*: SBM are based on multiple levels of social networks. Some aim to build on the patients' individual strengths (e.g., fostering own gratitude practice, Emmons & Stern, 2013), some on interpersonal relationships, and still others on community or environmental strengths (e.g., fostering social support; Hirani et al., 2018; Li et al., 2021).
- *SBM in the therapy room and/or outside of the therapy room*: SBM can be focused on in-session (micro-) skills (e.g., Flückiger et al., 2009) but also outside of the therapy room via strength-based homework and augmented online tools (e.g., de Vries et al., 2020; Scheel et al., 2004).

All of these definitions assume that a generally positive quality of SBM should be evident throughout the course of a therapy session. What counts is that therapists and patients get an explicit and collaborative focus on patients' strengths during sessions. Moreover, an explicit focus on SBM does not mean that there would not be time for problem-based methods during sessions (e.g., Yulish et al., 2017). The various definitions are in agreement that the major contraindication may be that therapists want to "make up" for previously neglected positive aspects in an exaggerated way afterwards and thus tend to make patients feel that they are no longer being taken seriously (e.g., "but, there are but quite a few positive things").

Assessment

Assessment of Strength-Based Therapist's and Patient's Behaviors

There are several video-rating systems to measure therapists' in-session use of SBM. These include overall rating of the overall positivity/resource activation at the end of sessions (von Consbruch et al., 2013); a moment-to-moment coding system in which innovative moments of the patient change process are assessed (Gonçalves et al., 2011); and resource-oriented microprocess analysis (ROMA; e.g., Flückiger et al., 2009), in which strength-based therapist (ROMA-T) and patient (ROMA-P) behaviors are assessed separately during 1-minute segments.

The ROMA-T version assesses the following strength-based categories (Flückiger & Grosse Holtforth, 2008): (a) immediate reinforcement of patient's specific strength, (b) emphasis on patient's self-directed change, (c) expression of confidence for improvement, (d) focus on personal skills, (e) emphasis on patient's positive emotions, (f) focus on interpersonal skills and social support, (g) focus on physical health, (h) emphasis on positive therapeutic process and relationship, (i) focus on treatment goals, (j) emphasis on solutions to problems, (k) emphasis on self-directed choice, (l) pick up a positive patient's metaphor, (m) exploring an exception, and (n) normalizing and reframing a targeted problem. An overall minute-by-minute rating of the quality of SBM is evaluated from −2 (e.g., therapist ignores positive aspects mentioned by the patient for at least several minutes) to +2 (e.g., therapist explores in detail the patient's strengths for more than several minutes) to +3 (e.g., excessive positivity, therapist appears overly enthusiastic or disingenuous).

Corresponding with the therapist categories, the ROMA-P rating system assesses the following strength-based categories of the patient at a minute-to-minute level: (a) mentioning of therapist's helpful behaviors, (b) focus on personal skills, (c) emphasis on positive emotions, (d) focus on interpersonal skills and social support, (e) focus on physical health, (f) focus on personal goals, (g) focus on problem-solving, (h) focus on self-directed choice, (i) using a positive metaphor, and (j) exploring an exception. An overall rating of the quality of SBM is evaluated on a 5-point scale from −2 (e.g., patient does not reflect on positive aspects mentioned several times by the therapist) to +2 (e.g., patient explores their strengths in detail over more than several minutes). Preferably, ROMA-T and ROMA-P are rated by different observers to maintain independence of raters.

Based on a 20-hour observer training, ROMA-T/P categories and quality can be assessed reliably (e.g., Cohen's $\kappa > 0.61$; Flückiger et al., 2009).

ROMA-T/P do not differentiate who initiates the strength-based therapeutic focus; it is assumed that both therapist and patient contribute to strength-based therapeutic talks, and the sum of the therapist's SBM may help keep a strength-based focus across several minutes. For example, a therapist may ask an open question and the patient may response in a manner in which the therapist starts to explore and reflect positive aspects more precisely. What matters is that therapist and patient successively include and appreciate strength-based aspects in the sessions.

Strength-Based Assessments Post-Session, Between Sessions, and Treatment Progress

The definition, repeated assessment, and monitoring of strength-based concepts comprise an SBM. There are post-session reports in which strength-based in-session experiences are assessed from both patient's and therapist's perspectives (e.g., Flückiger et al., 2010; Mander et al., 2015). Patient's positive experiences of well-being may also be assessed outside of the therapy room—for example, using intersession diaries or ecological momentary assessments/interventions (e.g., de Vries et al., 2020; Suhr et al., 2017; Vîslă et al., 2021).

We consider the World Health Organization's (WHO, 2018) definition of mental health as relevant to detecting strengths. Patient strengths may be optimally assessed in a broad measure battery that considers critical constructs of the "normal" human functioning and health, such as psychological and social well-being, positive affectivity, self-esteem, self-efficacy, and social support. Furthermore, the items and subscales of clinical questionnaires can be systematically discussed in terms of the patient's strengths, abilities, skills, needs, and motivation (e.g., item from the Inventory of Interpersonal Problems: "It is hard for me to trust other people"; patient answer: "Not at all"; Flückiger et al., 2016).

Many have also suggested using individualized assessments of progress toward mutually developed and well-defined treatment goals (e.g., criterion-oriented outcomes such as Goal Attainment Scaling [Kiresuk & Sherman, 1968] or Target Complaints [Battle et al., 1966]). It is hoped that a strength-based formulation of treatment goals would cover both what should be reduced (e.g., fewer symptoms, fewer interpersonal problems) and positive behaviors and functioning that should be increased/approached (e.g., Grosse & Grawe, 2002). Finally, reviewing therapy satisfaction (e.g., Seligman, 1995) is a critical SBM to validate patient-centered outcomes.

Clinical Example

Strength-based methods are characterized as a general attentional focus attuned to patient strengths. This attentional focus impacts the course of strength-based therapist (micro-)skills. Both are shown in the following recorded dialogue of a strength-based conversation early in a course of individual psychotherapy (the details have been altered to maintain confidentiality). The patient (P) and therapist (T) are exploring an item on a pre-session assessment: "I've had a positive experience since the last session." The patient answered, "Yes, a little bit." The ROMA ratings are provided for every minute of dialogue; the ratings cover the whole minute and not a single sentence.

T: There probably are different topics that are relevant today and that need attention. Interestingly, there were some positive experiences last week . . . "a little bit"? (Therapist makes the positive experience explicit even it is described as "a little bit" by the patient; ROMA-T: no rating)

P: Well, I would not say that I am a different person than last week, but yes, there were some positive aspects. (ROMA-P: no rating)

T: . . . mhm . . . (verbal affirmation) (Therapist validates patient's positive evaluation; ROMA-T: no rating)

P: Well, to be honest, I did not do the activity diary that we scheduled for this week. Basically, it worked without it. I was able to get up in the morning. Taking a shower worked well. I went to the office and that worked well. (ROMA-P: focus on personal skills)

T: Great! What exactly went well? (Therapist explores the strengths situation; ROMA-T: focus on patient's personal skills)

P: Well, the whole process of getting up. It almost went by itself. It wasn't a pressure from you, but already also knowing that you'll probably ask today. . . . Then to realize that yes, it works. (ROMA-P: mentioning of therapist's helpful behaviors, focus on personal skills)

T: It almost went by itself? (Therapist explores the positive causal attribution; ROMA-T: focus on patient's personal skills)

P: Yes, the point probably is that I just moved out of bed. Alarm clock on and then after five minutes at the second time I got out! So, we haven't even discussed that yet. I figured I could set the alarm with my favorite music. That helped. (ROMA-P: focus on personal skills) Whereas . . . if I think about it right now, . . . it was rather to escape this deadening. So, the feeling of still not being up.

T: It almost seems to me that you put a lot of thought into it and just tried things out. (Therapist highlights patient's proactivity and openness to plan and explore new behaviors; ROMA-T: focus on patient's personal skills)

P: Yes, there is a difference. I also went to my boss and told her directly that I wanted to stay on and finish the project. She was rather skeptical about giving me the responsibility in this situation. And she's right, and it would be stupid if I overextended myself and then keeled over and everything stopped working. But I also told her that I don't want to quit begging altogether and would like to try. (ROMA-P: focus on interpersonal skills and social support)

T: How did the boss react to that? (Therapist explores the assumed positive interpersonal reaction of the boss; ROMA-T: focus on interpersonal skills and social support)

P: Actually, she liked the idea and said I was welcome to come to her. That was always my fear that the boss would react badly. (ROMA-P: focus on interpersonal skills and social support)

T: It seems to me that your boss also has pretty good qualities and supports you in your goals? (Therapist emphasizes the positive patient evaluation of the unexpected strengths of the boss. ROMA-T: focus on interpersonal skills and social support)

P: Yes, that's true. Even though I like to make fun of the higher-ups, my boss is totally fine! (ROMA-P: focus on interpersonal skills and social support)

T: You checked "yes, a little bit" on the question. At the same time, these are pretty impressive experiences and may show that you are on a good path? (Therapist fosters the patient's positive outcome expectations; ROMA-T: express of confidence for improvement)

P: Well, I think I have to be honest with myself and reveal my doubts to you. (ROMA-P: focus on personal goals)

T: I very much appreciate your honesty with yourself and with me. That seems to me to be very important for our therapy. . . . What do you think are the next steps we should discuss in therapy? (Therapist highlights patient's honest engagement and fosters the patient's proactivity; ROMA-T: emphasis on positive therapeutic process and relationship; ROMA-T quality overall: +2)

P: I think what we are discussing right now might also be a good way to work on my fears, although getting out of bed is a different issue . . . but clearly, it feels like a first step and as you said before, we probably have to take this step by step. (ROMA-P: mentioning of therapist's helpful behaviors, focus on personal goals; ROMA-P quality overall: +2)

Some patients, especially in the beginning of treatment, may be ambivalent and fearful and, at the same time, have hope and trust in the treatment and the therapist. The therapist's openness to discuss their ambivalence is important in using SBM.

At first glance, the previous exchange may appear as a seamless "natural flow" of individual therapy. However, the therapist was successful in keeping the focus on the patient's positive experiences, although there were several opportunities to shift the focus to the patient's problems (e.g., Patient avoids what was scheduled for the week? Rigid ritual at the morning? External attributed change? Morning clock as a strategy to avoid facing the stressful work situation? Slight mistrust with other people?). A key therapist skill in the excerpt was to identify the patient's strengths and to explore them by making them explicit. This focus on the patient's positive experiences appears to have facilitated the patient's agency and growth.

Landmark Studies and Previous Reviews

Landmark Studies

In a qualitative study, Scheel and colleagues (2013) presented a summary of positive, strength-based processes that regularly occur in mainstream psychotherapies based on expert interviews of eight well-educated psychotherapists from different orientations. The authors identified 266 *pantheoretical statements* that were clustered into 18 units and five main themes through a consensus process. The themes were as follows:

- Amplification of strengths (exception finding, encouragement, therapist highlights client strengths)

- Contextual considerations (barriers to the use of client strengths such as acting in crisis, client characteristics such as help-seeking behaviors, matching strengths to client context)
- Strength-based processes (identification process such as small strengths as a starting point, therapeutic relationship as a source of strengths, the therapist as agent of change, client participation in identifying of strengths)
- Strength-based outcomes (goals and motivation foster strengths, instilling hope and empowerment, self-awareness as a strength)
- Positive meaning-making (balancing strengths and problems, use of metaphor to access strengths, resiliency as strength, generalization of strengths, reframing a deficit as a strength)

The authors concluded,

> Therapists reported using client strengths to broaden client perspectives and create hope and motivation, to create positive meanings through reframing and metaphors, to identify strengths through the interpersonal therapeutic process, to match client contexts through strengths, and to amplify strengths through encouragement and exception finding. (p. 392)

Gassmann and Grawe (2006) investigated the overall quality of SBM of therapists and patients in 120 sessions of CBT at a minute-by-minute level (each session lasting 50–60 minutes; overall approximately 6,000 minutes using a prior version of the ROMA-T overall rating). They contrasted 60 sessions with both low session and therapy outcome with 60 sessions with high session and therapy outcome. Results indicated higher global strength-based qualities in both patients and therapists in high-outcome sessions in comparison to low-outcome sessions. However, at the end of sessions with poor outcome cases, therapists showed an excessive focus on SBM while patients did not respond. The authors concluded that successive therapist attention to SBM during the whole sessions may be a characteristic of good outcomes cases.

Previous Meta-Analyses

Table 16.1 summarizes prior meta-analyses on the end-of-treatment outcomes of strength-based psychotherapies. Most of these meta-analyses contrasted strength-based psychotherapy with control conditions in terms of distal outcome. The majority of these contrasts indicated small to medium effects in favor of the positive/strength-based approaches. However, all meta-analyses investigated the absolute efficacy vis-à-vis control conditions that were not treatments designed to be fully therapeutic (i.e., bona fide psychotherapy; Wampold & Imel, 2015). Thus, these prior meta-analyses do not provide information on whether SBM increase or decrease preexisting psychotherapy efficacy under bona fide conditions.

To the best of our knowledge, there are no previous reviews or meta-analyses on the link between therapists' use of SBM and session outcomes. All the previous meta-analyses have focused on distal, end-of-treatment outcomes.

Table 16.1 Prior Meta-Analyses of Comparative Trials Investigating Strength-Based Treatments

Study	k	N	Targeted Mental Health Suffering	Treatment	Comparison	Primary Outcome	Effects
Bolier et al. (2013)	39	6,139	Psychosocial problems	PPI	NI, WL, TAU, PL	WB, DS	Effects after removing outliers (I^2 nonsignificant) Increase in subjective WB: $d = 0.26$, 95% CI [0.18, 0.33], $Z = 6.43$, $p < .01$ Increase in psychological WB: $d = 0.17$, 95% CI [0.09, 0.25], $Z = 4.18$, $p < .01$ Decrease in DS: $d = 0.18$, 95% CI [0.07, 0.28], $Z = 3.33$, $p < .01$
Chakhssi et al. (2018)	30	1,864	Mental and somatic disorders	PPI	AC, NI, WL	WB, DS	Effects after removing outliers and low-quality studies Increase in WB: $g = 0.19$, 95% CI [0.02, 0.37], $p = .030$, $I^2 = 40.9\%$ Decrease in DS: $g = 0.07$, 95% CI [−0.19, 0.32], $p = .598$, $I^2 = 66.1\%$
Munder et al. (2019)	10	918	Mental disorders	RFT	WL, AC	PS, IF, QoL	Superiority of RFT compared to TAU in 8 out of 11 comparisons $g_{PPWC} = 0.349$, 95% CI [0.576, 0.122], $p = .003$, $I^2 = 46.50\%$ $g_{POWC} = 0.190$, 95% CI [0.355, 0.025], $p = .024$, $I^2 = 0.00\%$
Sin & Lyubomirsky (2009)	51	4,266	Depressive symptoms	PPI	NT, PL, TAU, NC	WB, DS	Increase in WB: $Z_r = 0.29$ (range: −0.31, 0.84), $p = 4 \times 10^{-9}$, $\chi^2_{(48)} = 230.92$ Decrease in DS: $Z_r = 0.31$ (range: −0.28, 0.81), $p = 0.0001$, $\chi^2_{(24)} = 146.32$

White et al. (2019)	51/39	4,266/6,139	Depressive symptoms, psychosocial problems	PPI	NT, WL, TAU, PL	WB, DS	Replications accounting for SSSB and omitting outliers: Sin & Lyubomirsky (2009) Increase in WB: $r = .10$, 95% CI [−0.01, 0.20] ($Q(38) = 70.68, p < .001$) Decrease in DS: $r = -.03$, 95% CI [−0.17, 0.11] ($Q(19) = 26.82, p = .109$) Bolier et al. (2013) Increase of subjective WB: $r = .13$, 95% CI [0.00, 0.26] ($Q(22) = 57.39, p < .001$) Increase in psychological WB: $r = .02$, 95% CI [−0.09, 0.13] ($Q(15) = 18.41, p = .242$) Decrease in DS: $r = .15$, 95% CI [0.06, 0.24] ($Q(11) = 11.51, p = .402$)
Hoppen & Morina (2021)	20	1,360	Mental and somatic disorders	PPI	WL, active treatment		WL Increase in positive outcomes: $g = 0.72$, 95% CI [0.14, 1.31] Decrease in negative outcomes: $g = 0.48$, 95% CI [0.18, 0.78] Active treatment Increase in positive outcomes: $g = 0.92$, 95% CI [0.11, 1.74] Decrease in negative outcomes: $g = 0.94$, 95% CI [0.18, 1.70]

k, number of studies included; *N*, patient sample size; I^2, heterogeneity; *d*, Cohen's d; *g*, Hegdes' g Treatments; AC, active control group; NC, neutral control group; NT, no treatment; c, placebo; PPI, positive psychology intervention; RFT, resource-focused treatment; TAU, treatment as usual; WL, wait list.

Outcomes: BMI, body mass index; CI, confidence interval; *d*, Cohen's *d*; DS, depressive symptoms; *g*, Hedges' *g*; IF, interpersonal functioning; *OR*, odds ratio; POWC, post-test only with control; PPWC, pre–post with control; PS, primary symptoms; Q, Cochran's *Q* (residual heterogeneity); QoL, quality of life; SSSB, small study size bias; WB, well-being; Z_r, mean Fisher effect size.

Research Review

The goal of this systematic review and meta-analysis was twofold. First, we review the research evidence on strength-based process–outcome studies. We narratively reviewed studies that assess in-session SBM (comparable to the previously mentioned ROMA rating) under bona fide psychotherapy conditions and their connection to intermediate outcomes. Second, we conduct a comparative meta-analysis of trials that contrasted strength-based psychotherapies versus other bona fide psychotherapies. Most of these trials contrasted SBM with problem-focused methods within the same orientation, sometimes even using the same treatment manual/approach, but contrasting different degrees of using strengths.

Inclusion Criteria

The inclusion criteria include (a) the study author(s) referred to the individual psychotherapy as "strengths based" or "solution focused" or "resource oriented" or "resilience based"; (b) patients had a current mental health diagnosis; (c) treatments were bona fide psychotherapy; and (d) there was a comparable amount of treatment, supervision, and training sessions across the conditions. Studies were excluded if (a) the trials focused on children (younger than age 13 years) or couples or family therapy; and (b) the study design focused on prevention, aftercare, or at-risk programs usually using additive designs and exclusively for the comparative meta-analysis. Furthermore, the comparative meta-analysis, preliminary *pilot studies* consisted of treatment conditions with less than 10 patients and/or less than three therapists were excluded. When multiple treatments were available in the same study, we selected only those that met our criteria outlined above (e.g., medication conditions were excluded).

For the process–outcome studies, studies in which SBM were assessed directly at the in-session level (e.g., using ratings of video/audio recordings) were included. For the purpose of this chapter to review in-session processes, we did not consider studies in which the strength-based session experiences were assessed as overall ratings at post-session (e.g., using post-session reports).

The following criteria were used for bona fide psychotherapy (Wampold & Imel, 2015): Psychotherapists with at least a master's degree delivered the treatment, patients met diagnostic criteria, and two of the following four criteria were satisfied: (a) treatments were generally recognized as legitimate treatment, such as CBT or psychodynamic therapy, and therapists were not proscribed from well-accepted therapeutic actions, such as psychoeducation, being empathic, providing a treatment rationale; (b) description of treatment contained a reference to a psychological mechanism (e.g., operant conditioning); (c) a treatment manual/guide was used; and (d) treatment contained an active component that appeared in the psychological literature.

Search Strategy

For the systematic review and comparative meta-analysis, to locate comparative trials of strength-based psychotherapies, we searched (via EBSCO) the PsycInfo, ERIC,

MEDLINE, and PSYNDEX databases with the keywords «psychotherapy OR treatment» AND «strength based OR solution focused OR resource oriented OR resilience based» AND «RCT OR randomized control trial OR randomized controlled trial OR clinical trial» AND «disorder» in March 2021. In addition, we inspected the above-mentioned prior comparative meta-analyses (Carter et al., 2016 [s = 8]; Chakhssi et al., 2018 [s = 30]; Munder et al. 2019 [s = 10]; White et al., 2019 [s = 51/39]; Hoppen & Morina, 2021 [s = 20]). For the process–outcome studies, we examined the Introduction and Reference sections of included studies to detect further process–outcome studies. Furthermore, we checked the hits of a further systematic review with the keywords «resource activation OR Ressourcenaktivierung OR resource realization OR Ressourcenrealisierung» in April 2021 (Hummel, 2022).

The Figure 16.1 flowchart provides an overview of the extraction procedure. From the 534 and 2,353 articles, respectively (eight and 446 were duplicates), we identified eight process–outcome studies (representing 416 patients) and nine comparative trials (reporting 57 effect sizes at post assessment representing 729 patients with an average of 81 patients per study). The eight process–outcome studies and nine clinical trials are summarized in Tables 16.2 and 16.3 (for bona fide criteria and Risk of Bias 2, see https://osf.io/s7z2w). Agreement between raters of bona fide criteria for strength-based treatments and contrasting treatments was 92%. Coding disagreements were discussed

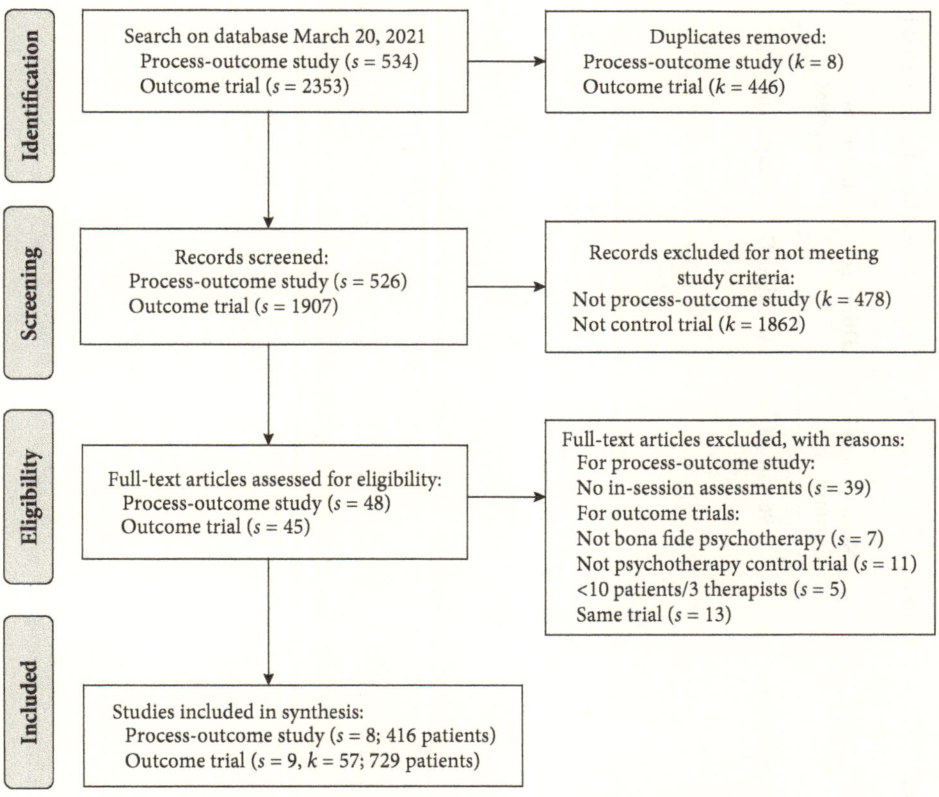

Figure 16.1 Flowchart of the included process–outcome studies and comparative trials.

Table 16.2 Summary of Strength-Based Process–Outcome Studies Investigating Bona Fide Psychotherapy

Study	No. of Sessions	*N*	Disorder	Inpatient/ Outpatient	Treatment	Process Measure	Summary of Immediate and Delayed In-Session Effects
Flückiger et al. (2009)	96	36	Mixed/SAD	Outpatient	ICBT	ROMA-T, ROMA-P	Comparable quality of SBM across two strength-based approaches. Personal skills highest associated with the patient's post-session evaluations of mastery ($r = .44$), personal goals highest association with clarification/insights ($r = .49$). Quality of SBM ($r = .39$, $p < .01$) correlated with the extent of goal achievement (GAS-R) at session 10.
Regli et al. (2000)	168	45	Mixed	Outpatient	ICBT	GCFA	Successful vs. less successful therapies: Significant difference in quality of SBM during the first few therapy sessions (higher quality of SBM in successful therapies). Therapy with above average alliance vs. below average alliance: Significantly higher quality of SBM in therapies with above average post-session alliance.
Kech (2008)	112	20	MDD	Inpatient	IPT	GCFA	Successful therapies: High emotional activation with simultaneous high quality of SBM ($r = .52$, $p < .001$). Opposite effect in unsuccessful therapies: High emotional activation but simultaneously low quality of SBM ($r = -.13$, $p = .30$).

Gassmann & Grawe (2006)	120	30	Mixed	Outpatient	ICBT	CMP	In successful therapy and therapy sessions: Quality of SBM positively associated with patient strength-based in-session talks ($r > .20$). In less successful therapies: high quality of SBM but low levels of patient strength-based talks at the end of sessions.
Flückiger & Studer (2009)	108	48	Mixed	Outpatient	ICBT	ROMA-T, ROMA-P	Personal skills and personal goals predicted shift into deeper emotional stages during sessions. After a shift, patients usually reframed or normalized their behavior.
Flückiger et al. (2014)	20	20	GAD	Outpatient	ICBT	ROMA-P	Personal skills at the beginning of sessions followed a more problem-focused stage that was characterized by a higher level of negative emotional expressions during therapy.
Schilling et al. (2021)	89	89	Mixed	Outpatient	ICBT	ROMA-T, ROMA-P	Sessions before a substantial increase of symptoms: Personal goals and positive reinterpretations significantly mentioned earlier in the sessions ($p < .01$).
E. Smith & Grawe (2003, 2005)	740	128	Mixed	Outpatient	ICBT	GCFA	Association of quality of SBM and session outcome composite ($d = 0.85$). In-session process: In situation in which the patient did not respond to the therapist's proposed method (20.92%), subsequent discussion about personal skills enhances the chance to turn into a productive session (51.1%).

CMP, Consistency Theory Micro-Process Analysis (Grawe, 1997); *d*, Cohen's *d*; GAD, generalized anxiety disorder; GAS-R, Goal Attainment Scaling—Revised; GCFA, general change factors (Grawe, 1997); ICBT, integrative cognitive–behavioral therapy; IPT, interpersonal psychotherapy; MDD, major depression disorder; *N*, patient sample size; ROMA-P/ROMA-T, Resource-Oriented Microprocess Analysis (Patient/Therapist Version); SAD, social anxiety disorder; SBM, strength-based methods (therapist).

Table 16.3 Comparative Trials Contrasting Strength-Based Methods with Bona Fide Psychotherapy

Study	Patient Population	Gender (% Male)	Mean Age (Years)	Depression or Anxiety Comorbidities Excluded	SUD Excluded	Bona Fide Strength-Based Psychotherapy	Bona Fide Comparison Psychotherapy	*N*	Effect Size[a]
Boyer et al. (2015)	ADHD	74	14.5	Yes	Yes	Solution-focused therapy + motivational interviewing	Manualized CBT (Plan My Life) + motivational interviewing	159	−0.07
Cheavens et al. (2012)	Major depression	41	37.0	No	Yes	Modular CBT for depression: Two treatment modules were selected to reflect individual patients' strengths.	Modular CBT for depression: Two treatment modules were selected to reflect individual patients' deficits.	42	0.52
Flückiger et al. (2008)	Multidiagnostic (depression and anxiety)	45	35.4	No	Yes	Custom-tailored CBT: (a) Case formulation of patients' strengths, (b) use of resource-focused methods (e.g., positive reframing, planning pleasure, imaginative techniques) in addition to CBT as usual	Custom-tailored CBT: (a) Case formulation without augmented focus on patients' strengths, (b) use of CBT as usual	40	0.39
Flückiger et al. (2016)	GAD	25	43.9	No	No	Manualized CBT for GAD (MAW): (a) Case formulation of patients' strengths, (b) tailoring CBT to match patients' strengths	Manualized CBT for GAD (MAW): (a) Case formulation of patients' GAD symptoms and comorbidities, (b) tailoring CBT to match patients' GAD symptoms	57	0.22

Flückiger et al. (2021)	GAD	25	31.4	No	No	Manualized CBT for GAD (MAW): (a) Case formulation of patients' strengths, (b) tailoring CBT to patients' change behaviors	Manualized CBT for GAD (MAW): (a) Case formulation of patients' GAD symptoms and comorbidities, (b) tailoring CBT to match patients' GAD symptoms	80	0.08
Knekt et al. (2008)	Multidiagnostic (depression and anxiety)	32	24.4	No	Yes	Solution-focused therapy	Short-time psychodynamic therapy	198	0.06
Kosfelder (2000)	Anxiety disorder	34	31	No	Yes	Custom-tailored CBT: CBT + solution-focused methods (focus on previous solution attempts, early change, compliments)	Custom-tailored CBT: Use of CBT as usual	75	−0.04
Teismann et al. (2011)	Major depression	33	46.0	No	Yes	Manualized CBT for depression: (a) Solution-focused methods (focus on previous solution attempts, early change, compliments), (b) strengths-oriented modification of CBT techniques (e.g., finding functional cognitions without elaborating dysfunctional cognitions)	Manualized CBT for depression: Use of CBT as usual	70	0.07
Willutzki et al. (2004)	SAD	58	38.2	Yes	Yes	Manualized CBT for SAD: (a) Solution-focused methods (focus on previous solution attempts, early change, compliments), (b) strengths-oriented modification of CBT techniques (finding functional cognitions without elaborating dysfunctional cognitions)	Manualized CBT for SAD: Use of CBT as usual	83	0.42

[a]Effect sizes in favor of strength-based methods.

ADHD, attention-deficit/hyperactivity disorder; CBT, cognitive–behavioral therapy; GAD, generalized anxiety disorder; MAW, Mastery of your Anxiety and Worry; SAD, social anxiety disorder; SUD, substance use disorder.

and resolved by reaching consensus. Effect size extractions and sample characteristics were coded, double-checked, and collaboratively discussed between the first and second author.

For the nine comparative trials, data included both peer-reviewed manuscripts ($s = 8$) and one thesis without peer review ($s = 1$; i.e., Kosfelder, 2000); data collected from randomized controlled trials ($s = 7$); and data from trials in which the patients were not randomized but, rather, grouped using propensity score methods on the basis of previously collected data ($s = 2$; i.e., Flückiger & Grosse Holtforth, 2008; Kosfelder, 2000). No trial with positive psychotherapy as a specific strength-based approach met the inclusion criteria (i.e., Andrewes et al. [2014] and Asgharipoor et al. [2012] treated five clients in the CBT control condition; Fava et al. [2005] and Chaves et al. [2017] considered less than three therapists; Uliaszek et al. [2016] investigated a subclinical student population; in Furchtlehner et al. [2020], group leaders were not psychotherapists).

Results: Review of Association of Strength-Based Methods with Immediate and Delayed In-Session Effects

The immediate and delayed in-session effects of SBM using video-based observer ratings are summarized in Table 16.2. These video ratings are primarily operationalized as a general positivity factor (e.g., ROMA-P/T overall quality ratings). These studies are variable in use of methods and samples (e.g., selection of particular sessions over a treatment course).

In the following paragraphs, we briefly summarize several of these eight studies and then provide a narrative synthesis of their collective results. Given their methodological heterogeneity, it is not surprising that the effects of SBM at the session level may be highly situational. At the same time, inspection of Table 16.2 reveals generally positive impacts of SBM on in-session effects, whereas in six studies there are in the majority positive associations of SBM with immediate and delayed in-session effects and two studies with mixed effects. No study indicated primarily negative associations of SBM with immediate and delayed in-session effects.

Using advanced analytic methods of decision trees (a machine learning algorithm), E. Smith and Grawe (2003, 2005) analyzed SBM in a sample of 613 sessions of 128 different cases to predict a composite score of session productivity evaluated at post-session (2,829 strength-based ratings of 10-minute sequences) in integrative CBT. The authors documented positive associations between strength-based therapist methods and immediate effects during the course of treatment. Of note, the correlative nature of the results precludes a definite causal interpretation: If a proposed therapeutic procedure was tailored to the individual skills and strengths of the patient so that they became actively involved, then the likelihood that the patient evaluated the session as productive was high (60.8%), in contrast to methods in which the patients were unable to respond adequately (20.9%). However, even in these sequences in which the patients did not respond well to the therapist-proposed methods (i.e., 20.9%), a subsequent discussion about the patient's positive skills and abilities enhanced the chance to turn the session into a productive one (51.1% of the 20.9%). These examples may exemplify that sessions in which SBM are used are often experienced as productive by patients.

With respect to potential specific effects of particular SBM, Flückiger and co-authors (2009) video-analyzed 96 sessions of two trials of strength-based CBT (Flückiger & Grosse Holtforth, 2008; Willutzki et al., 2004) using the ROMA-T/P minute-by-minute ratings. The results indicated that the global quality of SBM was higher in the strength-based psychotherapy conditions in comparison to the bona fide control conditions across the minutes. Both strength-based approaches showed comparable overall scores in the strength-based quality. The means of the overall strength-based quality predicted positive self-esteem evaluated by the patients at post-session. Overall, the results show that SBM do not contradict problem-oriented methods; in contrast, most ROMA-T categories were found to be positively related to higher levels of problem awareness at post-session ("problem actuation"; $r = .25–.48$).

In an explorative study with a preliminary sample of 20 severely distressed generalized anxiety disorder (GAD) outpatients, Flückiger and co-authors (2014) found that patients who were enabled by their therapists to speak about their personal skills (ROMA-P) early in sessions showed less resistance to discussing personal problems later in session (assessed by observers at a minute-by-minute level) and had better post-treatment outcomes. These results were in contrast to the a priori formulated hypothesis derived from the GAD literature that strength-based methods might increase experiential avoidance (i.e., SBM as a means of keeping patients away from painful experiences). In summary, the results of this study showed that therapist focus on personal skills is commonly observed in sessions even in a targeted disorder-specific population in which this hypothesized relationship is ambiguous.

In the previously mentioned landmark study by Gassmann and Grawe (2006), therapists' SBM were evident not only in the context of good outcome sessions but also in sessions in which therapeutic progress was challenged. Similar results were found in a study by Schilling and co-authors (2021) investigating sudden symptom gains and losses in patients receiving integrative CBT. The authors used ROMA-T ratings to compare the use of SBM in 30 therapy sessions before a sudden symptom gain with 29 sessions before a sudden loss. Whereas therapists' use of positive reinterpretations of problems was more often found in pre-gain sessions, positive reinforcements were frequent in pre-loss sessions. The results suggest that specific SBM can be experienced as unhelpful by patients in some cases. However, because of the correlational nature of these results, it cannot be ruled out that sudden loses happened despite, and not as a consequence of, the use of positive reinforcements.

Taken together, the results of these eight process–outcome studies (see Table 16.2) indicate that therapists use SBM with multiple client populations, across theoretical orientations, and with disparate disorders. Notably, despite their methodological variability, the general pattern of results was uniformly positive in that SBM were linked with more favorable intermediate, session-level patient outcomes. SBM consistently emerged as a therapeutic characteristic that is related to treatment progress across sessions. At the same time, and somewhat unexpected, the therapist use of SBM was also apparent in situations in which treatment progress was challenged (Gassmann & Grawe, 2006; Schilling et al., 2021). In these situations, the therapeutic function of SBM may be less straightforward as in successful sessions.

Results: Comparison of Strength-Based Psychotherapies to Other Bona Fide Psychotherapies

For the comparative multilevel meta-analysis, random effects restricted maximum-likelihood estimator was utilized. This analysis is based on the assumption that the studies in this meta-analysis were randomly sampled from a population of studies. Effect sizes were generated using the R statistical software "compute.es" package (Del Re, 2013), and the multilevel meta-analytic models and meta-analytic diagnostics (i.e., tests for outliers) used the R "metafor" package (Viechtbauer, 2010; for forest plot, see Fernández-Castilla et al., 2020).

To account for multiple outcomes per study (i.e., within-study effect sizes nested in a trial), we conducted multilevel meta-analytic models with three levels, where sampling variance of the extracted effect sizes at Level 1 was nested in *k* measures at Level 2 and *s* studies at Level 3 (e.g., Assink & Webbelink, 2016; Raudenbush & Bryk, 2002). The use of multilevel models in meta-analytic research enables integration of multiple outcomes and accounts for their interdependency because correlations between outcomes are rarely reported in primary studies and therefore difficult to obtain. In addition, the three-level approach allows examining outcome variance within studies (i.e., within-study heterogeneity) as well as between studies (i.e., between-study heterogeneity).

For the specific treatment contrasts, overall heterogeneity was assessed with the Q and I^2 statistics (Higgins & Thompson, 2002). I^2 is calculated as the percentage of variability due to true differences among effect sizes. We also tested whether within-study heterogeneity (i.e., various measures nested in a study) explained a significant proportion of the overall heterogeneity by comparing the full model with a reduced model, where the within-study variance was fixed as zero (Assink & Wibbelink, 2016).

Power calculations were estimated based on Jackson and Turner's (2017) recommendation using metapower package in R (Griffin, 2021). Given a small effect of d of 0.10, an average group size across studies of $n = 80$, and some heterogeneity of $I^2 = 20\%$, the power for meta-analytic random effects models was .86 for 57 effect sizes. That indicated that there was sufficient power to detect treatment differences).

The overall weighted average (omnibus) effect size contrasting strength-based psychotherapies versus bona fide psychotherapies based on 57 effect sizes nested in nine trials was $g = 0.166$ (95% confidence interval [CI] [0.027, 0.305], $p < .01$) in favor of strength-based psychotherapies (see Table 16.3). The omnibus effect size was computed while accounting for the sample size of each study, as well as within-study dependence between outcome measures. The forest plot (Figure 16.2) depicts the 57 effect sizes nested in nine studies. There was nonsignificant heterogeneity among the effect sizes ($Q(56) = 69.1$, $p = .11$, $I^2 = 19\%$, CI [16, 22]). A small amount of heterogeneity was primarily impacted by between-study variance ($\sigma^2_{\text{level 3}} = .03$), and within-study variance across particular outcome measures was marginal ($\sigma^2_{\text{level 2}} = .00$). That is, the small heterogeneity observed in this meta-analysis was primarily based on the various study contexts and relatively independent from the particular outcome measure used within studies.

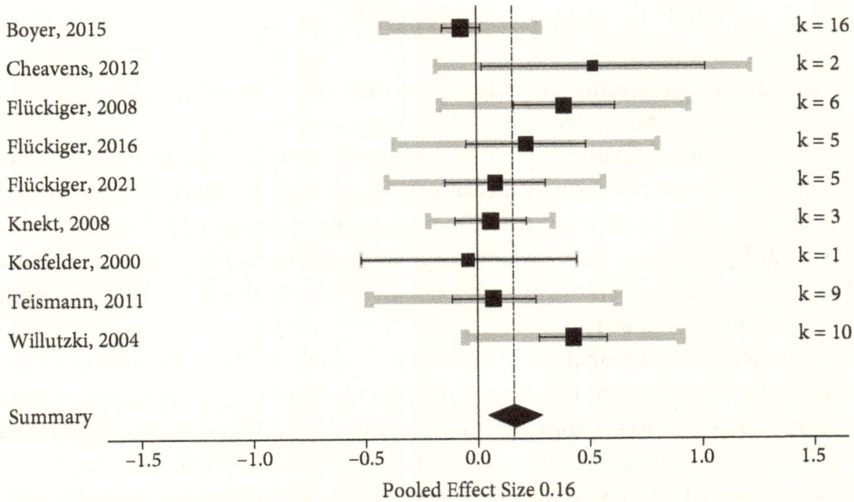

Note: Grey bars indicate variability at measurement level, black bars represent variability at study level

Figure 16.2 Forest plot: Relative efficacy in favor of strength-based methods vis-à-vis bona fide psychotherapy ($k = 57$ effect sizes).

The funnel plot (Figure 16.3) is a diagram that plots the standard error on the *y* axis and the effect size on the *x* axis. Due to the relatively small proportion of within-study heterogeneity, we provided the study-level estimates for illustrative purposes ($s = 9$). In the presence of bias, the plot would show a higher concentration of studies on one side of the mean than the other. There was no indication of publication bias in our sample (asymmetry, $p > .48$; trim and fill missing studies: 0). In addition, we computed how many unpublished nonsignificant studies it would take to reduce the overall effects size to $g = 0$. In this data set, this fail-safe value was greater than 11 studies.

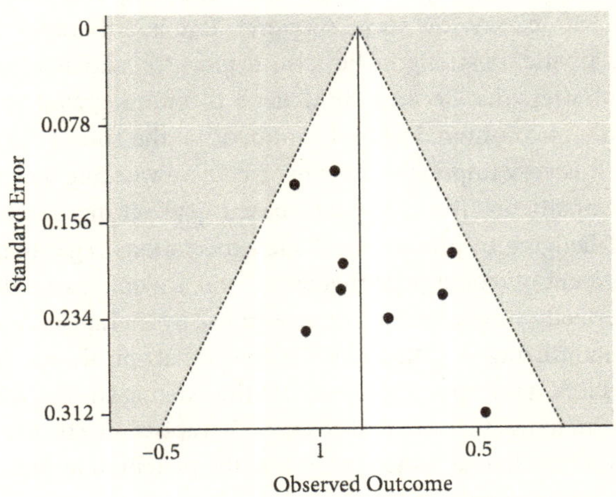

Figure 16.3 Funnel plot of the nine comparative trials.

Moderators of Meta-Analyses

We analyzed disorder-specific outcomes as potential moderator in the meta-analysis (1, targeted disorder-specific outcome measure; 0, general outcome). We considered that the disorder-specific measures (e.g., Beck Depression Inventory in depressed patients) might differ from overall distress measures (e.g., Symptom Check List-90, Working Ability Index). As a trend, targeted disorder-specific outcomes ($g = 0.178$, 95% CI [0.025, 0.332], $p < .05$, $k = 28$) revealed marginally higher effect sizes in strength-based studies than general outcomes ($g = 0.155$, 95% CI [0.003, 0.306], $p < .05$; $k = 29$; moderator: $F(2/55) = 2.95$, $p < .061$).

In summary, our meta-analysis of comparative trials indicated an additional small but significant benefit of SBM in comparison to other bona fide psychotherapies with a less systematized focus on SBM. Based on 57 effect sizes nested in nine trials, the effect size on distal, end-of-treatment outcomes was 0.166 in favor of strength-based psychotherapies. In all these trials, SBM were used as augmentation strategies within bona fide psychotherapies targeting clinical populations.

Possible Negative Effects and Harm

We are unaware of any specific research identifying the rates or types of negative effects of strength-based psychotherapies under bona fide conditions (as exceptions, in their GAD trials, Flückiger et al. [2016, 2021] monitored suicidal ideation as serious adverse events and took out insurance for any possible side effect; no suicidal ideation and no insurance cases were observed). Hence, we rely on our collective clinical and training experiences in addressing these potential effects.

Based on those experiences, we have noted several potential negative effects of SBM. First, therapists may have a diagnostic focus on patients' strengths at the expense of a comprehensive assessment of all domains of functioning. Strength-based assessments can also uncover important aspects of personal suffering (e.g., low well-being, low self-esteem, low self-efficacy, low social support). That is, a therapist may not only neglect to validate a patient's strengths but also neglect to validate a patient's problems and their lack of strengths. Second, SBM need to be integrated in the therapeutic process in an authentic fashion. Delayed comments at the end of challenging sessions (e.g., therapist: "It is very impressive how hard you are working") can be perceived as cynical and unempathetic. Third, strength-based goal setting can be too optimistic and thus too challenging to promote realistic expectations regarding the anticipated change and treatment outcome (e.g., therapist: "You are doing so well, fantastic! Your next steps are perfectly simple!"). Fourth, overpraise by therapists can be perceived as devaluating or infantilizing (e.g., therapist: "It's great that you always come on time, Mr. Perfectionist!"). Fifth, it is important to validate the existing strengths for what they are before putting them to use for potential change. Therapists may be tempted to focus on new behaviors and fast change, which could lead the patient to feel misunderstood and pressed to make changes for the therapist.

Therapists often are sensitized to not appear too positive or overzealous. For example, in a preliminary study in which therapists took a maximal focus on SBM, less than 10 minutes out of 6,230 minutes was perceived as "excessive positivity" by the observers (ROMA-T quality +3; Flückiger & Grosse Holtforth, 2008). Excess therapist enthusiasm may prove an error, but an uncommon one according to this research evidence.

Diversity Considerations

There is a small but growing literature on diversity consideration in SBM (e.g., Hendriks et al., 2018; Jankowski et al., 2020; Rao & Donaldson, 2015). Outside of the clinical context, Cohen and colleagues (2006, 2009) investigated a brief social psychological self-affirmation to close the minority achievement gap in tertiary education. White and African American students were randomly assigned to one of two conditions: (a) self-affirmation, which included writing a brief essay on their personal values and why they are important to them; and (b) a control condition, writing about why the least relevant personal goals might be important to others. The results in this study revealed that African Americans in the self-affirmation group academic performance were comparable to both of the White American groups (self-affirmation and control), whereas the African Americans in the control group performed worse than all other groups. These preliminary results highlighted the potential benefits of a strength-based approach among African Americans. Importantly, these findings have not been consistently replicated across minority populations (e.g., Cohen & Sherman, 2014; Sherman et al., 2021).

The reviewed studies primarily were conducted in Europe, where the participation of ethnic minorities usually is not quantified in study reports. Multicultural competence may require careful attention and awareness to the patient's background and experiences that integrate both mental health perspectives: the patient's sufferings and strengths (Cacioppo et al., 2012). The identities of individuals from sexual, racial, and ethnic minorities are shaped in the context of multiple stressors, experiences of marginalization, and systemic barriers. These individuals also frequently lack access to mental health care and often experience mistrust of the mental health system due to a history of negative experiences with health care professionals. Thus, therapists should acknowledge a patient's culture and social context by a strength-based attitude. Therapists should maintain a humble and curious approach, invite the patient to share their experiences and establish their own definitions of strengths. For example, people's concepts of well-being and life satisfaction may vary across language and culture (e.g., Diener & Diener, 2009; Jepp et al., 2020).

Limitations of the Research

This chapter is based on a systematic synthesis of the research. Although our team made an effort to locate the available research on SBM in psychotherapy, no systematic review or meta-analysis is truly exhaustive. To address the complexity in the comparative meta-analysis, we selected only comparative trials with treatment contrasts in which the comparison groups were conducted under at least minimal standards of a professional psychotherapy. However, we did not investigate particular strength-based outcomes such as treatment satisfaction (Seligman, 1995) and individual goal attainment (Kiresuk & Sherman, 1968). These questionnaires were simply (or not so simply) not included in the assessment plans of the trials (in parallel to potential negative side effects in recently published study protocols; e.g., Klatte et al., 2023).

Limitations of our review of process–outcome studies include a relatively small number of studies, which might be due, among other things, to our focus on direct assessments of SBM that led us to discard studies employing indirect assessments of SBM (e.g., post-session reports). Furthermore, most of the reviewed process–outcome studies used correlational designs and could not rule out alternative explanations for their findings (e.g., confound of SBM with other therapist or treatment variables). There is little knowledge about the potential short-term impact of strength-based micro methods using analogue experiments (for an exception, see Strauman et al., 2015). Finally, from a methodological perspective, there is a lack of qualitative process studies (for an exception, see Scheel et al., 2013).

Training Implications

Strength-based methods are rarely emphasized explicitly in clinical training (Jankowski et al., 2020). One possible reason is that they are often perceived as a professional competence of developing positive attitudes toward patients rather than specific skills that can be taught (e.g., Gelso & Woodhouse, 2003; Scheel et al., 2013). However, therapists in training can be sensitized to and learn SBM, particularly through learning to use assessment measures such as the ROMA-T.

Multiple psychotherapy manuals emphasize SBM for clinical training. These practice-based references include positive psychotherapy (e.g., Conoley & Scheel, 2018; Parks & Schueller, 2014; Rashid & Seligman, 2019Rashid, 2015), strength-based CBT (Cheavens et al., 2012; Padesky & Mooney, 2012), and resource activation (Flückiger et al., 2010; Willutzki & Teismann, 2013). Based on these manuals, we offer the following pantheoretical training recommendations:

- Include education regarding the risk of patient bias toward negative information as well as therapist bias toward problems and deficits (Smith et al., 2006).
- Address in clinical training both long-term perspectives (e.g., matching treatments to patients' preexisting capabilities and motivational readiness) and short-term perspectives (e.g., detection of patient's strengths during sessions, applying methods that foster patient's well-being and positive qualities).
- Consider discussions on the situation-specific nature of strengths because certain qualities can be adaptive and healthy in certain situations but maladaptive in others (e.g., the "always look on the bright side of life" video can be used to discuss cynical aspects of SBM: https://www.youtube.com/watch?v=SJUhlRoBL8M).
- Teach strength-based (micro-)skills by means of deliberate practice and using video-based feedback.
- Train students to monitor and balance their emphasis on distress and problems with their focus on client strengths. Psychotherapeutic methods should integrate both problem-focused and strength-based perspectives.

- Encourage trainees to be responsive to patients' expression of their own strengths, while leaving space to discuss their distress when needed.

Therapeutic Practices

Our systematic review of strength-based in-session studies and meta-analysis of comparative trials suggest that SBM produce meaningful psychotherapy effects. The meta-analytic evidence presented in this chapter indicates that strength-based psychotherapies prove as efficacious, and sometimes slightly more efficacious, than other bona fide psychotherapies. Based on this research evidence, we recommend that practitioners do the following:

- Consider providing SBM at every stage of therapy; not in every minute but in every session.
- Integrate the assessment of a patient's personal strengths into the clinical interview and standardized assessment.
- Discuss explicitly with patients both weaknesses and strengths identified in the clinical assessment.
- Individualize case formulations that integrate both patient's sufferings and strengths; SBM can provide a differentiated and balanced picture of the patient and situation.
- Be aware that the assessment of positive constructs might identify problematic aspects of functioning (e.g., low self-esteem, hope, gratitude, kindness).
- Collaborate with patients in defining and amplifying their strengths. Therapists and patients may disagree on the value or meaning of certain strengths and their role in patients' functioning.
- Consider obtaining an outside perspective from a significant other on the patient's strengths; it can sometimes provide beneficial information of which the patient is unaware.
- Use SBM to improve and broaden therapy success in terms of the WHO mental health definition (e.g., symptom reduction, well-being, social integration).
- Create wording or therapist slang that communicates inclusiveness and positive regard (e.g., "You just said *highlight moment*. What does this mean to you?"; "This voice of your *silly old man*, does it have something wise to say or is it just silly?").
- Monitor and validate positive change across the whole psychosocial functioning during therapy.
- Make an effort to find and discuss functional aspects in behaviors that are easily dismissed as dysfunctional (by either you or the patient).
- Identify preexisting problem-solving strategies to facilitate behavioral change and use them to build new skills.
- Incorporate patient strengths into homework assignment (e.g., observation of positive episodes during a week, planning enjoyment) and in fostering activities outside of the therapy room (e.g., recreation, physical movement, social support).
- Respect a patient's culture and social context in identifying strengths; a person's concept of well-being and life satisfaction varies across culture.

References

*Studies included in the process–outcome review and meta-analysis.

Andrewes, H. E., Walker, V., & O'Neill, B. (2014). Exploring the use of positive psychology interventions in brain injury survivors with challenging behaviour. *Brain Injury*, *28*(7), 965–971. https://doi.org/10.3109/02699052.2014.888764

Asgharipoor, N., Asgharnejad Farid, A., Arshadi, H., & Sahebi, A. (2012). A comparative study on the effectiveness of positive psychotherapy and group cognitive–behavioral therapy for the patients suffering from major depressive disorder. *Iranian Journal of Psychiatry and Behavioral Sciences*, *6*(2), 33–41.

Assink, M., & Wibbelink, C. J. M. (2016). Fitting three-level meta-analytic models in R: A step-by-step tutorial. *The Quantitative Methods for Psychology*, *12*, 154–174. https://www.tqmp.org/RegularArticles/vol12-3/p154

Bandura, A. (2006). Toward a psychology of human agency. *Perspectives on Psychological Science*, *1*(2), 164–180. https://doi.org/10.1111/j.1745-6916.2006.00011.x

Battle, C. C., Imber, S. D., Hoehn-Saric, R., Nash, E. R., & Frank, J. D. (1966). Target complaints as criteria of improvement. *American Journal of Psychotherapy*, *20*(1), 184–192. https://doi.org/10.1176/appi.psychotherapy.1966.20.1.184

Bohart, A. C. (2007). Insight and the active client. In L. G. Castonguay & C. Hill (Eds.), *Insight in psychotherapy* (pp. 257–277). American Psychological Association. https://doi.org/10.1037/11532-012

Bolier, L., Haverman, M., Westerhof, G. J., Riper, H., Smit, F., & Bohlmeijer, E. (2013). Positive psychology interventions: A meta-analysis of randomized controlled studies. *BMC Public Health*, *13*, Article 119. https://doi.org/10.1186/1471-2458-13-119

Bonanno, G. A. (2021). *The end of trauma: How the new science of resilience is changing how to think about PTSD*. Basic Books.

*Boyer, B. E., Geurts, H. M., Prins, P. J., & Van der Oord, S. (2015). Two novel CBTs for adolescents with ADHD: The value of planning skills. *European Child & Adolescent Psychiatry*, *24*(9), 1075–1090. https://doi.org/10.1007/s00787-014-0661-5

Cacioppo, J. T., Berntson, G. G., Norris, C. J., & Gollan, J. K. (2012). The evaluative space model. In P. A. M. Van Lange, A. W. Kruglanski, & E. T. Higgins (Eds.), *Handbook of theories of social psychology* (pp. 50–72). SAGE. https://doi.org/10.4135/9781446249215.n4

Carter, T., Morres, I. D., Meade, O., & Callaghan, P. (2016). The effect of exercise on depressive symptoms in adolescents: A systematic review and meta-analysis. *Journal of the American Academy of Child and Adolescent Psychiatry*, *55*(7), 580–590. https://doi.org/10.1016/j.jaac.2016.04.016

Catalino, L. I., & Fredrickson, B. L. (2011). A Tuesday in the life of a flourisher: The role of positive emotional reactivity in optimal mental health. *Emotion*, *11*(4), 938–950. https://doi.org/10.1037/a0024889

Chakhssi, F., Kraiss, J. T., Sommers-Spijkerman, M., & Bohlmeijer, E. T. (2018). The effect of positive psychology interventions on wellbeing and distress in clinical samples with psychiatric or somatic disorders: A systematic review and meta-analysis. *BMC Psychiatry*, *18*(1), Article 211. https://doi.org/10.1186/s12888-018-1739-2

Chaves, C., Lopez-Gomez, I., Hervas, G., & Vazquez, C. (2017). A comparative study on the efficacy of a positive psychology intervention and a cognitive behavioral therapy for clinical depression. *Cognitive Therapy and Research*, *41*(3), 417–433. https://doi.org/10.1007/s10608-016-9778-9

*Cheavens, J. S., Strunk, D. R., Lazarus, S. A., & Goldstein, L. A. (2012). The compensation and capitalization models: A test of two approaches to individualizing the treatment of depression. *Behaviour Research and Therapy*, *50*(11), 699–706. https://doi.org/10.1016/j.brat.2012.08.002

Cohen, G. L., Garcia, J., Apfel, N., & Master, A. (2006). Reducing the racial achievement gap: A social-psychological intervention. *Science*, *313*(5791), 1307–1310. https://doi.org/10.1126/science.1128317

Cohen, G. L., Garcia, J., Purdie-Vaughns, V., Apfel, N., & Brzustoski, P. (2009). Recursive processes in self-affirmation: Intervening to close the minority achievement gap. *Science, 324*(5925), 400–403. https://doi.org/10.1126/science.1170769

Cohen, G. L., & Sherman, D. K. (2014). The psychology of change: Self-affirmation and social psychological interventions. *Annual Review of Psychology, 65*, 333–371.https://doi.org/10.1146/annurev-psych-010213-115137

Conoley, C. W., & Scheel, M. J. (2018). *Goal focused positive psychotherapy: A strength-based approach*. Oxford University Press.

Cronbach, L. J., & Snow, R. E. (1977). *Aptitudes and instructional methods: A handbook for research on interactions*. Irvington.

Del Re, A. C. (2012). Compute.es. R-package statistical software.

De Vries, L. P., Baselmans, B. M. L., & Bartels, M. (2020). Smartphone-based ecological momentary assessment of wellbeing: A systematic review and recommendations for future studies. *Journal of Happiness Studies: An Interdisciplinary Forum on Subjective Wellbeing, 22*, 2361–2408. Advance online publication. https://doi.org/10.1007/s10902-020-00324-7

Diener, E., & Diener, M. (2009). Cross-cultural correlates of life satisfaction and self-esteem. In E. Diener (Eds.), *Culture and well-being* (pp. 71–91). Springer. https://doi.org/10.1007/978-90-481-2352-0_4

Emmons, R. A., & Stern, R. (2013). Gratitude as a psychotherapeutic intervention. *Journal of Clinical Psychology, 69*(8), 846–855. https://doi.org/10.1002/jclp.22020

Fava, G. A. (2016). *Well-being therapy: Treatment manual and clinical applications*. Karger.

Fava, G. A., Ruini, C., Rafanelli, C., Finos, L., Salmaso, L., Mangelli, L., & Sirigatti, S. (2005). Well-being therapy of generalized anxiety disorder. *Psychotherapy and Psychosomatics, 74*(1), 26–30. https://doi.org/10.1159/000082023

Fernández-Castilla, B., Declercq, L., Jamshidi, L., Beretvas, N., Onghena, P., & Van den Noortgate, W. (2020). Visual representations of meta-analyses of multiple outcomes: Extensions to forest plots, funnel plots, and caterpillar plots. *Methodology, 16*(4), 299–315. https://doi.org/10.5964/meth.4013

*Flückiger, C., Caspar, F., Holtforth, M. G., & Willutzki, U. (2009). Working with patients' strengths: a microprocess approach. *Psychotherapy Research, 19*(2), 213–223. https://doi.org/10.1080/10503300902755300

Flückiger, C., Del Re, A. C., Wampold, B. E., & Horvath, A. O. (2018). The alliance in adult psychotherapy: A meta-analytic synthesis. *Psychotherapy, 55*(4), 316–340. https://doi.org/10.1037/pst0000172

*Flückiger, C., Forrer, L., Schnider, B., Bättig, I., Bodenmann, G., & Zinbarg, R. E. (2016). A single-blinded, randomized clinical trial of how to implement an evidence-based treatment for generalized anxiety disorder [IMPLEMENT]: Effects of three different strategies of implementation. *EBioMedicine, 3*, 163–171. https://doi.org/10.1016/j.ebiom.2015.11.049

*Flückiger, C., & Grosse Holtforth, M. (2008). Focusing the therapist's attention on the patient's strengths: A preliminary study to foster a mechanism of change in outpatient psychotherapy. *Journal of Clinical Psychology, 64*(7), 876–890. https://doi.org/10.1002/jclp.20493

Flückiger, C., Grosse Holtforth, M., Del Re, A. C., Lutz, W. (2013). Working along sudden gains—Responsiveness on small and subtle early changes and exceptions. *Psychotherapy, 50*, 292–297. https://doi.org/10.1037/a0031940

*Flückiger, C., & Studer, R. (2009). Die Berner Ressourcen-Taskforce—Ressourcenaktivierung und Problembearbeitung unter der Lupe. *Verhaltenstherapie und Psychosoziale Praxis, 41*(4), 829–839.

*Flückiger, C., Vîslă, A., Wolfer, C., Hilpert, P., Zinbarg, R. E., Lutz, W., Grosse Holtforth, M., & Allemand, M. (2021). Exploring change in cognitive–behavioral therapy for generalized anxiety disorder: A two-arms ABAB crossed-therapist randomized clinical implementation trial. *Journal of Consulting and Clinical Psychology, 89*(5), 454–468. https://doi.org/10.1037/ccp0000639

Flückiger, C., Wüsten, G., Zinbarg, R. E., & Wampold, B. E. (2010). *Resource activation: Using clients' own strengths in psychotherapy and counseling*. Hogrefe.

*Flückiger, C., Zinbarg, R. E., Znoj, H., & Ackert, M. (2014). Resource activation in generalized anxiety: An observer-based microprocess analysis of patients' in-session outcomes. *Psychotherapy*, *51*(4), 535–545.

Flückiger, C., Znoj, H. J., & Vîslă, A. (2016). Detecting information processing bias toward psychopathology: Interpreting Likert scales at intake assessment. *Psychotherapy*, *53*, 284–290. https://doi.org/10.1037/pst0000081

Furchtlehner, L. M., Schuster, R., & Laireiter, A.-R. (2020). A comparative study of the efficacy of group positive psychotherapy and group cognitive behavioral therapy in the treatment of depressive disorders: A randomized controlled trial. *Journal of Positive Psychology*, *15*, 832–845, https://doi.org/10.1080/17439760.2019.1663250

Fredrickson, B. L. (2001). The role of positive emotions in positive psychology. The broaden-and-build theory of positive emotions. *American Psychologist*, *56*(3), 218–226. https://doi.org/10.1037//0003-066x.56.3.218

*Gassmann, D., & Grawe, K. (2006). General change mechanisms: The relation between problem activation and resource activation in successful and unsuccessful therapeutic interactions. *Clinical Psychology & Psychotherapy*, *13*(1), 1–11. https://doi.org/10.1002/cpp.442

Gelso, C. J., & Woodhouse, S. (2003). Toward a positive psychotherapy: Focus on human strength. In W. B. Walsh (Ed.), *Counseling psychology and optimal human functioning* (pp. 171–197). Erlbaum.

Gonçalves, M. M., Gabalda, I. C., Ribeiro, A. P., Pinheiro, P., Borges, R., Sousa, I., & Stiles, W. B. (2014). The Innovative Moments Coding System and the Assimilation of Problematic Experiences Scale: A case study comparing two methods to track change in psychotherapy. *Psychotherapy Research*, *24*(4), 442–455. https://doi.org/10.1080/10503307.2013.835080

Gonçalves, M. M., Ribeiro, P. A., Mendes, I., Matos, M., & Santos, A. (2011). Tracking novelties in psychotherapy process research: The Innovative Moments Coding System. *Psychotherapy Research*, *21*, 497–509. https://doi.org/10.1080/10503307.2011.560207

Grawe, K. (1997). Research-informed psychotherapy. *Psychotherapy Research*, *7*(1), 1–19, https://doi.org/10.1080/10503309712331331843

Griffin, J. (2021). Metapower—Computing and visualizing statistical power for meta-analysis. https://cran.r-project.org/web/packages/metapower/index.html

Grosse, M., & Grawe, K. (2002). Bern Inventory of Treatment Goals: Part 1—Development and first application of a taxonomy of treatment goal themes. *Psychotherapy Research*, *12*(1), 79–99. https://doi.org/10.1080/713869618

Helliwell, J. F., Layard, R., Sachs, J., De Neve, J.-E., Aknin, L.B., & Wang, S. (2021). World happiness report 2021. Sustainable Development Solutions Network.

Hendriks, T., Schotanus-Dijkstra, M., Hassankhan, A., Graafsma, T., Bohlmeijer, E., & de Jong, J. (2018). The efficacy of positive psychology interventions from non-Western countries: A systematic review and meta-analysis. *International Journal of Wellbeing*, *8*(1), 71–98. doi:10.5502/ijw.v8i1.711

Higgins, J. P., & Thompson, S. G. (2002). Quantifying heterogeneity in a meta-analysis. *Statistics in Medicine*, *21*(11), 1539–1558. https://doi.org/10.1002/sim.1186

Hill, C. E. (2018). *Meaning in life: A therapist's guide*. American Psychological Association.

Hirani, S. S., Norris, C. M., Van Vliet, K. J., Van Zanten, S. V., Karmaliani, R., & Lasiuk, G. (2018). Social support intervention to promote resilience and quality of life in women living in Karachi, Pakistan: A randomized controlled trial. *International Journal of Public Health*, *63*(6), 693–702. https://doi.org/10.1007/s00038-018-1101-y

Hobfoll, S. E. (1989). Conservation of resources: A new attempt at conceptualizing stress. *American Psychologist*, *44*, 513–524.

Hoppen, T. H., & Morina, N. (2021). Efficacy of positive psychotherapy in reducing negative and enhancing positive psychological outcomes: a meta-analysis of randomised controlled trials. *BMJ Open*, *11*(9), e046017. https://doi.org/10.1136/bmjopen-2020-046017

Hummel, L. (2021). *A systematic search of process studies on resource activation*. Unpublished Bachelor Thesis, University of Zürich, Switzerland.

Jackson, D., & Turner, R. (2017). Power analysis for random-effects meta-analysis. *Research Synthesis Methods*, *8*(3), 290–302. https://doi.org/10.1002/jrsm.1240

Jankowski, P. J., Sandage, S. J., Bell, C. A., Davis, D. E., Porter, E., Jessen, M., Motzny, C. L., Ross, K. V., & Owen, J. (2020). Virtue, flourishing, and positive psychology in psychotherapy: An overview and research prospectus. *Psychotherapy, 57*(3), 291–309. https://doi.org/10.1037/pst0000285

Jebb, A. T., Morrison, M., Tay, L., & Diener, E. (2020). Subjective well-being around the world: Trends and predictors across the life span. *Psychological Science, 31*(3) 293–305.

Kahneman, D., Diener, E., & Schwarz, N. (1999). *Well-being: The foundations of hedonic psychology*. Russell Sage Foundation.

*Kech, S. (2008). *Einflussfaktoren auf den Behandlungserfolg der Interpersonellen Psychotherapie bei stationären Depressionspatienten: Analyse der Wirkmechanismen* [Unpublished dissertational thesis]. University of Freiburg, Germany.

Kiresuk, T. J., & Sherman, R. E. (1968). Goal attainment scaling: A general method for evaluating comprehensive community mental health programs. *Community Mental Health Journal, 4*(6), 443–453. https://doi.org/10.1007/BF01530764

Klatte, R., Strauss, B., Flückiger, C., Färber, F., & Rosendahl, J. (2023). Defining and assessing adverse events and harmful effects in psychotherapy study protocols: A systematic review. *Psychotherapy, 60*(1), 130–148. https://doi.org/10.1037/pst0000359

*Knekt, P., Lindfors, O., Härkänen, T., Välikoski, M., Virtala, E., Laaksonen, M. A., Marttunen, M., Kaipainen, M., Renlund, C., & Helsinki Psychotherapy Study Group. (2008). Randomized trial on the effectiveness of long- and short-term psychodynamic psychotherapy and solution-focused therapy on psychiatric symptoms during a 3-year follow-up. *Psychological Medicine, 38*(5), 689–703. https://doi.org/10.1017/S003329170700164X

*Kosfelder, J. (2000). *Handlungsorientierung durch Lösungsfokus. Eine klinisch-psychologische Interventionsstudie*. Der Andere Verlag.

Lee, J. H., Nam, S. K., Kim, A.-R., Kim, B., Lee, M. Y., & Lee, S. M. (2013). Resilience: A meta-analytic approach. *Journal of Counseling & Development, 91*(3), 269–279. https://doi.org/10.1002/j.1556-6676.2013.00095.xe

Leendertse, J., Wierdsma, A. I., van den Berg, D., Ruissen, A. M., Slade, M., Castelein, S., & Mulder, C. L. (2021). Personal recovery in people with a psychotic disorder: A systematic review and meta-analysis of associated factors. *Frontiers in Psychiatry, 12*, 622628. https://doi.org/10.3389/fpsyt.2021.622628

Li, F., Luo, S., Mu, W., Li, Y., Ye, L., Zheng, X., Xu, B., Ding, Y., Ling, P., Zhou, M., & Chen, X. (2021). Effects of sources of social support and resilience on the mental health of different age groups during the COVID-19 pandemic. *BMC Psychiatry, 21*, Article 16. https://doi.org/10.1186/s12888-020-03012-1

Macdonald, J., & Muran, C. J. (2021). The reactive therapist: The problem of interpersonal reactivity in psychological therapy and the potential for a mindfulness-based program focused on "mindfulness-in-relationship" skills for therapists. *Journal of Psychotherapy Integration, 31*(4), 452–467. https://doi.org/10.1037/int0000200

Mander, J., Schlarb, A., Teufel, M., Keller, F., Hautzinger, M., Zipfel, S., Wittorf, A., & Sammet, I. (2015). The Individual Therapy Process Questionnaire: Development and validation of a revised measure to evaluate general change mechanisms in psychotherapy. *Clinical Psychology & Psychotherapy, 22*(4), 328–345. https://doi.org/10.1002/cpp.1892

Mittelmark, M. B., Sagy, S., Eriksson, M., Bauer, G. F., Pelikan, J. M., Lindström, B., & Espnes, G. A. (Eds.). (2017). *The handbook of salutogenesis*. Springer.

Munder, T., Karcher, A., Yadikar, Ö., Szeles, T., & Gumz, A. (2019). Focusing on patients' existing resources and strengths in cognitive–behavioral therapy and psychodynamic therapy: A systematic review and meta-analysis. *Zeitschrift fur Psychosomatische Medizin und Psychotherapie, 65*(2), 144–161. https://doi.org/10.13109/zptm.2019.65.2.144

Ng, T. H., Alloy, L. B., & Smith, D. V. (2019). Meta-analysis of reward processing in major depressive disorder reveals distinct abnormalities within the reward circuit. *Translational Psychiatry, 9*(1), 1–10.

Niemiec, R. M. (2018). *Character strengths interventions: A field guide for practitioners*. Hogrefe.

Padesky, C. A., & Mooney, K. A. (2012). Strength-based cognitive–behavioural therapy: A four-step model to build resilience. *Clinical Psychology & Psychotherapy, 19*(4), 283–290. https://doi.org/10.1002/cpp.1795

Parks, A. C., & Schueller, S. M. (Eds.). (2014). *The Wiley Blackwell handbook of positive psychological interventions*. Wiley Blackwell.

Phillips, A. (2015). *Unforbidden pleasures*. Hamish Hamilton.

Rao, M. A., & Donaldson, S. I. (2015). Expanding opportunities for diversity in positive psychology: An examination of gender, race, and ethnicity. *Canadian Psychology, 56*(3), 271–282. https://doi.org/10.1037/cap0000036

Rashid, T. (2015). Positive psychotherapy: A strength-based approach. *Journal of Positive Psychology, 10*(1), 25–40. https://doi.org/10.1080/17439760.2014.920411

Rashid, T., & Seligman, M. E. P. (2019). *Positive psychotherapy*. Oxford University Press.

Rathert, C., Wyrwich, M. D., & Boren, S. A. (2013). Patient-centered care and outcomes: A systematic review of the literature. *Medical Care Research and Review, 70*(4), 351–379. https://doi.org/10.1177/1077558712465774

Raudenbush, S. W., & Bryk, A. S. (2002). *Hierarchical linear models*. SAGE.

*Regli, D., Bieber, K., Mathier, F., & Grawe, K. (2000). Beziehungsgestaltung und Aktivierung von Ressourcen in der Anfangsphase von Therapien. *Verhaltenstherapie und Verhaltensmedizin, 21*(4), 399–420.

Riches, S., Schrank, B., Rashid, T., & Slade, M. (2016). WELLFOCUS PPT: Modifying positive psychotherapy for psychosis. *Psychotherapy, 53*(1), 68–77. https://doi.org/10.1037/pst0000013

Ryan, R. M., & Deci, E. L. (2008). A self-determination theory approach to psychotherapy: The motivational basis for effective change. *Canadian Psychology, 49*(3), 186–193. https://doi.org/10.1037/a0012753

Satir, V., Banmen, J., Gerber, J., & Gomori, M. (1991). *The Satir model: Family therapy and beyond*. Science and Behavior Books.

Scheel, M. J., Hanson, W. E., & Razzhavaikina, T. I. (2004). The process of recommending homework in psychotherapy: A review of therapist delivery methods, client acceptability, and factors that affect compliance. *Psychotherapy: Theory, Research, Practice, Training, 41*(1), 38–55. https://doi.org/10.1037/0033-3204.41.1.38

Scheel, M. J., Davis, C. K., & Hederson, J. D. (2013). Therapist use of client strengths: A qualitative study of positive processes. *The Counseling Psychologist, 41*, 392–427. https://doi.org/10.1177/0011000012439427

*Schilling, V. N. L. S., Boyle, K. S., Rubel, J. A., Flückiger, C., Zimmermann, D., & Lutz, W. (2021). Patients' and therapists' actions on the precipice of change: Session processes before sudden gains and sudden losses. *Journal of Psychotherapy Integration, 31*(3), 238–256. https://doi.org/10.1037/int0000242

Scholz, U., Doña, B. G., Sud, S., & Schwarzer, R. (2002). Is general self-efficacy a universal construct? Psychometric findings from 25 countries. *European Journal of Psychological Assessment, 18*(3), 242–251. https://doi.org/10.1027/1015-5759.18.3.242

Seligman, M. E. (1995). The effectiveness of psychotherapy. The *Consumer Reports* study. *American Psychologist, 50*(12), 965–974. https://doi.org/10.1037//0003-066x.50.12.965

Sherman, D. K., Lokhande, M., Müller, T., & Cohen, G. L. (2021). Self-affirmation interventions. In G. M. Walton & A. J. Crum (Eds.), *Handbook of wise interventions: How social psychology can help people change* (pp. 63–99). The Guilford Press.

Sin, N. L., & Lyubomirsky, S. (2009). Enhancing well-being and alleviating depressive symptoms with positive psychology interventions: A practice-friendly meta-analysis. *Journal of Clinical Psychology, 65*(5), 467–487. https://doi.org/10.1002/jclp.20593

*Smith, E. C., & Grawe, K. (2003). What makes psychotherapy sessions productive? A new approach to bridging the gap between process research and practice. *Clinical Psychology and Psychotherapy, 10*, 275–285.

*Smith, E. C., & Grawe, K. (2005). Which therapeutic mechanisms work when? A step towards the formulation of empirically validated guidelines for therapists' session-to-session decisions. *Clinical Psychology and Psychotherapy, 12*(2), 112–123.

Smith, N. K., Larsen, J. T., Chartrand, T. L., Cacioppo, J. T., Katafiasz, H. A., & Moran, K. E. (2006). Being bad isn't always good: Affective context moderates the attention bias toward negative information. *Journal of Personality and Social Psychology, 90*, 210–220. https://doi.org/10.1037/0022-3514.90.2.210

Solomonov, N., Victoria, L. W., Dunlop, K., Respino, M., Hoptman, M. J., Zilcha-Mano, S., Oberlin, L., Liston, C., Areán, P. A., Gunning, F. M., & Alexopoulos, G. S. (2020). Resting state functional connectivity and outcomes of psychotherapies for late-life depression. *American Journal of Geriatric Psychiatry*, *28*(8), 859–868.

Strauman, T. J., Socolar, Y., Kwapil, L., Cornwell, J. F., Franks, B., Sehnert, S., & Higgins, E. T. (2015). Microinterventions targeting regulatory focus and regulatory fit selectively reduce dysphoric and anxious mood. *Behaviour Research and Therapy*, *72*, 18–29. https://doi.org/10.1016/j.brat.2015.06.003

Suhr, M., Risch, A. K., & Wilz, G. (2017). Maintaining mental health through positive writing: Effects of a resource diary on depression and emotion regulation. *Journal of Clinical Psychology*, *73*(12), 1586–1598. https://doi.org/10.1002/jclp.22463

Tay, L., & Diener, E. (2011). Needs and subjective well-being around the world. *Journal of Personality and Social Psychology*, *101*(2), 354–365. https://doi.org/10.1037/a0023779

*Teismann, T., Dymel, W., Schulte, D., & Willutzki, U. (2011). Ressourcenorientierte Akutbehandlung unipolarer Depressionen: Eine randomisierte kontrollierte Psychotherapiestudie. *Psychotherapie, Psychosomatik und Medizinische Psychologie*, *61*(7), 295–302. https://doi.org/10.1055/s-0030-1270453

Tolpin, M. (2002). Doing psychoanalysis of normal development: Forward edge transferences. *Progress in Self-Psychology*, *18*, 167–190.

Uliaszek, A. A., Rashid, T., Williams, G. E., & Gulamani, T. (2016). Group therapy for university students: A randomized control trial of dialectical behavior therapy and positive psychotherapy. *Behaviour Research and Therapy*, *77*, 78–85. https://doi.org/10.1016/j.brat.2015.12.003

Viechtbauer, W. (2010). Conducting meta-analyses in R with the metafor package. *Journal of Statistical Software*, *36*(3), 1–48. https://doi.org/10.18637/jss.v036.i03

Vîslă, A., Zinbarg, R. E., Hilpert, P., Allemand, M., & Flückiger, C. (2021). Worry and positive episodes in the daily lives of individuals with generalized anxiety disorder: An ecological momentary assessment study. *Frontiers in Psychology*, *12*, 722881. https://doi.org/10.3389/fpsyg.2021.722881

von Consbruch, K., Flückiger, C., Stangier, U., Beutel, M. E., Herpertz, S., Hoyer, J., Leibing, E., Leichsenring, F., Salzer, S., Strauß, B., & Wiltink, J. (2013). WIFA-k: Ein neues Messinstrument zur zeitökonomischen Erfassung allgemeiner Wirkfaktoren nach Grawe [Assessing common factors in psychotherapy: Psychometric properties of a new time-economic instrument (WIFA-k)]. *Psychotherapie Psychosomatik Medizinische Psychologie*, *63*(7), 286–289. https://doi.org/10.1055/s-0032-1331206

Wampold, B. E., & Imel, Z. E. (2015). *The great psychotherapy debate: The evidence for what makes psychotherapy work* (2nd ed.). Routledge.

Werbrouck, A., Swinnen, E., Kerckhofs, E., Buyl, R., Beckwée, D., & De Wit, L. (2018). How to empower patients? A systematic review and meta-analysis. *Translational Behavioral Medicine*, *8*(5), 660–674. https://doi.org/10.1093/tbm/iby064

White, C. A., Uttl, B., & Holder, M. D. (2019). Meta-analyses of positive psychology interventions: The effects are much smaller than previously reported. *PLoS One*, *14*(5), e0216588. https://doi.org/10.1371/journal.pone.0216588

*Willutzki, U., Haas, H., Neumann, B., Koban, C., & Schulte, D. (2004). Zur Psychotherapie sozialer Ängste: Kognitive Verhaltenstherapie im Vergleich zu einem kombiniert ressourcenorientierten Vorgehen. Eine randomisierte kontrollierte Interventionsstudie. *Zeitschrift für Klinische Psychologie und Psychotherapie*, *33*, 42–50. https://doi.org/10.1026/1616-3443.33.1.42

Willutzki, U., & Teismann, T. (2013). *Ressourcenaktivierung in der Psychotherapie*. Hogrefe.

World Health Organization. (2018). *Metal health: Strengthening our response*. https://www.who.int/news-room/fact-sheets/detail/mental-health-strengthening-our-response

Yulish, N. E., Goldberg, S. B., Frost, N. D., Abbas, M., Oleen-Junk, N. A., Kring, M., Chin, M. Y., Raines, C. R., Soma, C. S., & Wampold, B. E. (2017). The importance of problem-focused treatments: A meta-analysis of anxiety treatments. *Psychotherapy*, *54*(4), 321–338. https://doi.org/10.1037/pst0000144

17

Enhancing Emotion Regulation

Shigeru Iwakabe, Kaori Nakamura, and Nathan C. Thoma

Emotion dysregulation is considered one of the common core mechanisms of psychopathology (Gratz et al., 2015) and is an emerging transdiagnostic focus of psychotherapy for a wide range of behavioral disorders. Frequent methods of enhancing patient emotion regulation (ER) across a variety of treatment packages include (a) undoing avoidance of negative emotions, (b) enhancing emotional awareness, (c) allowing the full experience of feared or avoided emotion, (d) learning effective cognitive reappraisal, and (e) learning behavioral and action strategies to modulate unpleasant emotions (Berking et al., 2008; McMain et al., 2010; Mennin & Fresco, 2014).

Psychotherapies that address patient ER can be roughly divided into two groups. The first group consists of structured psychoeducation and ER skills training rooted in the cognitive–behavioral tradition. These include the Unified Protocol (UP; Barlow et al., 2017), acceptance and commitment therapy (ACT; Hayes, 2004), dialectical behavior therapy (DBT; Linehan, 1993), and mindfulness-based cognitive therapy (MBCT; Kabat-Zinn, 1994). The methods developed specifically to address ER skills include Skills Training in Affect and Interpersonal Regulation (STAIR; Cloitre et al., 2002), acceptance-based behavioral therapy (Roemer et al., 2008), emotion regulation therapy (ERT; Mennin et al., 2015; Renna et al., 2017), and affect regulation training (Berking & Lukas, 2015).

The second group of psychotherapies is affect-focused, experiential treatments that aim to facilitate immediate patient ER, most often used in affect-focused therapies. These include emotion-focused therapy (EFT; Greenberg, 2021), accelerated experiential dynamic psychotherapy (AEDP; Fosha, 2021), and short-term dynamic psychotherapy (STDP; Abbass, 2015; Frederickson et al., 2018; McCullough et al., 2003). The therapist helps patients tolerate and regulate maladaptive emotions and transform them by facilitating the experience of adaptive emotions (Greenberg, 2021), ultimately resulting in decreased emotional arousal and greater calmness and well-being (Fosha, 2021).

Although these approaches have somewhat different therapeutic foci reflecting respective underlying theories of ER, they nonetheless address patient ER as one of the central targets of psychotherapy. In the structured methods, modules address each of the above ER components and progressively build ER capacities. In affect-focused methods, therapists try to be responsive to the patient's immediate emotional experiencing in selecting an optimally facilitative method.

Shigeru Iwakabe, Kaori Nakamura, and Nathan C. Thoma, *Enhancing Emotion Regulation* In: *Psychotherapy Skills and Methods That Work*. Edited by: Clara E. Hill and John C. Norcross, Oxford University Press. © Clara E. Hill and John C. Norcross 2023. DOI: 10.1093/oso/9780197611012.003.0017

Definitions

Emotion regulation refers to the process of modulating one or more aspects of an emotional experience or response (Gross, 1998). Regulated emotion keeps the individual within a window of tolerance in which optimal emotional functioning is possible (Greenberg, 2021; Siegel, 1999). ER is considered to be intrinsic to mental health and adaptive psychological functioning.

ER encompasses a combination of downregulation of negative emotions and upregulating positive emotions (Gross, 1998). It involves both internal and external actions to initiate, increase, maintain, decrease, or transform both positive and negative emotions in response to changing demands of emotion-evoking situations. Although often used to refer to a person's behaviors undertaken once distressing emotions have occurred, ER also includes emotion generation, which is how emotion occurs (e.g., Campos et al., 2004). Thus, therapeutic work is not only about teaching strategies to cope with emotions that have already occurred but also about transforming those aversive emotions so that more adaptive emotions are experienced in their place (Grecucci et al., 2020; Greenberg, 2021).

There is no singular therapist method directly associated with enhancing patient ER. Therefore, enhancing ER can be defined as a group of therapist methods and responses designed to build and strengthen patient ER capacity. That can be accomplished through a variety of means: providing relational and dyadic responses, facilitating emotional processing and transformation, and teaching skills for tolerating distressing emotions.

Clinical Description and Indications

Given that most people seeking psychotherapy have difficulties regulating emotions, facilitating effective ER is a common goal across psychotherapies (Grecucci et al., 2017; Leahy et al., 2011). Reviewing the clinical literature on emotion processing and regulation, McMain and associates (2010) detailed eight common principles: (a) Engage in an ongoing assessment of patient's capacity to modulate emotions; (b) develop a compassionate, accepting, and genuine therapeutic relationship; (c) educate patients about emotions and their function; (d) promote awareness and acceptance; (e) help patients reduce problematic avoidance and inhibition of emotions; (f) increase the capacity to adaptively express emotion; (g) increase positive emotional experiences; and (h) facilitate changes in emotional processes by providing opportunities for new experiences.

Structured Approaches

Structured methods frequently address ER skills by means of psychoeducation, skills training, and homework exercises. The outline of each session typically includes specific tasks to be completed with accompanying workbooks that patients use for homework.

The UP (Barlow et al., 2017; Farchione et al., 2021) teaches ER skills in 10–20 sessions of individual treatment. Four modules specifically target ER: (a) psychoeducation about the nature and function of emotions, including a detailed discussion of how the patient's avoidance of emotion is problematic because it reduces the emotion in the short term but reinforces the cycle of emotions in the long term; (b) teaching patients to observe, name. and let go of their emotions without evaluation; (c) learning cognitive ER strategies to change misappraisals related to negative emotions; and (d) modifying emotionally driven behaviors, which are a specific set of reactive behaviors associated with emotion to drive a person to withdraw, avoid, and escape with exposure to feared emotions.

In DBT (Linehan, 2015), the enhancement of ER is guided by three basic principles (McMain et al., 2001): (a) enhancing the ability to be aware of and accept emotional experience, (b) cultivating the ability to regulate emotions and tolerate distress, and (c) changing negative emotions through new learning experiences with exposure. DBT differentiates distress tolerance skills from ER skills. The goal of distress skills is to accept overwhelming emotions and survive through the crises by distracting themselves with pleasurable and self-soothing activities, but not to effect and change their environment as is the aim of ER skills. Mindfulness skills play a central role in both ER and distress tolerance skill learning. Patients learn to nonjudgmentally observe and describe the present moment through contemplative practice and develop wise mind, which is finding a middle path integrating their reason and emotion (Linehan, 2015).

In the first phase of ERT (Mennin et al., 2015; Renna et al., 2017), the therapist helps the patient cultivate mindful ER skills to increase awareness of emotional experiences and act flexibly to the intense emotional experiences. They then teach metacognitive regulation skills, such as decentering, reframing, and distancing to create a healthy distance and emotional clarity rather than being reactive and consumed by emotions. The therapist also uses a series of imagery exercises to have the patient vividly remember and experience triggers of their emotional response and facilitate "do-overs" in which the patient elaborates and enacts a sequence of more adaptive responses in the session. Patients are also taught breathing and other relaxation techniques. In the second phase, therapists teach patients to adopt a proactive orientation, consciously choosing to expose themselves to anxiety-provoking yet rewarding experiences to replace dysregulating patterns. The therapist uses imaginal exposure and chair dialogue with the patient so that the patient can rehearse taking actions toward their personal values rather than responding reactively through worry and rumination.

Affect-Focused Therapies

Emotion regulation is enhanced in affect-focused therapies by accessing and facilitating the experience of adaptive emotion whose experience has been previously inaccessible, blocked, or avoided (Greenberg, 2021). The therapist's consistent empathy, warmth, and validation, even in the face of the patient feeling upset or overwhelmed, is important because it is internalized by the patient and becomes a part of the way the patient subsequently responds to upsetting events. In addition, the moment-to-moment empathic attunement to the patient's emotional state creates a clear focus on the patient's here-and-now experiences as well as ongoing assessment of emotional processing. Therapists also help patients pay attention to physical signs of emotions, including changes in breathing, muscular tension, and other nonverbal signs; stay with and absorb/take in such experiences; and symbolize or find words to describe them.

In addition, therapists facilitate the experience of adaptive emotions through various expressive and evocative techniques (Medley, 2021). The therapist encourages the patient to stay with the emerging emotional experience, sometimes exaggerating and repeating certain actions or phrases so that these are vividly experienced. Dysregulated emotions are transformed by a new experience of adaptive emotions, which Greenberg (2021) called "changing emotion with emotion." The experience of adaptive emotions is followed by a reflective process of creating its new meaning. Therapists may also help patients reflect the relational experience of being accompanied by the therapist who bears witness to the transformation (Fosha, 2001).

Indications and Contraindications

When patients show signs of experiencing secondary emotions or maladaptive emotions that are highly distressing, therapists do not intensify or facilitate patient emotional experience but, rather, help patients modulate and bear these emotions. In-session markers for such dysregulation are when the patient is (a) overwhelmed; (b) unable to cognitively process the conversation (cognitive disorganization); (c) shaky, vulnerable, and fragile; (d) anxious/panicky; and/or (e) visibly upset and hyperventilating (Fosha et al., 2018). Methods to regulate and modulate overwhelming in-session emotional experiences include relational validation through empathy, explicit emotional support, somatic grounding, and cognitive regulative interventions.

Assessment

Assessing Emotion Regulation Methods

We know of no specific measures of ER methods. Early psychotherapy process researchers identified affect-focused therapist responses using categories of therapist verbal responses (Elliott et al., 1987), such as the revised Hill Counselor Verbal Response Modes Category System (Hill, 1985, 1986). These studies differentiate therapist responses that were facilitative of patient affect, such as reflection and minimum encourager, from those that were not directly related to facilitation of affect, such as provision of information, direct guidance, and advice-giving. In order to elaborate the rating of therapist response mode, therapist intention scales such as the 19-item Intentions List (Hill & O'Grady, 1985) were added. The Intentions List includes intentions to facilitate patient emotional change process such as "cathart" and "feelings-awareness."

Three rating scales used by trained judges include items that evaluate the extent of affect focus and some aspects of therapist methods for ER. For example, the Psychotherapy Process Q-set (Jones et al., 1988) has items such as "Therapist draws attention to patient's non-verbal behavior" and "Therapist is sensitive to the patient's feelings, attuned to the patient: empathic." These items are often used to rate the extent to which affect-focused methods were used. The Comparative Psychotherapy Process Scale (Hilsenroth et al., 2005) includes items such as "Therapist encourages patient to experience and express feelings in the session" and "Therapist addresses the patient's avoidance of important topics and shifts in mood." The Multitheoretical List of Interventions–30 (Solomonov et al., 2018) includes items that identify and label emotions, defenses, conflict splits, moment-to-moment experience, exploring personal meaning, and showing interest in the patient's experience.

Fosha et al. (2018) developed the AEDP 9+1 Change Process Scale, a therapist-rated measure of therapeutic methods used in AEDP. Five of the nine items (facilitating access to the bodily rooted experience and to the felt sense of experience, defense work, experientially processing core affective experience, metatherapeutic processing of transformational experience, and promoting integration and processing core state experience) relate to facilitating patient emotional process. Two items relate to responding to in-session emotion dysregulation (undoing aloneness, and working with overwhelming and highly distressing emotions and alleviating these emotions within the window of tolerance).

Assessing Outcomes of Emotion Regulation Work

Several observer-rated scales measure in-session behavioral indications of ER. Adequate interrater agreement or reliability have been demonstrated for all of them. The Observer-Measure of Affect Regulation (J. Watson et al., 2011) defines ER as consisting of level of awareness/labeling, modulation and arousal, modulation of expression, acceptance of affective experience, and reflection on experience. The Client Emotional Productivity Scale–Revised (Auszra et al., 2013) measures the degree to which a patient experiences a primary emotion in an effective and useful manner (attending, symbolization, congruence, acceptance, regulation, agency, and differentiation). The Classification of Affective-Meaning State (Pascual-Leone & Greenberg, 2005) classifies patient emotional state into primary or secondary emotions based on vocal tone, involvement, and meaning. The Achievement of Therapeutic Objectives Scale (Berggraf et al., 2012) includes a subscale of Activating Affects, and the Client Expressed Emotional Arousal Scale–III-R (Machado et al., 1999) measures expressed emotions in terms of its intensity and type (anger, fear, joy, love, sadness, and surprise) based on the vocal quality and nonverbal behaviors.

In addition, there are a number of self-report measures of ER that would typically be completed by patients post-session; adequate reliabilities and validities have been reported for all. These include the Emotion Regulation Questionnaire (Gross & John, 2003), Difficulties in Emotion Regulation Scale (Gratz & Roemer, 2004), Emotion Dysregulation Questionnaire (Gill et al., 2021), Action and Acceptance Questionnaire–II (Bond et al., 2011), Affective Style Questionnaire (Hofmann & Kashdan, 2010), Emotion Regulation Skills Questionnaire (Berking & Znoj, 2008), Cognitive Emotion Regulation Questionnaire (Garnefski et al., 2001), Affect Integration Inventory (Solbakken et al., 2011), Distress Tolerance Scale (Simons & Gaher, 2005), Meta-Emotion Scale (Mitmansgruber et al., 2008), Emotional Processing Difficulties

Scale–Revised (Faustino et al., 2022), Emotion Regulation Goals Scale (Brandão et al., 2022), and Dimensions of Openness to Emotions (Reicherts, 2007). Several scales tapping common positive and negative emotions are also sometimes used as client self-report measures of ER; these include the Positive and Negative Affect Schedule (D. Watson et al., 1988) and Profiles of Mood State Questionnaires (McNair et al., 1971). In addition, the Self-Compassion Scale (SCS; Neff, 2003) measures how individuals respond to emotionally distressing events.

Zelkowitz and Cole (2016) examined convergent and discriminant validity of eight self-report ER scales with a large university student sample. Exploratory factor analysis revealed three factors: *out-of-control negative emotions* representing the degree to which a person experiences strong negative emotions that are beyond one's ability to regulate; *emotional awareness and expression* representing the degree to which individuals are aware of, admit to, and express strong pro-social emotions ranging from joy to guilt; and *cognitive strategies for emotion regulation*, reflecting concrete cognitive strategies for regulating negative emotion such as positive reappraisal, refocusing on planning, and putting into perspective.

Clinical Examples

In the following, we present three examples of working with emotional regulation.

AEDP Methods for Working with Dysregulated Emotions

The first example is taken from Lamagna (2021, p. 308), who illustrates the work with emotion dysregulation in AEDP. While working with a therapist (T), a 60-year-old married White female patient (P) on the verge of leaving her husband was flooded with distressing emotions.

P: (*Getting more distressed*) It just hurts so much. (*tears up*) It's still so close—that feeling . . . (pause) and I feel afraid of it.

T: Yes. Let me help you with that feeling.

P: I don't know what I'm feeling. It's too hard for me (*increasingly agitated, gasping with tears in her eyes*).

T: Linda . . . can you just check in with me for a second? Can you feel me here with you?

P: *[Not registering the therapist's statement]* It all hurts too much. I miss my mother (*breaks into sobs*).

T: (*Softly*) Yes.

P: (*Sobbing*) I missed so much.

T: (*Slowly and with softness*) Yeah, you did. Keep breathing.

P: I keep telling myself I'm doing well. I have this wonderful world around me . . . (*sobs*)

T: Can you check in and see that I'm here with you? See if we can ask this distressed part of you if she would be willing to separate out—just a little bit. And if she won't, it's okay. We'll figure out other ways of helping.

P: I'm just surprised it's so deep.

T: Okay. Do you have a sense whether there is a willingness for the distress to step back? Did you feel any shifting in your body?

P: I'm just able to breathe. (*seems slightly calmer*)

T: Just notice that you can breathe now. (long pause) What are you noticing now?

The therapist first responded with calling attention to his empathic presence, using a gentle tone and slowed-down speech, to dyadically regulate the patient's dysregulation that exacerbated her sense of aloneness. Then he used physical regulation (breathing) to help the patient attend to and accept the somatic experience of her emotion, to which the patient responded partially. The therapist also used intrarelational method, which asked the patient to separate from the distressed part of her self. The patient finally made a meaningful contact with the therapist and partially regulated her distressing emotion.

Affect-Oriented Methods for Enhancing Emotional Awareness

In the following vignette (from Paivio & Pascual-Leone, 2010,p. 146), a male patient, who had complex post-traumatic stress disorder, felt he could never rely on others for support and had developed a fiercely independent style. Acknowledging his emerging sense of insecurity and neediness was uncomfortable and made him uneasy. The therapist oriented the patient's attention to emergent feelings and aimed to help him allow the emotional experience and increase his emotional awareness.

T: So, it's about feeling alone, that's the main concern, like you can't handle it?

P: It's not, "can't handle it," exactly, but . . . lonely. I hate it.

T: OK, stay with that lonely feeling. It's uncomfortable, I know, but let's explore it a bit.

P: Like, I hate coming home from work, the apartment is so empty, we used to talk about stuff. She always seemed to understand, well, at least listen (laughs) . . . Like now I'm just floundering around . . .

T: Floundering, directionless. So, she was like your anchor, it's like you were so very attached to her.

P: Yes, I guess I was.

T: And now she's gone, you've become unattached, not only lonely but kind of insecure?

P: Yes, I do feel insecure, less confident, it's weird. I never realized how much I depend on her.

T: Say more, depended on her for what?

The therapist helps the patient explore the feeling that he was experiencing in his body in the moment. The therapist uses empathic responding to describe the nuance of the patient's subjective emotional experience; as a result, the patient learns to differentiate his lonely feeling to enhance a sense of emotional clarity.

Unified Protocol Methods for Addressing Emotional Avoidance

The third example, taken from the UP for emotional disorders by Barlow et al. (2018, p. 93), addresses the patient's emotional avoidance and concerns about being more in the present with her emotional experiences in the module of mindful emotional awareness.

P: I don't like to sit still—it makes me more anxious.

T: Tell me more—what happens when you sit still?

P: I don't know—I just feel like I should be doing something. I feel like if I stop thinking about everything I need to do, my whole day will fall apart. I'm also afraid I'll start thinking about things I'd really rather not think about.

T: So by sitting still and focusing on the present, you're afraid you will be losing control of things that are supposed to happen today and that you might start thinking about things that have happened in the past?

P: Yeah, and that just makes me even more anxious.

T: So, you are not late for anything at the moment, but you are focusing on the possibility that you might be late later on. How does focusing on the possibility you might be late later on make you feel?

P: Anxious!

T: And what about the information that right now, in this moment, you are not running late?

P: Well, much less anxious. But I still could run late later!

T: The thing is, you have no way of knowing exactly what may happen later. You may hit traffic or your doctor's appointment might run over. Or, alternatively, you might find the roads are clear and your appointment only lasts 15 minutes instead of the scheduled 30 minutes. In other words, you just don't know. The only thing you do know for sure is that you are in this office right now, and at the moment you are not late for anything. This means that the only thing that is different about worrying about the future as opposed to paying attention to the present moment is that one makes you really anxious and the other makes you less anxious.

In this excerpt, the therapist uses a psychoeducational approach to help the patient focus on the present rather than worrying about the future. He thus tried to help her modulate her anxiety by differentiating the anxious thoughts from the external reality.

Landmark Studies and Previous Reviews

In this section, we feature two landmark ER studies. The first study concerned activation of adaptive emotions; the second focused on task analysis of corrective emotional experience.

Ulvenes et al. (2014)

Ulvenes and colleagues (2014) studied whether the therapist orienting patients toward affect produced an activation of adaptive emotion. They studied 24 patients receiving short-term dynamic psychotherapy and 23 receiving cognitive therapy for cluster C personality disorders with comorbid mood or anxiety disorders. Patients made significant improvements in both treatments. Therapist methods were rated using nine items on the Psychotherapy Process Q-Set (Jones et al., 1988) that assess patient orientation to affect. The patient's level of adaptive affect experience was rated using the Activating Affects and the Sense of Self subscales of the Achievement of Therapeutic Objectives Scale (ATOS; Berggraf et al., 2012), which was rated every 10 minutes of the session.

The therapist's use of affect-oriented methods and the patients' level of affect both gradually increased over the course of therapy. When a therapist used more affect-oriented methods for a particular patient than usual for that patient, the patient exhibited more affect. Patients whose therapist was more affect-oriented exhibited more activation of adaptive affect. In addition, patients who had a higher sense of self than when they started therapy experienced activating affect when the therapist used more affect-oriented methods than was typical for the patients.

The Ulvenes et al. (2014) study is significant in separating adaptive affect from inhibiting affect and examining the sense of self as a moderator. When patients were in their negative self state in which they did not recognize positive aspects of themselves, focusing on emotion did not bring activating affect. It may be inferred from this finding that therapist focus on affect when the patient's sense of self is negative might lead to an increase in the inhibiting affect but not activating affect. This study is also significant in that it confirmed the importance of affect-oriented methods across two therapies whose putative change mechanisms probably differ.

Nakamura and Iwakabe (2018)

Nakamura and Iwakabe (2018) conducted a task analysis of corrective emotional experience in six events from six patients who made clinically significant improvements in depression and anxiety. The therapist was an experienced male therapist who took an emotion-focused approach.

Nakamura and Iwakabe (2018) identified steps in patients' change process and the corresponding therapist's methods from an intensive process analysis. Two components of patient emotional change emerged from the analysis. The first was *intrapersonal change*, which started with the patient expressing emotional distress and eventually expressing stronger and more painful emotions such as shame, leading to the experience of relief. The second was *interpersonal change*, which consisted of processing of the immediate relational experience of successfully working through difficult emotions together. Patients then articulated their positive interpersonal experience by contrasting it with their previous hurtful experiences.

Nakamura and Iwakabe (2018) also identified two sets of therapist methods that facilitated the two above processes. First, there were experiential methods: (a) *empathic understanding*, in which the therapist tracked patient in-session experiences and verbally communicated his understanding; (b) *focusing on emotional/somatic experiences*, in which the therapist directed patients' attention on their somatic experience of emotion; and (c) *experiential directing*, in which the therapist provided specific guidance for processing patients' emotional experiences. Second, relational methods were (a) *affirming and valuing* the patient, in which the therapist explicitly communicated the patient's strength, resilience, and change; (b) *creating and maintaining a relational focus*, in which the therapist focused on the immediate relational experience; (c) *reciprocating disclosure*, in which the therapist verbalized his experience of the therapeutic relationship and the patient; and (d) *co-creating a relational meaning*, in which the therapist shared his experience of what just happened and invited the patient to reflect together.

Although a single event of corrective emotional experience cannot be the sole contributor to the improvement in ER, this is one of the few studies that examined in-session therapist methods addressing both positive and negative emotions with an ER outcome. The emergence of positive sense of self as well as adaptive emotions suggests that the distressing emotions were both regulated and transformed.

Previous Reviews

Sloan and associates (2017) identified 67 studies that measured changes in both ER and psychopathology following a psychological treatment, both individual and group. The treatments examined included affect-focused therapies such as EFT and STDP, as well as structured therapies such as ACT, cognitive–behavioral therapy (CBT), DBT, and MBCT. Both maladaptive ER strategies and overall emotion dysregulation significantly decreased at post-treatment in all but two studies regardless of (a) specific treatment, (b) the measure of ER, and (c) the patient's disorder.

Moltrecht and colleagues (2021) examined 21 randomized controlled trials (RCTs) of psychological treatments for improving ER in youth (aged 6–24 years). These treatments improved patients' ER, which in turn was associated with the improvements in psychopathology, but effect sizes were small.

A meta-analysis by Daros et al. (2021) included 90 RCTs on treating depression and anxiety among patients aged 14–24 years. Treatments included a variety of therapies, such as ACT, CBT, and DBT, as well as ERT. Patients' ER skills significantly improved, which was positively related to improvements in their depression and anxiety.

In summary, these meta-analyses generally showed the positive effect of affect-focused treatment packages on ER. They did not, however, review the specific components of treatments associated with the changes in ER.

Research Review

Search Strategy and Inclusion Criteria

We searched PubMed, PsycInfo, and Web of Science between August 2021 and May 2022 using the following terms: counseling or therapy, therapist response, therapist interventions, therapist strategies, ER, emotional experience, outcome, and emotional expression. We also asked colleagues for articles that might have been missed in the search.

The following inclusion criteria were used: (a) actual individual psychotherapy studies (no analogues); (b) published in English; (c) included adult patients (aged 18 years or older) with psychological problems; (d) included at least one validated self-report or observational measure of ER; and (e) included a measure of immediate, intermediate, or distal outcome. Studies were excluded if (a) the treatment was predominantly given in a group format or in an e-learning format; (b) they consisted of analogue sessions with college students or those within a normative population; and (c) they did not report sufficient data on above inclusion criteria (e.g., pre- and post-treatment means, standard deviations, sample sizes) or obvious errors in these values were found.

Identified publications were downloaded from the databases. If relevant literature was identified during the abstract screening, we manually screened each study's reference list for further eligible publications. The selected studies were appraised independently by the first two authors for methodological aspects, such as sampling and sample characteristics, instruments, and treatment used in primary studies, according to our inclusion and exclusion criteria. The two authors discussed and came to agreement when the eligibility of a study was unclear.

The flowchart shown in Figure 17.1 provides an overview of the extraction procedure. The initial web search identified 743 articles. We added 64 additional records identified from previous meta-analyses. From a total of 807 studies, 763 articles were excluded based on the abstract and method screening. An effectiveness study on AEDP (Iwakabe et al., 2022) was added because it included an ER measure. In total, 44 studies entered the full text screening. Of these, 13 papers had to be excluded due to insufficient data reported. Thirty-one studies matched the selection criteria and provided sufficient data. During the data extraction, three studies were excluded because some values were clearly wrong (e.g., effect size $d > 3.0$).

Emotion Regulation and Immediate and Intermediate Outcomes

We first reviewed the literature on immediate and intermediate in-session treatment outcomes. Immediate outcomes were typically assessed in the subsequent speaking turn or the same segment of a session in which a therapist method was used. Intermediate outcomes were assessed with self-report ER questionnaires administered at post session after a particular intervention module, such as an emotional awareness skills module, was used.

Table 17.1 summarizes a total of eight studies (84 clients and 33 therapists) of ER in association with immediate in-session outcomes and two studies (14 clients and 2 therapists) of intermediate outcomes. Most studies were multiple case studies, and one was a qualitative study. Given the small number of studies, we could not conduct a meta-analysis. Instead, we used box scores (our judgment based on the evidence of the outcomes) to aggregate the effects of ER methods across studies.

Table 17.1 contains the coded results of the 10 studies. For all outcomes, the three authors read each study and consensually arrived at a box score for each outcome: "+" denotes a positive effect, "=" denotes a neutral/no effect, and "–" denotes a negative effect. We assigned +1 to a positive box score, 0 to a neutral box score, and –1 to a negative box score in order to determine an overall box score for each outcome across samples. Furthermore, in order to account for sample size differences, we then multiplied the box score by the sample size for the finding, summed across the samples, and then divided by the total sample size to get a weighted box score for each immediate and intermediate

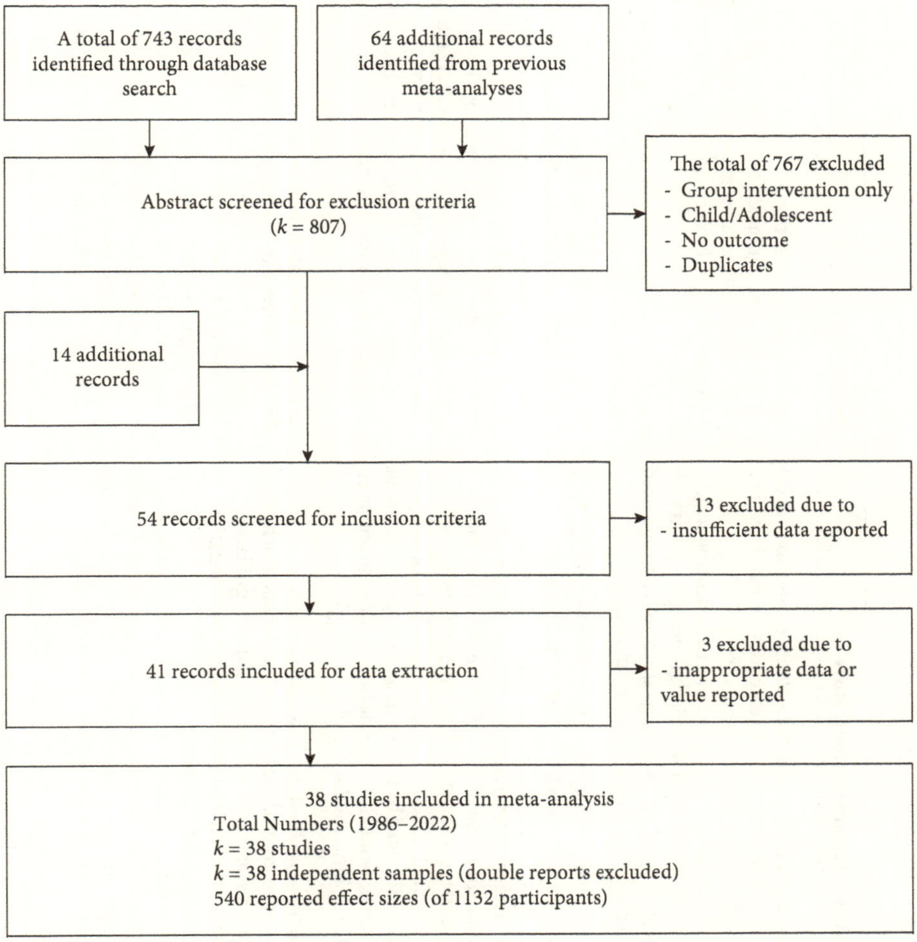

Figure 17.1 Flow diagram of the study selection process.

outcome. We considered scores between −1.00 and −0.50 negative, between −0.49 and + 0.49 neutral, and between 0.50 and +1.00 positive.

For immediate outcomes, we first looked at five studies of client experiencing. In two studies of short-term psychodynamic therapy, plan-compatible interpretations were associated with the higher level of client experiencing (Silberschatz & Curtis, 1993; Silberschatz et al., 1986). Similarly, in client-centered therapy, interpretations referring to feelings given with particular nonverbal qualities were associated with a higher level of experiencing (Gazzola & Stalikas, 1997). In Hill et al. (1988), however, interpretations did not have a higher experiencing level compared to other response modes, such as self-disclosure, open question, and approval. Similarly, Stalikas and Fitzpatrick (1996) did not find a significant relationship between therapist response modes and the client experiencing. There were thus three positive and two neutral box scores. The weighted box score across these five studies was .50 for interpretations on ER as measured with the Client Experiencing Scale.

Table 17.1 Studies of Immediate and Intermediate Outcomes of Emotion Regulation Methods

Study	Sample	Measures of ASR, Outcomes, Moderators	Results
Stalikas & Fitzpatrick (1996)	3 archival single sessions with 3 clients all from the United States, and 1 RET, 1 client-centered, 1 Gestalt therapist who is from South Africa.	Measure of therapist: HCVRCS-R (Friedlander, 1982) as coded by trained judges from transcripts; 8 categories were collapsed into 3 categories in terms of degree of structure. Measure of immediate in-session outcome: Experiencing scale (Klein et al., 1986) rated by trained judges using a 7-point scale (1 = impersonal, avoided; 7 = feelings are attended to and used for problem resolution and self-understanding).	Intermediate outcomes No relation was significant between degrees of structure of therapist responses and experiencing (= box score).
Gazzola & Stalikas (1997)	6 single sessions conducted by Carl Rogers; 2 male and 4 female clients, all apparently from the United States.	Measure of therapist: The category of Interpretation in HCVRCS-R (Friedlander, 1982) as coded by trained judges from transcripts: consensual qualitative research. A group of 3 judges independently described in writing about the nature of interpretation, the manner in which it was delivered, and the client immediate reactions following interpretation. Measure of immediate in-session outcome: The Experiencing scale (Klein et al., 1986) rated by trained judges using a 7-point scale (1 = impersonal, avoided; 7 = feelings are attended to and used for problem resolution and self-understanding).	Immediate in-session outcomes Interpretations occurred 17 times, and in 13 times they were followed by the occurrence of a higher experiencing (+ box score). Interpretations that were followed by client experiencing: (a) referred to specific client feelings, (b) were phrased tentatively, (c) delivered using the voice of the client, and (d) addressed immediate feelings.
Hill et al. (1988)	8 case studies of 12-session courses of psychotherapy in the United States. The 8 clients were adult and female and were depressed, anxious, and had self-esteem and relationship problems. The experienced therapists (4 male, 4 female, all White) came from a range of theoretical orientations.	Measure of therapist method: HCVRCS (Hill, 1985, 1986) as coded by trained judges from transcripts which has 10 categories: approval, information, direct, guidance, closed question, open question, paraphrase, interpretation, confrontation, and self-disclosure. Measure of immediate in-session outcome: Client Experiencing Scale (Klein et al., 1986) rated by trained judges using a 7-point scale (1 = impersonal, avoided; 7 = feelings are attended to and used for problem resolution and self-understanding).	Immediate in-session outcomes Ratings of client experiencing following speaking turns that included therapist self-disclosure averaged 2.49 (*SD* = 0.73) on a 7-point scale (7 = high) (+ box score). Followed by open question (*M* = 2.40, SD = 0.65), approval (*M* = 2.36, *SD* = 0.65), Paraphrase (*M* = 2.34, SD = 0.65), and interpretation (*M* = 2.34, *SD* = 0.67). (= box score for interpretation).

Silberschatz, et al. (1986)	3 adult patients with good, moderate, and poor outcome in a 16-session individual psychotherapy from the Mount Zion Brief Therapy Research Project. Therapists were experienced psychodynamic therapists. A multiple case study.	Measure of therapist method: Transference interpretations were classified using the Malan intervention typology defined as any interpretation directed toward the patient's feelings about the therapist or the therapy. Plan Compatibility of Intervention Scale was used to measure the extent to which a therapist response is suited to case formulation of the patient's plan on a 7-point Likert scale as coded by trained judges from audiotapes and transcripts. Measure of immediate in-session outcome: Client Experiencing Scale (Klein et al., 1986) rated by trained judges using a 7-point scale (1 = impersonal, avoided; 7 = feelings are attended to and used for problem resolution and self-understanding).	Immediate in-session outcomes The degree to which the therapist passed tests was significantly and positively related to the client experiencing immediately following the therapist statement in both cases. (+ box score for plan compatible interpretation).
Silberschatz & Curtis (1993)	2 adult patients with dysthymic disorder in a 16-session individual psychotherapy from the Mount Zion Brief Therapy Research Project. Therapists were experienced psychodynamic therapists. Both had an excellent outcome. A multiple case study.	Measure of therapist method: Patient Test Scale was used to identify segments of patient's testing the therapist. Patient Test Scale was used to identify segments that had included testing of a central pathogenic belief in the therapeutic relationship. Therapist Scale was then used to rate the extent to which the therapist passed or failed the patient's test on a 7-point Likert scale. Measure of immediate in-session outcome: Client Experiencing Scale (Klein et al., 1986) rated by trained judges using a 7-point scale (1 = impersonal, avoided; 7 = feelings are attended to and used for problem resolution and self-understanding). The Relaxation Scale (Curtis et al., 1986) was used to measure the patients' state of freedom, realization, and comfort (versus anxiety, drivenness on a 5-point scale). Measures of moderators: None.	Immediate in-session outcomes The degree to which the therapist passed tests was significantly and positively related to the client experiencing immediately following the therapist statement in both cases ($r = .67, .62$). (+ box score for plan compatible interpretation). The degree to which the therapist passed tests was significantly and positively related to the following patient relaxation in one case ($r = .55$). (+ box score for plan compatible interpretation).

(*continued*)

Table 17.1 Continued

Study	Sample	Measures of ASR, Outcomes, Moderators	Results
Town et al. (2012)	Twenty-four 10-minute segments from 6 adult patients with cluster C personality disorder receiving short-term psychodynamic psychotherapy for 36–60 sessions (mean 47 sessions; (4 female therapists, 2 male therapists; all White). The therapist, who was the originator of the STDP, treated all patients.	Measure of therapist ER method: The PICS as coded by trained judges from videotapes and transcripts has 8 categories: question, information, self-disclosure, clarification, directive, support, interpretation, and confrontation. The 4 content categories are defenses, anxieties, impulse/feeling, and no content. Measure of immediate ER outcome: Affect Experiencing Scale taken from the ATOS (McCullough et al., 2003), a 6-point scale (1 = no affect arousal, no report of feeling; 6 = full and complete affective arousal) rated by a group of 8 judges.	Immediate in-session outcomes The highest predicted levels of patient immediate affect experiencing were provided by confrontation-feeling (an average of 2.49 [$SD = 1.10$]). (+ box score), followed by confrontation-defense ($M = 2.33$, $SD = 0.96$) (+ box score) and then facilitative responses such as support ($M = 2.39$, $SD = 1.10$) (+ box score) and clarification ($M = 2.13$, $SD = 1.05$) (+ box score).
Ulvenes et al. (2014)	50 Norwegian patients with cluster C personality disorders in the RCT receiving either 40-session CT or STDP. 19 with major depression, 19 with dysthymia, 5 with panic disorder, 5 with agoraphobia, 7 with OCD, 28 with GAD, 4 with somatoform disorder. 8 dynamic therapists and 6 CBT therapists. Therapists had approximately 10 years of clinical experience, had 1 training case, and conducted their therapy according to the treatment manuals.	Measure of therapist ER method: Psychotherapy Q-Sort as coded by trained judges from videotapes and transcripts has 100 items. 9 items associated with Affect-focused interventions were selected to form Affect Orientation Scale such as "Th drawing attention to patient's nonverbal behavior," "Th sensitive to the patient's feelings, attuned to the patient," and "Th points out patient's attempts to ward off feelings." Measure of immediate ER outcome: Affect Experiencing Scale taken from the ATOS (McCullough et al., 2003), a 10-point scale (1 = no affect arousal, no report of feeling; 10 = full and complete affective arousal) rated by a group of trained judges for every 10 minutes of therapy. Moderator: Patient's sense of self, which is the interpersonal sense of self and ranges from a maladaptive negative view to an adaptive positive view of the self (1 = individuals deny or ignore their wants and needs and have little or no ability to identify their strengths and weaknesses; 10 = individuals acknowledge and affirm their wants and needs and are realistic about their strengths and weaknesses).	As therapy progressed, the therapists orienting the patient to affect increasingly elicited affect (+ box score). The patients whose therapist was orienting more to affect generally exhibited more activation of affect (between-patients level). When a therapist attempted to orient more to affect than what was normal for this particular patient (i.e., vis-à-vis the mean level of TAO for that patient), the patient exhibited more activation (within-patient level). Patients who had a higher sense of self than what they started therapy with were able to experience affect when the therapist oriented them to affect more than was typical for that patient.

Nakamura & Iwakabe (2018)	6 episodes of CEE taken from individual affect-focused therapy with adult patients (female = 4; male = 2), all Japanese. All patients achieved RCI on ER. 1 experienced therapist. A qualitative study.	Measure of therapist ER method: Task analysis of episodes of CEE. 2 researchers repeatedly watched videotaped segments and identified therapist methods to facilitate patient's CEE. Measure of therapist ER method: Task analysis of episodes of CEEs. 2 researchers watched videotaped segments and identified the essential patient steps toward the resolution of an emotional conflict from a distressed and dysregulated state to a positive emotionally regulated state.	2 groups of therapist methods were identified. One is experiential methods consisting of empathic understanding, focusing on emotional/somatic experiences, and experiential directing (+ box score). The other is relational methods consisting of affirming/valuing the client, creating/maintaining a relational focus, reciprocating disclosure, and co-creating a relational meaning. (+ box score). Patients started out from a state of secondary distress or emotional avoidance. Patients increasingly experienced and expressed more painful emotions and associated negative beliefs. Grief and self-soothing or self-compassion followed in which the patients projected warmth to themselves, which led to a sense of relief. This intrapersonal change process was followed by interpersonal change process in which the therapist and the patient shared their in-session experience. Mutual disclosure and sharing of positive emotions led to a sense of closeness and the patient articulated their experience in relation to their previous hurtful experiences.
Bentley et al. (2017)	10 adults with NSSI between 19 and 30 years old (female = 9; male = 1; Caucasian = 6; others = 4). All had comorbidity (MDD, GAD, SOC). 4 were on medication. Multiple case experiments. The therapist was a master student whose adherence was monitored.	Measure of therapist ER method: Adherence was monitored during weekly supervision meetings and 20% of session audio recordings were randomly selected and rated for adherence and competency by the lead developer of the UP treatment. Average adherence rating was 4.8 out of 5 (excellent). Two modules were differentiated: mindful emotional awareness and cognitive appraisal. Measure of intermediate ER outcome: The SMQ (Chadwick et al., 2008) is a 16-item self-report measure of mindful emotion awareness. Higher scores on the SMQ reflect greater levels of mindful awareness. The ERQ (Gross & John, 2003) is one of the most widely used research tools that classifies ER strategies into 2 subcategories, each with 10 items: cognitive reappraisal and expressive suppression.	9 of 10 patients demonstrated clinically reliable changes in at least one of the two emotion regulation skills. 2 patients showed module specificity of change based on visual inspection of changes in mindful emotion awareness and cognitive reappraisal. 6 patients who received only one intervention, 3 showed reliable change in only the targeted skill and 3 showed reliable change in both skills (= box score).

(*continued*)

Table 17.1 Continued

Study	Sample	Measures of ASR, Outcomes, Moderators	Results
Abasi et al. (2021)	4 patients with SAD with comorbidity of depression. All Iranian (female = 1; male = 3). Multiple case experiments. Therapist was a doctoral candidate under supervision.	Measure of therapist ER method: A treatment manual for ERT was used, and the treatment adherence was monitored by weekly supervision. ERT consists of 4 modules: awareness skills, emotion regulation skills, experiential exposure to promote the new contextual learning, and consolidating gains and relapse preventions. Measure of intermediate ER outcome: DERS (Gratz & Roemer, 2004) is a 36-item scale that assesses 6 facets of emotion dysregulation: non-acceptance of emotional responses, difficulties in engaging in goal direction, impulse control difficulties, lack of emotional awareness, limited access to emotion regulation strategies, and lack of emotional clarity on a 5-point Likert scale. AIM (Larsen et al., 1986): AIM is a self-report 40-item measure rated on a 6-point Likert scale (never = 1 to always = 6). Negative emotional subscale was used. The ERQ (Gross & John, 2003) is one of the most widely used research tools that classifies ER strategies into 2 subcategories each with 10 items: cognitive reappraisal and expressive suppression.	ER was measured weekly using DERS, ERQ, and AIM. All 4 patients achieved RCI on their ER by the end of treatment. No patient showed module specificity of change based on visual inspection of changes in DERS, ERQ, and AIM. The introduction of ER skills training in the mid-phase of treatment was not associated with the increased improvement of ER skills (= box score).

AIM, Affect Intensity Measure; ATOS, Achievement of Therapeutic Objectives Scale; CEE, corrective emotional experiences; CT, ; DERS, Difficulties in Emotion Regulation Scale; ER, emotion regulation; ERQ, Emotion Regulation Questionnaire; ERT, emotion regulation therapy; GAD, generalized anxiety disorder; HCVRCS, Hill Counselor Verbal Response Mode Category System; HCVRCS-R, Hill Counselor Verbal Response Mode Category System–Revised; MDD, major depressive disorder; NSSI, non-suicidal self-injuries; OCD, obsessive–compulsive disorder; PICS, Psychotherapy Interactional Coding System; RCI, Reliable Change Index; RCT, ; RET, ; SAD, social anxiety disorder; SMQ, Southampton Mindfulness Questionnaire; SOC, social anxiety disorder; STDP, short-term dynamic psychotherapy; TAO; UP, Unified Protocol for the Transdiagnostic Treatment of Emotional Disorders; +, positive effect; =, neutral/no effect; –, negative effect.

We also examined three short-term dynamic psychotherapy studies of therapist affect-oriented skills, including confrontation on affect, defenses, and facilitative/supportive methods (Town et al., 2012) and focusing on affects (Ulvenes et al., 2014) in association with adaptive affect. Therapist focus on affect was associated with a higher level of adaptive affect experiences, which is a part of ER via emotional transformation. In a qualitative study, Nakamura and Iwakabe (2018) found that the immediate outcome of experiential methods was arriving at an emotional resolution. For these three studies, there were three positive box scores; the average weighted box score was 1.

In terms of intermediate outcomes, Bentley and colleagues (2017) tested the introduction of mindful emotional awareness skills and emotion modulation skills related to improvements in specific areas of ER (the Southampton Mindfulness Questionnaire for mindful emotional awareness and the Emotion Regulation Questionnaire (ERQ) Reappraisal subscale for emotion modulation) in the Unified Protocol. The results showed no module-specific effects. Abasi et al. (2021) studied four cases of ERT for social anxiety disorder in which the introduction of the ER modulation skills component had an additive effect to the mindful emotional awareness component that was initially given. They used the Acceptance subscale of the Difficulties in Emotion Regulation Scale (DERS) for emotional awareness, the Affect Intensity Measure for emotional modulation, and the Reappraisal subscale of the ERQ for adaptive ER strategy for every session. Neither study found module-specific effects, although most patients achieved reliable change by the end of the course of treatment on these ER scales as well as their symptoms for social anxiety. Box scores for module-specific outcomes are neutral for three ER scales.

In summary, immediate outcomes (client experiencing and activating affect) were positive, indicating that interpretations focusing on immediate feelings with gentle and tentative manner of delivery and focusing on the patient immediate emotional experience resulted in a higher level of experiencing and adaptive affect. The experiencing level, however, does not specifically tell us about what aspects of ER are at work. On the other hand, Nakamura and Iwakabe (2018) showed that the process of emotional change leading to a regulated emotional state may involve qualitative shifts from secondary emotions, via more painful emotions to grief and self-compassion, followed by positive emotional experience with the therapist. This finding suggests that ER involves overcoming avoidance and defenses to allow the experience of difficult and painful emotions, facilitating the occurrence of underlying adaptive emotions, and reflecting on emotional experience in the therapeutic relationship.

In contrast, no module-specific effects of mindful emotional awareness or emotion modulation skills were found in studies on *intermediate* outcomes, although they were effective in improving ER. Bentley et al. (2017) suspected that different therapist methods may address the extinction of distress in response to intense emotions. They also suggested that individuals respond differently to different treatment modules.

Emotion Regulation and Distal Treatment Outcomes

From the search strategy detailed above, 28 independent studies encompassing a total of 1,034 patients and 201 therapists (the number of therapists was not cited in 10 studies) were included in the meta-analysis of distal outcomes. The main characteristics of the 28 included studies are summarized in Table 17.2. The data on which our analysis is based span more than 15 years (2007–2022) and consist of published studies using independent samples collected in naturalistic settings ($k = 18$) and RCTs ($k = 10$). The number of eligible studies ($k = 28$) included in this meta-analysis is smaller than the size of previous meta-analyses because we included only individual treatments with clinical samples. ACT ($k = 7$), DBT ($k = 3$), and UP ($k = 2$) were the most commonly employed treatment packages. These therapies had some group components ($k = 7$) in addition to individual therapy. Although one study compared online intervention with in-person intervention, we included only the in-person data in this meta-analysis. A variety of psychological disorders and problems were treated, including anxiety disorders, eating disorder, borderline personality disorder, and substance use disorder.

The most frequently used outcome scales were DERS ($k = 13$), Action and Acceptance Questionnaire (AAQ; $k = 10$), and ERQ ($k = 5$). Although they measure somewhat different aspects of ER, we combined them in one analysis given that moderate to high correlations have been reported among them. We report both overall mean scores and subscale means when they were available (Table 17.2). For the meta-analysis, we used effect sizes for the full scale unless specified.

We conducted a series of random effects models. This model is based on the assumption that the studies in this meta-analysis were randomly sampled from a population of studies. All analyses were conducted using Comprehensive Meta-Analysis (Borenstein et al., 2013). First, we tested an overall pre- and post-treatment difference in ER. Second, we examined potential moderators—whether effect sizes systematically varied due to (a) measures, (b) types of treatments, (c) types of control group, and (d) type of disorder. In addition, comparisons between the treatment group and different control groups were tested when available. Treatment effect was estimated using the weighted mean effect size Hedges' g.

The random effects model with all 28 independent studies resulted in a large treatment effect ($g = 0.82$), 95% confidence interval [CI] [0.71, –0.93], $p < .001$) compared to no treatment/wait list. That is, multiple therapies evidenced large improvements in patient ER compared to no treatment or pre- to post-treatment. At the same time, there was a large heterogeneity in the effect sizes, $I^2 = 82.66\%$ ($Q = 155.68$, $df = 27$, $p < .001$).

We also calculated the effect size of pretreatment to 2- to 6-month follow-up for the 10 studies that reported those data ($g = 0.86$, 95% CI [0.59, –1.14], $p < .001$; $I^2 = 74.06$; $Q = 34.69$, $df = 9$, $p < .001$) and pretreatment to 12-month follow-up for 3 studies ($g = 0.71$, 95% CI [0.26, –1.15], $p = .002$; $I^2 = 89.37$; $Q = 18.81$, $df = 2$, $p < .001$). The results indicate that treatment gains in ER were largely maintained; there was no significant deterioration from post-treatment to 2- to 6- and 12-month follow-up (for 2- to 6-month, $k = 10$; $g = -0.07$, 95% CI [–0.26, –0.12], $p = .456$; $I^2 = 58.02$; $Q = 21.44$, $df = 9$, $p = .011$; for 12-month, $k = 3$; $g = 0.03$, 95% CI [–0.29, –0.35], $p = .871$; $I^2 = 83.12$; $Q = 11.85$, $df = 2$, $p = .003$). Although the number of studies with the follow-up data was small, the treatment effect on ER was maintained after termination.

The fail-safe N indicated that approximately 6,811 studies with an effect size of 0 would need to be published in order to bring the weighted mean effect below .10, or practical significance. We also calculated Duval and Tweedie's trim and fill. The adjusted effect size for a random effects model was $g = 0.71$ (observed value $g = 0.82$, 95% CI

Table 17.2 Studies Included in Meta-Analysis of Treatments and Distal Effects on Patient Emotion Regulation

		Treatment Characteristics						ER Outcomes						
						N			Pre Mean (*SD*)		Post/Follow-Up Mean (*SD*)			
First Author, Year	Design	Disorder	Intervention	ER treatment components	Session	Treatment	Control	ER Measure	Treatment	Control	Treatment	Control	Effect Size[a]	Association
Dalrymple, 2007	Open trial	SAD	ACT	Mindfulness	12 × 60-min weekly sessions	19		AAQ-9	41.21 (7.74)		33.46 (8.86) 3-month: 34.92 (8.91)		Pre–post: $d = 0.93$ Pre–3-month: $d = 0.75$	Earlier changes in the AAQ predicted later changes in symptom severity ($\beta = -.48, p < .05$).
Petersen, 2009	Random assignment	AUD	ACT vs. TAU; common therapeutic interventions (e.g., group therapy)	Mindfulness	Mean 5.2 × 30-min biweekly sessions	12	12	AAQ-9	44.8 (5.1)	45.5 (6.3)	34.4 (10.6)	44.1 (5.7)	ACT: $d = 1.32$	Reductions in AAQ scores were significantly correlated with improvement on the HRS ($r = .57, p = .05$), but not the BDI-II ($r = .32, p = .31$).
Twohig, 2010	RCT	OCD	ACT vs. PRT	Contact with the present moment or mindfulness exercises	8 × 60-min weekly sessions	41	38	AAQ-16	59.76 (11.36)	57.16 (11.67)	73.69 (13.22) 3-month: 73.37 (14.44)	63.81 (7.69) 67.13 (10.74)	Pre–post ACT: $d = 1.06$ PRT: $d = 0.47$ Pre–3-month ACT: $d = 0.86$ PRT: $d = 0.64$	

(continued)

Table 17.2 Continued

First Author, Year	Design	Treatment Characteristics						ER Outcomes					Effect Size[a]	Association
						N			Pre Mean (*SD*)		Post/Follow-Up Mean (*SD*)			
		Disorder	Intervention	ER treatment components	Session	Treatment	Control	ER Measure	Treatment	Control	Treatment	Control		
Arch, 2012	RCT	Anxiety disorder	ACT vs. CBT	Acceptance, mindfulness	12 × 60-min weekly sessions	57	71	AAQ-16	59.01 (12.35)	58.49 (11.84)	70.82 (13.14)	69.43 (14.75)	Pre–post ACT: $d = 1.16$ CBT: $d = 0.90$	
											6-month: 72.14 (10.86)	6-month: 68.38 (13.76)	Post–6-month ACT: $d = 0.63$ CBT: $d = 0.45$	
											12-month: 71.71 (11.42)	12-month: 68.43 (11.65)	6-month–12-month ACT: $d = 0.10$ CBT: $d = 0.00$	
Dehlin, 2013	Case reports	OCD	ACT	Acceptance, mindfulness	8 × 60- to 90-min weekly sessions	5		AAQ-II	36.2 (5.2)		21.6 (4.8)		[Pre–post: $g = 2.32$]	When graphed, declining AAQ-II slopes appear to generally co-occur with declines in both compulsions and avoided valued activities.
											3-month: 20.6 (8.4)		[Pre–3-month: $g = 1.49$]	
Walser, 2015	Open trial	Depression	ACT	Acceptance, mindfulness	12–16 sessions	926		AAQ-II	30.93 (10.246)		38.92 (11.742)		[$g = 0.71$]	Interaction of time with experiential acceptance to predict depression severity was not significant ($b = 0.05$, $p = .362$).
Khoramnia, 2020	RCT	SAD	ACT vs. WL	Acceptance, mindfulness	12 × 90-min sessions	12	12	AAQ-II	79.72 (9.55)	82.27 (13.10)	94.45 (7.28)	83.00 (12.73)	MANCOVA ES = 0.43 [Pre-post: $g = 1.96$]	

											83.02 (16.46)	75.18 (15.89)	[Pre–2-month: $g = 1.02$]
								SCS	78.18 (12.70)	84.27 (14.93)	94.81 (6.21)	81.27 (10.09)	ES = 0.38 [Pre–post: $g = 2.71$]
											2-month: 96.77 (16.98)	2-month: 83.54 (16.57)	ES = 0.435 [Pre–2-month: $g = 2.85$]
								DERS	115.5 (13.71)	117.36 (9.78)	101.36 (9.26)	117.00 (10.86)	ES = 0.311 [Pre–post: $g = 1.80$]
											2-month: 98.54 (15.77)	2-month: 120.18 (10.60)	ES = 0.301 [Pre–2-month: $g = 2.40$]
Roemer, 2007	Open trial	GAD	ABBT	A variety of mindfulness practices, diaphragmatic breathing, and progressive muscle relaxation	16 × 60- to 90-min weekly to biweekly sessions	16		AAQ-9	44.56 (5.99)		29.81 (7.41)		Univariate ANOVA $\eta_p^2 = 0.76$ [Pre–post: $g = 2.04$]
											3-month: 34.17 (7.76)		$\eta_p^2 = 0.58$ [Pre–3-month: $g = 1.38$]
Kumar, 2008	Open trial	Depress-ion	EBCT	Mindfulness	20–24 sessions	29		AAQ-16	75.33 (13.30)		67.37 (12.94)		$d = 0.61$
Price, 2019	RCT	SUD	MABT + TAU vs. WHE + TAU vs. TAU only (including group sessions)	Developing the capacity to sustain interoceptive awareness as a mindful process to facilitate appraisal of interoceptive experiences	8–10 × 90-min sessions	74	WHE: 46	DERS	87.3 (25.1)	WHE: 88.2 (27.0)	77.4 (24.2)	WHE: 85.7 (28.0)	[MABT vs. TAU: $g = 0.76$]
							TAU: 67			TAU: 83.8 (27.3)		TAU: 83.6 (27.5)	

(*continued*)

Table 17.2 Continued

		Treatment Characteristics						ER Outcomes					
					N			Pre Mean (*SD*)		Post/Follow-Up Mean (*SD*)			
First Author, Year	Design	Disorder	Intervention	ER treatment components	Session	Treatment	Control	ER Measure	Treatment	Control	Treatment	Control	Effect Size[a]	Association
Axelrod, 2011	Open trial	BPD and substance depen- dence	DBT		60-min weekly individual sessions and 90-min weekly group sessions for 20 weeks	24		DERS	118.00 (18.47)		94.80 (17.89)		[$g = 1.23$]	Significant interactions were observed with frequency of substance use and emotion regulation, $F(1, 21) = 8.202$, $p = .009$, with changes in substance use losing significance when controlling for improvement in emotion regulation, $F(1, 21) = 0.112$, NS
Goodman, 2014	Open trial	BPD	DBT vs. healthy controls		50- to 60-min weekly individual sessions and 90-min weekly group sessions for 12 months	11	11	DERS	120.5 (24.2)	56.6 (14.9)	101.5 (25.7)	54.8 (14.4)	MANOVA $\eta^2 = 0.21$ [$g = 1.64$]	Reduction in amygdala activity to repeated unpleasant pictures following DBT was associated with improved emotion regulation as measured by the change in total DERS score ($r = 0.70$, $p < 0.02$).

Bianchini, 2019	RCT (a pilot study)	BPD	DBT vs. TAU	Core mindfulness skills, distress tolerance, emotional regulation	60-min weekly individual sessions and 120-min weekly group sessions for 12 months	10	11	DERS	56.6 (11.77)	52.9 (19.52)	65.6 (9.40)	65.1 (15.57)	[$g = 0.39$]
Ito, 2016	Open trial	Depressive and anxiety disorders	UP		Mean 18.13 × 50- to 90-min weekly sessions	17		ERQ: Reappraisal	16.2 (6.9)		23.8 (7.7)		Pre–post: $g = -0.92$
											3-month: 25.4 (4.9)		Pre–3-month: $g = -1.37$
								ERQ: Suppression	13.9 (6.0)		13.8 (3.5)		Pre–post: $g = 0.09$
											3-month: 13.4 (3.4)		Pre–3-month: $g = 0.15$
Sauer-Zavala, 2016	Case reports	BPD and comorbid anxiety and mood disorders	UP	Mindfulness (present-focused and nonjudgmental attention)	16–20 weekly sessions	5		DERS	112.00 (16.26)		84.40 (24.85)		$ES_{sg} = 1.29$ [$g = 0.83$]
Beaumont, 2012	Random assignment	Trauma-related symptoms	CBT + CMT vs. CBT	Developing empathy for themselves and acceptance of their distress	12 sessions	16	16	SCS-SF	2.13 (0.75)	1.94 (0.51)	3.72 (0.57)	3.21 (0.57)	[$g = 0.66$]
Wonderlich, 2014	RCT	BN	ICAT vs. CBT-E		21 × 50-min sessions for 19 weeks	40	40	DERS	100.6 (18.4)	98.4 (17.6)	88.9 (13.2)	90.5 (13.7)	[Pre–post: $g = 0.42$]
											4-month: 90.0 (13.8)	4-month: 93.0 (13.3)	[Pre–4-month: $g = 0.58$]

(*continued*)

Table 17.2 Continued

First Author, Year	Design	Treatment Characteristics					ER Outcomes						Effect Size[a]	Association
		Disorder	Intervention	ER treatment components	Session	N		ER Measure	Pre Mean (*SD*)		Post/Follow-Up Mean (*SD*)			
						Treatment	Control		Treatment	Control	Treatment	Control		
MacDonald, 2017	RCT	ED	CBT-RR vs. MI; day hospital including CBT group therapy	Distress tolerance, emotion regulation	4 × 60-min weekly sessions	23	21	DERS: Nonacceptance	20.87 (6.50)	20.10 (7.17)	14.56 (4.93)	15.41 (6.34)	Univariate time by condition interactions [*g* = 0.32]	
								DERS: Goals	20.52 (5.00)	19.33 (4.76)	15.90 (4.30)	19.15 (4.31)	[*g* = 1.19]	
								DERS: Impulse	27.57 (6.21)	27.48 (7.80)	20.55 (5.43)	24.01 (8.74)	[*g* = 0.53]	
								DERS: Awareness	16.52 (4.57)	15.24 (4.23)	13.02 (3.99)	15.23 (4.39)	Partial $\eta^2 = .16$ [*g* = 0.99]	
								DERS: Strategies	19.74 (6.05)	20.04 (7.68)	15.11 (4.77)	18.62 (6.98)	[*g* = 1.00]	
								DERS: Clarity	20.65 (3.93)	20.71 (3.66)	15.74 (3.89)	18.88 (5.10)	Partial $\eta^2 = .19$ [*g* = 1.09]	
Zalaznik, 2019	Open trial	PDA	CBT	Therapist encourages exploration of experiences of bodily sensations without suppression or avoidance	12 sessions	31		ERQ: Suppression	3.78 (1.29)		2.87 (1.28)		[*g* = 0.69]	

Monell, 2022	Open trial	ED	CBT or other therapies		12-month 44% treatment terminated 56% treatment ongoing	307		DERS	101.80 (25.45)		87.60 (29.58)		$d = -0.59$	Change in emotion dysregulation primarily had an indirect effect (through change in self-image), whereas change in self- image had a direct effect, on change in ED psychopathology improvement.
Jain, 2020	RCT	PTSD or depress-ion	STAIR vs. TAU	Emotion regulation skills, self-compassion	5 × 60-min sessions	13	13	DERS	103.9 (21.1)	110.5 (25.4)	79.3 (17.2) 3-month: 85.3 (19.0)	104.1 (21.4) 3-month: 102.7 (20.2)	Pre–post STAIR: $g = 1.38$ TAU: $g = 0.30$ Pre–3-month STAIR: $g = 0.90$ TAU: $g = 0.44$	
Doorn, 2014	Open trial	Moderate to severe emotional problems	EDT	The therapist helps the patient gradually experience more underlying feeling while regulating anxiety and reducing defensive behaviors.	One 2- to 3-hour initial session	31		SCS-SF	24.88 (8.10)		27.16 (7.85)		$d = 0.38$	

(continued)

Table 17.2 Continued

		Treatment Characteristics						ER Outcomes						
						N			Pre Mean (*SD*)		Post/Follow-Up Mean (*SD*)			
First Author, Year	Design	Disorder	Intervention	ER treatment components	Session	**Treatment**	**Control**	ER Measure	**Treatment**	**Control**	**Treatment**	Control	Effect Size[a]	Association
Chavooshi, 2017	RCT	MUP	ISTDP online vs. in-person[b]	Emotional awareness, tolerate and experience emotions	16 × 60-min weekly sessions	Online: 39	In-person: 42	ERQ: Reappraisal	16.2 (6.5)	17.91 (6.5)	16.2 (5.7)	24.12 (4.8)	Pre–post Online: $d = 0.48$ In-person: $d = 0.77$	
											12-month: 15.4 (5.6)	12-month: 24.1 (6.3)	Pre–12-month Online: $d = 0.49$ In-person: $d = 0.74$	
								ERQ: Suppression	12.3 (8.5)	11.15 (7.9)	11.9 (7.5)	5.52 (3.4)	Pre–post Online: $d = 0.48$ In-person: $d = 0.94$	
											12-month: 11.3 (7.2)	12-month: 7.51 (3.5)	Pre–12-month Online: $d = 0.42$ In-person: $d = 0.73$	

Iwakabe, 2022	Open trial	Trans-diagnostic	AEDP	Dyadic affect regulation	16 × 60-min sessions	63		DERS	94.62 (22.93)	76.97 (21.25)	Pre–post: $d = -0.77$
										6-month: 74.13 (22.48)	Pre–6-month: $d = -1.03$
										12-month: 71.02 (21.16)	Pre–12-month: $d = -0.92$
								SCS	15.53 (3.93)	19.44 (4.73)	Pre–post: $d = 0.99$
										6-month: 19.98 (5.00)	Pre–6-month: $d = 1.32$
										12-month: 19.71 (4.69)	Pre–12-month: $d = 0.94$
								AAQ-II	30.57 (6.61)	21.82 (8.24)	Pre–post: $d = -1.25$
										6-month: 19.90 (7.74)	Pre–6-month: $d = -1.77$
										12-month: 19.75 (8.63)	Pre–12-month: $d = -1.46$

(continued)

Table 17.2 Continued

First Author, Year	Design	Treatment Characteristics						ER Outcomes					Effect Size[a]	Association
						N			Pre Mean (*SD*)		Post/Follow-Up Mean (*SD*)			
		Disorder	Intervention	ER treatment components	Session	Treatment	Control	ER Measure	Treatment	Control	Treatment	Control		
Glisenti, 2018	Case reports	BED	EFT	Phase 1: Promoting awareness of emotions, welcoming and accepting emotions, putting emotions into words, identifying primary emotions Phase 2: Evaluating whether the primary emotion was adaptive or maladaptive, identifying destructive emotion schemes, accessing other adaptive emotions and needs, and transforming maladaptive emotion schemes	12 × 60-min weekly sessions	6		DERS	101.23 (18.75)		53.67 (8.69)		[g = 1.66]	

Normann-Eide, 2015	Open trial	BPD or APD	Step-down treatment or outpatient treatment		Step-down treatment[c]: Median 45 individual sessions Outpatient treatment: Median 46 individual sessions	52		ACI: Global AC	3.58 (0.50)		3-year: 4.00 (0.58)		$d = 0.84$	The AC change explained 7.7% of the variance in CIP ($p = .033$), 8.6% of the variance in identity integration ($p = .026$), and 8.7% of the variance in relational capacities ($p = .005$) at 3 years.
Mennin, 2018	RCT	GAD	ERT vs. MAC	Patients were encouraged to deploy regulation skills during in-session and out-of-session exposures.	20 × 60- to 90-min weekly sessions	28	25	ERQ: Reappraisal	22.6 (6.2)	21.6 (9.2)	Mid: 26.4 (5.2) Post: 29.7 (4.4)	Mid: 21.6 (9.7) Post: 24.0 (9.9)	$g = 0.54$	All proposed mediators showed an indirect effect of group on the primary outcomes. For example, GAD CSR was mediated by ERQ Reappraisal ($B = -.27$, $p < .05$) and DERS ($B = -.39$, $p < .05$).
								DERS	98.2 (23.1)	104.8 (22.4)	Mid: 82.3 (20.3) Post: 74.6 (19.0)	Mid: 102.2 (23.2) Post: 96.0 (22.0)	$g = 0.80$	

(continued)

Table 17.2 Continued

		Treatment Characteristics						ER Outcomes						
						N			Pre Mean (*SD*)		Post/Follow-Up Mean (*SD*)			
First Author, Year	Design	Disorder	Intervention	ER treatment components	Session	**Treatment**	**Control**	ER Measure	**Treatment**	**Control**	**Treatment**	Control	Effect Size[a]	Association
O'Toole, 2019	Open trial	GAD	ERT	The cultivation of emotion regulation skills	16 × 60- to 90-min weekly sessions	31		ERQ: Reappraisal	20.8 (7.8)		29.2 (7.3)		$d = 0.9$	Changes in cognitive reappraisal temporally preceded changes in all three outcomes (PSWQ, $z = -2.37, p = .018, r = .42$; STAI-7, $z = -2.43, p = .016, r = .43$; GAD-7, $z = -2.19, p = .029, r = .39$).

ER, emotion regulation; NS, not significant.

Disorders: APD, avoidant personality disorder; AUD, alcohol use disorder; BED, binge eating disorder; BN, bulimia nervosa; BPD, borderline personality disorder; ED, eating disorder; GAD, generalized anxiety disorder; MUP, medically unexplained pain; OCD, obsessive–compulsive disorder; PDA, panic disorder with agoraphobia; PTSD, post-traumatic stress disorder; SAD, social anxiety disorder; SUD, substance use disorder.

Interventions: ABBT, acceptance-based behavior therapy; ACT, acceptance and commitment therapy; AEDP, accelerated experiential dynamic psychotherapy; CBT, cognitive–behavioral therapy; CBT-E, cognitive–behavioral therapy–enhanced; CBT-RR, cognitive–behavior therapy for rapid response; CMT, compassionate mind training; DBT, dialectical behavior therapy; EBCT, exposure-based cognitive therapy; EDT, experiential dynamic therapy; EFT, emotion-focused therapy; ERT, emotion regulation therapy; ICAT, integrative cognitive–affective therapy; ISDP, intensive short-term dynamic psychotherapy; MABT, mindful awareness in body-oriented therapy; MAC, modified attention control; MI, motivational interviewing; PRT, progressive relaxation training; STAIR, Skills Training in Affective and Interpersonal Regulation; TAU, treatment as usual; UP, Unified Protocol for the Transdiagnostic Treatment of Emotional Disorders; WHE, women's health education; WL, waiting list.

Outcome measures: AAQ, Action and Acceptance Questionnaire; ACI, Affect Consciousness Interview; ANOVA, analysis of variance; BDI-II, Beck Depression Inventory–II; CIP, Circumplex of Interpersonal Problems (a 48-item version of the Inventory of Interpersonal Problems); CSR, Clinician's Severity Rating from the Anxiety Disorders Interview Schedule for DSM-IV, Lifetime Version; DERS, Difficulty in Emotion Regulation Scale; ERQ, Emotion Regulation Questionnaire; GAD-7, Generalized Anxiety Disorder–7; HRS, Hamilton Rating Scale; MANCOVA, multivariate analysis of covariance; PSWQ, Penn State Worry Questionnaire; SCS, Self-Compassion Scale; SCS-SF, Self-Compassion Scale–Short Form; STAI-7, State–Trait Anxiety Inventory–7.

[a]Effect sizes shown in brackets were calculated by the authors.

[b]This meta-analysis used in-person data only.

[c]Eighteen-week day-hospital treatment and then 90-minute weekly group therapy for a maximum of 4 years and weekly individual therapy for a maximum of 2.5 years.

[0.60, −0.83]). All our data are based on a search of electronic databases and included only published articles, which may have resulted in bias toward larger *N* studies and positive effect sizes. Figure 17.2 presents a funnel plot, which is a diagram of standard error on the *y* axis and the effect size on the *x* axis.

Given the large heterogeneity in effect sizes, we conducted a series of moderator analyses. The moderator analyses related to the ER measure, therapy type, comparison group, and patient type were all statistically significant. The effect sizes for each ER measure are presented in Table 17.2. The effect sizes for the DERS, AAQ, and SCS as outcome measures were similar (from 0.86 to 0.97), whereas effect sizes for the suppression subscale in ERQ were significantly smaller in comparison ($g = 0.49$). Table 17.3 also shows the average effect sizes for the psychological treatments on the ER outcome. ACT ($k = 7$; $g = 0.95$) and DBT ($k = 3$; $g = 1.11$) had slightly larger effect sizes than CBT and UP, but all were moderate to large effect sizes. The effect size comparing the ER treatment against active control ($k = 9$) was $g = 0.67$, 95% CI [0.39, −0.94], $p < .001$). Compared to the waiting-list group, the effect size was significantly larger ($k = 3$; $g = 1.51$, 95% CI [0.85, −2.18], $p < .001$). For the 16 studies with no control group, the effect size was also large ($g = 0.83$, 95% CI [0.70, −0.96], $p < .001$).

The psychological treatments were more effective for depression and anxiety ($k = 10$; $g = 0.82$, 95% CI [0.60, −1.05], $p < .001$), personality disorder ($k = 5$; $g = 0.93$, 95% CI [0.61, −1.26], $p < .001$; mostly of borderline personality disorder), and substance use disorder ($k = 2$; $g = 0.85$, 95% CI [0.47, −1.23], $p < .001$) than eating disorder ($k = 4$; $g = 0.81$, 95% CI [0.34, −1.27], $p = .001$). The number of sessions ($g = -0.001$), year of publication ($g = 0.006$), and number of participants ($g = -0.00$) bore no systematic relation to the ER effect sizes ($p > .3339$).

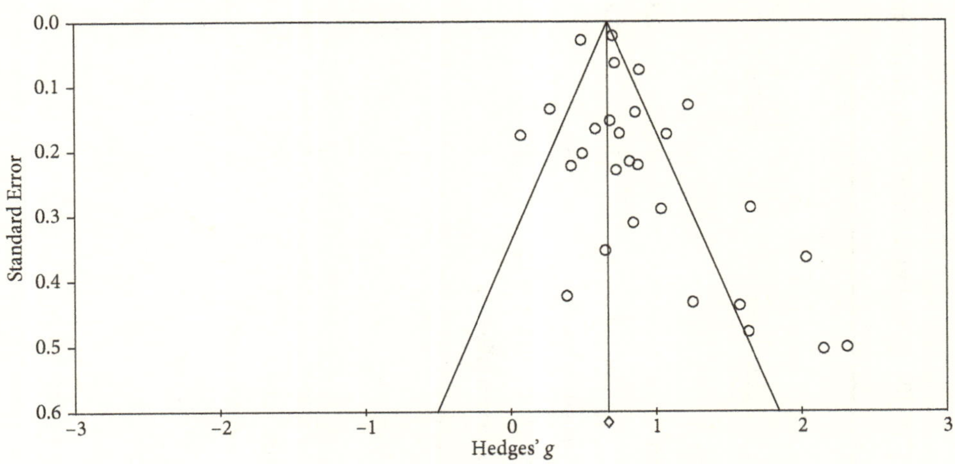

Figure 17.2 Funnel plot of treatment effects on emotion regulation outcomes.

Table 17.3 Effect Sizes by Outcome Assessment Time, Emotion Regulation Measure, Treatment Package, Control Group, and Disorder

Comparison	No. of Studies	Hedges' *g* and 95% CI				Heterogeneity			
		Point Estimate	Lower Limit	Upper Limit	*p* Value	*Q* Value	*df* (*Q*)	*p* Value	I^2
Time point									
Pre–post	28	0.82	0.71	0.93	< .001	155.68	27	< .001	82.66
Pre–2- to 6-month follow-up	10	0.86	0.59	1.14	< .001	34.69	9	< .001	74.06
Pre–12-month follow-up	3	0.71	0.26	1.15	.002	18.81	2	< .001	89.37
Post–2- to 6-month follow-up	10	−0.07	−0.26	0.12	.456	21.44	9	.011	58.02
Post–12-month follow-up	3	0.03	−0.29	0.35	.871	11.85	2	.003	83.12
ER measure									
AAQ	10	0.97	0.70	1.24	< .001	60.75	9	< .001	85.18
DERS	13	0.96	0.74	1.19	< .001	82.11	12	< .001	85.39
ERQ-Reappraisal	4	1.00	0.81	1.19	< .001	0.99	3	.804	0.00
ERQ-Suppression	3	0.49	0.08	0.90	.020	10.94	2	.004	81.72
SCS	4	0.86	0.35	1.38	.001	25.51	3	< .001	88.24
Treatment package									
ACT	7	0.95	0.57	1.32	< .001	33.46	6	< .001	82.07
DBT	3	1.11	0.54	1.67	< .001	4.55	2	.103	56.03
UP (ERQ-Combined and DERS)	2	0.66	0.34	0.98	< .001	1.20	1	.273	16.95

UP (ERQ-Reappraisal and DERS)	2	0.90	0.60	1.21	< .001	0.25	1	.619	0.00
CBT	3	0.56	0.40	0.72	< .001	2.83	2	.244	29.19
ERT	2	1.07	0.78	1.37	< .001	0.01	1	.909	0.00
Experiential (EDT, ISTDP, AEDP, and EFT)	4	0.87	0.47	1.26	< .001	25.29	3	< .001	88.14
Control									
Active control	9	0.67	0.39	0.94	< .001	18.71	8	.016	57.24
Waiting list	3	1.51	0.85	2.18	< .001	4.00	2	.135	50.03
No control	16	0.83	0.70	0.96	< .001	121.56	15	< .001	87.66
Disorder									
Depression/anxiety	10	0.82	0.60	1.05	< .001	42.16	9	< .001	78.65
OCD	2	1.46	0.09	3.01	.064	8.21	1	.004	87.82
PD	5	0.93	0.61	1.26	< .001	16.04	4	.003	75.06
ED	4	0.81	0.34	1.27	.001	17.44	3	.001	82.80
SUD	2	0.85	0.47	1.23	< .001	1.15	1	.283	13.14

AAQ, Action and Acceptance Questionnaire; ACT, acceptance and commitment therapy; AEDP, accelerated experiential dynamic psychotherapy; CBT, cognitive–behavioral therapy; DBT, dialectical behavior therapy; DERS, Difficulty in Emotion Regulation Scale; ED, eating disorder; EDT, experiential dynamic therapy; EFT, emotion-focused therapy; ER, emotion regulation; ERQ, Emotion Regulation Questionnaire; ERT, emotion regulation therapy; ISDP, intensive short-term dynamic psychotherapy; OCD, obsessive–compulsive disorder; PD, personality disorder; SCS, Self-Compassion Scale; SUD, substance use disorder; UP, Unified Protocol for the Transdiagnostic Treatment of Emotional Disorders.

Possible Negative Effects and Harm

Affect-focused methods are usually contraindicated for patients with impulse control problems, active substance abuse, and those whose dysregulation is exacerbated due to organic factors, including thought disorders (Greenberg, 2015). Individuals suffering from these disorders may harbor strong emotions and as a result act out on them. Affect-focused methods do not lead to patients' productive emotional experience when patients are feeling negative toward the self, such as shame, guilt, and self-contempt (Ulvenes et al., 2014).

There is no evidence that ER methods lead to higher risk for dropouts and negative effects than psychotherapy methods that do not directly focus on or evoke emotional experience. Nonetheless, future studies need to identify patient characteristics that are associated with non-improvement and deterioration.

Diversity Considerations

The vast majority of studies in our meta-analysis were conducted in the United States among samples of predominantly White individuals. However, ER and emotional expression are influenced by worldviews, values, and socially sanctioned rules (Mesquita et al., 2014). A review of 25 studies on racial and ethnic differences in ER showed that in 71% of the studies, ethnoracial minorities exhibited greater use of maladaptive ER strategies (Weiss et al., 2022). One study demonstrated that Asian individuals endorsed significantly greater suppression of negative emotions than Hispanic and White individuals (Kalibatseva & Leong, 2018).

When working with ER, therapists must consider how patients' cultural backgrounds inform display rules, as well as what might be considered adaptive or maladaptive ER (Markus & Kitayama, 1991). In collectivist cultures, suppressing one's emotions in the service of maintaining interpersonal harmony is often considered healthier than expressing one's emotions directly and freely. The expression of certain negative emotions can be damaging to one's social role and is thus inhibited even in the therapeutic relationship because of the fear of appearing disrespectful to the therapist, who is in a position of authority.

Gender differences, socioeconomic status, and other cultural identity factors have not been adequately examined in the ER research. Some studies suggest that there are gender differences in the use of ER strategies (e.g., Goubet & Chrysikou, 2019). This is an area in which further investigations are needed.

Limitations of the Research

Few studies have examined therapist moment-to-moment methods and their immediate, in-session, and intermediate effects on patient ER. Virtually all studies have examined the effects of multicomponents treatment packages on distal ER outcomes. The overall treatments prove effective in enhancing ER, but we do not know which specific components or methods account for the improvement. Affect-focused methods and structured methods are quite different. Common and different change processes according to each method should be delineated.

Another important task is to define ER and its multiple facets. There are several similar concepts, such as emotional processing and emotional experiencing, and their differences as well as overlaps have not yet been empirically delineated.

Future researchers can also examine the therapeutic relationship in ER work. Implicit ER is hypothesized to develop through internalizing an empathic therapist. One study showed that patients with therapists who had higher ER ability had significantly better improvements in ER (Abargil & Tishby, 2022). Future researchers could also examine common and unique factors associated with ER methods of different orientations in the context of particular therapeutic relationships.

The measurement of ER as an outcome has mostly been conducted using self-report scales; however, they may not capture the variability in how individuals spontaneously select and implement ER strategies (Aldao, 2013). Self-report questionnaires tend to overlook natural fluctuations of ER in response to daily environmental demands and emotional experiences. They are also subject to recall bias and do not necessarily correspond to the concurrent report of ER (Aldao et al., 2010; Solhan et al., 2009).

An alternative to self-report scales is ecological momentary assessment, a set of techniques that utilize repeated sampling of individuals' real-time behaviors by the use of mobile and internet technology (Shiffman et al., 2008). This might identify how a particular therapist method can affect a patient's ER in their daily life. In addition, the moment-to-moment measure of ER can be used to test the immediate effect of therapist methods and relationship behaviors. Common autonomic and electromygraphic measures may be used to track physiological arousal (Zaehringer et al., 2020). Motion energy analysis (Ramseyer, 2020) using an automated computer program may also be an effective way to track ER in a moment-to-moment manner. Nonverbal synchrony, or the coordination of the patient's and the therapist's bodily movements, has been shown to be associated with psychotherapy outcome and also with ER (Tschacher et al., 2014). Considering that ER occurs dyadically (Fosha, 2001), a combination of these measures may detect microprocesses of the therapist method and relational behaviors.

Training Implications

Given the meta-analytic evidence that multiple psychological treatments lead to improvement in ER for a range of psychological problems, trainees could benefit from learning about ER as well as its therapeutic methods. Students may familiarize themselves with observer rating scales, such as the Observer-Measure of Affect Regulation, to identify in-session markers for ER. They also can learn methods to increase emotional awareness, identify emotional avoidance, modulate dysregulated emotions, and transform maladaptive emotions with adaptive emotions as these are frequent components of ER work.

We suspect that deliberate practice might prove helpful in mastering affect-focused methods and related skills (Goldman et al., 2021). The therapist's use of voice and nonverbal behavior is critical in communicating empathy (Abargil & Tishby, 2022) and helping patients modulate their emotions (Paivio & Laurent, 2001). Trainees can practice these responses while focusing on their voice and nonverbals associated with ER, repeatedly watch their performance, receive feedback from supervisors, incorporate it, and practice the skill until it is mastered. In some affect-focused therapies, videotaped supervision is the norm, in which both supervisor and supervisee track the process of change as well as how therapists intervene moment-to-moment both verbally and nonverbally (e.g., Greenberg & Tomescue, 2017; Prenn & Fosha, 2017).

Finally, trainees can benefit from receiving training in treatments focusing on ER. ACT, AEDP, DBT, and EFT demonstrated larger effect sizes on ER in our meta-analysis. Specific instructions for structured exercises and homework will be helpful tools for trainees working with patients with emotional dysregulation.

Therapeutic Practices

The meta-analysis demonstrated large gains in patient ER from psychological treatments, but empirical evidence is lacking on the effectiveness of specific components or therapist methods. Hence, we offer recommendations based on the sparse research evidence and our clinical practice:

- Enhance patient ER capacity for a variety of behavioral disorders.
- Use either affect-oriented methods or structured psychoeducational and skill training methods to work with ER.
- Employ steps associated with enhancing patient ER: undoing experiential avoidance, enhancing emotional awareness, promoting a full emotional experience, understanding the meaning of experience, and learning strategies to cope with distress.
- Provide a therapeutic relationship characterized by empathy, validation, and support to help patients develop ER capacity. Such a relationship is frequently internalized by the patient and may function to change schemas that are putatively at the root of emotional dysregulation.
- Address patients' fearful avoidance or suppression of emotional experience via psychoeducation.
- Consider the patient's sense of self in focusing on ER in session: When patients are in their negative self-state, they frequently do not recognize positive aspects of themselves, and focusing on emotion is not likely to bring adaptive affects.
- Consider the patient's cultural identity and worldview as well as the context in which the patient's emotional experience occurs in evaluating the appropriateness of ER.

References

* Studies included in the meta-analyses.

Abargil, M., & Tishby, O. (2022). How therapists' emotion recognition relates to therapy process and outcome. *Clinical Psychology & Psychotherapy*, *29*(3), 1001–1019. https://doi.org/10.1002/cpp.2680

*Abasi, I., Pourshahbaz, A., Mohammadkhani, P., Dolatshahi, B., Moradveisi, L., & Mennin, D. S. (2021). Emotion regulation therapy for social anxiety disorder: A single case series study. *Behavioural and Cognitive Psychotherapy*, *49*(6), 658–672. https://doi.org/10.1017/S1352465821000175

Abbass, A. (2015). *Reaching through resistance: Advanced psychotherapy techniques*. Seven Leaves Press.

Aldao, A. (2013). The future of emotion regulation research: Capturing context. *Perspectives on Psychological Science, 8*(2), 155–172. https://doi.org/10.1177/1745691612459518

Aldao, A., Nolen-Hoeksema, S., & Schweizer, S. (2010). Emotion-regulation strategies across psychopathology: A meta-analytic review. *Clinical Psychology Review, 30*(2), 217–237. https://doi.org/10.1016/j.cpr.2009.11.004

*Arch, J. J., Eifert, G. H., Davies, C., Plumb Vilardaga, J. C., Rose, R. D., & Craske, M. G. (2012). Randomized clinical trial of cognitive behavioral therapy (CBT) versus acceptance and commitment therapy (ACT) for mixed anxiety disorders. *Journal of Consulting and Clinical Psychology, 80*(5), 750–765. https://doi.org/10.1037/a0028310

Auszra, L., Greenberg, L. S., & Herrmann, I. (2013). Client emotional productivity—Optimal client in-session emotional processing in experiential therapy. *Psychotherapy Research, 23*(6), 732–746. https://doi.org/10.1080/10503307.2013.816882

*Axelrod, S. R., Perepletchikova, F., Holtzman, K., & Sinha, R. (2011). Emotion regulation and substance use frequency in women with substance dependence and borderline personality disorder receiving dialectical behavior therapy. *American Journal of Drug and Alcohol Abuse, 37*(1), 37–42. https://doi.org/10.3109/00952990.2010.535582

Barlow, D. H., Farchione, T. J., Fairholme, C. P., Ellard, K. K., Boisseau, C. L., Allen, L. B., & Ehrenreich-May, J. (2017). *Unified Protocol for Transdiagnostic Treatment of Emotional Disorders: Therapist guide*. Oxford University Press.

Barlow, D. H., Farchione, T. J., Sauer-Zavala, S., Murray-Latin, H., Ellard, K. K., Bullis, J. R., Bentley, K., Boettcher, H., & Cassiello-Robbins, C. (2018). *Unified Protocol for Transdiagnostic Treatment of Emotional Disorders: Therapist guide* (2nd ed.). Oxford University Press.

*Beaumont, E., Galpin, A., & Jenkins, P. (2012). "Being kinder to myself": A prospective comparative study, exploring post-trauma therapy outcome measures, for two groups of clients, receiving either cognitive behaviour therapy or cognitive behaviour therapy and compassionate mind training. *Counselling Psychology Review, 27*(1), 31–43.

*Bentley, K. H., Nock, M. K., Sauer-Zavala, S., Gorman, B. S., & Barlow, D. H. (2017). A functional analysis of two transdiagnostic, emotion-focused interventions on nonsuicidal self-injury. *Journal of Consulting and Clinical Psychology, 85*(6), 632–646. https://doi.org/10.1037/ccp0000205

Berggraf, L., Ulvenes, P. G., Wampold, B. E., Hoffart, A., & McCullough, L. (2012). Properties of the Achievement of Therapeutic Objectives Scale (ATOS): A generalizability theory study. *Psychotherapy Research, 22*(3), 327–347. https://doi.org/10.1080/10503307.2011.653997

Berking, M., & Lukas, C. A. (2015). The Affect Regulation Training (ART): A transdiagnostic approach to the prevention and treatment of mental disorders. *Current Opinion in Psychology, 3*, 64–69. https://doi.org/10.1016/j.copsyc.2015.02.002

Berking, M., Wupperman, P., Reichardt, A., Pejic, T., Dippel, A., & Znoj, H. (2008). Emotion-regulation skills as a treatment target in psychotherapy. *Behaviour Research and Therapy, 46*(11), 1230–1237. https://doi.org/10.1016/j.brat.2008.08.005

Berking, M., & Znoj, H. (2008). Entwicklung und Validierung eines Fragebogens zur standardisierten Selbsteinscha¨tzung emotionaler Kompetenzen [Development and validation of a self-report measure for the assessment of emotion-regulation skills]. *Zeitschrift für Psychiatrie, Psychologie und Psychotherapie, 56*, 141–152.

*Bianchini, V., Cofini, V., Curto, M., Lagrotteria, B., Manzi, A., Navari, S., Ortenzi, R., Paoletti, G., Pompili, E., Pompili, P. M., Silvestrini, C., & Nicolò, G. (2019). Dialectical behaviour therapy (DBT) for forensic psychiatric patients: An Italian pilot study. *Criminal Behaviour and Mental Health, 29*(2), 122–130. https://doi.org/10.1002/cbm.2102

Bond, F. W., Hayes, S. C., Baer, R. A., Carpenter, K. M., Guenole, N., Orcutt, H. K., Waltz, T., & Zettle, R. D. (2011). Preliminary psychometric properties of the Acceptance and Action Questionnaire–II: A revised measure of psychological inflexibility and experiential avoidance. *Behavior Therapy, 42*(4), 676–688. https://doi.org/10.1016/j.beth.2011.03.007

Borenstein, M., Hedges, L., Higgins, J., & Rothstein, H. (2013). *Comprehensive Meta-Analysis version 3*. Biostat.

Brandão, T., Brites, R., Hipólito, J., & Nunes, O. (2022). The Emotion Regulation Goals Scale: Advancing its psychometric properties using item response theory analysis. *Journal of Clinical Psychology*, *78*(9), 1940–1957. https://doi.org/10.1002/jclp.23343

Campos, J. J., Frankel, C. B., & Camras, L. (2004). On the nature of emotion regulation. *Child Development*, *75*(2), 377–394. https://doi.org/10.1111/j.1467-8624.2004.00681.x

Chadwick, P., Hember, M., Symes, J., Peters, E., Kuipers, E., & Dagnan, D. (2008). Responding mindfully to unpleasant thoughts and images: Reliability and validity of the Southampton Mindfulness Questionnaire (SMQ). *British Journal of Clinical Psychology*, *47*(Pt. 4), 451–455. https://doi.org/10.1348/014466508X314891

*Chavooshi, B., Mohammadkhani, P., & Dolatshahee, B. (2017). Telemedicine vs. in-person delivery of intensive short-term dynamic psychotherapy for patients with medically unexplained pain: A 12-month randomized, controlled trial. *Journal of Telemedicine and Telecare*, *23*(1), 133–141. https://doi.org/10.1177/1357633X15627382

Cloitre, M., Koenen, K. C., Cohen, L. R., & Han, H. (2002). Skills training in affective and interpersonal regulation followed by exposure: A phase-based treatment for PTSD related to childhood abuse. *Journal of Consulting and Clinical Psychology*, *70*(5), 1067–1074. https://doi.org/10.1037//0022-006x.70.5.1067

Curtis, J. T., Ransohoff, P., Sampson, F., Brumer, S., & Bronstein, A. (1986). Expressing warded-off contents in behavior. In J. Weiss, H. Sampson, & the Mount Zion Psychotherapy Research Group (Eds.), *The psychoanalytic process: Theory, clinical observation, and empirical research* (pp. 187–205). Guilford.

*Dalrymple, K. L., & Herbert, J. D. (2007). Acceptance and commitment therapy for generalized social anxiety disorder: A pilot study. *Behavior Modification*, *31*(5), 543–568. https://doi.org/10.1177/0145445507302037

Daros, A. R., Haefner, S. A., Asadi, S., Kazi, S., Rodak, T., & Quilty, L. C. (2021). A meta-analysis of emotional regulation outcomes in psychological interventions for youth with depression and anxiety. *Nature Human Behaviour*, *5*(10), 1443–1457. https://doi.org/10.1038/s41562-021-01191-9

*Dehlin, J. P., Morrison, K. L., & Twohig, M. P. (2013). Acceptance and commitment therapy as a treatment for scrupulosity in obsessive compulsive disorder. *Behavior Modification*, *37*(3), 409–430. https://doi.org/10.1177/0145445512475134

*Doorn, K. A., Macdonald, J., Stein, M., Cooper, A. M., & Tucker, S. (2014). Experiential dynamic therapy: A preliminary investigation into the effectiveness and process of the extended initial session. *Journal of Clinical Psychology*, *70*(10), 914–923. https://doi.org/10.1002/jclp.22094

Elliott, R., Hill, C. E., Stiles, W. B., Friedlander, M. L., Mahrer, A. R., & Margison, F. R. (1987). Primary therapist response modes: Comparison of six rating systems. *Journal of Consulting and Clinical Psychology*, *55*(2), 218–223. https://doi.org/10.1037/0022-006X.55.2.218

Farchione, T. J., Tirpak, J. G. W., & Olesnycky, O. S. (2021). The Unified Protocol: A transdiagnostic treatment for emotional disorders. In A. Wenzel (Ed.), *Handbook of cognitive behavioral therapy: Overview and approaches* (pp. 701–730). American Psychological Association. https://doi.org/10.1037/0000218-024

Faustino, B., Vasco, A. B., Da Silva, A. N., & Barreira, J. (2022). Emotional Processing Difficulties Scale–Revised: Preliminary psychometric study. Person-Centered & Experiential Psychotherapies, *21*(4), 349–366. https://doi.org/10.1080/14779757.2022.2028661

Fosha, D. (2001). The dyadic regulation of affect. *Journal of Clinical Psychology*, *57*(2), 227–242. https://doi.org/10.1002/1097-4679(200102)57:2<227::AID-JCLP8>3.0.CO;2-1

Fosha, D. (Ed.). (2021). *Undoing aloneness & the transformation of suffering into flourishing: AEDP 2.0*. American Psychological Association. https://doi.org/10.1037/0000232-000

Fosha, D., Edlin, J., & Iwakabe, S. (2018). AEDP 9+1 Change Process Scale [Unpublished manuscript].

Frederickson, J. J., Messina, I., & Grecucci, A. (2018). Dysregulated anxiety and dysregulating defenses: Toward an emotion regulation informed dynamic psychotherapy. *Frontiers in Psychology*, *9*, 2054. https://doi.org/10.3389/fpsyg.2018.02054

Friedlander, M. L. (1982). Counseling discourse as a speech event: Revision and extension of the Hill Counselor Verbal Response Category System. *Journal of Counseling Psychology*, *29*(4), 425–429. https://doi.org/10.1037/0022-0167.29.4.425

Garnefski, N., Kraaij, V., & Spinhoven, P. (2001). Negative life events, cognitive emotion regulation and emotional problems. *Personality and Individual Differences*, *30*(8), 1311–1327. https://doi.org/10.1016/S0191-8869(00)00113-6

*Gazzola, N., & Stalikas, A. (1997). An investigation of counselor interpretations in client-centered therapy. *Journal of Psychotherapy Integration*, *7*(4), 313–327. https://doi.org/10.1023/B:JOPI.0000010886.33685.64

Gill, D., Warburton, W., Sweller, N., Beath, K., & Humburg, P. (2021). The Emotional Dysregulation Questionnaire: Development and comparative analysis. *Psychology and Psychotherapy*, *94*(Suppl 2), 426–463. https://doi.org/10.1111/papt.12283

*Glisenti, K., Strodl, E., & King, R. (2018). Emotion-focused therapy for binge-eating disorder: A review of six cases. *Clinical Psychology & Psychotherapy*, *25*(6), 842–855. https://doi.org/10.1002/cpp.2319

Goldman, R. N., Vaz, A., & Rousmaniere, T. (2021). Deliberate practice in emotion-focused therapy. American Psychological Association. https://doi.org/10.1037/0000227-000

*Goodman, M., Carpenter, D., Tang, C. Y., Goldstein, K. E., Avedon, J., Fernandez, N., Mascitelli, K. A., Blair, N. J., New, A. S., Triebwasser, J., Siever, L. J., & Hazlett, E. A. (2014). Dialectical behavior therapy alters emotion regulation and amygdala activity in patients with borderline personality disorder. *Journal of Psychiatric Research*, *57*, 108–116. https://doi.org/10.1016/j.jpsychires.2014.06.020

Goubet, K. E., & Chrysikou, E. G. (2019). Emotion regulation flexibility: Gender differences in context sensitivity and repertoire. *Frontiers in Psychology*, *10*, 935. https://doi.org/10.3389/fpsyg.2019.00935

Gratz, K. L., & Roemer, L. (2004). Multidimensional assessment of emotion regulation and dysregulation: Development, factor structure, and initial validation of the difficulties in emotion regulation scale. *Journal of Psychopathology and Behavioral Assessment*, *26*(1), 41–54. https://doi.org/10.1023/B:JOBA.0000007455.08539.94

Gratz, K. L., Weiss, N. H., & Tull, M. T. (2015). Examining emotion regulation as an outcome, mechanism, or target of psychological treatments. *Current Opinion in Psychology*, *3*, 85–90. https://doi.org/10.1016/j.copsyc.2015.02.010

Grecucci, A., Frederickson, J., & Job, R. (2017). Editorial: Advances in emotion regulation: From neuroscience to psychotherapy. *Frontiers in Psychology*, *8*, 985. https://doi.org/10.3389/fpsyg.2017.00985

Grecucci, A., Messina, I., Amodeo, L., Lapomarda, G., Crescentini, C., Dadomo, H., Panzeri, M., Theuninck, A., & Frederickson, J. (2020). A dual route model for regulating emotions: Comparing models, techniques and biological mechanisms. *Frontiers in Psychology*, *11*, 930. https://doi.org/10.3389/fpsyg.2020.00930

Greenberg, L. S. (2015). *Emotion-focused therapy: Coaching clients to work through their feelings* (2nd ed.). American Psychological Association. https://doi.org/10.1037/14692-000

Greenberg, L. S. (2021). Changing emotion with emotion: A practitioner's guide. American Psychological Association. https://doi.org/10.1037/0000248-000

Greenberg, L. S., & Tomescu, L. R. (2017). Supervision essentials for emotion-focused therapy. American Psychological Association. https://doi.org/10.1037/15966-000

Gross, J. J. (1998). The emerging field of emotion regulation: An integrative review. *Review of General Psychology*, *2*(3), 271–295.

Gross, J. J., & John, O. P. (2003). Individual differences in two emotion regulation processes: Implications for affect, relationships, and well-being. *Journal of Personality and Social Psychology*, *85*(2), 348–362. https://doi.org/10.1037/0022-3514.85.2.348

Hayes, S. C. (2004). Acceptance and commitment therapy, relational frame theory, and the third wave of behavioral and cognitive therapies. *Behavior Therapy*, *35*(4), 639–665. https://doi.org/10.1016/S0005-7894(04)80013-3

Hill, C. E. (1985). *Manual for Counselor Verbal Response Modes Category System* (Rev. ed.) [Unpublished manuscript]. University of Maryland at College Park.

Hill, C. E. (1986). An overview of the Hill Counselor and Client Verbal Response Modes Category Systems. In L. S. Greenberg & W. M. Pinsof (Eds.), *The psychotherapeutic process: A research handbook* (pp. 131–160). Guilford.

*Hill, C. E., Helms, J. E., Tichenor, V., Spiegel, S. B., O'Grady, K. E., & Perry, E. S. (1988). Effects of therapist response modes in brief psychotherapy. *Journal of Counseling Psychology, 35*(3), 222–233. https://doi.org/10.1037/0022-0167.35.3.222

Hill, C. E., & O'Grady, K. E. (1985). List of therapist intentions illustrated in a case study and with therapists of varying theoretical orientations. *Journal of Counseling Psychology, 32*(1), 3–22. https://doi.org/10.1037/0022-0167.32.1.3

Hilsenroth, M. J., Blagys, M. D., Ackerman, S. J., Bonge, D. R., & Blais, M. A. (2005). Measuring psychodynamic–interpersonal and cognitive–behavioral techniques: Development of the Comparative Psychotherapy Process Scale. *Psychotherapy: Theory, Research, Practice, Training, 42*(3), 340–356. https://doi.org/10.1037/0033-3204.42.3.340

Hofmann, S. G., & Kashdan, T. B. (2010). The Affective Style Questionnaire: Development and psychometric properties. *Journal of Psychopathology and Behavioral Assessment, 32*(2), 255–263. https://doi.org/10.1007/s10862-009-9142-4

*Ito, M., Horikoshi, M., Kato, N., Oe, Y., Fujisato, H., Nakajima, S., Kanie, A., Miyamae, M., Takebayashi, Y., Horita, R., Usuki, M., Nakagawa, A., & Ono, Y. (2016). Transdiagnostic and transcultural: Pilot study of Unified Protocol for depressive and anxiety disorders in Japan. *Behavior Therapy, 47*(3), 416–430. https://doi.org/10.1016/j.beth.2016.02.005

*Iwakabe, S., Edlin, J., Fosha, D., Thoma, N. C., Gretton, H., Joseph, A. J., & Nakamura, K. (2022). The long-term outcome of accelerated experiential dynamic psychotherapy: 6- and 12-month follow-up results. *Psychotherapy, 59*(3), 431–446. https://doi.org/10.1037/pst0000441

*Jain, S., Ortigo, K., Gimeno, J., Baldor, D. A., Weiss, B. J., & Cloitre, M. (2020). A randomized controlled trial of brief Skills Training in Affective and Interpersonal Regulation (STAIR) for veterans in primary care. *Journal of Traumatic Stress, 33*(4), 401–409. https://doi.org/10.1002/jts.22523

Jones, E. E., Cumming, J. D., & Horowitz, M. J. (1988). Another look at the nonspecific hypothesis of therapeutic effectiveness. *Journal of Consulting and Clinical Psychology, 56*(1), 48–55. https://doi.org/10.1037/0022-006X.56.1.48

Kabat-Zinn, J. (1994). *Wherever you go, there you are: Mindfulness meditation in everyday life.* Hyperion.

Kalibatseva, Z., & Leong, F. T. L. (2018). Cultural factors, depressive and somatic symptoms among Chinese American and European American college students. *Journal of Cross-Cultural Psychology, 49*(10), 1556–1572. https://doi.org/10.1177/0022022118803181

*Khoramnia, S., Bavafa, A., Jaberghaderi, N., Parvizifard, A., Foroughi, A., Ahmadi, M., & Amiri, S. (2020). The effectiveness of acceptance and commitment therapy for social anxiety disorder: A randomized clinical trial. *Trends in Psychiatry and Psychotherapy, 42*(1), 30–38. https://doi.org/10.1590/2237-6089-2019-0003

Klein, M. H., Mathieu-Coughlan, P., & Kiesler, D. J. (1986). The experiencing scales. In L. S. Greenberg & W. M. Pinsof (Eds.), *The psychotherapeutic process: A research handbook* (pp. 21–71). Guilford.

*Kumar, S., Feldman, G., & Hayes, A. (2008). Changes in mindfulness and emotion regulation in an exposure-based cognitive therapy for depression. *Cognitive Therapy and Research, 32*(6), 734–744. https://doi.org/10.1007/s10608-008-9190-1

Lamagna, J. (2021). Finding healing in the broken places: Intra-relational AEDP work with traumatic aloneness. In D. Fosha (Ed.), *Undoing aloneness & the transformation of suffering into flourishing: AEDP 2.0* (pp. 293–319). American Psychological Association. https://doi.org/10.1037/0000232-012

Larsen, R. J., Diener, E., & Emmons, R. A. (1986). Affect intensity and reactions to daily life events. *Journal of Personality and Social Psychology, 51*(4), 803–814. https://doi.org/10.1037/0022-3514.51.4.803

Leahy, R. L., Tirch, D., & Napolitano, L. A. (2011). *Emotion regulation in psychotherapy: A practitioner's guide*. Guilford.

Linehan, M. M. (1993). *Cognitive-behavioral treatment of borderline personality disorder*. Guilford.

Linehan, M. M. (2015). *DBT skills training handout and worksheets* (2nd. ed.). Guilford.

*MacDonald, D. E., McFarlane, T. L., Dionne, M. M., David, L., & Olmsted, M. P. (2017). Rapid response to intensive treatment for bulimia nervosa and purging disorder: A randomized controlled trial of a CBT intervention to facilitate early behavior change. *Journal of Consulting and Clinical Psychology*, *85*(9), 896–908. https://doi.org/10.1037/ccp0000221

Machado, P. P., Beutler, L. E., & Greenberg, L. S. (1999). Emotion recognition in psychotherapy: Impact of therapist level of experience and emotional awareness. *Journal of Clinical Psychology*, *55*(1), 39–57. https://doi.org/10.1002/(sici)1097-4679(199901)55:1<39::aid-jclp4>3.0.co;2-v

Markus, H. R., & Kitayama, S. (1991). Culture and the self: Implications for cognition, emotion, and motivation. *Psychological Review*, *98*(2), 224–253. https://doi.org/10.1037/0033-295X.98.2.224

McCullough, L., Larsen, A. E., Schanche, E., Andrews, S., Kuhn, N., & Hurley, C. L. (2003). *Achievement of Therapeutic Objectives Scale*. Short-Term Psychotherapy Research Program at Harvard Medical School. https://www.affectphobia.com

McMain, S., Korman, L. M., & Dimeff, L. (2001). Dialectical behavior therapy and the treatment of emotion dysregulation. *Journal of Clinical Psychology*, *57*(2), 183–196. https://doi.org/10.1002/1097-4679(200102)57:2<183::aid-jclp5>3.0.co;2-y

McMain, S., Pos, A., & Iwakabe, S. (2010). Facilitating emotion regulation: General principles for psychotherapy. *Psychotherapy Bulletin*, *45*, 16–21.

McNair, D. M., Lorr, M., & Droppleman, L. F. (1971). Manual for the profile of mood states.

Medley, B. (2021). Portrayals in work with emotion in AEDP: Processing core affective experience and bringing it to completion. In D. Fosha (Ed.), *Undoing aloneness & the transformation of suffering into flourishing: AEDP 2.0* (pp. 217–240). American Psychological Association. https://doi.org/10.1037/0000232-009

Mennin, D. S., & Fresco, D. M. (2014). Emotion regulation therapy. In J. J. Gross (Ed.), *Handbook of emotion regulation* (pp. 469–490). Guilford.

*Mennin, D. S., Fresco, D. M., O'Toole, M. S., & Heimberg, R. G. (2018). A randomized controlled trial of emotion regulation therapy for generalized anxiety disorder with and without co-occurring depression. *Journal of Consulting and Clinical Psychology*, *86*(3), 268–281. https://doi.org/10.1037/ccp0000289

Mennin, D. S., Fresco, D. M., Ritter, M., & Heimberg, R. G. (2015). An open trial of emotion regulation therapy for generalized anxiety disorder and cooccurring depression. *Depression and Anxiety*, *32*(8), 614–623. https://doi.org/10.1002/da.22377

Mesquita, B., De Leersnyder, J., & Albert, D. (2014). The cultural regulation of emotions. In J. J. Gross (Ed.), *Handbook of emotion regulation* (pp. 284–301). Guilford.

Mitmansgruber, H., Beck, T. N., & Schüßler, G. (2008). "Mindful helpers": Experiential avoidance, meta-emotions, and emotion regulation in paramedics. *Journal of Research in Personality*, *42*(5), 1358–1363. https://doi.org/10.1016/j.jrp.2008.03.012

Moltrecht, B., Deighton, J., Patalay, P., & Edbrooke-Childs, J. (2021). Effectiveness of current psychological interventions to improve emotion regulation in youth: A meta-analysis. *European Child & Adolescent Psychiatry*, *30*(6), 829–848. https://doi.org/10.1007/s00787-020-01498-4

*Monell, E., Clinton, D., & Birgegård, A. (2022). Emotion dysregulation and eating disorder outcome: Prediction, change and contribution of self-image. *Psychology and Psychotherapy*, *95*(3), 639–655. https://doi.org/10.1111/papt.12391

*Nakamura, K., & Iwakabe, S. (2018). Corrective emotional experience in an integrative affect-focused therapy: Building a preliminary model using task analysis. *Clinical Psychology & Psychotherapy*, *25*(2), 322–337. https://doi.org/10.1002/cpp.2150

Neff, K. D. (2003). Self-compassion: An alternative conceptualization of a healthy attitude toward oneself. *Self and Identity*, *2*(2), 85–101. https://doi.org/10.1080/15298860309032

*Normann-Eide, E., Johansen, M. S., Normann-Eide, T., Egeland, J., & Wilberg, T. (2015). Personality disorder and changes in affect consciousness: A 3-year follow-up study of patients with avoidant and borderline personality disorder. *PLoS One*, *10*(12), e0145625. https://doi.org/10.1371/journal.pone.0145625

*O'Toole, M. S., Renna, M. E., Mennin, D. S., & Fresco, D. M. (2019). Changes in decentering and reappraisal temporally precede symptom reduction during emotion regulation therapy for generalized anxiety disorder with and without co-occurring depression. *Behavior Therapy*, *50*(6), 1042–1052. https://doi.org/10.1016/j.beth.2018.12.005

Paivio, S. C., & Laurent, C. (2001). Empathy and emotion regulation: Reprocessing memories of childhood abuse. *Journal of Clinical Psychology*, *57*(2), 213–226. https://doi.org/10.1002/1097-4679(200102)57:2<213::aid-jclp7>3.0.co;2-b

Paivio, S. C., & Pascual-Leone, A. (2010). Emotion-focused therapy for complex trauma: An integrative approach. American Psychological Association. https://doi.org/10.1037/12077-000

Pascual-Leone, A., & Greenberg, L. (2005). Classification of affective-meaning states. In A. Pascual-Leone (Ed.), *Emotional processing in the therapeutic hour: "Why the only way out is through"* (pp. 289–367) [Unpublished doctoral thesis]. York University. https://www.uwindsor.ca/people/apl/sites/uwindsor.ca.people.apl/files/pascual-leone_greenberg_2005_cams_measure.pdf

*Petersen, C. L., & Zettle, R. D. (2009). Treating inpatients with comorbid depression and alcohol use disorders: A comparison of acceptance and commitment therapy versus treatment as usual. *The Psychological Record*, *59*(4), 521–536.

Prenn, N. C. N., & Fosha, D. (2017). *Supervision essentials for accelerated experiential dynamic psychotherapy*. American Psychological Association. https://doi.org/10.1037/0000016-000

*Price, C. J., Thompson, E. A., Crowell, S. E., Pike, K., Cheng, S. C., Parent, S., & Hooven, C. (2019). Immediate effects of interoceptive awareness training through Mindful Awareness in Body-Oriented Therapy (MABT) for women in substance use disorder treatment. *Substance Abuse*, *40*(1), 102–115. https://doi.org/10.1080/08897077.2018.1488335

Ramseyer, F. T. (2020). Exploring the evolution of nonverbal synchrony in psychotherapy: The idiographic perspective provides a different picture. *Psychotherapy Research*, *30*(5), 622–634. https://doi.org/10.1080/10503307.2019.1676932

Reicherts, M. (2007). Dimensions of openness to emotions (DOE): A model of affect processing, manual (Scientific report No. 168). University of Fribourg.

Renna, M. E., Quintero, J. M., Fresco, D. M., & Mennin, D. S. (2017). Emotion regulation therapy: A mechanism-targeted treatment for disorders of distress. *Frontiers in Psychology*, *8*, 98. https://doi.org/10.3389/fpsyg.2017.00098

*Roemer, L., & Orsillo, S. M. (2007). An open trial of an acceptance-based behavior therapy for generalized anxiety disorder. *Behavior Therapy*, *38*(1), 72–85. https://doi.org/10.1016/j.beth.2006.04.004

Roemer, L., Orsillo, S. M., & Salters-Pedneault, K. (2008). Efficacy of an acceptance-based behavior therapy for generalized anxiety disorder: Evaluation in a randomized controlled trial. *Journal of Consulting and Clinical Psychology*, *76*(6), 1083–1089. https://doi.org/10.1037/a0012720

*Sauer-Zavala, S., Bentley, K. H., & Wilner, J. G. (2016). Transdiagnostic treatment of borderline personality disorder and comorbid disorders: A clinical replication series. *Journal of Personality Disorders*, *30*(1), 35–51. https://doi.org/10.1521/pedi_2015_29_179

Shiffman, S., Stone, A. A., & Hufford, M. R. (2008). Ecological momentary assessment. *Annual Review of Clinical Psychology*, *4*, 1–32. https://doi.org/10.1146/annurev.clinpsy.3.022806.091415

Siegel, D. J. (1999). *The developing mind: How relationships and the brain interact to shape who we are*. Guilford.

*Silberschatz, G., & Curtis, J. T. (1993). Measuring the therapist's impact on the patient's therapeutic progress. *Journal of Consulting and Clinical Psychology*, *61*(3), 403–411. https://doi.org/10.1037/0022-006X.61.3.403

*Silberschatz, G., Fretter, P. B., & Curtis, J. T. (1986). How do interpretations influence the process of psychotherapy? *Journal of Consulting and Clinical Psychology*, *54*(5), 646–652. https://doi.org/10.1037/0022-006X.54.5.646

Simons, J. S., & Gaher, R. M. (2005). The Distress Tolerance Scale: Development and validation of a self-report measure. *Motivation and Emotion*, *29*(2), 83–102. https://doi.org/10.1007/s11031-005-7955-3

Sloan, E., Hall, K., Moulding, R., Bryce, S., Mildred, H., & Staiger, P. K. (2017). Emotion regulation as a transdiagnostic treatment construct across anxiety, depression, substance, eating and borderline personality disorders: A systematic review. *Clinical Psychology Review*, *57*, 141–163. https://doi.org/10.1016/j.cpr.2017.09.002

Solbakken, O. A., Hansen, R. S., Havik, O. E., & Monsen, J. T. (2011). Assessment of affect integration: Validation of the affect consciousness construct. *Journal of Personality Assessment*, *93*(3), 257–265. https://doi.org/10.1080/00223891.2011.558874

Solhan, M. B., Trull, T. J., Jahng, S., & Wood, P. K. (2009). Clinical assessment of affective instability: Comparing EMA indices, questionnaire reports, and retrospective recall. *Psychological Assessment*, *21*(3), 425–436. https://doi.org/10.1037/a0016869

Solomonov, N., McCarthy, K. S., Gorman, B. S., & Barber, J. P. (2018). The Multitheoretical List of Therapeutic Interventions–30 items (MULTI-30). *Psychotherapy Research*, *19*, 96–113 doi:10.1080/10503307.2017.1422216

*Stalikas, A., & Fitzpatrick, M. (1996). Relationships between counselor interventions, client experiencing, and emotional expressiveness: An exploratory study. *Canadian Journal of Counselling*, *30*(4), 262–271.

*Town, J. M., Hardy, G. E., McCullough, L., & Stride, C. (2012). Patient affect experiencing following therapist interventions in short-term dynamic psychotherapy. *Psychotherapy Research*, *22*(2), 208–219. https://doi.org/10.1080/10503307.2011.637243

Tschacher, W., Rees, G. M., & Ramseyer, F. (2014). Nonverbal synchrony and affect in dyadic interactions. *Frontiers in Psychology*, *5*, 1323. https://doi.org/10.3389/fpsyg.2014.01323

*Twohig, M. P., Hayes, S. C., Plumb, J. C., Pruitt, L. D., Collins, A. B., Hazlett-Stevens, H., & Woidneck, M. R. (2010). A randomized clinical trial of acceptance and commitment therapy versus progressive relaxation training for obsessive–compulsive disorder. *Journal of Consulting and Clinical Psychology*, *78*(5), 705–716. https://doi.org/10.1037/a0020508

*Ulvenes, P. G., Berggraf, L., Wampold, B. E., Hoffart, A., Stiles, T., & McCullough, L. (2014). Orienting patient to affect, sense of self, and the activation of affect over the course of psychotherapy with cluster C patients. *Journal of Counseling Psychology*, *61*(3), 315–324. https://doi.org/10.1037/cou0000028

*Walser, R. D., Garvert, D. W., Karlin, B. E., Trockel, M., Ryu, D. M., & Taylor, C. B. (2015). Effectiveness of acceptance and commitment therapy in treating depression and suicidal ideation in veterans. *Behaviour Research and Therapy*, *74*, 25–31. https://doi.org/10.1016/j.brat.2015.08.012

Watson, D., Clark, L. A., & Tellegen, A. (1988). Development and validation of brief measures of positive and negative affect: The PANAS scales. *Journal of Personality and Social Psychology*, *54*(6), 1063–1070. https://doi.org/10.1037//0022-3514.54.6.1063

Watson, J. C., McMullen, E. J., Prosser, M. C., & Bedard, D. L. (2011). An examination of the relationships among clients' affect regulation, in-session emotional processing, the working alliance, and outcome. *Psychotherapy Research*, *21*(1), 86–96. https://doi.org/10.1080/10503307.2010.518637

Weiss, N. H., Thomas, E. D., Schick, M. R., Reyes, M. E., & Contractor, A. A. (2022). Racial and ethnic differences in emotion regulation: A systematic review. *Journal of Clinical Psychology*, *78*(5), 785–808. https://doi.org/10.1002/jclp.23284

*Wonderlich, S. A., Peterson, C. B., Crosby, R. D., Smith, T. L., Klein, M. H., Mitchell, J. E., & Crow, S. J. (2014). A randomized controlled comparison of integrative cognitive–affective therapy (ICAT) and enhanced cognitive–behavioral therapy (CBT-E) for bulimia nervosa. *Psychological Medicine*, *44*(3), 543–553. https://doi.org/10.1017/S0033291713001098

Zaehringer, J., Jennen-Steinmetz, C., Schmahl, C., Ende, G., & Paret, C. (2020). Psychophysiological effects of downregulating negative emotions: Insights from a meta-analysis of healthy adults. *Frontiers in Psychology, 11*, 470. https://doi.org/10.3389/fpsyg.2020.00470

*Zalaznik, D., Weiss, M., & Huppert, J. D. (2019). Improvement in adult anxious and avoidant attachment during cognitive behavioral therapy for panic disorder. *Psychotherapy Research, 29*(3), 337–353. https://doi.org/10.1080/10503307.2017.1365183

Zelkowitz, R. L., & Cole, D. A. (2016). Measures of emotion reactivity and emotion regulation: Convergent and discriminant validity. *Personality and Individual Differences, 102*, 123–132. https://doi.org/10.1016/j.paid.2016.06.045

18
Chairwork

Antonio Pascual-Leone and Tabarak Baher

Chairwork, a therapeutic method used in psychotherapy for almost 100 years (Moreno, 1948), represents a group of enactment methods in which the client engages in an imaginal dialogue (Perls, 1973). These enactments are unscripted dialogues with varying degrees of structure (a) between the client and an aspect of themselves or (b) between the client and another (imagined) person with whom a relational conflict exists. The main objective of engaging in chairwork is to explore underlying feelings and their associated meaning for the purpose of reaching a resolution of personal difficulties (Greenberg et al., 1993; Perls, 1973).

Chairwork is prominently represented in many treatment packages for individual psychotherapy, including Gestalt therapy, emotion-focused therapy (EFT), schema therapy, and cognitive–behavioral therapy (CBT). However, research has not systematically explored its effects on proximal in-session (i.e., immediate) and distal treatment (i.e., long-term) outcomes. In this chapter, after providing definitions and clinical examples, we review the effect of chairwork on immediate and long-term outcomes in individual psychotherapy. We conclude with limitations of the research, diversity considerations, training implications, and therapeutic practices.

Definitions

Chairwork can be defined as the enactment of the relationship between parts of the self (Greenberg et al., 1993; Kellog, 2004; Perls, 1973). The purposes of these enactments are to gain a new perspective on one's experiences and to attain a resolution of conflict between parts of the self or between the self and an important other (Greenberg et al., 1993; Perls, 1973). At least four major types of chairwork have been identified: (a) the *two-chair task* for enacting internal dialogue between conflicting parts of the self; (b) the *two-chair task* for enacting otherwise automatic process of self-interruption or self-censorship; (c) the *empty-chair task* for enacting internal dialogues regarding conflict with a significant other person; and (d) *compassion-focused chairwork* for enacting affinity, compassion, or tenderness toward the self (Greenberg et al., 1993; Kellog, 2004; Perls, 1973).

Chairwork is typically understood in the literature in concrete and operational terms. Examples of that pragmatic definition include using a chair to help imagine talking to another person who is not actually present or shuttling between two chairs to help one speak from different positions. However, there is a wide range of physical manifestations and potential intervention targets (Greenberg et al., 1993; Paivio et al.,

Antonio Pascual-Leone and Tabarak Baher, *Chairwork* In: *Psychotherapy Skills and Methods That Work.*
Edited by: Clara E. Hill and John C. Norcross, Oxford University Press.
DOI: 10.1093/oso/9780197611012.003.0018

2010; Pugh & Broome, 2020). We propose that all types of chairwork include five essential elements: (a) an intentional but unscripted *enactment* for working through a personal difficulty; (b) exploration of each side of (typically two) *conflicting parts* (distinct positions, "voices"), which are in juxtaposition to one another; (c) vivid engagement through an *imaginal entry into a scene*; (d) *each perspective is independently elaborated in relation to the other*, often by dynamically switching between parts, positions, and perspectives; and (e) *integrating compatible aspects from each of the opposing parts*, combining them into a coherent whole. As such, completion of the method (resolution) is marked by the generation of a *new and overarching experience*, meaning, and/or change in emotion (a dialectic synthesis).

Our definition excludes several methods that may otherwise appear similar in presentation. Chairwork is not (a) *behavioral rehearsal* to prepare clients for an intended future conversation, confrontation, or assertiveness training; (b) *emotional role-play* (i.e., imagining how one would respond if one were diagnosed with lung cancer) without a juxtaposition of parts to be synthesized; (c) *exploring evidence* for or against some belief, without an imaginal entry and responding to some scenario "as if"; and (d) *weighing pros/cons*, where resolution is a "best choice" rather than a synthesis of parts. Furthermore, chairwork *does not have to involve chairs* or moving furniture; it can be a semistructured, internal, and imaginative process (Paivio et al., 2010). Finally, although chairwork may implicitly involve exposure to imagined stimuli (e.g., a perpetrator) or to feared emotional experiences (e.g., tolerating and engaging distress), chairwork is *not exposure without an intention to synthesize* opposing parts.

History of Chairwork

Enactments, which refer to the expression of one's thoughts and feelings into action through dramatization, resolve internal (intrapersonal) conflict between the client and an aspect of themself, and external (interpersonal) conflict between the client and an imagined other was first used in psychodrama group therapy (Moreno, 1948). During a session of group therapy, a client would be asked to role-play one side of their own conflict, while other members of the group role-played other parts of the client. Role-playing conflicts in psychodrama was later implemented in individual Gestalt therapy, in which the client was asked to play both sides of the presenting conflict (Perls, 1969, 1973). Later, steps involved in successful chairwork for individual therapy were elaborated in EFT using task analysis (e.g., Greenberg, 1983; Greenberg & Foerster, 1996). Since then, CBT and schema therapy have also come to incorporate a more cognitive rendition of chairwork (de Oliveira, 2008; Pugh, 2018).

Theoretical Development of Chairwork

The notion of conflict between parts of the self has been a core feature of numerous theoretical and cultural frameworks. However, the dialogical self theory succinctly captures this idea of a self that is composed of differentiated parts, known as *I-positions*, that make up the entire entity of the "self." Together, these parts of self make up a complex "society of mind" (Hermans et al., 1992). Each I-position holds different perspectives of thoughts and feelings that contribute to how an individual feels, thinks, and behaves in the world. These perspectives are expressed through dialogue between the I-positions, which help shape an individual's idea of what their self-image ought to be. These I-positions (parts) are experienced as the voice of the internal critic or the opinions that others are perceived to hold about the individual, which are often internalized as absolute truths about the self. These voices are then reflected in how one speaks to oneself (Hermans et al., 1992).

Interactions become problematic when one I-position is overly critical or coercive toward the rest of the self (known as the "experiencing self"), in an attempt to preserve the needs of the self-image (Perls, 1969). Emotional disturbances can also arise when apprehensiveness over encountering pain, typically from the experiential self, leads to unresolved and unexpressed negative emotions related to an interpersonal interaction. As a result, individuals may find themselves unable to adaptively respond to new situations (Perls, 1969, 1973). Accordingly, Gestalt's chairwork was developed based on the assumption that identifying and separating different parts of the self and facilitating dialogue between them can ameliorate the associated distressing emotions (Perls, 1973).

Clinical Description and Indications

Two-Chair Task to Resolve Conflicts Within the Self

Internal dialogue is facilitated through the two-chair task when it is evident that the internal conflict is being caused by a split between aspects of the self (Clarke & Greenberg, 1986; Greenberg & Watson, 2006). A *split* is said to occur when two distinct parts of the self (positions) are identifiable, the conflicting part is perpetuating negative self-treatment or actions against the self, and a client feels torn or a sense of struggle.

Self-splits can manifest as a *decisional split*, in which the client is undecided about something. The therapist helps the client explore some unspoken sense of obligation to certain values of beliefs in one chair (e.g., "I like the security of a job at the bank") versus a tacit sense of fundamentally unmet needs in the other chair (e.g., "I long to become a full-time artist"). Statements of indecision or personal dilemma (e.g., "Should I file for a divorce or not?") serve as in-session markers for introducing the two-chair task to work through a decisional split. Decisional splits in those with social anxiety present as catastrophic "if–then" statements, in which a client believes that a social consequence (e.g., rejection, embarrassment) will occur if they engage in a particular action (Elliot, 2013; Mendes et al., 2016).

A *negative self-evaluation split* could occur when a client actively treats themself badly, such as cases of punitive self-criticism or a habitual self-interruption that constrains and prohibits the healthy experience. The prototypic marker of this type of split is when a client describes a sense of rigid obligation to some value (e.g., "I should do more") or expresses contempt or hostility toward themself (e.g., "I'm such an idiot, it's pathetic"). When the self talk reveals an unrelenting or overbearing tone (e.g., [shaking head], "It's like, 'get it together!! You *have* to do this!'"), it serves as a marker for the two-chair task. These kinds of markers are frequently described in cases of depression (where the critical voice is critical and contemptuous; Greenberg & Watson, 2006) or anxiety (where the critical voice is controlling and restrictive; Watson & Greenberg, 2017).

In a split associated with anxiety symptoms, the critical and coercive self reinforces a fear or doubt of a consequence occurring if the experiencing self attempts to pursue an unmet need (Elliot et al., 2004; Greenberg & Watson, 2006). Specifically, the self-evaluative split serves to overcontrol and constrain the self as a form of self-protection (e.g., "You are weak and need to be protected against failure or disappointment, it is a dangerous world and you should not dare or take risks"; Elliot et al., 2004).

The *attributional split* represents a version of this same process, except a client refers to their own self disparagement in terms of the impact by another person (e.g., "My wife makes me feel belittled" or "People will think I'm a loser"). The criticism is projected, and the marker for two-chair work is salient in cases of social anxiety (Greenberg et al., 1993).

Irrespective of how a negative self-evaluation manifests, the therapist sets up a dialogue between the two chairs that brings the opposing parts into the client's awareness. The client is asked to actively embody and express their own negative self-treatment from the "critical chair" (e.g., "I tell myself: 'You're such a lazy piece of garbage!'") and then to elaborate what it is like to hear or receive the impact of that negative self-treatment in the "experiencing chair" (e.g., "That makes it feel worthless, ashamed, but also angry at the injustice"). Whatever the case, the two-chair task is used to consider each side in turn; the conflict is elaborated toward a rapprochement of opposing positions. The process is resolved through dialogue and enactment, switching between positions until some level of integration between the two chairs emerges to synthesize a higher level of meaning (Clarke & Greenberg, 1986; Kellogg, 2004; Perls, 1973).

Two-Chair Task to Resolve Self-Interruption

The *self-interruptive split* is an example of negative self-treatment. Rather than "putting myself down," this form of negative self-treatment is about "shutting myself down" or "constraining my self-expression." Identifying markers of the self-interruptive split often begins by focusing on implicit behaviors and conspicuous absence of feeling (e.g., "I hold myself back" or "I was going to stand up for myself . . . but there's no point"). This intrapersonal conflict is between the dominance of an "avoiding self" and the "experiencing self" (Clarke & Greenberg, 1986; Elliott et al., 2004). The interruption can take the form of verbalized statements that express feelings of resignation, numbness, or stagnation in one's emotions or nonverbal gestures (e.g., relaxing fist after a few seconds of it being clenched; Clarke & Greenberg, 1986; Greenberg & Watson, 2006). Others may express feelings of numbness or stagnation (e.g., "Something whelmed up inside, but it just went away, like an emergency shutoff . . ."). Self-interruptions related to avoiding painful emotions are a transdiagnostic phenomenon that can be found in anxiety, depression, complex trauma, eating disorders, and personality disorders (Werner et al., 2019).

The central objective of this kind of chairwork is in separating out parts of the self that precipitate a self-interruption, a process that often occurs outside of awareness. The therapist directs the client to enact the part that interrupts from one chair (e.g., "Be the emergency shut. What do you say to her? How to you turn off the feeling or sap her will to continue?"). Paradoxically, clients are encouraged to interrupt themselves on purpose until they gain an awareness of what has been an implicit process. Catastrophizing thoughts are elaborated (e.g., "Don't go there, you'll drown in your own tears") as well as nonverbal expressions (e.g., "I hold my breath, bite down hard and look at the ceiling, waiting for the feeling to go away"). As clients become aware of their role in this process, exercising it at will, they also gain control over whether they want to interrupt or not.

Empty-Chair Tasks to Resolve Conflicts in Relation to Others

The empty-chair task is indicated when a client expresses unresolved feelings of anger, hurt, or resentment toward a person of significance, known as *unfinished business* (Clarke & Greenberg, 1986; Greenberg & Goldman, 2019; Perls, 1973). Specific markers of the empty-chair task vary in their emotional arousal depending on the diagnostic concern. Clients who present with unfinished business or complex relational trauma typically express unresolved and lingering negative feelings toward a personal grievance (Clarke & Greenberg, 1986; Greenberg et al., 1993; Paivio & Pascual-Leone, 2023). The classic marker for an empty-chair task is when a client relays dialogue from a past conversation and literally speaks from the other's position (e.g., "He would say x"; "She would be, like, 'You . . .'"). The empty-chair task is used to work through unresolved feelings, which may range from long-standing interpersonal grievances to complex relational trauma (Greenberg et al., 1993). Although the task addresses interpersonal difficulties, resolution in relation to a significant other is not the same as an interpersonal process itself (e.g., resolving a conflict in couple's therapy). In an empty-chair task, a therapist facilitates the resolution of a relational injury by helping the client get closure for relational events, independently of the other person.

The person with whom the client has unfinished business is visualized as seated in the empty chair (Greenberg et al., 2008; Perls, 1973). The client may be asked to enact the hurtful actions of the target person from the empty chair, in a direct and immediate way toward the experiencing chair. When the client switches into the experiencing chair, they are asked to attend to and express the emerging emotions they actively experience in response to the hurtful actions and attitudes of the target person. The dialogue may consist of multiple shifts between the experiencing chair and the empty chair, in which the client is sometimes directed to speak as if they were the target person (e.g., Therapist: "Come over here and *be* your dad for a moment, what's the message being sent when he rolls his eye, put words to that. It's like he's saying . . .?"). Resolution often consists of fully expressing previously unresolved feelings toward the other person in the context of this imaginal dialogue, which helps the client change how they view the other person and leads to a healthier experience of themselves in relation to past interactions.

Compassion-Focused Chairwork

Given markers of self-neglect or other negative self-treatment, *compassion-focused chairwork* is used to foster positive affect (e.g., compassion, empathy, love, tender respect) for oneself and a broader connection to one's humanity. The markers for introducing compassionate chairwork may be a poignant negative self-treatment related to self-criticism, the client presents with intense vulnerable emotion related to trauma, or simply that there is a need for downregulation and self-soothing or self-care. In compassion-focused therapy, clients are introduced to "compassionate self practices" prior to chairwork (Bell et al., 2020; Gilbert, 2010; Gilbert & Irons, 2005). The method is then deployed prescriptively to focus on other parts of the self via chairwork. Such work may include focusing compassion toward an imagined other (e.g., as in empty-chair task) or creating a dialogue between the compassionate self and a vulnerable self (e.g., as in the two-chair task). The goal of compassion-based chairwork is not to fight against a punitive critic or perpetrator (cf, Arntz & Jacob, 2013; Pavio & Pascual-Leone, 2023) but, rather, to provide an additional lens of compassionate understanding and self-acceptance (Bell et al., 2020). The "compassionate chair" is intentionally evoked by therapists, who direct clients in adopting a care-based mentality, enacting compassionate attributes and skills.

The degree to which the compassionate chair represents a separate task or a segment of work embedded toward the end of other chairwork (and without preparatory practice) depends on one's treatment approach (see Arimitsu, 2016; Greenberg et al., 1993). Whatever the case, a client empathizes and shows compassion toward themself in light of, or in reaction to, the witnessing of their own negative self-treatment or past negative interpersonal events. In both stand-alone and part of conflict resolution, the compassionate self could be enacted as a third-party observer who expresses affinity toward the experiencing self and/or the opposing self/other (e.g., "What would an ideal mother say?" "What would God say?" "How might you encourage a small child?" "Can you respond to that with love and tenderness?").

Chairwork Across Different Therapeutic Approaches

Chairwork has predominantly been used in Gestalt, EFT, schema, CBT, and compassion-focused therapy. Chairwork in these treatments is typically carried out following a framework that resembles our five-point definition given above, but they are used to serve different purposes (Pugh, 2018). Therapists using chairwork in Gestalt therapy typically take an exploratory approach that allows the dialogue to be elaborated in a spontaneous way (Perls, 1973). That is, the direction of the method unfolds on a moment-to-moment basis with the only predetermined objective of increasing awareness and identifying underlying needs (Perls, 1973). In EFT, chairwork aims at facilitating emotional processing in the moment by viscerally activating a maladaptive emotion scheme, exploring unmet needs, and generating adaptive emotions (Greenberg & Watson, 2006; Pascual-Leone & Greenberg, 2007). Thus, imaginal dialogue in EFT is concerned with the impact of emotion-laden statements and interpersonal conflicts.

In schema or CBT, chairwork involves an internal dialogue that may focus the client's attention on confirmatory evidence that offers credence to a certain maladaptive belief (Kellogg, 2004). Thus, one chair represents the confirmatory evidence for a maladaptive schema, and the other represents disconfirmatory evidence against the maladaptive schema. The two-chair task can alternatively be facilitated by personifying the different characters involved in a judicial courtroom trial in different chairs (de Oliveira, 2008; de Oliveira et al., 2012a). The client alternates between the "internal prosecutor" and "defense attorney," while presenting confirmatory and disconfirming evidence about a maladaptive thought. At the end, both the client and the therapist take the "juror chair" to discuss the accuracy of the evidence. In this chapter, we refer to this as "trial-based chairwork."

Two-chair and empty-chair tasks can also be used in CBT to help clients enact certain problematic behavior in one chair and then practice generating more adaptive states of meaning in the other (Goldfried & Davison, 1976; Pugh, 2018). But rather than preparation for any anticipated real-life event, this exercise is done for the sole purpose of reinforcing more adaptive ways of construing and responding. It is an encoding and rehearsal of new meaning in the context of old problems.

Contraindications

Clients already in a state of emotional overarousal or dysregulation may not benefit from engaging in chairwork due to the highly evocative nature of the method. Overwhelming distress can disrupt the attentional abilities required of a client to make meaning related to emerging emotions (Briere & Scott, 2006). Excessive distress can also validate preexisting beliefs about the repercussions associated with engaging with evocative affects, which is counterproductive (Paivio & Pascual-Leone, 2023). Last, chairwork is not intended for clients who have a fragmented sense of self (e.g., dissociative identity disorder).

Assessment

Assessing the Presence and Quality of Chairwork

The presence and quality of chairwork have been assessed in EFT using the Levels of Engagement Scale (Paivio et al., 2001). Trained raters make a global appraisal of a client's quality of engagement during the task as a whole. The presence of chairwork is easily determined by the therapist proposing a task, setting up a chair, and inviting the client to speak directly to an imaged other or part of the self. This conspicuous act determines the frequency with which chairwork is introduced. Going further, the quality of engagement considers three components: A client's (a) involvement in the process of chairwork (e.g., willingness, enactment, spontaneous involvement), (b) expression and exploration of emotion (e.g., acknowledging emotion, expressive arousal), and (c) maintaining psychological contact with the object of emotion (e.g., vividness; using "I" and "you" language rather than speaking in third person; making "eye contact" with the imagined person, part of the self, or therapist. These criteria for the presence and quality of chairwork showed good interrater reliably ($\kappa = .80–.81$) in an EFT study of complex trauma (Paivio et al., 2001).

Assessing Immediate Outcomes

Short-term outcomes of chairwork can be understood as client responses that occur while engaged in the intervention. Examples of short-term outcomes hypothesized to be associated with chairwork include emotional awareness; expressive arousal; and sequential transformations of emotion, insight, and depth of experiencing. These constructs overlap and are each associated to varying degrees.

A number of instruments purposefully measure these within-session processes. These include, for example, observer ratings on the Client Experiencing Scale, the Client Emotional Arousal Scale, or client self reports on the credibility of their self-critical beliefs. There is no single construct (much less a single instrument) that has been established for the assessment of process outcomes related to chairwork. Because of (a) the complexity involved in chairwork, (b) the range of ways in which it has been implemented across treatment approaches, and (c) the fact that this research area remains exploratory, we aim only to illustrate how the field has approached the process assessment of chairwork.

The best candidate measure for the process assessment of chairwork is depth of client experiencing (Klein et al., 1986), the emerging moment-by-moment embodied experience of new subjective meaning-making. The level of experiencing for each client is determined by the verbal content and manner of a client's speech. This process is typically measured using an observer-rated measure known as the Client Experiencing Scale (Klein et al., 1986). The scale consists of seven levels, reflecting the extent to which clients are engaging with emerging emotions and sensations in a meaningful way. At low levels of experiencing (levels 1 and 2), clients discuss their inner experiences in an external and superficial manner (e.g., "Well, my phone calls with him are fairly short, I don't want to talk"). At medium levels of experiencing (levels 3 and 4), a client begins to label and even convey a portrait of their internal experience (e.g., "It's like I'm drowning in fear" or "I have the sense of betrayal, like he still owes me"). Finally, at higher levels of experiencing (levels 5–7), clients might actively puzzle and postulate about their own experience (e.g., "I wonder why I get so worked up? I guess it's the sense that I've never been part of a family") or encounter new insights and emerging emotions (e.g., "I need to feel like I matter, and I deserve that!"), experiencing them in the moment. A meta-analysis review of research using the measure shows it to have excellent interrater reliability and to be an important predictor of symptom outcomes across treatment approaches (Pascual-Leone & Yeryomenko, 2017).

Although depth of client experiencing is the most used instrument for measuring the effects of chairwork, a number of other measures have been explored as well. Such measures represent a range of constructs but typically have only been used once or twice. One of the reasons for this paucity in research is that the assessment of chairwork per se has not frequently been a research question in the available studies.

Emotional arousal refers to the intensity with which emotions are internally experienced, whereas *expression* is the articulation and symbolization of internal arousal through observable verbal and nonverbal behavior. In some studies, clients are asked to rate the intensity of some target emotion on a scale of 1 (low) to 10 (high) (as in Nardone et al., 2022; Narkiss-Guez et al., 2015), whereas others have used physiological measures or acoustic patterns (Diamond et al., 2010; Rochman & Diamond, 2008). Still other research has used observer-rated scales to assess verbal and nonverbal indicators of emotional arousal, including changes in facial expressions, tone of voice, gestures, posture, and speech patterns (e.g., Client Emotional Arousal Scale–III; as in Stiegler, Molde, et al., 2018a). Last, measuring arousal during chairwork has also focused on problem activation via client self-reports (e.g., Bern Post Session Report; as in Trachsel et al., 2012). When reported, these measurements showed good psychometrics.

Insight is defined as the ability to understand and make sense of one's experience in a meaningful way that often emerges through reflection (Castonguay & Hill, 2007). In the context of chairwork, insight may include recognizing the prominence of one's internal dialogue, how it contributes to the distress one experiences, or gaining an understanding of why one feels a certain way (Stiegler, Binde ret al., 2018). In chairwork, insight has primarily been assessed by directly asking clients about a newfound awareness or having clients reflect on their experience engaging in the intervention (e.g., Bell et al., 2020, 2021). An example of this kind of assessment is when clients are periodically given a single-item self-report to rate the perceived credibility of core self-critical beliefs (e.g., Delavechia et al., 2016; de Oliveira et al., 2012a; van Maarschalkerweerd et al., 2021).

Sequential transformation refers to the patterns in discrete emotions as a unique therapeutic process. This involves following maladaptive emotions with the evocation of adaptive emotions, known in EFT as changing emotion with emotion (Pascual-Leone, 2018). Temporally ordered patterns in discrete emotion have been studied as a process outcome of chairwork using minute-by-minute observer-rated codes based on a client's verbal and nonverbal expressions of emotion (e.g., Classification of Affective-Meaning States; Pascual-Leone & Greenberg, 2005; as in Khayyat-Abuaita et al., 2019, showing excellent interrater reliability). Other studies have similarly assessed specific shifts using single-item client self-reports on the intensity of discrete emotions provided while chairwork is being conducted (e.g., Narkiss-Guez et al., 2015; Rochman & Diamond, 2008).

Assessing Distal Outcomes

The effectiveness of chairwork in effecting distal treatment outcomes has been assessed over several domains. These include the extent to which individuals reach the resolution of target complaints identified by clients, change in psychological symptoms related to mental health conditions, increases in their self-esteem, and compassion toward the self. These outcomes are "distal" in the sense that there is a causal chain that is believed to begin with chairwork (or another therapeutic method).

The outcomes examined have also varied somewhat by treatment approach. For example, resolution, forgiveness, and closure have been more frequently represented in research on EFT and are typically measured using client self-reports (e.g., Resolution Scale, as in Paivio et al., 2001). Self-compassion, self-esteem, and identity are typically examined by compassion-focused and humanistic–experiential approaches using multi-item self-reports (e.g., Rosenberg Self-Esteem Scale or Self-Compassion Scale; as in Arimitsu, 2016; Goldman et al., 2006; Neff et al., 2007). However, psychological symptoms and distress comprise the most common domain for examining change because the distal effects of chairwork have been tied primarily to the treatment objectives rather than the aims of chairwork itself. Typical measures here include self-report measures of depression (Center for Epidemiologic Studies Depression Scale; Hautzinger & Bailer, 1993; as in Trachsel et al., 2012) or anxiety (State–Trait Anxiety Inventory–State-Form Subscale; Spielberger et al., 1970), target complaints (Target Complaint Discomfort Box Scale; Battle et al., 1966), or single-item and visual analogue scales regarding specific outcome changes (Valence of Punitive Belief; as in Delavechia et al., 2016; de Oliveira et al., 2012a; or Visual Analogue Scale–Dysphoria, as in Whelton, 2005).

Clinical Example

The following example of chairwork is from an abridged treatment session of EFT. The client gave consent for the publication of this example and was collaboratively involved in editing the text as well as decisions to suitably alter identifying variables. At this moment in the session, the client (C) presents a marker of *unfinished business*, the therapist (T) then introduces the chairwork method, and they engage in the process.

C: These days I can't even get my brother on the phone without me becoming caustic and bitter with him. I've always tried to support him, give him a leg up, but he's never really done anything for himself. He didn't even respond to my invitation to go on a vacation together. He's just been too passive for too many years, and I'm so frustrated by him.

T: Ok. Let's try something. Can you imagine him here in this room? What would that be like? . . . If you imagine him sitting in this chair. . . . What comes up inside for you?

C: Ugh! I can't even *look* at him. (frowns, shakes head) I can't believe it. I never thought it would come to this. . . . He's become so self-absorbed, totally unaccountable to anyone!

T: Do that some more, shake your head at him. Tell him: "I can't even look at you . . ."

C: It's true, I can't even look at you! I feel *so* disappointed by your lack of involvement or interest in me . . . or your nieces. I also feel angry. You are so self-involved, everything is a pity party for you, every conversation is about your "special-ness" and excuses. You're oblivious to your entitlement. You take what you want and don't give in return.

T: What's happening inside as you say this?

C: It feels unfair, I feel betrayed . . .

T: Betrayed . . . like, "You didn't have my back"? . . . or "This isn't want I hoped for" . . .?

C: Well, yeah . . . based on what I expected or hoped for from a family member. . . . I don't understand him. How can he be happy?! He's not. I don't even know if he wants more contact . . . he seems like he doesn't care.

T: Ok, switch chairs. Come over here and be your brother for a minute. What do you think it would be like for him to hear this?

C: I think he would feel overwhelmed but also get indignant. He has no accountability.

T: So, do that. Be the "indignant brother." How does he show that?

C: Oh, he's like: "You're always criticizing me, I'm not standing for this abuse bla bla bla and I have to protect myself, I have to manage myself. I can't handle it."

T: Oh, I see, it's like, "I can't handle your demands"? or . . .?

C: Yes, that's basically what he's really saying. . . . "I can't handle your demands . . . I don't want that kind of relationship. I have to do it my own way. It makes me anxious to be tied down. . . ." I mean he has all these problems, weird disabilities. He's not actually that functional. Some of it is cowardice, but some of it's *real* . . . and I *know* he's suffering.

T: So, what's that message being sent? Like, reading between the lines, say it in words for him. It's like, there's more meaning than he is saying. . . . Can you say it for him?

C: "I only have time for myself. I have so few resources. I'm sorry." And I think he *is* sorry.

T: Switch chairs. What's going on inside with you? This resonates somehow. . . .

C: Well, he's so scared of life, and he lives like a mouse, but he's also so sensitive and hangs onto stuff. He's so fragile for some reason. Well, there *are* reasons but it's complicated. And he feels so ashamed too . . . I wish I could help him, but he doesn't want my help.

T: Speak to him. When it isn't frustrating, what do you want to tell him?

C: (Heavy sigh) "You are so crippled by your own shame, and you do all this crazy-making defensive charade, but I know it's *hard* on you. I know you're hurting. . . . I love you. I don't know what to say, but I'm going to back off . . . and I'm here if you need me."

T: And I see the sadness in your eyes. . . . There is a loss for you. . . .

C: It's heartbreaking! . . . A loss for both of us, really. I wish he was more involved, in my life, in my kid's lives. . . . It must be lonely for him. And somehow, I need to respect him, his choices. . . . Maybe I don't need to work so hard. He's who he is. Either he'll find his way or . . . I don't know. It's not really mine to solve. He's still family. I hope he decides to live a little. . . . It's his life. And I'll make use of the middle-space with him.

T: (Long pause) So, as we step out of that dialogue with him . . . I guess I'm wondering, what's this like for you? How does it all sit with you?

C: It's a relief, in a weird way. I miss him but I need to get out more myself. Spend time with my own friends, make some space between us. Maybe it will be a relief for him too.

Landmark Studies and Previous Reviews

A landmark study uses a dismantling research design to identify whether chairwork contributes to long-term outcome. Using a between-subjects additive design, Goldman et al. (2006) randomly assigned 38 participants who met clinical criteria for depression to a person-centered therapy or EFT. Both therapies primarily used empathetic responding and the same relationship conditions, but EFT made additional use of chairwork (two-chair and empty-chair) as needed. The findings revealed a medium additive effect, in which chairwork plus empathetic responding led to a significantly greater alleviation of depressive symptoms ($d = 0.51$) and global symptoms of distress (d

= 0.56), while increasing interpersonal functioning ($d = 0.58$) and self-esteem ($d = 0.35$) relative to the impact of classic person-centered therapy.

The client experience of incorporating chairwork in the context of a strong therapeutic relationship has been explored using qualitative interviews (Stiegler, Binder, et al., 2018). Participants completed EFT in which chairwork was used as a central method. They reported that the unusual nature of having to speak to oneself was associated with increased anxiety and uncertainty about how well they performed during the task. Some clients reported feeling apprehensive, uncomfortable, and embarrassed about engaging in chairwork, but they also observed that the empathetic relationship helped assuage this concern. Clients reported that chairwork helped them experience painful emotions more intensely, clearly, and painfully than simply talking about their internal conflict. Such intensity was perceived as productive, in that it allowed internal difficulties to be concretized in the here and now, which facilitated awareness of the severity and harshness of one's critical voice and how the client was contributing to their own emotional difficulties in the ways they speak to themselves. As one participant summed up, "It's heavy, intensive, horrendous and nice" (Stiegler, Binder, et al., 2018, p. 139).

Despite a 100-year history of chairwork in psychotherapy and its incorporation across treatment approaches, to date there has been no systematic review on the impact of this therapeutic method. We attribute this absence to the lack of a universal definition (such as the one we propose), but even more so to the complexity and multistep nature of the method, as well as its wide range of outcome effects.

Research Review

Quantitative Meta-Analysis

We sought to synthesize the research evidence on chairwork in individual psychotherapy. The following three research questions were examined: What are the outcome effects of chairwork on (a) immediate processes and (b) distal symptom change? and (c) How does the effect of chairwork compare to the effects of other therapy methods?

Selection of Studies

The literature search was conducted using PsycInfo, ERIC, MEDLINE, and Social Sciences Abstracts databases in January 2022. To ensure that all relevant studies were included, the following search strings were used to identify articles and dissertations that included these terms in the title, abstract, key terms, methods, or test and measurement section: chairwork OR empty chair OR two chair OR imaginal confrontation OR imaginal dialogue OR hot seat AND psychotherapy OR therapy OR counselling OR counseling OR arousal OR experiencing OR emotion OR awareness OR reflection OR insight OR meaning making OR symptom OR change OR outcome OR effect. To attenuate potential publication bias, researchers were contacted for unpublished materials and relevant dissertations/theses that may not have been available through search databases.

We then screened all articles. No restrictions were placed on participant characteristics, meaning all clinical presentations, age, and race/ethnicity demographics were included as long as the studies were conducted in the context of an individual psychotherapy session(s) in which chairwork was facilitated (group, family, and couples therapies were excluded). Studies were required to make a comparison of chairwork through between-group (e.g., alternative or no treatment) or within the individual over the course of therapy (e.g., pre–post treatment, multiple baseline). In addition, qualitative studies that examined clients' accounts of helpful aspects of chairwork were retrieved.

Methodological quality of all primary studies that met inclusion criteria was carefully evaluated for internal validity. Doing so helped minimize the number of studies with overestimated or underestimated effect sizes that may have been the result of methodological shortcomings. All studies were assessed to ensure they (a) used reliable measures or reported adequate interrater reliability, (b) had nonsignificant rates of missing data and attrition, (c) did not introduce redundant data due to the use of a secondary data set from another article included in the current analysis, (d) provided appropriate comparison groups or measures, (e) used random assignment when needed, (f) were published in the English language, and (g) included an assessment or internal controls (e.g., task supervision or explicit protocols) for adherence to the way chairwork was conducted or for treatment packages as a whole that included chairwork.

The search produced 366 potential sources (Figure 18.1). Of these, 76 were duplicates, could not be accessed, or were not written in English. Another 214 consisted of articles not examining chairwork, chapters, case studies without comparisons or outcome measures, or review papers. Of the 76 studies retrieved, 53 did not meet the inclusion criteria (see Figure 18.1). The remaining 23 studies were included in the review. Those studies reflect data from a total of 693 clients and more than 197 therapists.

The 23 studies included the use of chairwork over a single session or the repetitive use of chairwork over multiple sessions in the context of a multi-session treatment. In contrast to treatment packages in which multiple methods are used, these multi-session studies were limited in the number of methods being facilitated in addition to chairwork, such that only those needed to prepare the client for chairwork were used. For instance, in EFT studies, this included using empathetic reflection and building therapeutic alliance prior to chairwork; whereas in studies of cognitive–behavioral models, this often included explaining the CBT model and generating a list of unhelpful thoughts that were later evaluated during chairwork. Data from single-session studies typically showed the impact of a one-time use of chairwork in addressing a clinically relevant issue, whereas multi-session studies were likely to reflect the impact of repeated sessions of chairwork in the context of other supporting methods. As such, single-session and multi-session studies were analyzed separately.

Coding

For each study retrieved, we coded factors related to (a) *treatment* (i.e., type of chairwork, therapeutic orientation, and laboratory setting vs. treatment setting), (b) *participant* (i.e., clinical presentation and outpatient vs. student research participants), (c) *comparison* (i.e., types of control groups being used), and (d) *outcome* (i.e., type of outcome measured and when). In addition, we coded means, standard deviations, and effect sizes. Single-session studies of chairwork were designed to examine presenting concerns of a clinical nature (i.e., levels of self-criticism, difficulty making vocational

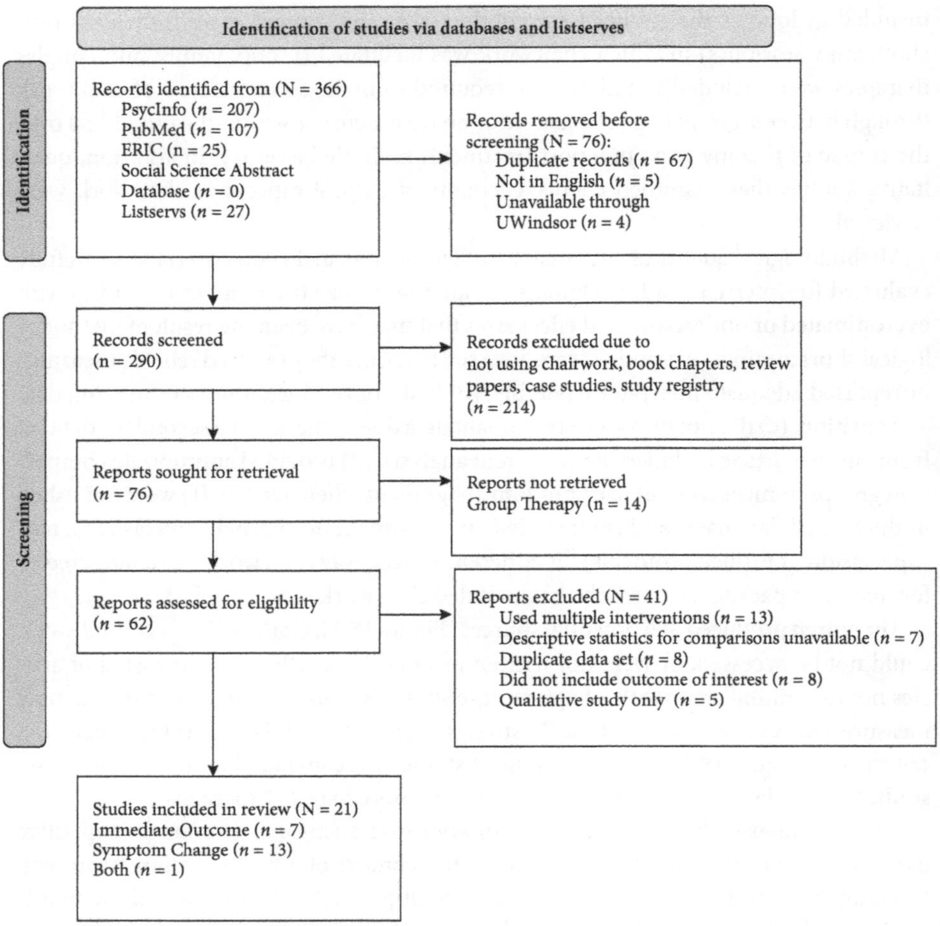

Figure 18.1 PRISMA diagram: Search results.

decisions, and unresolved anger toward an important other) rather than recruiting by clinical diagnosis. As such, symptom change was primarily associated with changes in distress regarding the presenting concern. When studies used multiple measures to assess outcomes in response to the presenting concern without a clear distinction in which was most relevant, the measure with the highest internal consistency was selected.

In contrast, multi-session treatments used patients who specifically met clinical diagnostic criteria for a particular disorder (i.e., social anxiety, post-traumatic stress disorder, obsessive–compulsive disorder, and depression). For the purposes of assessing whether chairwork is effective in treating presenting concerns, the outcome measure pertaining to a client's clinical presentation was selected. When samples consisted of comorbid disorders (e.g., depression and anxiety), the two target outcome measures were combined to produce a single effect.

Data Analysis

For primary studies that conducted between-group and/or within-group comparisons, a standardized mean difference (Cohen's *d*) was used as a measure of effect size (Cohen,

1969, 1977). For ease of interpretation, improvements in outcome were coded in the positive direction. Studies that report the effect size associated with the comparison of interest (e.g., pre–post therapy or between intervention groups) were directly extrapolated. Effect sizes that were reported as Pearson correlations and their associated variances were converted into *d* values. When not reported, established formulas were used to calculate effect sizes and standard error for between-group comparisons based on descriptive statistics reported (means and standard deviations for each condition post treatment; Cohen, 1969, 1977). In contrast, the formulas for calculating effect sizes and associated standard error for within-group comparisons are less clear.

Cohen's *d* was computed using mean difference and a pooled variance. In the context of within-group data, the pooled variance assumes homoscedasticity between the pre and post therapy scores. Homoscedasticity is often violated in psychotherapy research because clients do not typically improve in a uniform manner. Instead, improvements vary from one client to another regardless of whether overall significant improvements are observed, which contributes to larger variability among post-therapy scores. As such, the standard deviation of pre-therapy scores is recommended as an alternative measure of variance for calculating effect sizes for within-group data (Kline, 2013). The calculations of Cohen's *d* for within-group studies in the current syntheses are consistent with these recommendations.

The data set consists of within-subject designs that do not typically report the statistics (standard error, confidence intervals, standard deviation of the difference) necessary to conduct significance testing in a meta-analysis—that is, the standard error for each effect size is a function of the standard error of the original comparison test (e.g., repeated-measures analysis of variance or paired-sample *t*-test). The standard error from the original comparison test served as the starting point, which was then reduced in the percentage of change that the mean difference was reduced when calculating the individual effect sizes. However, the standard errors of comparison tests were not typically reported, and they require the standard deviation of the difference (SD_{diff}) to be calculated. To obtain a standard error, we calculated the SD_{diff} associated with pre-to-post therapy scores using the following formula:

$$SD_{diff} = SQRT\ [SD^2_{Time\ 1} + SD^2_{Time\ 2} - (2 \times Corr \times SD_{Time\ 1} \times SD_{Time2})]$$

where SQRT, square root.

The correlation between Time 1 and Time 2 represents the magnitude of improvement from pre to post therapy, with higher correlations representing small improvements and lower correlations representing larger improvements. Most of the primary studies reported a significant improvement in outcome, but the correlation was not reported and expected ranges were not found in the literature. Given that meta-analyses are not overly sensitive to precise estimates of standard error, the SD_{diff} was calculated using an estimated correlation of pre-to-post therapy scores. A sensitivity analysis using multiple correlations (i.e., .20, .30, .40, .50, .60, .70, .80, .90, and 1.00) revealed that higher correlations inflated standard error, which in turn decreased the probability of finding a significant summary effect in the meta-analysis. In the current study, .80 correlation was used because it balanced between attenuating Type I error and retaining some representation of the significant change reported in primary studies.

To ensure sufficient power, meta-analyses were conducted when three or more studies were available. When a sufficient number of studies were unavailable, findings were synthesized using a narrative review. The meta-analyses were conducted using Stata version 17. Summary effects were derived under the random-effects model with the inverse of the standard error as the weighting factor. A restricted maximum likelihood estimate (REML) was used to estimate the between-study variance (T^2). The usefulness of the REML method lies in its ability to use a set of contrast from the data set to create distribution, which is then used to calculate between-study variance (Veroniki et al., 2016). Heterogeneity was then examined using Cochrane's *Q* statistic and the I^2 statistic. Finally, funnel plots and Rosenthal's (1979) fail-safe *N* test were used to examine the number of additional studies needed to null the findings.

Immediate Process Outcomes

There was substantial variability in the measures used and the research designs of relevant studies: Two studies measured arousal, two studies examined the credibility of punitive core beliefs, and four studies measured the depth of client experiencing. Moreover, the studies that examined depth of client experiencing used between-subject designs of Gestalt therapy, whereas the other four used within-subject designs of various treatments. In contrast to the standard errors of the within-subjects' effects that were overestimated, the standard error of between-group effects could be more precisely calculated due to the availability of standardized formulas. As such, studies were separately synthesized according to the research design used to maximize the interpretability and precision of findings. We first explore the effects of chairwork on immediate outcomes in within-subject designs (subgroup $k = 4$) and then explore the effects on depth of experiencing from between-subject designs (subgroup $k = 4$).

Four studies using within-subjects design reported on the facilitation of arousal or credibility of core beliefs in a single session of chairwork. The results of these studies are summarized in Figure 18.2. The pooled chairwork effect revealed a nonsignificant effect in facilitating these immediate outcomes, $d = 0.10, p = .41$, 95% confidence interval (CI) [−0.14, 0.34]. The tests of heterogeneity indicated no significant variability among the individual effect sizes of the primary studies, $Q(3) = .02, p = 1.00, I^2 = 0$, meaning the magnitude of the effect sizes were relatively consistent across each of the studies. As such, no moderators could be meaningfully examined.

Nevertheless, the nonsignificant effect remains difficult to interpret and might be explained by a Type II error, the artifact of using overestimated standard errors, because it is inconsistent with effects reported within studies. Namely, the two studies that examined the impact of trial-based chairwork reported significant reductions in the credibility of core punitive beliefs (Delavechia et al., 2016; de Oliveira et al., 2012a; see Figure 18.2). By contrast, EFT chairwork did not produce greater emotional arousal intensity than other methods (e.g., relational reframe, empathetic responding; Diamond et al., 2010; Narkiss-Guez et al., 2015).

Only one study has examined arousal as process outcome over the course of multiple treatment sessions, and it was with return-to-work program clients who were suffering with depression or anxiety (Stiegler, Molde, et al., 2018a). This study used a multiple baseline design to compare emotional arousal as observed during a treatment phase that included chairwork to the process in another treatment phase without chairwork.

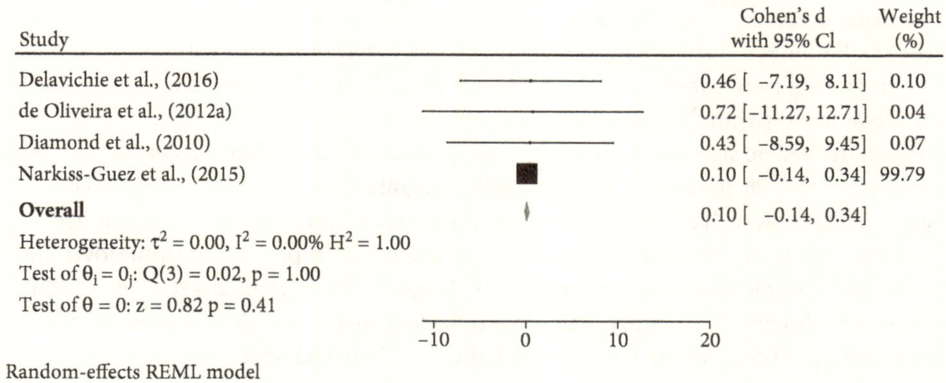

Note: The effect of a single session of chairwork on these immediate outcomes is non-significant. Two studies included in this analysis used EFT chairwork (Diamond et al., 2012; Narkiss-Guez et al., 2015), whereas two (Delavechia et al., 2016; de Oliveira et al., 2012a) used CBT-informed chairwork.

Figure 18.2 Meta-analysis: Does a single session of chairwork impact expressive arousal and credibility of punitive core beliefs?

Although the intensity of arousal was not different between phases, the number of segments that had high arousal was increased when treatment included chairwork.

Four studies using a Gestalt therapy approach to chairwork compared the proportion of time segments that clients spend in deeper levels of experiencing (i.e., ≥4) during single sessions of chairwork versus single sessions of empathetic reflection, in what represent between-subject dismantling designs. Figure 18.3 summarizes the results of these studies. The pooled intervention effect revealed a large effect of $d = 0.90$, $p < .001$, 95%

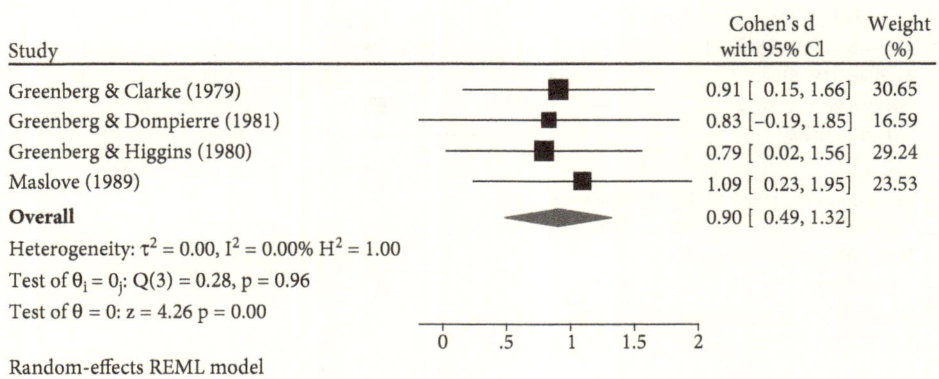

Note: A single session of chairwork has a large effect over empathic responding in increasing a client's depth of experiencing. All four studies included in this analysis used a gestalt therapy approach to chairwork and involved between-subject dismantling designs.

Figure 18.3 Meta-analysis: Does a single session of chairwork impact depth of experiencing more than empathic reflection?

CI [0.49, 1.32]. Although the funnel plots could not be accurately interpreted due to the small number of studies included, the fail-safe *N* test indicated that nine additional studies would be needed to null the summary effect. Thus, chairwork seems to be more effective in deepening experiencing than empathetic reflection. The tests of heterogeneity indicated no significant variability among the individual effect sizes of the primary studies, $Q(3) = .28, p = .96, I^2 = 0$, meaning the magnitude of the effect sizes was relatively consistent across each of the primary studies. As such, no moderators were examined.

Only one study examined depth of experiencing as a process outcome over the course of multiple treatment sessions of EFT (Stiegler, Molde, et al., 2018b). Introducing chairwork did not significantly change the trajectory in depth of client experience when comparing across phases of treatment that did or did not include chairwork.

Distal Symptom Outcomes

Seven studies compared the pre-to-post improvements in symptom reduction following a single session of chairwork, using within-subject designs. Their results are presented in Figure 18.4. The pooled chairwork effect revealed a large effect of $d = 1.73, p \leq .05$, 95% CI [0.03, 3.44] on the reduction of symptoms (distress, anxiety, and depression). The funnel plots could not be accurately interpreted due to the small number of studies included, but a fail-safe *N* test indicated that 54 additional studies would be needed to null the effect. Thus, chairwork seems to be effective in improving symptom change at the end of treatment. Tests of heterogeneity indicated significant variability among the individual effect sizes, $Q(6) = 261.07, p < .001, I^2 = 95.38$. In other words, the magnitude of the effect sizes was not consistent across the studies. Alas, the small number of studies did not allow for the formal assessment of moderators.

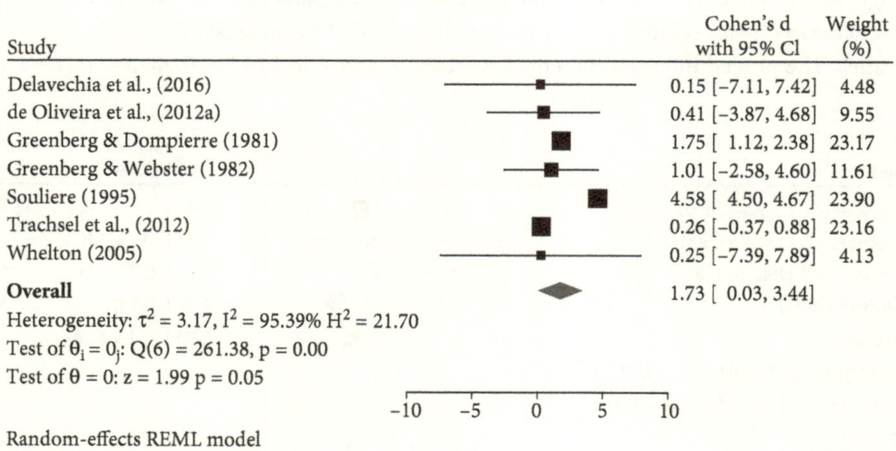

Note: A single session of chairwork has a large effect in reducing a client's psychological symptoms. Five studies included in this analysis used a gestalt therapy approach to chairwork, whereas two (Delavechia et al., 2016; de Oliveira et al., 2012a) used CBT-informed chairwork.

Figure 18.4 Meta-analysis: Does a single session of chairwork impact pre-to-post symptom reduction?

However, it is worth noting that the assessment of outcome allowed for two subgroups to be derived on conceptual grounds: Four studies used multi-item standardized symptom surveys (e.g., of anxiety or depression), whereas three studies used single-item subjective rankings (e.g., subjective units of distress). An exploratory moderation analysis showed no significant difference between the two for measuring symptom change, $Q(1) = .73$, $p = .39$, but a visual inspection of the forest plot suggested a possible pattern in which studies with standardized surveys produced a larger effect ($d = 2.03$) than studies with single-item subjective rankings ($d = 0.30$). Because significance testing of an effect depends on the standard errors of each primary study, the nonsignificant moderation may be a Type II error, an artifact of using overestimated standard errors. As such, the observed pattern suggests findings on the effectiveness of chairwork in producing symptom change may be influenced by the type of measure used.

One study examined EFT consisting almost entirely of chairwork, paring down the range of methods normally included in a complete treatment package in an effort to isolate the accumulated impact of chairwork. Whereas the previous analysis reported on the impact of a single session, this study speaks to the pre-to-post impact of ongoing treatment. Clients with high levels of self-criticism engaged in five to eight sessions using the two-chair task, in which the first session was used to build therapeutic alliance (Shahar et al., 2012). Results showed a significant improvement on anxiety ($n = 10$; $d = 0.71$) and depressive symptoms over the course of treatment ($d = 1.31$). Post-treatment reductions in anxiety and depression brought clients to a nonclinical range and were maintained at 6-month follow-up (Shahar et al., 2012).

Chairwork Compared to Treatment as Usual

Three studies compared the effects of single-session chairwork using various treatments to empathetic reflection or a decision-making task by way of between-subject designs. These results are displayed in Figure 18.5. The analyses revealed a nonsignificant effect on the reduction of symptoms (i.e., distress, anxiety, and depression) following a

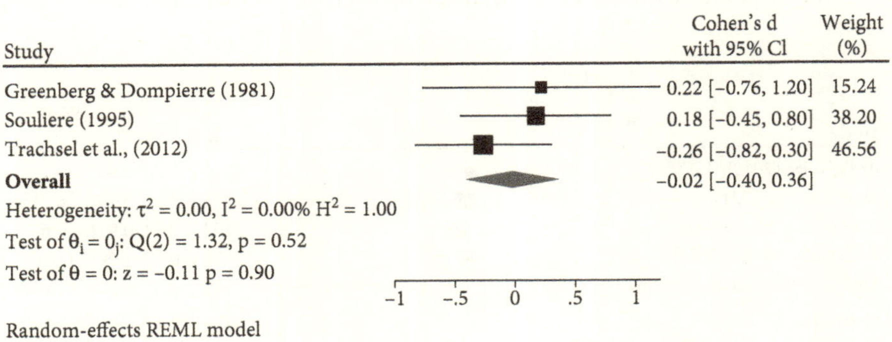

Note: A single session of chairwork has a non-significant impact over alternative interventions in changing psychological symptoms. Two studies included in this analysis used a gestalt therapy approach to chairwork, whereas the third (Trachsel et al., 2012) used an integrative approach. Two of these studies were also included in Figure 4's examination of within-subject effects.

Figure 18.5 Meta-analysis: Does a single session of chairwork impact pre-to-post symptom reduction more than alternative methods?

single session, $d = -0.02$, $p = .92$, 95% CI [−0.40, 0.36]. Thus, symptom changes following chairwork are comparable to changes related to either person-centered empathetic reflections or CBT-based decision-making tasks. Tests of heterogeneity showed no significant variability among the individual effect sizes, $Q(2) = 1.32$, $p = .52$, $I^2 = 0$, meaning the magnitude of the effects was fairly consistent across these single-intervention studies. Thus, no moderators were examined.

Studies have also examined the impact of chairwork over the course of ongoing treatment, thus offering evidence about the accumulated effect of this method. We conducted a meta-analysis of studies that typically used between-subject designs to compare the use of ongoing chairwork to established treatment methods (e.g., dismantling studies, alternate approaches within the same treatment framework) or multiple baseline controls. As shown in Figure 18.6, five studies compared the effectiveness of multi-session chairwork in reducing symptoms associated with the client's presentation concern. These studies reported on post-traumatic stress disorder, social anxiety, depression, obsessive–compulsive disorder, or both depression and anxiety. The comparison treatments were prolonged exposure, client-centered therapy, and automatic thought records. The meta-analysis revealed a small, statistically significant effect, $d = 0.40$, $p = .01$, 95% CI [0.12, 0.68], in the improvement in presenting concern following the use of chairwork over multiple sessions in comparison to the use of other treatments. The tests of heterogeneity suggested no significant variability among the individual effect sizes, $Q(2) = 4.38$, $p = .36$, $I^2 = 0$, meaning the magnitude of the effect sizes was relatively consistent across these treatment studies. The funnel plot could not be accurately interpreted due to the scarcity of studies, but a fail-safe *N* test indicated that five additional studies would be needed to null the effect.

Despite the overall significant effect, visual inspection of the forest plot revealed that three studies reported nonsignificant effect sizes, whereas two studies reported significant effect sizes (Figure 18.6). Although a quantitative moderation could not be conducted due to the small number of studies, a qualitative examination of the articles revealed that the studies comparing CBT-based chairwork treatments and conventional CBT interventions reported no significant difference between conditions (Duren et al., 2021; Oliveira et al.,

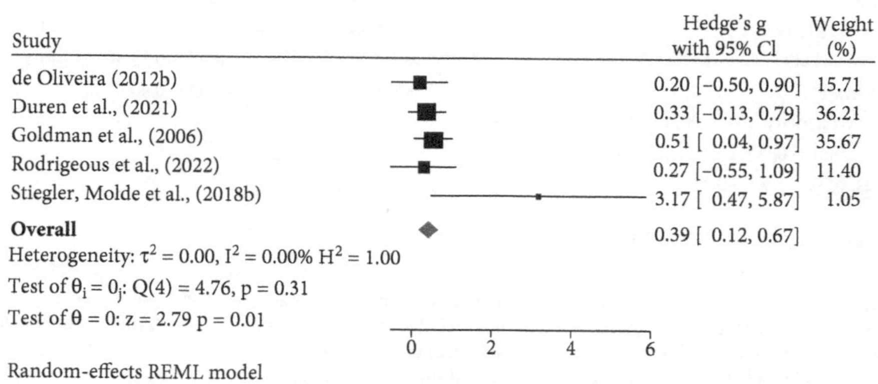

Figure 18.6 Meta-analysis: Does treatment using chairwork impact symptom reduction more than a treatment as usual?

2012b; Rodrigues et al., 2022). By contrast, in studies of EFT chairwork, there was significantly greater alleviation of clients' presenting concerns than in person-centered therapy (Goldman et al., 2006; Stiegler, Molde, et al., 2018b). These findings suggest that the extent to which chairwork produces greater symptom change over other methods is probably dependent on the therapeutic orientation being examined.

Furthermore, this apparent differential pattern in the effects of chairwork across treatment approaches seems to hold at follow-up. The positive symptom changes associated with CBT chairwork were maintained 12 months post-treatment (without further improvement), much like the effects of a conventional CBT comparison (de Oliveira et al., 2012b). However, not only were the symptom changes associated with EFT chairwork significantly better post-treatment but also clients continued to improve for another 18 months, while those receiving the person-centered comparison treatment were more likely to suffer a relapse (Ellison et al., 2009).

Evidence for Causality

Randomized experimental designs offered some evidence about the causal role that chairwork plays in facilitating depth of experiencing process and symptom change. Furthermore, the dismantling studies of treatment with versus without chairwork also point to unique effects that may be attributable to chairwork. However, no studies to date have used lagged correlations, structural equations, unconfounded regressions, or conducted growth curve analyses as evidence of causality.

Several *task analyses* have been conducted on the role of chairwork in EFT. This is a qualitative–quantitative hybrid method for developing descriptive as well as causal models of how a change process unfolds over time and relating it to outcome (Elliott, 2010). The process has been modeled for self-critical chairwork (Greenberg, 1983; Greenberg & Foerster, 1996), empty chairwork (Greenberg & Malcolm, 2002), and self-interruptive chairwork (Vrana, 2021). Each task analytic study generated a specific causal model of change, and each has subsequently been verified in its own right using hypothesis testing with samples from clinical trials. Although the models are unique and address different clinical problems, they suggest convergences at a more abstract level of analysis.

In a detailed review of these studies and drawing on the first author's expertise in task analysis as well as chairwork, we conducted a qualitative meta-synthesis of any commonalities observed across the study models. Descriptions of each model's set of ordered steps were interpreted and grouped thematically through a rational analysis to produce a general causal model. Six common components of chairwork were identified, and they are typically ordered in time. These ordered components are as follows:

1. Activating the problem state
2. Exploring one's inner reaction
3. Enacting the specific core concern
4. Expressing emotion in the service of an unmet need
5. A change in perspective on the original problem
6. Negotiating future engagements

A backwards comparison shows that the instantiations of our general causal model are operationalized slightly differently across the various applications of chairwork (Greenberg & Foerster, 1996; Greenberg & Malcolm, 2002; Vrana, 2021). Nevertheless, based on the original studies, a sequence of the six general components anticipated therapeutic outcomes in EFT and did so better than when components were either missing or not in order.

This synthesis remains to be tested more rigorously. Even so, the six components do figure prominently in qualitative research on clients' personal explanations of how chairwork helped them (Bell et al., 2020; Stiegler, Binder et al., 2018). Such client reports corroborate the original task analytic findings and support our meta-synthesis reported above. Client accounts further pointed to the helpful function served by specific aspects of chairwork, namely (a) physical chairs served as symbolic representation of parts, (b) enactments vivified and offered structure to the conflict, and (c) the imaginal dialogue brought out a covert process (Bell et al., 2020; Chadwick, 2003; Stiegler, Binder, et al., 2018). Taken together, these empirical findings and the rational synthesis provide some evidence of a causal link, demonstrating a temporal relation between the elements of chairwork in contributing to positive treatment outcomes.

Summary of Research Reviews

We reviewed the effects of chairwork on emotional processing and symptom change. The systematic search indicated the chairwork literature on process and symptom change to date is composed of a small number of studies ($k = 21$) that differ in the (a) types of outcomes measured, (b) research designs used, (c) number of sessions, and (d) assessment time points. Differences among studies prevented us from meaningfully aggregating across all studies into a single summary effect. Nevertheless, we found some evidence that chairwork was associated with noteworthy changes and fared well in comparison with alternative methods.

A meta-analysis revealed that a single session of chairwork was moderately more effective in deepening experience than empathic reflection on its own (i.e., $d = 0.90$). That is, adding chairwork increased the depth of patient experiencing, an important immediate outcome of psychotherapy.

In contrast, chairwork was not consistently associated with greater effectiveness in facilitating other kinds of immediate outcomes, such as emotional arousal or decreasing credibility of core beliefs, than other interventions. It remains uncertain whether the different implementation of chairwork in experiential approaches (e.g., EFT, Gestalt) compared to CBT (i.e., trial-based chairwork, decision cube) is related to their immediate outcomes, although some comparative process research (Watson & Bedard, 2006) has suggested this deserves careful consideration. Studies that provided data on pre–post or distal outcomes showed that patients regularly enjoyed symptom reductions after engaging in chairwork. The meta-analysis on single sessions of chairwork points to a large subsequent improvement in symptoms ($d = 1.73$), in absolute terms. However, when the effect after a single session of chairwork was compared to those of other therapy methods (i.e., empathetic reflection, problem-solving, and decision cube), its association with symptom change was no different.

The impact of ongoing chairwork over multiple treatment sessions was also examined. Compared to dismantled or alternative treatments, a small effect showed the advantage of including chairwork in ongoing treatment ($d = 0.40$). Thus, although the meta-analyses of single-session chairwork did not show superior outcomes compared to alternative methods, the repeated use of chairwork over a course of treatment seemed to generate a more pronounced and significant benefit.

Although the pool of studies was quite small, a closer examination points to treatment approach as a possible moderator. Both a dismantling study and a multiple baseline study showed that incorporating chairwork into EFT was associated with greater gains than person-centered empathic responding. In addition, two studies reported certain gains associated with EFT's chairwork continue to improve over time, beyond the conclusion of treatment (Ellison et al., 2009; Paivio et al., 2001). In contrast, multiple baseline studies and treatment -as-usual comparisons showed that the CBT version of chairwork maintained gains but without further improvement over time.

Finally, the evidence of causality related to chairwork relies on several independently conducted task analytic studies, all in the context of EFT. We provided a rational analysis that synthesizes those findings and suggests six process steps in a causal chain to explain how chairwork leads to positive therapeutic change. Qualitative reports from clients provide further evidence triangulating this understanding of the change process.

Possible Negative Effects and Harm

Because chairwork can be evocative, some therapists are alarmed by how poignantly emotions are activated and raise concerns about whether the enactments of chairwork may exacerbate or even introduce new negative emotions, such as self-contempt. However, research suggests the maladaptive emotions clients express during chairwork correspond to what they feel in everyday life, even if they do not typically disclose these feelings (Beuchat et al., 2022). In contrast, when clients do not experience such unhealthy emotions in their daily life, chairwork fails to elicit them (Beuchat et al., 2022; Kramer et al., 2022). This suggests there is little risk of introducing clients to novel harmful experiences via chairwork, although for those who do experience maladaptive emotions, the task will activate those feelings.

The novelty of chairwork may violate certain social norms, and the sheer evocative nature of such enactments can also lead clients to feel hesitant or even resistant to participating in it (Paivio & Pascual-Leone, 2023; Stiegler, Binder, et al., 2018). Across treatment approaches, clients reported in qualitative interviews that they experienced painful emotions more intensely when they fully engaged with the method. The interviews indicate that participating in chairwork is uncomfortable and intense but also helpful (Bell et al., 2020; Stiegler, Binder, et al., 2018; van Maarschalkerweerd et al., 2021). With that caveat in mind, there has been no research documentation of negative effects directly associated with chairwork.

Diversity Considerations

The diversity of the participants has not been reported in most quantitative studies to date, although some case study and qualitative research does speak to this, at least for EFT. At first consideration, there are cultural factors that may add to client's hesitancy about participating in such emotionally expressive methods that presume an individualistic understanding of personal conflict. Nevertheless, there is reason to believe the novelty and structure of chairwork create a special context for exploring feelings and voices that would otherwise be culturally taboo. Levitt and colleagues (2019) give examples of chairwork fruitfully adapted to culturally diverse clients, such as a Latin American lesbian living in the United States and a man in Japan who subscribed to traditional cultural and gender norms (see also Arimitsu, 2016).

A comparison of various treatments for loneliness and distress among runaway adolescent girls in Iran identified empty chairwork as a possible explanation for good treatment outcomes (Mahdavi et al., 2020). Chairwork has been found valuable in treating a female Mexican migrant worker to North America, who had been victim to human trafficking and presented with complex trauma (Pascual-Leone et al., 2017). Westmacott and Edmondstone (2020) argued that chairwork in EFT is a powerful tool for working with transgender and gender-diverse clients suffering minority stress or internalized homophobia. Taken together, these examples suggest that an advantage of chairwork is that it offers a physical structure that externalizes the "voices" of stigma and oppression and then re-engages them in a new kind of dialogue. Finally, survey results (Pugh et al., 2021) attest to the use of chairwork online ("tele-chairwork"), which increases its accessibility to those who may be otherwise restricted geographically, physically, or for health reasons.

Limitations of the Research

The major limitation of our research review is its lack of precision in calculating effect sizes and standard error and the limited conclusions that can be made about the effects of chairwork. These limitations are primarily due to the methodological shortcomings of the literature and reporting standards of the field. First, findings in the current study were conducted with an overestimated standard error. As such, the results lack precision and do not represent the true effectiveness of chairwork. Instead, we provide preliminary evidence of patterns associated with chairwork. Researchers are encouraged to directly report the effect sizes and their associated standard error for both within-group comparisons and between-group comparisons. Second, the unique effects of chairwork were examined in only a marginal number of studies. To study process, researchers need to consider multiple processes relevant to chairwork, examining these relative to each other and in contrast to alternative methods.

In addition, chairwork's role as a "fact-finding mission" in CBT or as an "open-ended meaning elaboration" in EFT suggests some fundamental differences that need to be considered. Regarding symptom change, dismantling studies are needed to examine the effects of incorporating chairwork into existing treatments. Given that chairwork might function via multiple mechanisms, which may be leveraged in different combinations depending on the treatment, both these kinds of studies are critical to providing an empirical illustration of chairwork's impact. Furthermore, the discrepancies among outcomes in our research review may be explained by the prominence of each outcome as activated by the respective treatments. Many CBT methods are already tailored toward helping clients effectively evaluate the credibility of thought patterns (Castonguay & Hill, 2007; Pugh, 2018). Where chairwork seems to differ most from alternative therapies is in the vividness of enactment and unscripted dialogue. These probably unique aspects of chairwork point to processes related to problem activation (Trachsel et al., 2012), expressed arousal (Stiegler, Molde, et al., 2018a), and the sequential transformations of emotion associated with heightening arousal (Nardone et al., 2022; Narkiss-Guez et al., 2015).

Last, the general task analytic model of six steps in a causal sequence needs to be further explored. It may serve a common basis for the further study of process steps in chairwork. Reducing the complexity of such a multistep method, particularly as it is implemented across treatment approaches, could greatly advance our understanding of this treatment method.

Training Implications

Findings of the current review highlight the potential impact that just one session of chairwork can have on emotional experiencing and symptom reduction. However, teaching therapists to introduce such a novel task is an initial challenge for training. Clinical observations suggest that a salient predictor of whether the client will agree to engage in chairwork may be the confidence with which that therapist introduces it (L. Greenberg, personal communication, 2006). Furthermore, given that the timing for switching chairs and deepening experience is highly contingent on the emergent meaning and flow of emotional arousal, we suggest training therapists to heighten their perceptual acuity to within-session markers of chairwork (Pascual-Leone & Andreescu, 2013).

Conducting chairwork also requires a therapist to monitor arousal and "strike while the iron is hot" to move clients to the next step (Nardone et al., 2022, p. 110), and the quality with which the client first engages in chairwork has a large effect on treatment outcomes (Paivio et al., 2001). So, therapists should be trained to foster clients' maximum engagement in the first introduction of chairwork. Finally, therapists need to be reassured by the research evidence that the task does not gratuitously introduce maladaptive emotion but, rather, that it lays bare a tacit reality of client experience (Beuchat et al., 2022; Kramer et al., 2022). As indicated by qualitative reports, although provocative and emotional, clients report the subjective experience that chairwork is helpful and worthwhile (Bell et al., 2020; Stiegler, Binder, et al., 2018).

Given the complexity and dynamic nature of the method, chairwork seems best learned through the study of video-recorded examples and in clinical training workshops. Feedback from trainees on what they valued in such trainings has supported our understanding that it is useful to get supervised practice in implementing the method but also to experience it subjectively in the role of "client." A variety of training workshops and supervision are available, but to our knowledge, no peer-reviewed research has been conducted on such programs.

Therapeutic Practices

Although tentative, the research findings recommend several therapeutic practices:

- Consider using one of the four types of chairwork for patients experiencing internal conflicts or unfinished business with significant others.
- Use chairwork to deepen client experiencing beyond empathetic responding.
- Incorporate chairwork into person-centered therapy and other talk therapies to bolster symptom reduction.
- Consider using chairwork for a session or two in CBT or other talk therapies because the research supports its effectiveness at least as much as alternative methods.
- Engage clients in chairwork over multiple session to improve distal treatment outcomes for clients.
- Counter initial fears that chairwork may precipitate intolerable emotions; instead, follow the research evidence that clients routinely find it helpful and worthwhile.

References

* Studies included in the meta-analysis.

Arimitsu, K. (2016). The effects of a program to enhance self-compassion in Japanese individuals: A randomized controlled pilot study. *Journal of Positive Psychology, 11*(6), 559–571. doi:10.1080/17439760.2016.1152593

Arntz, A., & Jacob, G. (2013). *Schema therapy in practice: An introductory guide to the schema mode approach.* Wiley-Blackwell.

Battle, C. C., Imber, S. D., Hoehn-Saric, R., Nash, E. R., & Frank, J. D. (1966). Target complaints as criteria of improvement. *American Journal of Psychotherapy, 20*(1), 184–192. https://doi.org/10.1176/appi.psychotherapy.1966.20.1.184

Bell, T., Montague, J., Elander, J., & Gilbert, P. (2020). "A definite feel-it moment": Embodiment, externalisation and emotion during chair-work in compassion-focused therapy. *Counselling & Psychotherapy Research, 20*(1), 143–153. http://dx.doi.org/10.1002/capr.12248

Bell, T., Montague, J., Elander, J., & Gilbert, P. (2021). Multiple emotions, multiple selves: Compassion focused therapy chairwork. *The Cognitive Behaviour Therapist, 14*, e22. http://dx.doi.org/10.1017/S1754470X21000180

Beuchat, H., Grandjean, L., Despland, J. N., Pascual-Leone, A., Gholam, M., Swendsen, J., & Kramer, U. (2022). Ecological momentary assessment of emotional processing: An exploratory analysis comparing daily life and a psychotherapy analogue session. *Counselling and Psychotherapy Research, 22*(2), 345–356. https://doi.org/10.1002/capr.12455

Briere, J., & Scott, C. (2006). *Principles of trauma therapy: A guide to symptoms, evaluation, and treatment.* SAGE.

Castonguay, L. G., & Hill, C. (Eds.). (2007). *Insight in psychotherapy.* American Psychological Association. https://doi.org/10.1037/11532-000

Chadwick, P. (2003). Two-chairs, self-schemata and a person-based approach to psychosis. *Behavioural and Cognitive Psychotherapy, 31*, 439–449.

Clarke, K. M., & Greenberg, L. S. (1986). Differential effects of the Gestalt two-chair intervention and problem solving in resolving decisional conflict. *Journal of Counseling Psychology, 33*(1), 11–15.

Cohen, J. (1969). *Statistical power analysis for the behavioral sciences.* Academic Press.

Cohen, J. (1977). *Statistical power analysis for the behavioral sciences* (Rev. ed.). Erlbaum.

*Delavechia, T. R., Velasquez, M. L., Duran, É. P., Matsumoto, L. S., & de Oliveira, I. R. (2016). Changing negative core beliefs with trial-based thought record. *Revista de Psiquiatria Clinica, 43*(2), 31–33. https://doi.org/10.1590/0101-60830000000078

de Oliveira, I. R. (2008). Trial-based thought record (TBTR): Preliminary data on a strategy to deal with core beliefs by combining sentence reversion and the use of analogy with a judicial process. *Revista Brasileira de Psiquiatria, 30*(1), 12–18. https://doi.org/10.1590/S1516-44462008000100003

*de Oliveira, I. R., Hemmany, C., Powell, V. B., Bonfim, T. D., Duran, E. P., Novais, N., Velasquez, M., Di Sarno, E., Alves, G., Cesnik, J.; Brazilian TBTR Study Group. (2012a). Trial-based psychotherapy and the efficacy of trial-based thought record in changing unhelpful core beliefs and reducing self-criticism. *CNS Spectrums, 17*, 16–23.

*de Oliveira, I. R., Powell, V. B., Wenzel, A., Caldas, M., Seixas, C., Almeida, C., Bonfim, T., Grangeon, M. C., Castro, M., Galvão, A., De Oliveira Moraes, R. & Sudak, D. (2012b). Efficacy of the trial-based thought record, a new cognitive therapy strategy designed to change core beliefs, in social phobia. *Journal of Clinical Pharmacy and Therapeutics, 37*(3), 328–334. https://doi.org/10.1111/j.1365-2710.2011.01299.x

*Diamond, G. M., Rochman, D., & Amir, O. (2010). Arousing primary vulnerable emotions in the context of unresolved anger: "Speaking about" versus "speaking to." *Journal of Counseling Psychology, 57*(4), 402–410. https://doi.org/10.1037/a0021115

*Duran, É. P., Corchs, F., Vianna, A., Araújo, Á. C., Del Real, N., Silva, C., Ferreira, A. P., De Vitto Francez, P., Godói, C., Silveira, H., Matsumoto, L., Gebara, C. M., De Barros Neto, T. P., Chilvarquer, R., De Siqueira, L. L., Bernik, M., & Neto, F. L. (2021). A randomized clinical trial to assess the efficacy of trial-based cognitive therapy compared to prolonged exposure for post-traumatic stress disorder: Preliminary findings. *CNS Spectrums, 26*(4), 427–434. https://doi.org/10.1017/S1092852920001455

Elliott, R. (2010). Psychotherapy change process research: Realizing the promise. *Psychotherapy Research, 20*(2), 123–135. https://doi.org/10.1080/10503300903470743

Elliott, R., Watson, J. C., Goldman, R. N., & Greenberg, L. S. (2004). *Learning emotion-focused therapy: The process–experiential approach to change*. American Psychological Association.

*Ellison, J. A., Greenberg, L. S., Goldman, R. N., & Angus, L. (2009). Maintenance of gains following experiential therapies for depression. *Journal of Consulting and Clinical Psychology, 77*(1), 103–112. https://doi.org/10.1037/a0014653

Gilbert, P. (2010). *Compassion focused therapy: Distinctive features*. Routledge.

Gilbert, P., & Irons, C. (2005). Focused therapies and compassionate mind training for shame and self-attacking. In P. Gilbert (Ed.), *Compassion: Conceptualisations, research and use in psychotherapy* (pp. 263–325). Routledge.

Goldfried, M. R., & Davison, G. C. (1976). *Clinical behavior therapy*. Holt, Rinehart & Winston.

*Goldman, R. N., Greenberg, L. S., & Angus, L. (2006). The effects of adding emotion-focused interventions to the client-centered relationship conditions in the treatment of depression. *Psychotherapy Research, 16*(5), 536–546. https://doi.org/10.1080/10503300600589456

Greenberg, L. (1983). Toward a task analysis of conflict resolution in Gestalt therapy. *Psychotherapy: Theory, Research & Practice, 20*, 190–201.

*Greenberg, L. S., & Clarke, K. M. (1979). Differential effects of the two-chair experiment and empathic reflections at a conflict marker. *Journal of Counseling Psychology, 26*(1), 1–8. https://doi.org/10.1037/0022-0167.26.1.1

*Greenberg, L. S., & Dompierre, L. M. (1981). Specific effects of Gestalt two-chair dialogue on intrapsychic conflict in counseling. *Journal of Counseling Psychology, 28*(4), 288–294. https://doi.org/10.1037/0022-0167.28.4.288

Greenberg, L. S., & Foerster, F. S. (1996). Task analysis exemplified: The process of resolving unfinished business. *Journal of Consulting and Clinical Psychology, 64*(3), 439–446. https://doi.org/10.1037/0022-006X.64.3.439

Greenberg, L. S., & Goldman, R. N. (2019). Theory of practice of emotion-focused therapy. In L. S. Greenberg & R. N. Goldman (Eds.), *Clinical handbook of emotion-focused therapy* (pp. 61–89). American Psychological Association. https://doi.org/10.1037/0000112-003

*Greenberg, L. S., & Higgins, H. M. (1980). Effects of two-chair dialogue and focusing on conflict resolution. *Journal of Counseling Psychology, 27*(3), 221–224. https://doi.org/10.1037/0022-0167.27.3.221

Greenberg, L. S., & Malcolm, W. (2002). Resolving unfinished business: Relating process to outcome. *Journal of Consulting and Clinical Psychology, 70*(2), 406–416. https://doi.org/10.1037/0022-006X.70.2.406

Greenberg, L. S., Rice, L. N., & Elliott, R. (1993). *Facilitating emotional change: The moment-by-moment process*. Guilford.

Greenberg, L. J., Warwar, S. H., & Malcolm, W. M. (2008). Differential effects of emotion-focused therapy and psychoeducation in facilitating forgiveness and letting go of emotional injuries. *Journal of Counseling Psychology, 55*(2), 185–196. https://doi.org/10.1037/0022-0167.55.2.185

Greenberg, L. S., & Watson, J. C. (2006). *Emotion-focused therapy for depression*. American Psychological Association. https://doi.org/10.1037/11286-000

*Greenberg, L. S., & Webster, M. C. (1982). Resolving decisional conflict by Gestalt two-chair dialogue: Relating process to outcome. *Journal of Counseling Psychology, 29*(5), 468–477. https://doi.org/10.1037/0022-0167.29.5.468

Hautzinger, M., & Bailer, M. (1993). *Allgemeine Depressions Skala* [The General Depression Scale]. Beltz.

Hermans, H., Kempen, H., & Van Loons, R. (1992). The dialogical self: Beyond individualism and rationalism. *American Psychologist, 47*, 23–33.

Kellogg, S. (2004). Dialogical encounters: Contemporary perspectives on "chairwork" in psychotherapy. *Psychotherapy: Theory Research, Practice, Training, 41*, 310–320.

Khayyat-Abuaita, U., Paivio, S., Pascual-Leone, A., & Harrington, S. (2019). Emotional processing of trauma narratives is a predictor of outcome in emotion focused therapy for complex trauma. *Psychotherapy, 56*(4), 526–536 http://dx.doi.org/10.1037/pst0000238

Klein, M. H., Mathieu-Coughlan, P., & Kiesler, D. J. (1986). The experiencing scales. In L. S. Greenberg & W. M. Pinsof (Eds.), *The psychotherapeutic process: A research handbook* (pp. 21–71). Guilford.

Kline, R. B. (2013). Beyond significance testing: Statistics reform in the behavioral sciences (2nd ed.). American Psychological Association. https://doi.org/10.1037/14136-000

Kramer, U., Beuchat, H., Grandjean, L., Despland, J.-N., & Pascual-Leone, A. (2022, March 28) Changes in emotional processing in daily life: Relationship with in-session self-esteem. *Counselling Psychology Quarterly*. https://doi.org/10.1080/09515070.2022.2029349

Levitt, H. M., Whelton, W. J., & Iwakabe, S. (2019). Integrating feminist–multicultural perspectives into emotion-focused therapy. In L. S. Greenberg & R. N. Goldman (Eds.), *Clinical handbook of emotion-focused therapy* (pp. 425–444). American Psychological Association. https://doi.org/10.1037/0000112-019

Mahdavi, A., Yaghoobi, A., Rashid, K., & Kordnoghabi, R. (2020). Comparison of the effect of compassion-based techniques and cognitive behavioral schema therapy techniques in reducing loneliness and emotion regulation difficulties in runaway adolescent girls. *Iranian Evolutionary and Educational Psychology, 2*(1), 33–45. http://ieepj.hormozgan.ac.ir/article-1-159-en.html

*Maslove, V. J. (1989). The differential effects of empathic reflection and the Gestalt empty-chair dialogue on depth of experiencing when used with an issue of unfinished business [Master's thesis]. University of British Columbia. https://open.library.ubc.ca/collections/ubctheses/831/items/1.0053761

Mendes, I., Rosa, C., Stiles, W. B., Caro Gabalda, I., Gomes, P., Basto, I., & Salgado, J. (2016). Setbacks in the process of assimilation of problematic experiences in two cases of emotion-focused therapy for depression. *Psychotherapy Research, 26*, 638–652. doi:10.1080/10503307.2015.1136443

Moreno, J. L. (1948). *Psychodrama* (Vol. 1). Beacon House.

Nardone, S., Pascual-Leone, A., & Kramer, U. (2022). "Strike while the iron is hot": Increased arousal anticipates unmet needs. *Counselling Psychology Quarterly, 35*(1), 110–128. https://doi.org/10.1080/09515070.2021.1955659

*Narkiss-Guez, T., Zichor, Y. E., Guez, J., & Diamond, G. M. (2015). Intensifying attachment-related sadness and decreasing anger intensity among individuals suffering from unresolved

anger: The role of relational reframe followed by empty-chair interventions. *Counselling Psychology Quarterly, 28*(1), 44–56.

Neff, K. D., Kirkpatrick, K. L., & Rude, S. S. (2007). Self-compassion and adaptive psychological functioning. *Journal of Research in Personality, 41*(1), 139–154. https://doi.org/10.1016/j.jrp.2006.03.004

Paivio, S. C., Hall, I. E., Holowaty, K. A. M., Jellis, J. B., & Tran, N. (2001). Imaginal confrontation for resolving child abuse issues. *Psychotherapy Research, 11*(4), 433–453.

Paivio, S. C., Jarry, J. L., Chagigiorgis, H., Hall, I., & Ralston, M. (2010). Efficacy of two versions of emotion-focused therapy for resolving child abuse trauma. *Psychotherapy Research, 20*(3), 353–366.

Paivio, S. C., & Pascual-Leone, A. (2023). *Emotion focused therapy for complex trauma: An integrative approach* (2nd ed.). American Psychological Association.

Pascual-Leone, A. (2018). How clients "change emotion with emotion": A programme of research on emotional processing. *Psychotherapy Research, 28*(2), 165–182. https://doi.org/10.1080/10503307.2017.1349350

Pascual-Leone, A., & Andreescu, C. (2013). Repurposing process measures to train psychotherapists: Training outcomes using a new approach. *Counselling and Psychotherapy Research, 13*(3), 210–219. doi:10.1080/14733145.2012.739633

Pascual-Leone, A., & Greenberg. L. (2005). Classification of affective-meaning states. In *Emotional processing in the therapeutic hour: "Why the only way out is through"* (pp. 289–367) [Unpublished doctoral thesis]. York University.

Pascual-Leone, A., & Greenberg, L. S. (2007). Emotional processing in experiential therapy: Why "the only way out is through." *Journal of Consulting and Clinical Psychology, 75*(6), 875–887. https://doi.org/10.1037/0022-006X.75.6.875

Pascual-Leone, A., Kim, J., & Morrison, O.-P. (2017). Working with victims of human trafficking. *Journal of Contemporary Psychotherapy, 47*(1), 41–59. doi:10.1007/s10879-016-9338-3

Pascual-Leone, A., & Yeryomenko, N. (2017). The client "experiencing" scale as a predictor of treatment outcomes: A meta-analysis on psychotherapy process. *Psychotherapy Research, 27*(6), 653–665. doi:10.1080/10503307.2016.1152409

Perls, F. S. (1969). *Gestalt therapy verbatim*. Real People Press.

Perls, F. S. (1973). *Gestalt approach, and eye witness to therapy*. Bantam.

Pugh, M. (2018). Cognitive behavioural chairwork. *International Journal of Cognitive Therapy, 11*(1), 100–116. https://doi.org/10.1007/s41811-018-0001-5

Pugh, M., Bell, T., & Dixon, A. (2021). Delivering tele-chairwork: A qualitative survey of expert therapists. *Psychotherapy Research, 31*(7), 843–858. https://doi.org/10.1080/10503307.2020.1854486

Pugh, M., & Broome, N. (2020). Dialogical coaching: An experiential approach to personal and professional development. *Consulting Psychology Journal: Practice and Research, 72*(3), 223–241.

Rochman, D., & Diamond, G. M. (2008). From unresolved anger to sadness: Identifying physiological correlates. *Journal of Counseling Psychology, 55*(1), 96–105. https://doi.org/10.1037/0022-0167.55.1.96

*Rodrigues, E. P., Fechine, A., Oliveira, A. C., Matos, C., Passarela, C. M., Hemanny, C., Dias, F. M., Batista, J. W., Albuquerque, L. N., Soares, M. S., Coelho Neto, P. E., Araújo, V. P., Ayres, Z. M., & Oliveira, I. R. (2022). Randomized clinical trial of the efficacy of trial-based cognitive therapy for obsessive–compulsive disorder: Preliminary findings. *Trends in Psychiatry and Psychotherapy, 44*. Advance online publication. https://doi.org/10.47626/2237-6089-2021-0247

Rosenthal, R. (1979). The file drawer problem and tolerance for null results. *Psychological Bulletin, 86*(3), 638–641. https://doi.org/10.1037/0033-2909.86.3.638

*Shahar, B., Carlin, E. R., Engle, D. E., Hegde, J., Szepsenwol, O., & Arkowitz, H. (2012). A pilot investigation of emotion-focused two-chair dialogue intervention for self-criticism. *Clinical Psychology and Psychotherapy, 19*(6), 496–507. https://doi.org/10.1002/cpp.762

*Souliere, M. (1995). The differential effects of the empty chair dialogue and cognitive restructuring on the resolution of lingering angry feelings [Doctoral dissertation, University of Ottawa, 1994]. Dissertation Abstracts International, 56, 2342B. (University Microfilms No. AAT NN95979)

Spielberger, C. D., Gorsuch, R. L. & Lushene, R. E. (1970). *Manual for the State–Trait Anxiety Inventory*. Consulting Psychologists Press.

Stiegler, J. R., Binder, P. E., Hjeltnes, A., Stige, S. H., & Schanche, E. (2018). "It's heavy, intense, horrendous and nice": Clients' experiences in two-chair dialogues. *Person-Centered and Experiential Psychotherapies*, *17*(2), 139–159. https://doi.org/10.1080/14779757.2018.1472138

*Stiegler, J., Molde, H., & Schanche, E. (2018a). Does an emotion-focused two-chair dialogue add to the therapeutic effect of the empathic attunement to affect? *Clinical Psychology and Psychotherapy*, *25*, e86–e95. https://doi.org/10.1002/cpp.2144

*Stiegler, J. R., Molde, H., & Schanche, E. (2018b). Does the two-chair dialogue intervention facilitate processing of emotions more efficiently than basic Rogerian conditions? *European Journal of Psychotherapy & Counselling*, *20*(3), 337–355. https://doi.org/10.1080/13642537.2018.1495245

*Trachsel, M., Ferrari, L., & Holtforth, M. G. (2012). Resolving partnership ambivalence: A randomized controlled trial of very brief cognitive and experiential interventions with follow-up. *Canadian Journal of Counselling and Psychotherapy*, *46*(3), 239–258.

van Maarschalkerweerd, F., Engelmoer, I. M., Simon, S., & Arntz, A. (2021). Addressing the punitive parent mode in schema therapy for borderline personality disorder: Short-term effects of the empty chair technique as compared to cognitive challenging. *Journal of Behavior Therapy and Experimental Psychiatry*, *73*, 101–138.

Veroniki, A. A., Jackson, D., Viechtbauer, W., Bender, R., Bowden, J., Knapp, G., Kuss, O., Higgins, J. P., Langan, D., & Salanti, G. (2016). Methods to estimate the between-study variance and its uncertainty in meta-analysis. *Research Synthesis Methods*, *7*(1), 55–79. https://doi.org/10.1002/jrsm.1164

Vrana, G. C. (2021). *Resolution of self-interruption in emotion-focused therapy: A model of client process* [Unpublished dissertation]. York University. https://yorkspace.library.yorku.ca/xmlui/bitstream/handle/10315/39140/Vrana_Genevieve_C_2021_PhD.pdf?sequence=2&isAllowed=y

Watson, J. C., & Bedard, D. L. (2006). Clients' emotional processing in psychotherapy: A comparison between cognitive-behavioral and process-experiential therapies. *Journal of Consulting and Clinical Psychology*, *74*, 152–159.

Watson, J. C., & Greenberg, L. S. (2017). Emotion-focused therapy for generalized anxiety. American Psychological Association. https://doi.org/10.1037/0000018-000

Werner, Tibubos, A. N., Rohrmann, S., & Reiss, N. (2019). The clinical trait self-criticism and its relation to psychopathology: A systematic review—Update. *Journal of Affective Disorders*, *246*, 530–547. https://doi.org/10.1016/j.jad.2018.12.069

Westmacott, R., & Edmondstone, C. (2020). Working with transgender and gender diverse clients in emotion focused therapy: Targeting minority stress. *Person-Centered & Experiential Psychotherapies*, *19*(4), 331–349. doi:10.1080/14779757.2020.1717986

*Whelton, W. J. (2005). *Emotion in self-criticism* (Order No. AAINQ67926). APA PsycInfo (619957364; 2002-95020-268).

19

Dream Work and Nightmare Treatments

Patricia T. Spangler and Wonjin Sim

Authors' Note: The opinions and assertions expressed herein are those of the author(s) and do not necessarily reflect the official policy or position of the Uniformed Services University or the Department of Defense. The contents of this publication are the sole responsibility of the author(s) and do not necessarily reflect the views, opinions or policies of The Henry M. Jackson Foundation for the Advancement of Military Medicine, Inc. Mention of trade names, commercial products, or organizations does not imply endorsement by the U.S. Government.

Working with dreams in psychotherapy is a method as old as psychotherapy itself. Freud (1900/1966) characterized the power of dream interpretation as the *via regia* to knowledge of the unconscious. Theoretical orientations view the importance and clinical utility of dreams differently and thus have different methods. For example, psychodynamic dream interpretation (e.g., Adler, 1936, 1938, 1958; Freud, 1900/1966) focuses on understanding the meaning of the dream via free association, *symbolic* interpretation of the whole dream, and *decoding* each sign. The Jungian method (Jung, 1964, 1974) uses both subjective (i.e., everything in the dream personifies the dreamers' personality) and objective (i.e., the dream ego or characters in the dream represent outer-world events) interpretation (Vaughan, 2016). In Gestalt psychotherapy, dreams are considered a metaphor of current or ongoing unresolved life events of dreamers (Perls, 1969).

The therapeutic goals of dream work vary markedly. Psychotherapists sometimes use dream work to help clients gain insight into themselves or their relationships; at other times, it may be to alleviate post-traumatic nightmares. In this chapter, we describe methods for working with both dreams and nightmares, provide clinical examples, and summarize the research evidence of these methods' efficacy. We then discuss the limitations of this evidence and conclude with diversity considerations, training implications, and therapeutic practices.

Definitions

Although we found no specific definitions of dream work or of working with nightmares, for this chapter we define these methods as using the client's experience of a dream or nightmare in session to address their presenting concerns—for example, gaining insight into themselves or decreasing the frequency of nightmares. Further definition varies according to clinical approach. Dreams are defined as "a physiologically and psychologically conscious state that occurs during sleep and is often characterized by a rich array of endogenous sensory, motor, emotional, and other experiences" (American

Patricia T. Spangler and Wonjin Sim, *Dream Work and Nightmare Treatments* In: *Psychotherapy Skills and Methods That Work*. Edited by: Clara E. Hill and John C. Norcross, Oxford University Press. © Clara E. Hill and John C. Norcross 2023.
DOI: 10.1093/oso/9780197611012.003.0019

Psychological Association, 2022). Nightmares can be distinguished from dreams in that they are vivid, emotionally distressing dreams that typically awaken the sleeper.

Clinical Descriptions and Indications

Cognitive–Experiential Dream Model

To date, only one method of dream work has a substantial body of research on its process and outcome. The Hill cognitive–experiential dream model (CEDM; Hill, 2004) is an eclectic approach that incorporates humanistic–experiential, psychoanalytic, Gestalt, cognitive, and behavioral theories. Although in ongoing psychotherapy, therapists rarely follow the method exactly (see Hill et al., 2013), Hill (2004) provided a structured approach that has been used to test the dream model empirically. The model comprises three stages: exploration, insight, and action.

The exploration stage of CEDM is based on client-centered therapy but is more structured than the traditional client-centered approach. Therapists help clients activate their cognitive schema to facilitate the activation of thoughts, feelings, and experiences associated with their dreams. Similar to other types of therapy, the therapist starts by building rapport and trust with the client to help the client feel safe to explore their dream experiences with the therapist. The therapist then asks the client to tell their dream in the firstperson, present tense as if it is happening now and to choose three to five of the most salient images in the dream. They then explore each image in depth following the four DRAW steps: *d*escribe the images in detail, *r*e-experience emotion related to the image, *a*ssociate the image to earlier experiences, and determine any *w*aking life triggers for the image.

To begin the DRAW steps, the therapist asks the client to describe the first image in great detail so that they can re-create and relive the dream scene. The therapist may ask the client to use all five senses (e.g., visual cues, smell, sound, touch) to describe each image. In the re-experience step, the therapist asks the client to share their emotions and feelings at the moment of each image, and the therapist may reflect their feelings to help them clarify and deepen their emotional experience. For example, the therapist might ask, "How are you feeling at this moment when you see the old house in your dream?" In the association step, the client is asked to discuss their memories, thoughts, and feelings associated with each image. For example, the therapist may ask, "What comes to your mind when you think of a loose tooth?" After the client comes up with associations, the therapist helps the client explore further for each association. Last, the therapist asks the client to discuss potential waking life triggers for each image. For example, the therapist may ask, "What is going on in your life that might trigger the image of the faceless man?" After the therapist and client finish the four DRAW steps for the first image, they follow the DRAW steps for the second image, etc.

In the insight stage, the client works with the therapist to construct a meaning of their dream based on what they learned in the exploration stage. The therapist asks the client what they think the dream means, which helps the therapist understand the client's perspective or level of understanding and interpretation of their dream. Hill (2004) then suggested that the therapist work with the client using at least one of four ways of interpreting the dream. The therapist may ask the client to understand their dreams as the experience itself rather than focusing on what reflects (e.g., "If we just take this dream as an experience that you have lived through, what did you learn about yourself?" p. 49). Second, the therapist could focus on how the dream as a whole reflects what is happening in the client's waking life. Third, the therapist could help the client understand the dream as something that represents parts of self or childhood conflict (e.g., maladaptive interpersonal patterns with their parents). Last, the client can be asked to explore how the dream might reflect spiritual concerns or existential issues (e.g., death anxiety or meaning of life).

In the action stage, the therapist asks the client to change the dream as if they are the director of their dreams (e.g., asking their partner to fight the monster together). Next, the client is asked to bridge the changes in their dream to the changes they would like to make in their waking life (e.g., opening up to their partner regarding their current concerns and asking for help). The therapist can help the client come up with specific behavioral changes, such as developing skills to ask for help or developing their assertiveness skills. If the client cannot think of behavioral changes based on their dreams, then the therapist can ask the client to discuss ideas for a ritual to honor the meaning of the dream (e.g., artwork or other symbolic art).

Methods for Working with Nightmares

In this section, we review three methods for working nightmares: imagery rehearsal therapy (IRT; Krakow & Zadra, 2006); exposure, relaxation, and rescripting therapy (ERRT; Davis, 2009); and nightmare deconstruction and reprocessing (NDR; Spangler & West, 2018). Before describing the three major approaches, we present several common skills the three approaches share. We present them in the order they are typically used within the nightmare methods.

All of the methods for working with nightmares begin with *psychoeducation* to provide information to clients about nightmares and their relationship to trauma, anxiety, and insomnia; to help clients understand their own nightmares as a symptom; and to orient them to the treatment.

Imagery skills are developed and practiced in IRT in preparation for imagery rescripting. The therapist guides the client through imagining a pleasant or neutral image or task in session and assists with working through obstacles including persistent negative images.

Exposure to nightmare content is used in ERRT and NDR for the purpose of activating nightmare-related emotions in session and identifying maladaptive thoughts and schemas.

Relaxation skills such as diaphragmatic breathing and progressive muscle relaxation (PMR) are used to modulate physiological arousal symptoms in clients with anxiety, panic disorder, and post-traumatic stress disorder (PTSD). Relaxation skills reduce hyperarousal and insomnia symptoms in PTSD clients (Kim et al., 2013). Relaxation methods are used in ERRT and NDR.

Identifying themes/making meaning facilitates gaining a deeper understanding of the client's nightmare. Understanding why the client has a nightmare, which parts are especially distressing, and how the nightmare may be different from the actual trauma are helpful in making meaning and identifying themes. In ERRT (Davis, 2009), themes are identified in one of five areas that are common in trauma survivors: safety, trust, power, esteem, and intimacy (Resick et al., 2016). For nightmare themes that do not fall within one of these five areas (e.g., grief, racial trauma, moral injury), another approach to meaning-making is called for. As an adaptation of CEDM, NDR's second stage focuses on making meaning derived from the client experience rather than fitting the meaning to a predetermined theme, which allows for a broader range of possible meanings.

Reprocessing, used in NDR, involves activating a stored memory; working in session to associate it with connections to emotion, memory, sensation, and insights; and connecting to adaptive memory networks and changing the nature of the memory (Shapiro, 2001).

Imagery rescripting was developed as a treatment for PTSD as an addition to imaginal exposure (Arntz et al., 2013). The aim of imagery rescripting is to decrease traumatic stress symptoms and change early trauma-related schemas by helping clients develop a sense of control over their trauma story by replacing problematic schema with a neutral or positive script without denying the trauma. Imagery rescripting has been used effectively to rescript nightmares in IRT, ERRT, and NDR.

Rehearsal involves having the client repeat new information or behaviors to focus attention on the new material in order to alter maladaptive thoughts and behaviors. In nightmare treatments, rehearsal of a rescripted dream is done in session and assigned as homework with the goal of maximizing the amount of time the client thinks about the new dream. Rehearsal is used in IRT, ERRT, and NDR.

Imagery Rehearsal Therapy

Imagery rehearsal therapy is a psychoeducational intervention that carefully limits exposure to nightmare content (Krakow & Zadra, 2006). Krakow posited that experiencing nightmares is a learned sleep behavior and that discussing them in session would reinforce this behavior. In addition to psychoeducation, another component of IRT is development of the client's imagery skills to enable them to *rescript* nightmares with neutral or positive images through repeated *rehearsal*.

IRT was originally developed as a four-session treatment, with each session lasting approximately 2 hours. In the first IRT session, the therapist provides psychoeducation, specifically that (a) nightmares fragment sleep; (b) fragmented sleep disrupts normal sleep architecture, resulting in poor sleep quality; (c) poor sleep quality is the result of psychological and physiological processes; (d) trying to improve sleep quality will maximize relief; and (e) treating nightmares is a critical component of treating trauma-related sleep disturbance. Nightmares are discussed as a natural response to a trauma, with reference to research indicating that nightmares assist with emotional processing and may serve an evolutionary purpose of keeping alert to other possible dangers.

In the second IRT session, information is presented on how nightmares "take on a life of their own." Clients are asked to estimate the extent to which nightmares can be attributed to trauma or to habit (between 0% and 100%). The therapist introduces the principles of imagery. Specific points are that (a) imagery is a natural part of mental functioning, (b) images are often the last conscious activity prior to sleep, (c) waking imagery may be a bridge to sleep imagery, and (d) imagery is like intensive daydreaming. The therapist tests the client's imagery skills, and the client practices imagery for 1, 5, or 15 minutes, depending on ability. The therapist helps the client overcome obstacles to practice, with six possible strategies for managing negative images: (a) clapping and saying "Stop!"; (b) relaxed breathing; (c) grounding by focusing on the physical environment; (d) talking with the therapist, a friend, or family member about images; (e) writing down images; and (f) acknowledging unpleasant images and then turning attention to a positive or neutral image. The client is given homework of practicing imagery for 5–20 minutes a day.

In the third IRT session, the therapist trains the client to use imagery to change mental habits. For example, the client is instructed to recall a recent major change in their life, such as moving to a new home. The role of imagery in how they made this change is examined. The client recognizes that they pictured the move before thinking about it, and long before actually moving, thus emphasizing the importance of imagery to change. The client then selects something they would like to change and spends 5–10 minutes picturing the components of the change. The session then shifts to facilitating a change in identity. The client is asked to picture themself as someone who does not have nightmares and discuss what it would mean to let go of their identity as a nightmare sufferer. The client then selects a nightmare to change and writes it down. The therapist instructs the client to begin rescripting the dream by changing the images in any way they would like. Changes to the dream are rehearsed both in session and as homework.

In the fourth session, the therapist works with the client to develop a plan to practice newly learned imagery and to use it if they experience new nightmares after termination. The therapist emphasizes that the change process is incremental and that clients should continue to practice positive imagery to address negative images that arise.

Exposure, Relaxation, and Rescripting Therapy

Exposure, relaxation, and rescripting therapy is a cognitive–behavioral method for treating post-traumatic nightmares. It is based on a modification of IRT for the purpose of increasing *exposure* to nightmare content (Davis, 2009). ERRT was originally developed as three 90-minute sessions (Davis, 2009), but recent adaptations have included four or five 90-minute sessions to allow inclusion of psychoeducation and to provide more time in session for exposure and rescripting (Pruiksma et al., 2020).

The first ERRT session begins with the therapist providing the client with an overview. The therapist then focuses on psychoeducation on healthy sleep, followed by stimulus control therapy and implementing sleep hygiene habits. The therapist assigns homework, including practicing PMR on a nightly basis, changing a minimum of one unhealthy sleep habit, and completing a sleep diary with a nightmare log. Subsequent sessions begin with a review of the assigned homework.

The second session begins with the therapist providing further psychoeducation about psychological trauma and how nightmares develop and are maintained. Then the therapist leads the client through further practice of PMR and then assigns homework of reviewing the session content, practicing PMR, and choosing another unhealthy sleep habit to modify.

The third session begins with the therapist exposing the client to the content of one of their nightmares. The therapist directs the client to write a detailed description of the nightmare and to read it aloud in order to activate the fear memory network. The therapist then guides the client in identifying one or more of the trauma-related themes used in cognitive processing therapy (Resick et al., 2017)—power/control, esteem, trust, intimacy, and safety—and using that theme to rescript the narrative. The therapist then teaches diaphragmatic breathing. Homework includes modification of another sleep habit, rehearsal of the rescripted dream by reading it aloud, visualizing it, and practice of diaphragmatic breathing before sleep.

In the fourth session, the therapist asks the client to describe their experience of imagery rehearsal. If further rescripting is necessary, the dream is again rescripted as in Session 3, with the client writing a description and reading it aloud. This can be done either with the original nightmare or with another nightmare in order to reinforce the effect of imagery rehearsal. Similar homework as in Session 3 is again prescribed.

In the final session, the therapist discusses the treatment, asking the client to identify the skills in ERRT that were most effective for them. The therapist and client also make a plan for further improvement of symptoms.

Nightmare Deconstruction and Reprocessing

Nightmare deconstruction and reprocessing was adapted from CEDM (Hill, 2004; Hill & Spangler, 2016) by integrating psychoeducation, exposure, distress monitoring, relaxation, reprocessing, and rehearsal components into five or six sessions. The first NDR session consists of psychoeducation on nightmares, sleep, PTSD, and memory; an overview of NDR; motivation assessment; and introduction of relaxation skills. Because exposure to nightmare images can be distressing, it is helpful to describe NDR and assess the client's motivation for treatment and exposure tolerance.

In the second session, the therapist uses the three NDR stages. In Stage 1, the therapist guides the client through deconstructing three to five key nightmare images using the DRAWS steps, adapted from CEDM, with the addition of an "S" step for use of the Subjective Units of Distress Scale (SUDS; Wolpe, 1969) to monitor distress levels. The client should be engaged enough to activate the distressing memory but not so engaged that the emotional experience of the memory is unmanageable. In Stage 2, the goal is to *make meaning* of the nightmare and how it relates to the client's trauma memory. *Reprocessing* the nightmare may be centered on resolving grief; evaluating fear and anxiety; or challenging negative self-image related to guilt, shame, or moral injury. Reprocessing focuses on expressing and alleviating emotional distress and challenging thoughts through the use of probes, Socratic questioning, clarifications, and analysis of expected consequences. In Stage 3, the goal is to help the client gain mastery by *rescripting* the nightmare to decrease distress and facilitate reconsolidation of the trauma memory. There are three key components: (a) constructing a detailed description of changes to dream images based on work done in the first two stages, (b) helping the client emotionally engage with the new images through behavioral rehearsal of the changes, and (c) recording the rescripted dream. Homework assignments are to listen to the rescripted dream twice each day, including once immediately before sleep each night; to record any nightmares that occur; and to use a relaxation skill if awakened by a nightmare.

In the next two or three sessions, the tasks are to review the homework and any obstacles to completing it. Then the therapist asks the client to describe changes to the dream and helps the client deconstruct the changes to the nightmare by going through the three stages. As the client's nightmare severity and frequency decrease, the therapist can begin to bridge from changes to the dream to making changes in the client's waking life. Waking life changes should be based on understanding of the dream and may include (a) changing specific behaviors, such as interacting more with a spouse, participating in activities that help the client feel less isolated, or delaying angry reactions; (b) creating a ritual to honor the dream, which can be particularly meaningful when loss or grief is involved; or (c) continuing to work on the dream through journaling or talking with others.

The final session focuses on preparing the client to master their dreams independently. The therapist and client review changes made to nightmares and in waking life and then discuss which proposed changes have worked and why, which changes have not worked and why, and what future changes the client hopes to make.

Indications and Contraindications

The Hill cognitive–experiential dream model has been widely used with multiple client populations. CEDM generally works well with clients who can recall their dreams, are interested in learning about the meaning of their dreams, and have positive attitudes toward dreams (Crook & Hill, 2003; Crook-Lyon & Hill, 2004; Hill et al., 2013). In other words, CEDM may not work well with clients who cannot recall their dreams or are not interested in learning about their dreams.

IRT has been used with clients suffering from nightmare disorder as well as with those who have post-traumatic nightmares, including sexual assault survivors and military personnel and veterans with combat trauma. ERRT and NDR were developed primarily for post-traumatic nightmares and have been used with military personnel and veterans with combat trauma and with survivors of sexual assault. Because recall and description of nightmares are essential components of ERRT and NDR, these methods are contraindicated in clients who cannot recall nightmare content.

Assessment

Assessment of CEDM and Outcomes

Some studies on CEDM have included adherence and therapist competence measures to assess the use of CEDM in session. For example, therapists, clients, and/or judges rated how competent the therapist was in each stage of the CEDM session, and therapist adherence was measured by asking clients and therapists how much therapists used skills associated with each stage (e.g., re-experiencing the feelings in the exploration stage; Diemer et al., 1996, Hill et al., 2006; Wonnell & Hill, 2000). One measure that has been used to assess immediate delayed outcome of CEDM sessions is the Depth Scale of the Session Evaluation Questionnaire (SEQ-D; Stiles & Snow, 1984), a widely used psychometrically sound measure of client perception of session quality. Gains from Dream Interpretation (GDI; Heaton et al., 1998) assesses how clients perceive exploration, insight, and action gains from dream work.

A measure of distal outcome for CEDM studies is the single-item Insight into dream question (Hill et al., 2006). Clients are asked to write a dream and give an interpretation, responding to the questions, "What do you now think that dream means? How would you interpret it?" Judges are trained to rate insight using a 9-point scale (1 = no insight, 9 = high insight). Interrater reliability (internal consistency α) for insight ratings ranged from .86 to .94 for teams of two to five judges on CEDM studies. In addition, the Quality of Action Ideas (Hill et al., 2006) measures the quality of action plans. Clients are asked to write an action idea, responding to the questions, "Based on this dream, what changes would you like to make in your current life? How would you go about making those changes?" Judges are trained to rate the quality of action ideas using a 9-point scale (1 = low quality, 9 = high quality). Interrater reliability for the quality of action ideas ranged from .93 to .96 (Hill et al., 2006). Last, client Target Problem (Hill et al., 2006) is also a distal outcome measure for CEDM studies. After dream sessions, clients are asked to write down problems that are reflected in their presenting dreams. They then rate their post-session functioning and retrospectively rate their pre-session functioning on the target problem using a 13-point scale (1 = worst possible functioning, 13 = best possible functioning).

Assessment of Nightmare Treatments and Outcomes

Assessment of therapist adherence to methods of working with nightmares has not been consistent. Most trials of IRT to date have not included an adherence check, as has been noted in previous reviews (Harb et al., 2013; Hansen et al., 2013). Two trials of ERRT systematically tracked therapist adherence by adapting a judge-rated adherence measure from PTSD clinical trials (Resick et al., 2008) for components that are unique and essential to each session. Sessions were audio recorded and judges independently rated adherence. In one study (Pruiksma et al., 2018), more than 95% of components were included in all sessions, and in another study (Miller et al., 2018) all unique or essential components were rated as satisfactory or better. Thus, it appears that therapists can adhere to ERRT.

Immediate outcome has been studied rarely in nightmare treatment studies. Spangler and colleagues' (2022) pilot trial of NDR utilized SUDS to assess clients' distress levels at multiple time points during the session to determine change in in-session distress over the course of treatment. In addition, they monitored client heart rate and electrodermal activity using the Empatica E4 wristband (Garbarino et al., 2014) to assess immediate physiological outcome measures.

Distal outcome assessments used in nightmare treatment research include the Disturbing Dream and Nightmare Severity Index (Krakow et al., 2002), the Trauma-Related Nightmare Survey (Cranston et al., 2017), and the Nightmare Distress

Questionnaire (Belicki, 1992). These instruments assess the frequency and intensity of nightmares, how frequently the nightmares cause sleep disturbance (from fear of going to sleep, waking from nightmare, and not being able to return to sleep after a nightmare), as well as effect on daytime functioning (mood, cognition, and relationships). Insomnia is also typically assessed as an outcome in nightmare treatment studies, primarily with the Pittsburgh Sleep Quality Index (Buysse et al., 1989) or the Insomnia Severity Index (Bastien et al., 2001). The Pittsburgh Sleep Quality Index–Addendum (Germain et al., 2005) is often used as a measure of trauma-related sleep disturbance. Because nightmares and insomnia are symptoms of PTSD, two PTSD instruments are often used in nightmare treatment studies: the Clinician-Administered PTSD Scale for DSM-5 (Weathers et al. 2015) and the self-reported PTSD Checklist for DSM-5 (Weathers et al., 2013). Both measures include items asking about the 20 diagnostic symptoms of PTSD, including items assessing frequency and severity of nightmares and insomnia. In addition, polysomnography has been used as an outcome measure of nightmare treatment studies.

Clinical Examples

Cognitive Experiential Dream Model

Following is a clinical example of a dream session using the CEDM from the study by Ahn and Sim (2014). The client was a 22-year-old cisgender Asian American male. The therapist was a 25-year-old cisgender White female graduate student in a master's program in counseling psychology. The client presented the following dream, told in the first-person present tense:

> I am in a large wooden room with a woman and the entire floor is an atlas. We are able to fly at will and are kind of like thieves although I am unsure of what my relationship to her is. We pick a spot on the atlas and are transported to a museum. We steal a painting and the police begin to chase us. They seem to recognize us. We are really worried and scared that we will be caught. We almost get caught, but then return to the atlas room, escaping at the last second, and feel relieved and free.

In the exploration stage, the therapist guided the client through the DRAW steps: the woman, the room, and the scene where they almost got caught. The woman seemed familiar, and she made him feel comfortable, excited, energetic, and carefree. She reminded him of a childhood friend and of his mother, of his ideal self or how he strives to be, and of how he felt while dancing—light and free. The room felt comfortable, familiar, safe, and exciting and reminded him of his passions and interests. The room was associated with feeling comfortable starting his graduate program and looking forward to what is to come. Last, in the image in which he was almost caught, he felt fearful, unsure, scared, but also thrilled by the chase, which he associated with deadlines and getting caught doing something wrong when he was younger. He thought this image might be associated with having deadlines and not being organized, starting graduate school, growing up, and losing freedom.

The therapist began the insight stage by asking the client what he thought the dream might mean following their exploration of the three images. The client reported that the dream reflected his current goals and things that he did not want to happen, such as missing a deadline, feeling late, or not being able to fit everything he wants into his life. The therapist probed for additional insights and asked what he learned about himself from the dream. He said he enjoyed the adventure and the thrill of the chase, but he still worried about deadlines. Then, the therapist asked how different images of the dream represent parts of the client. The client said the neat and elegant room represents his ideal self. When the therapist asked for an existential meaning of the dream, the client indicated that the dream made him think of his desire to be better about his ideal self and achieve more and his transition from college to graduate school.

In the action stage, the therapist asked the client what changes he would like to make to the dream. The client said he would do more adventure and would change almost getting caught to having a cleaner getaway. When the therapist asked how he would translate the changes in the dream into the changes in his waking life, the client said he wanted to engage in passions and interests more and make an effort to do the things that make him carefree and happy. He also reported that he wanted to be more open and comfortable socially and make new friends. In addition, he wanted to be more organized, manage time better, and be more focused. For each change, the therapist asked how difficult the change would be for him and what obstacles he expected to happen while he made changes in his waking life. The therapist then helped the client prepare for implementing the action plan.

After the completion of the dream session, the client reported that he was satisfied with the session (5 out of 5 on the Session Evaluation Scale) and gained a lot from the dream interpretation (8.14 out of 9 on Gains from Dream Interpretation). Specifically, he reported that he learned more about the meaning of his dream and gained ideas for how to change some aspects of himself and his life. Because it was a single session of dream work, the therapist and researcher could not assess what changes the client was able to make after the dream session.

Nightmare Treatments

We use a single case to illustrate the use of IRT, ERRT, and NDR. The case is based on an actual research participant, who granted permission to use the dream content for purposes of this chapter. Identifying information has been modified to preserve confidentiality. The client was a 55-year-old, African American, cisgender male Coast Guard veteran with a history of chronic nightmares and insomnia subsequent to an incident that occurred during a patrol in the Arctic 20 years prior. The polar icebreaker to which he was assigned was caught on an ice sheet, tearing a long gash in the hull and causing the ship to take on water. The ship, listing severely, made it to port for repairs after a long, harrowing journey. The client reported that he had a recurring nightmare about the incident four or five nights a week:

> I'm on deck, and we're patrolling as usual when I hear the alarm bell and realize that we're drifting into an ice shelf. I can hear and feel the ship's hull make contact with

> the ice, just as it did when it actually happened. We're hung up on the ice shelf, and compartments belowdecks begin to fill with water. I order two crew members to move to their assigned positions, but they ignore me. I go below myself and hear my buddy calling out. He's struggling to make his way to the hatch, but the force of the incoming water keeps him from escaping. It's weird because the force of the water should be pushing him toward the hatch. I can't reach him. I yell for him. I wake up.

Imagery Rehearsal Therapy

In the first IRT session, during the psychoeducation, the client is relieved when the therapist tells him that he will not have to talk about his trauma or the content of his nightmare. He is not surprised to learn that military personnel are at risk for developing traumatic stress symptoms, particularly sleep disturbances. He also learns that his nightmares were a normal response to his trauma like his but that after 20 years, they no longer serve a healing purpose. He identifies one sleep habit he will try to change—watching television while in bed.

In the second IRT session, the client learns that chronic nightmares are a learned behavior, and he estimates that his nightmares are probably approximately 90% due to habit rather than trauma response. The client then learns about the imagery system, and he comes up with positive images of a leafy hiking trail near his home. The client practices pleasant imagery, increasing the duration by extending the imagined trail and giving more detail about autumn colors and coolness of the air. He practices the hiking trail imagery between sessions.

In the third IRT session, the client chooses building a garden shed, imagining the steps and rehearsing them in order. The client is guided to think about changing his identity from someone who has the same nightmare nearly every night to someone who has pleasant dreams or no dreams he can recall. The client writes out his nightmare but does not read it aloud. He chooses the hike as a replacement for the nightmare and rehearses the images in session. Homework is rehearsing the new dream daily before bed.

In the final session, the client reports that he had only one nightmare in the past week, which is an improvement but a little disappointing. The therapist emphasizes the change process is incremental and encourages the client to continue rehearsing the new dream and enhancing it with additional positive images.

Exposure, Relaxation, and Rescripting Therapy

In the first and second sessions of ERRT, the client learns about stimulus control and sleep hygiene and quickly identifies not watching television in bed as a means of stimulus control. He is familiar with PMR and looks forward to practicing it again. He is surprised by having to keep a nightmare log because he has no problem recalling his nightmare. The client is assigned homework of reviewing the session content, practicing PMR, and choosing another unhealthy sleep habit to modify.

In the third ERRT session, the client writes a detailed description of his recurrent nightmare and reads it aloud, identifying the strongest theme as safety because the collision and difficult journey to port were so harrowing. He also identifies power/control as an important theme because of the crew members who disobeyed him and his inability to pull his buddy out of swirling water. The client writes the rescripted nightmare and reads aloud the alternative narrative in which the crew members obey his orders and help him pull his buddy out of the frigid swirling water. The therapist teaches the client diaphragmatic breathing. Homework includes rehearsing the rescripted dream and visualizing the images each night before going to sleep, practicing diaphragmatic breathing or PMR before bed every night, and maintaining a regular bedtime.

At the fourth session, the client reports that he has had only one disturbing dream in the past week, which was about difficulty with his supervisees at work. The client quickly identifies the dream as having a power/control theme similar to the one in his original nightmare. The client rescripts a dream in which he communicates clearly with the supervisees and asks if they have questions or issues following his directions. The client knows his homework will be to rehearse the rescripted dream, practice relaxation, and continue with sleep hygiene and stimulus control.

In the final ERRT session, the client reports no distressing dreams in the past week. He tells the therapist that relaxation, rescripting, and rehearsal were most helpful because of how quickly he returned to sleep after any nightmares and how quickly his nightmares decreased when he rehearsed the rescripted dream. He will continue stimulus control, sleep hygiene, and relaxation skills nightly and to rescript any future disturbing dreams.

Nightmare Deconstruction and Reprocessing

As he learns about NDR in Session 1, the client is concerned that giving a detailed description of his nightmare might make it more intense. The therapist explains that this is why they will meet twice a week in the first 2 weeks—to provide sufficient support and expedite his mastery over the nightmares. The client's preferred relaxation skill is relaxed breathing, which they practice in session and is assigned as homework, along with keeping a nightmare diary.

In the second NDR session, the client tells the dream in the first-person, present tense. Four key images are identified: the impact of the icebreaker with the ice, the disobedient crew members, his buddy trapped in the swirling water, and his inability to reach his buddy. They use the DRAW steps on each image. The image with the highest SUDS level was his not being able to help his buddy, which was an 85 on the 0 to 100 SUDS. The client describes feeling extremely frustrated when he could not reach his buddy and fearful that his buddy would die in the frigid water. It is notable that the image of his being unable to reach his buddy did not actually happen during the collision. In Stage 2, meaning-making and reprocessing, the client says he thinks the dream reflects his worry about the crew and fear for himself during the collision. In exploring why the nightmare did not accurately depict the actual collision, the therapist asks whether the frustration might represent similar earlier experiences in life. The client says he feels frustrated when he is the only person who takes responsibility on group tasks. He associates this frustration with trying to learn new tasks as a child, and his father insisted that he figure it out for himself. The client is able to identify times when others have stepped forward to help, such as his church group that works together at Habitat for Humanity sites. The client rescripts the dream so that the crew members are replaced by church group members, who help pull his buddy to safety. The client records the rescripted dream and listens to it twice a day.

In Sessions 3–5, the client reports changes to the dream in which crew members are reliable and the image of his trapped buddy is no longer in the dream. The new dream images are deconstructed with the DRAWS steps, and the client's SUDS levels decrease to a maximum of 30. Transitioning to making changes in his waking life, the client says he would like to focus on relationships with unsupportive workmates. In the final session, the client reports that understanding his pattern of frustration with being the only person to step up helped him see that he actually does have people he can call on for support. In considering potential triggers for future nightmares, the client states that in the past his nightmares became more intense when he had a tight deadline at work. The therapist recommends using a relaxation skill during difficult work periods and to remember the NDR stages for any future disturbing dreams.

Landmark Studies and Previous Reviews

CEDM Reviews

Hill and Goates (2004) and Hill and Knox (2010) reviewed 19 studies on CEDM, finding that in comparison with normative data, clients rated CEDM sessions as having greater depth (i.e., quality, satisfaction) than non-dream-focused sessions. One of the most consistent outcomes across studies was increased insight into dreams as expressed in sessions (Hill & Goates, 2004). In terms of moderators, they found that clients who were psychologically minded, had a positive attitude toward dreams, and had good dream recall were most likely to benefit from working with dreams.

One study highlighted in that review (Hill et al., 2006) examined predictors of the process and outcome of dream sessions using CEDM. A total of 157 clients participated in single dream sessions with 42 psychotherapists in three university settings. Results suggested that clients gained insight (i.e., understood the meaning of their dreams) and developed better quality action plans based on their understanding of their dreams. Clients also reported better functioning on their target problems, reflected in their presenting dreams. In addition, therapist competence and adherence in the exploration and insight stages were positively associated with the average of the Relationship Scale (Hill & Kellems, 2002), Session Evaluation Scale (Hill & Kellems, 2002), and GDI (Heaton et al., 1998) ($t = 5.90^{***}$ for exploration stage client-rated adherence and competence, and $t = 4.36^{***}$ for insight stage client-rated adherence and competence; t, test of significance of variables; $^{***}p < .001$). Furthermore, when clients' level of functioning on the target problem reflected on their presenting dream was low before their dream sessions, clients were more likely to rate the quality of the insight and action stages highly and made the most changes in their target problem. Finally, clients with low initial insight and with low action ideas gained the most insight and action, respectively.

IRT and ERRT

Since 2012, five meta-analyses have been conducted that included IRT or ERRT as methods for treating nightmares (Augedal et al., 2013; Casement & Swanson, 2012; Hansen et al., 2013; Seda et al., 2015; Yücel et al., 2020). There is considerable overlap among these meta-analyses in the studies included for analysis. However, some of the meta-analyses included studies that were not of either IRT or ERRT (Augedal et al., 2013; Hansen et al., 2013; Yücel et al., 2020) or involved self-guided IRT (Seda et al., 2015).

Given the purpose of this chapter, we thus review only Casement and Swanson's (2012) meta-analysis, which examined the effects of studies that included therapist-delivered IRT or ERRT as at least one treatment method for 511 clients in 13 studies on nightmare frequency, sleep quality, and post-traumatic stress. Casement and Swanson analyzed data from eight IRT studies, three ERRT studies, one study of imagery rescripting and exposure therapy (an adaptation of ERRT), and one study of IRT combined with cognitive–behavioral treatment for insomnia (CBT-I). Effects for nightmare frequency were moderate for both pre- to post-treatment (g = .69) and 6- to 12-month follow-up (g = .72). There were also moderate effects for sleep quality for pre- to post-treatment (g = .68) and 6- to 12-month follow-up (g = .62). Effects of IRT/ERRT on post-traumatic stress were moderate for pre- to post-treatment (g = .72) and large for 6- to 12-month follow-up (g = .93). Effect sizes between IRT/ERRT and control were moderate for nightmare frequency (g = .59), sleep quality (g = .64), and post-traumatic stress (g = .67). These results provide a reference for comparison with the box score analyses reported below. However, because the studies in Casement and Swanson (2012) included both individual and group treatment studies, we do not include them in the summary table.

Research Review

CEDM Meta-Analysis

The two prior reviews of CEDM (Hill & Goates, 2004; Hill & Knox, 2010) concluded that dream work using the Hill model resulted in greater session depth and increased insight into the target dream. Hence, we focused the current meta-analysis on these two outcome variables. A review of the literature was conducted from November 2021 to January 2022 using the search engines PsycInfo, PubMed, PsycARTICLE, Cochrane, and ERIC using the following keywords: "cognitive-experiential," "dream," "Hill," "intervention," "therapy," and "treatment." Reference lists were examined from the articles that met inclusion criteria for the meta-analysis. The search was limited to studies published in English and reported in journals, theses, and dissertations.

Twenty-three studies were found in the initial search, including 21 peer-reviewed journal articles and two dissertations. Both authors reviewed the study titles and abstracts for common variables that were likely to yield data on session depth and insight into the dream. Articles were rejected if they were case studies, studies of group or couples CEDM, did not measure session depth or insight into the dream, or did not report results necessary for calculating effect size. Two authors were contacted in an attempt to access means and standard deviations, but one author was unresponsive and the other no longer had access to the study data set.

Thus, studies were included in the meta-analysis if they involved individual psychotherapy that had CEDM as a treatment; included a measure of session depth (immediate outcome) or a measure of insight into the dream (distal outcome); included enough detail to calculate effect sizes; were written in English; and were published or in press by August 31, 2022. Treatments were classified as CEDM if they included all three stages of the model and included at least one standard, in-person session with a therapist. Based on these inclusion criteria, a total of eight studies were included in the meta-analysis, with 514 clients (Table 19.1).

Table 19.1 Studies Included in the CEDM Meta-Analysis

Study	Design	Clients	*N*	Depth ES 1	Depth ES 2	Insight ES 1	Insight ES 2
Diemer et al. (1996)	Within- and between-subjects analysis; 2 CEDM sessions vs. 2 event sessions using Hill model	Moderately distressed adult community dwellers	25	–0.04	0.14	0.26	—
Heaton et al. (1998)	Between-treatment analysis; participants each got 1 therapist-facilitated CEDM session and 1 self-guided dream session	University undergraduates	25	1.54	—	—	—
Hill et al. (2000)	Between-subjects analysis; 8–10 sessions with several sessions of CEDM vs. several sessions focused on loss	Distressed adult community dwellers with a recent loss	14	1.43	—	—	—
Wonnell & Hill (2000)	Between-subjects analysis; single session of full CEDM vs. CEDM without action stage	University undergraduates	43	0.08	—	—	—
Hill et al. (2001)	Within- and between-subjects analysis; single session of CEDM with insight focused on waking life vs. parts-of-self	University undergraduates	105	—	—	0.37	—
Hill et al. (2003)	Between-subjects analysis; single session of CEDM with therapist empathy + input vs. with therapist empathy vs. computer assisted	University undergraduates	94	0.38	1.17	—	—
T. Davis & Hill (2005)	Within- and between-group analysis; CEDM with waking life interpretation vs. CEDM with spiritual interpretation	Adults from the community self-identifying as spiritual	51	—	—	0.99	0.90
Hill et al. (2006)	Within-subject analysis; single session of CEDM; predictors of outcome	Undergraduates, graduate students, and community dwellers	157	—	—	1.07	—

CEDM, cognitive experiential dream model; ES, effect size.

The following information was extracted from each of the eight studies: identification (title, authors, year of publication, journal title), sample characteristics (size, demographic information), number of sessions, insight measure used, session depth measure used, and means and standard deviations. The single-item Insight question (Falk & Hill, 1995) was used for all studies. For session depth, data from the SEQ-D (Stiles & Snow, 1984) were extracted.

All eight studies included in the meta-analysis were studies of CEDM published between 1996 and 2006. Of these, five studies included comparisons of SEQ-D between treatment groups, and four included pre- to post-treatment change in Insight into dream (one study included both SEQ-D and Insight into dream). Table 19.1 shows the descriptive characteristics of the analyzed studies. The SEQ-D studies included 201 participants, and the Insight studies included 338 participants.

Data were coded by one author (PS) and quality checked by the other (WS) to ensure accuracy. Between-group effect sizes were calculated for session depth, and within-group effects for Insight into dream were calculated for each study. Computation of mean effect sizes (Hedges' *g*) and 95% confidence intervals (CIs) were calculated in R (Viechtbauer, 2010) using a random effects model. Given the small sample size, robust variance estimation model was used in R to adjust for dependency among the effects.

For the between-treatment studies, random effects model analysis showed a moderate effect size for CEDM on session depth (SEQ-D), Hedges' $g = 0.70$, 95% CI [−0.16, 1.56], $p < .10$, with substantial heterogeneity, $I^2 = 78\%$. This result indicates that standard CEDM sessions had greater depth than comparator treatment sessions. Comparator treatments varied across the studies and included focusing on spirituality, focusing on loss, computer-guided CEDM, event interpretation, unstructured sessions, and self-guided dream interpretation.

For pre- to post-treatment change in insight into the dream, there was also a moderate effect size for CEDM: Hedges' $g = .67$, 95% CI [−1.34, 0.007], $p < .10$, with substantial heterogeneity, $I^2 = 83\%$. This result indicated that judges rated the clients' insight into their dream higher after the CEDM session than prior to the session.

In summary, these meta-analytic results support the conclusions of the previous CEDM reviews (Hill & Goates, 2004; Hill & Knox, 2010). Specifically, working with dreams using the CEDM helps clients gain insight into their dreams, and clients perceive these sessions as deeper than sessions not using the full CEDM.

Review of Methods for Working with Nightmares

Given that five meta-analyses of IRT and ERRT have been conducted since 2012, with the most recent published in 2020, no meta-analysis on nightmare treatments was conducted for this chapter. The studies reviewed here are those not analyzed by Casement and Swanson (2012) and that included individual, therapist-delivered IRT, ERRT, or NDR for adults as at least one method for treating nightmares. We review three studies of IRT, three studies of ERRT, and two studies of NDR/CEDM for nightmares. Box scores were determined by calculating the number of positive, negative, and neutral outcomes for each study. Although some of these studies included a variety of outcome measures, in the interest of brevity and consistency across studies, we report outcomes only on nightmare frequency, nightmare severity/distress, sleep quality, insomnia, and post-traumatic stress symptoms. Some of these outcomes were analyzed both as pretreatment to post-treatment and as compared against a bona fide treatment. We tallied by outcome type (e.g., nightmare severity, sleep disturbance) rather than by the total number of analyses; for example, if there was a large effect for pre- to post-treatment and large effect for between-treatment on nightmare severity, this counted as one positive box score.

IRT

van Schagen and colleagues (2015) randomized 86 clients with moderate to severe psychiatric disorders to either IRT plus treatment as usual (TAU) or TAU alone. The IRT supplement included six sessions of IRT written in Dutch. Therapist adherence to the protocol was monitored but not reported in this article. Results showed a moderate effect for IRT at post-treatment for nightmare frequency ($d = 0.50$), nightmare distress ($d = 0.70$), and post-traumatic stress symptoms ($d = 0.70$). Hence, there are three positive box scores for this study.

Belleville and colleagues (2018) compared the efficacy of IRT combined with CBT to CBT alone for treating PTSD in sexual assault survivors. Forty-two patients were randomized to either IRT + CBT or CBT alone. For nightmare frequency, there was a large effect for pre- to post-IRT ($d = 0.91$) and a moderate effect between treatment types ($d = 0.58$). For nightmare distress, there was a large effect for pre- to post-IRT ($d = 1.13$) and a moderate effect between treatment types ($d = 0.63$). For sleep quality, there was a large effect for pre- to post-IRT ($d = 0.91$) and a small effect between treatment types ($d = 0.45$). For post-traumatic stress symptoms, there was a large effect for pre- to post-IRT ($d = 2.93$) and a moderate effect between treatment types ($d = 0.67$). Hence, there were four positive and one neutral box scores for this study.

Putois and colleagues (2019) tested teletherapy IRT for both post-traumatic and idiopathic nightmares. The pre-to-post design included assessment at baseline, post-treatment, and 3-month follow-up. Forty-eight patients completed a four-session IRT adapted for video teleconference with a psychologist in individual therapy. No training or adherence information was reported. Results showed large pre- to post-treatment effects for nightmare frequency ($d = 1.32$), sleep disturbance ($d = 0.90$), insomnia ($d = 0.98$), and post-traumatic stress symptoms ($d = 0.37$–0.48). Hence, this study yielded four positive box scores.

ERRT

A 2018 pilot study (Miller et al., 2018) tested ERRT-B for patients with bipolar disorder. Seven adults diagnosed with bipolar I or II disorder with a history of trauma and nightmares received five 90-minute sessions of ERRT modified to include psychoeducation about bipolar disorder and sleep and development of a plan to respond to potential worsening of bipolar symptoms. There was good therapist adherence, with the unique and essential elements of ERRT-B included and rated satisfactory or better. One participant dropped out after the first session (12.5% attrition). Pretreatment to 3-month follow-up results showed large effects for nightmare frequency ($d = 2.07$), nightmare severity ($d = 2.09$), and post-traumatic stress symptoms ($d = 1.44$ and 1.07); a moderate effect for sleep quality ($d = 0.50$); and a small effect for insomnia. Hence, this study yielded five positive box scores.

Pruiksma and colleagues' (2018) dismantling study compared standard ERRT against ERRT with no exposure (NEX) in 70 community-dwelling adults with frequent nightmares (≥1 per week). Therapist adherence to both treatment protocols was high, with 96% of unique and essential elements rated as good or excellent for ERRT and 98% for the NEX group, and there was low participant dropout (17.65%). In this sample, 64.3 of participants met criteria for PTSD. Results showed there were no significant differences between ERRT and NEX on any of these distal outcome measures. For ERRT, baseline to 6-month follow-up showed large effects for nightmare severity (d = 0.95), sleep quality (d = 1.25), and insomnia (d = 1.61) and moderate effects for nightmare frequency (d = 0.61) and post-traumatic stress (d = 0.65). Although linear mixed model results showed no significant differences between ERRT and NEX on any of these outcomes, because NEX was not a bona fide treatment, we do not consider the effect sizes in our box score analyses. Hence, this study yielded four positive box scores.

Pruiksma and colleagues' (2020) pilot tested ERRT-M, which was adapted for military personnel. Forty active duty service members were randomized to ERRT-M or to a minimal contact control group. There was high therapist adherence to treatment protocol, with 87% of the unique and essential elements and 97% of essential but not unique elements rated as good or excellent, and there was low participant dropout (17.5%). Results showed that for nightmare frequency, there were moderate effects for pretreatment to 1-month follow-up (d = 0.52) and between treatments (d = 0.53). For nightmare severity, there were also moderate pretreatment to follow-up effects (d = 0.55) and between-treatment effects (d = 0.60). For insomnia, results showed moderate pretreatment to follow-up effects (d = 0.59) and between-treatment effects (d = 0.52). Finally, for post-traumatic stress symptoms, there was a moderate pretreatment to follow-up effect (d = 0.58) and a small between-group effect (d = 0.12). Hence, this study yielded four positive box scores.

CEDM/NDR

Heaton (2002) conducted a randomized trial of CEDM adapted for nightmares that included 29 clients. Treatment consisted of two to four 60- to 90-minute sessions. Participants were randomized to immediate treatment (n = 17) or 1-month delay (n = 12). Analysis of variance results showed that the immediate treatment group did not have a greater decrease in nightmare frequency or nightmare intensity compared to the wait-list control group. Effect sizes for nightmare frequency and nightmare severity were small ($\eta^2 = 0.03$ and $\eta^2 = 0.05$, respectively). Hence, this study yielded two neutral box scores.

Spangler and colleagues (2022) conducted a single-arm pilot trial of NDR. Treatment consisted of eight sessions of NDR over 8 weeks. Participants were 11 active duty military service members and veterans with post-traumatic nightmares. Pretreatment to follow-up results for distal outcomes showed a large effect for nightmare frequency (d = 0.93), a small effect for sleep quality (d = 0.41), and a small effect for post-traumatic stress (d = 0.48). Immediate outcome variables included in-session physiologic data collected via wristband device, and analysis of the difference in electrodermal activity (as an indicator of distress) between Visit 0 (psychoeducation visit) and Visit 1 (initial exposure to nightmare content) showed a moderate effect size (d = 0.58). There was also a moderate effect (d = 0.57) for the difference between Visit 1 and Visit 7 (final exposure to nightmare content). These results indicate that NDR may have some efficacy in decreasing nightmare frequency and sleep disturbance and that electrodermal activity is a reliable physiologic indicator of client emotional engagement during activation of trauma memory through nightmare content and of their decreasing reactivity to their original nightmare narrative over the course of therapy. Hence, this study yielded four positive box scores.

Summary

Results from seven of the eight studies reviewed here provide evidence for the efficacy of these methods for working with nightmares. The three IRT studies with 176 clients resulted in 11 positive box scores. When putting these results in conjunction with the results of Casement and Swanson (2012; $g = .59–.72$), there appears to be moderate to strong evidence for the efficacy of IRT for nightmare frequency and severity, sleep disturbance, insomnia, and post-traumatic stress symptoms. In addition, these studies provide evidence of IRT's efficacy across diagnoses and when delivered by teleconference. van Schagen and colleagues' (2015) study of IRT was important because it provided evidence of IRT's efficacy for nightmares related to a variety of psychiatric disorders comorbid with PTSD and that the IRT protocol could be translated and used in Dutch. It is interesting to note that the virtual IRT study (Putois et al., 2019) reported large effect sizes for nightmare frequency, sleep disturbance, and insomnia. Additional research, particularly on conducting IRT virtually, is needed.

The three studies of ERRT included 117 clients and resulted in 14 positive box scores across five distal outcomes. In considering these results together with those of the meta-analysis by Casement and Swanson (2012), which reviewed four ERRT or adapted ERRT studies with 110 clients, there appears to be moderate to strong evidence of the efficacy of ERRT for nightmare frequency and severity, sleep disturbance, insomnia, and post-traumatic stress symptoms. All of the ERRT studies reviewed here include data on therapist adherence and participant dropout, with high levels of adherence and low dropout, which strengthens the validity of the results. In addition, the pilot study conducted by Miller and colleagues (2018) provides preliminary evidence that ERRT can be adapted for clients with bipolar disorder with a history of trauma, which may be an indicator of its adaptability for other diagnoses. Finally, although the between-group results were null, the dismantling study conducted by Pruiksma and colleagues (2018) nevertheless addresses the vital question of response variability among nightmare methods, with implications for future studies.

There is less evidence for the efficacy of NDR/adapted CEDM. The pilot trial conducted by Spangler and colleagues (2022) showed large effects for nightmare severity and small effects for sleep disturbance and post-traumatic stress, which are consistent with other exposure-based nightmare treatments such as ERRT. However, the sample size was small ($N = 11$). Results reported by Heaton (2002) were limited to between-group effect sizes because means and standard deviations were not reported. Possible reasons for the wide variability in response to exposure methods are unclear. Immediate outcomes may have been a factor, but only one study (Spangler et al., 2022) reported in-session outcomes, so it is not possible to compare the study results on immediate outcomes. It would expand understanding of mechanisms of action if future studies of exposure and non-exposure methods for working with nightmares include both immediate and distal outcomes.

Possible Negative Effects and Harm

There have been no reported negative effects or harm in using CEDM to work with dreams. However, some clients may find the depth of dream work difficult if they are not prepared for it or it is not characterologically or culturally suited to them.

Although there is no research evidence of exposure to nightmare content causing harm, there is a high dropout rate for exposure-based, trauma-focused therapies such as prolonged exposure and cognitive processing therapy (Najavits, 2015). Given the high dropout rate for exposure methods, nightmare methods that use exposure may likewise induce premature termination and result in truncated care. One of the nightmare meta-analyses reported an attrition rate of 26%, slightly higher than that for CBT (Casement & Swanson, 2012). Another meta-analysis reported a larger range of attrition of 23.4–51.9% (Augedal et al., 2013); however, the attrition rates were not specified for each treatment.

Finally, there is a growing body of research that indicates an association between nightmares and suicidality, even after controlling for other mental health diagnoses (Bernert & Joiner, 2007; Harris et al., 2020; Pigeon et al., 2012). There is little research on the impact of nightmare-exposure treatment on suicidality. One secondary analysis of data from two ERRT studies found a decrease in suicide ideation from baseline to post-treatment (Cogan et al., 2019); however, suicidality was assessed with one item, and it was not assessed during the initial weeks of treatment, when distress at exposure is likely highest and patient mastery of nightmare material has not yet been developed. In addition, individuals with significant ideation and intent to act were excluded from these studies. Thus, until further evidence is available, it is recommended that a thorough assessment of suicidality be done prior to starting work with nightmares, and it should be monitored during treatment for those at elevated risk.

Diversity Considerations

Several studies examined the process and outcome of the CEDM with diverse populations, including Taiwanese college students, Asian American students, and international students in the United States. Results suggested that clients completing CEDM sessions showed similar gains to the U.S. samples (Sim et al., 2010; Sim et al., 2021; Tien et al., 2006). Asian clients reported all three components of CEDM (exploration, insight, and action stages) were helpful. In addition, Asian American clients responded differently to therapist input (i.e., high and low therapist input) depending on their level of attachment anxiety and Asian values (Hill et al., 2007).

Among the nightmare method studies, more than half of the studies analyzed in the prior meta-analysis and the eight additional studies were conducted in veteran or military samples. The ranges of effect sizes for civilian and military/veteran samples were approximately equivalent (see Tables 19.1 and 19.2; Casement & Swanson, 2012). No study to date has compared the immediate or distal effects of working with nightmares in military versus civilian samples. Nevertheless, military culture has unique aspects that may impact working with nightmares. For example, stoicism is a military cultural value that may cause some clients to underreport their SUDS level in session, making it difficult for the therapist to ascertain the client's engagement with the nightmare content. Nightmares may, however, present an opportunity for service members and veterans to seek treatment for post-traumatic stress by seeking help for a sleep problem rather than a mental health problem, which may carry more stigma for them.

Reporting of demographics in the meta-analyses of nightmare work was mixed. One study (Casement & Swanson, 2012) reported that of the studies which reported race, 61% of the samples were White. A review of the demographics of 13 studies included in the meta-analysis and the eight nightmare treatment studies showed that the percentage of women clients varied from 0% to 100%, with studies of sexual assault nightmares including predominantly women and studies with military service members or veterans including predominantly men. The studies published since the last meta-analysis included predominantly women, except for the two studies that sampled military personnel and veterans. Thus, results can be generalized with regard to gender. With regard to race and ethnicity, although the participants of the studies with civilian samples were predominantly White (62–100%), participants in the 11 studies of military personnel and veterans were more ethnically diverse, with 33–63% self-identifying as White.

Limitations of the Research

Although CEDM has been widely studied, results of the current meta-analysis should be interpreted with caution given the small number of studies in the analysis. In addition, the components of the comparator treatments were similar to CEDM for some studies but different for others. This variability in comparators may have been a factor in the high heterogeneity; some comparators were partial CEDM or self- or computer-assisted, so the elements of CEDM were still present. In future studies of CEDM, we encourage researchers to include pre- and post-session ratings of insight into the dream, session depth, and perhaps other distal outcomes, such as actual changes in behavior or reduction of distress. In addition, given that clients may perceive greater depth in CEDM sessions, and thus may be more involved, attention could be given to process variables such as the working alliance, which has been investigated in a few CEDM studies and may be a useful process measure in future studies. Most empirical studies of dream work have investigated CEDM; more empirical research on other dream work methods will probably prove helpful.

With regard to nightmare treatment research, conclusions are also limited due to insufficient reporting of critical variables, such as therapist adherence to treatment and group versus individual therapy. In addition, few nightmare treatment studies have investigated immediate outcomes, which is important when considering the in-session

Table 19.2 Nightmare Treatment Effect Sizes and Box Scores

Study	Description	*N*	NM Frequency (Distal) (*d*) Box Score	NM Severity/ Distress (Distal) (*d*) Box Score	Sleep Quality (Distal) (*d*) Box Score	Insomnia (Distal) (*d*) Box Score	PTS (Distal) (*d*) Box Score	EDA (Immediate)	Box Score Total
van Schagen et al. (2015)	RCT; TAU compared to IRT + TAU in Dutch patients with comorbid psychiatric disorders	86	Pre to post ($d = 0.81$) Between ($d = 0.39$) 1+	Pre to post ($d = 0.78$) Between ($d = 0.57$) 1+	—	—	Pre to post ($d = 0.62$) Between ($d = 0.60$) 1+	—	3+
Belleville et al. (2018)	RCT; IRT + CBT compared to CBT alone in Canadian sexual assault survivors	42	Pre to post ($d = 0.91$) Between ($d = 0.58$) 1+	Pre to post ($d = 1.13$) Between ($d = 0.63$) 1+	Pre to post ($d = 0.91$) Between ($d = 0.45$) 1+	—	Pre to post ($d = 2.39$) Between ($d = 0.67$) 1+	—	4+
Putois et al. (2019)	Pilot of IRT via teletherapy in adults with idiopathic or PTS nightmares	48	Pre to post ($d = 1.32$) 1+	—	Pre to post ($d = 0.90$) 1+	Pre to post ($d = 0.98$) 1+	Pre to post ($d = 0.37$ to 0.48) 1+	—	4+
IRT total		176	3+	2+	2+	1+	3+		11+
Miller et al. (2018)	Pilot study of ERRT adapted for adults with bipolar disorder	7	Pre to post ($d = 2.07$) 1+	Pre to post ($d = 2.09$) 1+	Pre to post ($d = 0.50$) 1+	Pre to post ($d = 0.37$) 1+	Pre to post ($d = 1.44$ to 1.07) 1+	—	5+

Pruiksma et al., (2018)	Dismantling study; ERRT compared to NEX in adults with nightmares	70	Pre to post ($d = 0.61$) 1+	Pre to post ($d = 0.95$) 1+	Pre to post ($d = 1.25$) 1+	Pre to post ($d = 1.61$) 1+	Pre to post ($d = 0.65$) 1+	—	5+
Pruiksma et al. (2020)	RCT; ERRT compared to minimal contact control in active-duty military personnel	40	Pre to post ($d = 0.52$) Between ($d = 0.53$) 1+	Pre to post ($d = 0.55$) Between ($d = 0.60$) 1+	—	Pre to post ($d = 0.59$) Between ($d = 0.52$) 1+	Pre to post ($d = 0.58$) Between ($d = 0.12$) 1+	—	4+
ERRT total		117	3+	3+	3+	2+	3+		14+
Heaton (2002)	RCT; CEDM for nightmares compared to 1-month delay in U.S. adults with nightmares and no trauma	29	Between $\eta^2 = 0.03$ 1=	Between $\eta^2 = 0.05$ 1=				—	2=
Spangler et al. (2022)	Single-arm pilot trial of NDR; in military personnel and veterans with post-trauma nightmares	11	Pre to post ($d = 0.93$) 1+		Pre to post ($d = 0.41$) 1+		Pre to post ($d = 0.48$) 1+	Pre to post ($d = 0.57$ to 0.58) 1+	4+
NDR total		40							4+ 2=

CBT, cognitive–behavioral therapy; CEDM, cognitive experiential dream model; ERRT, exposure, relaxation, and rescripting therapy; IRT, imagery rehearsal therapy; NDR, nightmare deconstruction and reprocessing; NM, nightmare; PTS, post-traumatic stress; RCT, randomized controlled trial; TAU, treatment as usual.

impact of trauma activation. Indeed, prior nightmare treatment meta-analyses have analyzed exposure treatments and non-exposure treatments as a single approach. However, trauma activation (and eventual habituation) through in-session exposure is believed to be the mechanism of change in exposure-based PTSD treatments (Haubrich & Nader, 2018), and treatments that activate trauma memory through exposure to nightmare content will of course have different effects than one that avoids exposure, such as IRT (Krakow & Zadra, 2006). Thus, future researchers can not only focus on testing outcomes of exposure versus non-exposure treatments but also examine session-level factors, especially those related to trauma activation. In addition, greater consideration can be given to integrating physiologic markers of distress, which is becoming increasingly feasible with the widespread use of wearable technology to track cardiovascular output and electrodermal activity.

Training Implications

Dream work often is not a core component of graduate training programs, but educators can consider adding training on dream work. In one study of training in CEDM (Crook-Lyon et al., 2009), therapists who received a 3-hour workshop on CEDM reported an increase in their self-efficacy in using CEDM and positive attitudes toward dreams. Two useful resources for CEDM training are the book *Dream Work in Therapy: Facilitating Exploration, Insight, and Action* (Hill, 2004) and the videotape *Dream Work in Practice* (Hill, 2013).

Although there is no empirical evidence supporting the efficacy of IRT training methods, the developer of IRT, Barry Krakow offers training resources at https://barrykrakowmd.com/product-category/imagery-rehearsal-therapy. For additional information on working with post-traumatic nightmares, Uniformed Services University's Center for Deployment Psychology has information web pages and regularly conducts training in IRT and CBT-I (https://deploymentpsych.org/psychological-training).

Therapeutic Practices

On the basis of our meta-analysis of CEDM studies and the previous meta-analyses on nightmare treatments, we offer the following research-supported practices:

- Invite clients to bring a dream to session to facilitate insight gains.
- Consider using CEDM to facilitate greater depth in dreams.
- In selecting a method of working with nightmares, consider client potential or demonstrated response to exposure—some clients cannot tolerate it.
- In working with nightmares, consider which approach might be best suited to client culture and experience. For example, racial or refugee trauma reflected in a nightmare might be approached using a method with more latitude in interpretation.
- Assess client suicidality among nightmare sufferers, particularly in the early sessions of exposure-based treatments.
- Consider using SUDS ratings when working with nightmare content; what you think is the most distressing image may not be for the client.

References

* Studies included in the meta-analysis.

Adler, A. (1936). On the interpretation of dreams. *International Journal of Individual Psychology, 2*, 3–16.

Adler, A. (1938). *Social interest: A challenge to mankind*. Faber & Faber.

Adler A. (1958). *What life should mean to you*. Capricorn.

Ahn, C., & Sim, W. (2014, August 7–10). Dream work in the US and Korea: A cross-cultural investigation [Conference presentation]. APA 2014 Convention, Washington, DC.

American Psychological Association. (2022). Dream. In *APA dictionary of psychology*. American Psychological Association. https://dictionary.apa.org/dream

Arntz, A., Sofi, D., & van Breukelen, G. (2013). Imagery rescripting as treatment for complicated PTSD in refugees: A multiple baseline case series study. *Behaviour Research and Therapy, 51*(6), 274–283. https://doi.org/10.1016/j.brat.2013.02.009

Augedal, A. W., Hansen, K. S., Kronhaug, C. R., Harvey, A. G., & Pallesen, S. (2013). Randomized controlled trials of psychological and pharmacological treatments for nightmares: A meta-analysis. *Sleep Medicine Reviews, 17*(2), 143–152. https://doi.org/10.1016/j.smrv.2012.06.001

Bastien, C. H., Vallières, A., & Morin, C. M. (2001). Validation of the Insomnia Severity Index as an outcome measure for insomnia research. Sleep Medicine, 2(4), 297–307. https://doi.org/10.1016/S1389-9457(00)00065-4

Belicki, K. (1992). The relationship of nightmare frequency to nightmare suffering with implications for treatment and research. *Dreaming, 2*(3), 143–148.

*Belleville, G., Dubé-Frenette, M., & Rousseau, A. (2018). Efficacy of imagery rehearsal therapy and cognitive behavioral therapy in sexual assault victims with posttraumatic stress disorder: A randomized controlled trial. *Journal of Traumatic Stress, 31*(4), 591–601. https://doi.org/10.1002/jts.22306

Bernert, R. A., & Joiner, T. E. (2007). Sleep disturbances and suicide risk: A review of the literature. *Neuropsychiatric Disease and Treatment, 3*(6), 735–743. https://doi.org/10.2147/ndt.s1248

Buysse, D. J., Reynolds, C. F., Monk, T. H., Berman, S. R., & Kupfer, D. J. (1989). The Pittsburgh Sleep Quality Index (PSQI): A new instrument for psychiatric research and practice. *Psychiatry Research, 28* (20), 193–213.

Casement, M. D., & Swanson, L. M. (2012). A meta-analysis of imagery rehearsal for post-trauma nightmares: Effects on nightmare frequency, sleep quality, and posttraumatic stress. *Clinical Psychology Review, 32*(6), 566–574. https://doi.org/10.1016/j.cpr.2012.06.002

Cogan, C. M., Lee, J. Y., Cranston, C. C., Pruiksma, K. E., Rhudy, J. L., & Davis, J. L. (2019). The impact of exposure, relaxation, and rescripting therapy for post-trauma nightmares on suicidal ideation. *Journal of Clinical Psychology, 75*(12), 2095–2105. https://doi.org/10.1002/jclp.22852

Cranston, C. C., Miller, K. E., Davis, J. L., & Rhudy, J. L. (2017). Preliminary validation of a brief measure of the frequency and severity of nightmares: The Trauma-Related Nightmare Survey. *Journal of Trauma & Dissociation, 18*(1), 88–99. https://doi.org/10.1080/15299732.2016.1191578

Crook, R. E., & Hill, C. E. (2003). Working with dreams in psychotherapy: The therapists' perspective. *Dreaming, 13*(2), 83–93. https://doi.org/10.1023/A:1023350025033

Crook-Lyon, R. E., & Hill, C. E. (2004). Client reactions to working with dreams in psychotherapy. *Dreaming, 14*(4), 207–219. https://doi.org/10.1037/1053-0797.14.4.207

Crook-Lyon, R. E., Hill, C. E., Wimmer, C. L., Hess, S. A., & Goates-Jones, M. K. (2009). Therapist training, feedback, and practice for dream work: A pilot study. *Psychological Reports, 105*(1), 87–98. https://doi.org/10.2466/pr0.105.1.87-98

Davis, J. L. (2009). *Treating post-trauma nightmares: A cognitive behavioral approach*. Springer.

*Davis, T. L., & Hill, C. E. (2005). Spiritual and nonspiritual approaches to dream work: Effects on clients' well-being. *Journal of Counseling & Development, 83*(4), 492–503. https://doi.org/10.1002/j.1556-6678.2005.tb00371.x

*Diemer, R. A., Lobell, L. K., Vivino, B. L., & Hill, C. E. (1996). Comparison of dream interpretation, event, interpretation, and unstructured sessions in brief therapy. *Journal of Counseling Psychology, 43*(1), 99–112. https://doi.org/10.1037//0022-0167.43.1.99

Falk, D. R., & Hill, C. E. (1995). The effectiveness of dream interpretation groups for women undergoing a divorce transition. *Dreaming, 5*(1), 29–42. https://doi.org/10.1037/h0094421

Freud, S. (1966). The interpretation of dreams. Avon. (Original work published 1900)

Garbarino, M., Lai, M., Bender, D., Picard, R. W., & Tognetti, S. (2014). Empatica E3—A wearable wireless multi-sensor device for real-time computerized biofeedback and data acquisition. In *2014 4th International Conference on Wireless Mobile Communication and Healthcare—Transforming Healthcare Through Innovations in Mobile and Wireless Technologies (MOBIHEALTH)* (pp. 39–42). IEEE. doi:10.1109/MOBIHEALTH.2014.7015904

Germain, A., Hall, M., Krakow, B., Katherine Shear, M., & Buysse, D. J. (2005). A brief sleep scale for posttraumatic stress disorder: Pittsburgh Sleep Quality Index Addendum for PTSD. *Journal of Anxiety Disorders, 19*(2), 233–244. https://doi.org/10.1016/j.janxdis.2004.02.001

Hansen, K., Höfling, V., Kröner-Borowik, T., Stangier, U., & Steil, R.(2013). Efficacy of psychological interventions aiming to reduce chronic nightmares: A meta-analysis. *Clinical Psychology Review, 33*(1), 146–155. https://doi.org/10.1016/j.cpr.2012.10.012

Harb, G. C., Phelps, A. J., Forbes, D., Ross, R. J., Gehrman, P. R., & Cook, J. M. (2013). A critical review of the evidence base of imagery rehearsal for posttraumatic nightmares: Pointing the way for future research. *Journal of Traumatic Stress, 26*(5), 570–579. https://doi.org/10.1002/jts.21854

Harris, L. M., Huang, X., Linthicum, K. P., Bryen, C. P., & Ribeiro, J. D. (2020). Sleep disturbances as risk factors for suicidal thoughts and behaviours: A meta-analysis of longitudinal studies. *Scientific Reports, 10*(1), 13888. https://doi.org/10.1038/s41598-020-70866-6

Haubrich, J., & Nader, K. (2018). Memory reconsolidation. *Current Topics in Behavioral Neurosciences, 37*, 151–176. https://doi.org/10.1007/7854_2016_463

*Heaton, K. J. (2002). An investigation of nightmare-focused treatment using the Hill cognitive–experiential method of dream work [Proquest Information & Learning]. *Dissertation Abstracts International: Section B: The Sciences and Engineering, 64*(1-B), 420.

*Heaton, K. J., Hill, C. E., Peterson, D. A., Rochlen, A. B., & Zack, J. S. (1998). A comparison of therapist-facilitated and self-guided dream interpretation sessions. *Journal of Counseling Psychology, 45*(1), 115–122. https://doi.org/10.1037/0022-0167.45.1.115

Hill, C. E. (2013). *Dream work in practice* [DVD]. Washington, DC: American Psychological Association. ISBN: 978-1-4338-1308-5

Hill, C. E. (Ed.). (2004). Dream work in therapy: Facilitating exploration, insight, and action. American Psychological Association. https://doi.org/10.1037/10624-000

*Hill, C. E., Crook-Lyon, R., Hess, S., Goates-Jones, M., Roffman, M., Stahl, J., Sim, W., & Johnson, M. (2006). Prediction of session process and outcome in the Hill dream model: Contributions of client characteristics and the process of the three stages. *Dreaming, 16*, 159–185. https://doi.org/10.1037/1053-0797.16.3.159

Hill, C. E., Gelso, C. J., Gerstenblith, J., Chui, H., Pudasaini, S., Burgard, J., Baumann, E., & Huang, T. (2013). The dreamscape of psychodynamic psychotherapy: Dreams, dreamers, dream work, consequences, and case studies. *Dreaming, 23*(1), 1–45.

Hill, C. E., & Goates, M. K. (2004). Research on the Hill cognitive–experiential dream model. In C. E. Hill (Ed.), *Dream work in therapy: Facilitating exploration, insight, and action* (pp. 245–288). American Psychological Association. https://doi.org/10.1037/10624-014

Hill, C. E., & Kellems, I. S. (2002). Development and use of the Helping Skills Measure to assess client perceptions of the effects of training and of helping skills in sessions. *Journal of Counseling Psychology, 49*, 264–272. https://doi.org/10.1037/0022-0167.49.2.264

*Hill, C. E., Kelley, F. A., Davis, T. L., Crook, R. E., Maldonado, L. E., Turkson, M. A., Wonnell, T. L., Suthakaran, V., Zack, J. S., Rochlen, A. B., Kohchakian, M. R., & Codrington, J. N. (2001). Predictors of outcome of dream interpretation sessions: Volunteer client characteristics, dream characteristics, and type of interpretation. *Dreaming, 11*, 53–72. https://doi.org/10.1023/A:1009420619940

Hill, C. E., & Knox, S. (2010). The use of dreams in modern psychotherapy. *International Review of Neurobiology, 92*, 291–317. https://doi.org/10.1016/S0074-7742(10)92013-8

*Hill, C. E., Rochlen, A. B., Zack, J. S., McCready, T., & Dematatis, A. (2003). Working with dreams using the Hill cognitive–experiential model: A comparison of computer-assisted, therapist empathy, and therapist empathy + input conditions. *Journal of Counseling Psychology, 50*(2), 211–220. https://doi.org/10.1037/0022-0167.50.2.211

Hill, C. E., & Spangler, P. T. (2016). Hill cognitive–experiential method. In J. E. Lewis & S. Krippner (Eds.), *Working with dreams and PTSD nightmares: 14 approaches for psychotherapists and counselors* (pp. 133–142). ABC-CLIO.

Hill, C. E., Tien, H.-L. S., Sheu, H.-B., Sim, W., Ma, Y., Choi, K.-H., & Tashiro, T. (2007). Predictors of outcome of dream work for East Asian volunteer clients: Dream factors, attachment anxiety, Asian values, and therapist input. *Dreaming, 17*(4), 208–226. https://doi.org/10.1037/1053-0797.17.4.208

*Hill, C. E., Zack, J. S., Wonnell, T. L., Hoffman, M. A., Rochlen, A. B., Goldberg, J. L., Nakayama, E. Y., Heaton, K. J., Kelley, F. A., Eiche, K., Tomlinson, M. J., & Hess, S. (2000). Structured brief therapy with a focus on dreams or loss for clients with troubling dreams and recent loss. *Journal of Counseling Psychology, 47*(1), 90–101. https://doi.org/10.1037/0022-0167.47.1.90

Jung, C. G. (1964). *Man and his symbols*. Dell.

Jung, C. G. (1974). *Dreams* (R. F. C. Hull, Trans.). Princeton University Press.

Kim, S. H., Schneider, S. M., Kravitz, L., Mermier, C., & Burge, M. R. (2013). Mind–body practices for posttraumatic stress disorder. *Journal of Investigative Medicine, 61*(5), 827–834. https://doi.org/10.2310/JIM.0b013e3182906862

Krakow, B. J., Melendrez, D. C., Johnston, L. G., Clark, J. O., Santana, E. M., Warner, T. D., Hollifield, M. A., Schrader, R., Sisley, B. N., & Lee, S. A. (2002). Sleep dynamic therapy for Cerro Grande Fire evacuees with posttraumatic stress symptoms: A preliminary report. *Journal of Clinical Psychiatry, 63*(8), 673–684. https://doi:10.4088/jcp.v63n0804

Krakow, B. J., & Zadra, A. (2006). Clinical management of chronic nightmares: Imagery rehearsal therapy. *Behavioral Sleep Medicine, 4*(1), 45–70. https://doi.org/10.1207/s15402010bsm0401_4

*Miller, K. E., Davis, J. L., & Rhudy, J. L. (2018). Pilot study: Brief posttrauma nightmare treatment for persons with bipolar disorder. *Dreaming, 28*(2), 150–161. https://doi.org/10.1037/drm0000082

Najavits, L. M. (2015). The problem of dropout from "gold standard" PTSD therapies. *F1000prime Reports, 7*, 43. https://doi.org/10.12703/P7-43

Perls, F. S. (1969). *Gestalt therapy verbatim*. Real People Press.

Pigeon, W. R., Pinquart, M., & Conner, K. (2012). Meta-analysis of sleep disturbance and suicidal thoughts and behaviors. *Journal of Clinical Psychiatry, 73*(9), e1160–e1167. https://doi.org/10.4088/JCP.11r07586

*Pruiksma, K., Cranston, C. C., Rhudy, J. L., Micol, R. L., & Davis, J. L. (2018). Randomized controlled trial to dismantle exposure, relaxation, and rescripting therapy (ERRT) for trauma-related nightmares. *Psychological Trauma, 10*(1), 67–75. https://doi.org/10.1037/tra0000238

*Pruiksma, K., Taylor, D. J., Mintz, J., Nicholson, K. L., Rodgers, M., Young-McCaughan, S., Hall-Clark, B. N., Fina, B. A., Dondanville, K. A., Cobos, B., Wardle-Pinkston, S., Litz, B. T., Roache, J. D., & Peterson, A. L. (2020). A pilot randomized controlled trial of cognitive behavioral treatment for trauma-related nightmares in active duty military personnel. *Journal of Clinical Sleep Medicine, 16*(1), 29–40. https://doi.org/10.5664/jcsm.8116

*Putois, B., Peter-Derex, L., Leslie, W., Braboszcz, C., El-Hage, W., & Bastuji, H. (2019). Internet-based intervention for posttraumatic stress disorder: Using remote imagery rehearsal therapy to treat nightmares. *Psychotherapy and Psychosomatics, 88*(5), 315–316. https://doi.org/10.1159/000501105

Resick, P. A., Galovski, T. E., Uhlmansiek, M. O. B., Scher, C. D., Clum, G. A., & Young-Xu, Y. (2008). A randomized clinical trial to dismantle components of cognitive processing therapy for posttraumatic stress disorder in female victims of interpersonal violence. *Journal of Consulting and Clinical Psychology, 76*, 243–258. http://dx.doi.org/10.1037/0022-006X.76.2.243

Resick, P. A., Monson, C. M., & Chard, K. M. (2016). *Cognitive processing therapy for PTSD: A comprehensive manual*. Guilford.

Seda, G., Sanchez-Ortuno, M. M., Welsh, C. H., Halbower, A. C., & Edinger, J. D. (2015). Comparative meta-analysis of prazosin and imagery rehearsal therapy for nightmare frequency, sleep quality, and posttraumatic stress. *Journal of Clinical Sleep Medicine, 11*(1), 11–22. https://doi.org/10.5664/jcsm.4354

Shapiro, F. (2001). *Eye movement desensitization and reprocessing: Basic principles, protocols, and procedures* (2nd ed.). Guilford.

Sim, W., Hill, C. E., Chowdhury, S., Huang, T., Zaman, N., & Talavera, P. (2010). Problems and action ideas discussed by first- and second-generation female East Asian students during dream sessions. *Dreaming, 20*(1), 42–59. https://doi.org/10.1037/a0018993

Sim, W., Hill, C. E., Duan, C., An, M., Gupta, S., & Prass, M. (2021). Working on dreams to facilitate Asian international university students' transition to the United States. *Dreaming, 31*(2), 100–116. https://doi.org/10.1037/drm0000170

*Spangler, P. T., Dempsey, C., Nissan, D., Phares, A., West, J., Willing, M., & Winslow, B. (2022, September 12–15). *Nightmare deconstruction and reprocessing: Final pilot results of a treatment for trauma-related nightmares and insomnia* [Poster presentation]. 2022 Military Health Systems Research Symposium, Kissimmee, FL.

Spangler, P. T., & West, J. C. (2018). Nightmare deconstruction and reprocessing for PTSD nightmares. In E. Vermetten, A. Germain, & T. Neylan (Eds.), *Sleep and combat-related posttraumatic stress disorder* (pp. 311–316). Springer.

Stiles, W. B., & Snow, J. S. (1984). Dimensions of psychotherapy session impact across sessions and across clients. *British Journal of Clinical Psychology, 23*(1), 59–63. https://doi.org/10.1111/j.2044-8260.1984.tb00627.x

Tien, H.-S., Lin, C.-H., & Chen, S.-C. (2006). Dream interpretation session for college students in Taiwan: Who benefits and what volunteer clients view as most and least helpful. *Dreaming, 16*, 246–257.

*van Schagen, A. M., Lancee, J., de Groot, I. W., Spoormaker, V. I., & van den Bout, J. (2015). Imagery rehearsal therapy in addition to treatment as usual for patients with diverse psychiatric diagnoses suffering from nightmares: A randomized controlled trial. *Journal of Clinical Psychiatry, 76*(9), e1105–e1113. https://doi.org/10.4088/JCP.14m09216

Vaughan, A. G. (2016). Jungian dreamwork. In J. Lewis & S. Krippner. (Eds.), *Working with dreams and PTSD nightmares: 14 approaches for psychotherapists and counselors* (pp. 1–21). ABC-CLIO.

Viechtbauer, W. (2010). Conducting meta-analyses in R with the metafor package. *Journal of Statistical Software, 36*(3), 1–48. doi:10.18637/jss.v036.i03

Weathers, F. W., Blake, D. D., Schnurr, P. P., Kaloupek, D. G., Marx, B. P., & Keane, T. M. (2015). The Clinician-Administered PTSD Scale for DSM-5 (CAPS-5)—Past Month [Measurement instrument]. Available from http://www.ptsd.va.gov

Weathers, F. W., Litz, B., Keane, T., Palmieri, P., Marx, B., & Schnurr, P. (2013). *The PTSD checklist for DSM-5 (PCL-5)*. Available from http://www.ptsd.va.gov

Wolpe, J. (1969). *The practice of behavior therapy*. Pergamon.

*Wonnell, T. L., & Hill, C. E. (2000). Effects of including the action stage in dream interpretation. *Journal of Counseling Psychology, 47*(3), 372–379. https://doi.org/10.1037/0022-0167.47.3.372

Yücel, D. E., van Emmerik, A. A., Souama, C., & Lancee, J. (2020). Comparative efficacy of imagery rehearsal therapy and prazosin in the treatment of trauma-related nightmares in adults: A meta-analysis of randomized controlled trials. *Sleep Medicine Reviews, 50*, 101248. https://doi.org/10.1016/j.smrv.2019.101248

20

Meditation, Mindfulness, and Acceptance

Simon B. Goldberg, Christopher Anders, Shannon L. Stuart-Maver, and D. Martin Kivlighan, III

Authors' Note: We have no known conflicts of interest to disclose. SBG was supported by the National Center for Complementary & Integrative Health of the National Institutes of Health (K23AT010879). The authors are grateful for correspondence with Dr. Kate Morrison regarding the role of acceptance in third-wave cognitive–behavioral therapies.

> For after all, the best thing one can do when it is raining, is to let it rain.
>
> —Henry Wadsworth Longfellow (1900, p. 398)

During the past three decades, there has been a dramatic increase in both scientific and popular interest in what have been defined as the *third wave* of cognitive and behavioral therapies (Hayes, 2004). Widely studied third-wave therapies include acceptance and commitment therapy (ACT; Hayes et al., 1999), dialectical behavior therapy (DBT; Linehan, 1993), and mindfulness meditation-based therapies such as mindfulness-based stress reduction (MBSR; Kabat-Zinn, 2013) and mindfulness-based cognitive therapy (MBCT; Segal et al., 2013). Of course, various forms of meditation have existed for thousands of years in contemplative traditions throughout the world (Smith, 1991). The secularized forms of mindfulness meditation found in MBSR and MBCT are derived from Buddhist practices (Kabat-Zinn, 2011). Whereas prior waves of cognitive–behavioral therapy (CBT) focused on symptom reduction, these third-wave therapies instead emphasize promotion of behaviors associated with psychological health and well-being. Thus, patients are encouraged to shift their emphasis from making unpleasant experiences go away to moving in psychologically healthy and value-driven directions regardless of painful thoughts, emotions, and events that may occur (Block-Lerner et al., 2009).

Meditation, mindfulness, and acceptance (MMA) are three central methods included to varying degrees across these third-wave therapies. There is clear evidence these methods have gained strong footholds within the psychotherapy world and broader Western culture (Davis & Hayes, 2011; Michalak et al., 2020; Van Dam et al., 2018). Hundreds of randomized controlled trials (RCTs) have been conducted investigating mindfulness meditation-based interventions alone (Goldberg et al., 2022), and ACT, DBT, and MBCT are all listed as evidence-based treatments by the American Psychological Association's Society of Clinical Psychology (n.d.). Meditation-based smartphone apps are far and away the most popular mental health apps (Wasil et al., 2020). To date, the bulk of scientific research on MMA in psychotherapy has

Simon B. Goldberg, Christopher Anders, Shannon L. Stuart-Maver, and D. Martin Kivlighan, III, *Meditation, Mindfulness, and Acceptance* In: *Psychotherapy Skills and Methods That Work.* Edited by: Clara E. Hill and John C. Norcross, Oxford University Press.
 DOI: 10.1093/oso/9780197611012.003.0020

emphasized testing treatment packages (e.g., ACT, DBT, MBCT). Consistent with the broader psychotherapy literature (Wampold & Imel, 2015), these therapies generally improve psychological symptoms to a similar degree as other interventions that are intended to be therapeutic (i.e., bona fide psychotherapies; Galante et al., 2021; Goldberg et al., 2018; Öst, 2008, 2014).

While treatment packages have been invaluable for popularizing MMA within psychotherapy, these methods may hold promise for implementation outside of the context of a specific or manualized treatment package. Therapists commonly use a wide variety of methods in actual clinical practice (Cook et al., 2010), and many are already using mindfulness (Michalak et al., 2020). This chapter focuses on the narrower MMA methods themselves rather than the treatment packages within which these methods are commonly implemented (e.g., ACT, DBT, MBCT).

Definitions

Meditation has been defined as "a family of complex emotional and attentional regularly training regimes developed for various ends, including the cultivation of well-being and emotional balance" (Lutz et al., 2008, p. 163). Various forms of meditation have been studied scientifically, primarily drawn from Eastern contemplative traditions (e.g., Tibetan, Theravaden, Zen Buddhism, Hinduism; Harrington & Dunne, 2015; Nidich et al., 2018). These include practices designed to develop attention regulation (e.g., meta-awareness or awareness of the processes of consciousness), cultivate cognitive and affective patterns conducive to well-being (e.g., kindness, compassion), and foster insight into the nature of the self (e.g., self-inquiry practices; Dahl et al., 2015). A wide variety of specific practices are used to support these changes and may include focusing on a single object (e.g., the breath coming in and out of the body), generating feelings of kindness and compassion (e.g., using the repetition of phrases and visualizing directing feelings toward particular people), or reflecting on the changing nature of moment-to-moment experience (Dahl et al., 2015).

Mindfulness has been defined as a way of purposefully attending to present-moment experience without judgment (Kabat-Zinn, 1994). Mindfulness meditation is a specific form of meditation practice aimed at cultivating the capacity to orient attention nonjudgmentally toward the present moment.

Acceptance methods enhance patients' experiential acceptance, defined as having or allowing private events (including painful ones) free of attempts at regulation (Block-Lerner et al., 2009)—in other words, allowing things to be experienced without needing to change them or push them away. This orientation contrasts with experiential avoidance, in which one is "unwilling to remain in contact with particular private experiences (e.g., bodily sensations, emotions, thoughts, memories, behavioral predispositions) and takes steps to alter the form or frequency of these events and the contexts that occasion them" (Hayes et al., 1996, p. 1154).

There are many forms of meditation in practice, including mindfulness meditation designed to train one's capacity for experiential acceptance by attending to present-moment private experiences without effort to change them (Block-Lerner et al., 2009). Broader still, experiential acceptance has been proposed as a common factor across various forms of psychotherapy that, through methods such as therapists' unconditional positive regard for their patients, patients turn toward rather than away from painful private experiences (Block-Lerner et al., 2009). In contrast, mindfulness meditation, unlike acceptance alone, trains both acceptance and present-moment awareness (i.e., monitoring with acceptance; Lindsay & Creswell, 2017).

Clinical Description and Indications

Meditation, mindfulness, and acceptance methods can be implemented in multiple ways within individual psychotherapy of different theoretical orientations (for guidelines for implementing mindfulness meditation, see Michalak et al., 2019). Formal meditation practice (in contrast to informal practice implemented in daily life; Kabat-Zinn, 2013) involves taking a few moments (or longer) in a session to engage in a specific meditation practice. For example, a therapist may guide the patient in a body scan, in which one turns their attention to the physical sensations occurring in the body (Kabat-Zinn, 2013), or a lovingkindness meditation, in which one generates feelings of kindness toward oneself or others (Salzberg, 2004). The initial introduction of formal meditation will probably occur with an extended guided practice in the session followed by inquiry, during which the therapist supports the patient reflecting on their practice experience (Michalak et al., 2019). This inquiry could start with discussion of physical sensations and allow patients the opportunity to draw linkages between body states and affective experiences.

Mindfulness can also take the form of a guided meditation practice (e.g., body scan). But it may be introduced less formally by inviting patients to pay attention to their internal experience (i.e., physical sensations, affective state, cognitions) with curiosity and acceptance.

Acceptance can likewise be implemented through formal meditation practice or a wide range of other methods. Both ACT and DBT include numerous acceptance methods to provide patients a direct experience of experiential acceptance. These may involve stories or images to express the drawbacks of non-acceptance (e.g., characterizing the relationship between anxiety and struggle as a volleyball game; Forsyth & Eifert, 2007), as well as conceptual frameworks (e.g., willingness vs. willfulness) and behavioral methods (e.g., half-smiling) to promote experiential acceptance (Linehan, 2015).

As will be discussed, there is limited research evidence to guide the use of meditation within psychotherapy sessions outside of third-wave treatment packages. And, importantly, much of the research on third-wave treatment packages, especially mindfulness, has occurred in group settings (although see studies investigating individual MBCT; e.g., Tovote et al., 2014). There are elements in the group setting that may make MMA methods particularly helpful (e.g., opportunity to learn from others' experience, sense of shared humanity with others experiencing similar difficulties; Yalom & Leszcz, 2005). To the extent to which evidence from treatment packages (often delivered in groups) generalizes to implementation in individual therapy, there is evidence that all three methods may effectively reduce common forms of psychological distress (e.g., depression, anxiety, stress) and may be helpful for chronic pain and substance use (Galante et al., 2021; Goldberg et al., 2021; Goyal et al., 2014; Öst, 2008, 2014).

In terms of other specific indications, DBT was designed for patients with borderline personality disorder, although it includes many other treatment ingredients beyond acceptance (e.g., training in emotion regulation and interpersonal effectiveness skills; Linehan, 2015). There is some evidence that individuals with greater severity of depression may benefit more from MBCT (Kuyken et al., 2016). However, on the whole, moderators of method effectiveness are generally unknown.

Formal meditation and mindfulness methods may calm some patients and enhance a sense of alliance, collaboration, and a healing setting. For example, MBCT (Segal et al., 2013) conceptualizes mindfulness as a method to detect early signs of relapse and prevent worsening of symptoms through increased awareness and decentering (i.e., ability to dis-identify with internal experience; Bernstein et al., 2015).

Using MMA methods may be particularly important for individuals who find meditation practice aversive and even triggering (Baer et al., 2019; Goldberg, Lam, et al., 2022). Particular care should be taken when implementing formal meditation practice for those with trauma histories (Treleaven, 2018). Specific forms of meditation (e.g., compassion practice) may be triggering for patients prone to rumination, who may feel discouraged by their inability to immediately embody the qualities being cultivated through practice (Segal et al., 2013).

With acceptance strategies, the therapist establishes a validating environment prior to introducing acceptance methods. Indeed, methods for validating and responding to invalidation are included in DBT (Linehan, 2015), as many patients with borderline personality disorder are sensitive to perceived emotional invalidation. Patients may reasonably wish to (and be encouraged to) make changes to factors contributing to their distress. Thus, acceptance is best focused on both immediate (e.g., distress in the current moment) and persistent experiences (e.g., chronic illness) that cannot be constructively resolved in another way (i.e., accepting the things one cannot change, changing the things one can; Block-Lerner et al., 2009). Therapists implementing acceptance should be sensitive to their patients' resistance to the perceived message that their life cannot be better. Of course, acceptance does not imply that change will not occur (and Eastern contemplative traditions clearly acknowledge that change is inevitable; Bodhi, 2005), and there is strong evidence that acceptance strategies can, somewhat counterintuitively, decrease distress and other symptoms (e.g., pain, substance use; Goldberg et al., 2021; Öst, 2008).

Beyond these general suggestions, the research literature has largely not yet established the specific patient characteristics, in-session markers, or clinical circumstances for which acceptance and mindfulness are most indicated (Michalak et al., 2019).

Assessment

Several adherence and competence measures have been designed to assess implementation of treatment packages emphasizing MMA methods (e.g., Chawla et al., 2010; Hanley & Garland, 2021; Harned et al., 2021; Segal et al., 2002). However, to our knowledge, these measures have not been used to evaluate implementation outside the treatment package. In theory, these measures may include relevant items for implementing them in individual psychotherapy. However, it will be vital for future researchers to investigate this possibility directly (e.g., by administering items drawn from existing adherence and competence measures). Developing measures specifically for evaluating the implementation of MMA methods in individual psychotherapy and outside of a treatment package is also an essential step in this area.

In a study investigating the inclusion of mindfulness within psychotherapy, a measure of general psychotherapeutic presence (Therapeutic Presence Inventory; Geller et al., 2010) was used to assess therapists' in-session mindfulness and acceptance based on patient and therapist ratings (Mander et al., 2019). Mander et al. (2019) also included observer-rated items assessing the therapists' provision of specific methods (mindfulness or progressive muscle relaxation in this particular study). The authors of this study used a measure designed to assess mindfulness practice quality (Practice Quality–Mindfulness [PQ-M]; Del Re et al., 2013) to evaluate patients' perceived quality of their mindfulness practice. Although Mander et al. (2019) conceptualized the PQ-M as a measure of mindfulness implementation, it could also reasonably be viewed as a measure of outcome (i.e., patient's mindfulness practice quality being an outcome of an effective implementation of a mindfulness method).

Far greater work has focused on developing measures to evaluate the distal (e.g., trait mindfulness) and proximal (e.g., state mindfulness) outcomes of MMA methods. Widely used self-report measures of trait mindfulness (as opposed to mindfulness occurring in the moment, which would be state mindfulness) that could evaluate the distal effects of these methods include the Mindful Attention Awareness Scale (MAAS; Brown & Ryan, 2003) and the Five Facet Mindfulness Questionnaire (FFMQ; Baer et al., 2006). These measures are responsive to mindfulness meditation training (Goldberg et al., 2019; Quaglia et al., 2016), and the FFMQ has also been shown to respond to informal mindfulness practice (Hanley et al., 2015). Both measures have shown desirable psychometric properties, including acceptable internal consistency, as well as evidence for construct validity (convergent and discriminant validity) and structural validity (Baer et al., 2006; Brown & Ryan, 2003). However, it is worth noting that these measures not only may be responsive to mindfulness training but also appear to increase in the context of psychological treatments (Baer et al., 2019; Goldberg et al., 2019). The Self-Compassion Scale (Neff, 2003) is widely used to measure compassion toward self and has been shown to be responsive to brief lovingkindness meditation training (Smeets et al., 2014). The Acceptance and Action Questionnaire–II (Bond et al., 2011) is designed to assess experiential avoidance (e.g., "I'm afraid of my feelings") and is commonly used within the context of ACT.

Although some of these measures have shown responsiveness to short-term training (e.g., mindfulness inductions), they are considered trait measures (i.e., measures that do not vary from moment to moment). There has been parallel development of state measures of mindfulness which may be relevant to assessing the impact of mindfulness or meditation methods in a particular session. These include a state version of the MAAS (Brown & Ryan, 2003), the Toronto Mindfulness Scale (Lau et al., 2006), and the State Mindfulness Scale (Tanay & Bernstein, 2013). As noted above, the PQ-M (Del Re et al., 2013) has been used to evaluate within-session implementation of mindfulness practice. Changes in the PQ-M have been linked to improvements in psychological symptoms and trait mindfulness within mindfulness interventions (Del Re et al., 2013; Goldberg et al., 2014; Goldberg, et al., 2020).

Clinical Example

We provide a fictional vignette to illustrate how one might implement MMA methods in individual psychotherapy.

Linda was a 39-year-old African American, cisgender, heterosexual woman. She was employed as a lawyer at a law firm. She came to psychotherapy struggling with depressed mood, anhedonia, intense worry, difficult sleeping, fatigue, and recent back pain that was interfering with her recreational activities. She was happily married and the mother of two children aged 5 and 8 years, both diagnosed with autism spectrum disorder. Linda regularly attended services at a local church, and her religion was an important part of her worldview and support system.

The therapist (T), Dr. Chen, had seen Linda (the patient [P]) for three sessions. Dr. Chen focused on building rapport, gathering background information, setting norms and expectations for psychotherapy, and providing cognitive–behavioral methods for managing mood (e.g., behavioral activation), sleep (e.g., sleep hygiene), and chronic pain (e.g., encouraged consultation with medical provider and physical therapist). Linda benefitted some from these strategies, but she remained distressed and discouraged by her life challenges.

This vignette is from the fourth session of their therapy:

T: Linda, I want to acknowledge all of the efforts you have been putting into improving your mental health, especially in the past few weeks. I know this can be really challenging to do, particularly when you're not feeling so great to begin with. It's clear you want to feel better.

P: Thank you, Dr. Chen. I have been trying to follow up on the suggestions you have given me. I think what we're doing has been helpful. But I also know there's a long way to go and sometimes it just feels like things are never really going to get better for me.

T: It's true that there are some pretty major stressors in your life right now. I'm sure most people in your situation would feel overwhelmed. And some of these stressors are probably going to be around for a while. Along with the strategies we've discussed already in therapy, I was wondering if you might be open to exploring another method that some of my patients have found really helpful. Have you ever tried mindfulness meditation?

P: No, not really, but I have heard of it before. I do go to church every Sunday and try to pray a few times a week. That's kind of like meditation for me.

T: Definitely. For many people, prayer can be a way to center themselves, and there is good scientific evidence that prayer can be really helpful for mental health.

P: I know my connection to God really helps me. But maybe this meditation thing could be helpful too?

T: Maybe. We could explore it a bit in here together, if you like.

P: Sure.

T: Okay. Well, in a nutshell, mindfulness involves practicing being with our moment-to-moment experience, just as it is. Of course, this can be challenging when the way things are going is painful or unpleasant. With some practice, we can build our capacity to stay with things, even those that are painful, without having to push them away. There's been a lot of research done on mindfulness and it has been shown, somewhat paradoxically, to decrease the distress associated with the painful things one may experience, including some of the things you're struggling with. If you're open to it, I could guide us in a brief mindfulness practice together now.

P: I'm curious. Let's try it.

T: Great. So if you're comfortable, feel free to close your eyes (short pause). Find a comfortable position to sit in your chair—ideally one that is both relaxed but also alert. It can be helpful to keep the back straight, if that feels comfortable to you. Take a few, deep breaths (pause). We can start just paying attention to how it feels in the body to be sitting here. What do the feet feel like on the floor (short pause)? What does the chair feel like? Are there other sensations happening in the body—maybe pain, tightness, heat, or cold? There's no need to evaluate any of these experiences, just to get a little curious about what physical sensation is like (pause). See if you can get the mind curious about these very ordinary experiences (pause). Take a moment to see what's happening emotionally. How are you feeling? Tired, anxious, sad, excited, relaxed (pause)? Our job with this practice is simply to notice what's here. If a strong emotion is present—maybe anxiety or sadness—see if it's possible to connect with this feeling with a sense of care and curiosity. If the feeling becomes overwhelming, you can move your attention back to the body, maybe the feet on the floor (short pause).Let's take a few minutes just noticing what's happening in the body and the heart (longer pause). Great. That's it. How was that for you?

P: Wow, I can't believe how hard it was to pay attention to my body! Is everybody's mind so cluttered?

T: In my experience, yes. And it can be a lot to see that, especially at the beginning. What was it like to try to stay with what was happening in your body and your emotions? What did you notice? (initiating brief inquiry, could be longer in actual practice)

P: It was intense, especially for the first few minutes. I could feel my heart beating fast and some pain in my back. Then I started to worry about my kids, who have been having a tough week. But I think I calmed down a little by the end. There's just so much happening in my life right now (soft crying).

T: There is so much happening in your life right now. And, it takes a huge amount of courage to turn towards that, like you're doing right now.

P: I just wish I could make some of my problems go away.

T: I'm sure. And I do think some of the changes you've started making like not going on social media right before sleeping will help. And, like you've said, life is hard and some of the hard parts of life are not going away anytime soon. What would you think of incorporating a few minutes of a practice like this into your daily routine, maybe as a complement to the other things you're trying?

P: I could give that a try. I can see how it might be helpful. Maybe I could do this for a few minutes before I pray. I could see them going nicely together.

T: I love that idea. We could even start our sessions together with a minute or two of mindfulness. I can give you some suggestions for apps you can use at home.

Landmark Studies and Previous Reviews

There are dozens of RCTs testing MMA methods as part of larger treatment packages. Meta-analyses of these RCTs have concluded that these treatment packages, like various forms of psychotherapy (Wampold & Imel, 2015), tend to produce moderate- to large-magnitude effects on psychological symptoms when compared to no treatment and produce nonsignificant effects when compared to other forms of psychotherapy (Goldberg et al., 2021; Goyal et al., 2014; Öst, 2008, 2014).

Meta-analyses have also examined the effects of stand-alone, without-therapy mindfulness exercises delivered outside of the context of a mindfulness meditation-based intervention as well as brief mindfulness inductions. Results from these meta-analyses suggest that stand-alone mindfulness exercises produce reductions in depression and anxiety relative to controls (standardized mean differences = 0.41, 0.39, respectively; Blanck et al., 2018). Brief mindfulness inductions may also reduce negative affect, although this effect may be exaggerated due to the lack of publication of nonsignificant findings (i.e., publication bias; Schumer et al., 2018).

Despite these promising findings, research on the impact of MMA methods outside a treatment package is just beginning. Here, we review two landmark studies that examined the impact of adding these strategies to psychotherapy.

One RCT directly evaluated the impact of including MMA methods in individual psychotherapy outside the context of a treatment package (Mander et al., 2019). This study included 162 adults with depressive or anxiety disorders who were being treated by 48 therapists in an outpatient CBT training clinic in Germany. Patients were randomly assigned to receive 5-minute introductions to audio-guided mindfulness meditation (adaptation of the breathing space from MBCT), audio-guided progressive muscle relaxation, or treatment-as-usual (therapist and patient were free to use the first 5 minutes of sessions however they would like) at the beginning of each session over a 25-session course of treatment. Therapists were trained to deliver the active interventions through two expert-led workshops, separated by 6 weeks, during which the therapists were asked to practice the method (mindfulness meditation or progressive muscle relaxation) at home.

The primary outcome of the 5-minute psychotherapy session introductions was patients' general clinical symptoms assessed at four time points. The study had a large sample to detect small effects for between-group differences. Several secondary outcomes were assessed, including therapeutic alliance, depression, anxiety, and mindfulness. Therapists' adherence (self-report and observer rated) was also assessed on their assigned session introduction, therapeutic presence, mindfulness practice quality, allegiance, and CBT competence.

This was an exemplary study in many respects. It included random assignment conducted by an independent research assistant; assessed clinically relevant outcomes in a clinical sample (Mander et al., 2015); featured patient-, therapist-, and observer-rated outcomes; provided training from experts and opportunities for therapist home practice; had an adequate sample size (i.e., was statistically powered) to detect small effects; and incorporated statistical analyses accounting for the nested data structure (multilevel models).

Within this unusually rigorous context, Mander et al. (2019) reported no evidence for differences across types of session introductions. All groups showed moderate to large improvements across their primary outcome and all secondary outcomes. Moreover, the researchers found no evidence that assignment to the mindfulness condition moderated the alliance–outcome association, nor that baseline demographic or mindfulness-related measures moderated the impact of condition assignment on outcomes.

The effect sizes for between-group differences on the primary outcome (general clinical symptoms) were Cohen's $d = 0.00$ (for mindfulness vs. progressive muscle relaxation) and $d = 0.12$ (for mindfulness vs. treatment-as-usual). Across the secondary outcomes, the maximum between-group difference for mindfulness versus progressive muscle relaxation was $d = 0.31$ (for therapist-rated therapeutic alliance) and for mindfulness versus treatment-as-usual $d = 0.20$ (for patient-rated mindfulness). Although between-group effects were not significant, these effect sizes were in the small range (i.e., $d \geq 0.20$; Cohen, 1988). This raises the question (not raised by Mander et al., 2019) as to whether statistical power may have impacted Mander et al.'s detection of certain between-group contrasts—in other words, the same magnitude effect may have been statistically significant in a larger sample. Understandably, Mander et al. were conservative in not testing and reporting between-group differences when omnibus tests of differences were not significant.

Rigorously obtained evidence that all introductions worked equally well should, of course, be taken seriously. Thus, the most conservative interpretation is that mindfulness as an introduction to a psychotherapy session did not improve clinical outcomes or alliance relative to other active introductions. Furthermore, this study provided no indication that some patients may benefit more from mindfulness than the other interventions tested (treatment-as-usual and progressive muscle relaxation). In other words, no patient-level characteristics (e.g., mindfulness-related, demographic, or diagnostic variables) moderated the treatment effects (Mander et al., 2019).

From our perspective, a key question in interpreting the results of Mander et al. (2019) is did their study test whether integrating mindfulness meditation into individual psychotherapy proved helpful. There are probably more individualized and flexible ways of including these methods. In routine practice, therapists can flexibly apply mindfulness (or meditation, acceptance) within the course of psychotherapy for a particular patient and/or at a particular time. This naturalistic implementation is, of course, more difficult to study experimentally. In addition, the study included a relatively modest dose of mindfulness training—just 5 minutes at the beginning of each session. Thus, it is unclear whether a more intensive inclusion of mindfulness training (perhaps coupled with home practice assignments) would have yielded different results.

Nonetheless, a future study could randomly assign therapists to integrate one or more MMA methods within their course of treatment with specific patients and not others. Similar to Mander et al. (2019), such a study could include assessments of adherence and competence as means for characterizing whether this "looser" operationalization of mindfulness impacted what occurred in psychotherapy.

We found two qualitative studies in our systematic review on the use of MMA methods in individual therapy (Horst et al., 2013; Michaelis et al., 2018). Horst et al. most directly examined the impact of incorporating mindfulness in individual psychotherapy. This study was conducted with trainee therapists and adult psychotherapy patients. The authors recruited five therapist–patient dyads in which the therapist had implemented a mindfulness exercise at least twice. The trainee therapists had some training in mindfulness before implementing these methods in session, either in the form of an 8-week group practicum or through their own independent study (e.g., books, other resources).

On the whole, both therapists and patients in the Horst et al. (2013) study found these practices to be helpful. The dyads reported numerous ways in which mindfulness facilitated the therapeutic experience, including reducing the presenting problem (e.g., managing pain), helping with transitions (starting and ending sessions), facilitating conversations, producing a calming effect, and slowing the session pace. Both patients and therapists, however, noted a lack of confidence in their ability to effectively implement mindfulness, particularly the first time, although they became more comfortable with practice.

Patients and therapists identified features that made these practices more or less successful (Horst et al., 2013). The helpful features included having mindfulness as a shared experience (therapists and patients practicing together and discussing their shared apprehensions), continued practice, mutual trust, and the importance of flexibility (e.g., "moving on" from the exercise if a patient did not find it helpful). It also appeared helpful to preface/process the experience in the form of conversations before and after the experience. Echoing concerns raised with implementing lovingkindness practice for patients with depression (Segal et al., 2013), one patient remarked that "you don't want to make someone feel like they aren't doing this right" (Horst et al., 2013, p. 377).

In addition to the Horst et al. (2013), a second qualitative study examined the use of mindfulness-based relaxation methods within individual CBT-informed treatment for managing seizures in nine adults (Michaelis et al., 2018). Patients were given the option of learning about mindfulness during the initial session and were then advised to practice it regularly. Seven of the nine patients chose to learn about mindfulness. All patients were encouraged to practice acceptance, specifically of uncomfortable feeling states. Adherence to home practice was not reported.

Michaelis et al.'s (2018) qualitative analysis focused on patients' sense of self-efficacy and mastery. Interestingly, mention of mindfulness was rare within the data reported. Two participants noted benefits from mindfulness under a theme focused on "shaping everyday life in a way that is good for oneself," while one mentioned mindfulness exercises were not necessary as they were engaging in yoga practice. Acceptance appeared more frequently. One participant remarked that "the word 'accepting' has become my mantra" (Michaelis et al., 2018, p. 157). Several participants mentioned acceptance as a helpful strategy under the "coping with seizures" theme. Self-acceptance also appeared under the "epilepsy as a means of increasing self-knowledge and control over one's life" theme: "I accept epilepsy.. . .It is still an illness, . . . but people with epilepsy are valuable anyway" (Michaelis et al., 2018, p. 158).

Research Review

Distal Outcomes of Treatment Packages

As noted above, many RCTs and meta-analyses of RCTs have examined the efficacy of treatment packages implementing MMA methods. The body of research examining mindfulness meditation is particularly large. A recent meta-review examined the evidence for mindfulness-based interventions seen in 44 meta-analyses of RCTs (Goldberg,

Riordan, et al., 2022). This review identified 160 different effect sizes characterizing the effects of mindfulness-based interventions from 336 RCTs (N = 30,483 participants). The mindfulness-based interventions included in these studies all involved the repeated practice of mindfulness meditation. The authors identified effect sizes representing the largest number of studies for a particular combination of population, intervention, comparison group, and outcome (e.g., studies testing MBCT for depressive relapse in adults; Kuyken et al., 2016).

Although it is not possible to summarize the details of this vast literature in brief, there were several patterns of findings. On the whole, mindfulness-based interventions produced small to moderate magnitude effects relative to passive control conditions (e.g., wait-list controls) at post-treatment, with many effects persisting although often decreasing at follow-up (Goldberg, Riordan, et al., 2022). These effects were observed across a range of populations, types of mindfulness interventions, and outcomes, although they tended to be most robust for common psychological symptoms (e.g., depression, anxiety). Effect sizes tended to diminish when mindfulness-based interventions were compared with active controls (i.e., other interventions intended to be therapeutic or "placebo" controls that were designed to control for attention but not include therapeutic ingredients), although there was still evidence for superiority in some instances (e.g., on common psychological symptoms). When compared directly, mindfulness-based interventions performed very similarly to frontline, evidence-based treatments (CBT, antidepressants; e.g., Kuyken et al., 2016).

In-Session Impact of MMA Methods

We designed our search terms to identify articles investigating one or more of the MMA methods. The search terms were ("mindful*" OR "meditate*" OR "acceptance" OR "dialectical") AND ("psychother*" OR "in session"). The search was conducted on January 18, 2021, using PubMed. Two doctoral students in counseling psychology supervised by two counseling psychology professors with experience in systematic reviews and meta-analysis completed inclusion/exclusion coding.

Retrieved references were first coded at the title and abstract level. Full-text articles were retrieved for studies that passed the title and abstract level of screening. Studies were eligible if they (a) investigated the use of MMA methods during individual psychotherapy and (b) were conducted using an adult sample. Both qualitative and quantitative studies were eligible. Studies were excluded if they (a) focused on a treatment package (e.g., MBSR, MBCT, DBT, ACT, or stand-alone modules from these packages that were not delivered in the context of general psychotherapy), (b) implemented MMA as an intervention for therapists (i.e., not patients), (c) occurred outside psychotherapy (e.g., analogue studies, mindfulness induction), and (d) examined mindfulness and/or acceptance as a mechanism (e.g., changes in trait mindfulness) but did not manipulate these characteristics (e.g., changes in trait mindfulness measured in routine psychotherapy within application of an MMA method). All coding was done independently by the two coders, with disagreements discussed by all four authors.

Our search returned 4,671 references, which were reviewed at the title and abstract level. Forty-five of these were reviewed at the full-text level. Three studies were ultimately deemed eligible for inclusion, two of which were qualitative studies and one of which was quantitative. Figure 20.1 presents the Preferred Reporting Items for Systematic Reviews and Meta-Analyses (PRISMA) flow diagram. Thus, there were an insufficient number of studies to perform a meta-analysis.

In lieu of a meta-analysis, we estimated box scores (i.e., summary judgment of the evidence for effects of MMA methods on in-session outcomes) for each of the three studies. We used +1, −1, and 0 to denote positive, neutral, and negative effects, respectively. To get a weighted box score, we multiplied the box score by the sample size for each finding and then computed an average box score across the studies. We interpreted box scores between −1.00 and −0.50 as negative, between 0.50 and +1.00 as positive, and between −0.49 and +0.49 as neutral. For the one quantitative study (Mander et al., 2019), we assigned a score of 0 to reflect the null effects observed for the use of mindfulness as a session-introducing exercise in a sample of 162 patients. For Horst et al. (2013), we assigned a score of +1 for mindfulness in a sample of five therapy dyads (n = 10). For Michaelis et al. (2018), we assigned a score of 0 for mindfulness and +1 for

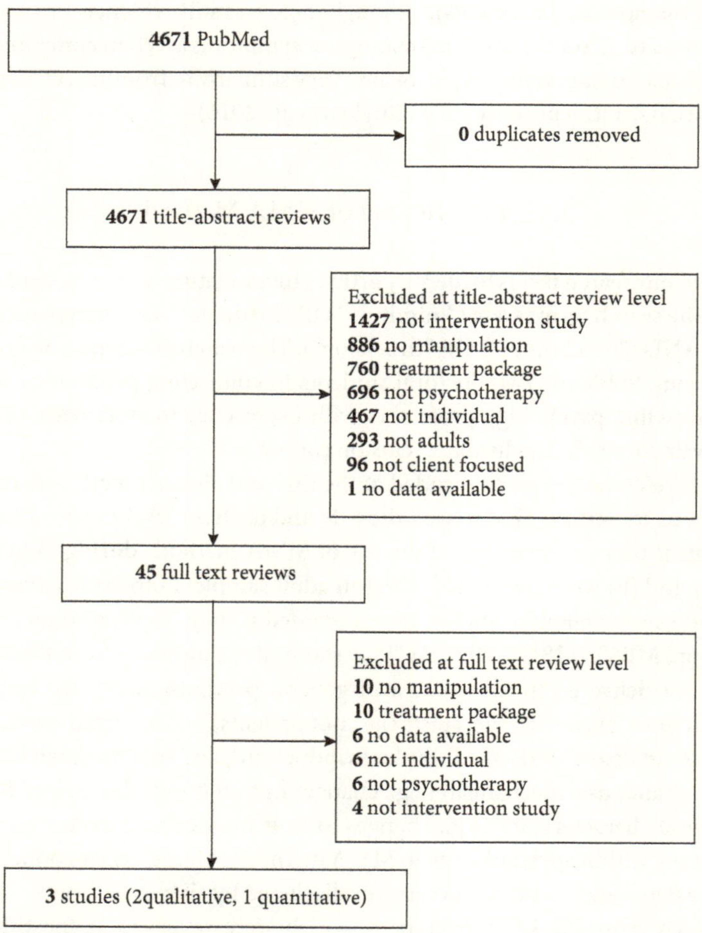

Figure 20.1 PRISMA flow diagram.

acceptance in a sample of nine people with epilepsy. The weighted box score for mindfulness was neutral [(0 × 162 = 0 for Mander et al.) + (+1 × 10 = 10 for Horst et al.) + (0 × 9 = 0 for Michaelis et al.) = 10/181 across both studies = 0.06 weighted box score]. The weighted box score for acceptance was positive [(1 × 9 = 9 for Michaelis et al.) = 9/9 across one study = 1 weighted box score]. Taken together, these studies provide inconclusive evidence regarding the impact of these methods on in-session outcomes.

Possible Negative Effects and Harm

Systematic evaluation of harm and adverse effects in meditation-based methods is lacking (Baer et al., 2019). To our knowledge, no systematic evaluation of harm and adverse effects of informal mindfulness or acceptance methods implemented outside of a treatment package exists. Thus, we focus here on what is known about meditation practice generally.

It is widely recognized within the contemplative traditions that these practices can have challenging consequences (Lindahl et al., 2017). There is now strong scientific evidence that intensive meditation practice (i.e., meditation retreats), in particular, can produce a host of perceptual, affective, and behavioral shifts that can cause varying degrees of distress, even as these experiences may be viewed as natural consequences of spiritual development and even as indicators of spiritual progress (Baer et al., 2019; Lindahl et al., 2017).

It does appear that "unpleasant experiences" are fairly common within meditation-based methods (e.g., 67–73% of participants in MBCT). The estimates of harm (defined as worsening) range from 2% to 7% (Baer et al., 2020; Britton et al., 2021; Hirshberg et al., 2022). Moreover, 32–50% of individuals in the general population who have been exposed to meditation report having had meditation-related challenges, most commonly anxiety, traumatic re-experiencing, and increased emotional sensitivity (Goldberg, Lam, et al., 2022). These experiences seem to be more common for individuals with proneness toward negative affect (depression, anxiety, loneliness) and with early childhood adversity (Goldberg, Lam, et al., 2022).

These results highlight the need for clinicians to apply meditation with caution and sensitivity, especially when patients have a trauma history. In our view, the available data suggest the benefits of meditation generally outweigh the potential harm. Indeed, these negative consequences are not associated with whether an individual feels glad to have practiced meditation (Goldberg, Lam, et al., 2022), suggesting distressing consequences usually do not overshadow the potential benefits. Furthermore, results from RCTs testing meditation apps indicate that they decrease (rather than increase) risk for symptom worsening relative to wait-list controls (Goldberg, Imhoff-Smith, et al., 2020; Hirshberg et al., 2021).

Diversity Considerations

Diversity has been understudied within research on meditation (Eichel et al., 2021). There is a small body of research investigating mindfulness-based methods for racial/

ethnic participants in the United States, indicating that these interventions produce modest benefits (standardized mean differences = 0.26 and 0.11 for comparisons with inactive controls and active controls at post-treatment, respectively) with effect sizes potentially smaller than those seen for similar interventions in the general population (Sun et al., 2022).

A growing number of RCTs have investigated mindfulness in non-Western samples (Asia, Middle East, South America; Galante et al., 2021). Additional dimensions of diversity (gender, sexual orientation, socioeconomic status) remain understudied in relation to these methods, although women are more likely than men to enroll in community-based mindfulness training (Hirshberg et al., 2022). Furthermore, it is generally unknown which, if any, demographic characteristics moderate the impact of these methods, although the one RCT testing the addition of MMA methods to general psychotherapy did not find that patient demographics moderated treatment effects (Mander et al., 2019). Nonetheless, there are reasons to believe that these approaches may be culturally resonant for some cultural groups (e.g., alignment with African American spiritual values and beliefs; Biggers et al., 2020; Woods-Giscombé & Black, 2010).

Given the limited research related to diversity, clinicians may be advised to apply research-informed principles from the broader multicultural counseling and cultural adaptation (Benish et al., 2011; D. M. Davis et al., 2018; Sue et al., 2019). Although these methods were intentionally secularized for their application in biomedical and health settings (Kabat-Zinn, 2011), it is nonetheless important to consider the ways in which they may relate to (and may potentially be perceived as contradicting) patients' spiritual or religious beliefs. Clinicians are advised to approach such discussions with cultural humility and curiosity (Hook et al., 2013).

Limitations of the Research

Research on the use of MMA methods in individual psychotherapy outside of treatment packages is just beginning. The three studies we identified investigating the use of MMA in this way had important limitations, some of which were discussed above. Mander et al. (2019) used a brief (5-minute) audio-guided mindfulness meditation practice but did not examine either a more flexible or a therapist-led implementation of mindfulness nor the impact of more intensive mindfulness practice (e.g., longer session introductions, home practice assigned to patients). The two qualitative studies (Horst et al., 2013; Michaelis et al., 2018) included small samples and did not involve randomization, making causal inferences not possible. An important limitation across all three studies was a lack of evaluation of MMA effects on outcomes theoretically sensitive to MMA methods immediately following their implementation. The closest to this was Mander et al., who assessed therapeutic alliance at the end of each psychotherapy session. However, this was following a 50-minute session (not immediately following the mindfulness practice), and therapeutic alliance may or may not be sensitive to mindfulness training. It may well be that there are short-term but nonetheless important effects of these methods that are not captured by retrospective assessments. Taken together, it remains scientifically uncertain whether promising findings drawn from the treatment package literature will apply.

We highlight several future directions for future research on MMA methods. There is a need to clarify the optimal dosage for incorporating these methods, as they could range from very minimal (e.g., mentioning a meditation app as adjunctive support, including an informal acceptance method) to central (e.g., applying these methods once or more every session). It may be valuable to investigate the impact of assigning homework outside of session. As noted, examining effects on more proximal outcomes (e.g., immediately following the application of a MMA method) may be helpful here. It will also be important to clarify when and for whom these methods may be most effective as well as when they may be contraindicated. It is also important to investigate cultural adaptation of these methods (Sun et al., 2022), given that culturally adapted treatments outperform non-adapted treatments for racial/ethnic minority groups in psychotherapy generally (Benish et al., 2011). Last, it will be important to clarify the necessary therapist training for implementing these strategies (Michalak et al., 2019), including whether and how training might be incorporated into graduate education.

Training Implications

There are widely available clinical training programs for learning to implement the treatment packages (e.g., MBSR, MBCT, DBT, ACT) from which these MMA methods are drawn. Interested clinicians would be well served by participating in MBSR or MBCT as participants, trainees, or co-therapists (Michalak et al., 2019). Personal practice probably enhances implementing meditation strategies and skillfully managing challenges that arise for patients. As with most novel strategies, clinicians may benefit from working with supervisors who have experience implementing these methods in individual therapy.

Therapeutic Practices

The plentiful research evidence on the effectiveness of MMA methods embedded within omnibus treatment packages indicates that they can be used successfully. The scant research on in-session outcomes on using these methods in individual therapy also suggests that patients may find the methods helpful, as do their clinicians. Based on this research evidence, we offer the following practice recommendations:

- Consider offering MMA methods to patients seeking to "accept" or "lean into" presenting problems.
- Recommend MMA to patients with common psychological symptoms (e.g., depression, anxiety) as well as those seeking to improve their well-being; these groups may be most likely to benefit. Consider integrating MMA methods into individual psychotherapy of various theoretical orientations.

- Monitor potential adverse reactions, especially to formal meditation practice, because approximately half of those practicing meditation experience some "unpleasant" effects along with their benefits.
- Consider obtaining personal experience and training with MMA methods because they may enable you to anticipate and manage these unpleasant experiences among clients.
- Consider administering instruments to assess the effects of MMA methods, monitor client progress, and adjust interventions accordingly (routine outcome monitoring).

References

* Studies included in the systematic review.

Baer, R., Crane, C., Miller, E., & Kuyken, W. (2019). Doing no harm in mindfulness-based programs: Conceptual issues and empirical findings. *Clinical Psychology Review*, *71*, 101–114. doi:10.1016/j.cpr.2019.01.001

Baer, R., Crane, C., Montero-Marin, J., Phillips, A., Taylor, L., Tickell, A., & Kuyken, W. (2020). Frequency of self-reported unpleasant events and harm in a mindfulness-based program in two general population samples. *Mindfulness*, *12*(3), 763–775. https://doi.org/10.1007/s12671-020-01547-8

Baer, R., Gu, J., Cavanagh, K., & Strauss, C. (2019). Differential sensitivity of mindfulness questionnaires to change with treatment: A systematic review and meta-analysis. *Psychological Assessment*, *31*(10), 1247–1263. http://dx.doi.org/10.1037/pas0000744

Baer, R. A., Smith, G. T., Hopkins, J., Krietemeyer, J., & Toney, L. (2006). Using self-report assessment methods to explore facets of mindfulness. *Assessment*, *13*, 27–45.

Benish, S. G., Quintana, S., & Wampold, B. E. (2011). Culturally adapted psychotherapy and the legitimacy of myth: A direct-comparison meta-analysis. *Journal of Counseling Psychology*, *58*(3), 279–289. doi:10.1037/a0023626

Bernstein, A., Hadash, Y., Lichtash, Y., Tanay, G., Shepherd, K., & Fresco, D. M. (2015). Decentering and related constructs: A critical review and metacognitive processes model. *Perspectives on Psychological Science*, *10*(5), 599–617. doi:10.1177/1745691615594577

Biggers, A., Spears, C. A., Sanders, K., Ong, J., Sharp, L. K., & Gerber, B. S. (2020). Promoting mindfulness in African American communities. *Mindfulness*, *11*(10), 2274–2282.

Blanck, P., Perleth, S., Heidenreich, T., Kröger, P., Ditzen, B., Bents, H., & Mander, J. (2018). Effects of mindfulness exercises as stand-alone intervention on symptoms of anxiety and depression: Systematic review and meta-analysis. *Behaviour Research and Therapy*, *102*, 25–35.

Block-Lerner, J., Wulfert, E., & Moses, E. (2009). ACT in context: An exploration of experiential acceptance. *Cognitive and Behavioral Practice*, *16*(4), 443–456.

Bodhi, B. (2005). *In the Buddha's words: An anthology of discourses from the Pali canon*. Wisdom Publications.

Bond, F. W., Hayes, S. C., Baer, R. A., Carpenter, K. M., Guenole, N., Orcutt, H. K., Waltz, T., & Zettle, R. D. (2011). Preliminary psychometric properties of the Acceptance and Action Questionnaire–II: A revised measure of psychological inflexibility and experiential avoidance. *Behavior Therapy*, *42*(4), 676–688.

Britton, W. B., Lindahl, J. R., Cooper, D. J., Canby, N. K., & Palitsky, R. (2021). Defining and measuring meditation-related adverse effects in mindfulness-based programs. *Clinical Psychological Science*, *9*(6), 1185–1204. https://doi.org/10.1177/2167702621996340

Brown, K., & Ryan, R. (2003). The benefits of being present: Mindfulness and its role in psychological well-being. *Journal of Personality and Social Psychology*, *84*(4), 822–848.

Chawla, N., Collins, S., Bowen, S., Hsu, S., Grow, J., Douglass, A., & Marlatt, G. (2010). The Mindfulness-Based Relapse Prevention Adherence and Competence Scale: Development, interrater reliability, and validity. *Psychotherapy Research*, *20*(4), 388–397.

Cohen, J. (1988). *Statistical power analysis for the behavioral sciences* (2nd ed.). Hillsdale, NJ: Erlbaum.

Cook, J., Biyanova, T., Elhai, J., Schnurr, P., & Coyne, J. (2010). What do psychotherapists really do in practice? An internet study of over 2000 practitioners. *Psychotherapy Theory, Research, Practice, Training*, *47*(2), 260–267.

Dahl, C. J., Lutz, A., & Davidson, R. J. (2015). Reconstructing and deconstructing the self: Cognitive mechanisms in meditation practice. *Trends in Cognitive Sciences*, *19*(9), 515–523. doi:10.1016/j.tics.2015.07.001

Davis, D. E., DeBlaere, C., Owen, J., Hook, J. N., Rivera, D. P., Choe, E., Van Tongeren, D., Worthington, E., Jr., & Placeres, V. (2018). The multicultural orientation framework: A narrative review. *Psychotherapy*, *55*(1), 89–100.

Davis, D. M., & Hayes, J. A. (2011). What are the benefits of mindfulness? A practice review of psychotherapy-related research. *Psychotherapy*, *48*(2), 198–208. doi:10.1037/a0022062

Del Re, A. C., Flückiger, C., Goldberg, S. B., & Hoyt, W. T. (2013). Monitoring mindfulness practice quality: An important consideration in mindfulness practice. *Psychotherapy Research*, *23*(1), 54–66. doi:10.1080/10503307.2012.729275

Eichel, K., Gawande, R., Acabchuk, R. L., Palitsky, R., Chau, S., Pham, A., Cheaito, A., Yam, D., Lipsky, J., Dumais, T., Zhu, Z., King, J., Fulwiler, C., Schuman-Olivier, Z., Moitra, E., Proulx, J., Alejandre-Lara, A., & Britton, W. (2021). A retrospective systematic review of diversity variables in mindfulness research, 2000–2016. *Mindfulness*, *12*, 2573–2592.

Forsyth, J. P., & Eifert, G. H. (2007). *The mindfulness and acceptance workbook for anxiety: A guide to breaking free from anxiety, phobias, and worry using acceptance and commitment therapy*. New Harbinger.

Galante, J., Friedrich, C., Dawson, A. F., Modrego-Alarcón, M., Gebbing, P., Delgado-Suárez, I., Gupta, R., Dean, L., Dalgleish, T., White, I., & Jones, P. B. (2021). Mindfulness-based programmes for mental health promotion in adults in nonclinical settings: A systematic review and meta-analysis of randomized controlled trials. *PLoS Medicine*, *18*(1), e1003481.

Geller, S. M., Greenberg, L. S., & Watson, J. C. (2010). Therapist and client perceptions of therapeutic presence: The development of a measure. *Psychotherapy Research*, *20*(5), 599–610.

Goldberg, S. B., Del Re, A. C., Hoyt, W. T., & Davis, J. M. (2014). The secret ingredient in mindfulness interventions? A case for practice quality over quantity. *Journal of Counseling Psychology*, *61*(3), 491–497. doi:10.1037/cou0000032

Goldberg, S. B., Imhoff-Smith, T., Bolt, D. M., Wilson-Mendenhall, C. D., Dahl, C. J., Davidson, R. J., & Rosenkranz, M. A. (2020). Testing a multi-component, self-guided, smartphone-based meditation app: Three-armed randomized controlled trial. *JMIR Mental Health*, *7*(11), e23825. doi:10.2196/23825

Goldberg, S. B., Knoeppel, C., Davidson, R. J., & Flook. L. (2020). Does practice quality mediate the relationship between practice time and outcome in mindfulness-based stress reduction? *Journal of Counseling Psychology*, *67*(1), 115–122. doi:10.1037/cou0000369

Goldberg, S. B., Lam, S. U., Britton, W. B., & Davidson, R. J. (2022). Prevalence of meditation-related adverse effects in a population-based sample in the United States. *Psychotherapy Research*, *32*(3), 291–305.

Goldberg, S. B., Riordan, K., Sun, S., & Davidson, R. J. (2022). The empirical status of mindfulness-based interventions: A systematic review of 44 meta-analyses of randomized controlled trials. *Perspectives on Psychological Science*, *17*(1), 108–130. doi:10.1177/1745691620968771

Goldberg, S. B., Tucker, R. P., Greene, P. A., Davidson, R. J., Wampold, B. E., Kearney, D. J., & Simpson, T. L. (2018). Mindfulness-based interventions for psychiatric disorders: A systematic review and meta-analysis. *Clinical Psychology Review*, *59*, 52–60. doi:10.1016/j.cpr.2017.10.011

Goldberg, S. B., Tucker, R. P., Greene, P. A., Simpson, T. L., Hoyt, W. T., Kearney, D. J., & Davidson, R. J. (2019). What can we learn from randomized clinical trials about the construct validity of self-report measures of mindfulness? A meta-analysis. *Mindfulness, 10*(5), 775–785. doi:10.1007/s12671-018-1032-y

Goyal, M., Singh, S., Sibinga, E. M., Gould, N. F., Rowland-Seymour, A., Sharma, R., Berger, Z., Sleicher, D., Maron, D., Shihab, H., Ranasinghe, P., Linn, S., Saha, S., Bass, E., & Haythornthwaite, J. A. (2014). Meditation programs for psychological stress and well-being: A systematic review and meta-analysis. *JAMA Internal Medicine, 174*(3), 357–368. doi:10.1001/jamainternmed.2013.13018

Hanley, A. W., & Garland, E. L. (2021). The Mindfulness-Oriented Recovery Enhancement Fidelity Measure (MORE-FM): Development and validation of a new tool to assess therapist adherence and competence. *Journal of Evidence-Based Social Work, 18*(3), 308–322.

Hanley, A. W., Warner, A. R., Dehili, V. M., Canto, A. I., & Garland, E. L. (2015). Washing dishes to wash the dishes: Brief instruction in an informal mindfulness practice. *Mindfulness, 6*(5), 1095–1103.

Harned, M. S., Korslund, K. E., Schmidt, S. C., & Gallop, R. J. (2021). The Dialectical Behavior Therapy Adherence Coding Scale (DBT ACS): Psychometric properties. *Psychological Assessment, 33*(6), 552–561. https://doi.org/10.1037/pas0000999

Harrington, A., & Dunne, J. D. (2015). When mindfulness is therapy: Ethical qualms, historical perspectives. *American Psychologist, 70*(7), 621–631. doi:10.1037/a0039460

Hayes, S. C. (2004). Acceptance and commitment therapy, relational frame theory, and the third wave of behavioral and cognitive therapies. *Behavior Therapy, 35*(4), 639–665.

Hayes, S. C., Strosahl, K., & Wilson, K. (1999). *Acceptance and commitment therapy: An experiential approach to behavior change*. Guilford.

Hayes, S. C., Wilson, K. G., Gifford, E. V., Follette, V. M., & Strosahl, K. (1996). Experiential avoidance and behavioral disorders: A functional dimensional approach to diagnosis and treatment. *Journal of Consulting and Clinical Psychology, 64*(6), 1152–1168.

Hirshberg, M. J., Frye, C., Dahl, C. J., Riordan, K. M., Vack, N. J., Sach, J., Goldman, R., Davidson, R. J., & Goldberg, S. B. (2022). A randomized controlled trial of a smartphone-based well-being training in public school system employees during the COVID-19 pandemic. *Journal of Educational Psychology*. doi:10.1037/edu0000739

Hirshberg, M. J., Goldberg, S., Rosenkranz, M. A., & Davidson, R. J. (2022). Prevalence of harm in mindfulness-based stress reduction. *Psychological Medicine, 52*(6), 1080–1088. doi:10.1017/S0033291720002834

Hook, J. N., Davis, D. E., Owen, J., Worthington, E. L., Jr., & Utsey, S. O. (2013). Cultural humility: Measuring openness to culturally diverse clients. *Journal of Counseling Psychology, 60*(3), 353–366.

*Horst, K., Newsom, K., & Stith, S. (2013). Client and therapist initial experience of using mindfulness in therapy. *Psychotherapy Research, 23*(4), 369–380.

Kabat-Zinn, J. (1994). *Wherever you go, there you are: Mindfulness meditation in everyday life*. Hyperion.

Kabat-Zinn, J. (2011). Some reflections on the origins of MBSR, skillful means, and the trouble with maps. *Contemporary Buddhism, 12*(1), 281–306.

Kabat-Zinn, J. (2013). *Full catastrophe living: How to cope with stress, pain and illness using mindfulness meditation* (Rev. ed.). Piatkus.

Kuyken, W., Warren, F. C., Taylor, R. S., Whalley, B., Crane, C., Bondolfi, G., Hayes, R., Huijbers, M., Ma, H., Schweizer, S., Segal, Z., Speckens, A., Teasdale, J., Van Heeringen, K., Williams, M., Byford, S., Byng, R., & Dalgeish, T. (2016). Efficacy of mindfulness-based cognitive therapy in prevention of depressive relapse: An individual patient data meta-analysis from randomized trials. *JAMA Psychiatry, 73*(6), 565–574. doi:10.1001/jamapsychiatry.2016.0076

Lau, M. A., Bishop, S. R., Segal, Z. V., Buis, T., Anderson, N. D., Carlson, L., Shapiro, S., Carmody, J., Abbey, S.,& Devins, G. (2006). The Toronto Mindfulness Scale: Development and validation. *Journal of Clinical Psychology, 62*(12), 1445–1467. doi:10.1002/jclp.20326

Lindahl, J. R., Fisher, N. E., Cooper, D. J., Rosen, R. K., & Britton, W. B. (2017). The varieties of contemplative experience: A mixed-methods study of meditation-related challenges in Western Buddhists. *PLoS One, 12*(5), e0176239. doi:10.1371/journal.pone.0176239

Lindsay, E. K., & Creswell, J. D. (2017). Mechanisms of mindfulness training: Monitor and acceptance theory (MAT). *Clinical Psychology Review*, *51*, 48–59.

Linehan, M. M. (1993). *Cognitive-behavioral treatment of borderline personality disorder*. Guilford.

Linehan, M. M. (2015). *DBT skills training manual* (2nd ed.). Guilford.

Longfellow, H. W. (1900). *Poems of Henry W. Longfellow*. New York: A. L. Burt Company.

Lutz, A., Slagter, H., Dunne, J., & Davidson, R. (2008). Attention regulation and monitoring in meditation. *Trends in Cognitive Science*, *12*(4), 163–169.

*Mander, J., Blanck, P., Neubauer, A. B., Kröger, P., Flückiger, C., Lutz, W., Barnow, S., Bents, H., & Heidenreich, T. (2019). Mindfulness and progressive muscle relaxation as standardized session- introduction in individual therapy: A randomized controlled trial. *Journal of Clinical Psychology*, *75*(1), 21–45.

Mander, J., Kröger, P., Heidenreich, T., Flückiger, C., Lutz, W., Bents, H., & Barnow, S. (2015). The Process–Outcome Mindfulness Effects in Trainees (PrOMET) study: Protocol of a pragmatic randomized controlled trial. *BMC Psychology*, *3*(1), 1–13.

*Michaelis, R., Niedermann, C., Reuber, M., Kuthe, M., & Berger, B. (2018). "Seizures have become a means of somehow learning things about myself"—A qualitative study of the development of self-efficacy and mastery during a psychotherapeutic intervention for people with epilepsy. *Epilepsy & Behavior*, *84*, 152–161.

Michalak, J., Crane, C., Germer, C. K., Gold, E., Heidenreich, T., Mander, J., Meibert, P., & Segal, Z. V. (2019). Principles for a responsible integration of mindfulness in individual therapy. *Mindfulness*, *10*(5), 799–811.

Michalak, J., Steinhaus, K., & Heidenreich, T. (2020). (How) do therapists use mindfulness in their clinical work? A study on the implementation of mindfulness interventions. *Mindfulness*, *11*(2), 401–410.

Neff, K. (2003). The development and validation of a scale to measure self-compassion. *Self and Identity*, *2*, 223–250.

Nidich, S., Mills, P. J., Rainforth, M., Heppner, P., Schneider, R. H., Rosenthal, N. E., Salerno, J., Gaylord-King, C., & Rutledge, T. (2018). Non-trauma-focused meditation versus exposure therapy in veterans with post-traumatic stress disorder: A randomised controlled trial. *Lancet Psychiatry*, *5*(12), 975–986.

Öst, L. G. (2008). Efficacy of the third wave of behavioral therapies: A systematic review and meta-analysis. *Behaviour Research and Therapy*, *46*(3), 296–321.

Öst, L. G. (2014). The efficacy of acceptance and commitment therapy: An updated systematic review and meta-analysis. *Behaviour Research and Therapy*, *61*, 105–121.

Quaglia, J. T., Braun, S. E., Freeman, S. P., McDaniel, M. A., & Brown, K. W. (2016). Meta-analytic evidence for effects of mindfulness training on dimensions of self-reported dispositional mindfulness. *Psychological Assessment*, *28*(7), 803–818. doi:10.1037/pas0000268

Salzberg, S. (2004). *Lovingkindness: The revolutionary art of happiness*. Shambala.

Schumer, M. C., Lindsay, E. K., & Creswell, J. D. (2018). Brief mindfulness training for negative affectivity: A systematic review and meta-analysis. *Journal of Consulting and Clinical Psychology*, *86*(7), 569–583.

Segal, Z. V., Teasdale, J. D., Williams, J. M., & Gemar, M. C. (2002). The Mindfulness-Based Cognitive Therapy Adherence Scale: Inter-rater reliability, adherence to protocol and treatment distinctiveness. *Clinical Psychology and Psychotherapy*, *9*, 131–138. doi:10.1002/cpp.320

Segal, Z. V., Williams, J. M. G., & Teasdale, J. D. (2013). *Mindfulness-based cognitive therapy for depression* (2nd ed.). Guilford.

Smeets, E., Neff, K., Alberts, H., & Peters, M. (2014). Meeting suffering with kindness: Effects of a brief self-compassion intervention for female college students. *Journal of Clinical Psychology*, *70*(9), 794–807. doi:10.1002/jclp.22076

Smith, H. (1991). *The world's religions*. HarperCollins.

Society of Clinical Psychology. (n.d.). *Psychological treatments*. https://div12.org/treatments

Sue, D. W., Sue, D., Neville, H. A., & Smith, L. (2019). *Counseling the culturally diverse: Theory and practice* (8th ed.). Wiley.

Sun, S., Goldberg, S. B., Loucks, E. B., & Brewer, J. A. (2022). Mindfulness-based interventions among people of color: A systematic review and meta-analysis. *Psychotherapy Research, 32*(3), 277–290.

Tanay, G., & Bernstein, A. (2013). State Mindfulness Scale (SMS): Development and initial validation. *Psychological Assessment, 25*(4), 1286–1299.

Tovote, K. A., Fleer, J., Snippe, E., Peeters, A. C., Emmelkamp, P. M., Sanderman, R., Links, T., & Schroevers, M. J. (2014). Individual mindfulness-based cognitive therapy and cognitive behavior therapy for treating depressive symptoms in patients with diabetes: Results of a randomized controlled trial. *Diabetes Care, 37*(9), 2427–2434.

Treleaven, D. A. (2018). *Trauma-sensitive mindfulness: Practices for safe and transformative healing*. Norton.

Van Dam, N. T., van Vugt, M. K., Vago, D. R., Schmalzl, L., Saron, C. D., Olendzki, A., Meissner, T., Lazar, S., Kerr, C., Gorchov, J., Fox, K., Field, B., Britton, W., Brefcyznski-Lewis, J., & Meyer, D. E. (2018). Mind the hype: A critical evaluation and prescriptive agenda for research on mindfulness and meditation. *Perspectives on Psychological Science, 13*(1), 36–61. doi:10.1177/1745691617709589

Wampold, B., & Imel, Z. E. (2015). *The great psychotherapy debate: The evidence for what makes psychotherapy work* (2nd ed.). Routledge.

Wasil, A. R., Gillespie, S., Patel, R., Petre, A., Venturo-Conerly, K. E., Shingleton, R. M., Weisz, J., & DeRubeis, R. J. (2020). Reassessing evidence-based content in popular smartphone apps for depression and anxiety: Developing and applying user-adjusted analyses. *Journal of Consulting and Clinical Psychology, 88*(11), 983–993.

Woods-Giscombé, C. L., & Black, A. R. (2010). Mind–body interventions to reduce risk for health disparities related to stress and strength among African American women: The potential of mindfulness-based stress reduction, loving-kindness, and the NTU therapeutic framework. *Complementary Health Review, 15*(3), 115–131. doi:10.1177/1533210110386776

Yalom, I. D., & Leszcz, M. (2005). *The theory and practice of group psychotherapy* (5th ed.). Basic Books.

21

Facilitating Behavioral Activation

Pim Cuijpers, Eirini Karyotaki, Mathias Harrer, and Yvonne Stikkelbroek

With more than 300 million people suffering from depressive disorders, depression is the most prevalent mental disorder (World Health Organization, 2017). Furthermore, depression is associated with considerable excess mortality and morbidity. Apart from the personal suffering by patients and their relatives, depression is also associated with huge economic costs. Because it affects people of working age, the costs associated with production losses are especially high (Herrman et al., 2022). Depression is considered to be one of the main major public health challenges of the coming decades (World Health Organization, 2017).

Several psychological treatments are available for depression, which are usually considered to be first-line treatments. These include cognitive–behavioral therapy (CBT), interpersonal psychotherapy, nondirective counseling, problem-solving therapy, psychodynamic therapy, and behavioral activation (Cuijpers, Quero, et al., 2021).

In this chapter, we focus on behavioral activation (BA), one of the best examined methods for treating depression. We first define BA and describe its components, the assessments used to measure progress, and a detailed case example illustrating how it works with actual patients. We also give an overview of the outcome research on treatment packages including BA and provide a meta-analysis of randomized controlled trials on the distal, end-of-treatment outcomes for such BA treatments. Thereafter, we narratively review the results of several studies on the immediate and intermediate outcomes of BA. The chapter concludes with research limitations, diversity considerations, and training and practice implications. In this chapter, we mostly focus on BA as an independent treatment and only briefly discuss treatment packages in which BA is only one of the components.

Definitions

Behavioral activation can be briefly defined as a psychological method aimed at increasing positive interactions between a person and the environment (Cuijpers, Karyotaki, et al., 2020). A more extensive and precise definition was given in an authoritative review of the origins and current status of BA (Dimidjian et al., 2011):

> a structured, brief psychotherapeutic approach that aims to (a) increase engagement in adaptive activities (which often are those associated with the experience of pleasure or mastery), (b) decrease engagement in activities that maintain depression or increase risk for depression, and (c) solve problems that limit access to reward or that maintain or increase aversive control. (pp. 3–4)

Pim Cuijpers, Eirini Karyotaki, Mathias Harrer, and Yvonne Stikkelbroek, *Facilitating Behavioral Activation* In: *Psychotherapy Skills and Methods That Work*. Edited by: Clara E. Hill and John C. Norcross, Oxford University Press. © Clara E. Hill and John C. Norcross 2023. DOI: 10.1093/oso/9780197611012.003.0021

Building on Ferster's (1973) behavioral theory of depression, BA was developed as a treatment in the 1960s and 1970s by Lewinsohn (1974) and colleagues. In the same period, cognitive restructuring was developed by Beck and colleagues (1979), and several early pilot studies examined whether one of the two was more effective (e.g., McNamara & Horan, 1986; Taylor & Marshall, 1977; Wilson, et al., 1983). However, because these studies were underpowered, researchers were not capable of identifying differences between the two. In the end, Beck and colleagues (1979) included their own version of BA in their cognitive therapy manual, and BA was more or less "forgotten" as a separate method.

Currently, four types of BA can be distinguished (Mazzucchelli et al., 2009; Cuijpers, Karyotaki, et al., 2020):

1. Pleasant activity (consisting of monitoring and scheduling pleasant activities, sometimes including social skills training; Lewinsohn, 1974)
2. Self-control (monitoring of activities and mood, goal setting, self-evaluation of performance, and self-administering rewards; Rehm, 1984)
3. Contextual BA (activity scheduling, self-monitoring, graded task assignment, role-playing, functional analysis, mental rehearsal and mindfulness; Jacobson et al., 2001; Martell et al., 2001)
4. Behavioral activation treatment for depression (contracting to change immediate environmental contingencies, goal setting and graduated task assignment, monitoring, and self-administering rewards; Lejuez et al., 2001)

One of the most interesting aspects of BA is that it is relatively simple compared to full CBT. The basic idea of BA is that therapists help patients find which activities are related to a better mood and then work to build more of these pleasant activities into the patients' lives. This method does not require higher level patterns of thoughts, which for many patients are quite complicated and require an intensive learning process. Therapists do not need, therefore, necessarily to be fully trained psychotherapists or clinical psychologists. One seminal randomized trial conducted in the United Kingdom showed that BA delivered by nurses in primary care was not inferior to full CBT delivered by highly trained therapists (Richards et al., 2016).

Because BA is relatively easy for both therapists and patients, it has also been used with patients suffering from other disorders and more complicated populations. These groups include caregivers of dementia patients (Teri et al., 1997), children with physical disabilities (Suh et al., 2021), adults with post-traumatic stress disorder (Wagner et al., 2019), bereavement (Acierno et al., 2021), anxiety and depression in cancer survivors, concurrent methamphetamine dependence and sexual risk for HIV acquisition among men who have sex with men (Mimiaga et al., 2019), and as a preventive intervention in college students (Fazzino et al., 2020).

Clinical Description and Indications

Behavioral activation consists of several components: psychoeducation, mood monitoring, identifying pleasant and unpleasant activities, monitoring of activities, and activity scheduling.

Psychoeducation

In BA, it is assumed that how you feel is caused by what you do. If you feel depressed, then you do not have enough pleasant activities in your life. BA therapists start by explaining this principle to patients.

In the early versions of activity scheduling, it was explained that someone gets depressed because they get into a negative vicious circle. The person starts doing fewer pleasant activities than before, which makes them somewhat depressed, which then causes the person to do even fewer pleasant activities, which makes the person even more depressed, and so on. The therapist also explains to the patient that the goal of the method is to turn this circle around in the positive direction. By doing a small thing that you like (or used to like before becoming depressed), you feel a little more positive, which stimulates you to do some more things you like, which again makes you feel somewhat better, and so on.

Such a rationale makes sense to most patients, although some patients feel that is a very simple explanation of their depression. They believe their depression is much more complicated and has to do with all kinds of other things, such as their family history, personality, childhood traumas, or recent stressors. In these cases, it is important to explain that the rationale for BA may be simple, but that does not mean that it is simple to do, and that many elements of learning how to build pleasant activities are directly related to the more complicated dynamics.

Mood Monitoring

With *mood monitoring*, patients are asked to rate their own mood at least once a day. Sometimes this is done separately for the mornings, afternoons, and evenings so that the patient has three ratings for one day. More recently, this mood monitoring is done through *ecological momentary assessment*, such that the patient gets random signals from their mobile phone during the day to rate mood at that moment.

Mood monitoring has several goals in BA. First, it gives the patient an instrument to become aware of their mood during the day and over time. Second, mood monitoring gives patients an instrument to verify whether the treatment works. If their mood improves over time, then they can assume that the treatment is successful. Third, and possibly the most important goal of mood monitoring, it helps patients explore why their mood varies over time. Why was your mood so low on Sunday evening, and why not that bad on Tuesday morning? What happened? Where were you? What were you doing? This can help the patient become aware of causes and triggers for a low or high mood. A patient could say, for example, "When I think about Monday morning and that I have to go to meet this colleague I hate, I feel depressed" and "On Tuesday morning I still feel good, because I always go to yoga on Monday evening and manage to forget all the stresses of the day."

Identifying Pleasant and Unpleasant Activities

The core of BA is that a patient increases the number of activities that improve mood. The patient makes a list of activities that they like to do or used to like (before the depression). Pleasant activities can range from physically active activities, such as cycling, walking in the country, or swimming, to physically inactive activities, such as talking about sports, reading a book, or watching television. The only criterion is whether the patient experiences it as a pleasant event.

For some patients, it can be difficult to make a list of such pleasant activities. To help them, the Pleasant Events Schedule can be used. This questionnaire includes 307 activities that may be experienced as pleasant by patients (MacPhillamy & Lewinsohn, 1982). The questionnaire was developed and validated specifically for identifying pleasant events and for use in BA. There is also a comparable questionnaire to identify unpleasant events, the Unpleasant Events Schedule (Lewinsohn et al., 1985).

Monitoring of Activities

Monitoring of activities is a core element of BA. Patients have a diary in which they record when pleasant and unpleasant activities occur, how pleasant or unpleasant they were, and their mood. The patient can be asked to rate pleasantness and mood on a scale ranging from 0 (worst) to 10 (best ever). After 1 or 2 weeks of monitoring mood and activities, therapists can make graphical summaries of the data. For example, in the clinical example discussed later, "Ann" made a list of 15 pleasant activities (using the Pleasant Activities Schedule) and then rated for 2 weeks the frequency of these activities and her mood. It was difficult to give one overall rating for her mood for each whole day because her mood varied, but she was able to give one overall rating for the entire time period.

Activity Scheduling

After enough information is collected on activities that generate a better or worse mood, it is time to start changing daily activities to improve mood. In this step, the therapist helps the patient develop a plan of how pleasant activities can be built into the patient's daily life while at the same time unpleasant activities are reduced. This *activity scheduling* is the phase in which the major improvements of mood in the patient should be expected.

In simple versions of BA, the patient is expected to plan more pleasant activities into daily life and make a goal of how many pleasant activities should be had every day of the coming week. In more complicated versions, the patient and therapist work through the antecedents–behavior–consequences (ABCs) in an individualized way. The ABCs are worked through, and the patient is helped to change them in such a way that they no longer result in decreased mood.

Solving problems in building more pleasant activities is a key element of activity scheduling. For example, a patient can be very busy because of work during the day and family in the evenings, nights, and mornings. They may feel unable to build pleasant activities into such a busy life. Discussing such problems and working on concrete solutions is a key part of BA—for example, in this case, doing something during lunch time, when the children are in bed, or devising a better task division with the partner.

Assessment

There are no validated and published instruments to measure the occurrence and quality of BA as conducted by therapists. There is one scale, the Quality of Behavioral Activation Scale, but this has not yet been published, nor have its content and goals (Dimidjian et al., in preparation), although it has been used in at least one study (McCauley et al., 2016).

Likewise, we know of no measures of immediate outcome—that is, how clients respond to components of BA during sessions. Hence, we focus on intermediate (i.e., throughout therapy) and distal (end-of-treatment) outcomes.

Regarding intermediate outcomes, there are several important patient-rated assessment measures, especially assessment of mood and pleasant activities because these are fully integrated into BA. Mood ratings can vary over time and depend on the moment. Because these ratings are based on one item and simply ask the patient to rate mood, the pleasantness of activities, or how often they do these activities, the psychometric properties cannot be clearly established. Two other patient-reported measures for assessing mood, depression, and pleasant activities have better psychometric properties: the Pleasant Events Schedule (MacPhillamy & Lewinsohn, 1982) and the Unpleasant Events Schedule (Lewinsohn et al., 1985). Both of these are validated but simple lists of activities. It has been argued, however, that counting the frequency of pleasant and interpersonal events is not necessarily effective (Kanter et al., 2007). For example, going to see a movie is arguably pleasant, but for a particular client this behavior could function as an escape from aversive schoolwork.

In terms of distal outcomes, the Behavioral Activation for Depression Scale (BADS) measures when and how clients become more activated over the course of BA (Kanter et al., 2007). Many recent trials have used BADS as a secondary outcome measure. Although BA can also be used in other mental health problems, the primary outcome of BA is usually depression. The most used self-report measures include the Beck Depression Inventory (BDI; Beck et al., 1961) and the BDI-II (Beck et al., 1996), which are well validated and can give a good indication of the severity of depression. In an increasing number of studies, the Patient Health Questionnaire–9 (Kroenke et al., 2001) is used. Other self-report instruments often used for measuring outcome include the Center for Epidemiologic Studies Depression scale (Radloff, 1977), the Hospital Anxiety and Depression Scale (Zigmond, & Snaith, 1983; usually in people who also have comorbid general medical disorders), the Geriatric Depression Scale (Yesavage et al., 1982) for depression in older adults, and the Revised Child Anxiety and Depression Scale (Chorpita et al., 2000) and the Childhood Depression Inventory (Kovacs, 1985) for measuring depression in children and adolescents. The most used clinician-rated instruments are the Hamilton Rating Scale for Depression (Hamilton, 1960) and the Montgomery–Åsberg Depression Rating Scale (Montgomery & Åsberg, 1979).

Another category of distal outcome measures is aimed at examining whether a patient meets criteria for a depressive disorder. This assessment can be done with several structured clinical interviews, including the Structured Clinical Interview for DSM-5 (First et al., 2015), the World Health Organization Composite International Diagnostic Interview (Robins et al., 1988), the Mini-International Neuropsychiatric Interview (Sheehan et al., 1998), and the Schedule for Affective Disorders and Schizophrenia for

School—Age Children (Puig-Antich & Chambers, 1978) for diagnoses in children and adolescents.

Clinical Example

The following describes a fictional example of a patient, based on our experience working with BA with patients.

"Ann" is a 23-year-old cisgender woman living with her boyfriend, "Clark." Two years ago, for Clark's job, they moved away from the town where they were both born. Ann seemed to cope well in the beginning of their relocation, but after 1 year she got the flu and was sick for 3 weeks. She went back to work as a librarian but suffered from tiredness. Her relations with her colleagues had been good, but then she was assigned a new manager, and he pressured her to get more work done. Sometimes he picked on her, and Ann did not get support from her colleagues. Her concentration and sleep were decreasing. She started to worry, and that diminished her sleep further. Work consumed her energy, and even on holidays she could not experience pleasure anymore.

Her family doctor tested for possible physical causes but could not find any. Then he screened Ann for depression. He offered to prescribe antidepressant medication, but Ann wanted to try psychological treatment first. He referred Ann to a psychologist.

The psychologist concluded that Ann was suffering from depression. Her score on the BDI was 29, above the clinical cutoff of 19 for moderate to severe depression. At that time, Ann had been on sick leave for 2½ months and stayed in bed frequently. She spent most of her time on social media, which made her feel even more worthless. She tried to prepare meals when Clark returned home after work. Most of the time she failed to do so.

Clark tried to cheer Ann up, but without much success. She reacted irritably and complained he did not fully grasp how she felt. Sometimes she said, "You don't understand anything." Afterwards she felt guilty for being so rude to him. Clark was glad that a clear diagnosis was established and hoped that the treatment would be successful. He tried to motivate Ann to work with the psychologist on her problems. Ann experienced his encouragement as a clear sign that Clarke thought she was crazy. The psychologist suggested BA because Ann was so passive. Ann understood this rationale. She missed her life as it was before she got the flu, and she wanted to be able to manage her mood and energy.

Psychoeducation

Ann (Patient [P]) was educated about the connection among activities, mood, and thoughts because she was not convinced that doing pleasant things could change her problem. She thought the therapist (T) did not understand her depression. If she would have found anything pleasant, she would have immediately done it by herself.

T: Ann, can you rate your mood, from 0 to 10, yesterday at 12.00 o'clock?

P: (Silence) I think it was a three.

T: That must be very difficult for you to bear. How did you figure out what mood you were in?

P: I had to think about yesterday. I remembered what I was doing. I was still in bed and did not have the energy to get out.

T: So, you remembered where you were and what you were doing. At that moment you knew how to rate your mood. This is exactly what I mean. We have to figure what activities influence your mood in a positive way. Maybe you think that it is impossible to improve your mood so easily because if it was you should have done that by now.

P: Yeah, it feels so stupid if it is so simple.

T: Yeah, exactly. A depressed mood can fool you and make you think that nothing is going to help. Take the three components—act, think and feeling. Which of the three do you want to change first?

P: Feeling.

T: Of course, but the problem is that you cannot decide to feel different. If so, you would have done that. Maybe Clark also said at some point, "Cheer up, this should be nice."

P: Yes, it makes me feel so hopeless and I think I am a bad wife and he would be better off without me.

T: I can understand it is exactly what you both don't want. It is impossible to decide to feel different on purpose. What you *can* do is to decide to do small activities which have proven in the past to be pleasant. Also try to watch your mood.

P: Does this really work?

T: Yes, it is possible that if you systematically gather information on your mood and activities, the depressed mood can be influenced step by step. We will encounter difficulties on the way, but we can address them and this can lead to a better understanding of how the depression got hold of you.

Mood Monitoring

Ann was asked to daily rate her mood every day at 7 p.m. (Figure 21.1). Ann was indecisive on how she felt. She was asked to compare her mood to her mood during the happiest (10) or worst (1) moment. In the beginning, Ann thought she experienced almost no differences in her mood and that she always felt gloomy. After several days of monitoring, however, she noticed that her mood was not always the same. Small differences appeared and were discussed during the therapy sessions.

Identifying Pleasant Activities

Ann made a list of activities supposed to be pleasant. It was difficult for her because she could not imagine activities to be pleasant, although they used to be pleasant. The therapist helped her choose small activities that were available and easy to do. For instance, cut a flower in the garden and put it in a vase. She also chose checking Facebook for messages, such that checking for 10 minutes was scored as one pleasant activity. Watching television shows or series for 30 minutes was also rated as one pleasant activity. In addition, she remembered that as a student she liked to plant cuttings and see

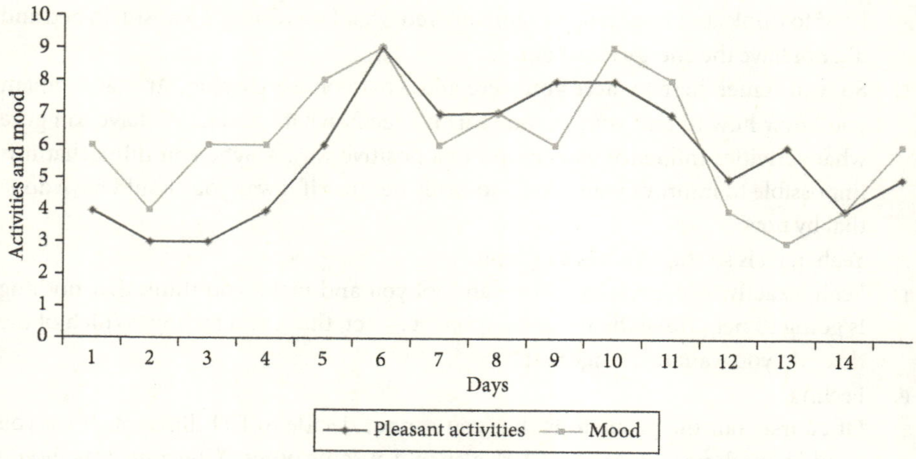

Figure 21.1 Patient's mood and number of pleasant activities during a 2-week period.

if they would grow. Ann made a list of 15 such pleasant activities using the Pleasant Activities Schedule.

Monitoring of Activities

Ann used a physical booklet to monitor the occurrence of the pleasant activities. Ann was passive at the beginning of therapy, and the therapist did not ask much of Ann in order to create early success in the first tasks. Ann rated how many times she did a pleasant activity during the day. After monitoring her mood and pleasant activities for 2 weeks, the therapist and Ann discussed the results:

T: I see you did a really good job of monitoring your mood and activities.
P: I think I made some mistakes. I sometimes forgot to rate pleasant activities.
T: Exactly. It is difficult to think of scoring the mood and pleasant activities but you scored your mood every day. That is very good.

Ann discovered fluctuations in her mood and also noticed that waiting to do pleasant activities until she felt like it did not lead to anything. But when she ignored her mood and started a pleasant activity, then something changed in her mood. Not a major improvement, but it was better than staying in bed. Looking at the graph in Figure 21.1, her mood was better when she conducted more pleasant activities. Ann was surprised to see it.

T: Let's see what the graph is telling us.
P: I thought this monitoring was helping. Finally, I could do something to get better. On day 12, I had a really bad day and it remained bad for three days. The pleasant activities ceased.
T: What happened on day 12 or maybe the day before?

P: Clark went on a business trip, and I felt abandoned. I knew he had to go but I could not get over it. I stayed in bed and watched television.

T: Did you anticipate this feeling?

P: No, not at all. I used to enjoy some time alone and would read books for hours without being disturbed. But I cannot concentrate anymore to read a book.

T: Yes, a depression can deplete your concentration but it will return when the depression diminishes. Feeling depressed can make you doubt about everything, even your relationship with Clark, as if he already was leaving you. Now that you know this can happen, what would you do next time to prevent feeling like this?

P: I do not know. I just gave up.

T: Maybe you should not be alone when you are depressed. Could you make special plans for yourself?

P: Yes, I could visit my mother or ask her to come over to have some time together. That would be something. I do miss her.

Activity Scheduling

Some activities that Ann had listed on the activities list turned out not to be pleasant, so Ann modified her pleasant activity list. Watching television and Facebook checking were removed from the pleasant activity list because they did not improve her mood. She added bird-watching in the garden and folding towels to her list. The list was on her mobile phone, and she could look at it any moment for ideas. Ann also planned when to do pleasant activities and put those plans on the calendar. For instance, getting out of bed was a major task for Ann. She scheduled having fresh coffee with Clark in the morning at the kitchen counter before he went to work. Clark left the bedroom doors open so that Ann could smell the fresh coffee. It gave her mood a boost and helped her approach the rest of the day.

Ann had enjoyed spending time with friends before she got depressed, but she did not have friends in her current town. She thus scheduled FaceTime meetings with old friends. At first, she felt guilty for being out of contact for a long time. After the first positive response, however, she felt reassured that she was doing the right thing.

A neighbor offered several times to join the tennis association with her. Clark supported Ann and went with her to check it out. Ann was overwhelmed by the friendly welcome, and she started lessons for beginners. Step by step, with the support of the therapist and Clark, Ann discovered how to manage her mood and energy better, as well as how to manage obstacles. Fourteen sessions and 4 months after she had her first meeting with her therapist, her depression was in remission with a BDI score of 5, and Ann was back at work.

Landmark Studies and Previous Reviews

Although the effects of BA were examined in several randomized trials in the 1970s, all of these early studies were small and did not have sufficient statistical power to find small effects. Several later trials have proven important for the development of BA. The study by Jacobson and colleagues (1996) was relatively large compared to the previous studies and found no indication that BA was less effective than CBT. Building on these results, another influential trial was conducted and again found no significant difference between BA and CBT, although BA was more effective with more severe depression (Dimidjian et al., 2006). A third significant trial conducted in the United Kingdom with 440 randomized patients showed that BA delivered by junior mental health workers in primary care was as effective as CBT delivered by psychotherapists (Richards et al., 2016).

Several recent meta-analyses have integrated the findings from randomized trials of BA as an independent treatment package on distal, end-of-treatment outcomes. The largest, most recent meta-analysis included 28 trials and found a pooled effect size (Hedges' *g*) of 0.83 on depression, 0.37 on anxiety, and 0.64 on activation (Stein et al., 2021). Although the quality of most of the trials was modest, this meta-analysis suggested that BA is an effective treatment for depression as well as other outcomes.

A larger network meta-analyses included 331 randomized controlled trials comparing eight major types of psychotherapy for depression with each other or with control groups (wait list, usual care, pill placebo) on distal, end-of-treatment outcomes (Cuijpers, Quero, et al., 2021). A total of 36 trials included a BA treatment arm. No significant difference was found between BA and other types of therapy (except for nondirective counseling, which may have been an artifact given that nondirective counseling was often used as the control condition).

A more specific but smaller network meta-analysis included studies that compared treatments including BA (as independent treatment package), cognitive restructuring (CR), or the combination of BA and CR for depression, with each other or with wait-list or usual care (Ciharova et al., 2021). This meta-analysis suggested that all three had comparable effects on depression, and no significant outcome differences were found.

In recent years, several smaller meta-analytic studies of treatments including BA have been conducted. Most of these meta-analyses focused on specific target groups, such as older adults (Orgeta et al., 2017), young people (Tindall et al., 2017), and dementia and informal caregivers (Zabihi et al., 2020). Other meta-analyses focused on specific treatment formats of BA, including internet-based BA (Huguet et al., 2018) and group BA (Simmonds-Buckley et al., 2019). Another recent meta-analysis focused on BA for patients with co-occurring depression and substance use disorders (Pott et al., 2022). The number of randomized trials included in these narrower meta-analyses was relatively small, but most found moderate to large effects when comparing BA to usual care or wait-list control groups and confirmed the results of the larger (network) meta-analyses (although the effects in co-occurring depression and substance use disorders were small and nonsignificant; Pott et al., 2022).

All of the previous meta-analyses focused on BA in groups and guided self-help, but none focused on BA in individual psychotherapy. In this chapter, we conduct a meta-analysis of individual BA on distal, end-of-treatment outcomes.

Research Review

Identification and Selection of Studies

The current study is part of a larger meta-analytic project on psychological treatments of depression that was registered at the Open Science Framework (Cuijpers, Karyotaki, et al., 2020). Supplemental materials are available at the project's website (https://www.metapsy.org). This database has been used in a series of earlier published meta-analyses (Cuijpers, 2017).

The studies included in the current review were identified through the larger, already existing database of randomized trials on the psychological treatment of depression. For this database, we searched four major bibliographical databases (PubMed, PsycInfo, Embase, Cochrane Library) by combining terms (both index terms and text words) indicative of depression and psychotherapies, with filters for randomized controlled trials. The full search strings can be found at the project's website (www.metapsy.org). Furthermore, we checked the references of earlier meta-analyses on psychological treatments of depression. The database is continuously updated and was developed through a comprehensive literature search (from 1966 to January 1, 2022). All records were screened by two independent researchers, and all papers that could possibly meet inclusion criteria according to one of the researchers were retrieved as full text. The decision to include or exclude a study in the database was also done by the two independent researchers, and disagreements were resolved through discussion.

For this meta-analysis, we included randomized controlled trials in which BA for patients with depression were compared with a control condition (wait-list, care-as-usual, other). Depression could be defined as meeting criteria for a depressive disorder according to a diagnostic interview or as a score above the cutoff on a self-report depression measure. We only included trials in which BA was administered individually.

Quality Assessment and Data Extraction

We assessed the validity of included studies using four criteria of the Risk of Bias (RoB) assessment tool (Version 1, developed by Cochrane Collaboration; Higgins et al., 2011). The RoB tool assesses possible sources of bias in randomized trials, including the adequate generation of allocation sequence, the concealment of allocation to conditions, the prevention of knowledge of the allocated intervention (masking of assessors), and dealing with incomplete outcome data (this was assessed as positive when intention-to-treat analyses were conducted, meaning that all randomized patients were included in the analyses). Assessment of the validity of the included studies was conducted by two independent researchers, and disagreements were solved through discussion.

We coded participant characteristics (diagnostic method, recruitment method, target group, mean age, proportion of women), characteristics of BA (number of sessions), as well as general characteristics of the studies (type of control group, publication year, country where the study was conducted).

Outcome Measures

For each comparison between BA and a control condition, the effect size indicating the difference between the two groups at post-test in terms of distal outcomes (depressive symptoms) was calculated (Hedges' *g*; Hedges & Olkin, 1985). Effect sizes were calculated by subtracting (at post-test) the average score of the BA group from the average score of the control group and dividing the result by the pooled standard deviation. Because some studies had relatively small sample sizes, we corrected the effect size for small sample bias. When means and standard deviations were not reported, we calculated the effect size using dichotomous outcomes; if these were not available either, we used other statistics (e.g., *t* value or *p* value) to calculate the effect size.

Meta-Analyses

The meta-analyses were conducted with the meta packages in R (Version 4.1.1) and R studio (Version 1.1.463 for Mac). The metapsyTools package (Harrer et al., 2021) was specifically developed for the meta-analytic project of which this study is a part.

We calculated the pooled effect sizes in several different ways so that we could explore if different methods of pooling outcomes resulted in different outcomes. We pooled all outcomes within a study, before pooling across studies. To pool effect sizes within studies, an intra-study correlation coefficient of $\rho = 0.5$ was assumed. This method of pooling the effect sizes was the main method of analyses. We also conducted several sensitivity analyses. The details of these analyses are given later in Table 21.2, in which the results of each of these analyses, as well as a brief explanation of the exact method, are provided.

Random effects models were conducted in which the between-study heterogeneity variance was estimated using the restricted maximum likelihood method. We applied the Knapp–Hartung method to obtain robust confidence intervals and significance tests of the overall effect (IntHout et al., 2014). As a test of homogeneity of effect sizes, we calculated the I^2 statistic and its 95% confidence interval (CI), which is an indicator of heterogeneity in percentages. A value of 0% indicates no observed heterogeneity, and larger values indicate increasing heterogeneity, with 25% as low, 50% as moderate, and 75% as high heterogeneity (Higgins et al., 2003). Because I^2 cannot be interpreted as an absolute measure of the between-study heterogeneity, we also added the prediction interval, which indicates the range in which the true effect size of 95% of all populations will fall (Borenstein et al., 2009, 2017).

In addition to Hedges' *g*, we also calculated the numbers needed to treat (NNT; Furukawa, 1999), in which the control group's event rate was set at a conservative 17% (based on the pooled response rate of 50% reduction of symptoms across trials in psychotherapy for depression; 0).

In addition to calculating the effect size after adjustment for publication bias trim and fill procedure, we tested for publication bias by inspecting the funnel plot on primary outcome measures and by Egger's test of the intercept to quantify the bias captured by the funnel plot and to test whether it was significant.

Because the number of included studies was low and subgroup analyses usually have low statistical power (Cuijpers, Griffin, et al., 2021), we conducted only a small number of subgroup analyses that we considered essential: type of control group, diagnosed mood disorder versus a cutoff on a self-report measure, recruitment method, adults in general versus a more specific target group, and risk of bias (low vs. other).

Results

Selection and Inclusion of Studies

After examining a total of 30,889 records (21,563 after removal of duplicates), we retrieved 3,584 full-text papers for further consideration. We excluded 3,563 of the retrieved papers. The Preferred Reporting Items for Systematic Reviews and Meta-Analyses (PRISMA) flowchart describing the inclusion process, including the reasons for exclusion, is presented in Figure 21.2. A total of 22 randomized controlled trials with 819 patients (399 in the BA conditions and 420 in the control conditions) met inclusion criteria for this meta-analysis.

Characteristics of Included Studies

A summary of key characteristics of the 22 included studies is presented in Table 21.1. In 7 trials, participants met criteria for a depressive disorder according to a diagnostic interview, whereas the other 15 trials included participants who scored above a cutoff on a self-report depression scale. In 13 studies, usual care was used as control group, 5 studies used a wait-list control group, and the 4 remaining studies used another control group. Ten studies were conducted in the United States, 6 in Europe, and 6 in other countries. The number of sessions ranged from 1 to 24, with the majority (18 interventions) between 4 and 12 sessions.

Sixteen of the 22 studies reported that the random numbers were generated correctly (adequate sequence generation; 73%); 11 reported allocation to conditions by an independent party (50%); four reported using blinded outcome assessors (18%), whereas 14 used only self-report outcomes (64%). In 17 studies, intent-to-treat analyses were conducted (77%). Nine studies (41%) met all criteria for low risk of bias, nine other studies (41%) met two or three criteria, and four studies met only one criterion (18%).

Distal Outcomes for Individual Behavioral Activation on Depression

The results of the meta-analysis according to the different models are presented in Table 21.2. The forest plot is given in Figure 21.3. The main analyses indicated a large effect of BA on depression compared with control groups. Hedges' g was 0.85 (95% CI: 0.57, 1.1), which corresponds to an NNT of 3.48. Heterogeneity was high (75%; 95% CI: 62, 83), and the prediction interval was broad (−0.25, 1.94).

The majority of the other models indicated comparable pooled outcomes for BA, with only small differences from the main model. The overall outcomes of individual BA on distal, end-of-treatment outcomes were robust. However, the effect size was considerably smaller when only studies with low risk of bias were considered, although the effect size was still significant ($g = 0.56$; 95% CI: 0.09, 1.03). Heterogeneity was still high in these analyses ($I^2 = 80\%$; 95% CI: 66, 89; prediction interval: −0.85, 1.98). Excluding outliers and influential cases did not reduce heterogeneity much.

We also found significant indications for publication bias. Egger's test was significant ($p = .02$), and the effect size was considerably reduced after adjusting through trim and fill procedure ($g = 0.60$; 95% CI: 0.29, 0.92). Heterogeneity was still high after this adjustment ($I^2 = 79\%$; 95% CI: 70, 85; prediction interval: −0.85, 2.06).

Table 21.1 Selected Characteristics of Randomized Trials Comparing Individual Behavioral Activation to Control Groups

Study	Diagnosis	N_{int}	N_{ctr}	N_{sess}	Control	Mean Age (Years)	Proportion of Women	Recruitment	Target Group	SG	AC	BA	ITT	RoB	Country
Choi, 2020	Self-report	90	94	5	Other	69	0.73	Other	Elderly	+	–	–	+	2	United States
Chowdhary et al. (2016)	Self-report	24	31	7	CAU	41	0.69	Other	Adults	+	–	sr	+	3	India
Dimidjian et al. (2006)	Diagnosed mood disorder	43	53	24	Other	40	0.66	Community	Adults	+	–	sr	+	3	United States
Dimidjian et al. (2017)	Self-report	86	77	10	CAU	29	1.00	Other	Perinatal	+	+	sr	+	4	United States
Ekers et al. (2011)	Diagnosed mood disorder	23	24	12	WL	45	0.62	Clinical	Adults	+	+	sr	+	4	United Kingdom
Funderburk et al. (2021)	Self-report	68	72	4	CAU	53	0.09	Clinical	Veterans	–	+	sr	+	3	United States
Gawrysiak et al. (2009)	Self-report	14	16	1	CAU	18	0.80	Community	Students	–	–	sr	+	2	United States
Hemanny et al. (2019)	Diagnosed mood disorder	24	26	12	CAU	40	0.86	Community	Adults	+	–	+	+	3	Brazil
Jordans et al. (2019)	Diagnosed mood disorder	60	60	4	CAU	nr	0.85	Other	Adults	+	+	sr	+	4	Nepal
Kanter et al. (2015)	Diagnosed mood disorder	21	22	8	CAU	38	0.79	Clinical	Minority	+	–	sr	+	3	United States

McIndoo et al. (2016)	Self-report	16	14	4	WL	19	0.62	Community	Students	+	–	–	+	2	United States
Nasrin et al. (2017)	Diagnosed mood disorder	19	17	1	WL	36	0.59	Clinical	Adults	+	+	sr	–	3	United Kingdom
Pagoto et al. (2013)	Diagnosed mood disorder	68	76	18	Other	46	1.00	Community	Over-weight women	+	+	+	+	4	United States
Patel et al. (2017)	Self-report	230	236	6	CAU	43	0.77	Clinical	Adults	+	+	sr	+	4	India
Raue et al. (2019)	Self-report	8	10	12	CAU	76	0.83	Other	Elderly	–	–	–	–	0	United States
Richards et al. (2018)	Self-report	15	14	8	CAU	65	0.48	Other	General medical patients	+	+	sr	+	4	United Kingdom
Taylor& Marshall (1977)	Self-report	7	7	6	WL	22	0.71	Community	Students	–	–	sr	–	1	Canada
Thomas et al. (2019)	Self-report	15	12	8	CAU	66	0.40	Community	General medical patients	+	+	sr	+	4	United Kingdom
Turner et al. (1979)	Self-report	17	17	5	CAU	25	0.50	Community	Adults	–	–	sr	–	1	United States
Vázquez et al. (2017)	Self-report	22	19	4	CAU	58	0.93	Other	Caregivers	+	+	sr	+	4	Europe
Vázquez et al. (2020)	Self-report	70	80	4	CAU	55	0.96	Other	Caregivers	+	+	sr	+	4	Europe
Wilson et al. (1983)	Self-report	8	9	8	WL	40	0.80	Community	Adults	–	–	sr	–	1	Australia

AC, allocation concealment; MA: masking of assessors; CAU, care-as-usual; ITT, intention-to-treat analyses; N_{ctr}, number of participants in the control group; N_{int}, number of participants in the intervention group; N_{sess}, number of sessions; nr, ; RoB, risk of bias total score; SG, sequence generation; sr, self-report; WL, wait list.

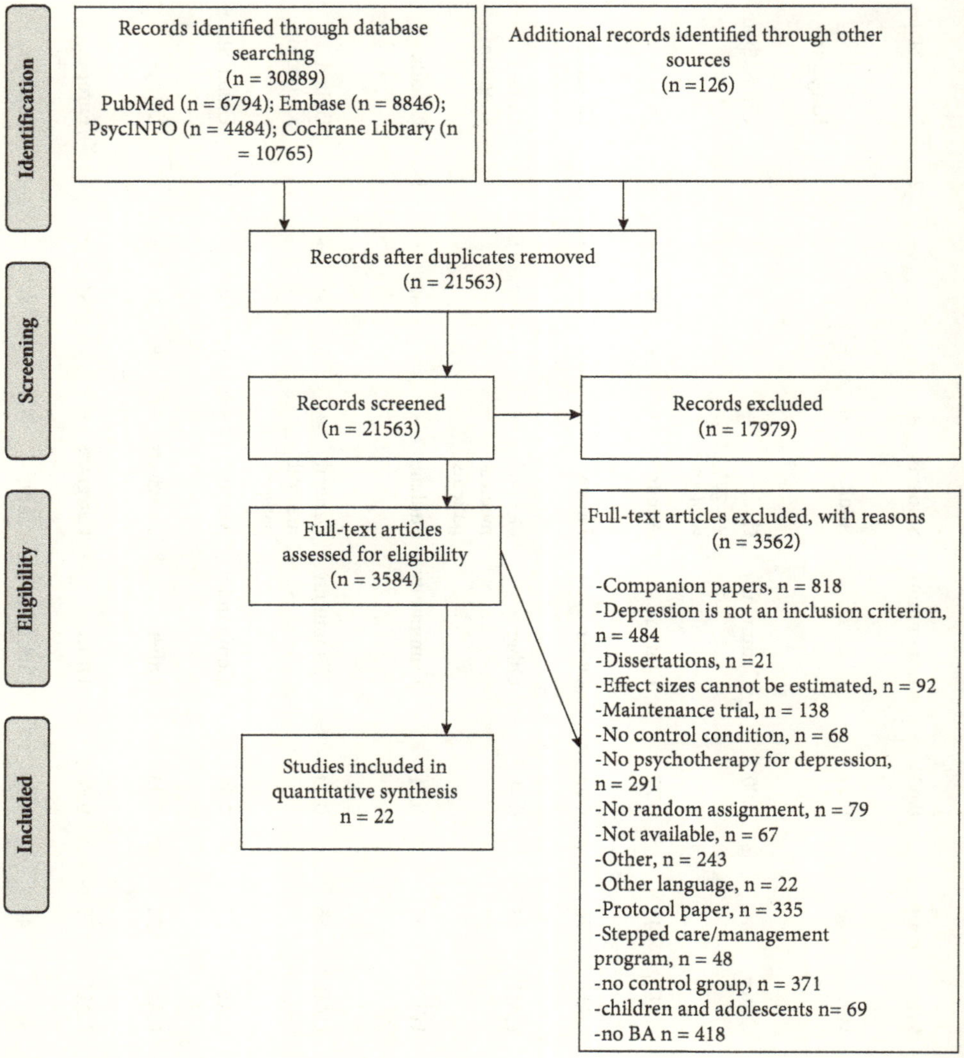

Figure 21.2 PRISMA flow diagram.

The results of the subgroup analyses are reported in Table 21.3. We found a significant difference between studies using different types of control groups ($p < .001$). Studies that used a wait-list control had a considerably larger effect size than studies using usual care or other groups. The other subgroup analyses examined the type of control group, diagnosis (mood disorder vs. scoring above a cutoff), recruitment, target group, and risk of bias. None of these analyses pointed at significant differences between subgroups.

Summary

This meta-analysis shows that individual BA has significant end-of-treatment effects on depression. Although these effects may be somewhat overestimated because of publication bias and the suboptimal quality of several trials, the effects are still statistically

Table 21.2 The Effects of Individual Behavioral Activation for Depression According to Different Models

Model	*k*	*g*	CI	I^2	CI	PI	NNT
Main outcomes[a]	22	0.83	[0.55, 1.1]	76.05	[63.92, 84.1]	[−0.28, 1.93]	3.57
Three-level model (CHE)[b]	30	0.82	[0.54, 1.1]	83.10	—	[−0.34, 1.99]	3.60
One effect size per study (lowest effect size)	22	0.76	[0.46, 1.06]	76.27	[64.29, 84.23]	[−0.44, 1.96]	3.95
One effect size per study (highest effect size)	22	0.87	[0.58, 1.16]	75.50	[63.01, 83.78]	[−0.26, 2.01]	3.35
Outliers removed[c]	25	0.82	[0.62, 1.02]	64.27	[45.29, 76.67]	[0.04, 1.6]	3.59
Influence analysis[d]	30	0.82	[0.57, 1.07]	74.01	[62.85, 81.82]	[−0.3, 1.94]	3.62
Adjusted for publication bias[e]	28	0.60	[0.29, 0.92]	78.60	[69.6, 84.9]	[−0.85, 2.06]	5.22
Only studies with low risk of bias	11	0.56	[0.09, 1.03]	80.46	[65.94, 88.79]	[−0.85, 1.98]	5.62
Assuming independence of effects[f]	30	0.82	[0.57, 1.07]	74.01	[62.85, 81.82]	[−0.3, 1.94]	3.62

[a]When one study had more effect sizes, these were pooled within the study before pooling across studies.

[b]Outcomes according to a multilevel (three-level) model (effect sizes nested in studies), using the three-level correlated and hierarchical effects model (Pustejovsky & Tipton, 2022); parameter tests and confidence intervals of which are also calculated using robust variance estimation to guard against model misspecification. We assumed an intra-study correlation of $\rho = 0.5$. For this model, we calculated a multilevel extension of I^2, describing the total variability attributable to heterogeneity within studies (Level 2) and heterogeneity between studies (Level 3) (Cheung, 2014; Harrer et al., 2021).

[c]Outliers were excluded with the non-overlapping confidence intervals approach, in which a study is defined as an outlier when the 95% CI of the effect size does not overlap with the 95% CI of the pooled effect size (Harrer et al., 2021).

[d]The pooled effect size with influential cases excluded (Viechtbauer & Cheung, 2010).

[e]Adjustment according to the trim and fill procedure (Duval & Tweedie, 2000).

[f]Effect sizes were pooled as if they are all independent of each other and not clustered within studies.

NNT, number needed to treat; PI, prediction interval.

significant and clinically meaningful after adjusting for these problems. The type of control group also affected the effect size, with waiting lists possibly overestimating the actual effects, which is in line with previous research on psychotherapies for depression (Cuijpers, Quero, et al., 2021; Furukawa et al., 2014). However, several sensitivity analyses indicated that the effects found for BA are robust.

Immediate In-Session and Intermediate Outcomes for Behavioral Activation

Minimal research has focused on in-session outcomes of BA. In one study examining in-session outcomes of BA (Santos et al., 2017), it was found that in 79% of the patients

Study	Comparison	Instrument	g	S.E.
Choi, 2020	bat vs. other ctr	hdrs	0.65	0.1513
Chowdhary, 2016	bat vs. cau	bdi-1	0.45	0.2754
Dimidjian, 2006	bat vs. other ctr	hdrs	0.96	0.2458
Dimidjian, 2017	bat vs. cau	phq-9	0.33	0.1715
Ekers, 2011	bat vs. wl	bdi-2	1.15	0.3552
Funderburk, 2021	bat vs. cau	phq-9	0.22	0.1687
Gawrysiak, 2009	bat vs. cau	bdi-2	1.66	0.4269
Hemanny, 2019	bat vs. cau	hdrs	1.29	03118
Jordans, 2019	bat vs. cau	phq-9	0.41	0.1845
Kanter, 2015	bat vs. cau	hdrs	0.19	0.3058
Mclndoo, 2016	bat vs. wl	hdrs	1.36	0.4082
Nasrin, 2017	bat vs. wl	phq-9	1.74	0.3944
Pagoto, 2013	bat vs. other ctr	hdrs	0.30	0.1929
Patel, 2017	bat vs. cau	bdi-2	0.52	0.0942
Raue, 2019	bat vs. cau	hdrs	0.79	0.5634
Richards, 2018	bat vs. cau	bdi-2	−0.42	0.3897
Taylor, 1977	bat vs. wl	bdi-1	1.63	0.6272
Thomas, 2019	bat vs. cau	phq-9	0.70	0.3313
Turner, 1979	bat vs. other ctr		1.45	0.5326
Vazquez, 2017	bat vs. cau	ces-d	2.03	0.3877
Vazquez, 2020	bat vs. cau	ces-d	1.25	0.1791
Wilson, 1983	bat vs. wl	hdrs	1.83	0.5874
RE Model				
95% PI				

Heterogeneity: $\chi^2_{21} = 84.04$ ($P < .001$), $I^2 = 75\%$

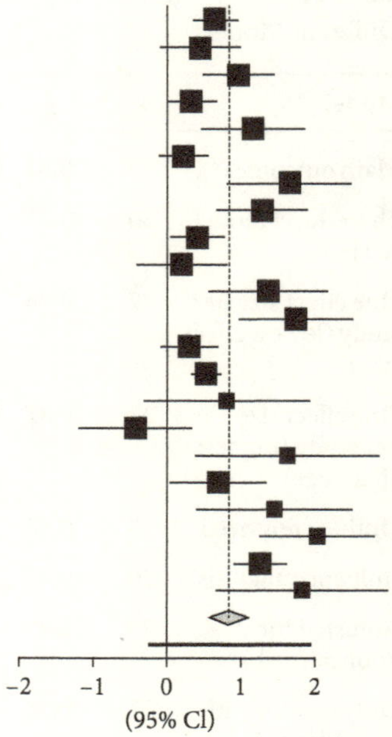

Figure 21.3 Forest plot.

Table 21.3 Subgroup Analyses

	k	*g*	CI	I^2	CI	NNT	
Control group							
Usual care	13	0.69	[0.31, 1.08]	78.7	[64.1, 87.3]	4.43	<0.001
Wait list	5	1.47	[1.11, 1.83]	0	[0, 79.2]	1.90	
Other	4	0.70	[0.06, 1.34]	58.2	[0, 86.1]	4.35	
Diagnosis							
Mood	7	0.81	[0.29, 1.33]	73.6	[43.4, 87.7]	3.67	0.81
Cutoff	15	0.87	[0.5, 1.25]	77.2	[62.6, 86]	3.37	
Recruitment							
Community	9	1.11	[0.71, 1.51]	62	[21.5, 81.6]	2.55	0.25
Clinical	5	0.70	[−0.09, 1.49]	76.5	[42.8, 90.4]	4.35	
Other	8	0.68	[0.1, 1.25]	81.2	[64, 90.2]	4.50	
Target group							
Adults in general	9	0.95	[0.55, 1.35]	69	[37.9, 84.5]	3.05	0.46
Other	13	0.76	[0.35, 1.18]	79.3	[65.3, 87.7]	3.95	
Risk of bias							
Low	9	0.68	[0.17, 1.18]	81.4	[65.7, 89.9]	4.50	0.27
Other	13	0.98	[0.63, 1.34]	68.9	[44.8, 82.5]	2.94	

NNT, number needed to treat.

participating in BA, changes in activation preceded or co-occurred with changes in depression, whereas this was not the case in patients receiving usual care. In another study, it was found that sudden gains predicted lower depression scores after treatment (O'Mahen et al., 2017) and that participants with higher social functioning at baseline, who did not experience a stressful life event during therapy, and who completed more online modules were more likely to have a sudden gain. It was also found in this study that therapists focused on specific, concrete content more in the session preceding the sudden gain than in the yoked sessions with women who did not have sudden gains. However, a more concrete therapist focus was only associated with having a sudden gain, not with the outcome on depressive symptoms at post-test. In another study of BA, it was found that enactment of activities was significantly related to the likelihood of remission at post-treatment and of maintaining improvement at 3-month follow-up (Meeks et al., 2019). More research is clearly needed to understand in-session processes and outcomes of BA.

Possible Negative Effects and Harms

Unfortunately, minimal research has focused on the negative effects of BA. Some of the trials in our meta-analysis report negative effects in patients receiving BA. Ekers and colleagues (2011) reported that none of the patients receiving BA deteriorated, whereas 16% in patients receiving usual care deteriorated. In another study (Funderbunk et al., 2021), the symptoms worsened in 10% of participants receiving BA, whereas 7% worsened in the control group. Other studies also reported serious adverse events (Patel et al., 2017; Raue et al., 2019; Richards et al., 2018; Thomas et al., 2019), but these numbers are very low (<5%) and in most cases not related to the treatment, such as hospital admissions, or equally divided across the treatment and control groups. Because of the small number of trials reporting negative effects, it is unfortunately not possible to make a reliable estimate of the proportion of patients who deteriorate during BA. Meta-analyses of psychotherapies in general show that this proportion is low and significantly smaller in treatment than in control conditions (Cuijpers et al., 2018; Cuijpers, Karyotaki, et al., 2021).

Diversity Considerations

The studies included in our meta-analysis varied considerably in terms of target samples. Only six of the 22 studies were aimed at adults in general, whereas one study was specifically aimed at Latinos in the United States (Kanter et al., 2015), one at veterans (Funderbunk et al., 2021), one at women with obesity (Pagoto et al., 2013), two at older adults (Choi et al., 2020; Raue et al., 2019), two at college students (Gawrysiak et al., 2009; McIndoo et al., 2016), two at nonprofessional caregivers (Vázquez et al., 2017, 2020), and two at patients with comorbid general medical disorders (Richards et al., 2018; Thomas et al., 2019). Although most studies were conducted in the United States and Europe, four studies were conducted in low- and middle-income countries, two in India (Chowdhary et al., 2016; Patel et al., 2017), one in Nepal (Jordans et al., 2019), and one in Brazil (Hemanny et al., 2019). There were not enough studies in each of these specific groups to examine whether the effect sizes differed from those in other groups.

Limitations of the Research

The number of trials examining the effects of individual BA is relatively small, and the quality of many of these trials is suboptimal. Although our meta-analysis indicated significant effects of individual BA treatment packages on distal outcomes, these results should be considered with caution because of the modest number and the low quality of these trials. However, overall individual BA is effective in the treatment of depression, and previous research has shown that there are few indications that BA is less effective than other methods.

We know that the entire BA treatment package works on distal outcomes, but we know little of its effects on immediate session or intermediate outcomes. Virtually all of the research conducted has focused on distal, end-of-treatment outcomes.

Nor do we know which of the components of BA are responsible for its salutatory impact. The science has not made enough progress to determine which of the components prove necessary. Research on working mechanisms and mediators of therapies has mostly been correlational, and currently, no mechanism of BA or any other therapy has been sufficiently empirically validated (Cuijpers, Reijnders, et al., 2019). Therefore, it is still unknown how BA works. Additional research using additive or dismantling designs is probably necessary.

Training Implications

Individual BA is a relatively easy treatment, and its principles are easily understood by patients and clinicians. The COBRA trial in the United Kingdom showed that BA can effectively be delivered by junior mental health workers, and other trials have shown that it can be effectively delivered by lay health counselors (e.g., Jordans et al., 2019; Patel et al., 2017). BA is also one of the components of several therapies that are delivered by lay health counselors in low- and middle-income countries, such as Problem Management Plus developed by the World Health Organization (2016).

Research has found that BA can be effectively trained using resource-sensitive and -accessible methods, such as online modular training. In one study, an online modular, active learning model for training community mental health professionals in the use of BA was examined (Puspitasari et al., 2013). In a within-subject design with eight participants, trainees reported increased implementation of BA methods in actual sessions. In a second study, the same online learning package was improved by incorporating more active learning strategies to the training protocol (Puspitasari et al., 2013). Also, a role-play to assess BA was added for a more objective rather than self-report measure of trainees' performance. Results of the second study indicated that the skills at implementing two of the three core BA methods (providing the rationale and activity scheduling) increased significantly in the nine participants. Their performance was maintained at follow-up. In both studies, participants reported high satisfaction with the training.

Therapeutic Practices

- Consider conducting individual BA for the treatment of adult depression.
- Add BA to your clinical repertoire because it is as effective as other psychotherapies for depression, such as CBT and interpersonal psychotherapy. It can be used briefly in a few sessions as part of a more extensive treatment package or more extensively as an independent treatment.
- Use BA especially in severe depression, when more insight-oriented therapies are not feasible, because it is a straightforward method that can be used across severity levels.
- Conduct more clinical and diagnostic evaluations in cases of comorbidity because there is no evidence whether BA is also effective with comorbid disorders.
- Identify patients' pleasant and unpleasant activities, monitor such activities, and conduct activity scheduling.
- Account for the personal preferences and cultural identities of patients because BA is flexible and can be adapted to patients' situations and needs.
- Do not stop too soon with BA when patients experience problems in changing behavior. First try to motivate patients and solve problems in the application.

References

* Studies included in the meta-analysis.

Acierno, R., Kauffman, B., Muzzy, W., Tejada, M. H., & Lejuez, C. (2021). Behavioral activation and therapeutic exposure vs. cognitive therapy for grief among combat veterans: A randomized clinical trial of bereavement interventions. *American Journal of Hospice and Palliative Medicine*, *38*, 1470–1478.

Beck, A. T., Rush, A. J., Shaw, B. F., & Emery, G. (1979). *Cognitive therapy of depression*. Guilford.

Beck, A. T., Steer, R. A., & Brown, G. K. (1996). *Manual for the Beck Depression Inventory–II*. Psychological Corporation.

Beck, A. T., Ward, C. H., Mendelson, M., Mock, J., & Erbaugh, J. (1961). An inventory for measuring depression. *Archives of General Psychiatry*, *4*, 561–571.

Borenstein, M., Hedges, L. V., Higgins, J. P. T., & Rothstein, H. R. (2009). *Introduction to meta-analysis*. Wiley.

Borenstein, M., Higgins, J. P. T., Hedges, L. V., & Rothstein, H. R. (2017). Basics of meta-analysis: I^2 is not an absolute measure of heterogeneity. *Research Synthesis Methods*, *8*, 5–18.

Cheung, M. W. L. (2014). Modeling dependent effect sizes with three-level meta-analyses: A structural equation modeling approach. *Psychological Methods*, *19*, 211–229.

*Choi, N. G., Marti, C. N., Wilson, N. L., Chen, G. J., Sirrianni, L., Hegel, M. T., Bruce, M. B., & Kunik, M. E. (2020). Effect of telehealth treatment by lay counselors vs by clinicians on depressive symptoms among older adults who are homebound: A randomized clinical trial. *JAMA Network Open*, *3*, e2015648.

Chorpita, B. F., Yim, L. M., Moffitt, C. E., Umemoto L. A., & Francis, S. E. (2000). Assessment of symptoms of DSM-IV anxiety and depression in children: A Revised Child Anxiety and Depression Scale. *Behaviour Research and Therapy*, *38*, 835–855.

*Chowdhary, N., Anand, A., Dimidjian, S., Shinde, S., Weobong, B., Balaji, M., Hollon, S., Rahman, A., Wilson, G., Verdeli, H., Araya, R., King, M., Jordans, M., Fairburn, C., Kirkwood, B., & Patel, V. (2016). The Healthy Activity Program lay counsellor delivered treatment for severe depression in India: Systematic development and randomised evaluation. *British Journal of Psychiatry, 208*, 381–388.

Ciharova, M., Furukawa, T. A., Efthimiou, O., Karyotaki, E., Miguel, C., Noma, H., Cipriani, A., Riper, H., & Cuijpers, P. (2021). Cognitive restructuring, behavioral activation and cognitive-behavioral therapy in the treatment of adult depression: A network meta-analysis. *Journal of Consulting and Clinical Psychology, 89*, 563–574.

Cuijpers, P. (2017). Four decades of outcome research on psychotherapies for adult depression: An overview of a series of meta-analyses. *Canadian Psychology, 58*, 7–19.

Cuijpers, P., Cristea, I. A., Karyotaki, E., Reijnders, M., & Hollon, S. D. (2019). Component studies of psychological treatments of adult depression: A systematic review and meta-analysis. *Psychotherapy Research, 29*, 15–29.

Cuijpers, P., Griffin, J. W., & Furukawa, T. A. (2021). The lack of statistical power of subgroup analyses in meta-analyses: A cautionary note. *Epidemiology and Psychiatric Sciences, 30*, e78.

Cuijpers, P., Karyotaki, E., Ciharova, M., Miguel, C., Noma, H., & Furukawa, T. A. (2021). The effects of psychotherapies for depression on response, remission, reliable change, and deterioration: A meta-analysis. *Acta Psychiatrica Scandinavica, 144*, 288–299

Cuijpers, P., Karyotaki, E., de Wit, L., & Ebert, D. D. (2020). The effects of fifteen evidence-supported therapies for adult depression: A meta-analytic review. *Psychotherapy Research, 30*, 279–293.

Cuijpers, P., Muñoz, R. F., Clarke, G. N., & Lewinsohn, P. M. (2009). Psychoeducational treatment and prevention of depression: The "Coping with Depression" course thirty years later. *Clinical Psychology Review, 29*, 449–458.

Cuijpers, P., Noma, H., Karyotaki, E., Cipriani, A., & Furukawa, T. (2019). Individual, group, telephone, self-help and internet-based cognitive behavior therapy for adult depression; A network meta-analysis of delivery methods. *JAMA Psychiatry, 76*, 700–707.

Cuijpers, P., Noma, H., Karyotaki, E., Vinkers, C. H., Cipriani, A., & Furukawa, T. A. (2020). A network meta-analysis of the effects of psychotherapies, pharmacotherapies and their combination in the treatment of adult depression. *World Psychiatry, 19*, 92–107.

Cuijpers, P., Quero, S., Noma, H., Ciharova, M., Miguel, C., Karyotaki, E., Cipriani, A., Cristea, I., & Furukawa, T. A. (2021). Psychotherapies for depression: A network meta-analysis covering efficacy, acceptability and long-term outcomes of all main treatment types. *World Psychiatry, 20*, 283–293.

Cuijpers, P., Reijnders, M., & Huibers, M. J. H. (2019). The role of common factors in psychotherapy outcome. *Annual Review of Clinical Psychology, 15*, 207–231.

Cuijpers, P., Reijnders, M., Karyotaki, E., de Wit, L., & Ebert, D. D. (2018). Negative effects of psychotherapies for adult depression: A meta-analysis of deterioration rates. *Journal of Affective Disorders, 239*, 138–145.

Dimidjian, S., Barrera, M., Martell, C., Muñoz, R. F., & Lewinsohn, P. M. (2011). The origins and current status of behavioral activation treatments for depression. *Annual Review of Clinical Psychology, 7*, 1–38.

*Dimidjian, S., Goodman, S., Sherwood, N., Simon, G., Ludman, E., Gallop, R., Shaw Welch, S., Boggs, J., Metcalf, C., Hubley, S., Powers, D., & Beck, A. (2017). A pragmatic randomized clinical trial of behavioral activation for depressed pregnant women. *Journal of Consulting and Clinical Psychology, 85*, 26–36.

*Dimidjian, S., Hollon, S. D., Dobson, K. S., Schmaling, K. B., Kohlenberg, R. J., Addis, M. E., Gallop, R., McGlinchey, J., Markley, D., Gollan, J., Atkins, D., Dunner, D., & Jacobson, N. (2006). Randomized trial of behavioral activation, cognitive therapy, and antidepressant medication in the acute treatment of adults with major depression. *Journal of Consulting and Clinical Psychology, 74*, 658–670.

Dimidjian, S., Hubley, S., Martell, C., Herman, R., & Dobson, K. (n.d.). Quality of Behavioral Activation Scale [Unpublished manuscript]. University of Colorado Boulder.

Duval, S., & Tweedie, R. (2000). Trim and fill: A simple funnel-plot-based method of testing and adjusting for publication bias in meta-analysis. *Biometrics, 56*, 455–463.

*Ekers, D., Richards, D., McMillan, D., Bland, J. M., & Gilbody, S. (2011). Behavioural activation delivered by the non-specialist: Phase II randomised controlled trial. *British Journal of Psychiatry, 198*, 66–72.

Fazzino, T. L., Lejuez, C. W., & Yi, R. (2020). A behavioral activation intervention administered in a 16-week freshman orientation course: Study protocol. *Contemporary Clinical Trials, 90*, 105950.

Ferster, C. B. (1973). A functional analysis of depression. *American Psychologist, 28*, 857–870.

First, M. B., Williams, J. B. W., Karg, R. S., & Spitzer, R. L. (2015). *Structured Clinical Interview for DSM-5–Research Version (SCID-5 for DSM-5, Research Version; SCID-5-RV)*. American Psychiatric Association.

*Funderburk, J. S., Pigeon, W. R., Shepardson, R. L., Wadea, M., Ackera, J., Fivecoat, H., Wray, L. O., & Maisto, S. A. (2021). Treating depressive symptoms among veterans in primary care: A multi-site RCT of brief behavioral activation. *Journal of Affective Disorders, 283*, 11–19.

Furukawa, T. A. (1999). From effect size into number needed to treat. *Lancet, 353*, 1680.

Furukawa, T. A., Noma, H., Caldwell, D. M., Honyashiki, M., Shinohara, K., Imai, H., Chen, P., Hunot, V., & Churchill, R. (2014). Waiting list may be a nocebo condition in psychotherapy trials: A contribution from network meta-analysis. *Acta Psychiatrica Scandinavica, 130*, 181–192.

*Furukawa, T. A., Shinohara, K., Sahker, E., Karyotaki, E., Miguel, C., Ciharova, M., Bockting, C. L. H., Breedvelt, J. J. F., Tajika, A., Imai, H., Ostinelli, E. G., Sakata, M., Toyomoto, R., Kishimoto, S., Ito, M., Furukawa, Y., Cipriani, A., Hollon, S. D., & Cuijpers, P. (2021). Initial treatment choices to achieve sustained response in major depression: A systematic review and network meta-analysis. *World Psychiatry, 20*, 387–396.

*Gawrysiak, M., Nicholas, C., & Hopko, D. R. (2009). Behavioral activation for moderately depressed university students: Randomized controlled trial. *Journal of Counseling Psychology, 56*, 468–475.

Hamilton, M. (1960). A rating scale for depression. *Journal of Neurology, Neurosurgery and Psychiatry, 23*, 56–62.

Harrer, M., Cuijpers, P., Furukawa, T. A., & Ebert, D. D. (2021). *Doing meta-analysis in R: A practical guide*. Protect Lab, Friedrich-Alexander University Erlangen-Nuremberg.

Hedges, L. V., & Olkin, I. (1985). *Statistical methods for meta-analysis*. Academic Press.

*Hemanny, C., Carvalho, C., Maia, N., Reis, D., Botelho, A. C., Bonavides, D., Seixas, C., & de Oliveira, I. (2020). Efficacy of trial-based cognitive therapy, behavioral activation and treatment as usual in the treatment of major depressive disorder: Preliminary findings from a randomized clinical trial. *CNS Spectrums, 25*, 535–544. doi:10.1017/S1092852919001457

Herrman, H., Patel, V., Kieling, C., Berk, M., Buchweitz, C., Cuijpers, P., Furukawa, T., Kessler, R., Kohrt, B., Maj, M., McGorry, P., Reynolds, C., 3rd, Weissman, M., Chibanda, D., Dowrick, C., Howard, L., Hoven, C., Knapp, M., Mayberg, H., . . . Wolpert, M. (2022). Time for united action on depression: A Lancet–World Psychiatric Association Commission. *Lancet, 399*(10328), 857–1022. https://doi.org/10.1016/S0140-6736(21)02141-3

Higgins, J. P. T., Altman, D. G., Gøtzsche, P. C., Jüni, P., Moher, D., Oxman, A. D., Savovic, J., Schulz, K., Weeks, L., Sterne, J.; Cochrane Bias Methods Group; Cochrane Statistical Methods Group. (2011). The Cochrane Collaboration's tool for assessing risk of bias in randomised trials. *BMJ, 343*, d5928.

Higgins, J. P. T., Thompson, S. G., Deeks, J. J., & Altman, D. G. (2003). Measuring inconsistency in meta-analyses. *BMJ, 327*, 557–560.

Huguet, A., Miller, A., Kisely, S., Rao, S., Saadat, N., & McGrath, P. J. (2018). A systematic review and meta-analysis on the efficacy of internet-delivered behavioral activation. *Journal of Affective Disorders, 235*, 27–38.

Jacobson, N. S., Dobson, K. S., Truax, P. A., Addis, M. E., Koerner, K., Gollan, J. K., Gortner, E., & Prince, S. (1996). A component analysis of cognitive–behavioral treatment for depression. *Journal of Consulting and Clinical Psychology*, *85*(1), 26–36.

Jacobson, N. S., Martell, C. R., & Dimidjian, S. (2001). Behavioral activation treatment for depression: Returning to contextual roots. *Clinical Psychologist*, *8*, 255–270.

*Jordans, M. J. D., Luitel, N. P., Garman, E., Kohrt, B. A., Rathod, S. D., Shrestha, P., Kompoe, I., Lund, C., & Patel, V. (2019). Effectiveness of psychological treatments for depression and alcohol use disorder delivered by community-based counsellors: Two pragmatic randomised controlled trials within primary healthcare in Nepal. *British Journal of Psychiatry*, *215*, 485–493.

*Kanter, J. W., Mulick, P. S., Busch, A. M., Berlin, K. S., & Martell, C. R. (2007). The Behavioral Activation for Depression Scale (BADS): Psychometric properties and factor structure. *Journal of Psychopathology and Behavioral Assessment*, *29*, 191–202.

*Kanter, J. W., Santiago-Rivera, A. L., Santos, M. M., Nagy, G., López, M., Hurtado, G. D., & West, P. (2015). A randomized hybrid efficacy and effectiveness trial of behavioral activation for Latinos with depression. *Behavior Therapy*, *46*(2), 177–192.

Karyotaki, E., Efthimiou, O., Miguel, C., Maas genannt Bermpohl, F., Furukawa, T. A., & Cuijpers, P., for the Individual Patient Data Meta-Analyses for Depression (IPDMA-DE) Collaboration. (2021). Internet-based cognitive behavioral therapy for depression: An individual patient data network meta-analysis. *JAMA Psychiatry*, *78*, 361–371.

Karyotaki, E., Kemmeren, L., Riper, H., Twisk, J., Hoogendoorn, A., Kleiboer, A., Mira, A., Mackinnon, A., Meyer, B., Botella, C., Littlewood, E., Andersson, G., Christensen, H., Klein, J., Schroder, J., Breton-Lopez, J., Scheider, J., Griffiths, K., Farrer, L., . . . Cuijpers, P. (2018). Is self-guided internet-based cognitive behavioural therapy (iCBT) harmful? An individual participant data meta-analysis. *Psychological Medicine*, *48*(15), 2456–2466.

Karyotaki, E., Riper, H., Twisk, J., Hoogendoorn, A., Kleiboer, A., Mira, A., Mackinnon, A., Meyer, B., Botella, C., Littlewood, E., Andersson, G., Christensen, H., Klein, J., Schroder, J., Breton-Lopez, J., Scheider, J., Griffiths, K., Farrer, L., Huibers, M., . . . Cuijpers, P. (2017). Efficacy of self-guided internet-based cognitive behavioral therapy (iCBT) in treatment of depressive symptoms: An individual participant data meta-analysis. *JAMA Psychiatry*, *74*(4), 351–359.

Kovacs, M. (1985). The Children's Depression Inventory (CDI). *Psychopharmacology Bulletin*, *21*, 995–998.

Kroenke, K., Spitzer, R. L., & Williams, J. B. (2001). The PHQ-9: Validity of a brief depression severity measure. *Journal of General Internal Medicine*, *16*, 606–613.

Lejuez, C. W., Hopko, D. R., & Hopko, S. D. (2001). A brief behavioral activation treatment for depression treatment manual. *Behavior Modification*, *25*, 255–286.

Lejuez, C. W., Hopko, D. R., LePage, J. P., Hopko, S. D., & McNeil, D. W. (2001). A brief behavioral activation treatment for depression. *Cognitive and Behavioral Practice*, *8*, 164–175.

Lewinsohn, P. M. (1974). A behavioral approach to depression. In R. J. Friedman & M. M. Katz (Eds.), *The psychology of depression: Contemporary theory and research* (pp. 157–185). Winston-Wiley.

Lewinsohn, P. M., Mermelstein, R. M., Alexander, C., & MacPhillamy, D. J. (1985). The Unpleasant Events Schedule: A scale for the measurement of aversive events. *Journal of Clinical Psychology*, *41*, 483–498.

MacPhillamy, D. J., & Lewinsohn, P. M. (1982). The Pleasant Events Schedule: Studies on reliability, validity, and scale intercorrelation. *Journal of Consulting and Clinical Psychology*, *50*(3), 363–380.

Martell, C. R., Addis, M. E., & Jacobson, N. S. (2001). *Depression in context: Strategies for guided action*. Norton.

Mazzucchelli, T., Kane, R., & Rees, C. (2009). Behavioral activation treatments for depression in adults: A meta-analysis and review. *Clinical Psychology: Science and Practice*, *16*(4), 383–411.

McCauley, E., Gudmundsen, G., Schloredt, K., Martell, C., Rhew, I., Hubley, S., & Dimidjian, S. (2016). The Adolescent Behavioral Activation Program: Adapting behavioral activation as a treatment for depression in adolescence. *Journal of Clinical Child and Adolescent Psychology, 45*, 291–304.

*McIndoo, C. C., File, A. A., Preddy, T., Clark, C. G., & Hopko, D. R. (2016). Mindfulness-based therapy and behavioral activation: A randomized controlled trial with depressed college students. *Behaviour Research and Therapy, 77*, 118–128.

McNamara, K., & Horan, J. J. (1986). Experimental construct validity in the evaluation of cognitive and behavioral treatments for depression. *Journal of Counseling Psychology, 33*(1), 23–30.

Meeks, S., Van Haitsma, K., & Shryock, S. K. (2019). Treatment fidelity evidence for BE-ACTIV—a behavioral intervention for depression in nursing homes. *Aging and Mental Health, 23*, 1192–1202.

Mimiaga, M. J., Pantalone, D. W., Biello, K. B., White Hughto, J. M., Frank, J., O'Cleirigh, C., Reisner, S. L., Restar, A., Mayer, K. H., & Safren, S. A. (2019). An initial randomized controlled trial of behavioral activation for treatment of concurrent crystal methamphetamine dependence and sexual risk for HIV acquisition among men who have sex with men. *AIDS Care, 31*, 1083–1095.

Montgomery, S. A., & Åsberg, M. (1979). A new depression scale designed to be sensitive to change. *British Journal of Psychiatry, 134*, 382–389.

*Nasrin, F., Rimes, K., Reinecke, A., Rinck, M., & Barnhofer, T. (2017). Effects of brief behavioural activation on approach and avoidance tendencies in acute depression: Preliminary findings. *Behavioural and Cognitive Psychotherapy, 45*(1), 58–72.

O'Mahen, H. A., Wilkinson, E., Bagnall, K., Richards, D. A., & Swales, A. (2017). Shape of change in internet based behavioral activation treatment for depression. *Behaviour Research and Therapy, 95*, 107–116.

Orgeta, V., Brede, J., & Livingston, G. (2017). Behavioural activation for depression in older people: Systematic review and meta-analysis. *British Journal of Psychiatry, 211*(5), 274–279.

*Pagoto, S., Schneider, K. L., Whited, M. C., Oleski, J. L., Merriam, P., Appelhans, B., Ma, Y., Olendzk, B., Waring, M., Busch, A., Lemon, S., Ockene, I., & Crawford, S. (2013). Randomized controlled trial of behavioral treatment for comorbid obesity and depression in women: The Be Active Trial. International Journal of Obesity, 37, 1427–1434.

*Patel, V., Weobong, B., Weiss, H., Anand, A., Bhat, B., Katti, B., Dimidjian, S., Araya, R., Hollon, S., King, M., Vijayakumar, L., Park, A., McDaid, D., Wilson, T., Velleman, R., Kirkwood, B., & Fairburn, C. (2017). The Healthy Activity Program (HAP), a lay counsellor-delivered brief psychological treatment for severe depression, in primary care in India: A randomised controlled trial. *Lancet, 389*(10065), 176–185.

Pott, S. L., Delgadillo, J., & Kellett, S. (2022). Is behavioral activation an effective and acceptable treatment for co-occurring depression and substance use disorders? A meta-analysis of randomized controlled trials. *Journal of Substance Abuse Treatment, 132*, 108478.

Puig-Antich, J., & Chamber, W. (1978). *The Schedule for Affective Disorders and Schizophrenia for School-Age Children (Kiddie-SADS)*. New York State Psychiatric Institute.

Puspitasari, A., Kanter, J. W., Murphy, J., Crowe, A., & Koerner, K. (2013). Developing an online, modular, active learning training program for behavioral activation. *Psychotherapy, 50*(2), 256–265.

Pustejovsky, J. E., & Tipton, E. (2022). Meta-analysis with robust variance estimation: Expanding the range of working models. *Prevention Science, 23*, 425–438.

Radloff, L. S. (1977). The CES-D scale: A self-report depression scale for research in the general population. *Applied Psychological Measurement, 1*, 385–401.

*Raue, P. J., Sirey, J. A., Dawson, A., Berman, J., & Bruce, M. L. (2019). Lay-delivered behavioral activation for depressed senior center clients: Pilot RCT. *International Journal of Geriatric Psychiatry, 34*(11), 1715–1723.

Rehm, L. P. (1984). Self-management therapy for depression. *Advances in Behaviour Research and Therapy, 6*, 83–98.

Richards, D. A., Ekers, D., McMillan, D., Taylor, R. S., Byford, S., Warren, F. C., Barrett, B., Farrand, P. A., Gilbody, S., Kuyken, W., O'Mahen, H., Watkins, E. R., Wright, K. A., Hollon, S. D., Reed, N., Rhodes, S., Fletcher, E., & Finning, K. (2016). Cost and Outcome of Behavioural

Activation versus Cognitive Behavioural Therapy for Depression (COBRA): A randomised, controlled, non-inferiority trial. *Lancet, 388*(10047), 871–880.

*Richards, S. H., Dickens, C., Anderson, R., Richards, D. A., Taylor, R. S., Ukoumunne, O. C., Kessler, D., Turner, K., Kuyken, W., Gandhi, M., Knight, L., Gibson, A., Davey, A., Warren, F., Winder, R., Wright, C., & Campbell, J. (2018). Assessing the effectiveness of enhanced psychological care for patients with depressive symptoms attending cardiac rehabilitation compared with treatment as usual (CADENCE): A pilot cluster randomised controlled trial. *Trials, 17*, 59.

Robins, L. N., Wing, J., Wittchen, H. U., Helzer, J. E., Babor, T. F., Burke, J., Farmer, A., Jablenski, A., Pickens, R., Regier, D. A., Sartorius, N., & Towle, L. H. (1988). The Composite International Diagnostic Interview: An epidemiologic instrument suitable for use in conjunction with different diagnostic systems and in different cultures. *Archives of General Psychiatry, 45*, 1069–1077.

Santos, M. M., Rae, J. R., Nagy, G. A., Manbeck, K. E., Hurtado, G. D., West, P., Santiago-Rivera, A., & Kanter, J. W. (2017). A client-level session-by-session evaluation of behavioral activation's mechanism of action. *Journal of Behavior Therapy and Experimental Psychiatry, 54*, 93–100.

Sheehan, D. V., Lecrubier, Y., Sheehan, K. H., Amorim, P., Janavs, J., Weiller, E., Hergueta, T., Baker, R., & Dunbar, G. (1998). The Mini-International Neuropsychiatric Interview (M.I.N.I.): The development and validation of a structured diagnostic psychiatric interview for DSM-IV and ICD-10. *Journal of Clinical Psychiatry, 59*(Suppl. 20), 22–33.

Simmonds-Buckley, M., Kellett, S., & Waller, G. (2019). Acceptability and efficacy of group behavioral activation for depression among adults: A meta-analysis. *Behavior Therapy, 50*, 864–885.

Stein, A. T., Carl, E., Cuijpers, P., Karyotaki, E., & Smits, J. A. J. (2021). Looking beyond depression: A meta-analysis of the effect of behavioral activation on depression, anxiety, and activation. *Psychological Medicine, 51*(9), 1491–1504.

Suh, J. W., Lee, E. B., Han, Y., Lee, M. G., & Choi, K. H. (2021). The effects of brief behavioral activation (BA) on children with physical disabilities: A randomized controlled trial. *American Journal of Orthopsychiatry, 91*(1), 86–95.

*Taylor, F. G., & Marshall, W. L. (1977). Experimental analysis of a cognitive–behavioral therapy for depression. *Cognitive Therapy and Research, 1*(1), 59–72.

Teri, L., Logsdon, R. G., Uomoto, J., & McCuryy, S. M. (1997). Behavioral treatment of depression in dementia patients: A controlled clinical trial. *Journal of Gerontology: Psychological Sciences, 52B*, P159–P166.

*Thomas, S. A., Drummond, A. E., Lincoln, N. B., Palmer, R. L., das Nair, R., Latimer, N. R., Hackney, G., Mmandefield, L., Walters, S., Hatton, R., Cooper, C., Chater, T., England, T., Callaghan, P., Coates, E., Sutherland, K., Eshtan, S., & Topcu, G. (2019). Behavioural activation therapy for post-stroke depression: The BEADS feasibility RCT. *Health Technology Assessment, 23*(47), 1–176.

Tindall, L., Mikocka-Walus, A., McMillan, D., Wright, B., Hewitt, C., & Gascoyne, S. (2017). Is behavioural activation effective in the treatment of depression in young people? A systematic review and meta-analysis. *Psychology and Psychotherapy, 90*(4), 770–796.

*Turner, R. W., Ward, M. F., & Turner, D. J. (1979). Behavioral treatment for depression: An evaluation of therapeutic components. *Journal of Clinical Psychology, 35*(1), 166–175.

*Vázquez, F. L., López, L., Torres, Á. J., Otero, P., Blanco, V., Diaz, O., & Paramo, M. (2020). Analysis of the components of a cognitive–behavioral intervention for the prevention of depression administered via conference call to nonprofessional caregivers: A randomized controlled trial. *International Journal of Environmental Research and Public Health, 17*(6), 2067.

*Vázquez, F. L., Torres, Á., Otero, P., Blanco, V., Díaz, O., & Estévez, L. E. (2017). Analysis of the components of a cognitive–behavioral intervention administered via conference call for preventing depression among non-professional caregivers: A pilot study. *Aging and Mental Health, 21*(9), 938–946.

Viechtbauer, W., & Cheung, M. W. L. (2010). Outlier and influence diagnostics for meta-analysis. *Research Synthesis Methods, 1*, 112–125.

Wagner, A. W., Jakupcak, M., Kowalski, H. M., Bittinger, J. N., & Golshan, S. (2019). Behavioral activation as a treatment for posttraumatic stress disorder among returning veterans: A randomized trial. *Psychiatric Services, 70*(10), 867–873.

*Wilson, P. H., Goldin, J. C., & Charbonneau-Powis, M. (1983). Comparative efficacy of behavioral and cognitive treatments of depression. *Cognitive Therapy and Research, 7*(2), 111–124.

World Health Organization. (2016). *Problem Management Plus (PM+): Individual psychological help for adults impaired by distress in communities exposed to adversity.*

World Health Organization. (2017). *Depression and other common mental disorders: Global health estimates* (License: CC BY-NC-SA 3.0 IGO).

Yesavage, J. A., Brink, T. L., Rose, T. L., Lum, O., Huang, V., Adey, M., & Leirer, V. O. (1982). Development and validation of a geriatric depression screening scale: A preliminary report. *Journal of Psychiatric Research, 17*, 37–49.

Zabihi, S., Lemmel, F. K., & Orgeta, V. (2020). Behavioural activation for depression in informal caregivers: A systematic review and meta-analysis of randomised controlled clinical trials. *Journal of Affective Disorders, 274*, 1173–1183.

Zigmond, A. S., & Snaith, R. P. (1983). The Hospital Anxiety and Depression Scale. *Acta Psychiatrica Scandinavica, 67*, 361–370.

22

Cognitive Restructuring

Iony D. Ezawa and Steven D. Hollon

Authors' Note: Iony D. Ezawa was supported in part from a National Institute of Mental Health training grant (T32-MH18921) during completion of this work.

One method that is hypothesized to play a role in the process of change across many psychotherapies is cognitive restructuring (CR), which refers to a set of techniques used to help clients identify, evaluate, and correct inaccurate beliefs (Beck et al., 1979). CR is a focal method for a variety of disorders, including major depressive disorder, panic disorder, social anxiety disorder, obsessive–compulsive disorder, and post-traumatic stress disorder.

In this chapter, we provide an overview of CR, including how it is defined, applied, and measured within individual psychotherapy. We provide a review of the extant research on CR, with a particular emphasis on therapist provision of CR within sessions and its effect on therapeutic outcomes. As a part of this review, we discuss landmark studies, diversity considerations, and limitations of the current research. Last, we discuss the implications of the research for psychotherapy training and practice.

Definitions

Cognitive theory posits that cognitions are a key determinant of human behavior and emotion. These cognitions stem from *schemas*, which are the assumptions and attitudes derived from previous experience. It is hypothesized that when these schemas are maladaptive, the associated biased cognitions lead to the etiology and maintenance of psychopathology (Beck, 1987, 1996). In line with this theory, cognitive therapies aim to teach clients how to identify, evaluate, and correct their inaccurate beliefs and their underlying dysfunctional schemas (Beck et al., 1979). The collection of methods targeted at achieving these aims is referred to as CR (e.g., Beck et al., 1979; D. A. Clark & Beck, 2010; D. Dobson & Dobson, 2009). We thus define CR as a collection of techniques aimed at teaching clients how to identify, evaluate, and correct their inaccurate beliefs and their underlying dysfunctional schemas.

CR may be applied differently across the cognitive–behavior therapies. For instance, cognitive therapy (CT) tends to focus on clients' idiosyncratic belief systems and the kinds of evidence it would take to change those beliefs. This focus can result in a personalized application of CR that aims to produce meaningful change in those beliefs. On the other hand, cognitive–behavioral therapy (CBT) integrates cognitive strategies with behavioral methods. The distinction in how CT and CBT therapists tend to employ CR is between what a given belief means to a client and whether a client thinks a given

Iony D. Ezawa and Steven D. Hollon, *Cognitive Restructuring* In: *Psychotherapy Skills and Methods That Work.*
Edited by: Clara E. Hill and John C. Norcross, Oxford University Press.
DOI: 10.1093/oso/9780197611012.003.0022

thought. It is possible to believe something without actually thinking it at a given moment versus thinking something at a given moment without actually believing it. CT tends to emphasize the former and CBT tends to emphasize the latter (Hollon, 2021).

Given the broad assortment and utilization of CR, it has often been referred to under different labels, such as cognitive methods, schema modification, or cognitive change procedures. CR is thought to be necessary for effective application of CT and CBT, leading to the proposed mechanism of cognitive change and subsequent symptom improvements. Rather than being defined as a single method, CR refers to the collection of therapeutic techniques aimed at helping clients identify, challenge, and correct biased and maladaptive automatic interpretations of events. In other words, if the intention of a method is to promote cognitive change or schema modification, and if it is presented to the client in that fashion, the technique can be considered CR. An overview of these techniques is provided in Table 22.1.

The generic process of CR—teaching clients how to identify, evaluate, and correct their inaccurate beliefs and their underlying dysfunctional schemas—is employed in multiple forms of individual psychotherapy. Virtually all mental health professionals address their clients' beliefs in some way. However, in this chapter, we focus on CR in the CBT tradition and research.

Clinical Description and Indications

Cognitive restructuring is often instantiated through use of a thought record, which describes the process of identifying, evaluating, and considering alternatives to automatic negative thoughts (i.e., thoughts that seem to occur instantaneously and on the "fringe" of awareness that affect mood and behavior). In completing the thought record, the therapist helps clients record specific thoughts and examine the relation between their feelings and behaviors. Once clients can elicit specific thoughts and record these thoughts, therapists can help clients "distance" themselves affectively from the beliefs—that is, to recognize that their beliefs are efforts to represent reality, not reality itself. That is facilitated by treating their thoughts as testable hypotheses rather than as established facts. The goal is not just to examine the accuracy of clients' beliefs for them but also to teach them how to do so for themselves.

In CT, there is a basic distinction between thoughts and beliefs. Thoughts are actual events that pass through the sensorium that may or may not be believed, whereas beliefs are perceptions of reality that do not actually have to be processed at any given moment to influence affect and behavior. A person may like to "think" that they are competent, but if they do not "believe" that it is true, they will experience distress and hesitate in performance situations. CT emphasizes the idiosyncratic meaning of the belief whether it is present in the sensorium or not, whereas cognitive–behavioral approaches tend to take a more concrete focus on whether a thought occurred whether it was believed or not.

The process of evaluating thoughts often includes three questions pertaining to evidence, alternatives, and implications of automatic thoughts. Specifically, therapists may pose the first question listed at the bottom of the thought record, "What is the evidence that the automatic thought is true or not true?" to help clients examine available

Table 22.1 Examples of Cognitive Restructuring

Technique	Description
Report thoughts	Asking the client to report specific thoughts (verbatim if possible) that the client experienced in the session *or* in a situation that occurred prior to the session
Relate thoughts and mood	Encouraging the client to relate affective states that the client has experienced (*or* will experience in the future) to the client's ongoing thoughts
Distancing from beliefs	Encouraging the client to view their thoughts as beliefs which may or may not be true (representations of reality) rather than as established fact (reality itself)
Examine available evidence	Helping the client to use available evidence (including the client's prior experiences) to test the validity of their beliefs
Search for alternative explanations	Helping the client to consider alternative explanations for events besides their initial explanation
Think about implications of beliefs	Helping the client to determine the realistic consequences if the client's belief proved to be true
Consider different perspectives	Encouraging the client to see their thoughts or problems from a different perspective
Recognize cognitive errors	Helping the client to identify specific types of cognitive distortions or errors (e.g., all-or-none thinking, overgeneralization) present in the client's thinking
Explore personal meaning	Probing for underlying beliefs related to a thought the client reported to explore the idiosyncratic personal meaning associated with the client's initial thought
Test beliefs prospectively	Encouraging the client to engage in specific behaviors for the purpose of testing the validity of their beliefs *or* make explicit predictions about external events and test those predictions to evaluate their accuracy

Note. Descriptions were previously outlined in Hollon et al. (1988).

evidence to test the validity of their automatic thoughts. The second question, "Are there alternative explanations for that event?" is used to help clients generate explanations for an event other than the original explanation. The third question, "What are the implications if the thought is true?" is used to help the client determine what the implications or realistic consequences would be if their automatic thoughts proved to be true. These three questions, as prescribed in the thought record tool, help clients evaluate the accuracy of their automatic thoughts. Additional helpful CR techniques include recognizing cognitive errors in their thinking (e.g., all-or-none thinking), encouraging clients to see their thoughts from a different perspective (e.g., "What would you say to a friend who was in the same situation?"), and considering the personal meaning of such thoughts (e.g., "What does that thought mean about you?").

Although many CR methods are logical and conversational in nature, CR may also include behavioral techniques that have the intention to promote cognitive change. Most notably, therapists can collaborate with clients to design behavioral experiments to test their beliefs prospectively. Crafting behavioral experiments can be personalized to examine each client's idiosyncratic beliefs, focusing on the kinds of evidence needed to effectively test each client's beliefs, and being conducted in real-world settings. It is important to make a distinction between behavioral experiments intended to test a belief and pure behavioral exposure techniques intended to reduce affective distress.

Behavioral exposure involves subjecting a client to a conditioned stimulus that extinguishes (or habituates) the conditioned fear or anxiety response, with a consequential reduction in avoidance behavior. Strictly speaking, this would not be considered CR given that it does not have an explicit aim to identify and disconfirm erroneous negative beliefs. However, if exposure is suggested to the client to test the accuracy of that belief, then it is considered CR. For instance, in the treatment of specific phobia, if exposure is presented as a behavioral experiment to test the accuracy of the client's belief that he would jump off the bridge to his death (something that the second author once believed), then his forcing himself to run across the Golden Gate Bridge would serve as a behavioral experiment that also was an instance of CR. Exposure may influence what we believe, but unless it is undertaken to test those beliefs, then it does not meet our definition as a CR therapy method.

When the second author (SDH) described this anecdote concerning testing the accuracy of the belief behind his fear of running over bridges during a workshop back in the early 2000s, Chris Fairburn, an Oxford Don with a wicked sense of humor, asked if the author planned to run up the steps of the Eiffel Tower, which was visible through the window behind the presenter. When SDH answered that he had no such plan, since what he had had was a fear of bridges and that he had conquered that, Fairburn suggested that what he really had was a fear of jumping from high places and that his disconfirmation with respect to bridges might not generalize to towers. SDH of course spent the afternoon running up and down the steps at the Eiffel Tower, and Fairburn turned out to be right. SDH was seized with a sense of panic as he started up the steps that lasted over the first 30 steps or so, but he persevered, and the fear gave way to a sense of mastery and a feeling of euphoria (just as he had experienced on the Golden Gate Bridge). Score one for Professor Fairburn and the idiosyncratic nature of cognitions.

In the treatment of social phobia, social exposures are used to test whether safety behaviors (behaviors that are used to minimize or prevent a feared interpersonal outcome) help or hinder the clients in social situations (D. M. Clark & Wells, 1995). Clients with social phobia typically fear that they will behave in ways in social interactions that will expose them to ridicule or censor and thus engage in a variety of safety behaviors intended to forestall the dreaded consequences. Someone who is concerned that they will come across as boring may scan the newspapers in the morning to find interesting things to say, or someone who fears saying something "stupid" may try to monitor what they say as they say it (spectating). Clients who fear blushing will cover their face with their hands, and clients who fear sweating through their shirts will wear jackets or sweaters even in warm weather to cover up the stains. Therapists can determine what is most concerning to the client and have them interact with others both with and without the "safety behaviors," often videotaping the interactions. What clients typically learn is that they come across in a more competent fashion when they drop the safety behaviors and focus instead on the other person in the interaction. Such behavioral experiments (exposures) are designed to test their idiosyncratic beliefs but involve little effort to logically dispute those notions in advance. A recent network meta-analysis found that individual cognitive therapy based on the Clark and Wells model produced larger effect sizes than any other approach, including antidepressant medications or more conventional group CBT (Mayo-Wilson et al., 2014).

In the treatment of panic disorder, the therapist first asks the client what it is that they most fear happening (e.g., a heart attack, psychotic decompensation, or extreme social embarrassment) and then encourages them to drop whatever safety behaviors they typically use to prevent the feared catastrophe from occurring (D. M. Clark, 1997). Clients who are afraid of having a heart attack are encouraged to drop their typical safety behaviors (laying down and controlling their breathing) and to do whatever they think it takes to bring on one (e.g., engage in rapid shallow breathing or run up and down a flight of stairs or spin around in an office chair). When the catastrophic event does not occur, they have powerful evidence that they were never at risk in the first place. This exercise is a clear instance of CR via use of a behavioral experiment. Simple interoceptive exposure in the absence of a rationale connecting the non-occurrence of the catastrophic event as evidence that the individual was not at risk is exposure only and not CR.

Clients who suffer from post-traumatic stress disorder usually do everything they can not to think about the trauma, but that paradoxically appears to be what brings the symptoms (flashbacks, night terrors, and the like) about. Any of the trauma-focused cognitive or behavioral approaches encourage clients to relive the traumatic experience, but whereas a more purely behavioral approach such as prolonged exposure requires dozens of repeated (and excruciating) instances to extinguish (or habituate) the distress, a more purely cognitive approach requires only reliving the experience a time or two for the purpose of finding the meaning the client has ascribed. A variety of cognitive and behavioral strategies are then applied to examine the accuracy of that belief. For example, one of the authors once worked with a client who had been raped as a teen and who concluded that no decent man that she was interested in would reciprocate her interest if he ever knew what had happened to her. Both CR and behavioral experiments (disclosing the secret to a girlfriend in preparation for disclosure to her new boyfriend) were used to help her move beyond the disconcerting belief. CT is not necessarily more efficacious than prolonged exposure in the treatment of post-traumatic stress disorder, but it is less distressing to the client and appears to produce comparable symptomatic outcomes with fewer sessions and far less attrition (Lewis, Roberts, Andrew, et al., 2020; Lewis, Roberts, Gibson, et al., 2020).

CR is emphasized as a core element in many treatments for several disorders, including in cognitive treatments of depressive disorders, anxiety disorders, obsessive–compulsive disorder, post-traumatic stress disorder, and psychosis. Given the broad assortment of CR methods, therapists can select the individual CR techniques that best fit each client's case conceptualization and treatment goals. These methods can be introduced as early as the first session and continued to be practiced throughout and beyond a course of therapy.

Assessment

Cognitive Restructuring Measures

We review three measures that assess CR within session. Two of these measures are observer-rated measures, which involve intensively trained raters concurrently watching recordings of therapy sessions and coding CR usage within that session. The third measure is a client-report assessment of CR used within session. Although each assesses CR within session, these measures only provide estimates of the amount of CR that occurred in a session and have not been used to determine exactly where in the session the CR occurred.

Collaborative Study Psychotherapy Rating Scale

The Cognitive Methods subscale of the Collaborative Study Psychotherapy Rating Scale (CSPRS; Hollon et al., 1988) is an observer-rated measure of therapist's adherence to CR during a session. The CSPRS was originally developed to distinguish therapist behaviors among CBT, interpersonal psychotherapy, and clinical management of medication in the National Institute of Mental Health's Treatment of Depression Collaborative Research Program (Elkin, 1994). A factor analysis conducted on a sample of 176 adults with depression receiving CBT identified a 10-item Cognitive Methods subscale (for details, see Strunk et al., 2012). The CSPRS Cognitive Methods subscale has demonstrated acceptable interrater reliability and good internal consistency (e.g., Sasso et al., 2016; Schmidt et al., 2019; Strunk et al., 2010).

Performance of CT Strategies

The Performance of CT Strategies (PCTS) is also an observer-rated measure of client's cognitive behavioral skills used within a session (Strunk et al., 2007). The PCTS contains three subscales: a three-item Behavioral Activation subscale, a 10-item Automatic Thought Work subscale, and a two-item Schema or Core Belief Work subscale. The latter two subscales represent CR. All items are rated on 7-point Likert scales. The PCTS has demonstrated good interrater reliability, internal consistency, and validity with respect to predicting relapse independent from a measure of CT skill competency (Strunk et al., 2007).

Bern Post-Session Report

The Bern Post-Session Report (BPSR; Flückiger et al., 2010) includes three self-report items that clients complete after a session to assess the extent to which they used CR in the session that was just finished. The CR portion of the BPSR has demonstrated adequate internal consistency (Gómez Penedo et al., 2020). A comparison between therapist and observer ratings on this measure has demonstrated acceptable discriminant and convergent validity (Flückiger et al., 2009, 2010).

Measures of Cognitive Restructuring Effectiveness

The effectiveness of therapeutic methods can be evaluated with immediate outcomes (measured in-session), intermediate outcomes (measured post- or between-session), or distal outcomes (measured post-treatment). We review four specific outcomes (including three intermediate and two distal outcomes) that have been used to evaluate the effectiveness of CR in the research literature.

Intermediate Outcomes

Cognitive Change–Immediate Scale

The Cognitive Change–Immediate Scale is a five-item self-report measure administered at post-session that assesses clients' experience of cognitive change within the session that just occurred (Schmidt et al., 2019). This measure asks clients to indicate the extent to which they agreed with items on 7-point Likert scales, with higher scores indicating greater agreement. This measure has demonstrated excellent internal consistency and convergent validity with a measure of CBT skills (Schmidt et al., 2019).

Beck Depression Inventory–II

The Beck Depression Inventory–II (BDI-II) is a 21-item self-report measure that assesses a client's depressive symptoms (Beck et al., 1996). This measure is completed at the start of each session on 0- to 3-point scales. The BDI-II has demonstrated excellent reliability and validity (Beck et al., 1996).

World Health Organization Well-Being Index

The World Health Organization Well-Being Index (WHO-5) is a five-item self-report measure that was designed to assess subjective psychological well-being. The items on the measure are rated on 0- to 5-point Likert scales. The measure has been validated as a screening tool for depression (Topp et al., 2015).

Distal Outcomes

Relapse Risk

One study has assessed relapse risk during a post-treatment follow-up period in relation to CR (Strunk et al., 2007) in a sample of clients who responded to treatment. In this sample of treatment responders, clients met relapse criteria if they scored 14 or greater on the Hamilton Rating Scale for Depression (Hamilton, 1960) for 2 consecutive weeks at any point during a 1-year follow-up period.

Dropout

One study examined dropout in relation to CR (Ezawa & Strunk, 2022a). In this study, dropout was defined as a patient prematurely discontinuing treatment.

Clinical Examples

In the hypothetical vignettes below, we illustrate common CR methods that therapists use with clients in sessions. In the first example, we describe a situation in which the therapist (T) is helping the client (C) complete a thought record. In the second example, we describe a therapist helping the client review a prospective test of their belief.

Completing a Thought Record

C: My partner does not like talking or spending time with me anymore. He must be starting to lose interest in me.

T: How do you know your partner does not like talking or spending time with you anymore?

C: Because I am boring and depressed all the time.

T: Well, let's check that thought out. Let's see what evidence you have that your partner doesn't like you anymore. What evidence do you have to support that thought?

C: He doesn't talk with me as often after work. We also haven't gone on a date night in a long while.

T: What happens after work?

C: Well, he comes home late. Then, we usually just eat a late dinner, watch TV, and go to bed.

T: And why does he come home late?

C: He was recently promoted, and he said he has been given more responsibilities than before, which has been stressful for him.

T: So, your partner is working longer hours after the recent promotion. When did you start feeling like he doesn't like you anymore?

C: I guess it started around the time of that promotion.

T: Hmm. . . . It sounds like there might be other possible explanations for why your partner has been talking or spending less time with you lately besides your initial thought that he is losing interest in you. What evidence do you have against that thought your partner doesn't like you anymore?

C: Well, I have asked him directly if he has lost interest, and he denies it.

T: So, he has directly told you he has not lost interest. Interesting . . .

C: Yes, but he might be lying or trying to protect my feelings.

T: What are the implications if he was lying, and it is true that he has lost interest?

C: Well, I guess I would be sad, and that I would have to move on.

T: Okay, so that is one possibility. Is there anything you could do that might help rekindle that interest?

C: Yes, I suppose so. When we were first dating, we spent a lot of time together and went on fun dates. That seemed to make our relationship stronger.

T: Great, well let's make sure to jot this down on your thought record.

Thought Record

THOUGHT RECORD

Directions: When you notice your mood getting worse, ask yourself, "What' s going through my mind right now?" and as soon as possible jot down the thought or mental image in the Automatic Thoughts column. Then consider how realistic those thoughts are.

Date	**Situation** Where were you – and what was going on – when you got upset?	**Emotions** What emotions did you feel (sad, anxious, angry, etc.)? Rate intensity (0-100%).	**Automatic Thoughts** What thoughts and/or images went through your mind? Rate your belief in each (0-100%).	**Alternative Responses** Use the questions at the bottom to compose responses to the automatic thoughts. Rate your belief in each (0-100%). Also, consult the list of possible distortions.	**Outcome** Rerate belief in your automatic thoughts (0-100%) and in the intensity of your emotions (0-100%).
11/1	*Partner came home from work and did not spend time with me before going to bed.*	*Sad – 90%* *Frustrated – 50%*	*My partner does not like talking or spending time with me anymore. (90%) {mind-reading}* *He must be starting to lose interest in me. (100%) {jumping to conclusions}*	*I have asked my partner if he has lost interest, and he denies it. (80%) {evidence}* *Partner was recently promoted, and he has been given more responsibilities than before, which has been stressful for him. (95%) {alternative explanations}* *If my partner has lost interest in me, there are things that I can do to rekindle that interest or move beyond the relationship. (90%) {implications}*	*Sad – 20%* *Frustrated – 10%*

(1) What is the **evidence** that the automatic thought is true? What is the evidence that it is not true?
(2) Are there **alternative explanations** for that event, or alternative ways to view the situation?
(3) What are the **implications** if the thought is true? What' s most upsetting about it? What' s most realistic? What can I do about it?
(4) What would I tell a good friend in the same situation?

Possible Distortions: All-or-none Thinking; Overgeneralizing; Discounting the Positives; Jumping to Conclusions; Mind-reading; Fortune-telling; Magnifying/Minimizing; Emotional Reasoning; Making "Should" Statements; Labelling; Inappropriate Blaming

Testing Beliefs Prospectively

T: Last week we discussed how you tend to think that strangers will notice how anxious you are, so you engage in the safety behaviors, such as avoiding eye contact or putting your hands on your face when you are talking to a stranger. Tell me about how your experiment went to test out your belief that a barista would notice your anxiety if you ordered a coffee without engaging in your safety behaviors?

C: It went much better than I predicted. I was able to focus on the barista more than on myself, and the barista did not give any indication that she noticed my anxiety. If anything, the barista treated me like every other customer and was very friendly!

T: Wow, so what did you learn about yourself in this interaction?

C: I learned my anxiety was not as obvious as I thought, or at least that a stranger did not treat me any differently even if she noticed I was anxious. Also, maybe my safety behaviors make me more focused on my own anxiety, and they may draw more attention to my discomfort.

T: So how can you build on this?

C: I can keep practicing engaging with strangers without using my safety behaviors.

T: That sounds like an excellent plan!

Behavioral Experiments Record Sheet

BEHAVIORAL EXPERIMENTS RECORD SHEET

Date	Situation	Prediction What do you think will happen? How much do you believe it will, 0-100? How would you know if it had? e.g., how would you predict other people would react?	Experiment What can you do to test the prediction? Remember to focus on what actually happens rather than your feelings & let go of Safety Behaviours.	Outcome Where was your attention focused? What actually happened? Was the prediction correct?	Learning What I learned in general about myself in social interactions. How can I build on this?
11/1	*Order a coffee from a barista at a local coffee shop.*	*If I do not use my safety behaviors (i.e., avoid eye contact, cover face with hands), then the barista will see me blush and notice my voice is shaky.* *(85%)* *The barista will stare at me or ask me if something is wrong.*	*Go to a local coffee shop and order a coffee while keeping my hands at my sides and making eye contact with the barista.*	*My attention was focused on the barista.* *I ordered the coffee and felt like my voice was 10% shaky. The barista did not stare at me or ask if something was wrong. The barista treated me like a regular customer and was really friendly.* *The prediction was wrong.*	*My anxiety was not as noticeable as I thought it was, or at least strangers do not care enough to treat me any different than anyone else.* *I can try dropping my safety behaviors again when talking to new strangers.*

Landmark Studies and Previous Reviews

Little literature has focused on examining the direct impact of CR applied within session. This is likely in part due to the intensive training and resources needed to repeatedly measure CR within and outcomes after each session. Instead, most research efforts have examined the effect of CR across sessions using component analysis or mediation analysis. *Component analysis* examines the impact of CR on outcome experimentally by dismantling treatment packages and then comparing interventions containing a CR component with interventions that do not contain a CR component. The rationale behind these studies is that dismantling permits examination of the additive effect of CR. *Mediation analysis*, on the other hand, relies on correlational analyses across time to determine whether the implementation of CR leads to subsequent cognitive change. Although these studies do measure CR within sessions, they do not necessarily relate it to cognitive or symptom change within that same session. Nonetheless, these methods elucidate the role of CR in the overall therapeutic process and are worthy of review.

Component Analysis

Among the earliest studies to utilize component analysis was a comparison of a behavioral activation alone (BA; focused on increasing behaviors to activate positive affect) versus a treatment that included both BA and automatic thought work (AT; focused on modifying automatic dysfunctional thoughts) versus a full CT treatment (which included BA, AT, and schema change work [SC] focused on modifying broader thought patterns and schema change) in a sample of 150 outpatients with major depressive disorder (MDD; Jacobson et al., 1996). There were no significant outcome differences among the three treatments at post-treatment or 6-month follow-up. At the 2-year follow-up, there were also no significant differences between treatment conditions on depressive relapse (Gortner et al., 1998). In interpreting the results of these studies, the authors questioned the necessity of CR in the treatment of depression.

In a subsequent trial, 241 adults with MDD were randomized to a BA (which excluded cognitive interventions) versus CT (which included BA and cognitive interventions) and each versus paroxetine alone (a selective serotonin reuptake inhibitor) in the context of an 8-week pill placebo condition (Dimidjian et al., 2006). All active conditions were equally effective at post-treatment for mild to moderate MDD, but the BA and paroxetine condition were found to be significantly more effective than CT and pill placebo in treating severe MDD. A 2-year follow-up showed that CT and BA were as efficacious as continuation medication and more efficacious than medication withdrawal (K. Dobson et al., 2008). These results suggest that CR may contribute little to the efficacy of treatment and thus is not a necessary treatment component. This interpretation, however, depends on the quality of the CR provided, and there were indications in the latter trial that the cognitive therapists essentially "gave up" and provided largely supportive therapy with interpersonally difficult patients who were more severely depressed (Coffman et al., 2007).

Component analysis has also examined the role of CR in the treatment of anxiety disorders, particularly in relation to exposure. Like component analyses in the treatment of depression, purely behavioral interventions and combined cognitive–behavioral interventions have been shown to be equally effective in the treatment of anxiety symptoms (for a more comprehensive review, see Deacon & Abramowitz, 2004). Also like the depression treatment literature, few studies have examined purely cognitive interventions. Regarding panic disorder specifically, CR alone and exposure alone have both been shown to lead to symptom improvement; however, combined exposure and CR do not lead to significantly stronger effects than exposure alone (for a review, see Gould et al., 1995). Regarding social anxiety disorder, past studies have failed to find significant differences in post-treatment outcomes between cognitive–behavioral and exposure only treatments (for a review, see Feske & Chambless, 1995).

Regarding obsessive–compulsive disorder, component analyses have most often been used to test exposure and response prevention (ERP; a behavioral therapy that exposes clients to situations that provoke their obsessions) against ERP plus CR. Some studies have found CBT to have comparable outcomes to ERP (Cottraux et al., 2001; Whittal et al., 2005). However, some studies have found ERP alone to be more effective than CBT (McLean et al., 2001). Others have found that the addition of CR to ERP did not have significantly different outcomes than ERP alone (O'Connor et al., 2005). Given these findings, it appears CR is less effective than ERP, and that adding CR to ERP does not improve outcome (Abramowitz et al., 2005). Again, questions can be raised as to how adequately CR was provided by essentially behavioral investigators at the time these trials were conducted. Incidentally, early proponents of exposure therapy for obsessive–compulsive disorder have come to focus on the disconfirmation of idiosyncratic beliefs regarding personal responsibility in recent years (Salkovskis, 1999).

In post-traumatic stress disorder treatment research, component analysis has been used extensively to examine the role of CR in relation to trauma exposure. CBT (with exposure) has been found to be as efficacious as trauma exposure alone, leading some researchers to conclude that CR is not effective because it adds little or no additional benefit to treatment (Longmore & Worrell, 2007). However, more recent systematic and meta-analytic reviews have concluded that exposure, CR, and CBT (including both exposure and CR) are all equally effective in the treatment of post-traumatic stress disorder (Hassija & Gray, 2010; Ponniah & Hollon, 2009) and that CR may have a more enduring effect than exposure alone (Tarrier & Sommerfield, 2004). Component analyses of cognitive processing therapy have shown that CR may be the most effective component of the larger treatment package (Resick et al., 2008; Stein et al., 2012; Walter et al., 2014).

A meta-analysis of 20 randomized controlled trials that compared CT alone (without exposure) and exposure alone in the treatment of anxiety disorders revealed similar effect sizes for the treatment of post-traumatic stress disorder, obsessive–compulsive disorder, and panic disorder (Ougrin, 2011). On the other hand, the effect size for the treatment of social anxiety disorder was significantly greater for CT when looking at both acute and long-term outcomes. Taken together, these component analyses suggest that CR is an effective method for depression and anxiety, at least as effective as behavioral components. CR may be especially important in some cases, such as in the treatment of social anxiety disorder, albeit in the indirect form of behavioral experiments.

Mediation Analysis

The cognitive mediation hypothesis states that cognitive change is what accounts for symptom change (D. A. Clark & Beck, 2010). Given that the aim of CR is to produce cognitive change, many researchers measure cognitive change as a proxy for the quality or success of CR (instead of measuring the implementation of CR directly). For example, the Ways of Responding Scale (WOR; Barber & DeRubeis, 1992) assesses client's cognitive change by coding their written responses to a series of hypothetical negative events. Greater change on the WOR has been found to predict greater depressive symptom improvement across the course of cognitive and psychodynamic psychotherapies (Barber & DeRubeis, 2001; Connolly Gibbons et al., 2009).

Reviews of the literature on cognitive mediation have yielded mixed conclusions. Longmore and Worrell (2007) conducted a review on studies examining cognitive mediation in CBT and concluded that there was limited evidence for the cognitive mediation hypothesis. Hofmann (2008) critiqued this review for the selective scope of studies included in the review. In a separate review focused on examining cognitive mediation in the treatment of depression specifically, Garratt et al. (2007) concluded that cognitive change predicted change in depressive symptoms, but that this relation was not specific to cognitive treatments. More recent comprehensive reviews have suggested the available evidence is consistent with cognitive mediation for a variety of disorders (Clark, 2014; Hofmann et al., 2018; Lorenzo-Luaces et al., 2015). While reviewing the literature according to criteria for statistical mediation (i.e., evidence of a statistical mediational relation of cognitions on symptoms, an effect of CBT on cognitive change, and cognitive change temporally preceding symptom change), Hofmann et al. (2018) found considerable support for the cognitive mediation hypothesis in the treatment of panic disorder, social anxiety disorder, and post-traumatic stress disorder and preliminary support for generalized anxiety disorder and MDD.

Limitations of Component and Mediation Analyses

Component analysis can further understanding on whether CR provides additional therapeutic effect above and beyond the components to which it is being compared; however, a significant limitation is that this type of analysis cannot speak to the direct effect of CR. Similarly, mediation analyses based on the cognitive mediation hypothesis do not allow researchers to draw conclusions about CR in session because it relies on the untested assumption that the cognitive changes measured are indeed the result of CR alone. It is conceivable that cognitive changes can be the product (or byproduct) of methods other than CR (e.g., exposure might lead to symptom improvement by both behavioral and cognitive change). Relatedly, CR may not always or exclusively lead to cognitive changes. Therefore, it is critical to examine CR applied within session and its relation to intermediate and distal therapeutic outcomes.

Research Review

In this section, we present a systematic review of studies examining the effect of CR *within* session on psychotherapy outcomes.

Search Strategy

Our inclusion criteria for studies in this review were (a) written in English, (b) appearing in peer-reviewed journals, (c) measured CR as a specific *within-session* method, (d) assessed some measure of outcome, (e) conducted as individual therapy, (f) in a face-to-face setting, and (g) contained sufficient information to examine the relation between CR and that outcome.

We used several search strategies to identify studies for inclusion in this review. First, we conducted a search of the PsycInfo database. We examined studies that included at least one of the terms listed in each of these three following categories: (a) cognitive restructuring, cognitive methods, cognitive change procedures, cognitive intervention, schema modification, automatic thought modification, modify automatic thoughts; (b) outcome, symptom; and (c) therapy, psychotherapy. The final PsycInfo database search resulted in 629 results. After removing duplicates, 419 unique articles remained. In addition, we searched the reference section of previous reviews (Clark, 2014; Hofmann et al., 2018; Lorenzo-Luaces et al., 2015). We then inspected each of the individual study abstracts for the inclusion criteria. We identified eight articles for in-depth examination that appeared to meet the inclusion criteria based on their abstracts.

After reviewing these studies, we identified five studies that fully met our inclusion criteria. The reasons the other three articles did not meet inclusion criteria were that they did not contain a measure of CR as a specific within-session method ($k = 1$; Teasdale & Fennell, 1982), did not contain sufficient information to examine the relation between CR and outcome ($k = 1$; Mohlman, 2013), and was a re-analysis of a data set that already examined the relation between CR and an outcome (Sasso et al., 2016). Table 22.2 provides a list of the studies included in the review.

Review of the Studies

Strunk et al. (2007) examined CR within session in a sample of 35 patients with moderate to severe depression who responded to a course of CT. In this study, the PCTS was used to assess automatic thought and schema/core belief work at sessions recorded during the 12th week, 14th week, and last week of acute treatment. Due to missing data, the analyses in this study concerning the PCTS were limited to 32 patients. While controlling for study site and pretreatment CBT skill use, the overall PCTS was significantly related to reduced risk of relapse during the year-long follow-up period (χ^2 (1, $N = 32$) = 5.46, hazard = 3.37, confidence interval [CI] = 1.22, 9.32, $p = .02$). However, the PCTS is a composite measure that includes a measure of behavioral activation along with the two cognitive restructuring indices. When looking at the individual CR-related subscales, neither was significantly associated with risk of relapse, although each was in the expected direction: PCTS-AT (χ^2 (1, $N = 32$) = 1.11, hazard = 1.68, CI = 0.64, 4.41, $p = .29$); PCTS-SC (χ^2 (1, $N = 32$) = 3.80, hazard = 1.82, CI = 1.00, 3.34, $p = .05$).

Table 22.2 Studies in the Research Review

Source	*N*	CR Measure	Outcome	Treatment	Results	*r*	*d*
Strunk et al., 2007	32	PCTS-AT	Relapse Risk	CBT	+	.19	0.39
	32	PCTS-SC	Relapse Risk	CBT	+	.35	0.75
Strunk et al., 2010	60	CSPRS-CM	Symptoms	CBT	+	.44	0.98
Schmidt et al., 2019	126	CSPRS-CM	Cognitive Change	CBT	+	.20	0.41
Gómez Penedo et al., 2020	71	BPSR-CR	Symptoms	CBT	+	.41	0.90
	70	BSPR-CR	Symptoms	EBCT	+	.42	0.93
Ezawa et al., 2021	229	CSPRS-CM	Symptoms	CBT	+	.39	0.85
	229	CSPRS-CM	Dropout	CBT	+	.47	1.07

BPSR-CR, Bern Post-Session Report–Cognitive Restructuring questionnaire; CBT, cognitive–behavioral therapy; CR, cognitive restructuring; CSPRS-CM, Collaborative Study Psychotherapy Rating Scale–Cognitive Methods subscale; EBCT, exposure-based cognitive therapy; PCTS-AT, Performance of Cognitive Therapy Strategies–Automatic Thought Work subscale; PCTS-SC, Performance of Cognitive Therapy Strategies–Schema or Core Belief Work subscale; +, relation between CR and therapeutic outcome in the expected direction.

Strunk et al. (2010) measured CR using the CSPRS for the first four therapy sessions of 60 clients who participated in a course of CBT for depression. Symptoms were also assessed before each session using the BDI-II (Beck et al., 1996). The authors found CR significantly predicted lower symptom scores in the next session while controlling for current symptoms ($r = .44$, $t = 3.67$, $p < .001$). CR remained a significant predictor of next-session symptom change even when controlling for the alliance ($r = .42$, $t = 3.49$, $p = .0009$).

In a re-analysis of the same data set, Sasso et al. (2016) disaggregated the within- and between-person variation of CR. The authors then examined the within- and between-person components of CR as predictors of next-session symptom improvements and found that both components significantly predicted next-session improvements (between: $b = 1.58$, $SE = 0.51$, $t(54) = 3.14$, $p = .003$; within: $b = 3.58$, $SE = 1.14$, $t(156) = 3.15$, $p = .002$). Relations focused on the within-person variability of predictor variables can ensure stable patient characteristics are not accountable for the relation.

Schmidt et al. (2019) also used the CSPRS to measure CR for the first five sessions of 126 clients who participated in a course of CT. CR was then disaggregated into within- and between-person components and examined as predictors of same-session cognitive change, which was assessed using the Cognitive Change–Immediate scale (Schmidt et al., 2019). Higher values of within- and between-person CR predicted greater immediate cognitive change (within: $b = .97$, $SE = 0.57$, $t(351) = 3.43$, $p = .001$; between: $b = 3.10$, $SE = 1.32$, $t(119) = 2.34$, $p = .02$).

Gómez Penedo et al. (2020) measured CR using the BPSR in a sample of clients randomized to exposure-based CT (EBCT; $n = 71$) or CT for depression ($n = 70$). CR was assessed after each session. After treatment completion, 3-month, 6-month, and 12-month follow-up, clients also completed measures of avoidance (measured with the Cognitive–Behavioral Avoidance Scale; Ottenbreit & Dobson, 2004), self-efficacy (measured with the Generalized Self-Efficacy Scale; Schwarzer & Jerusalem, 1999), and depressive symptoms (measured with the BDI-II). Across both treatments, greater increases in CR were related to lower avoidance and greater self-efficacy, and both lower avoidance and greater self-efficacy were associated with lower levels of depressive symptoms at the 12-month follow-up. In addition, CR was directly related to decreased depressive symptom scores at the 12-month follow-up. Although the original publication did not report the direct relation between CR and outcomes, Gómez Penedo reported in a personal communication that CR (modeled as a Level 1 predictor in a three-level multilevel model) predicted next-session symptoms (measured with the WHO-5, coded with greater scores indicating lower depression severity) in both the EBCT and CBT samples (EBCT sample: $b_{standardized} = 0.37$; CBT sample: $b_{standardized} = 0.36$).

Ezawa and Strunk (2022a) examined within-person components of CR, behavioral methods, and the therapeutic alliance as predictors of next-session symptom change across the early sessions of 229 clients who participated in a course of CBT (while controlling for within-client current symptoms and including therapist as a random effect). CR was assessed using the CSPRS, and symptoms were assessed using the BDI-II. In that study, higher values of within-client CR predicted lower next-session symptoms ($b_{standardized} = -0.39$, $b = -0.78$, $SE = 0.29$, $t(212) = -2.72$,

p = .01) and lower risk of dropout ($b_{standardized}$ = 1.93, b = 1.93, SE = 0.49, OR = 6.85, 95% CI = 2.59, 18.11, $p < 0.001$). Neither the within-person component of behavioral methods nor the therapeutic alliance predicted next-session symptoms. This study incorporated data from three prior studies of CBT for depression, two of which were Strunk et al. (2010) and Schmidt et al. (2019). Moreover, the sample used in Ezawa and Strunk (2022a) (composed of only White therapists) was restricted to Black and White patients because the primary test included examining differences in CBT delivery between the races. Thus, there was partial but not complete overlap in samples with the studies already reported. Interestingly, CR use differed markedly between groups such that therapists utilized significantly less CR with Black patients than White patients. However, the effect of CR use on next-session symptoms did not differ based on the race of the patient.

In summary, this systematic review identified five studies that examined the effect of CR as a within-session method on intermediate or distal psychotherapy outcomes. Each of these studies was conducted in the context of providing a cognitive treatment for depression. Measurement of CR varied markedly across studies, as did the therapeutic outcome of interest. Yet, in all identified studies (see Table 22.2), therapist use of CR was positively related to therapeutic outcome (i.e., lower risk of relapse, lower next-session depressive symptoms, greater cognitive change, and lower attrition).

Meta-Analysis

We then conducted a meta-analysis of studies included in the research review that contained sufficient information to estimate r and Cohen's d effect sizes of the relation between CR and a therapeutic outcome. To keep observations independent, we chose not to include Ezawa and Strunk (2022a) given the overlap of this study's participants with Strunk et al. (2007) and Schmidt et al. (2019), although the effect size for the relation between CR and next-session symptoms from Ezawa and Strunk is presented in the forest plot for purposes of comparison. Relatedly, we included only one of the relations between CR and relapse risk for Strunk et al. (2007) (instead of the two CR measures). Due to the small number of studies, we conducted a single meta-analysis with datasets examining both intermediate and distal outcomes in relation to CR. Peterson and Brown's (2005) formula was used to impute the associated r values for studies that only reported standardized βs. To calculate the pooled mean effect size, we employed a random effects model and calculated effect size intervals using Comprehensive Meta-Analysis Version 3 software. We calculated the I^2 statistic to assess the heterogeneity of effect sizes. We also calculated Egger's and Begg's tests for indication of publication bias. Tests for publication bias assume symmetry in the distribution of studies around the observed mean with smaller studies contributing more extreme scores in either direction. When publication bias occurs, it is usually smaller studies with weaker findings that fail to make it into the literature. This pattern is reflected in a deficit of studies in the lower left quadrant of the normal curve and can be detected by either of the two tests of symmetry that we conducted and is usually depicted visually with a funnel plot.

Table 22.3 Studies Included in the Meta-Analysis

Source	*N*	CR Measure	Outcome	*r*	*d*	95% CI for r
Strunk et al., 2007	32	PCTS-SC	Relapse Risk	.35	0.75	0.00, 0.62
Strunk et al., 2010	60	CSPRS-CM	Symptoms	.44	0.98	0.25, 0.43
Schmidt et al., 2019	126	CSPRS-CM	Cognitive Change	.20	0.41	0.02, 0.37
Gómez Penedo et al., 2020[1]	71	BPSR-CR	Symptoms	.41	0.90	0.20, 0.59
Gómez Penedo et al., 2020[2]	70	BSPR-CR	Symptoms	.42	0.93	0.21, 0.60
Total (random effects)	359	CR	Positive Outcome	.34	0.72	0.25, 0.43
Ezawa et al., 2021	229	CSPRS-CM	Symptoms	.39	0.85	0.28, 0.50

Note. Positive effect sizes reflect relations between CR and the respective therapeutic outcome in the expected positive direction.

BPSR-CR, Bern Post-Session Report–Cognitive Restructuring questionnaire; CBT, cognitive-behavioral therapy; CR, cognitive restructuring; CSPRS-CM, Collaborative Study Psychotherapy Rating Scale–Cognitive Methods subscale; EBCT, exposure-based cognitive therapy; PCTS-SC, Performance of Cognitive Therapy Strategies–Schema or Core Belief Work subscale; Gómez Penedo et al. (2020)[1], CBT sample; Gómez Penedo et al. (2020)[2], EBCT sample.

The overall *r* effect size of the studies examining the relation between CR and therapeutic outcomes was .35 (95% CI = .24 – .44; Cohen's $d = 0.85$) with low heterogeneity ($I^2 = 11.40$). A list of the studies included in the meta-analysis is found in Table 22.3. A forest plot of study *r* effect sizes is found in Figure 22.1. There was no significant evidence of publication bias according to Egger's ($P = 0.14$) and Begg's tests ($P = 0.16$). The total number of clients was 353.

The outcomes among studies included in the meta-analysis varied considerably, but the findings were robust across these different intermediate (i.e., depressive symptoms, cognitive change) and distal outcomes (i.e., relapse risk). In addition, the smallest

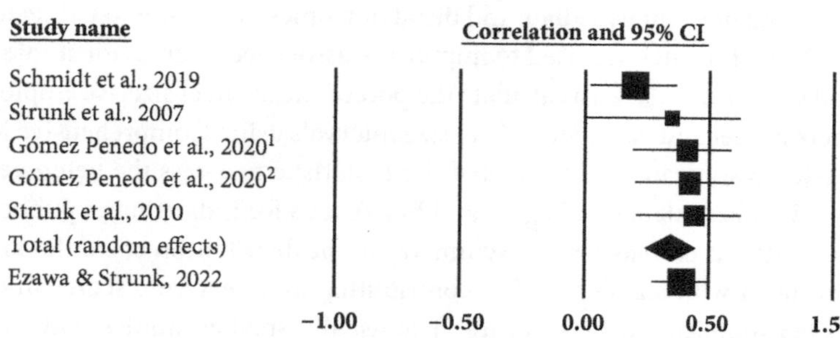

Note: Positive effect sizes reflect relations between CR and treatment outcomes in the expected direction. Gómez Penedo et al., 2020[1] = CBT sample; Gómez Penedo et al., 2020[2] = EBCT sample.

Figure 22.1 Forest plot.

effect sizes listed in Table 22.3 (Schmidt et al., 2019, and Ezawa & Strunk, 2022a) were those belonging to the two studies that disaggregated the within- and between-patient components of the CR variable. By doing so, these studies ruled out any relations involving the within-patient components of CR as being accounted for by stable patient characteristics (Curran & Bauer, 2011; Wang & Maxwell, 2015).

Possible Negative Effects and Harm

We are not aware of any reported negative effects of CR. Nor did any of the reviewed studies directly report any harm as a result of CR. At the same time, it is important to consider when CR might be appropriate for thoughts and contexts. For example, if a client has a fear about walking alone at night, a therapist might target that fear as irrational. However, if the client is a woman or a person of color, this fear might reflect plausible detections of gender- or racism-related threats. If the therapist were to directly challenge thoughts around these plausible threats, the client may not find this helpful or may find it invalidating. Instead, a therapist might use CR to identify and examine thoughts surrounding what it means to the client that they are facing this plausible threat. In this way, CR is still utilized but with thoughts that may be more likely linked to the client's experience of psychopathology. The goal of CR is not to minimize existing threats but rather to get an accurate sense of what they might be.

Diversity Considerations

Psychotherapists are often encouraged to adapt or flexibly implement psychotherapy to meet each client's unique cultural needs (e.g., Hays, 2009). One of the studies included in our systematic review examined whether therapists differed in their delivery of CR when providing CBT to Black or White patients. Interestingly, the therapists (who were all White in that study) provided significantly less CR to Black than White patients (Ezawa & Strunk, 2022a). A subsequent experimental study examining 218 therapist's decision-making in response to clinical case vignettes revealed that therapists viewed CR as less therapeutic for Black as compared to White patients (Ezawa & Strunk, 2022b). However, Ezawa and Strunk (2022a) did not find that patient race moderated the relation between CR and symptoms, suggesting that CR was equally effective for both Black and White patients. More research is needed to understand how cultural dimensions (e.g., client gender, sexual orientation, socioeconomic status) may impact the beliefs, use, and effectiveness of CR.

Limitations of the Research

There are several methodological difficulties in examining the therapeutic effect of CR within sessions, which likely relates to the small number of studies (Lorenzo-Luaces et al., 2015). First, measuring CR within a session is resource intensive. Besides the number of hours needed to rate therapy sessions, training a single rater can take upwards of 70 hours (Strunk et al., 2007), and often multiple raters are needed to reach acceptable reliability (Ezawa et al., 2021). Future researchers might consider automating training procedures to increase the reliability of and reduce the resources needed to utilize current observer-rated CR measures (e.g., Ezawa et al., 2021). Another possibility is for future researchers to adapt the current observer-rated measures of CR (e.g., the CSPRS) into therapist and client self-report measures of CR use within session. Likely related to the methodological difficulties of assessing CR, none of the studies included in our review examined immediate within-session effects of CR. More research is critically needed to examine CR's immediate impacts on client cognition, behaviors, and moods in session. This information would provide a clearer understanding of when it would be most useful to utilize CR in session. Recent breakthroughs in technology (such as machine learning and artificial intelligence) may pave the way for computerized coding of CR and outcomes in therapy sessions.

Second, our review did not cover CR use in between sessions. CR is often assigned as homework for clients to complete on their own and then bring back into the subsequent session on the assumption that these skills account for CBT's enduring effect. A few self-report measures of client CR skill use outside of session have been developed, including the Skills of CT scale (Jarrett et al., 2011), the CBT Skills Questionnaire (Jacob et al., 2011), and the Competencies of CT Scale (Strunk et al., 2014). We encourage studies examining CR use outside of sessions as a future direction.

Third, many of the studies examining the effect of CR have relied on naturalistic studies that cannot establish causality. While manipulating single variables (such as therapist application of CR) can be difficult to achieve, it is essential that researchers consider the timing of assessments to ensure that CR and outcomes are not measured concurrently and are aligned with a causal relation. For example, if one were to find a significant relationship between two variables assessed at a single time point, it would not be known whether variable A causes variable B, whether variable B causes variable A, if there was a reciprocal relation between the two variables, or if there was an unmeasured variable causing changes in variable A or B. In the absence of a controlled experiment, researchers are encouraged to consider the timing of assessments to ensure that the measurement of variables are independent and consistent with the direction of the hypothesized relation.

Fourth, there is a need to investigate mediators of the relation between therapist methods and treatment outcomes such as symptoms. It would be more consistent with the cognitive theory to measure CR as a predictor of cognitive changes, as opposed to direct predictors of symptom outcomes. There might also be other mediational pathways, and moderators of such pathways, that researchers ought to consider when designing future studies to investigate the impact of CR within session.

Training Implications

While we are unaware of any training protocols for CR specifically (as opposed to cognitive therapy generally), we recommend that psychotherapists first attain a comprehensive understanding of the cognitive model (Beck, 1976, 1979). When providing CR, clients are most likely to receive a therapeutic benefit when they too understand the cognitive model, specifically that the way in which they interpret events drives their mood and behaviors. Furthermore, CR is first used to identify and challenge negative automatic thoughts in specific situations, but over time, therapists may amplify the impact of CR by using these methods to help identify and challenge client's underlying core beliefs.

Training in CR typically involves didactic instruction, active modeling, role playing with feedback, and supervision, usually but not necessarily as part of a formal training program in cognitive (or cognitive-behavioral) therapy. For therapeutic manuals describing how to implement CR in session, please see Beck et al. (1979) and J. S. Beck (2020).

Therapeutic Practices

There is initial evidence that CR promotes positive outcomes in individual psychotherapy. In the current review of all identified studies (Table 22.2), therapist use of CR was positively related to intermediate (i.e., lower next-session depressive symptoms and greater cognitive change) and distal treatment outcomes (i.e., lower risk of relapse and lower attrition). These studies examining the therapeutic impact of CR within session have been limited to the treatment of depression. However, component analyses that have examined the additive effect of CR in relation to behavioral components have found CR to be at least as equally effective as behavioral components in the treatment of anxiety disorders and obsessive-compulsive disorder. In addition, evidence from component analyses suggest that CR may be more therapeutic than behavioral components in the treatment of social anxiety disorder and posttraumatic stress disorder (Clark, 2014). In a complementary body of work, mediation analyses have found cognitive change (i.e., the expected product of CR) to lead to symptom improvement across a variety of disorders (Hofmann et al., 2018; Lorenzo-Luaces et al., 2015). Thus, we offer the following practices based on this body of research evidence:

- Utilize cognitive restructuring by helping clients identify, challenge, and correct negative inaccuracies in their thinking.
- Promote cognitive restructuring in the treatment of several disorders, including depression, anxiety, social anxiety disorder, obsessive-compulsive disorder, and posttraumatic stress disorder.
- Consider the use of cognitive restructuring in any clinical circumstances when working with clients to foster cognitive change and subsequent symptom improvement.
- Beware of possible biases in under-utilizing CR with members of marginalized populations.
- Recall that the goal of CR is not to minimize existing threats but rather to get an accurate sense of what they might be.

References

* Studies included in the meta-analysis.

Abramowitz, J. S., Taylor, S., & McKay, D. (2005). Potentials and limitations of cognitive treatments for obsessive–compulsive disorder. *Cognitive Behaviour Therapy*, *34*, 140–147. https://doi.org/10.1080/16506070510041202

Barber, J. P., & DeRubeis, R. J. (1992). The ways of responding: A scale to assess compensatory skills taught in cognitive therapy. *Behavioral Assessment*, *14*, 93–115.

Barber, J. P., & DeRubeis, R. J. (2001). Change in compensatory skills in cognitive therapy for depression. *Journal of Psychotherapy Practice and Research*, *10*, 8–13.

Beck, A. T. (1976). *Cognitive therapy and the emotional disorders*. International Universities Press.

Beck, A. T. (1987). Cognitive models of depression. *Journal of Cognitive Psychotherapy*, *1*, 5–37.

Beck, A. T. (1996). Beyond belief: A theory of modes, personality, and psychopathology. In P. M. Salkovskis (Ed.), *Frontiers of cognitive therapy* (pp. 1–25). Guilford.

Beck, A. T., Rush, A. J., Shaw, B. F., & Emery, G. (1979). *Cognitive therapy of depression*. Guilford.

Beck, A. T., Steer, R. A., & Brown, G. K. (1996). *Manual for the Beck Depression Inventory* (2nd ed.). Psychological Corporation.

Beck, J. S. (2020). *Cognitive behavior therapy: Basics and beyond* (3rd ed.). Guilford.

Clark, D. A. (2012). Cognitive restructuring. In S. G. Hofmann, D. J. Dozois, W. E. Rief, & J. A. Smits (Eds.), *The Wiley handbook of cognitive behavioral therapy* (pp. 1–22). Wiley Blackwell. https://doi.org/10.1002/9781118528563.wbcbt02

Clark, D. A. (2014). Cognitive restructuring. In S. G. Hofmann (Ed.), *The Wiley handbook of cognitive behavioral therapy* (pp. 1–22). Wiley Blackwell. https://doi.org/10.1002/9781118528563.wbcbt02

Clark, D. A., & Beck, A. T. (2010). *Cognitive therapy of anxiety disorders: Science and practice*. Guilford.

Clark, D. M. (1997). Panic disorder and social phobia. In D. M. Clark & C. G. Fairburn (Eds.), *Science and practice of cognitive behaviour therapy* (pp. 119–153). Oxford University Press.

Clark, D. M., & Wells, A. (1995). A cognitive model of social phobia. In R. G. Heimberg, M. R. Liebowitz, D. A. Hope, & F. R. Schneier (Eds.), *Social phobia: Diagnosis, assessment and treatment* (pp. 69–93). Guilford.

Coffman, S., Martell, C. R., Dimidjian, S., Gallop, R., & Hollon, S. D. (2007). Extreme nonresponse in cognitive therapy: Can behavioral activation succeed where cognitive therapy fails? *Journal of Consulting and Clinical Psychology*, *75*, 531–541.

Cottraux, J., Note, I., Yao, S. N., Lafont, S., Note, B., Mollard, E., Bouvard, M., Sauteraud, A., Bourgeois, M., & Dartiques, J. F. (2001). A randomized controlled trial of cognitive therapy versus intensive behavior therapy in obsessive compulsive disorder. *Psychotherapy and Psychosomatics*, *70*, 288–297. https://doi.org/10.1159/000056269

Curran, P. J., & Bauer, D. J. (2011). The disaggregation of within-person and between-person effects in longitudinal models of change. *Annual Review of Psychology*, 62, 583–619. http://dx.doi.org/10.1146/annurev.psych.093008.100356

Deacon, B. J., & Abramowitz, J. S. (2004). Cognitive and behavioral treatments for anxiety disorders: A review of meta-analytic findings. *Journal of Clinical Psychology*, *60*, 429–441. https://doi.org/10.1002/jclp.10255

Dimidjian, S., Hollon, S. D., Dobson, K. S., Schmaling, K. B., Kohlenberg, R. J., Addis, M. E., Gallop, R., McGlinchey, J., Markley, D., Gollan, J., Atkins, D., Dunner, D., & Jacobson, N. S. (2006). Randomized trial of behavioral activation, cognitive therapy, and antidepressant medication in the acute treatment of adults with major depression. *Journal of Consulting and Clinical Psychology*, *74*, 658–670. https://doi.org/10.1037/0022-006X.74.4.658

Dobson, D., & Dobson, K. S. (2009). *Evidence-based practice of cognitive–behavioral therapy*. Guilford.

Dobson, K. S., Hollon, S. D., Dimidjian, S., Schmaling, K. B., Kohlenberg, R. J., Gallop, R. J., Rizvi, S. L., Gollan, J. K., Dunner, D. L., & Jacobson, N. S. (2008). Randomized trial of behavioral activation, cognitive therapy, and antidepressant medication in the prevention of relapse and recurrence in major depression. *Journal of Consulting and Clinical Psychology. 76*, 468–477.

Elkin, I. (1994). The NIMH Treatment of Depression Collaborative Research Program: Where we began and where we are. In A. E. Bergin & S. L. Garfield (Eds.), *Handbook of psychotherapy and behavior change* (pp. 114–139). Wiley.

Ezawa, I. D., Bartels, G. C., Pfeifer, B., J., & Strunk. D. R. (2021). Pay no attention to the man behind the curtain: The overlooked issue of rater selection in psychotherapy observer ratings. *Psychotherapy Research, 31*, 548–556. https://doi.org/10.1080/10503307.2020.1780510

*Ezawa, I. D., & Strunk, D. R. (2022a). Differences in the delivery of cognitive behavioral therapy for depression when therapists work with Black and White patients. *Cognitive Therapy and Research, 46*, 104–113. https://doi.org/10.1007/s10608-021-10254-0

Ezawa, I. D., & Strunk, D. R. (2022b). Working with Black vs. White patients: An experimental test of therapist decision-making in cognitive behavioral therapy for depression. *Cognitive Behaviour Therapy, 51*, 229–242. https://doi.org/10.1080/16506073.2021.1970799

Feske, U., & Chambless, D. L. (1995). Cognitive behavioral versus exposure only treatment for social phobia: A meta-analysis. *Behavior Therapy, 26*, 695–720. https://doi.org/10.1016/S0005-7894(05)80040-1

Flückiger, C., Caspar, F., Holtforth, M. G., & Willutzki, U. (2009). Working with patients' strengths: A microprocess approach. *Psychotherapy Research, 19*, 213–223. http://dx.doi.org/10.1080/10503300902755300

Flückiger, C., Regli, D., Zwahlen, D., Hostettler, S., & Bern, U. (2010). Der Berner Patienten–und Therapeutenstundenbogen 2000 Ein Instrument zur Erfassung von Therapieprozessen. *Zeitschrift für Klinische Psychologie und Psychotherapie, 39*, 71–79. http://dx.doi.org/10.1026/1616-3443/a000015

Garratt, G., Ingram, R. E., Rand, K. L., & Sawalani, G. (2007). Cognitive processes in cognitive therapy: Evaluation of the mechanisms of change in the treatment of depression. *Clinical Psychology: Science and Practice, 14*, 224–239. http://dx.doi.org/10.1111/j.1468-2850.2007.00081.x

Gibbons, M. B. C., Crits-Christoph, P., Barber, J. P., Wiltsey Stirman, S., Gallop, R., Goldstein, L. A., Temes, C. M., & Ring–Kurtz, S. (2009). Unique and common mechanisms of change across cognitive and dynamic psychotherapies. *Journal of Consulting and Clinical Psychology, 77*, 801–813. https://doi.org/10.1037/a0016596

*Gómez Penedo, J. M., Coyne, A. E., Constantino, M. J., Krieger, T., & Hayes, A. M. (2020). Theory-specific client change processes and mechanisms in different cognitive therapies for depression. *Journal of Consulting and Clinical Psychology, 88*, 774–785. https://doi.org/10.1037/ccp0000502

Gortner, E. T., Gollan, J. K., Dobson, K. S., & Jacobson, N. S. (1998). Cognitive–behavioral treatment for depression: Relapse prevention. *Journal of Consulting and Clinical Psychology, 66*, 377–384. https://doi.org/10.1037/0022-006X.66.2.377

Gould, R. A., Otto, M. W., & Pollack, M. H. (1995). A meta-analysis of treatment outcome for panic disorder. *Clinical Psychology Review, 15*, 819–844. https://doi.org/10.1016/0272-7358(95)00048-8

Hamilton, M. (1960). A rating scale for depression. *Journal of Neurology, Neurosurgery & Psychiatry, 23*, 56–62. https://doi.org/10.1136/jnnp.23.1.56

Hassija, C. M., & Gray, M. J. (2010). Are cognitive techniques and interventions necessary? A case for the utility of cognitive approaches in the treatment of PTSD. *Clinical Psychology: Science and Practice, 17*, 112–127. https://doi.org/10.1111/j.1468-2850.2010.01201.x

Hays, P. A. (2009). Integrating evidence-based practice, cognitive–behavior therapy, and multicultural therapy: Ten steps for culturally competent practice. *Professional Psychology: Research and Practice, 40*, 354–360. https://doi.org/10.1037/a0016250

Hofmann, S. G. (2008). Common misconceptions about cognitive mediation of treatment change: A commentary to Longmore and Worrell (2007). *Journal of Consulting and Clinical Psychology, 28*, 67–70. https://doi.org/10.1016/j.cpr.2007.03.003

Hofmann, S. G., Carpenter, J. K., & Curtiss, J. (2018). Cognitive mediation of symptom change in cognitive–behavioral therapy: A review of the evidence. In R. L. Leahy (Ed.), *Science and practice in cognitive therapy: Foundations, mechanisms, and applications* (pp. 124–141). Guilford.

Hollon, S. D. (2021). Aaron Beck and the history of cognitive therapy: A tale of two cities (and one institute). In W. Pickren (Ed.), *Oxford research encyclopedia of psychology*. Oxford University Press.

Hollon, S. D., Evans, M. D., Auerbach, A., DeRubeis, R. J., Elkin, I., Lowery, A., Kris, M. R., Grove, W. M., Tuason, V. B., & Piasecki, J. M. (1988). *Development of a system for rating therapies for depression: Differentiating cognitive therapy, interpersonal psychotherapy and clinical management pharmacotherapy* [Unpublished manuscript]. Vanderbilt University.

Jacob, K. L., Christopher, M. S., & Neuhaus, E. C. (2011). Development and validation of the cognitive–behavioral therapy skills questionnaire. *Behavior Modification, 35*, 595–618. https://doi.org/10.1177/0145445511419254

Jacobson, N. S., Dobson, K. S., Truax, P. A., Addis, M. E., & Koerner, K. (1996). A component analysis of cognitive–behavioral treatment of depression. *Journal of Consulting and Clinical Psychology, 64*, 295–304. https://doi.org/10.1037/0022-006X.64.2.295

Jarrett, R. B., Vittengl, J. R., Clark, L. A., & Thase, M. E. (2011). Skills of Cognitive Therapy (SoCT): A new measure of patients' comprehension and use. *Psychological Assessment, 23*, 578–586. https://doi.org/10.1037/a0022485

Lewis, C., Roberts, N. P., Andrew, M., Starling, E., & Bisson, J. I. (2020). Psychological therapies for post-traumatic stress disorder in adults: Systematic review and meta-analysis. *European Journal of Psychotraumatology, 11*, 1729633. https://doi.org/10.1080/20008198.2020.1729633

Lewis, C., Roberts, N. P., Gibson, S., & Bisson, J. I. (2020). Dropout from psychological therapies for post-traumatic stress disorder (PTSD) in adults: Systematic review and meta-analysis. *European Journal of Psychotraumatology, 11*, 1709709. https://doi.org/10.1080/20008198.2019.1709709

Longmore, R. J., & Worrell, M. (2007). Do we need to challenge thoughts in cognitive behavior therapy? *Clinical Psychology Review, 27*, 173–187. https://doi.org/10.1016/j.cpr.2006.08.001

Lorenzo-Luaces, L., German, R. E., & DeRubeis, R. J. (2015). It's complicated: The relation between cognitive change procedures, cognitive change, and symptom change in cognitive therapy for depression. *Clinical Psychology Review, 41*, 3–15. https://doi.org/10.1016/j.cpr.2014.12.003

Mayo-Wilson, E., Dias, S., Mavranezouli, I., Kew, K., Clark, D. M., Ades, A. E., & Pilling, S. (2014). Psychological and pharmacological interventions for social anxiety disorder in adults: A systematic review and network meta-analysis. *Lancet Psychiatry, 1*(5), 368–376.

McLean, P. D., Whittal, M. L., Thordarson, D. S., Taylor, S., Sochting, I., Koch, W. J., Paterson, R., & Anderson, K. W. (2001). Cognitive versus behavior therapy in the group treatment of obsessive–compulsive disorder. *Journal of Consulting and Clinical Psychology, 69*, 205–214. https://doi.org/10.1037/0022-006X.69.2.205

Mohlman, J. (2013). Executive skills in older adults with GAD: Relations with clinical variables and CBT outcome. *Journal of Anxiety Disorders, 27*, 131–139. https://doi.org/10.1016/j.janxdis.2012.12.001

O'Connor, K. P., Aardema, F., Bouthillier, D., Fournier, S., Guay, S., Robillard, S., Pelissier, M., Landry, P., Todorov, C., Tremblay, M., & Pitre, D. (2005). Evaluation of an inference-based approach to treating obsessive–compulsive disorder. *Cognitive Behaviour Therapy, 34*, 148–163. https://doi.org/10.1080/16506070510041211

Ottenbreit, N. D., & Dobson, K. S. (2004). Avoidance and depression: The construction of the Cognitive–Behavioral Avoidance Scale. *Behaviour Research and Therapy, 42*(3), 293–313. https://doi.org/10.1016/S0005-7967(03)00140-2

Ougrin, D. (2011). Efficacy of exposure versus cognitive therapy in anxiety disorders: Systematic review and meta-analysis. *BMC Psychiatry, 11*, Article 200. https://doi.org/10.1186/1471-244X-11-200

Peterson, R. A., & Brown, S. P. (2005). On the use of beta coefficients in meta-analysis. *Journal of Applied Psychology, 90*, 175–181. https://doi.org/10.1037/0021-9010.90.1.175

Ponniah, K., & Hollon, S. D. (2009). Empirically supported psychological treatments for adult acute stress disorder and posttraumatic stress disorder: A review. *Depression and Anxiety*, *26*, 1086–1109. https://doi.org/10.1002/da.20635

Resick, P. A., Galovski, T. E., Uhlmansiek, M. O., Scher, C. D., Clum, G. A., & Young-Xu, Y. (2008). A randomized clinical trial to dismantle components of cognitive processing therapy for posttraumatic stress disorder in female victims of interpersonal violence. *Journal of Consulting and Clinical Psychology*, *76*, 243–258. https://doi.org/10.1037/0022-006X.76.2.243

Salkovskis, P. M. (1999). Understanding and treating obsessive–compulsive disorder. *Behaviour Research and Therapy*, *37*(Suppl. 1), S29–S52.

Sasso, K. E., Strunk, D. R., Braun, J. D., DeRubeis, R. J., & Brotman, M. A. (2016). A re-examination of process–outcome relations in cognitive therapy for depression: Disaggregating within-patient and between-patient effects. *Psychotherapy Research*, *26*, 387–398. http://dx.doi.org/10.1080/10503307.2015.1026423

*Schmidt, I. D., Pfeifer, B. J., & Strunk, D. R. (2019). Putting the "cognitive" back in cognitive therapy: Sustained cognitive change as a mediator of in-session insights and depressive symptom improvement. *Journal of Consulting and Clinical Psychology*, *87*, 446–456. https://doi.org/10.1037/ccp0000392

Stein, N. R., Dickstein, B. D., Schuster, J., Litz, B. T., & Resick, P. A. (2012). Trajectories of response to treatment for posttraumatic stress disorder. *Behavior Therapy*, *43*, 790–800. https://doi.org/10.1016/j.beth.2012.04.003

*Strunk, D. R., Brotman, M. A., & DeRubeis, R. J. (2010). The process of change in cognitive therapy for depression: Predictors of early inter-session symptom gains. *Behaviour Research and Therapy*, *48*, 599–606. https://doi.org/10.1016/j.brat.2010.03.011

Strunk, D. R., Cooper, A. A., Ryan, E. T., DeRubeis, R. J., & Hollon, S. D. (2012). The process of change in cognitive therapy for depression when combined with antidepressant medication: Predictors of early intersession symptom gains. *Journal of Consulting and Clinical Psychology*, *80*, 730–738. https://doi.org/10.1037/a0029281

*Strunk, D. R., DeRubeis, R. J., Chiu, A. W., & Alvarez, J. (2007). Patients' competence in and performance of cognitive therapy skills: Relation to the reduction of relapse risk following treatment for depression. *Journal of Consulting and Clinical Psychology*, *75*, 523–530. https://doi.org/10.1037/0022-006X.75.4.523

Strunk, D. R., Hollars, S. N., Adler, A. D., Goldstein, L. A., & Braun, J. D. (2014). Assessing patients' cognitive therapy skills: Initial evaluation of the Competencies of Cognitive Therapy Scale. *Cognitive Therapy and Research*, *38*, 559–569. https://doi.org/10.1007/s10608-014-9617-9

Tarrier, N., & Sommerfield, C. (2004). Treatment of chronic PTSD by cognitive therapy and exposure: 5-year follow-up. *Behavior Therapy*, *35*, 231–246. https://doi.org/10.1016/S0005-7894(04)80037-6

Teasdale, J. D., & Fennell, M. J. (1982). Immediate effects on depression of cognitive therapy interventions. *Cognitive Therapy and Research*, *6*, 343–351. https://doi.org/10.1007/BF01173582

Topp, C. W., Østergaard, S. D., Søndergaard, S., & Bech, P. (2015). The WHO-5 Well-Being Index: A systematic review of the literature. *Psychotherapy and Psychosomatics*, *84*, 167–176. https://doi.org/10.1159/000376585

Walter, K. H., Dickstein, B. D., Barnes, S. M., & Chard, K. M. (2014). Comparing effectiveness of CPT to CPT-C among US veterans in an interdisciplinary residential PTSD/TBI treatment program. *Journal of Traumatic Stress*, *27*, 438–445. https://doi.org/10.1002/jts.21934

Wang, L. P., & Maxwell, S. E. (2015). On disaggregating between-person and within-person effects with longitudinal data using multilevel models. *Psychological Methods*, *20*, 63–83. http://dx.doi.org/10.1037/met0000030

Whittal, M. L., Thordarson, D. S., & McLean, P. D. (2005). Treatment of obsessive–compulsive disorder: Cognitive behavior therapy vs. exposure and response prevention. *Behaviour Research and Therapy*, *43*, 1559–1576. https://doi.org/10.1016/j.brat.2004.11.012

23

Skills and Methods That Work in Psychotherapy

Research Results, Training Implications, Therapeutic Practices, and Task Force Conclusions

Clara E. Hill, John C. Norcross, and the Steering Committee

The interorganizational Task Force on Psychotherapy Skills and Methods That Work was commissioned to identify, compile, and disseminate the research evidence on psychotherapist skills and methods used across theoretical orientations. The contributors of the preceding chapters in this volume have carefully examined the research evidence for the impact of skills/methods on immediate, intermediate, and distal treatment outcomes. We are grateful to the contributors for undertaking the enormous task of disentangling and summarizing the literature, which was often messy and disjointed.

Based on this research evidence, the contributors concluded their respective chapters with possible negative effects, diversity issues, research limitations, training implications, and therapeutic practices. Their chapters provided valuable information for practitioners on how to use the skills/methods, guidance for trainers on how to help students learn the skills/methods, inspiration for future researchers on how to study the skills/methods better, encouragement for research funders to provide more funding for studying skills/methods, and cautions to policymakers about using the current evidence to set restrictive policies about psychotherapy.

No book could include all the possible skills and methods of psychotherapy. In fact, we commissioned chapters on therapist challenges, behavioral rehearsal/role-playing, development of mentalization, exposure methods, and working with cultural diversity, but for a number of reasons, these did not come to fruition. We could have included dozens of additional chapters, for example, on interruptions, clarifications, summary statements, confrontations, imagery, hypnosis, and more. Hence, we have included only a subset of possible skills/methods, and others might indeed prove effective.

In this chapter, we take on the ambitious task of summarizing what we have learned and integrating what the Task Force has concluded from this multiyear endeavor. Following the format of the preceding research chapters, we summarize our lessons in five sections. We start with the foundations of the skills/methods: definitions, clinical descriptions, assessments, and clinical examples. In the second section, we recap the research evidence for the effectiveness of the skills/methods in terms of immediate in-session, intermediate, and distal outcomes, including the consensual judgment of the Task Force Steering Committee on which skills/methods work. We also address possible negative effects, diversity considerations, and caveats in interpreting the research

Clara E. Hill, John C. Norcross, and the Steering Committee, *Skills and Methods That Work in Psychotherapy*
In: *Psychotherapy Skills and Methods That Work.* Edited by: Clara E. Hill and John C. Norcross, Oxford University Press.
 DOI: 10.1093/oso/9780197611012.003.0023

findings. In the third section, we consider in more detail the training implications. Fourth are the recommendations for therapeutic practices. In the fifth and final section, we present the conclusions of the Task Force from the entire project. We direct new readers to Chapter 1 for the rationale of the Task Force and the background on the constructs involved in the research reviews and Task Force conclusions.

Foundations of the Skills/Methods

In all the chapters, contributors adeptly presented the theoretical and clinical foundations for the skills and methods under consideration. Indeed, there were rich literatures for each skill/method, as these are all commonly used within psychotherapy.

In terms of definitions, most contributors had a relatively easy time, particularly with skills that were defined by their grammatical structure (e.g., questions, advice, empathic reflections) or with methods that were defined by their structure (e.g., role induction). A few contributors had more difficulty with operationalizing their skills or methods because they were more expansive or used differently by clinicians (e.g., Socratic questions, metaphors, dream work, strength-based methods).

For some chapters, it was relatively straightforward and easy to categorize the clinician behavior either as a skill (e.g., questions, advice) or a method (e.g., cognitive restructuring, role induction). But others proved problematic. For example, interpretations can be coded as a microprocess but are often conceptualized clinically as a sequence of skills (e.g., clarification followed by challenges followed by interpretations), which is closer to a method. Similarly, some of what we considered methods (e.g., dream work, chairwork, collaborative assessment methods) were composed of multiple steps, although these components were rarely tested individually. Furthermore, some of the methods have sometimes been tested as whole treatment packages (e.g., strength-based methods, meditation/mindfulness/acceptance, behavioral activation, cognitive restructuring) rather than as a separate method within a treatment package.

A problem that arose in at least two chapters (e.g., silences, dyadic synchrony) involved contributors having difficulty attributing the skill or method to the psychotherapist when it is so clearly co-constructed between the therapist and client. This problem was also encountered occasionally in the previous Task Force on Psychotherapy Relationships That Work (Norcross & Lambert, 2019); relationships are obviously the product of two people. Much like parenting, the influences are bidirectional, but we expect therapists to "lead" and "shape." It is indeed challenging to disentangle who contributed what, but we focused this book on the psychotherapist's contribution because of the need to determine what therapists do to lead and shape and what trainers can do to improve their effectiveness.

In terms of the assessment of the specific skill/method, contributors to the skills chapters (e.g., questions, empathic reflections, advice) had a relatively easy task as verbal response modes have been systematized and categorized going back as far as the mid-20th century (e.g., Snyder, 1945). The problem is that these assessments are often simplistic and lack clinical nuance. Contributors of chapters on multifaceted methods experienced more difficulty as their methods (e.g., emotion regulation, strength-based methods) have not been examined operationally in terms of actual behavior or adherence within sessions. Clearly, new and better ways of assessing both skills and methods are needed so that we can study what is occurring in sessions.

In terms of the assessment of outcomes, they were divided into immediate in-session (e.g., clients offering new memories in sessions after therapist interpretations) and delayed (e.g., based on clients or therapists reviewing the videotape of the session and rating the effectiveness of specific events), intermediate (e.g., client post-session ratings of alliance), and distal (e.g., end-of-treatment changes in symptomatology). (Although not addressed in the research reviews in this volume, long-term follow-up assessments, months or years after termination, also prove useful but difficult to connect with specific skills/behaviors.) Contributors frequently noted the utter lack of immediate in-session measures that could assess expected client responses to their skills/methods. They noted that global measures, such as client experiencing or involvement, might not capture the intended or unintended reactions to empathic reflections, advice, mindfulness, and the like.

Similarly, most measures of intermediate outcome (e.g., working alliance, session evaluation) and distal outcome (e.g., changes in symptomatology) were not designed to assess the intended or desired effects of specific skills or methods. We, and the contributors, bemoaned such generic and crude assessments of the subtle impacts of specific clinician behaviors. We hope that clinicians will think about what researchers should be looking for in these assessments of specific skills/methods and provide guidance to researchers for improved tools.

In terms of clinical examples, contributors offered rich descriptions of how these skills and methods are typically implemented in practice. This clinical abundance reflects how psychotherapy practice develops long before researchers evaluate the research evidence of efficacy. These clinical descriptions also remind us of the complexity, lushness, and individuality of how these skills and methods are used across client populations and theoretical orientations.

Research Evidence for the Effectiveness of the Skills/Methods

All contributors cited landmark studies on their specific skills/methods, and these are noteworthy as the best the field has to offer at this time. Future researchers can build from these landmark studies to improve the literature.

For several well-defined *methods* (e.g., between-session homework, role induction, collaborative assessment methods, routine outcome monitoring), contributors also identified previous meta-analytic reviews, typically of distal outcomes. Notably, however, no previous research reviews or meta-analyses existed on the effectiveness of most of the therapy *skills*.

Association Between Therapy Skills/Methods and Treatment Outcomes

All contributors conducted a thorough review of the literature. Many initially dismissed the few studies on immediate in-session outcomes but were encouraged to return to the literature and be as inclusive as possible in their final research review.

Alas, only a couple of contributors included studies published outside English-language journals. Like most of psychological science (Henrich et al., 2010), psychotherapy research continues to emanate primarily from WEIRD (Western, educated, industrialized, rich and democratic) societies. What is known about the relation between therapy skills/methods and treatment outcomes is thus limited to a WEIRD socio-historical-cultural context. The current evidence base largely excludes other ways of understanding the constructs themselves and the relations between them.

Several contributors provided quantitative meta-analyses on the association of their therapy method to outcome. These quantitative meta-analyses were typically for distal outcomes, mostly of methods (e.g., role induction, collaborative assessment methods, routine outcome monitoring, strength-based methods, meditation/mindfulness/acceptance, behavioral activation, emotion regulation). These quantitative meta-analyses have become increasingly the "gold standard" for systematically reviewing the efficacy of treatment methods on distal, end-of-therapy outcomes, although they also have their flaws (Baldwin & Goldberg, 2021).

Far more challenging was locating empirical studies involving immediate in-session outcomes, especially of the methods, and then determining how to review these few studies. Given the paucity of studies, especially for immediate outcomes, contributors often resorted to box scores (see Chapter 1) to summarize the evidence (e.g., questions, interpretations, advice/suggestions/ recommendations, dyadic synchrony, paradoxical interventions, Socratic questions, metaphors). Box scores certainly do not provide as robust evidence as quantitative meta-analyses, but probably are superior to narrative reviews alone. Many people are not familiar with box scores, and there appears not to be good sources in the literature, so we developed some rules and examples as the Task Force evolved (see Chapter 1).

Not all the research evidence was amenable to quantitative syntheses. In these instances (self-disclosure, immediacy, empathic reflections, silences, rupture repair, and chairwork), contributors summarized some or all of the evidence qualitatively.

Once the research reviews were completed, at least four members of the Task Force's Steering Committee independently judged the research evidence for the immediate, intermediate, and distal outcomes for each skill or method. They determined whether the research evidence was demonstrably effective, probably effective, neutral or mixed evidence, not effective, or had insufficient research to judge. They based their judgments on six criteria (similar to those used for *Psychotherapy Relationships That Work*; Norcross & Lambert, 2019): number of empirical studies, consistency of empirical results, independence of supportive studies, magnitude of association between the skill/method and outcome, evidence for a causal link between the skill/method and outcome, and ecological or external validity of the findings.

The Task Force co-chairs/co-editors then aggregated and reviewed the Task Force's 47 judgments of the research evidence (18 on immediate outcomes, 8 on intermediate outcome, and 21 on distal outcomes). The majority judgment was honored in all instances. In cases of divided judgments, the co-chairs again reviewed the criteria, discussed the research evidence, and arrived at a consensus judgment. The multiple judges, the explicit criteria, and the recursive process of reaching consensus added rigor to the final determination.

Table 23.1 summarizes the results reported by contributors for the associations between the therapy skills/methods and patient outcomes. The table also provides the Steering Committee's consensus judgments on the typical effectiveness of these psychotherapy skills and methods.

Table 23.1 Summary of associations between psychotherapist skills/methods and psychotherapy outcomes.

Skill/Method	Type of Outcome	# Studies	# Clients/ Patients	Type of Analysis	Results of Research Review	Consensus on Research Evidence
Affirmation/ Validation (skill)	Distal	64	3,528	Meta-analysis	$g = 0.28–0.36$	Demonstrably Effective
Self-disclosure (skill)	Immediate	5	99	Qualitative meta-analysis	Improved relationship (64%) Gained insight (46%) Better mental health (45%) Helpful (37%)	Insufficient Research
Immediacy (skill)	Immediate	15	78	Qualitative meta-analysis	Improved relationship (40%) Opened up (40%) Not helpful (39%)	Insufficient Research
Rupture Repair (method)	Immediate	5	21	Task analysis	Acknowledged & explored rupture	Insufficient Research
		3	10	Task analysis	Renegotiated goal	
	Distal	11	1,318	Meta-analysis	$d = 0.51–0.62$	Probably Effective
	Training	6	407	Meta-analysis	$d = 0.22$	
Questions (skill)	Immediate	10	328	Box score	5+, 5=, 6 -	Neutral/Mixed
Socratic Questioning (method)	Immediate	6	39	Box score	6+, 0 = , 0-	Insufficient Research
	Distal	1	55	Box score	2+, 0 = , 0-	Insufficient Research
Empathic Reflections (skill)	Immediate					Neutral/Mixed
	In-Session	24	1,217	Meta-analysis	$d = 0.05$	
		4	44	Qual: Narrative	Increased self-understanding	
		21	(1,152 egs)	Conver. analysis	Positive if therapist responds to empathic opportunity, reflects client's stance, and makes a correction	
	Delayed	3	72	Meta-analysis	$d = 0.04$	
	Distal	22	1,734	Meta-analysis	$d = 0.04$	Neutral/Mixed

Metaphors (skill)	Immediate					Insufficient Research
	In-Session	5	9	Box score	5+, 0=, 0-	
	Delayed	5	17	Box score	4+, 0=, 3-	
	Distal	5	80	Box score	3+, 5=, 0-	Insufficient Research
Interpretations (skill)	Immediate In-Session	6	88	Box score	10+. 6=, 4-	Neutral/Mixed
	Intermediate	4	288	Box score	8+, 5=, 3-	Neutral/Mixed
	Distal	12	866	Box score	9+, 19=, 3-	Neutral/Mixed
Paradoxical Interventions (method)	Intermediate	12	35	Box score	12+, 0=, 1-	Probably Effective
	Distal					Demonstrably Effective
	Pre-post	17	422	Meta-analysis	$d = 1.1$	
	Compared to non-PI	17	471	Meta-analysis	$d = 0.49$	
Advice, Suggestions, Recommendations (skill)	Immediate					Neutral/Mixed
	In-Session	5	141	Box score	2+, 14=, 4-	
	Delayed	3	22	Box score	0+, 10=, 1-	
	Intermediate	2	123	Box score	2+, 0=. 0-	Insufficient Research
Homework (method)	Immediate					Neutral/Mixed
	In-Session	9	322	Box score	3+, 0=, 6-, WBS = .26	
	Intermediate	16	982	Box Score	10+, 2=, 4-, WBS = .53	Probably Effective
	Distal (previous review)	14	477	Meta-analysis	$d = 0.53$	Demonstrably Effective
Silences (method)	In-dialogue silences					Probably Effective
	Immediate	17	276	Integrative Meta-analysis	Therapist allowing productive pauses was associated with more client emotional attunement, new symbolization, meaning making, lowered emotional distress, and increased collaboration. Therapist permitting obstructive pauses was associated with client withdrawal, relational rifts, greater emotional distress, and poorer alliance.	

(continued)

Table 23.1 Continued

Skill/Method	Type of Outcome	# Studies	# Clients/ Patients	Type of Analysis	Results of Research Review	Consensus on Research Evidence
	Extended silences					Probably Effective
	Immediate	16	33	Qualitative meta-analysis	Therapist support as well understanding and identifying client experiences during silences was associated with increases in client insight/self-understanding, capacity for relationships, containment of emotions, and autonomy.	
Dyadic Synchrony (method)	Intermediate	8	323	Box score	WBS = .257	Neutral/Mixed
	Movement	6	259	Box score	WBS = .214	
	Physiological	2	64	Box score	WBS = .479	
	Distal	14	786	Box score	WBS = .343	Neutral/Mixed
	Movement	10	667	Box score	WBS = .389	
	Vocal	2	116	Box score	WBS = -.222	
	Physiological	1	60	Box score	WBS = .500	
	Linguistic	1	7	Box score	WBS = 0	
Role Induction (method)	Immediate					Probably Effective
	In-session	8	651	Meta-analysis	$d = 0.64$	
	Delayed	3	151	Box score	3+, 0=, 0-	
	Distal					Probably Effective
	Dropout	15	1,307	Meta-analysis	$OR = 1.64$	
	Mid-Treatment	5	288	Meta-analysis	$d = 0.26$	
	End-Treatment	8	662	Meta-analysis	$d = 0.33$	
Collaborative Assessment Methods (method)	Distal					Probably Effective
	Process	7	320	Meta-analysis	$d = 0.59$	
	Symptoms	7	332	Meta-analysis	$d = 0.19$	
	Growth	5	264	Meta-analysis	$d = 0.42$	
	Cases	6	6	Box score	6+, 0=, 0-	

Routine Outcome Monitoring (method)	Distal (All clients)					
	End-treatment	58	21,699	Meta-analysis	$d = 0.15$	Demonstrably Effective
	Follow-up					
	Dropout	4	1,027	Meta-analysis	$d = 0.18$	
	Deterioration	39	14,369	Meta-analysis	$OR = 1.19$	
	Distal (Not-on-track)	26	10,413	Meta-analysis	$OR = 1.16$	
	End-treatment	27	15,146	Meta-analysis	$d = 0.17$	
Strength-based Methods (method, treatment)	Immediate	8	416	Box score	6+, 2=, 0-	Probably Effective
	Distal					Demonstrably Effective
	Disorder-specific					
	Previous combined	10–51	max 6,139	Meta-analysis	$g = 0.07–0.94$	
	Current bona fide	9	729	Meta-analysis	$g = 0.18$	
	Other Outcomes					
	Previous combined	10–51	Max 6,139	Meta-analysis	$g = 0.02–0.92$	
	Current bona fide	9	729	Meta-analysis	$g = 0.16$	
Emotion Regulation (method, treatment)	Immediate	8	84	Box score	6+, 2=, 0-	Probably Effective
	Intermediate	2	14	Box score	0+, 3=, 0-	Insufficient Research
	Distal	28	1,034	Meta-analysis	$g = 0.82$	Demonstrably Effective
Chairwork (method, treatment)	Immediate					Neutral/Mixed
	Btwn groups	4	295	Meta-analysis	$d = 0.10$	
	Btwn groups	4	98	Meta-analysis	$d = 0.90$	
	Distal					Probably Effective
	Pre-post single sess	7	326	Meta-analysis	$d = 1.73$	
	Btwn grps, post-sess	3	105	Meta-analysis	$d = -0.02$	
	Btwn grps, post-tx	5	238	Meta-analysis	$d = 0.40$	
		4	100	Task analysis	Step 1: activate problem state Step 2: explore inner reaction Step 3: enact core concern Step 4: express emotion Step 5: change perspective Step 6: negotiate engagement	

(*continued*)

Table 23.1 Continued

Skill/Method	Type of Outcome	# Studies	# Clients/ Patients	Type of Analysis	Results of Research Review	Consensus on Research Evidence
Dream Work and Nightmare Treatment (method, treatment)	Dream work CEDM					
	Intermediate	8	539	Meta-analysis	$g = 0.67–0.70$	Demonstrably Effective
	Nightmare Tx					
	IRT/ERRT					Demonstrably Effective
	Distal					
	Previous	13	511	Meta-analysis	$g = .59$ to $.93$	
	Current	6	293	Box score	24+, 1=, 0-	Insufficient Research
	NDR					
	Immediate	1	11	Box score		
	Distal	2	40	Box score	4+, 2=, 0-	Insufficient Research
Meditation, Mindfulness, Acceptance (methods, treatment)	Immediate					Insufficient Research
	In-session	3	176	Box score	WBS = .06	
		1	9	Box score	WBS = 1.0	
	Distal					Demonstrably Effective
	Previous reviews (pre-post)	28	3,009	Meta-analysis	$g = 0.40–0.95$	
	MMA vs no tx	89	5,748	Meta-analysis	$g = 0.55$	
	MMA vs bona fide active control	42	3,810	Meta-analysis	$g = 0.23$	
	MMA vs evidence-based tx	28	2,806	Meta-analysis	$g = -0.004$	
Behavioral Activation (method, treatment)	Distal	22	819	Meta-analysis	$g = 0.85$	Demonstrably Effective (for depression)

Cognitive Restructuring (method, treatment)	Intermediate and Distal	4	353	Meta-analysis	$d = 0.85$	
	Intermediate	4	550	Box score	5+, 0=, 0-	Demonstrably Effective (for depression)
	Distal	2	261	Box score	3+, 0=, 0-	Demonstrably Effective (for depression)

Note. Skill = discrete verbal response mode; Method = a collection of skills oriented toward a specific aim which is implemented within an overall treatment approach; Treatment (tx) = entire treatment package focusing on and inseparable from the methods.

For Type of Outcome: Immediate includes both Immediate In-Session outcomes (typically judged by trained raters) and Immediate Delayed (ratings of in-session process typically made after sessions by therapists, clients, and trained judges); Intermediate = outcomes rated at post-session or between sessions; Distal = end-of-treatment outcome.

Tx: treatment; egs: excerpts; Qual.: Qualitative; Previous: previous published review.

For Type of Analysis: Box scores: + is a positive score, = is a neutral score, - is a negative score. WBS = weighted box score (between −1.00 to −0.50 is considered negative; between −0.49 to +0.49 is considered neutral, and between +0.50 to +1.00 is considered positive); Conver. analysis = conversational analysis.

Under Dream Work and Nightmare Tx, CEDM = cognitive-experiential dream model, IRT = imagery rehearsal therapy, ERRT = exposure, relaxation, and rescripting therapy, CDR = nightmare deconstruction and reprocessing therapy.

Consensus on Research Evidence: the consensus judgment of the Task Force Steering Committee about the strength of the research evidence for the effectiveness of each type of outcome for each skill/method: demonstrably effective, probably effective, neutral or mixed evidence, not effective, insufficient research to judge.

Research Evidence for the Effectiveness of Skills

For the eight skills reviewed in this volume, contributors located at least some research studies for seven skills for immediate, two skills for intermediate, and four skills for distal outcomes. Hence, immediate outcomes have been the most often studied for therapy *skills*.

- For immediate outcomes, there was a sufficient amount of research to make judgments about four skills. Questions, empathic reflections, interpretations, and advice/suggestions/recommendations were all judged to be neutral/mixed in terms of effectiveness.
- For intermediate outcomes, there was a sufficient amount of research evidence to make judgments about one skill. Interpretations were judged to be neutral/mixed in terms of effectiveness.
- For distal outcomes, there was a sufficient amount of research evidence to make judgments about three skills. Affirmation/validation was judged to be demonstrably effective; empathic reflections and interpretations were judged to be neutral/mixed.

In summary, we have evidence that, on average, therapist affirmation/validation was demonstrably effective in terms of distal outcomes. The only skill (interpretations) that was tested across all types of outcomes was judged as having neutral/mixed evidence for all three. The remaining research evidence on the effectiveness of the other six discrete therapy skills was decidedly mixed or neutral.

Research Evidence for the Effectiveness of Methods

For the 19 methods reviewed in this volume, contributors located at least some research studies for 11 for immediate, six for intermediate, and 16 for distal outcomes in their searches. Hence, distal outcomes have been the most often studied type of outcomes for *methods*.

- For immediate outcomes, there was a sufficient amount of research to make judgments about seven methods. Both in-dialogue and extended silences, role induction, strength-based methods, and emotion regulation were judged to be probably effective; homework and chairwork were judged to be neutral/mixed in terms of effectiveness.
- For intermediate outcomes, there was a sufficient amount of evidence to make judgments about five methods. Cognitive experiential dream work and cognitive restructuring were judged to be demonstrably effective, paradoxical interventions and homework were judged as probably effective, and dyadic synchrony was judged as neutral/mixed.
- For distal outcomes, there was a sufficient amount of evidence to make judgments about 14 methods. Nine (homework, paradoxical interventions, routine outcome monitoring, strength-based methods, emotion regulation, imagery rehearsal therapy/exposure/relaxation/rescripting therapy for nightmares, meditation/mindfulness/acceptance, behavioral activation, cognitive restructuring) were judged to be demonstrably effective. Four (rupture repair, role induction,

collaborative assessment methods, chairwork) were judged to be probably effective, and one (dyadic synchrony) was judged to be neutral/mixed across both of its two types of outcomes.

In short, there was evidence for probable or demonstrable effectiveness for 17 of the 19 methods (all but dyadic synchrony and Socratic questioning). In fact, six therapy methods (paradoxical interventions, role induction, strength- based methods, emotion regulation, homework, cognitive restructuring) evidenced probable or demonstrable effectiveness across two types of outcomes.

Research Evidence on Type of Outcomes

The strength of the research evidence systematically varied as a function of the type of therapy outcome, which itself was confounded with the type of statistical analysis. Of the judgments rendered by the Steering Committee on therapy skills and methods (see Table 23.1), 12 were of demonstrable effectiveness, 11 of probable effectiveness, 11 of neutral/mixed effectiveness, and 13 of insufficient research. Interestingly, 10 of the 12 judgments of demonstrable effectiveness were based completely on quantitative meta-analyses conducted on distal, end-of-treatment outcomes, and one used a quantitative meta-analysis on intermediate outcomes. On the other end of the spectrum, no therapy skill or method was determined to be demonstrably effective for immediate outcomes; these were rarely analyzed by quantitative meta-analyses. As noted in Chapter 1, it is easier to study distal outcomes (which are typically based on patient self-report of symptom changes) than immediate in-session outcomes (which typically require labor-intensive coding of microprocesses by trained judges).

Possible Negative Effects

Although difficult to define and assess harm and adverse effects, "some patients are clearly worse at the time therapy is terminated than when they started" (Barkham & Lambert, 2021, p. 170). If, indeed, some patients get worse and if the decline cannot be attributed to a progressive decline that started prior to treatment or to traumatic life events during therapy, it makes sense that what therapists do in sessions could lead to clients' worsening (e.g., if therapists do no work to repair ruptures, it makes sense that clients could be harmed).

Investigation into the negative effects of psychotherapy has lagged behind the study of its positive effects. In six of the chapters, however, contributors reported some empirical evidence for possible negative effects and harm (although this evidence was typically found in only one or two studies and is thus in need of replication):

- Empathic reflections have been found to have negative effects when they deviate too far from client experiences, are not expressed tentatively enough or with enough empathy, fail to adequately represent the intensity of feelings, or are not repaired after clients signal disagreement (Elliott et al., Chapter 5).
- Adverse effects have been reported in assigning homework that causes clients to feel pressure, anxiety, worsened mood, resistance, and ruptures. The use of

structured worksheets (e.g., thought and activity diaries) as homework seems to be particularly difficult for depressed clients, and some clients experienced suicidal thoughts from watching recorded videotapes at home of their own treatment sessions as part of exposure homework (Ryum et al., Chapter 10).
- For interpretations, some evidence shows that inaccurate interpretations can be harmful. Furthermore, a high dose of transference interpretations can be harmful because they make patients feel attacked, accused, and misunderstood; they are considered "high-risk, high-gain" methods (Zilcha-Mano et al., Chapter 7).
- Obstructive silences (moments in which clients withdraw from the relationship, avoid pressing issues, or disengage from therapeutic tasks) have been associated with poor alliances and outcomes. Clients with histories of feeling criticized, rejected, paranoid, psychotic, highly disturbed, or personality disorders might interpret long and frequent silences as being judgmental and interfering with the therapeutic relationship (Levitt & Morrill, Chapter 11).
- Evidence was found in one study that persons with schizophrenia had difficulty comprehending emotionally laden metaphors. Some clients might find the use of such metaphors to be off-putting or confusing; they might judge metaphoric language as less efficient, direct, or concrete than literal language (McMullen & Tay, Chapter 6).
- Negative effects in behavioral activation (BA) ranged from 0% to 10% across six studies. "Because of the small number of trials reporting negative effects, it is unfortunately not possible to make a reliable estimate of the proportion of patients who deteriorate during BA" (Cuijpers et al., Chapter 21).

For the other skills and methods reviewed in this volume, the chapter contributors reported no research on negative effects. The typical summary was something along the lines of, "Unfortunately, possible negative effects of CAM [collaborative assessment methods] have not been studied to date" (Aschieri et al., Chapter 14).

Despite not having empirical evidence, contributors suggested possible uninvestigated ways in which their skill/method could potentially lead to negative effects or harm. Williams (Chapter 3) suggested that therapists' emotional reactions and emotional regulation could influence the delivery of questions, and clients' emotional reactivity could negatively affect their response to questions. Overholser and Beale (Chapter 4) noted that Socratic questions could become overly abstract for clients who struggle with cognitive complexity, and clients might feel interrogated if Socratic questions were the only skill used throughout a therapy session. Peluso and Freund (Chapter 8) observed that clinicians are often concerned about using paradoxical interventions because they seem manipulative and gimmicky. Hill and colleagues (Chapter 9) suggested that negative effects might occur after advice/suggestions/recommendations if clients become passive and expect that therapists will solve their problems. Atzil-Slonim and colleagues (Chapter 12) suggested that context is undoubtedly crucial to when synchrony leads to positive or negative outcomes; for instance, it would not prove helpful when both therapist and client are depressed, anxious, or physiologically aroused. Aschieri and colleagues (Chapter 14) noted that client discomfort and micro-ruptures are possible negative effects of collaborative assessment methods; such methods are particularly challenging in forensic and mandatory assessments. Barkham and colleagues (Chapter 15) suggested that patients with severe psychopathology and cluster B personality disorders might experience negative effects of routine outcome monitoring, especially when clinical support tools are not available. In strength-based methods, Flückiger and colleagues (Chapter 16) noted that therapists can sometimes focus too much on strengths, be too optimistic and unrealistic, and come across as devaluing and infantilizing. Pascual-Leone and Baher (Chapter 18) stated that because chairwork violates social norms and is evocative, clients sometimes feel hesitant or even resistant to participating in it. Spangler and Sim (Chapter 19) cautioned that the prolonged exposure and cognitive processing of nightmare treatments might result in high dropout rates as found in other exposure-based therapies. Ezawa and Hollon (Chapter 22) suggested that cognitive restructuring may not prove useful for all thoughts and contexts, particularly that rational fears should not be discounted or minimized.

Diversity Considerations

As with negative effects and harm, minimal research has been conducted on the effectiveness of therapy skills and methods with culturally diverse patients and practitioners. In this section, only three of the chapters offered evidence for the effects of client cultural diversity on treatment outcome (and again, these results were based on few studies):

- Levitt and Morrill (Chapter 11) cited a study in which male therapists and clients more often than female therapists and clients used silence as a "shield" or boundary between each other in therapy (Hill et al., 2003).
- Swift et al. (Chapter 13) found that role induction was generally more effective in samples that had more non-Hispanic White clients than diverse racial and ethnic minorities.
- For cognitive restructuring, Ezawa and Hollon (Chapter 22) reported a study in which White therapists delivered less cognitive restructuring to Black than White patients even though cognitive restructuring has been found to be equally effective for Black and White patients (Ezawa & Strunk, 2022a). They also cited a study in which therapists viewed cognitive restructuring as less therapeutic for Black than White patients (Ezawa & Strunk, 2022b).

Similar outcomes were reported across cultural groups for three other skills/methods. Elliott and colleagues (Chapter 5) noted that similar results have been found for motivational interviewing across sociocultural dimensions for empathic reflections, although most of the research was conducted with Black and Hispanic clients. For between-session homework, Ryum et al. (Chapter 10) found that the impact of client characteristics was mostly negligible, but added that most research has been conducted with Western clients. Spangler and Sim (Chapter 19) reported that cognitive–experiential dream work produced similar benefit for university clients in both the United States and Taiwan.

For the other skills and methods included in this book, there was no empirical evidence for the impact of patient diversity on treatment outcomes. Nevertheless, all these contributors expressed their conviction that diversity makes a difference in the outcomes of their respective skills and methods. For example, Levitt and Morrill (Chapter 11) theorized that silence means something different to therapists and clients from diverse cultures and provided anecdotal evidence for their assertion.

Where might the field look more sensitively for the effects of cultural diversity? Four places, we suggest. One: Follow the lead of research on cultural adaptations and other means of personalizing psychotherapy (Cohen et al., 2021; Norcross & Wampold, 2019). Adapt the skill or method to salient cultural identities of patients and compare the results to those obtained with generic implementations.

Two: Avoid simply looking at race/ethnicity, sexual orientation, or country of origin as moderators of distal outcome, as these are proxy measures that do not directly address culture and likely obscure cultural effects (Betancourt & López, 1993). We are probably more likely to find cultural differences through qualitative methods examining inner experiences. Using recall methods that play back specific events in sessions (e.g., perceived microaggressions, discussing cultural differences) and asking for reactions might prove helpful, and conversation analyses might reveal interesting dynamics.

Three: Proactively test theoretically derived cultural differences in psychotherapy. For example, given that Asian cultures are theorized to be more collectivist and less individualistically oriented than Western cultures (Duan et al., 2012; Sue et al., 2022), researchers could test whether individualistically oriented patients respond differently to therapists' suggestions to strive to achieve for oneself rather than to honor the family.

Four: Examine the conceptual equivalence (Brislin, 1993) of psychotherapy phenomena and the ways in which these phenomena do or do not manifest in an equivalent manner in differing societal and cultural contexts. The previous three suggestions all center on constructs and assumptions created in the WEIRD frame of reference. It is hoped that future research will consider constructs and assumptions from other frames of reference that address questions about intersectionality and power as well.

Caveats in Interpreting the Results

The contributors all bemoaned the flaws and inadequacies of the research in their respective literature reviews. Such limitations can guide future researchers as well as caution practitioners and policymakers from reaching premature conclusions about "what works" and "what does not."

In addition to the research limitations in any single chapter, there were obvious restrictions in the scope and magnitude of a single task force. We desire to be forthright and proactive in articulating these limitations. Here, we present several compelling caveats in interpreting the results of the preceding chapters and of the entirety of the Task Force.

Low Power

To have adequate evidence from which to draw conclusions, we need multiple studies with many psychotherapists and clients so that extraneous factors can be minimized across studies. Unfortunately, however, for most of the skills and methods reviewed in this volume, there were shockingly few studies. Furthermore, even for those skills/methods that had a sufficient number of studies, different definitions, measures, and analytic methods were often employed across studies, making it questionable whether it was valid to summarize across studies. The source of strength in psychotherapy research—its diversity in designs, outcomes, and measures—also proved the root of the problem. In statistical terms, most of the meta-analyses and research syntheses struggled with low power.

Absence of Moderators

The summary numbers in Table 23.1 apply strictly to the average or typical client. There were scattered reports in the chapters of moderators, but these were hardly ever replicated across studies. Combining all clients and disorders obscures what works when with whom. There are occasions when every skill or method used by some therapists proves helpful and other occasions when harmful. Practitioners need to know more than what works on average; practitioners need to know for which clients and which situations each skill/method is effective. We need, in short, tests of moderation, particularly with populations rarely studied.

Complexity of Psychotherapy Not Captured

Psychotherapy is a dynamic and complex process, experienced differently by each participant in varying contexts. Some of the therapy skills (particularly the response modes) might have received consensual judgments as neutral/mixed or insufficient research because they were considered out of context. The paucity of context in the research reviews might also explain certain adverse effects—for instance, the ineffective use of the skills in a given moment.

To capture the individual nature of this complex phenomenon, researchers would need to conduct intensive case studies, with input from therapists, clients, significant others, and external observers, using measures unique to the individuals involved, taking into account historical, contextual, and cultural factors. Instead, most of the research represented in this book focused on the frequency of a particular therapist skill/method in relation to distal outcomes, using only patient self-report measures, disregarding the context and nuance of how psychotherapy operates, and neglecting the evidence that clients often conceal, distort, and even lie about their therapeutic experiences (Farber et al., 2019).

We can all recount personal experiences as clinicians and clients when empathic reflections, interpretations, silence, and the rest of the skills and methods covered in this book had profound positive or negative effects. Yet, the research literature disappoints by not reflecting these experiences. At times, there were glimpses in how the research summaries accurately encapsulated clinical experiences, and we hope that in the future, we refine our ability to study these phenomena.

Patterns and Sequences Not Revealed

Many of the skills and methods were researched as if they occur in isolation, rather than in sequence or in interactions with other variables. An interpretation, for instance, is often preceded by multiple exchanges of exploration (e.g., questions, reflections) and asking the client about their understanding before a tentative interpretation is offered. The therapist then follows with questions about accuracy, and the interpretation is co-constructed between the therapist and client (i.e., reshaped, reformulated, and repeated in subsequent sessions). It is probably the lengthy sequence and repetition of skillful interpretations rather than the single interpretation that is helpful. Alas, most of the chapters and research summaries did not explicate the chain or pattern of therapeutic events.

Cannot Claim Causality

To assert causality between a skill/method and an outcome, researchers usually need to conduct experimental studies (e.g., manipulating whether metaphors are used or not used). But (and this is a huge "but") experimentally manipulating many of these therapist skills/methods changes the very nature of the psychotherapy itself. For example, the metaphors provided by therapists probably need to be tailored to the individual patient and provided at the optimal moment when the patient is "ready." Response to a metaphor undoubtedly depends on the timing and the manner in which it is presented (e.g., empathically and tentatively vs. as "Truth"). With few prominent exceptions in this volume (e.g., role induction and routine outcome monitoring), the research did not afford confident causal connections between the respective skill or method and the treatment outcome. We join those advocating for evidentiary pluralism in identifying casual relationships in psychotherapy (e.g., Oddli et al., 2022).

Cannot Reliably Separate Therapist and Client Contributions

As noted eloquently in the chapters on silence and dyadic synchrony (Chapters 11 and 12), most skills and methods are not uniquely a product of the therapists' work but, rather, are products of the interaction between the therapist and client at a particular time and place. Hence, these research syntheses have not, and perhaps cannot, reliably separate the therapist's contribution from the client's contribution to the process. In the future, researchers can investigate how therapists and clients co-create the processes that facilitate progress in psychotherapy.

Results Depend on Type of Outcome

As noted in Chapter 1, immediate in-session assessment allows for perhaps the best research evidence on the effectiveness of a particular skill or method given the temporal link between what the therapist did and how the client responded. But even here, caution is needed because we know clinically that outcomes vary when assessed at different points. For example, a client might have an immediate negative reaction to a therapist's advice, but later reconsider it and decide to implement it and find the advice to be helpful. Intermediate and distal outcomes are most suspect because of the difficulty in clearly linking the skill/method to the intermediate (e.g., the association between the skill/method and working alliance is tenuous given that many factors together lead to developing, maintaining, and repairing the working alliance) and the distal outcomes (e.g., the association between a particular question and symptom change cannot be made given the distance in time and the interaction with many other variables).

Indeed, it seems that psychotherapy researchers have done things backwards: We probably should have first examined the effects of particular skills/methods on immediate outcomes and then tested distal outcomes by including mediators and moderators. We suspect that professionals conducted research backwards for urgent pragmatic reasons: to prove the efficacy of psychotherapy for insurance reimbursement, for public and legal recognition, for external grant funding, and for acceptance as health care aligned with a biomedical model.

In addition, the research evidence looks more "solid" for distal outcomes than for immediate and intermediate outcomes. It is easier to collect and quantitatively summarize these studies, often conducted with large numbers of participants using self-report data and sophisticated meta-analyses. Table 23.1 convincingly bears out this pattern: 10 of the 11 therapy methods determined to be demonstrably effective were reviewed by meta-analyses on distal outcomes. By contrast, no therapy skill or method was determined to be demonstrably effective for immediate outcomes and only one for intermediate outcomes.

Research on immediate in-session outcomes requires time-intensive coding of psychotherapy sessions, fewer participants are involved, and often qualitative analyses are used. That made it more difficult (and less compelling) to aggregate results across studies. In fact, there was often an insufficient number of research studies to perform meta-analyses on immediate and intermediate outcomes; authors had to rely on box scores as a way of summarizing the research.

A related caveat is that researchers sometimes chose non–bona fide comparisons to test the effects of their methods. In other words, they compared a genuine psychotherapy method (e.g., a strength-based method) to a non-psychotherapy method (e.g., a discussion between strangers). Of course, it is easier to find positive effects in such a comparison than comparing the skill/method to another bona fide skill/method.

Not All Skills and Methods Were Reviewed

As noted previously in this chapter, not all possible skills and methods were covered. Hence, this volume should not be construed as generalizing to all possible skills and methods used in psychotherapy. Furthermore, most researchers did not systematically consider subtypes of the skills; for example, questions can be open or closed; focused on facts, thoughts, or feelings; oriented toward the past, present, or future; and presented with different levels of quality. Averaging across all these subtypes potentially obscured the effectiveness of particular subtypes.

Training Implications

In the general literature on training and supervision, there is some evidence for the effectiveness of helping skills programs for beginning trainees as well as of training in treatment packages as part of randomized clinical trials (Knox & Hill, 2021). Based on a summary of the chapters in this book, however, there is considerably less evidence for the effectiveness of training on specific skills and methods.

The contributors to this volume were eloquent and specific in describing *what* trainees should learn about their respective therapy skills and methods, but not so much *how* trainees could actually learn and competently provide those skills and methods. There was even less empirical research demonstrating the efficacy of such training. That pattern adheres to a long, undistinguished history in psychotherapy training where it is presumed that once the key behaviors are identified, students will magically absorb the skill via didactic instruction and expert modeling (Norcross & Popple, 2017). Psychotherapeutic competence has typically been assumed rather than verified.

We aimed to distill the collective expertise of the chapter contributors on training students in these critical psychotherapy behaviors. Hence, we read, reread, coded, and recoded the training processes recommended by the chapter authors for the skills and methods reviewed in this book (for this analysis, we collapsed therapist self-disclosure and immediacy into one skill given that their training implications were presented together, and we kept imagery rehearsal therapy and exposure/relaxation/rescripting therapy for nightmares as separate methods as they were presented in that chapter). The recommended training processes were coded into categories of *instruction*, *modeling*, *practice*, and *feedback* (along with an "other" category) based on Bandura's framework for these four essential components of learning (Bandura, 1969, 1997; Hill & Lent, 2006).

Almost all of the contributors recommended some form of *instruction* in their skill or method: 61% recommended didactic instruction, 35% recommended imparting knowledge about that specific skill/method, 35% assigned a specific reading or manual on the skill/method, and 35% suggested a clinical training workshop. The authors could advance more than one instructional process, of course, but virtually all (96%) recommended that training should include some form of instruction, which makes sense given that trainees need some information about what they are learning.

About half (52%) of the contributors also explicitly recommended *modeling* of some kind. The modeling took the form of observing an expert's or model's videotape of the skill or method (31% of authors), watching a professor or supervisor model the behavior (17%), or observing their own recorded use of the behavior in question (17%). The assumption is that watching someone else's or one's own performance provides the trainee with an experience of what it would be like to deliver or receive the skill or method.

More than half (60%) of the contributors, in addition, explicitly recommended that trainees *practice* the therapy skill or method in question. Specifically, they recommended role-play or behavioral rehearsal of the skill/method (43%), deliberate practice (26%), practice administering assessments or measures of the skill/method (13%), or structured exercises (9%). We were surprised that more contributors did not focus on deliberate practice given recent evidence about its effectiveness (e.g., Chow et al., 2015; Hill et al., 2014, 2020; Rousmaniere et al., 2017).

Contributors may have inferred or assumed that *feedback* would follow student practice of the behaviors, but only about a third of them (35%) explicitly mentioned the need for feedback. Usually the feedback was related to the trainee role-play, practice, or performance of the indicated skill/method. Surprisingly, the contributors almost never advocated for the use of observer rating scales to provide feedback, or focusing on coding or rating trainee behavior to identify the method and its in-session markers to establish fidelity or adherence. Similarly, contributors almost never explicitly mentioned ensuring that students reach a competence threshold in the method or skill.

Several contributors explicitly advanced additional training processes that did not neatly cluster under instruction, modeling, practice, and feedback. These *other* recommendations entailed two calls for emphasizing trainee responsiveness to patients when utilizing the skill/method and two recommendations to incorporate active learning strategies in training. Both accord with the growing literature on what works in training and supervising health care professionals (Norcross et al., 2017).

On average, three or four specific recommendations were made in each chapter about how clinical training should proceed on acquiring these therapy skills and methods. Surprisingly, however, research evidence for the effectiveness of training in those skills and methods was rarely offered. Specific evidence was presented in only four chapters:

- For rupture repairs, Eubanks and Muran (in Chapter 2) summarized a meta-analysis that training therapists in rupture repairs led to modest improvements in subsequent treatment outcomes. Critical components of the alliance-focused training included increasing therapist awareness of ruptures and improving therapists' abilities to regulate their emotions around ruptures. Training involved analyzing rupture moments via videotape analysis, role-plays, mindfulness training, reading, watching tapes of experienced therapists, and training in process measures such as the Rupture Resolution Rating System or 3RS (Eubanks et al., 2023; Muran & Eubanks, 2020). Evidence showed that rupture resolution training proved especially valuable for cognitive behavior therapists, perhaps because they have not received explicit training in processing relationship dynamics with patients.
- Elliott and associates (Chapter 5) discussed the evidence for the effectiveness of training in the broader field of empathy and empathy-related skills (Ngo et al., 2022), although they did not present specific evidence for training on empathic reflections. They also noted that the impact of empathy training on client outcome remains unknown, and curricula have often promulgated simplistic ideas about empathic reflections and led to their indiscriminate use.
- Barkham and colleagues (Chapter 15) reported evidence that training in routine outcome monitoring (ROM) has resulted in fewer deteriorated cases but no changes in symptom reduction or dropout (De Jong et al., 2021), as well as more positive attitudes toward ROM (Edbrooke-Childs et al., 2016) and rates of ROM adoption (Persons et al., 2016). The training ranged from a 2-hour introduction to a full-day workshop followed by booster sessions and monthly supervision. In learning ROM, Barkham et al. noted that although passive learning (e.g., reading, workshops) increases knowledge, behavioral rehearsal and modeling of interactions with patients (e.g., responding to patients' reactions to data, addressing adaptations to treatment) were more likely to enhance the delivery of ROM (Beidas et al., 2014). In addition, they suggested that training the trainers as well as trainees was integral to securing the systemic adoption of ROM (see Swift et al., 2015).
- In one study of training in cognitive–experiential dream work (CEDM), Spangler and Sim (Chapter 19) reported that psychotherapists who received a 3-hour workshop on CEDM increased their self-efficacy in using CEDM and positive attitudes toward dreams (Crook-Lyon et al., 2009).

A final observation about training. We coded the contributors' recommended training processes according to Bandura's (1969, 1997) four-component model of learning (instruction, modeling, practice, and feedback), but this may not be the most comprehensive list. Ngo and colleagues (2022) proposed six components for training (didactic, rehearsal, reflection, observation, feedback, and mindfulness). Combining these two systems produces seven components (instruction/didactic, modeling, observation, practice/rehearsal, feedback, reflection, and mindfulness) that could be used for training as well as for research on training.

Therapeutic Practices

The contributors finished their respective chapters with bulleted, action-oriented therapeutic practices. They routinely concluded that the skill or method in question should be learned, added to therapists' repertoires, and employed judiciously. We were, as a rule, impressed by their clinical sagacity and grateful for their therapeutic guidance.

The clinical imperative for practitioners is to know what works when with whom. The research evidence in this book, by contrast, attests largely that these skills and methods are effective sometimes, but we typically do not yet know what works for whom and when. The clinical need for research-driven specificity has proven once again elusive.

Still, there were promising leads in the research, and the psychotherapy field has inched closer to the desired goal of evidence-based clinical guidance. Below we summarize and integrate these promising leads, candidly acknowledging that these are tentative leads requiring empirical verification and replication. Until then, practice will continue to lead research.

We found replicated research evidence for "moderators" in five skills/methods: rupture repair (worse if client had personality disorders, and cognitive behavior therapists did better than psychodynamic psychotherapists in training, Chapter 2); role induction (better results for older non-Hispanic White male clients and with experienced over inexperienced therapists, Chapter 13); routine outcome monitoring (more effective with trained than untrained therapists, and clinical support tools better than other methods, Chapter 15); emotion regulation (patients with several disorders fared better than those with eating disorders, Chapter 17); and chairwork (emotion-focused therapists had better outcomes than cognitive behavior therapists did, Chapter 18). Unfortunately, there was little consistency across skills/methods in terms of which moderators were tested and replicated.

In addition, several of these clinical methods were developed for (or tested on) specific disorders. The encouraging results of the meta-analyses on cognitive restructuring (Chapter 22) and behavioral activation (Chapter 21), for example, were based on studies of depressed patients. The positive results of research conducted on treatments for nightmares, for another example, were tested primarily on military personnel experiencing nightmares. Thus, these treatments might need to be adapted in order to work with other disorders.

Other promising leads for "what works when for whom" emanated from clinical expertise with a gleaning of research support. Here, we encapsulate a sampling of these clinical gems from the respective chapters in *Psychotherapy Skills and Methods That Work*:

- Employ Socratic questioning to prompt clients to engage more fully in the therapeutic work in general, and with clients struggling with depression, pessimism, and without psychotropic medications in particular (Chapter 4).
- Offer empathic reflections particularly when clients are confused or uncertain about their feelings; such reflections regularly enhance their self-understanding. As well, strive to match your reflections to their distance from the client's main message: The further away a reflection is from the client's expressed experience, the more careful, tentative, or humble it should be (Chapter 5).
- Refrain from the overzealous use of stock (pre-prepared) metaphors and pay particular attention to key metaphors spontaneously repeated by the client (Chapter 6).
- Attend to patients' quality of object relations when using interpretations. Patients with poorer object relations tend to benefit more from interpretations compared to patients with high quality of object relations (Chapter 7).
- The use of paradoxical interventions remains controversial. The research evidence, however, indicates that they are especially effective for anxiety disorders, sleep difficulties, and highly reactant patients (Chapter 8).
- Remember that clients are more likely to complete between-session homework congruent with the content they want to remember from a session. Also, remind clients that engaging in homework is an opportunity to learn something new—even when the task does not proceed as planned (Chapter 10).
- Consider reassuring clients that they are welcome to take their time with introspective silence. Clients sometimes cut short productive silence because they are worried about therapists waiting for them, so reassurance can prove useful (Chapter 11).
- Allow yourself to move flexibly in and out of synchrony with patients. Consider especially the emotional context: Some contexts call for high synchrony (e.g., when clients experience adaptive emotions), whereas others call for relatively low synchrony (e.g., when clients experience maladaptive emotions; Chapter 12).
- Collaborative assessment methods (CAMs) exert, in a couple of sessions, positive effects on distal treatment outcomes, but their primary mechanism of action may be a function of therapist respect, collaboration, and empathic understanding rather than in the exact sequence in which they are implemented. Moreover, CAMs tend to work best when therapists assist clients in developing a more compassionate and useful view of themselves (Chapter 14).
- Incorporate patient strengths into homework assignments (e.g., observation of positive episodes during a week, planning enjoyment) and in fostering activities outside of the therapy room (e.g., recreation, physical movement, social support). Therapists can integrate strength-based methods into all forms of psychotherapy (Chapter 16).
- Counter clients' initial fears that chairwork may precipitate overwhelming or intolerable emotions. Rather, follow the research evidence that clients routinely find the method helpful and worthwhile (Chapter 18).
- Given that several treatment methods are available to reduce the terror of nightmares, consider which method best suits the patient's culture, experiences, and tolerance for exposure methods (Chapter 19).

- Do not prematurely discontinue behavioral activation when patients experience problems in changing their behavior. Instead, try to motivate the patient, provide research-driven hope that the method works, and solve problems in its application (Chapter 21).

Task Force Conclusions

In bringing the work of this interorganizational, multiyear Task Force to an end, we are reminded of Jonas Salk's sage observation that "the reward for work well done is the opportunity to do more." Indeed, much has been done and done well, but more must be done before we can be confident about the effectiveness of therapy skills and methods, especially in terms of immediate in-session and intermediate outcomes.

The Steering Committee has drawn the following conclusions from the Task Force on Psychotherapy Skills and Methods That Work. These statements do not constitute the formal policies of any organization nor are they considered practice or treatment standards. Rather, they represent current scientific knowledge and the consensual judgment of the Steering Committee.

- Mental health professionals regularly use multiple skills and methods to facilitate client behavior and personality change.
- These therapy skills and methods are largely transdiagnostic (used across patient diagnoses or disorders) and pantheoretical (employed across diverse theoretical orientations).
- Efforts to promulgate best practices or compile evidence-based treatments without attending to the effectiveness of their constituent methods and skills are clinically dubious and potentially misleading.
- Understanding psychotherapy effectiveness requires attention to impacts on patients at four temporal intervals: immediate in-session, intermediate (end of session or between sessions), distal (end of treatment), and follow-up (post-treatment).
- These skills and methods are not offered by therapists at random but, rather, are implemented in response to perceived client needs (in that moment, in a session, or as part of an overarching treatment plan).
- Therapists vary in the way that they present the skills/methods to be responsive to the needs of clients/patients at the moment.
- The absolute and relative amount of outcome variance accounted for by therapist skills and methods (relative to the treatment approach, the therapeutic relationship, client factors, therapist effects, responsiveness, and other factors) cannot be determined at present because of insufficient research evidence.
- In terms of distal (end-of-treatment) outcomes, nine skills and methods can be characterized as demonstrably effective: affirmation/validation, paradoxical interventions, homework, routine outcome monitoring, strength-based methods, emotional regulation, meditation/mindfulness/acceptance, behavioral activation, and cognitive restructuring. An additional five can be categorized as probably effective: rupture repair, role induction, collaborative assessment methods, chairwork, and imagery rehearsal therapy for nightmares.

- In terms of intermediate (post-session or mid-treatment), one method can be characterized as demonstrably effective (cognitive experiential dream work) and two as probably effective (paradoxical interventions, homework).
- In terms of immediate (in-session) outcomes, five methods can be categorized as probably effective: in-dialogue and extended silences, role induction, strength-based methods, and emotion regulation.
- These research-supported or evidence-based skills and methods complement and extend evidence-based psychotherapy relationships and treatment packages.
- Four therapy skills and methods lack sufficient research evidence for determining their effectiveness on any of the outcomes at this time (self-disclosure, immediacy, Socratic questioning, metaphors). There is a need for empirical research on these skills/methods, especially assessing specific outcomes that therapists intend to facilitate when using them.
- Most of these research results address average findings for typical patients, thus masking individual variability and obscuring the clinical reality that these skills and methods prove sometimes helpful and sometimes harmful for particular patients and circumstances.
- There is also an urgent need for extending the scope of this research base beyond WEIRD societies and cultures. Failure to do so will increase the irrelevance of this work.
- A determination or classification of any psychotherapeutic skill, method, and treatment package as effective must necessarily refer to the temporal interval (e.g., immediate, intermediate, distal), the type of outcome (e.g., symptom reduction, well-being), and the comparator group (e.g., within vs. between groups, bona fide psychotherapy comparisons vs. nonclinical controls).
- Research is urgently needed on immediate in-session outcomes to establish at least a temporal link between the skill/method and the client response. Promising approaches include task analyses and conversation analyses. Such research is admittedly laborious, but such investigations will bring us closer to clinical reality.
- The clinical implementation of any therapy skill and method must prove responsive to the cultural identities, singular situations, and clinical needs of the individual client at specific moments in therapy.
- Future practice and research should prioritize the "what works for whom under which conditions" imperative that guides psychotherapy.
- Additional research is sorely required on training processes to ensure students competently provide these skills and methods.

References

Baldwin, S. A., & Goldberg, S. B. (2021). Methodological foundations and innovations in quantitative psychotherapy research. In M. Barkham, W. Lutz, & L. G. Castonguay (Eds.), *Bergin and Garfield's handbook of psychotherapy and behavior change* (50th anniversary ed., pp. 19–50). Wiley.

Bandura, A. (1969). *Principles of behavior modification.* Holt, Rinehart & Winston.

Bandura, A. (1997). *Self-efficacy: The exercise of control.* Freeman.

Barkham, M., & Lambert, M. J. (2021). The efficacy and effectiveness of psychological therapies. In M. Barkham, W. Lutz, & L. G. Castonguay (Ed.), *Bergin and Garfield's handbook of psychotherapy and behavior change* (50th anniversary ed., pp. 135–189). Wiley.

Beidas, R. S., Cross, W., & Dorsey, S. (2014). Show me, don't tell me: Behavioral rehearsal as a training and analogue fidelity tool. *Cognitive and Behavioral Practice*, *21*, 1–11. http://doi.org/10.1016/j.cbpra.2013.04.002

Betancourt, H., & López, S. R. (1993). The study of culture, ethnicity, and race in American psychology. *American Psychologist*, *48*(6), 629–637. https://doi.org/10.1037/0003-066X.48.6.629

Brislin, R. W. (1993). *Understanding culture's influence on behavior*. Harcourt Brace Jovanovich.

Chow, D. L., Miller, S. D., Seidel, J. A., Kane, R. T., Thornton, J. A., & Andrews, W. P. (2015). The role of deliberate practice in the development of highly effective psychotherapists. *Psychotherapy*, *52*(3), 337–345. https://doi.org/10.1037/pst0000015

Cohen, Z. D., Delgadillo, J., & DeRubeis, R. J. (2021). Personalized treatment approaches. In M. Barkham, W. Lutz, & L. G. Castonguay (Eds.), *Bergin and Garfield's handbook of psychotherapy and behavior change* (50th anniversary ed., pp. 673–704). Wiley.

Crook-Lyon, R. E., Hill, C. E., Wimmer, C. L., Hess, S. A., & Goates-Jones, M. K. (2009). Therapist training, feedback, and practice for dream work: A pilot study. *Psychological Reports*, *105*(1), 87–98. https://doi.org/10.2466/pr0.105.1.87-98

De Jong, K., Conijn, J. M., Gallagher, R., Reshetnikova, A. S., Heij, M., & Lutz, M. C. (2021). Using progress feedback to improve outcomes and reduce drop-out, treatment duration, and deterioration: A multilevel meta-analysis. *Clinical Psychology Review*, *85*, 102002. https://doi.org/10.1016/j.cpr.2021.102002

Duan, C., Hill, C., Jiang, G., Hu, B., Chui, H., Hui, K., Liu, J., & Yu, L. (2012). Therapist directives: Use and outcomes in China. *Psychotherapy Research*, *22*(4), 442–457. https://doi.org/10.1080/10503307.2012.664292

Edbrooke-Childs, J., Wolpert, M., & Deighton, J. (2016). Using Patient Reported Outcome Measures to Improve Service Effectiveness (UPROMISE): Training clinicians to use outcome measures in child mental health. *Administration and Policy in Mental Health*, *43*(3), 302–308. https://doi.org/10.1007/s10488-014-0600-2

Eubanks, C. F., Muran, J. C., & Samstag, L. W. (2023). Alliance-focused training: Teaching therapists to navigate alliance ruptures. In L. G. Castonguay & C. E. Hill (Eds.), *Advancing training and supervision in psychotherapy*. American Psychological Association.

Ezawa, I. D., & Strunk, D. R. (2022a). Differences in the delivery of cognitive behavioral therapy for depression when therapists work with Black and White patients. *Cognitive Therapy and Research*, *46*, 104–113. https://doi.org/10.1007/s10608-021-10254-0

Ezawa, I. D., & Strunk, D. R. (2022b). Working with Black vs. White patients: An experimental test of therapist decision-making in cognitive behavioral therapy for depression. *Cognitive Behaviour Therapy*, *51*, 229–242. https://doi.org/10.1080/16506073.2021.1970799

Farber, B. A., Blanchard, M., & Love, M. (2019). *Secrets and lies in psychotherapy*. American Psychological Association.

Henrich, J., Heine, S. J., & Norenzayan, A. (2010). Most people are not WEIRD. *Nature*, *466*(7302), 29. https://doi.org/10.1038/466029a

Hill, C. E., & Lent, R. W. (2006). A narrative and meta-analytic review of helping skills training: Time to revive a dormant area of inquiry. *Psychotherapy*, *43*(2), 154–172. https://doi.org/10.1037/0033-3204.43.2.154

Hill, C. E., Kivlighan, D. M., III, Rousmaniere, T., Kivlighan, D. M., Jr., Gerstenblith, J. A., & Hillman, J. W. (2020). Deliberate practice: Effects on doctoral student therapists and clients. *Psychotherapy*, *57*(4), 587–597. https://doi.org/10.1037/pst0000247

Hill, C. E., Spangler, P. T., Jackson, J., & Chui, H. (2014). Training undergraduate students to use insight skills: Integrating results across three studies. *The Counseling Psychologist*, *42*(6), 800–820. https://doi.org/10.1177/0011000014542602

Hill, C. E., Thompson, B. J., & Ladany, N. (2003). Therapist use of silence in therapy. *Journal of Clinical Psychology*, *59*, 513–524. http://dx.doi.org/10.1002/jclp.10155

Knox, S., & Hill, C. E. (2021). Training and supervision in psychotherapy: What we know and what we need to know. In M. Barkham, W. Lutz, & L. G. Castonguay (Eds.), *Bergin and Garfield's handbook of psychotherapy and behavior change* (50th anniversary ed., pp. 327–349). Wiley.

Muran, J. C., & Eubanks, C. F. (2020). *Therapist performance under pressure: Negotiating emotion, difference, and rupture*. American Psychological Association.

Ngo, H., Sokolovic, N., Coleman, A., & Jenkins, J. M. (2022). Teaching empathy to mental health practitioners and trainees: Pairwise and network meta-analyses. *Journal of Consulting and Clinical Psychology, 90*(11), 851–860. https://doi.org/10.1037/ccp0000773

Norcross, J. C., Hogan, T. P., Koocher, G. P., & Maggio, L. A. (2017). *Clinician's guide to evidence-based practices: Behavioral health and addictions* (2nd ed.). Oxford University Press.

Norcross, J. C., & Lambert, M. J. (2019). *Psychotherapy relationships that work: Volume 1. Evidence-base therapist contributions*. Oxford University Press.

Norcross, J. C., & Popple, L. M. (2017). *Supervision essentials for integrative psychotherapy*. American Psychological Association.

Norcross, J. C., & Wampold, B. E. (Eds.) (2019). *Psychotherapy relationships that work Volume 2: Evidence-based therapist responsiveness*. Oxford University Press.

Oddli, H. W., Stänicke, E., Halvorsen, M. S., & Lindstad, T. G. (2022). Causality in psychotherapy research: Towards evidential pluralism. *Psychotherapy Research*.

Persons, J. B., Koerner, K., Eidelman, P., Thomas, C., & Liu, H. (2016). Increasing psychotherapists' adoption and implementation of the evidence-based practice of progress monitoring. *Behaviour Research and Therapy, 76*, 24–31. https://doi.org/10.1016/j.brat.2015.11.004

Rousmaniere, T., Goodyear, R. K., Miller, S. D., & Wampold, B. E. (Eds.). (2017). *The cycle of excellence: Using deliberate practice to improve supervision and training*. Wiley.

Snyder, W. U. (1945). An investigation of the nature of nondirective psychotherapy. *Journal of General Psychology, 33*, 193–223. https://doi.org/10.1037/10841-035

Sue, D. W., Sue, D., Neville, H. A., & Smith, L. (2022). *Counseling the culturally diverse: Theory and practice* (9th ed.). Wiley.

Swift, J. K., Callahan, J. L., Rousmaniere, T. G., Whipple, J. L., Dexter, K., & Wrape, E. R. (2015). Using client outcome monitoring as a tool for supervision. *Psychotherapy, 52*(2), 180–184. https://doi.org/10.1037/a0037659

Index

For the benefit of digital users, indexed terms that span two pages (e.g., 52–53) may, on occasion, appear on only one of those pages

Tables, figures, and boxes are indicated by *t*, *f*, and *b* following the page number